Life Span Development

A Topical Approach

Fourth Edition

Robert S. Feldman
University of Massachusetts Amherst

Senior Producer and Strategy Manager: Kelli Strieby
Content Producer: Lisa Mafrici
Portfolio Manager Assistant: Caroline Fassett
Content Developer: Cathy Murphy
Senior Executive Product Marketing Manager: Christopher Brown
Senior Field Marketing Manager: Debi Henion
Content Producer Manager: Amber Mackey
Content Development Manager: Marita Sermolins Bley

Art/Designer: Integra-Chicago
Digital Studio Course Producer: Elissa Senra-Sargent
Full-Service Project Manager: Integra-Chicago
Compositor: Integra-Chicago
Printer/Binder: LSC Communications, Inc.
Cover Printer: LSC Communications
Cover Art Director: Cate Rickard Barr
Cover Designer: Gary Pikovsky/Piko Design LLC
Cover Image: A-Digit/Getty Images

Library of Congress Cataloging-in-Publication Data:

Names: Feldman, Robert S. (Robert Stephen), author.
Title: Life span development : a topical approach / Robert S. Feldman.
Description: Fourth Edition. | New York, NY : Pearson, [2020] | Includes bibliographical references and index.
Identifiers: LCCN 2018041997 | ISBN 9780135188033 (pbk. : alk. paper)
Subjects: LCSH: Developmental psychology. | Life cycle, Human. | Human growth. | MESH: Human Development | Personality Development
Classification: LCC BF713 .F48 2020 | DDC 155–dc23
LC record available at https://lccn.loc.gov/2018041997

1 19

Revel Access Code Card
ISBN 10:   0-135-21221-9
ISBN 13: 978-0-135-21221-9

Revel Combo Card
ISBN 10:   0-13-546481-1
ISBN 13: 978-0-13-546481-6

Rental Edition
ISBN 10:   0-135-18803-2
ISBN 13: 978-0-135-18803-3

Loose-Leaf Edition
ISBN 10:   0-135-17872-X
ISBN 13: 978-0-135-17872-0

Instructor's Review Copy
ISBN 10:   0-135-17870-3
ISBN 13: 978-0-135-17870-6

Pearson

Brief Contents

Contents

Preface

*L*ife Span Development: A Topical Approach is the outgrowth of conversations and survey data drawing on the thinking of literally hundreds of instructors. These instructors voiced two main challenges in teaching life span development, reaching a surprising degree of consensus. First, almost every instructor acknowledged that the breadth of life span development is so vast that it is difficult to cover the entire field within the confines of a traditional college term. Consequently, many instructors saw most life span development texts as too long. Their students were concerned about the length of the texts and had trouble completing the entire book.

Second, many instructors expressed the concern that traditional, chronologically based life span development books were arranged in a way that made it difficult for students to understand the scope of development within particular topical areas (such as social or personality development across the entire life span) without skipping from one chapter to another.

Life Span Development: A Topical Approach addresses both of these concerns. This book, which is based on the chronologically organized, highly popular *Development Across the Life Span*, is shorter than traditional life span books, and it is arranged in a way that helps students to see the "big picture" of development across the entire life span within a specific topical area.

Life Span Development: A Topical Approach maintains the student-friendliness that has been the hallmark of the original. It is rich in examples and illustrates the applications that can be derived from the research and theory of life span developmentalists. It pays particular attention to the applications that can be drawn from theory and research in the field.

To optimize student learning and to provide instructors with maximum flexibility, the book uses a modular approach. Each chapter is divided into three modules focusing on particular subtopics. Consequently, rather than facing long, potentially daunting chapters, students encounter material that is divided into smaller, more manageable chunks. Of course, presenting material in smaller chunks represents a structure that research long ago found to be optimum for promoting learning.

The modular approach has another advantage: It allows instructors to customize instruction by assigning only those modules that fit their course. Because the modules are self-contained, instructors can pick and choose which modules best contribute to their course. Because of the flexibility of this structure, instructors who wish to highlight a particular topic can do so easily and—equally important— have the option of not including specific modules.

Overview of the Fourth Edition

This edition of *Life Span Development: A Topical Approach*— like its predecessors—provides a broad overview of the field of human development. It covers major topics, such as physical development, cognitive development, and social and personality development. In addition, separate chapters focus on health and wellness, language development, intelligence, development of the self, moral development and aggression, gender and sexuality, relationships, living in a multicultural world, and death and grieving.

The book seeks to accomplish the following four major goals:

- First and foremost, the book is designed to provide a broad, balanced overview of the field of life span development. It introduces readers to the theories, research, and applications that constitute the discipline, examining both the traditional areas of the field and more recent innovations. It pays particular attention to the applications developed by life span development specialists, demonstrating how life span developmentalists use theory, research, and applications to help solve significant social problems.

- The second goal of the text is to explicitly tie development to students' lives. Findings from the study of life span development have a significant degree of relevance to students, and this text illustrates how these findings can be applied in a meaningful, practical sense. Applications are presented in a contemporaneous framework, including current news items, timely world events, and contemporary uses of life span development that draw readers into the field. Numerous descriptive scenarios and vignettes reflect everyday situations in people's lives, explaining how they relate to the field.

- The third goal is to highlight both the commonalities and the diversity of today's multicultural society. Consequently, the book incorporates material relevant to diversity in all its forms—racial, ethnic, gender, sexual orientation, religion, and cultural—throughout every chapter. In addition, every chapter has at least one *Developmental Diversity and Your Life* section. These features explicitly consider how cultural factors relevant to development both unite and diversify our contemporary global society.

- Finally, the fourth goal is one that is implicit in the other three: making the field of life span development engaging, accessible, and interesting to students. Life span development is a joy both to study and to teach because so much of it has direct, immediate meaning for our lives. Because all of us are involved in our own developmental paths, we are tied in very personal ways to the content areas covered by the book. *Life Span Development: A Topical Approach*, then, is meant to engage and nurture this interest, planting a seed that will develop and flourish throughout readers' lifetimes.

In accomplishing these goals, the book strives to be user friendly. Written in a direct, conversational voice, it duplicates as much as possible a dialogue between author and student. The text is meant to be understood and mastered on its own by students of every level of interest and motivation. To that end, it includes a variety of pedagogical features that promote mastery of the material and encourage critical thinking.

In short, the book blends and integrates theory, research, and applications, focusing on the breadth of human development. Furthermore, rather than attempting to provide a detailed historical record of the field, it focuses on the here and now, drawing on the past where appropriate, but with a view toward delineating the field as it now stands and the directions toward which it is evolving. Similarly, while providing descriptions of classic studies, the emphasis is on current research findings and trends.

Life Span Development: A Topical Approach is meant to be a book that readers will want to keep in their own personal libraries, one that they will take off the shelf when considering problems related to that most intriguing of questions: How do people come to be the way they are?

Special Features of the Fourth Edition

In addition to its modular structure, *Life Span Development: A Topical Approach* includes a set of features designed to engage students and help them learn the material effectively. These include:

Chapter-Opening Prologues
Each chapter begins with a short vignette, describing an individual or situation that is relevant to the basic developmental issues being discussed in the chapter.

Looking Ahead Sections
These opening sections orientate readers to the topics to be covered, bridging the opening prologue with the remainder of the chapter.

Learning Objectives
Each major section includes explicit learning objectives. These numbered learning objectives provide a means for instructors to evaluate student mastery of specific content. These learning objectives anchor the module reviews and chapter summary.

From Research to Practice
Each chapter includes a section that describes current developmental research applied to everyday problems, helping students to see the impact of developmental research throughout society. All of these sections are new in this edition. Each *From Research to Practice* box concludes with a Shared Writing prompt, which students can respond to, as well as respond to peers' responses, and instructors can moderate.

Developmental Diversity and Your Life
Every chapter has at least one *Developmental Diversity and Your Life* section incorporated into the text. These sections highlight issues relevant to today's multicultural society.

Neuroscience and Development
Special sections exploring what we know about development through the lens of neuroscience appear in many chapters. Most of these features have been revised for the fourth edition to reflect cutting-edge research.

Running Glossary
Key terms are defined in the margins of the page on which the term is presented.

Development in Your Life
Every chapter includes information on specific uses that can be derived from research conducted by developmental investigators. These boxes, formerly titled *Are You an Informed Consumer of Development?*, are now titled *Development in Your Life*.

Review and Journal Prompt Sections
Interspersed throughout each chapter are three module reviews—short recaps of the chapter's main points—as well as Journal Prompts designed to elicit critical thinking about the subject matter through written responses.

End-of-Chapter Material
Each chapter ends with a summary and an epilogue that refers back to the opening prologue and that ties the chapter together. The Looking Back summary is keyed to the learning objectives provided at the start of major sections of each chapter.

Career Prompts
Students will encounter frequent questions throughout the text designed to show the applicability of the material to a

variety of professions, including education, nursing, social work, and health care providers.

What's New in the Fourth Edition?

This edition includes a number of significant changes and additions.

One figure in each chapter now includes a *Thinking About the Data* prompt, which encourages the reader to think about what is behind the data they see in graphs and tables. This critical thinking question in the figure caption is a jumping-off point to a data-driven Social Explorer activity in Revel.

Furthermore, all *From Research to Practice* boxes—which describe a contemporary developmental research topic and its applied implications—are new to this edition. Boxes formerly called *Are You an Informed Consumer of Development?* are now titled *Development in Your Life*. Many of the *Developmental Diversity and Your Life* boxes, as well as the *Neuroscience and Development* boxes, have been revised in this edition.

In addition, module reviews are now tied to learning objectives to help students organize section reviewing around the objectives.

Finally, the fourth edition of **Life Span Development: A Topical Approach** incorporates a significant amount of new and updated information. For instance, advances in such areas as behavioral genetics, brain development, evolutionary perspectives, and cross-cultural approaches to development receive expanded and new coverage. Dozens of figures and photos have been revised or replaced, and hundreds of new citations have been added, with most of those from articles and books published in the past few years.

New topics were added to every chapter. The following sample of new and revised topics featured in this edition provides a good indication of the currency of the revision:

Chapter 1: Introduction to Lifespan Development

- Revised prologue on *in vitro fertilization*
- Additional material on Vygotsky and scaffolding
- Revised material on culture, ethnicity, and race, including two new *Developmental Diversity and Your Life* sections:
  - "How Culture, Ethnicity, and Race Influence Development" discusses cultural, ethnic, racial, socioeconomic, and gender considerations in the study of development.
  - "Choosing Research Participants Who Represent the Diversity of Humanity" emphasizes the importance of truly representing the general population when studying development.

- **Table 1-1**, Approaches to Lifespan Development, now includes sex and gender topics in the questions asked by development researchers
- Refined explanation of critical period
- Figure 1-1 on brain differences in a person with autism
- Refined explanation of cognitive neuroscience approaches
- Updated Figure 1-5 on longitudinal vs. cross-sectional research
- Figure 1-3 on scientific method
- Using lifespan development research for public policy

Chapter 2: Genetics, Prenatal Development, and Birth

- Prologue on genetic testing
- *From Research to Practice* section on transgenerational epigenetic inheritance
- Updated Table 2-1 on the genetic basis of various disorders
- Updated Table 2-3 on DNA-based genetic tests
- Cultural and religious concerns about reproductive technologies
- Abortion statistics
- Cross-cultural differences in abortion
- Statistics on percentage of women facing physical abuse during pregnancy
- Smoking as the single most preventable cause of death of infants and mothers
- Rate of twins by geographical region
- Miscarriage aftermaths
- Opioid use during pregnancy
- Revised art in Figures 2-3, 2-4, and 2-6
- Statistics on length of hospital stay
- Statistics on survival rates for very pre-term babies
- Figure 2-13 on international rates of infant mortality
- Figure 2-15 on rates of infant mortality in the United States by race

Chapter 3: Physical Growth and Aging Across the Lifespan

- Statistics on shaken baby syndrome, with new Figure 3-9 showing damage to the brain of a shaken baby
- Causes of cultural differences in sleep patterns in infants
- Figure 3-11 showing myelin development over time
- Figure 3-12 on pruning of gray matter

Chapter 4: Health and Wellness

- Prologue on stress in emerging adulthood
- *From Research to Practice* box on the banning of crib bumpers in several states
- *Neuroscience and Development* box on exercise and depression
- Mindfulness as a stress reduction technique
- Figure 4-2, world hunger map
- Updated statistics on poverty and hunger in the United States
- Updated statistics on obesity in the United States, with new Figure 4-4
- Updated statistics on parents' perception of children's health
- Effects of lead poisoning, including the lead poisoning that occurred in Flint, Michigan
- Introduction of SUID, along with the discussion of SIDS
- Figure 4-8 on reduction in instances of SIDS and SUID
- Updated statistics on rates of Alzheimer's disease
- Benefits of breastfeeding
- Introduction of solid foods in infancy
- Just-right phenomenon in nutrition

Chapter 5: Cognitive Growth: Piaget and Vygotsky

- Prologue on early language development
- Change in key term from scheme to schema
- *From Research to Practice* box on screen time and the video deficit

Chapter 6: Cognitive Growth: Information Processing Approaches

- Prologue on information processing, learning to work as a barista
- *Neuroscience and Development* box on sleep and memory, including new Figure 6-6 showing differences in hippocampal activity in sleep-deprived study participants
- *From Research to Practice* box on smartphones and memory

Chapter 7: Language Development

- Prologue on toddler speech
- *From Research to Practice* section on improving language skills for preschoolers from low-income families
- *Developmental Diversity and Your Life* section on first words spoken across the world

Chapter 8: Intelligence

- Prologue on sibling aptitude differences
- *Neuroscience and Development* box on the "eureka" moment
- *From Research to Practice* box on the impact of child neglect on intelligence
- Relationship between age and creativity

Chapter 9: Social and Emotional Development

- Prologue on modeling emotions to children
- *From Research to Practice* section on the Second Step program, focusing on emotional control and empathy
- *Neuroscience and Development* box on the effect of therapy on the brain
- Adolescent anxiety disorders

Chapter 10: Development of the Self

- Prologue on rethinking careers in mid-life
- *From Research to Practice* section on social comparison and self-esteem in the digital age
- More on the development of socioeconomic awareness
- Emerging adulthood
- Millennials' views of work and career
- Social comparison
- Figure 10-3 on gap in wages between men and women
- Immigration rates and impacts
- Figure 10-5 on occupational prestige—millennials and the older generation
- Table 10-2: high-burnout careers
- Reducing career burnout

Chapter 11: Moral Development and Aggression

- Prologue on making good decisions
- Hispanic parental values
- Cultural differences in childrearing practices
- New data on child abuse and neglect
- Additional signs of child abuse
- *From Research to Practice* section on helping teens with aggressive behavior

Chapter 12: Gender and Sexuality

- Prologue on a non-gender-conforming child
- *From Research to Practice* section on sexting and social media

- Transgender individuals
- Updated Figure 12-1 on age at which adolescents have sex for the first time
- Updated statistics and Figure 12-2 on teenage pregnancy rates
- Figure 12-3 on reported frequency of sexual intercourse
- Dating via social media
- Cultural norms and intercultural dating
- Emerging adulthood
- Figure 12-12, update on divorce rates
- Figure 12-13, living patterns of older Americans

Chapter 13: Friends and Family

- Prologue on retirement
- *Neuroscience and Development* box on positive endorsements and social media
- *From Research to Practice* box on guiding children through the divorce of parents
- Figure 13-5, Benefits of Growing Older
- Correlation of poverty and physical and mental health problems
- Updated statistics on labor force participation of mothers
- Updated statistics on child poverty
- Figure 13-9, Living Arrangements of Children
- Multigenerational families
- Gay and lesbian parents
- Figure 13-11, Poverty in Late Adulthood

Chapter 14: Schooling, Culture, and Society: Living in a Multicultural World

- Prologue on choosing a child care situation
- Updates on Head Start and other preschool environments
- Figure 14-1 on child care of preschool children
- Grade inflation
- *From Research to Practice* section on racial diversity on college campuses
- Figure 14-7, racial makeup of college students
- Figure 14-10, social media use among teens
- Digital divide

Chapter 15: Death and Dying

- Prologue on a good death
- *From Research to Practice* section on grief after spouse death

- Professional mourners in China
- Displays of grief in Egypt
- Additional ways of helping children deal with grief
- New statistics on assisted suicides and jurisdictions
- Treatment of dying across cultures
- Updated statistics on infant mortality in the United States and other countries
- Figure 15-4 on predictions of lifespan versus reality

Revel™

Revel is an interactive learning environment that deeply engages students and prepares them for class. Media and assessment integrated directly within the authors' narrative lets students read, explore interactive content, and practice in one continuous learning path. Thanks to the dynamic reading experience in Revel, students come to class prepared to discuss, apply, and learn from instructors and from each other.

Learn more about Revel:

www.pearson.com/revel

The fourth edition includes integrated videos and media content throughout, allowing students to explore topics more deeply at the point of relevancy. Revel makes the content come alive as students respond to "Myth or Truth" and "Fun Facts and a Lie" interactives. Each chapter also includes at least one "Trending Topic" feature, which explores cutting-edge research or current events.

Highly engaging interactives encourage student participation. Interactive scenarios invite students into "choose your own path"–type activities. Other interactives lead them through how a health care professional, counselor, teacher, or parent might react to a specific developmental situation or solve a problem. Students can also explore interactive figures using drag-and-drop and predictive graphing tools, as well as hotspot images.

Each chapter includes a *Thinking About the Data* prompt, which encourages the student to think about what is behind the data they see in graphs and tables using a data-driven Social Explorer activity in Revel.

Finally, a set of carefully curated videos builds on text content, exploring developmental psychology from a variety of perspectives, including a deeper look at diversity and the latest in neuroscience.

Revel also offers the ability for students to assess their content mastery by taking multiple-choice quizzes that offer instant feedback and by participating in a variety of writing assignments, such as peer-reviewed questions and auto-graded assignments.

MyVirtualLife integration enables students to apply developmental concepts in a simulated environment within their Revel™ course. MyVirtualLife is an interactive simulation that allows students to parent a child from birth to age 18, making decisions on the child's behalf. Once the virtual child turns 18, the student user's perspective flips for the second half of the program, which enables students to live a simulated life and see the impact of their first-person decisions over the course of a lifetime.

Revel Combo Card

The Revel Combo Card provides an all-in-one access code and loose-leaf print reference (delivered by mail).

Ancillaries

Life Span Development: A Topical Approach, Fourth Edition, is accompanied by a superb set of teaching and learning materials.

- **Instructor's Resource Manual** (ISBN: 0135178673). The Instructor's Resource Manual has been thoroughly reviewed and revised for the fourth edition. It includes learning objectives, key terms and concepts, self-contained lecture suggestions, and class activities for each chapter. The Instructor's Resource Manual is available for download via the Pearson Instructor's Resource Center (www.pearsonhighered.com) and Revel.

- **Video Enhanced PowerPoint Slides** (ISBN: 0135178819). These slides bring the Feldman design right into the classroom, drawing students into the lecture and providing wonderful interactive activities, visuals, and videos.

- **PowerPoint Lecture Slides** (ISBN: 0135178681). The lecture slides provide an active format for presenting concepts from each chapter and feature prominent figures and tables from the text. The PowerPoint Lecture Slides are available for download via the Pearson Instructor's Resource Center (www.pearsonhighered.com) or Revel.

- **Test Bank** (ISBN: 013517869X). For the fourth edition, each question was checked for accuracy to ensure that the correct answer was marked and the page reference was accurate. The test bank contains 1000 multiple-choice, true/false, and essay questions, each correlated to chapter topic and learning objectives. The test bank features the identification of each question as factual, conceptual, applied, or analytical. Finally, each item is also identified in terms of difficulty level to allow professors to customize their tests and ensure a balance of question types. Each chapter of the test item file begins with the Total Assessment Guide: an easy-to-reference grid that makes creating tests easier by organizing the test questions by text section, question type, and whether it is factual, conceptual, applied, or analytical. Each chapter ends by listing the Revel assessment questions featured in the digital Revel textbook product.

- **MyTest** (ISBN: 0135178665). The test bank comes with the Pearson MyTest, a powerful assessment generation program that helps instructors easily create and print quizzes and exams. Questions and tests can be authored online, allowing instructors ultimate flexibility and the ability to efficiently manage assessments anytime, anywhere. For more information, go to www.PearsonMyTest.com.

- **Pearson Teaching Films Lifespan Development Video (ISBN: 0205656021)** engages students and brings to life a wide range of topics spanning prenatal through the end of the life span. International videos shot on location allow students to observe similarities and differences in human development across various cultures.

- **Supplementary Texts.** Contact your Pearson representative to package any of these supplementary texts with *Life Span Development*, Fourth Edition.

  - *Current Directions in Developmental Psychology* (ISBN: 0205597505). Readings from the American Psychological Society. This exciting reader includes over 20 articles that have been carefully selected for the undergraduate audience, and taken from the very accessible *Current Directions in Psychological Science* journal. These timely, cutting-edge articles allow instructors to bring their students a real-world perspective about today's most current and pressing issues in psychology. The journal is discounted when packaged with this text for college adoptions.

  - *Twenty Studies That Revolutionized Child Psychology* **by Wallace E. Dixon, Jr.** (ISBN: 0130415723). Presenting the seminal research studies that have shaped modern developmental psychology, this brief text provides an overview of the environment that gave rise to each study, its experimental design, its findings, and its impact on current thinking in the discipline.

  - *Human Development in Multicultural Contexts: A Book of Readings* (ISBN: 0130195235). Written by Michele A. Paludi, this compilation of readings highlights cultural influences in developmental psychology.

  - *The Psychology Major: Careers and Strategies for Success* (ISBN: 0205684688). Written by Eric Landrum (Idaho State University), Stephen Davis (Emporia State University), and Terri Landrum (Idaho State University), this 160-page paperback provides valuable information on career options available to psychology majors, tips for improving academic performance, and a guide to the APA style of research reporting.

Acknowledgments

I am grateful to the following reviewers who have provided a wealth of comments, constructive criticism, and encouragement:

Jessica Lee, Sam Houston State University; Debra Hollister, Valencia College, Lake Nona campus; Suzanne Gibson,

Meridian Community College; Michael Poulakis, University of Indianapolis; Jim Hanson, Grand View University; Kimberly DuVall, James Madison University; Brian Sexton, Kean University; Eirini Papafratzeskakou, Mercer County Community College; Gloria Anderson, Troy University; Jackie Goldstein, Samford University; Stefanie Keen, University of South Carolina Upstate; Dawn Kriebel, Immaculata University; Lakshmi Raman, Oakland University; Diane Wille, Indiana University Southeast; Lola Aagaard, Morehead State University; Kristine Anthis, Southern Connecticut State University; Mitchell Baker, Moraine Valley Community College; Jonathan Bates, Hunter College; Manolya Bayar, University of Hartford; Janine Buckner, Seton Hall University; Michael Caruso, University of Toledo; Elaine Cassel, Lord Fairfax Community College—Fauquier; Jean Choi, Humber College; Michelle Clark, James Madison University; Jeff Cookston, San Francisco State University; Brent Costleigh, Brookdale Community College; Lisa End-Berg, Kennesaw State University; Carolyn Fallahi, Central Connecticut State; Lisa Fozio-Thielk, Waubonsee Community College; Troianne Grayson, Florida Community College at Jacksonville; James Guinee, University of Central Arkansas; Tomo Imamichi, Borough of Manhattan Community College; Marsha Ironsmith, East Carolina University; Alisha Janowsky, University of Central Florida; Laura Johnson, Davidson County Community College; Tara Johnson, Indiana University of Pennsylvania; Linda Jones, Blinn College; Franz Klutschkowski, North Central Texas College; Jonathan Lang, Borough of Manhattan Community College; Ann Lim-Brand, Brookdale Community College; Geri Lotze, Virginia Commonwealth University; Pei-Wen Ma, William Paterson University; Salvador Macias, University of South Carolina; Nicole Martin, Kennesaw State University; Ronnie Naramore, Angelina College; Lisa Newell, Indiana University of Pennsylvania; Kathleen Rudasill, University of Louisville; Lynne Schmelter-Davis, Brookdale Community College; Sandy Sego, American International College; Jenessa Steele, Radford University; Barry Stennett, Athens Technical College & Gainesville State College; Timothy Trant, Louisiana State University; Larry Venuk, Northern Virginia Community College; Christine Ziegler, Kennesaw State University.

Many others deserve a great deal of thanks. I am indebted to the numerous people who provided me with a superb education, first at Wesleyan University and later at the University of Wisconsin. Specifically, Karl Scheibe played a pivotal role in my undergraduate education, and Vernon Allen acted as mentor and guide through my graduate years. It was in graduate school that I learned about development, being exposed to such experts as Ross Parke, John Balling, Joel Levin, Herb Klausmeier, and many others. My education continued when I became a professor. I am especially grateful to my colleagues at the University of Massachusetts, who make the university such a wonderful place in which to teach and do research.

Several people played central roles in the development of this book. The thoughtful and creative Stephen Hupp and Jeremy Jewell of Southern Illinois University—Edwardsville were partners in developing the Revel materials, and their input was critical. John Bickford of the University of Massachusetts Amherst provided important research and editorial support, and I am thankful for his help and superb writing skills. I am also grateful to Christopher Poirier of Stonehill College, who produced the wonderful Instructor Resource Manual and Test Bank that accompany *Life Span Development*. Finally, John Graiff and Michelle Goncalves were essential in juggling and coordinating the multiple aspects of working on a project such as this, and I am very grateful for the substantial role they played.

I also am grateful to the superb Pearson team that was instrumental in the inception and development of this book. Kelli Streiby, senior producer and strategy manager, was an enthusiastic and thoughtful advocate for the book. Managing Editor Marita Sermolins Bley went beyond the call of duty to provide guidance as this book became a reality. I am grateful for their support. Most of all, I want to thank the always thoughtful, creative, responsive, and extremely organized Cathy Murphy, who played a critical role in bringing this book to fruition.

On the production end of things, Program Manager Jane Lee Kaddu and Project Manager Valerie Iglar-Mobley helped in bringing all the aspects of the text together. I am also perennially grateful to Jeff Marshall, whose many ideas permeate this book. Finally, I'd like to thank (in advance) marketing manager Chris Brown, on whose skills I'm counting.

I also wish to acknowledge the members of my family, who play such an essential role in my life. My brother, Michael, my sisters-in-law and brother-in-law, my nieces and nephews—all make up an important part of my life. In addition, I am always indebted to the older generation of my family, who led the way in a manner I can only hope to emulate. I will always be obligated to Harry Brochstein, Mary Vorwerk, and Ethel Radler. Most of all, the list is headed by my father, Saul Feldman, and my mother, Leah Brochstein.

In the end, it is my immediate family who deserve the greatest thanks. My terrific kids, Jonathan and wife Leigh; Joshua and wife Julie; and Sarah and husband Jeff not only are nice, smart, and good-looking, but my pride and joy. My wonderful grandchildren, Alex, Miles, Naomi, and Lilia, have brought immense happiness from the moment of their births. And ultimately my wife, Katherine Vorwerk, provides the love and grounding that makes everything worthwhile. I thank them, with all my love.

Robert S. Feldman

University of Massachusetts Amherst

About the Author

Robert S. Feldman is professor of psychological and brain sciences and deputy chancellor of the University of Massachusetts, Amherst. A recipient of the College Distinguished Teacher Award, he teaches psychology classes ranging in size from 15 to nearly 500 students. During the course of three decades as a college instructor, he has taught both undergraduate and graduate courses at Mount Holyoke College, Wesleyan University, and Virginia Commonwealth University in addition to the University of Massachusetts.

Professor Feldman, who initiated the Minority Mentoring Program at the University of Massachusetts, also has served as a Hewlett Teaching Fellow and Senior Online Teaching Fellow. He initiated distance learning courses in psychology at the University of Massachusetts.

A Fellow of the American Psychological Association, the Association for Psychological Science, and the American Association for the Advancement of Science, Professor Feldman received a B.A. with High Honors from Wesleyan University (from which he received the Distinguished Alumni Award). He has an M.S. and Ph.D. from the University of Wisconsin-Madison. He is a winner of a Fulbright Senior Research Scholar and Lecturer award, and he has written more than 200 books, book chapters, and scientific articles.

Professor Feldman has edited *Development of Nonverbal Behavior in Children* and *Applications of Nonverbal Behavioral Theory and Research*, and co-edited *Fundamentals of Nonverbal Behavior*. He is also author of *Child Development, Understanding Psychology*, and *P.O.W.E.R. Learning: Strategies for Success in College and Life*. His books have been translated into a number of languages, including Spanish, French, Portuguese, Dutch, Chinese, Korean, and Japanese. His research interests include honesty and deception in everyday life, work that he described in *The Liar in Your Life*, a trade book published in 2009. His research has been supported by grants from the National Institute of Mental Health and the National Institute on Disabilities and Rehabilitation Research.

Professor Feldman is past-president of the Federation of Associations of Behavioral and Brain Sciences Foundation, a consortium of social, behavioral, and brain science societies. In addition, he is president of the board of New England Public Radio.

Professor Feldman loves music, is an enthusiastic pianist, and enjoys cooking and traveling. He has three children, four grandchildren, and he and his wife, a psychologist, live in western Massachusetts in a home overlooking the Holyoke Mountain Range.

Chapter 1
An Orientation to Lifespan Development

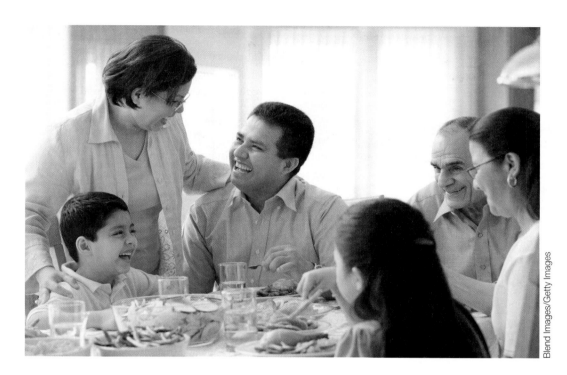

Blend Images/Getty Images

⌄ Learning Objectives

LO 1.1 Define the field of lifespan development and describe what it encompasses.

LO 1.2 Describe the areas that lifespan development specialists cover.

LO 1.3 Describe some of the basic influences on human development.

LO 1.4 Summarize four key issues in the field of lifespan development.

LO 1.5 Describe how the psychodynamic perspective explains lifespan development.

LO 1.6 Describe how the behavioral perspective explains lifespan development.

LO 1.7 Describe how the cognitive perspective explains lifespan development.

LO 1.8 Describe how the humanistic perspective explains lifespan development.

LO 1.9 Describe how the contextual perspective explains lifespan development.

LO 1.10 Describe how the evolutionary perspective explains lifespan development.

LO 1.11 Discuss the value of applying multiple perspectives to lifespan development.

LO 1.12 Describe the role that theories and hypotheses play in the study of development.

LO 1.13 Compare the two major categories of lifespan development research.

LO 1.14 Identify different types of correlational studies and their relationship to cause and effect.

LO 1.15 Explain the main features of an experiment.

LO 1.16 Distinguish between theoretical research and applied research.

LO 1.17 Compare longitudinal research, cross-sectional research, and sequential research.

LO 1.18 Describe some ethical issues that affect psychological research.

Chapter Overview

Prologue: New Conceptions

In many ways, the first meeting of Louise Brown and Elizabeth Carr was unremarkable: just two women, one in her 30s, the other in her 40s, chatting about their lives and their own children.

But in another sense the meeting was extraordinary. For Louise Brown was the world's first "test-tube baby," born by in vitro fertilization (IVF), a procedure in which fertilization of a mother's egg by a father's sperm takes place outside of the mother's body. And Elizabeth Carr was the first baby born by IVF in the United States.

Louise was a preschooler when her parents told her how she was conceived, and throughout her childhood she was bombarded with questions. It became routine to explain to her classmates that she, in fact, was not born in a laboratory. At times, she felt completely alone. For Elizabeth, too, growing up was not easy as she experienced bouts of insecurity.

Today, however, Louise and Elizabeth are hardly unique. They are among the more than 5 million babies that have been born using the procedure, one that has almost become routine. And both became mothers themselves, giving birth to babies who were conceived, incidentally, the old-fashioned way (Falco, 2012; Gagneux, 2016; Simpson, 2017). ∎

Looking Ahead

Louise Brown's and Elizabeth Carr's conceptions may have been novel, but their development, from infancy onward, has followed predictable patterns. While the specifics of our own development vary—some of us encounter economic deprivation or live in war-torn territories; others contend with family issues like divorce and stepparents—the broad strokes of the development that is set in motion the moment we are conceived are remarkably similar for all of us. Like LeBron James, Bill Gates, and, yes, Louise Brown and Elizabeth Carr, each and every one of us has traversed the territory known as child development.

IVF is just one of the brave new worlds of the 21st century. Issues ranging from cloning and the consequences of poverty on development to the effects of culture and race raise significant developmental concerns. Underlying these are even more fundamental issues. How do children develop physically? How does their understanding of the world grow and change over time? And how do our personalities and our social world develop as we move from birth through adolescence?

Louise Brown (left) and Elizabeth Carr (right).

These questions and many others are central to lifespan development. The field encompasses a broad span of time and a wide range of topics. Think about the range of interests that different specialists might focus on when considering Louise Brown and Elizabeth Carr:

- Lifespan development researchers who investigate behavior at the level of biological processes might determine whether Louise and Elizabeth's functioning prior to birth was affected by their conception outside the womb.
- Specialists in lifespan development who study genetics might examine how the genetic endowment from their parents affects their later behavior.
- Lifespan development specialists who investigate thinking processes might examine how Louise and Elizabeth's understanding of the circumstances of their conception changed as they grew older.
- Other researchers in lifespan development, who focus on physical growth, might consider whether their growth rates differed from that of children conceived more traditionally.
- Lifespan development experts who specialize in the social world and social relationships might look at the ways that Louise and Elizabeth interacted with others and the kinds of friendships they developed.

Although their interests take many forms, these specialists in lifespan development share one concern: understanding the growth and change that occur during the course of life. Taking many differing approaches, developmentalists study how both the biological inheritance from our parents and the environment in which we live jointly affect our behavior.

Whether they focus on heredity or environment, all developmental specialists acknowledge that neither one alone can account for the full range of human development. Instead, we must look at the interaction of heredity and environment, attempting to grasp how both underlie human behavior.

In this chapter, we orient ourselves to the field of lifespan development. We begin with a discussion of the scope of the discipline, illustrating the wide array of topics it covers and the full range of ages it examines. We also survey the key issues and controversies of the field and consider the broad perspectives that developmentalists take. Finally, we discuss the ways developmentalists use research to ask and answer questions. Many of the questions that developmentalists ask are, in essence, the scientist's version of the questions that parents ask about their children and themselves: how the genetic legacy of parents plays out in their children; how children learn; why they make the choices they make; whether personality characteristics are inherited and whether they change or are stable over time; how a stimulating environment affects development; and many others. To pursue their answers, of course, developmentalists use the highly structured, formal scientific method, while parents mostly use the informal strategy of waiting, observing, engaging, and loving their kids.

DETERMINING THE NATURE—AND NURTURE—OF LIFESPAN DEVELOPMENT

Have you ever wondered how it is possible that an infant tightly grips your finger with tiny, perfectly formed hands? Or marveled at the way an adolescent can make involved decisions about whom to invite to a party? Or wondered what it is that makes a grandfather at 80 so similar to the father he was when he was 40?

If you've ever contemplated such things, you are asking the kinds of questions that scientists in the field of *lifespan development* pose. In this section, we'll examine how the field of lifespan development is defined and the scope of the field, as well as some basic influences on human development.

Defining Lifespan Development

LO 1.1   Define the field of lifespan development and describe what it encompasses.

lifespan development
the field of study that examines patterns of growth, change, and stability in behavior that occur throughout the entire life span.

Lifespan development is the field of study that examines patterns of growth, change, and stability in behavior that occur throughout the entire life span. In its study of growth, change, and stability, lifespan development takes a *scientific* approach. Like members of other scientific disciplines, researchers in lifespan development test their assumptions about the nature and course of human development by applying scientific methods. They develop theories about development, and they use methodical, scientific techniques to validate the accuracy of their assumptions systematically.

Lifespan development focuses on *human* development. Although there are developmentalists who study the course of development in nonhuman species, the vast majority study people. Some seek to understand universal principles of development, whereas others focus on how cultural, racial, and ethnic differences affect development. Still others aim to understand the traits and characteristics that differentiate one person from another. Regardless of approach, however, all developmentalists view development as a continuing process throughout the life span.

As developmental specialists focus on change during the life span, they also consider stability. They ask in which areas, and in what periods, people show change and growth, and when and how their behavior reveals consistency and continuity with prior behavior.

Finally, developmentalists assume that the process of development persists from the moment of conception and until death, with people changing in some ways right up to the end of their lives and in other ways exhibiting remarkable stability. They believe that no single period governs all development, but instead that people maintain the capacity for substantial growth and change throughout their lives.

The Scope of the Field of Lifespan Development

LO 1.2   Describe the areas that lifespan development specialists cover.

Clearly, the definition of lifespan development is broad and the scope of the field is extensive. Typically, lifespan development specialists cover several quite diverse areas, choosing to specialize in both a topical area and an age range.

physical development
development involving the body's physical makeup, including the brain, nervous system, muscles, and senses, and the need for food, drink, and sleep.

TOPICAL AREAS IN LIFESPAN DEVELOPMENT.   Some developmentalists focus on **physical development**, examining the ways in which the body's makeup—the brain, nervous system, muscles, and senses, and the need for food, drink, and sleep—helps determine behavior. For example, one specialist in physical development might examine the effects of malnutrition on the pace of growth in children, while another might look at how athletes' physical performance declines during adulthood (Fell & Williams, 2008; Muiños & Ballesteros, 2014).

Other developmental specialists examine **cognitive development**, seeking to understand how growth and change in intellectual capabilities influence a person's behavior. Cognitive developmentalists examine learning, memory, problem-solving skills, and intelligence. For example, specialists in cognitive development might want to see how problem-solving skills change over the course of life, or whether cultural differences exist in the way people explain their academic successes and failures (Dumka et al., 2009; Penido et al., 2012; Coates, 2016).

Finally, some developmental specialists focus on personality and social development. **Personality development** is the study of stability and change in the enduring characteristics that differentiate one person from another over the life span. **Social development** is the way in which individuals' interactions and relationships with others grow, change, and remain stable over the course of life. A developmentalist interested in personality development might ask whether there are stable, enduring personality traits throughout the life span, whereas a specialist in social development might examine the effects of racism or poverty or divorce on development (Lansford, 2009; Tine, 2014; Manning et al., 2017). These four major topic areas—physical, cognitive, social, and personality development—are summarized in Table 1-1.

AGE RANGES AND INDIVIDUAL DIFFERENCES.   In addition to choosing to specialize in a particular topical area, developmentalists also typically look at a particular age range. The life span is usually divided into broad age ranges: the prenatal period (the period from conception to birth); infancy and toddlerhood (birth to age 3); the preschool period (ages 3 to 6); middle childhood (ages 6 to 12); adolescence (ages 12 to 20); young adulthood (ages 20 to 40); middle adulthood (ages 40 to 65); and late adulthood (age 65 to death).

It's important to keep in mind that these broad periods—which are largely accepted by lifespan developmentalists—are social constructions. A *social construction* is a shared notion of reality, one that is widely accepted but is a function of society and culture at a given time. Consequently, the age ranges within a period—and even the

cognitive development
development involving the ways that growth and change in intellectual capabilities influence a person's behavior.

personality development
development involving the ways that the enduring characteristics that differentiate one person from another change over the life span.

social development
the way in which individuals' interactions with others and their social relationships grow, change, and remain stable over the course of life.

Table 1-1 Approaches to Lifespan Development

Orientation	Defining Characteristics	Examples of Question Asked*
Physical development	Emphasizes how the brain, nervous system, muscles, sensory capabilities, and needs for food, drink, and sleep affect behavior	• What determines the sex of a child? (2) • What are the long-term results of premature birth? (2) • What are the benefits of breast milk? (4) • What are the consequences of early or late sexual maturation? (3) • What leads to obesity in adulthood? (4) • How do adults cope with stress? (4) • What are the outward and internal signs of aging? (3) • What is the relationship between aging and illness? (4)
Cognitive development	Emphasizes intellectual abilities, including learning, memory, problem solving, and intelligence	• What are the earliest memories that can be recalled from infancy? (6) • What are the intellectual consequences of watching television? (14) • What is intelligence, and how is it measured? (8) • Are there benefits to bilingualism? (7) • What are the fundamental elements of information processing? (6) • Are there ethnic and racial differences in intelligence? (8) • What is cognitive development, and how did Piaget revolutionize its study? (5) • How does creativity relate to intelligence? (8)
Personality and social development	Emphasizes enduring characteristics that differentiate one person from another, and how interactions with others and social relationships grow and change over the lifetime	• Do newborns respond differently to their mothers than to others? (9) • What is the best procedure for disciplining children? (11) • When does a sense of gender identity develop, and how do sex and gender provide a context for development? (12) • How can we promote cross-race friendships? (13) • What are the emotions involved in confronting death? (15) • How do we choose a romantic partner? (14) • What sorts of relationships are important in late adulthood? (13) • What are typical patterns of marriage and divorce in middle adulthood? (12) • In what ways are people affected by culture and ethnicity? (13)

*Numbers in parentheses indicate in which chapter the question is addressed.

periods themselves—are in many ways arbitrary and often culturally derived. For example, later in the book we'll discuss how the concept of childhood as a separate period did not even exist prior to the 17th century. At that time, children and adults were seen as little different from one another except in terms of size. Furthermore, while some periods have a clear-cut boundary (infancy begins with birth, the preschool period ends with entry into elementary school, and adolescence starts with sexual maturity), others don't.

For instance, consider the period of young adulthood, which at least in Western cultures is typically assumed to begin at age 20. That age, however, is notable only because it marks the end of the teenage period. In fact, for many people, such as those enrolled in higher education, the age change from 19 to 20 has little special significance, coming as it does in the middle of the college years. For them, more substantial changes may occur when they leave college and enter the workforce, which is more likely to happen around age 22. Furthermore, in some non-Western cultures, adulthood may be considered to start much earlier, when children whose educational opportunities are limited begin full-time work.

In fact, some developmentalists have proposed entirely new developmental periods. For instance, psychologist Jeffrey Arnett argues that adolescence extends into *emerging adulthood*, a period beginning in the late teenage years and continuing into the mid-20s. During emerging adulthood, people are no longer adolescents, but they haven't fully taken on the responsibilities of adulthood. Instead, they are still trying out different identities and engaging in self-focused exploration (Arnett, 2011, 2016; de Dios, 2012; Sumner, Burrow, & Hill, 2015).

In short, there are substantial *individual differences* in the timing of events in people's lives. In part, this is a biological fact of life: People mature at different rates and reach developmental milestones at different points. However, environmental factors also play a significant role in determining the age at which a particular event is likely to occur. For example, the typical age of marriage varies substantially from one culture to another, depending in part on the functions that marriage plays in a given culture.

THE LINKS BETWEEN TOPICS AND AGES.   Each of the broad topical areas of lifespan development—physical, cognitive, social, and personality development—plays a role throughout the life span. Consequently, some developmental experts focus on physical development during the prenatal period, and others during adolescence. Some might specialize in social development during the preschool years, while others look at social relationships in late adulthood. And still others might take a broader approach, looking at cognitive development through every period of life.

In this book, we take a comprehensive approach to lifespan development, proceeding topically across the life span through physical, cognitive, and social and personality development. Within each developmental area, we consider various topics related to that area as a way to present an overview of the scope of development through the life span.

One of the first observations that we make is that no one develops alone, without interacting with others who share the same society and the same time period. This universal truth leads not to unity, but to the great diversity that we find in cultures and societies across the world and—on a smaller scale—within a larger culture, as we discuss in the next section.

Influences on Lifespan Development

LO 1.3   Describe some of the basic influences on human development.

Bob, born in 1947, is a baby boomer; he was born soon after the end of World War II, when returning soldiers caused an enormous bulge in the birth rate. He was an adolescent at the height of the civil rights movement and the beginning of protests against the Vietnam War. His mother, Leah, was born in 1922 and is still alive at 96; her generation passed its childhood and teenage years in the shadow of the Depression. Bob's son, Jon, was born in 1975. Now established in a career after graduating from college and starting his own family, he is a member of what has been called Generation X.

Jon's younger sister, Sarah, who was born in 1982, is part of the next generation, which sociologists have called the Millennial Generation. She now is raising a preschooler of her own after finishing graduate school and starting her career. She sees post-Millennials—the generation that followed her—as being engrossed in social media and their iPhones.

These people are in part products of the social times in which they live. Each belongs to a particular **cohort**, a group of people born at around the same time in the same place. Such major social events as wars, economic upturns and depressions, famines, and epidemics (like the one due to the AIDS virus) work similar influences on members of a particular cohort (Dittmann, 2005; Twenge, Gentile, & Campbell, 2015).

Cohort effects provide an example of *history-graded influences*, which are biological and environmental influences associated with a particular historical moment. For instance, people who lived in New York City during the 9/11 terrorist attack on the World Trade Center experienced shared biological and environmental challenges due to the attack. Their development is going to be affected by this normative history-graded influence (Laugharne, Janca, & Widiger, 2007; Park, Riley, & Snyder, 2012; Kim, Bushway & Tsao, 2016).

In contrast, *age-graded influences* are biological and environmental influences that are similar for individuals in a particular age group, regardless of when or where they are raised. For example, biological events such as puberty and menopause are universal events that occur at relatively the same time throughout all societies. Similarly, a sociocultural event such as entry into formal education can be considered an age-graded influence because it occurs in most cultures around age 6.

cohort
a group of people born at around the same time in the same place.

From *an educator's* perspective

How would a student's cohort membership affect his or her readiness for school? For example, what would be the benefits and drawbacks of coming from a cohort in which Internet use was routine, compared with earlier cohorts prior to the appearance of the Internet?

Development is also affected by *sociocultural-graded influences*, the social and cultural factors present at a particular time for a particular individual, depending on such variables as ethnicity, social class, and subcultural membership. For example, sociocultural-graded influences will be considerably different for children who are white and affluent than for children who are members of a minority group and living in poverty (Rose et al., 2003).

Finally, *non-normative life events* are specific, atypical events that occur in a person's life at a time when such events do not happen to most people. For example, a child whose parents die in an automobile accident when she is 6 years old has experienced a significant non-normative life event.

Key Debates in Lifespan Development

LO 1.4   Summarize four key issues in the field of lifespan development.

Today, several key issues and questions dominate the field. Among the major issues are the nature of change, the importance of critical and sensitive periods, lifespan approaches versus more focused approaches, and the nature–nurture issue.

CONTINUOUS CHANGE VERSUS DISCONTINUOUS CHANGE.   One of the primary issues challenging developmentalists is whether development proceeds in a continuous or discontinuous fashion. In **continuous change**, development is gradual, with achievements at one level building on those of previous levels. Continuous change is quantitative in nature; the basic underlying developmental processes that drive change remain the same over the course of the life span. Continuous change, then, produces changes that are a matter of degree, not of kind. Changes in height prior to adulthood, for example, are continuous. Similarly, as we'll see later in the chapter, some theorists suggest that changes in people's thinking capabilities are also continuous, showing gradual quantitative improvements rather than developing entirely new cognitive processing capabilities.

continuous change
gradual development in which achievements at one level build on those of previous levels.

discontinuous change
development that occurs in distinct steps or stages, with each stage bringing about behavior that is assumed to be qualitatively different from behavior at earlier stages.

In contrast, one can view development as being made up of primarily **discontinuous change**, occurring in distinct stages. Each stage or change brings about behavior that is assumed to be qualitatively different from behavior at earlier stages. Consider the example of cognitive development again. We'll see later in the chapter that some cognitive developmentalists suggest that as we develop, our thinking changes in fundamental ways, and that such development is not just a matter of quantitative change but of qualitative change.

Most developmentalists agree that taking an either/or position on the continuous–discontinuous issue is inappropriate. While many types of developmental change are continuous, others are clearly discontinuous.

CRITICAL AND SENSITIVE PERIODS: GAUGING THE IMPACT OF ENVIRONMENTAL EVENTS.   If a woman comes down with a case of rubella (German measles) in the first 20 weeks of pregnancy, the consequences for the child she is carrying are likely to be devastating: They include the potential for blindness, deafness, and heart defects. However, if she comes down with the exact same strain of rubella in the 30th week of pregnancy, damage to the child is unlikely.

critical period
a specific time during development when a particular event has its greatest consequences and the presence of certain kinds of environmental stimuli is necessary for development to proceed normally.

The differing outcomes of the disease in the two periods demonstrate the concept of critical periods. A **critical period** is a specific time during development when a particular event has its greatest consequences. Critical periods occur when the presence of certain kinds of environmental stimuli enable development to proceed normally, or when exposure to certain stimuli results in abnormal development. For example, mothers who take drugs at particular times during pregnancy may cause permanent harm to their developing child (Mølgaard-Nielsen, Pasternak, & Hviid, 2013; Nygaard et al., 2017).

Although early specialists in lifespan development placed great emphasis on the importance of critical periods, more recent thinking suggests that in many realms, individuals are more malleable than was first thought, particularly in the domain of personality and social development. For instance, rather than suffering permanent damage from a lack of certain kinds of early social experiences, there is increasing evidence that people can use later experiences to their benefit, to help them overcome earlier deficits.

sensitive period
a point in development when organisms are particularly susceptible to certain kinds of stimuli in their environments, but the absence of those stimuli does not always produce irreversible consequences.

Consequently, developmentalists are now more likely to speak of sensitive periods rather than critical periods. In a **sensitive period**, organisms are particularly susceptible to certain kinds of stimuli in their environment. A sensitive period represents the optimal period for particular capacities to emerge, and children are particularly sensitive to environmental influences.

It is important to understand the difference between the concepts of critical periods and sensitive periods. In critical periods, it is assumed that the absence of certain kinds of environmental influences is likely to produce permanent, irreversible consequences for the developing individual. In contrast, although the absence of particular environmental influences during a sensitive period may hinder development, it is possible for later experiences to overcome the earlier deficits. In other words, the concept of sensitive period recognizes the plasticity of developing humans (Armstrong, et al., 2006; Hooks & Chen, 2008; Hartley & Lee, 2015).

LIFESPAN APPROACHES VERSUS A FOCUS ON PARTICULAR PERIODS.   On which part of the life span should developmentalists focus their attention? For early developmentalists, the answers tended to be infancy and adolescence. Most attention was clearly concentrated on those two periods, largely to the exclusion of other parts of the life span.

Today, the story is different. Developmentalists now believe that the entire life span is important, for several reasons. One is the discovery that developmental growth and change continue during every part of life—as we'll discuss throughout this book.

Furthermore, an important part of every person's environment is the presence of other people around him or her—the person's social environment. To fully understand the social influences on people of a given age, we need to understand the people who are in large measure providing those influences. For instance, to understand development

Developmental Diversity and Your Life
How Culture, Ethnicity, and Race Influence Development

In the United States, parents praise young children who ask a lot of questions for being "intelligent" and "inquisitive." The Dutch consider such children "too dependent on others." Italian parents judge inquisitiveness as a sign of social and emotional competence, not intelligence. Spanish parents praise character far more than intelligence, and Swedes value security and happiness above all.

What are we to make of the diverse parental expectations cited above? Is one way of looking at children's inquisitiveness right and the others wrong? Probably not, if we take into consideration the cultural contexts in which parents operate. In fact, different cultures and subcultures have their own views of appropriate and inappropriate methods and interpretations of childrearing, just as they have different developmental goals for children (Feldman & Masalha, 2007; Huijbregts et al., 2009; Chen, Chen, & Zheng, 2012).

Specialists in child development must take into consideration broad cultural factors. For example, as we'll discuss further in Chapter 10, children growing up in Asian societies tend to have a *collectivistic orientation*, focusing on the interdependence among members of society. In contrast, children in Western societies are more likely to have an *individualistic orientation*, in which they concentrate on the uniqueness of the individual.

Similarly, child developmentalists must also consider ethnic, racial, socioeconomic, and gender differences if they are to achieve an understanding of how people change and grow throughout the life span. If these specialists succeed in doing so, not only can they attain a better understanding of human development, but they may also be able to derive more precise applications for improving the human social condition. To complicate the study of diverse populations, the terms *race* and *ethnic group* are often used inappropriately. *Race* originated as a biological concept, and initially referred to classifications based on physical and structural characteristics of species. But such a definition has little validity in terms of humans, and research shows that it is not a meaningful way to differentiate people.

For example, depending on how race is defined, there are between 3 and 300 races, and no race is genetically distinct. The fact that 99.9 percent of genetic makeup is identical in all humans makes the question of race seem insignificant. Thus, race today is generally thought of as a social construction, something defined by people and their beliefs (Helms, Jernigan, & Mascher, 2005; Smedley & Smedley, 2005; Alfred & Chlup, 2010).

In contrast, *ethnic group* and *ethnicity* are broader terms for which there is greater agreement. They relate to cultural background, nationality, religion, and language. Members of ethnic groups share a common cultural background and group history.

In addition, there is little agreement about which names best reflect different races and ethnic groups. Should the term *African American*—which has geographical and cultural implications—be preferred over *black*, which focuses primarily on race and skin color? Is *Native American* preferable to *Indian*? Is *Hispanic* more appropriate than *Latino*? And how can researchers accurately categorize people with multiracial backgrounds?

In order to fully understand development, then, we need to take the complex issues associated with human diversity into account. It is only by looking for similarities and differences among various ethnic, cultural, and racial groups that developmental researchers can distinguish principles of development that are universal from principles that are culturally determined. In the years ahead, then, it is likely that lifespan development will move from a discipline that focuses primarily on North American and European development to one that encompasses development around the globe (Matsumoto & Yoo, 2006; Kloep et al., 2009).

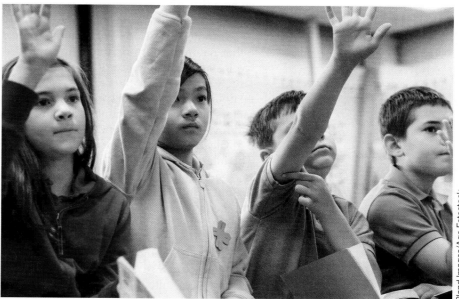

Culture, ethnicity, and race have significant effects on development.

Blend Images/Age Fotostock

in infants, we need to unravel the effects of their parents' ages on their social environments. A 15-year-old first-time mother will provide parental influences of a very different sort from those provided by an experienced 37-year-old mother. Consequently, infant development is in part an outgrowth consequence of adult development.

In addition, as lifespan developmentalist Paul Baltes points out, development across the life span involves both gains and losses. With age, certain capabilities become more refined and sophisticated, while others involve loss of skill and capacity. For example, vocabulary tends to grow throughout childhood and continues this growth through most of adulthood. At the same time, certain physical abilities, like reaction time, improve until early and middle adulthood, when they begin to decline (Ghisletta et al., 2010).

People also shift in how they invest their resources (in terms of motivation, energy, and time) at different points during the life span. Early in life, more of one's personal resources are devoted to activities involving growth, such as studying or learning new skills. As one grows older, more resources are devoted to dealing with the losses people face during late adulthood (Staudinger & Leipold, 2003).

THE RELATIVE INFLUENCE OF NATURE AND NURTURE ON DEVELOPMENT. One of the enduring questions of development involves how much of people's behavior is due to their genetically determined nature and how much is due to nurture, the influences of the physical and social environment in which a child is raised. This issue, which has deep philosophical and historical roots, has dominated much work in lifespan development (Wexler, 2006).

In this context, *nature* refers to traits, abilities, and capacities that are inherited from one's parents. It encompasses any factor that is produced by the predetermined unfolding of genetic information—a process known as **maturation**. These genetic, inherited influences are at work as we move from the one-cell organism that is created at the moment of conception to the billions of cells that make up a fully formed human. Nature influences whether our eyes are blue or brown, whether we have thick hair throughout life or eventually go bald, and how good we are at athletics. Nature allows our brains to develop in such a way that we can read the words on this page.

In contrast, *nurture* refers to the environmental influences that shape behavior. Some of these influences may be biological, such as the impact of a pregnant mother's use of cocaine on her unborn child or the amount and kind of food available to children. Other environmental influences are more social, such as the ways parents discipline their children and the effects of peer pressure on an adolescent. Finally, some influences are a result of larger, societal-level factors, such as the socioeconomic circumstances in which people find themselves.

Although developmentalists reject the notion that behavior is the sole result of either nature or nurture, the nature–nurture question can cause heated debate. Take, for instance, intelligence. If intelligence is primarily determined by heredity and is largely fixed at birth, then efforts to improve intellectual performance later in life may be doomed to failure. In contrast, if intelligence is primarily a result of environmental factors, such as the amount and quality of schooling and home stimulation, then an improvement in social conditions could cause intelligence to increase.

Clearly, neither nature nor nurture stands alone in most developmental matters. The interaction of genetic and environmental factors is complex, in part because certain genetically determined traits have not only a direct influence on children's behavior but also an indirect influence in shaping children's environments. For example, children who cry a great deal—a trait that may be produced by genetic factors—may influence their environment by making their parents rush to comfort them whenever they cry. The parents' responsivity to their children's genetically determined behavior becomes an environmental influence on the children's subsequent development (Bradley & Corwyn, 2008; Stright, Gallagher, & Kelley, 2008; Barnes & Boutwell, 2012).

Similarly, although our genetic background orients us toward particular behaviors, those behaviors will not necessarily occur in the absence of an appropriate environment. People with similar genetic backgrounds (such as identical twins) may behave in very different ways, and people with highly dissimilar genetic backgrounds

maturation
the predetermined unfolding of genetic information.

can sometimes behave quite similarly (Kato & Pedersen, 2005; Segal et al., 2015; Sudharsanan, Behrman, & Kohler, 2016).

In sum, the nature–nurture question is challenging. Ultimately, we should consider the two sides of the issue as ends of a continuum, with particular behaviors falling somewhere between the ends. The same can be said of the other controversies that we have considered. For instance, continuous versus discontinuous development is not an either/or proposition; some forms of development fall toward the continuous end of the continuum, while others lie closer to the discontinuous end. In short, few statements about development involve either/or absolutes (Rutter, 2006; Deater-Deckard & Cahill, 2007).

Module 1.1 Review

LO 1.1   Define the field of lifespan development and describe what it encompasses.

Lifespan development, a scientific approach to understanding human growth and change throughout life, encompasses physical, cognitive, social, and personality development.

LO 1.2   Describe the areas that lifespan development specialists cover.

Developmentalists focus on physical development, cognitive development, and personality and social development. In addition to choosing to specialize in a particular topical area, developmentalists also typically look at a particular age range.

LO 1.3   Describe some of the basic influences on human development.

Membership in a cohort, based on age and place of birth, subjects people to influences based on historical events

(history-graded influences). People are also subject to age-graded influences, sociocultural-graded influences, and non-normative life events. Culture and ethnicity also play an important role in development—both broad culture and aspects of culture, such as race, ethnicity, and socioeconomic status.

LO 1.4   Summarize four key issues in the field of lifespan development.

Four important issues in lifespan development are continuity versus discontinuity in development, the importance of critical periods, whether to focus on certain periods or on the entire life span, and the nature–nurture controversy.

Journal Writing Prompt

Applying Lifespan Development: What are some examples of the ways culture (either broad culture or aspects of culture) affects human development?

MODULE 1.2

THEORETICAL PERSPECTIVES ON LIFESPAN DEVELOPMENT

Until the 17th century in Europe, there was no concept of "childhood." Instead, children were simply thought of as miniature adults. They were assumed to be subject to the same needs and desires as adults, to have the same vices and virtues as adults, and to warrant no more privileges than adults. They were dressed the same as adults, and their work hours were the same as those of adults. Children also received the same punishments for misdeeds. If they stole, they were hanged; if they did well, they could achieve prosperity, at least so far as their station in life or social class would allow.

This view of childhood seems wrong-headed now, but at the time it was what passed for lifespan development. From this perspective, there were no differences due to age; except for size, people were assumed to be virtually unchanging, at least on a psychological level, throughout most of the life span (Ariès, 1962; Acocella, 2003; Hutton, 2004; Wines, 2006).

Although, looking back over several centuries, it is easy to reject the medieval view of childhood, it is less clear how to formulate a contemporary substitute.

Should our view of development focus on the biological aspects of change, growth, and stability over the life span? The cognitive or social aspects? Or some other factors?

People who study lifespan development approach the field from a number of different perspectives. Each general perspective encompasses one or more *theories*—broad, organized explanations and predictions concerning phenomena of interest. A theory provides a framework for understanding the relationships among a seemingly unorganized set of facts or principles.

We all develop theories about development, based on our experience, folklore, and stories in the media. However, theories in lifespan development are different. Whereas our own personal theories are built on unverified observations that are developed haphazardly, developmentalists' theories are more formal, based on a systematic integration of prior findings and theorizing. These theories allow developmentalists to summarize and organize prior observations, and they also permit them to move beyond existing observations to draw deductions that may not be immediately apparent. In addition, these theories are then subject to rigorous testing in the form of research. By contrast, the developmental theories of individuals are not subject to such testing and may never be questioned at all (Thomas, 2001).

We will consider six major theoretical perspectives used in lifespan development: the psychodynamic, behavioral, cognitive, humanistic, contextual, and evolutionary perspectives. Each emphasizes somewhat different aspects of development and steers developmentalists in particular directions. Furthermore, each perspective continues to evolve and change, as befits a growing and dynamic discipline.

The Psychodynamic Perspective: Focusing on the Inner Person

LO 1.5 Describe how the psychodynamic perspective explains lifespan development.

psychodynamic perspective
the approach stating that behavior is motivated by inner forces, memories, and conflicts that are generally beyond people's awareness and control.

When Marisol was 6 months old, she was involved in a bloody automobile accident—or so her parents tell her, since she has no conscious recollection of it. Now, however, at age 24, she is having difficulty maintaining relationships, and her therapist is seeking to determine whether her current problems are a result of the earlier accident.

Looking for such a link might seem a bit far-fetched, but to proponents of the **psychodynamic perspective**, it is not so improbable. Advocates of the psychodynamic perspective believe that much of behavior is motivated by inner forces, memories, and conflicts of which a person has little awareness or control. The inner forces, which may stem from one's childhood, continually influence behavior throughout the life span.

psychoanalytic theory
the theory proposed by Sigmund Freud that suggests that unconscious forces act to determine personality and behavior.

FREUD'S PSYCHOANALYTIC THEORY. The psychodynamic perspective is most closely associated with Sigmund Freud. Freud, who lived from 1856 to 1939, was a Viennese physician whose revolutionary ideas ultimately had a profound effect not only on the fields of psychology and psychiatry but also on Western thought in general (Greenberg, 2012; Roth, 2016).

Freud's **psychoanalytic theory** suggests that unconscious forces act to determine personality and behavior. To Freud, the *unconscious* is a part of the personality about which a person is unaware. It contains infantile wishes, desires, demands, and needs that, because of their disturbing nature, are hidden from conscious awareness. Freud suggested that the unconscious is responsible for a good part of our everyday behavior.

According to Freud, everyone's personality has three aspects: id, ego, and superego. The *id* is the raw, unorganized, inborn part of personality that is present at birth. It represents primitive drives related to hunger, sex, aggression, and irrational impulses.

The *ego* is the part of personality that is rational and reasonable. The ego acts as a buffer between the real world outside of us and the primitive id. Finally, the *superego*

Sigmund Freud.

Table 1-2 Freud's and Erikson's Theories

Approximate Age	Freud's Stages of Psychosexual Development	Major Characteristics of Freud's Stages	Erikson's Stages of Psychosocial Development	Positive and Negative Outcomes of Erikson's Stages
Birth to 12–18 months	Oral	Interest in oral gratification from sucking, eating, mouthing, biting	Trust vs. mistrust	*Positive:* Feelings of trust from environmental support *Negative:* Fear and concern regarding others
12–18 months to 3 years	Anal	Gratification from expelling and withholding feces; coming to terms with society's controls relating to toilet training	Autonomy vs. shame and doubt	*Positive:* Self-sufficiency if exploration is encouraged *Negative:* Doubts about self, lack of independence
3 to 5–6 years	Phallic	Interest in the genitals; coming to terms with Oedipal conflict, leading to identification with same-sex parent	Initiative vs. guilt	*Positive:* Discovery of ways to initiate actions *Negative:* Guilt from actions and thoughts
5–6 years to adolescence	Latency	Sexual concerns largely unimportant	Industry vs. inferiority	*Positive:* Development of sense of competence *Negative:* Feelings of inferiority, no sense of mastery
Adolescence to adulthood (Freud); Adolescence (Erikson)	Genital	Reemergence of sexual interests and establishment of mature sexual relationships	Identity vs. role diffusion	*Positive:* Awareness of uniqueness of self, knowledge of role to be followed *Negative:* Inability to identify appropriate roles in life
Early adulthood (Erikson)			Intimacy vs. isolation	*Positive:* Development of loving, sexual relationships and close friendships *Negative:* Fear of relationships with others
Middle adulthood (Erikson)			Generativity vs. stagnation	*Positive:* Sense of contribution to continuity of life *Negative:* Trivialization of one's activities
Late adulthood (Erikson)			Ego-integrity vs. despair	*Positive:* Sense of unity in life's accomplishments *Negative:* Regret over lost opportunities of life

represents a person's conscience, incorporating distinctions between right and wrong. It begins to develop around age 5 or 6 and is learned from an individual's parents, teachers, and other significant figures.

Freud also addressed personality development during childhood. He argued that **psychosexual development** occurs as children pass through a series of stages in which pleasure, or gratification, is focused on a particular biological function and body part. As illustrated in Table 1-2 (which also contains material on Erik Erikson, who we discuss later), he suggested that pleasure shifts from the mouth (the *oral stage*) to the anus (the *anal stage*) and eventually to the genitals (the *phallic stage* and the *genital stage*).

According to Freud, if children are unable to gratify themselves sufficiently during a particular stage, or conversely, if they receive too much gratification, fixation may occur. *Fixation* is behavior reflecting an earlier stage of development due to an unresolved conflict. For instance, fixation at the oral stage might produce an adult who is unusually absorbed in oral activities—eating, talking, or chewing gum.

ERIKSON'S PSYCHOSOCIAL THEORY. Psychoanalyst Erik Erikson, who lived from 1902 to 1994, provided an alternative psychodynamic view in his theory of psychosocial development, emphasizing our social interaction with other people. In Erikson's view, society and culture both challenge and shape us. **Psychosocial development** encompasses changes in our interactions with and understandings of one another as well as in our knowledge and understanding of ourselves as members of society (Erikson, 1963; Malone, et al., 2016; Knight, 2017).

Erikson's theory suggests that developmental change occurs throughout our lives in eight distinct stages (see Table 1-2). The stages emerge in a fixed pattern and are similar for all people. Erikson argued that each stage presents a crisis or conflict that the individual must resolve. Although no crisis is ever fully resolved, making life increasingly

psychosexual development according to Freud, a series of stages that children pass through in which pleasure, or gratification, focuses on a particular biological function and body part.

psychosocial development the approach that encompasses changes in our interactions with and understandings of one another, as well as in our knowledge and understanding of ourselves as members of society.

Erik Erikson.

complicated, the individual must at least address the crisis of each stage sufficiently to deal with demands made during the next stage of development. Unlike Freud, who regarded development as relatively complete by adolescence, Erikson suggested that growth and change continue throughout the life span (de St. Aubin, McAdams, & Kim, 2004).

ASSESSING THE PSYCHODYNAMIC PERSPECTIVE. Freud's insight that unconscious influences affect behavior was a monumental accomplishment, and the fact that it seems at all reasonable to us shows how extensively the idea of the unconscious has pervaded thinking in Western cultures. In fact, work by contemporary researchers studying memory and learning suggests that we unconsciously carry with us memories that have a significant impact on our behavior.

However, many of the basic principles of Freud's psychoanalytic theory have been called into question because they have not been validated by subsequent research. In particular, the notion that childhood stages determine adult personalities has little research support. In addition, because much of Freud's theory was based on a limited population of upper-middle-class Austrians living during a strict, puritanical era, its application to broad, multicultural populations is questionable. Finally, because Freud's theory focuses primarily on male development, it has been criticized as sexist and may be interpreted as devaluing women (Schachter, 2005; Gillham, Law, & Hickey, 2010; O'Neil & Denke, 2016).

Erikson's view that development continues throughout the life span is highly important—and has received considerable support. However, the theory also has its drawbacks. Like Freud's theory, it focuses more on men's than women's development. It is also vague in some respects, making it difficult for researchers to test rigorously. And, as is the case with psychodynamic theories in general, it is difficult to make definitive predictions about a given individual's behavior using the theory. In sum, then, the psychodynamic perspective provides good descriptions of past behavior but imprecise predictions of future behavior (de St. Aubin & McAdams, 2004).

The Behavioral Perspective: Focusing on Observable Behavior

LO 1.6   Describe how the behavioral perspective explains lifespan development.

When Elissa Sheehan was 3, a large brown dog bit her, and she needed dozens of stitches and several operations. From the time she was bitten, she broke into a sweat whenever she saw a dog, and in fact never enjoyed being around any pet.

To a lifespan development specialist using the behavioral perspective, the explanation for Elissa's behavior is straightforward: She has a learned fear of dogs. Rather than looking inside the organism at unconscious processes, the **behavioral perspective** suggests that the keys to understanding development are observable behavior and outside stimuli in the environment. If we know the stimuli, we can predict the behavior. In this respect, the behavioral perspective reflects the view that nurture is more important to development than nature.

behavioral perspective
the approach suggesting that the keys to understanding development are observable behavior and outside stimuli in the environment.

> **From the perspective of *a child-care provider***
>
> How important do you think it is to have an understanding of the behavioral perspective, and how would you apply it to your daily work?

Behavioral theories reject the notion that people universally pass through a series of stages. Instead, people are assumed to be affected by the environmental stimuli to which they happen to be exposed. Developmental patterns, then, are personal, reflecting a particular set of environmental stimuli, and behavior is the result of continuing exposure to specific factors in the environment. Furthermore, developmental change is viewed in quantitative, rather than qualitative, terms. For instance, behavioral theories hold that advances in problem-solving capabilities as children age are largely a result of greater mental *capacities* rather than changes in the *kind* of thinking that children are able to bring to bear on a problem.

John B. Watson.

CLASSICAL CONDITIONING: STIMULUS SUBSTITUTION

> *Give me a dozen healthy infants, well-formed, and my own specified world to bring them up in and I'll guarantee to take any one at random and train him to become any type of specialist I might select—doctor, lawyer, artist, merchant-chief, and yes, even beggar-man and thief, regardless of his talents, penchants, tendencies, abilities.* (Watson, 1925)

With these words, John B. Watson, one of the first American psychologists to advocate a behavioral approach, summed up the behavioral perspective. Watson, who lived from 1878 to 1958, believed strongly that we could gain a full understanding of development by carefully studying the stimuli that composed the environment. In fact, he argued that by effectively controlling a person's environment, it was possible to produce virtually any behavior.

Classical conditioning occurs when an organism learns to respond in a particular way to a neutral stimulus. For instance, if the sound of a bell is paired with the presentation of meat, a dog will learn to react to the bell alone in the same way it reacts to the meat—by salivating and wagging its tail. The behavior is a result of conditioning, a form of learning in which the response associated with one stimulus (food) comes to be connected to another—in this case, the bell.

classical conditioning
a type of learning in which an organism responds in a particular way to a neutral stimulus that normally does not bring about that type of response.

The same process of classical conditioning explains how we learn emotional responses. In the case of dog-bite victim Elissa Sheehan, for instance, Watson would say that one stimulus has been substituted for another: Elissa's unpleasant experience with a particular dog (the initial stimulus) has been transferred to other dogs and to pets in general.

OPERANT CONDITIONING. In addition to classical conditioning, there are other types of learning, especially what behaviorists call operant conditioning. **Operant conditioning** is a form of learning in which a voluntary response is strengthened or weakened by its association with positive or negative consequences. It differs from classical conditioning in that the response being conditioned is voluntary and purposeful rather than automatic (such as salivating). In operant conditioning, formulated and championed by psychologist B. F. Skinner (1904–1990), individuals learn to *operate* on their environments to bring about desired consequences (Skinner, 1975).

operant conditioning
a form of learning in which a voluntary response is strengthened or weakened by its association with positive or negative consequences.

Whether children and adults will seek to repeat a behavior depends on whether it is followed by reinforcement. *Reinforcement* is the process by which a behavior is followed by a stimulus that increases the probability that the behavior will be repeated. Hence, a student is apt to work harder if he or she receives good grades; workers are likely to labor harder if their efforts are tied to pay increases; and people are more apt to buy lottery tickets if their buying habits are reinforced by winning occasionally. In addition, *punishment*, the introduction of an unpleasant or painful stimulus or the removal of a desirable stimulus, will decrease the probability that a preceding behavior will occur in the future.

Behavior that is reinforced, then, is more likely to be repeated, while behavior that receives no reinforcement or is punished is likely to be *extinguished*, in the language of operant conditioning. Principles of operant conditioning are used in **behavior modification**, a formal technique for promoting the frequency of desirable behaviors and decreasing the incidence of unwanted ones. Behavior modification has been used in situations ranging from teaching people with severe developmental disabilities basic language to helping people with self-control problems stick to diets (Wupperman et al., 2012; Wirth, Wabitsch, & Hauner, 2014; Miltenberger, 2016).

behavior modification
a formal technique for promoting the frequency of desirable behaviors and decreasing the incidence of unwanted ones.

SOCIAL-COGNITIVE LEARNING THEORY: LEARNING THROUGH IMITATION.

A 5-year-old boy seriously injures his 22-month-old cousin while imitating a violent wrestling move he had seen on television. Although the baby sustained spinal cord injuries, he improved and was discharged 5 weeks after his hospital admission (Reuters Health eLine, 2002; Ray & Heyes, 2011).

What form of learning is being demonstrated in this picture?

Cause and effect? We can't know for sure, but it certainly seems possible, especially to social-cognitive learning theorists. According to developmental psychologist Albert Bandura and colleagues, a significant amount of learning is explained by **social-cognitive learning theory**, an approach that emphasizes learning by observing the behavior of another person, called a *model* (Bandura, 1994, 2002).

If operant conditioning makes learning a matter of trial and error, social-cognitive learning theory makes learning a product of observation. Social-cognitive learning theory holds that when we see the behavior of a model being rewarded, we are likely to imitate that behavior. For instance, in one classic experiment, children who were afraid of dogs were exposed to a model, nicknamed the "Fearless Peer," who was seen playing happily with a dog (Bandura, Grusec, & Menlove, 1967). After exposure, the children who previously had been afraid were more likely to approach a strange dog than children who had not seen the model.

Bandura suggests that social-cognitive learning proceeds in four steps (Bandura, 1986). First, an observer must pay attention and perceive the most critical features of a model's behavior. Second, the observer must successfully recall the behavior. Third, the observer must reproduce the behavior accurately. Finally, the observer must be motivated to learn and carry out the behavior.

From *a social worker's* perspective

How do the concepts of social learning and modeling relate to the mass media, and how might exposure to mass media influence a child's family life?

social-cognitive learning theory

learning by observing the behavior of another person, called a model.

ASSESSING THE BEHAVIORAL PERSPECTIVE. Research using the behavioral perspective has made significant contributions, ranging from techniques for educating children with severe intellectual disabilities to identifying procedures for curbing aggression. At the same time, some controversies surround the behavioral perspective. For example, although they are part of the same general behavioral perspective, classical and operant conditioning and social learning theory diverge in some basic ways. Both classical and operant conditioning present learning in terms of external stimuli and responses, in which the only important factors are the observable features of the environment. In such an analysis, people and other organisms are like inanimate "black boxes": Nothing that occurs inside the box is understood—nor much cared about, for that matter.

To social learning theorists, such an analysis is an oversimplification. They argue that what makes people different from rats and pigeons is the occurrence of mental activity, in the form of thoughts and expectations. A full understanding of people's development, they maintain, cannot occur without moving beyond external stimuli and responses.

In many ways, social learning theory has come to predominate in recent decades over classical and operant conditioning theories. In fact, another perspective that focuses explicitly on internal mental activity has become enormously influential. This is the cognitive approach, which we consider next.

The Cognitive Perspective: Examining the Roots of Understanding

LO 1.7   Describe how the cognitive perspective explains lifespan development.

When 3-year-old Jake is asked why it sometimes rains, he answers "so the flowers can grow." When his 11-year-old sister Lila is asked the same question, she responds "because of evaporation from the surface of the earth." And when their cousin Ajima, who is studying meteorology in graduate school, considers the same question, her extended answer includes a discussion of cumulonimbus clouds, the Coriolis effect, and synoptic charts.

To a developmental theorist using the cognitive perspective, the difference in the sophistication of the answers is evidence of a different degree of knowledge and understanding, or cognition. The **cognitive perspective** focuses on the processes that allow people to know, understand, and think about the world.

The cognitive perspective emphasizes how people internally represent and think about the world. By using this perspective, developmental researchers hope to understand how children and adults process information and how their ways of thinking and understanding affect their behavior. They also seek to learn how cognitive abilities change as people develop, the degree to which cognitive development represents quantitative and qualitative growth in intellectual abilities, and how different cognitive abilities are related to one another.

cognitive perspective
the approach that focuses on the processes that allow people to know, understand, and think about the world.

PIAGET'S THEORY OF COGNITIVE DEVELOPMENT.   No one has had a greater impact on the study of cognitive development than Jean Piaget (1896–1980), a Swiss psychologist. Piaget proposed that all people pass through a fixed sequence of universal stages of cognitive development—and not only does the *quantity* of information increase in each stage, but the *quality* of knowledge and understanding changes as well. His focus is on the change in cognition that occurs as children move from one stage to the next (Piaget, 1962, 1983).

Broadly speaking, Piaget suggests that human thinking is arranged into *schemes*—organized mental patterns that represent behaviors and actions. In infants, schemes represent concrete behavior—a scheme for sucking, for reaching, and for each separate behavior. In older children, the schemes become more sophisticated and abstract, such as the skills involved in riding a bike or playing an interactive video game. Schemes are like intellectual computer software that directs and determines how data from the world are looked at and dealt with.

Piaget suggests that the growth in children's understanding of the world can be explained by two basic principles: assimilation and accommodation. *Assimilation* is the process by which people understand a new experience in terms of their current stage of cognitive development and existing ways of thinking. In contrast, *accommodation* refers to changes in existing ways of thinking in response to encounters with new stimuli or events. Assimilation and accommodation work in tandem to bring about cognitive development.

Assessing Piaget's Theory.   Piaget has profoundly influenced our understanding of cognitive development and is one of the towering figures in lifespan development. He provided masterful descriptions of how intellectual growth proceeds during childhood—descriptions that have stood the test of literally thousands of investigations. Broadly, then, Piaget's broad view of the sequence of cognitive development is accurate. However, the specifics of the theory have been questioned. For instance, some cognitive skills clearly emerge earlier than Piaget suggested. Furthermore, the universality of Piaget's stages has been disputed. Growing evidence suggests that particular cognitive skills emerge according to a different timetable in non-Western cultures. And in every culture, some people never seem to reach Piaget's highest level of cognitive sophistication: formal, logical thought (Genovese, 2006; De Jesus-Zayas, Buigas, & Denney, 2012; Siegler, 2016).

Ultimately, the greatest criticism is that cognitive development is not necessarily as discontinuous as Piaget's stage theory suggests. Many developmental researchers argue that growth is considerably more continuous. These critics have suggested an alternative perspective, known as the information processing approach, that focuses on the processes that underlie learning, memory, and thinking throughout the life span.

INFORMATION PROCESSING APPROACHES.   Information processing approaches have become an important alternative to Piagetian approaches. **Information processing approaches** to cognitive development seek to identify the ways individuals take in, use, and store information.

Information processing approaches grew out of developments in computers. They assume that even complex behavior such as learning, remembering, categorizing, and thinking can be broken down into a series of individual, specific steps. They contend that children, like computers, have limited capacity for processing information. As children develop, though, they employ increasingly sophisticated strategies that allow them to process information more efficiently.

information processing approaches
models that seek to identify the ways individuals take in, use, and store information.

In stark contrast to Piaget's view, information processing approaches assume that development is marked more by quantitative advances than qualitative ones. Our capacity to handle information changes with age, as does our processing speed and efficiency. Furthermore, information processing approaches suggest that as we age, we are better able to control the nature of processing and the strategies we choose to process information.

An information processing approach that builds on Piaget's research is known as neo-Piagetian theory. In contrast to Piaget's original work, which viewed cognition as a single system of increasingly sophisticated general cognitive abilities, *neo-Piagetian theory* considers cognition as being made up of different types of individual skills. Using the terminology of information processing approaches, neo-Piagetian theory suggests that cognitive development proceeds quickly in certain areas and more slowly in others. For example, reading ability and the skills needed to recall stories may progress sooner than the sorts of abstract computational abilities used in algebra or trigonometry. Furthermore, neo-Piagetian theorists believe that experience plays a greater role in advancing cognitive development than traditional Piagetian approaches claim (Case, Demetriou, & Platsidou, 2001; Loewen, 2006; Barrouillet & Gaillard, 2011).

Assessing Information Processing Approaches.   Information processing approaches have become a central part of our understanding of development, but they do not offer a complete explanation for behavior. For example, they have paid little attention to behavior such as creativity, in which the most profound ideas often are developed in a seemingly nonlogical, nonlinear manner. In addition, they do not take into account the social context in which development takes place—and theories that do this have become increasingly popular.

cognitive neuroscience approaches

approaches that examine cognitive development through the lens of brain processes.

COGNITIVE NEUROSCIENCE APPROACHES.   Among the most recent additions to the array of approaches taken by lifespan developmentalists, **cognitive neuroscience approaches** look at cognitive development at the level of brain processes. Like other cognitive perspectives, cognitive neuroscience approaches consider internal mental processes, but they focus specifically on the neurological activity that underlies thinking, problem solving, and other cognitive behavior.

Cognitive neuroscientists seek to identify actual locations and functions within the brain that are related to different types of cognitive activity. For example, using sophisticated brain scanning techniques, cognitive neuroscientists have demonstrated that thinking about the meaning of a word activates different areas of the brain than thinking about how the word sounds when spoken.

Cognitive neuroscientists are also providing clues to the cause of *autism spectrum disorder*, a major developmental disability that can produce profound language deficits and self-injurious behavior in young children. For example, neuroscientists have found that the brains of children with the disorder show explosive, dramatic growth in the first year of life, making their heads significantly larger than those of children without the disorder (see Figure 1-1). By identifying children with the disorder very early in their lives, health-care practitioners can provide crucial early intervention (Lewis & Elman, 2008; Howard et al., 2014; Grant, 2017).

Cognitive neuroscience approaches are also on the forefront of cutting-edge research that has identified genes associated with disorders ranging from physical problems such as breast cancer to psychological disorders such as schizophrenia. Identifying the genes that make one vulnerable to such disorders is the first step in genetic engineering in which gene therapy can reduce severity or even prevent the disorder from occurring (Strobel et al., 2007; Ranganath, Minzenberg, & Ragland, 2008; Rodnitzky, 2012). (Also see the *Neuroscience and Development* box on page 20.)

Assessing Cognitive Neuroscience Approaches.   Cognitive neuroscience approaches represent a new frontier in child and adolescent development. Using sophisticated measurement techniques that many of them developed only in the last few years, cognitive neuroscientists are able to peer into the inner functioning of the brain. Advances in our understanding of genetics also have opened a new window into both normal and abnormal development and suggested a variety of treatments for abnormalities.

Figure 1-1 The Autistic Brain

Researchers have found abnormalities in the temporal lobe of the brain in some children diagnosed with autism spectrum disorder.

(**Source:** Boddaert, N. et al. [2009]. "MRI Findings in 77 Children with Non-Syndromic Autistic Disorder", *PLoS ONE*. 2009; 4[2]: e4415.).

Critics of the cognitive neuroscience approach have suggested that it sometimes provides a better *description* than *explanation* of developmental phenomena. For instance, finding that children with autism have larger brains than those without the disorder does not explain why their brains became larger—that's a question that remains to be answered. Still, such work not only offers important clues to appropriate treatments but, ultimately, can also lead to a full understanding of a range of developmental phenomena.

The Humanistic Perspective: Concentrating on the Unique Qualities of Human Beings

LO 1.8   Describe how the humanistic perspective explains lifespan development.

The unique qualities of humans are the central focus of the humanistic perspective, the fourth of the major theories used by lifespan developmentalists. Rejecting the notion that our behavior is largely determined by unconscious processes, by learning from our environment, or by rational cognitive processing, the **humanistic perspective** contends that people have a natural capacity to make decisions about their lives and to control their behavior. According to this approach, each individual has the ability and motivation to reach more advanced levels of maturity, and people naturally seek to reach their full potential. The humanistic perspective emphasizes *free will*, the ability of humans to make choices and come to decisions about their lives instead of relying on societal standards.

Carl Rogers, one of the major proponents of the humanistic perspective, suggests that all people have a need for positive regard that results from an underlying wish to be loved and respected. Because positive regard comes from other people, we become dependent on them. Consequently, our view of ourselves and our self-worth is a reflection of how we think others view us (Rogers, 1971; Motschnig & Nykl, 2003; Malchiodi, 2012). Rogers, along with another key figure in the humanistic perspective, Abraham Maslow, suggests that self-actualization is a primary goal in life. *Self-actualization* is a state of self-fulfillment in which people achieve their highest potential in their own unique way (Maslow, 1970; Sheldon, Joiner, & Pettit, 2003; Machiodi, 2012).

humanistic perspective
the theory contending that people have a natural capacity to make decisions about their lives and control their behavior.

Neuroscience and Development

The Essential Principles of Neuroscience

It is quiet in the computer lab as three students download assignments in preparation for upcoming midterm exams. Jonathan, a business major, reviews an article on how advertising influences buying behavior; Christina, a music and special education major, reads about how music helps motor control in children with cerebral palsy; and Marisha, a criminal justice major, takes notes on an article about variables that influence early release from prison. None of these students is enrolled in a bioscience program, yet they all have one thing in common as they prepare for their tests: neuroscience

Contemporary neuroscience and its sub-areas addresses an array of relevant problems with methods and insights from brain research and encourages translation of this research to the application of new scientific knowledge to every facet of the human condition. In order to address awareness of our increasing understanding of neuroscience, the Society for Neuroscience (SfN) has spearheaded an effort in which hundreds of neuroscientists and educators across the United States developed eight concepts within four overarching concepts that contain fundamental principles (named *Neuroscience Core Concepts*) they believe everyone should know about the brain and the nervous system.

Answer "true" or "false" to the statements below to learn how much you know about the brain and its workings.

True or False?

1. The most complex organ in the body is the brain.
2. There are 100 billion neurons in the brain.
3. All body systems are influenced by the nervous system.
4. Communication between neurons occurs using both electrical and chemical signaling.
5. Every thought, perception, and behavior is the result of combinations of signals among neurons.
6. The foundation of the nervous system is based on circuits that are determined by genetics.
7. The nervous system is changed by the experiences a person has.
8. Challenging the brain with mental and physical activity maintains its structure and function.
9. Some neurons continue to be created throughout the life span.
10. Intelligence is the outcome of the brain's reasoning, planning, and solving problems.
11. The brain allows us to communicate using language.
12. The brain creates curiosity.

For more information, go to the SfN Brain Facts website (http://www.brainfacts.org/).

Source: Society for Neuroscience (SfN) (2015). *Brain Facts*. Washington, DC: SfN.

Answers: All of these statements are true. Score one point for each correct answer.

ASSESSING THE HUMANISTIC PERSPECTIVE. Despite its emphasis on important and unique human qualities, the humanistic perspective has not had a major impact on the field of lifespan development. Its lack of influence is primarily due to its inability to identify any sort of broad developmental change that is the result of increasing age or experience. Still, some of the concepts drawn from the humanistic perspective, such as self-actualization, have helped describe important aspects of human behavior and are widely discussed in areas ranging from health care to business (Zalenski & Raspa, 2006; Elkins, 2009; Beitel et al., 2014).

The Contextual Perspective: Taking a Broad Approach to Development

LO 1.9   Describe how the contextual perspective explains lifespan development.

Although lifespan developmentalists often consider development in terms of physical, cognitive, personality, and social factors separately, this categorization has one serious drawback: In the real world, none of these broad influences occurs in isolation from any other. Instead, the different types of influence interact constantly.

contextual perspective
the theory that considers the relationship between individuals and their physical, cognitive, personality, and social worlds.

The **contextual perspective** considers the relationship between individuals and their physical, cognitive, personality, and social worlds. It suggests that a person's unique development cannot be properly viewed without seeing how that person is enmeshed within a rich social and cultural context. We'll consider two major theories that fall under this category, Bronfenbrenner's bioecological approach and Vygotsky's sociocultural theory.

THE BIOECOLOGICAL APPROACH TO DEVELOPMENT. In acknowledging the problem with traditional approaches to lifespan development, psychologist Urie Bronfenbrenner (1989, 2000, 2002) has proposed an alternative perspective, called the bioecological approach. The **bioecological approach** suggests that five levels of the environment simultaneously influence individuals. Bronfenbrenner suggests that we cannot fully understand development without considering how a person is influenced by each of these levels (illustrated in Figure 1-2).

bioecological perspective
the perspective suggesting that different levels of the environment simultaneously influence individuals.

- The *microsystem* is the everyday, immediate environment in which children lead their daily lives. Homes, caregivers, friends, and teachers all are influences that are part of the microsystem, but the child is not just a passive recipient. Instead, children actively help construct the microsystem, shaping their immediate world. The microsystem is the level at which most traditional work in child development has been directed.

- The *mesosystem* connects the various aspects of the microsystem. The mesosystem binds children to parents, students to teachers, employees to bosses, and friends to friends. It acknowledges the direct and indirect influences that bind us to one another, such as those that affect a mother or father who has a bad day at the office and then is short-tempered with her or his son or daughter at home.

- The *exosystem* represents broader influences, encompassing societal institutions such as local government, the community, schools, places of worship, and the local media. Each of these institutions can have an immediate, and major, impact on personal development, and each affects how the microsystem and mesosystem operate. For example, the quality of a school will affect a child's cognitive development and potentially can have long-term consequences.

Figure 1-2 Bronfenbrenner's Approach to Development

Urie Bronfenbrenner's bioecological approach to development offers five levels of the environment that simultaneously influence individuals: the macrosystem, exosystem, mesosystem, microsystem, and chronosystem.

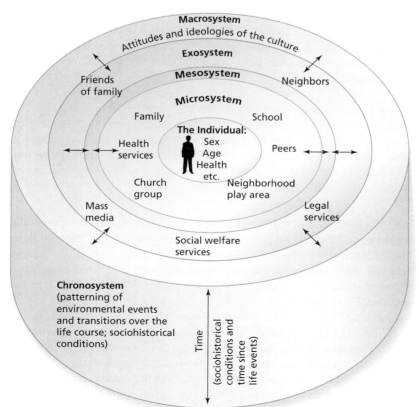

- The *macrosystem* represents the larger cultural influences on an individual, including society in general, types of governments, religious and political value systems, and other broad, encompassing factors. For example, the value a culture places on education affect the values of the people who live in that culture. Children are both part of a broader culture (such as Western culture) and members of one or more subcultures (for instance, Mexican American subculture).

- Finally, the *chronosystem* underlies each of the previous systems. It involves the way the passage of time, including historical events (such as the terrorist attacks in September 2001) and more gradual historical changes (such as changes in the number of women who work outside of the home), affect children's development.

The bioecological approach emphasizes the *interconnectedness of the influences on development*. Because the various levels are related to one another, a change in one part of the system affects other parts of the system. For instance, a parent's loss of a job (involving the mesosystem) has an impact on a child's microsystem.

Conversely, changes on one environmental level may make little difference if other levels are not also changed. For instance, improving the school environment may have a negligible effect on academic performance if children receive little support for academic success at home. Similarly, the influences among family members are multidirectional. Parents don't just influence their child's behavior—the child also influences the parents' behavior.

Finally, the bioecological approach stresses the importance of broad cultural factors that affect development. Researchers in lifespan development increasingly look at how membership in cultural and subcultural groups influences behavior.

Consider, for instance, whether you agree that children should be taught that their classmates' assistance is essential to getting good grades in school, or that they should plan to continue their fathers' businesses, or that they should take their parents' advice in choosing a career. If you have been raised in the most widespread North American culture, you would likely disagree with all three statements, since they violate the premises of *individualism*, the dominant Western philosophy that emphasizes personal identity, uniqueness, freedom, and the worth of the individual.

However, if you were raised in a traditional Asian culture, your agreement with the three statements would be considerably more likely because the statements reflect the value orientation known as *collectivism*—the notion that the well-being of the group is more important than that of the individual. People raised in collectivistic cultures tend to emphasize the welfare of the groups to which they belong, sometimes even at the expense of their own personal well-being (Yu & Stiffman, 2007; Cheung et al., 2016; Sparrow, 2016).

Assessing the Bioecological Approach. Although Bronfenbrenner regards biological influences as an important component of the bioecological approach, ecological influences are central to the theory. In fact, some critics argue that the perspective pays insufficient attention to biological factors. Still, the bioecological approach is important because it suggests the multiple levels at which the environment affects children's development.

sociocultural theory
the approach that emphasizes how cognitive development proceeds as a result of social interactions between members of a culture.

VYGOTSKY'S SOCIOCULTURAL THEORY. To Russian developmentalist Lev Semenovich Vygotsky, a full understanding of development was impossible without taking into account the culture in which people develop. Vygotsky's **sociocultural theory** emphasizes how cognitive development proceeds as a result of social interactions between members of a culture (Vygotsky, 1926/1997; Göncü & Gauvain, 2012; Fleer, Gonzalez, & Veresov, 2017).

Vygotsky, who lived a brief life from 1896 to 1934, argued that children's understanding of the world is acquired through their problem-solving interactions with adults and other children. As children play and cooperate with others, they learn what is important in their society and, at the same time, advance cognitively in their understanding of the world. Consequently, to understand the course of development, we must consider what is meaningful to members of a given culture.

More than most other theories, sociocultural theory emphasizes that development is a *reciprocal transaction* between the people in a child's environment and the child. Vygotsky believed that people and settings influence the child, who in turn influences the people and settings. This pattern continues in an endless loop, with children being both recipients of socialization influences and sources of influence. For example, a child raised with his or her extended family nearby will grow up with a different sense of family life than a child whose relatives live a considerable distance away. Those relatives, too, are affected by that situation and that child, depending on how close and frequent their contact is with the child.

Theorists who built on Vygotsky's work have used the example of *scaffolds*, the temporary platforms used by construction workers when building a structure, to describe how children learn. Scaffolding is the temporary support that teachers, parents, and others provide children as they are learning a task. As children become increasingly competent and master a task, the scaffolding can be withdrawn, allowing children to carry out the task on their own (Lowe et al., 2013; Peralta et al., 2013; Dahl et al., 2017).

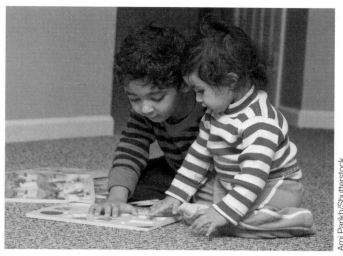

According to Vygotsky, children can develop cognitively in their understanding of the world, and learn what is important in society, through play and cooperation with others.

Assessing Vygotsky's Theory. Sociocultural theory has become increasingly influential, despite Vygotsky's death more than eight decades ago. The reason is the growing acknowledgment of the central importance of cultural factors in development. Children do not develop in a cultural vacuum. Instead, their attention is directed by society to certain areas, and as a consequence, they develop particular kinds of skills that are an outcome of their cultural environment. Vygotsky was one of the first developmentalists to recognize and acknowledge the importance of culture, and—as today's society becomes increasingly multicultural—sociocultural theory is helping us to understand the rich and varied influences that shape development (Rogan, 2007; Frie, 2014; van der Veer & Yasnitsky, 2016).

Sociocultural theory is not without its critics, however. Some suggest that Vygotsky's strong emphasis on the role of culture and social experience led him to ignore the effects of biological factors on development. In addition, his perspective seems to minimize the role that individuals play in shaping their environment.

Evolutionary Perspective: Our Ancestors' Contributions to Behavior

LO 1.10 Describe how the evolutionary perspective explains lifespan development.

One increasingly influential approach is the evolutionary perspective, the sixth and final developmental perspective that we will consider. The **evolutionary perspective** seeks to identify behavior that is the result of our genetic inheritance from our ancestors (Buss & Reeve, 2003; Bjorklund & Ellis, 2005; Goetz & Shackelford, 2006; Tomasello, 2011).

Evolutionary approaches have grown out of the groundbreaking work of Charles Darwin. In 1859, Darwin argued in his book *On the Origin of Species* that a process of natural selection creates traits in a species that are adaptive to its environment. Using Darwin's arguments, evolutionary approaches contend that our genetic inheritance determines not only such physical traits as skin and eye color, but certain personality traits and social behaviors as well. For instance, some evolutionary developmentalists suggest that behaviors such as shyness and jealousy are produced in part by genetic causes, presumably because they helped increase the survival rates of humans' ancient relatives (Easton, Schipper, & Shackelford, 2007; Buss, 2012; Geary & Berch, 2016).

The evolutionary perspective draws heavily on the field of *ethology*, which examines the ways in which our biological makeup influences our behavior. A primary proponent of ethology was Konrad Lorenz (1903–1989), who discovered that newborn geese are

evolutionary perspective
the theory that seeks to identify behavior that is a result of our genetic inheritance from our ancestors.

Konrad Lorenz, seen here with geese who from their birth have followed him, considered the ways in which behavior reflects inborn genetic patterns.

genetically preprogrammed to become attached to the first moving object they see after birth. His work, which demonstrated the importance of biological determinants in influencing behavior patterns, ultimately led developmentalists to consider the ways in which human behavior might reflect inborn genetic patterns.

The evolutionary perspective encompasses one of the fastest-growing areas within the field of lifespan development: behavioral genetics. *Behavioral genetics* studies the effects of heredity on behavior. Behavioral geneticists seek to understand how we might inherit certain behavioral traits and how the environment influences whether we actually display such traits. It also considers how genetic factors may produce psychological disorders such as schizophrenia. (Bjorklund & Ellis, 2005; Rembis, 2009; Plomin et al., 2016).

ASSESSING THE EVOLUTIONARY PERSPECTIVE. There is little argument among lifespan developmentalists that Darwin's evolutionary theory provides an accurate description of basic genetic processes, and the evolutionary perspective is increasingly visible in the field of lifespan development. However, applications of the evolutionary perspective have been subjected to considerable criticism.

Some developmentalists are concerned that because of its focus on genetic and biological aspects of behavior, the evolutionary perspective pays insufficient attention to the environmental and social factors involved in producing children's and adults' behavior. Other critics argue that there is no good way to experimentally test theories derived from this approach because humans evolved so long ago. For example, it is one thing to say that jealousy helped individuals to survive more effectively and another thing to prove it. Still, the evolutionary approach has stimulated research on how our biological inheritance influences at least partially our traits and behaviors (Baptista et al., 2008; Del Giudice, 2015; Barbaro et al., 2017).

Why It Is Wrong to Ask "Which Approach Is Right?"

LO 1.11 Discuss the value of applying multiple perspectives to lifespan development.

We have considered the six major perspectives used in lifespan development—psychodynamic, behavioral, cognitive, humanistic, contextual, and evolutionary—summarized in Table 1-3, which applies the theories to the case of a young adult who is overweight. It would be natural to wonder which of the six provides the most accurate account of human development.

For several reasons, this is not an appropriate question. For one thing, each perspective emphasizes different aspects of development. For instance, the psychodynamic approach emphasizes unconscious determinants of behavior, while behavioral perspectives emphasize overt behavior. The cognitive and humanistic perspectives look more at what people think than at what they do. The contextual perspective examines social and cultural influences on development, and the evolutionary perspective focuses on how inherited biological factors underlie development.

Each perspective is based on its own premises and focuses on different aspects of development—the way different maps of the same geographical area focus on different aspects and features of that area. In the same way, the same developmental phenomenon can be looked at from a number of perspectives. In fact, some lifespan developmentalists use an eclectic approach, drawing on several perspectives simultaneously.

Table 1-3 Major Perspectives on Lifespan Development

Perspective	Key Ideas about Human Behavior and Development	Major Proponents	Example
Psychodynamic	Behavior throughout life is motivated by inner, unconscious forces, stemming from childhood, over which we have little control.	Sigmund Freud, Erik Erikson	This view might suggest that a young adult who is overweight has a fixation in the oral stage of development.
Behavioral	Development can be understood through studying observable behavior and environmental stimuli.	John B. Watson, B. F. Skinner, Albert Bandura	In this perspective, a young adult who is overweight might be seen as not being rewarded for good nutritional and exercise habits.
Cognitive	Emphasis on how changes or growth in the ways people know, understand, and think about the world affect behavior.	Jean Piaget	This view might suggest that a young adult who is overweight hasn't learned effective ways to stay at a healthy weight and doesn't value good nutrition.
Humanistic	Behavior is chosen through free will and motivated by our natural capacity to strive to reach our full potential.	Carl Rogers, Abraham Maslow	In this view, a young adult who is overweight may eventually choose to seek an optimal weight as part of an overall pattern of individual growth.
Contextual	Development should be viewed in terms of the interrelationship of a person's physical, cognitive, personality, and social worlds.	Urie Bronfenbrenner, Lev Vygotsky	In this perspective, being overweight is caused by a number of interrelated factors in that person's physical, cognitive, personality, and social worlds.
Evolutionary	Behavior is the result of genetic inheritance from our ancestors; traits and behavior that are adaptive for promoting the survival of our species have been inherited through natural selection.	Influenced by early work of Charles Darwin, Konrad Lorenz	This view might suggest that a young adult might have a genetic tendency toward obesity because extra fat helped his or her ancestors to survive in times of famine.

The various theoretical perspectives provide different ways of looking at development. Considering them together paints a fuller portrait of the many ways humans change and grow over the life span. However, not all theories and claims derived from the various perspectives are accurate. How do we choose among competing explanations? The answer is *research*, which we consider in the final module of this chapter.

Module 1.2 Review

LO 1.5 Describe how the psychodynamic perspective explains lifespan development.

The psychodynamic perspective looks primarily at the influence of internal, unconscious forces on development.

LO 1.6 Describe how the behavioral perspective explains lifespan development.

The behavioral perspective focuses on external, observable behaviors as the key to development.

LO 1.7 Describe how the cognitive perspective explains lifespan development.

The cognitive perspective focuses on the processes that allow people to know, understand, and think about the world.

LO 1.8 Describe how the humanistic perspective explains lifespan development.

The humanistic perspective concentrates on the theory that each individual has the ability and motivation to reach more advanced levels of maturity and that people naturally seek to reach their full potential.

LO 1.9 Describe how the contextual perspective explains lifespan development.

The contextual perspective focuses on the relationship between individuals and the social context in which they lead their lives.

LO 1.10 Describe how the evolutionary perspective explains lifespan development.

The evolutionary perspective seeks to identify behavior that is a result of our genetic inheritance from our ancestors.

LO 1.11 Discuss the value of applying multiple perspectives to lifespan development.

The various theoretical perspectives provide different ways of looking at development. An eclectic approach paints a more complete picture of the ways humans change over the life span.

Journal Writing Prompt

Applying Lifespan Development: What examples of human behavior have you seen that seem to have been inherited from our ancestors because they helped individuals survive and adapt more effectively? Why do you think they are inherited?

MODULE 1.3

RESEARCH METHODS

The Greek historian Herodotus wrote of an experiment conducted by Psamtik, the King of Egypt, in the seventh century B.C. Psamtik was eager to prove a cherished Egyptian belief, that his people were the oldest race on earth. To test this notion, he developed a hypothesis: If a child was never exposed to the language of his elders, he would instinctively adopt the primal language of humanity—the original language of the first people. Psamtik was certain this would be Egyptian.

For his experiment, Psamtik entrusted two Egyptian infants to the care of a herdsman in an isolated area. They were to be well looked after but not allowed to leave their cottage. And they were never to hear anyone speak a single word.

When Herodotus investigated the story, he learned that Psamtik sought to learn what the first word the children would say. Herodotus claims the experiment worked, but not as Psamtik had hoped. One day, when the children were 2 years old, they greeted the herdsman with the word "Becos!" The herdsman didn't know this word but when the children continued to use it, he contacted Psamtik. The king sent for the children who repeated the strange word to him. Psamtik did some research. Becos, it turned out, was "bread" in Phrygian. Psamtik had to conclude the Phrygians had preceded the Egyptians.

scientific method
the process of posing and answering questions using careful, controlled techniques that include systematic, orderly observation and the collection of data.

With the perspective of several thousand years, we can easily see the shortcomings—both scientific and ethical—in Psamtik's approach. Yet his procedure represents an improvement over mere speculation and as such is sometimes seen as the first developmental experiment in recorded history (Hunt, 1993).

Theories and Hypotheses: Posing Developmental Questions

theories
explanations and predictions concerning phenomena of interest, providing a framework for understanding the relationships among an organized set of facts or principles.

LO 1.12 **Describe the role that theories and hypotheses play in the study of development.**

Questions such as those raised by Psamtik drive the study of development. In fact, developmentalists are still studying how children learn language. Others are working on such questions as: What are the effects of malnutrition on later intellectual performance? How do infants form relationships with their parents, and does day care disrupt such relationships? Why are adolescents particularly susceptible to peer pressure? Can mentally challenging activities reduce declines in intellectual abilities related to aging? Do any mental faculties improve with age?

hypothesis
a prediction stated in a way that permits it to be tested.

To answer such questions, developmentalists, like all psychologists and other scientists, rely on the scientific method. The **scientific method** is the process of posing and answering questions using careful, controlled techniques that include systematic, orderly observation and the collection of data. The scientific method involves three major steps: (1) identifying questions of interest, (2) formulating an explanation, and (3) carrying out research that either lends support to the explanation or refutes it (Figure 1-3).

Figure 1-3 The Scientific Method

A cornerstone of research, the scientific method is used by psychologists as well as researchers from all other scientific disciplines.

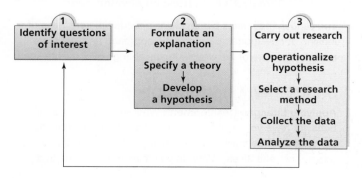

The scientific method involves the formulation of **theories**, the broad explanations and predictions about phenomena of interest that scientists create. For instance, the idea that there is a crucial bonding period between parent and child immediately after birth is a theory.

Developmental researchers use theories to form hypotheses. A **hypothesis** is a prediction stated in a way that permits it to be tested. For instance, someone who subscribes to the general theory that bonding is crucial might derive the hypothesis that effective bonding occurs only if it lasts for a certain length of time.

Choosing a Research Strategy: Answering Questions

LO 1.13 Compare the two major categories of lifespan development research.

Once researchers have formed a hypothesis, they must develop a research strategy for testing its validity. There are two major categories of research: correlational research and experimental research. **Correlational research** seeks to identify whether an association or relationship between two factors exists. As we'll see, correlational research cannot be used to determine whether one factor *causes* changes in the other. For instance, correlational research could tell us if there is an association between the number of minutes a mother and her newborn child are together immediately after birth and the quality of the mother–child relationship when the child reaches age 2. Such correlational research indicates whether the two factors are *associated* or *related* to one another, but not whether the initial contact caused the relationship to develop in a particular way (Schutt, 2001).

In contrast, **experimental research** is designed to discover *causal* relationships between various factors. In experimental research, researchers deliberately introduce a change in a carefully structured situation in order to see the consequences of that change. For instance, a researcher conducting an experiment might vary the number of minutes that mothers and children interact immediately following birth, in an attempt to see whether the amount of bonding time affects the mother–child relationship.

Because experimental research is able to answer questions of causality, it is fundamental to finding answers to various developmental hypotheses. However, some research questions cannot be answered through experiments, for either technical or ethical reasons (e.g., it would be unethical to design an experiment in which a group of infants was offered no chance to bond with a caregiver at all). In fact, a great deal of pioneering developmental research—such as that conducted by Piaget and Vygotsky—employed correlational techniques. Consequently, correlational research remains an important tool in the developmental researcher's toolbox.

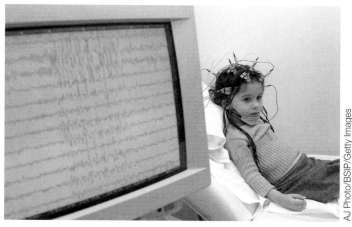

In experimental research, one uses controlled conditions to attempt to discover causal relationships between various factors.

AJ Photo/BSIP/Getty Images

correlational research research that seeks to identify whether an association or relationship between two factors exists.

experimental research research designed to discover causal relationships between various factors.

Correlational Studies

LO 1.14 Identify different types of correlational studies and their relationship to cause and effect.

As we've noted, correlational research examines the relationship between two variables to determine whether they are associated, or *correlated*. For instance, researchers interested in the relationship between televised aggression and subsequent behavior have found that children who watch a good deal of aggression on television—murders, crimes, shootings, and the like—tend to be more aggressive than those who watch only a little. In other words, viewing of aggression and actual aggression are strongly associated, or correlated (Singer & Singer, 2000; Feshbach & Tangney, 2008; Qian, Zhang, & Wang, 2013; Coyne, 2016).

But can we conclude that the viewing of televised aggression *causes* the more aggressive behavior? Not at all. Consider some of the other possibilities: It might be that being aggressive in the first place makes children more likely to choose to watch violent programs. In this case, the aggressive tendency causes the viewing behavior, not the other way around.

Or consider that there may be a *third* factor operating on both the viewing and the aggression. Suppose, for example, that children of lower socioeconomic status are more likely to behave aggressively *and* to watch higher levels of aggressive television than those raised in more affluent settings. In this case, a third

Figure 1-4 Finding a Correlation

Finding a correlation between two factors does not imply that one factor causes the other factor to vary. For instance, suppose a study found that viewing television shows with high levels of aggression is correlated with actual aggression in children. The correlation may reflect at least three possibilities: (a) watching television programs containing high levels of aggression causes aggression in children; (b) children who behave aggressively choose to watch TV programs with high levels of aggression; or (c) some third factor, such as a child's socioeconomic status, leads both to higher aggression and to choosing to watch television programs with high levels of aggression. **THINKING ABOUT THE DATA:** What other factors, besides socioeconomic status, might be plausible third factors? Other than correlational research designs, what other types of research designs could be used to examine the relationship between watching a TV show with high levels of aggression and the actual behavior of children? (Hint: look ahead in the chapter).

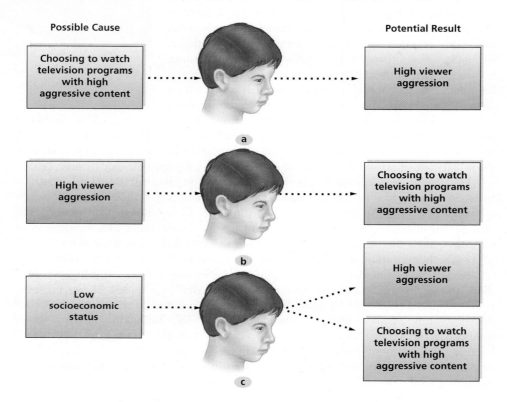

variable—socioeconomic status—causes both the aggressive behavior and the television viewing. (The various possibilities are illustrated in Figure 1-4.)

In short, finding that two variables are correlated proves nothing about causality. Although the variables may be linked causally, this is not necessarily the case. Still, we have learned a lot from correlational studies. For instance, we have learned that the closer the genetic link between two people, the more highly associated is their intelligence. We have learned that the more parents speak to their young children, the more extensive are the children's vocabularies. And we have learned that the better the nutrition that infants receive, the fewer the cognitive and social problems they experience later (Hart, 2004; Colom, Lluis-Font, & Andrès-Pueyo, 2005; Robb, Richert, & Wartella, 2009).

THE CORRELATION COEFFICIENT. The strength and direction of a relationship between two factors is represented by a mathematical score, called a *correlation coefficient*, that ranges from +1.0 to −1.0. A positive correlation indicates that as the value of one factor increases, it can be predicted that the value of the other will also increase. For instance, if we find that the more money people make in their first job after college, the higher their scores on a survey of job satisfaction, and that people who make less money have lower scores when surveyed about their job satisfaction, we have found a positive correlation. (Higher values of the factor "salary" are associated with higher values of the factor "job satisfaction," and lower values of "salary" are associated with lower values of "job satisfaction.") The correlation coefficient, then, would be indicated by a positive number, and the stronger the association between salary and job satisfaction, the closer the number would be to +1.0.

In contrast, a correlation coefficient with a negative value informs us that as the value of one factor increases, the value of the other factor declines. For example, suppose we found that the greater the number of hours adolescents spend texting, the worse their academic performance is. Such a finding would result in a negative correlation, ranging between 0 and −1.0. More texting would be associated with lower performance, and less texting would be associated with better performance. The stronger the association between texting and school performance, the closer the correlation coefficient would be to −1.0 (Figure 1-4).

Finally, it may be that two factors are unrelated to one another. For example, it is unlikely that we would find a correlation between school performance and shoe size. In this case, the lack of a relationship would be indicated by a correlation coefficient close to 0.

It is important to repeat that, even if a correlation coefficient is very strong, there is no way we can know whether one factor *causes* the other factor to vary. It simply means that the two factors are associated with one another in a predictable way.

TYPES OF CORRELATIONAL STUDIES. There are several types of correlational studies. **Naturalistic observation** is the observation of a naturally occurring behavior without intervention in the situation. For instance, an investigator who wishes to learn how often preschool children share toys with one another might observe a classroom over a three-week period, recording how often the preschoolers spontaneously share with one another. The key point about naturalistic observation is that the investigator simply observes the children, without interfering with the situation whatsoever (e.g., Fanger, Frankel, & Hazen, 2012; Nilsen et al., 2014; Snowdon & Burghardt, 2017).

naturalistic observation
a type of correlational study in which some naturally occurring behavior is observed without intervention in the situation.

Though naturalistic observation has the advantage of identifying what children do in their "natural habitat," there is an important drawback to the method: Researchers are unable to exert control over factors of interest. For instance, in some cases researchers might find so few naturally occurring instances of the behavior of interest that they are unable to draw any conclusions at all. In addition, children who know they are being watched may modify their behavior as a result of the observation. Consequently, their behavior may not be representative of how they would behave if they were not being watched.

Increasingly, naturalistic observation employs *ethnography*, a method borrowed from the field of anthropology and used to investigate cultural questions. In ethnography, a researcher's goal is to understand a culture's values and attitudes through careful, extended examination. Typically, researchers using ethnography act as participant observers, living for a period of weeks, months, or even years in another culture. By carefully observing everyday life and conducting in-depth interviews, researchers are able to obtain a deep understanding of the nature of life within another culture (Dyson, 2003).

Case studies involve extensive, in-depth interviews with a particular individual or a small group of individuals. They often are used not just to learn about the individual being interviewed but also to derive broader principles or draw tentative conclusions that might apply to others. For example, case studies have been conducted on children who display unusual genius and on children who have spent their early years in the wild, apparently without human contact. These case studies have provided important information to researchers and have suggested hypotheses for future investigation (Cohen & Cashon, 2003; Wilson, 2003; Ng & Nicholas, 2010; Halkier, 2013).

case study
study that involves extensive, in-depth interviews with a particular individual or a small group of individuals.

Using *diaries*, participants are asked to keep a record of their behavior on a regular basis. For example, a group of adolescents may be asked to record each time they interact with friends for more than 5 minutes, thereby providing a way to track their social behavior.

Surveys represent another sort of correlational research. In **survey research**, a group of people chosen to represent some larger population are asked questions about their attitudes, behavior, or thinking on a given topic. For instance, surveys have been conducted about parents' use of punishment on their children and on attitudes toward breastfeeding. From the responses, inferences are drawn regarding the larger population represented by the individuals being surveyed.

survey research
a type of study where a group of people chosen to represent some larger population are asked questions about their attitudes, behavior, or thinking on a given topic.

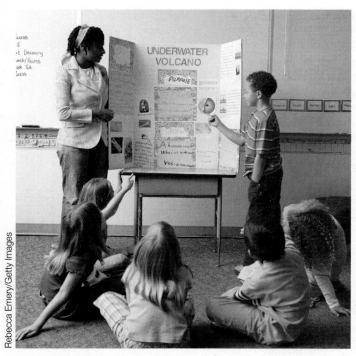

Naturalistic observation is utilized to examine a situation in its natural habitat without interference of any sort. What are some disadvantages of naturalistic observation?

psychophysiological methods

research that focuses on the relationship between physiological processes and behavior.

PSYCHOPHYSIOLOGICAL METHODS. Some developmental researchers, particularly those using a cognitive neuroscience approach, make use of psychophysiological methods. **Psychophysiological methods** focus on the relationship between physiological processes and behavior. For instance, a researcher might examine the relationship between blood flow within the brain and problem-solving capabilities. Similarly, some studies use infants' heart rate as a measure of their interest in stimuli to which they are exposed (Field, Diego, & Hernandez-Reif, 2009; Mazoyer et al., 2009; Jones & Mize, 2016).

Among the most frequently used psychophysiological measures are the following:

- *Electroencephalogram (EEG).* The EEG reports electrical activity within the brain recorded by electrodes placed on the outside of the skull. That brain activity is transformed into a pictorial representation of the brain, permitting the representation of brain wave patterns and diagnosis of disorders such as epilepsy and learning disabilities.

- *Computerized axial tomography (CAT) scan.* In a CAT scan, a computer constructs an image of the brain by combining thousands of individual X-rays taken at slightly different angles. Although it does not show brain activity, it does illuminate the structure of the brain.

- *Functional magnetic resonance imaging (fMRI) scan.* An fMRI provides a detailed, three-dimensional computer-generated image of brain activity by aiming a powerful magnetic field at the brain. It offers one of the best ways of learning about the operation of the brain, down to the level of individual nerves.

Experiments: Determining Cause and Effect

LO 1.15 Explain the main features of an experiment.

experiment

a process in which an investigator, called an experimenter, devises two different experiences for participants and then studies and compares the outcomes.

In an **experiment**, an investigator or experimenter typically devises two different conditions (or *treatments*) and then studies and compares the outcomes of the participants exposed to those two different conditions in order to see how behavior is affected. One group, the *treatment* or *experimental group*, is exposed to the treatment variable being studied; the other, the *control group*, is not.

For instance, suppose you want to see if exposure to movie violence makes viewers more aggressive. You might show a group of adolescents a series of movies with a great deal of violent imagery. You would then measure their subsequent aggression. This group would constitute the treatment group. For the control group, you might show a second group of adolescents movies that contain no aggressive imagery, and measure their subsequent aggression. By comparing the amount of aggression displayed by members of the treatment and control groups, you would be able to determine whether exposure to violent imagery produces aggression in viewers. In fact, this describes an experiment conducted at the University of Louvain in Belgium. Psychologist Jacques-Philippe Leyens and his colleagues found that the level of aggression rose significantly for the adolescents who had seen the movies containing violence (Leyens et al., 1975).

The central feature of this experiment—and all experiments—is the comparison of the consequences of different treatments. The use of both treatment and control groups allows researchers to rule out the possibility that something other than the experimental manipulation produced the results found in the experiment. For instance, if a control group was not used, experimenters could not be certain that some other factor, such as the time of day the movies were shown, the need to sit still during the movie, or even the mere passage of time, produced the changes that were observed. By using a control group, then, experimenters can draw accurate conclusions about causes and effects.

INDEPENDENT AND DEPENDENT VARIABLES. The **independent variable** is the variable that researchers manipulate in the experiment (in our example, it is the type of movie participants saw—violent or nonviolent). In contrast, the **dependent variable** is the variable that researchers measure to see if it changes as a result of the experimental manipulation. In our example, the degree of aggressive behavior shown by the participants after viewing violent or nonviolent films is the dependent variable. (Here is one way to remember the difference: A hypothesis predicts how a dependent variable *depends* on the manipulation of the independent variable.) Every experiment has an independent and dependent variable.

Experimenters must make sure their studies are not influenced by factors other than those they are manipulating. For this reason, they take great care to make sure that the participants in both the treatment and control groups are not aware of the purpose of the experiment (which could affect their responses or behavior) and that the experimenters do not influence who is chosen for the control and treatment groups. The procedure that is used for this is known as random assignment. In *random assignment*, participants are assigned to different experimental groups or "conditions" purely on the basis of chance. This way the laws of statistics ensure that personal characteristics that might affect the outcome of the experiment are divided proportionally among the participants in the different groups, making the groups equivalent. Equivalent groups achieved by random assignment allow an experimenter to draw conclusions with confidence.

Given these advantages, why aren't experiments always used? The answer is that there are some situations that a researcher, no matter how ingenious, simply cannot control. And there are some situations in which control would be unethical, even if it were possible. For instance, no researcher would be able to assign different groups of infants to parents of high and low socioeconomic status in order to learn the effects of such status on subsequent development. In situations in which experiments are logistically or ethically impossible, developmentalists employ correlational research.

Furthermore, keep in mind that a single experiment is insufficient to answer a research question definitively. Before complete confidence can be placed in a conclusion, research must be *replicated*, or repeated, sometimes using other procedures and techniques with other participants. Sometimes developmentalists use a procedure called *meta-analysis*, which permits them to combine the results of many studies into one overall conclusion (Peterson & Brown, 2005; Le et al., 2010).

CHOOSING A RESEARCH SETTING. Deciding *where* to conduct a study may be as important as determining *what* to do. In the Belgian experiment on the influence of exposure to media aggression, the researchers used a real-world setting—a group home for boys who had been convicted of juvenile delinquency. They chose this **sample**, the group of participants selected for the experiment, because it was useful to have adolescents whose normal level of aggression was relatively high and because they could incorporate showing the films into the everyday life of the home with minimal disruption.

Using a real-world setting (as in the aggression experiment) is the hallmark of a field study. A **field study** is a research investigation carried out in a naturally occurring setting. Field studies capture behavior in real-life settings, where research participants may behave more naturally than in a laboratory.

Field studies may be used in both correlational studies and experiments. They typically employ naturalistic observation, the technique in which researchers observe a naturally occurring behavior without intervening or changing the situation. A researcher might examine behavior in a child-care center, view the groupings of adolescents in high school corridors, or observe elderly adults in a senior center.

Because it is often difficult to control the situation and environment enough to run an experiment in a real-world setting, field studies are more typical of correlational designs than experimental designs. Most developmental research experiments are conducted in laboratory settings. A **laboratory study** is a research investigation conducted in a controlled setting explicitly designed to hold events constant. The laboratory may be a room or building designed for research, as in a university psychology department. Researchers can exert enough control in a laboratory study to learn how their treatments affect participants.

independent variable
the variable that researchers manipulate in an experiment.

dependent variable
the variable that researchers measure in an experiment and expect to change as a result of the experimental manipulation.

sample
the group of participants chosen for the experiment.

field study
a research investigation carried out in a naturally occurring setting.

laboratory study
a research investigation conducted in a controlled setting explicitly designed to hold events constant.

Developmental Diversity and Your Life

Choosing Research Participants Who Represent the Diversity of Humanity

In order for lifespan development to represent the full range of the human condition, its research must incorporate individuals of different races, ethnicities, cultures, genders, and other categories. The field of lifespan development is increasingly concerned with issues of human diversity, but its actual progress in this domain has been slow. For instance, although our understanding of the development of non-white children has grown substantially over the past three decades, it is still as not as complete as for nonminority children (McLoyd, 2006; Cabera, 2013).

Even when members of minority groups are included in research, the particular participants may not represent the full range of variation that actually exists within the group. For example, African American infants used in a research

study might well be disproportionally upper and middle class, because parents in higher socioeconomic groups may be more likely to have the time and transportation capabilities to bring their infants into a research center. In contrast, African Americans (as well as members of other groups) who are relatively poor will face more hurdles when it comes to participating in research.

Something is amiss when a science that seeks to explain people's behavior—as is the case with lifespan development—disregards significant groups of individuals. Lifespan developmentalists are aware of this issue, and they have become increasingly sensitive to the importance of using participants who are fully representative of the general population (Fitzgerald, 2006; Nypaver & Shambley-Ebron, 2016).

Theoretical and Applied Research: Complementary Approaches

LO 1.16 Distinguish between theoretical research and applied research.

theoretical research
research designed specifically to test some developmental explanation and expand scientific knowledge.

Developmental researchers typically focus on either theoretical research or applied research. **Theoretical research** is designed specifically to test some developmental explanation and expand scientific knowledge, whereas **applied research** is meant to provide practical solutions to immediate problems. For instance, if we were interested in the processes of cognitive change during childhood, we might carry out a study of how many digits children of various ages can remember after one exposure to multidigit numbers—a theoretical approach. Alternatively, we might focus on how children learn by examining ways in which elementary school instructors can teach children to remember information more easily. Such a study would represent applied research, because the findings are applied to a particular setting and problem.

applied research
research meant to provide practical solutions to immediate problems.

There is not always a clear distinction between theoretical and applied research. For instance, is a study that examines the consequences of ear infections in infancy on later hearing loss theoretical or applied? Because such a study may help illuminate the basic processes involved in hearing, it can be considered theoretical. But if it helps to prevent hearing loss, it may be considered applied research (Lerner, Fisher, & Weinberg, 2000).

In fact, as we discuss in the *From Research to Practice* box, research of both a theoretical and an applied nature has played a significant role in shaping and resolving a variety of public policy questions.

Measuring Developmental Change

LO 1.17 Compare longitudinal research, cross-sectional research, and sequential research.

How people grow and change through their life spans is central to the work of all developmental researchers. Consequently, one of the thorniest research issues they face concerns the measurement of change and differences over age and time. To solve this problem, researchers have developed three major research strategies: longitudinal research, cross-sectional research, and sequential research.

LONGITUDINAL STUDIES: MEASURING INDIVIDUAL CHANGE. If you were interested in learning how a child's moral development changes between the ages of

From Research to Practice

Using Lifespan Developmental Research to Improve Public Policy

Does the Head Start preschool program enhance children's cognitive and social development?

How does the use of social media affect the self-esteem of adolescents?

How are soldiers and their families affected when they return from war?

What are some effective ways to bolster schoolgirls' confidence in their math and science aptitude?

Should children with developmental disabilities be schooled in regular classrooms, or are they better off in special classrooms with other children who are similarly disabled?

How should society best address the opioid epidemic affecting adolescents and adults in the United States?

Each of these questions represents a national policy issue that can be answered only by considering the results of relevant research studies. By conducting controlled studies, developmental researchers have made a number of important contributions affecting education, family life, and health on a national scale. Consider, for instance, the variety of ways that public policy issues have been informed by various types of research findings (Cramer, Song, & Drent, 2016; Crupi & Brondolo, 2017; Kennedy-Hendricks et al., 2017):

■ *Research findings can provide policymakers a means of determining what questions to ask in the first place.* For example, the winding down of the wars in Iraq and Afghanistan has prompted questions about the impact on returning U.S. service members, with research showing that war has a lasting impact not only on them but also on their partners, children, and other family members whose needs should be considered in any interventions supporting the health and adjustment of veterans. Research has also disconfirmed the widespread belief that childhood vaccinations are linked to autism, contributing invaluable evidence to the controversy over the risks and benefits of mandatory child immunization (Price et al., 2010; Lester, et al., 2013; Young, Elliston, & Ruble, 2016).

■ *Research findings and the testimony of researchers are often part of the process by which laws are drafted.* A good deal of legislation has been passed based on findings from developmental researchers. For example, research revealed that children with developmental disabilities benefit from exposure to children without special needs, ultimately leading to passage of national legislation mandating that children with disabilities be placed in regular school classes as often as possible. Research showing that children raised by same-sex couples fare just as well as children raised by a mother and father has undermined an often-used but baseless argument that same-sex marriage is harmful to children (Gartrell & Bos, 2010; Bos et al., 2016).

■ *Policymakers and other professionals use research findings to determine how best to implement programs.* Research has shaped programs designed to reduce the incidence of unsafe sex among teenagers, to increase the level of prenatal care for pregnant mothers, to encourage and support women in the pursuit of math and science studies, and to promote flu shots for older adults. The common thread among such programs is that many of the details of the programs are built on basic research findings.

■ *Research techniques are used to evaluate the effectiveness of existing programs and policies.* Once a public policy has been implemented, it is necessary to determine whether it has been effective and successful in accomplishing its goals. To do this, researchers employ formal evaluation techniques, developed from basic research procedures. For instance, careful studies of DARE, a popular program meant to reduce children's use of drugs, began to find that it was ineffective. Using the research findings of developmentalists, DARE instigated new techniques, and preliminary findings suggest that the revised program is more effective. Other research on intervention strategies to prevent online harassment of adolescents shows that monitoring teens' Internet access is actually many times more effective than attempting to restrict it (Phillips, Gormley, & Anderson, 2016; Barlett, Chamberlin, & Witkower, 2017; Cline & Edwards, 2017).

Shared Writing Prompt

Despite the existence of research data that might inform policy about development, politicians rarely discuss such data in their speeches. Why do you think that is the case?

---

3 and 5, the most direct approach would be to take a group of 3-year-olds and follow them until they were 5, testing them periodically.

Such a strategy illustrates longitudinal research. In **longitudinal research**, the behavior of one or more study participants is measured as they age. Longitudinal research measures change over time. By following many individuals over time, researchers can understand the general course of change across some period of life.

The granddaddy of longitudinal studies, which has become a classic, is a study of gifted children begun by Lewis Terman about 90 years ago. In the study a group

longitudinal research
research in which the behavior of one or more participants in a study is measured as they age.

Cross-sectional research allows researchers to compare representatives of different age groups at the same time.

of 1,500 children with high IQs were tested about every five years. The participants have provided information on everything from intellectual accomplishment to personality and longevity (McCullough, Tsang, & Brion, 2003; Subotnik, 2006; Warne & Liu, 2017).

Longitudinal research has also provided great insight into language development. For instance, by tracing how children's vocabularies increase on a day-by-day basis, researchers have been able to understand the processes that underlie the human ability to become competent in using language (Childers, 2009; Fagan, 2009 Kelloway & Francis, 2013).

Assessing Longitudinal Studies.   Longitudinal studies can provide a wealth of information about change over time. However, they have several drawbacks. For one thing, they require a tremendous investment of time, because researchers must wait for participants to age. Furthermore, participants often drop out over the course of the research, move away, or become ill or even die as the research proceeds.

In addition, participants may become "test-wise" and perform better each time they are assessed as they become more familiar with the procedure. Finally, they may be affected by the repeated presence of an experimenter or observer.

Consequently, despite the benefits of longitudinal research, particularly its ability to look at change within individuals, developmental researchers often turn to other methods in conducting research. The alternative they choose most often is the cross-sectional study.

CROSS-SECTIONAL STUDIES.   Suppose again that you want to consider how children's moral development—their sense of right and wrong—changes from ages 3 to 5. Instead of following the same children over several years, we might look simultaneously at three groups of children: 3-year-olds, 4-year-olds, and 5-year-olds, perhaps presenting each group with the same problem and then seeing how they respond to it and explain their choices.

cross-sectional research
research in which people of different ages are compared at the same point in time.

Such an approach typifies cross-sectional research. In **cross-sectional research**, people of different ages are compared at the same point in time. Cross-sectional studies provide information about differences in development between different age groups.

Assessing Cross-Sectional Studies.   Cross-sectional research takes far less time than longitudinal research: Participants are tested at just one point in time. Terman's study might have been completed decades ago if Terman had simply looked at a group of gifted 15-year-olds, 20-year-olds, 25-year-olds, and so forth, up to 80-year-olds. Because the participants would not be periodically tested, there would be no chance that they would become test-wise, and problems of participant attrition would not occur.

However, cross-sectional research brings its own difficulties. Recall that every person belongs to a particular *cohort* of individuals born at around the same time in the same place. If we find that people of different ages vary along some dimension, the differences may be due to differences in cohort membership, not age *per se*.

Consider a concrete example: If we find in a correlational study that people who are 25 perform better on a test of intelligence than those who are 75, there are several alternative explanations other than that intelligence declines in old age. Instead, the finding may be attributable to cohort differences. The 75-year-olds may have had less formal education than the 15-year-olds because members of the older cohort were less likely to finish high school than members of the younger one. Or perhaps the older group received less adequate nutrition as infants than the younger group. In short, we cannot rule out the possibility that age-related differences in cross-sectional studies are actually cohort differences.

Cross-sectional studies also may suffer from *selective dropout*, in which participants in some age groups are more likely to quit participating in a study than others. For example,

Mat Hayward/Shutterstock

suppose a study of cognitive development in preschoolers includes a lengthy assessment of cognitive abilities. It is possible that young preschoolers would find the task more difficult and demanding than older preschoolers. As a result, the younger children would be more likely to discontinue participation in the study than the older preschoolers.

Finally, cross-sectional studies have an additional, and more basic, disadvantage: They are unable to inform us about changes in individuals or groups. If longitudinal studies are like videos taken of a person at various ages, cross-sectional studies are like snapshots of entirely different groups. Although we can establish differences related to age, we cannot fully determine whether such differences are related to change over time.

SEQUENTIAL STUDIES. Because both longitudinal and cross-sectional studies have drawbacks, researchers have turned to some compromise techniques. Among the most frequently employed are sequential studies, which are essentially a combination of longitudinal and cross-sectional studies.

In **sequential studies**, researchers examine a number of different age groups at several points in time. For instance, an investigator interested in children's moral behavior might begin a sequential study by examining the behavior of three groups of children who are 3 years old, 4 years old, or 5 years old at the time the study begins.

The study continues for the next several years, with each participant tested annually. Thus, the 3-year-olds would be tested at ages 3, 4, and 5; the 4-year-olds at ages 4, 5, and 6, and the 5-year-olds at ages 5, 6, and 7. By combining the advantages of longitudinal and cross-sectional research, this approach permits developmental researchers to tease out the consequences of age *change* versus age *difference*. The major research techniques for studying development are summarized in Figure 1-5.

Ethics and Research

LO 1.18 Describe some ethical issues that affect psychological research.

In the "research study" conducted by Egyptian King Psamtik, two children were removed from their mothers and held in isolation in an effort to learn about the roots of language. If you found yourself thinking this was extraordinarily cruel, you are in good company. Clearly, such an experiment raises blatant ethical concerns, and nothing like it would ever be done today.

In order to help researchers avoid ethical problems, the major organizations of developmentalists, including the Society for Research in Child Development and the American Psychological Association, have developed comprehensive ethical guidelines for researchers. Among the basic principles that must be followed are those involving freedom from harm, informed consent, the use of deception, and maintenance of participants' privacy (American Psychological Association, 2002; Toporek, Kwan, & Williams, 2012; Joireman & Van Lange, 2015):

- **Researchers must protect participants from physical and psychological harm.** Their welfare, interests, and rights come before those of researchers. In research, participants' rights always come first (Sieber, 2000; Fisher, 2004).

- **Researchers must obtain informed consent from participants before their involvement in a study.** If they are over age 7, participants must voluntarily agree to be in a study. For those under 18, their parents or guardians must also provide consent.

The requirement for informed consent raises some difficult issues. Suppose, for instance, researchers want to study the psychological effects of abortion on adolescents. Although they may be able to obtain the consent of an adolescent who has had an abortion, the researchers may need to get her parents' permission as well because she is a minor. But if the adolescent hasn't told her parents about the abortion, the mere request for permission from the parents would violate her privacy—leading to a breach of ethics.

From the perspective of *a health-care provider*

Do you think there are some special circumstances involving adolescents, who are not legally adults, that would justify allowing them to participate in a study without obtaining their parents' permission? What might such circumstances involve?

Figure 1-5 Research Techniques for Studying Development

In a *cross-sectional study*, 3-, 4-, and 5-year-olds are compared at a similar point in time (in the year 2019). In *longitudinal research*, a set of participants who are 3 years old in 2019 are studied when they are 4 years old (in 2020) and when they are 5 years old (in 2021). Finally, a *sequential study* combines cross-sectional and longitudinal techniques; here, a group of 3-year-olds would be compared initially in 2019 with 4- and 5-year-olds but would also be studied one and two years later, when they themselves were 4 and 5 years old. Although the graph does not illustrate this, researchers carrying out this sequential study might also choose to retest the children who were 4 and 5 in 2019 for the next two years. What advantages do the three kinds of studies offer?

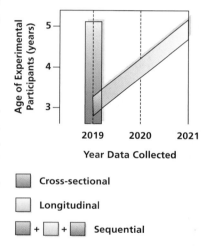

Cross-sectional

Longitudinal

+ + Sequential

sequential studies
research in which researchers examine a number of different age groups over several points in time.

- **The use of deception in research must be justified and cause no harm.** Although deception to disguise the true purpose of an experiment is permissible, any experiment that uses deception must undergo careful scrutiny by an independent panel before it is conducted. Suppose, for example, we want to know the reaction of participants to success and failure. It is ethical to tell participants that they will be playing a game when the true purpose is actually to observe how they respond to doing well or poorly on the task. However, such a procedure is ethical only if it causes no harm to participants, has been approved by a review panel, and ultimately includes a full debriefing, or explanation, for participants when the study is over (Underwood, 2005).

- **Participants' privacy must be maintained.** If participants are videotaped during the course of a study, for example, they must give their permission for the videotapes to be viewed. Furthermore, access to the tapes must be carefully restricted.

Development in Your Life

Thinking Critically About "Expert" Advice

If you immediately comfort crying babies, you'll spoil them.
If you let babies cry without comforting them, they'll be untrusting and clingy as adults.
Spanking is one of the best ways to discipline your child.
Never hit your child.
If a marriage is unhappy, children are better off if their parents divorce than if they stay together.
No matter how difficult a marriage is, parents should avoid divorce for the sake of their children.

There is no lack of advice on the best way to raise a child or, more generally, to lead one's life. From best-sellers such as *Chicken Soup for the Soul: On Being a Parent* to magazine and newspaper columns that provide advice on every imaginable topic, each of us is exposed to tremendous amounts of information.

Yet not all advice is equally valid. The mere fact that something is in print or on television or the Internet does not make it legitimate or accurate. Fortunately, some guidelines can help distinguish when recommendations and suggestions are reasonable and when they are not:

- **Consider the source of the advice.** Information from established, respected organizations such as the American Medical Association, the American Psychological Association, and the American Academy of Pediatrics is likely to be the result of years of study, and its accuracy is probably high. If you don't know the organization, investigate further to find out more about its goals and philosophy.

- **Evaluate the credentials of the person providing advice.** Information coming from established, acknowledged researchers and experts in a field is likely to be more accurate than that coming from a person whose credentials are obscure. Consider where the author is employed and whether he or she has a particular political or personal agenda.

- **Understand the difference between anecdotal evidence and scientific evidence.** Anecdotal evidence is based on one or two instances of a phenomenon, haphazardly discovered or encountered; scientific evidence is based on careful, systematic procedures. If an aunt tells you that all her children slept through the night by 2 months of age and therefore so can your child, that is quite different from reading a report that 75 percent of children sleep through the night by 9 months. Of course, even with such a report, it would be a good idea to find out how large the study was or how this number was arrived at.

- **If advice is based on research findings, there should be a clear, transparent description of the studies on which the conclusion is based.** Who were the participants in the study? What were the methods used? What do the results show? Think critically about the way in which the findings were obtained before accepting them.

- **Do not overlook the cultural context of the information.** Although an assertion may be valid in some contexts, it may not be true in all situations. For example, it is typically assumed that providing infants the freedom to move about and exercise their limbs facilitates their muscular development and mobility. Yet in some cultures, infants spend most of their time closely bound to their mothers—with no apparent long-term damage (Tronick, 1995).

- **Don't assume that because many people believe something, it is necessarily true.** Scientific evaluation has often proved that some of the most basic presumptions about the effectiveness of various techniques are invalid.

In short, the key to evaluating information relating to human development is to maintain a healthy dose of skepticism. No source of information is invariably, unfailingly accurate. By keeping a critical eye on the statements you encounter, you'll be in a better position to determine the very real contributions made by developmentalists to understanding how humans develop over the course of their life spans.

Module 1.3 Review

LO 1.12 Describe the role that theories and hypotheses play in the study of development.

Theories in development are systematically derived explanations of facts or phenomena. Theories suggest hypotheses, which are predictions that can be tested.

LO 1.13 Compare the two major categories of lifespan development research.

Correlational research seeks to identify whether an association or relationship between two factors exists. Experimental research is designed to discover *causal* relationships between various factors.

LO 1.14 Identify different types of correlational studies and their relationship to cause and effect.

Naturalistic observation, case studies, and survey research are types of correlational studies. Some developmental researchers also make use of psychophysiological methods.

LO 1.15 Explain the main features of an experiment.

Experimental research seeks to discover cause-and-effect relationships by the use of a treatment group and a control group. By manipulating the independent variable and observing changes in the dependent variable, researchers find evidence of causal links between variables. Research studies may be conducted in field settings, where participants are subject to natural conditions, or in laboratories, where conditions can be controlled.

LO 1.16 Distinguish between theoretical research and applied research.

Theoretical research is designed specifically to test some developmental explanation and expand scientific knowledge, whereas applied research is meant to provide practical solutions to immediate problems.

LO 1.17 Compare longitudinal research, cross-sectional research, and sequential research.

Researchers measure age-related change through longitudinal studies, cross-sectional studies, and sequential studies.

LO 1.18 Describe some ethical issues that affect psychological research.

Developmental researchers must follow ethical standards for conducting research. Ethical guidelines for researchers cover freedom from harm, informed consent, the use of deception, and preservation of participant privacy.

Journal Writing Prompt

Applying Lifespan Development: Formulate a theory about one aspect of human development and a hypothesis that relates to it.

Epilogue

As we've seen, the scope of lifespan development is broad, touching on a wide range of topics that address how people grow and change through the course of life. We've also found that there are a variety of techniques by which developmentalists seek to answer questions of interest.

Before proceeding to the next chapter, take a few minutes to reconsider the prologue of this chapter—about the case of Louise Brown and Elizabeth Carr, among the first children to be born through in vitro fertilization. Based on what you now know about child development, answer the following questions:

1. What are some of the potential benefits, and the costs, of the type of conception—in vitro fertilization—that was carried out for Louise's and Elizabeth's parents?

2. What are some questions that developmentalists who study either physical, cognitive, or personality and social development might ask about the effects on Louise and Elizabeth of being conceived via in vitro fertilization?

3. The creation of complete human clones—exact genetic replicas of an individual—is still in the realm of science fiction, but the theoretical possibility does raise some important questions. For example, what would be the psychological consequences of being a clone?

4. If clones could actually be produced, how might they help scientists understand the relative impact of heredity and environment on development?

Looking Back

LO 1.1 Define the field of lifespan development and describe what it encompasses.

Lifespan development is a scientific approach to questions about growth, change, and stability in the physical, cognitive, social, and personality characteristics at all ages from conception to death.

LO 1.2 Describe the areas that lifespan development specialists cover.

Some developmentalists focus on physical development, examining the ways in which the body's makeup helps determine behavior. Other developmental specialists examine cognitive development, seeking to understand how growth and change in intellectual capabilities influence a person's behavior. Still other developmental specialists focus on personality and social development. In addition to choosing to specialize in a particular topical area, developmentalists also typically look at a particular age range.

LO 1.3 Describe some of the basic influences on human development.

Each individual is subject to normative history-graded influences, normative age-graded influences, normative sociocultural-graded influences, and non-normative life events. Culture—both broad and narrow—is an important issue in lifespan development. Many aspects of development are influenced not only by broad cultural differences but also by ethnic, racial, and socioeconomic differences within a particular culture.

LO 1.4 Summarize four key issues in the field of lifespan development.

Four key issues in lifespan development are as follows: (1) whether developmental change is continuous or discontinuous; (2) whether development is largely governed by critical periods during which certain influences or experiences must occur for development to be normal; (3) whether to focus on certain particularly important periods in human development or on the entire life span; and (4) the nature–nurture controversy, which focuses on the relative importance of genetic versus environmental influences.

LO 1.5 Describe how the psychodynamic perspective explains lifespan development.

The psychodynamic perspective is exemplified by the psychoanalytic theory of Sigmund Freud and the psychosocial theory of Erik Erikson. Freud focused attention on the unconscious and on stages through which children must pass successfully to avoid harmful fixations. Erikson identified eight distinct stages of development, each characterized by a conflict, or crisis, to work out.

LO 1.6 Describe how the behavioral perspective explains lifespan development.

The behavioral perspective typically concerns stimulus–response learning, exemplified by classical conditioning, the operant conditioning of B. F. Skinner, and Albert Bandura's social-cognitive learning theory.

LO 1.7 Describe how the cognitive perspective explains lifespan development.

Within the cognitive perspective, the most notable theorist is Jean Piaget, who identified developmental stages through which all children are assumed to pass. Each stage involves qualitative differences in thinking. In contrast, information processing approaches attribute cognitive growth to quantitative changes in mental processes and capacities, and cognitive neuroscience approaches focus on biological brain processes.

LO 1.8 Describe how the humanistic perspective explains lifespan development.

The humanistic perspective contends that people have a natural capacity to make decisions about their lives and control their behavior. The humanistic perspective emphasizes free will and the natural desire of humans to reach their full potential.

LO 1.9 Describe how the contextual perspective explains lifespan development.

The contextual perspective considers the relationship between individuals and their physical, cognitive, personality, and social worlds. The bioecological approach stresses the interrelatedness of developmental areas and the importance of broad cultural factors in human development. Lev Vygotsky's sociocultural theory emphasizes the central influence on cognitive development exerted by social interactions between members of a culture.

LO 1.10 Describe how the evolutionary perspective explains lifespan development.

The evolutionary perspective attributes behavior to genetic inheritance from our ancestors, contending that genes determine not only traits such as skin and eye color, but certain personality traits and social behaviors as well.

LO 1.11 Discuss the value of applying multiple perspectives to lifespan development.

The various theoretical perspectives provide different ways of looking at development. An eclectic approach paints a more complete picture of the ways humans change over the life span.

LO 1.12 Describe the role that theories and hypotheses play in the study of development.

Theories are broad explanations of facts or phenomena of interest, based on a systematic integration of prior findings and theories. Hypotheses are theory-based predictions that can be tested. The process of posing and answering questions systematically is called the scientific method.

LO 1.13 Compare the two major categories of lifespan development research.

Researchers test hypotheses by correlational research (to determine whether two factors are associated) and experimental research (to discover cause-and-effect relationships).

LO 1.14 Identify different types of correlational studies and their relationship to cause and effect.

Correlational studies use naturalistic observation, case studies, and survey research to investigate whether certain characteristics of interest are associated with other characteristics. Some developmental researchers also make use of psychophysiological methods. Correlational studies lead to no direct conclusions about cause and effect.

LO 1.15 Explain the main features of an experiment.

Typically, experimental research studies are conducted on participants in a treatment group who receive the experimental treatment and participants in a control group who do not. Following the treatment, differences between the two groups can help the experimenter to determine the effects of the treatment. The independent variable is the variable that researchers manipulate in the experiment, whereas the dependent variable is the variable that researchers measure in an experiment and expect to change as a result of the experimental manipulation. Experiments may be conducted in a laboratory or in a real-world setting.

LO 1.16 Distinguish between theoretical research and applied research.

Theoretical research is designed specifically to test some developmental explanation and expand scientific knowledge, while applied research is meant to provide practical solutions to immediate problems.

LO 1.17 Compare longitudinal research, cross-sectional research, and sequential research.

To measure change across human ages, researchers use longitudinal studies of the same participants over time, cross-sectional studies of different-age participants conducted at one time, and sequential studies of different-age participants at several points in time.

LO 1.18 Describe some ethical issues that affect psychological research.

Ethical issues that affect psychological research include the protection of participants from harm, informed consent of participants, limits on the use of deception, and the maintenance of privacy.

Key Terms and Concepts

lifespan development 4
physical development 4
cognitive development 5
personality development 5
social development 5
cohort 7
continuous change 7
discontinuous change 8
critical period 8
sensitive period 8
maturation 10
psychodynamic perspective 12
psychoanalytic theory 12
psychosexual development 13
psychosocial development 13
behavioral perspective 14

classical conditioning 15
operant conditioning 15
behavior modification 15
social-cognitive learning theory 16
cognitive perspective 17
information processing approaches 17
cognitive neuroscience approaches 18
humanistic perspective 19
contextual perspective 20
bioecological perspective 21
sociocultural theory 22
evolutionary perspective 23
scientific method 26
theories 26
hypothesis 26
correlational research 27

experimental research 27
naturalistic observation 29
case study 29
survey research 29
psychophysiological methods 30
experiment 30
independent variable 31
dependent variable 31
sample 31
field study 31
laboratory study 31
theoretical research 32
applied research 32
longitudinal research 33
cross-sectional research 34
sequential studies 35

Chapter 2
Genetics, Prenatal Development, and Birth

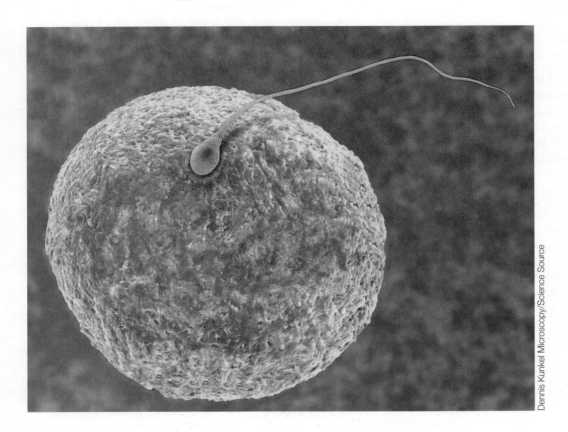

Dennis Kunkel Microscopy/Science Source

∨ Learning Objectives

LO 2.1 Describe how genes and chromosomes provide our basic genetic endowment.

LO 2.2 Compare monozygotic twins with dizygotic twins.

LO 2.3 Describe how the sex of a child is determined.

LO 2.4 Explain the mechanisms by which genes transmit information.

LO 2.5 Describe the field of behavioral genetics.

LO 2.6 Describe the major inherited disorders.

LO 2.7 Describe the role of genetic counselors and differentiate between different forms of prenatal testing.

LO 2.8 Explain how the environment and genetics work together to determine human characteristics.

LO 2.9 Summarize the methods by which researchers study the interaction of genetic and environmental factors in development.

LO 2.10 Examine how genetics and the environment jointly influence physical traits, intelligence, and personality.

LO 2.11 Describe ways in which genes influence the environment.

LO 2.12 Describe the process of fertilization.

LO 2.13 Summarize the three stages of prenatal development.

LO 2.14 Describe major physical and ethical challenges that relate to pregnancy.

LO 2.15 Analyze threats to the fetal environment, and explain what can be done about them.

LO 2.16 Describe the normal process of labor.

LO 2.17 Describe the process of birth and analyze current approaches to childbirth.

LO 2.18 Recognize threats and complications that may accompany childbirth, and explain how they can be addressed.

LO 2.19 Describe the process of cesarean delivery, and explain why its use is increasing.

LO 2.20 Describe infant mortality rates, and explain factors that affect those rates.

Chapter Overview

Module 2.1 Earliest Development and the Foundations of Genetics

Genes and Chromosomes: The Code of Life

Multiple Births: Two—or More—for the Genetic Price of One

Boy or Girl? Establishing the Sex of the Child

The Basics of Genetics: The Mixing and Matching of Traits

The Human Genome and Behavioral Genetics: Cracking the Genetic Code

Inherited and Genetic Disorders: When Development Deviates from the Norm

Genetic Counseling: Predicting the Future from the Genes of the Present

Module 2.2 The Interaction of Heredity and Environment

The Role of the Environment in Determining the Expression of Genes: From Genotypes to Phenotypes

Studying Development: How Much Is Nature, How Much Is Nurture?

From Research to Practice: When Nurture Becomes Nature

Genetics and the Environment: Working Together

Can Genes Influence the Environment?

Module 2.3 Prenatal Growth and Birth

Fertilization: The Moment of Conception

The Stages of the Prenatal Period: The Onset of Development

Neuroscience and Development: Autism and the Toddler Brain

Pregnancy Problems

The Prenatal Environment: Threats to Development

Development in Your Life: Optimizing the Prenatal Environment

Labor: The Process of Birth Begins

Approaches to Childbirth: Where Medicine and Attitudes Meet

Birth Complications

Caesarean Delivery: Intervening in the Process of Birth

Stillbirth and Infant Mortality: The Tragedy of Premature Death

Developmental Diversity and Your Life: Overcoming Racial and Cultural Differences in Infant Mortality

Prologue: Going with the Odds

In every respect, Stephen Monaco seemed to be a healthy and normal 3-year-old. Yet one day, he developed a stomach virus that led to severe brain damage and the terrible diagnosis of a rare disease called isovaleric acidemia (IVA). IVA makes the body unable to metabolize a common amino acid found in protein. Unbeknownst to them, Stephen's parents were carriers of the disease, which struck Stephen without warning. Stephen became permanently disabled.

The case was different when Jana became pregnant again. Her daughter, Caroline, received prenatal testing before birth. Learning that she carried the mutation that led to Stephen's illness, doctors were able to give her medication the day she was born, and immediately put her on a special diet. Although Stephen will never be able to talk, walk, or feed himself, Caroline is an active, normal child. Genetic testing, says Jana, "gave Caroline the future that Stephen didn't get to have." (Kalb, 2006, p. 52; Spinelli, 2015) ∎

Prenatal tests have become increasingly sophisticated.

monkeybusinessimages/Getty Images

Looking Ahead

A hidden genetic disorder robbed Jana and Tom Monaco's first child of a normal, healthy life. Their second child was spared the same fate by advances in genetic testing, which gave the Monacos a chance to intervene before the damage was done. They were able to stop Caroline's inherited disorder from doing the same damage by controlling aspects of her environment.

In this chapter, we'll examine what developmental researchers and other scientists have learned about ways that heredity and the environment work in tandem to create and shape human beings, and how that knowledge is being used to improve people's lives. We begin with the basics of heredity, the genetic transmission of characteristics from biological parents to their children, by examining how we receive our genetic endowment. We'll consider an area of study, behavioral genetics, which specializes in the consequences of heredity on behavior. We'll also discuss what happens when genetic factors cause development to go off track, and how such problems are dealt with through genetic counseling and gene therapy.

But genes are only one part of the story of prenatal development. We'll also consider the ways in which a child's genetic heritage interacts with the environment in which he or she grows up—how one's family, socioeconomic status, and life events can affect a variety of characteristics, including physical traits, intelligence, and even personality.

Finally, we'll focus on the very first stages of development, tracing prenatal growth and birth. We'll review some of the alternatives available to couples who find it difficult to conceive. We'll also talk about the stages of the prenatal period and how the prenatal environment offers both threats to—and the promise of—future growth. We will then discuss the birth process, including some alternatives to the traditional model of birthing that has dominated American life for decades, and we will finish with a discussion of some of the complications that can cloud the birth process.

MODULE 2.1

EARLIEST DEVELOPMENT AND THE FOUNDATIONS OF GENETICS

We humans begin the course of our lives simply. Like individuals from tens of thousands of other species, we start as a single cell, a tiny speck probably weighing no more than one twenty-millionth of an ounce. But, as we'll see in this section, from this humble beginning, in a matter of just several months if all goes well, a living, breathing individual infant is born.

Genes and Chromosomes: The Code of Life

LO 2.1 Describe how genes and chromosomes provide our basic genetic endowment.

The single cell we described above is created when a male reproductive cell, a *sperm*, pushes through the membrane of the *ovum*, the female reproductive cell. These *gametes*, as the male and female reproductive cells are also known, each contain huge amounts of genetic information. About an hour or so after the sperm enters the ovum, the two gametes suddenly fuse, becoming one cell, a **zygote**. The resulting combination of their genetic instructions—over 2 billion chemically coded messages—is

zygote

the new cell formed by the process of fertilization.

sufficient to begin creating a whole person. The blueprints for creating a person are stored and communicated in our **genes**, the basic units of genetic information. The roughly 25,000 human genes are the biological equivalent of "software" that programs the future development of all parts of the body's "hardware."

All genes are composed of specific sequences of **DNA (deoxyribonucleic acid) molecules**. The genes are arranged in specific locations and in a specific order along 46 **chromosomes**, rod-shaped portions of DNA that are organized in 23 pairs. However, sex cells—the ova and the sperm—contain half this number, so that a child's mother and father each provide one of the two chromosomes in each of the 23 pairs. The 46 chromosomes (in 23 pairs) in the new zygote contain the genetic blueprint that will guide cell activity for the rest of the individual's life (Pennisi, 2000; Celera Genomics: International Human Genome Sequencing Consortium, 2001; see Figure 2-1). Through a process called *mitosis*, which accounts for the replication of most types of cells, nearly all the cells of the body will contain the same 46 chromosomes as the zygote.

Specific genes in precise locations on the chain of chromosomes determine the nature and function of every cell in the body. For instance, genes determine which cells will ultimately become part of the heart and which will become part of the muscles of the leg. Genes also establish how different parts of the body will function: how rapidly the heart will beat, or how much strength a muscle will have.

If each parent provides just 23 chromosomes, where does the potential for the vast diversity of human beings come from? The answer resides primarily in the nature of the processes that underlie the cell division of the gametes. When gametes—sperm and ova—are formed in the adult human body in a process called *meiosis*, each gamete receives one of the two chromosomes that make up each of the 23 pairs. Because for each of the 23 pairs it is largely a matter of chance which member of the pair is contributed, there are 2^{23}, or some 8 million, different combinations possible. Furthermore, other processes, such as random transformations of particular genes, add to the variability of the genetic brew. The outcome: tens of *trillions* of possible genetic combinations.

With so many possible genetic mixtures provided by heredity, there is no likelihood that someday you'll bump into a genetic duplicate of yourself—with one exception: an identical twin.

Multiple Births: Two—or More—for the Genetic Price of One

LO 2.2 Compare monozygotic twins with dizygotic twins.

Although it doesn't seem surprising when dogs and cats give birth to several offspring at one time, in humans multiple births are cause for comment. They should be: Less than 3 percent of all pregnancies produce twins, and the odds are even slimmer for three or more children.

Why do multiple births occur? Sometimes a cluster of cells in the ovum splits off within the first 2 weeks after fertilization. The result is two genetically identical zygotes, which, because they come from the same original zygote, are called monozygotic. **Monozygotic twins** are twins who are genetically identical. Any differences in their future development can be attributed only to environmental factors, since genetically they are exactly the same.

There is a second, and actually more common, mechanism that produces multiple births. In these cases, two separate ova are fertilized by two separate sperm at roughly the same time. Twins produced in this fashion are known as **dizygotic twins**. Because they are the result of two separate ovum–sperm combinations, they are no more genetically similar than two siblings born at different times.

Of course, not all multiple births produce only two babies. Triplets, quadruplets, and even higher-order births are produced by either (or both) of the mechanisms that yield twins. Thus, triplets may be some combination of monozygotic, dizygotic, or trizygotic.

Although the chances of having a multiple birth are typically slim, the odds rise considerably when couples use fertility drugs to improve the probability they will conceive a child. For example, 1 in 10 couples using fertility drugs have dizygotic

Figure 2-1 The Contents of a Single Human Cell

At the moment of conception, humans receive about 25,000 genes, contained on 46 chromosomes in 23 pairs.

genes
the basic units of genetic information.

DNA (deoxyribonucleic acid) molecules
the substance that genes are composed of that determines the nature of every cell in the body and how it will function.

chromosomes
rod-shaped portions of DNA that are organized in 23 pairs.

monozygotic twins
twins who are genetically identical.

dizygotic twins
twins who are produced when two separate ova are fertilized by two separate sperm at roughly the same time.

Figure 2-2 Rising Multiples

The number and rate of twin births has risen considerably over the past three decades.

(**Source:** NCHS Data Brief Number 80, January 2012. *Three Decades of Twin Births in the United States, 1980–2009.*)

At the moment of conception, humans receive 23 pairs of chromosomes, half from the mother and half from the father. These chromosomes contain thousands of genes.

twins, compared to an overall figure of 1 in 86 for all Caucasian couples in the United States. Older women, too, are more likely to have multiple births, and multiple births are also more common in some families than in others. The increased use of fertility drugs and rising average age of mothers giving birth has meant that multiple births have increased in the past 25 years (see Figure 2-2; Martin et al., 2005).

There are also racial, ethnic, and national differences in the rate of multiple births, probably due to inherited differences in the likelihood that more than one ovum will be released at a time. One out of 70 African American couples has a dizygotic birth, compared with the 1 out of 86 figure for white American couples. Furthermore, in some areas of central Africa, the rate of dizygotic births is among the highest in the world (Choi, 2017). Mothers carrying multiple children run a higher-than-average risk of premature delivery and birth complications. Consequently, these mothers must be particularly concerned about their prenatal care.

Boy or Girl? Establishing the Sex of the Child

LO 2.3   Describe how the sex of a child is determined.

Recall that there are 23 matched pairs of chromosomes. In 22 of these pairs, each chromosome is similar to the other member of its pair. The one exception is the pair that determines the sex of the child. In females, the 23rd pair consists of two matching, relatively large X-shaped chromosomes, appropriately identified as XX. In males, the members of the pair are dissimilar. One consists of an X-shaped chromosome, but the other is a shorter, smaller Y-shaped chromosome. This pair is identified as XY.

As we discussed earlier, each gamete carries one chromosome from each of the parent's 23 pairs of chromosomes. Since a female's 23rd pair of chromosomes are both Xs, an ovum will always carry an X chromosome, no matter which chromosome of the 23rd pair it gets. A male's 23rd pair is XY, so each sperm could carry either an X or a Y chromosome.

If the sperm contributes an X chromosome when it meets an ovum (which, remember, will always contribute an X chromosome), the child will have an XX pairing on the 23rd chromosome—and will be a female. If the sperm contributes a Y chromosome, the result will be an XY pairing—a male (see Figure 2-3).

It is clear from this process that the father's sperm determines the sex of the child. This fact is leading to the development of techniques that will allow parents to increase the chances of specifying the sex of their child. In one new technique, lasers measure the DNA in sperm. By discarding sperm that harbor the unwanted sex chromosome, the chances of having a child of the desired sex increase dramatically (Van Balen, 2005).

Of course, procedures for choosing a child's sex raise ethical and practical issues. For example, in cultures that value one sex over the other, might there be a kind of sex discrimination prior to birth? Furthermore, a shortage of children of the less-preferred sex might ultimately emerge. Many questions remain, then, before sex selection becomes routine (Bhagat, Laskar, & Sharma, 2012).

The Basics of Genetics: The Mixing and Matching of Traits

LO 2.4 Explain the mechanisms by which genes transmit information.

What determined the color of your hair? Why are you tall or short? What made you susceptible to hay fever? And why do you have so many freckles? To answer these questions, we need to consider the basic mechanisms involved in the way that the genes we inherit from our parents transmit information.

We can start by examining the discoveries of an Austrian monk, Gregor Mendel, in the mid-1800s. In a series of simple yet convincing experiments, Mendel cross-pollinated pea plants that always produced yellow seeds with pea plants that always produced green seeds. The result was not, as one might guess, a plant with a combination of yellow and green seeds. Instead, all of the resulting plants had yellow seeds. At first it appeared that the green-seeded plants had had no influence.

However, additional research on Mendel's part proved this was not true. He bred together plants from the new, yellow-seeded generation that had resulted from his original crossbreeding of the green-seeded and yellow-seeded plants. The consistent result was a ratio of three-quarters yellow seeds to one-quarter green seeds.

Why did this 3-to-1 ratio of yellow to green seeds appear so consistently? It took Mendel's genius to provide an answer. Based on his experiments with pea plants, he argued that when two competing traits, such as a green or yellow coloring of seeds, were both present, only one could be expressed. The one that was expressed was called a **dominant trait**. Meanwhile, the other trait remained present in the organism, but unexpressed. This was called a **recessive trait**. In the case of Mendel's original pea plants, the offspring plants received genetic information from both the green-seeded and yellow-seeded parents. However, the yellow trait was dominant, and consequently the recessive green trait did not assert itself.

Keep in mind, however, that genetic material relating to both parent plants is present in the offspring, even though it cannot be seen. The genetic information is known as the organism's genotype. A **genotype** is the underlying combination of genetic material present (but outwardly invisible) in an organism. In contrast, a **phenotype** is the observable trait, the trait that actually is seen.

Although the offspring of the yellow-seeded and green-seeded pea plants all have yellow seeds (i.e., they have a yellow-seeded phenotype), the genotype consists of genetic information relating to both parents.

And what is the nature of the information in the genotype? To answer that question, let's turn from peas to people. In fact, the principles are the same not just for plants and humans but for the majority of species.

Recall that parents transmit genetic information to their offspring via the chromosomes they contribute through the gamete they provide during fertilization. Some of the genes form pairs called *alleles*, genes governing traits that may take alternate forms, such as hair or eye color. For example, brown eye color is a dominant trait (B); blue eyes are recessive (b). A child's allele may contain similar or dissimilar genes from

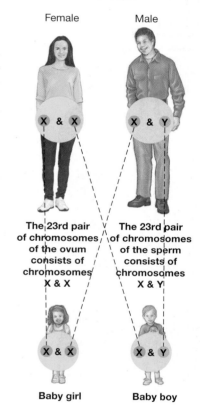

Figure 2-3 Determining Sex

When an ovum and sperm meet at the moment of fertilization, the ovum is certain to provide an X chromosome, while the sperm will provide either an X or a Y chromosome. If the sperm contributes its X chromosome, the child will have an XX pairing on the 23rd chromosome and will be a girl. If the sperm contributes a Y chromosome, the result will be an XY pairing—a boy. Does this mean that girls are more likely to be conceived than boys?

dominant trait
the one trait that is expressed when two competing traits are present.

recessive trait
a trait within an organism that is present, but is not expressed.

genotype
the underlying combination of genetic material present (but not outwardly visible) in an organism.

phenotype
an observable trait; the trait that actually is seen.

homozygous

inheriting from parents similar genes for a given trait.

heterozygous

inheriting from parents different forms of a gene for a given trait.

each parent. If the child receives similar genes, he or she is said to be **homozygous** for the trait. However, if the child receives different forms of the gene from the parents, he or she is said to be **heterozygous**. In the case of heterozygous alleles (Bb), the dominant characteristic, brown eyes, is expressed. However, if the child happens to receive a recessive allele from each of the parents and therefore lacks a dominant characteristic (bb), the child will display the recessive characteristic, such as blue eyes.

AN EXAMPLE OF THE TRANSMISSION OF GENETIC INFORMATION. We can see this process at work in humans by considering the transmission of *phenylketonuria (PKU)*, an inherited disorder in which a child is unable to make use of phenylalanine, an essential amino acid present in proteins found in milk and other foods. If left untreated, PKU allows phenylalanine to build up to toxic levels, causing brain damage and intellectual disabilities (Widaman, 2009; Deon et al., 2015; Palermo et al., 2017).

PKU is produced by a single allele, or pair of genes. As shown in Figure 2-4, we can label each gene of the pair with a *P* if it carries a dominant gene, which causes the normal production of phenylalanine, or a *p* if it carries the recessive gene that produces PKU. In cases in which neither parent is a PKU carrier, both the mother's and the father's pairs of genes are the dominant form, symbolized as *PP* (Figure 2-4a). Consequently, no matter which member of the pair is contributed by the mother and father, the resulting pair of genes in the child will be *PP*, and the child will not have PKU.

However, consider what happens if one of the parents has a recessive *p* gene. In this case, which we can symbolize as *Pp*, the parent will not have PKU, since the normal *P* gene is dominant. But the recessive gene can be passed down to the child (Figure 2-4b). This is not so bad: If the child has only one recessive gene, he or she will not suffer from PKU. But what if both parents carry a recessive *p* gene (Figure 2-4c)? In this case, although neither parent has the disorder, it is possible for the child to receive a recessive gene from both parents. The child's genotype for PKU then will be *pp*, and he or she will have the disorder.

Remember, though, that even children whose parents both have the recessive gene for PKU have only a 25 percent chance of inheriting the disorder. Due to the laws of probability, 25 percent of children with *Pp* parents will receive the dominant gene from each parent (these children's genotype would be *PP*), and 50 percent will receive the dominant gene from one parent and the recessive gene from the other (their genotypes would be either *Pp* or *pP*). Only the unlucky 25 percent who receive the recessive gene from each parent and end up with the genotype *pp* will suffer from PKU.

POLYGENIC TRAITS. The transmission of PKU is a good way to illustrate the basic principles of how genetic information passes from parent to child, although the case of PKU is simpler than most. In reality, relatively few traits are governed by a single pair of genes;

Figure 2-4 PKU Probabilities

PKU, a disease that causes brain damage and developmental disabilities, is produced by a single pair of genes inherited from one's mother and father. If neither parent carries a gene for the disease (a), a child cannot develop PKU. Even if one parent caries the recessive gene, but the other doesn't (b), the child cannot inherit the disease. However, if both parents carry the recessive gene (c), there is a one in four chance the child will have PKU.

instead, most traits are the result of **polygenic inheritance**, through which a combination of multiple gene pairs is responsible for the production of a particular trait.

Furthermore, some genes come in several alternate forms, and still others act to modify the way that particular genetic traits (produced by other alleles) are displayed. Genes also vary in terms of their *reaction range*, the potential degree of variability in the actual expression of a trait due to environmental conditions. And some traits, such as blood type, are produced by genes in which neither member of a pair of genes can be classified as purely dominant or recessive. Instead, the trait is expressed in terms of a combination of the two genes—such as type AB blood.

A number of recessive genes, called **X-linked genes**, are located only on the X chromosome. Recall that in females, the 23rd pair of chromosomes is an XX pair, while in males it is an XY pair. One result is that males have a higher risk for a variety of X-linked disorders, since males lack a second X chromosome that can counteract the genetic information that produces the disorder. For example, males are significantly more apt to have red-green color blindness, a disorder produced by a set of genes on the X chromosome. Similarly, *hemophilia*, a blood disorder, is produced by X-linked genes.

polygenic inheritance
inheritance in which a combination of multiple gene pairs is responsible for the production of a particular trait.

X-linked genes
genes that are considered recessive and are located only on the X chromosome.

The Human Genome and Behavioral Genetics: Cracking the Genetic Code

LO 2.5   Describe the field of behavioral genetics.

Mendel's achievements in recognizing the basics of genetic transmission of traits were trailblazing. However, they mark only the beginning of our understanding of the ways those particular sorts of characteristics are passed on from one generation to the next.

The most recent milestone in understanding genetics was reached in early 2001, when molecular geneticists succeeded in mapping the specific sequence of genes on each chromosome. This accomplishment stands as one of the most important moments in the history of genetics, and, for that matter, of all biology (Celera Genomics: International Human Genome Sequencing Consortium, 2001).

Already, the mapping of the gene sequence has provided important advances in our understanding of genetics. For instance, the number of human genes, long thought to be 100,000, has been revised downward to 25,000—not many more than organisms that are far less complex (see Figure 2-5). Furthermore, scientists have discovered that 99.9 percent of the gene sequence is shared by all humans. What this means is that we humans are far more similar to one another than we are different. It also indicates that many of the differences that seemingly separate people—such as race—are, literally, only skin-deep. Mapping of the human genome will also help in the identification of particular disorders to which a given individual is susceptible (Levenson, 2012; Goldman & Domschke, 2014; Caplan & Kunzler, 2015).

The mapping of the human gene sequence is supporting the field of behavioral genetics. As the name implies, **behavioral genetics** studies the effects of heredity on behavior and psychological characteristics. Rather than simply examining stable, unchanging characteristics such as hair or eye color, behavioral genetics takes a broader approach, considering how our personality and behavioral habits are affected by genetic factors (Li, 2003; Judge, Ilies, & Zhang, 2012; Johnson & Penke, 2015; Krüger, Korsten, & Hoffman, 2017).

Personality traits, such as shyness or sociability, moodiness, and assertiveness, are among the areas being studied. Other behavior geneticists study psychological disorders, such as depression, attention-deficit/hyperactivity disorder, and schizophrenia, looking for possible genetic links (Haeffel et al., 2008; Wang et al., 2012; Plomin et al., 2016; see Table 2-1).

Behavioral genetics holds substantial promise. For one thing, researchers working within the field have gained a better understanding of the specifics of the genetic code that underlie human behavior and development.

Even more important, researchers are seeking to identify how genetic defects may be remedied (Miller et al., 2008; Bleidorn, Kandler, & Caspi, 2014). To understand how that might come about, we need to consider the ways in which genetic factors, which normally cause development to proceed so smoothly, may falter.

behavioral genetics
the study of the effects of heredity on behavior.

Figure 2-5 Uniquely Human?

Humans have about 25,000 genes, making them not much more genetically complex than some primitive species.

(**Source:** International Human Genome Sequencing Consortium (2001) "Initial Sequencing and Analysis of the Human Genome," *Nature*, 409, 860–921.

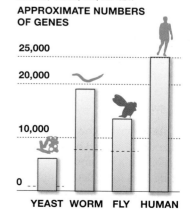

Estimated percentage of each creature's total genes found in humans are indicated by the dotted line.

Table 2-1 Current Understanding of the Genetic Basis of Selected Behavioral Disorders and Traits

Behavioral Trait	Current Beliefs About Genetic Basis
Huntington's disease	Mutations in HTT gene
Obsessive-compulsive disorder (OCD)	Several potentially relevant genes have been identified, but environment plays an important role
Fragile X intellectual disability	Mutations in the FMR gene
Early onset (familial) Alzheimer's disease	Three distinct genes identified; at least 11 mutations in the PSEN2 gene are related
Attention-deficit/hyperactivity disorder (ADHD)	Evidence in some studies has linked ADHD with dopamine-receptor D4 and D5 genes, but the complexity of the disease makes it difficult to identify a specific gene
Alcoholism	Research suggests that genes affecting the activity of the neurotransmitters serotonin and GABA likely are involved in risk for alcoholism
Schizophrenia spectrum disorder	There is no agreement, but deletions or duplications are related to the disorder; links to chromosomes 1, 5, 6, 10, 13, 15, and 22 have also been reported

(**Source:** Based on McGuffin, Riley, & Plomin, 2001; Genetics Home Reference, 2017).

Inherited and Genetic Disorders: When Development Deviates from the Norm

LO 2.6   Describe the major inherited disorders.

PKU is just one of several disorders that may be inherited. Like a bomb that is harmless until its fuse is lit, a recessive gene responsible for a disorder may be passed on unknowingly from one generation to the next, revealing itself only when, by chance, it is paired with another recessive gene. It is only when two recessive genes come together like a match and a fuse that the gene will express itself and a child will inherit the genetic disorder.

But there is another way that genes are a source of concern: In some cases, genes become physically damaged. For instance, they may break down due to wear and tear or chance events occurring during the cell division processes of meiosis and mitosis. Sometimes genes, for no known reason, spontaneously change their form, a process called *spontaneous mutation*.

Alternatively, certain environmental factors, such as exposure to X-rays or even highly polluted air, may produce a malformation of genetic material. When such damaged genes are passed on to a child, the results can be disastrous in terms of future physical and cognitive development (Samet, DeMarini, & Malling, 2004; Tucker-Drob & Briley, 2014).

In addition to PKU, which occurs once in 10,000 to 20,000 births, other inherited and genetic disorders include:

Down syndrome
a disorder produced by the presence of an extra chromosome on the 21st pair; once referred to as mongolism.

fragile X syndrome
a disorder produced by injury to a gene on the X chromosome, producing mild to moderate intellectual disability.

sickle-cell anemia
a blood disorder that gets its name from the shape of the red blood cells in those who have it.

- *Down syndrome*. As we noted earlier, most people have 46 chromosomes, arranged in 23 pairs. One exception is individuals with **Down syndrome**, a disorder produced by the presence of an extra chromosome on the 21st pair. Once referred to as mongolism, Down syndrome is the most frequent cause of intellectual disabilities. It occurs in about 1 out of 700 births, although the risk is much greater in mothers who are unusually young or old (Davis, 2008; Channell et al., 2014; Glasson et al., 2016).
- *Fragile X syndrome*. **Fragile X syndrome** occurs when a particular gene is injured on the X chromosome. The result is mild-to-moderate intellectual disability (Cornish, Turk, & Hagerman, 2008; Hocking, Kogan, & Cornish, 2012; Shelton et al., 2017).
- *Sickle-cell anemia*. Around one-tenth of people of African descent carry genes that produce sickle-cell anemia, and 1 in 400 actually has the disease. **Sickle-cell anemia** is a blood disorder that gets its name from the shape of the red blood cells in those who have it. Symptoms include poor appetite, stunted growth, swollen stomach, and yellowish eyes. People afflicted with the most severe form of the disease rarely live beyond childhood. However, for those with less severe cases, medical advances have produced significant increases in life expectancy.

- *Tay-Sachs disease*. Occurring mainly in Jews of eastern European ancestry and in French-Canadians, **Tay-Sachs disease** usually causes death before its victims reach school age. There is no treatment for the disorder, which produces blindness and muscle degeneration prior to death.

- *Klinefelter's syndrome*. One male out of every 500 is born with **Klinefelter's syndrome**, the presence of an extra X chromosome. The resulting XXY complement produces underdeveloped genitals, extreme height, and enlarged breasts. Klinefelter's syndrome is one of a number of genetic abnormalities that result from receiving the improper number of sex chromosomes. For instance, there are disorders produced by an extra Y chromosome (XYY), a missing second chromosome (X0, called *Turner syndrome*), and three X chromosomes (XXX). Such disorders are typically characterized by problems relating to sexual characteristics and by intellectual deficits (Murphy, 2009; Hong et al., 2014; Turriff et al., 2016).

It is important to keep in mind that the mere fact that a disorder has genetic roots does not mean that environmental factors do not also play a role (Rolland & Willams, 2006; Finn, 2008). Consider, for instance, sickle-cell anemia, which primarily afflicts people of African descent. Because the disease can be fatal in childhood, we'd expect that those who suffer from it would be unlikely to live long enough to pass it on. And this does seem to be true, at least in the United States: Compared with parts of West Africa, the incidence in the United States is much lower.

But why shouldn't the incidence of sickle-cell anemia also be gradually reduced for people in West Africa? This question proved puzzling for many years, until scientists determined that carrying the sickle-cell gene raises immunity to malaria, which is a common disease in West Africa. This heightened immunity meant that people with the sickle-cell gene had a genetic advantage (in terms of resistance to malaria) that offset, to some degree, the disadvantage of being a carrier of the sickle-cell gene (Mohammed et al., 2006).

The lesson of sickle-cell anemia is that genetic factors are intertwined with environmental considerations and can't be looked at in isolation. Furthermore, we need to remember that although we've been focusing on inherited factors that can go awry, in the vast majority of cases the genetic mechanisms with which we are endowed work quite well. Overall, 95 percent of children born in the United States are healthy and normal. For the 250,000 who are born with some sort of physical or mental disorder, appropriate intervention often can help treat and, in some cases, cure the problem.

Moreover, due to advances in behavioral genetics, genetic difficulties increasingly can be forecast, anticipated, and planned for before a child's birth, enabling parents to take steps before the child is born to reduce the severity of certain genetic conditions. In fact, as scientists' knowledge regarding the specific location of particular genes expands, predictions of what the genetic future may hold are becoming increasingly exact, as we discuss next (Fransen, Meertens, & Schrander-Stumpel, 2006).

Tay-Sachs disease
a disorder that produces blindness and muscle degeneration prior to death; there is no treatment.

Klinefelter's syndrome
a disorder resulting from the presence of an extra X chromosome that produces underdeveloped genitals, extreme height, and enlarged breasts.

genetic counseling
the discipline that focuses on helping people deal with issues relating to inherited disorders.

Genetic Counseling: Predicting the Future from the Genes of the Present

LO 2.7 **Describe the role of genetic counselors and differentiate between different forms of prenatal testing.**

If you knew that your mother and grandmother had died of Huntington's disease—a devastating, always fatal inherited disorder marked by tremors and intellectual deterioration—to whom could you turn to learn your own chances of coming down with the disease? The best person to turn to would be a member of a field that, just a few decades ago, was nonexistent: genetic counseling. **Genetic counseling** focuses on helping people deal with issues relating to inherited disorders.

Genetic counselors use a variety of data in their work. For instance, couples contemplating having a child may seek to determine the risks involved in a future pregnancy. In such a case, a counselor will take a thorough family history, seeking any familial incidence of birth defects that might indicate a pattern of recessive or X-linked genes. In addition, the counselor will take into account factors such as the age of the mother and father and

Sickle-cell anemia, named for the presence of misshapen red blood cells, is carried in the genes of 1 in 10 African Americans.

any previous abnormalities in other children they may have already had (O'Doherty, 2014; Austin, 2016; Madlensky et al., 2017).

Typically, genetic counselors suggest a thorough physical examination. Such an exam may identify physical abnormalities that potential parents may have and not be aware of. In addition, samples of blood, skin, and urine may be used to isolate and examine specific chromosomes. Possible genetic defects, such as the presence of an extra sex chromosome, can be identified by assembling a *karyotype*, a chart containing enlarged photos of each of the chromosomes.

PRENATAL TESTING.   If the woman is already pregnant, there are a variety of techniques to assess the health of her unborn child. The earliest test is a *first-trimester screen*, which combines a blood test and ultrasound sonography in the 11th to 13th week of pregnancy and can identify chromosomal abnormalities and other disorders, such as heart problems. In **ultrasound sonography**, high-frequency sound waves bombard the mother's womb. These waves produce a rather indistinct, but useful, image of the unborn baby, whose size and shape can then be assessed. Repeated use of ultrasound sonography can reveal developmental patterns. Although the accuracy of blood tests and ultrasound in identifying abnormalities is not high early in pregnancy, it becomes more accurate later on.

A more invasive test, **chorionic villus sampling (CVS)**, can be employed in the 10th to 13th week of the first trimester if blood tests and ultrasound have identified a potential problem or if there is a family history of inherited disorders. CVS involves inserting a thin needle into the fetus and taking small samples of hairlike material that surrounds the embryo. The test can be done between the 8th and 11th week of pregnancy. However, it produces a risk of miscarriage of 1 in 100 to 1 in 200 cases. Because of the risk, its use is relatively infrequent.

In **amniocentesis**, a small sample of fetal cells is drawn by a tiny needle inserted into the amniotic fluid surrounding the unborn fetus. Carried out 15 to 20 weeks into the pregnancy, amniocentesis allows the analysis of the fetal cells that can identify a variety of genetic defects with nearly 100 percent accuracy. In addition, it can determine the sex of the child. Although there is always a danger to the fetus in an invasive procedure such as amniocentesis, it is generally considered safe, with the risk of miscarriage of 1 in 200 to 1 in 400 cases.

After the various tests are complete and all possible information is available, the couple will meet with the genetic counselor again. Typically, counselors avoid giving specific recommendations. Instead, they lay out the facts and present various options, ranging from doing nothing to taking more drastic steps, such as terminating the pregnancy through abortion. Ultimately, it is the parents who must decide what course of action to follow.

ultrasound sonography

a process in which high-frequency sound waves scan the mother's womb to produce an image of the unborn baby, whose size and shape can then be assessed.

chorionic villus sampling (CVS)

a test used to find genetic defects that involves taking samples of hairlike material that surrounds the embryo.

amniocentesis

the process of identifying genetic defects by examining a small sample of fetal cells drawn by a needle inserted into the amniotic fluid surrounding the unborn fetus.

SCREENING FOR FUTURE PROBLEMS.   The newest role of genetic counselors involves testing people to identify whether they themselves, rather than their children, are susceptible to future disorders because of genetic abnormalities. For instance, Huntington's disease typically does not appear until people reach their 40s. However, genetic testing can identify much earlier whether a person carries the flawed gene that produces Huntington's disease. Presumably, people's knowledge that they carry the gene can help them prepare themselves for the future (Cina & Fellmann, 2006; Tibben, 2007; Sánchez-Castañeda et al., 2015).

In amniocentesis, a sample of amniotic fluid surrounding the fetus is examined to identify genetic defects.

BSIP SA/Alamy Stock Photo

From the perspective of *a health-care provider*

What are some ethical and philosophical questions that surround the issue of genetic counseling? Might it sometimes be unwise to know ahead of time about possible genetically linked disorders that might afflict your child or yourself?

Table 2-2 Some Currently Available DNA-Based Gene Tests

Disease	Description
Alzheimer's disease	Late-onset variety of senile dementia
Amyotrophic lateral sclerosis (Lou Gehrig's disease)	Progressive motor function loss leading to paralysis and death
Breast and ovarian cancer (inherited)	Early-onset tumors of breasts and ovaries
Congenital hypothyroidism	Thyroid gland disorder
Cystic fibrosis	Thick mucus accumulations in lungs and chronic infections in lungs and pancreas
Duchenne muscular dystrophy (Becker muscular dystrophy)	Severe to mild muscle wasting, deterioration, weakness
Fragile X syndrome	Intellectual disability
Hemophilia A and B	Bleeding disorders
Hereditary nonpolyposis colon cancer[a]	Early-onset tumors of colon and sometimes other organs
Huntington's disease	Progressive neurological degeneration, usually beginning in midlife
Neurofibromatosis, type 1	Multiple benign nervous system tumors that can be disfiguring; cancers
Phenylketonuria	Progressive intellectual disability due to missing enzyme; correctable by diet
Sickle-cell disease	Blood cell disorder, chronic pain, and infections
Spinal muscular atrophy	Severe, usually lethal progressive muscle-wasting disorder in children
Tay-Sachs disease	Seizures, paralysis, fatal neurological disease of early childhood

[a] These are susceptibility tests that provide only an estimated risk for developing the disorder.

(**Sources:** Human Genome Project, 2010; Genetics Home Reference, 2017.)

In addition to Huntington's disease, more than a thousand disorders can be predicted on the basis of genetic testing (see Table 2-2). Although such testing may bring welcome relief from future worries—if the results are negative—positive results may produce just the opposite effect. In fact, genetic testing raises difficult practical and ethical questions (Human Genome Project, 2006; Twomey, 2006; Klitzman, 2012).

Suppose, for instance, a woman who thought she was susceptible to Huntington's disease was tested in her 20s and found that she carried the flawed gene and would therefore get the disease. She might experience depression and remorse. In fact, some studies show that 10 percent of people who find they have the flawed gene that leads to Huntington's disease never recover fully on an emotional level (Myers, 2004; Wahlin, 2007).

Genetic testing clearly is a complicated issue. It rarely provides a simple yes or no answer as to whether an individual will be susceptible to a disorder. Instead, typically it presents a range of probabilities. In some cases, the likelihood of actually becoming ill depends on the type of environmental stressors to which a person is exposed. Personal differences also affect a given person's susceptibility to a disorder (Bonke et al., 2005; Lucassen, 2012; Crozier, Robertson, & Dale, 2015; Djurdjinovic & Peters, 2017).

Module 2.1 Review

LO 2.1 **Describe how genes and chromosomes provide our basic genetic endowment.**

In humans, the male sex cell (the sperm) and the female sex cell (the ovum) provide the developing baby with 23 chromosomes each.

LO 2.2 **Compare monozygotic twins with dizygotic twins.**

Monozygotic twins are twins who are genetically identical. Dizygotic twins are two separate ova that are fertilized by two separate sperm at roughly the same time.

LO 2.3 **Describe how the sex of a child is determined.**

When an ovum and sperm meet at the moment of fertilization, the ovum provides an X chromosome, while the sperm provides either an X or a Y chromosome. If the sperm contributes its X chromosome, the child will have an XX pairing and will be a girl. If the sperm contributes a Y chromosome, the result will be an XY pairing—a boy.

LO 2.4 **Explain the mechanisms by which genes transmit information.**

A genotype is the underlying combination of genetic material present in an organism, but invisible; a phenotype is the visible trait, the expression of the genotype.

LO 2.5 **Describe the field of behavioral genetics.**

The field of behavioral genetics, a combination of psychology and genetics, studies the effects of genetics on behavior and psychological characteristics.

LO 2.6   **Describe the major inherited disorders.**

Several inherited and genetic disorders are due to damaged or mutated genes.

LO 2.7   **Describe the role of genetic counselors and differentiate between different forms of pre-natal testing.**

Genetic counselors use a variety of data and techniques to advise future parents of possible genetic risks to their unborn children. A variety of techniques can be used to assess the health of an unborn child if a woman is already pregnant, including ultrasound, CVS, and amniocentesis.

Journal Writing Prompt

Applying Lifespan Development: How can the field of behavioral genetics help researchers understand human development?

MODULE 2.2

THE INTERACTION OF HEREDITY AND ENVIRONMENT

Like many other parents, Jared's mother, Leesha, and his father, Jamal, tried to figure out which one of them their new baby resembled the most. He seemed to have Leesha's big, wide eyes, and Jamal's generous smile. As he grew, Jared grew to resemble his mother and father even more. His hair grew in with a hairline just like Leesha's, and his teeth, when they came, made his smile resemble Jamal's even more. He also seemed to act like his parents. For example, he was a charming little baby, always ready to smile at people who visited the house—just like his friendly, jovial dad. He seemed to sleep like his mom, which was lucky since Jamal was an extremely light sleeper who could do with as little as four hours a night, while Leesha liked a regular seven or eight hours.

Were Jared's ready smile and regular sleeping habits something he just luckily inherited from his parents? Or did Jamal and Leesha provide a happy and stable home that encouraged these welcome traits? What causes our behavior? Nature or nurture? Is behavior produced by inherited, genetic influences, or is it triggered by factors in the environment?

The simple answer is: There is no simple answer.

The Role of the Environment in Determining the Expression of Genes: From Genotypes to Phenotypes

LO 2.8   **Explain how the environment and genetics work together to determine human characteristics.**

As developmental research accumulates, it is becoming increasingly clear that to view behavior as due to *either* genetic *or* environmental factors is inappropriate. A given behavior is not caused just by genetic factors; nor is it caused solely by environmental forces. Instead, as we first discussed in Chapter 1, the behavior is the product of some combination of the two.

temperament

patterns of arousal and emotionality that represent consistent and enduring characteristics in an individual.

For instance, consider **temperament**, patterns of arousal and emotionality that represent consistent and enduring characteristics in an individual. Suppose we found—as increasing evidence suggests is the case—that a small percentage of children are born with temperaments that produce an unusual degree of physiological reactivity. Having a tendency to shrink from anything unusual, such infants react to novel stimuli with a rapid increase in heartbeat and unusual excitability of the limbic system of the brain. Such heightened reactivity to stimuli at the start of life, which seems to be linked to inherited factors, is also likely to cause children, by the time they are 4 or 5, to be considered shy by their parents and teachers. But not always: some of them behave indistinguishably from their peers at the same age (De Pauw & Mervielde, 2011; Pickles et al., 2013; Smiley et al., 2016).

What makes the difference? The answer seems to be the environment in which the children are raised. Children whose parents encourage them to be outgoing by arranging new opportunities for them may overcome their shyness. In contrast, children raised in a stressful environment marked by marital discord or a prolonged illness may be more likely to retain their shyness later in life. Jared, described earlier, may have been born with an easy temperament, which was easily reinforced by his caring parents (Kagan, 2010; Casalin et al., 2012; Merwin et al., 2017).

INTERACTION OF FACTORS. Such findings illustrate that many traits reflect **multifactorial transmission**, meaning that they are determined by a combination of both genetic and environmental factors. In multifactorial transmission, a genotype provides a particular range within which a phenotype may achieve expression. For instance, people with a genotype that permits them to gain weight easily may never be slim, no matter how much they diet. They may be *relatively* slim, given their genetic heritage, but they may never be able to reach a certain degree of thinness. In many cases, then, it is the environment that determines the way in which a particular genotype will be expressed as a phenotype (Plomin, 2016).

By contrast, certain genotypes are relatively unaffected by environmental factors. In such cases, development follows a preordained pattern, relatively independent of the specific environment in which a person is raised. For instance, research on pregnant women who were severely malnourished during famines caused by World War II found that their children were, on average, unaffected physically or intellectually as adults (Stein et al., 1975). Similarly, no matter how much health food people eat, they are not going to grow beyond certain genetically imposed limitations in height. Little Jared's hairline was probably affected very little by any actions on the part of his parents.

Ultimately, of course, it is the unique interaction of inherited and environmental factors that determines people's patterns of development.

The more appropriate question, then, is *how much* of the behavior is caused by genetic factors, and *how much* by environmental factors? (See, for example, the range of possibilities for the determinants of intelligence, illustrated in Figure 2-6.) At one extreme is the idea that opportunities in the environment are solely responsible for intelligence; on the other, that intelligence is purely genetic—you either have it or you don't. The usefulness of such extremes seems to be to point us toward the middle— that intelligence results from some combination of natural mental ability and environmental opportunity (Asbury & Plomin, 2014).

multifactorial transmission
the determination of traits by a combination of both genetic and environmental factors in which a genotype provides a range within which a phenotype may be expressed.

Figure 2-6 Possible Sources of Intelligence

Intelligence may be explained by a range of differing possible sources, spanning the nature–nurture continuum. Which of these explanations do you find most convincing, given the evidence discussed in the chapter?

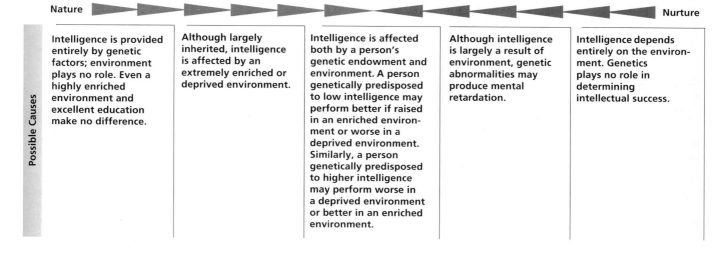

Studying Development: How Much Is Nature, How Much Is Nurture?

LO 2.9 **Summarize the methods by which researchers study the interaction of genetic and environmental factors in development.**

Developmental researchers use several strategies to try to resolve the question of the degree to which traits, characteristics, and behavior are produced by genetic or environmental factors. Their studies involve both nonhuman species and humans.

NONHUMAN ANIMAL STUDIES: CONTROLLING BOTH GENETICS AND ENVIRONMENT. It is relatively simple to develop breeds of animals that are genetically similar to one another in terms of specific traits. The people who raise Butterball turkeys for Thanksgiving do it all the time, producing turkeys that grow especially rapidly so that they can be brought to market inexpensively. Similarly, strains of laboratory animals can be bred to share similar genetic backgrounds.

By observing animals with similar genetic backgrounds in different environments, scientists can determine, with reasonable precision, the effects of specific kinds of environmental stimulation. For example, to determine the effects of living in different settings, animals can be raised in unusually stimulating environments, with lots of items to climb over or through, or in relatively barren environments. Conversely, researchers can examine groups of animals that have been bred to have significantly *different* genetic backgrounds on particular traits. Then, by exposing such animals to identical environments, they can determine the role of genetic background.

From Research to Practice
When Nurture Becomes Nature

A fundamental assumption about genetic inheritance has long been that environmental alterations of an organism's health cannot be passed down to future generations; if we cut off a mouse's tail, we do not expect its offspring to be tailless. Only genetic mutations—not lifestyle choices such as poor diet nor environmental insults such as exposure to toxins—were thought to be heritable. But recent research finds that an individual's life experiences can be passed down to children, grandchildren, and subsequent generations.

It's a phenomenon called *transgenerational epigenetic inheritance*, and it works a bit differently from usual inheritance. Instead of changing the genetic code itself, life experiences change the parts of DNA that switch individual genes on or off. Not every gene is active everywhere in the body; the DNA that is responsible for making insulin, for example, is only "switched on" in certain cells of the pancreas. When an event such as malnourishment or drug use affects the DNA "switches" in sperm or eggs, the alterations can be passed on to future generations (Daxinger & Whitelaw, 2012; Babenko, Kovalchuk, & Metz, 2015; Nestler, 2016).

In one study, healthy male rats were fed a high-fat diet that caused them to put on weight and develop symptoms consistent with type 2 diabetes, such as insulin resistance. Although these rats did not have a preexisting genetic tendency to be diabetic, their daughters also developed symptoms of type 2 diabetes as adults—even though they ate normal diets. Some researchers think that transgenerational epigenetic inheritance could partly explain the epidemic of childhood obesity: Our high-fat diets may not only put us at risk, but perhaps our children as well (Skinner, 2010; Crews et al., 2012).

Happily, it's not just harmful effects that can be passed on this way. One study showed that mice developed better memory after being exposed to an enriched and stimulating environment, as previous research showed would be the case, and that the mice's offspring also showed the beneficial memory effect even though they didn't experience the same enriched environment.

The implications of this research are astounding—it may well be the case that the poor life choices we make in our youth have consequences for our progeny as well as ourselves (Arai et al., 2009; Nestler, 2011; Heard & Martienssen, 2014).

Shared Writing Prompt:
Why would the poor life choices we make in our youth, rather than those we might make later in life, have possible consequences for our children?

Of course, the drawback to using nonhumans as research subjects is that we can't be sure how well the findings we obtain can be generalized to people. Still, the opportunities that animal research offers are substantial. (Also see the *From Research to Practice* box.)

CONTRASTING RELATEDNESS AND BEHAVIOR: ADOPTION, TWIN, AND FAMILY STUDIES. Clearly, researchers can't control either the genetic backgrounds or the environments of humans in the way they can with nonhumans. However, nature conveniently has provided the potential to carry out various kinds of "natural experiments"—in the form of twins. Recall that monozygotic twins are identical genetically. Because their inherited backgrounds are precisely the same, any variations in their behavior must be due entirely to environmental factors.

It would be rather simple for researchers to make use of identical twins to draw unequivocal conclusions about the roles of nature and nurture. For instance, by separating identical twins at birth and placing them in totally different environments, researchers could assess the impact of environment unambiguously. Of course, ethical considerations make this impossible. What researchers can—and do—study, however, are cases in which identical twins have been put up for adoption at birth and are raised in substantially different environments. Such instances allow us to draw fairly confident conclusions about the relative contributions of genetics and environment (Agrawal & Lynskey, 2008; Nikolas, Klump, & Burt, 2012; Strachan et al., 2017).

The data from such studies of identical twins raised in different environments are not always without bias. Adoption agencies typically take the characteristics (and wishes) of birth mothers into account when they place babies in adoptive homes. For instance, children tend to be placed with families of the same race and religion. Consequently, even when monozygotic twins are placed in different adoptive homes, there are often similarities between the two home environments, making it often impossible to attribute differences in behavior to differences in the environment.

Studies of dizygotic twins also present opportunities to learn about the relative contributions of nature and nurture. Recall that dizygotic twins are genetically no more similar than siblings in a family born at different times. By comparing behavior within pairs of dizygotic twins with that of pairs of monozygotic twins (who are genetically identical), researchers can determine if monozygotic twins are more similar on a particular trait, on average, than dizygotic twins. If so, they can assume that genetics plays an important role in determining the expression of that trait.

Still another approach is to study people who are totally unrelated to one another and who therefore have dissimilar genetic backgrounds but who share an environmental background. For instance, a family that adopts, at the same time, two very young unrelated children probably will provide them with quite similar environments throughout their childhood. In this case, similarities in the children's characteristics and behavior can be attributed with some confidence to environmental influences (Segal, 2000; Segal et al., 2007; van den Berg et al., 2008).

Finally, developmental researchers have examined groups of people in light of their degree of genetic similarity. For instance, on the one hand, if we find a high association on a particular trait between biological parents and their children, but a weaker association between adoptive parents and their children, we have evidence for the importance of genetics in determining the expression of that trait. On the other hand, if there is a stronger association on a trait between adoptive parents and their children than between biological parents and their children, we have evidence for the importance of the environment in determining that trait (Plomin, 2007).

Developmental researchers have used all these approaches, and more, to study the relative impact of genetic and environmental factors. What have they found? Based on decades of research, they have concluded that virtually all traits, characteristics, and behaviors are the joint result of the combination and interaction of nature and nurture. Genetic and environmental factors work in tandem, each affecting and being affected by the other, creating the unique individual that each of us is and will become (Robinson, 2004; Waterland & Jirtle, 2004; Kendler et al., 2017).

Monozygotic and dizygotic twins present opportunities to learn about the relative contributions of heredity and situational factors. What can psychologists learn from studying twins?

Genetics and the Environment: Working Together

LO 2.10 Examine how genetics and the environment jointly influence physical traits, intelligence, and personality.

Let's look at ways in which genetics and the environment influence our physical traits, intelligence, and personality.

PHYSICAL TRAITS: FAMILY RESEMBLANCES. Monozygotic twins are merely the most extreme example of the fact that the more genetically similar two people are, the more likely they are to share physical characteristics. Tall parents tend to have tall children, and short ones tend to have short children. Obesity also has a strong genetic component (Bouchard et al., 1990). For example, in one study, pairs of identical twins were put on diets that contained an extra 1,000 calories a day—and ordered not to exercise. Over a three-month period, the twins gained almost identical amounts of weight. Moreover, different pairs of twins varied substantially in how much weight they gained, with some pairs gaining almost three times as much weight as other pairs.

Other, less obvious physical characteristics also show strong genetic influences. For instance, blood pressure, respiration rates, and even the age at which life ends are more similar in closely related individuals than in those who are less genetically alike (Melzer, Hurst, & Frayling, 2007; Wu, Treiber, & Snieder, 2013; Falcone et al., 2014).

INTELLIGENCE: MORE RESEARCH, MORE CONTROVERSY. No issue involving the relative influence of heredity and environment has generated more research than intelligence. Why? The main reason is that intelligence, generally measured in terms of an IQ score, is a central characteristic that differentiates humans from other species. In addition, intelligence is strongly related to success in scholastic endeavors and, somewhat less strongly, to other types of achievement.

Genetics plays a significant role in intelligence. In studies of both overall or general intelligence and of specific subcomponents of intelligence (such as spatial skills, verbal skills, and memory), as can be seen in Figure 2-7, the closer the genetic link between two individuals, the greater the correspondence of their overall IQ scores.

Not only is genetics an important influence on intelligence, but the impact increases with age. For instance, as fraternal (i.e., dizygotic) twins move from infancy to adolescence, their IQ scores become less similar. In contrast, the IQ scores of identical (monozygotic) twins become increasingly similar over the course of time. These opposite patterns suggest the intensifying influence of inherited factors with increasing age (Silventoinen et al., 2012; Madison et al., 2016).

Although it is clear that heredity plays an important role in intelligence, investigators are much more divided on the question of the degree to which it is inherited. One of the more extreme views was held by psychologist Arthur Jensen (2003), who argued that as much as 80 percent of intelligence is a result of heredity. Others have suggested more modest figures, ranging from 50 to 70 percent. It is critical to keep in mind that such figures are averages across large groups of people, and that any particular individual's degree of inheritance cannot be predicted from these averages (Brouwer et al., 2014; Schmiedek, 2017).

It is important to keep in mind that although heredity clearly plays an important role in intelligence, environmental factors such as exposure to books, good educational experiences, and intelligent peers are profoundly influential. Even those like

Figure 2-7 Genetics and IQ

The closer the genetic link between two individuals, the greater the correspondence between their IQ scores. **THINKING ABOUT THE DATA:** Why is there a difference in the median correlation of IQ's between children reared together and siblings reared together? Alternatively, why is there a difference in the median correlation of IQ's between children reared together and siblings reared apart? How would you characterize the influence of genetics and environment on IQ?
(**Source:** Bouchard & McGue, 1981.)

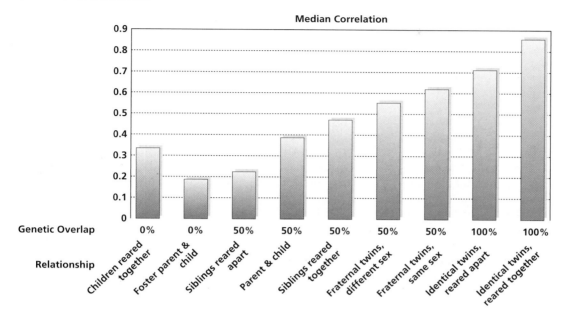

Jensen who make the most extreme estimates of the role of genetics still admit that environmental factors play a significant role. In fact, in terms of public policy, environmental influences are the focus of efforts geared toward maximizing people's intellectual success. As developmental psychologist Sandra Scarr suggests, we should be asking what can be done to maximize the intellectual development of each individual (Bouchard, 1997; Garcia et al., 2005).

From *an educator's* perspective

Some people have used the proven genetic basis of intelligence to argue against strenuous educational efforts on behalf of individuals with below-average IQs. Does this viewpoint make sense based on what you have learned about heredity and environment? Why or why not?

GENETIC AND ENVIRONMENTAL INFLUENCES ON PERSONALITY: BORN TO BE OUTGOING? Do we inherit our personality? At least in part. There's increasing research evidence suggesting that some of our most basic personality traits have genetic roots. For example, two of the key "Big Five" personality traits, neuroticism and extroversion, have been linked to genetic factors. *Neuroticism*, as used by personality researchers, is the degree of emotional stability an individual characteristically displays. *Extroversion* is the degree to which a person seeks to be with others, to behave in an outgoing manner, and generally to be sociable. For instance, Jared, the baby described earlier in this chapter, may have inherited a tendency to be outgoing from his extroverted father, Jamal (Horwitz, Luong, & Charles, 2008; Zyphur et al., 2013; Briley & Tucker-Drob, 2017).

How do we know which personality traits reflect genetics? Some evidence comes from direct examination of genes themselves. For instance, it appears that a specific gene is very influential in determining risk-taking behavior. This novelty-seeking gene affects the production of the brain chemical dopamine, making some people more prone than others to seek out novel situations and to take risks (Ray et al., 2009; Veselka et al., 2012 Reichborn-Kjennerud et al., 2015).

Other evidence for the role of genetics in the determination of personality traits comes from studies of twins. For instance, in one major study, researchers looked at the personality traits of hundreds of pairs of twins. Because a good number of the twins were genetically identical but had been raised apart, it was possible to determine with some confidence the influence of genetic factors (Tellegen et al., 1988). The researchers found that certain traits reflected the contribution of genetics considerably more than others. As you can see in Figure 2-8, social potency (the tendency to be a masterful, forceful leader who enjoys being the center of attention) and traditionalism (strict endorsement of rules and authority) are strongly associated with genetic factors (Harris, Vernon, & Jang, 2007; South et al., 2015).

Even less basic personality traits are linked to genetics. For example, political attitudes, religious interests and values, and even attitudes toward human sexuality have genetic components (Bouchard, 2004; Koenig et al., 2005; Kandler, Bleidorn, & Riemann, 2012).

Clearly, genetic factors play a role in determining personality. At the same time, the environment in which a child is raised also affects personality development. For example, some parents encourage high activity levels, seeing activity as a manifestation of independence and intelligence. Other parents may encourage lower levels of activity on the part of their children, feeling that more passive children will get along better in society. In part, these parental attitudes are culturally determined: Parents in the United States may encourage higher activity levels, while parents in Asian cultures may encourage greater passivity. In both cases, children's personalities will be shaped in part by their parents' attitudes (Cauce, 2008; Luo et al., 2017).

Figure 2-8 Inheriting Traits

These traits are among the personality factors that are related most closely to genetic factors. The higher the percentage, the greater the degree to which the trait reflects the influence of heredity. Do these figures mean that "leaders are born, not made"? Why or why not?
(**Source:** Adapted from Tellegen et al., 1988.)

Social potency 61%
A person high in this trait is masterful, a forceful leader who likes to be the center of attention.

Traditionalism 60%
Follows rules and authority, endorses high moral standards and strict discipline.

Stress reaction 55%
Feels vulnerable and sensitive and is given to worries and is easily upset.

Absorption 55%
Has a vivid imagination readily captured by rich experience; relinquishes sense of reality.

Alienation 55%
Feels mistreated and used, that "the world is out to get me."

Well-being 54%
Has a cheerful disposition, feels confident and optimistic.

Harm avoidance 50%
Shuns the excitement of risk and danger, prefers the safe route even if it is tedious.

Aggression 48%
Is physically aggressive and vindictive, has taste for violence and is "out to get the world."

Achievement 46%
Works hard, strives for mastery, and puts work and accomplishment ahead of other things.

Control 43%
Is cautious and plodding, rational and sensible, likes carefully planned events.

Social closeness 33%
Prefers emotional intimacy and close ties, turns to others for comfort and help.

Can Genes Influence the Environment?

LO 2.11 Describe ways in which genes influence the environment.

According to developmental psychologist Sandra Scarr (1998), the genetic endowment provided to children by their parents not only determines their genetic characteristics but also actively influences their environment. Scarr suggests three ways a child's genetic predisposition might influence his or her environment.

Children tend to actively focus on those aspects of their environment that are most connected with their genetically determined abilities. For example, an active, more aggressive child will gravitate toward sports, while a more reserved child will be more engaged by academics or solitary pursuits, like computer games or drawing. They also pay less attention to those aspects of the environment that are less compatible with their genetic endowment. For instance, two girls may be reading the same school bulletin board. One may notice the sign advertising tryouts for Little League baseball, while her less coordinated but more musically endowed friend might be more apt to spot the notice recruiting students for an after-school chorus. In each case, the child is attending to those aspects of the environment in which her genetically determined abilities can flourish.

In some cases, the gene-environment influence is more passive and less direct. For example, a particularly sports-oriented parent, who has genes that promote good physical coordination, may provide many opportunities for a child to play sports.

Finally, the genetically driven temperament of a child may *evoke* certain environmental influences. For instance, an infant's demanding behavior may cause parents to be more attentive to the infant's needs than they would be if the infant were less demanding. Or a child who is genetically inclined to be well coordinated may play ball with anything in the house so often that her parents notice. They may then decide that she should have some sports equipment.

In sum, determining whether behavior is primarily attributable to nature or nurture is a bit like shooting at a moving target. Not only are behaviors and traits a joint outcome of genetic and environmental factors, but the relative influence of genes and environment for specific characteristics shifts over the course of people's lives. Although the pool of genes we inherit at birth sets the stage for our future development, the constantly shifting scenery and the other characters in our lives determine just how our development eventually plays out. The environment both influences our experiences and is molded by the choices we are temperamentally inclined to make.

Module 2.2 Review

LO 2.8 Explain how the environment and genetics work together to determine human characteristics.

Human characteristics and behavior often reflect multifactorial transmission, meaning that they are a joint outcome of genetic and environmental factors.

LO 2.9 Summarize the methods by which researchers study the interaction of genetic and environmental factors in development.

Developmental researchers use a number of strategies to examine the extent to which traits and behavior are due to genetic factors or environmental factors. Strategies include animal studies and research on twins, adopted siblings, and families.

LO 2.10 Examine how genetics and the environment jointly influence physical traits, intelligence, and personality.

Genetic influences have been identified in physical characteristics, intelligence, and personality traits and behaviors. Environmental factors, such as family dispositions and habits, also play a role in such traits as intelligence and personality.

LO 2.11 Describe ways in which genes influence the environment.

Children may influence their environment through genetic traits that cause them to construct—or influence their parents to construct—an environment that matches their inherited dispositions and preferences.

Journal Writing Prompt

Applying Lifespan Development: How might an environment different from the one you experienced have affected the development of personality characteristics that you believe you inherited from one or both of your parents?

PRENATAL GROWTH AND BIRTH

Robert accompanied Lisa to her first appointment with the midwife. The midwife checked the results of tests done to confirm the couple's own positive home pregnancy test. "Yep, you're going to have a baby," she confirmed, speaking to Lisa. "You'll need to set up monthly visits for the next 6 months, then more frequently as your due date approaches. You can get this prescription for prenatal vitamins filled at any pharmacy, and here are some guidelines about diet and exercise. You don't smoke, do you? That's good." Then she turned to Robert. "How about you? Do you smoke?" After giving lots of instructions and advice, she left the couple feeling slightly dazed but ready to do whatever they could to have a healthy baby.

From the moment of conception, development proceeds relentlessly. As we've seen, many aspects are guided by the complex set of genetic guidelines inherited from the parents. Of course, prenatal growth, like all development, is also influenced from the start by environmental factors. As we'll see, both parents, like Lisa and Robert, can take part in providing a good prenatal environment.

Fertilization: The Moment of Conception

LO 2.12 Describe the process of fertilization.

When most of us think about the facts of life, we tend to focus on the events that cause a male's sperm cells to begin their journey toward a female's ovum. Yet the act of sex that brings about the potential for conception is both the consequence and the start of a long string of events that precede and follow **fertilization**, or conception: the joining of sperm and ovum to create the single-celled zygote from which life begins.

Both the male's sperm and the female's ovum come with a history of their own. Females are born with around 400,000 ova located in the two ovaries. However, the ova do not mature until the female reaches puberty. From that point until she reaches menopause, the female will ovulate about every 28 days. During ovulation, an egg is released from one of the ovaries and pushed by minute hair cells through the fallopian tube toward the uterus. If the ovum meets a sperm in the fallopian tube, fertilization takes place (Stella, Verrischi, & Lipay, 2008).

Sperm, which look a little like microscopic tadpoles, have a shorter life span. They are created by the testicles at a rapid rate: An adult male typically produces several hundred million sperm a day. Consequently, the sperm ejaculated during sexual intercourse are of considerably more recent origin than the ovum to which they are heading.

When sperm enter the vagina, they begin a winding journey that takes them through the cervix, the opening into the uterus, and into the fallopian tube, where fertilization may take place. However, only a tiny fraction of the 300 million cells that are typically ejaculated during sexual intercourse ultimately survive the arduous journey. That's usually okay, though: It takes only one sperm to fertilize an ovum, and each sperm and ovum contain all the genetic data necessary to produce a new human.

The Stages of the Prenatal Period: The Onset of Development

LO 2.13 Summarize the three stages of prenatal development.

The prenatal period consists of three stages: the germinal, embryonic, and fetal stages. They are summarized in Table 2-3.

THE GERMINAL STAGE: FERTILIZATION TO 2 WEEKS. In the **germinal stage**, the first—and shortest—stage of the prenatal period, the zygote begins to divide and grow in complexity during the first 2 weeks following conception. During the germinal stage,

fertilization

the process by which a sperm and an ovum—the male and female gametes, respectively—join to form a single new cell.

germinal stage

the first—and shortest—stage of the prenatal period, which takes place during the first 2 weeks following conception.

Table 2-3 Stages of the Prenatal Period

Germinal	Embryonic	Fetal
Fertilization to 2 Weeks	2 Weeks to 8 Weeks	8 Weeks to Birth

Dr. Yorgos Nikas/Science Source · Petit Format/Science Source · Neil Bromhall/Science Source

The germinal stage is the first and shortest, characterized by methodical cell division and the attachment of the organism to the wall of the uterus. Three days after fertilization, the zygote consists of 32 cells, a number that doubles by the next day. Within a week, the zygote multiplies to 100 to 150 cells. The cells become specialized, with some forming a protective layer around the zygote.

The zygote is now designated an embryo. The embryo develops three layers, which ultimately form a different set of structures as development proceeds. The layers are as follows:

Ectoderm: Skin, hair teeth, sense organs, brain, spinal cord

Endoderm: Digestive system, liver, pancreas, respiratory system

Mesoderm: Muscles, bones, blood, circulatory system

At 8 weeks, the embryo is 1 inch long.

The fetal stage formally starts when the differentiation of the major organs has occurred. Now called a fetus, the individual grows rapidly as length increases 20 times. At 4 months, the fetus weighs an average of 4 ounces; at 7 months, 3 pounds; and at the time of birth, the average child weighs just over 7 pounds.

the fertilized egg (now called a *blastocyst*) travels toward the *uterus*, where it becomes implanted in the uterus's wall, which is rich in nutrients. The germinal stage is characterized by methodical cell division, which gets off to a quick start: Three days after fertilization, the organism consists of some 32 cells, and by the next day the number doubles. Within a week, it is made up of 100 to 150 cells, and the number rises with increasing rapidity.

In addition to increasing in number, the cells of the organism become increasingly specialized. For instance, some cells form a protective layer around the mass of cells, while others begin to establish the rudiments of a placenta and umbilical cord. When fully developed, the **placenta** serves as a conduit between the mother and fetus, providing nourishment and oxygen via the *umbilical cord*, which also removes waste materials from the developing child. The placenta also plays a role in fetal brain development (Kalb, 2012).

THE EMBRYONIC STAGE: 2 TO 8 WEEKS. By the end of the germinal period—just 2 weeks after conception—the organism is firmly secured to the wall of the mother's uterus. At this point, the child is called an *embryo*. The **embryonic stage** is the period from 2 to 8 weeks following fertilization. One of the highlights of this stage is the development of the major organs and basic anatomy.

At the beginning of the embryonic stage, the developing child has three distinct layers, each of which will ultimately form a different set of structures as development proceeds. The outer layer of the embryo, the *ectoderm*, will form skin, hair, teeth, sense organs, and the brain and spinal cord. The *endoderm*, the inner layer, produces the digestive system, liver, pancreas, and respiratory system. Sandwiched between the ectoderm and endoderm is the *mesoderm*, from which the muscles, bones, blood, and circulatory system are forged. Every part of the body is formed from these three layers.

If you were looking at an embryo at the end of the embryonic stage, you might be hard-pressed to identify it as human. Only an inch long, an 8-week-old embryo has what appear to be gills and a tail-like structure. However, a closer look reveals several familiar features. Rudimentary eyes, nose, lips, and even teeth can be recognized, and the embryo has stubby bulges that will form arms and legs.

The head and brain undergo rapid growth during the embryonic period. The head begins to represent a significant proportion of the embryo's size, encompassing about 50 percent of its total length. The growth of nerve cells, called *neurons*, is astonishing: During pregnancy, an average of 250,000 neurons are produced every minute! The nervous system begins to function around the 5th week, emitting weak brain waves (Nelson & Bosquet, 2000; Stiles & Jernigan, 2010).

placenta
a conduit between the mother and fetus, providing nourishment and oxygen via the umbilical cord.

embryonic stage
the period from 2 to 8 weeks following fertilization, during which significant growth occurs in the major organs and body systems.

Figure 2-9 Body Proportions

During the fetal period, the proportions of the body change dramatically. At 2 months, the head represents about half the fetus, but by the time of birth, it is one-quarter of its total size.

1/2	3/8	1/4

| 2 months after conception | 5 months after conception | Newborn |

fetal stage

the stage that begins at about 8 weeks after conception and continues until birth.

fetus

a developing child, from 8 weeks after conception until birth.

THE FETAL STAGE: 8 WEEKS TO BIRTH. It is not until the final period of prenatal development, the fetal stage, that the developing child becomes easily recognizable. The **fetal stage** starts at about 8 weeks after conception and continues until birth. The fetal stage formally starts when the differentiation of the major organs has occurred.

Now called a **fetus**, the developing child undergoes astoundingly rapid change during the fetal stage. For instance, it increases in length some 20 times, and its proportions change dramatically. At 2 months, around half the fetus is what will ultimately be its head; by 5 months, the head accounts for just over a quarter of its total size (see Figure 2-9). The fetus also substantially increases in weight. At 4 months, the fetus weighs an average of about 4 ounces; at 7 months, it weighs about 3 pounds; and at the time of birth the average child weighs just over 7 pounds.

At the same time, the developing child is rapidly becoming more complex. Organs become more differentiated and start to work. By 3 months, for example, the fetus swallows and urinates. In addition, the interconnections between the different parts of the body become more complex and integrated. For example, arms develop hands; hands develop fingers; fingers develop nails.

As this is happening, the fetus makes itself known to the outside world. In the earliest stages of pregnancy, mothers may be unaware that they are, in fact, pregnant. As the fetus becomes increasingly active, however, most mothers certainly take notice. By 4 months, a mother can feel the movement of her child, and several months later others can feel the baby's kicks through the mother's skin. In addition to the kicks that alert its mother to its presence, the fetus can turn, do somersaults, cry, hiccup, clench its fist, open and close its eyes, and suck its thumb.

The brain becomes increasingly sophisticated during the fetal stage. The two symmetrical left and right halves of the brain, known as *hemispheres*, grow rapidly, and the interconnections between neurons become more complex. The neurons become coated with an insulating material called *myelin*, which helps speed the transmission of messages from the brain to the rest of the body.

By the end of the fetal period, brain waves are produced that indicate the fetus passes through different stages of sleep and wakefulness. The fetus is also able to hear (and feel the vibrations of) sounds to which it is exposed. For instance, researchers Anthony DeCasper and Melanie Spence (1986) asked a group of pregnant mothers to read aloud the Dr. Seuss story *The Cat in the Hat* two times a day during the latter months of pregnancy. Three days after the babies were born, they appeared to recognize the story they had heard, responding more to it than to another story that had a different rhythm.

In weeks 8 to 24 following conception, hormones are released that lead to the increasing differentiation of male and female fetuses. For example, high levels of androgen are produced in males that affect the size of brain cells and the growth of neural connections, which, some scientists speculate, ultimately may lead to differences in male and female brain structure and even later variations in gender-related behavior (Knickmeyer & Baron-Cohen, 2006; Burton et al., 2009; Jordan-Young, 2012).

Just as no two adults are alike, no two fetuses are the same. Although development during the prenatal period follows the broad patterns outlined here, there are significant differences in the specific nature of individual fetuses' behavior. Some fetuses are exceedingly active, while others are more sedentary. (The more active fetuses will probably be more active after birth.) Some have relatively quick heart rates, while others' heart rates are slower, with the typical range varying between 120 and 160 beats per minute (DiPietro et al., 2002; Niederhofer, 2004; Tongsong et al., 2005).

Such differences in fetal behavior are due in part to genetic characteristics inherited at the moment of fertilization. Other kinds of differences, though, are brought about by the nature of the environment in which the child spends its first 9 months of life. As we will see, there are numerous ways in which the prenatal environment of infants affects their development—in good ways and bad. (Also see the *Neuroscience and Development* box.)

Neuroscience and Development

Autism and the Toddler Brain

Jeffery arrived in the world with signs of good health. An uneventful pregnancy and birth gave no clue about what Jeffery would be like in only 3 years. By 6 months, the little boy's parents noted he did not smile like other children; by his first birthday he had not yet babbled, pointed, or waved. At age 3, Jeffrey regressed and was withdrawn, even to caring family members. It was at this time that Jeffery was diagnosed with autism spectrum disorder (ASD).

Autism spectrum disorder (ASD) is a neurodevelopmental disorder characterized by abnormal brain development and functioning. Although its cause remains unknown, researchers hypothesize that ASD is related to problems with the function or structure of the central nervous system, especially the amygdala.

The amygdala is an almond-shaped complex cluster of neurons located deep within the inner side of each temporal lobe of the brain. In the past, scientists theorized that the amygdala, using sensory input from visual, auditory, and somatosensory systems, helps humans to process and respond to many kinds of events, particularly those involving fear and panic. More recent evidence suggests that fluctuations in the amygdala also occur when people are exposed to subtle, biologically relevant emotional and social information, such as facial expressions (Whalen et al., 2009).

Furthermore, new evidence suggests that the development of the amygdala in people with ASD undergoes a specific growth pattern in which the amygdala early in life is larger than typical, but later is smaller compared people without ASD. To investigate this pattern, a team of researchers used imaging scans to measure amygdala size and collected social and communication function information from 89 toddlers between the ages of 1 and 5.

Follow-up scanning and testing were completed after 5 years. Toddlers who were later diagnosed with ASD had significantly larger right and left amygdala compared with typically developing toddlers. Amygdala size was also related to the severity of social and communication impairments as measured by standardized tests in boys but not in girls with ASD.

Early life amygdala overgrowth may provide an early clue to later diagnosis of ASD. In addition, differential social and communication impairments for boys and girls may potentially be revealed by studying the size of the amygdala.

■ Based on these research findings, do you think all toddlers should be screened early in life for amygdala size? Why or why not?

Pregnancy Problems

LO 2.14 Describe major physical and ethical challenges that relate to pregnancy.

For some couples, conception presents a major challenge. Let's consider some of the challenges—both physical and ethical—that relate to pregnancy.

INFERTILITY. Some 15 percent of couples suffer from **infertility**, the inability to conceive after 12 to 18 months of trying to become pregnant. Fertility is negatively correlated with age: The older the parents, the more likely infertility will occur; see Figure 2-10.

In men, infertility is typically a result of producing too few sperm. Use of illicit drugs or cigarettes and previous bouts of sexually transmitted diseases also increase infertility. For women, the most common cause of infertility is failure to release an egg through ovulation. This may occur because of a hormone imbalance, a damaged fallopian tube or uterus, stress, or abuse of alcohol or drugs (Lewis, Legato, & Fisch, 2006; Malik et al., 2015).

Several treatments for infertility exist. Some difficulties can be corrected through the use of drugs or surgery. Another option may be **artificial insemination**, a procedure in which a man's sperm is placed directly into a woman's vagina by a physician. In some situations, the woman's husband provides the sperm, while in others it is an anonymous donor from a sperm bank.

In other cases, fertilization takes place outside of the mother's body. **In vitro fertilization (IVF)** is a procedure in which a woman's ova are removed from her ovaries, and a man's sperm are used to fertilize the ova in a laboratory. The fertilized egg is then implanted in a woman's uterus. Similarly, *gamete intrafallopian transfer (GIFT)*

infertility
the inability to conceive after 12 to 18 months of trying to become pregnant.

artificial insemination
a process of fertilization in which a man's sperm is placed directly into a woman's vagina by a physician.

in vitro fertilization (IVF)
a procedure in which a woman's ova are removed from her ovaries, and a man's sperm are used to fertilize the ova in a laboratory.

Figure 2-10 Older Women and Risks of Pregnancy

Not only does the rate of infertility increase as women get older, but the risk of chromosomal abnormality increases as well.

(**Source:** Reproductive Medicine Associates of New Jersey, 2002.)

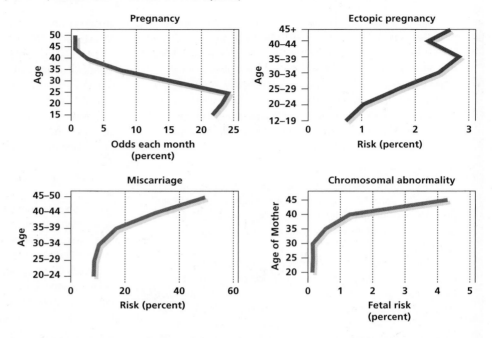

and *zygote intrafallopian transfer (ZIFT)* are procedures in which an egg and sperm or fertilized egg are implanted in a woman's fallopian tubes. In IVF, GIFT, and ZIFT, implantation is done either in the woman who provided the donor eggs or, in rarer instances, in a *surrogate mother*, a woman who agrees to carry the child to term. Surrogate mothers may also be used in cases in which the mother is unable to conceive; the surrogate mother is artificially inseminated by the biological father, and she agrees to give up rights to the infant (Frazier et al., 2004; Kolata, 2004; Hertz & Nelson, 2015).

IVF is increasingly successful, with pregnancy rates as high as 48 percent for women under 35 (but with lower rates for older women). (Actual live birth rates are lower, since not all pregnancies ultimately result in birth.) It is also becoming more commonplace, with the procedure being used and publicized by women such as actress Nicole Kidman. Worldwide, more than 3 million babies have been created through IVF (SART, 2012).

ETHICAL ISSUES. The use of surrogate mothers, in vitro fertilization, and sex selection techniques presents a web of ethical and legal issues, as well as many emotional concerns. In some cases, surrogate mothers have refused to give up the child after its birth, while in others the surrogate mother has sought to have a role in the child's life. In such cases, the rights of the mother, the father, the surrogate mother, and ultimately the baby are in conflict.

Even more troubling are concerns raised by sex selection techniques. Is it ethical to terminate the life of an embryo based on its sex? Do cultural pressures that may favor boys over girls make it permissible to seek medical intervention to produce male offspring? And—even more disturbing—if it is permissible to intervene in the reproductive process to obtain a favored sex, what about other characteristics determined by genetics that it may be possible in the future to preselect for? For instance, assuming the technology advances, would it be ethical to select for a favored eye or hair color, a certain level of intelligence, or a particular kind of personality? That's not feasible now, but it is not out the realm of possibility in the future.

For the moment, many of these ethical issues remain unresolved. But they raise important philosophical questions. Moreover, they involve cultural and religious issues. For example, in some religions, such as Catholicism, the use of some reproductive technologies such as IVF and surrogate mothers are prohibited because they are seen as violating the dignity of the child and marriage.

But the answer to one question is clear: How do children conceived using emerging reproductive technologies such as in vitro fertilization fare?

Research shows that they do quite well. In fact, some studies find that the quality of family life for those who have used such techniques may be superior to that in families with naturally conceived children. Furthermore, the later psychological adjustment of children conceived using IVF and artificial insemination is no different from that of children conceived using natural techniques (Dipietro, Costigan, & Gurewitsch, 2005; Hjelmstedt, Widstrom, & Collins, 2006; Siegel, Dittrich, & Vollmann, 2008).

However, the increasing use of IVF techniques by older individuals (who might be quite elderly when their children reach adolescence) may change these positive findings. Because widespread use of IVF is still a recent phenomenon, we just don't know yet what will happen with aging parents (Colpin & Soenen, 2004).

MISCARRIAGE AND ABORTION. A *miscarriage*—medically known as a spontaneous abortion—occurs when pregnancy ends before the developing child is able to survive outside the mother's womb. The embryo detaches from the wall of the uterus and is expelled.

Some 15 to 20 percent of all pregnancies end in miscarriage, usually in the first several months of pregnancy. Many occur so early that the mother is not even aware she was pregnant and may not even know she has suffered a miscarriage. Typically, miscarriages are attributable to some sort of genetic abnormality in the fetus. In addition, hormonal problems, infections, or maternal health problems can lead to miscarriage. Whatever the cause, women who suffer miscarriage frequently experience anxiety, depression, and grief. Because their bodies may continue to look pregnant for a period of several weeks before they go back to their pre-pregnant state, grief over the loss may be intensified and prolonged (Zucker & Alexander-Tanner, 2017).

Even after subsequently having a healthy child, women who have had a miscarriage in the past still have a higher risk for depression. In addition, the aftereffects may linger, sometimes for years, and the woman may have difficulty caring for her healthy child (Leis-Newman, 2012; Murphy, Lipp, & Powles, 2012; Sawicka, 2016).

About one in five pregnancies worldwide end in *abortion*, in which a mother voluntarily chooses to terminate pregnancy. Women in developing countries are more likely to have abortions than women in more developed countries, and the number of abortions in developed countries has declined significantly over the past several decades (Guttmacher Institute, 2017).

Involving a complex set of physical, psychological, legal, and ethical issues, abortion is a difficult choice for every woman. A task force of the American Psychological Association (APA), which looked at the aftereffects of abortion, found that, following an abortion, most women experienced a combination of relief over terminating an unwanted pregnancy and regret and guilt. In most cases, for adult women with an unplanned pregnancy who had an elective, first-trimester abortion, the risk of mental health problems was not higher than for women who actually deliver that pregnancy (APA Reproductive Choice Working Group, 2000; Sedgh et al., 2012).

Other research finds that abortion may be associated with an increased risk of future psychological problems. Clearly, there are significant individual differences in how women respond to the experience of abortion, and in all cases, abortion is a difficult decision (Cockrill & Gould, 2012; van Ditzhuijzen et al., 2013; Guttmacher Institute, 2017).

The Prenatal Environment: Threats to Development

LO 2.15 **Analyze threats to the fetal environment, and explain what can be done about them.**

According to the Siriono people of South America, if a pregnant woman eats the meat of certain kinds of animals, she runs the risk of having a child who may act and look like those animals. According to opinions offered on daytime talk shows, a pregnant mother should avoid getting angry in order to spare her child from entering the world with anger (Cole, 1992).

Such views are largely the stuff of folklore, although there is some evidence that a mother's anxiety during pregnancy may affect the sleeping patterns of the fetus prior to birth. However, there are certain aspects of a mother's and father's behavior, both before and after conception, that can produce lifelong consequences for the child. Some consequences show up immediately, but half the possible problems aren't apparent before birth. Other problems, more insidious ones, may not manifest until years after birth (Couzin, 2002; Tiesler & Heinrich, 2014).

Some of the most profound consequences are brought about by teratogenic agents. A **teratogen** is an environmental agent such as a drug, chemical, virus, or other factor that produces a birth defect. Although it is the job of the placenta to keep teratogens from reaching the fetus, the placenta is not entirely successful at this, and probably every fetus is exposed to some teratogens.

The timing and quantity of exposure to a teratogen are crucial. At some phases of prenatal development, a certain teratogen may have only a minimal impact. At other periods, however, the same teratogen may have significant consequences. Generally, teratogens have their most significant effects during periods of especially rapid prenatal development. Sensitivity to specific teratogens is also related to racial and cultural background. For example, Native American fetuses are more susceptible to the effects of alcohol than those of European American descent (Kinney et al., 2003; Winger & Woods, 2004; Rentner, Dixon, & Lengel, 2012).

Furthermore, different organ systems are vulnerable to teratogens at different times during development. For example, the brain is most susceptible 15 to 25 days after conception, while the heart is most vulnerable 20 to 40 days following conception (see Figure 2-11; Kolb, 1993).

When considering the findings relating to specific teratogens, as we'll do next, we need to keep in mind the broader social and cultural context in which teratogen exposure occurs. For example, living in poverty increases the chances of exposure to teratogens. Mothers who are poor may not be able to afford adequate nutrition, and they may not be able to afford adequate medical care, making them more susceptible to illness that can damage a developing fetus. They are more likely to be exposed to pollution. Consequently, it is always important to consider the context of exposure to teratogens.

MOTHER'S DIET. Most of our knowledge of the environmental factors that affect the developing fetus comes from the study of the mother. For instance, as the midwife pointed out in the example of Lisa and Robert, a mother's diet clearly plays an important role in bolstering the development of the fetus. A mother who eats a varied diet high in nutrients is apt to have fewer complications during pregnancy, an easier labor, and a generally healthier baby than a mother whose diet is restricted in nutrients (Guerrini, Thomson, & Gurling, 2007; Marques et al., 2014).

With 800 million hungry people in the world, the problem of diet is of immense global concern. Even worse, the number of people vulnerable to hunger is close to 1 *billion*. Clearly, restrictions in diet that bring about hunger on such a massive scale affect millions of children born to women living in those conditions (United Nations, 2015).

MOTHER'S AGE. More women are giving birth later in life than was true just two or three decades ago. The cause for this change is largely transformations in society, as more women choose to pursue advanced degrees and to start careers before giving birth to their first child (Gibbs, 2002; Wildberger, 2003; Bornstein et al., 2006).

Consequently, the number of women who give birth in their 30s and 40s has grown considerably. However, this delay in childbirth has potential consequences for both mothers' and children's health. Women who give birth when over age 30 are at greater risk for a variety of pregnancy and birth complications than younger ones. For instance, they are more apt to give birth prematurely, and their children are more likely to have low birthweights. This occurs in part because of a decline in the condition of a woman's eggs. For example, by the time they are 42 years old, 90 percent of a woman's eggs are no longer normal (Gibbs, 2002; Moore & deCosta, 2006). Older

teratogen

an environmental agent, such as a drug, chemical, virus, or other factor that produces a birth defect.

Figure 2-11 Teratogen Sensitivity

Depending on their state of development, some parts of the body vary in their sensitivity to teratogens. (**Source:** Moore, 1974.)

Most common site of birth defect

■ Heart ■ Central nervous system ■ Eye ■ Arm ■ Leg

■ Ear ■ Teeth ■ Palate ■ External genitalia ■ Brain

mothers are also considerably more likely to give birth to children with Down syndrome, a form of intellectual disability. About 1 out of 100 babies born to mothers over 40 has Down syndrome; for mothers over 50, the incidence increases to 25 percent, or one in four (Weijerman et al., 2008). However, some research shows that older mothers are not automatically at risk for more pregnancy problems. For instance, one study found that when women in their 40s who had not experienced health difficulties were considered, they were no more likely to have prenatal problems than those in their 20s (Kirchengast & Hartmann, 2003; Carson et al., 2016).

The risks involved in pregnancy are greater not only for older mothers but for atypically young women as well. Women who become pregnant during adolescence—and such pregnancies actually encompass 20 percent of all pregnancies—are more likely to have premature deliveries. Furthermore, the mortality rate of infants born to adolescent mothers is double that for mothers in their 20s (Kirchengast & Hartmann, 2003).

MOTHER'S PRENATAL SUPPORT.   Keep in mind, though, that the higher mortality rate for babies of adolescent mothers reflects more than just physiological problems related to the mothers' youth. Young mothers often face adverse social and economic factors that can affect infant health. Many teenage mothers do not have enough money or social support, a situation that prevents them from getting good prenatal care and parenting support after the baby is born. Poverty or social circumstances, such as a lack of parental involvement or supervision, may even have set the stage for the adolescent to become pregnant in the first place (DePietro, 2004; Huizink, Mulder, & Buitelaar, 2004).

MOTHER'S HEALTH. Depending on when it strikes, an illness in a pregnant woman can have devastating consequences. For instance, the onset of *rubella* (German measles) in the mother prior to the 11th week of pregnancy is likely to cause serious consequences in the baby, including blindness, deafness, heart defects, or brain damage. In later stages of a pregnancy, however, adverse consequences of rubella become increasingly less likely.

Several other diseases may affect a developing fetus, again depending on when the illness is contracted. For instance, *chicken pox* may produce birth defects, while *mumps* may increase the risk of miscarriage. Furthermore, some sexually transmitted infections such as *syphilis* can be transmitted directly to the fetus, who will be born suffering from the disease. In some cases, sexually transmitted diseases such as *gonorrhea* are transmitted to the child as it passes through the birth canal to be born. *AIDS (acquired immune deficiency syndrome)*, too, may be passed on to the fetus through the blood that reaches the placenta (Nesheim et al., 2004).

MOTHER'S DRUG USE. A pregnant woman's use of many kinds of drugs—both legal and illegal—poses serious risks to the unborn child. Even over-the-counter remedies for common ailments can have surprisingly injurious consequences. For instance, aspirin taken for a headache can lead to fetal bleeding and growth impairments (Finnegan & Kandall, 2008; Tsantefski, Humphreys, & Jackson, 2014).

Some drugs taken by mothers cause difficulties in their children literally decades after they are taken. As recently as the 1970s, the artificial hormone *DES (diethylstilbestrol)* was frequently prescribed to prevent miscarriage. Only later was it found that the daughters of mothers who took DES stood a much higher than normal chance of developing a rare form of vaginal or cervical cancer and had more difficulties during their pregnancies. Sons of the mothers who had taken DES had their own problems, including a higher rate than average of reproductive difficulties (Adams Hillard, 2001; Schecter, Finkelstein, & Koren, 2005).

Birth control or fertility pills taken by pregnant women before they are aware of their pregnancy can also cause fetal damage. Such medicines contain sex hormones that affect developing brain structures in the fetus. These hormones, which when produced naturally are related to sexual differentiation in the fetus and gender differences after birth, can cause significant damage (Brown, Hines, & Fane, 2002).

Illicit drugs may pose equally great, and sometimes even greater, risks for the environments of prenatal children. For one thing, the purity of drugs purchased illegally varies significantly, so drug users can never be quite sure what specifically they are ingesting. Furthermore, the effects of some commonly used illicit drugs such as marijuana and cocaine can be particularly devastating (Williams & Ross, 2007; Goldschmidt et al., 2008; Willford, Richardson, & Day, 2012).

The most recent drug problem involving pregnant mothers is the opioid epidemic in the United States. Opioids are highly addictive, and some are relatively inexpensive to obtain. Many pregnant women who are addicted to opioids such as heroin or oxycodone face barriers when they seek treatment, because the kinds of drug treatments that would normally be used to help recovery may be dangerous to the unborn child. In fact, some drug treatment facilities turn pregnant women away. It is a health crisis of growing proportions (Ockerman, 2017).

MOTHER'S USE OF ALCOHOL AND TOBACCO. A pregnant woman who reasons that having a drink every once in a while or smoking an occasional cigarette has no appreciable effect on her unborn child is kidding herself: Increasing evidence suggests that even small amounts of alcohol and nicotine can disrupt the development of the fetus.

Mothers' use of alcohol can have profound consequences for the unborn child. The children of alcoholics, who consume substantial quantities of alcohol during pregnancy, are at the greatest risk. Approximately 1 out of every 750 infants is born with **fetal alcohol spectrum disorder (FASD)**, a disorder that may include below-average intelligence and sometimes intellectual disability, delayed growth, and facial deformities. FASD is now the primary preventable cause of intellectual disability (Calhoun & Warren, 2007; Bakoyiannis et al., 2014; Wilhoit, Scott, & Simecka, 2017).

Even mothers who use smaller amounts of alcohol during pregnancy place their child at risk. **Fetal alcohol effects (FAE)** is a condition in which children display some, although not all, of the problems of FASD due to their mother's consumption of alcohol during pregnancy (Baer, Sampson, & Barr, 2003).

Children who do not have FAE may still be affected by their mothers' use of alcohol. Studies have found that maternal consumption of an average of just two alcoholic drinks a day during pregnancy is associated with lower intelligence in their offspring at age 7. Other research concurs, suggesting that relatively small quantities of alcohol taken during pregnancy can have future adverse effects on children's behavior and psychological functioning. Furthermore, the consequences of alcohol ingestion during pregnancy are long-lasting. For example, one study found that 14-year-olds' success on a test involving spatial and visual reasoning was related to their mothers' alcohol consumption during pregnancy. The more the mothers reported drinking, the less accurately their children responded (Mattson, Calarco, & Lang, 2006; Streissguth, 2007; Chiodo et al., 2012).

Because of the risks associated with alcohol, physicians today counsel pregnant women (and even those who are trying to become pregnant) to avoid drinking any alcoholic beverages. In addition, they caution against another practice proven to have an adverse effect on an unborn child: smoking.

Smoking produces several consequences, none of which are good. For starters, smoking reduces the oxygen content and increases the carbon monoxide of the mother's blood, which quickly reduces the oxygen available to the fetus. In addition, the nicotine and other toxins in cigarettes slow the respiration rate of the fetus and speed up its heart.

The ultimate result is an increased possibility of miscarriage and a higher likelihood of death during infancy. In fact, estimates suggest that smoking by pregnant women leads to more than 100,000 miscarriages and the deaths of 5,600 babies in the United States alone each year (Haslam & Lawrence, 2004).

Smokers are two times as likely as nonsmokers to have babies with an abnormally low birthweight, and smokers' babies are shorter, on average, than those of nonsmokers. Furthermore, women who smoke during pregnancy are 50 percent more likely to have children with intellectual disabilities. Finally, mothers who smoke are more likely to have children who exhibit disruptive behavior during childhood (Wakschlag et al., 2006; Alshaarawy & Anthony, 2015).

DO FATHERS AFFECT THE PRENATAL ENVIRONMENT? It would be easy to reason that once the father has done his part in the sequence of events leading to conception, he would have no role in the *prenatal* environment of the fetus. In fact, developmental researchers have in the past generally shared this view, and there is relatively little research investigating fathers' influence on the prenatal environment.

However, it is becoming increasingly clear that fathers' behavior may well influence the prenatal environment. Consequently, health practitioners are applying the research to suggest ways fathers can support healthy prenatal development (Martin et al., 2007; Vreeswijk et al., 2013).

For instance, fathers-to-be should avoid smoking. Secondhand smoke from a father's cigarettes may affect the mother's health, which in turn influences her unborn child. The greater the level of a father's smoking, the lower the birthweight of his children (Delpisheh et al., 2006; da Veiga & Wilder, 2008).

From *a health-care provider's* perspective

In addition to avoiding smoking, what else might fathers-to-be do to help their unborn children develop normally in the womb?

fetal alcohol spectrum disorder (FASD)
a disorder caused by the pregnant mother consuming substantial quantities of alcohol during pregnancy, potentially resulting in intellectual disability and delayed growth in the child.

fetal alcohol effects (FAE)
a condition in which children display some, although not all, of the problems of fetal alcohol syndrome due to the mother's consumption of alcohol during pregnancy.

Monkey Business Images/Shutterstock

Pregnant women who drink alcohol place their unborn children at significant risk.

Similarly, a father's use of alcohol and illegal drugs can have significant effects on the fetus. Alcohol and drug use impairs sperm and may lead to chromosomal damage that may affect the fetus at conception. In addition, alcohol and drug use during pregnancy may also affect the prenatal environment by creating stress in the mother and generally producing an unhealthy environment. Environmental toxins in the father's workplace—such as lead or mercury—may bind to sperm and cause birth defects (Dare et al., 2002; Choy et al., 2002; Guttmannova et al., 2016).

Finally, fathers who are physically or emotionally abusive to their pregnant wives can damage their unborn children. By increasing the level of maternal stress, or actually causing physical damage, abusive fathers increase the risk of harm to their unborn children. In fact, around 5 percent of women face physical abuse during pregnancy (Bacchus, Mezey, & Bewley, 2006; Martin, et al., 2006).

Labor: The Process of Birth Begins

LO 2.16 Describe the normal process of labor.

About 266 days after conception, a protein called *corticotropin-releasing hormone* (CRH) triggers (for some still unknown reason) the release of various hormones, and the process that leads to birth begins. One critical hormone is *oxytocin*, which is released by the mother's pituitary gland. When the concentration of oxytocin becomes high enough, the mother's uterus begins periodic contractions (Terzidou, 2007; Tattersall et al., 2012; Gordon et al., 2017).

Development in Your Life

Optimizing the Prenatal Environment

If you are contemplating ever having a child, you may be overwhelmed, at this point, by the number of things that can go wrong. Don't be. Although both genetics and the environment pose their share of risks, in the vast majority of cases, pregnancy and birth proceed without mishap. Moreover, there are several things that women can do—both before and during pregnancy—to optimize the probability that pregnancy will progress smoothly. (Centers for Disease Control and Prevention, 2017). Among them:

- **For women who are planning to become pregnant, several precautions are in order.** First, they should have non-emergency X-rays only during the first 2 weeks after their menstrual periods. Second, they should be vaccinated against rubella (German measles) at least 3, and preferably 6, months before getting pregnant. Finally, they should avoid birth control pills at least 3 months before trying to conceive, because of disruptions to hormonal production caused by the pills.

- **Eat well, both before and during (and after, for that matter!) pregnancy.** Pregnant mothers are, as the old saying goes, eating for two. This means that it is more essential than ever to eat regular, well-balanced meals. In addition, physicians typically recommend taking prenatal vitamins that include folic acid, which can decrease the likelihood of birth defects (Amitai et al., 2004).

- **Don't use alcohol and other drugs.** The evidence is clear that many drugs pass directly to the fetus and may cause birth defects. It is also clear that the more one drinks, the greater the risk to the fetus. The best advice, whether you are already pregnant or planning to have a child: Don't use *any* drug unless directed by a physician. If you are planning to get pregnant, encourage your partner to avoid using alcohol or other drugs too (O'Connor & Whaley, 2006).

- **Monitor caffeine intake.** Although it is still unclear whether caffeine produces birth defects, it is known that the caffeine found in coffee, tea, and chocolate can pass to the fetus, acting as a stimulant. Because of this, you probably shouldn't drink more than a few cups of coffee a day (Wisborg et al., 2003).

- **Whether pregnant or not, don't smoke.** This holds true for mothers, fathers, and anyone else in the vicinity of the pregnant mother, since research suggests that smoke in the fetal environment can affect birthweight. Smoking is the single most preventable cause of illness and death among infants and their mothers.

- **Exercise regularly.** In most cases, pregnant women can continue to exercise, particularly exercises involving low-impact routines. However, extreme exercise should be avoided, especially on very hot or very cold days. (Evenson, 2011; DiNallo, Downs, & Le Masurier, 2012; Centers for Disease Control and Prevention, 2017).

During the prenatal period, the uterus, which is composed of muscle tissue, slowly expands as the fetus grows. Although for most of the pregnancy it is inactive, after the fourth month it occasionally contracts in order to ready itself for the eventual delivery. These contractions, called *Braxton-Hicks contractions*, are sometimes called "false labor," because while they can fool eager and anxious expectant parents, they do not signify that the baby will be born soon.

When birth is actually imminent, the uterus begins to contract intermittently. Its increasingly intense contractions act as if it were a vise, opening and closing to force the head of the fetus against the *cervix*, the neck of the uterus that separates it from the vagina. Eventually, the force of the contractions becomes strong enough to propel the fetus slowly down the birth canal until it enters the world as a **neonate**—the term used for a newborn. It is this exertion and the narrow birth passageway that often gives newborns the battered, cone-head appearance.

The process of labor produces a range of emotions.

Labor proceeds in three stages (see Figure 2-12). In the *first stage of labor*, the uterine contractions initially occur around every 8 to 10 minutes and last about 30 seconds. As labor proceeds, the contractions occur more frequently and last longer. Toward the end of labor, the contractions may occur every 2 minutes and last almost 2 minutes. During the final part of the first stage of labor, the contractions increase to their greatest intensity, a period known as *transition*. The mother's cervix fully opens, eventually expanding enough (usually to around 10 cm) to allow the baby's head (the widest part of the body) to pass through.

neonate
the term used for a newborn

This first stage of labor is the longest. Its duration varies significantly, depending on the mother's age, race, ethnicity, number of prior pregnancies, and a variety of other factors involving both the fetus and the mother. Typically, labor takes 16 to 24 hours for firstborn children, but there are wide variations. Births of subsequent children usually involve shorter periods of labor.

During the *second stage of labor*, which typically lasts around 90 minutes, the baby's head emerges further from the mother with each contraction, increasing the size

Figure 2-12 Three Stages of Labor

Stage 1

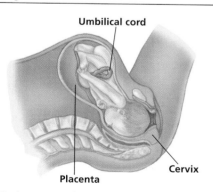

Umbilical cord

Placenta

Cervix

Uterine contractions initially occur every 8 to 10 minutes and last 30 seconds. Toward the end of labor, contractions may occur every 2 minutes and last as long as 2 minutes. As the contractions increase, the cervix, which separates the uterus from the vagina, becomes wider, eventually expanding to allow the baby's head to pass through.

Stage 2

The baby's head starts to move through the cervix and birth canal. Typically lasting around 90 minutes, the second stage ends when the baby has completely left the mother's body.

Stage 3

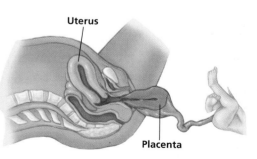

Uterus

Placenta

The child's umbilical cord (still attached to the neonate) and the placenta are expelled from the mother. This stage is the quickest and easiest, taking just a few minutes.

episiotomy

an incision sometimes made to increase the size of the opening of the vagina to allow the baby to pass.

of the vaginal opening. Because the area between the vagina and rectum must stretch a good deal, an incision called an **episiotomy** is sometimes made to increase the size of the opening of the vagina. However, this practice has been increasingly criticized in recent years as potentially causing more harm than good, and the number of episiotomies has fallen drastically in the past decade. The second stage of labor ends when the baby has completely left the mother's body (Dudding, Vaizey, & Kamm, 2008; Manzanares et al., 2013; Ballesteros-Meseguer, 2016).

Finally, the *third stage of labor* occurs when the child's umbilical cord (still attached to the neonate) and the placenta are expelled from the mother. This stage is the quickest and easiest, taking just a few minutes.

Approaches to Childbirth: Where Medicine and Attitudes Meet

LO 2.17 Describe the process of birth and analyze current approaches to childbirth.

The exact moment of birth occurs when the fetus, having left the uterus through the cervix, passes through the vagina to emerge fully from its mother's body. In most cases, babies automatically make the transition from taking in oxygen via the placenta to using their lungs to breathe air. Consequently, as soon as they are outside the mother's body, most newborns spontaneously cry. This helps them clear their lungs and breathe on their own.

What happens next varies from situation to situation and from culture to culture. In Western cultures, health-care workers are almost always on hand to assist with the birth. In the United States, 99 percent of births are attended by professional health-care workers, but in many less-developed countries less than half of births have professional health-care workers in attendance (United Nations Statistics Division, 2012).

THE BIRTHING PROCESS: A MENU OF CHOICES.

In her second pregnancy, Alma Juarez knew she wanted something other than traditional obstetrics. No drugs. No lying flat on her back for the delivery (which had slowed her contractions and made an oxygen mask necessary). This time, Juarez took control. She joined an exercise class for pregnant women and read books on childbirth. She also chose a nurse-midwife instead of an obstetrician. She wanted someone to work with her, not dictate to her.

When Juarez went into labor, she called the midwife, who met her at the hospital. Juarez was determined to stay on her feet, making use of gravity to hasten the birth. Her husband and the midwife took turns walking with her as the contractions got stronger. When she was fully dilated, she got on her hands and knees, a posture she knew would minimize the effort of pushing. Thirty minutes later, her daughter was born. No drugs, no extra oxygen. Juarez says, "The first birth, I was exhausted. The second birth, I was elated."

Parents in the Western world have developed a variety of strategies—and some very strong opinions—to help them deal with something as natural as giving birth, which occurs apparently without much thought throughout the nonhuman animal world. Today parents need to decide: Should the birth take place in a hospital or in the home? Should a physician, a nurse, or a midwife assist? Is the father's presence desirable? Should siblings and other family members be on hand to participate in the birth?

Most of these questions cannot be answered definitively, primarily because the choice of childbirth techniques often comes down to a matter of values and opinions. No single procedure will be effective for all mothers and fathers, and no conclusive research evidence has proven that one procedure is significantly more effective than another. As we'll see, there is a wide variety of different issues and options involved, and certainly one's culture plays a role in choices of birthing procedures.

The abundance of choices is largely due to a reaction to traditional medical practices that had been common in the United States until the early 1970s. Before that time, the typical birth went something like this: A woman in labor was placed in a room with many other women, all of whom were in various stages of childbirth, and some of whom were screaming in pain. Fathers and other family members were not allowed to be present. Just before delivery, the woman was rolled into a delivery room, where the birth took place. Often she was so drugged that she was not aware of the birth at all.

At the time, physicians argued that such procedures were necessary to ensure the health of the newborn and the mother. However, critics charged that alternatives were available that not only would maximize the medical well-being of the participants in the birth but also would represent an emotional and psychological improvement (Curl et al., 2004; Hotelling & Humenick, 2005).

ALTERNATIVE BIRTHING PROCEDURES. Not all mothers give birth in hospitals, and not all births follow a traditional course. Among the major alternatives to traditional birthing practices are the following:

- *Lamaze birthing techniques.* The Lamaze method has achieved widespread popularity in the United States. Based on the writings of Dr. Fernand Lamaze, the method makes use of breathing techniques and relaxation training (Lamaze, 1970). Typically, mothers-to-be participate in a series of weekly training sessions in which they learn exercises that help them relax various parts of the body on command. A "coach," most typically the father or the mother's partner, is trained along with the future mother. The training allows women to cope with painful contractions by concentrating on their breathing and producing a relaxation response, rather than by tensing up, which can make the pain more acute. Women learn to focus on a relaxing stimulus, such as a tranquil scene in a picture. The goal is to learn how to deal positively with pain and to relax at the onset of a contraction.

  Does the procedure work? Most mothers, as well as fathers, report that a Lamaze birth is a very positive experience. They enjoy the sense of mastery that they gain over the process of labor, a feeling of being able to exert some control over what can be a formidable experience. Given that, we can't be sure that parents who choose the Lamaze method aren't already more highly motivated about the experience of childbirth than parents who do not choose the technique. It is therefore possible that the accolades they express after Lamaze births are due to their initial enthusiasm and not to the Lamaze procedures themselves (Larsen, O'Hara, & Brewer, 2001; Zwelling, 2006).

- *Bradley Method.* The Bradley Method, which is sometimes known as "husband-coached childbirth," is based on the principle that childbirth should be as natural as possible and involve no medication or medical interventions. Women are taught to "tune into" their bodies in order to deal with the pain of childbirth. To prepare for childbirth, mothers-to-be are taught muscle relaxation techniques, similar to Lamaze procedures, and good nutrition and exercise during pregnancy are seen as important to prepare for delivery. Parents are urged to take responsibility for childbirth, and the use of physicians is viewed as unnecessary and sometimes even dangerous. As you might expect, the discouragement of traditional medical interventions is quite controversial (Reed, 2005).

- *Hypnobirthing.* Hypnobirthing is a new, but increasingly popular, technique. It involves a form of self-hypnosis during delivery, which creates a sense of peace and calm, thereby reducing pain. The basic concept is to produce a state of focused concentration in which a mother relaxes her body while focusing inward. Increasing research evidence shows the technique can be effective in reducing pain (Olson, 2006; White, 2007; Alexander, Turnbull, & Cyna, 2009).

- *Water Birthing.* Still relatively uncommon in the United States, water birthing is a practice in which a woman enters a pool of warm water to give birth. The theory is that the warmth and buoyancy of the water is soothing, easing the length and pain of labor and childbirth, and the entry into the world is soothed for the infant, who moves from the watery environment of the womb to the birthing pool. Although there is some evidence that water birthing reduces pain and the length of labor, there is a risk of infection from the unsterile water (Thoni, Mussner, & Ploner, 2010; Jones et al., 2012).

CHILDBIRTH ATTENDANTS: WHO DELIVERS? Traditionally, *obstetricians*, physicians who specialize in delivering babies, have been the childbirth attendants of choice. In the past few decades, more mothers have chosen to use a *midwife*, a childbirth attendant who stays with the mother throughout labor and delivery. Midwives—most often nurses specializing in childbirth—are used primarily for pregnancies in which no complications are expected. The use of midwives has increased steadily in the United States—there are now 7,000 of them—and they are employed in 10 percent of births. Midwives help deliver some 80 percent of babies in other parts of the world, often at home. Home birth is common in countries at all levels of economic development. For instance, a third of all births in the Netherlands occur at home (Ayoub, 2005; Klein, 2012; Sandall, 2014).

From *a health-care worker's* perspective

While 99 percent of U.S. births are attended by professional medical workers or birthing attendants, this is the case in only about half of births worldwide. What do you think are some reasons for this, and what are the implications of this statistic?

The newest trend in childbirth assistance is also one of the oldest: the doula (pronounced doo-lah). A *doula* is trained to provide emotional, psychological, and educational support during birth. A doula does not replace an obstetrician or midwife, and does not do medical exams. Instead, doulas, who are often well-versed in birthing alternatives, provide the mother with support and make sure parents are aware of alternatives and possibilities regarding the birth process.

Although the use of doulas is new in the United States, they represent a return to an older tradition that has existed for centuries in other cultures. Although they may not be called "doulas," supportive, experienced older women have helped mothers as they give birth in non-Western cultures for centuries.

A growing body of research indicates that the presence of a doula is beneficial to the birth process, speeding deliveries and reducing reliance on drugs. Yet concerns remain about their use. Unlike certified midwives, who are nurses and receive an additional year or two of training, doulas do not need to be certified or have any particular level of education (Humphries, & Korfmacher, 2012; Simkin, 2014; Darwin et al., 2017).

USE OF ANESTHESIA AND PAIN-REDUCING DRUGS. Among the greatest advances of modern medicine is the ongoing discovery of drugs that reduce pain. However, the use of medication during childbirth is a practice that holds both benefits and pitfalls (Williams, Povey, & White, 2008).

About half of women who give birth receive anesthesia do so in the form of *epidural anesthesia*, which produces numbness from the waist down. Traditional epidurals produce an inability to walk and in some cases prevent women from helping to push the baby out during delivery. However, a newer form of epidural, known as a *walking epidural* or *dual spinal-epidural*, uses smaller needles and a system for administering continuous doses of anesthetic. It permits women to move about more freely during labor and has fewer side effects than traditional epidural anesthesia (Simmons et al., 2007; Osterman & Martin, 2011).

It is clear that drugs hold the promise of greatly reducing, and even eliminating, pain associated with labor, which can be extreme and exhausting. But pain reduction comes at a cost: Drugs administered during labor reach not just the mother but the fetus as well. The stronger the drug, the greater its effects on the fetus and neonate. Because of the small size of the fetus relative to the mother, drug doses that might have only a minimal effect on the mother can have a magnified effect on the fetus.

Anesthetics may temporarily depress the flow of oxygen to the fetus and slow labor. In addition, newborns whose mothers have been anesthetized are less physiologically responsive, show poorer motor control during the first days after birth, cry more, and may have more difficulty initiating breastfeeding (Ransjö-Arvidson et al., 2001; Torvaldsen et al., 2006).

Still, most research suggests that drugs, as they are currently employed during labor, produce only minimal risks to the fetus and neonate. Guidelines issued by the

American College of Obstetricians and Gynecologists suggest that a woman's request for pain relief at any stage of labor should be honored, and that the proper use of minimal amounts of drugs for pain relief is reasonable and has no significant effect on a child's later well-being (ACOG, 2002; Albers et al., 2007; Costa-Martins et al., 2014).

Birth Complications

LO 2.18 Recognize threats and complications that may accompany childbirth, and explain how they can be addressed.

When Ivy Brown's son was stillborn, a nurse told her that sad as it was, nearly 1 percent of births in her city, Washington, DC, ended in death. That statistic spurred Brown to become a grief counselor, specializing in infant mortality. She formed a committee of physicians and city officials to study the capital's high infant mortality rate and find solutions to lower it. "If I can spare one mother this terrible grief, my loss will not be in vain," Brown says.

The infant mortality rate in Washington, DC, capital of the richest country in the world, is 8 deaths per 1,000 births, exceeding the rate of countries such as Hungary, Cuba, and Ireland. Overall, nearly 50 countries have better birth rates than the United States (*World Factbook*, 2016; Vinik, 2015; see Figure 2-13).

Why is infant survival less likely in the United States than in quite a few less developed countries? To answer this question, we need to consider the nature of the problems that can occur during labor and delivery.

PRETERM INFANTS: TOO SOON, TOO SMALL.   Around one out of 10 infants are born earlier than normal. **Preterm infants**, or premature infants, are born prior to 38 weeks after conception. Because they have not had time to develop fully as fetuses, preterm infants are at high risk for illness and death.

The extent of danger faced by preterm babies largely depends on the child's weight at birth, which has great significance as an indicator of the extent of the baby's development. Although the average newborn weighs around 3,400 grams (about 7 1/2 pounds), **low-birthweight infants** weigh less than 2,500 grams (around 5 1/2 pounds). Although only 7 percent of all newborns in the United States fall into the low-birthweight category, they account for the majority of newborn deaths (DeVader et al., 2007).

Although most low-birthweight infants are preterm, some are small-for-gestational-age babies. **Small-for-gestational-age infants** are infants who, because of delayed fetal growth, weigh 90 percent (or less) of the average weight of infants of the same gestational age. Small-for-gestational-age infants are sometimes also preterm, but may not be (Bergmann, Bergmann, & Dudenhausen, 2008; Salihu et al., 2013).

If the degree of prematurity is not too great and weight at birth is not extremely low, the threat to the child's well-being is relatively minor. In such cases, the main treatment may be to keep the baby in the hospital to gain weight. Additional weight is critical because fat layers help prevent chilling in neonates, who are not particularly efficient at regulating body temperature.

Research also shows that preterm infants who receive more responsive, stimulating, and organized care are apt to show more positive outcomes than those children whose care is not as good. Some of these interventions are quite simple.

preterm infants
infants who are born prior to 38 weeks after conception (also known as premature infants).

low-birthweight infants
infants who weigh less than 2,500 grams (around 5 1/2 pounds) at birth.

small-for-gestational-age infants
infants who, because of delayed fetal growth, weigh 90 percent (or less) of the average weight of infants of the same gestational age.

Figure 2-13 International Infant Mortality

While the United States has greatly reduced its infant mortality rate in the past 25 years, it ranks below many other industrialized countries. What are some of the reasons for this?
(Source: *World Factbook*, 2016.)

Preterm infants stand a much greater chance of survival today than they did even a decade ago.

For example, "kangaroo care," in which infants are held skin-to-skin against their parents' chests, appears to be effective in helping preterm infants develop. Massaging preterm infants several times a day triggers the release of hormones that promote weight gain, muscle development, and the ability to cope with stress (Kaffashi et al., 2013; Athanasopoulou & Fox, 2014; Nobre et al., 2017).

Newborns who are born more prematurely and who have birthweights significantly below average face a tougher road. For them, simply staying alive is a major task. For instance, low-birthweight infants are highly vulnerable to infection, and because their lungs have not had sufficient time to develop completely, they have problems taking in sufficient oxygen. As a consequence, they may experience *respiratory distress syndrome (RDS)*, with potentially fatal consequences.

To deal with RDS, low-birthweight infants are often placed in incubators, enclosures in which temperature and oxygen content are controlled. The exact amount of oxygen is carefully monitored. Too low a concentration of oxygen will not provide relief, and too high a concentration can damage the delicate retinas of the eyes, leading to permanent blindness.

The immature development of preterm neonates makes them unusually sensitive to stimuli in their environment. They can easily be overwhelmed by the sights, sounds, and sensations they experience, and their breathing may be interrupted or their heart rates may slow. They are often unable to move smoothly; their arm and leg movements are uncoordinated, causing them to jerk about and appear startled. Such behavior is quite disconcerting to parents (Miles et al., 2006; Valeri et al., 2015).

Despite the difficulties they experience at birth, the majority of preterm infants eventually develop normally. However, the tempo of development often proceeds more slowly for preterm children compared to children born at full term, and more subtle problems sometimes emerge later. For example, by the end of their first year, only 10 percent of prematurely born infants display significant problems, and only 5 percent are seriously disabled. By age 6, however, approximately 38 percent have mild problems that call for special educational interventions. For instance, some preterm children show learning disabilities, behavior disorders, or lower-than-average IQ scores. They also may be at greater risk for mental illness. Others have difficulties with physical coordination. Still, around 60 percent of preterm infants are free of even minor problems (Hall et al., 2008; Nosarti et al., 2012; El Ayoubi et al., 2016).

VERY-LOW-BIRTHWEIGHT INFANTS: THE SMALLEST OF THE SMALL. The story is less positive for the most extreme cases of prematurity—very-low-birthweight infants. **Very-low-birthweight infants** weigh less than 1,250 grams (around 2 1/4 pounds) or, regardless of weight, have been in the womb less than 30 weeks.

very-low-birthweight infants infants who weigh less than 1,250 grams (around 2.25 pounds) or, regardless of weight, have been in the womb less than 30 weeks.

Very-low-birthweight infants not only are tiny—some fitting easily in the palm of the hand at birth—they hardly seem to belong to the same species as full-term newborns. Their eyes may be fused shut and their earlobes may look like flaps of skin on the sides of their heads. Their skin is a darkened red color, whatever their race.

Very-low-birthweight babies are in grave danger from the moment they are born, due to the immaturity of their organ systems. Before the mid-1980s, these babies would not have survived outside their mothers' wombs. However, medical advances have led to a higher chance of survival, pushing the *age of viability*, the point at which an infant can survive prematurely, to about 22 weeks—some 4 months earlier than the term of a normal delivery. Of course, the longer the period of development beyond conception, the higher are a newborn's chances of survival. A baby born earlier than 25 weeks has less than a 50–50 chance of survival. As medical capabilities progress and developmental researchers come up with new strategies for dealing with preterm infants and improving their lives, the age of viability is likely to be pushed even earlier (see Figure 2-14; Seaton et al., 2012).

Figure 2-14 Survival and Gestational Age

Chances of a fetus surviving greatly improve after 28 to 32 weeks. Rates shown are the number per thousand of babies born in the United States after specified lengths of gestation who survive the first year of life. **THINKING ABOUT THE DATA:** How does the U.S. infant mortality rate compare with other countries at 24–27 weeks gestation? What about at 37 weeks or more gestation?

(**Source:** MacDorman & Mathews, 2009.)

	United States	Austria	Denmark	England and Wales[2]	Finland	Northern Ireland	Norway	Poland	Scotland	Sweden
22–23 weeks[1]	707.7	888.9	947.4	880.5	900.0	1,000.0	555.6	921.1	1,000.0	515.2
24–27 weeks	236.9	319.6	301.2	298.2	315.8	268.3	220.2	530.6	377.0	197.7
28–31 weeks	45.0	43.8	42.2	52.2	58.5	54.5	56.4	147.7	60.8	41.3
32–36 weeks	8.6	5.8	10.3	10.6	9.7	13.1	7.2	23.1	8.8	12.8
37 weeks or more	2.4	1.5	2.3	1.8	1.4	1.6	1.5	2.3	1.7	1.5

1 Infant mortality rates at 22–23 weeks of gestation may be unreliable due to reporting differences.
2 England and Wales provided 2005 data.
NOTE: Infant mortality rates are per 1,000 live births in specified group.
SOURCE: NCHS linked birth/infant death data set (for U.S. data), and *European Perinatal Health Report* (for European data).

The physical and cognitive problems experienced by low-birthweight and pre-term babies are even more pronounced in very-low-birthweight infants, with astonishing financial consequences. A 3-month stay in an incubator in an intensive care unit can run hundreds of thousands of dollars, and about half of these newborns ultimately die, despite massive medical intervention (Institute of Medicine, 2007).

Even if a very-low-birthweight preterm infant survives, the medical costs can continue to mount. For instance, one estimate suggests that the average monthly cost of medical care for such infants during the first 3 years of life may be between 3 and 50 times higher than the medical costs for a full-term child. Such astronomical costs have raised ethical debates about the expenditure of substantial financial and human resources in cases in which a positive outcome may be unlikely (Prince, 2000; Doyle, 2004; Petrou, 2006).

As medical capabilities progress and developmental researchers come up with new strategies for dealing with preterm infants and improving their lives, the age of viability is likely to be pushed even earlier. Emerging evidence suggests that high-quality care can provide protection from some of the risks associated with prematurity, and that in fact by the time they reach adulthood, premature babies may be little different from other adults. Still, the costs of caring for preterm infants are enormous: The U.S. government estimates that caring for premature infants is $26 billion a year (Hack et al., 2002; Saul, 2009).

WHAT CAUSES PRETERM AND LOW-BIRTHWEIGHT DELIVERIES? About half of preterm and low-birthweight births are unexplained, but several known causes account for the remainder. In some cases, premature labor results from difficulties relating to the mother's reproductive system. For instance, mothers carrying twins have unusual stress placed on them, which can lead to early labor. In fact, most multiple births are preterm to some degree (Luke & Brown, 2008; Saul, 2009; Habersaat et al., 2014).

In other cases, preterm and low-birthweight babies are a result of the immaturity of the mother's reproductive system. Young mothers—under age 15—are more prone to deliver prematurely than older ones. In addition, a woman who becomes pregnant within 6 months of a previous delivery is more likely to deliver a preterm or low-birthweight infant than a woman whose reproductive system has had a chance to recover from a prior delivery. Father's age matters, too: Pregnant women with older male partners are more likely to have preterm deliveries (Branum, 2006; Blumenshine et al., 2011; Teoli, Zullig, & Hendryx, 2015).

Finally, factors that affect the general health of the mother, such as nutrition, level of medical care, amount of stress in the environment, and economic support, all are related to prematurity and low birthweight. Rates of preterm births differ between racial groups, not because of race per se but because members of racial minorities have disproportionately lower incomes and higher stress as a result. For instance, the percentage of low-birthweight infants born to African American mothers is double that for Caucasian American mothers (Bergmann, Bergmann, & Dudenhausen, 2008; Butler, Wilson, & Johnson, 2012; Teoli, Zullig, & Hendryx, 2015).

POSTMATURE BABIES: TOO LATE, TOO LARGE.   One might imagine that a baby who spends extra time in the womb might have some advantages, given the opportunity to continue growth undisturbed by the outside world. Yet **postmature infants**—those still unborn 2 weeks after the mother's due date—face several risks.

postmature infants

infants still unborn 2 weeks after the mother's due date.

For example, the blood supply from the placenta may become insufficient to nourish the still-growing fetus adequately. Consequently, the blood supply to the brain may be decreased, leading to the potential of brain damage. Similarly, labor becomes riskier (for both the child and the mother) as a fetus who may be equivalent in size to a 1-month-old infant has to make its way through the birth canal (Fok et al., 2006).

Difficulties involving postmature infants are more easily prevented than those involving preterm babies, since medical practitioners can induce labor artificially if the pregnancy continues too long. Not only can certain drugs bring on labor, but physicians also have the option of performing cesarean deliveries, a form of delivery we consider next.

Cesarean Delivery: Intervening in the Process of Birth

LO 2.19 Describe the process of cesarean delivery, and explain why its use is increasing.

cesarean delivery

a birth in which the baby is surgically removed from the uterus, rather than traveling through the birth canal (sometimes known as a c-section).

As Elena entered her 18th hour of labor, the obstetrician who was monitoring her progress began to look concerned. She told Elena and her husband, Pablo, that the fetal monitor revealed that the fetus's heart rate had begun to repeatedly fall after each contraction. After trying some simple remedies, such as repositioning Elena on her side, the obstetrician came to the conclusion that the fetus was in distress. She told them that the baby should be delivered immediately, and to accomplish that, she would have to carry out a cesarean delivery.

Elena became one of the more than 1 million mothers in the United States who have a Cesarean delivery each year. In a **cesarean delivery** (sometimes known as a *c-section*), the baby is surgically removed from the uterus rather than traveling through the birth canal.

Cesarean deliveries occur most frequently when the fetus shows distress of some sort. For instance, if the fetus appears to be in danger, as indicated by a sudden rise in its heart rate or if blood is seen coming from the mother's vagina during labor, a cesarean may be performed. Mothers over age 40 are more likely to have cesarean deliveries than younger ones. Overall, cesarean deliveries in the United States now make up 32 percent of all deliveries (Tang et al., 2006; Romero, Coulson, & Galvin, 2012).

Cesarean deliveries are also used in some cases of *breech position*, in which the baby is positioned feet first in the birth canal. Breech position births, which occur in about 1 out of 25 births, place the baby at risk, because the umbilical cord is more likely to be compressed, depriving the baby of oxygen. Cesarean deliveries are also more likely in *transverse position* births, in which the baby lies crosswise in the uterus, or when the baby's head is so large it has trouble moving through the birth canal.

Tyler Olson/Fotolia

Routine use of fetal monitors has led to an increase in cesarean deliveries.

The routine use of a **fetal monitor**, a device that measures the baby's heartbeat during labor, has contributed to a soaring rate of cesarean deliveries. Nearly a third of all children in the United States are born in this way, up some 500 percent from the early 1970s, when the rate stood at 5 percent (Hamilton, Martin, & Ventura, 2011; Paterno, McElroy, & Regan, 2016).

fetal monitor
a device that measures the baby's heartbeat during labor.

Are cesareans an effective medical intervention? Other countries have substantially lower rates of cesarean deliveries, and there is no association between successful birth consequences and the rate of cesarean deliveries. In addition, cesarean deliveries carry dangers. Cesarean delivery represents major surgery, and the mother's recovery can be relatively lengthy, particularly when compared to a normal delivery. In addition, the risk of maternal infection is higher with cesarean deliveries (Porter et al., 2007).

Finally, a cesarean delivery presents some risks for the baby. Because cesarean babies are spared the stresses of passing though the birth canal, their relatively easy passage into the world may deter the normal release of certain stress-related hormones, such as catecholamines, into the newborn's bloodstream. These hormones help prepare the neonate to deal with the stress of the world outside the womb, and their absence may be detrimental to the newborn child. In fact, research indicates that babies born by cesarean delivery are more likely to experience breathing problems upon birth than those who experience at least some labor prior to being born via a cesarean delivery. Finally, mothers who deliver by cesarean are less satisfied with the birth experience, although their dissatisfaction does not influence the quality of mother–child interactions (MacDorman et al., 2008; Xie et al., 2015; Kjerulff & Brubaker, 2017).

Because the increase in cesarean deliveries is, as we have said, connected to the use of fetal monitors, medical authorities now currently recommend that they not be used routinely. There is evidence that outcomes are no better for newborns who have been monitored than for those who have not been monitored. In addition, monitors tend to indicate fetal distress when there is none—false alarms—with disquieting regularity. Monitors do, however, play a critical role in high-risk pregnancies and in cases of preterm and postmature babies (Freeman, 2007; Sepehri & Guliani, 2017).

Stillbirth and Infant Mortality: The Tragedy of Premature Death

LO 2.20 **Describe infant mortality rates, and explain factors that affect those rates.**

The joy that accompanies the birth of a child is completely reversed when a newborn dies. The relative rarity of their occurrence makes infant deaths even harder for parents to bear.

Sometimes a child does not even live beyond its passage through the birth canal. **Stillbirth**, the delivery of a child who is not alive, occurs in less than 1 delivery out of 100. Sometimes the death is detected before labor begins. In this case, labor is typically induced, or physicians may carry out a cesarean delivery in order to remove the body from the mother as soon as possible. In other cases of stillbirth, the baby dies during its travel through the birth canal.

stillbirth
the delivery of a child who is not alive, occurring in less than 1 delivery in 100.

In the United States, the overall rate of **infant mortality** (defined as death within the first year of life) is 6.17 deaths per 1,000 live births. Infant mortality generally has been declining since the 1960s, and declined 12 percent from 2005 to 2011 (McDormatt, Hoyert, & Matthews, 2013; Loggins & Andrade, 2014; Prince et al., 2016).

infant mortality
death within the first year of life.

Whether the death is a stillbirth or occurs after the child is born, the loss of a baby is tragic, and the impact on parents is enormous. The loss and grief parents feel, and their passage through it, is similar to that experienced when an older loved one dies. The juxtaposition of the first dawning of life and an unnaturally early death may make the death particularly difficult to accept and handle. Depression is common, and it is often intensified owing to a lack of support. Some parents even experience post-traumatic stress disorder (Badenhorst et al., 2006; Cacciatore & Bushfield, 2007; Turton, Evans, & Hughes, 2009). There are also differences related to race, socioeconomic, and culture in infant mortality, as we discuss in the *Developmental Diversity and Your Life* section.

Developmental Diversity and Your Life

Overcoming Racial and Cultural Differences in Infant Mortality

Even though there has been a general decline in the infant mortality rate in the United States over the past several decades, African American babies are more than twice as likely to die before age 1 than white babies. This difference is largely the result of socioeconomic factors: African American women are significantly more likely to be living in poverty than Caucasian women and to receive less prenatal care. As a result, their babies are more likely to be of low birthweight—the factor most closely linked to infant mortality—than infants of mothers of other racial groups (see Figure 2-15; Duncan & Brooks-Gunn, 2000; Grady, 2006 Rice et al., 2017).

But it is not just members of particular racial groups in the United States who suffer from poor mortality rates. As mentioned earlier, the rate of infant mortality in the United States is higher than the rate in many other countries. For example, the mortality rate in the United States is almost double that of Japan.

Why does the United States fare so poorly in terms of newborn survival? One answer is that the United States has a higher rate of low-birthweight and preterm deliveries than many other countries. When U.S. infants are compared to infants of the same weight who are born in other countries, the differences in mortality rates disappear (MacDorman et al., 2005; Davis & Hofferth, 2012).

Another reason for the higher U.S. mortality rate relates to economic diversity. The United States has a higher proportion of people living in poverty than many other countries. Because people in lower economic categories are less likely to have adequate medical care and tend to be less healthy, the relatively high proportion of economically deprived individuals in the United States has an impact on the overall mortality rate (Bremner & Fogel, 2004; MacDorman et al., 2005; Close et al., 2013).

Many countries do a significantly better job than the United States in providing prenatal care to mothers-to-be. For instance, low-cost and even free care, both before and after delivery, is often available in other countries. Furthermore, paid maternity leave is frequently provided to pregnant women, lasting in some cases as long as 51 weeks. The opportunity to take an extended maternity leave can be important: Mothers who spend more time on maternity leave may have better mental health and higher-quality interactions with their infants (Waldfogel, 2001; Feldman, Sussman, & Zigler, 2004).

Better health care is only part of the story. In certain European countries, in addition to a comprehensive package of services involving general practitioner, obstetrician, and midwife, pregnant women receive many privileges, such as transportation benefits for visits to health care providers. In Norway, pregnant women may be given living expenses for up to 10 days so that they can be close to a hospital when it is time to give birth. And when their babies are born, new mothers receive the assistance of trained home helpers for just a small payment (DeVries, 2005).

In the United States, the story is very different. About one out of every six pregnant women has insufficient prenatal care. Some 20 percent of white women and close to 40 percent of African American women receive no prenatal care early in their pregnancies. Five percent of white mothers and 11 percent of African American mothers do not see a health-care provider until the last 3 months of pregnancy; some never see a health-care provider at all (Hueston, Geesey, & Diaz, 2008; Friedman, Heneghan, & Rosenthal, 2009; Cogan et al., 2012).

Figure 2-15 Race and Infant Mortality

Although infant mortality is dropping for both African American and white children, the death rate is still more than twice as high for African American children. These figures show the number of deaths in the first year of life for every 1,000 live births.
Source: ChildStats.gov, 2017.

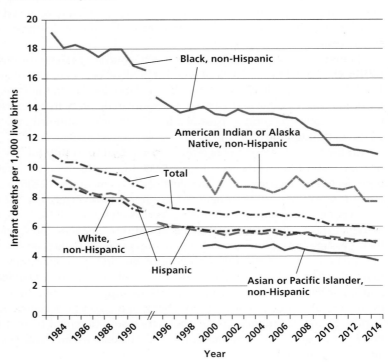

Ultimately, the lack of prenatal services results in a higher mortality rate. Yet this situation can be changed if greater support is provided. A start would be to ensure that all economically disadvantaged pregnant women have access to free or inexpensive high-quality medical care from the very beginning of pregnancy. Furthermore, barriers that prevent poor women from receiving such care should be reduced. For instance, programs can be developed that help pay for transportation to a health facility or for the care of older children while the mother is making a health-care visit. The cost of these programs is likely to be offset by the savings they make possible—healthy babies cost less than infants with chronic problems as a result of poor nutrition and prenatal care (Kronenfeld, 2002).

Jake Lyell/Alamy Stock Photo

Racial and cultural differences are related to prenatal health care.

Module 2.3 Review

LO 2.12 Describe the process of fertilization.

When sperm enter the vagina, they begin a journey that takes them through the cervix, the opening into the uterus, and into the fallopian tube, where fertilization may take place. Fertilization joins the sperm and ovum to start prenatal development.

LO 2.13 Summarize the three stages of prenatal development.

The prenatal period consists of three stages: germinal, embryonic, and fetal.

LO 2.14 Describe major physical and ethical challenges that relate to pregnancy.

Infertility is the inability conceive after 12 to 18 months of trying to become pregnant. It may be overcome by artificial insemination, in vitro fertilization, or the use of surrogate mothers, which present certain ethical issues.

LO 2.15 Analyze threats to the fetal environment, and explain what can be done about them.

A teratogen is an environmental agent such as a drug, chemical, virus, or other factor that produces a birth defect. The diet, age, prenatal support, and illnesses of mothers can affect their babies' health and growth. Mothers' use of drugs, alcohol, tobacco, and caffeine can adversely affect the health and development of the unborn child. Fathers' and others' behaviors (e.g., smoking) can also affect the health of the unborn child.

LO 2.16 Describe the normal process of labor.

In the first stage of labor, contractions increase in frequency, duration, and intensity until the baby's head is able to pass through the cervix. In the second stage, the baby moves through the cervix and birth canal and leaves the mother's body. In the third stage, the umbilical cord and placenta emerge.

LO 2.17 Describe the process of birth, and analyze current approaches to childbirth.

Many birthing options are available to parents today. They may weigh the advantages and disadvantages of anesthetic drugs during birth, and they may choose alternatives to traditional hospital birthing, including the Lamaze method, the use of a birthing center, and the use of a midwife.

LO 2.18 Recognize threats and complications that may accompany childbirth, and explain how they can be addressed.

Largely because of low birthweight, preterm infants may have substantial difficulties after birth and later in life. Very-low-birthweight infants are in special danger because of the immaturity of their organ systems. Preterm and low-birthweight deliveries can be caused by health, age, and pregnancy-related factors in the mother. Income (and, because of its relationship with income, race) is also an important factor. Many preterm babies spend weeks or months in the neonatal intensive care unit receiving specialized care to help them develop.

LO 2.19 Describe the process of cesarean delivery, and explain why its use is increasing.

Cesarean deliveries are performed with postmature babies or when the fetus is in distress, in the wrong position, or unable to progress through the birth canal. The routine use of a fetal monitor has contributed to a soaring rate of cesarean deliveries.

LO 2.20 **Describe infant mortality rates, and explain factors that affect those rates.**

The overall rate of infant mortality is 6.17 deaths per 1,000 live births. In the United States, African American babies are more than twice as likely to die before age 1 than white babies. Infant mortality rates can be affected by the availability of inexpensive health care and good education programs for mothers-to-be.

Journal Writing Prompt

Applying Lifespan Development: What are some ethical considerations relating to providing intensive medical care to very-low-birthweight babies? Do you think such interventions should be routine practice? Why or why not?

Epilogue

In this chapter, we have discussed the basics of heredity and genetics, including the way in which the code of life is transmitted across generations through DNA. We have also seen how genetic transmission can go wrong, and we have discussed ways in which genetic disorders can be treated—and perhaps prevented—through new interventions such as genetic counseling.

One important theme in this chapter has been the interaction between hereditary and environmental factors in determining a number of human traits. While we have encountered a number of surprising instances in which heredity plays a part—including in the development of personality traits and even personal preferences and tastes—we have also seen that heredity is virtually never the sole factor in any complex trait. Environment nearly always plays an important role.

Next, we proceeded to a review of the main stages of prenatal growth—germinal, embryonic, and fetal—and examined threats to the prenatal environment and ways to optimize that environment for the fetus. Then we examined the process of labor and birth, touching on threats

and complications that can arise during childbirth and ways in which those threats can be lessened. We looked at the phenomenon of cesarean delivery and discussed factors that can affect infant mortality rates.

Before moving on, return to the prologue—about the Monaco children with IVA—and answer the following questions based on your understanding of genetics and prenatal development.

1. How could Jana and Tom Monaco have passed on a rare genetic disease to their children without knowing that they were carriers of it?

2. From the Monacos' story, would you guess that IVA is an X-linked trait or not?

3. What evidence is there in the story of the Monacos' children that the debilitating effects of IVA are determined by a combination of both genetic and environmental factors?

4. Could the Monacos have learned that they were carriers of IVA before their son Stephen was born? How?

Looking Back

LO 2.1 **Describe how genes and chromosomes provide our basic genetic endowment.**

A child receives 23 chromosomes from each parent. These 46 chromosomes provide the genetic blueprint that will guide cell activity for the rest of the individual's life.

LO 2.2 **Compare monozygotic twins with dizygotic twins.**

Monozygotic twins are twins who are genetically identical. Dizygotic twins result when two separate ova are fertilized by two separate sperm at roughly the same time.

LO 2.3 **Describe how the sex of a child is determined.**

When an ovum and a sperm meet at the moment of fertilization, the ovum provides an X chromosome, while the sperm provides either an X or a Y chromosome. If the sperm contributes its X chromosome, the child will have an XX pairing and will be a girl. If the sperm

contributes a Y chromosome, the result will be an XY pairing—a boy.

LO 2.4 **Explain the mechanisms by which genes transmit information.**

Gregor Mendel discovered how plants transmit traits and also explained the means by which dominant and recessive traits are formed and passed on. A genotype is the underlying combination of genetic material present in an organism, but invisible; a phenotype is the visible trait, the expression of the genotype.

LO 2.5 **Describe the field of behavioral genetics.**

The field of behavioral genetics, a combination of psychology and genetics, studies the effects of genetics on behavior and psychological characteristics. Among the goals of the field are to increase our understanding of the origins of genetic defects and to devise possible techniques for preventing or remedying them.

LO 2.6   Describe the major inherited disorders.

Genes may become physically damaged or may spontaneously mutate. If damaged genes are passed on to the child, the result can be a genetic disorder. Major genetic disorders include Down syndrome, fragile X syndrome, sickle-cell anemia, Tay-Sachs disease, and Klinefelter's syndrome.

LO 2.7   Describe the role of genetic counselors and differentiate between different forms of prenatal testing.

Genetic counselors use a variety of data and techniques to advise future parents of possible genetic risks to their unborn children. A variety of techniques can be used to assess the health of an unborn child if a woman is already pregnant, including ultrasound, CVS, and amniocentesis.

LO 2.8   Explain how the environment and genetics work together to determine human characteristics.

Behavioral characteristics are often determined by a combination of genetics and environment. Genetically based traits can be influenced by environmental conditions and factors in a process referred to as multifactorial transmission. The genotype provides a range within which the phenotype can achieve expression.

LO 2.9   Summarize the methods by which researchers study the interaction of genetic and environmental factors in development.

To work out the different influences of heredity and environment, researchers use nonhuman studies and human studies, particularly of twins.

LO 2.10   Examine how genetics and the environment jointly influence physical traits, intelligence, and personality.

Virtually all human traits, characteristics, and behaviors are the result of the combination and interaction of nature and nurture. Many physical characteristics show strong genetic influences. Intelligence contains a strong genetic component but can be significantly influenced by environmental factors. Some personality traits, including neuroticism and extroversion, have been linked to genetic factors, and even attitudes, values, and interests have a genetic component. Some personal behaviors may be genetically influenced through the mediation of inherited personality traits.

LO 2.11   Describe ways in which genes influence the environment.

Children may influence their environment through genetic traits that cause them to construct—or influence their parents to construct—an environment that matches their inherited dispositions and preferences.

LO 2.12   Describe the process of fertilization.

When sperm enter the vagina, they begin a journey that takes them through the cervix, the opening into the uterus, and into the fallopian tube, where fertilization may take place. Fertilization joins the sperm and ovum to start prenatal development.

LO 2.13   Summarize the three stages of prenatal development.

The germinal stage (fertilization to 2 weeks) is marked by rapid cell division and specialization, and the attachment of the zygote to the wall of the uterus. During the embryonic stage (2 to 8 weeks), the ectoderm, the mesoderm, and the endoderm begin to grow and specialize. The fetal stage (8 weeks to birth) is characterized by a rapid increase in complexity and differentiation of the organs. The fetus becomes active, and most of its systems become operational.

LO 2.14   Describe major physical and ethical challenges that relate to pregnancy.

Some couples need medical aid to help them conceive. Among the alternate routes to conception are artificial insemination and in vitro fertilization (IVF). Some women may also experience miscarriage or opt for an abortion.

LO 2.15   Analyze threats to the fetal environment, and explain what can be done about them.

A teratogen is an environmental agent, such as a drug, chemical, virus, or other factor that produces a birth defect. Factors in the mother that may affect the unborn child include diet, age, illnesses, and drug, alcohol, and tobacco use. The behaviors of fathers and others in the environment may also affect the health and development of the unborn child.

LO 2.16   Describe the normal process of labor.

In the first stage of labor contractions occur about every 8 to 10 minutes, increasing in frequency, duration, and intensity until the mother's cervix expands. In the second stage of labor, which lasts about 90 minutes, the baby begins to move through the cervix and birth canal and ultimately leaves the mother's body. In the third stage of labor, which lasts only a few minutes, the umbilical cord and placenta are expelled from the mother.

LO 2.17   Describe the process of birth, and analyze current approaches to childbirth.

After it emerges, the newborn, or neonate, is usually inspected for irregularities, cleaned, and returned to its mother and father. It also undergoes newborn screening tests. Today, parents have a wide range of birthing techniques from which to choose, such as Lamaze techniques, the Bradley Method, hypnobirthing, and water birthing.

LO 2.18 **Recognize threats and complications that may accompany childbirth, and explain how they can be addressed.**

Preterm, or premature, infants, born less than 38 weeks following conception, generally have low birthweight, which can cause chilling, vulnerability to infection, respiratory distress syndrome, and hypersensitivity to environmental stimuli. Preterm infants may even show adverse effects later in life, including slowed development, learning disabilities, behavior disorders, below-average IQ scores, and problems with physical coordination. Very-low-birthweight infants are in special danger because of the immaturity of their organ systems. However, medical advances have pushed the age of viability of the infant back to about 24 weeks following conception. Postmature babies, who spend extra time in their mothers' wombs, are also at risk. However, physicians can artificially induce labor or perform a cesarean delivery to address this situation.

LO 2.19 **Describe the process of cesarean delivery, and explain why its use is increasing.**

Cesarean deliveries are performed when the fetus is in distress, in the wrong position, or unable to progress through the birth canal. The routine use of a fetal monitor has contributed to a soaring rate of cesarean deliveries.

LO 2.20 **Describe infant mortality rates, and explain factors that affect those rates.**

The infant mortality rate in the United States is higher than the rate in many other countries, and is higher for low-income families than for higher-income families.

Key Terms and Concepts

zygote   42
genes   43
DNA (deoxyribonucleic acid) molecules   43
chromosomes   43
monozygotic twins   43
dizygotic twins   43
dominant trait   45
recessive trait   45
genotype   45
phenotype   45
homozygous   46
heterozygous   46
polygenic inheritance   47
X-linked genes   47
behavioral genetics   47
Down syndrome   48

fragile X syndrome   48
sickle-cell anemia   48
Tay-Sachs disease   49
Klinefelter's syndrome   49
genetic counseling   49
ultrasound sonography   50
chorionic villus sampling (CVS)   50
amniocentesis   50
temperament   52
multifactorial transmission   53
fertilization   60
germinal stage   60
placenta   61
embryonic stage   61
fetal stage   62
fetus   62
infertility   63

artificial insemination   63
in vitro fertilization (IVF)   63
teratogen   66
fetal alcohol spectrum disorder (FASD)   69
fetal alcohol effects (FAE)   69
neonate   71
episiotomy   72
preterm infants   75
low-birthweight infants   75
small-for-gestational-age infants   75
very-low-birthweight infants   76
postmature infants   78
cesarean delivery   78
fetal monitor   79
stillbirth   79
infant mortality   79

Chapter 3
Physical Growth and Aging Across the Life Span

Monkey Business Images/Shutterstock

Learning Objectives

LO 3.1 Describe infants' physical development in the first 2 years of life.

LO 3.2 Summarize the physical development that occurs during the preschool and middle childhood years and the factors that affect this development.

LO 3.3 Identify the physical changes adolescents experience as the body reaches puberty.

LO 3.4 Describe the physical changes that occur from early to late adulthood and how they affect adults' capabilities.

LO 3.5 Distinguish functional age from chronological age.

LO 3.6 Discuss the role of neurons in brain development.

LO 3.7 Explain what is meant by brain lateralization and describe how it develops in early childhood.

LO 3.8 Identify the reflexes that infants are born with that help them adapt to their surroundings and protect themselves.

LO 3.9 Summarize the gross motor skills that emerge during infancy and the preschool years, and explain how they are related to brain development.

LO 3.10 Give examples of fine motor skills, and describe their developmental pattern in infants and young children.

LO 3.11 Describe the capabilities of infants regarding each of the five senses.

LO 3.12 Recognize the sensory difficulties school-age children may experience and how they can affect children's learning.

LO 3.13 Discuss the changes in sensory perception in middle adulthood and the factors that may affect these changes.

LO 3.14 Give examples of the decline in various sense organs experienced in late adulthood and how these changes affect the lives of the elderly.

Chapter Overview

Prologue: Dreaming of Sleep

Liz and Seth Kaufman are so exhausted they have a hard time staying awake through dinner. The problem? Their 3-month-old son, Evan, who shows no signs of adopting normal patterns of eating and sleeping anytime soon. "I thought babies were these big sleep fanatics, but Evan takes little cat naps of an hour throughout the night, and then stays awake all day," Liz says. "I'm running out of ways to entertain him because all I want to do is sleep."

Evan's feeding schedule was hard on Liz, too. "He wants to nurse every hour for 5 hours in a row, which makes it hard to keep up my milk supply. Then he goes another 5 hours *not* wanting to nurse, and I'm positively, painfully engorged." Seth tries to help out, walking at night with Evan when he won't sleep, offering him a bottle of Liz's expressed milk at 3 a.m. "But sometimes he just refuses the bottle," Seth says. "Only Mommy will do."

The pediatrician has assured the Kaufmans that their son is healthy and blossoming. "We're pretty sure Evan will come out of this just fine," Liz says. "It's us we're wondering about." ■

Looking Ahead

Evan's parents can relax. Their son will settle down. Sleeping through the night is just one of the succession of milestones that characterize the dramatic physical attainments of infancy. In this chapter, we focus on physical growth and aging across the life span. We begin by discussing the growth of the body from birth to old age, covering the major body changes along the life span. We also address height and weight change, maturation and puberty in adolescence, and the onset of aging and the physical changes it brings.

The chapter then examines brain growth and motor development, showing how the connections that the brain makes during early life influence development and the reflexes and motor skills that children develop as they age. We look at some surprising cultural differences, as well as differences between males and females. Along the way, we discuss toilet training, and we ask why some people prefer their left hand and others their right.

Finally, the chapter turns to perceptual development. We discuss the development and progress of sensory perception early in life, and we see how the senses change later in life. We track the relationship of the senses to such school topics as reading, writing, and self-esteem, and, in considering adulthood and old age, we look at the effects on daily life activities of sensory changes and the tendency to slow down.

Sleep is vital for normal physical growth and change across the life span.

MODULE 3.1

PHYSICAL GROWTH AND CHANGE

Let's begin our look at physical development by looking at the changes that occur during the first two years of life.

Physical Growth in Infancy

LO 3.1   Describe infants' physical development in the first 2 years of life.

Evan's sleep patterns were the beginning of a succession of physical milestones that humans experience following birth. The period of infancy, which starts at birth and continues until the second birthday, is a time of obvious changes in height and weight and less apparent changes in the nervous system. Infants quickly develop increasingly stable patterns in such basic activities as sleeping, eating, and attending to the world.

The average newborn weighs just over 7 pounds, which is less than the weight of the average Thanksgiving turkey. The average newborn is about 20 inches long, shorter than a loaf of French bread. Newborns are helpless; if left to fend for themselves, they could not survive.

Yet after just a few years, the story is very different. Babies become much larger, they are mobile, and they grow increasingly independent. How does this growth happen? We can answer this question first by describing the changes in weight and height that occur over the first 2 years of life.

RAPID ADVANCES.   Infants grow rapidly over their first 2 years (see Figure 3-1). By 5 months, the average infant's birthweight has doubled to around 15 pounds. By the first birthday, the baby's weight has tripled to about 22 pounds. Although the pace of weight gain slows during the second year, by the end of his or her second year, the average child weighs around four times as much as he or she did at birth. Of course, there is a good deal of variation among infants. Height and weight measurements, which are taken regularly during physicians' visits during a baby's first year, provide a way to spot problems in development.

The weight gains of infancy are matched by increased length. By the end of the first year, the typical baby grows almost a foot and is about 30 inches tall. By the second birthday, children average 3 feet.

Not all parts of an infant's body grow at the same rate. For instance, at birth the head accounts for one-quarter of the newborn's entire body size. During the first 2 years of life, the rest of the body begins to catch up. By age 2 the baby's head is only one-fifth of body length, and by adulthood it is only one-eighth (see Figure 3-2).

There are also gender and ethnic differences in weight and length. Girls generally are slightly shorter and weigh slightly less than boys, and these differences remain throughout childhood (and, as we will see later, the disparities become considerably greater during adolescence). Furthermore, Asian infants tend to be slightly smaller than North American Caucasian infants, and African American infants tend to be slightly bigger than North American Caucasian infants.

INTEGRATING THE BODILY SYSTEMS: THE LIFE CYCLES OF INFANCY.   If you happen to overhear new parents discussing their newborns, chances are one or several bodily

Figure 3-1 Height and Weight

Although the greatest increase in height and weight occurs during the first year of life, children continue to grow throughout infancy and toddlerhood. (**Source:** Cratty, 1979.)

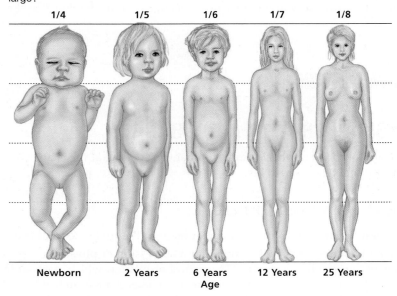

Figure 3-2 Decreasing Proportions

At birth, the head represents one-quarter of the neonate's body. By adulthood, the head is only one-eighth the size of the body. Why is the neonate's head so large?

1/4	1/5	1/6	1/7	1/8
Newborn	2 Years	6 Years	12 Years	25 Years

Age

functions will be the subject. In the first days of life, infants' body rhythms—waking, eating, sleeping, and elimination—govern the infant's behavior, often at seemingly random times.

These most basic activities are controlled by a variety of bodily systems. Although each behavioral pattern probably is functioning effectively, it takes some time and effort for infants to integrate the separate behaviors. One of the neonate's major missions is to make its individual behaviors work in harmony, helping it, for example, to sleep through the night (Waterhouse & DeCoursey, 2004).

rhythms

repetitive, cyclical patterns of behavior.

RHYTHMS AND STATES. One of the most important ways that behavior becomes integrated is through the development of various **rhythms**, which are repetitive, cyclical patterns of behavior. Some rhythms are immediately obvious, such as the change from wakefulness to sleep. Others are more subtle but still easily noticeable, such as breathing and sucking patterns. Still others may require careful observation to be noticed. For instance, newborns may go through periods in which they jerk their legs in a regular pattern every minute or so. Although some of these rhythms are apparent just after birth, others emerge slowly over the first year as the neurons of the nervous system become increasingly integrated (Harvey, Mullin, & Hinshaw, 2006; Upshaw, Bernier, & Sommerville, 2015).

state

degree of awareness an infant displays of both internal and external stimulation.

One of the major body rhythms is an infant's **state**, the degree of awareness of both internal and external stimulation. As can be seen in Table 3-1, such states include various levels of wakeful behaviors, such as alertness, fussing, and crying, and different levels of sleep as well. Each change in state brings about an alteration in the amount of stimulation required to get the infant's attention (Diambra & Menna-Barreto, 2004).

SLEEP: PERCHANCE TO DREAM? At the beginning of infancy, the major state that occupies a baby's time is sleep—much to the relief of exhausted parents, who often regard sleep as a welcome respite from caregiving responsibilities. On average, newborn infants sleep some 16 to 17 hours a day, with wide variations from 10 to 20 or more (de Graag et al., 2012; Blumberg, Gall, & Todd, 2014; Korotchikova et al., 2016).

Infants sleep a lot, but you shouldn't ever wish to "sleep like a baby." Their sleep comes in spurts of around 2 hours, followed by periods of wakefulness. Because of this, infants—and their sleep-deprived parents—are "out of sync" with the rest of the world, for whom sleep comes at night and wakefulness during the day. Most babies do not sleep through the night for several months (Sadeh, 2007; James-Roberts et al., 2015; Blomqvist et al., 2017).

Table 3-1 Primary Behavioral States

States	Characteristics	Percentage of Time When Alone in State
Awake States		
Alert	Attentive or scanning, the infant's eyes are open, bright, and shining.	6.7
Nonalert Waking	Eyes are usually open, but dull and unfocused. Varied but typically high motor activity.	2.8
Fuss	Fussing is continuous or intermittent, at low levels.	1.8
Cry	Intense vocalizations occurring singly or in succession.	1.7
Transition States Between Sleep and Waking		
Drowse	Infant's eyes are heavy-lidded, but opening and closing slowly. Low level of motor activity.	4.4
Daze	Open, but glassy and immobile eyes. State occurs between episodes of Alert and Drowse. Low level of activity.	1.0
Sleep-Wake Transition	Behaviors of both wakefulness and sleep are evident. Generalized motor activity; eyes may be closed, or they open and close rapidly. State occurs when baby is awakening.	1.3
Sleep States		
Active Sleep	Eyes closed; uneven respiration; intermittent rapid eye movements. Other behaviors: smiles, frowns, grimaces, mouthing, sucking, sighs, and sigh-sobs.	50.3
Quiet Sleep	Eyes are closed, and respiration is slow and regular. Motor activity limited to occasional startles, sigh-sobs, or rhythmic mouthing.	28.1
Transitional Sleep States		
Active-Quiet Transition Sleep	During this state, which occurs between periods of Active Sleep and Quiet Sleep, the eyes are closed, and there is little motor activity. Infant shows mixed behavioral signs of Active Sleep and Quiet Sleep.	1.9

(**Source:** Adapted from Thoman & Whitney, 1990.)

Luckily for their parents, infants gradually settle into a more adult-like pattern. After a week, babies sleep a bit more at night and are awake for slightly longer periods during the day. Typically, by the age of 16 weeks, infants begin to sleep as much as 6 continuous hours at night, and daytime sleep falls into regular napping patterns. Most infants sleep through the night by the end of the first year, and the total amount of sleep they need each day is down to about 15 hours (Mao et al., 2004; Magee, Gordon, & Caputi, 2014).

Hidden beneath the supposedly tranquil sleep of infants is another cyclic pattern. During periods of sleep, infants' heart rates increase and become irregular, their blood pressure rises, and they begin to breathe more rapidly. Sometimes, though not always, their closed eyes begin to move in a back-and-forth pattern, as if they were viewing an action-packed scene. This period of active sleep is similar, although not identical, to the **rapid eye movement, or REM, sleep** that is found in older children and adults and is associated with dreaming (Blumberg et al., 2013).

At first, this active, REM-like sleep takes up around one-half of an infant's sleep, compared with just 20 percent of an adult's sleep. However, the quantity of active sleep quickly declines, and by the age of 6 months amounts to just one-third of total sleep time (Burnham et al., 2002; Staunton, 2005; Ferri, Novelli, & Bruni, 2017).

The appearance of active sleep periods that are similar to REM sleep in adults raises the intriguing question of whether infants dream during those periods. No one knows the answer, although it seems unlikely. First of all, young infants do not have much to dream about, given their relatively limited experiences. Furthermore, the brain waves of sleeping infants appear to be qualitatively different from those of adults who are dreaming. It is not until the baby reaches 3 or 4 months of age that the wave patterns become similar to those of dreaming adults (Zampi et al., 2002).

What is the function of REM sleep in infants? Some researchers think it provides a means for the brain to stimulate itself—a process called *autostimulation* (Roffwarg, Muzio, & Dement, 1966). Stimulation of the nervous system would be particularly important in infants, who spend so much time sleeping and relatively little in alert states.

Infants' sleep cycles seem largely preprogrammed by genetic factors, but environmental influences also play a part. For instance, among the Kipsigis of Africa, infants sleep with their mothers at night and are allowed to nurse whenever they wake. In the daytime, they accompany their mothers during daily chores, often napping while strapped to their mothers' backs. Because they are often out and on the go,

rapid eye movement, or REM, sleep

the period of sleep that is found in older children and adults and is associated with dreaming.

Kipsigis infants do not sleep through the night until much later than babies in Western societies, and for the first 8 months of life, they seldom sleep longer than 3 hours at a stretch. In comparison, 8-month-old infants in the United States may sleep as long as 8 hours at a time. One reason for these cultural differences may relate to the use of artificial light and shades used to manage natural light that varies across cultures (Super & Harkness, 1982; Rothrauff, Middlemiss, & Jacobson, 2004; Owens, 2008).

Physical Growth During the Preschool and Middle Childhood Years

LO 3.2 **Summarize the physical development that occurs during the preschool and middle childhood years and the factors that affect this development.**

Although growth slows through the preschool and middle childhood years, considerable—and important—development still occurs during this time.

DEVELOPMENT IN THE PRESCHOOL YEARS. Infancy presents challenges of its own—but add to these the ability to move about, and the preschool years give caregivers a wealth of worries. In addition to worrying about colds and other illnesses and, especially in recent years, about what and how much their child eats, they must insist on quiet time and a bedtime that will afford their child adequate sleep, just at the time when their child becomes most active. If this seems like a long list of worries, remember that the list of delights that the preschool years bring is far longer.

During the preschool years, children experience rapid advances in their physical abilities that are nothing short of astounding. Just how far they develop is apparent when we look at the changes they undergo in their size, shape, and physical abilities.

By age 2, the average child in the United States weighs around 25 to 30 pounds and is close to 36 inches tall. By the time children are 6 years old, they weigh about 46 pounds and stand 46 inches tall (see Figure 3-3).

These averages mask significant individual differences. For instance, 10 percent of 6-year-olds weigh 55 pounds or more, and 10 percent weigh 36 pounds or less. Furthermore, average differences between boys and girls increase during the preschool years. Although at age 2 the differences are relatively small, during the preschool years boys start becoming taller and heavier, on average, than girls.

Changes in Body Shape and Structure. The bodies of a 2-year-old and a 6-year-old vary not only in height and weight but also in shape. During the preschool years, boys and girls become less round and more slender. Moreover, their arms and legs lengthen, and the size relationship between the head and the rest of the body becomes more adult-like. By the time children reach age 6, their proportions are similar to those of adults.

Other physical changes occur internally. Muscle size increases, and children grow stronger. Bones become sturdier, and the sense organs continue to develop. For instance, the *eustachian tube* in the ear changes its orientation so radically that it may cause the earaches that are so typical of the preschool years.

Figure 3-3 Gaining Height and Weight

The preschool years are marked by steady increases in height and weight. The figures show the median point for boys and girls at each age, in which 50 percent of children in each category are above this height or weight level and 50 percent are below.

(**Source:** National Center for Health Statistics, 2000.)

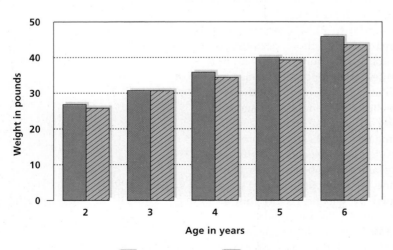

Economic Factors. Economics also affects these averages. The better nutrition and health care typically received by children in developed countries translates into differences in growth. For instance, the average Swedish 4-year-old is as tall as the average 6-year-old in Bangladesh. Within the United States, children in families with incomes below the poverty level are more likely to be shorter than children raised in more affluent homes (Zhang & Wang, 2004; Leathers & Foster, 2004; Mendoza et al., 2007).

DEVELOPMENT IN MIDDLE CHILDHOOD

Cinderella, dressed in yella,
Went upstairs to kiss her fella.
But she made a mistake and she kissed a snake.
How many doctors did it take?
One, two, . . .

While the other girls chanted this jump-rope rhyme, Kat proudly displayed her new ability to jump backward. In second grade, Kat was becoming quite good at jumping rope. In first grade, she simply had not been able to master it. But over the summer, she had spent many hours practicing, and now that practice was paying off.

Variations of 6 inches in height between children of the same age are not unusual and are well within normal ranges.

As Kat is gleefully experiencing, children make great physical strides in middle childhood, mastering many new skills. How does this progress occur? We'll first consider typical physical growth during this period and then turn our attention to variations in cultural patterns.

Slow but steady—these words characterize the nature of growth during middle childhood. In contrast to the swift growth from birth to age 5 and the remarkable growth spurt of adolescence, middle childhood is relatively tranquil. The body has not shifted into neutral; physical growth continues but at a more stately pace than in the preschool years.

Height and Weight Changes. In elementary school, children in the United States grow, on average, 2 to 3 inches a year. By age 11, the average height for girls is 4 feet, 10 inches while boys average 4 feet, 9 1/2 inches. This is the only period in life when girls tend to be taller than boys. This pattern reflects the slightly more rapid physical development of girls, who start their adolescent growth spurt around age 10.

Weight gain in middle childhood follows a similar pattern; boys and girls both gain around 5 to 7 pounds a year. Weight is also redistributed. As "baby fat" disappears, children's bodies become more muscular and their strength increases.

Cultural Patterns of Growth. Most children in North America receive sufficient nutrients to grow to their full potential. In other parts of the world, however, inadequate nutrition and disease take their toll, producing children who are shorter and weigh less. The discrepancies can be dramatic: Poor children in cities such as Calcutta, Hong Kong, and Rio de Janeiro are smaller than affluent children in the same cities.

In the United States, most variations in height and weight are the result of people's unique genetic inheritance, including genetic factors relating to racial and ethnic background. Asian and Oceanic Pacific children tend to be shorter than those of northern and central European ancestry. In addition, the rate of growth is generally more rapid for black children than for white (Deurenberg, Deurenberg-Yap, Guricci, 2002; Deurenberg et al., 2003).

Even within racial and ethnic groups, individuals vary significantly. We cannot attribute racial and ethnic differences solely to genetic factors because dietary customs as well as variations in levels of affluence may also contribute to differences. In addition, severe stress—brought on by factors such as parental conflict or alcoholism—can affect the pituitary gland, thereby affecting growth (Koska et al., 2002; Dobrova-Krol et al., 2008; Emack et al., 2008).

Note the changes that have occurred in just a few years in these pre- and post-puberty photos of the same boy.

Physical Changes in Adolescence

LO 3.3 **Identify the physical changes adolescents experience as the body reaches puberty.**

> *For young males of the Awa tribe, adolescence begins with an elaborate and—to Western eyes—gruesome ceremony to mark the passage from childhood to adulthood. The boys are whipped for 2 or 3 days with sticks and prickly branches. Through the whipping, the boys atone for their previous infractions and honor tribesmen who were killed in warfare. This ritual continues for days.*

We are no doubt grateful we were spared such physical trials when we entered adolescence. But members of Western cultures have their own rites of passage, admittedly less fearsome, such as bar mitzvahs and bat mitzvahs at age 13 for Jewish boys and girls, and confirmation ceremonies in many Christian denominations (Eccles, Templeton, & Barber, 2003; Hoffman, 2003).

From *an educator's* perspective

Why do you think many cultures regard the passage to adolescence as a significant transition that calls for unique ceremonies?

Regardless of their nature, the underlying purpose of these ceremonies tends to be the same across cultures: symbolically celebrating the physical changes that transform a child's body into an adult body capable of reproduction.

THE RAPIDLY MATURING ADOLESCENT. In only a few months, adolescents can grow several inches as they are transformed, at least physically, from children to young adults. During such a growth spurt—a period of very rapid growth in height and weight—boys, on average, grow 4.1 inches a year and girls 3.5 inches. Some adolescents grow as much as 5 inches in a single year (Tanner, 1972; Caino et al., 2004).

Boys' and girls' growth spurts begin at different ages. As you can see in Figure 3-4, girls' spurts begin around age 10, while boys' start around age 12. During the 2-year period starting at age 11, girls tend to be taller than boys, but then the situation reverses itself and males, on average, are taller than females for the remainder of the life span.

puberty
the period of growth during which the sexual organs mature.

PUBERTY. **Puberty**, the period when the sexual organs mature, begins when the pituitary gland in the brain signals other glands to begin producing the sex hormones, *androgens* (male hormones) or *estrogens* (female hormones), at adult levels. (Males and females produce both types of sex hormones, but males have higher levels of androgens and females have higher levels of estrogens.) The pituitary gland also signals the body to produce more growth hormones. These interact with the sex hormones to cause the growth spurt and puberty. The hormone *leptin*, too, appears to play a role in the onset of puberty.

Like the growth spurt, puberty begins earlier for girls, starting at around age 11 or 12, whereas boys begin at about age 13 or 14. However, this time frame varies widely. Some girls begin puberty as early as 7 or 8 or as late as age 16.

menarche
the onset of menstruation.

Puberty in Girls.   Although it is not clear why puberty begins when it does, environmental and cultural factors play a role. For example, **menarche**, the onset of menstruation and probably the most obvious sign of puberty in girls, varies greatly around the world. In poorer, developing countries, menstruation begins later than in more economically advantaged countries. Even within wealthier countries, more affluent girls begin to menstruate earlier than less affluent girls.

It appears that girls who are better nourished and healthier tend to start menstruation earlier. Some studies have suggested that weight or the proportion of fat to muscle in the body plays a key role in the onset of menarche. For example, in the United States, athletes with a low percentage of body fat may start menstruating later than less active girls. Conversely, obesity—which increases the secretion of leptin, a hormone related to the onset of menstruation—leads to earlier puberty (Woelfle, Harz, & Roth, 2007; Sanchez-Garrido, & Tena-Sempere, 2013; Shen et al., 2016).

Figure 3-4 Growth Patterns

Patterns of growth are depicted in two ways. The first figure shows height at a given age, while the second shows the height *increase* that occurs from birth through the end of adolescence. Notice that girls begin their growth spurt around age 10, while boys begin their growth spurt at about age 12. However, by age 13, boys tend to be taller than girls. What are the social consequences for boys and girls of being taller or shorter than average? **THINKING ABOUT THE DATA:** For both height and weight, girls are on average taller and heavier than boys for two years out of their lives. During what two-year age range are they taller? During what two-year age range do they weigh more?
(**Source:** Adapted from Cratty, 1986.)

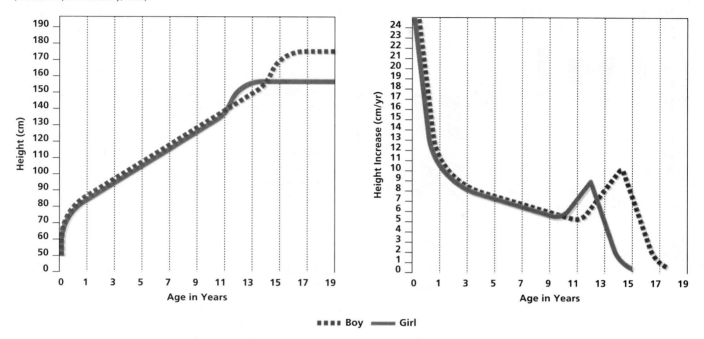

■■■■ Boy ━━━ Girl

Other factors can affect the timing of menarche. For example, environmental stress from parental divorce or intense family conflict can be a factor in an early onset (Ellis, 2004; Belsky et al., 2007; Rodgers et al., 2015).

Over the past century or so, girls in the United States and other cultures have been entering puberty at earlier ages. In the late 19th century, menstruation began, on average, around age 14 or 15, compared with today's 11 or 12. The average age for other indicators of puberty, such as the attaining of adult height and sexual maturity, has also dropped, probably due to reduced disease and improved nutrition (Harris, Prior, & Koehoorn, 2008; James et al., 2012; Sun et al., 2017).

Menstruation is one of several changes in puberty related to the development of primary and secondary sex characteristics. **Primary sex characteristics** are associated with the development of the organs and body structures related directly to reproduction. **Secondary sex characteristics** are the visible signs of sexual maturity that do not involve the sex organs directly.

In girls, primary sex characteristics pertain to changes in the vagina and uterus. Secondary sex characteristics include the development of breasts and pubic hair. Breasts begin to grow around age 10, and pubic hair appears at about age 11. Underarm hair appears about 2 years later.

For some girls, signs of puberty start unusually early. One out of seven Caucasian girls develops breasts or pubic hair by age 8. For African American girls, the figure is one out of two. The reasons for this earlier onset are unclear, and what defines normal and abnormal onset is a controversy among specialists (Ritzen, 2003; Mensah et al., 2013; Mrug et al., 2014).

Puberty in Boys. Boys' sexual maturation follows a somewhat different course. Growth of the penis and scrotum accelerates around age 12, with the organs reaching adult size about 3 or 4 years later. As boys' penises enlarge, other primary sex

primary sex characteristics
characteristics associated with the development of the organs and structures of the body that directly relate to reproduction.

secondary sex characteristics
the visible signs of sexual maturity that do not directly involve the sex organs.

Figure 3-5 Sexual Maturation

The changes in sexual maturation that occur for males and females during early adolescence.
(**Source:** Based on Tanner, 1978.)

characteristics develop. The prostate gland and seminal vesicles, which produce semen (the fluid that carries sperm), enlarge. A boy's first ejaculation, known as *spermarche*, usually occurs around age 13, more than a year after the body begins producing sperm. At first, the semen contains relatively few sperm, but the sperm count increases significantly with age. Secondary sex characteristics are also developing. Pubic hair begins to grow around age 12, followed by the growth of underarm and facial hair. Finally, boys' voices deepen as the vocal cords become longer and the larynx grows larger. (Figure 3-5 summarizes the changes that occur in sexual maturation during early adolescence.)

The surge in hormones that triggers puberty may also lead to rapid mood swings. Boys may have feelings of anger and annoyance associated with higher hormone levels. In girls, higher levels of hormones are associated with depression as well as anger (Hyde, Mezulis, & Abramson, 2008; Van den Bergh et al., 2008; Fujisawa & Shinohara, 2011).

Physical Changes in Adulthood

LO 3.4 **Describe the physical changes that occur from early to late adulthood and how they affect adults' capabilities.**

As Anton ate his lunch one sunny day in Bryant Part, he idly watched two young men playing a high-speed chess game at the next table. One of the players was sitting in a wheelchair. As the game proceeded, with first one player then the other announcing his moves and slamming his timer, Anton found himself hoping that the guy in the wheelchair would win the match.

No such luck. After only a few more moves, the opponent loudly and triumphantly called "Check," and the handicapped player, after surveying the board, tipped his king and conceded defeat. Anton was disappointed: He had hoped that the able-bodied player would go easy on his opponent.

But Anton almost choked on his sandwich when he saw the winner reach for his cane as he rose to shake the hand of the man in the wheelchair. The winner was blind. Both players had a disability, and the one who couldn't even see the board had won the match.

As Anton learned, many people have disabilities, and focusing on what they lack instead of what they have is itself a kind of blindness. It is also a mistake to offer sympathy for the handicap instead of understanding the individual who has it.

Most people are at their physical peak in early adulthood, which starts at the end of adolescence (around age 20) and continues until roughly the start of middle age (around age 40). For them, the body acts as if it's on automatic pilot: Physical health and fitness are never better. Still, there are others who have mild or severe disabilities, and they too are developing during this period. And often, aside from the area of their disability, they too are at their peak.

THE UPS AND DOWNS OF PHYSICAL TRANSITIONS. In most respects, physical development and maturation are complete at early adulthood. Most people have attained their full height, with limbs proportional to their size, rendering the gangliness of adolescence a memory. People in their early 20s tend to be healthy, vigorous, and energetic. Although **senescence**, the natural physical decline brought about by increasing age, has begun, age-related changes are not usually obvious until later in life. At the same time, some growth continues; for example, some people, particularly late maturers, continue to gain height in their early 20s.

senescence

the natural physical decline brought about by increasing age.

NEGATIVE CHANGE. For many people, early adulthood is the first time—but by no means the last—that they have to deal seriously with the negative consequences of developmental change. As middle adulthood continues, people become aware of the gradual physical changes that aging brings. Some are the result of senescence, or naturally occurring declines; others are related to lifestyle choices, such as diet, exercise, smoking, and alcohol or drug use.

Although physical changes occur throughout life, these changes take on new significance in midlife, particularly in Western cultures that highly value a youthful appearance. The psychological significance of aging may far exceed the relatively minor and gradual changes a person experiences. A woman may have had gray hairs in her 20s, but in her 40s they may multiply to an extent she cannot ignore. She may feel no longer young.

People's emotional reactions to midlife's physical changes depend in part on their self-concepts. When self-image is tied closely to one's physical attributes—as it is for very athletic men and women or those who are physically quite attractive—middle adulthood can be particularly difficult. The changes the mirror reveals signal aging and mortality as well as a loss of physical attractiveness. However, because most people's self-concept is not so closely tied to physical attributes, middle-aged adults generally report no less satisfaction with their body image than younger adults (McKinley, 2006; Hillman, 2012; Murray & Lewis, 2014).

From *a social worker's* perspective

When older people win praise and attention for being "vigorous," "active," and "youthful," is this a message that combats or supports stereotypes about aging?

LATE ADULTHOOD

> *"Feel the burn."* That's what the teacher says, and many of the 14 women in the class are doing just that. As the teacher continues through a variety of exercises, the women participate to varying degrees. Some stretch and reach vigorously, while others just move in time to the beat of the music. It's not much different from thousands of exercise classes all over the United States, yet to the youthful observer there is one surprise: The youngest woman in this class is 66 years old, and the oldest, dressed in a sleek black leotard, is 81.

The surprise registered by this observer reflects the stereotype that people over 65 are sedentary, incapable of vigorous exercise. The reality, however, is different. Although the physical capabilities of elderly people are not the same as they were in earlier stages of life, many older persons remain remarkably agile and physically fit in later life. Still, the outer and inner changes that began subtly during middle adulthood become unmistakable during old age (Riebe, Burbank, & Garber, 2002; Sargent-Cox, Anstey, & Luszcz, 2012).

As we discuss aging, we should take note of the distinction between primary and secondary aging. As we saw earlier, **primary aging**, or *senescence*, involves universal and irreversible changes due to genetic programming. In contrast, **secondary aging** encompasses changes that are due to illness, health habits, and other individual factors, which are not inevitable. Although the physical and cognitive changes of secondary aging are common, they are potentially avoidable and can sometimes be reversed.

OUTWARD SIGNS OF AGING.   One of the most obvious indicators of aging is the hair, which usually becomes distinctly gray and eventually white, and may thin out. The face and other parts of the body become wrinkled as the skin loses elasticity and *collagen*, the protein that forms the basic fibers of body tissue (Lesnoff-Caravaglia, 2007).

People may become noticeably shorter, with some shrinking as much as 4 inches. Although this shortening is partially due to changes in posture, the primary cause is that the cartilage in the discs of the backbone has become thinner. This is particularly true for women, who are more susceptible than men to **osteoporosis**, or thinning of the bones, largely because of reduced production of estrogen.

As we have seen, osteoporosis, which affects 25 percent of women over 60, is a primary cause of broken bones among older people. It is largely preventable if exercise is adequate and calcium and protein intake is sufficient earlier in life. Osteoporosis can be treated and even prevented with drugs such as Fosamax (alendronate) (Tadic et al., 2012; Hansen et al., 2014).

Although negative stereotypes against appearing old affect both genders, they are particularly potent for women. In Western cultures there is a *double standard* for appearance,

primary aging
aging that involves universal and irreversible changes that, due to genetic programming, occur as people get older.

secondary aging
changes in physical and cognitive functioning that are due to illness, health habits, and other individual differences, but that are not due to increased age itself and are not inevitable.

osteoporosis
a condition in which the bones become brittle, fragile, and thin, often brought about by a lack of calcium in the diet.

by which women are judged more harshly than men. For instance, gray hair in men is often viewed as "distinguished"; in women it is a sign of being "over the hill" (Frerking, 2006).

As a consequence of the double standard, women are considerably more likely than men to feel compelled to hide the signs of aging. For instance, older women are much more likely than men to dye their hair and to have cosmetic surgery, and women's use of cosmetics is designed to make them look younger. This is changing, however. Men are also becoming more interested in maintaining a youthful appearance, another sign of the dominance of a youth orientation in Western culture (Unger & Crawford, 2003; Clarke & Griffin, 2007).

INTERNAL AGING. As the outward signs of aging become more apparent, changes also take place in the internal functioning of the organ systems (Whitbourne, 2001; Aldwin & Gilmer, 2004).

The brain becomes smaller and lighter. As it shrinks, it pulls away from the skull, and the space between brain and skull doubles from age 20 to age 70. The brain uses less oxygen and glucose, and blood flow is reduced. The number of neurons, or brain cells, declines in some parts of the brain, although not as much as was once thought. Recent research suggests that the number of cells in the cortex may drop only minimally or not at all. In fact, some evidence suggests that certain types of neuronal growth may continue throughout the life span (Raz et al., 2007; Gattringer et al., 2012; Jäncke et al., 2015).

The reduced flow of blood in the brain is due in part to the heart's diminished ability to pump blood through hardening and shrinking blood vessels. A 75-year-old man pumps less than three-quarters of the blood that he could pump during early adulthood (Yildiz, 2007).

Other bodily systems also work at lower capacity. The respiratory system is less efficient, and the digestive system produces less digestive juice and is less efficient in pushing food through the system—thereby increasing the incidence of constipation. Some hormones are produced at lower levels. Muscle fibers decrease both in size and in amount, and they become less efficient at using oxygen from the bloodstream and storing nutrients (Vecchiet, 2002; Morley, 2012).

Although these changes are normal, they often occur earlier in people who have less healthy lifestyles. For example, smoking accelerates declines in cardiovascular capacity at any age.

Lifestyle factors can also slow the changes associated with aging. For instance, people whose exercise program includes weightlifting may lose muscle fiber at a slower rate than those who are sedentary. Similarly, physical fitness is related to better performance on mental tests, may prevent a loss of brain tissue, and may even aid in the development of new neurons. Studies suggest that sedentary older adults who begin aerobic fitness training ultimately show cognitive benefits (Pereira et al., 2007; Lin et al., 2014; Bonavita & Tedeschi, 2017).

The Myth and Reality of Aging

LO 3.5 Distinguish functional age from chronological age.

Astronaut-turned-senator John Glenn was 77 years old when he returned to space on a 10-day mission to help NASA study how the elderly adjust to space travel. Although sheer altitude sets Glenn apart from others, many people lead active, vigorous lives during late adulthood, fully engaged with life.

Old age used to be equated with loss: loss of brain cells, intellectual capabilities, energy, sex drive. That view is being displaced as **gerontologists**, specialists who study aging, paint a very different picture. Rather than a period of decline, late adulthood is seen as a stage in which people continue to change—to grow in some areas and, yes, to decline in others.

gerontologists
specialists who study aging.

Even the definition of "old" is changing. Many people in late adulthood, which begins around age 65 and continues to death, are as vigorous and involved with life as people several decades younger. We can no longer define old age by chronological years alone; we must also take into account people's physical and psychological well-being, their *functional age*. Some researchers divide people into three groups according to functional ages: the *young old* are healthy and active; the *old old* have some health problems and difficulties with daily activities; and the *oldest old* are frail and need care. According to functional age, an active, healthy 100-year-old would be considered young old, while a 65-year-old in the late stages of emphysema would be among the oldest old.

Late adulthood holds a unique distinction among life's stages: Because people are living longer, late adulthood is getting longer. Whether we start counting at 65 or 70, a greater proportion of people are alive in late adulthood today than at any time in world history. Demographers have taken to dividing the period using the same terms—but with different meanings—as researchers of functional aging. For demographers, the terms are purely chronological. The *young old* are 65 to 74 years old. The *old old* are between 75 and 84, and the *oldest old* are 85 and older.

THE DEMOGRAPHICS OF LATE ADULTHOOD.   One out of every eight Americans is 65 or older, and projections suggest that by 2050 nearly one-quarter of the population will be 65 and older. The number of people over 85 is projected to increase from 4 million to 18 million by 2050 (Ortman, Velkoff, & Hogan, 2014).

The fastest-growing segment of the population is the oldest old—people 85 or older. In the past two decades, the size of this group has nearly doubled. The population explosion among older people is not limited to the United States. As can be seen in Figure 3-6, the number of elderly is increasing substantially in countries around the globe. By 2050, the number of adults worldwide over 60 will exceed the number of people under 15 for the first time in history (Sandis, 2000; United Nations, 2013).

Figure 3-6 The Elderly Population Worldwide

Longer life is transforming population profiles worldwide, with the proportion of those over age 60 predicted to increase substantially by the year 2050.
(**Source:** Based on United Nations, 2013.)

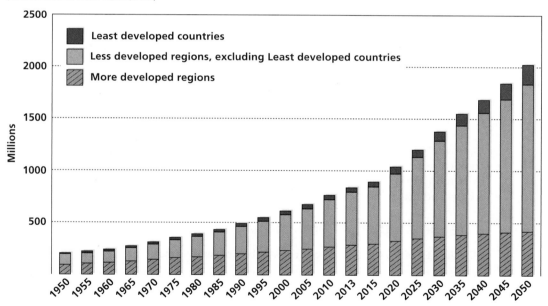

Module 3.1 Review

LO 3.1   **Describe infants' physical development in the first 2 years of life.**

The pattern of physical development is rapid growth over the first 2 years. Infants integrate their behavior through the development of various rhythms and states, and within a year they develop the ability to sleep through the night.

LO 3.2   **Summarize the physical development that occurs during the preschool and middle childhood years and the factors that affect this development.**

The pattern of physical development in preschool and middle childhood is slow and steady. Economics and culture affect the patterns of growth.

LO 3.3 Identify the physical changes adolescents experience as the body reaches puberty.

The key physical change of adolescence is puberty, which can have powerful effects on adolescents depending on whether they are male or female and late maturing or early maturing.

LO 3.4 Describe the physical changes that occur from early to late adulthood and how they affect adults' capabilities.

In general, early adulthood is the first time that people have to deal seriously with negative changes. While many physical changes associated with aging are universal and irreversible, such as thinning cartilage in the spine or reduced blood flow to the brain, changes referred to as secondary aging are often the result of poor lifestyle and health habits.

LO 3.5 Distinguish functional age from chronological age.

Because many older adults are as vigorous and involved with life as people several decades younger, we cannot define old age by chronological years alone; we also must take into account people's physical and psychological well-being, their *functional age*.

Journal Writing Prompt

Applying Lifespan Development: How might biology and environment combine to affect the physical growth of a child adopted as an infant from a developing country and reared in a more industrialized one?

MODULE 3.2

BRAIN GROWTH AND MOTOR DEVELOPMENT

It is a hot summer day in Atlanta, Georgia. Adults move slowly through the humid air, but not 8-year-old Suzanne McGuire. A look of triumph crosses her face as she rounds the corner from third base to home plate.

Moments before, she was waiting for the pitcher to throw the ball. Her first two turns at bat, Suzanne had struck out, leaving her unhappy and a bit humiliated.

On her third at-bat, though, the pitch looked perfect. She swung at it with confidence and high hope. When the bat connected with the ball, lobbing it well beyond the left fielder for a home run, it created a moment she would never forget.

Suzanne McGuire has come a long way since the preschool years, when quick, coordinated running and batting to the mark were not possible. As a child's motor and brain development proceeds from infancy onward, parents watch in awe as skills emerge that eventually will allow their kids to roll over, take their first step, and pick up a cookie crumb from the floor. And these skills will ultimately form the basis of later, even more complex behaviors as the child develops gross motor skills—like swinging a bat—and fine motor skills—like playing scales on a piano.

The Nervous System and Brain: Making Connections

LO 3.6 Discuss the role of neurons in brain development.

When their first baby is born, parents marvel at the infant, oohing and aahing at every sneeze and smile and whimper, trying to guess their meaning. Whatever feelings, movements, and thoughts the baby is experiencing, they are all brought about by the same complex network: the infant's nervous system. The *nervous system* comprises the brain and the nerves that extend throughout the body.

THE GROWING BRAIN. The brain grows at a faster rate than any other part of the body. Two-year-olds have brains that are about three-quarters the size and weight of an adult brain. By age 5, children's brains weigh 90 percent of average adult brain weight. In comparison, the average 5-year-old's total body weight is just 30 percent of average adult body weight (Alosco et al., 2014).

Why does the brain grow so rapidly? One reason is an increase in the number of interconnections among cells, which supports more complex communication between neurons and permits the rapid growth of cognitive skills. In addition, the amount of protective myelin increases, which speeds the transmission of electrical impulses along brain cells.

Figure 3-7 The Neuron

The basic element of the nervous system, the neuron, has a number of components.
(**Source:** Van de Graaf, 2000.)

Neurons are the basic cells of the nervous system. Figure 3-7 shows the structure of an adult neuron. Like all cells in the body, neurons have a cell body containing a nucleus. But unlike other cells, neurons have a distinctive ability: They can communicate with other cells, using a cluster of fibers called *dendrites* at one end. Dendrites receive messages from other cells. At their opposite end, neurons have a long extension called an *axon*, the part of the neuron that carries messages destined for other neurons. Neurons do not actually touch one another. Rather, they communicate with other neurons by means of chemical messengers, *neurotransmitters*, which travel across the small gaps, known as synapses, between neurons.

Although estimates vary, infants are born with between 100 billion and 200 billion neurons. In order to reach this number, neurons multiply at an amazing rate prior to birth. At some points in prenatal development, cell division creates some 250,000 additional neurons every minute.

At birth, most neurons in an infant's brain have relatively few connections to other neurons. During the first 2 years of life, however, a baby's brain will establish billions of new connections between neurons. Furthermore, the network of neurons becomes increasingly complex, as illustrated in Figure 3-8. The intricacy of neural connections continues to increase throughout life. In fact, in adulthood a single neuron is likely to have a minimum of 5,000 connections to other neurons or other body parts.

SYNAPTIC PRUNING.   Babies are actually born with many more neurons than they need. In addition, although synapses are formed throughout life based on our changing

Figure 3-8 Neuron Networks

Over the first 2 years of life, networks of neurons become increasingly complex and interconnected. Why are these connections important?
(**Source:** Based on Conel, 1939/1975.)

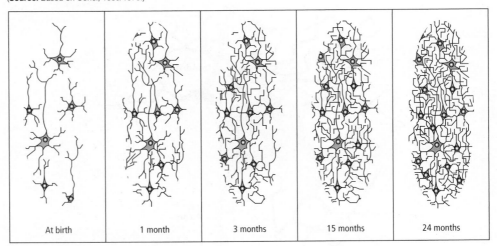

| At birth | 1 month | 3 months | 15 months | 24 months |

synaptic pruning
the elimination of neurons as the result of nonuse or lack of stimulation.

myelin
protective insulation that surrounds parts of neurons, increasing the speed of transmission of electrical impulses along brain cells.

cerebral cortex
the upper layer of the brain.

Figure 3-9 Shaken Baby Syndrome

This CAT scan shows severe brain injury in an infant suspected of being abused by a caretaker who shook the infant.

Scott Camazine/Alamy

experiences, the billions of new synapses infants form during the first 2 years are more numerous than necessary. What happens to the extra neurons and synaptic connections?

Like a farmer who, to strengthen the vitality of a fruit tree, prunes away unnecessary branches, brain development enhances certain capabilities in part by "pruning down" unnecessary neurons. Neurons that do not become interconnected with other neurons as the infant's experience of the world increases eventually die out, enhancing the efficiency of the nervous system.

Similarly, if a baby's experiences do not stimulate certain nerve connections, these, like unused neurons, are eliminated—a process called **synaptic pruning**. The result of synaptic pruning is to allow established neurons to build more elaborate communication networks with other neurons. Unlike most other aspects of growth, then, the development of the nervous system proceeds most effectively through the loss of cells (Schafer & Stevens, 2013; Gomez-Nicola & Perry, 2015; Athanasiu et al., 2017).

After birth, neurons continue to increase in size. In addition to growth in dendrites, the axons of neurons become coated with **myelin**, a fatty substance that, like the insulation on an electric wire, provides protection and speeds the transmission of nerve impulses. So, even though many neurons are lost, the increasing size and complexity of the remaining ones contribute to impressive brain growth. A baby's brain triples its weight during his or her first 2 years of life, and it reaches more than three-quarters of its adult weight and size by age 2.

As they grow, the neurons also reposition themselves, becoming arranged by function. Some move into the **cerebral cortex**, the upper layer of the brain, while others move to *subcortical levels*, which are below the cerebral cortex. The subcortical levels, which regulate such fundamental activities as breathing and heart rate, are the most fully developed at birth. As time passes, however, the cells in the cerebral cortex, which are responsible for higher-order processes such as thinking and reasoning, become more developed and interconnected.

Although the brain is protected by the bones of the skull, it is highly sensitive to some forms of injury. One particularly devastating injury comes from a form of child abuse called *shaken baby syndrome* in which an infant is shaken by a caretaker, usually out of frustration or anger caused by a baby's crying. Shaking can lead the brain to rotate within the skull, causing blood vessels to tear and destroying the intricate connections between neurons, producing severe medical problems, long-term physical and learning disabilities, and often death (see Figure 3-9). Estimates of the incidence of shaken baby syndrome range from 1,000 to 3,000 cases a year in the United States. One-quarter of babies who are shaken ultimately die, and 80 percent of survivors have permanent brain damage (American Association of Neurological Surgeons, 2012; Narang & Clarke, 2014; Grinkevičiūtė et al., 2016; Centers for Disease Control and Prevention, 2017).

ENVIRONMENTAL INFLUENCES ON BRAIN DEVELOPMENT. Brain development, much of which unfolds automatically because of genetically predetermined patterns, is also strongly susceptible to environmental influences. The brain's **plasticity**, the degree to which a developing structure or behavior is modifiable due to experience, is relatively great. For instance, as we've seen, an infant's sensory experience affects both the size of individual neurons and the structure of their interconnections. Consequently, compared with those brought up in more enriched environments, infants raised in severely restricted settings are likely to show differences in brain structure and weight (Cirulli, Berry, & Alleva, 2003; Couperus & Nelson, 2006; Glaser, 2012).

Furthermore, researchers have found that there are sensitive periods during development. A **sensitive period** is a specific but limited time, usually early in an organism's life, during which the organism is particularly susceptible to environmental influences relating to some particular facet of development. A sensitive period may be associated with a behavior—such as the development of vision—or with the development of a structure of the body, such as the configuration of the brain (Uylings, 2006; Hartley & Lee, 2015).

> **From *a social worker's* perspective**
>
> What are some cultural or subcultural influences that might affect parents' childrearing practices?

The existence of sensitive periods suggests that if deprived of a certain level of early environmental stimulation during a sensitive period, the infant may suffer damage or fail to develop capabilities that can never be fully remedied. If this is true, providing successful later intervention for such children may prove challenging (Gottlieb & Blair, 2004).

The opposite question also arises: Does an unusually high level of stimulation during sensitive periods produce developmental gains beyond what a more commonplace level of stimulation would provide?

There is no simple answer. Determining how unusually impoverished or enriched environments affect later development is one of the major questions addressed by developmental researchers as they look for ways to maximize opportunities for developing children. In the meantime, many developmentalists suggest that simple activities can provide a stimulating environment that will encourage healthy brain growth, including cuddling, talking and singing, and playing with babies to help enrich their environment (Garlick, 2003; Shoemark, 2014).

Brain Lateralization

LO 3.7 Explain what is meant by brain lateralization and describe how it develops in early childhood.

By the end of the preschool period, the *corpus callosum,* a bundle of nerve fibers that connects the two hemispheres of the brain, becomes considerably thicker, developing as many as 800 million individual fibers that help coordinate brain functioning between the two hemispheres. At the same time, the two halves of the brain become increasingly differentiated and specialized. **Lateralization,** the process in which certain functions are located more in one hemisphere than the other, becomes more pronounced during the preschool years.

For most people, the left hemisphere is primarily involved with tasks that necessitate verbal competence, such as speaking, reading, thinking, and reasoning. The right hemisphere develops its own strengths, especially in nonverbal areas such as comprehension of spatial relationships, recognition of patterns and drawings, music, and emotional expression (see Figure 3-10; Pollak, Holt, & Wismer Fries, 2004; Watling & Bourne, 2007; Dundas, Plaut, & Behrmann, 2015).

plasticity
the degree to which a developing structure or behavior is modifiable due to experience.

sensitive period
a point in development when organisms are particularly susceptible to certain kinds of stimuli in their environments, but the absence of those stimuli does not always produce irreversible consequences.

lateralization
the process in which certain cognitive functions are located more in one hemisphere of the brain than in the other.

Figure 3-10 Looking into the Brain

This set of PET brain scans illustrates that activity in the right or left hemisphere of the brain differs according to the task in which a person is engaged. How might educators use this finding in their approach to teaching?

Left   Right

ZEPHYR/Getty Images

Each hemisphere also begins to process information in a slightly different manner. The left hemisphere processes data sequentially, one piece at a time. The right hemisphere processes information in a more global manner, reflecting on it as a whole (Geschwind & Iacoboni, 2007; Barber et al., 2012).

While there is some specialization, in most respects the two hemispheres act in tandem and are interdependent. In fact, each hemisphere can perform most of the tasks of the other. For example, the right hemisphere does some language processing and plays an important role in language comprehension (Hall, Neal, & Dean, 2008; Jahagirdar, 2014; Hodgson, Hirst, & Hudson, 2016).

Individual Differences in Lateralization. There are also individual and cultural differences in lateralization. For example, many of the 10 percent of people who are left-handed or ambidextrous (able to use both hands interchangeably) have language centered in the right hemisphere or have no specific language center (Isaacs et al., 2006; Szaflarski et al., 2012; Porac, 2016).

Among the most controversial findings relating to the specialization of the hemispheres of the brain is evidence that lateralization is related to gender and culture. For instance, starting during the first year of life and continuing in the preschool years, boys and girls show some hemispheric differences associated with lower body reflexes and the processing of auditory information. Boys also clearly tend to show greater specialization of language in the left hemisphere; among girls, language is more evenly divided between the two hemispheres. Such differences may help explain why girls' language development proceeds at a more rapid pace during the preschool years than boys' language development (Bourne & Todd, 2004; Huster, Westerhausen, & Herrmann, 2011; Allan, Joye & Lonigan, 2017).

According to psychologist Simon Baron-Cohen, the differences between male and female brains may help explain the puzzling riddle of *autism*, the profound developmental disability that produces language deficits and great difficulty in interacting with others. Baron-Cohen argues that children with autism (who are predominately male) have what he calls an "extreme male brain." The extreme male brain, though relatively good at systematically sorting out the world, is poor at understanding the emotions of others and experiencing empathy for others' feelings. To Baron-Cohen, individuals with an extreme male brain have traits associated with the normal male brain but display the traits to such an extent that their behavior is viewed as autistic (Auyeung & Baron-Cohen, 2012; Lau et al., 2013; Ruigrok et al., 2014).

Although Baron-Cohen's theory is quite controversial, it is clear that some kind of gender differences exist in lateralization. But we still don't know the extent of the differences and why they occur. One explanation is genetic: Female brains and male brains are predisposed to function in slightly different ways. Such a view is supported by data suggesting the existence of minor structural differences between the male and female brain. For instance, a section of the corpus callosum is proportionally larger in women than in men. Furthermore, studies conducted among other species, such as primates, rats, and hamsters, have found size and structural differences in the brains of males and females (Colibazzi et al., 2008; Redcay & Courchesne, 2008; Luders, Toga, & Thompson, 2014).

Before we accept a genetic explanation for the differences between female and male brains, we need to consider an equally plausible alternative: It may be that verbal abilities emerge earlier in girls because girls receive greater encouragement for verbal skills than boys do. For instance, even as infants, girls are spoken to more than boys. Such higher levels of verbal stimulation may produce growth in particular areas of the brain that does not occur in boys. Consequently, environmental factors rather than genetic ones may lead to the gender differences we find in brain lateralization (Hohm et al., 2007; Rosenberg, 2013).

Lateralization by Culture. Not only may there be differences in brain lateralization between boys and girls, but the culture in which they are raised may also be related to brain lateralization. For instance, native speakers of Japanese process information related to vowel sounds primarily in the left hemisphere of the brain. In comparison, North and South Americans and Europeans—as well as people of Japanese ancestry who learn Japanese as a second language—process vowel sounds primarily in the brain's right hemisphere.

The explanation for this cultural difference in processing of vowels seems to rest on the nature of the Japanese language. Specifically, the Japanese language allows for the expression of complex concepts using only vowel sounds. Consequently, a specific type of brain lateralization may develop while learning and using Japanese at a relatively early age (Hiser & Kobayashi, 2003).

This explanation, which is speculative, does not rule out the possibility that some type of subtle genetic difference may also be at work in determining the difference in lateralization. Once again, then, we find it challenging to tease out the relative impact of heredity and environment.

THE LINKS BETWEEN BRAIN GROWTH AND COGNITIVE DEVELOPMENT. Neuroscientists are just beginning to understand the ways in which brain development is related to cognitive development. For example, it appears that there are periods during childhood in which the brain shows unusual growth spurts, and these periods are linked to advances in cognitive abilities. One study that measured electrical activity in the brain across the life span found unusual spurts at between 18 months and 2 years, a time when language abilities increase rapidly. Other spurts occurred around other ages when cognitive advances are particularly intense (see Figure 3-11; Mabbott et al., 2006; Westermann et al., 2007).

Other research has suggested that increases in myelin may be related to preschoolers' growing cognitive capabilities. For example, myelination of the *reticular formation*, an area of the brain associated with attention and concentration, is completed by the time children are about 5. This may be associated with children's growing attention spans as they approach school age. The improvement in memory that occurs during the preschool years may also be associated with myelination: During the preschool years, myelination is completed in the hippocampus, an area associated with memory (Rolls, 2000; de Bellis et al., 2001).

We do not yet know the direction of causality. (Does brain development produce cognitive advances, or do cognitive accomplishments fuel brain development?) However, it is clear that increases in our understanding of the physiological aspects of the brain will eventually have important implications for parents and teachers.

During the rest of the life span, brain development and cognitive growth are interrelated. Teenagers tend to assert themselves more as they gain greater independence. This independence is, in part, the result of changes in the brain that bring significant advances in cognitive abilities. As the number of neurons continues to grow, and their interconnections become richer and more complex, adolescent thinking becomes more sophisticated (Toga & Thompson, 2003; Blakemore, 2012; Konrad, Firk, & Uhlhaas, 2013).

The brain produces an oversupply of gray matter during adolescence, which is later pruned back by 1 to 2 percent each year (see Figure 3-12). Myelination increases, making the transmission of neural messages more efficient. Both pruning and increased myelination contribute to the growing cognitive abilities of adolescents (Sowell et al., 2001; Sowell et al., 2003; Li, 2012; Mychasiuk & Metz, 2016).

The prefrontal cortex of the brain, which is not fully developed until the early 20s, undergoes considerable development during adolescence. The *prefrontal cortex* allows people to think, evaluate, and make complex judgments in a uniquely human way. It underlies the increasingly complex intellectual achievements that are possible during adolescence.

Figure 3-11 Myelin in Newborns' Brains

Myelin, the protective insulation that surrounds parts of neurons, increases with age and may be related to cognitive development. These composite scans show the distribution of myelin at birth.

Neil M. Borden/Photo Researchers, Inc. / Science Source

Figure 3-12 Pruning Gray Matter

As children grow into adulthood, gray matter is pruned from the brain. These composite scans show changes in gray matter and other physical changes in the cortex from age 5 through 20. (**Source:** Gogtay et al. 2004.)

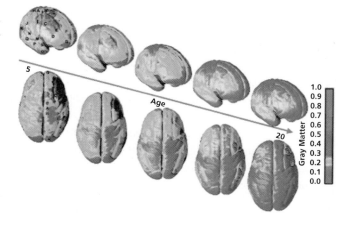

At this stage, the prefrontal cortex becomes increasingly efficient in communicating with other parts of the brain, creating a communication system that is more distributed and sophisticated, which permits the different areas of the brain to process information more effectively (Scherf, Sweeney, & Luna, 2006; Wiggins et al., 2014).

The prefrontal cortex also provides impulse control. An individual with a fully developed prefrontal cortex is able to inhibit the desire to act on such emotions as anger or rage. In adolescence, however, the prefrontal cortex is biologically immature; the ability to inhibit impulses is not fully developed. This brain immaturity may lead to the risky and impulsive behaviors that characterize adolescence—and some behaviors that are even more extreme.

Furthermore, some researchers theorize that not only do adolescents underestimate the risks of risky behavior, but they also overestimate the rewards that will come from the behavior. Regardless of the causes of risk-taking in adolescents, it has led to a heated discussion of whether the death penalty should be applied to adolescents (Steinberg & Scott, 2003; Casey, Jones, & Somerville, 2011; Gopnik, 2012).

Brain development also produces changes in regions involving dopamine sensitivity and production. As a result, adolescents may become less affected by alcohol, requiring more drinks to experience its effects—leading to higher alcohol intake. Changes in dopamine sensitivity may also increase sensitivity to stress, leading to further alcohol use (Spear, 2002).

Teenagers tend to assert themselves more as they gain greater independence. This independence is, in part, the result of changes in the brain that bring significant advances in cognitive abilities. As the number of neurons (the cells of the nervous system) continues to grow, and their interconnections become richer and more complex, adolescent thinking becomes more sophisticated (Thompson & Nelson, 2001; Toga & Thompson, 2003; Also see the *From Research to Practice* box).

reflexes
unlearned, organized involuntary responses that occur automatically in the presence of certain stimuli.

From Research to Practice
Young Adult Brains Are Still Developing

Once you have reached young adulthood, you're free to explore a variety of new experiences from which society shields children and adolescents because their so-called impressionable minds are still developing. Parental guidance, consent, or supervision are no longer required. Your access to very violent movies, bars and nightclubs, and all kinds of other adult-only situations is increasingly unfettered. But is your brain really done developing?

Research indicates that it actually isn't, and it won't be until later in your 20s. Rather than being fully grown, the young adult brain continues to grow new neural connections and to prune away unused pathways. This is generally a good thing—it means that young adults' minds are still malleable and adaptive to new experiences. For example, learning a new language, musical instrument, or job skill is easier for young adults than it is for older adults (Whiting, Chenery, & Copland, 2011).

One part of the brain in particular, the prefrontal cortex, doesn't mature until well into young adulthood. This region is responsible for such higher-order mental functions as planning, decision making, and impulse control. It's little wonder, then, that the greatest risks to health and well-being in this stage of life mainly involve poor judgment—motor vehicle accidents, violence, drug abuse, and excessive drinking chief among them. But it's also a time of opportunity when young adults can instill such highly beneficial traits as resilience, self-control, and self-regulation (Raznahan et al., 2011; Giedd, 2012; Steinberg, 2014).

What you do with this time can have important implications going forward. For example, recent research found that the more that young adults used Facebook, the worse they felt at the time and the more their satisfaction with life declined over time. This fits with a broader concern expressed by scientists who study young adult brain development: The choice of activities in young adulthood can have lasting consequences, for better or worse (Beck, 2012; Giedd, 2012; Kross et al., 2013).

Shared Writing Prompt
What could young adults do to optimize their ongoing brain development?

Reflexes: Protective Reactions

LO 3.8 **Identify the reflexes that infants are born with that help them adapt to their surroundings and protect themselves.**

(a)

When her father pressed 3-day-old Christina Michaelson's palm with his finger, she responded by tightly winding her small fist around his finger and grasping it. When he moved his finger upward, she held on so tightly that it seemed he might be able to lift her completely off her crib floor.

In fact, her father was right: Christina probably could have been lifted in this way. The reason for her resolute grip was activation of one of the dozens of reflexes with which infants are born. Newborns enter the world with a repertoire of reflexive behavioral patterns that help them adapt to their new surroundings and serve to protect them.

(b)

Reflexes are unlearned, organized involuntary responses that occur automatically in the presence of certain stimuli. As we can see from the list of reflexes in Table 3-2, many reflexes clearly represent behavior that has survival value, helping to ensure the well-being of the infant. For instance, the *swimming reflex* makes a baby who is lying facedown in a body of water paddle and kick in a sort of swimming motion. The obvious consequence of such behavior is to help the baby move from danger and survive until a caregiver can come to its rescue. Similarly, the *eye blink reflex* seems designed to protect the eye from too much direct light, which might damage the retina.

Given the protective value of many reflexes, it might seem beneficial for them to remain with us for our entire lives. In fact, some do: The eye-blink reflex remains functional throughout the full life span. Quite a few reflexes, however, such as the swimming reflex, disappear after a few months. Why should this be the case?

(c)

Infants showing (a) the grasping reflex, (b) the startle reflex, and (c) the Moro reflex.

Researchers who focus on evolutionary explanations of development attribute the gradual disappearance of reflexes to the increase in voluntary control over behavior that occurs as infants become more able to control their muscles. In addition, it may be that reflexes form the foundation for future, more complex behaviors. As these more intricate behaviors become well learned, they encompass the earlier reflexes. Finally, it is possible that reflexes stimulate parts of the brain responsible for more complex behaviors, helping them develop (Lipsitt, 2003).

Table 3-2 Some Basic Reflexes in Infants

Reflex	Approximate Age of Disappearance	Description	Possible Function
Rooting reflex	3 weeks	Neonate's tendency to turn its head toward things that touch its cheek.	Food intake
Stepping reflex	2 months	Movement of legs when held upright with feet touching the floor.	Prepares infants for independent locomotion
Swimming reflex	4–6 months	Infant's tendency to paddle and kick in a sort of swimming motion when lying facedown in a body of water.	Avoidance of danger
Grasping reflex	5–6 months	Infant's fingers close around an object placed in its hands.	Provides support
Moro reflex	6 months	Activated when support for the neck and head is suddenly removed. The arms of the infant are thrust outward and then appear to grasp onto something.	Similar to primates' protection from falling
Babinski reflex	8–12 months	An infant fans out its toes in response to a stroke on the outside of its foot.	Unknown
Startle reflex	Remains in different form	An infant, in response to a sudden noise, flings out its arms, arches its back, and spreads its fingers.	Protection
Eye-blink reflex	Remains	Rapid shutting and opening of eye on exposure to direct light.	Protection of eye from direct light
Sucking reflex	Remains	Infant's tendency to suck at things that touch its lips.	Food intake
Gag reflex	Remains	An infant's reflex to clear its throat.	Prevents choking

ETHNIC AND CULTURAL DIFFERENCES AND SIMILARITIES IN REFLEXES. Although reflexes are, by definition, genetically determined and universal throughout all infants, there are actually some cultural variations in the ways they are displayed. For instance, consider the *Moro reflex*, which is activated when support for the neck and head is suddenly removed. The Moro reflex consists of the infant's arms thrusting outward and then appearing to seek to grasp onto something. Most scientists feel that the Moro reflex represents a leftover response that we humans have inherited from our nonhuman ancestors. The Moro reflex is an extremely useful behavior for monkey babies, who travel about by clinging to their mothers' backs. If they lose their grip, they fall down unless they are able to grasp quickly onto their mother's fur—using a Moro-like reflex (Zafeiriou, 2004; Rousseau et al., 2017).

The Moro reflex is found in all humans, but it appears with significantly different vigor in different children. Some differences reflect cultural and ethnic variations (Freedman, 1979). For instance, Caucasian infants show a pronounced response to situations that produce the Moro reflex. Not only do they fling out their arms, but they also cry and respond in a generally agitated manner. In contrast, Navajo babies react to the same situation much more calmly. Their arms do not flail out as much, and they cry only rarely.

Gross Motor Skills

LO 3.9 **Summarize the gross motor skills that emerge during infancy and the preschool years, and explain how they are related to brain development.**

Anya sat in the sandbox at the park, chatting with the other parents and playing with her two children, 5-year-old Nicholai and 13-month-old Sofia. While she chatted, she kept a close eye on Sofia, who would still put sand in her mouth sometimes if she wasn't stopped. Today, however, Sofia seemed content to run the sand through her hands and try to put it into a bucket. Nicholai, meanwhile, was busy with two other boys, rapidly filling and emptying the other sand buckets to build an elaborate sand city, which they would then destroy with toy trucks.

When children of different ages gather at a playground, it's easy to see that preschool children have come a long way in their motor development since infancy. Both their gross and their fine motor skills have become increasingly fine-tuned. Sofia, for example, is still mastering putting sand into a bucket, while her brother, Nicholai, uses that skill easily as part of his larger goal of building a sand city.

Probably no physical changes are more obvious—and more eagerly anticipated—than the increasing array of motor skills that babies acquire during infancy. Most parents can remember their child's first steps with a sense of pride and awe at how quickly she or he changed from a helpless infant, unable even to roll over, into a person who could navigate quite effectively in the world.

Even though the motor skills of newborn infants are not terribly sophisticated, at least compared with attainments that will soon appear, young infants are still able to accomplish some kinds of movement. For instance, when placed on their stomachs they wiggle their arms and legs and may try to lift their heavy heads. As their strength increases, they are able to push hard enough against the surface on which they are resting to propel their bodies in different directions. They often end up moving backward rather than forward, but by the age of 6 months they become rather accomplished at moving themselves in particular directions. These initial efforts are the forerunners of crawling, in which babies coordinate the motions of their arms and legs and propel themselves forward. Crawling appears typically between 8 and 10 months. (Figure 3-13 provides a summary of some of the milestones of normal motor development.)

Walking comes later. At around the age of 9 months, most infants are able to walk by supporting themselves on furniture, and half of all infants can walk well by the end of their first year of life.

At the same time infants are learning to move around, they are perfecting the ability to remain in a stationary sitting position. At first, babies cannot remain seated upright without support. But they quickly master this ability, and most are able to sit without support by the age of 6 months.

Figure 3-13 Milestones of Motor Development

Fifty percent of children are able to perform each skill at the month indicated in the figure. However, the specific timing at which each skill appears varies widely. For example, one-quarter of children are able to walk well at 11.1 months; by 14.9 months, 90 percent of children are walking well. Is knowledge of such average benchmarks helpful or harmful to parents?
(**Source:** Adapted from Frankenburg et al., 1992.)

| 3.2 months: rolling over | 3.3 months: grasping rattle | 5.9 months: sitting without support | 7.2 months: standing while holding on | 8.2 months: grasping with thumb and finger |

| 11.5 months: standing alone well | 12.3 months: walking well | 14.8 months: building tower of two cubes | 16.6 months: walking up steps | 23.8 months: jumping in place |

By the time they are 3 years old, children have mastered a variety of skills: jumping, hopping on one foot, skipping, and running. By ages 4 and 5, their skills have become more refined as they have gained greater control over their muscles. For instance, at age 4 they can throw a ball with enough accuracy that a friend can catch it, and by age 5 they can toss a ring and have it land on a peg 5 feet away. Five-year-olds can learn to ride bikes, climb ladders, and ski downhill—activities that all require considerable coordination (Williams & Monsma, 2007). Figure 3-14 summarizes major gross motor skills that emerge during the preschool years.

ACTIVITY LEVEL. The advances in gross motor skills are related to brain development and myelination of neurons in areas of the brain related to balance and coordination. Another reason motor skills develop at such a rapid clip during the preschool years is that children spend a great deal of time practicing them. During this period, the general level of activity is extraordinarily high: Preschoolers seem to be perpetually in motion. In fact, the activity level is higher at age 3 than at any other point in the entire life span. In addition, as they age, preschoolers' general physical agility increases (Planinsec, 2001).

Despite generally high activity levels, there are also significant variations among children. Some differences are related to inherited temperament. Because of temperamental factors, children who are unusually active during infancy tend to continue to be so during the preschool years, whereas those who are relatively docile during infancy generally remain fairly docile during those years. Furthermore, monozygotic (identical) twins tend to show more similar activity levels than do dizygotic twins, a fact that suggests the importance of genetics in determining activity level (Wood et al., 2007).

Of course, genetics is not the sole determinant of preschoolers' activity levels. Environmental factors, such as a parent's style of discipline and, more broadly, a particular culture's view of what is appropriate and inappropriate behavior, also play a role. Some cultures are fairly lenient in allowing preschoolers to play vigorously, whereas others are considerably more restrictive.

Figure 3-14 Significant Gross Motor Skills in Early Childhood
(**Source:** Based on Corbin, 1973.)

Age 3

Able to walk up
stairs, alternating
feet

Unable to stop or
turn suddenly

Able to jump a length
of 15–24 inches

Age 4

Able to walk down a
long staircase, alternating
feet, with assistance

Have some control in starting,
stopping, and turning

Length of jump
increases to 24–33 inches

Age 5

Able to walk down a
long staircase, alternating
feet

Capable of starting, stopping,
and turning in games

Able to make a running
jump of 28–36 inches

Ultimately, a combination of genetic and environmental factors determines just how active a child will be. But the preschool period generally represents the most active time of the child's entire life.

From *an educator's* perspective

How might culture influence activity level in children? What might the long-term effects be on children influenced in this way?

CONTINUED DEVELOPMENT OF GROSS MOTOR SKILLS.   Later, during the school years, muscle coordination in particular improves. Watching a softball player pitch a ball past a batter to her catcher, a runner reach the finish line in a race, or a jump-roper execute complex movements involving the feet, legs, body, and arms, we are struck by the huge strides that these children have made since the more awkward days of preschool.

During middle childhood, children master many types of skills that earlier they could not perform well. For instance, most school-age children can readily learn to ride a bike, ice skate, swim, and skip rope (see Figure 3-15).

GENDER DIFFERENCES IN GROSS MOTOR SKILLS.   Girls and boys differ in several aspects of gross motor coordination. In part, this difference is produced by variations in muscle strength, which is somewhat greater in boys than in girls. For instance, boys can typically throw a ball better and jump higher. Furthermore, boys' overall activity levels are generally greater than girls' (Olds et al., 2009).

Although they are not as strong as boys and have lower overall activity levels, girls generally surpass boys in tasks that involve the coordination of their arms and legs. For instance, at age 5, girls are better than boys at performing jumping jacks and balancing on one foot (Largo, Fischer, & Rousson, 2003; Spessato et al., 2013).

The gender differences on some tasks involving gross motor skills are due to a number of factors. In addition to genetically determined differences in strength and activity levels, social factors likely play a role. As we will discuss later, gender increasingly determines the sorts of activities that society views as appropriate for girls and appropriate for boys. For instance, if the games that are considered acceptable for

Figure 3-15 Gross Motor Skills Developed Between Ages 6 and 12

Why would it be important that a social worker be aware of this period of development?

(**Source:** Adapted from Cratty, 1978, p. 222.)

6 Years	7 Years	8 Years	9 Years	10 Years	11 Years	12 Years
Girls superior in accuracy of movement; boys superior in more forceful, less complex acts.	Can balance on one foot with eyes closed.	Can grip objects with 12 pounds of pressure.	Girls can jump vertically 8.5 inches over their standing height plus reach; boys can jump vertically 10 inches.	Can judge and intercept directions of small balls thrown from a distance.	Boys can achieve standing broad jump of 5 feet; girls can achieve standing broad jump of 4.5 feet.	Can achieve high jump of 3 feet.
Can throw with the proper weight shift and step.	Can walk on a 2-inch-wide balance beam without falling off.	Can engage in alternate rhythmical hopping in a 2-2, 2-3, or 3-3 pattern.	Boys can run 16.6 feet per second; girls can run 16 feet per second.	Both girls and boys can run 17 feet per second.		
Acquire the ability to skip.	Can hop and jump accurately into small squares (hopscotch).	Girls can throw a small ball 33 feet; boys can throw a small ball 59 feet.				
	Can correctly execute a jumping-jack exercise.	The number of games participated in by both sexes is the greatest at this age.				

preschool boys tend to involve gross motor skills more than the games deemed appropriate for girls, boys will have more practice than girls in gross motor activities and ultimately be more proficient in them (Haines, 2003).

Regardless of their gender, however, children typically show significant improvement in their gross motor skills during the preschool years. Such improvement permits them by the time they are 5 to climb ladders, play follow-the-leader, and snowboard with relative ease. And when comparisons are made between boys and girls who regularly take part in similar activities—such as softball—gender variations in gross motor skills are minimal (Jurimae & Saar, 2003; Müller et al., 2015).

Why the change? Expectations probably played a role. Society did not expect girls to be highly active physically and told girls that they would do worse than boys in sports, and the girls' performance reflected that message.

Today, however, society's message has changed, at least officially. For instance, the American Academy of Pediatrics suggests that boys and girls should engage in the same sports and games, and that they can do so together in mixed-gender groups. There is no reason to separate the sexes in physical exercise and sports until puberty, when the smaller size of females begins to make them more susceptible to injury in contact sports (American Academy of Pediatrics, 2004; Kanters et al., 2013; Deaner, Balish, & Lombardo, 2016).

POTTY WARS.   Another aspect of muscular skills—one that parents of toddlers often find most problematic—is bowel and bladder control. The timing and nature of toilet training are controversial issues.

Sharon Bell was amazed when her daughter, Leah, just 2, announced she didn't want to wear diapers anymore. From now on, Leah said, she would only use the potty. She was even more amazed when Leah woke up with dry pajamas the next morning, and every morning after that. Three months passed without a single accident. Bell had to admit, her 2-year-old was toilet-trained.

Leah's determination and success had another surprising effect. Her brother, Adam, age 4, who had never been able to give up his nighttime diaper, suddenly stopped needing one. "I'm older than she is," Adam explained when Bell asked him about the sudden change. "If Leah doesn't wear a diaper anymore, then I'm not wearing one."

Few child-care issues raise as much concern among parents as toilet training. And on few issues are there so many opposing opinions from experts and laypersons. Often the various viewpoints are played out in the media. On the one hand, some pediatricians suggest a flexible approach to toilet training, advocating that it be put off until the child shows signs of readiness. On the other hand, other pediatricians argue for a more rigid approach, saying that toilet training should be done early and quickly.

What is clear is that the age at which toilet training takes place has been rising over the past few decades. For example, in 1957, most children were toilet trained by 18 months. Today, the average age at which children are toilet trained is around 30 months. Two percent were still not toilet-trained at age 4 (Turner & Matlock, 2013).

The current guidelines of the American Academy of Pediatrics support Brazelton's position, suggesting that there is no single time to begin toilet training and that training should begin only when children show that they are ready. Children have no bladder or bowel control until the age of 12 months and only slight control for 6 months after that. Although some children show signs of readiness for toilet training between 18 and 24 months, some are not ready until 30 months or older (Fritz & Rockney, 2004; Connell-Carrick, 2006).

Fine Motor Skills

LO 3.10 Give examples of fine motor skills, and describe their developmental pattern in infants and young children.

As infants are perfecting their gross motor skills, such as sitting upright and walking, they are also making advances in their fine motor skills (see Table 3-3). For instance, by the age of 3 months, infants show some ability to coordinate the movements of their limbs.

Furthermore, although infants are born with a rudimentary ability to reach toward an object, this ability is neither very sophisticated nor very accurate, and it disappears around the age of 4 weeks. A different, more precise, form of reaching reappears at 4 months. It takes some time for infants to coordinate successful grasping after they reach out, but in fairly short order they are able to reach out and hold onto an object of interest (Daum, Prinz, & Aschersleben, 2011; Foroud, & Whishaw, 2012; Libertus, Joh, & Needham, 2016).

The sophistication of fine motor skills continues to grow. By the age of 11 months, infants are able to pick up off the ground objects as small as marbles—something caregivers need to be concerned about since the next place such objects often go is the mouth. By the time they are 2 years old, children can carefully hold a cup, bring it to their lips, and take a drink without spilling a drop.

Grasping, like other motor advances, follows a sequential developmental pattern in which simple skills are combined into more sophisticated ones. For example, infants first begin picking things up with their whole hand. As they get older, they use a *pincer grasp*, where thumb and index finger meet to form a circle. The pincer grasp

Table 3-3 Milestones of Fine Motor Development

Age (months)	Skill
3	Opens hand
3	Holds on to rattle
8	Grasps with finger and thumb
11	Holds crayon
16	Puts pegs in board
24	Imitates lines on a paper
33	Copies figures like a circle

(**Source:** Based on Frankenburg et al., 1992.)

allows for considerably more precise motor control (Thoermer et al., 2013; Bhatia, Davis, & Shamas-Brandt, 2015).

As children move further into the preschool and school years, their ability to use fine motor skills, which involve smaller, more delicate body movements, grows apace. After infancy, fine motor skills encompass such varied activities as using a fork and spoon, cutting with scissors, tying one's shoelaces, typing at a keyboard, writing in cursive, and playing the piano.

The skills involved in fine motor movements require a good deal of practice, as anyone knows who has watched a 4-year-old struggling painstakingly to copy letters of the alphabet. Yet fine motor skills show clear developmental patterns (see Table 3-4). At age 3, children can undo their clothes when they go to the bathroom, they can put a simple jigsaw puzzle together, and they can fit blocks of different shapes into matching holes. However, they do not show much polish in accomplishing such tasks; for instance, they may try to force puzzle pieces into place.

By age 4, their fine motor skills are considerably better. For example, they can fold paper into triangular designs and print their name with a crayon. And by the time they are 5, most children are able to hold and manipulate a thin pencil properly.

By ages 6 and 7, children are able to tie their shoes and fasten buttons; by age 8, they can use each hand independently; and by 11 and 12, they can manipulate objects with almost as much capability as they will show in adulthood.

One reason for advances in fine motor skills is that the amount of myelin in the brain increases significantly between the ages of 6 and 8. Myelin provides protective insulation that surrounds parts of nerve cells. Because increased levels of myelin raise the speed at which electrical impulses travel between neurons, messages can reach muscles more rapidly and control them better. (Also see the *Developmental Diversity and Your Life* box.)

Table 3-4 Fine Motor Skills in Early Childhood

3-Year-Olds	4-Year-Olds	5-Year-Olds
Cuts paper	Folds paper into triangles	Folds paper into halves and quarters
Pastes using finger	Prints name	Draws triangle, rectangle, circle
Builds bridge with three blocks	Strings beads	Uses crayons effectively
Draws O and +	Copies X	Creates clay objects
Draws doll	Builds bridge with five blocks	Copies letters
Pours liquid from pitcher without spilling	Pours from various containers	Copies two short words
Completes simple jigsaw puzzle	Opens and positions clothespins	

Developmental Diversity and Your Life
The Cultural Dimensions of Motor Development

Among the Ache people, who live in the rain forest of South America, infants face an early life of physical restriction. Because the Ache lead a nomadic existence, living in a series of tiny camps in the rain forest, open space is at a premium. Consequently, for the first few years of life, infants spend nearly all their time in direct physical contact with their mothers. Even when they are not physically touching their mothers, they are permitted to venture no more than a few feet away.

Infants among the Kipsigis people, who live in a more open environment in rural Kenya, Africa, lead quite a different existence. Their lives are filled with activity and exercise. Parents seek to teach their children to sit up, stand, and walk from the earliest days of infancy. For example, very young infants are

placed in shallow holes in the ground designed to keep them in an upright position. Parents begin to teach their children to walk starting at the eighth week of life. The infants are held with their feet touching the ground, and they are pushed forward.

Clearly, the infants in these two societies lead very different lives (Super, 1976). But do the relative lack of early motor stimulation for Ache infants and the efforts of the Kipsigis to encourage motor development really make a difference?

The answer is both yes and no. It's yes in that Ache infants tend to show delayed motor development, relative both to Kipsigis infants and to children raised in North American and European societies. Although their social abilities are no different, Ache children tend to begin walking at around 23 months, about a year later than the typical child in the United States. In contrast, Kipsigis children, who are encouraged in their motor development, learn to sit up and walk several weeks earlier, on average, than U.S. children.

In the long run, however, the differences between Ache, Kipsigis, and North American and European children disappear. By about age 6, there is no evidence of differences in general, overall motor skills.

As we see with the Ache and Kipsigis babies, variations in the timing of motor skills seem to depend in part on parental expectations of what is the "appropriate" schedule for the emergence of specific skills. For instance, one study examined the motor skills of infants who lived in a single city in England, but whose mothers varied in ethnic origin. In the research, English, Jamaican, and Indian mothers' expectations were first assessed regarding several markers of their infants' motor skills. The Jamaican mothers expected their infants to sit and walk significantly earlier than the English and Indian mothers, and the actual emergence of these activities was in line with their expectations. The source of the Jamaican infants' earlier mastery seemed to lie in the treatment of the children by their parents. For instance, Jamaican mothers

gave their children practice in stepping quite early in infancy (Hopkins & Westra, 1990).

In sum, cultural factors help determine the time at which specific motor skills appear. Activities that are an intrinsic part of a culture are more apt to be purposely taught to infants in that culture, leading to the potential of their earlier emergence (Nugent, Lester, & Brazelton, 1989; Nixon-Cave, 2001).

Cultural influences affect the rate of the development of motor skills.

HANDEDNESS: SEPARATING RIGHTIES FROM LEFTIES. How do preschoolers decide which hand to hold the pencil in as they work on their copying and other fine motor skills? For many, their choice was established soon after birth.

By the end of the preschool years, most children show a clear preference for the use of one hand over the other—the development of **handedness**. Actually, some signals of future handedness are seen early in infancy, when infants may show a preference for one side of the body over the other. By the age of 7 months, some infants seem to favor one hand by grabbing more with it than the other. Many children, however, show no preference until the end of the preschool years (Segalowitz & Rapin, 2003).

By age 5, most children display a clear tendency to use one hand over the other, with 90 percent being right-handed and 10 percent left-handed. More boys than girls are left-handed.

Much speculation has been devoted to the meaning of handedness, fueled in part by long-standing myths about the sinister nature of left-handedness. (The word *sinister* itself is derived from a Latin word meaning "on the left.") In Islamic cultures, for instance, the left hand is generally used when going to the toilet, and it is considered uncivilized to serve food with that hand. In Christian art, portrayals of the devil often show him as left-handed.

However, there is no scientific basis for myths that suggest that there is something wrong with being left-handed. In fact, some evidence exists that left-handedness may be associated with certain advantages. For example, a study of 100,000 students who took the SAT college admissions test showed that 20 percent in the highest-scoring category were left-handed, double the proportion of left-handed people in the general population. Such gifted individuals as Michelangelo, Leonardo da Vinci, Benjamin Franklin, and Pablo Picasso were left-handed (Bower, 1985; Li et al., 2015).

handedness
the preference for using one hand over the other.

ART: THE PICTURE OF DEVELOPMENT. It is a basic feature of many kitchens: the refrigerator covered with recent art created by the children of the house. Yet the art that children create is far more important than mere kitchen decoration. Developmentalists suggest that art plays an important role in honing fine motor skills, as well as in several other aspects of development (Morra, 2008).

At the most basic level, the production of art involves practice with tools such as paintbrushes, crayons, pencils, and markers. As preschoolers learn to manipulate these tools, they gain motor control skills that will help them as they learn to write.

But art also teaches several important lessons. For example, children learn the importance of planning, restraint, and self-correction. When 3-year-olds pick up a brush, they tend to swish it across the page, with little thought of the ultimate product. By the time they are 5, however, children spend more time thinking about and planning the final product. They are more likely to have a goal in mind when they start out, and when they are finished, they examine their creation to see how successful they have been. Older children will also produce the same artwork over and over, seeking to overcome their previous errors and improve the final product.

According to developmental psychologist Howard Gardner, the rough, unformed art of preschoolers represents the equivalent of linguistic babbling in infants. He argues that the random marks that young preschoolers make contain all the building blocks of more sophisticated creations that will be produced later (Golumb, 2002, 2003; Gardner, 2011).

Other researchers suggest that children's art proceeds through a series of stages during the preschool years (Winner, 2006). The first is the *scribbling* stage, in which the end product appears to be random scrawls across a paper. But this is not the case: Instead, scribbles can be categorized, consisting of 20 distinct types, such as horizontal lines and zigzags.

The *shape* stage, which is reached around age 3, is marked by the appearance of shapes, such as squares and circles. In this stage, children draw shapes of various sorts, as well as Xs and plus signs. After reaching this stage, they soon move into the *design* stage, which is characterized by the ability to combine more than one simple shape into a more complex one. Finally, children enter the *pictorial* stage between ages 4 and 5. At this point, drawings begin to approximate recognizable objects.

The depiction of recognizable real-world objects, known as representational art, may appear to be a substantial advance over previous art, and adults often strongly encourage its creation. However, in some respects this change to representational art is regrettable, for it marks a shift in focus away from an interest in form and design. Because form and design are important and in some ways essential, a focus on representation may ultimately have disadvantages. As the famous artist Pablo Picasso once remarked, "It has taken me a whole lifetime to learn to draw like children" (Winner, 1989).

DEVELOPMENTAL NORMS: COMPARING THE INDIVIDUAL TO THE GROUP. Keep in mind that the timing of the milestones in motor development that we have been discussing is based on norms. **Norms** represent the average performance of a large sample of children of a given age. They permit comparisons between a particular child's performance on a particular behavior and the average performance of the children in the norm sample.

For instance, one of the most widely used techniques to determine infants' normative standing is the **Brazelton Neonatal Behavior Assessment Scale (NBAS)**, a measure designed to determine infants' neurological and behavioral responses to their environment.

Taking about 30 minutes to administer, the NBAS includes 27 separate categories of responses that constitute four general aspects of infants' behavior: interactions with others (such as alertness and cuddliness), motor behavior, physiological control (such as the ability to be soothed after being upset), and responses to stress (Canals et al., 2003; Ohta & Ohgi, 2013).

Although the norms provided by scales such as the NBAS are useful in making broad generalizations about the timing of various behaviors and skills, they must be interpreted with caution. Because norms are averages, they mask substantial individual differences in the times when children attain various achievements.

Norms are useful only to the extent that they are based on data from a large, heterogeneous, culturally diverse sample of children. Unfortunately, many of the norms on which developmental researchers have traditionally relied have been based on groups of infants who are predominantly Caucasian and from the middle and upper socioeconomic strata (e.g., Gesell, 1946). The reason: Much of the research was conducted on college campuses, using the children of graduate students and faculty.

norms
the average performance of a large sample of children of a given age.

Brazelton Neonatal Behavioral Assessment Scale (NBAS)
a measure designed to determine infants' neurological and behavioral responses to their environment.

This limitation would not be critical if no differences existed in the timing of development in children from different cultural, racial, and social groups. But they do. For example, as a group, African American babies show more rapid motor development than Caucasian babies throughout infancy. Moreover, there are significant variations related to cultural factors, as we discuss next (de Onis et al., 2007; Wu et al., 2008; Mendonça, Sargent, & Fetters, 2016).

Module 3.2 Review

LO 3.6 **Discuss the role of neurons in brain development.**

Brain growth is very fast during infancy, mostly because of a startling increase in the number of interconnections among neurons and the amount of myelin produced. Billions of connections form immediately after birth, and the brain shows a great deal of plasticity, or susceptibility to environmental influences. Later, the number of neurons and connections decreases as a result of the infant's experiences.

LO 3.7 **Explain what is meant by brain lateralization and describe how it develops in early childhood.**

Brain growth is rapid during the preschool years. In addition, the brain develops lateralization, a tendency of the two hemispheres to adopt specialized tasks.

LO 3.8 **Identify the reflexes that infants are born with that help them adapt to their surroundings and protect themselves.**

Infants are born with an array of reflexes that protect the baby through involuntary behavior until it can protect itself. In addition, reflexes may form the foundation of future, more complex behaviors.

LO 3.9 **Summarize the gross motor skills that emerge during infancy and the preschool years, and explain how they are related to brain development.**

From newborns with little mobility or strength, children quickly learn to push their bodies up, sit up, crawl, walk, jump, hop, run, and eventually perform sports activities that rely on both gross and fine motor skills. Motor development and control continue late into the life span.

LO 3.10 **Give examples of fine motor skills and describe their developmental pattern in infants and young children.**

As infants are perfecting their gross motor skills, they are also making advances in their fine motor skills. For instance, by the age of 3 months, infants show some ability to coordinate the movements of their limbs. As children move into the preschool and school years, their ability to use fine motor skills, which involve smaller, more delicate body movements, grows apace.

Journal Writing Prompt

Applying Lifespan Development: Do you think that differences in males' and females' motor skills are primarily innate or environmental? Why? Will differences eventually disappear?

MODULE 3.3

PERCEPTUAL DEVELOPMENT

William James, one of the founding fathers of psychology, believed that the world of the infant is a "blooming, buzzing confusion" (James, 1890/1950). Was he right?

In this case, James's wisdom failed him. The newborn's sensory world does lack the clarity and stability that we can distinguish as adults, but day by day the world grows increasingly comprehensible as the infant's ability to sense and perceive the environment develops. Babies appear to thrive in an environment enriched by pleasing sensations.

sensation
the physical stimulation of the sense organs.

The Development of the Senses

perception
the sorting out, interpretation, analysis, and integration of stimuli involving the sense organs and brain.

LO 3.11 Describe the capabilities of infants regarding each of the five senses.

The processes that underlie infants' understanding of the world around them are sensation and perception. **Sensation** is the physical stimulation of the sense organs, and **perception** is the mental process of sorting out, interpreting, analyzing, and integrating stimuli from the sense organs and brain.

INFANTS' CAPABILITIES.   The study of infants' capabilities in the realm of sensation and perception challenges the ingenuity of investigators. As we'll see, researchers have developed a number of procedures for understanding sensation and perception in different realms.

Infants' Eyesight.   From the time of Lee Eng's birth, everyone who met him felt that he gazed at them intently. His eyes seemed to meet those of visitors. They seemed to bore deeply and knowingly into the faces of people who looked at him.

How good in fact was Lee's vision, and what, precisely, could he make out of his environment? Quite a bit, at least up close. According to some estimates, a newborn's distance vision ranges from 20/200 to 20/600, which means that an infant can only see with accuracy visual material up to 20 feet that an adult with normal vision is able to see with similar accuracy from a distance of between 200 and 600 feet (Cavallini et al., 2002; Xiao et al., 2015; Jones et al., 2015).

These figures indicate that infants' distance vision is one-tenth to one-third that of the average adult. This isn't so bad, actually: The vision of newborns provides the same degree of distance acuity as the uncorrected vision of many adults who wear eyeglasses or contact lenses. Furthermore, infants' distance vision grows increasingly acute. By 6 months of age, the average infant's vision is already 20/20—in other words, identical to that of adults (Cavallini et al., 2002; Corrow et al., 2012).

Depth perception is a particularly useful ability, helping babies acknowledge heights and avoid falls. In a classic study, developmental psychologists Eleanor Gibson and Richard Walk (1960) placed infants on a sheet of heavy glass. A checkered pattern appeared under one-half of the glass sheet, making it seem that the infant was on a stable floor. However, in the middle of the glass sheet, the pattern dropped down several feet, forming an apparent "visual cliff." The question Gibson and Walk asked was whether infants would willingly crawl across the cliff when called by their mothers (see Figure 3-16).

The results were clear: Most of the infants in the study, who ranged in age from 6 to 14 months, could not be coaxed over the apparent cliff. Clearly, most of them had already developed the ability to perceive depth by that age (Gibson & Walk, 1960; Kretch & Adolph, 2013; Adolph, Kretch, & LoBue, 2014).

Infants also show clear visual preferences, preferences that are present from birth. Given a choice, infants reliably prefer to look at stimuli that include patterns than to look at simpler stimuli (see Figure 3-17). How do we know? Developmental

(a)

(b)

(c)

A neonate's view of the world is limited to 8 to 14 inches. (a) Objects beyond that distance are fuzzy. (b) By 3 months, objects are seen with clarity. (c) A month after birth, newborns' vision has improved, but still lacks clarifying detail.

Figure 3-16 Visual Cliff

The "visual cliff" experiment examines the depth perception of infants. Most infants in the age range of 6 to 14 months cannot be coaxed to cross the cliff, apparently responding to the fact that the patterned area drops several feet.

Figure 3-17 Preferring Complexity

In a classic experiment, researcher Robert Fantz found that 2- and 3-month-old infants preferred to look at more complex stimuli than simple ones.

(**Source:** Based on Fantz, 1961.)

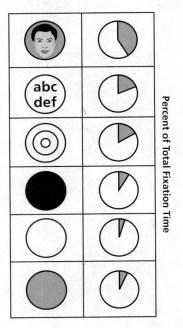

Percent of Total Fixation Time

psychologist Robert Fantz (1963) created a classic test. He built a chamber in which babies could lie on their backs and see pairs of visual stimuli above them. Fantz could determine which of the stimuli the infants were looking at by observing the reflections of the stimuli in their eyes.

Fantz's work was the impetus for a great deal of research on the preferences of infants, most of which points to a critical conclusion: Infants are genetically preprogrammed to prefer particular kinds of stimuli. For instance, just minutes after birth they show preferences for certain colors, shapes, and configurations of various stimuli. They prefer curved to straight lines, three-dimensional figures to two-dimensional ones, and human faces to nonfaces. Such capabilities may point to the existence of highly specialized cells in the brain that react to stimuli of a particular pattern, orientation, shape, and direction of movement (Hubel & Wiesel, 2004; Kellman & Arterberry, 2006; Gliga et al., 2009).

Genetics is not the sole determinant of infant visual preferences. Just a few hours after birth, infants have already learned to prefer their own mother's face to other faces. Similarly, between the ages of 6 and 9 months, infants become more adept at distinguishing between the faces of humans, while they become less able to distinguish the faces of members of other species. They also distinguish between male and female faces. Such findings provide another clear piece of evidence of how heredity and environmental experiences are woven together to determine an infant's capabilities (Quinn et al., 2008; Otsuka et al., 2012; Bahrick et al., 2016).

Auditory Perception: Sound in Infancy.   What is it about a mother's lullaby that helps soothe a crying baby? Some clues emerge when we look at the capabilities of infants in the realm of auditory sensation and perception.

Infants hear from the time of birth—and even before, as the ability to hear begins prenatally. Even in the womb, the fetus responds to sounds outside of its mother. Furthermore, infants are born with preferences for particular sound combinations (Trehub, 2003; Pundir et al., 2012; Missana, Altvater-Mackensen, & Grossmann, 2017).

Because they have had some practice in hearing before birth, it is not surprising that infants have reasonably good auditory perception after they are born. Infants actually are more sensitive to certain very high and very low frequencies than adults—a sensitivity that seems to increase during the first 2 years of life. However, infants are initially less sensitive than adults to middle-range frequencies, though eventually their capabilities within the middle range improve (Fernald, 2001; Lee & Kisilevsky, 2014).

In addition to the ability to detect sound, infants need several other abilities in order to hear effectively. For instance, *sound localization* permits us to pinpoint the direction from which a sound is emanating. Compared to adults, infants have a slight handicap in this task because effective sound localization requires the use of the slight difference in the times at which a sound reaches our two ears. Sound that we hear first in the right ear tells us that the source of the sound is to our right. Because infants' heads are smaller than those of adults, the difference in timing of the arrival of sound at the two ears is less than it is in adults, so they have difficulty determining from which direction sound is coming (Winkler, 2016).

Despite the potential limitation brought about by their smaller heads, infants' sound localization abilities are fairly good even at birth, and they reach adult levels of success by age 1. Furthermore, young infants are capable of making the fine discriminations that their future understanding of language will require (Werner et al., 2007; Slugocki & Trainor, 2014).

Smell and Taste in Infancy.   What do infants do when they smell a rotten egg? Pretty much what adults do—crinkle their noses and generally look unhappy. However, the scent of bananas and butter evokes a pleasant reaction from infants (Pomares, Schirrer, & Abadie, 2002).

The sense of smell is so well developed, even among very young infants, that at least some 12- to 18-day-old babies can distinguish their mothers on the basis of smell alone. For instance, in one experiment infants were exposed to the smell of gauze pads worn under the arms of adults the previous evening. Infants who were being breast-fed were able to distinguish their mothers' scent from those of other adults. However, not all infants could do this: Those who were being bottle-fed were unable to make the distinction. Moreover, both breast-fed and bottle-fed infants were unable to distinguish their fathers on the basis of odor (Mizuno & Ueda, 2004; Lipsitt & Rovee-Collier, 2012).

Infants seem to have an innate sweet tooth (even before they have teeth!), and they show facial expressions of disgust when they taste something bitter. Very young infants smile when a sweet-tasting liquid is placed on their tongues. They also suck harder at a bottle if it is sweetened. Since breast milk has a sweet taste, it is possible that this preference may be part of our evolutionary heritage, retained because it offered a survival advantage (Porges, Lipsitt, & Lewis, 1993; Blass & Camp, 2015).

Infants' Sensitivity to Pain and Touch. Today, it is widely acknowledged that infants are born with the capacity to experience pain. Obviously, no one can be sure if the experience of pain in children is identical to that in adults, any more than we can tell if an adult friend who complains of a headache is experiencing pain that is more or less severe than our own pain when we have a headache. What we do know is that pain produces distress in infants. Their heartbeat increases, they sweat, they show facial expressions of discomfort, and they change the intensity and tone of crying when they are hurt (Kohut & Riddell, 2009; Rodkey & Riddell, 2013; Pölkki et al., 2014).

There appears to be a developmental progression in reactions to pain. For example, a newborn infant who has her heel pricked for a blood test responds with distress, but it takes her several seconds to show the response. In contrast, only a few months later, the same procedure brings a much more immediate response. It is possible that the delayed reaction in infants is produced by the relatively slower transmission of information within the newborn's less developed nervous system (Puchalsi & Hummel, 2002; also see the *Neuroscience and Development* box).

Neuroscience and Development

Beyond Band-Aids: How Pain in Infancy Affects Pain in Adulthood

Over a decade ago, researchers discovered that newborns exposed to painful stimuli early in life experience changes in their later sensory processing. For example, premature infants exposed to painful medical procedures in the neonatal intensive care unit are less sensitive to pain at 18 months of age.

Is this a lasting effect? To help answer this question, neuroscientists Jamie LaPrairie and Anne Murphy administered the drug naloxone to laboratory rats injured at birth. Naloxone blocks the actions of endogenous opioid peptides, a substance in the brain that is released following an injury and that inhibits pain. These peptides also play an important role in motivation, emotion, and stress responses (LaPrairie & Murphy, 2009; Victoria, Karom, & Murphy, 2015).

The birth-injured rats were again tested as adult animals, and their midbrain gray matter was examined to see if the birth trauma had altered the functioning of natural opioids. The researchers found that the level of endogenous opioid peptides in birth-injured rats was two times higher than that in non-birth-injured rats. Apparently, their painful early-life trauma created a brain response with fewer receptors to permit optimal sensitivity to pain medications later in life.

One critical question is whether these findings can be generalized to humans, particularly to premature infants who may experience dozens of procedures after birth. Since neonatal procedures cause such discomfort, it is conceivable that it may produce a change in the wiring of children's brains in adulthood (Simons et al., 2003; LaPrairie & Murphy, 2009).

■ Are there any factors that may arise during development across the life span that might counter these findings?

Responding to Touch.   It clearly does not take the sting of pain to get an infant's attention. Even the youngest infants respond to gentle touches, such as a soothing caress, which can calm a crying, fussy infant (Hertenstein, 2002; Gitto et al., 2012; Aznar & Tenenbaum, 2016).

Touch is one of the most highly developed sensory systems in a newborn. It is also one of the first to develop; there is evidence that by 32 weeks after conception, the entire body is sensitive to touch. Furthermore, several of the basic reflexes present at birth, such as the rooting reflex, require touch sensitivity to operate: Infants must sense a touch near their mouths in order to automatically seek a nipple to suck (Haith, 1986; Byrd, Nelson, & Manthey, 2006).

Infants' abilities in the realm of touch are particularly helpful in their efforts to explore the world. Several theorists have suggested that one of the ways children gain information about the world is through touching. As mentioned earlier, at the age of 6 months, infants are apt to place almost any object in their mouths, apparently taking in data about the object's configuration from their sensory responses to the feel of it in their mouths (Byrd, Nelson, & Manthey, 2006).

Multimodal Perception: Combining Individual Sensory Inputs.   When Eric Pettigrew was 7 months old, his grandparents presented him with a squeaky rubber doll. As soon as he saw it, he reached out for it, grasped it in his hand, and listened as it squeaked. He seemed delighted with the gift.

One way of considering Eric's sensory reaction to the doll is to focus on each of the senses individually: what the doll looked like to Eric, how it felt in his hand, and what it sounded like. This approach has dominated the study of sensation and perception in infancy.

Let's consider another approach, however: We might examine how the various sensory responses are integrated with one another. Instead of looking at each individual sensory response, we could consider how the responses work together and are combined to produce Eric's ultimate reaction. The **multimodal approach to perception** considers how information that is collected by various individual sensory systems is integrated and coordinated (Farzin, Charles, & Rivera, 2009).

multimodal approach to perception
the approach that considers how information that is collected by various individual sensory systems is integrated and coordinated.

> **From *a health-care provider's* perspective**
>
> Persons who are born without the use of one sense often develop unusual abilities in one or more other senses. What can health-care professionals do to help infants who are lacking in a particular sense?

Although the multimodal approach is a relatively recent innovation in the study of how infants understand their sensory world, it raises some fundamental issues about the development of sensation and perception. For instance, some researchers argue that sensations are initially integrated with one another in the infant, while others maintain that the infant's sensory systems are initially separate and that brain development leads to increasing integration (Lickliter & Bahrick, 2000; Lewkowicz, 2002; Flom & Bahrick, 2007).

We do not know yet which view is correct. However, it does appear that by an early age infants are able to relate what they have learned about an object through one sensory channel to what they have learned about it through another. For instance, even one-month-old infants are able to recognize by sight objects that they have previously held in their mouths but never seen. Clearly, some cross-talk between various sensory channels is already possible a month after birth (Streri, 2003).

Infants' multimodal perception showcases their sophisticated perceptual abilities, which continue to grow throughout the period of infancy. Such perceptual growth is aided by infants' discovery of **affordances**, the options that a given situation or stimulus provides. For example, infants learn that they might potentially fall when walking down a steep ramp—that is, the ramp *affords* the possibility of falling. Such knowledge is crucial as infants make the transition from crawling to walking. Similarly, infants learn that an object shaped in a certain way can slip out of their hands if not grasped correctly. For example, Eric is learning that his toy has several affordances: He can grab it and squeeze it, listen to it squeak, and even chew comfortably on it if he is teething (Wilcox et al., 2007; Huang, 2012; Rocha et al., 2013). (Also see the *Development in Your Life* box.)

affordances
the option that a given situation or stimulus provides.

Development in Your Life

Exercising Your Infant's Body and Senses

Recall how cultural expectations and environments affect the age at which various physical milestones, such as the first step, occur. Although most experts feel that attempts to accelerate physical and sensory-perceptual development yield little advantage, parents should ensure that their infants receive sufficient physical and sensory stimulation. There are several specific ways to accomplish this goal:

■ Carry a baby in different positions—Switching among a backpack, a frontpack, or a football hold with the infant's head in the palm of your hand and its feet lying on your arm lets the infant view the world from several perspectives.

■ Let infants explore their environment. Don't contain them too long in a barren environment. Let them crawl or wander around—after first making the environment "childproof" by removing dangerous objects.

■ Engage in "rough-and-tumble" play. Wrestling, dancing, and rolling around on the floor—if not violent—are activities that are fun and that stimulate older infants' motor and sensory systems.

■ Let babies touch their food and even play with it. Infancy is too early to start teaching table manners.

■ Provide toys that stimulate the senses, particularly toys that can stimulate more than one sense at a time. For example, brightly colored, textured toys with movable parts are enjoyable and help sharpen infants' senses.

SENSORY DEVELOPMENT IN PRESCHOOLERS. The increasing development of the brain permits improvements in the senses during the preschool period. For instance, brain maturation leads to better control of eye movements and focusing. Still, preschoolers' eyes are not as capable as they will be in later stages of development. Specifically, preschool-age children are unable to easily and precisely scan groupings of small letters, as is required when reading small print. Consequently, preschoolers who start to read often focus on just the initial letter of a word and guess at the rest—leading, as you might expect, to relatively frequent errors. It is not until they are approximately 6 years old that children can effectively focus and scan. Even at this point, however, they still don't have the capabilities of adults (Burgund & Abernathy, 2008).

Preschool-age children also begin a gradual shift in the way they view objects made up of multiple parts. For instance, consider the rather unusual vegetable–fruit–bird combination shown in Figure 3-18. Rather than identifying it as a bird, as most adults do, preschool-age children see the figure in terms of the parts that make it up ("carrots" and "cherries" and "a pear"). Not until they reach middle childhood, about the age of 7 or 8, do they begin to look at the figure in terms of both its overall organization and its parts ("a bird made of fruit").

Preschoolers' judgments of objects may reflect the way in which their eyes move when perceiving figures (Zaporozhets, 1965). Until age 3 or 4, preschoolers devote most of their looking to the insides of two-dimensional objects they are scanning, concentrating on the internal details and largely ignoring the perimeter of the figure. In contrast, 4- and 5-year-olds begin to look more at the surrounding boundaries of the figure, and at 6 and 7, they look at the outside systematically, with far less scanning of the inside. The result is a greater awareness of the overall organization of the figure.

Vision is not the only sense that improves during the preschool period. For instance, *auditory acuity*, or the sharpness of hearing, improves as well. However, because hearing is more fully developed at the start of the preschool period, the improvement is not as significant as with vision.

One area in which preschoolers' auditory acuity does show some deficits is in their ability to isolate specific sounds when many sounds are heard simultaneously. This deficiency may account for why some preschoolers are easily distracted by competing sounds in group situations, such as classrooms (McAdams & Drake, 2002).

Figure 3-18 Sensory Development

Preschool-age children who view this odd vegetable–fruit–bird combination focus on the components that make it up. Not until they reach middle childhood do they begin to look at the figure as a whole in addition to its parts. (**Source:** Elkind, 1978.)

Sensory Difficulties in the School Years: Visual, Auditory, and Speech Problems

LO 3.12 Recognize the sensory difficulties school-age children may experience and how they can affect children's learning.

Anyone who has lost his or her eyeglasses or a contact lens knows how difficult even basic, everyday tasks must be for the sensory impaired. To function without adequate vision, hearing, or speech poses a tremendous challenge.

Visual impairment has both a legal and an educational meaning. Legal impairment is defined precisely: *Blindness* is visual acuity below 20/200 after correction (meaning the inability to see at 20 feet what is typically seen at 200 feet), while *partial sightedness* is visual acuity of less than 20/70 after correction.

Even if a child is not legally blind, visual problems may seriously affect schoolwork. For one thing, the legal criterion pertains solely to distance vision, while most school tasks require close-up vision. The legal definition does not consider abilities in the perception of color, depth, and light either—all of which might influence a student's success. About 1 student in 1,000 requires special education services due to visual impairment.

Most severe visual problems are identified fairly early, but an impairment can go undetected. Visual problems can also emerge gradually as development brings changes in the apparatus of the eye.

Auditory impairments can cause social as well as academic problems since much peer interaction involves informal conversation. Hearing loss affects 1 to 2 percent of the school-age population (Yoshinaga-Itano, 2003; Smith, Bale, & White, 2005; Martin-Prudent et al., 2016).

In some cases, hearing is impaired at only certain frequencies, or pitches. For example, the loss may be great at pitches in the normal speech range yet minimal in other frequencies, such as those of very high or low sounds. Different levels of amplification at different frequencies may be required; a hearing aid that amplifies all frequencies equally may be ineffective, amplifying sounds the child can hear to an uncomfortable degree.

How a child adapts depends on when the hearing loss begins. The effects will likely be more severe in a child with little or no exposure to the sound of language, producing an inability to understand or produce speech. For a child who has learned language, hearing loss will not seriously affect subsequent linguistic development.

Severe and early loss of hearing can impair abstract thinking. Concrete concepts can be visually illustrated, but abstract concepts depend on language for meaning. For example, it is difficult to explain the concept of "freedom" or "soul" without use of language (Marschark, Spencer, & Newsom, 2003; Meinzen-Derr et al., 2014; Fitzpatrick et al., 2017).

Auditory difficulties may be accompanied by **speech impairments**, one of the most public types of exceptionality: Speech that deviates from the norm is obvious whenever the child speaks. It also interferes with communication and may produce maladjustment in the speaker. Speech impairments occur in around 3 to 5 percent of the school-age population (Bishop & Leonard, 2001).

Childhood-onset fluency disorder, or *stuttering,* involves a substantial disruption in the rhythm and fluency of speech and is the most common speech impairment. Despite much research, no specific cause has been identified. Occasional stuttering is not unusual in young children—or even in normal adults—but chronic

---

visual impairment
a special need that involves significant loss of sight.

auditory impairment
a special need that involves the loss of hearing or some aspect of hearing.

speech impairment
speech that deviates so much from the speech of others that it calls attention to itself, interferes with communication, or produces maladjustment in the speaker.

childhood-onset fluency disorder (or *stuttering***)**
substantial disruption in the rhythm and fluency of speech; the most common speech impairment.

AMELIE-BENOIST/BSIP/Getty Images

Auditory impairments can produce both academic and social difficulties, and may lead to speech difficulties.

stuttering can be a severe problem. Stuttering hinders communication and can be embarrassing or stressful for children, who may come to fear conversation and speaking aloud in class (Altholz & Golensky, 2004; Sasisekaran, 2014).

Parents and teachers can help children who stutter by not drawing attention to the issue and by giving them sufficient time to finish what they are saying, no matter how protracted the statement becomes. It does not help stutterers to finish their sentences for them or otherwise correct their speech (Ryan, 2001; Beilby, Byrnes, & Young, 2012).

The Senses in Middle Adulthood

LO 3.13 Discuss the changes in sensory perception in middle adulthood and the factors that may affect these changes.

Soon after turning 40, Sharon Boker-Tov noticed that it took longer to bounce back from minor illnesses such as colds and the flu. Then she noticed changes in her eyesight: She needed more light to read fine print, and she had to adjust how far she held newspapers from her face in order to read them easily. Finally, she couldn't deny that the gray strands in her hair, which had first appeared in her late 20s, were becoming a virtual forest.

The vision changes Sharon Boker-Tov experienced are so common that reading glasses and bifocals have become a stereotypical emblem of middle age. Like Sharon, most people notice changes in the sensitivity not only of their eyes but also of other sense organs. All the organs seem to shift at about the same rate, but the changes are particularly marked in vision and hearing.

VISION.   Starting at around age 40, *visual acuity*—the ability to discern fine spatial detail in both close and distant objects—begins to decline. The shape of the eye's lens changes and its elasticity deteriorates, which makes it harder to focus images sharply onto the retina. The lens becomes less transparent, so less light passes through the eye (Uttl, 2006).

A nearly universal change in midlife is the loss of near vision, called **presbyopia**. Even people who have never needed glasses or contact lenses find themselves holding print at an increasing distance in order to bring it into focus. Eventually, they need reading glasses. For those who were already near-sighted, presbyopia may require bifocals or two sets of glasses (Kalsi, Heron, & Charman, 2001; Koopmans & Kooijman, 2006; Kemper, 2012).

presbyopia
a nearly universal change in eyesight during middle adulthood that results in some loss of near vision.

Midlife brings other vision changes. Depth perception, distance perception, and the ability to see in three dimensions all decline. The loss of elasticity in the lens also impairs people's ability to adapt to darkness, making it more difficult to navigate a dark room (Stuen & Fischer, 2007; Andrews, d'Avossa, & Sapir, 2017).

Although normal aging brings changes in vision, in some cases disease is involved. One of the most frequent eye problems is glaucoma, which may, if left untreated, lead to blindness. **Glaucoma** occurs when pressure in the fluid of the eye increases, either because the fluid cannot drain properly or because too much is produced. Around 1 to 2 percent of people over age 40 are afflicted, and African Americans are particularly susceptible.

glaucoma
a condition in which pressure in the fluid of the eye increases, either because the fluid cannot drain properly or because too much fluid is produced.

Initially, the increased pressure may constrict the neurons involved in peripheral vision and lead to tunnel vision. Ultimately, the pressure can become so high that all nerve cells are constricted, which causes complete blindness. Fortunately, with early detection, glaucoma can be treated. Medication can reduce the pressure, as can surgery to restore normal drainage of eye fluid (Plosker & Keam, 2006; Lambiase et al., 2009; Sleath et al., 2017).

HEARING.   Hearing declines in acuity in midlife, though the changes tend to be less evident than those affecting vision.

Visual impairments can have profound effects on daily living.

presbycusis

loss of the ability to hear sounds of high frequency.

Environmental factors cause some of the hearing losses. People who work near loud noises—such as airplane mechanics and construction workers—are more apt to suffer debilitating and permanent hearing loss.

Many changes are simply related to aging. Age brings a loss of *cilia* or *hair cells* in the inner ear, which transmit neural messages to the brain when vibrations bend them. Like the lens of the eye, the eardrum becomes less elastic with age, reducing sensitivity to sound (Wiley et al., 2005).

The ability to hear high-pitched, high-frequency sounds usually degrades first, a problem called **presbycusis**. About 12 percent of people between 45 and 65 suffer from presbycusis. Men are more prone to hearing loss than women, starting at around age 55. People with hearing problems may also have trouble identifying the direction and origin of a sound, a process called sound localization (Veras & Mattos, 2007; Gopinath et al., 2012; Koike, 2014).

Declines in hearing do not markedly affect most people in middle age. Many compensate for any losses relatively easily—by asking people to speak up, turning up the volume of a television set, or paying closer attention to what others are saying.

REACTION TIME IN ADULTHOOD: NOT-SO-SLOWING DOWN. One common concern is that people slow down once they reach middle adulthood. Such a worry is not valid in most cases. Reaction time does increase (i.e., it takes longer to react to a stimulus), but usually the increase is mild and hardly noticeable. For instance, reaction time in responding to a loud noise increases by about 20 percent from age 20 to 60. Tasks requiring the coordination of various skills—such as driving a car—show less of an increase. Still, it takes more time to move the foot from the gas pedal to the brake when a driver faces an emergency situation. Changes in the speed at which the nervous system processes nerve impulses increase reaction time (Roggeveen, Prime, & Ward, 2007; Wolkorte, Kamphuis, & Zijdewind, 2014).

Despite increased reaction time, middle-aged drivers have fewer accidents than younger ones, partly because they tend to be more careful and take fewer risks. Moreover, older drivers' greater experience benefits them. The minor slowing of reaction time is compensated by their expertise (Cantin et al., 2009; Endrass, Schreiber, & Kathmann, 2012; Meador, Boyd, & Loring, 2017).

Lifestyle choices can retard the slowing-down process. An active exercise program counteracts the effects of aging, improving health, muscle strength, and endurance. Developmentalists would agree: "Use it or lose it" (Conn et al., 2003).

Sensory Changes in Late Adulthood

LO 3.14 Give examples of the decline in various sense organs experienced in late adulthood and how these changes affect the lives of the elderly.

Old age brings declines in the sense organs; this has major psychological consequences because the senses are people's link with the world.

VISION. Age-related changes in the physical apparatus of the eye—the cornea, lens, retina, and optic nerve—lead to a decrease in visual abilities. The lens becomes less transparent, allowing only a third as much light to reach the retina at 60 as at 20. The optic nerve also becomes less efficient in transmitting nerve impulses (Gawande, 2007). As a result, vision declines along several dimensions. We see distant objects less well, need more light to see clearly, and take longer to adjust from dark to light and vice versa.

These changes cause everyday problems. Driving, particularly at night, becomes more challenging. Reading requires more light, and eye strain comes more easily. Of course, eyeglasses and contact lenses can correct many of these problems, and the majority of older people see reasonably well (Owsley, Stalvey, & Phillips, 2003).

Several eye diseases become more common during late adulthood. For instance, *cataracts*—cloudy or opaque areas on the lens of the eye that interfere with the passage of light—frequently develop. Cataracts bring blurred vision and glare in bright light. If cataracts are left untreated, the lens becomes milky white and blindness results. However, cataracts can be surgically removed, and eyesight can be restored with eyeglasses, contact lenses, or *intraocular lens implants*, in which a plastic lens is permanently placed in the eye (Walker, Anstey, & Lord, 2006).

Another serious problem among elderly individuals is glaucoma. As we noted earlier, *glaucoma* occurs when pressure in the fluid of the eye increases, either because the fluid cannot drain properly or too much fluid is produced. Glaucoma can be treated by drugs or surgery if it is detected early enough.

The most common cause of blindness in people over 60 is *age-related macular degeneration (AMD)*, which affects the *macula*, a yellowish area near the retina at which visual perception is most acute. When a portion of the macula thins and degenerates, the eyesight gradually deteriorates (see Figure 3-19). If diagnosed early, macular degeneration can sometimes be treated with medication or lasers. There is also some evidence that a diet rich in antioxidant vitamins (C, E, and A) can reduce the risk of AMD (Wiggins & Uwaydat, 2006; Coleman et al., 2008; Jager, Mieler, & Miller, 2008).

HEARING. Around 30 percent of adults between 65 and 74 have some hearing loss, and the figure rises to 50 percent among people over 75. Overall, more than 10 million elderly people in the United States have hearing impairments of one kind or another (Chisolm, Willott, & Lister, 2003; Pacala & Yueh, 2012; Bainbridge & Wallhagen, 2014).

Aging particularly affects the ability to hear higher frequencies. This makes it hard to hear conversations amid background noise or when several people are speaking simultaneously. Some elderly persons actually find loud noises painful.

Although hearing aids would probably be helpful around 75 percent of the time, only 20 percent of elderly people wear them. One reason is that hearing aids are far from perfect. They amplify background noises as much as conversations, making it difficult for wearers to separate what they want to hear from other sounds.

Figure 3-19 The World Through Macular Degeneration

(a) Age-related macular degeneration affects the macula, a yellowish area of the eye located near the retina. Eyesight gradually deteriorates once the portion of the macula thins and degenerates. (b) Macular degeneration leads to a gradual deterioration of the center of the retina, leaving only peripheral vision. This is an example of what a person with macular degeneration might see. (**Source:** AARP, 2005, p. 34.)

Paul Parker/Science Source

Pearson Education

Furthermore, many people feel that hearing aids make them appear even older and encourage others to treat them as if they were disabled (Lesner, 2003; Meister & von Wedel, 2003).

TASTE AND SMELL. Elderly people who have always enjoyed eating may experience a real decline in the quality of life because of changes in sensitivity to taste and smell. Both senses become less discriminating, causing food to be less appetizing than it was earlier (Kaneda et al., 2000; Nordin, Razani, & Markison, 2003).

The decrease in taste and smell sensitivity has a physical cause. The tongue loses taste buds over time, making food less tasty. The problem is compounded as the olfactory bulbs in the brain begin to shrivel. Because taste depends on smell, this makes food taste even blander.

The loss of taste and smell sensitivity has an unfortunate side effect: Because food does not taste as good, people eat less and open the door to malnutrition. They may also oversalt their food, thereby increasing their risk of *hypertension*, or high blood pressure, one of the most common health problems of old age (Smith et al., 2006).

GAME OVER?

> *Karl winced as the "game over" message came up on his grandsons' video game system. He enjoyed trying out their games, but he just couldn't shoot down those bad guys as quickly as his grandkids could.*

As people get older and reach late adulthood, they take longer: longer to put on a tie, to reach a ringing phone, to press the buttons in a video game. One reason is a lengthening of reaction time, which begins to increase in middle age and by late adulthood may rise significantly (Benjuya, Melzer, & Kaplanski, 2004; Der & Deary, 2006).

It is not clear why people slow down. One explanation, known as the **peripheral slowing hypothesis**, suggests that the peripheral nervous system, which encompasses the nerves that branch from the spinal cord and brain to the extremities of the body, becomes less efficient with age. As a result, it takes longer for information from the environment to reach the brain and for commands from the brain to be transmitted to the muscles (Salthouse, 2006).

According to the **generalized slowing hypothesis**, by contrast, processing in all parts of the nervous system, including the brain, is less efficient. As a consequence, slowing occurs throughout the body, including the processing of both simple and complex stimuli and the transmission of commands to the muscles (Harada, Natelson Love, & Triebel, 2013).

Although we don't know which explanation is more accurate, it is clear that the slowing of reaction time and general processing results in a higher incidence of accidents for elderly persons. Slowed reaction and processing time means they can't efficiently receive information from the environment that may indicate a dangerous situation. Slowed decision-making processes impair their ability to remove themselves from harm's way. Drivers over 70 have as many fatal accidents per mile driven as teenagers.

Although response time slows, the *perception* of time seems to speed up with age. The days and weeks seem to go by more quickly, and time seems to rush by faster for older adults, perhaps because of changes in the way the brain coordinates its internal time clock (Mangan, 1997; Coelho et al., 2004; Facchini & Rampazi, 2009).

peripheral slowing hypothesis
the theory that suggests that overall processing speed declines in the peripheral nervous system with increasing age.

generalized slowing hypothesis
the theory that processing in all parts of the nervous system, including the brain, is less efficient.

Module 3.3 Review

LO 3.11 Describe the capabilities of infants regarding each of the five senses.

Infants' sensory abilities are surprisingly well developed at or shortly after birth. Very early, infants can see depth and motion, distinguish colors and patterns, localize and discriminate sounds, and recognize the sound and smell of their mother. Infants are sensitive to pain, which manifests itself after a slight delay, and touch, which is one of the most highly developed sensory systems in the newborn. Infants largely use touch to explore their world.

LO 3.12 Recognize the sensory difficulties school-age children may experience and how they can affect children's learning.

School-age children experience sensory impairments that may interfere with their learning and academic success.

LO 3.13 Discuss the changes in sensory perception in middle adulthood and the factors that may affect these changes.

In middle age, most people notice changes in the sensitivity of their eyes and other sense organs. All the organs seem to shift at about the same rate, but the changes are particularly marked in vision and hearing.

LO 3.14 Give examples of the decline in various sense organs experienced in late adulthood and how these changes affect the lives of the elderly.

Old age brings many changes in sensory perception that can cause social and psychological difficulties for older people, such as hearing impairments that can hamper one's social life and the loss of taste and smell sensitivity that can make food unappealing and lead to malnutrition. In old age people slow down, and their reaction time increases. Two explanations generated to explain this phenomenon are the nervous-system-oriented peripheral slowing hypothesis and the whole-body-oriented generalized slowing hypothesis.

Journal Writing Prompt

Applying Lifespan Development: Should older people, who are susceptible to slowing, be subject to strict examinations to renew their driver's licenses? Should such tests cover more than eyesight (e.g., response time, mental abilities)? What issues should be taken into consideration?

Epilogue

In this chapter, we discussed the nature and pace of physical growth and change across the life span. We next looked at brain growth, the development and uses of reflexes, and the development of motor skills. We closed the chapter with a look at perceptual development and adults' sensory abilities.

Turn back for a moment to the prologue, which describes Evan Kaufman's unsettled sleeping and eating patterns, and answer these questions.

1. Evan's parents are wondering if he will ever sleep through the night. What could you tell them about the development of rhythms in infancy to reassure them their son will eventually adopt more conventional behavior?

2. Evan's mother mentions that she's running out of ways to entertain her son because he's awake all day long. Do you think that Evan's wakefulness could be caused, in part, by too much stimulation in his environment?

3. What advice could you give his mother that might help both her and Evan to relax?

4. Based on what you learned about cross-cultural research on sleep patterns, what reassurance could you provide Evan's parents about his sleeping patterns?

Looking Back

LO 3.1 Describe infants' physical development in the first 2 years of life.

Babies integrate their individual behaviors by developing rhythms—repetitive, cyclical patterns of behavior. A major rhythm relates to the infant's state—the awareness he or she displays to internal and external stimulation.

LO 3.2 Summarize the physical development that occurs during the preschool and middle childhood years and the factors that affect this development.

Children grow very rapidly over their first 2 years. During the middle childhood years, the body grows at a slow but steady pace that is influenced by both genetic and social factors.

LO 3.3 Identify the physical changes adolescents experience as the body reaches puberty.

Adolescence is a period of rapid physical growth, including the major changes associated with puberty.

LO 3.4 Describe the physical changes that occur from early to late adulthood and how they affect adults' capabilities.

By young adulthood, the body and the senses are at their peak, but growth is still proceeding, particularly in the brain. Old age brings both external and internal changes. During adulthood, people experience gradual declines in physical characteristics and appearance.

LO 3.5 Distinguish functional age from chronological age.

Some researchers divide people into three groups according to functional ages: The *young old* are healthy and active; the *old old* have some health problems and difficulties with daily activities; and the *oldest old* are frail and need care. For demographers, the terms are purely chronological. The *young old* are 65 to 74 years old. The *old old* are between 75 and 84, and the *oldest old* are 85 and older.

LO 3.6 Discuss the role of neurons in brain development.

The development of the nervous system first entails the development of billions of neurons and interconnections among them. Later, the numbers of both neurons and connections decrease in a process called synaptic pruning as a result of the infant's experiences. Brain plasticity, the susceptibility of a developing organism to environmental influences, is relatively high. Researchers have identified sensitive periods during the development of body systems and behaviors—limited periods when the organism is particularly susceptible to environmental influences.

LO 3.7 Explain what is meant by brain lateralization and describe how it develops in early childhood.

Brain growth is rapid during the preschool years. In addition, the brain develops lateralization, a tendency of the two hemispheres to adopt specialized tasks.

LO 3.8 Identify the reflexes that infants are born with that help them adapt to their surroundings and protect themselves.

Babies are born with reflexes—unlearned, organized involuntary responses to particular environmental stimuli. Reflexes include the swimming reflex, the eye-blink reflex, and the Moro reflex. The function of reflexes appears to be to protect the infant from sudden threats until a voluntary system of responses develops.

LO 3.9 Summarize the gross motor skills that emerge during infancy and the preschool years, and explain how they are related to brain development.

Infants progress from a state of few motor skills to the ability to sit up, crawl, and eventually stand and walk. Both gross and fine motor development is rapid during the first 4 years. During the school years, muscle coordination improves to the extent that athletic activities become possible. These skills constantly improve through the school years, adolescence, and at least young adulthood. During middle childhood, boys generally surpass girls in muscle strength, while girls' muscle coordination is often more advanced than that of boys.

LO 3.10 Give examples of fine motor skills, and describe their developmental pattern in infants and young children.

The fine motor skills follow a predetermined pattern of development of steadily increasing ability to use the hands and fingers. As their motor skills develop, children develop handedness and artistic skills.

LO 3.11 Describe the capabilities of infants regarding each of the five senses.

Infants' sensory abilities are reasonably good at birth. For example, they can see depth, motion, color, and patterns, and they can distinguish and locate sounds in their environment. By 6 months eyesight equals that of most adults. Infants can smell and taste, and they are sensitive to touch, which is their main sense for exploring and interpreting the world.

LO 3.12 Recognize the sensory difficulties school-age children may experience and how they can affect children's learning.

Even if a child is not legally blind, visual problems may seriously affect schoolwork. Auditory impairments can cause social as well as academic problems since much peer interaction involves informal conversation. Auditory difficulties may be accompanied by speech impairments.

LO 3.13 Discuss the changes in sensory perception in middle adulthood and the factors that may affect these changes.

In middle age, most people notice changes in the sensitivity of their eyes and other sense organs. All the organs seem to shift at about the same rate, but the changes are particularly marked in vision and hearing

LO 3.14 Give examples of the decline in various sense organs experienced in late adulthood and how these changes affect the lives of the elderly.

Aging brings many changes in the senses, most of which represent deterioration and many of which can cause social isolation. In addition, the decrease in taste and smell sensitivity among older adults can lead to under-eating and malnutrition. In middle and late adulthood, reaction time increases as older people simply slow down. However, most people learn ways to compensate for diminished sensation by increased attention and care.

Key Terms and Concepts

rhythms 88
state 88
rapid eye movement, or REM, sleep 89
puberty 92
menarche 92
primary sex characteristics 93
secondary sex characteristics 93
senescence 94
primary aging 95
secondary aging 95
osteoporosis 95
gerontologists 96
synaptic pruning 100

myelin 100
cerebral cortex 100
plasticity 101
sensitive period 101
lateralization 101
reflexes 105
handedness 112
norms 113
Brazelton Neonatal Behavioral
    Assessment Scale (NBAS) 113
sensation 114
perception 114
multimodal approach to perception 118

affordances 118
visual impairment 120
auditory impairment 120
speech impairment 120
childhood-onset fluency disorder or
    stuttering 120
presbyopia 121
glaucoma 121
presbycusis 122
peripheral slowing hypothesis 124
generalized slowing hypothesis 124

Chapter 4
Health and Wellness

Corey Jenkins/Alamy

Learning Objectives

LO 4.1 Explain the experience of stress across the life span.

LO 4.2 Analyze the consequences of stress.

LO 4.3 Describe strategies for coping with stress.

LO 4.4 Analyze the importance of proper nutrition to human development.

LO 4.5 Examine threats to health and wellness faced by children and adolescents.

LO 4.6 Discuss the general health concerns of adults.

LO 4.7 Describe the health risks confronting older adults.

LO 4.8 Describe how good nutrition in childhood promotes wellness later in life.

LO 4.9 Explain how exercise can affect health and longevity.

LO 4.10 Examine the nature of sexuality in later life.

LO 4.11 Explain how wellness can be maintained in old age.

Chapter Overview

Prologue: Graduating from Stress

Elsa graduated near the top of her class two years ago and looked forward to entering the
professional world. She believed she would finally be stress-free upon landing her first
real job. She was wrong. Learning the ropes at work turned out to be a lot harder than she
imagined, and she was putting in more hours than she anticipated. She felt good about her
salary, but paying back loans ate up a large portion of her paycheck.

    Stress affected her personal life as well. When her long-time romantic relationship
ended, she decided to try online dating for the first time. Choosing the right person turned
out to be just as challenging online as it was in the real world, even with endless possibilities
to scroll through. Finding time for dating was one part of the issue; finding the energy was
the other.

    Elsa's stress was interfering with her sleep, and she now had less time to go to the
gym. She also noticed her eating choices were taking a turn for the worse. She even started
worrying that she was becoming too reliant many nights on a glass of wine to help her relax.

    Luckily her sister, who was also her best friend, was the person she could talk to about
everything. "I finally graduated from college," Elsa told her sister, "but when will I graduate
from stress?" ∎

Looking Ahead

Elsa's difficulties in her work and personal life are not at all unusual. People in early
adulthood are at the height of their physical and cognitive abilities, but they can also experience tremendous stress as they launch themselves into the adult world.

    In this chapter, we focus on the physical aspects of health and
wellness. We begin by considering stress, a potential barrier to wellness. We discuss the origins and consequences of stress, as well as
effective techniques for coping. We take a look at ways stress now affects even school-age children.

    We turn from stress to illness. We consider malnutrition, which is
mainly a problem in developing countries, and we examine obesity,
which is very much an issue in the United States. We see the effects of
obesity as well as those of eating disorders. We then turn to a discussion of the major threats to wellness and health throughout the life
span. We continue with a consideration of common physical and psychological disorders in adulthood, including the influence of personality type and cultural factors on such health issues as coronary heart

Stress can affect people of all ages.

disease and cancer, which rank at the top of people's fears as they age. We end the module with a discussion of Alzheimer's disease.

The final module of the chapter covers ways to promote health and wellness. We examine the effects of a good diet and exercise as means to improve wellness. Finally, we discuss typical changes in men's and women's sexuality as they age, as well as how older adults can maintain wellness.

MODULE 4.1

STRESS AND COPING

Our lives are crowded with events and circumstances, known as *stressors*, that threaten our equilibrium. Stressors need not be unpleasant events: Even the happiest events—starting a long-sought job, planning a wedding—can produce stress. In this section, we'll look at the origins and consequences of stress, as well as ways to handle stress. As we'll see, how well people cope with stress depends on a complex interplay of physical and psychological factors (Shimizu & Pelham, 2004; Snyder, Barry, & Valentino, 2015).

The Stages and Origins of Stress

LO 4.1 Explain the experience of stress across the life span.

Experienced job interviewers, college counselors, and owners of bridal shops all know that not everyone reacts the same way to a potentially stressful event. What makes the difference?

STAGES OF STRESS.   According to psychologists Arnold Lazarus and Susan Folkman, people move through a series of stages that determine whether they will experience stress (Lazarus & Folkman, 1984; Lazarus, 1991).

primary appraisal
an individual's assessment of an event to determine whether its implications are positive, negative, or neutral.

Primary appraisal is the first step—the individual's assessment of an event to determine whether its implications are positive, negative, or neutral. If a person sees the event as primarily negative, he or she appraises it in terms of the harm that it has caused in the past, how threatening it is likely to be, and how likely it is that the challenge can be resisted successfully. For example, you are likely to feel differently about an upcoming French test if you passed the last one with flying colors than you would if you did poorly.

secondary appraisal
a person's answer to the question, "Can I handle it?"—an assessment of whether the coping abilities and resources on hand are adequate.

Secondary appraisal follows. **Secondary appraisal** is the person's answer to the question, "Can I handle it?"—an assessment of whether the coping abilities and resources on hand are adequate. If resources are lacking and the threat is great, the person will feel stress. A traffic ticket is always upsetting, but if you can't afford the fine, the stress is greater.

Stress varies with the person's appraisal, and that appraisal varies with the person's temperament and circumstances. Some general principles help predict when an event will be appraised as stressful. Psychologist Shelley Taylor (2010) suggests the following characteristics of events that have a high likelihood of producing stress:

- Events and circumstances that produce negative emotions—for example, dealing with the illness of a loved one produces more stress than planning for the adoption of a new baby.

- Situations that are uncontrollable or unpredictable—for example, professors who give surprise quizzes produce more stress than those who schedule them in advance.

- Events and circumstances that are ambiguous and confusing—for example, a new job that does not have a clear job description is likely to produce more stress than a well-defined position.

- Having to simultaneously accomplish many tasks that strain a person's capabilities—for example, a graduate student who is expecting her first child the same month she is scheduled to submit her dissertation is likely to feel more stress than a student with less on her agenda.

In addition, each period in life brings with it its own types of stressors.

STRESS IN CHILDHOOD: THE PRESSURE TO MAKE THE GRADE

Brian and Tiffany Aske of Oakland, California, desperately want their daughter, Ashlyn, to succeed in first grade.... When they started Ashlyn in kindergarten last year, they had no reason to worry. A bright child with twinkling eyes, Ashlyn was eager to learn, and the neighborhood school had a great reputation. But by November, Ashlyn, then 5, wasn't measuring up. No matter how many times she was tested, she couldn't read the 130-word list her teacher gave her: words like "our," "house," and "there." She became so exhausted and distraught over homework—including a weekly essay on "my favorite animal" or "my family vacation"—that she would put her head down on the dining-room table and sob. "She would tell me, 'I can't write a story, Mama. I just can't do it,'" said Tiffany. (Tyre, 2006, p. 34)

The No Child Left Behind Act of 2002 aimed to ensure that all children would be able to read by the time they reached the third grade. The law requires school principals to meet this goal or risk losing their jobs and their school funding. Although the intentions of this law may have been good, in some cases there has been an unforeseen outcome: So much focus is placed on reading that other important topics such as social studies and music and activities such as recess have been excluded from the school day. Worse, some schools' reading programs have become so intense that some children, such as Ashlyn in our story above, are simply burning out (Abril & Gault, 2006; Paige, 2006).

Whereas kindergarten was once a time for finger painting, story time, and free play, children are increasingly beginning reading lessons at that level. Frequent testing to ensure that children are meeting short-term and long-term literacy goals has become more commonplace. The experience of failure—and of competitive pressure to be at the top of the class—is hitting children at younger ages than before.

From *an educator's* perspective

Do you accept the view that children in U.S. society are "pushed" academically to the extent that they feel too much stress and pressure at a young age? Why?

One trend that has many parents and educators concerned is an increase in the amount of homework assigned. A study conducted by the Institute for Social Research at the University of Michigan determined that children are spending a lot more time on academics today than they did 20 years ago. The time spent in school for children ages 6 to 8 has increased from about 5 hours to about 7 hours per weekday. Time spent studying and reading has increased over that time period, while playtime, sports, and other outdoor activities have decreased (Juster, Ono, & Stafford, 2004).

But is the extra homework worth the cost? While time spent on homework is associated with greater academic achievement in secondary school, the relationship weakens for the lower grades; below grade five, the relationship disappears. Experts explain this finding in terms of younger children's inability to tune out distractions, as well as their yet undeveloped study skills. Moreover, research with older children shows that more homework is not necessarily better. In fact, the benefits of homework may reach a plateau beyond which additional time spent on homework produces no further benefits (Cooper & Valentine, 2001; Trautwein et al., 2006; Farrell & Danby, 2015).

Some educational experts fear that the social and emotional development of children is taking a back seat to literacy education, and that the pressure, the testing, the accelerated programs, and the time spent in school—as well as in after-school programs and on homework—may be robbing kids of opportunities to just be kids and causing considerable stress. Some parents, such as the Askes, whom we encountered

For younger children, homework may not have the benefits it has for older children—and it may cause stress.

above, are worried that their children are simply becoming frustrated and discouraged with learning (Kohn, 2006).

Ultimately, the Askes found their own solution to the stress that Ashlyn was facing: They moved to a different state, where Ashlyn could attend a less intense public school that offered more flexibility and less pressure. But this option is not open to everyone, and most kids have to cope as well as they can with the pressure cookers that schools have become.

ADOLESCENT STRESS: LATE TO BED, EARLY TO RISE. In view of the increasing academic and social stresses they experience, children—and especially adolescents—go to bed later and get up earlier, leaving them sleep-deprived. This deprivation coincides in adolescence with a shift in their internal clocks. Older adolescents have a need to go to bed later and to sleep later in the morning, requiring 9 hours of sleep to feel rested. In the conflict between late nights and early morning classes, however, they get far less sleep than their bodies crave (Wolfson & Richards, 2011; Dagys et al., 2012).

Why does this matter? For one, sleep-deprived teens have lower grades, are more depressed, and have greater difficulty controlling their moods. They are also at great risk for auto accidents (Fredriksen et al., 2004; Roberts, Roberts, & Xing, 2011; Louca & Short, 2014; also see the *Neuroscience and Development* box on the genetic underpinnings of sleep).

In addition to academic stresses, adolescents experience social stress related to body image and fitting in. As we will see when we discuss eating disorders later in the chapter, some experts suggest that adolescent eating disorders are a result of such stressful situations as perfectionistic, overdemanding parents or other family difficulties.

From *a health-care provider's* perspective

Do people of all ages experience stress? How do stressors differ from age to age?

THE STRESSES OF ADULTHOOD. The nature of what is stressful changes as people age. For example, in young adulthood, many people are caught up with the stresses involved with getting an education and a job and establishing long-term relationships. Later, marriage, ongoing career goals, and parenthood can cause stress. And the stresses of adult parents change too: In the beginning, parents may worry about whether their toddler is ready to give up a pacifier, whereas later, parents may experience stress over their adolescent children's potential drug use.

In later adulthood, stresses may change. Retirement and health issues may cause significant stress, as can declining strength and energy, worries about loss of memory, and a feared decrease in intelligence or sexual passion. Sometimes the worry becomes intense and affects significant relationships with others: with parents and children, siblings and friends, supervisors and coworkers.

The Consequences of Stress

LO 4.2 Analyze the consequences of stress.

psychoneuroimmunology (PNI) the study of the relationship among the brain, the immune system, and psychological factors.

No matter what events trigger stress, the results are similar. Researchers in the new field of **psychoneuroimmunology (PNI)**—the study of the relationship among the brain, the immune system, and psychological factors—have examined the outcomes of stress. They have found that stress produces three main consequences, summarized in Figure 4-1.

First, stress has direct physiological outcomes. The most immediate outcome is a biological reaction, as hormones secreted by the adrenal glands cause a rise in heart rate, blood pressure, respiration rate, and sweating. In some situations, these

Figure 4-1 The Consequences of Stress

Stress produces three major consequences: direct physiological effects, harmful behaviors, and indirect health-related behaviors.

(**Source:** Adapted from Baum, 1994.)

immediate effects are beneficial because the "emergency reaction" they produce in the sympathetic nervous system enables people to defend themselves from a sudden, threatening situation (Janusek, Cooper, & Mathews, 2012; Irwin, 2015).

However, as stress-related hormones are constantly secreted, the heart, blood vessels, and other body tissues may deteriorate. As a consequence, people become more susceptible to diseases as their ability to fight off germs declines (Lundberg, 2006; Rohleder, 2012).

In addition, the immune system—the organs, glands, and cells that are the body's line of defense against disease—may be damaged by stress. Stress can interfere with the immune system's ability to stop germs from reproducing or cancer cells from spreading. In addition, stress may overstimulate the immune system into attacking the body itself and damaging healthy tissue (Caserta et al., 2008; Connor, 2008; Liu et al., 2012; Ménard et al., 2017).

Over the long run, the constant wear and tear of fighting off stress can have other formidable costs. Headaches, backaches, skin rashes, indigestion, chronic fatigue, and even the common cold are stress-related illnesses (Suinn, 2001; McGrady, 2007).

Stress may also lead to **psychosomatic disorders**, medical problems caused by the interaction of psychological, emotional, and physical difficulties. For instance, ulcers, asthma, arthritis, and high blood pressure may sometimes be produced by stress (Davis et al., 2008; Marin et al., 2009).

The direct physiological effects of stress are just the first major consequence. As shown in Figure 4-1, the second major consequence of stress is that it leads people to engage in *harmful behaviors*, such as cutting back on sleep, increasing smoking and drinking, eating poorly, or taking drugs.

Finally, another major consequence of stress is that it has *indirect effects on health-related behavior*. For example, people under a lot of stress may be less likely to seek out good medical care or may delay doing so. They are also less likely to exercise or to comply with medical advice. All of these failures can lead to or affect serious health conditions, including such major problems as heart disease, which we will discuss in greater detail next (Zellner et al., 2006; Ihle et al., 2012; Andreotti et al., 2015).

To get a sense of how much stress you have in your own life, complete the questionnaire in Table 4-1.

psychosomatic disorders
medical problems caused by the interaction of psychological, emotional, and physical difficulties.

Table 4-1 How Stressed Are You?

The statements below will help you determine your level of stress. Mark the appropriate number in each box, then add up those numbers to find your score. Your answers should reflect your experiences in the past month only. To help you rate the extent of your stress, use the key at the bottom.

1. I become upset when something happens unexpectedly.

☐ 0 = never, 1 = almost never, 2 = sometimes, 3 = fairly often, 4 = very often

2. I feel I'm unable to control the things that are most important in my life.

☐ 0 = never, 1 = almost never, 2 = sometimes, 3 = fairly often, 4 = very often

3. I feel nervous and "stressed."

☐ 0 = never, 1 = almost never, 2 = sometimes, 3 = fairly often, 4 = very often

4. I feel confident about my ability to handle my personal problems.

☐ 4 = never, 3 = almost never, 2 = sometimes, 1 = fairly often, 0 = very often

5. In general, I feel things are going my way.

☐ 4 = never, 3 = almost never, 2 = sometimes, 1 = fairly often, 0 = very often

6. I'm able to control irritations in my life.

☐ 4 = never, 3 = almost never, 2 = sometimes, 1 = fairly often, 0 = very often

7. I feel I cannot cope with all the things I need to do.

☐ 0 = never, 1 = almost never, 2 = sometimes, 3 = fairly often, 4 = very often

8. Generally, I feel on top of things.

☐ 4 = never, 3 = almost never, 2 = sometimes, 1 = fairly often, 0 = very often

9. I get angry at things that are beyond my control.

☐ 0 = never, 1 = almost never, 2 = sometimes, 3 = fairly often, 4 = very often

10. I feel problems pile up to such an extent that I cannot overcome them.

☐ 0 = never, 1 = almost never, 2 = sometimes, 3 = fairly often, 4 = very often

How Do You Measure Up?

Stress levels vary from person to person, but you can compare your total score to the averages below:

Age		Gender	
18–29	14.2	Men	12.1
30–44	13.0	Women	13.7
45–54	12.6		
55–64	11.9		
65 and older	12.0		

Marital Status

Widowed	12.6
Married or living with partner	12.4
Single or never wed	14.1
Divorced	14.7
Separated	16.6

(**Source:** Based on Cohen., Kamarck, & Mermelstein, 1983. Dept. of Psychology, Carnegie Mellon University.)

Coping with Stress

LO 4.3   Describe strategies for coping with stress.

Ally McKennon, 17, never seems to catch up. She works dawn til dusk at her schoolwork and has a part-time job as a waitress on weekends. She has her heart set on a small eastern liberal arts college, and though she knows it is listed as "highly competitive," she thinks she has the grades and the standardized test scores to get in, and she chose four courses that would impress college admissions officers. If she can only manage to stay up a few hours longer each night to study and can avoid entanglements with boys....

Todd Comins, also 17 and a student at the same school as Ally, always seems rested, fed, and happy. He works a part-time job at the same restaurant as Ally but always seems cheerful and has lots of friends of both sexes. He has a list of highly challenging colleges that he would be happy to attend, along with a couple of "safety schools," any one of which would suit him fine. He never seems overworked and doesn't much care about his test scores or grades. Paradoxically, he gets As in his courses and scored high on his standardized tests.

Ally knows that Todd is no brighter than she, but his approach to life seems different. She can't seem to be relaxed; he can't seem to get anxious. What gives?

COPING STRATEGIES.   Stress is a normal part of every life. But some people are better than others at coping—the effort to control, reduce, or learn to tolerate the threats that lead to stress. What's the secret to coping? It turns out that people use a variety of strategies.

Some people use *problem-focused coping*—managing a threatening situation by directly changing it to make it less stressful. For example, a man having difficulties on the job may ask his boss to change his responsibilities, or he may look for another job.

Other people employ *emotion-focused coping*—the conscious regulation of emotion. For instance, a mother having trouble finding appropriate care for her child while she is at work may tell herself that she should look at the bright side: At least she has a job in a difficult economy (Greenberg, 2008; Master et al., 2009).

Sometimes people acknowledge that they are in a stressful situation that cannot be changed, but they cope by managing their reactions. For example, they may take up meditation or exercise to reduce their physical reactions.

Coping is also aided by the presence of *social support*—assistance and comfort supplied by others. Turning to others can provide both emotional support (in the form of a shoulder to cry on) and practical, tangible support (such as a temporary loan) (Green, DeCourville, & Sadava, 2012; Vallejo-Sánchez & Pérez-García, 2015).

Finally, even if people do not consciously cope with stress, some psychologists suggest that they may unconsciously use **defensive coping** mechanisms. Defensive coping involves unconscious strategies that distort or deny the true nature of a situation. For instance, people may trivialize a life-threatening illness or tell themselves that failing a major test is unimportant.

defensive coping
unconscious strategies that distort or deny the true nature of a situation.

Another type of defensive coping is *emotional insulation*, through which people unconsciously try to block emotions and thereby avoid pain. But if defensive coping becomes a habitual response to stress, the person's reliance on avoidance can stand in the way of dealing with the reality of the situation (Ormont, 2001).

In some cases, people use drugs or alcohol to escape from stressful situations. Like defensive coping, drinking and drug use do not help address the situation causing the stress, and they can increase a person's difficulties. For example, people may become addicted to the substances that initially provided them with a pleasurable sense of escape.

HARDINESS, RESILIENCE, AND COPING. The success with which people deal with stress depends in part on their *coping style*, their general tendency to deal with stress in a particular way. For example, people with a "hardy" coping style are especially successful. **Hardiness** is a personality characteristic associated with a lower rate of stress-related illness.

hardiness
a personality characteristic associated with a lower rate of stress-related illness.

Hardy individuals are take-charge people who revel in life's challenges. People who are high in hardiness are more resistant to stress-related illness than those with less hardiness. Hardy people react to stressors with optimism, convinced that they can respond effectively. By turning threats into challenges, they are less apt to experience high levels of stress (Andrew et al., 2008; Maddi, 2014).

For people who face the most profound difficulties—such as the unexpected death of a loved one—a key factor in their reactions is their level of resilience. *Resilience* is the ability to withstand, overcome, and even thrive after profound adversity (Werner, 2005; Kim-Cohen, 2007; Lipsitt & Demick, 2012).

Resilient people tend to be easygoing and good-natured, with good social and communication skills. They are independent, feeling that they can shape their own fate and are not dependent on others or luck. They work with what they have and make the best of any situation (Deshields et al., 2005; Friborg et al., 2005; Galluccio & Safran, 2015; also see the *Development in Your Life* box.)

Assistance and comfort by others in times of stress can provide both emotional and practical support.

Antonio Guillem/iStock/Getty Images Plus

Development in Your Life

Coping with Stress

General guidelines that can help people cope with stress include the following:

- **Seek control over the situation.** Taking charge of a situation that is producing stress can take you a long way toward coping with it. For example, if you are feeling stress about a test, do something about it—such as forming a study group or starting to study more intensively.

- **Redefine "threat" as "challenge."** Changing the definition can make a situation seem less threatening. "Look for the silver lining" is not bad advice. For example, if you're fired, look at it as an opportunity to get a new and better job.

- **Use mindfulness.** Mindfulness stress reduction techniques involve learning to become aware of one's surroundings, making every moment count, and observing one's thoughts and feelings without judging them. Research has demonstrated that getting into a mindful state helps manage and reduce stress responses (Meland et al., 2015; Ramasubramanian, 2017).

- **Find social support.** Almost any difficulty can be faced more easily with the help of others. Friends, family members, and even telephone hot lines staffed by trained counselors can provide significant support. (For help in identifying appropriate hot lines, the U.S. Public Health Service maintains a "master" toll-free number that can provide phone numbers and addresses of many national groups. Call 800-336-4794.)

- **Use relaxation techniques.** Reducing the physiological arousal brought about by stress can be effective in coping with stress. Techniques that produce relaxation, such as transcendental meditation, Zen and yoga, progressive muscle relaxation, and even hypnosis, have been shown to be effective. One that works particularly well was devised by physician Herbert Benson and is illustrated in Table 4-2 (Benson, 1993; Menezes et al., 2015).

- **Maintain a healthy lifestyle that will reinforce your body's natural coping mechanisms.** Exercise, eat nutritiously, get enough sleep, and avoid or reduce use of alcohol, tobacco, or other drugs.

- **If all else fails, keep in mind that a life without stress would be dull.** Stress is natural, and successfully coping with it can be gratifying.

Table 4-2 How to Elicit the Relaxation Response

Some general advice on regular practice of the relaxation response:

- Try to find 10 to 20 minutes in your daily routine; before breakfast is a good time.
- Sit comfortably.
- For the period you will practice, try to arrange your life so you won't have distractions. Turn off your phone and computer, and ask someone else to watch the kids.
- Time yourself by glancing periodically at a clock or watch (but don't set an alarm). Commit yourself to a specific length of practice, and try to stick to it.

There are several approaches to eliciting the relaxation response. Here is one standard set of instructions:

Step 1. Pick a focus word or short phrase that's firmly rooted in your personal belief system. For example, a nonreligious individual might choose a neutral word like *one* or *peace* or *love*. A Christian person desiring to use a prayer could pick the opening words of Psalm 23, *The Lord is my shepherd*; a Jewish person could choose *Shalom*.

Step 2. Sit quietly in a comfortable position.

Step 3. Close your eyes.

Step 4. Relax your muscles.

Step 5. Breathe slowly and naturally, repeating your focus word or phrase silently as you exhale.

Step 6. Throughout, assume a passive attitude. Don't worry about how well you're doing. When other thoughts come to mind, simply say to yourself, "Oh, well," and gently return to the repetition.

Step 7. Continue for 10 to 20 minutes. You may open your eyes to check the time, but do not use an alarm. When you finish, sit quietly for a minute or so, at first with your eyes closed and later with your eyes open. Then do not stand for 1 or 2 minutes.

Step 8. Practice the technique once or twice a day.

(**Source:** Benson, 1993.)

Module 4.1 Review

LO 4.1 Explain the experience of stress across the life span.

Not everyone responds to stress the same way. People move through stages—primary appraisal and secondary appraisal—to determine whether they will experience stress. Stress may appear at any time of life. Some educational initiatives, for example, have caused students and teachers to experience stress.

LO 4.2 Analyze the consequences of stress.

Long-term exposure to stressors may cause deterioration in the heart, blood vessels, and other body tissues. Stress is linked to many common ailments.

LO 4.3 Describe strategies for coping with stress.

Strategies for coping with stress include problem-focused coping, emotion-focused coping, the use of social support, and defensive coping. People who react effectively to stress have a positive coping style, which may involve hardiness and/or resilience. Less successful strategies include resorting to drugs or drink.

Journal Writing Prompt

Applying Lifespan Development: Why might it be the case that students who spend a lot of time doing homework tend not to have better academic success than students who spend a moderate amount of time?

MODULE 4.2

ILLNESS AND WELL-BEING

Stress affects health across the life span, and as noted above, it can contribute to illness and disease. In this section, we'll look at other factors related to illness and well-being, including malnutrition, obesity, and eating disorders, as well as the particular health concerns at different ages.

Malnutrition, Obesity, and Eating Disorders

LO 4.4   Analyze the importance of proper nutrition to human development.

At 20 pounds and 27 inches long, Zachary Miller was a happy and healthy, but not especially active, baby. "The pediatrician told me, 'The big ones don't like to move,'" says Zach's mom, Ellie. "She told me to put him on the floor and on his tummy as often as possible. He hates that. But it does get him to push up on his arms and roll over."

At 7 months, Zach was already overweight. (Sachs, 2006, p. 112)

As this situation shows, concerns with nutrition and eating take center stage from a very early age. Although worrying about the weight of a 7-month-old baby may seem extreme to many, as we'll see in this section, the consequences of malnutrition, overeating, and eating disorders stretch across the entire life span.

MALNUTRITION.   While babies like Zach may be overweight, *malnutrition*, the condition of having an improper amount and balance of nutrients, is more common among children living in many developing countries, where overall 10 percent of infants are severely malnourished (see Figure 4-2).

Undernutrition is a problem across the globe, and is particularly widespread in Asia and Africa. For example, 60 percent of North Korean children age 6 months to 7 years are suffering moderate to severe malnutrition (Chaudhary & Sharma, 2012; United Nations World Food Programme, 2016; UNICEF, WHO, 2016).

Sadly, malnutrition produces several results, none of them good. Malnourished children in developing countries begin to show a slower growth rate by the age of 6 months. By the time they reach the age of 2 years, their height and weight are only 95 percent that of children in more industrialized countries. In addition, children who have been chronically malnourished during infancy later score lower on IQ tests and tend to do less well in school. These effects may linger even after the children's diet has improved substantially (Ratanachu-Ek, 2003; Waber et al., 2014; Peter et al., 2016).

From *a health-care provider's* perspective

How might biology and environment combine to affect the nutritional habits of a child adopted as an infant from a developing country and reared in a more industrialized one?

Malnourishment at an early age can lower IQ scores, even if diet improves later. How might this deficit be overcome?

Chris Hondros/Getty Images

Problems of malnourishment are not restricted to developing countries, however. In the United States, around 20 percent of children live in poverty, which puts them at risk for malnutrition. Overall, some 26 percent of families who have children 3 years

Figure 4-2 Undernourished in the Population

Prevalence of undernourishment in the population (percent) in 2012–2014. **THINKING ABOUT THE DATA:** What countries in Africa have higher and lower rates of underweight children? What about Asia?
(**Source:** UNICEF, WHO, 2016.)

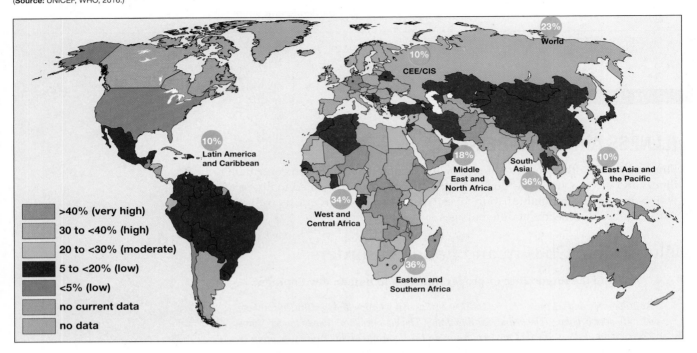

old and younger live in poverty, and 6 percent of Americans live in extreme poverty, meaning their income is $10,000 a year or less. And, as shown in Figure 4-3, the poverty rates are even higher for black, Hispanic, and American Indian families (National Center for Children in Poverty, 2013).

Social service programs mean that these children rarely become severely malnourished, but such children remain susceptible to *undernutrition*, in which there is some deficiency in diet. Some surveys find that as many as a quarter of 1- to 5-year-old

Figure 4-3 Children Living in Poverty

Members of black, American Indian, and Hispanic households are more likely to live in poverty than members of white and Asian families.
(**Source:** National Center for Children in Poverty, 2013.)

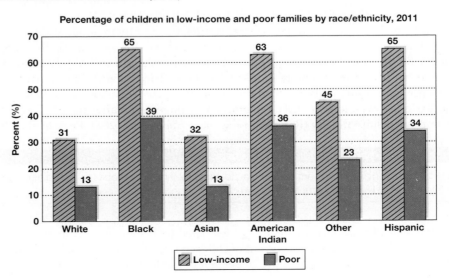

children in the United States have diets that fall below the minimum caloric intake recommended by nutritional experts. Although the consequences are not as severe as those of malnutrition, undernutrition also has long-term costs. For instance, cognitive development later in childhood is affected by even mild to moderate undernutrition (Tanner & Finn-Stevenson, 2002; Lian et al., 2012).

Severe malnutrition during infancy may lead to several disorders. Malnutrition during the first year can produce *marasmus*, a disease in which infants stop growing. Marasmus, attributable to a severe deficiency in proteins and calories, causes the body to waste away and ultimately results in death. Older children are susceptible to *kwashiorkor*, a disease in which a child's stomach, limbs, and face swell with water. To a casual observer, it appears that a child with kwashiorkor is actually chubby. However, this is an illusion: The child's body is in fact struggling to make use of the few nutrients that are available (Douglass & McGadney-Douglass, 2008).

In some cases, infants who receive sufficient nutrition act as though they have been deprived of food. Looking as though they suffer from marasmus, they are underdeveloped, listless, and apathetic. The real cause, though, is emotional: They lack sufficient love and emotional support. In such cases, known as **nonorganic failure to thrive**, children stop growing not for biological reasons but owing to a lack of stimulation and attention from their parents. Usually occurring by the age of 18 months, nonorganic failure to thrive can be reversed through intensive parent training or by placing children in a foster home where they can receive emotional support.

nonorganic failure to thrive
a disorder in which infants stop growing due to a lack of stimulation and attention as the result of inadequate parenting.

From *an educator's* perspective

What might be some of the reasons that malnourishment, which slows physical growth, also harms IQ scores and school performance? How might malnourishment affect education in developing countries?

OBESITY.   In spite of a widely held view that thinness is a virtue, at least in the United States, increasing numbers of children are becoming obese. **Obesity** is defined as a BMI at or above the 95th percentile for children of the same age and sex. (BMI is calculated by dividing a child's weight in kilograms by the square of their height in meters). By this definition, 17 percent of U.S. children are obese—a proportion that has more than tripled since the 1970s. And it's not only a problem in the United States; the number of children ages 5–19 who are obese has increased 1,000 percent from 1975 to 2016 (see Figure 4-4; Ogden et al., 2015; NCD Risk Factor Collaboration, 2017).

It is clear that malnourishment has potentially disastrous consequences for an infant. Less clear, however, are the effects of obesity. Although there is no demonstrable

obesity
a BMI at or above the 95th percentile for children of the same age and sex.

Figure 4-4 Obesity in Children

Percentage of children ages 2 to 19 who are obese, by age.
(**Source:** Ogden, et al., 2014.)

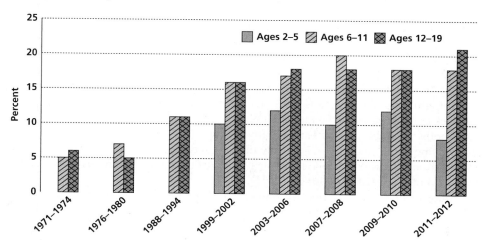

association between obesity during infancy and obesity at age 16, some research suggests that overfeeding during infancy may lead to the creation of an excess of fat cells, which remain in the body throughout life and may predispose a person to be overweight. Weight gains during infancy are associated with weight at age 6. Other research shows an association between obesity after age 6 and adult obesity, suggesting that obesity in babies ultimately may be found to be associated with adult weight problems. A clear link between overweight babies and overweight adults, however, has not yet been found (Carnell et al., 2013; Murasko, 2015; Mallan et al., 2016).

Although the evidence linking infant obesity to adult obesity is inconclusive, it's plain that the old view that "a fat baby is a healthy baby" may well be incorrect. Indeed, cultural myths about food clearly lead to overfeeding. But other factors are related to obesity in infants. For example, infants delivered via cesarean section are twice as likely to become obese as those born vaginally (Huh et al., 2012).

Obesity in Adolescence. Obesity remains the most common nutritional concern in adolescence and adulthood. One in five adolescents is overweight, and 1 in 20 can be classified as obese (more than 20 percent above average body weight). Furthermore, the proportion of females who are classified as obese increases over the course of adolescence (Critser, 2003; Kimm et al., 2003).

Adolescents are obese for the same reasons as younger children, but special concerns with body image may have severe psychological consequences at this age. The potential health consequences of obesity during adolescence are also problematic. Obesity taxes the circulatory system, increasing the risk of high blood pressure and type 2 diabetes. Obese adolescents also have an 80 percent chance of becoming obese adults (Blaine, Rodman, & Newman, 2007; Morrison et al., 2015).

Obesity in Adulthood. Obesity is particularly prevalent in the United States. The world average weight for adults is 137 pounds; in the United States, the average is 180 (Walpole, 2012; see Figure 4-5). As in childhood, obesity is on the rise. From 1998 to 1999, obesity increased 6 percent. Some 12 percent of those age 18 to 29 are obese, and the numbers edge up throughout adulthood (Centers for Disease Control and Prevention, 2010).

The Causes of Obesity. Poor diets contribute to obesity not just in childhood, but in adolescence and adulthood as well. During childhood, many parents provide their children with too few fruits and vegetables and more fats and sweets than recommended. School lunch programs may contribute to the problem, failing to provide nutritious options. Adults continue the trend when they grow up.

Given how energetic children can be, it is surprising that a major factor in childhood obesity is a lack of exercise. School-age children tend to engage in relatively little exercise and are not particularly fit. Around 40 percent of boys 6 to 12 are unable to do more than one pull-up, and a quarter can't do any.

Furthermore, children have shown little or no improvement in the amount of exercise they get, despite national efforts to increase the fitness of school-age children, in part because many schools have reduced the time available for recess and gym classes. From 6 to 18, boys decrease their physical activity by 24 percent and girls by 36 percent (Moore, Gao, & Bradlee, 2003; Sallis & Glanz, 2006; Weiss & Raz, 2006).

For school-age girls, the lack of exercise may reflect a lack of organized sports or good athletic facilities for women. It may be the result of lingering cultural norms that suggest athletic participation is more the realm of boys than girls. Whatever the reason, lack of exercise feeds the increase in obesity.

Another possible answer is that many kids spend a lot of time watching television and playing computer games. Not only do such sedentary activities prevent exercise, but children often snack while viewing TV or surfing the Web (Anderson & Butcher, 2006; Taveras et al., 2006; Goldfield, 2012).

In terms of adolescent obesity, one survey found that by the end of the teenage years, few females get much exercise outside of school physical education classes; the older they get, the less they exercise. This is especially true for older black female

Figure 4-5 First in Obesity

Obesity is particularly prevalent in the United States. The world average weight for adults is 137 pounds; in the United States, the average is 180.

(**Source:** Walpole, 2012.)

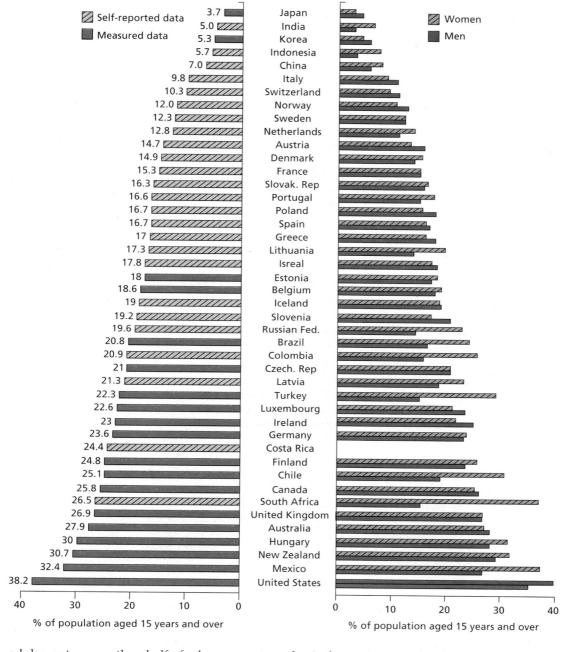

adolescents, more than half of whom report *no* physical exercise outside of school, compared with about a third of white adolescents (Delva, O'Malley, & Johnston, 2006; Nicholson & Browning, 2012).

Genetic and social characteristics as well as diet influence obesity. Particular inherited genes predispose certain children to be overweight. For example, adopted children's weights tend to reflect those of their birth parents rather than their adoptive parents (Whitaker et al., 1997; Skledar et al., 2012).

The Cost of Obesity. People pay the costs of childhood obesity throughout their lives. Obese children are more likely to be overweight as adults and have a greater risk of heart disease, type 2 diabetes, and other diseases. Some scientists believe an epidemic of obesity may be leading to a decline in life span in the United States (Olshansky et al., 2005; Krishnamoorthy, Hart, & Jelalian, 2006; An, 2015).

EATING DISORDERS

At 16, Ariel Porter was pretty, outgoing, and popular, but when a boy she liked kidded her about being "too fat" to take out, she took it seriously. She began to obsess about food, using her mom's food scale to plan her meals compulsively. She kept charts of portion sizes, weights, and calories, cutting her food into tiny morsels and placing minuscule amounts of meat, vegetables, and fruit into an array of zip-up bags labeled with the days of the week and acceptable times of consumption.

In a few months, Ariel went from 101 pounds to 83. Her hips and ribs became clearly visible, and her fingers and knees ached constantly. Her menstrual periods stopped flat, her hair developed split ends, and her fingernails broke easily. Still, Ariel insisted she was overweight, pinching imaginary pockets of fat on her body to prove her point. What finally got her to accept that she had a problem was the return of her older sister from college. At first sight of Ariel, her sister gasped audibly, dropped to her knees, and broke down crying.

This young woman suffers from anorexia nervosa, a severe eating disorder in which people refuse to eat, while denying that their behavior and appearance are out of the ordinary.

anorexia nervosa

a severe eating disorder in which individuals refuse to eat, while denying that their behavior and appearance, which may become skeletal, are out of the ordinary.

A dramatic increase in food consumption fuels the rapid physical growth of adolescence. During the growth spurt, the average girl requires some 2,200 calories a day, and the average boy 2,800. For most adolescents, the major issue is eating a sufficient balance of nutritious foods. However, for adolescents like Ariel Porter, **anorexia nervosa**—a severe eating disorder in which individuals refuse to eat—takes control of their lives. Clearly, Ariel Porter is not alone. The prevalence of serious eating disorders has increased significantly over the past 20 years. Even girls as young as 6 worry about becoming "fat," and some 40 percent of girls ages 9 to 10 are trying to lose weight. Their concern with weight often reflects the U.S. preoccupation with slimness, which permeates the entire society (Greenwood & Pietromonaco, 2004).

Anorexia Nervosa. Anorexia is a dangerous psychological disorder; some 15 to 20 percent of its victims starve themselves to death. It primarily afflicts women between the ages of 12 and 40; intelligent, successful, and attractive white adolescent girls from affluent homes are the most susceptible. Anorexia is also becoming a problem for boys; about 10 percent of victims are male. This percentage is rising and is associated with the use of steroids (Ricciardelli & McCabe, 2004; Crisp et al., 2006; Schecklmann et al., 2012).

Though they eat little, anorexics tend to focus on food. They may shop often, collect cookbooks, talk about food, or cook huge meals for others. They may be incredibly thin, but their body image is so distorted that they see themselves as disgustingly fat and try to lose more weight. Even when they grow skeletal, they cannot see what they have become.

bulimia

an eating disorder characterized by binges on large quantities of food, followed by purges of the food through vomiting or the use of laxatives.

Bulimia. **Bulimia**, another eating disorder, is characterized by *binge eating*, consuming large amounts of food, followed by *purging* through vomiting or the use of laxatives. Bulimics may eat an entire gallon of ice cream or a whole package of tortilla chips, but then feel such powerful guilt and depression that they intentionally rid themselves of the food. The disorder poses real risks. Though a bulimia sufferer's weight remains fairly normal, the constant vomiting and diarrhea of the binge-and-purge cycles may produce a chemical imbalance that triggers heart failure.

Causes of Eating Disorders. Why eating disorders occur is not clear, but several factors are implicated. Dieting often precedes the onset of eating disorders, as society exhorts even normal-weight individuals to be ever thinner. Losing weight may lead to feelings of control and success that encourage more dieting. Girls who mature early and have a higher level of body fat are more susceptible to eating disorders in later adolescence as they try to trim their mature bodies to fit the cultural ideal of a thin, boyish physique. Clinically depressed adolescents are also prone to develop eating disorders later (Wade & Watson, 2012; Thompson-Brenner, 2015).

Some experts suggest that a biological cause lies at the root of both anorexia nervosa and bulimia. Twin studies suggest that genetic components are involved. In addition, hormonal imbalances sometimes are involved (Kaye et al., 2004).

Other explanations emphasize psychological and social factors. As noted earlier, some experts suggest that perfectionist, overdemanding parents or other family difficulties lead to the disorders. Culture also plays a role. For example, anorexia nervosa is found only in cultures that idealize slender female bodies. Because this standard is not widespread, anorexia is not prevalent outside the United States (Harrison & Hefner, 2006; Bodell, Joiner, & Ialongo, 2012). For example, it is nonexistent in Asia, with two exceptions: the upper classes of Japan and Hong Kong, where Western influence is greatest.

Furthermore, anorexia nervosa is a fairly recent disorder. Anorexia nervosa was not seen in the 17th and 18th centuries, when the ideal female body was plump. The increasing number of boys with anorexia in the United States may reflect a male ideal that emphasizes muscles and spurns body fat (Mangweth, Hausmann, & Walch, 2004; Makino et al., 2006; Greenberg, Cwikel, & Mirsky, 2007).

Because anorexia nervosa and bulimia have both biological and environmental causes, treatment typically requires a mix of approaches, for example, both psychological therapy and dietary modifications. In more extreme cases, hospitalization may be necessary (Porzelius, Dinsmore, & Staffelbach, 2001; Stice & Shaw, 2004; Robergeau, Joseph, & Silber, 2006).

Threats to Wellness and Health in Childhood and Adolescence

LO 4.5 Examine threats to health and wellness faced by children and adolescents.

Let's now look at some of the threats to health and wellness that children and adolescents face.

THREATS IN CHILDHOOD. The majority of children in the United States are reasonably healthy. In fact, 88 percent of parents of children 4 or younger report their children are in excellent or very good health (National Health Interview Survey, 2015).

A runny nose due to the common cold is the most frequent—and happily, the most severe—health problem during the preschool years. For example, the average preschooler experiences 7 to 10 colds and other minor respiratory illnesses in each of the years from age 3 to 5 (Kalb, 1997). Although the sniffles and coughs that are the symptoms of such illnesses are certainly distressing to children, the unpleasantness is usually not too severe, and the illnesses usually last only a few days.

Actually, such minor illnesses may offer some unexpected benefits: Not only may they help children build up immunity to more severe illnesses to which they may be exposed in the future, but they also may provide some emotional benefits. Specifically, some researchers argue that minor illness permits children to understand their bodies better. It may also permit them to learn coping skills that will help them deal more effectively with future, more severe diseases. Furthermore, it gives them the ability to understand better what others who are sick are going through. This ability to put oneself in another's shoes, known as empathy, may teach children to be more sympathetic and better caretakers (Notaro, Gelman, & Zimmerman, 2002; Raman & Winer, 2002; Williams & Binnie, 2002).

Behavioral Problems.   Although physical illness is typically a minor problem during the preschool and school years, an increasing number of children are being treated with drugs for emotional disorders, such as depression. In fact, the use of drugs such as antidepressants and stimulants has grown significantly (see Figure 4-6). Although it is not clear why the increase has occurred, some experts believe that parents and teachers may be seeking a quick fix for behavior problems that may, in fact, represent normal difficulties (Pozzi-Monzo, 2012; Muller, 2013; Whalen, Sylvester, & Luby, 2017).

The danger of injuries during the preschool years is in part a result of children's curiosity. It is important to take protective measures to reduce the hazards.

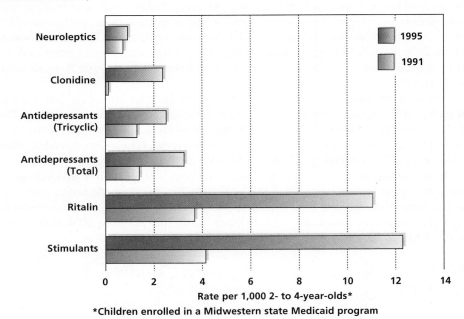

Figure 4-6 Numbers of Preschool Children Taking Medication for Behavioral Problems

Although there is no clear explanation as to why the use of stimulants and antidepressants has increased among children, some experts believe that medication is a quick-fix solution for behavior problems that may in fact represent normal difficulties.
(**Source:** Zito et al., 2000.)

Rate per 1,000 2- to 4-year-olds*
*Children enrolled in a Midwestern state Medicaid program

Accidents. The greatest risk that children face comes from neither illness nor mental health problems but from accidents: Before age 10, children are twice as likely to die from an injury as from an illness. U.S. children have a one in three chance every year of receiving an injury that requires medical attention (Field & Behrman, 2003).

The danger of injuries is in part a result of high levels of physical activity. Combine the physical activity, curiosity, and lack of judgment that characterize this age group, and it is no wonder that preschoolers are accident-prone.

Furthermore, some children are more apt than others to take risks and consequently to be injured. Boys, who are more active than girls and tend to take more risks, have a higher rate of injuries. Economic factors also play a role. Children raised under conditions of poverty in urban areas, whose inner-city neighborhoods may contain more hazards than more affluent areas, are two times more likely to die of injuries than children living in affluence (Morrongiello, Midgett, & Stanton, 2000; Morrongiello & Hogg, 2004; Sengoelge, Hasselberg, & Ormandy, 2014).

Safeguarding the Childhood Environment. Many threats to children can be prevented entirely, or at least limited and lessened. For instance, parents and caregivers can take precautions to prevent injuries, starting by "child-proofing" homes and classrooms with electrical outlet covers and child locks on cabinets. Car seats and bike helmets can help prevent injuries from accidents. Parents and teachers also need to be aware of the dangers from long-term hazards.

For example, lead poisoning is a significant danger for many children. Some 14 million children are at risk for lead poisoning due to exposure to lead, according to the Centers for Disease Control and Prevention. Despite stringent legal restrictions on the amount of lead in paint and gasoline, lead is still found on painted walls and window frames—particularly in older homes—and in ceramics, lead-soldered pipes, automobile and truck exhaust, and even dust and water (Fiedler, 2012; Dozor & Amler, 2013; Herendeen & MacDonald, 2014).

Even tiny amounts of lead in the water drunk by children can lead to permanent health and developmental problems. This point was made apparent, tragically, in the case of Flint, Michigan, where the city water supply became contaminated with lead when water was rerouted through water pipes that allowed lead to leak into the water supply starting in 2014. Residents had to use bottled water until the situation could be remedied (Goodnough & Atkinson, 2016).

Because small amounts of lead can permanently harm children, the U.S. Department of Health and Human Services has called lead poisoning the most severe health threat to children younger than age 6. Exposure to lead has been linked to lower intelligence, problems in verbal and auditory processing, and hyperactivity and distractibility. High lead levels have also been linked to higher levels of antisocial behavior, including aggression and delinquency in school-age children (see Figure 4-7). At yet higher levels of exposure, lead poisoning results in illness and death (Zhang et al., 2013; Earl et al., 2016).

SIDS: An Ill-Understood Killer. For a tiny percentage of infants, the rhythm of sleep is interrupted by a deadly affliction: sudden infant death syndrome. **Sudden infant death syndrome (SIDS)** is a disorder in which seemingly healthy infants die in their sleep. Put to bed for a nap or for the night, an infant simply never wakes up.

SIDS strikes about 1 in 2,500 infants in the United States each year. Although it seems to occur when normal breathing patterns during sleep are interrupted, scientists have been unable to discover why. It is clear that infants don't smother or choke; they die a peaceful death, simply ceasing to breathe.

Although no reliable way to prevent the syndrome has been found, the American Academy of Pediatrics now suggests that babies sleep on their backs rather than on their sides or stomachs—called the back-to-sleep guideline. In addition, they suggest that parents consider giving their babies a pacifier during naps and bedtime (Task Force on Sudden Infant Death Syndrome, 2005). Recent guidelines also make other recommendations for parents, as we discuss in the *From Research to Practice* box.

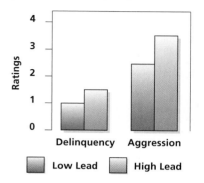

Figure 4-7 The Consequence of Lead Poisoning

High levels of lead have been linked to higher levels of antisocial behavior, including aggression and delinquency, in school-age children. (**Source:** Needleman et al., 1996.)

sudden infant death syndrome (SIDS)
a disorder in which seemingly healthy infants die in their sleep.

From Research to Practice

Sale of Crib Bumpers Banned in Two States

Crib bumpers, or paddings that surround the inside perimeter of the crib, were originally created to fill the wide gaps between slats in older cribs. Beginning in the 1970s, however, safety regulations required that companies make cribs with more closely spaced slats, reducing the chance that an infant's head would become lodged between them. At that point, crib bumpers were no longer needed. However, because many parents considered crib bumpers to be a safety device, they continued to use them even though they were obsolete (Gabler, 2011).

The reality is that in addition to being unnecessary, crib bumpers also pose a physical risk because they can cause infants to die from entrapment, strangulation, and suffocation. Research into accidental infant deaths found that 27 deaths were caused by crib bumpers from 1985 to 2005. Even more recent research continues to document the risk of infant deaths due to crib bumpers. (Thach, Rutherford, & Harris, 2007; Scheers, Woodard, & Thach, 2016).

As a result of research showing these risks, the American Academy of Pediatrics (AAP) has discouraged parents from using crib bumpers as part of their recommendations to encourage a safe sleep environment. Chicago became the first American city to ban the sale of crib bumpers in 2011, and Maryland became the first state to ban

their sale in 2013. In 2017, Ohio also banned the sale of crib bumpers (American Academy of Pediatrics, 2011; Gabler, 2011; George, 2017).

The AAP provides several other recommendations for creating a safe sleep environment. For example, the AAP cautions against having any soft objects in the crib and encourages room sharing (but not bed sharing) for the first 6–12 months (American Academy of Pediatrics, 2016).

Although the rate of SIDS has declined in recent decades, it continues to be the leading cause of death for infants. Also, rates of accidental suffocation and unintentional strangulation have been on the rise. Recommendations from the AAP have the goal of decreasing infant deaths due to factors in the sleep environment. Thus, it is important for parents to talk to pediatricians about safe sleep habits and to seek out additional information provided by the AAP (Centers for Disease Control and Prevention, 2017).

Shared Writing Prompt

Why do some parents ignore the research-backed sleep recommendations from the American Academy of Pediatrics? What can be done to get more parents to follow these recommendations?

Figure 4-8 Declining Rates of SIDS in the United States

SIDS rates have dropped dramatically as parents have become more informed and put babies to sleep on their backs instead of their stomachs.
(**Source:** Centers for Disease Control and Prevention, 2017.)

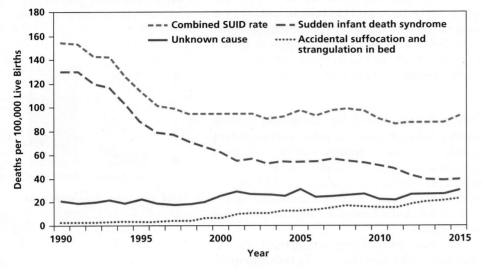

Figure 4-9 Downward Trend in Marijuana Use

According to an annual survey, the proportion of students reporting marijuana use over the past 12 months has decreased since 1999. What might account for the decline in drug use?
(**Source:** Johnston et al., 2015.)

The number of deaths from SIDS has decreased significantly since these guidelines were developed (see Figure 4-8). Still, SIDS is the leading cause of death in children under age 1 (Eastman, 2003; Daley, 2004; Blair, et al., 2006).

THREATS TO ADOLESCENTS. The use of drugs, alcohol, and tobacco and the incidence of sexually transmitted infections may sometimes threaten health during adolescence, usually one of the healthiest periods of life. While the extent of risky behavior is difficult to gauge, preventable problems can be serious problems for adolescents' health and well-being.

Drugs. How common is illegal drug use during adolescence? Very. For example, 1 in 15 high school seniors smokes marijuana on a daily or near-daily basis. Furthermore, marijuana usage has remained at fairly high levels over the past decade, and attitudes about its use have become more positive (Nanda & Konnur, 2006; Tang & Orwin, 2009; Johnston et al., 2015; see Figure 4-9).

Adolescents have a variety of reasons for using drugs. Some use them for the pleasurable experience they supposedly provide. Others use them to try to escape from the pressures of everyday life, however temporarily. Some adolescents try drugs simply for the thrill of doing something illegal.

One of the newest reasons for using drugs is to enhance academic performance. A growing number of high school students are using drugs such as Adderall, an amphetamine prescribed for attention-deficit/hyperactivity disorder. When used illegally, Adderall is assumed to increase focus and is thought to increase the ability to study and allow users to study for long hours (Schwarz, 2012).

The drug use of well-known celebrities also contributes to drug use. Finally, peer pressure plays a role: Adolescents are particularly susceptible to the perceived standards of their peer groups (Nation & Heflinger, 2006; Young et al., 2006).

The use of illegal drugs is dangerous in several respects. For instance, some drugs are addictive. **Addictive drugs** are drugs that produce a biological or psychological dependence in users, leading to increasingly powerful cravings for them.

When drugs produce a biological addiction, their presence in the body becomes so common that the body is unable to function in their absence. Furthermore, addiction causes actual physical—and potentially lingering—changes in the nervous system. In such cases, drug intake no longer may provide a "high" but may be necessary simply to maintain the perception of everyday normalcy (Cami & Farré, 2003; Munzar, Cami, & Farré, 2003).

In addition to physical addiction, drugs also can produce psychological addiction. In such cases, people grow to depend on drugs to cope with the everyday stress of life. If drugs are used as an escape, they may prevent adolescents from confronting—and potentially solving—the problems that led them to drug use in the

addictive drugs

drugs that produce a biological or psychological dependence in users, leading to increasingly powerful cravings for them.

first place. Finally, drugs may be dangerous because even casual use of less hazardous drugs can escalate to more dangerous forms of substance abuse (Teesson & Mewton, 2015).

Alcohol: Use and Abuse.   More than 60 percent of college students have something in common: They've consumed at least one alcoholic drink during the past 30 days. Twelve percent of college students engaged in heavy drinking (five or more drinks on an occasion on five or more occasions per month) in the past month. High school students, too, are drinkers: Some two-thirds of high school seniors report having had an alcoholic drink in the past year, and in some groups—such as male athletes—the proportion of drinkers is even higher (Johnston, et al., 2014).

Binge drinking is a particular problem on college campuses. For men, it is defined as drinking five or more drinks in one sitting; for women, who tend to weigh less and whose bodies absorb alcohol less efficiently, binge drinking is defined as four drinks in one sitting. Surveys find that almost half of male college students and over 40 percent of female college students say they participated in binge drinking during the previous 2 weeks (see Figure 4-10).

Binge drinking affects even those who don't drink or drink very little. Two-thirds of lighter drinkers reported that they had been disturbed by drunken students while sleeping or studying. Around a third had been insulted or humiliated by a drunken student, and 25 percent of women said they had been the target of an unwanted sexual advance by a drunk classmate. Furthermore, brain scans show damaged tissue in teenage binge drinkers compared to non-binge drinkers (Wechsler et al., 2009; Squeglia et al., 2012; Spear, 2014).

Why do adolescents start to drink? There are many reasons. For some—especially male athletes, whose rate of drinking tends to be higher than that of the adolescent general population—drinking is seen as a way of proving they can drink as much as anybody. Others drink for the same reason that some use drugs: It releases inhibitions and tension and reduces stress. Many begin because the conspicuous examples of drunkenness strewn around campus cause them to assume that everyone is drinking heavily, a phenomenon known as the *false consensus effect* (Weitzman, Nelson, & Wechsler, 2003; Dunn et al., 2012; Archimi & Kuntsche, 2014).

For some adolescents, alcohol use becomes a habit that cannot be controlled. **Alcoholics**, those with alcohol problems, learn to depend on alcohol and are unable to control their drinking. They also become increasingly able to tolerate alcohol and therefore need to drink ever-larger amounts of liquor in order to bring about the positive effects they crave. Some drink throughout the day, while others go on binges in which they consume huge quantities of alcohol.

The reasons that some adolescents—or anyone—become alcoholics are not fully understood. Genetics plays a role: Alcoholism runs in families. For some adolescents, alcoholism may be triggered by efforts to deal with the stress that having an alcoholic parent or family member can cause. Yet not all alcoholics have family members with alcohol problems (Berenson, 2005).

Tobacco: The Dangers of Smoking.   Most adolescents are well aware of the dangers of smoking, but many still indulge in it. Recent figures show that, overall, a smaller proportion of adolescents smoke than in prior decades, but the numbers remain substantial; and within certain groups they are increasing. Smoking is on the rise among girls, and in several countries, including Austria, Norway, and Sweden, the proportion of girls who smoke is higher than the proportion of boys. There are racial differences as well: White children and children in lower-socioeconomic-status households are more likely to experiment with cigarettes and to start smoking earlier than African American children and children living in higher socioeconomic status households. Also, significantly more white males of high school age smoke than do African American males in high school, although the differences have narrowed in recent years (Baker, Brandon, & Chassin, 2004; Fergusson et al., 2007; Proctor, Barnett, & Muilenburg, 2012).

Figure 4-10 Binge Drinking Among College Students

For men, binge drinking was defined as consuming five or more drinks in one sitting; for women, the total was four or more. Why is binge drinking popular? (**Source:** Wechsler et al., 2003.)

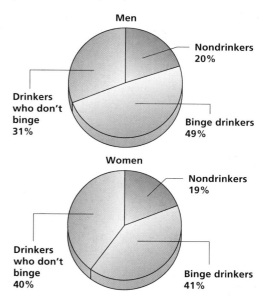

alcoholics

persons with alcohol problems who have learned to depend on alcohol and are unable to control their drinking.

Smoking is becoming a habit that is harder and harder to maintain. There are growing social sanctions against it. And as more places, including schools and places of business, have become "smoke-free," it's becoming more difficult to find a comfortable place to smoke. Even so, a good number of adolescents still smoke, despite knowing the dangers of smoking and of secondhand smoke.

Why do adolescents begin to smoke and maintain the habit? For one thing, adolescents are influenced by advertisements for cigarettes in the media, even if the ads aren't targeting their age group. In addition, the number of images of attractive, popular actors smoking in films viewed by adolescents is increasing. As a result, among at least some adolescents, smoking is viewed as a "cool" activity (Golmier, Chebat, & Gelinas-Chebat, 2007; Sargent, Tanski, & Gibson, 2007).

Cigarettes are also very addicting. Nicotine, the active chemical ingredient of cigarettes, can produce biological and psychological dependency very quickly. Although one or two cigarettes do not usually produce a lifetime smoker, it takes only a little more to start the habit. People who smoke as few as 10 cigarettes early in their lives stand an 80 percent chance of becoming habitual smokers (Stacy et al., 1992; Haberstick et al., 2007).

One of the newest trends in smoking is the use of *e-cigarettes,* battery-powered cigarette-shaped devices that deliver nicotine that is vaporized to form a mist. Although they appear to be less harmful than traditional cigarettes, we still don't know their long-term effects, and the U.S. government has sought to regulate their sale (Tavernise, 2014; Hecht et al., 2015).

Despite their potential dangers, they have become increasingly popular. Some 13 percent of high school students used e-cigarettes in 2014, and the number of users appears to be increasing. At the same time, use of traditional tobacco cigarettes declined significantly among high school students, suggesting that e-cigarette use might be a substitute for traditional cigarettes (Gray, 2013; Tavernise, 2013; Centers for Disease Control and Prevention, 2015).

Sexually Transmitted Infections

When her doctor informed her that she had AIDS, Cheryl Mundt, age 17, thought immediately of her first boyfriend. He had broken up with her a year ago without any explanation, and Cheryl could never contact him afterward. Now she was faced with having to tell her new boyfriend about her condition, and she wasn't sure what his reaction would be. She only knew that she had to tell him right away, whatever the consequences.

Cheryl Mundt was not alone: *Acquired immunodeficiency syndrome,* or *AIDS,* is one of the leading causes of death among young people worldwide. AIDS has no cure and ultimately brings death to those who are infected with the human immunodeficiency virus (HIV) that produces the disease.

Because AIDS is spread primarily through sexual contact, it is classified as a **sexually transmitted infection (STI)**. Although it began as a problem that primarily affected gay men, it has spread to other populations, including heterosexuals and intravenous drug users. Minorities have been particularly hard hit: African Americans and Hispanics account for 70 percent of new AIDS cases, and African American males have almost eight times the prevalence of AIDS as white males. Already, over 20 million people have died due to AIDS worldwide, and the number of people living with the disease numbers almost 34 million worldwide (Centers for Disease Control and Prevention, 2006; UNAIDS, 2011).

Although AIDS is the deadliest of sexually transmitted infections, there are a number of other STIs that are far more common (see Figure 4-11). In fact, one out of four adolescents contracts an STI before graduating from high school. Overall, around 2.5 million teenagers contract an STI, such as the ones listed in the figure (Weinstock, Berman, & Cates, 2004).

The most common STI is *human papilloma virus (HPV).* HPV can be transmitted through genital contact without intercourse. Most infections do not have symptoms, but HPV can produce genital warts and in some cases lead to cervical cancer. A vaccine

sexually transmitted infection (STI)

a disease that is spread through sexual contact.

that protects against some kinds of HPV is now available. The U.S. Centers for Disease Control and Prevention recommends it be routinely administered to girls and boys ages 11 to 12—a recommendation that has provoked considerable political reaction (Friedman et al., 2006; Kahn, 2007; Schwarz et al., 2012).

Another common STI is *trichomoniasis*, an infection in the vagina or penis, which is caused by a parasite. Initially without symptoms, it can eventually cause a painful discharge. *Chlamydia*, a bacterial infection, initially has few symptoms, but later it causes burning urination and a discharge from the penis or vagina. It can lead to pelvic inflammation and even to sterility. Chlamydial infections can be treated successfully with antibiotics (Fayers et al., 2003).

Genital herpes is a virus not unlike the cold sores that sometimes appear around the mouth. The first symptoms of herpes are often small blisters or sores around the genitals, which may break open and become quite painful. Although the sores may heal after a few weeks, the infection often recurs after an interval, and the cycle repeats itself. When the sores reappear, the infection, for which there is no cure, is contagious.

Gonorrhea and *syphilis* are the STIs that have been recognized for the longest time; cases were recorded by ancient historians. Until the advent of antibiotics, both infections were deadly. However, today both can be treated quite effectively.

Contracting an STI is not only an immediate problem during adolescence, but could become a problem later in life, too. Some infections increase the chances of future infertility and cancer.

Short of abstinence, there is no certain way to avoid STIs. Even when adolescents have been exposed to substantial sex education, the use of safer sex practices is far from universal because teens are prone to feel invulnerable and are therefore more likely to engage in risky behavior. This is particularly true when adolescents perceive that their partner is "safe"—someone they know well and with whom they are involved in a relatively long-term relationship (Lefkowitz, Sigman, & Kit-fong Au, 2000; Tinsley, Lees, & Sumartojo, 2004).

Unfortunately, unless an individual knows the complete sexual history and STI status of a partner, unprotected sex remains a risky business. And learning a partner's complete sexual history is difficult. Not only is it embarrassing to ask, but partners may not be accurate reporters, whether from ignorance of their own exposure, embarrassment, a sense of privacy, or simply forgetfulness. As a result, STIs remain a significant problem.

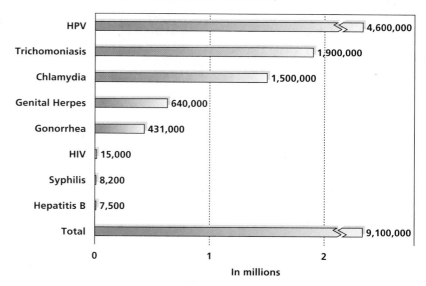

Figure 4-11 Sexually Transmitted Infections (STIS) Among Adolescents

Why are adolescents in particular danger of contracting an STI?

(**Source:** Guttmacher Institute, 2004; Weinstock, Berman, & Cates, 2006.)

The Health Concerns of Adulthood

LO 4.6   Discuss the general health concerns of adults.

We've discussed the particular health concerns related to childhood and adolescents. Although most young and middle-aged adults are healthy in these years, changes do occur. Let's look at some factors relating to health for adults as they age.

HEIGHT, WEIGHT, AND STRENGTH.   Most people reach their maximum height in their 20s and remain close to that height until around 55. People then begin a "settling" process in which the bones attached to the spinal column become less dense. Although the loss of height is very slow, women average a 2-inch decline and men a 1-inch decline over the rest of the life span (Rossman, 1977).

osteoporosis

a condition in which the bones become brittle, fragile, and thin, often brought about by a lack of calcium in the diet.

Women are more prone to this decline because they are at greater risk of osteoporosis. **Osteoporosis**, a condition in which the bones become brittle, fragile, and thin, is often caused by a lack of calcium in the diet. Although it has a genetic component, osteoporosis is one aspect of aging that can be affected by lifestyle choices. Women—and men—can reduce the risk of osteoporosis by eating a calcium-rich diet (calcium is found in milk, yogurt, cheese, and other dairy products) and by exercising regularly (Alvarez-Leon, Roman-Vinas, & Serra-Majem, 2006; Prentice et al., 2006; Azari & Gupta, 2015).

Body fat tends to increase in middle adulthood. Even those who have always been slim may begin to gain weight. Because height is not increasing, and actually may be declining, these gains increase the incidence of obesity.

This weight gain can often be avoided. As we'll see later, lifestyle choices play a major role. People who exercise regularly tend to avoid obesity, as do those who live in cultures where life is more active than it is in many Western cultures.

Declines in strength accompany height and weight changes. Strength gradually decreases, particularly in the back and leg muscles. By age 60, people average a 10 percent loss of their maximum strength. Still, such a loss is relatively minor, and most people are easily able to compensate.

HEALTH. Health concerns become increasingly important to people as they age. Surveys show that not only are adults worried about specific health issues (such as obesity and cancer), but they are even more concerned about access to health care and its cost (Jones, 2008; see Figure 4-12).

Adults in their 20s and 30s stand a higher risk of dying from accidents, primarily car accidents, than from most other causes. But there are other killers: Among the leading sources of death for people 25 to 34 are AIDS, cancer, heart disease, and suicide. Amid the grim statistics of mortality, age 35 represents a significant milestone. It is at that point that illness and disease overtake accidents as the leading cause of death—the first time this is true since infancy.

For most people, however, midlife is a period of health. According to census figures, the vast majority of middle-aged adults report no chronic health difficulties and face no limitations on their activities. In fact, adults are less susceptible to colds and other minor illnesses than they were as children, and they recover quickly from those that they do come down with.

In some ways health is even better in middle adulthood than in earlier periods of life. People ages 45 to 65 are less likely than younger adults to experience infections, allergies, respiratory diseases, and digestive problems. They may contract fewer of these diseases because they have already experienced them and built up immunities.

Certain chronic diseases do begin to appear in middle adulthood. Arthritis typically begins after age 40, and type 2 diabetes is most likely to occur between ages 50 and 60, particularly in those who are overweight. Hypertension (high blood pressure) is one of the most frequent chronic disorders. Often called the "silent killer" because it is symptomless, hypertension, if left untreated, greatly increases the risk of strokes and heart disease. For such reasons, many preventive and diagnostic medical tests are routinely recommended for midlife adults (see Table 4-3).

The onset of chronic diseases in middle age boosts the death rate above that of earlier periods. Still, death remains rare: Only 3 out of every 100 40-year-olds are expected to die before age 50, and 8 out of every 100 50-year-olds are expected to die before age 60. And the death rate for people between 40 and 60 has declined dramatically over the past

Figure 4-12 Health Worries of Adulthood

During adulthood, health care cost and access are significant concerns—even greater than specific health problems, such as obesity and cancer.
(**Source:** Jones 2008.)

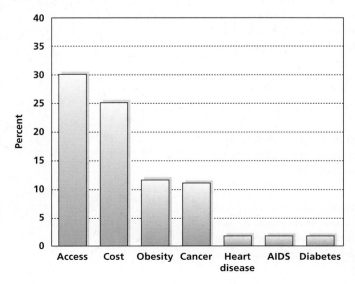

Table 4-3 Adult Preventive Health Care Screening Recommendations

These are general guidelines for healthy adults who have no symptoms of disease.				
Screening	**Description**	**Ages 40–49**	**Ages 50–59**	**Age 60+**
All Adults				
Blood Pressure	Used to detect hypertension, which can lead to heart attack, stroke, or kidney disease	Every 2 years	Every 2 years	Every 2 years; every year if family history of hypertension
Cholesterol—Total/HDL	Used to detect high cholesterol levels, which increase risk of heart disease	All adults should receive total cholesterol screening, HDL cholesterol, LDL cholesterol, and triglycerides AT LEAST ONCE; cardiac risk factors and lipoprotein results will determine frequency of follow-up by your health-care provider		
Eye Examination	Used to determine if glasses required and to check for eye disease	Every 2–4 years; diabetics—every year	Every 2–4 years; diabetics—every year	Every 2–4 years; at age 65 and over, every 1–2 years; diabetics—every year
Flexible Sigmoidoscopy or Double Contrast Barium Enema or Colonoscopy	A procedure using a scope or X-ray to detect cancer of the colon and rectum		Baseline at age 50; every 3–5 years after initial test	Every 3–5 years; age to stop depends on health; follow up normal colonoscopy in 8–10 years
Fecal Occult Blood Screening	Detects unseen blood in stool, which is an early warning sign for colon cancer		Every year	Every year
Rectal Exam (Digital)	Examination of prostate or ovaries to detect cancer		Every year	Every year
Urinalysis Screening	Examination to detect presence of excess protein in urine	Every 5 years	Every 5 years	Every 3–5 years
Immunizations (Shots): Tetanus	Protection against infection after injury	Every 10 years	Every 10 years	Every 10 years
Influenza (Flu)	Protection against the influenza virus	Any person with chronic medical conditions, such as heart, lung, kidney disease, diabetes	Annually, age 50 and over	Annually, age 65 and over
Pneumococcal	Protection against pneumonia			At age 65, then every 6 years
Additional Guidelines for Women				
Breast Self-Exam/Breast Exam by Provider	Examination to detect changes in breast that may indicate cancer	Every month/every year	Every month/every year	Every month/every year
Mammogram	Low-dose X-ray used to locate tumors for early detection of breast cancer	Every year	Every year	Every year
Pap Smear	Test that takes small sample of cells to detect cervical cancer or precancer cells	After 3 normal tests in a row, screen every 2–3 years unless at special risk	After 3 normal tests in a row, screen every 2–3 years unless at special risk	Women 70 and older with 3 normal tests in a row and no abnormal tests in the 10 years prior to age 70 may cease having Pap test
Pelvic Exam	Examination to detect pelvic abnormality	Every year (if ovaries remain after hysterectomy)	Every year (if ovaries remain after hysterectomy)	Every year (if ovaries remain after hysterectomy)
Additional Guidelines for Men				
Prostate-Specific Antigen	Blood test used to detect cancer of the prostate gland	Positive family history cancer: every year; African Americans: every year	Every year upon doctor's advice	Until age 75, every year upon doctor's advice
Testicular Self-Exam	Examination to detect changes in testicles that may indicate cancer	Every month	Every month	Every month

50 years. It now stands at just half of what it was in the 1940s. There are also cultural variations in health, as we consider next (Smedley & Syme, 2000).

Not all adults fare equally well, however. Lifestyle decisions, such as the use—or abuse—of alcohol, tobacco, or drugs or engaging in unprotected sex can hasten *secondary aging*, physical declines brought about by environmental factors or behavioral choices. In addition, cultural factors play a role in aging.

CULTURAL AND OTHER FACTORS AFFECTING HEALTH. Overall figures for the health of middle-aged adults mask vast individual differences. While most people are healthy, some are beset by a variety of ailments. Genetics plays a role. For instance, hypertension often runs in families. Other factors are important as well.

SES. Socioeconomic status (SES) is a significant factor affecting the health of adults. For whites and African Americans of the same SES level, the death rate for African Americans is lower than for whites. Members of lower-income families of any race, however, are more likely to experience a disabling illness. There are many reasons for this. People in lower-SES households are more apt to work in dangerous occupations, such as mining or construction work. Lower-income people also often have inferior or no health care coverage. The crime rates and environmental pollutants are generally higher in lower-income neighborhoods. A higher incidence of accidents and health hazards, and thus a higher death rate, are linked to lower levels of income (Daly, Boyce, & Wood, 2015).

Gender. Gender also makes a difference. Men in midlife are more apt to die than women of the same age (e.g., in automobile accidents), a trend that holds true from birth.

Still, the incidence of illness among women is higher than among men. Women are more susceptible to minor, short-term illness and chronic but non-life-threatening diseases such as migraine headaches, whereas men are more susceptible to serious illnesses such as heart disease. Fewer women smoke than men, which reduces their risk for cancer and heart disease; women drink less alcohol than men, which lowers the incidence of cirrhosis of the liver and auto accidents; and they work at less dangerous jobs.

Another reason for the higher rate of illness in women may be that more medical research targets men and the disorders they suffer. The vast majority of medical research money goes to preventing life-threatening diseases faced mostly by men rather than to chronic conditions such as heart disease that may cause disability and suffering but not necessarily death. Typically, research on diseases that strike both men and women focuses on men as subjects rather than women. This bias is now being addressed in initiatives by the U.S. National Institutes of Health, but the historical pattern has been one of gender discrimination by a male-dominated research community (Vidaver et al., 2000).

Race and Violence. Another major cause of death is violence. The murder rate is significantly higher in the United States than in any other developed country (see Figure 4-13). The U.S. murder rate of 4.5 per 100,000 men is more than nine times greater than that of Japan (Smith-Rosenberg, 2010).

Murder rates also depend significantly on racial factors. African Americans have twice the death rate of Caucasians, and minorities in general have a higher likelihood of dying through homicide than the Caucasian majority. In fact, whereas murder is the fifth most frequent cause of death for young adult white Americans, it is the most likely cause of death for African Americans, and it is a significant factor for Hispanic Americans. In some areas of the country, a young black male has a higher probability of dying violently than a soldier in the Iraq War

Figure 4-13 Tracking Murder

The murder rate is far higher in the United States than in many other developed countries. What features of U.S. society contribute to this state of affairs?
(**Source:** Based on UNDOC, 2013.)

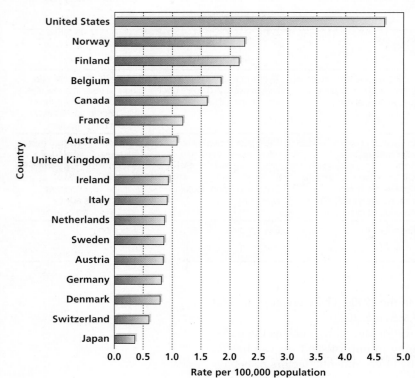

Developmental Diversity and Your Life

How Cultural Beliefs Influence Health and Health Care

Manolita recently suffered a heart attack. She was advised by her doctor to change her eating and activity habits or face the risk of another life-threatening heart attack. During the period that followed, Manolita dramatically changed her eating and activity habits. She also began going to church and praying extensively. After a recent checkup, Manolita is in the best shape of her life. What are some of the reasons for Manolita's amazing recovery? (Murguia, Peterson, & Zea, 1997, p. 16)

After reading this passage, would you conclude that Manolita recovered her health because (a) she changed her eating and activity habits, (b) she became a better person, (c) God was testing her faith, or (d) her doctor prescribed the correct changes?

When asked this question in a survey, more than two-thirds of Latino immigrants from Central America, South America, or the Caribbean believed that "God was testing her faith" had a moderate or great effect on her recovery, although most also agreed that a change in eating and activity habits was important.

According to psychologists Alejandro Murguia, Rolf Peterson, and Maria Zea (1997), who conducted the survey, cultural health beliefs, along with demographic and psychological barriers, can affect the use of physicians and medical care. They suggest that Latinos are more likely than non-Hispanic whites to believe in supernatural causes of illness, which may explain why Latinos are the least likely of any Western ethnic group to seek the help of a physician when they are ill.

Health-care providers need to take cultural beliefs into account when treating members of different cultural groups. For example, if a patient believes that the source of his or her illness is a spell cast by a jealous romantic rival, the patient may not comply with medical regimens that ignore that perceived source. To provide effective health care, then, health-care providers must be sensitive to such cultural health beliefs.

had. Overall, the murder rate for African Americans is four times the national average (Sugarmann, 2014).

Cultural factors also influence younger adults' lifestyles and health-related behavior, as we examine in the *Developmental Diversity and Your Life* box.

CORONARY HEART DISEASE. We've discussed a number of factors that affect the health of middle-aged adults. However, more men die in middle age from heart and circulatory system diseases than from any other cause. Women are less vulnerable, but they are not immune. Each year such diseases kill around 200,000 people under age 65, and they are responsible for more loss of work and disability days due to hospitalization than any other cause.

Although heart and circulatory diseases are a major problem, some people have a much lower risk than others. The death rate in some countries, such as Japan, is only a quarter the rate in the United States. A few other countries have a considerably higher death rate. Why?

The answer is both genetics and environment. Some people seem genetically predisposed to heart disease. If a person's parents suffered from it, the likelihood is greater that she or he will too. Similarly, sex and age are risk factors: Men are more likely to suffer from heart disease, and the risk rises as people age.

Environment and lifestyle choices are also important. Cigarette smoking, a diet high in fats and cholesterol, and a lack of physical exercise all increase the risk of heart disease. Such factors may explain country-to-country variations in the rate of heart disease. For example, the death rate from heart disease in Japan is relatively low and may be due to differences in diet: The typical Japanese diet is much lower in fat than it is in the United States (De Meersman & Stein, 2007; Scarborough et al., 2012; Platt et al., 2014).

Diet is not the only factor. Psychological factors—particularly how stress is perceived and experienced—appear to be related to heart disease. For instance, a set of personality characteristics, known as Type A behavior, appears to be a factor in the development of coronary heart disease. Consider the following vignette:

> *It was a normal exercise session for Jerome Yanger. Up at 5:30 a.m., he climbed onto his exercise bike and began vigorously peddling, hoping to meet, and exceed, his average speed of 14 miles per hour. Stationed in front of the television, he used the remote control to tune to the morning business news. Occasionally glancing up at the television, he began reading a report he had begun the night before, silently cursing at some of the poor sales figures he was seeing. By the time his half-hour of exercise was over, he had finished the report, signed a few letters his administrative assistant had typed for him, and left two voicemail messages for some colleagues.*

Most of us would be ready for a nap after such a packed half-hour. For Jerome Yanger, however, it was routine: He always tried to multitask, thinking it more efficient. Developmentalists might see it as symptomatic of the Type A behavior pattern, which puts Jerome at risk for coronary heart disease.

Type A behavior pattern
behavior characterized by competitiveness, impatience, and a tendency toward frustration and hostility.

The **Type A behavior pattern** is characterized by competitiveness, impatience, and a tendency toward frustration and hostility. Type A people are extremely ambitious, and they engage in *polyphasic activities*—multiple activities carried out simultaneously. They are the true multitaskers whom you see talking on their phones while working on their laptop computers while riding the commuter train—and eating breakfast. Easily angered, they become both verbally and nonverbally hostile if prevented from reaching their goals.

Type B behavior pattern
behavior characterized by non-competitiveness, patience, and a lack of aggression.

In contrast, many people have virtually the opposite characteristics in what is known as the Type B behavior pattern. The **Type B behavior pattern** is characterized by non-competitiveness, patience, and a lack of aggression. In contrast to Type As, Type Bs experience little sense of time urgency, and they are rarely hostile.

Most people are not purely Type A or Type B. In fact, these types represent the ends of a continuum, with most people falling somewhere in between. Still, the majority come close to one or the other of the two categories. These categories become important in midlife because research suggests that the distinction is related to the risk of coronary heart disease. Type A men have twice the rate of coronary heart disease, a greater number of fatal heart attacks, and five times as many heart problems as Type B men (Wielgosz & Nolan, 2000).

THE THREAT OF CANCER. Few diseases are as frightening as cancer, and many middle-aged adults view a cancer diagnosis as a death sentence. Although the reality is different—many forms of cancer respond well to medical treatment, and 40 percent of those diagnosed are still alive 5 years later—the disease raises many fears. And there is no denying that cancer is the second-leading cause of death in the United States (Smedley & Syme, 2000).

The precise trigger for cancer is still not known, but the process by which it spreads is clear. Certain cells in the body begin to multiply rapidly and uncontrollably. As they increase in number, these cells form tumors. Unimpeded, they draw nutrients from healthy cells and body tissue. Eventually, they destroy the body's ability to function.

Like heart disease, cancer is associated with a variety of genetic and environmental risk factors. Some cancers have clear genetic components. For example, a family history of breast cancer—the most common cause of cancer death among women—raises the risk for a woman.

Several environmental and behavioral factors are also related to the risk of cancer. Poor nutrition, smoking, alcohol use, exposure to sunlight, exposure to radiation, and particular occupational hazards (such as exposure to certain chemicals or asbestos) are all known to increase the chances of developing cancer.

After a diagnosis, several forms of treatment are possible, depending on the type of cancer. One treatment is *radiation therapy*, in which radiation targets the tumor in an attempt to destroy it. Patients undergoing *chemotherapy* ingest controlled doses of toxic substances meant to poison the tumor. Finally, surgery is used to remove the tumor (and often the surrounding tissue). The form of treatment is determined by how far the cancer has spread when it is first identified.

Because early detection improves a patient's chances, diagnostic techniques that help identify the first signs of cancer are of great importance. This is especially true in middle adulthood, when the risk of certain cancers increases.

Physicians urge that women do routine breast exams and men regularly check their testicles for signs of cancer. Mammograms provide internal scans of women's breasts to help identify early-stage cancer. However, at what age women should begin to routinely have the procedure has been controversial. Cancer of the prostate gland, the most common type of cancer in men, can be detected by routine rectal exams and by a blood test that identifies prostate-specific antigen (PSA).

Health Risks Facing Older Adults

LO 4.7   Describe the health risks confronting older adults.

Despite common misconceptions, most people are healthy in adulthood, and most of the illnesses and diseases found in late adulthood are not peculiar to old age; people of all ages suffer from cancer and heart disease, for instance. However, the *incidence* of these and many other diseases rises with age, raising the odds that an elderly person will be ill during the period. Moreover, whereas younger people can readily rebound from a variety of health problems, older persons bounce back more slowly from illnesses. And ultimately, the illness may get the best of an older person, preventing a full recovery.

COMMON PHYSICAL DISORDERS IN OLDER ADULTS.   The leading causes of death in older adults are heart disease, cancer, and stroke. In fact, close to three-quarters of people in late adulthood die from these problems. Because aging is associated with a weakening of the body's immune system, older adults are also more susceptible to infectious diseases (Feinberg, 2000).

In addition to their risk of fatal diseases and conditions, most older people have at least one chronic, long-term condition. For instance, *arthritis*, an inflammation of one or more joints, afflicts roughly half of older people. Arthritis can cause painful swelling in various parts of the body, and it can be disabling. Sufferers can find themselves unable to carry out the simplest of everyday activities, such as unscrewing the cap of a jar of food or turning a key in a lock. Although aspirin and other drugs can relieve some of the swelling and reduce the pain, the condition cannot be cured (Sun, Wu, & Kalunian, 2007).

Around one-third of older people have *hypertension*, or high blood pressure. Many people who have high blood pressure are unaware of their condition because it does not have any symptoms, which makes it more dangerous. Over time, higher tension within the circulatory system can result in deterioration of the blood vessels and heart, and can raise the risk of cerebrovascular disease, or stroke, if it is not treated (Wiggins & Uwaydat, 2006).

PSYCHOLOGICAL AND MENTAL DISORDERS IN OLDER ADULTS.   Some 15 to 25 percent of those over age 65 are thought to show some symptoms of psychological disorder, although this represents a lower prevalence rate than in younger adults. The behavioral symptoms related to these disorders are sometimes different in those over 65 than those displayed by younger adults (Whitbourne, 2001).

One of the more prevalent problems is major depression, which is characterized by feelings of intense sadness, pessimism, and hopelessness. One obvious reason older people may become depressed is their experience of cumulative losses with the death of spouses and friends. Their own declining health and physical capabilities, which may make them feel less independent and in control, may also contribute to the prevalence of depression (Menzel, 2008; Vink et al., 2009; Taylor, 2014).

These explanations make sense, but it is not yet entirely clear that depression is a significantly worse problem in late adulthood than it is earlier in life. Some studies suggest that the rate of depression actually may be lower during late adulthood. One reason for this contradictory finding is that there may be two kinds of depression in older adulthood: depression that continues from earlier stages of life and depression that occurs as a result of aging (Gatz, 1997).

It is not unusual for some elderly people to suffer from drug-induced psychological disorders brought about by combinations of drugs they may be taking for various medical conditions. Because of changes in metabolism, a dose of a particular drug that would be appropriate for a 25-year-old might be much too large for a person of 75. The effects of drug interactions can be subtle, and they can manifest themselves in a variety of psychological symptoms, such as drug intoxication or anxiety. Because of these possibilities, older people who take medications must be careful to inform their physicians and pharmacists of every drug they take. They should also avoid medicating themselves with over-the-counter drugs because a combination of nonprescription and prescription drugs may be dangerous, or even deadly.

dementia
the most common mental disorder of the elderly, covering several diseases, each of which includes serious memory loss accompanied by declines in other mental functioning.

The most common mental disorder of elderly people is **dementia**, a broad category of serious memory loss accompanied by declines in other mental functioning, which encompasses a number of diseases. Although dementia has many causes, the symptoms are similar in all cases: declining memory, lessened intellectual abilities, and impaired judgment. The chances of experiencing dementia increase with age. Less than 2 percent of people between 60 and 65 are diagnosed with dementia, but the percentages double for every 5-year period past 65. There are some ethnic differences, too, with African Americans and Hispanics showing higher levels of dementia than Caucasians (Alzheimer's Association, 2017).

The most common form of dementia is Alzheimer's disease.

ALZHEIMER'S DISEASE

Sandra Frye passes around a photo of her father. "He was 75 when this was taken. He looks great and he could still sail back then, but he was already forgetting things like what he'd done yesterday or what he'd eaten for breakfast."

Frye takes part in a support group for family members of Alzheimer's patients. The second picture she shares shows her father 10 years later. "It was sad. He'd start talking to me and his words would jumble. Then he'd forget who I was. He forgot he had a younger brother or that he'd been a pilot in World War II. A year after this photo, he was bedridden. Six months later, he died."

Alzheimer's disease
a progressive brain disorder that produces loss of memory and confusion.

When Sandra Frye's father was diagnosed with **Alzheimer's disease**, he joined the 4.5 million Americans who suffer from this debilitating brain disorder that produces loss of memory and confusion and saps both the physical and mental powers of its victims.

Alzheimer's leads to the deaths of 100,000 people in the United States each year and represents one of the most serious mental health problems faced by the aging population. One in 10 people age 65 and older has Alzheimer's; 19 percent of those age 75 to 84 have the disease, and nearly half of people over age 85 are affected by the disease. Unless a cure is found, some 14 million people will be victims of Alzheimer's by 2050—more than three times the current number (Park et al., 2015; Alzheimer's Association, 2017).

The symptoms of Alzheimer's disease develop gradually. Generally, the first sign is unusual forgetfulness. A person may stop at a grocery store several times during the week, forgetting that he or she has already done the shopping. People may also have trouble recalling particular words during conversations. At first, recent memories are affected, and then older memories fade. Eventually, people with the disease are totally confused, unable to speak intelligibly or to recognize even their closest family and friends. In the final stages of the disease, they lose voluntary control of their muscles and are bedridden. Because victims of the disorder are initially aware that their memories are failing and often understand quite well the future course of the disease, they may suffer from anxiety, fear, and depression—emotions not difficult to understand, given the grim prognosis.

Biologically, Alzheimer's occurs when production of *beta amyloid precursor protein*—a protein that normally helps the production and growth of neurons—goes awry, producing large clumps of cells called plaque that trigger inflammation and deterioration of nerve cells. The brain shrinks, and several areas of the hippocampus and frontal and temporal lobes show deterioration. Furthermore, certain neurons die, which leads to a shortage of various neurotransmitters, such as acetylcholine (Wolfe, 2006; Medeiros et al., 2007; Bredesen, 2009).

Although the physical changes in the brain that produce the symptoms of Alzheimer's are clear, what is not known is what triggers the problem in the first place. Several explanations have been advanced. Genetics clearly plays a role, with some families showing a much higher incidence of Alzheimer's than others. In certain families, half the children appear to inherit the disease from their parents. Furthermore, years before the actual symptoms of Alzheimer's emerge, people who are genetically at high risk for the disease show differences in brain functioning (see Figure 4-14) (Coon et al., 2007; Nelson et al., 2007; Thomas & Fenech, 2007).

Most evidence suggests that Alzheimer's is an inherited disorder, but nongenetic factors such as high blood pressure or diet may increase susceptibility to the disease. In one cross-cultural study, poor black residents in a Nigerian town were less likely to develop Alzheimer's than a comparable sample of African Americans living in the United States. The researchers speculate that variations in diet between the two groups—the residents of Nigeria ate mainly vegetables—might account for the differences in the Alzheimer's rates (Lahiri et al., 2007; Fuso et al., 2012; Roussotte et al., 2014).

Other explanations for the disease have also been investigated. For example, scientists are studying certain kinds of viruses, dysfunctions of the immune system, and hormonal imbalances that may produce the disease. Other studies have found that lower levels of linguistic ability in the early 20s are associated with declines in cognitive capabilities due to Alzheimer's much later in life (Alisky, 2007; Carbone et al., 2014).

As victims lose the ability to feed and clothe themselves, or even to control bladder and bowel functions, they must be cared for 24 hours a day. Because such care is typically impossible for even the most dedicated families, most Alzheimer's victims end their lives in nursing homes. Patients with Alzheimer's make up some two-thirds of residents in nursing homes (Prigerson, 2003).

People who care for the victims of Alzheimer's often become secondary victims of the disease. It is easy to become frustrated, angry, and exhausted by the demands of Alzheimer's patients, whose needs may be overpowering. In addition to the physical chore of providing total care, caregivers face the loss of a loved one, who not only is visibly deteriorating but can act emotionally unstable and even fly into rages. The burdens of caring for a person with Alzheimer's can be overwhelming (Ott, Sanders, & Kelber, 2007; Sanders et al., 2008; Iavarone et al., 2014).

Figure 4-14 A Different Brain?

Brain scans show differences between the brains of those with Alzheimer's disease and those who do not suffer from it.

(Photo Researchers, Inc. / Science Source)

Development in Your Life

Caring for People with Alzheimer's Disease

Alzheimer's disease is one of the most difficult illnesses to deal with, as a friend or loved one progressively deteriorates both mentally and physically. However, several steps can be taken to help both patient and caregiver deal with Alzheimer's.

■ Make patients feel secure in their home environments by keeping them occupied in the everyday tasks of living as long as possible.

■ Provide labels for everyday objects, furnish calendars and detailed but simple lists, and give oral reminders of time and place.

■ Keep clothing simple. Provide clothes with few zippers and buttons, and lay them out in the order in which they should be put on.

■ Put bathing on a schedule. People with Alzheimer's may be afraid of falling and of hot water, and may therefore avoid needed bathing.

- Prevent people with the disease from driving. Although patients often want to continue driving, their accident rate is high—some 20 times higher than average.

- Monitor the use of the telephone. Alzheimer's patients who answer the phone have been victimized by agreeing to requests of telephone salespeople and investment counselors.

- Provide opportunities for exercise, such as a daily walk. This prevents muscle deterioration and stiffness.

- Caregivers should remember to take time off. Although caring for an Alzheimer's patient can be a full-time chore, caregivers need to lead their own lives. Seek out support from community service organizations.

- Call or write the Alzheimer's Association, which can provide support and information. The association can be reached at 225 N. Michigan Ave. Fl. 17, Chicago, IL 60601-7633; Tel. 1-800-272-3900; http://www.alz.org.

Module 4.2 Review

LO 4.4 **Analyze the importance of proper nutrition to human development.**

Adequate nutrition is important for physical, social, and cognitive development. Malnutrition can slow growth, affect intellectual performance, and cause diseases. Obesity is a common problem in the United States across the life span. Adolescents are particularly susceptible to eating disorders, especially anorexia nervosa and bulimia.

LO 4.5 **Examine threats to health and wellness faced by children and adolescents.**

Children are relatively healthy, with the greatest health risk being accidents. Adolescents also tend to be healthy but are susceptible to unhealthy, addictive habits (e.g., use of drugs, alcohol, or tobacco) and sexually transmitted infections.

LO 4.6 **Discuss the general health concerns of adults.**

Young adults are generally as fit and healthy as they will ever be. Accidents present the greatest risk of death, and violence is a significant risk, particularly for nonwhite males. Heart disease is a risk for middle-aged adults. Both genetic and environmental factors contribute to heart disease, including the Type A behavior pattern. The incidence of cancer begins to be significant in middle adulthood. Therapies such as radiation therapy, chemotherapy, and surgery can successfully treat cancer.

LO 4.7 **Describe the health risks confronting older adults.**

Although most older people are healthy, the incidence of some serious diseases rises in old age, and most people have at least one chronic ailment, such as depression, before they die. The most prevalent and damaging brain disorder among older people is Alzheimer's disease.

Journal Writing Prompt

Applying Lifespan Development: How can societal and environmental influences contribute to the emergence of an eating disorder?

MODULE 4.3

PROMOTING HEALTH AND WELLNESS

Juana Sandino sighed as she sat down to nurse the baby—again. She had fed 4-week-old Juan about every hour today, and he still seemed hungry. Some days, it seemed like all she did was breast-feed her baby. "Well, he must be going through a growth spurt," she decided, as she settled into her favorite rocking chair and put the baby to her nipple.

Good Diet: The Foundation of Wellness

LO 4.8 **Describe how good nutrition in childhood promotes wellness later in life.**

As we saw in the previous module, malnutrition has serious and long-lasting consequences. The opposite can also be true: The habits formed in infancy support to a surprising extent the robust physical growth that occurs during infancy and continues—now rapidly, now slowly—through the life span.

Without proper nutrition, infants cannot reach their physical potential, and they may suffer cognitive and social consequences as well. Although there are vast individual differences in what constitutes appropriate nutrition—infants differ in terms of growth rates, body composition, metabolism, and activity levels—some broad guidelines do hold. In general, infants should consume about 50 calories per day for each pound they weigh—an allotment that is twice the suggested caloric intake for adults (Costello et al., 2003; Gregory, 2005; Skinner et al., 2004).

Typically, though, it's not necessary to count calories for infants. Most infants regulate their caloric intake quite effectively on their own. If they are allowed to consume as much as they seem to want and are not pressured to eat more, they will do fine.

BREAST OR BOTTLE? Fifty years ago, if a mother asked her pediatrician whether breastfeeding or bottle-feeding was better, she would have received a simple and clear-cut answer: Bottle-feeding was the preferred method. Starting around the 1940s, the general belief among child-care experts was that breastfeeding was an obsolete method that put children unnecessarily at risk.

With bottle-feeding, the argument went, parents could keep track of the amount of milk their baby was receiving and could thereby ensure that the child was taking in sufficient nutrients. In contrast, mothers who breast-fed their babies could never be certain just how much milk their infants were getting. Use of the bottle was also supposed to help mothers keep their feedings to a rigid schedule of one bottle every 4 hours, the recommended procedure at that time.

Today a mother would get a very different answer to the same question. Child-care authorities agree: For the first 12 months of life, there is no better food for an infant than breast milk. Breast milk not only contains all the nutrients necessary for growth, but it also seems to offer some immunity to a variety of childhood diseases, such as respiratory illnesses, ear infections, diarrhea, and allergies. Breastfeeding for as little as 4 months reduces infections by an average of 45 percent, and the reduction in infection is 65 percent lower for 6 months of breastfeeding compared to formula-fed babies. Breast milk is more easily digested than cow's milk or formula, and it is convenient for the mother to dispense. There is even some evidence that breast milk may enhance cognitive growth, leading to high adult intelligence (Duijts et al., 2010; Julvez et al., 2014; Rogers & Blissett, 2017).

Breast milk also contains complex carbohydrates called *oligosaccharides* (which are also found in such foods as asparagus, onions, wheat, and barley). Humans can't digest oligosaccharides, but bacteria can, pointing to the role of breast milk in nurturing the bacteria that normally thrive in the human gut and provide important protective functions. It turns out that these oligosaccharides are very specific: Only one species of bacterium, called *B. longum* bv. *infantis*, has all the enzymes necessary to digest them. This enables that species of bacteria to dominate any others inhabiting the infant gut, crowding out other, potentially harmful, species of bacteria. In short, the oligosaccharides found in breast milk may provide long-term health benefits and allow the avoidance of future problems such as diabetes and immune system difficulties (Vinukonda et al., 2016; Qiu et al., 2016).

Breastfeeding is not a cure-all for infant nutrition and health, and the millions of individuals who have been raised on formula should not be concerned that they have suffered irreparable harm. But it does continue to be clear that the popular slogan used by groups advocating the use of breastfeeding is right on target: "Breast is best" (Birch et al., 2000; Rabin, 2006; Ludlow et al., 2012).

SOLID FOODS: WHEN AND WHAT? Although pediatricians agree that breast milk is the ideal initial food, at some point infants require more nutrients than breast milk alone can provide. Although the American Academy of Pediatrics and the American Academy of Family Physicians recommend exclusive breastfeeding for about 6 months, followed by continued breastfeeding for 1 year or longer, solid foods can begin to be introduced after 6 months (American Academy of Pediatrics, 2013).

Solid foods are introduced into an infant's diet gradually, one at a time, in order to permit monitoring of preferences and allergies. Most often cereal comes first, followed

Breast or bottle? Although infants receive adequate nourishment from breast- or bottle-feeding, most authorities agree that "breast is best."

by strained fruits. Vegetables and other foods typically are introduced next, although the order varies significantly from one infant to another.

The timing of *weaning*, the gradual cessation of breast- or bottle-feeding, varies greatly. In developed countries such as the United States, weaning frequently occurs as early as 3 or 4 months. Some mothers, however, continue breastfeeding for 2 or 3 years. The American Academy of Pediatrics recommends that infants be fed breast milk for the first 12 months (American Academy of Pediatrics, 2013; Lee, 2017).

Because the rate of growth is slower than during infancy, preschoolers need less food, which may cause parents to worry. However, children tend to be adept at eating enough if they are provided with nutritious meals. In fact, anxiously encouraging children to eat more than they want may lead to obesity.

EFFECTS OF DIET. In general, popular wisdom holds that the more a baby eats, the stronger and healthier he or she will become. Although there is a relationship between size and nutrition, it is not all positive. Diet has many effects, and size isn't the only area affected. For instance, diet is related to social and emotional functioning at school age. Children who receive more nutrients are more involved with their peers, show more positive emotion, and have less anxiety than children with less adequate nutrition.

Diet is also linked to cognitive performance. For example, in one study, children in Kenya who were well nourished performed better on a test of verbal abilities and other cognitive measures than those who had mild to moderate undernutrition. As noted earlier, malnutrition may influence cognitive development by dampening children's curiosity, responsiveness, and motivation to learn (Brown & Pollitt, 1996; Wachs, 2002; Grigorenko, 2003).

EATING THE RIGHT FOODS. As we discussed earlier, obesity is a major problem across the life span, often driven by nutritional issues. How do parents ensure that their children have good nutrition without turning mealtimes into a tense, adversarial situation? In most cases, the best strategy is to make sure that a variety of foods, low in fat and high in nutritional content, is available. Because of the danger of iron deficiency anemia, foods that have a relatively high iron content are particularly important. Iron deficiency anemia is one of the most prevalent nutritional problems in developed countries, such as the United States. High-iron foods include dark green vegetables (such as broccoli), whole grains, and some kinds of meat such as lean beef. It is also important to avoid foods with high sodium content and to include foods with low fat content (Jalonick, 2011).

Because preschool children, like adults, will not find all foods equally appealing, children should be given the opportunity to develop their own natural preferences. As long as their overall diet is adequate, no single food is indispensable. Exposing children to a wide variety of foods by encouraging them to take just one bite of new foods is a relatively low-stress way of expanding children's diets (Busick et al., 2008; Struempler et al., 2014).

In behavior called the *just-right phenomenon,* some preschool children develop strong rituals and routines about the kinds of foods they will eat. They may only eat certain foods that are prepared in a particular way and presented to them in a particular manner on a plate. In adults, such rigidity would be a sign of a psychological disorder, but it is normal in young children. Almost all preschoolers eventually outgrow it (Curtin et al., 2015).

Exercise: Use It or Lose It?

LO 4.9   Explain how exercise can affect health and longevity.

As we've seen throughout this chapter, when it comes to health throughout the life span, lifestyle choices matter. Especially important is regular exercise, which tends to make people feel stronger and more able to compensate for any losses.

Only a small time commitment is enough to yield significant health benefits. According to the American College of Sports Medicine and the Centers for Disease Control and Prevention, people should accumulate at least 30 minutes of moderate physical activity at least 5 days a week. Exercise time can be continuous or in bouts

Figure 4-15 The Benefits of Exercise

Many benefits accrue from maintaining a high level of physical activity throughout life.
(**Source:** DiGiovanna, 1994.)

The Advantages of Exercise

Muscle System

Slower decline in energy molecules, muscle cell thickness, number of muscle cells, muscle thickness, muscle mass, muscle strength, blood supply, speed of movement, stamina

Slower increase in fat and fibers, reaction time, recovery time, development of muscle soreness

Nervous System

Slower decline in processing impulses by the central nervous system

Slower increase in variations in speed of motor neuron impulses

Circulatory System

Maintenance of lower levels of LDLs and higher HDL/cholesterol and HDL/LDL ratios

Decreased risk of high blood pressure, atherosclerosis, heart attack, stroke

Skeletal System

Slower decline in bone minerals

Decreased risk of fractures and osteoporosis

Psychological Benefits

Enhanced mood

Feelings of well-being

Reduces stress

of at least 10 minutes, as long as the daily total reaches 30 minutes. Moderate activity includes walking briskly at 3 to 4 mph, biking at speeds up to 10 mph, golfing while carrying or pulling clubs, fishing by casting from shore, playing ping-pong, or canoeing at 2 to 4 mph. Even common household chores, such as weeding, vacuuming, and mowing with a power mower, provide moderate exercise (Geirsdottir et al., 2015).

The advantages of exercise are many (see Figure 4-15). Exercise increases cardiovascular fitness, meaning that the heart and circulatory system operate more efficiently. Furthermore, lung capacity increases, raising endurance. Muscles become stronger, and the body is more flexible and maneuverable. The range of movement is greater, and the muscles, tendons, and ligaments are more elastic. Moreover, exercise helps reduce *osteoporosis*, the thinning of the bones, in later life.

Figure 4-16 The Result of Fitness: Longevity

The greater the fitness level, as measured by adherence to the Health and Human Services (HHS) guidelines met, the higher the gains in life expectancy due to physical activity.

(**Source:** National Institutes of Health, 2012.)

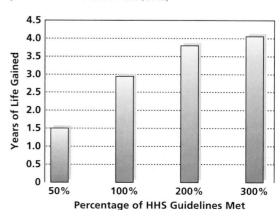

From *an educator's* perspective

Can people be taught the lifelong advantages of regular exercise? Should school-based physical education programs be changed to foster a lifelong commitment to exercise?

Exercise may also optimize the immune response of the body, helping it fight off disease. It may even decrease stress and anxiety and reduce depression. It can provide a sense of control over the body and a feeling of accomplishment (Harris, Cronkite, & Moos, 2006; Wise et al., 2006; Treat-Jacobson, Bronäs, & Salisbury, 2014). Even better is its ultimate reward: It is associated with increased longevity (see Figure 4-16; Stevens et al., 2002).

Neuroscience and Development
Exercise, Depression, and the Brain: Moving Your Way Toward a Better Mood

Has a friend ever encouraged you to go get some exercise when you're feeling blue? If so, they've given you good advice based on neuroscience. There are good reasons to expect that exercise can help people cope with feelings of depression.

In research comparing an exercise-based treatment group to a control group, people in the exercise-based group reported significantly fewer symptoms of depression. Both aerobic exercise (e.g., running) and resistance exercise (e.g., weightlifting) appeared to be effective. These findings have been replicated in several studies (Cooney, Dwan, & Mead, 2014).

One reason exercise might help with depression has to do with the effect it has on the brain. For example, people with depression tend to have a smaller hippocampus, part of the brain that plays a role in the regulation of stress. Exercise has been shown to increase hippocampal size. Similarly, exercise appears to affect other parts of the brain related to depression as well (Gujral et al., 2017).

So the next time you're feeling down in the dumps, a surprisingly good strategy could be playing basketball with friends, going for a run, or any other activity that gets your blood pumping. Better yet, exercise might be a good way to help prevent depressive symptoms in the first place (Harvey et al., 2017).

■ **Other treatments for depression include medication and cognitive-behavioral therapy. What might be the advantages and disadvantages to recommending exercise for depression instead of one of these other options?**

Sexuality

LO 4.10 Examine the nature of sexuality in later life.

For those who can—or choose to—enjoy it, sex contributes to wellness across the life span, a fact that applies to old age as well as to younger periods of life. Of course, there are some changes in sexual functioning related to age.

Testosterone, the male hormone, declines during adulthood, with some research finding a decrease of approximately 30 to 40 percent from the late 40s to the early 70s. It takes a longer time, and more stimulation, for men to get a full erection. The refractory period—the time following an orgasm during which men are unable to become aroused again—may last as long as a day or even several days.

Women's vaginas become thin and inelastic, and they produce less natural lubrication, making intercourse more difficult (Seidman, 2003). For most women, though, the changes do not reduce sexual pleasure. Those women who do find intercourse less enjoyable can seek help from an increasing array of drugs, such as topical creams and testosterone patches, designed to increase sexual pleasure (Freedman & Ellison, 2004).

Let's look at some of the factors that affect men's and women's sexuality in midlife, and the roles both attitude and prescription drugs can play in alleviating some of the problems commonly associated with this life stage.

THE CLIMACTERIC AND MENOPAUSE

At age 51, Elaine was looking forward to her postmenopausal life. Her youngest child had just left home to study art, and she had recently reduced her work schedule to 30 hours a week. She envisioned the year to come as an opportunity for a "second honeymoon" with her husband, Greg, with no need for contraceptives or fears of becoming pregnant.

Her imagined honeymoon quickly evaporated in a heat wave of hot flashes and night sweats. Though Elaine recognized these as normal symptoms of menopause, she was having to change her clothing three or more times a day. And she was having more headaches. Her doctor prescribed hormone therapy to replace the estrogen she was losing through menopause. As she was not a likely candidate for any of the drug's negative side effects, she took her doctor's recommendation. The hormone therapy eased her symptoms and revitalized her spirits. Four months later, she and Greg booked a month's romantic getaway in Greece.

Women enter a period, around age 45, known as the climacteric, which lasts for 15 to 20 years. The **female climacteric** marks the transition that ends the childbearing years.

The most notable sign of this transition is menopause. **Menopause** is the cessation of menstruation. Menstrual periods begin to occur irregularly and less frequently during a 2-year period starting at around age 47 or 48, although this may begin as early as age 40 or as late as age 60. Menopause is completed when a woman passes a year without a menstrual period.

Menopause is important because it marks the end of a woman's natural fertility (although eggs implanted in a postmenopausal woman can produce a pregnancy). In addition, levels of estrogen and progesterone—the female sex hormones—begin to drop (Schwenkhagen, 2007).

These changes in hormone production may produce a variety of symptoms, although they vary significantly for individuals. One of the most prevalent symptoms is "hot flashes," in which women experience a surge of heat above the waist. A woman may get red and begin to sweat when a hot flash occurs. Afterward, she may feel chilled. Some women have hot flashes several times a day; others, not at all.

During menopause, headaches, feelings of dizziness, heart palpitations, and aching joints are relatively common, though not universal. In one survey, only half of the women reported having hot flashes, and only about one-tenth of all women experienced severe distress during menopause. Many women—perhaps as many as half—have no significant symptoms at all (Ishizuka, Kudo, & Tango, 2008; Levin, 2015; Guérin, Goldfield, & Prud'homme, 2017).

For many women, menopause symptoms may begin a decade before menopause actually occurs. *Perimenopause* describes this period prior to menopause when hormone production begins to change. It is marked by sometimes radical fluctuations in hormone levels, resulting in some of the same symptoms found in menopause (Winterich, 2003; Shea, 2006). For some women, the symptoms of perimenopause and menopause are considerable, and treating these problems can be challenging.

THE PSYCHOLOGICAL CONSEQUENCES OF MENOPAUSE. Traditionally, many people, including experts, believed that menopause was linked directly to depression, anxiety, crying spells, lack of concentration, and irritability. Some researchers estimated that as many as 10 percent of menopausal women suffered severe depression. It was assumed that the physiological changes of menopause caused such problems (Ayers, Forshaw, & Hunter, 2010; DeAngelis, 2010).

From *a health-care provider's* perspective

What cultural factors in the United States might contribute to a woman's negative experience of menopause? How?

Today, most researchers take a different view, regarding menopause as a normal part of aging that does not, by itself, produce psychological symptoms. Some women do experience psychological difficulties, but they do so at other times in life as well (Matthews et al., 2000; Freeman, Sammel, & Liu, 2004; Somerset et al., 2006).

Research shows that a woman's expectations can significantly affect her experience of menopause. Women who expect to have difficulties are more likely to attribute every physical symptom and emotional swing to menopause, while those with more positive attitudes are less apt to do so. A woman's attribution of physical symptoms, then, may affect her perception of menopause—and thus her actual experience of the period (Breheny & Stephens, 2003; Strauss, 2011).

THE MALE CLIMACTERIC. Do men experience the equivalent of menopause? Not really. Lacking anything akin to menstruation, they cannot experience its discontinuation. But men do experience changes in midlife that are referred to as the male climacteric. The **male climacteric** is the period of physical and psychological change in the reproductive system that occurs late in midlife, typically in a man's 50s.

female climacteric
the period that marks the transition from being able to bear children to being unable to do so.

menopause
the cessation of menstruation.

DavidDennisPhotos/Getty Images

While women in some cultures anticipate menopause with dread, Mayan women have no notion of hot flashes, and they generally look forward to the end of their childbearing years.

male climacteric
the period of physical and psychological change relating to the male reproductive system that occurs during late middle age.

Because the changes are gradual, it is hard to pinpoint the exact period of the male climacteric. For instance, despite declines in testosterone levels and sperm count, men are able to father children throughout middle age. And it is no easier for men than women to attribute psychological symptoms to subtle physiological changes.

One physical change that occurs frequently is enlargement of the *prostate gland*. By age 40, about 10 percent of men have enlarged prostates, and the percentage increases to half of all men by age 80. Enlargement of the prostate produces problems with urination, including difficulty starting urination or a need to urinate frequently at night.

Sexual problems also increase as men age. In particular, *erectile dysfunction*, in which men are unable to achieve or maintain an erection, becomes more common. Drugs such as Viagra, Levitra, and Cialis, as well as patches that deliver doses of testosterone, often prove an effective treatment (Abdo et al., 2008; Glina, Cohen, & Vieira, 2014; Wentzell, 2017).

Men, like women, undergo psychological development in middle adulthood, but the extent to which psychological changes are related to reproductive or other physical changes remains an open question.

Wellness in Old Age: Avoiding the Inevitable?

LO 4.11 Explain how wellness can be maintained in old age.

Is getting sick an inevitable part of growing old? Not necessarily. As we'll discuss in this section, whether an older person is ill or well depends less on age than on a variety of factors, including genetic predisposition, past and present environmental factors, and psychological factors.

FACTORS AFFECTING HEALTH IN OLD AGE. Certain diseases, such as cancer and heart disease, have a clear genetic component. Some families have a higher incidence of breast cancer, for instance, than others. At the same time, however, a genetic predisposition does not automatically mean that a person will get a particular illness. People's lifestyles—whether or not they smoke, the nature of their diet, their exposure to cancer-causing agents such as sunlight or asbestos—may raise or lower their chances of coming down with such a disease.

Furthermore, economic well-being also plays a role. For instance, as at all stages of life, living in poverty restricts access to medical care. Even relatively well-off people may have difficulties finding affordable health care. Because the United States has until recently lacked a health-care insurance system that provides for universal medical coverage, many elderly individuals have faced financial burdens in obtaining affordable health care. As a result, many have received inadequate care. They are less likely to have regular checkups, and when they finally go for treatment, their illnesses may be more advanced (Administration on Aging, 2003; Rudowitz & Antonisse, 2018).

Finally, psychological factors play an important role in determining people's susceptibility to illness—and ultimately the likelihood of death. For example, having a sense of control over one's environment, even over choices involving everyday matters, leads to a better psychological state and superior health outcomes (Levy et al., 2002; Montpetit & Bergeman, 2007; Taylor, 2015).

PROMOTING GOOD HEALTH IN OLD AGE. People can do specific things to enhance their physical well-being—as well as their longevity—during old age. It is probably no surprise that the right things to do are no different from what people should do during the rest of the life span: Eat a proper diet, exercise, and avoid obvious threats to health, such as smoking. Medical and social service providers who work with elderly people have begun to emphasize the importance of these lifestyle choices. The goal of many such professionals has become not just to ward off illness and death, but to extend people's *active life spans*, the amount of time they remain healthy and able to enjoy their lives (Sawatzky & Naimark, 2002; Gavin & Myers, 2003; Katz & Marshall, 2003).

Sometimes, however, older people experience difficulties that prevent them from following even these simple guidelines. For instance, varying estimates suggest that between 15 and 50 percent of elderly people do not have adequate nutrition, and several million experience hunger every day (deCastro, 2002; Donini, Savina, & Cannella, 2003; Strohl, Bednar, & Longley, 2012).

The reasons for such malnutrition and hunger are varied. Some elderly people are too poor to purchase adequate food, and some are too frail to shop or cook for themselves. Others feel little motivation to prepare and eat proper meals, particularly if they live alone or are depressed. For those who have experienced significant declines in taste and smell sensitivity, eating well-prepared food may no longer be enjoyable. And some older people may never have eaten well-balanced meals in earlier periods of life.

Obtaining sufficient exercise may also prove problematic for older persons. As we noted above, physical activity increases muscle strength and flexibility, reduces blood pressure and the risk of heart attack, and produces several other benefits, but many older people do not get sufficient exercise to experience any of these benefits. For instance, illness may prevent older adults from exercising, and even inclement weather during the winter may restrict a person's ability to get out of the house. Furthermore, problems can combine: A poor person with insufficient money to eat properly may as a consequence have little energy to put into physical activity.

SEX IN OLD AGE. Although it may surprise you, increasing evidence suggests that people are sexually active well into their 80s and 90s—and that being sexually active may provide health benefits. Two major factors determine whether an elderly person will engage in sexual activity. One is good physical and mental health. People need to be physically healthy and to hold generally positive attitudes about sexual activity in order for sex to take place. The other determinant of sexual activity during old age is previous regular sexual activity. The longer elderly men and women have gone without sexual activity, the less likely is future sexual activity. Furthermore, there's some intriguing evidence that having sex may have some unexpected side benefits: One study found that having sex regularly is associated with a lower risk of death (Huang et al., 2009; Hillman, 2012; McCarthy & Pierpaoli, 2015)!

Module 4.3 Review

LO 4.8   **Describe how good nutrition in childhood promotes wellness later in life.**

Parents have to decide whether to feed their infants via the breast or the bottle, and when to introduce solid foods into the diet. An unhealthy diet has negative effects on the social and emotional functioning of school-age children. To encourage children to expand their food choices, they should be provided with a variety of healthy foods and allowed to develop their own preferences.

LO 4.9   **Explain how exercise can affect health and longevity.**

Exercise is another important factor in wellness across the life span, and its benefits are many.

LO 4.10   **Examine the nature of sexuality in later life.**

Sexuality can contribute to wellness throughout the life span. Some changes in sexual functioning occur as people

age. Menopause, the cessation of menstruation, may last quite a long time and may be accompanied by physically uncomfortable symptoms. In some cases the symptoms are so severe that women and their physicians may consider hormone therapy, but despite its effectiveness, this treatment bears decided risks. Men also experience a climacteric, typically in the 50s. The prostate gland may become enlarged, and some men may experience erectile dysfunction.

LO 4.11   **Explain how wellness can be maintained in old age.**

Wellness and illness in old age depend on many factors, such as genetic predisposition, environmental factors, and psychological factors. Economic well-being also plays a role.

Journal Writing Prompt

Applying Lifespan Development: Can wellness and sexuality be maintained in old age? If so, how?

Epilogue

We have surveyed a significant landscape of health, illness, and stress in this chapter, considering their causes and looking into ways to deal with many of them. We have covered stress, nutrition, several serious diseases, and Alzheimer's, a grievous psychological disease. We have looked at the upside and downside of nutrition and sexuality throughout the life span, and we have discovered that well-being and good health depend to a large extent on a good diet and ongoing exercise.

Return to the prologue, in which we meet Elsa, a recent college graduate who has been struggling with feelings of stress. In light of what you now know about physical and cognitive development in early adulthood, answer the following questions.

1. What lies at the root of Elsa's stress? How might a psychoneuroimmunologist describe her situation and the long-term consequences it poses?

2. What considerations should Elsa take into account when it comes to drinking wine to cope with stress?

3. How could Elsa use problem-focused coping to manage her stress? How could she use emotion-focused coping?

4. What diet and exercise routines would you recommend to keep her healthy? How might these recommendations also help with her feelings of stress?

Looking Back

LO 4.1   Explain the experience of stress across the life span

People move through stages—primary appraisal and secondary appraisal—to determine whether what they face will be stressful. Different stages in the life span bring about different stressors.

LO 4.2   Analyze the consequences of stress.

Long-term exposure to stressors may cause deterioration in the heart, blood vessels, and other body tissues. Stress is linked to many common ailments.

LO 4.3   Describe strategies for coping with stress.

Strategies for coping with stress include problem-focused coping, emotion-focused coping, the use of social support, and defensive coping. People who react effectively to stress have a positive coping style, which may involve hardiness and/or resilience.

LO 4.4   Analyze the importance of proper nutrition to human development.

Adequate nutrition is important for physical, social, and cognitive development. Malnutrition can slow growth, affect intellectual performance, and cause diseases. The high incidence of obesity in the United States is unhealthy because obesity taxes the circulatory system and increases the risk of high blood pressure and type 2 diabetes. Anorexia leads its victims to cut out food so radically that they become skeletal. Some 15 to 20 percent of anorexics starve themselves to death. People with bulimia undergo cycles of binging and purging, which may cause heart failure.

LO 4.5   Examine threats to health and wellness faced by children and adolescents.

Children face their greatest risk from accidents, leading parents and caregivers to take special pains to childproof their environments. Sudden infant death syndrome (SIDS) is ill-understood, but since experts began recommending that babies sleep on their backs, the incidence is down. Adolescents' risky behavior can lead them to take up an unhealthy, addictive habit (e.g., use of drugs, alcohol, or tobacco) or contract a sexually transmitted infection.

LO 4.6   Discuss the general health concerns of adults.

Young adults are generally as fit and healthy as they will ever be, but for some an unhealthy diet and a low level of exercise combine to cause obesity. Women are susceptible to osteoporosis, in which the bones become brittle, fragile, and thin. A calcium-rich diet can combat osteoporosis. The health of adults is partly determined by genetics. Socioeconomic status is a significant contributor to health because lower-SES households are likelier to work in hazardous occupations and to have inadequate health care. Americans are more likely to die from violence than are residents of any other developed country, and African Americans have twice the death rate of Caucasians. Heart disease is a risk for middle-aged adults. Both genetic and environmental factors contribute to heart disease, including the Type A behavior pattern. The incidence of cancer begins to be significant in middle adulthood. Therapies such as radiation therapy, chemotherapy, and surgery can successfully treat cancer.

LO 4.7   Describe the health risks confronting older adults.

Although most older people are healthy, the incidence of some serious diseases rises in old age, and most people have at least one chronic ailment, such as depression, before they die. The most prevalent and damaging brain disorder among older people is Alzheimer's disease.

LO 4.8   Describe how good nutrition in childhood promotes wellness later in life.

An unhealthy diet has negative effects on the social and emotional functioning of school-age children. To encourage children to expand their food choices, they should be provided with a variety of healthy foods and allowed to develop their own preferences.

LO 4.9 **Explain how exercise can affect health and longevity.**

Even moderate exercise of at least 30 minutes of moderate physical activity at least 5 days a week can lead to health benefits and increases in longevity. Regular exercise helps makes people feel stronger and more able to compensate for any losses due to aging.

LO 4.10 **Examine the nature of sexuality in later life.**

Sexuality can contribute to wellness all along the life span. Some changes in sexual functioning occur as people age.

Menopause, the cessation of menstruation, may last quite a long time and may be accompanied by physically uncomfortable symptoms. In some cases, the symptoms are so severe that women and their physicians may consider hormone therapy, but despite its effectiveness, this treatment bears decided risks. Men also experience a climacteric, typically in their 50s. The prostate gland often becomes enlarged, and some men may experience erectile dysfunction. Several effective drug treatments have been developed to deal with erectile dysfunction.

LO 4.11 **Explain how wellness can be maintained in old age.**

Wellness and illness in old age depend on genetic, environmental, psychological, and economic factors.

Key Terms and Concepts

primary appraisal   130
secondary appraisal   130
psychoneuroimmunology (PNI)   132
psychosomatic disorders   133
defensive coping   135
hardiness   135
nonorganic failure to thrive   139
obesity   139

anorexia nervosa   142
bulimia   142
sudden infant death syndrome (SIDS)   145
addictive drugs   146
alcoholics   147
sexually transmitted infection (STI)   148

osteoporosis   150
Type A behavior pattern   154
Type B behavior pattern   154
dementia   156
Alzheimer's disease   156
female climacteric   163
menopause   163
male climacteric   163

Chapter 5
Cognitive Growth: Piaget and Vygotsky

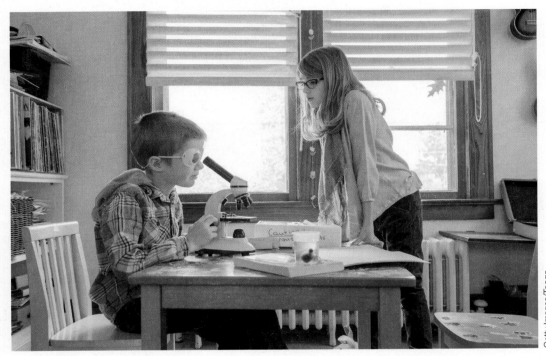

Getty Images/Tooga

Learning Objectives

LO 5.1 Summarize the fundamental features of Piaget's theory of cognitive development.

LO 5.2 Describe infants' cognitive development across the six substages of Piaget's sensorimotor stage.

LO 5.3 Define what Piaget meant by preoperational thought, and describe the cognitive characteristics of this stage.

LO 5.4 Describe the cognitive advances children make during Piaget's concrete operational and formal operational stages.

LO 5.5 Summarize the arguments for and against Piaget's theory of cognitive development.

LO 5.6 Compare and contrast Labouvie-Vief's, Perry's, and Schaie's theories of cognitive development to that of Piaget.

LO 5.7 Explain Vygotsky's view of cognitive development and contrast it to Piaget's theory.

LO 5.8 Define Vygotsky's zone of proximal development and explain the role it plays in children's cognitive development.

LO 5.9 Summarize the strengths and weaknesses of Vygotsky's theory of cognitive development in children.

Chapter Overview

Prologue: Making Things Happen

Alejandro Castillo laughs as he describes his 18-month old daughter Maria. "Every day is an adventure with her. I never know what she's going to think or say next." Maria seems to be learning so many new words every day, and she uses those words to label the world around her. Recently, at the playground, Maria encountered someone walking a dog. Although she was scared at first, Alejandro comforted her, saying "It's okay, it's a doggy. Doggy."

The next day, when the family went to the zoo, Alejandro was surprised that Maria remembered the word "doggy," but also realized that she still has a lot to learn. "That day at the zoo, everything was a 'doggy.' Monkeys, a cheetah, even a bear—they were all 'doggies' to Maria," Alejandro says with a grin. ∎

Looking Ahead

How do young children learn to understand the world around them? How do social interactions influence cognitive development? In this chapter, we consider cognitive development during childhood and adolescence from two important theoretical perspectives. First, we examine in detail the work of Swiss psychologist Jean Piaget, whose highly influential stage theory of development has served as the impetus for a considerable amount of research on cognitive development. We'll look at the foundations of Piaget's theory, including his description of schemas and the processes of assimilation and accommodation, and we will trace cognitive development through the four stages that Piaget identified and defined through his observations of children and adolescents.

Next, we will evaluate Piaget's theory, considering both its enormous contributions to developmental research and the many criticisms of his approach that have been voiced by researchers in the field. We will also consider competing theories of postformal thinking advanced by Gisela Labouvie-Vief, William Perry, K. Warner Schaie, and others.

Finally, we will conclude with a discussion of the work of Lev Vygotsky, a Russian psychologist. Vygotsky's views on the importance of culture to cognitive development have become increasingly influential, particularly in his focus on the social and cultural aspects of development and learning. Our discussions of Piaget and Vygotsky pave the way for consideration of the information processing approaches to cognitive development to which we turn in the next chapter.

Children experience cognitive advances that develop at breathtaking speed throughout childhood.

Swiss psychologist Jean Piaget.

MODULE 5.1

PIAGET'S APPROACH TO COGNITIVE DEVELOPMENT

Action = Knowledge.

If a simple equation could summarize a comprehensive theory of cognitive development, this one might encapsulate the ideas of Swiss psychologist Jean Piaget (1896–1980) about how we begin to understand the world. Unlike previous theorists, Piaget argued that infants acquire knowledge neither from facts communicated by others nor through sensation and perception. Instead, Piaget suggested that knowledge is the product of direct motor behavior. Although many of his basic explanations and propositions have been challenged by subsequent research, as we'll discuss later, the view that in significant ways infants learn by doing remains unquestioned (Piaget, 1983; Brandone, 2015; Zuccarini et al., 2016).

Fundamentals of Piaget's Theory

LO 5.1 **Summarize the fundamental features of Piaget's theory of cognitive development.**

Piaget's background and training influenced both the development of his theory and the methods he used to investigate it. Piaget was educated as a biologist and philosopher, and he received a Ph.D. in zoology. His initial work was aimed at producing an account of how knowledge was related to biology, which ultimately led to a theory of how children's understanding of the world develops. In doing research, Piaget relied on methods that are common among investigations of nonhuman species. For instance, his studies would often intensively focus on only a few children, including his own offspring. Furthermore, he frequently would observe children in their "natural habitat," such as while they were playing games. His goal was to understand *how* children think rather than characterizing whether their thinking was right or wrong at a given age.

As we first noted in Chapter 1, Piaget's theory is based on a stage approach to development. He assumed that all children pass through a series of four universal stages in a fixed order from birth through adolescence: *sensorimotor, preoperational, concrete operational*, and *formal operational*. He also suggested that movement from one stage to the next occurs when a child reaches an appropriate level of physical maturation and is exposed to relevant experiences. Without such experience, Piaget assumed that children were incapable of reaching their cognitive potential. Some approaches to cognition focus on changes in the content of children's knowledge about the world, but Piaget argued that it was critical to also consider the changes in the quality of children's knowledge and understanding as they move from one stage to another.

For instance, as they develop cognitively, infants experience changes in their understanding about what can and cannot occur in the world. Consider a baby who participates in an experiment during which she is exposed to three identical versions of her mother all at the same time, thanks to some well-placed mirrors. A 3-month-old infant will interact happily with each of these images of her mother. However, by 5 months of age, the child becomes quite agitated at the sight of multiple mothers. Apparently by this time, the child has figured out that she has but one mother, and viewing three at a time is thoroughly alarming (Bower, 1977). To Piaget, such reactions indicate that a baby is beginning to master principles regarding the way the world operates, indicating that she has begun to construct a mental sense of the world that she didn't have 2 months earlier.

Piaget believed that the basic building blocks of the way we understand the world are mental structures called **schema**, organized patterns of functioning that adapt and change with mental development. At first, schemas are related to physical, or sensorimotor, activity, such as picking up or reaching for toys. As children develop, their schemas move to a mental level, reflecting thought. Schemas are similar to computer

schema
an organized pattern of sensorimotor functioning.

software: They direct and determine how data from the world, such as new events or objects, are considered and dealt with (Rakison & Krogh, 2012; Lawson, Fisher, & Rakison, 2015; Di Paolo, Buhrmann & Barandiaran, 2017).

If you give a baby a new cloth book, for example, he or she will touch it, mouth it, perhaps try to tear it or bang it on the floor. To Piaget, each of these actions represents a schema, and they are the infant's way of gaining knowledge and understanding of this new object.

Piaget suggested that two principles underlie the growth in children's schemas: assimilation and accommodation. **Assimilation** is the process by which people understand an experience in terms of their current stage of cognitive development and way of thinking. Assimilation occurs, then, when a stimulus or an event is acted upon, perceived, and understood in accordance with existing patterns of thought. For example, an infant who tries to suck on any toy in the same way is assimilating the objects to her existing sucking schema. Similarly, a child who encounters a flying squirrel at a zoo and calls it a "bird" is assimilating the squirrel to his existing schema of bird.

In contrast, **accommodation** refers to changes in existing ways of thinking, understanding, or behaving in response to encounters with new stimuli or events. For instance, when a child sees a flying squirrel and calls it "a bird with a tail," he is beginning to accommodate new knowledge, modifying his schema of bird.

Piaget believed that the earliest schemas are primarily limited to the reflexes with which we are all born, such as sucking and rooting. Infants start to modify these simple early schemas almost immediately, through the processes of assimilation and accommodation, in response to their exploration of the environment. Schemas quickly become more sophisticated as infants become more advanced in their motor capabilities—to Piaget, a signal of the potential for more advanced cognitive development.

Cognitive Development in Infancy: Piaget's Sensorimotor Stage

LO 5.2 **Describe infants' cognitive development across the six substages of Piaget's sensorimotor stage.**

> *Olivia's dad is wiping up the mess around the base of her high chair—for the third time today! It seems to him that 14-month-old Olivia takes great delight in dropping food from the high chair. She also drops toys, spoons—anything, it seems—just to watch how it hits the floor. She almost appears to be experimenting to see what kind of noise or what size of splatter is created by each different thing she drops.*

Piaget probably would have said that Olivia's dad is right in theorizing that Olivia is conducting her own series of experiments to learn more about the workings of her world. As we noted at the beginning of this module, Piaget's views of the ways infants learn can be summed up in a simple equation: Action = Knowledge.

Piaget's theory, as noted earlier, is based on a stage approach to development, with the **sensorimotor stage** being the initial major stage of cognitive development. This stage can be broken down into six substages, summarized in Table 5-1. It is important to keep in mind that although the specific substages of the sensorimotor period may at first appear to unfold with great regularity, as though infants reach a particular age and smoothly proceed into the next substage, the reality of cognitive development is somewhat different. First, the ages at which infants actually reach a particular stage vary a good deal among children. The exact timing of a stage reflects an interaction between the infant's level of physical maturation and the nature of the social environment in which the child is being raised.

Piaget viewed development as a more gradual process than the notion of different stages might seem to imply. Infants do not go to sleep one night in one substage and wake up the next morning in the next one. Instead, there is a rather steady shifting of behavior as a child moves toward the next stage of cognitive development. Infants also pass through periods of transition, in which some aspects of their behavior reflect the next higher stage, while other aspects indicate their current stage (see Figure 5-1).

123RF/szefei

According to Piaget, a baby will use a sensorimotor schema, such as mouthing or banging, to understand a new object.

assimilation

the process in which people understand an experience in terms of their current stage of cognitive development and way of thinking.

accommodation

changes in existing ways of thinking that occur in response to encounters with new stimuli or events.

sensorimotor stage (of cognitive development)

Piaget's initial major stage of cognitive development, which can be broken down into six substages.

Table 5-1 Piaget's Six Substages of the Sensorimotor Stage

Substage	Age	Description	Example
Substage 1: Simple reflexes	First month of life	During this period, the various reflexes that determine the infant's interactions with the world are at the center of the infant's cognitive life.	The sucking reflex causes the infant to suck at anything placed on his lips.
Substage 2: First habits and primary circular reactions	From 1 to 4 months	At this age infants begin to coordinate what were separate actions into single, integrated activities.	An infant might combine grasping an object with sucking on it, or staring at something with touching it.
Substage 3: Secondary circular reactions	From 4 to 8 months	During this period, infants take major strides in shifting their cognitive horizons beyond themselves and begin to act on the outside world.	A child who repeatedly picks up a rattle in her crib and shakes it in different ways to see how the sound changes is demonstrating her ability to modify her cognitive schema about shaking rattles.
Substage 4: Coordination of secondary circular reactions	From 8 to 12 months	In this stage infants begin to use more calculated approaches to producing events, coordinating several schemas to generate a single act. They achieve object performance during this stage.	An infant will push one toy out of the way to reach another toy that is lying, partially exposed, under it.
Substage 5: Tertiary circular reactions	From 12 to 18 months	At this age infants develop what Piaget regards as the deliberate variation of actions that bring desirable consequences. Rather than just repeating enjoyable activities, infants appear to carry out miniature experiments to observe the consequences.	A child will drop a toy repeatedly, varying the position from which he drops it, carefully observing each time to see where it falls.
Substage 6: Beginnings of thought	From 18 months to 2 years	The major achievement of Substage 6 is the capacity for mental representation or symbolic thought. Piaget argued that only at this stage can infants imagine where objects that they cannot see might be.	Children can even plot in their heads unseen trajectories of objects, so that if a ball rolls under a piece of furniture, they can figure out where it is likely to emerge on the other side.

SUBSTAGE 1: SIMPLE REFLEXES (FIRST MONTH).   The first substage of the sensorimotor period is *Substage 1: Simple reflexes*, encompassing the first month of life. During this time, various inborn reflexes are at the center of infants' physical and cognitive lives, determining the nature of their interactions with the world. At the same time, some of the reflexes begin to accommodate the infant's experience with the nature of the world. For instance, an infant who is being breast-fed but who also receives supplemental bottles may start to change the way he or she sucks, depending on whether a nipple is on a breast or a bottle.

Figure 5-1 Transitions.

Infants do not suddenly shift from one stage of cognitive development to the next. Instead, Piaget argues that there is a period of transition in which some behavior reflects one stage, while another behavior reflects the more advanced stage. Does this gradualism argue against Piaget's interpretation of stages?

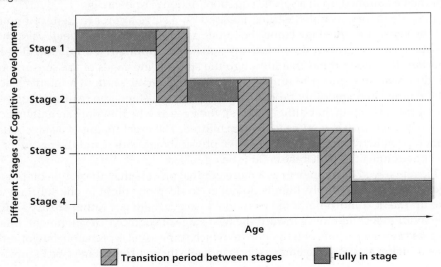

SUBSTAGE 2: FIRST HABITS AND PRIMARY CIRCULAR REACTIONS (1 TO 4 MONTHS).

Substage 2: First habits and primary circular reactions, the second substage of the sensorimotor period, occurs from 1 to 4 months of age. In this period, infants begin to coordinate what were separate actions into single, integrated activities. For instance, an infant might combine grasping an object with sucking on it, or staring at something with touching it.

If an activity engages a baby's interests, he or she may repeat it over and over, simply for the sake of continuing to experience it. This repetition of a chance motor event helps the baby start building cognitive schemas through a process known as a *circular reaction. Primary circular reactions* are schemas reflecting an infant's repetition of interesting or enjoyable actions—just for the enjoyment of doing them—which focus on the infant's own body.

Infants in Substage 4 can coordinate their secondary circular reactions, displaying an ability to plan or calculate how to produce a desired outcome.

SUBSTAGE 3: SECONDARY CIRCULAR REACTIONS (4 TO 8 MONTHS).

In *Substage 3: Secondary circular reactions*, the infant's actions are more purposeful. According to Piaget, this third stage of cognitive development in infancy occurs from 4 to 8 months of age. During this period, a child begins to act upon the outside world. For instance, infants now seek to repeat enjoyable events in their environments if they happen to produce them through chance activities. A child who repeatedly picks up a rattle in her crib and shakes it in different ways to see how the sound changes is demonstrating her ability to modify her cognitive schema about shaking rattles. She is engaging in what Piaget calls *secondary circular reactions*, which are schemas regarding repeated actions that bring about a desirable consequence.

SUBSTAGE 4: COORDINATION OF SECONDARY CIRCULAR REACTIONS (8 TO 12 MONTHS).

Some major leaps forward occur in *Substage 4: Coordination of secondary circular reactions*, which lasts from around 8 months to 12 months. In Substage 4, infants begin to employ **goal-directed behavior**, in which several schemas are combined and coordinated to generate a single act to solve a problem. For instance, they will push one toy out of the way to reach another toy that is lying, partially exposed, under it.

Infants' newfound purposefulness, their ability to use means to attain particular ends, and their skill in anticipating future circumstances owe their appearance in part to the developmental achievement of object permanence that emerges in Substage 4. **Object permanence** is the realization that people and objects exist even when they cannot be seen. It is a simple principle, but its mastery has profound consequences.

Consider, for instance, 7-month-old Chu, who has yet to learn the idea of object permanence. Chu's mother shakes a rattle in front of him, then takes the rattle and places it under a blanket. To Chu, who has not mastered the concept of object permanence, the rattle no longer exists. He will make no effort to look for it.

goal-directed behavior
behavior in which several schemas are combined and coordinated to generate a single act to solve a problem.

object permanence
the realization that people and objects exist even when they cannot be seen.

From a *caregiver's* perspective

In general, what are some implications for childrearing practices of Piaget's observations about the ways children gain an understanding of the world? Would you use the same approaches in childrearing for a child growing up in a non-Western culture? Why or why not?

Several months later, when he reaches Substage 4, the story is quite different (see Figure 5-2). This time, as soon as his mother places the rattle under the blanket, Chu tries to toss the cover aside, eagerly searching for the rattle. Chu clearly has learned that the object continues to exist even when it cannot be seen. For the infant who achieves an understanding of object permanence, then, out of sight is decidedly not out of mind.

The attainment of object permanence extends not only to inanimate objects but to people, too. It gives Chu the security that his father and mother still exist even when they have left the room.

Figure 5-2 Object Permanence.

Before an infant has understood the idea of object permanence, he will not search for an object that has been hidden right before his eyes. But several months later, he will search for it, illustrating that he has attained the concept of object permanence. Why would the concept of object permanence be important to a caregiver?

Before Object Permanence

After Object Permanence

SUBSTAGE 5: TERTIARY CIRCULAR REACTIONS (12 TO 18 MONTHS). *Substage 5: Tertiary circular reactions* is reached at around the age of 12 months and extends to 18 months. As the name of the stage indicates, during this period, infants develop tertiary circular reactions, which are schemas regarding the deliberate variation of actions that bring desirable consequences. Rather than just repeating enjoyable activities, as they do with secondary circular reactions, infants appear to carry out miniature experiments to observe the consequences.

For example, Piaget observed his son Laurent dropping a toy swan repeatedly, varying the position from which he dropped it, carefully observing each time to see where it fell. Instead of just repeating the action each time, Laurent made modifications in the situation to learn about their consequences. As you may recall from our discussion of research methods in Chapter 1, this behavior represents the essence of the scientific method: An experimenter varies a situation in a laboratory to learn the effects of the variation.

What is most striking about infants' behavior during Substage 5 is their interest in the unexpected. Unanticipated events are treated not only as interesting but also as something to be explained and understood. Infants' discoveries can lead to newfound skills, some of which may cause a certain amount of chaos. For instance, an infant may pull at a tablecloth in order to reach a plate of cookies or throw a water toy into the tub with increasing vigor to see how high the water splashes.

SUBSTAGE 6: BEGINNINGS OF THOUGHT (18 MONTHS TO 2 YEARS). The final stage of the sensorimotor period is *Substage 6: Beginnings of thought*, which lasts from around 18 months to 2 years. The major achievement of Substage 6 is the capacity for mental representation, or symbolic thought. A **mental representation** is an internal image of a past event or object. Piaget argued that by this stage infants can imagine where objects might be that they cannot see. They can even plot in their heads unseen trajectories of objects, so if a ball rolls under a piece of furniture, they can figure out where it is likely to emerge on the other side.

Because of children's new abilities to create internal representations of objects, their understanding of causality also becomes more sophisticated. For instance, consider Piaget's description of his son Laurent's efforts to open a garden gate:

mental representation
an internal image of a past event or object.

Laurent tries to open a garden gate but cannot push it forward because it is held back by a piece of furniture. He cannot account either visually or by any sound for the cause that prevents the gate from opening, but after having tried to force it he suddenly seems to understand; he goes around the wall, arrives at the other side of the gate, moves the armchair which holds it firm, and opens it with a triumphant expression. (Piaget, 1954, p. 296)

The attainment of mental representation also permits another important development: the ability to pretend. Using the skill of what Piaget refers to as **deferred imitation**, in which a person who is no longer present is imitated later, children are able to pretend that they are driving a car, feeding a doll, or cooking dinner long after they have witnessed such scenes played out in reality.

Infants begin to use goal-directed behavior in Substage 4 of the sensorimotor stage.

Cognitive Development in the Preschool Years

LO 5.3 **Define what Piaget meant by preoperational thought, and describe the cognitive characteristics of this stage.**

Three-year-old Sam was talking to himself in two very different voices. "Find your shoes," he said in a low voice. "Not today. I'm not going. I hate the shoes," he said in a higher-pitched voice. The lower voice answered, "You are a bad boy. Find the shoes, bad boy." The higher-voiced response was "No, no, no."

Sam's parents realized that he was playing a game with his imaginary friend, Gill—a bad boy who often disobeyed his mother. In fact, according to Sam's musings, Gill often was guilty of the very same misdeeds for which his parents blamed Sam.

Piaget saw the preschool years as a time of both stability and change. He placed the preschool years into a single stage of cognitive development—the preoperational stage—which lasts from 2 until around 7.

PIAGET'S STAGE OF PREOPERATIONAL THINKING (AGES 2 TO 7). During the **preoperational stage**, children's use of symbolic thinking grows, mental reasoning emerges, and the use of concepts increases. Seeing Mom's car keys may prompt a question, "Go to store?" as the child comes to see the keys as a symbol of a car ride. In this way, children become better at representing events internally and less dependent on sensorimotor activity to understand the world around them. Yet they are still not capable of **operations**: organized, formal, logical mental processes.

According to Piaget, a key aspect of preoperational thought is **symbolic function**, the ability to use a mental symbol, a word, or an object to stand for or represent something that is not physically present. For example, preschoolers can use a mental symbol for a car (the word *car*), and they understand that a small toy car is representative of the real thing. They have no need to get behind the wheel of an actual car to understand its basic purpose and use.

THE RELATIONSHIP BETWEEN LANGUAGE AND THOUGHT. Symbolic function is at the heart of one of the major advances of the preoperational period: the increasingly sophisticated use of language. Piaget suggests that the advances in language during the preschool years reflect improvements over the type of thinking that is possible during the earlier sensorimotor period. Instead of slow sensorimotor-based thinking, symbolic thought, which relies on improved linguistic ability, allows preschoolers to represent actions virtually, at much greater speed.

Even more important, language allows children to think beyond the present to the future. Rather than being grounded in the here-and-now, preschoolers can imagine future possibilities through language in the form of fantasies and daydreams.

CENTRATION: WHAT YOU SEE IS WHAT YOU THINK. Place a dog mask on a cat, and what do you get? According to 3- and 4-year-old preschoolers, a dog. To them, a

deferred imitation
an act in which a person who is no longer present is imitated by children who have witnessed a similar act.

preoperational stage
according to Piaget, the stage from approximately age 2 to age 7 in which children's use of symbolic thinking grows, mental reasoning emerges, and the use of concepts increases.

operations
organized, formal, logical mental processes.

symbolic function
the ability to use a mental symbol, a word, or an object to stand for or represent something that is not physically present.

Figure 5-3 Which Row Contains More Buttons?

When preschoolers are shown these two rows and asked which row has more buttons, they usually respond that the lower row of buttons contains more because it looks longer. They answer in this way even though they know quite well that 10 is greater than 8. Do you think preschoolers can be *taught* to answer correctly?

cat with a dog mask ought to bark like a dog, wag its tail like a dog, and eat dog food. In every respect, the cat has been transformed into a dog.

To Piaget, the root of this belief is centration, a key element—and limitation—of thinking in the preoperational period. **Centration** is the process of concentrating on one limited aspect of a stimulus—typically its superficial elements—and ignoring others. These elements come to dominate preschoolers' thinking, leading to inaccuracy.

Centration is the cause of the error illustrated in Figure 5-3 above. Asked which row contains more buttons, children who are 4 or 5 usually choose the row that looks longer rather than the one that actually contains more buttons. This occurs even though children of this age know quite well that 10 is more than 8. Rather than taking into account their understanding of quantity, they focus on appearance.

Preschoolers' focus on appearances might be related to another aspect of preoperational thought, the lack of conservation.

centration
the process of concentrating on one limited aspect of a stimulus and ignoring other aspects.

CONSERVATION: LEARNING THAT APPEARANCES ARE DECEIVING.   Consider the following scenario:

Four-year-old Jaime is shown two drinking glasses of different shapes. One is short and broad; the other is tall and thin. A teacher half-fills the short, broad glass with apple juice. The teacher then pours the juice into the tall, thin glass. The juice fills the tall glass almost to the brim. The teacher asks Jaime a question: Is there more juice in the second glass than there was in the first?

If you view this as an easy question, so do children like Jaime. The problem is that they almost always get it wrong.

conservation
the knowledge that quantity is unrelated to the arrangement and physical appearance of objects.

Most 4-year-olds say that there is more apple juice in the tall, thin glass than there is in the short, broad one. In fact, if the juice is poured back into the shorter glass, they are quick to say that there is now less juice than there was in the taller glass (see Figure 5-4).

The reason is that children of this age have not mastered conservation. **Conservation** is the knowledge that quantity is unrelated to the arrangement and physical appearance of objects.

Why do children in the preoperational stage make conservation errors? Piaget suggests that the main reason is that their tendency toward centration prevents them from focusing on the relevant features of the situation. Furthermore, they cannot follow the sequence of transformations that accompanies changes in the appearance of a situation.

Figure 5-4 Which Glass Contains More?

Most 4-year-old children believe that the amount of liquid in these two glasses differs because of the differences in the containers' shapes, even though they may have seen equal amounts of liquid being poured into each.

INCOMPLETE UNDERSTANDING OF TRANSFORMATION.
A preoperational, preschool child who sees several worms during a walk in the woods may believe that they are all the same worm. The reason: She views each sighting in isolation, unable

to understand that a transformation would be necessary for a worm to move quickly from one location to the next.

As Piaget used the term **transformation** to describe the process by which one state is changed into another. For instance, adults know that if a pencil that is held upright is allowed to fall down, it passes through a series of successive stages until it reaches its final, horizontal resting spot. In contrast, children in the preoperational period are unable to envision or recall the successive transformations that the pencil followed in moving from the upright to the horizontal position.

transformation
the process in which one state is changed into another.

EGOCENTRISM: THE INABILITY TO TAKE OTHERS' PERSPECTIVES. Another hallmark of the preoperational period is egocentric thinking. **Egocentric thought** is thinking that does not take into account the viewpoints of others. Preschoolers do not understand that others have different perspectives. Egocentric thought takes two forms: lack of awareness that others see things from a different physical perspective and failure to realize that others may hold thoughts, feelings, and points of view that differ from theirs. (Note what egocentric thought does *not* imply: that preoperational children intentionally think in a selfish or inconsiderate manner.)

egocentric thought
thinking that does not take into account the viewpoints of others.

Egocentric thinking lies behind children's lack of concern over their nonverbal behavior and the impact it has on others. For instance, a 4-year-old who receives a gift of socks may frown as he opens the package, unaware that his face can be seen by others and reveals his true feelings (Nilsen & Graham, 2009).

Egocentrism largely explains why many preschoolers talk to themselves, even in the presence of others, and often ignore what others are telling them. This behavior illustrates the egocentric nature of preoperational children's thinking: the lack of awareness that their behavior acts as a trigger to others' reactions and responses. Consequently, much of preschoolers' verbal behavior has no social motivation but is meant purely for their own consumption.

Egocentrism can also be seen in hiding games. In hide-and-seek, 3-year-olds may "hide" by covering their faces with a pillow—even though they remain in plain view. Their reasoning: If they cannot see others, others cannot see them. They assume that everyone else shares their view.

THE EMERGENCE OF INTUITIVE THOUGHT. Because Piaget labeled this the "preoperational period" and focused on cognitive deficiencies, it is easy to assume that preschoolers are marking time, but during this period they are far from idle. Cognitive development proceeds steadily, and new abilities emerge, including intuitive thought.

Intuitive thought refers to preschoolers' use of primitive reasoning and their avid acquisition of world knowledge. From about age 4 through 7, curiosity blossoms. Children ask "Why?" questions about nearly everything. At the same time, they may act as if they are authorities on particular topics, certain that they have the final word on an issue. Their intuitive thought leads them to believe that they know answers to all kinds of questions, with little or no logical basis for this confidence.

intuitive thought
thinking that reflects preschoolers' use of primitive reasoning and their avid acquisition of knowledge about the world.

In the late stages of the preoperational period, children's intuitive thinking prepares them for more sophisticated reasoning. For instance, preschoolers come to understand that pushing harder on the pedals makes a bicycle move faster or that pressing a button on a remote control makes the television change channels. By the end of the preoperational stage, preschoolers begin to grasp functionality, the idea that actions, events, and outcomes are related to one another in fixed patterns. They also become aware of identity, the understanding that certain things stay the same, regardless of changes in shape, size, and appearance—for instance, that a lump of clay contains the same amount of clay whether it is clumped into a ball or stretched out like a snake. Comprehension of identity is necessary for children to develop an understanding of conservation (the understanding, as we discussed earlier, that quantity is not related to physical appearances). For suggestions on promoting cognitive development in preschooler, see the *Development in Your Life* feature on the next page.

Cognitive Development in Middle Childhood and Adolescence

LO 5.4 **Describe the cognitive advances children make during Piaget's concrete operational and formal operational stages.**

As we have seen, from Piaget's perspective preschoolers think preoperationally. They are largely egocentric and lack the ability to use *operations*—organized, formal, logical mental processes.

concrete operational stage
the period of cognitive development between ages 7 and 12, which is characterized by the active, and appropriate, use of logic.

THE RISE OF CONCRETE OPERATIONAL THOUGHT (AGES 7 TO 12). All this changes during the school years in what Piaget calls the concrete operational stage. Occurring between ages 7 and 12, the **concrete operational stage** is characterized by the active, and appropriate, use of logic. Concrete operational thought applies logical operations to concrete problems. For instance, when children in this stage confront a conservation problem (such as determining whether the amount of liquid poured from one container to another of a different shape stays the same), they use cognitive and logical processes to answer, no longer judging solely by appearance. They are able to reason correctly that since none of the liquid has been lost, the amount stays the same. Being less egocentric, they can consider multiple aspects of a situation, an ability known as decentering.

The shift from preoperational to concrete operational thought takes time. Children shift between these modes of thought before concrete operations take a firm hold, able to answer conservation problems but unable to explain why. When asked for their reasoning, they may simply respond, "Because."

Once concrete operations take hold, however, children make several cognitive leaps, such as the concept of *reversibility*—the notion that transformations to a stimulus

Development in Your Life

Promoting Cognitive Development in Preschoolers: From Theory to the Classroom

Piaget's theory has had enormous influence on educational practice, particularly during the preschool years. Among the suggestions for parents and preschool teachers that arise out of the Piagetian approach are the following:

- Both parents and teachers should be aware of which general stage of cognitive development, with its capabilities and limitations, each individual child has reached. Unless they are aware of a child's current level of development, it will be impossible to provide appropriate materials and experiences.

- Instruction should take place at a level that reflects—but is just slightly higher than—each student's current level of cognitive development. For instance, Piaget suggests that cognitive growth is more likely to occur when information and material are of moderate novelty. With too little novelty, children will be bored; with too much, they will be confused.

- Instruction should be individualized as much as possible. Because children of the same age may hover around different levels of cognitive development, curriculum materials that are prepared individually stand a better chance of success.

- Students should be kept actively engaged in learning, and they should be allowed to pace themselves as they move through new material.

- Opportunities for social interaction—both with other students and with adults—should be provided. By receiving feedback from others and observing how others react in given situations, children learn new approaches and ways of thinking about the world.

- Students should be allowed to make mistakes. Cognitive growth often flows from confronting errors.

- Because cognitive development can occur only when children have achieved the appropriate level of maturation, children should not be pushed too far ahead of their current state of cognitive development. For instance, although it may be possible through intensive training to get preoperational children to recite, in a rote manner, the correct response to a conservation problem, this does not mean that they will have true comprehension of what they are verbalizing.

can be reversed. Grasping this notion, children realize that a ball of clay squeezed into a long, thin rope can become a ball again. More abstractly, this concept allows children to understand that if $3 + 5 = 8$, then $5 + 3$ also $= 8$—and, later, that $8 - 3 = 5$.

Concrete operational thinking also permits children to grasp such concepts as the relationship between time and speed. For instance, consider the problem in which two cars traveling different-length routes start and finish at the same points in the same amount of time. Children entering the concrete operational period reason that the cars' speed is the same. However, between ages 8 and 10, children begin to understand that for both cars to arrive simultaneously at the finish point, the car traveling the longer route must be moving faster.

Despite these advances, children still have one critical thinking limitation. They remain tied to concrete, physical reality. Furthermore, they cannot understand truly abstract or hypothetical questions, or questions involving formal logic, such as the concept of free will or determinism.

PIAGET'S FORMAL OPERATIONAL STAGE (AGES 12 TO 15).

Mrs. Kirby smiled as she read a highly creative paper. As part of her eighth-grade American Government class, she asked students to write about what their lives would be like if America had not won its war for independence from Britain. She had tried a similar task with her sixth-graders, but many of them were unable to imagine anything other than what they knew. Her eighth-graders, however, were inventing some very interesting scenarios. One boy imagined himself as Lord Lucas; a girl imagined that she would serve a rich landowner; another that she would plot to overthrow the government.

The ability to think beyond the concrete, current situation to what might or could be distinguishes adolescents' thinking from that of younger children. Adolescents are able to consider a variety of abstract possibilities; they can see issues in relative, as opposed to absolute, terms. When problems arise, they can perceive shadings beyond the black-and-white solutions of younger days (Keating, 1980, 1990; Lehalle, 2006).

There are several explanations for adolescents' cognitive development. According to Piaget, with adolescence comes the formal operational stage. In a problem devised by Piaget, 14-year-old Leigh is asked to solve the problem: What determines the speed at which a pendulum moves back and forth? Leigh is given a weight hanging from a string and told that she can vary several things: the length of the string, the weight of the object, the amount of force used to push the string, and the height to which the weight is raised in an arc before it is released.

Leigh doesn't remember, but she was asked to solve the same problem at age 8 as part of a longitudinal research study. She was then in the concrete operational period, and her efforts were not very successful. Her haphazard approach showed no systematic plan of action. For instance, she simultaneously tried to push the pendulum harder and shorten the length of the string and increase the weight on the string. Because she varied so many factors at once, when the pendulum's speed changed, she had no way of knowing what had made the difference.

Now, Leigh is more systematic. Rather than immediately pushing and pulling at the pendulum, she stops to think about which factors to consider. She ponders how she might test which factor is important, forming a hypothesis. Then, as a scientist conducts an experiment, she varies only one factor at a time. By examining each variable separately and systematically, she comes to the correct solution: The length of the string determines the speed of the pendulum.

Using Formal Operations to Solve Problems. Leigh's approach to the pendulum question shows she has moved into the formal operational period of cognitive development (Piaget & Inhelder, 1958). In the **formal operational stage**, people develop the ability to think abstractly. Piaget suggested that people reach this stage at the start of adolescence, around age 12.

formal operational stage
the stage at which people develop the ability to think abstractly.

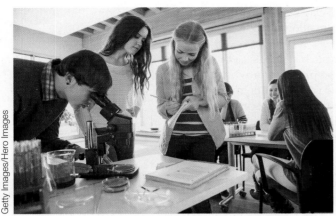

Like scientists who form hypotheses, adolescents in the formal operational stage use systematic reasoning. They start with a general theory about what produces a particular outcome and then deduce explanations for specific situations in which they see that particular outcome.

Adolescents can consider problems in abstract rather than concrete terms by using formal principles of logic. They can test their understanding by systematically conducting rudimentary experiments and observing the results. Thus, the adolescent Leigh could think about the pendulum problem abstractly, and she understood how to test her hypotheses.

Adolescents are able to use formal reasoning, starting with a general theory about what causes a certain outcome, and then deducing explanations for the situations in which that outcome occurs. Like scientists who form hypotheses, discussed in Chapter 1, they can test their theories. What distinguishes this kind of thinking from earlier stages is the ability to start with the abstract and move to the concrete; in previous stages, children are tied to the concrete present. At age 8, Leigh just moved things around to see what would happen in the pendulum problem, a concrete approach. At age 12, she began with the abstract idea that each variable should be tested separately.

Adolescents also can use propositional thought during this stage. *Propositional thought* is reasoning that uses abstract logic in the absence of concrete examples. Such thinking allows adolescents to understand that if certain premises are true, then a conclusion must also be true. For example:

> All men are mortal. [*premise*]
> Socrates is a man. [*premise*]
> Therefore, Socrates is mortal. [*conclusion*]

Adolescents understand that if both premises are true, then so is the conclusion. They are capable of using similar reasoning when premises and conclusions are stated more abstractly, as follows:

> All As are B. [*premise*]
> C is an A. [*premise*]
> Therefore, C is a B. [*conclusion*]

Although Piaget proposed that the formal operational stage begins at the onset of adolescence, he also hypothesized that—as with all the stages—full cognitive capabilities emerge gradually through a combination of physical maturation and environmental experiences. It is not until around age 15, Piaget says, that adolescents fully settle into the formal operational stage.

In fact, evidence suggests that many people hone these skills at a later age, and some never fully employ them at all. Most studies show that only 40 to 60 percent of college students and adults achieve formal operational thinking completely, with some estimates as low as 25 percent. But many adults who do not use formal operational thought in every domain are fully competent in some aspects of their lives (Sugarman, 1988; Commons & Richards, 2003).

The culture in which they are raised affects how adolescents use formal operations. People with little formal education, who live in isolated, technologically unsophisticated societies, are less likely to use formal operations than formally educated persons in more sophisticated societies (Oesterdiekhoff, 2007; Asadi, Amiri, & Molavi, 2014).

It is not that adolescents (and adults) from cultures using few formal operations are incapable of attaining them. It is more likely that what characterizes formal operations—scientific reasoning—is not equally valued in all societies. If everyday life does not require or promote a certain type of reasoning, it is not likely that people will use such reasoning when confronting a problem (Gauvain, 1998; Smorti, 2008).

The Consequences of Adolescents' Use of Formal Operations. The ability to reason abstractly, to use formal operations, changes adolescents' everyday behavior. Whereas earlier they may have blindly accepted rules and explanations, their increased abstract reasoning abilities may lead to strenuous questioning of their parents and other authority figures.

In general, adolescents become more argumentative. They enjoy using abstract reasoning to poke holes in others' explanations, and their increased critical thinking abilities zero in on parents' and teachers' perceived shortcomings. For instance, they may see their parents' arguments against using drugs as inconsistent if their parents used drugs in adolescence without consequence. But adolescents can be indecisive, too, as they are able to see the merits of multiple sides to issues (Kuhn & Franklin, 2006).

Coping with these new critical abilities can be challenging for parents, teachers, and other adults who deal with adolescents. But it makes adolescents more interesting, as they actively seek to understand the values and justifications they encounter.

Module 5.1 Review

LO 5.1   Summarize the fundamental features of Piaget's theory of cognitive development.

Jean Piaget argued that infants acquire knowledge directly through motor behavior, organizing their world into mental structures called schemas and subsequently either assimilating experiences into their current level of understanding or accommodating their ways of thinking to include the new experience. Piaget's theory is based on a stage approach to development in which children pass through a series of stages in a fixed order from birth through adolescence: sensorimotor, preoperational, concrete operational, and formal operational. As people move from one stage to another, the way they understand the world changes. The key way in which Piaget differs from many theorists who preceded him is in his observation that children experience *qualitative* changes in knowledge and understanding as they move from stage to stage, not just *quantitative* changes.

LO 5.2   Describe infants' cognitive development across the six substages of Piaget's sensorimotor stage.

The sensorimotor stage, from birth to about 2 years, involves a gradual progression through simple reflexes, single coordinated activities, interest in the outside world, purposeful combinations of activities, manipulation of actions to produce desired outcomes, and symbolic thought. These are the six substages of the sensorimotor stage.

LO 5.3   Define what Piaget meant by preoperational thought, and describe the cognitive characteristics of this stage.

According to Piaget, children in the preoperational stage develop symbolic function, a change in their thinking that is the foundation of further cognitive advances, but they are hampered by a tendency toward egocentric thought.

LO 5.4   Describe the cognitive advances children make during Piaget's concrete operational and formal operational stages.

Individuals in middle childhood are in the concrete operational stage of cognitive development, characterized by the application of logical processes to concrete problems and by "decentering"—the ability to take multiple aspects of a situation into account. As they enter Piaget's formal operational stage, adolescents begin to think abstractly, use logic, and perform systematic experiments to answer questions.

Journal Writing Prompt

Applying Lifespan Development: Think of a common children's toy with which you are familiar. How might its use be affected by the principles of assimilation and accommodation?

MODULE 5.2

APPRAISING PIAGET: SUPPORT, CHALLENGES, AND ALTERNATIVES

Most developmental researchers would probably agree that in many significant ways, Piaget's descriptions of how cognitive development proceeds are largely accurate. Yet there is substantial disagreement over the validity of the theory and many of its specific predictions (Marcovitch, Zelazo, & Schmuckler, 2003; Müller, Ten Eycke & Baker, 2015; Barrouillet, 2015).

Let's start with what is clearly correct about the Piagetian approach. Piaget was a virtuoso observer and masterly reporter of children's behavior, and his descriptions of growth remain a monument to his powers of observation. His many books contain brilliant, careful observations of children at work and play.

Furthermore, literally thousands of studies have supported Piaget's view that children learn much about the world by acting on objects in their environment. Finally, the broad outlines sketched out by Piaget of the sequence of cognitive development and the increasing cognitive accomplishments that occur during infancy and the preschool years, in particular, are generally accurate. His theories have had powerful educational implications, and many schools use his principles to guide instruction (Bibace, 2013; Müller, Ten Eycke, & Baker, 2015; Fowler, 2017).

The Critics Weigh In

LO 5.5   Summarize the arguments for and against Piaget's theory of cognitive development.

Despite the powerful influence of Piaget's work, specific aspects of his theory have come under increasing scrutiny—and criticism—in the decades since he carried out his pioneering work. For example, some researchers question the concept of stages that forms the basis of Piaget's theory. Although even Piaget acknowledged that children's transitions between stages are gradual, critics, particularly those who favor the information processing approach, contend that development proceeds in a much more continuous fashion. Rather than showing major leaps of competence at the end of one stage and the beginning of the next, improvement comes in more gradual increments, growing step by step in a skill-by-skill manner (Siegler, 2012; Siegler & Lortie-Forgues, 2014; Siegler, 2016).

Regarding infants in particular, some critics dispute Piaget's notion that cognitive development is grounded in motor activities. They charge that Piaget overlooked the importance of the sensory and perceptual systems that are present from a very early age in infancy—systems about which Piaget knew little, since so much of the research illustrating how sophisticated they are even in infancy was done relatively recently (Johnson, 2009; Houwen et al., 2016).

In addition, critics point to other drawbacks to Piaget's perspective:

- **Timing of Mastery of Object Permanence.** Piaget's critics also point to more recent studies that cast doubt on Piaget's view that infants are incapable of mastering the concept of object permanence until they are close to a year old. For instance, some work suggests that younger infants did not appear to understand object permanence because the techniques used to test their abilities were not sensitive enough to their true capabilities (Bremner, Slater, & Johnson, 2015; Baillargeon, 2008; Baillargeon & Dejong, 2017).

  It may be that a 4-month-old doesn't search for a rattle hidden under a blanket because she hasn't learned the motor skills necessary to do the searching—not because she doesn't understand that the rattle still exists. Similarly, the apparent inability of young infants to comprehend object permanence may reflect more about their memory deficits than their lack of understanding of the concept: The memories of young infants may be poor enough that they simply do not recall the earlier concealment of the toy. In fact, when more age-appropriate tasks are employed, some researchers have found indications of object permanence in children as young as 3 months (Wang, Baillargeon, & Paterson, 2005; Ruffman, Slade, & Redman, 2006; Sim & Xu, 2017).

  Many researchers contend that Piaget underestimated children's capabilities generally, in part due to the limitations of the mini-experiments he conducted. Subjected to a broader array of experimental tasks, children show less consistency within stages than Piaget predicted. Increasing evidence suggests that children's cognitive abilities emerge earlier than supposed; for example, some children demonstrate concrete operational thinking before age 7, the age at which Piaget suggested these abilities first appear (Dawson-Tunik, Fischer, & Stein, 2004).

- **Children's Understanding of Numbers.** Piaget may also have erred in asserting that preschoolers have little understanding of numbers, as shown by their inability to grasp conservation and reversibility (the understanding that a transformation can be reversed to return something to its original state). Recent experimental work calls that assertion into question. For instance, developmental psychologist Rochel Gelman has found that children as young as 3 can easily tell the difference between rows of two and three toy animals, regardless of the animals' spacing. Older children are able to identify which of two numbers is larger and show a rudimentary understanding of addition and subtraction (Vilette, 2002; Brandone et al., 2012; Dietrich et al., 2016).

  Gelman concludes that children have an innate ability to count, akin to the ability to use language that some theorists see as universal and genetically determined. This is clearly at odds with Piagetian notions, which suggest that children's numerical abilities do not blossom until after the preoperational period (i.e., after about age 7).

- **Conservation.** There are further difficulties with Piaget's contention that conservation does not emerge until the end of the preoperational period. This contention has not stood up to experimental scrutiny. Children can learn to answer conservation tasks correctly if they are given certain training and experiences. The fact that one can improve children's performance argues against the Piagetian view that children in the preoperational period have not reached a level of cognitive maturity to understand conservation (Halford & Andrews, 2006).

- **Cultural Issues.** Piaget's work also seems to describe children from developed, Western countries better than those in non-Western cultures. For instance, some evidence suggests that cognitive skills emerge on a different timetable for children in non-Western cultures than for children living in Europe and the United States. Infants raised in the Ivory Coast of Africa, for example, reach the various substages of the sensorimotor period at an earlier age than infants reared in France (Dasen et al., 1978; Mistry & Saraswathi, 2003; TamisLeMonda et al., 2012).

Despite these criticisms—which research has shown to be valid—we cannot dismiss Piaget. Although some early cross-cultural research implied that children in certain cultures remain preoperational, failing to master conservation and develop concrete operations, more recent research suggests otherwise. For instance, with proper training in conservation, children in non-Western cultures who do not conserve learn to do so. In one study, urban Australian children—who develop concrete operations on Piaget's timetable—were compared to rural Aborigine children, who typically do not conserve at the age of 14 (Dasen, Ngini, & Lavallee, 1979; Maynard & Greenfield, 2003). With training, the rural Aborigine children showed conservation skills similar to those of their urban counterparts, although about 3 years later (see Figure 5-5).

When children are interviewed by researchers from their own culture, who share their language and customs, and whose reasoning tasks relate to important cultural domains, the children are much more likely to display concrete operational thinking. Such research suggests that Piaget was right in arguing that concrete operations are universally achieved during middle childhood. Performance differences between Western and some non-Western children on Piagetian measures of conservation and concrete operations probably reflect a difference in experiences. The progress of cognitive development cannot be understood without considering a child's culture (Lau, Lee, & Chiu, 2004; Maynard, 2008; Wang et al., 2016).

Appraising Piaget: Research on babies in non-Western cultures suggests that Piaget's stages are not universal but are to some degree culturally derived.

Figure 5-5 Conservation Training.

Rural Australian Aborigine children trail their urban counterparts in the development of their understanding of conservation; with training, they later catch up. Without training, around half of 14-year-old Aborigines do not have an understanding of conservation. What can be concluded from the fact that training influences the understanding of conservation? (**Source:** Based on Dasen, Ngini, & Lavallee, 1979.)

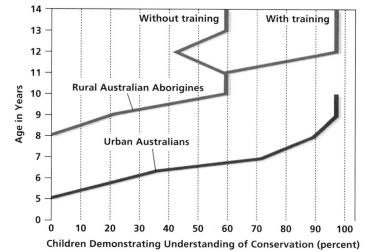

Children Demonstrating Understanding of Conservation (percent)

The nature of thought changes qualitatively during early adulthood.

A FINAL SUMMATION. Even Piaget's most passionate critics concede that he has provided us with an ingenious description of the broad outlines of cognitive development during infancy. His failings seem to be in underestimating the capabilities of younger infants and in his claims that sensorimotor skills develop in a consistent, fixed pattern.

Still, his influence has been enormous. Piaget's theories have inspired countless studies on the development of thinking capacities and processes, and they have spurred much classroom reform. His bold statements about the nature of cognitive development sparked opposition that brought forth new approaches, such as the information processing perspective we examine later in the chapter. Piaget remains a towering, pioneering figure in the field of development (Roth, Slone, & Dar, 2000; Kail, 2004).

Beyond Piaget

LO 5.6 Compare and contrast Labouvie-Vief's, Perry's, and Schaie's theories of cognitive development to that of Piaget.

As we've seen, Piaget, for all his brilliance and influence, has drawn his share of criticism. Let's look at several contemporary approaches that differ from Piaget's on the question of when cognitive development comes to an end. The developmentalists who espouse these approaches all agree on one thing: that Piaget underestimated the portion of the life span during which cognitive development occurs.

Consider the following scenario drawn from research by Adams and Labouvie-Vief (1986).

> Ben is known to be a heavy drinker, especially when he goes to parties. Tyra, Ben's wife, warns him that if he comes home drunk one more time, she will leave him and take the children. Tonight Ben is out late at an office party. He comes home drunk. Does Tyra leave Ben?

To the typical adolescent this case is open-and-shut: Tyra leaves Ben. But in early adulthood, the answer is less clear. People become less concerned with sheer logic and instead take into account real-life concerns that may influence and temper behavior.

To Piaget, the first stage of development is the sensorimotor stage, achieved in infancy, and the final stage is the formal operations stage, reached in adolescence. If we subscribed to the traditional Piagetian view of cognitive development, we would expect to find little intellectual growth in early adulthood.

Piaget argued that by the time people left adolescence, their thinking, at least qualitatively, had largely become what it would be for the rest of their lives. They might gather more information, but the ways in which they thought about it would not change. But this view of development seems overly limited. Does development really stop in adolescence?

LABOUVIE-VIEF AND POSTFORMAL THOUGHT. Gisela Labouvie-Vief and several other modern developmentalists have begun to conclude that the answer is no. They have found that cognitive development continues beyond adolescence because people are faced with dealing with the complexities of life throughout adulthood.

Labouvie-Vief suggests that the nature of thinking changes during early adulthood. She asserts that thinking based solely on formal operations is insufficient to meet the demands placed on young adults. The complexity of society, which requires specialization, and the challenge of finding one's way through that complexity, require thought that transcends logic to include practical experience, moral judgments, and values (Labouvie-Vief, 2009, 2015; Hamer & Van Rossum, 2016).

For example, imagine a young, single woman in her first job. Her boss, a married man whom she respects greatly and who is in a position to help her career, invites her to go with him to make an important presentation to a client. When the presentation, which has gone very well, is over, he suggests they go out to dinner and celebrate. Later that evening, after sharing a bottle of wine, he asks if he can walk her back to her hotel room to make sure she gets back safely. How should she handle the situation?

Logic alone doesn't answer such questions. Labouvie-Vief suggests that young adults' thinking must develop to handle ambiguous situations like these. She suggests that young adults learn to use analogies and metaphors to make comparisons, confront society's paradoxes, and become comfortable with a more subjective understanding. This requires weighing all aspects of a situation according to one's values and beliefs. It allows for interpretive processes and reflects the fact that the reasons behind events in the real world are painted in shades of gray rather than black and white (Labouvie-Vief, 2015; Sinnott et al., 2017).

To demonstrate how this sort of thinking develops, Labouvie-Vief presented experimental subjects, ranging in age from 10 to 40, with scenarios similar to the Ben and Tyra scenario above. Each story had a clear, logical conclusion, but it could be interpreted differently if real-world demands and pressures were taken into account.

In responding to the scenarios, adolescents relied heavily on the logic of formal operations. They tended to predict that Tyra would immediately pack up her bags and leave with the children when Ben came home drunk. After all, that's what she said she would do. In contrast, young adults were more apt to consider various real-life possibilities: Would Ben be apologetic and beg Tyra not to leave? Did Tyra really mean it when she said she would leave? Does Tyra have someplace to go?

Young adults exhibited what Labouvie-Vief calls postformal thinking. **Postformal thought** is thinking that goes beyond Piaget's formal operations. Rather than being based on purely logical processes, with absolutely right and wrong answers to problems, postformal thought acknowledges that adult predicaments must sometimes be solved in relativistic terms.

postformal thought
thinking that acknowledges that adult predicaments must sometimes be solved in relativistic terms.

From an *educator's* perspective

Can you think of situations that you would deal with differently as an adult than as an adolescent? Do the differences reflect postformal thinking?

According to psychologist Jan Sinnott (2014), postformal thinkers shift back and forth between an abstract, ideal solution and real-world constraints that might prevent implementation of that solution. Postformal thinkers understand that just as there can be multiple causes of a situation, there can be multiple solutions to it.

PERRY'S APPROACH TO POSTFORMAL THINKING. To psychologist William Perry (1981), the developmental growth of early adulthood involves mastering new ways of understanding the world. To examine intellectual and moral growth during college, Perry interviewed students at Harvard University. He found that students entering college tended to use *dualistic thinking* in their views of the world: Something was either right or wrong; people were either good or bad; others were either for them or against them.

However, as these students encountered new ideas and points of view from other students and their professors, their dualistic thinking declined. Consistent with postformal thinking, they understood that it is possible to hold multiple perspectives on an issue. Their attitude toward authorities also changed: Instead of assuming that experts had all the answers, they began to realize that their own thinking had validity if their position was well thought out and rational.

In fact, according to Perry, they had reached a stage in which knowledge and values were regarded as relativistic. Rather than seeing the world as having absolute standards and values, they argued that different societies, cultures, and individuals could have different standards and values, and all of them could be equally valid.

It's important to keep in mind that Perry's theory is based on a sample of interviews conducted with well-educated students attending an elite college. His findings may not apply as well to people who have never learned how to examine multiple points of view.

acquisitive stage

according to Schaie, the first stage of cognitive development, encompassing all of childhood and adolescence, in which the main developmental task is to acquire information.

achieving stage

the point reached by young adults in which intelligence is applied to specific situations involving the attainment of long-term goals regarding careers, family, and societal contributions.

responsible stage

the stage where the major concerns of middle-aged adults relate to their personal situations, including protecting and nourishing their spouses, families, and careers.

executive stage

the period in middle adulthood when people take a broader perspective than they had previously, including concerns about the world.

reintegrative stage

the period of late adulthood during which the focus is on tasks that have personal meaning.

SCHAIE'S STAGES OF COGNITIVE DEVELOPMENT. Developmental psychologist K. Warner Schaie offers another perspective on postformal thought. Taking up where Piaget left off, Schaie suggests that adults' thinking follows a set pattern of stages (illustrated in Figure 5-6). But Schaie focuses on the ways in which information is used during adulthood, rather than on changes in the acquisition and understanding of new information, as in Piaget's approach (Schaie & Zanjani, 2006; Hülür et al., 2015 Schaie, 2016).

Schaie suggests that before adulthood, the main cognitive developmental task is acquisition of information. Consequently, he labels the first stage of cognitive development, which encompasses all of childhood and adolescence, the **acquisitive stage**. Information gathered before we grow up is largely squirreled away for future use. Much of the rationale for education during childhood and adolescence, then, is to prepare people for future activities.

The situation changes considerably in early adulthood when the focus shifts from the future to the here-and-now. According to Schaie, young adults are in the **achieving stage**, applying their intelligence to attain long-term goals regarding their careers, family, and contributions to society. During the achieving stage, young adults must confront and resolve several major issues, and the decisions they make—such as what job to take and who to marry—have implications for the rest of their lives.

During the late stages of early adulthood and in middle adulthood, people move into the responsible and executive stages. In the **responsible stage**, middle-aged adults are mainly concerned with protecting and nourishing their spouses, families, and careers.

Sometime later, further into middle adulthood, many people (but not all) enter the **executive stage** in which they take a broader perspective, becoming more concerned about the larger world. People in the executive stage put energy into nourishing and sustaining societal institutions. They may become involved in town government, religious congregations, service clubs, charitable groups, factory unions—organizations that have a larger purpose in society (Sinnott, 1997, 2003).

Finally, the **reintegrative stage** is the period of late adulthood during which people focus on tasks that have personal meaning. They no longer focus on acquiring knowledge to solve potential problems that they may encounter. Instead, they acquire information about issues that specifically interest them. Furthermore, they have less interest in—and patience for—things that they do not see as having some immediate application to their lives.

Figure 5-6 Schaie's Stages of Adult Development
(**Source:** Schaie, 1977–1978.)

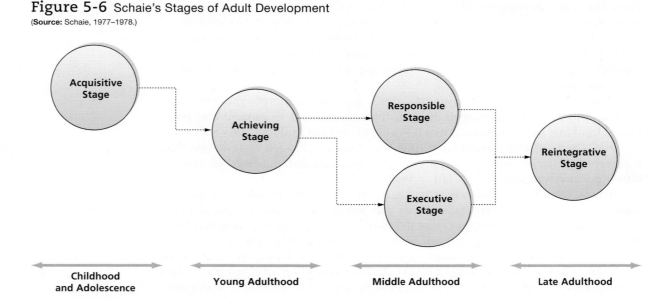

Module 5.2 Review

LO 5.5   **Summarize the arguments for and against Piaget's theory of cognitive development.**

Recent developmentalists, while acknowledging Piaget's acute observational ability and his pioneering contributions to cognitive development, have questioned many of his conclusions, including the boundaries between his stages, the severe limits he attached to preschoolers' abilities, the universality of cognitive development across cultures, and his judgment that cognitive development is essentially complete by the end of adolescence.

LO 5.6   **Compare and contrast Labouvie-Vief's, Perry's, and Schaie's theories of cognitive development to that of Piaget.**

In contrast to Piaget, Gisela Labouvie-Vief maintains that adults engage in postformal thought, in which predicaments must sometimes be solved in relativistic terms, rather than as absolute rights and wrongs. William Perry suggests that people move from dualistic thinking to relativistic thought during early adulthood. K. Warner Schaie argues that adults pass through five stages of information: acquisitive, achieving, responsible, executive, and reintegrative.

Journal Writing Prompt

Applying Lifespan Development: Do adults use schemas to organize their environment? Do the principles of assimilation and accommodation apply to adult learning as well as children's learning? How?

MODULE 5.3

VYGOTSKY'S VIEW OF COGNITIVE DEVELOPMENT: TAKING CULTURE INTO ACCOUNT

> *As her daughter watches, a member of the Chilcotin Indian tribe prepares a salmon for dinner. When the daughter asks a question about a small detail of the process, the mother takes out another salmon and repeats the entire process. According to the tribal view of learning, understanding and comprehension can come only from grasping the total procedure, and not from learning about the individual subcomponents of the task. (Tharp, 1989)*

The Chilcotin view of how children learn about the world contrasts with the prevalent view of Western society, which assumes that only by mastering the separate parts of a problem can one fully comprehend it. Do differences in the ways particular cultures and societies approach problems influence cognitive development? According to Russian developmental psychologist Lev Vygotsky, who lived from 1896 to 1934, the answer is a clear yes.

Cognitive Development and Social Interactions

LO 5.7   **Explain Vygotsky's view of cognitive development and contrast it to Piaget's theory.**

Vygotsky viewed cognitive development as the product of social interactions. Instead of concentrating on individual performance, Vygotsky's increasingly influential view focuses on the social aspects of development and learning.

Vygotsky sees children as apprentices, learning cognitive strategies and other skills from adult and peer mentors who not only present new ways of doing things but also provide assistance, instruction, and motivation. Consequently, he focuses on the child's social and cultural world as the source of cognitive development. According to Vygotsky, children gradually grow intellectually and begin to function on their own because of the assistance that adult and peer partners provide (Vygotsky, 1926/1997; Tudge & Scrimsher, 2003).

From Research to Practice

Screen Time and the Video Deficit

In a world that is increasingly saturated with technology designed to entertain us or keep us connected to each other, it is not surprising that mobile devices are being used by very young children. For example, in restaurants it's commonplace to see toddlers seated with their parents at a table, wearing earbuds and watching their favorite show on their parent's smartphone or playing a video game on a tablet. Many parents expect that using this technology will provide some sort of educational benefit for their child. But do young children learn as well from a screen as they would from interacting directly with an adult?

No, they do not, because of what has been termed the *video deficit*. Research has consistently found that for many learning tasks such as word-learning and imitation, young children learn much more quickly when interacting with an adult in person than they do watching instruction on a screen. For example, one study found that 12- to 18-month-olds learned many more new words when taught through live parent interaction compared to children who watched a popular DVD that attempted to teach the same words (DeLoache et al., 2010).

We don't yet fully understand what causes the video deficit in young children. However, a recent study looked at how toddlers' eye movements differ when they are being taught where to find a hidden object that was presented either on a screen or by a person. Researchers found that the toddlers interacting with a screen actually looked *more* at the place where the object was hidden and yet were *less likely* to find the object than were the toddlers interacting with a real person. This study and many like it underscore the importance of in-person interactions for young children and perhaps caution us not to rely on technology for education (Kirkorian et al., 2016).

Shared Writing Prompt

How might awareness of the video deficit influence strategies that parents and teachers use to educate young children?

Vygotsky contends that culture and society establish the institutions, such as preschools and play groups, that promote development by providing opportunities for cognitive growth. Furthermore, by emphasizing particular tasks, culture and society shape the nature of specific cognitive advances. Unless we look at what is important and meaningful to members of a given society, we may seriously underestimate the nature and level of cognitive abilities that ultimately will be attained (Balakrishnan & Claiborne, 2012; Nagahashi, 2013; Veraksa et al., 2016).

For example, children's toys reflect what is important and meaningful in a particular society. In Western societies, preschoolers commonly play with toy wagons, automobiles, and other vehicles, in part reflecting the mobile nature of the culture. In this way, a society subtly communicates to children a great deal about its expectations and characteristics.

In much the same way, societal expectations about gender play a role in how children come to understand the world. For example, one study conducted at a science museum found that parents provided more detailed scientific explanations to boys than to girls at museum displays. Such differences in level of explanation may lead to more sophisticated understanding of science in boys and ultimately may produce later gender differences in science learning (Crowley et al., 2001).

Vygotsky's approach is therefore quite different from Piaget's. Where Piaget looked at children and saw junior scientists, working by themselves to develop an independent understanding of the world, Vygotsky saw cognitive apprentices, learning from master teachers the skills valued in the child's culture. Where Piaget saw preschoolers who were egocentric, looking at the world from their own limited vantage point, Vygotsky saw preschoolers as using others to gain an understanding of the world (Halford, 2005; Karpov, 2006).

Getty Images/Tim Pannell

Students working in cooperative groups benefit from the insights of others.

The Zone of Proximal Development

LO 5.8 Define Vygotsky's zone of proximal development, and explain the role it plays in children's cognitive development.

Vygotsky proposed that children's cognitive abilities increase through exposure to information that is new enough to be intriguing but not too difficult to contend with. He called this the **zone of proximal development (ZPD)**, the level at which a child can almost, but not fully, perform a task independently, but can do so with the assistance of someone more competent. For cognitive development to occur, new information must be presented—by parents, teachers, or more skilled peers—within the zone of proximal development. For example, a preschooler might not be able to figure out by herself how to stick a handle on the clay pot she's making, but she can do it with advice from her child-care teacher (Zuckerman & Shenfield, 2007; Norton & D'Ambrosio, 2008; Warford, 2011).

The concept of the zone of proximal development suggests that even though two children might be able to achieve the same amount without help, if one child receives aid, he or she may improve substantially more than the other. The greater the improvement that comes with help, the larger the zone of proximal development.

SCAFFOLDING. The assistance or structuring provided by others has been termed **scaffolding**, after the temporary scaffolds that aid in building construction. Scaffolding is the support for learning and problem solving that encourages independence and growth. As in construction, the scaffolding that older people provide, which facilitates the completion of identified tasks, is removed once children can solve a problem on their own (Puntambekar & Hübscher, 2005; Warwick & Maloch, 2003; Radford et al., 2015).

To Vygotsky, scaffolding not only helps children solve specific problems, it also aids in the development of their overall cognitive abilities. In education, scaffolding involves, first of all, helping children think about and frame a task appropriately. In addition, a parent or teacher is likely to provide clues to task completion that fit the child's level of development and to model behavior that can lead to task completion.

To illustrate how scaffolding operates, consider the following conversation between mother and son:

Mother: Do you remember how you helped me make the cookies before?

Child: No.

Mother: We made the dough and put it in the oven. Do you remember that?

Child: When Grandma came?

Mother: Yes, that's right. Would you help me shape the dough into cookies?

Child: Okay.

Mother: Can you remember how big we made the cookies when Grandma was here?

Child: Big.

Mother: Right. Can you show me how big?

Child: We used the big wooden spoon.

Mother: Good boy, that's right. We used the wooden spoon, and we made big cookies. But let's try something different today by using the ice cream scoop to form the cookies.

Although this conversation may not appear to be a particularly sophisticated specimen of teaching and learning, it illustrates the practice of scaffolding. The mother is supporting her son's efforts, and she gets him to respond conversationally. In the

zone of proximal development (ZPD)
according to Vygotsky, the level at which a child can *almost,* but not fully, perform a task independently, but can do so with the assistance of someone more competent.

scaffolding
the support for learning and problem solving that encourages independence and growth.

process, she not only expands her son's abilities by using a different tool (the scoop instead of the spoon), she models how conversations proceed.

In some societies parental support for learning differs by gender. In one study, Mexican mothers were found to provide more scaffolding than fathers. A possible explanation is that mothers may be more aware of their children's cognitive abilities than are fathers (Tamis-LeMonda & Cabrera, 2002; de Oliveira & Jackson, 2017).

CULTURAL TOOLS.   One key aspect of the aid that more accomplished individuals provide to learners comes in the form of cultural tools. Cultural tools are actual, physical items (e.g., pencils, paper, calculators, computers, and so forth), as well as an intellectual and conceptual framework for solving problems. The framework includes the language that is used within a culture, its alphabetical and numbering schemas, its mathematical and scientific systems, and even its religious systems. These cultural tools provide a structure that can be used to help children define and solve specific problems, as well as an intellectual point of view that encourages cognitive development.

For an example of the pervasive influence of culture on thinking and action, consider the *Developmental Diversity and Your Life* box below.

Evaluating Vygotsky's Contributions

LO 5.9   **Summarize the strengths and weaknesses of Vygotsky's theory on cognitive development in children.**

Vygotsky's view has become increasingly influential, which is surprising given that he died over 80 years ago at age 37 (Winsler, 2003). His influence has grown because his writings are only now becoming widely disseminated in the United States due to the growing availability of good English translations. For most of the 20th century, Vygotsky was not widely known even within his native land. His work was banned for some time, and it was not until the breakup of the Soviet Union in the 1990s that it became freely available in the former Soviet countries. Thus, Vygotsky, long hidden from his fellow developmentalists, didn't emerge onto the scene until long after his death (Wertsch, 2008).

Developmental Diversity and Your Life

A Walk Through a Cultural Landscape

"Dad, how far is it to school?"

"It's about three blocks past the supermarket."

"School is about a 20-minute ride downtown on the subway that stops across the street from our apartment."

"If you walk to the public well, and then walk that distance again, and then again, you will reach the school."

"You know how the boys and girls all race to that tall tree in the grove by the river? The school is maybe two of those races from our house, in the direction of the morning sun."

Our culture is all around us, as invisible and as much taken for granted as water is to fish. No matter what we do or think about, we are expressing ourselves in terms of our culture.

Consider the cultural differences in how people talk about distance. In cities, distance is usually measured in blocks ("the store is about 15 blocks away"). To a child from a rural background, more culturally meaningful terms are needed, such as yards or miles, such practical rules of thumb as "a stone's throw," or references to known distances and landmarks ("about half the distance to town"). To make matters more complicated, "how far" questions are sometimes answered in terms not of distance, but of time ("it's about 15 minutes to the store"), which will be understood variously to refer to walking or riding time, depending on context—and, if riding time, to different forms of riding—by oxcart, bicycle, bus, canoe, or automobile, again depending on cultural context.

In short, not only is the nature of the tools available to children to solve problems and perform tasks highly dependent on the culture in which they live, but also the ways they think about problems and questions, and the ways they use those tools.

Even more important, though, is the quality of Vygotsky's ideas. They represent a consistent theoretical system and help explain a growing body of research on the importance of social interaction in promoting cognitive development. The idea that children's comprehension of the world flows from their interactions with their parents, peers, and other members of society is increasingly well supported. It is also consistent with a growing body of multicultural and cross-cultural research, which finds evidence that cognitive development is shaped, in part, by cultural factors (Hedegaard & Fleer, 2013; Friedrich, 2014; van der Veer & Yasnitsky, 2016).

Of course, not every aspect of Vygotsky's theory has been supported, and he can be criticized for a lack of precision in his conceptualization of cognitive growth. For instance, such broad concepts as the zone of proximal development are not terribly precise, and they do not always lend themselves to experimental tests (Daniels, 2006).

Furthermore, aside from his observations about the social function that children's private speech serves and his approach to the development of intelligence, both of which we will discuss in a later chapter, Vygotsky was largely silent on how basic cognitive processes such as attention and memory develop and how children's natural cognitive capabilities unfold. Because of his emphasis on broad cultural influences, he did not focus on how individual bits of information are processed and synthesized. These processes, essential to a complete understanding of cognitive development, are more directly addressed by information processing theories.

Still, Vygotsky's melding of the cognitive and social worlds of children has marked an important advance in our understanding of cognitive development.

Module 5.3 Review

LO 5.7 Explain Vygotsky's view of cognitive development and contrast it to Piaget's theory.

Lev Vygotsky proposed that the nature and progress of children's cognitive development are dependent on the children's social and cultural context. According to Vygotsky, culture and society determine how people engage in thought and set the agenda for education and the cognitive abilities that their members are expected to attain.

LO 5.8 Define Vygotsky's zone of proximal development, and explain the role it plays in children's cognitive development.

Vygotsky's theory features the concepts of the zone of proximal development and scaffolding. Vygotsky suggests that schoolchildren should have the opportunity to experiment and participate actively with their peers in their learning.

LO 5.9 Summarize the strengths and weaknesses of Vygotsky's theory of cognitive development in children.

Vygotsky's ideas have influenced educational practices in the United States and other nations. In particular, the practice of cooperative learning and the technique of reciprocal teaching owe their development to his insights about how teachers can best help students learn. Despite a lack of precision about basic cognitive processes, Vygotsky has become, in the years since his death, an influential figure in the study of cognitive development and the practice of education.

Journal Writing Prompt

Applying Lifespan Development: If children's cognitive development is dependent on interactions with others, what obligations does society have regarding such social settings as preschools and neighborhoods?

Epilogue

We have examined the work of two major cognitive development researchers, Jean Piaget and Lev Vygotsky, as well as several critics of their approaches. We have seen the weighty influence of Piaget's work on subsequent theoretical approaches and experimental work, and we have marveled at the ability of a Russian psychologist to construct a structure of theory and thought that has recently gained a strong footing in American education.

Before we proceed to social and personality development in the next chapter, turn back to the prologue of this chapter, about Maria Castillo, the toddler who recently learned the word "doggy" and seems to be applying it to every animal with fur, and answer the following questions.

1. According to Piaget, when Maria says "doggy" while pointing to a cheetah in the zoo, is that an example of assimilation or accommodation? Explain your reasoning.

2. What sensorimotor substage does Maria appear to be in? Explain your answer.

3. Vygotsky emphasized the importance of social interaction in cognitive development. How does the story of Maria support this theory?

4. Specifically describe how Maria's cognitive development might be compromised if she were raised in an environment with much less social interaction.

Looking Back

LO 5.1 Summarize the fundamental features of Piaget's theory of cognitive development.

Cognitive development focuses on changes in behavior that correspond to changes in an individual's intellectual abilities, with special attention to intelligence, language, and similar topics. Piaget theorized that the foundations of the way we understand the world are mental structures called schemas, organized patterns of functioning, that adapt and change with mental development. Two underlying principles explain how children's schemas grow. Assimilation consists of fitting stimuli or events into existing patterns of thought, while accommodation consists of expanding existing patterns of thought to fit stimuli or events. Piaget's theory is based on a stage approach to development, with children and adolescents passing through four universal stages in a predetermined sequence: sensorimotor, preoperational, concrete operational, and formal operational.

LO 5.2 Describe infants' cognitive development across the six substages of Piaget's sensorimotor stage.

In the six substages of the sensorimotor period, simple reflexes at first determine behaviors, then the infant's earliest habits become circular reactions, which eventually become goal-oriented problem-solving activities. In the next substage, infants deliberately vary their actions as if conducting experiments, and in the final substage, they begin to produce mental representations of events or objects.

LO 5.3 Define what Piaget means by preoperational thought, and describe the cognitive characteristics of this stage.

The preoperational stage occurs during the preschool years, as children's use of symbolic thinking, reasoning, and concepts increases. The preoperational stage has several limitations, including centration, a failure to conserve, an incomplete understanding of transformation, and egocentrism.

LO 5.4 Describe the cognitive advances children make during Piaget's concrete operational and formal operational stages.

Concrete operational thought develops during middle childhood. This stage is characterized by the active and appropriate use of logic. However, individuals in this stage are still limited to concrete reality and are unable to deal with abstract or hypothetical questions. Piaget's final stage, the formal operational period, occurs in later adolescence as people develop the ability to think abstractly.

LO 5.5 Summarize the arguments for and against Piaget's theory of cognitive development.

Despite Piaget's great influence on the field, specific aspects of his theory have been criticized, including the concept of stages that forms the basis of his theory and what many critics perceive as his persistent underestimation of children's abilities. Piaget has also been criticized for neglecting any consideration of development beyond the end of adolescence. Several cognitive researchers extend the stage approach to adulthood.

LO 5.6 Compare and contrast Labouvie-Vief's, Perry's, and Schaie's theories of cognitive development to that of Piaget.

Gisela Labouvie-Vief maintains that postformal thought develops in young adulthood. Postformal thinking surpasses logic to encompass interpretive and subjective thinking. William Perry suggests that people move from dualistic thinking to relativistic thought during early adulthood. K. Warner Schaie argues that adults pass through the acquisitive, achieving, responsible, executive, and reintegrative stages in the way they use information.

LO 5.7 Explain Vygotsky's view of cognitive development and contrast it to Piaget's theory.

In Vygotsky's view, cognitive development is the product of culture and of social interactions. Vygotsky believed that societal expectations about gender play a role in shaping how children come to understand the world.

LO 5.8 Define Vygotsky's zone of proximal development, and explain the role it plays in children's cognitive development.

Vygotsky notes that children learn best by participating in active learning through child–adult and child–child interactions that fall within each child's zone of proximal development. He also observes that learners need support—a process called scaffolding—to encourage their learning and problem solving until they achieve independence and growth.

LO 5.9 Summarize the strengths and weaknesses of Vygotsky's theory of cognitive development in children.

Vygotsky's views are respected because they represent a consistent theoretical system and are consistent with modern research on learning and cognitive development. Critics contend that Vygotsky's theories lack precision and lend themselves only with difficulty to experimental tests. Furthermore, Vygotsky never addressed some of the major topics in cognitive development, such as attention and memory, and he dealt only slightly with intelligence.

Key Terms and Concepts

schema   170

assimilation   171

accommodation   171

sensorimotor stage (of cognitive development)   171

goal-directed behavior   173

object permanence   173

mental representation   174

deferred imitation   175

preoperational stage   175

operations   175

symbolic function   175

centration   176

conservation   176

transformation   177

egocentric thought   177

intuitive thought   177

concrete operational stage   178

formal operational stage   179

postformal thought   185

acquisitive stage   186

achieving stage   186

responsible stage   186

executive stage   186

reintegrative stage   186

zone of proximal development (ZPD)   189

scaffolding   189

Chapter 6
Cognitive Growth: Information Processing Approaches

FatCamera/Getty Images/E+

Learning Objectives

LO 6.1 Describe how information is taken in, held, and used, according to information processing theorists.

LO 6.2 Explain how the architecture of the human information processing system functions.

LO 6.3 Compare the information processing approaches to Piaget's theory of cognitive development.

LO 6.4 Explain why attention is important for children's cognitive development.

LO 6.5 Describe memory improvements during childhood and analyze how childhood memories change over time.

LO 6.6 Analyze how memory changes as people age, and describe strategies for developing and improving memory.

LO 6.7 Describe applications of information processing approaches to the recall of events for legal purposes.

LO 6.8 Apply insights from information processing theory to classroom instruction.

LO 6.9 Compare the strengths and weaknesses of the information processing approach and other approaches to cognitive development.

Chapter Overview

Prologue: The Overwhelmed Barista

Eighteen-year-old Justin Daley was excited to start his first day working at the local coffee shop, but he had no idea it would be such a disaster. Learning how to operate the electronic register was daunting to say the least. With several dozen color-coded tabs and buttons on the screen representing drink categories and ingredients, there seemed to be no end to the possible combinations people could order.

When Justin took his first few orders, he sensed his customers' mounting impatience as he searched through each screen for the correct button. But he was no match for the evening rush as the line of customers began to stretch to the door. Thankfully, his 16-year-old co-worker Jasmine stepped in to help him take the orders. He stood in awe as she effortlessly navigated through each screen, her fingers almost a blur. "Remember that all the seasonal drinks have a yellow button," she reminded him.

As the crowd began to thin out, Justin thanked her for her help and commented "You were great, I don't know how you can remember where everything is on that register." Jasmine laughed and reassured him, "Don't worry, you'll be a pro in a few days. Then you'll get to move on to the toughest part of the job—actually making the drinks."

Justin smiled weakly, wondering if he'd even last a week. ■

Looking Ahead

Life demands that all of us learn new information every day, like the new barista Justin. But in this chapter, we diverge from the roads that Jean Piaget and Lev Vygotsky laid out for us. Rather than seeking to identify the universal milestones in cognitive development, as Piaget tried to do, or to recognize the contribution of the social world to thinking, as Vygotsky attempted, we now take a different approach based on *information processing*. According to the information processing approach, we can best understand cognitive development by considering the processes by which individuals acquire and use the information to which they are exposed. We need, then, to focus less on the qualitative changes in a person's cognitive development and to consider more closely their quantitative capabilities.

In this chapter, we'll first consider the foundations of information processing in three elementary functions—encoding, storage, and retrieval—that are involved in any processing of information, whether by humans or computers. We'll also consider the topic of attention, discussing the functions and development of attention in children, the use of planning and control strategies to focus attention, and the ways that attention affects our ability to accomplish our goals and complete our tasks. We will also discuss an increasingly prevalent attention disorder that affects learning and normal life functioning.

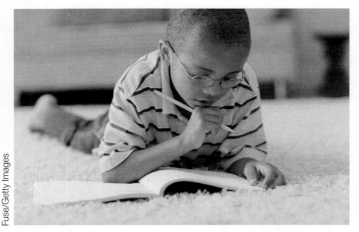

School-age children begin to use strategies for remembering information.

Next we'll consider memory, discussing first the development of basic memory capabilities in infancy and the surprising retention of information even at very young ages. We will discuss how infants' memories become lost or corrupted, and we will examine the reliability of children's memories of their own experiences. We'll then consider how and why memory improves as children age, and we'll discuss strategies that people use to control and improve cognitive processing. We'll also discuss whether culture affects the quality of memory—and the difficulty of conducting sound studies of memory across cultures.

Finally, we conclude the chapter with a look at some practical applications of information processing theory in the courtroom, the classroom, and the home. We also offer a general appraisal of the information processing perspective and its contributions to our understanding of human cognition.

MODULE 6.1

THE BASICS OF INFORMATION PROCESSING

"Who is the president of the United States?" "When is your birthday?" "Where did you leave your gloves?"

They're not very hard questions for an adult, or even for a 5-year-old. But whether someone is able to answer them depends on a series of processing steps that are hardly simple.

Encoding, Storage, and Retrieval: The Foundations of Information Processing

LO 6.1 **Describe how information is taken in, held, and used, according to information processing theorists.**

information processing approaches

approaches to cognitive development that seek to identify the ways that individuals take in, use, and store information.

Information processing approaches to cognitive development seek to identify the way that individuals take in, use, and store information. According to this approach, the quantitative changes in infants' abilities to organize and manipulate information represent the hallmarks of cognitive development.

According to this perspective, cognitive growth is characterized by increasing sophistication in information processing, similar to the way a computer program becomes more sophisticated and useful as the programmer modifies it and as the capacity of the computer's memory and its computational sophistication increase. Information processing approaches, then, focus on the types of "mental programs" that people use when they seek to solve problems (Fagan & Ployhart, 2015).

Whether someone is able to answer the questions posed at the start of this module depends on several basic processes of information processing (see Figure 6-1). For instance, it is necessary for the information to be encoded in memory. *Encoding* is the process by which information is initially recorded in a form usable to memory. All of us are exposed to a massive amount of information; if we tried to process it all, we would be overwhelmed. Consequently, people encode selectively, picking and choosing the information to which they will pay attention. The ability to answer questions such as the preceding, then, depends first on whether someone has been exposed to the information in the first place and subsequently on whether he or she has encoded it in a meaningful way.

Figure 6-1 Information Processing

The process by which information is encoded, stored, and retrieved.

Even if an individual has been exposed to the information initially and has encoded it in an appropriate way, there is still no guarantee that he or she will be able to answer questions about it correctly. Information must also have been stored in memory adequately. *Storage* refers to the maintenance of material saved in memory. If, for example, we have not adequately stored information about the name of the U.S. president, we will be unable to recall it later.

Finally, the success of an individual in answering informational questions will depend on retrieval processes. *Retrieval* is the process by which material in memory storage is located, brought into awareness, and used. Success in responding to the questions posed earlier, then, is a result of how well the material can be retrieved from storage.

Information processing approaches suggest that the processes of encoding, storage, and retrieval are analogous to different parts of a computer. Encoding can be thought of as a computer's keyboard, through which one inputs information; storage is the computer's hard drive or other local disk drive, where information is stored; and retrieval is analogous to the delivery of data to a computer's screen, where information is displayed. Only when all three processes—encoding, storage, and retrieval—are operating can information be processed.

AUTOMATIZATION.   In some cases, encoding, storage, and retrieval are relatively automatic, whereas in other cases they are deliberate. *Automatization* is the degree to which an activity requires attention. Processes that require relatively little attention are automatic; processes that require relatively large amounts of attention are controlled.

Automatic processes help us in our initial encounters with the world by "automatically" priming us to process information in particular ways. For instance, by age 5, children automatically encode information in terms of frequency. They automatically become aware of how often they have encountered various people, permitting them to differentiate familiar from unfamiliar people (Homae et al., 2012; Lie, 2015; Seyfarth & Cheney, 2013).

Furthermore, without intending to and without being aware of it, they develop a sense of how often different stimuli are found together simultaneously. This permits them to develop an understanding of *concepts*, categorizations of objects, events, or people that share common properties. For example, by encoding the information that four legs, a wagging tail, and barking are often found together, children are able to acquire the concept of "dog." Children—as well as adults—are rarely aware of how they learn such concepts, and they are often not able to articulate the features that distinguish one concept (such as a dog) from another (such as cat). Instead, learning tends to occur automatically.

Automatization also provides the benefit of permitting more efficient information processing, allowing children to concentrate on other mental problems. At the same time, automatization can backfire: In some situations a nonautomatic response is required, but an automatic response, which occurs readily, is employed instead. For instance, a young child who encounters a cat for the first time, but who automatically categorizes it as a dog because it has four legs and a tail, is a victim of automaticity.

Cognitive Architecture: The Three-System Approach

LO 6.2 **Explain how the architecture of the human information processing system functions.**

Although the ability to encode, store, and retrieve material is central to information processing, these processes are not the whole story. In fact, they don't provide an explanation of how information actually moves through the cognitive architecture. *Cognitive architecture* refers to the basic, enduring structures and features of information processing that are relatively constant over the course of development.

Cognitive architecture determines the specific steps through which material is processed as it travels through the human mind. Information processing theorists assume that the basic architecture of information processing systems is constant over the course of development, although the speed and capacity of the system are thought to grow. In short, developmental change is reflected not in changes in cognitive architecture but in the efficiency and capacity of information processing over time (Siegler, 1998; Lavelle, 2015).

The *three-system approach* is the oldest—and most influential—of the approaches to information processes. According to cognitive psychologists Richard Atkinson and Richard Shiffrin (1968), there are several steps in the overall process that permit a person to encode, store, and retain information. Atkinson and Shiffrin describe the process in much the same way that we illustrated information processing by comparing it to a computer that passes information through a sequential series of steps. The three-system model consists of a sensory store, short-term memory, and long-term memory (see Figure 6-2).

Before we consider the three-system model, keep this idea in mind: Although the three-part description of memory may seem to imply the existence of separate memory storage areas in the brain where each system is located, in fact this view is oversimplified and largely erroneous. Instead, the three types of memory represent abstract systems that describe distinct components or functions of memory as opposed to actual physical locations.

sensory store
the initial, momentary storage of information, lasting only an instant.

THE SENSORY STORE. According to the Atkinson–Shiffrin three-system model, information first encounters what is called a sensory store. The **sensory store** is the initial, momentary storage of information, lasting only an instant. Sensory memories are simply a cognitive representation of some stimulus, unfiltered and unevaluated. Because they are a raw representation of the stimulus, they are not analyzed in terms of their meaning.

There are actually several types of sensory stores. Information can be initially registered as a visual image, a sound, a smell, or even a twinge of pain. However, unless the information is processed and passed to the next stage, it is lost almost immediately and forever. Still, despite its rapid decay, the sensory store is highly accurate, representing an almost identical replica of every stimulus to which it is exposed. It is as if we take a sequential series of snapshots of the world around us. However, only a few of the snapshots are preserved, while the rest are destroyed upon the arrival of each new one. The few snapshots that are maintained are preserved only because they are transferred to the next information way station: short-term memory.

Figure 6-2 An Information Processing Model

According to the Atkinson and Shiffrin model, there are several steps in the process that permit the encoding, storage, and retention of information, similar to a computer that passes information through a sequential series of steps. The three-system model consists of a sensory store, short-term memory, and long-term memory.

(**Source:** Adapted from Atkinson & Shiffrin, 1968.)

SHORT-TERM MEMORY. **Short-term memory** is the short-duration, limited-capacity memory component in which selected input from the memory store is worked on. It is in short-term memory that thoughtful, deliberate information processing first takes place, giving meaning to the raw, nonmeaningful information from the sensory store. It is not clear how the transfer from the sensory store to short-term memory takes place. Some researchers suggest that the sensory information is first translated into images or graphical representations, while others argue that the transfer takes place when sensory stimuli are changed into words (Baddeley & Wilson, 1985). Whatever the exact process, **short-term memory** begins the process of storing information in terms of meaning.

Storage in short-term memory, though longer than in the sensory store, is still relatively short, lasting from 15 to 25 seconds. In addition, the capacity of short-term memory is limited. In adults, short-term memory can hold up to seven items, or "chunks," of information, with variations of plus or minus two chunks. A *chunk* is a meaningful group of stimuli that can be stored as a unit in short-term memory. A chunk might be a letter or number, a word, or even a well-known maxim ("two's company, three's a crowd"). The important point about the definition of a chunk is that it relates less to physical size than to meaningfulness. Consequently, a group of seven maxims may be held in short-term memory as effectively as seven unrelated letters.

The capacity of short-term memory increases with age. For instance, in one frequently used experimental task, lists of stimuli such as the numbers from zero through nine are presented in a random order, typically at a pace of one per second. Experimental participants of different ages are then asked to repeat the numbers. Results of such research clearly show that short-term memory capacity increases with age. Whereas 2- and 3-year-old children can remember only around two numbers, 7-year-old children can recall around five. But with increasing age, the increase in the quantity of numbers that can be recalled slows down. For instance, there is only a one-number increase from age 12 (where, on average, six numbers can be recalled) to adulthood, when the quantity of numbers that can be recalled reaches seven (see Figure 6-3).

Performance of other memory tasks also improves with age. For instance, children are increasingly able to listen to a string of digits ("1-5-6-3-4") and then repeat the string in reverse order ("4-3-6-5-1"). At the start of the preschool period, they can remember and reverse only about two digits; by the beginning of adolescence they can perform the task with as many as six digits (Klibanoff et al., 2006; Jack, Simcock, & Hayne, 2012; Jarrold & Hall, 2013).

The capacity of short-term memory is also affected by the nature of the material being remembered. For example, lists of single numbers are usually remembered slightly better than lists of single letters. Recall that the capacity of short-term memory is not based on the physical size of the material being encoded but on whether it forms meaningful chunks of information. Thus, a list of five random letters (c, s, h, t, c) will be considered five chunks, while a list of five words (cat, son, hand, tree, car) is also stored as five chunks. Clearly, the words contain more physical information and yet are just as easily memorized. The specific nature of what constitutes a chunk depends on an individual's prior experience (Miller, 1956).

Why does memory capacity (which in short-term memory is also called *memory span*) increase? One important reason is that with increasing age we are able to rehearse material in short-term memory more rapidly, and the shorter the time lag between repetitions of a stimulus, the less likely it is to be forgotten. This simple fact explains why older

short-term memory
the short-duration, limited-capacity memory component in which selected input from the memory store is worked on.

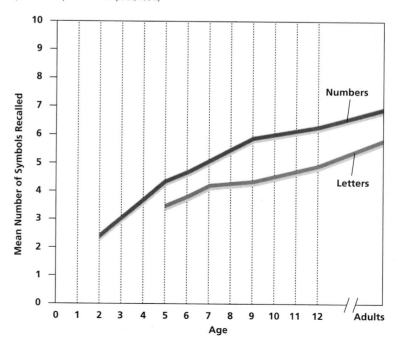

Figure 6-3 Increases in Memory Span
Memory span increases with age both for numbers and letters.
(**Source:** Adapted from Dempster, 1981.)

children, who are able to pronounce words more quickly, are also able to remember more: Their greater pronunciation speed permits them to rehearse words more quickly than younger children. According to some research, when speed of repetition is taken into account, the memory span of 6-year-olds is as great as that of young adults (Pertzov et al., 2015).

Although capacity and speed of processing change with age, the process used to handle material in short-term memory—rehearsal—is assumed to be constant. *Rehearsal* is the repetition of information that has entered short-term memory. As long as information in short-term memory is rehearsed, it is kept alive and is not lost. Even more important, rehearsal permits the transfer of material into long-term memory.

From *an educator's* perspective

What are some educational implications of the short attention spans of young children?

working memory

a set of temporary memory stores that actively manipulate and rehearse information.

WORKING MEMORY. Contemporary researchers view short-term memory as an information processing system that is highly active. In this perspective, short-term memory is referred to as **working memory**, a set of memory stores that actively manipulate and rehearse information (Bayliss et al., 2005a, 2005b; Unsworth & Engle, 2005).

According to the working memory view, the way in which we process information in working memory is determined by a "central executive." The *central executive* controls the functions of short-term memory, coordinating the processing of material, determining problem-solving strategies, directing attention, and selecting strategies for remembering in short-term memory.

long-term memory

the memory component in which information is stored on a relatively permanent basis.

LONG-TERM MEMORY. If it is sufficiently processed in short-term memory, information passes into the third and final information processing unit, long-term memory. **Long-term memory** is the memory component in which information is stored on a relatively permanent basis. In a process similar to the one that attends the arrival of a new book at a library, information arriving in long-term memory is filed and cataloged so that—at least in theory—it can be retrieved when it is needed.

Long-term memory is a repository that is nearly limitless in capacity. Even when they are young, children can remember a huge amount of information about the world. When they are older, the capacity is even greater. For instance, if you're like the average college student, your vocabulary consists of some 50,000 words, you know thousands of facts, and you have little trouble recalling sights, sounds, and even smells from your childhood.

If long-term memory is so large, why don't we remember everything that is stored there? The reason is that we suffer from retrieval problems. *Retrieval* is the process of locating and bringing information stored in memory into awareness. We are able to recall information through the use of *retrieval cues*, stimuli that permit people to recall information. Retrieval cues are like a library's catalog; they guide people to the location of a specific memory.

Retrieval cues may take the form of a word, an image, a smell, or a sound. When triggered by a retrieval cue, a memory comes to mind. For example, the smell of freshly baked chocolate chip cookies may trigger memories of one's childhood, including the emotions that are attached to specific recollections.

LONG-TERM MEMORY MODULES. In the same way that short-term memory can be viewed as working memory, contemporary researchers view long-term memory as having different components called *memory modules* representing different memory systems in the brain.

For example, researchers distinguish between *declarative memory*, memory for factual information such as names, dates, and facts, and *procedural memories*, memories relating to skills and habits, such as how to ice skate or ride a bike. We remember information about *things* in declarative memory, while we remember information about *how to do things* in procedural memory.

Comparing Information Processing Approaches to Alternative Theories of Cognitive Development

LO 6.3   **Compare the information processing approaches to Piaget's theory of cognitive development.**

It should be clear that information processing approaches differ significantly from other theories of cognitive development, particularly those of Piaget. Piaget's theory ties cognitive development to particular stages. At each stage, children are presumed to have developed a particular set of cognitive structures that determines the quality of their thinking. When children move to another stage, according to Piaget, the quality of their thinking changes significantly. Developmental changes, then, are largely qualitative.

In contrast, information processing approaches attribute cognitive development to gradual, continuous improvements in the ways children perceive, understand, and remember information. With age and practice, children process information more efficiently and with greater sophistication, and they are able to handle increasingly complex problems. Although some information processing theories do propose that cognitive development proceeds in a stagelike fashion, the stages to which they refer apply to specific subtypes of cognitive skills and are far narrower than Piaget's broad stages (Case & Okamoto, 1996). For the proponents of information processing approaches, then, it is quantitative advances in information processing skills—and not the qualitative changes suggested by Piaget—that constitute cognitive development. In the remainder of this chapter, we'll consider the specific nature of some of these changes.

Module 6.1 Review

LO 6.1   **Describe how information is taken in, held, and used, according to information processing theorists.**

The fundamental elements of information processing are encoding, storage, and retrieval. Automatization refers to the degree to which these processes require attention.

LO 6.2   **Explain how the architecture of the human information processing system functions.**

The three-system model proposes that information processing involves the sensory store, short-term memory, and long-term memory. The sensory store is the initial, momentary storage of nonmeaningful information. Selected information is passed to short-term memory, in which deliberate information processing first takes place and meaning is added. Contemporary approaches consider short-term memory as working memory, in which a central executive processor coordinates the processing of information. Information that has been sufficiently processed in short-term memory is passed to long-term memory, where it is stored on a relatively permanent basis for later retrieval. Long-term memories can be considered as memory modules, each of which is related to separate memory systems.

LO 6.3   **Compare the information processing approaches to Piaget's theory of cognitive development.**

Information processing models assume that development is quantitative in nature, rather than qualitative, as Piaget assumes.

Journal Writing Prompt

Applying Lifespan Development: It has been said that poets and artists process information differently than other people. Do you agree? Why? If you agree, in which of the three basic processes—encoding, storage, or retrieval—do you think the difference mostly lies?

MODULE 6.2

ATTENTION AND MEMORY

Two-month-old Meredith lies in her crib. Her gaze shifts from the mobile that is slowly moving above her head, repeatedly playing "Mary Had a Little Lamb," to her father, who is singing along with the tune. At the same time, her father strokes the wisps of hair on her head, as her older brother calls out from the next room, "Dad, where are you?"

Consider the multiple sources of information in Meredith's environment: the sights of the mobile and her father, the sound of the mobile and her father's and brother's voices, and the touch of her father's hand on her head. To which of these stimuli does she pay attention?

Attention

LO 6.4 Explain why attention is important for children's cognitive development.

attention

information processing involving the ability to strategically choose among and sort out different stimuli in the environment.

The choices Meredith makes are determined by **attention**, information processing involving the ability to strategically choose among and sort out different stimuli in the environment. Attention is the first step in information processing. If a child doesn't attend to a stimulus, or is unaware of it in the first place, that material cannot be processed further. Furthermore, if children are constantly distracted by incoming stimuli, they will be unable to sustain focus on their current activity.

From the time of birth, infants pay more attention to some objects and less to others. What they attend to and how long they attend to it are largely a result of the nature of the stimuli in the environment and the alternatives that are available. Some stimuli act as *attention-getting* stimuli due to their physical characteristics. Other stimuli are *attention-holding*; it is their meaningfulness that sustains attention.

From *a day-care worker's* perspective

What kinds of activities and toys would best promote the cognitive development of an infant for whom you were caring?

The properties that make a stimulus attention-getting are fairly constant throughout the life span. For instance, a loud noise or sudden movement is apt to evoke attention in both an infant and an adult. However, attention-holding stimuli vary across the life span according to an individual's age and experience. Thus, a toy truck is more of an attention-holding stimulus to a 4-year-old than it would be to a 12-year-old, while a book is obviously of greater interest to an older reader than to a child who has not yet learned to read.

Are differences in attention the result of younger children's lack of sensory capabilities? Although it seems plausible that the less well-developed sensory store of young children would render them incapable of initially taking in as much information as older individuals, in fact this does not seem to be the case (Morrison, Holmes, & Haith, 1974). Experiments have found that initial encoding of information in the sensory store is little different between 5-year-olds and adults. However, when 5-year-olds are asked to recall what they have been exposed to, they remember significantly less than older children and adults.

In short, children and adults seem to initially record information in the sensory store in the same way. Failures of information processing, then, are more likely caused by the inability to draw out information from the sensory store and to processing deficiencies in short-term memory. Several attentional factors determine whether and how effectively information is processed, including the control and planning of attention.

CONTROL OF ATTENTION. When we watch children of different ages react to their environments, it seems obvious that as they get older, their attention becomes more concentrated and lasting. A 2-year-old is more apt to leap from one activity to another than a 6-year-old. Older children are better able to concentrate on a particular activity for a longer period of time, ignoring extraneous distractions. Yet even 5- and 6-year-olds don't have long attention spans, averaging only 7 minutes on a single activity during preschool play periods.

The increasing ability to tune into certain stimuli, while tuning out of others, is an indication of increasing cognitive *control* of attention. With age, children become increasingly aware of their sensory and memory limitations, and they develop strategies for responding to stimuli of interest (Gallotta et al., 2015).

With age, children become more effective not only at controlling what they are attending to but also at excluding irrelevant or extraneous stimuli. For instance, children who are completing a task become better at focusing on what is central to the task and ignoring elements of the situation that will not further its completion. Thus, a preschool child might focus on the brightly colored pin worn by an individual who is giving directions on how to complete at task rather than on the directions themselves, as would an older child.

planning

the ability to allocate attentional resources on the basis of goals that one wishes to achieve.

PLANNING. With increasing age, people not only learn to control their attention in the face of irrelevant stimuli; they also become more proficient at mapping out and devising strategies for using their attention effectively; that is, they become better at planning. **Planning** is the ability to allocate attentional resources on the basis of goals that one wishes to achieve.

Even infants show their ability to plan. They are able to anticipate when routine child-care procedures are going to take place, beginning to shift attention according to what they expect to happen.

Despite early indications of "planfulness," young children are not highly proficient at planning, and the ability to plan effectively develops throughout the course of childhood and adolescence. For example, young children are unable to take into account all the steps that will be involved in solving complex problems. They are also less systematic than older children. In one experiment, children were asked to compare whether complex stimuli consisting of two houses were different (as in the top row of Figure 6-4) or the same (as in the bottom row of Figure 6-4). Examination of the eye movements of preschoolers comparing the two houses showed that they did not systematically compare the features of the two houses (Vurpillot, 1968). Instead, their eyes moved back and forth in a disorderly fashion, missing key features of the houses. As a result, they frequently said two different houses were the same. In contrast, school-age children used a more systematic strategy, comparing window-to-window, and they were much more accurate in determining whether the two were the same or different.

Several factors explain why younger children are deficient in planning, even when they may know that planning will help them reach a goal. For one thing, planning requires considering not only what one must do but also what one must *not* do. However, the ability to refrain from acting develops relatively slowly throughout childhood.

In addition, children frequently are more optimistic about their ability to reach their goal than is warranted. Their over-optimism leaves them unmotivated to engage in planning. Furthermore, planning may require coordination with others, and young children may not have the skills to cooperate effectively with others.

Still, children's ability to determine how they will allocate their attentional resources, as well as their general ability to control attention, grow significantly over the course of development. By the time they reach adolescence, they are more adept at effectively dividing their attention across more than one stimulus at a time—such as simultaneously studying for a biology test and listening to a Miley Cyrus tune.

Figure 6-4 Planning

When preschoolers compared two houses such as these to determine whether they were different from one another, their eye movements showed that they did not systematically compare the features of the two houses in order to make their determination. In contrast, school-age children's eye movements showed that they systematically compared the features of the houses on a window-by-window basis, and they were considerably more accurate than the younger children. **(Source:** Vurpillot, 1968.)

Memory and Its Duration

LO 6.5 Describe memory improvements during childhood and analyze how childhood memories change over time.

The improvements that occur in the control of attention and planning related to attention are likely produced by increases in maturation of the brain, as well as by the increasing educational demands placed on children.

THE DEVELOPMENT OF BASIC MEMORY CAPABILITIES. The ability of infants to distinguish new stimuli from old implies that some memory of the old must be present.

Figure 6-5 Early Signs of Memory

Infants who had learned the association between a moving mobile and kicking showed surprising recall ability if they were exposed to a reminder of the early memory.

infantile amnesia

the lack of memory for experiences that occurred prior to age 3.

Unless the infants had some memory of an original stimulus, it would be impossible for them to recognize that a new stimulus differed from an earlier one.

Other evidence confirms the ability of infants to remember. In one study, a string was tied to infants' ankles so that when they kicked that leg, an enticing mobile above their crib moved and made noise (see Figure 6-5). It took only a few days for 2-month-old infants to forget their training, but 6-month-old infants still remembered for as long as 3 weeks (Bearce & Rovee-Collier, 2006; Oakes & Kovack-Lesh, 2013; Fisher-Thompson, 2017).

Furthermore, infants who were later prompted to recall the association between kicking and moving the mobile showed evidence that the memory continued to exist even longer. Infants who had received just two training sessions lasting 9 minutes each still recalled about a week later, as illustrated by the fact that they began to kick when placed in the crib with the mobile. Two weeks later, however, they made no effort to kick, suggesting that they had forgotten entirely.

But they hadn't: When the babies saw a reminder—a moving mobile—their memories were apparently reactivated. In fact, the infants could remember the association, following prompting, for as long as an additional month. Other evidence confirms these results, suggesting that hints can reactivate memories that at first seem lost and that the older the infant, the more effective such prompting is (Bearce & Rovee-Collier, 2006; Moher, Tuerk, & Feigenson, 2012; Ross-Sheehy & Newman, 2015).

Is infant memory qualitatively different from that in older children and adults? Researchers generally believe that information is processed similarly throughout the life span, even though the kind of information being processed changes and different parts of the brain may be used. According to memory expert Carolyn Rovee-Collier, people, regardless of their age, gradually lose memories, although, just like babies, they may regain them if reminders are provided. Moreover, the more times a memory is retrieved, the more enduring the memory becomes (Hsu & Rovee-Collier, 2006; Turati, 2008; Bell, 2012).

THE DURATION OF MEMORIES. Although the processes that underlie memory retention and recall seem similar throughout the life span, the quantity of information stored and recalled does differ markedly as infants develop. Older infants can retrieve information more rapidly, and they can remember it longer. But just how long? Can memories from infancy be recalled, for example, after babies grow up?

Researchers disagree on the age from which memories can be retrieved. Although early research supported the notion of **infantile amnesia**—the lack of memory for experiences occurring before age 3—more recent research shows that infants do retain memories. For example, in one study, 6-month-old infants were shown a series of unusual events, such as intermittent periods of light and dark and strange sounds. When the children were later tested at the age 1½ or 2½, they demonstrated that they recalled the experience. Other research substantiates that infants show memory for behavior and situations that they have seen only once (Neisser, 2004; Callaghan, Li, & Richardson, 2014; Bucci & Stanton, 2017).

Such findings are consistent with evidence that the physical trace of a memory in the brain appears to be relatively permanent; this suggests that memories, even from infancy, may be enduring. However, memories may not be easily, or accurately, retrieved. For example, memories are susceptible to interference from other, newer information, which may displace or block out the older information, thereby preventing its recall.

One reason why infants appear to remember less may be because language plays a key role in determining the way memories from early in life can be recalled: Older children and adults may be able to report memories using only the vocabulary that they had available at the time of the initial event, when the memories were stored. Because their vocabulary at the time of initial storage may have been quite limited, they are unable to describe the event later in life, even though it is actually in their memories (Bauer et al., 2000; Simcock & Hayne, 2002; Heimann et al., 2006).

The question of how well memories formed during infancy are retained in adulthood remains not fully answered. Although infants' memories may be highly detailed and can be enduring if the infants experience repeated reminders, it is still not clear how accurate those memories remain over the course of the life span. Early memories are susceptible to incorrect recollection if people are exposed to related, and contradictory, information following the initial formation of the memory. Not only does such new information potentially impair recall of the original material, but the new material may also be inadvertently incorporated into the original memory, thereby corrupting its accuracy (Cordon et al., 2004).

In sum, the data suggest that although it is at least theoretically possible for memories to remain intact from a very young age—if subsequent experiences do not interfere with their recollection—in most cases memories of personal experiences in infancy do not last into adulthood. Current findings suggest that memories of personal experience do not seem to become accurate before age 18 to 24 months (Howe, Courage, & Edison, 2004; Bauer, 2007; Taylor, Liu, & Herbert, 2016.; also see the accompanying *Neuroscience and Development* box).

AUTOBIOGRAPHICAL MEMORY. Think back to your earliest memory. If you are like most people, the memory is an **autobiographical memory**, a memory of particular events from one's own life. For most people, autobiographical memories relate to an event that occurred around the age of 3 or later (Ross & Wilson, 2003; De Roten, Favez, & Drapeau, 2004; Nelson & Fivush, 2004).

autobiographical memory
memory of particular events from one's own life.

Neuroscience and Development

Sleep and Memory: Making the Case for Naps

More than half of adults in America don't get the minimum 7 hours of sleep per night recommended by the U.S. Centers for Disease Control and Prevention. But how important is a good night's sleep, or even a daytime nap, when it comes to your memory and ability to learn? Actually, it's much more important than you might think (National Sleep Foundation, 2013; Panel et al., 2015).

In a recent study, researchers with Harvard Medical School randomly assigned participants into two groups and then examined their ability to encode memories of pictures. One group was deprived of sleep by staying awake the night before the test; the other group had adequate sleep. As expected, the sleep-deprived participants performed much worse on a later test of what they remembered. MRI scans of both groups taken while they were exposed to the visual learning task illustrate how sleep deprivation negatively impacts the brain and memory encoding. Specifically, researchers found that hippocampal activity on both sides of the brain was much lower for the sleep-deprived participants than for those who got a good night's sleep (see Figure 6-6).

Getting sufficient sleep *after* learning a new skill is also essential. Researchers have found that the speed and accuracy of procedural memory—such as learning how to play the piano—improves greatly during NREM sleep. In fact, gains in motor skills can be acquired from shorter periods of additional sleep as well, even if it is just a 1-hour nap in the middle of the day (Walker & Stickgold, 2006; Abel et. al, 2013).

So the next time someone criticizes you for taking a nap, tell them you're really learning—with your eyes closed.

■ When considering this research on sleep and memory, what recommendations would you make to parents or school administrators?

Figure 6-6 The Impact of Sleep Deprivation on the Brain

Different views of the brain compare the sleep deprived group to the control group. Areas in blue represent reduced activation in the sleep deprived group compared to the control group.
(**Source:** Yoo et al., 2007.)

(a)   (b)

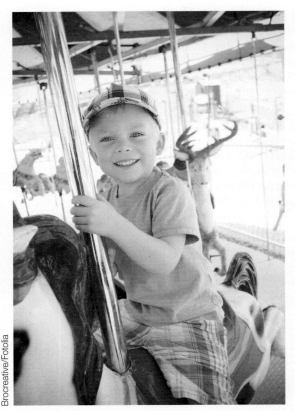

This preschooler may recall this ride in 6 months, but by the time he is 12, it will probably be forgotten. Can you explain why?

Preschool children's recollections of events that happened to them are sometimes, but not always, accurate. For instance, 3-year-olds can remember fairly well the central features of routine occurrences, such as the sequence of events involved in eating at a restaurant. In addition, preschoolers are typically accurate in their responses to open-ended questions, such as "What rides did you like best at the amusement park?" (Pathman et al., 2013; Valentino et al., 2014; McDonnell et al., 2016).

The accuracy of preschoolers' memories is partly determined by how soon the memories are accessed. Unless an event is particularly vivid or meaningful, it is not likely to be remembered at all. Moreover, not all autobiographical memories last into later life. For instance, a child may remember the first day of kindergarten 6 months or a year later, but later in life might not remember that day at all.

Memories are also affected by cultural factors. For example, Chinese college students' memories of early childhood are more likely to be unemotional and reflect activities involving social roles, such as working in their family's store, whereas U.S. college students' earliest memories are more emotionally elaborate and focus on specific events such as the birth of a sibling (Wang, 2006; Peterson, Wang, & Hou, 2009; Stevenson, Heiser, & Resing, 2016). (Also see the *Developmental Diversity and Your Life* box.)

Not only do preschoolers' autobiographical memories fade, but what is remembered may not be wholly accurate. For example, if an event happens often, such as a trip to a grocery store, it may be hard to remember one specific time it happened (Sutherland, Pipe, & Schick, 2003).

Adults, too, show errors in their autobiographical memories. For example, they forget information about their past that conflicts with their view of themselves in the present. If they feel well adjusted as adults, they view themselves as having been well-adjusted children—even if the reality was that they suffered from emotional problems. Similarly, college students are much more apt to accurately remember their good grades, while inaccurately remembering their bad ones (Walker, Skowronski, & Thompson, 2003; Kemps & Tiggemann, 2007).

Developmental Diversity and Your Life
Memory and Culture

When psychologist Michael Cole and colleagues presented rural Liberian children who did not attend school with a group of objects, one at a time, and asked them to recall as many as they could, they found a clear—and puzzling—result: Unlike children in Western, industrialized countries, the Liberian children showed no improvement in memory during middle childhood. (Cole et al., 1971)

At first glance, it might appear that the Liberian children had deficient memories compared to Western children. Fortunately, however, Cole and his colleagues also tried the same task with a group of children who did go to school in Liberia, and the results were quite different. In this case, there was little difference between the educated Liberian children and children who were raised in the United States. The schooled Liberian children showed the same increases in memory over the middle school years as were typically found in Western cultures.

The findings of this study are consistent with other research: When appropriate comparisons are made between members of different cultures, generally few memory differences arise. What are appropriate comparisons? Notably, the populations must be comparable in terms of educational level, the information people are seeking to recall must be equally meaningful to children in both cultures, and children must be similarly motivated to perform well on the task. When these criteria are met, differences in memory are generally not found.

Most memory experts conclude that there are both similarities and differences in memory across cultures. Basic memory processes are universal, regardless of the culture in which children are raised. In contrast, cultural factors affect what information is attended to, learned, rehearsed, and retrieved from memory. Consequently, there are *apparent* differences in memory, relating to the experiences that children have been presented within their own cultural context.

Memory Development and Control

LO 6.6 **Analyze how memory changes as people age, and describe strategies for developing and improving memory.**

Despite the occasional failures of autobiographical memory, it is clear that memory improves throughout the course of childhood and adolescence. But why? First, there are improvements in the basic processes and capacities related to memory. Although there is little evidence to suggest that the capacity of either sensory memory or long-term memory changes during childhood, it does appear that short-term, or working, memory does improve with age. To explain this improvement, developmental psychologist Robbie Case (Case & Okamoto, 1996; Case, 2007), who is known as a *neo-Piagetian* theorist, has blended information processing and Piagetian approaches.

Case suggests that cognitive development proceeds because of increases in working memory capabilities. As we mentioned earlier, the number of chunks of information that can be held in working memory increases throughout childhood, suggesting an increase in its capacity. But increased capacity does not necessarily imply increased size. Case suggests that observed improvements in working memory are due to increases in the operating efficiency of working memory.

According to the *operating efficiency hypothesis*, people are able to remember material better with age because they process information more quickly and use more effective, suitable strategies. Memory improvements are *not* due to increases in the size of working memory. Yet, even though the storage capacity of short-term memory is not expanding with age, less effort is needed to process information, and more cognitive resources are available to store information. The ultimate result is that, with age, more information can be processed in working memory (Case & Okamoto, 1996).

The greater efficiency of processing is indicated by increases in speed of processing with age. As individuals become older, they are able to process the same material with greater speed (see Figure 6-7). One important reason is that increases in brain maturation permit the faster manipulation of letters and numbers.

But improvements in the efficiency of processing are not the full story of memory improvement. As we see next, increases in the use of memory control strategies and the growth of metamemory and general knowledge also lead to improvements in memory.

MEMORY CONTROL STRATEGIES. Children's understanding of memory becomes more sophisticated as they grow older and increasingly engage in *control strategies*—conscious, intentionally used tactics to improve cognitive processing. For instance, school-age children are aware that rehearsal, the repetition of information, is a useful strategy for improving memory, and they increasingly employ it over the course of middle childhood.

Similarly, children progressively make more effort to organize material into coherent patterns, a strategy that permits them to recall it better. For instance, when faced with remembering a list including cups, knives, forks, and plates, older school-age children are more likely to group the items into coherent patterns—cups and plates, forks and knives—than children just entering the school age.

Children also begin to use strategies that are explicitly taught. For instance, a technique called the keyword strategy can

Figure 6-7 Information Processing and Age

As this figure, which represents a summary of many studies, indicates, people are increasingly able to process the same quantity of information in less time with increasing age. For example, it takes a 5-year-old about 3 seconds to process the information that a 16-year-old processes in just over 1 second.
(**Source:** Kail, 1991.)

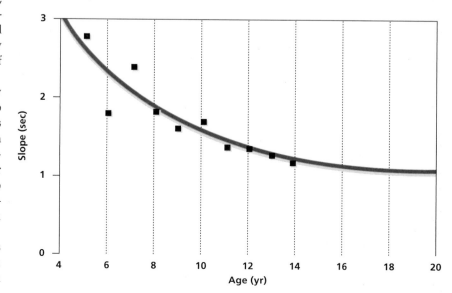

help students learn the vocabulary of a foreign language, the capitals of the states, or other information in which two sets of words or labels are paired. In the *keyword strategy*, one word is paired with another that sounds like it.

For example, in learning foreign language vocabulary, a foreign word is paired with a common English word that has a similar sound. The English word is the keyword. Thus, to learn the Spanish word for duck (*pato*, pronounced *pot-o*), the keyword might be "pot"; for the Spanish word for horse (*caballo*, pronounced *cob-eye-yo*), the keyword might be "eye." Once the keyword is chosen, children then form a mental image of the two words interacting with one another. For instance, a student might use an image of a duck taking a bath in a pot to remember the word *pato*, or a horse with bulging eyes to remember the word *caballo* (Pressley, 1987).

In addition to increasingly using explicit strategies as they get older, children also begin to recall memories more frequently in terms of **scripts**, general representations in memory of a sequence or series of events. For instance, when preschoolers experience the same activity or event repeatedly—such as being driven to preschool 5 days a week—the activity becomes remembered in terms of a general script. Subsequently, unless something unusual occurs, such as seeing an accident, it is difficult to recall anything specific about any particular ride to school because it is remembered in terms of the general script (Bohn & Berntsen, 2014).

scripts
general representations in memory of a sequence or series of events.

THE GROWTH OF METAMEMORY AND CONTENT KNOWLEDGE. The more you know, the better you're able to remember. At least that's the theory—largely supported by research—behind work on metamemory, as well as on the role of increasing general knowledge in memory capabilities.

metamemory
an understanding about the processes that underlie memory, which emerges and improves during middle childhood.

Metamemory is the understanding and knowledge that children and adults have about memory and the processes that underlie it. The simple fact that people forget is almost universally realized by age 6. Before then, though, many children deny that they ever forget anything! By the time they enter first grade, children have a general notion of what memory is. Furthermore, they know that some people have "good" memories and others have "bad" memories.

Development of metamemory skills helps children know how much time is needed to study material in order to remember it accurately. The amount of time that children say they need to understand material increases from age 4 up until adolescence. Presumably, children come to realize their memory limitations and that these limitations can be overcome by spending more time examining and studying the material.

Teaching metamemory skills to children has produced positive results. For example, teaching children to monitor how well they are comprehending material as they are studying helps them to understand the material better (Muldner & Conati, 2010).

It's not just knowledge of how memory operates that leads to improvements in memory. The increasing knowledge of children in all domains also leads to increases in how much they recall as well as what they remember. As the amount of material on a given topic stored in memory grows, it becomes easier to learn new, but related, material. The process of memorizing becomes more efficient, as prior memories provide a context for new information. Furthermore, when children are familiar with information that is being remembered, they are more likely to employ control strategies effectively. In short, the greater content knowledge that older children possess helps them to recall information better than younger children, who have less overall content knowledge.

PERSPECTIVES ON MEMORY DEVELOPMENT. We've seen that memory improves throughout the course of childhood and adolescence. Several processes account for this improvement. First, the amount of information that can be remembered in working memory increases with age, primarily because the processing of information becomes more efficient. At the same time, the use of control strategies improves as people get older. Older individuals know more strategies, and they can apply them more effectively and efficiently.

Finally, memory improvement occurs through growth in metamemory, understanding and knowledge about how memory works, as well as knowledge in general. As children come to understand more about memory, they begin to choose appropriate

Table 6-1 Contributions of Three Aspects of Memory During Several Periods of Development

Source of Development	AGE		
	0–5	5–10	10–Adulthood
Basic capacities	Many capacities present: association, generalization, recognition, etc. By age 5, if not earlier, absolute capacity of sensory memory at adult-like levels.	Speed of processing increases.	Speed of processing continues to increase.
Strategies	A few rudimentary strategies such as naming, pointing, and selective attention.	Acquisition and increasing use of many strategies: rehearsal, organization, etc.	Continuing improvement in quality of all strategies.
Metamemory and content knowledge	Little factual knowledge about memory. Some monitoring of ongoing performance. Steadily increasing content knowledge helps memory in areas in which the knowledge exists.	Increasing factual knowledge about memory. Improved monitoring of ongoing performance. Steadily increasing content knowledge helps memory in areas in which the knowledge exists. Also helps in learning of new strategies.	Continued improvements in knowledge.

(**Source:** Adapted from Siegler, 1998.)

control strategies. Furthermore, older children simply know more than younger children, and this increased knowledge permits them to learn new but related material more efficiently. As we have noted, the more children know about a given topic, the better they can remember it and the faster they can learn new material that relates to it.

In short, memory improvements come about through several types of developmental change, summarized in Table 6-1. It is important to remember that these underlying processes do not all produce memory improvements at the same time but take on varying levels of importance across different periods of childhood. Together, however, they result in astonishing improvements in the amount and kind of information that children are able to remember.

MEMORY IN ADULTHOOD: YOU MUST REMEMBER THIS. Whenever Mary Donovan can't find her car keys, she mutters to herself that she is "losing her memory." Mary probably believes that memory loss is pretty common in middle age and later adulthood.

During early adulthood, most adults' memory abilities are at their peak. Both sensory memory and short-term memory show virtually no weakening during middle adulthood. The story is a bit different for long-term memory, which declines with age for some people. It appears, however, that the reason for the decline is not a fading or a complete loss of memory but rather that with age, people register and store information less efficiently. In addition, age makes people less efficient in retrieving information that is stored in memory. In other words, even if the information was adequately stored in long-term memory, it may become more difficult to locate or isolate it.

Memory declines in middle age are relatively minor, and most can be compensated for by various cognitive strategies. As mentioned earlier, paying greater attention to material when it is first encountered can aid in its later recall. Your lost car keys may have relatively little to do with memory declines but may instead reflect your inattentiveness when you put them down.

Still, at least in middle adulthood, most people show only minimal memory losses, and many exhibit none at all. Furthermore, because of societal stereotypes about aging, people in middle adulthood may be prone to attribute their absentmindedness to aging, even though they have been absentminded throughout their lives. Consequently, it is the *meaning* they give to their forgetfulness that changes, rather than their actual ability to remember (Phillips & Henry, 2008).

Furthermore, adults whose memory ability begins to show actual signs of decline often develop or exercise strategies for remaining at the peak of competence for many years. We will look at this compensatory ability when we turn to practical intelligence—the kind of intelligence that IQ tests don't measure. It is possible for older people to remain competent because they have developed particular kinds of expertise and particular competencies. These competencies do not mask a loss of memory; they compensate for it. (See also the *Development in Your Life* box.)

mnemonics

formal strategies for organizing material in ways that make it more likely to be remembered.

Development in Your Life

Effective Strategies for Remembering

All of us are forgetful at one time or another. However, certain techniques can help us remember more effectively and make it less likely that we will forget things we want to remember. **Mnemonics** (pronounced "nee-MON-iks") are formal strategies for organizing material in ways that make it more likely to be remembered. The following are mnemonics that work not only in middle adulthood but at other points of the life span (Bloom & Lamkin, 2006; Morris & Fritz, 2006):

■ *Get organized.* For people who have trouble keeping track of where they left their keys or remembering appointments, the simplest approach is for them to become more organized. Using an appointment book, hanging one's keys on a hook, or using Post-it notes can help jog one's memory.

■ *Pay attention.* You can improve your recall by initially paying attention when you are exposed to new information and by purposefully thinking that you wish to recall it in the future. If you are particularly concerned about remembering something, such as where you parked your car, pay particular attention at the moment you

park the car and remind yourself that you really want to remember.

■ *Use the encoding specificity phenomenon.* According to the encoding specificity phenomenon, people are most likely to recall information in environments that are similar to those in which they initially learned ("encoded") it (Tulving & Thompson, 1973). For instance, people are best able to recall information on a test if the test is held in the room in which they studied.

■ *Visualize.* Making mental images of ideas can help you recall them later. For example, if you want to remember that global warming may lead to a rise in the sea level, think of yourself on a beach on a hot day, with the waves coming closer and closer to where you've set out your beach blanket.

■ *Rehearse.* In the realm of memory, practice makes perfect, or if not perfect, at least better. Adults of all ages can improve their memory if they expend more effort in rehearsing what they want to remember. By practicing what they wish to recall, people can substantially improve their recall of the material.

Module 6.2 Review

LO 6.4 Explain why attention is important for children's cognitive development.

Attention, which involves being aware of and interested in stimuli, is responsible for differences in information processing between young children and adults. Some failures of information processing appear to relate to the control and planning of attention.

LO 6.5 Describe memory improvements during childhood and analyze how childhood memories change over time.

As they age, children become increasingly aware of their sensory and memory limitations and develop strategies to control their attention to stimuli of interest and exclude extraneous stimuli. With age, children also become more adept at planning the use of attention, allocating attentional resources to meet their goals. Infants have memory capabilities from the earliest ages, but the parts of the brain involved in memory may change as they age and their ability to store and retrieve memories efficiently will increase. The phenomenon of infantile amnesia is probably not as absolute as once supposed, but the accuracy of infants' and young children's memories is questionable. Autobiographical memory does not achieve much accuracy until after the age of three.

LO 6.6 Analyze how memory changes as people age, and describe strategies for developing and improving memory.

Short-term memory increases in capacity during childhood, largely because of increases in operating efficiency that result in greater availability of resources to store information. In addition, memory functioning improves as children use more sophisticated control strategies to improve cognitive processing. The use of scripts to store and recall information also conserves memory resources. Metamemory, the understanding of memory and its functioning, permits children to plan and monitor memory use to meet goals. Furthermore, children's increasing knowledge of the world permits them to memorize and recall information more efficiently and effectively.

Journal Writing Prompt

Applying Lifespan Development: Recently, there has been interest in reviving memories from early childhood and even infancy through hypnosis or other treatments. What dangers do you see in such practices? Can the accuracy of revived memories be verified?

MODULE 6.3

APPLYING INFORMATION PROCESSING APPROACHES

Let's now look at some applications of information processing approaches.

Children's Eyewitness Testimony: Memory on Trial

LO 6.7 Describe applications of information processing approaches to the recall of events for legal purposes.

Would you trust the memory of a 4-year-old who was testifying in court?

You probably shouldn't. A growing body of research suggests that young children may recall things quite mistakenly, but with great conviction, contending that events occurred that never really happened and forgetting events that did occur.

Children's memories are especially susceptible to the suggestions of adults asking them questions. This is particularly true of preschoolers, who are considerably more vulnerable to suggestion than either adults or school-age children. Preschoolers are also more prone to make inaccurate inferences about the reasons behind others' behavior and are less able to draw appropriate conclusions based on their knowledge of a situation (Loftus, 2004; Goodman & Melinder, 2007; Havard & Memon, 2013).

From *a lawyer's* perspective

In what ways might children's tendency to make inaccurate inferences about the reasons behind people's behavior make them unreliable witnesses?

Of course, preschoolers recall many things accurately; as we discussed earlier in the chapter, children as young as 3 recall some events in their lives without distortion. However, not all recollections are accurate, and some events that are seemingly recalled with accuracy never occurred.

The error rate for children is further heightened when the same question is asked repeatedly. False memories actually may be more persistent than their actual memories (Loftus & Bernstein, 2005; Goodman & Quas, 2008; Boseovski, 2012).

How, then, can children be questioned in order to produce the most accurate recollections? One way is to question them as soon as possible after an event has occurred. The longer the time between the actual event and questioning, the less firm are children's recollections. Furthermore, more specific questions are answered more accurately than vague questions. Asking the questions outside of a courtroom is also preferable, as the courtroom setting can be intimidating and frightening (Landstrom, Granhag, & Hartwig, 2007; Hanna et al., 2013).

Although some experts have advocated the use of anatomically correct dolls, on which children can point out where they have may have experienced sexual contact, in fact careful research has not been supportive of the technique. In some instances, children make claims, using anatomically correct dolls, that they have touched another person in particular places that are wholly implausible—such as when a child claims to have touched a female's penis (Everson & Boat, 2002; Hungerford, 2005).

Ultimately, no foolproof way exists to test the accuracy of children's recollections. Testimony needs to be evaluated on a case-by-case basis, and judges must ensure that children are questioned in a low-key, nonthreatening manner by impartial questioners.

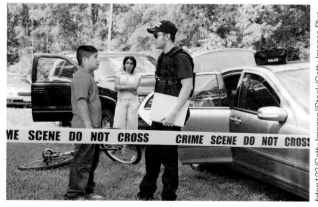

It is easy to influence children's recollections of events, depending on the questions that are posed to them.

It's not only children's memories that are easily influenced and subject to bias. Adults, too, are prone to significant error when they try to remember details of crimes they have witnessed. Even when people are highly confident, their memories can be remarkably wrong (Zaragoza, Belli, & Payment, 2007).

As in the case of children, the specific wording of questions can affect adult eyewitness testimony. For example, in one classic experiment (Loftus & Palmer, 1974), participants watched a film of two cars crashing into each other. Those viewers who were later asked how fast the cars were going when they *smashed* into each other responded, on average, with a speed of 41 miles per hour. In contrast, viewers asked how fast they were traveling when they *contacted* each other estimated the speed at only 32 miles per hour on average.

Information Processing Contributions to the Classroom

LO 6.8   Apply insights from information processing theory to classroom instruction.

Some of the most significant applications of information processing approaches have been made in the classroom. Not only has instruction in fundamental academic subjects been influenced by research in information processing, but efforts to teach children to think critically have also received a significant boost from researchers employing the information processing perspective.

HOW SHOULD WE TEACH READING?   Educators have long been engaged in an ongoing debate regarding the most effective means of teaching reading. At the heart of this debate is a disagreement about the nature of the mechanisms by which information is processed during reading. According to proponents of *code-based approaches to reading*, reading should be taught by presenting the basic skills that underlie reading. Code-based approaches emphasize the components of reading, such as the sounds of letters and their combinations—phonics—and how letters and sounds are combined to make words. They suggest that reading consists of processing the individual components of words, combining them into words, and then using the words to derive the meaning of written sentences and passages (Rego, 2006; Hagan-Burke et al., 2013; Cohen et al., 2016).

In contrast, some educators argue that reading is taught most successfully by using a whole-language approach. In *whole-language approaches to reading*, reading is viewed as a natural process, similar to the acquisition of oral language. According to this view, children should learn to read through exposure to complete writing—sentences, stories, poems, lists, charts, and other examples of actual uses of writing. Instead of being taught to sound out words, children are encouraged to make guesses about the meaning of words based on the context in which they appear. Through such a trial-and-error approach, children come to learn whole words and phrases at a time, gradually becoming proficient readers (Shaw, 2003; Sousa, 2005; Donat, 2006).

A growing body of data, based on careful research, suggests that code-based approaches are superior to whole-language approaches. For example, one study found that not only did a group of children tutored in phonics for a year improve substantially in their reading, compared to a group of good readers, but also that the neural pathways involved in reading became closer to those of good readers (Shapiro & Solity, 2008, 2016; Vaish, 2014).

Based on research such as the Shaywitz study, the National Reading Panel and National Research Council now support reading instruction using code-based approaches. Their position may signal an end to the debate over which approach to teaching reading is more effective (Rayner et al., 2002; Brady, 2011). Furthermore, developmental researchers have found that there are ways for parents to prepare their children for reading.

Whatever approach is used to teach reading, reading produces significant changes in the wiring of the brain. It boosts the organization of the visual cortex of the brain, and it improves the processing of spoken language (Dehaeme et al., 2007).

TEACHING CRITICAL THINKING. "There's no cereal that has more vitamins than Wheaties." "Using Crest toothpaste is the best way to fight cavities." "Be the first to buy Barbie's new playhouse."

The way that children evaluate such statements, which are typical of arguments made in commercials targeted to children, is dependent on their critical thinking skills. **Critical thinking** is thinking that makes use of cognitive skills and strategies that increase the likelihood of solving problems, forming inferences, and making decisions appropriately and successfully. It involves not jumping to conclusions on the basis of limited facts but considering information, weighing the alternatives, and coming to a reasoned decision. Critical thinkers scrutinize the assumptions that underlie their decisions, beliefs, and actions, and they pay attention to the contexts in which ideas are implemented.

critical thinking
thinking that makes use of cognitive skills and strategies that increase the likelihood of solving problems, forming inferences, and making decisions appropriately and successfully.

Although all of us naturally use thinking, it is often not *critical* thinking. We jump to conclusions on the basis of limited facts and make mistakes in logic. Children, especially, are more willing to take statements, such as those made in commercials, at face value. They respond to complex questions with simple answers. Even older children and adolescents often do not take all relevant information into account, and sometimes they are unaware what significant information is missing from a problem in order to come to a reasonable conclusion.

Although educators acknowledge the importance of critical thinking, in fact the critical thinking skills of students are not terribly high. For instance, one study found that less than 40 percent of 17-year-olds can find, summarize, and explain information. Another study comparing Japanese and U.S. students on mathematical problem solving found that the best students from the United States scored lower than the worst Japanese students. The differences can best be attributed to a lack of critical thinking skills in the U.S. students (Izawa & Hayden, 1993).

What are the ingredients of critical thinking? Four primary principles must be used in order for thinking to be appropriately critical. First, thinkers must identify and challenge the assumptions underlying a statement or contention. Second, they must check for factual accuracy and logical consistency among statements. Third, they need to take into account the context of a situation. Finally, they need to imagine and explore alternatives.

Although many children and adults could not be characterized as critical thinkers, such skills can be taught. In fact, teaching critical thinking is becoming a recommended part of the curriculum in many schools, beginning at the elementary level and running all the way up to the college level.

Reconsidering the Information Processing Perspective

LO 6.9 Compare the strengths and weaknesses of the information processing approach and other approaches to cognitive development.

Throughout this chapter we've considered the information processing perspective on cognitive development. For many child developmentalists, information processing approaches represent the dominant, most comprehensive, and ultimately the most accurate explanation of how children develop cognitively.

According to information processing approaches, cognitive development consists of gradual improvements in the ways people perceive, understand, and remember information. With age and practice, preschoolers process information more efficiently and with greater sophistication, and they are able to handle increasingly complex problems. In the eyes of proponents of information processing approaches, it is these quantitative advances in information processing—and not the qualitative changes suggested by Piaget—that constitute cognitive development (Zhe & Siegler, 2000).

For supporters of information processing approaches, the reliance on well-defined processes that can be tested by research studies with relative precision is one of the perspective's most important features. Rather than relying on concepts that are relatively vague, such as Piaget's notions of assimilation and accommodation or Vygotsky's ideas on the zone of proximal development and scaffolding, information processing approaches provide a comprehensive, logical set of concepts, focusing on the processes that underlie children's thinking. The focus on individual processes and skills, such as processing speed and memory, permits information processing researchers to use more precise measures of cognitive abilities and to produce more readily verifiable results.

Proponents of information processing theory have also been successful in focusing on important cognitive processes to which alternative approaches traditionally have paid little attention. For example, Piaget wrote relatively little about memory, and Vygotsky paid scant attention to the way information is processed mentally. In contrast, information processing comes to a different solution to some of Piaget's observations.

For instance, as preschoolers grow older, they have longer attention spans, can monitor and plan what they are attending to more effectively, and become increasingly aware of their cognitive limitations. These advances may be due to brain development. Such increasing attentional abilities place some of Piaget's findings in a different light. For instance, increased attention allows older children to attend to both the height *and* the width of tall and short glasses into which liquid is poured. This permits them to understand that the amount of liquid in the glasses stays the same when it is poured back and forth. Preschoolers, in contrast, are unable to attend to both dimensions simultaneously and thus are less able to conserve (Stock, Desoete, & Roeyers, 2007).

Yet information processing approaches have their detractors, who raise significant points. For one thing, the focus on a series of single, individual cognitive processes leaves out of consideration some important factors that appear to influence cognition. For instance, information processing theorists pay relatively little attention to social and cultural factors—a deficiency that Vygotsky's approach attempts to remedy.

An even more important criticism is that information processing approaches "lose the forest for the trees." In other words, information processing approaches pay so much attention to the detailed, individual sequence of processes that compose cognitive processing and development that they never adequately paint a whole, comprehensive picture of cognitive development—which Piaget did uniquely well.

Information processing theories have also been criticized as providing too sterile an account of what goes on in children's minds. Where, for instance, are the hopes, the dreams, the aspirations that inform so much of people's thinking? Because of their use of computer analogies, information processing proponents have been accused of forgetting about the qualities of thinking that set humans apart from other animals and focusing excessively on people as cold processing machines.

Of course, developmentalists using information processing approaches have responded to such criticisms. They contend that their model of cognitive development has the advantage of being precisely stated and capable of leading to testable hypotheses. They also argue that far more research supports their approach than alternative theories of cognitive development. In short, they suggest that their approach provides a more accurate account than any other.

Are they right? While it is tempting to try to answer the question "Which theory is best?" it is also premature to ask such a question, at least at this point in our understanding of cognitive development. Information processing theories remain just that—theories. It is too early to say whether the approach will provide a better description of cognitive development than the alternatives.

What is clear is that information processing approaches have been highly influential over the past two decades. They have been the impetus for a tremendous amount of research that has given us a better understanding of how children develop cognitively. Furthermore, it is clear that the information processing perspective will continue to be an important guide as we seek to understand how people make such remarkable cognitive strides as they move from infancy through childhood into adulthood.

From Research to Practice

Smartphones and Memory: A Complicated Relationship

While the advent and expansion of the Internet has made an almost infinite amount of information available to us, smartphones have put all of it in our pockets.

Instant access to information is convenient, but is it hurting our memory? Many researchers argue that smartphone use is undermining the brain's ability to make memories because of what is termed *cognitive offloading*. In other words, we tend to make an effort to remember information that we believe will not be easily accessible in the future, but we tend to forget information that we know we'll be able to find later because we have "offloaded" it somewhere, such as a smartphone (Wilmer, Sherman, & Chein, 2017).

For example, evidence from one study indicates that using a GPS app on a smartphone impairs our ability to learn how to travel a new route. In this study, a team of researchers from the University of Tokyo randomly assigned college student participants to one of three groups who used different strategies to learn the route. One group used a GPS smartphone app, while another group used a paper map to navigate. The third group, known as the direct experience group, was guided along the route by a researcher and then required to walk the route again themselves. The results indicated that the GPS group traveled farther, traveled more slowly, made more stops and direction errors, and

had a less accurate memory of the route, compared to the direct experience group. Even the group using a paper map traveled less distance and made fewer stops than the GPS group. Researchers believe that when we use GPS we pay less attention to driving a new route and therefore spend less cognitive energy encoding and storing the new information. Of course, we usually do this because we believe that if we ever need to return to that destination we will be able to rely on our GPS software again (Ishikawa, Fujiwara, Imai, & Okabe, 2008).

Although instant access to information may cause us to rely on our smartphones, some researchers believe that doing so may actually make us more cognitively efficient. For example, researchers have found that when we know we will have access to newly learned information, it improves our ability to learn more information in the future. Thus, remembering *how to find* information may be more important than remembering the actual information itself (Storm & Stone, 2015).

Shared Writing Prompt

What are some examples of how using a smartphone has helped or hurt your memory? Compare the benefits of smartphones with their effect on cognitive functioning.

Module 6.3 Review

LO 6.7   **Describe applications of information processing approaches to the recall of events for legal purposes.**

Because young children's memories are highly subject to suggestion and distortion, they can be unreliable witnesses in emotionally charged law cases.

LO 6.8   **Apply insights from information processing theory to classroom instruction.**

In the classroom, information processing approaches have supported approaches to reading instruction that are based on children's progression from low-level cognitive skills to higher-level skills. Information processing has been used to support both code-based and whole-language approaches to reading, and the best approach is probably a combination of the two.

Information processing approaches have also been used to develop critical thinking instruction, which focuses on the use of cognitive skills and strategies to analyze

assumptions, evaluate arguments, solve problems, and make decisions.

LO 6.9   **Compare the strengths and weaknesses of the information processing approach and other approaches to cognitive development.**

The information processing perspective has proven fruitful in offering explanations of cognitive phenomena and suggesting additional research through its generation of testable hypotheses. It is less successful in accounting for social and cultural factors that affect cognitive processes and in producing a rich, comprehensive picture of cognitive development.

Journal Writing Prompt

Applying Lifespan Development: Based on your knowledge about children's critical thinking skills, do you think advertising directed to children should be closely regulated or even prohibited? Why?

Epilogue

We have taken a look at information processing approaches to the study of cognitive development, discussing the basics of information processing compared with Piaget's and Vygotsky's theories. We have seen how information processing's practical, experimental methods have illuminated our understanding of memory and enlightened us as we considered some of the important issues of the day, including the reliability of children's testimony in court and the usefulness of information processing's insights and findings for education.

Look back to the prologue, about Justin Daley's first day at work, and answer the following questions:

1. What is going on in Justin's brain as he takes customer orders? What roles do encoding, storage, and retrieval play?

2. What practical strategies could Justin use to transfer information from his short-term to his long-term memory?

3. How can automatization explain the differences in Justin's performance and that of his co-worker Jasmine?

4. To be successful on the job, what are a few examples of concepts or processes that Justin must commit to long-term memory?

5. How can Jasmine use both declarative and procedural memory while training Justin to use the electronic register?

Looking Back

LO 6.1 Describe how information is taken in, held, and used, according to information processing theorists.

The three elements of information processing are encoding, storage, and retrieval. Encoding is the process by which information is initially recorded in a form usable to memory. Storage refers to the maintenance of material saved in memory. Retrieval is the process by which stored material is located, brought to awareness, and used. Automatization refers to the degree to which the processes of encoding, storage, and retrieval require attention. Processes that require little attention are automatic; those that require relatively large amounts of attention are controlled.

LO 6.2 Explain how the architecture of the human information processing system functions.

Cognitive architecture refers to the basic, enduring mental structures and features that determine the steps through which information is processed. According to the three-system model, information processing involves the sensory store, short-term memory, and long-term memory. The sensory store is where information is momentarily stored without meaning. Short-term memory receives selected information from the sensory store and begins processing it, adding meaning. Sufficiently processed information then is passed to long-term memory, where it is stored on a relatively permanent basis for later retrieval.

LO 6.3 Compare the information processing approaches to Piaget's theory of cognitive development.

The three-system model assumes that both the size of the processing system and the type of processing it engages in develop over time. It holds that development involves quantitative changes in cognitive processes, rather than qualitative changes in the nature of thinking, as Piaget assumes.

LO 6.4 Explain why attention is important for children's cognitive development.

Attention—awareness of and interest in stimuli—is the first step in information processing. Although the ability to take in information through the senses is constant from childhood to adulthood, the ability to control and plan attention improves with age. As they age, people become increasingly aware of their sensory and memory limitations and develop strategies to control attention. They also become better at planning and allocating attentional resources to meet their goals.

LO 6.5 Describe memory improvements during childhood and analyze how childhood memories change over time.

Infants have memory capabilities from the earliest ages, but it is possible that infantile memory depends on the hippocampus rather than additional brain structures that will be involved as the child develops. The gradual loss of information, and its return in response to appropriate stimuli, operate similarly throughout life. Infantile amnesia generally makes it unlikely that events that occurred before age 3 will be recalled. The phenomenon is probably not as absolute as was once supposed, but memories from infancy and early childhood, including autobiographical memories, are highly unreliable until after age 3.

LO 6.6 Analyze how memory changes as people age, and describe strategies for developing and improving memory.

Memory improvements in childhood and adolescence appear to be largely attributable to increased capabilities within short-term memory. According to the operating efficiency hypothesis, memory improves because individuals learn to process information more quickly and use more appropriate strategies. The use of scripts to store and recall information also conserves memory resources.

Metamemory, the understanding of memory and its underlying processes, helps children understand the need to plan and monitor memory use to meet goals. In addition, the increasing knowledge of the world that children acquire permits them to learn and remember information more efficiently and effectively.

LO 6.7 **Describe applications of information processing approaches to the recall of events for legal purposes.**

Reliance on the memories of young children in the courtroom has been shown to be risky. because they are highly subject to suggestion and distortion. Recall of events is most reliable if it is obtained soon after the events. Specific questions asked in a nonthreatening setting elicit the most trustworthy results, but even so, the memories of young children must be carefully evaluated before being used.

LO 6.8 **Apply insights from information processing theory to classroom instruction.**

The information processing approach has provided insight into the way children learn to read, which has influenced the nature of reading instruction. Children progress from low-level cognitive skills to higher-level skills. The debate between code-based and whole-language approaches to reading is not decided by information processing research, and the best approach is probably a combination of the two. Critical thinking is an important skill that information processing approaches have illuminated. As children grow, they become increasingly able to think critically, using cognitive skills and strategies to analyze assumptions, evaluate arguments, solve problems, and make decisions. However, the development of critical thinking skills is not automatic or universal; explicit instruction appears to be necessary.

LO 6.9 **Compare the strengths and weaknesses of the information processing approach and other approaches to cognitive development.**

The information processing perspective has contributed significantly to our understanding of cognitive phenomena and development. It provides a coherent, logical, relatively complete account of cognitive processes in terms that permit scientific testing. The perspective has been criticized for failing to address social and cultural factors that affect cognitive processes and for yielding an overly mechanistic, atomistic view of cognition.

Key Terms and Concepts

information processing
  approaches 196
sensory store 198
short-term memory 199
working memory 200

long-term memory 200
attention 202
planning 203
infantile amnesia 204
autobiographical memory 205

scripts 208
metamemory 208
mnemonics 210
critical thinking 213

Chapter 7
Language Development

IE200/Alamy

 Learning Objectives

LO 7.1 Identify the formal characteristics of language, and describe how prelinguistic communication develops.

LO 7.2 Explain how speech develops in infancy and how early language differs from that used by adults.

LO 7.3 Summarize the rapid advances made by preschoolers in their comprehension and production of language, and distinguish private speech from social speech.

LO 7.4 Describe the development of language in middle childhood and the role metalinguistic awareness plays in understanding how language works.

LO 7.5 Identify the major perspectives on language acquisition, and summarize the strengths and weaknesses of each.

LO 7.6 Compare and contrast the different theories about the relationship between language and thought.

LO 7.7 Describe how infant-directed speech affects children's language development.

LO 7.8 Explain how socioeconomic status influences language development in children.

LO 7.9 Compare bilingual education to the immersion approach, and identify the cognitive benefits of being bilingual.

Chapter Overview

Prologue: Early Infant Sounds

Brooke was quite surprised the first time she heard her 6-month-old daughter say "mama." She wasn't expecting to hear Riley's first word for several more months, but she was delighted that she accidentally caught the moment on video. When she shared the video on social media, her friends and family were equally amazed, and those closest to her suggested that she might just have a little genius on her hands. But at the same time, Brooke also wondered if she was just hearing the word "mama" among other random vocalizations her daughter was making. Ultimately, Brooke decided to just focus on enjoying her daughter's babbling, whether or not she was really saying "mama." ∎

Looking Ahead

Mama, Dada, Baba. Parents commonly wonder if some of the sounds their babies make are actually words or just more examples of babbling. Even before infants do say their first actual words they begin to understand the language used by others to make sense of the world around them. How do these linguistic abilities develop? For that matter, what is language, and what are its characteristics? What is the pattern and sequence of language development? And how does the use of language transform the cognitive world of infants and their parents?

In this chapter, we address these questions as we trace the ways that language develops. We begin by considering the route of language development, examining how the use of language changes as children grow older. We consider children's first words and how children rapidly build up a vocabulary and move from phrases to complex sentences and, ultimately, to an understanding of grammar and the pragmatic aspects of language use in social situations.

We then consider the roots of language. We present several different perspectives, and we also consider the relationship between language and thought.

Finally, we conclude with a look at the ways in which adults speak to children and the influences that these adult speech patterns may have on children's later development. We also examine some social issues in language development, including the relationship between poverty and language, bilingualism, and a controversy concerning the use of nonstandard English in the classroom.

Although we tend to think of language in terms of the production of words and then groups of words, infants can begin to communicate linguistically well before they say their first word.

MODULE 7.1

THE COURSE OF LANGUAGE DEVELOPMENT

When an infant utters his or her first word, no matter what it is, it marks the start of a dramatic transformation from an entity seemingly not so different from animals of many other species to an entity with skills that are, arguably, unique to human beings.

But those initial words are just the first and most obvious manifestations of language. Many months earlier, infants started using language to comprehend the world around them. How does this linguistic ability develop? What are the pattern and sequence of language development? And how does the use of language mark a transformation in the cognitive world of children and their parents? We'll consider these questions, and others, as we address the development of language through the course of childhood.

The Fundamentals of Language and Prelinguistic Communication

LO 7.1   Identify the formal characteristics of language, and describe how prelinguistic communication develops.

language

the systematic, meaningful arrangement of symbols, which provides the basis for communication.

Language, the systematic, meaningful arrangement of symbols, provides the basis for communication. But it does more than that: It closely relates to the way infants think about and understand the world. It enables them to reflect on people and objects, and to convey their thoughts to others.

Language has several formal characteristics that children must master as they develop linguistic competence. They include:

- **Phonology.** Phonology refers to the basic sounds of language, called *phonemes*, that can be combined to produce words and sentences. For instance, the "a" in "mat" and the "a" in "mate" represent two different phonemes in English, the first with a short "a" sound and the second with a long "a." Although English employs just 40 phonemes to create every word in the language, other languages have as many as 85 phonemes—and some as few as 15.

- **Morphemes.** Morphemes are the smallest language unit that has meaning. Some morphemes encompass complete words, while others add information necessary for interpreting a word, such as the endings "-s" for plural or "-ed" for past tense.

- **Semantics.** Semantics are the rules that govern the meaning of words and sentences. As their knowledge of semantics develops, children are able to understand the distinction between "Ellie was hit by a car" (an answer to the question of why Ellie has not been in school for the past week) and "A car hit Ellie" (used to announce an emergency situation).

In considering the development of language, we also need to distinguish between linguistic *comprehension*, the understanding of speech, and linguistic *production*, the use of language to communicate. One principle underlies the relationship between the two: Comprehension precedes production. An 18-month-old girl may be able to understand a complex series of directions ("pick up your coat from the floor and put it on the chair by the fireplace") but may not yet have strung more than two words together herself.

Comprehension, then, begins earlier than production, and throughout infancy comprehension increases at a faster rate than production. For instance, during infancy, comprehension of words expands at a rate of 22 new words a month, while production of words increases at a rate of about nine new words a month. Other forms of language ability show the same pattern, with comprehension consistently preceding production (Werker & Fennell, 2009; Shafto et al., 2012; Phung, Milojevich, & Lukowski, 2014; see Figure 7-1).

Figure 7-1 Comprehension Precedes Production

Throughout infancy, the comprehension of speech precedes the production of speech. THINKING ABOUT THE DATA: Choose one vocalization/speech skill and compare it to a corresponding language comprehension skill. Which skills emerges first and what is the length of time between the emergence of both skills? How might one skill rely on the other? (**Source:** Based on Bornstein & Lamb, 1992.)

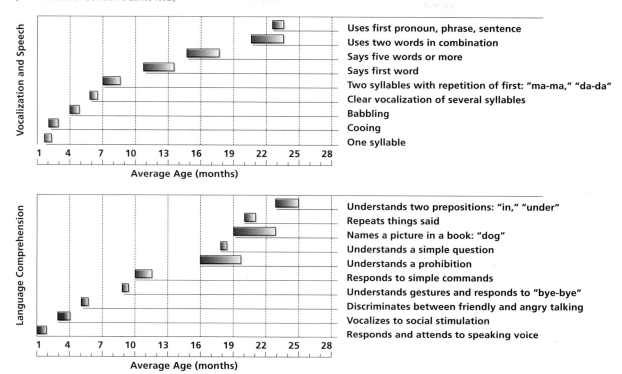

Let's turn now to the course that language development typically follows.

PRELINGUISTIC COMMUNICATION. Consider the following "dialogue" between a mother and her 3-month-old child:

Mother	Infant
	[Smiles]
Oh, what a nice little smile!	
Yes, isn't that pretty?	
There now.	
There's a nice little smile.	
	[Burps]
What a nice burp!	
Yes, that's better, isn't it?	
Yes.	
Yes.	
	[Vocalizes]
Yes!	
There's a nice noise.	

Although we tend to think of language in terms of the production first of words and then of groups of words, infants actually begin to communicate linguistically well before they say their first word. Spend 24 hours with even a very young infant, and you will hear a variety of sounds: cooing, crying, gurgling, murmuring, and various

prelinguistic communication
communication through sounds, facial expressions, gestures, imitation, and other nonlinguistic means.

babbling
making speechlike but meaningless sounds.

types of other noises. These sounds, though not meaningful in themselves, play an important role in linguistic development, paving the way for true language (Swingley, 2008; Martin, Onishi, & Vouloumanos, 2012).

Prelinguistic communication is communication through sounds, facial expressions, gestures, imitation, and other nonlinguistic means. When a father responds to his daughter's "ah" with an "ah" of his own, and then the daughter repeats the sound, and the father responds once again, they are engaged in prelinguistic communication. Clearly, the "ah" sound has no particular meaning. However, its repetition, which mimics the give-and-take of conversation, teaches the infant something about turn-taking (Tomasello, Carpenter, & Liszkowski, 2007; Ferry, Hespos, & Gentner, 2015).

The most obvious manifestation of prelinguistic communication is babbling. **Babbling**, making speechlike but meaningless sounds, starts at the age of 2 or 3 months and continues until around the age of 1 year. When they babble, infants repeat the same vowel sound over and over, changing the pitch from high to low (as in "ee-ee-ee," repeated at different pitches). After the age of 5 months, the sounds of babbling begin to expand, reflecting the addition of consonants (such as "bee-bee-bee-bee").

Babbling is a universal phenomenon, accomplished in the same way throughout all cultures. While they are babbling, infants spontaneously produce all of the sounds found in every language, not just the language they hear people around them speaking. In fact, even deaf children display their own form of babbling.

Babbling, which follows a prelinguistic stage of cooing, follows a progression from sounds that are the simplest to those that are more complex. Furthermore, although at first exposure to a particular language does not seem to influence babbling, experience eventually does make a difference. By the age of 6 months, babbling differs according to the language to which infants are exposed. The difference between cultures is so noticeable that even untrained listeners can distinguish between babbling infants who have been raised in cultures in which French, Arabic, or Cantonese languages are spoken. Furthermore, the speed at which infants begin homing in on their own language is related to the speed of later language development (Masapollo, Polka, & Ménard, 2015; Plummer & Beckman, 2015; McGillion et al., 2017).

Babbling may be the most obviously language-like achievement of early infancy, but there are other indications of prelinguistic speech. For instance, consider 5-month-old Marta, who spies her red ball just beyond her reach. After reaching for it and finding that she is unable to get to it, she makes a cry of anger that alerts her parents that something is amiss, and her mother hands it to her. Communication, albeit prelinguistic, has occurred.

Four months later, when Marta faces the same situation, she no longer bothers to reach for the ball and doesn't respond in anger. Instead, she holds out her arm in the direction of the ball, but now, with great purpose, seeks to catch her mother's eye. When her mother sees the behavior, she knows just what Marta wants. Clearly, Marta's communicative skills—though still prelinguistic—have taken a leap forward.

Even these prelinguistic skills are supplanted in just a few months, as we shall see next, when the gesture gives way to a new communication skill: producing an actual word. Marta's parents clearly hear her say "ball."

First Words: The Production of Speech

LO 7.2 Explain how speech develops in infancy and how early language differs from that used by adults.

When a mother and father first hear their child say "Mama" or "Dada," or even "baba," as in the case of Maura, the baby described in the prologue, it is hard to be anything but delighted. But their initial enthusiasm may be dampened a bit when they find that the same sound is used to ask for a cookie, a doll, and a ratty old blanket.

First words generally are spoken somewhere around the age of 10 to 14 months but may occur as early as 9 months. Once an infant starts to produce words, vocabulary increases at a rapid rate. By the age of 15 months, the average child has a vocabulary of 10 words and methodically expands his or her repertoire until the one-word stage of language development ends at around 18 months. Once that happens, a sudden spurt in vocabulary occurs. In just a short period—a few weeks somewhere between 16 and 24 months of age—there is an explosion of language, in which a child's vocabulary typically increases from 50 to 400 words (McMurray, Aslin, & Toscano, 2009; Koenig & Cole, 2013; Dehaene-Lambertz, 2017).

The first words in children's early vocabularies typically regard objects and things, both animate and inanimate. Most often they refer to people or objects who constantly appear and disappear ("Mama"), to animals ("kitty"), or to temporary states ("wet"). These first words are often **holophrases**, one-word utterances that stand for a whole phrase, whose meaning depends on the particular context in which they are used. For instance, a youngster may use the phrase "ma" to mean, depending on the context, "I want to be picked up by Mom" or "I want something to eat, Mom" or "Where's Mom?" (O'Grady & Aitchison, 2005).

holophrases
one-word utterances that depend on the particular context in which they are used to determine meaning.

Culture also has an effect on the type of first words spoken, as we consider in the *Developmental Diversity and Your Life* box; Tardif, 1996; Andruski, Casielles, & Nathan, 2014).

FIRST SENTENCES.   When Aaron was 19 months old, he heard his mother coming up the back steps, as she did every day just before dinner. Aaron turned to his father and distinctly said, "Ma come." In stringing those two words together, Aaron took a giant step in his language development.

The explosive increase in vocabulary that comes at around 18 months is accompanied by another accomplishment: the linking together of individual words into sentences that convey a single thought.

The linguistic advance represented by two-word combinations is important because the linkage not only provides labels for things in the world but also indicates the relations between them. For instance, the combination may declare something about possession ("Mama key") or recurrent events ("Dog bark"). Interestingly, most early sentences don't represent demands or even necessarily require a response. Instead, they are often merely comments and observations about events occurring in the child's world (O'Grady & Aitchison, 2005; Rossi et al., 2012).

Developmental Diversity and Your Life
First Words Across the World

Does the culture and language to which infants are exposed affect their first words? The answer is clearly yes.

For example, one study looked at the first 10 words produced by infants in three cultures: North America, Hong Kong, and Beijing, who spoke English, Putonghua, and Cantonese. The researchers found that although there were commonalities ("Daddy" and "Mommy" were among the first words used in all three cultures), there were also differences. For instance, among the English-speaking infants, there were three people-related and four animal-related terms, but there were eight and nine people-related terms and no animal terms for the Cantonese and Putonghua speakers (Tardif et al., 2008; Tardif et al, 2012).

Moreover, culture has an effect on the *type* of first words spoken. For example, unlike North American English-speaking infants, who are more apt to use nouns initially, Chinese Mandarin-speaking infants use more verbs than nouns. However, by the age of 20 months, there are remarkable cross-cultural similarities in the types of words spoken. For example, a comparison of 20-month-olds in Argentina, Belgium, France, Israel, Italy, and the Republic of Korea found that children's vocabularies in every culture contained greater proportions of nouns than other classes of words (Tardif, 1996; Bornstein, Cote, & Maital, 2004; Andruski, Casielles & Nathan, 2014).

In short, there are both similarities and differences in the earliest words spoken by infants due to the culture in which they are raised and the language spoken in their environments.

Table 7-1 Children's Imitation of Sentences Showing Decline of Telegraphic Speech

Sample Sentences	Speaker	26 months	29 months	32 months	35 months
I put on my shoes	Kim	Shoes	My shoes	I put on shoes	A
	Darden	Shoes on	My shoes on	Put on shoes	Put on my shoes
I will not go to bed	Kim	No bed	Not go bed	I not go bed	I not go to bed
	Darden	Not go bed	I not go bed	I not go to bed	I will not go bed
I want to ride the pony	Kim	Pony, pony	Want ride pony	I want ride pony	I want to ride pony
	Darden	Want pony	I want pony	I want the pony	A

A = accurate imitation.
(**Source:** Based on R. Brown & Fraser, 1963.)

Two-year-olds using two-word combinations tend to employ particular sequences that are similar to the ways in which adult sentences are constructed. For instance, sentences in English typically follow a pattern in which the subject of the sentence comes first, followed by the verb, and then the object ("Josh threw the ball"). Children's speech most often uses a similar order, although not all the words are initially included. Consequently, a child might say "Josh threw" or "Josh ball" to indicate the same thought. What is significant is that the order is typically not "threw Josh" or "ball Josh," but rather the usual order of English, which makes the utterance much easier for an English speaker to comprehend (Masataka, 2003; Ninio, 2014).

LINGUISTIC INACCURACIES. Although the creation of two-word sentences represents an advance, the language used by children still is by no means adultlike. As we've just seen, 2-year-olds tend to leave out words that aren't critical to the message, in the same way we might write a telegram for which we were paying by the word. For that reason, their talk is often called **telegraphic speech**. Rather than saying, "I put on my shoes," a child using telegraphic speech might say, "My shoes on." "I want to ride the pony" might become "I want pony" (see Table 7-1).

telegraphic speech
speech in which words not critical to the message are left out.

Early language has other characteristics that differentiate it from the language used by adults. For instance, consider Sarah, who refers to the blanket she sleeps with as "blankie." When her Aunt Ethel gives her a new blanket, Sarah refuses to call the new one a "blankie," restricting the word to her original blanket.

Sarah's inability to generalize the label of "blankie" to blankets in general is an example of *underextension*, using words too restrictively, which is common among children just mastering spoken language. Underextension occurs when language novices think that a word refers to a specific instance of a concept, instead of to all examples of the concept (Caplan & Barr, 1989; Masataka, 2003).

As infants like Sarah grow more adept with language, the opposite phenomenon sometimes occurs. In *overextension*, words are used too broadly, overgeneralizing their meaning. For example, when Sarah refers to buses, trucks, and tractors as "cars," she is guilty of overextension, making the assumption that any object with wheels must be a car. Although overextension reflects speech errors, it also shows that advances are occurring in the child's thought processes: The child is beginning to develop general mental categories and concepts (McDonough, 2002; Wałaszewska, 2011).

Infants also show individual differences in the style of language they use. For example, some use a referential style, in which language is used primarily to label objects. Others tend to use an expressive style, in which language is used mainly to express feelings and needs about oneself and others (Bornstein, 2000).

Language styles reflect, in part, cultural factors. For example, mothers in the United States label objects more frequently than do Japanese mothers, encouraging a more referential style of speech. In contrast, mothers in Japan are more apt to speak about social interactions, encouraging a more expressive style of speech (Fernald & Morikawa, 1993).

Kokhanchikov/Fotolia

By age 2, most children use two-word phrases, such as "ball play."

Language Advances During the Preschool Years

LO 7.3 **Summarize the rapid advances made by preschoolers in their comprehension and production of language, and distinguish private speech from social speech.**

I tried it out and it was very great!
This is a picture of when I was running through the water with Mommy.
Where you are going when I go to the fireworks with Mommy and Daddy?
I didn't know creatures went on floats in pools.
We can always pretend we have another one.
And the teacher put it up on the counter so no one could reach it.
I really want to keep it while we're at the park.
You need to get your own ball if you want to play "hit the tree."
When I grow up and I'm a baseball player, I'll have my baseball hat, and I'll put it on, and I'll play baseball. (Schatz, 1994, p. 179)

Listen to Ricky, at age 3. In addition to recognizing most letters of the alphabet, printing the first letter of his name, and writing the word *HI*, he is readily capable of producing the complex sentences quoted here.

During the preschool years, children's language skills reach new heights of sophistication. They begin the period with reasonable linguistic capabilities, though with significant gaps in both comprehension and production. In fact, no one would mistake the language used by a 3-year-old for that of an adult. However, by the end of the preschool years, they can hold their own with adults, both comprehending and producing language that has many of the qualities of adults' language. How does this transformation occur?

The two-word utterances of the 2-year-old soon increase in both number of words and scope. Language blooms so rapidly between the late 2s and the mid-3s that researchers have yet to understand the exact pattern. What is clear is that sentence length increases steadily, and the number of ways children combine words and phrases to form sentences—known as **syntax**—doubles each month. By the time a preschooler is 3, the various combinations reach into the thousands.

syntax
the combining of words and phrases to form sentences.

From *a preschool teacher's* perspective

How would you go about teaching new words to preschoolers, knowing how they develop language?

There are also enormous leaps in the number of words children use. By age 6, the average child has a vocabulary of around 14,000 words, acquired at a rate of nearly one new word every 2 hours, 24 hours a day. They manage this feat through a process known as **fast mapping**, in which new words are associated with their meaning after only a brief encounter (Kan & Kohnert, 2009; Marinellie & Kneile, 2012; Venker, Kover, & Weismer, 2016).

By age 3, preschoolers routinely use plurals and possessive forms of nouns (such as "boys" and "boy's"), the past tense (adding "-ed" at the end of words), and articles ("the" and "a"). They can ask, and answer, complex questions ("Where did you say my book is?" and "Those are trucks, aren't they?").

Preschoolers' skills extend to the appropriate formation of words that they have never before encountered. For example, in one classic experiment, preschool children were shown cards with drawings of a cartoon-like bird, such as those shown in Figure 7-2 (Berko, 1958). The experimenter told the children that the figure was a "wug," and then showed them a card with two of the cartoon figures. "Now there are two of them," the children were told, and they were then asked to supply the missing word in the sentence, "There are two _____" (the answer to which, of course, is "wugs").

Not only did the children show that they knew the rules about forming plural nouns, but also that they understood the possessive forms of nouns and the third-person singular and past-tense forms of verbs—all for words they had never encountered before, since they were nonsense words with no real meaning (O'Grady & Aitchison, 2005).

fast mapping
the process in which new words are associated with their meaning after only a brief encounter.

Figure 7-2 Forming Plurals

Even though preschoolers—like the rest of us—are unlikely to have ever before encountered a wug, they are able to produce the appropriate word to fill in the blank (which, for the record, is *wugs*).

(**Source:** Adapted from Berko, 1958.)

This animal is called a wug.

**We added another wug.
Now there are two _____.**

grammar

the system of rules that determine how our thoughts can be expressed.

pragmatics

the aspect of language relating to communicating effectively and appropriately with others.

private speech

spoken language that is not intended for others, commonly used by children during the preschool years.

social speech

speech directed toward another person and meant to be understood by that person.

Preschoolers also learn what *cannot* be said as they acquire the principles of grammar. **Grammar** is the system of rules that determine how our thoughts can be expressed. (*Grammar* is a broad, general term that encompasses syntax and other linguistic rules.) For instance, preschoolers come to learn that "I am sitting" is correct, while the similarly structured "I am knowing [that]" is incorrect. Although they still make frequent mistakes of one sort or another, 3-year-olds follow the principles of grammar most of the time. Some errors are very noticeable—such as the use of "mens" and "catched"—but these errors (called, as we saw, *overextension*) are actually quite rare. Young preschoolers are correct in their grammatical constructions more than 90 percent of the time (Guasti, 2002; Musolino & Lidz, 2006; Graf et al., 2015).

Finally, preschoolers' pragmatic abilities grow. **Pragmatics** is the aspect of language relating to communicating effectively and appropriately with others. The development of pragmatic abilities permits children to understand the basics of conversations—turn-taking, sticking to a topic, and what should and should not be said, according to the conventions of society. When children are taught that the appropriate response to receiving a gift is "thank you," they are learning the pragmatics of language.

PRIVATE SPEECH AND SOCIAL SPEECH. Over the course of the preschool years, children's use of **private speech**, spoken language that is not intended for others, is common. As much as 20 to 60 percent of what children say is private speech, and such speech is a normal practice during even later stages of childhood. Some research suggests that its use grows over the preschool years, peaking between the ages of 4 and 7. Notably, private speech becomes more secretive as children grow older and realize that society discourages talking to oneself. Consequently, older children tend to whisper private speech or silently move their lips, rather than speaking out loud (Manfra & Winsler, 2006).

Some developmentalists suggest that private speech performs an important function. For instance, as we discussed in Chapter 5, developmental psychologist Lev Vygotsky suggests that private speech facilitates children's thinking and helps them control their behavior. (Have you ever said to yourself, "Take it easy" or "Calm down," when trying to control your anger over some situation?) In Vygotsky's view, then, private speech ultimately serves an important social function, allowing children to solve problems and reflect upon difficulties they encounter. He also suggested that private speech is a forerunner to the internal dialogues that we use when we reason with ourselves during thinking (Al-Namlah, Meins, & Fernyhough, 2012; McGonigle-Chalmers, Slater, & Smith, 2014; Sawyer, 2017).

The preschool years also mark the growth of social speech. **Social speech** is speech directed toward another person and meant to be understood by that person. Before age 3, children may seem to be speaking only for their own entertainment, apparently not caring whether anyone else can understand. However, during the preschool years, children begin to direct their speech to others, wanting others to listen and becoming frustrated when they cannot make themselves understood. As a result, they begin to adapt their speech to others. Recall that Jean Piaget contended that most speech during the preoperational period was egocentric: Preschoolers were seen as taking little account of the effect their speech was having on others. However, more recent experimental evidence suggests that children are somewhat more adept in taking others into account than Piaget initially suggested.

Language Development During Middle Childhood: Mastering Language

LO 7.4 Describe the development of language in middle childhood and the role metalinguistic awareness plays in understanding how language works.

Listen to a pair of school-age children conversing with one another. Their speech, at least at first hearing, probably doesn't sound too different from that of adults.

In reality, however, the apparent similarity is deceiving. The linguistic sophistication of children—particularly at the start of the school-age period—still requires refinement to reach adult levels of expertise.

For instance, vocabulary continues to grow during the school years. Although children know thousands of words, they continue to add new words to their vocabularies, and at a fairly rapid clip. The average 6-year-old has a vocabulary of from 8,000 to 14,000 words, whereas the vocabulary grows by another 5,000 words between ages 9 and 11.

Furthermore, school-age children's mastery of grammar improves. For instance, the use of the passive voice is rare during the early school-age years (as in "The dog was walked by Lee," compared with the active-voice "Lee walked the dog"). Six- and 7-year-olds only infrequently use conditional sentences, such as, "If Sarah will set the table, I will wash the dishes." However, over the course of middle childhood, the use of both passive voice and conditional sentences increases. In addition, children's understanding of syntax grows during middle childhood.

By the time they reach first grade, most children pronounce words quite accurately. However, certain phonemes (units of sound) remain troublesome. For instance, the ability to pronounce *j, v, th,* and *zh* sounds develops later than the ability to pronounce other phonemes.

School-age children also may have difficulty decoding sentences when the meaning depends on *intonation*, or tone of voice. For example, consider the sentence, "George gave a book to Roberto, and he gave one to Bill." If the word *he* is emphasized, the meaning is "George gave a book to Roberto, and Roberto gave a different book to Bill." But if the intonation emphasizes the word *and*, then the meaning changes to "George gave a book to Roberto, and George also gave a book to Bill." Such subtleties are not easily sorted out by school-age children (Meng & Jijia, 2006; Verhagen, Leseman, & Messer, 2015).

Children also become more competent during the school years in their use of pragmatics. Pragmatics concern children's ability to use appropriate and effective language in a given social setting. For example, although children are aware of the rules of conversational turn-taking at the start of the early childhood period, their use of these rules is sometimes primitive. Consider the following conversation between 6-year-olds Yonnie and Ali:

Yonnie: My dad drives a FedEx truck.

Ali: My sister's name is Molly.

Yonnie: He gets up really early in the morning.

Ali: She wet her bed last night.

Later, however, conversations show more give-and-take, with the second child actually responding to the comments of the first. For instance, this conversation between 11-year-olds Mia and Yan reflects a more sophisticated mastery of pragmatics:

Mia: I don't know what to get Claire for her birthday.

Yan: I'm getting her earrings.

Mia: She already has a lot of jewelry.

Yan: I don't think she has that much.

METALINGUISTIC AWARENESS: LEARNING SELF-CONTROL.   One of the most significant developments in middle childhood is the increasing metalinguistic awareness of children. **Metalinguistic awareness** is an understanding of one's own use of language. By the time they are 5 or 6, children understand that language is governed by a set of rules. Whereas in the early years these rules are learned and comprehended implicitly, during middle childhood children come to understand them more explicitly (Merriman & Lipko, 2008).

metalinguistic awareness
an understanding of one's own use of language.

Metalinguistic awareness helps children achieve comprehension when information is fuzzy or incomplete. For instance, when preschoolers are given ambiguous or unclear information, they rarely ask for clarification, and they tend to blame themselves if they do not understand. By the time they reach age 7 or 8, children realize that miscommunication may be due to factors attributable not only to themselves but to the person communicating with them as well. Consequently, school-age children are more likely to ask for clarification of information that is unclear to them (Zipke, 2007; Merriman & Lipko, 2008; van den Herik, 2017).

Development in Your Life
Assessing Early Language Development

Given the critical role that language plays in cognitive development, parents often are concerned about whether their child's language development is proceeding on schedule. Although there are no hard-and-fast rules, given the wide variability in the timing of children's first words and the ways their vocabularies develop, there are several guidelines that indicate whether language development is normal. An infant who shows the following abilities is probably developing normally (American Speech-Language-Hearing Association, 2017).

- **Understanding at least some things that are heard.** This means that, at the minimum, the child has some receptive language and can hear. For instance, most children can discriminate between friendly and angry speech by the age of 6 months.

- **Producing sounds, such as a raspberry noise, at around 6 or 7 months.** Children who are deaf may cease producing prelinguistic speech at this point, even if they

produced it earlier, because they cannot hear themselves speaking.

- **Using gestures to communicate.** Pointing and reaching are often forerunners of language. By the age of 9 months, most children look toward an object that an adult is pointing to, and most use pointing themselves before the end of their first year.

- **Pretending to use language.** Even if the words make no sense, children may pretend to use language before they actually begin to speak, indicating that they at least know how language functions.

What if you cannot observe any of these indicators? It would be reasonable to have a pediatrician evaluate your child. Keep in mind, however, the wide range of variations in language development among different children, and the fact that the vast number of children develop quite normally.

The growing sophistication of their language also helps school-age children control their behavior. For instance, in one experiment, children were told that they could have one marshmallow treat if they chose to eat one immediately, but two treats if they waited. Most of the children, who ranged in age from 4 to 8, chose to wait, but the strategies they used while waiting differed significantly.

The 4-year-olds often chose to look at the marshmallows while waiting, a strategy that was not terribly effective. In contrast, 6- and 8-year-olds used language to help them overcome temptation, though in different ways. The 6-year-olds spoke and sang to themselves, reminding themselves that if they waited they would get more treats in the end. The 8-year-olds focused on aspects of the marshmallows that were not related to taste, such as their appearance, which helped them to wait. (Also see the *Development in Your Life* box on assessing early language development above.)

Module 7.1 Review

LO 7.1 Identify the formal characteristics of language, and describe how prelinguistic communication develops.

Before they *produce* their first word, infants *comprehend* many adult utterances and engage in several forms of prelinguistic communication, including the use of facial expressions, gestures, and babbling.

LO 7.2 Explain how speech develops in infancy and how early language differs from that used by adults.

Children typically produce their first words between 10 and 14 months, and rapidly increase their vocabularies from that point on. Language development proceeds through a pattern of holophrases,

two-word combinations, and telegraphic speech, and reflects a growing sense of the relations between objects in the world, and the acquisition of general mental categories and concepts.

LO 7.3 Summarize the rapid advances made by preschoolers in their comprehension and production of language, and distinguish private speech from social speech.

In the preschool years, linguistic ability increases rapidly, including advances in sentence length, vocabulary, and syntax. Children also develop a strong sense of the grammar of their language, knowing which forms and utterances are permissible and which are not, and improve their use of pragmatics, the appropriate use of language in social situations. Another linguistic development is a gradual shift from private speech to social speech. Jean Piaget regards private speech as a sign of immaturity and egocentrism; Lev Vygotsky views it as a useful cognitive mechanism that ultimately serves a social function.

LO 7.4 **Describe the development of language in middle childhood and the role metalinguistic awareness plays in understanding how language works.**

Language development in middle childhood is characterized by improvements in vocabulary, syntax, and pragmatics; by the use of language as a self-control device; and by the growth of metalinguistic awareness.

Journal Writing Prompt

Applying Lifespan Development: We have noted that deaf children babble with their hands. What other similarities and differences do you think there might be between the development of language—spoken and signed—in hearing and nonhearing children?

THE ORIGINS OF LANGUAGE DEVELOPMENT

The immense strides in language development during childhood raise a fundamental question: How does proficiency in language come about? Linguists are deeply divided on how to answer this question. They've considered two major aspects of the question: how language is acquired and what relationship exists between language and thought.

Language Acquisition

LO 7.5 **Identify the major perspectives on language acquisition, and summarize the strengths and weaknesses of each.**

Three major approaches have guided thinking on language acquisition. One is based on learning theory, the second centers on innate and genetically determined capabilities, and the third represents a combination of the first two approaches.

LEARNING THEORY APPROACHES: LANGUAGE AS A LEARNED SKILL. One view of language development emphasizes the basic principles of learning. According to the **learning theory approach**, language acquisition follows the fundamental laws of reinforcement and conditioning discussed in the first chapter (Skinner, 1957). For instance, a child who articulates the word *da* may be hugged and praised by her father, who jumps to the conclusion that she is referring to him. This reaction reinforces the child, who is more likely to repeat the word. In sum, the learning theory perspective on language acquisition suggests that children learn to speak by being rewarded for making sounds that approximate speech. Through the process of *shaping*, language becomes more and more similar to adult speech.

learning theory approach
the theory that language acquisition follows the basic laws of reinforcement and conditioning.

There's a problem, though, with the learning theory approach. It doesn't seem to adequately explain how children acquire the rules of language as readily as they do. For instance, young children are reinforced when they make errors. Parents are apt to be just as responsive if their child says, *Why the dog won't eat?* as they are if the child phrases the question more conventionally (*Why won't the dog eat?*). Both forms of the question are understood correctly, and both elicit the same response; reinforcement is provided for both correct and incorrect language usage. Under such circumstances, learning theory falls short of explaining satisfactorily how children learn to speak properly.

Children are also able to move beyond specific utterances they have heard and produce novel phrases, sentences, and constructions, an ability that also cannot be explained by learning theory. Furthermore, children can apply linguistic rules to nonsense words. In one study, 4-year-old children heard the nonsense verb "to pilk" in the sentence "the bear is pilking the horse." Later, when asked what was happening to the horse, they responded by placing the nonsense verb in the correct tense and voice: "He's getting pilked by the bear."

nativist approach

the theory that a genetically determined, innate mechanism directs the development of language.

universal grammar

a similar underlying structure shared by all the world's languages, according to linguist Noam Chomsky.

language-acquisition device (LAD)

a neural system of the brain hypothesized to permit understanding of language structure and provide strategies for learning the particular characteristics of a language.

NATIVIST APPROACHES: LANGUAGE AS AN INNATE SKILL. Such conceptual difficulties with the learning theory approach have led to the development of an alternative, championed by the linguist Noam Chomsky (2005) and known as the nativist approach. The **nativist approach** argues that there is a genetically determined, innate mechanism that directs the development of language. According to Chomsky, people are born with an innate capacity to use language, which emerges, more or less automatically, through maturation.

Chomsky's analysis of different languages suggests that all the world's languages share a similar underlying structure, which he calls **universal grammar**. In this view, the human brain is wired with a neural system called the **language-acquisition device (LAD)** that permits the understanding of language structure and provides a set of strategies and techniques for learning the particular characteristics of the language to which a child is exposed. In this view, language is uniquely human, made possible by a genetic predisposition to both comprehend and produce words and sentences (Wonnacott, 2013; Bolhuis et al., 2014; Yang et al., 2017).

Support for Chomsky's nativist approach comes from recent findings identifying a specific gene related to speech production. Further support comes from research showing that language processing in infants involves brain structures similar to those in adult speech processing, suggesting an evolutionary basis to language (Enard et al., 2002; Dehaene-Lambertz, Hertz-Pannier, & Dubois, 2006).

The view that language is an innate ability unique to humans also has its critics. For instance, some researchers argue that certain primates are able to learn at least the basics of language, an ability that calls into question the uniqueness of the human linguistic capacity. Furthermore, some critics believe that infants' use of general cognitive abilities underlies their language learning. Still others point out that although humans may be genetically primed to use language, its efficient use still requires significant social experience (Goldberg, 2004; Ibbotson & Tomasello, 2016).

THE INTERACTIONIST PERSPECTIVE ON LANGUAGE DEVELOPMENT. Neither the learning theory nor the nativist perspective fully explains language acquisition. As a result, some theorists have turned to a theory that combines both schools of thought. The *interactionist approach to language development* suggests that language development is produced through a combination of genetically determined predispositions and environmental circumstances that help teach language.

The interactionist perspective accepts that innate factors shape the broad outlines of language development. However, interactionists also argue that the specific course of language development is determined by the language to which children are exposed and the reinforcement they receive for using language in particular ways. Social factors are considered to be key to development, since the motivation provided by one's membership in a society and culture and one's interactions with others leads to the use of language and the growth of language skills (Dixon, 2004; Yang, 2006; Graf Estes, 2014).

> **From *a speech pathologist's* perspective**
>
> How important is it to understand the origin of language? Would it be the same across cultures? Why or why not?

Just as there is support for some aspects of learning theory and nativist positions, the interactionist perspective has also received some support. We don't know, at the moment, which of these positions will ultimately provide the best explanation. More likely, different factors play different roles at different times during childhood.

How Are Language and Thought Related?

LO 7.6 **Compare and contrast the different theories about the relationship between language and thought.**

It seems reasonable that Eskimo children, whose experience with freezing precipitation is far more extensive than that of children growing up in warmer climates, would have many words in their vocabulary to describe "snow." At least that was the thinking of linguist Benjamin Lee Whorf in the early 1900s. He argued that because snow was so much a part of Eskimo lives, Eskimos had a richer snow-related vocabulary than, for example, English speakers. Whorf's account seemed to be supported by data, and at least one expert contended that there were no fewer than 400 snow-related words in the Eskimo vocabulary—far more than in English.

Not so fast. Contemporary research has found that Whorf's claims regarding the Eskimo vocabulary were greatly exaggerated. Eskimos have no more words for "snow" than do English speakers. In fact, English contains many words of its own relating to snow: *Sleet, slush, blizzard, dusting, powder,* and *avalanche* are just a few examples (Chiu, Leung, & Kwan, 2007; Chabal & Marian, 2014).

The early contention that the Eskimo language was particularly rich in snowrelated words was used to support an influential proposition called the linguistic-relativity hypothesis. The **linguistic-relativity hypothesis** states that language shapes and may even determine the way people of a particular culture perceive and understand the world (Whorf, 1956; Casasanto, 2008). The hypothesis suggests that language provides categories that help children construct their perceptions of people and events in their surroundings. In short, the notion is that language shapes and produces thinking.

linguistic-relativity hypothesis the theory that language shapes and may determine the way people of a given culture perceive and understand the world.

The view that language shapes and produces thought is not the only plausible sequence, however. Consider an alternative: that instead of language being the *cause* of thought, the relationship works in the opposite direction, with language being the *result* of thinking about the world in particular ways and undergoing certain experiences. In this view, thought *produces* language.

The view that thinking shapes language is consistent with Piaget's views of the development of language. Piaget argued that the emergence of symbolic function (the ability to use mental symbols, words, and objects to represent something that is not physically present) during the preoperational period is a key aspect of the development of language skill. In short, advances in the sophistication of thinking permit language development.

Some developmentalists reject both the view that language shapes thought *and* the view that thought shapes language. Instead, they support an intermediate position: that language and thought are intertwined and influence one another. For instance, Vygotsky (1962) argues that although in the early stages of life, language and thinking develop independently, by age 2 they become interdependent. From that point, each influences the other. More precise thought permits language to become increasingly sophisticated, and more refined language capabilities allow more advanced thought.

We now have three views about the relationship between language and thought: Language shapes thought (the linguistic-relativity hypothesis), thought shapes language, and thought and language influence one another. Research supports all three views. Although most linguists would reject the notion that language is the *predominant* influence on thought, there is evidence that language does shape at least some kinds of thinking. For instance, the way in which information is stored and retrieved in memory is related to language, and the way that people evaluate others is influenced by the linguistic categories they have available to them (Gleitman & Papafragou, 2005; Casasanto, 2008).

However, there is also experimental support for the opposite position, that thinking shapes language. For instance, the experiences that children have shape their first words, which are usually about people, animals, and foods in their environment, regardless of the language they speak. Furthermore, cross-cultural research shows that even if there is no word for particular colors in a given language, people speaking that language can still distinguish the different colors, suggesting that language is not a prerequisite for thought (Rosch, 1974; Zhang, He, & Zhang, 2007).

The existence of evidence supporting both the languageshapes-thought and thought-shapes-language sequences suggests that the third position—that thought and language jointly influence one another—may ultimately prove to be the most accurate. Such a position seems plausible and is supported by direct experimental evidence (Riley, 2008). Most developmentalists, then, suggest that although initially language and thought may develop more or less independently, by the time children are 2 years old, language and thinking work in tandem, as Vygotsky suggested.

Module 7.2 Review

LO 7.5 **Identify the major perspectives on language acquisition, and summarize the strengths and weaknesses of each.**

The way language develops is a complex and controversial question. Several theoretical perspectives have been adopted to explain the phenomenon, including the learning theory, the nativist approach, and the interactionist approach. According to the learning theory, language acquisition is little different from learning of any sort, with children's language reinforced and shaped by adults. The emergence of a sense of grammar is not well explained by this approach. The nativist approach, developed by Noam Chomsky, claims that humans have an innate language capacity that naturally facilitates language development. The existence of sensitive periods for learning language, the lack of language among nonhuman species, and the existence of areas of the brain associated with language support the nativist approach, while the failure to specify a truly universal grammar weakens it. A compromise position is held by the interactionists, who argue that language development,

though innate, is determined by social factors, such as children's linguistic environment and the reinforcement they receive from others.

LO 7.6 **Compare and contrast the different theories about the relationship between language and thought.**

The linguistic-relativity hypothesis, advanced by Benjamin Lee Whorf, holds that language shapes thought. However, the opposite view, that thought shapes language, as Piaget believed, is also a prevalent view, and the truth is probably that language and thought influence one another.

Journal Writing Prompt

Applying Lifespan Development: If humans have a language-acquisition device, why do children raised in isolation fail to develop language naturally? Why do adults have such difficulty learning a new language?

MODULE 7.3

CHILDREN'S CONVERSATIONS: SPEAKING TO AND WITH CHILDREN

Say the following sentence aloud: Do you like the apple dumpling?

Now pretend that you are going to ask the same question of an infant, and speak it as you would for the child's ears.

Chances are that several things happened when you translated the phrase for the infant. First of all, the wording probably changed, and you may have said something like, "Does baby like the apple dumpling?" At the same time, the pitch of your voice probably rose, your general intonation most likely had a singsong quality, and you probably separated your words carefully.

The change in your language illustrates just one facet of the nature of conversations involving children. We turn now to several aspects of language involving children's conversations, beginning with speech directed at infants.

The Language of Infant-Directed Speech

LO 7.7 **Describe how infant-directed speech affects children's language development.**

infant-directed speech
a type of speech directed toward infants that is characterized by short, simple sentences.

In the example above, the shift in your language was due to your use of **infant-directed speech**, a style of speech that characterizes much of the verbal communication directed toward infants. This type of speech pattern used to be called *motherese*, because it was assumed that it applied only to mothers. However, that assumption was wrong, and the gender-neutral term *infant-directed speech* is now used more frequently.

Infant-directed speech is characterized by short, simple sentences. Pitch becomes higher, the range of frequencies increases, and intonation is more varied. There is also repetition of words, and topics are restricted to items that are assumed to be comprehensible to infants, such as concrete objects in the baby's environment. (Infants are not

Motherese, or, more precisely, infant-directed speech, includes the use of short, simple sentences and is said in a pitch that is higher than that used with older children and adults. Infant-directed speech is similar across cultures.

the only ones who are the recipients of a specific form of speech: We change our style of speech when speaking to foreigners, as well; Scott & Henderson, 2013; Wang, Seidl, & Cristia, 2015; Hartman, Ratner & Newman, 2017).

Sometimes infant-directed speech includes amusing sounds that are not even words, imitating the prelinguistic speech of infants. In other cases, it has little formal structure but is similar to the kind of telegraphic speech that infants use as they develop their own language skills.

Infant-directed speech changes as children become older. Around the end of the first year, infant-directed speech takes on more adultlike qualities. Sentences become longer and more complex, although individual words are still spoken slowly and deliberately. Pitch is also used to focus attention on particularly important words (Soderstrom et al., 2008; Kitamura & Lam, 2009).

Infant-directed speech plays an important role in infants' acquisition of language. As discussed next, infant-directed speech occurs all over the world, though there are cultural variations. Newborns prefer such speech to regular language, which suggests that they may be particularly receptive to it. Furthermore, some research indicates that babies who are exposed to a great deal of infant-directed speech early in life seem to begin to use words and exhibit other forms of linguistic competence earlier (Werker et al., 2007; Bergelson & Swingley, 2012; Eaves et al., 2016). (For a discussion of infant-directed speech across cultures, see the *Developmental Diversity and Your Life* box feature.)

Developmental Diversity and Your Life
Is Infant-Directed Speech Similar in All Cultures?

Do mothers in the United States, Sweden, and Russia speak the same way to their infants?

In some respects, they clearly do. Although the words themselves differ across languages, the way the words are spoken to infants is quite similar. According to a growing body of research, infant-directed speech is basically similar across cultures (Werker et al., 2007; Broesch & Bryant, 2015).

Even deaf mothers use a form of infant-directed speech: When communicating with their infants, deaf mothers use sign language at a significantly slower tempo than when communicating with adults, and they frequently repeat the signs (Masataka, 2000).

The cross-cultural similarities in infant-directed speech are so great, in fact, that they appear in some facets of language specific to particular types of interactions. For instance, evidence comparing American English, German, and Mandarin Chinese speakers shows that in each of the languages, pitch rises when a mother is attempting to get an infant's attention or produce a response, while pitch falls when she is trying to calm an infant (Papousek & Papousek, 1991).

Why do we find such similarities across very different languages? One hypothesis is that the characteristics of infant-directed speech activate innate responses in infants. As we have noted, infants seem to prefer infant-directed speech over adult-directed speech, suggesting that their perceptual systems may be more responsive to such characteristics. Another explanation is that infant-directed speech facilitates language development, providing cues as to the meaning of speech before infants have developed the capacity to understand the meaning of words (Trainor & Desjardins, 2002; Falk, 2004; Hayashi & Mazuka, 2017).

Despite the similarities in the style of infant-directed speech across diverse cultures, there are some important cultural differences in the *quantity* of speech that infants hear from their parents. For example, although the Gusii of Kenya care for their infants in an extremely close, physical way, they speak to them less than American parents do.

More precise comparisons, across a broader range of languages, reveal other similarities. For instance, Table 7-2 shows the remarkable similarities in speech pitch among speakers of different languages when they are directing speech to infants, as opposed to adults (Fernald et al., 1989). It is particularly interesting that in every case mothers raise their pitch more than fathers when speaking to infants. Furthermore, speakers of American English show the greatest differences between speech to an infant and speech to an adult.

In addition, the language parents employ with their children differs depending on the child's sex. By the age of 32 months, girls hear twice as many diminutives (words such as *kitty* or *dolly* instead of *cat* or *doll*) as boys hear. Although the use of diminutives declines with increasing age, their use consistently remains higher in speech directed at girls than in that directed at boys (see Figure 7-3; Gleason et al., 1994; Gleason & Ely, 2002; Arnon & Ramscar, 2012).

From *an educator's* perspective

What are some implications of differences in the ways adults speak to boys and girls? How might such speech differences contribute to later differences not only in speech but also in attitudes?

Parents are also more apt to respond differently to children's requests depending on the child's gender. For instance, when turning down a child's request, mothers are likely to respond with a firm "no" to a male child but to soften the blow to a female child by providing a diversionary response ("Why don't you do this instead?") or by somehow making the refusal less direct. Consequently, boys tend to hear firmer, clearer language, while girls are exposed to warmer phrases, often referring to inner emotional states (Perlmann & Gleason, 1990).

Do such differences in language directed at boys and girls during infancy affect their behavior as adults? There is

Table 7-2 The Most Common Features of Infant-Directed Speech

English	Spanish
1. Stronger intonation	1. Strong intonation
2. Exaggerated breathiness	2. Repetition
3. Higher pitch	3. Higher pitch
4. More repetition	4. More instructional
5. Lower volume	5. Use of attentionals
6. Vowel sounds lengthened	6. Volume is lower
7. Creakiness in voice	7. Higher volume
8. More instruction	8. Vowel sounds lower
9. Tenseness	9. Faster speed
10. Use of falsetto	10. More substitutions of personal pronouns

(**Source:** Based on Blount, 1982.)

Figure 7-3 Gender Differences in Language: Diminishing Diminutives

Although the use of diminutives toward both male and female infants declines with age, they are consistently used more often in speech directed at females. What do you think is the cultural significance of this?
(**Source:** Gleason et al., 1994.)

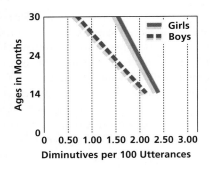

no direct evidence that plainly supports such an association, but men and women do use different sorts of language as adults. For instance, as adults, women tend to use more tentative, less assertive language ("Maybe we should try to go to a movie") than men ("I know, let's go to a movie!"). Though we don't know if these differences are a reflection of early linguistic experiences, such findings are certainly intriguing (Tenenbaum & Leaper, 2003; Hartshorne & Ullman, 2006; Plante et al., 2006).

Of course, gender is not the only factor that influences children's use of language. Increasing evidence suggests that the sheer quantity of speech that occurs in a household influences children's language development, and that quantity is associated with the economic well-being of the family environment, as we see next.

The Links Between Language Development and Poverty

LO 7.8   Explain how socioeconomic status influences language development in children.

Although it has long been assumed that the language that preschoolers hear at home has profound implications for their future cognitive success, only recently has research addressed the issue in actual home settings. In a landmark study, psychologists Betty Hart and Todd Risley (1995) studied the language used over a two-year period by a group of parents of varying levels of affluence as they interacted with their children. Coding some 1,300 hours of everyday interactions between parents and children produced several major findings:

- The rate at which language was addressed to children varied significantly according to the economic level of the family. As can be seen in Figure 7-4, the greater the affluence of the parents, the more they spoke to their children.

- In a typical hour, parents classified as professionals spent almost twice as much time interacting with their children as parents who received welfare assistance.

- By age 4, children in families that received welfare assistance were likely to have been exposed to some 13 million fewer words than those in families classified as professionals.

- There were differences in the kind of language used in the home by the various types of families. Children in families that received welfare assistance were apt to hear prohibitions ("no" or "stop," for example) twice as frequently as those in families classified as professionals.

Ultimately, the study found that the type of language to which children were exposed was associated with their performance on tests of intelligence. The greater the number and variety of words children heard, for instance, the better their performance at age 3 on a variety of measures of intellectual achievement (Hart & Risley, 1995; Fowler et al., 2006).

Figure 7-4 Different Language Exposure

Parents at differing levels of economic affluence provide different language experiences. Professional parents and working parents address more words to their children on average than parents on welfare. Why do you think this is so?
(**Source:** Hart & Risley, 1995.)

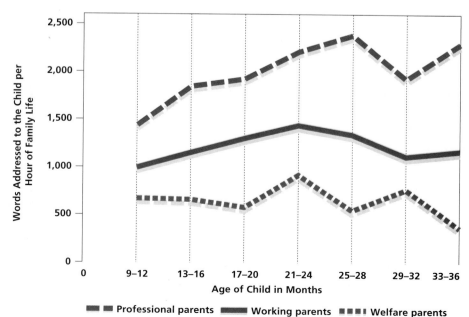

From Research to Practice

Can Language Skills Be Improved for Preschoolers Living in Families with Low Incomes?

Toddlers commonly say their first word sometime around their first birthday, and just a few months later the explosion of new word acquisition begins. By the end of the preschool years children typically have thousands of words in their vocabulary.

However, vocabulary size and comprehension can vary widely from one preschooler to the next. Family income has been identified as one variable associated with differences in language ability. That is, children living in poverty tend to use significantly fewer words. This difference is evident by the time a toddler reaches 18 months of age, if not sooner (Hart & Risley, 1995; Fernald, Marchman, & Weisleder, 2013; Betancourt, Brodsky, & Hurt, 2015).

Can anything be done to help promote language development in preschoolers who live in impoverished environments? Fortunately, programs for preschoolers from low-income families have shown promising results in terms of improving the children's oral language skills as well as their understanding of spoken language.

In these programs, researchers institute language interventions, conducted by teachers, teaching assistants, or paraprofessionals. Typically occurring over 12 to 30 weeks (about 60–80 minutes per week), the programs use techniques such as interactive reading (e.g., asking questions about stories), phonics activities (e.g., rhyming games), and direct instruction (e.g., specifically teaching new words). The results of these studies are positive: Children improved in skills such as vocabulary use and listening comprehension. The children also continued to show improvements when tested several months later (Phillips et al., 2016; Fricke et al., 2017; Hagen, Melby-Lervåg, & Lervåg, 2017).

Language is a critical area of development because it influences other forms of cognitive and social-emotional development. Thus, programs that improve language in preschoolers may have far-reaching positive consequences.

Shared Writing Prompt

What would be the advantages and challenges of incorporating parents in interventions designed to improve their children's language skills?

Several factors may explain why children raised in more affluent homes are spoken to more frequently than children in more financially impoverished households. For instance, more affluent parents may have the luxury of spending more time with their children, as well as more flexible hours. Furthermore, there may be less household stress, thereby permitting more freewheeling interactions and fewer situations in which parents are simply exhausted.

Although the findings are correlational, and thus cannot be interpreted in terms of cause and effect, they suggest the importance of early exposure to language, in terms of both quantity and variety. They also suggest that intervention programs that teach parents to speak to their children more often and to use more varied language may help alleviate some of the potentially damaging consequences of poverty.

From *a social worker's* perspective

What do you think are the underlying reasons for differences between poorer and more affluent households in the use of language, and how do such language differences affect a family's social interactions?

The research is also consistent with an increasing body of evidence showing that family income and poverty have powerful consequences for children's general cognitive development and behavior. By age 5, children raised in poverty tend to have lower IQ scores and perform less well on other measures of cognitive development than children raised in affluence. Furthermore, the longer children live in poverty, the more severe are the consequences. Poverty not only reduces the educational resources available to children, but it also has such negative effects on *parents* that it limits the psychological support they can provide their families. In short, the consequences of poverty are severe, and they linger (Kim, Curby, & Winsler, 2014; Sharkins, Leger, & Ernest, 2016; Lipina & Evers, 2017).

English Language Learners: Bilingual Education Versus Immersion

LO 7.9 **Compare bilingual education to the immersion approach, and identify the cognitive benefits of being bilingual.**

Children who enter school with little or no English proficiency must learn both the standard curriculum and the language in which that curriculum is taught. Known as *English-language learners (ELLs)*, these students face special challenges. Their lack of English language skills may significantly slow their academic progress and isolate them from other children. In addition, their specific cultural background may lead ELLs to understand the educational process differently. For example, in some cultures it is considered disrespectful to ask teachers questions about material they are presenting (Klingner & Artiles, 2006; Stipek & Hakuta, 2007).

BILINGUAL EDUCATION. One approach to educating students whose first language is not English is *bilingual education*, in which students are initially taught in their native language, while at the same time learning English. With bilingual instruction, students are able to develop a strong foundation in basic subject areas using their native language. The ultimate goal of most bilingual education programs is to gradually shift instruction to English.

An alternative approach is to immerse students in English, teaching solely in that language. According to proponents of this approach, initially teaching students in a language other than English hinders their efforts to learn English and slows their integration into society.

The two quite different approaches have been highly politicized, with some politicians arguing in favor of "English-only" laws and others urging school systems to respect the challenges faced by students who do not speak English by offering some instruction in their native language. Still, the psychological research clearly suggests that knowing more than one language offers several cognitive advantages. Because they have a wider range of linguistic possibilities to choose from as they assess a situation, speakers of two languages show greater cognitive flexibility. They can solve problems with increased creativity and versatility. Furthermore, learning in one's native tongue is associated with higher self-esteem in minority students (Hermanto, Moreno & Bialystok, 2012; Hsin & Snow, 2017).

In fact, bilingualism may do even more: It can provide significant cognitive advantages (Chen & Bond, 2007; Bialystok & Viswanathan, 2009; Hermanto, Moreno, & Bialystok, 2012).

Module 7.3 Review

LO 7.7 **Describe how infant-directed speech affects children's language development.**

When talking to infants, adults of all cultures tend to use infant-directed speech. This type of speech seems to appeal to infants and to facilitate their linguistic development. According to some research, adults tend to speak more indirectly to girls and more directly to boys, which may contribute to behavioral differences later in life.

LO 7.8 **Explain how socioeconomic status influences language development in children.**

Economic factors in the home have a significant influence on language development. Children raised in affluence hear a greater quantity and variety of language from their parents than do children raised in poverty, with positive effects on later measures of intellectual achievement.

LO 7.9 **Compare bilingual education to the immersion approach, and identify the cognitive benefits of being bilingual.**

Students who speak more than one language show greater cognitive flexibility, metalinguistic awareness, and even intelligence test performance, but immersion in the language of the dominant culture can be problematic for children of other cultures.

Journal Writing Prompt

Applying Lifespan Development: What are some implications of differences in the ways adults speak to boys and girls? How might such speech differences contribute to later differences not only in speech but also in attitudes?

Epilogue

We have examined the development of speech in children, observing how they progress from inaccurate users of language to accomplished speakers. The process by which children reach competence in language is complex but seems to come naturally to them. Their capabilities are so apparent that they can easily learn two or more languages if they hear them frequently and naturally—an ability envied by any school-age student or adult who has struggled with *Beginning French* or *Mandarin Made Easy*.

In the prologue, we encountered Brooke, who was wondering if her 6-month-old daughter, Riley, actually said "mama" or if this word was just part of her random vocalizations. Before we proceed to the next chapter, think about Brooke and Riley, and answer the following questions.

1. Why do you think Brooke is fascinated by the possible emergence of Riley's first word?

2. What role does infant-directed speech play in infants' language development? Is the influence of infant-directed speech on children's language learning similar in all cultures?

3. If Brooke and her family lived in an impoverished environment, what would be some possible effects of poverty on Riley's language development?

4. Would Riley benefit from learning multiple languages during early childhood?

Looking Back

LO 7.1 Identify the formal characteristics of language, and describe how prelinguistic communication develops.

Infants engage in prelinguistic communication, the use of sounds, gestures, facial expressions, imitation, and other nonlinguistic means to express thoughts and states. Babbling is a form of prelinguistic communication, which proceeds through regular stages and, with other forms of prelinguistic communication, prepares the infant for speech.

LO 7.2 Explain how speech develops in infancy and how early language differs from that used by adults.

Infants typically produce their first words between the ages of 10 and 14 months. Thereafter, vocabulary increases rapidly, especially during a spurt at around 18 months. At about the same time, children typically begin to link words together into primitive sentences that express single thoughts. Features of the child's native language begin to emerge as early as the babbling stage, when sounds other than those of the home language gradually disappear. In addition, the structure of the home language begins to be reflected even in telegraphic speech, when word order mirrors that used by mature speakers of the home language. Beginning speech is characterized by the use of holophrases, in which a single word conveys more complex meaning based on its context; telegraphic speech, in which only essential sentence components are used; underextension, in which an overly restrictive meaning is assigned to a word; and overextension, in which an overly generalized meaning is assigned to a word.

LO 7.3 Summarize the rapid advances made by preschoolers in their comprehension and production of language, and distinguish private speech from social speech.

The burst in language ability that occurs during the preschool years is dramatic. Children rapidly progress from two-word utterances to longer, more sophisticated expressions that reflect their growing vocabularies, sense of syntax, and emerging grasp of grammar. They also proceed along a continuum from private speech to more social speech. A process known as fast mapping develops in which children associate new words with their meanings after only a brief encounter.

LO 7.4 Describe the development of language in middle childhood and the role metalinguistic awareness plays in understanding how language works.

The language development of children in the school years is substantial, with improvements in vocabulary, syntax, and pragmatics. Despite these advances, school-age children's language is still not as proficient as it will become in adulthood, and some pronunciation and comprehension difficulties are normal. Improvements in language help children control their behavior through linguistic strategies. Moreover, their growing metalinguistic awareness permits them to realize that language use is rule-governed and is subject to breakdowns for which they are not solely responsible, and which can be remedied by seeking clarification.

LO 7.5 Identify the major perspectives on language acquisition, and summarize the strengths and weaknesses of each.

One theory of how humans develop language is the learning theory, which assumes that adults and children use basic behavioral processes—such as conditioning, reinforcement, and shaping—in language learning. The fact that people spontaneously develop a natural grammatical sense argues against this perspective. A radically different approach—the nativist approach—is proposed by Noam Chomsky, who holds that humans are genetically endowed with a language-acquisition device, which permits them to detect and use the principles of universal grammar that underlie all languages. Support for this view is derived from the existence of sensitive periods for learning language, the lack of language among non-human species, and the existence of areas of the brain associated with language, while the failure to specify a truly universal grammar weakens it. An intermediate approach—the interactionist perspective—holds that children have innate linguistic capabilities that are shaped by social factors such as the language to which children are exposed and the interactions that they have with others in their environment.

LO 7.6   Compare and contrast the different theories about the relationship between language and thought.

According to Benjamin Lee Whorf's linguistic-relativity hypothesis, the language that people speak influences the ways they perceive and understand the world. This view—that language shapes thought—is controversial; the opposite view—that thought shapes language—which is held by developmentalists such as Jean Piaget, is more mainstream but also controversial. An intermediate position—that thought and language jointly influence one another—is growing in acceptance and appears to be most accurate.

LO 7.7   Describe how infant-directed speech affects children's language development.

Infant-directed speech takes on characteristics, surprisingly invariant across cultures, that make it appealing to infants and that probably facilitate language development. There is some evidence that infants are especially—and perhaps

innately—attuned to the characteristics of infant-directed speech. Adult language also exhibits differences based on the gender of the child to whom it is directed.

LO 7.8   Explain how socioeconomic status influences language development in children.

Language development and economic circumstances are significantly linked. Preschool children raised in poverty tend to hear a smaller quantity and variety of language from their parents and caregivers than children raised in affluence. This linguistic difference in turn is linked to later differential performance on a variety of measures of intellectual achievement.

LO 7.9   Compare bilingual education to the immersion approach, and identify the cognitive benefits of being bilingual.

Bilingualism is an increasingly prevalent phenomenon in the school years. There is evidence that many children who are taught all subjects in the first language, with simultaneous instruction in English, experience few deficits and several linguistic and cognitive advantages. Immersion programs work well when majority children are immersed during the school day in a minority language but do not work as well the other way around: when minority children are immersed in the language of the majority. Bilingual children exhibit many positive traits, including greater metalinguistic awareness, a more explicit understanding of the rules of language, and a high level of cognitive sophistication.

Key Terms and Concepts

language   220
prelinguistic communication   222
babbling   222
holophrases   223
telegraphic speech   224
syntax   225
fast mapping   225

grammar   226
pragmatics   226
private speech   226
social speech   226
metalinguistic awareness   227
learning theory approach   229

nativist approach   230
universal grammar   230
language-acquisition device
    (LAD)   230
linguistic-relativity hypothesis   231
infant-directed speech   232

Chapter 8
Intelligence

DGLimages/Shutterstock

⌄ Learning Objectives

LO 8.1 Describe traditional methods for measuring intelligence.

LO 8.2 Examine current methods of intelligence testing.

LO 8.3 Explore key issues surrounding intelligence testing.

LO 8.4 Analyze alternative definitions of intelligence.

LO 8.5 Describe recent approaches to measuring intelligence in infants.

LO 8.6 Define achievement and aptitude tests and compare their uses.

LO 8.7 Analyze the sources of score differences achieved by different groups on IQ and other tests.

LO 8.8 Describe the effects of aging on intelligence.

LO 8.9 Explain the meaning of the term *least restrictive environment*.

LO 8.10 Analyze the characteristics and effects of intellectual disability.

LO 8.11 Describe the characteristics and effects of giftedness.

Chapter Overview

Prologue: A Meeting of Minds

Twins Darius and Jayden Johnson had always been compared to each other. As toddlers, Darius was "rambunctious" while Jayden was "so polite." But they were always close to one another in most ways.

However, Darius began to feel different from his twin, and even the rest of his family, when they started school. Darius struggled with learning to read, while Jayden loved to show off his "straight A" report card to his parents. As time passed, Darius began to think of Jayden as "the smart twin" and himself as only "the other twin."

The differences between the two only became more profound in middle school: Darius was assigned to special education classes; Jayden did accelerated coursework through the gifted program. But in high school everything seemed to change when Darius walked into his first day of automotive technology class. Not only was he a natural at learning how each mechanical part worked, but for the first time in his life Darius felt that he was really good at something. After high school, Darius would go on to start his own shop—Johnson Automotive Repair. And when Jayden struggled to find a job after graduating from college with a business degree, Darius hired him to help manage the thriving business, telling Jayden, "Mom always said everyone has their own path to success—and she was right." ■

Looking Ahead

The roads to success achieved by Darius and Jayden raise a number of issues, addressed in this chapter, about the nature of intelligence. How can we define intelligent behavior? Are people like Jayden smarter than others, and does that intelligence always pay off? Are people like Darius in some way deficient or disabled? What makes one person more, or less, intelligent than others?

To answer these questions, we first consider the ways that have been developed to differentiate children on the basis of intelligence. We discuss traditional measures of intelligence—IQ tests—and examine newer alternatives such as those suggested by Lev Vygotsky and information processing approaches to intelligence.

We then explore some of the controversial issues in the realm of intelligence. We consider how to measure intelligence in infancy and the meaning of racial differences

Understanding precisely what is meant by the concept of intelligence has proven to be a major challenge for researchers.

in IQ scores. We also look at the contested topic of intelligence among adults and examine whether the picture of declining cognitive competence is an empty stereotype or has some truth to it. We then suggest ways that adults can maintain their cognitive functioning.

The chapter ends with an examination of the two groups that show the extremes of intelligence: people with intellectual disabilities and gifted people. We consider the nature of the exceptionality of each of these populations and focus on the question of how exceptional children should best be integrated into society.

MODULE 8.1

INTELLIGENCE: DETERMINING INDIVIDUAL STRENGTHS

"Why should you tell the truth?" "How far is Los Angeles from New York?" "A table is made of wood; a window of ____."

As 10-year-old Hyacinth sat hunched over her desk, trying to answer a long series of questions like these, she tried to guess the point of the test she was taking in her fifth-grade classroom. Clearly, the test didn't cover material that her teacher, Ms. White-Johnston, had talked about in class.

"What number comes next in this series: 1, 3, 7, 15, 31, ____?"

As she continued to work her way through the questions, she gave up trying to guess the rationale for the test. She'd leave that to her teacher, she sighed to herself. Rather than attempting to figure out what it all meant, she simply tried to do her best on the individual test items.

Hyacinth might be surprised to learn that she was not alone in questioning the meaning and import of the items on the test she was taking. For although the test items were painstakingly developed, many developmentalists would admit to harboring their own doubts as to whether questions such as these are appropriate to the task of assessing what they are designed to measure: intelligence.

Intelligence Benchmarks: Differentiating the Intelligent from the Unintelligent

LO 8.1 Describe traditional methods for measuring intelligence.

Understanding precisely what is meant by the concept of intelligence has proven to be a major challenge for researchers interested in delineating what separates intelligent from unintelligent behavior. Although nonexperts have their own conceptions of intelligence (one survey found, for instance, that laypersons believe that intelligence consists of three components: problem-solving ability, verbal ability, and social competence), it has been more difficult for experts to concur. Still, a general definition of intelligence is possible: **Intelligence** is the capacity to understand the world, think with rationality, and use resources effectively when faced with challenges.

Part of the difficulty in defining intelligence stems from the many—and sometimes unsatisfactory—paths that have been followed over the years in the quest to distinguish more intelligent people from less intelligent ones. To understand how researchers have approached the task of devising batteries of assessments called *intelligence tests*, we need to consider some of the historical milestones in the area of intelligence.

BINET'S PIONEERING EFFORTS. The Paris school system was faced with a problem in the early 1900s: A significant number of children were not benefiting from regular instruction. Unfortunately, these children—many of whom we would now say had intellectual disabilities—were generally not identified early enough to shift them to

intelligence
the capacity to understand the world, think with rationality, and use resources effectively when faced with challenges.

special classes. The French minister of instruction approached psychologist Alfred Binet with the problem of devising a technique for the early identification of students who might benefit from instruction outside the regular classroom.

Binet tackled his task in a thoroughly practical manner. His years of observing school-aged children suggested to him that previous efforts to distinguish intelligent from unintelligent students—some of which were based on reaction time or keenness of sight—were off the mark. Instead, he launched a trial-and-error process in which items and tasks were administered to students who had been previously identified by teachers as being either "bright" or "dull." Tasks that the bright students completed correctly and the dull students failed to complete correctly were retained for the test. Tasks that did not discriminate between the two groups were discarded. The end result of this process was a test that reliably distinguished students who had previously been identified as fast or slow learners.

Binet's pioneering efforts in intelligence testing left three important legacies. The first was his pragmatic approach to the construction of intelligence tests. Binet did not have theoretical preconceptions about what intelligence was. Instead, he used a trial-and-error approach to psychological measurement that continues to serve as the predominant approach to test construction today. His definition of intelligence as that which his test measured has been adopted by many modern researchers, and it is especially popular among test developers who respect the widespread utility of intelligence tests but wish to avoid arguments about the underlying nature of intelligence.

Our second inheritance from Binet stems from his focus on linking intelligence and school success. Binet's reliance on teachers as the backbone for his procedure of constructing an intelligence test ensured that intelligence—defined as performance on the test—and school success—predicted by teachers—would be virtually one and the same. Binet's intelligence test and its current successors, then, have become reasonable indicators of the degree to which students possess attributes that contribute to successful school performance. Unfortunately, they do not provide particularly useful information regarding a vast number of other attributes that are largely unrelated to academic proficiency.

Finally, Binet developed a procedure of assigning each intelligence test score to a mental age, the age of the children taking the test who, on average, achieved that score. For example, if a 6-year-old girl received a score of 30 on the test, and this was the average score received by 10-year-olds, her mental age would be considered 10 years. Similarly, a 15-year-old boy who scored a 90 on the test—thereby matching the mean score for 15-year-olds—would be assigned a mental age of 15 years.

Although assigning a mental age to students indicates whether they are performing at the same level as their peers, it does not permit adequate comparisons between students of different chronological (or physical) ages. By using mental age alone, for instance, one might assume that a 15-year-old responding with a mental age of 17 years would be as bright as a 6-year-old responding with a mental age of 8 years, when actually the 6-year-old would be showing a much greater relative degree of brightness.

DEVELOPING THE MEASURE OF INTELLIGENCE. A solution to this problem comes in the form of the **intelligence quotient (IQ)**, a score that takes into account a student's mental and chronological age. The traditional method of calculating an IQ score uses the following formula, in which MA stands for mental age and CA for chronological age:

intelligence quotient (IQ)
a score that takes into account a student's mental and chronological age.

$$\text{IQ Score} = \frac{\text{MA}}{\text{CA}} \times 100$$

As a bit of trial-and-error with this formula demonstrates, people whose mental age (MA) is equal to their chronological age (CA) will always have an IQ of 100. Furthermore, if the chronological age exceeds the mental age—implying below-average intelligence—the score will be below 100; and if the chronological age is lower than the mental age—suggesting above-average intelligence—the score will be above 100.

Using this formula, we can return to our earlier example of a 15-year-old who scores at a 17-year-old mental age. This student's IQ is $17/15 \times 100$, or 113. In comparison, the IQ of a 6-year-old scoring at a mental age of 8 is $8/6 \times 100$, or 133—a higher IQ score than the 15-year-old's.

Figure 8-1 IQ Scores

The most common and average IQ score is 100, with 68.3 percent of all people falling within 15 points of 100. About 95 percent of the population has scores that are within 30 points above or below 100; fewer than 3 percent score below 55 or above 145.

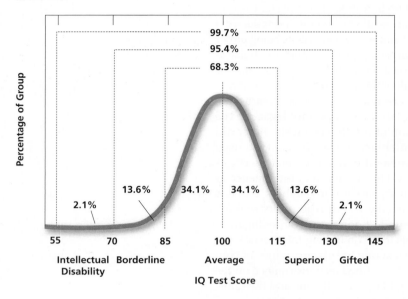

Although the basic principles behind the calculation of an IQ score still hold, scores today are calculated in a more mathematically sophisticated manner and are known as *deviation IQ scores*. Rather than comparing performance to children who are younger and older, deviation IQ scores are computed by comparing other children of the same age. The average deviation IQ score remains set at 100, and tests are now statistically constructed so that approximately two-thirds of children of a given age fall within 15 points of the average score of 100, achieving scores between 85 and 115. As scores rise or fall beyond this range, the percentage of children in the same score category drops significantly (see Figure 8-1).

Measuring IQ: Present-Day Approaches to Intelligence

LO 8.2 **Examine current methods of intelligence testing.**

Since the time of Binet, tests of intelligence have become increasingly accurate measures of IQ. Most of them can still trace their roots to his original work in one way or another. For example, one of the most widely used tests—the **Stanford-Binet Intelligence Scale, Fifth Edition (SB5)**—began as an American revision of Binet's original test. The test consists of a series of items that vary according to the age of the person being tested. For instance, young children are asked to answer questions about everyday activities or to copy complex figures. Older people are asked to explain proverbs, solve analogies, and describe similarities between groups of words. The test is administered orally, and test-takers are given progressively more difficult problems until they are unable to proceed.

The **Wechsler Intelligence Scale for Children-IV (WISC-IV)** and its adult version, the **Wechsler Adult Intelligence Scale-IV (WAIS-IV)**, are two other widely used intelligence tests. The tests provide separate measures of verbal and performance (or nonverbal) skills, as well as a total score. As you can see from the items similar to those actually on the test in Figure 8-2, the verbal tasks are traditional word problems that test skills such as understanding a passage, while typical nonverbal tasks include copying a complex design, arranging pictures in a logical order, and assembling objects. The separate portions of the test allow for easier identification of any specific problems a test-taker may have. For example, significantly higher scores on the performance part of the test than on the verbal part may indicate difficulties in linguistic development.

The **Kaufman Assessment Battery for Children (KABC-II)** takes a different approach than the Stanford-Binet, WISC-IV, and WAIS-IV. In the KABC-II, children are tested on their ability to integrate different kinds of stimuli simultaneously and to use step-by-step thinking. A special virtue of the KABC-II is its flexibility. It allows the person giving the test to use alternative wording or gestures, or even to pose questions in a different language, in order to maximize a test-taker's performance. This makes testing more valid and equitable for children for whom English is a second language (Kaufman et al., 2005; Singer et al., 2012).

In addition to individualized IQ tests, there are also several tests designed to be administered to groups of children. Such group IQ tests require written answers to a series of written questions. Their great advantage over other types of IQ tests is the ease with which they can be administered.

Stanford-Binet Intelligence Scale, Fifth Edition (SB5)
a test that consists of a series of items that vary according to the age of the person being tested.

Wechsler Intelligence Scale for Children-IV (WISC-IV)
a test for children that provides separate measures of verbal and performance (nonverbal) skills, as well as a total score.

Wechsler Adult Intelligence Scale-IV (WAIS-IV)
a test for adults that provides separate measures of verbal and performance (nonverbal) skills, as well as a total score.

Kaufman Assessment Battery for Children (KABC-II)
a children's intelligence test permitting unusual flexibility in its administration.

Figure 8-2 Measuring Intelligence

The Wechsler Intelligence Scale for Children-IV (WISC-IV) includes items such as these. What do such items cover? What do they miss?

Name	Goal of Item	Example
Information	Assess general information	How many nickels make a dime?
Comprehension	Assess understanding and evaluation of social norms and past experience	What is the advantage of keeping money in the bank?
Arithmetic	Assess math reasoning through verbal problems	If two buttons cost 15 cents, what will be the cost of a dozen buttons?
Similarities	Test understanding of how objects or concepts are alike, tapping abstract reasoning	In what way are an hour and a week alike?
Digit symbol	Assess speed of learning	Match symbols to numbers using key.
Picture completion	Visual memory and attention	Identify what is missing.
Object assembly	Test understanding of relationship of parts to wholes	Put pieces together to form a whole.

Central Issues in Intelligence Testing

LO 8.3 **Explore key issues surrounding intelligence testing.**

Let's examine some key issues and controversies surrounding intelligence testing.

GROUP ADMINISTRATION. Despite their advantages, group IQ tests have several disadvantages. For one thing, the questions asked on group tests tend to be more restricted than those administered individually. In addition, children are often more motivated when they are asked questions individually by a test administrator than when they are responding in a group. Finally, outside factors, such as being distracted by other students, having their pencils break, or not paying attention to instructions, may interfere with children's performance. Ultimately, group-administered IQ tests may provide a far less accurate assessment of IQ than individually administered tests.

BIAS. As we'll discuss later in the chapter, IQ tests have been criticized for discriminating against members of minority racial, ethnic, and cultural groups. In order to overcome this bias, some IQ tests have been specifically designed to overcome the potential

Figure 8-3 The Raven Progressive Matrices Test

In the Raven Progressive Matrices Test, examinees are shown an abstract figure with a missing piece. They are asked to choose from several possibilities to identify which piece would complete the figure. The Raven is designed to be free of cultural bias because it is assumed that no group is more or less familiar with the task.

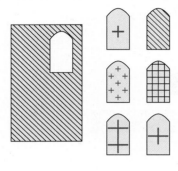

reliability
a quality of tests that measure consistently what they are trying to measure.

validity
a quality of tests that actually measure what they are supposed to measure.

specific learning disorders
difficulties in the acquisition and use of listening, speaking, reading, writing, reasoning, or mathematical abilities.

for cultural bias. For instance, *culture-fair IQ tests* are designed to be independent of the cultural background of test-takers. An example is the Raven Progressive Matrices Test, which asks test-takers to examine abstract designs that have a missing piece and choose the missing piece from several possibilities (see Figure 8-3).

The assumption behind culture-fair IQ tests is that no particular cultural group will be more or less acquainted with the test content, and consequently the test results will be free from cultural bias. Unfortunately, the culture-fair tests have not been very successful, and the disparities based on minority group membership still occur. A true culture-fair IQ test has yet to be developed (Ostrosky-Solis & Oberg, 2006).

RELIABILITY AND VALIDITY. Every time we measure our weight on our bathroom scale, we assume that any changes we find are due to fluctuations in our actual weight and not produced by inaccuracies in the scale. In the same fashion, testing experts who produce IQ tests construct them to have reliability. **Reliability** exists when a test measures consistently what it is trying to measure. If we assume that IQ is a stable characteristic, then a test that has reliability will produce the same score each time it is administered to a particular person. If a test produced a score of 105 at one time, but the next time it produced a score of 130, then it is not reliable. However, if each time the test is administered to the same individual it yielded a score of 105, then the test is reliable.

Even if a test is reliable, it is not necessarily valid. A test has **validity** when it actually measures what it is supposed to measure. For instance, just as a valid bathroom scale should measure a person's weight correctly and unambiguously, a valid IQ test should measure an individual's underlying intelligence correctly and unambiguously.

Tests can be reliable without being valid. For example, we could devise a completely reliable test for intelligence if we made the assumption that skull circumference was related to intelligence. Because measuring skull size precisely is fairly easy, we would then have a very reliable measure. But would such a test of intelligence be valid? Hardly, because it seems far-fetched that skull size would have much to do with anyone's intelligence. Well, not far-fetched to everyone: There have been serious efforts in the past to match skull configuration to psychological attributes such as intelligence, although such attempts have, not surprisingly, proved unsuccessful (Deary et al., 2007).

To assess intelligence accurately, IQ tests must be both reliable *and* valid. Although there is wide agreement that well-established IQ tests meet the formal requirements of reliability, their validity, as we will see, is far more controversial.

THE MEANING OF IQ SCORES. What do IQ scores mean? For most children, they are reasonable predictors of school performance. That's not surprising, given that intelligence tests were developed to identify students who were having difficulties (Sternberg & Grigorenko, 2002).

But the story differs for performance outside of school. Although people with higher scores tend to finish more years of schooling, once this is statistically controlled for, IQ scores do not closely relate to income and later success in life. Two people with different scores may both earn bachelor's degrees at the same college, but the person with a lower IQ might have a higher income and a more successful career. These difficulties with traditional IQ scores have led researchers to consider alternative approaches (Zagorsky, 2007; Naglieri, 2015).

But even within the academic sphere, IQ scores aren't always accurate predictors of school performance. For instance, 2.6 million school-age children in the United States are officially labeled as having learning disorders. **Specific learning disorders** are characterized by difficulties in the acquisition and use of listening, speaking, reading, writing, reasoning, or mathematical abilities. A somewhat ill-defined, grab-bag category, specific learning disorders are diagnosed when there is a discrepancy between children's actual academic performance and their apparent potential to learn (Kozey & Siegel, 2008; Schwab, 2014).

Several types of specific learning disorders have been identified. The most common is *attention-deficit/hyperactivity disorder (ADHD)*. Children with ADHD are inattentive and impulsive, with a low tolerance for frustration and generally a great deal of inappropriate activity. Yet their IQ scores are either normal or above. Other children with specific learning disorders suffer from *dyslexia*, a reading disability that can result in the misperception of letters during reading and writing, unusual difficulty in sounding out letters, confusion between left and right, and difficulties in spelling. For these children, taking a traditional IQ test is a challenging task in itself, regardless of their underlying intelligence, and artificially low IQ scores can result. In these ways, normal IQ scores can fail to detect abnormal learning (Byrne, Shankweiler, & Hine, 2008; Nicolson & Fawcett, 2008; Rohrer-Baumgartner et al., 2014).

In short, despite the frequent measurement and use of traditional IQ scores, their usefulness is not always apparent. Because of these difficulties with IQ scores, researchers have turned to alternative approaches to intelligence (Pascual-Leon & Johnson, 2005).

What IQ Tests Don't Tell: Alternative Conceptions of Intelligence

LO 8.4   Analyze alternative definitions of intelligence.

The intelligence tests schools use most today regard intelligence as a single factor, a unitary mental ability. This attribute is commonly called *g* (Spearman, 1927; Lubinski, 2004). Assumed to underlie performance on every aspect of intelligence, the *g* factor is what IQ tests presumably measure.

However, many theorists disagree that intelligence is unidimensional. Some developmentalists suggest that two kinds of intelligence exist: fluid and crystallized (Cattell, 2004). **Fluid intelligence** reflects information processing capabilities, reasoning, and memory; for example, a student asked to group a series of letters according to some criterion or to remember a set of numbers would be using fluid intelligence (Ziegler et al., 2012; Geary, 2015; Kenett et al., 2016).

In contrast, **crystallized intelligence** is the cumulative information, skills, and strategies people have learned and can apply in solving problems. A student would likely use crystallized intelligence to solve a puzzle or find the solution to a mystery (Hill et al., 2013; Thorsen, Gustafsson, & Cliffordson, 2014; Hülür et al., 2017).

Other theorists divide intelligence into even more parts. Psychologist Howard Gardner suggests that we have at least eight distinct intelligences, each of them relatively independent of the others (see Figure 8-4). Gardner suggests that, for example, some people may be particularly skilled in linguistic intelligence, while others may be particularly skilled in musical intelligence. Others, in contrast, may show the opposite pattern (Chen & Gardner, 2005; Gardner & Moran, 2006; Roberts & Lipnevich, 2012; also see the *Neuroscience and Development* box).

fluid intelligence
intelligence that reflects information processing capabilities, reasoning, and memory.

crystallized intelligence
the store of information, skills, and strategies that people have acquired through education and prior experiences and through their previous use of fluid intelligence.

From *an educator's* perspective

Does Howard Gardner's theory of multiple intelligences suggest that classroom instruction should be modified from an emphasis on the traditional 3Rs of reading, writing, and arithmetic?

Russian psychologist Lev Vygotsky took a very different approach to intelligence. He suggested that we should assess intelligence by looking not only at fully developed cognitive processes but at processes in development as well. To do this, he contended that assessment tasks should involve cooperative interaction between the assessed individual and the assessor—a process called *dynamic assessment*. In short, intelligence is reflected both in how children perform on their own and how they perform when helped by adults (Vygotsky, 1927/1976; Lohman, 2005).

Psychologist Robert Sternberg (2003a), taking another approach, suggests that intelligence is best viewed as information processing. In this view, how people store material in memory and later use it to solve intellectual tasks provides the most precise concept of intelligence. Rather than focusing on the subcomponents that make up the *structure* of intelligence, information processing approaches examine the *processes* underlying intelligent behavior.

Figure 8-4 Gardner's Eight Intelligences

Howard Gardner has theorized that there are eight distinct intelligences, each relatively independent of the others. How do you fit into this categorization?

(**Source:** Based on Walters & Gardner, 1986.)

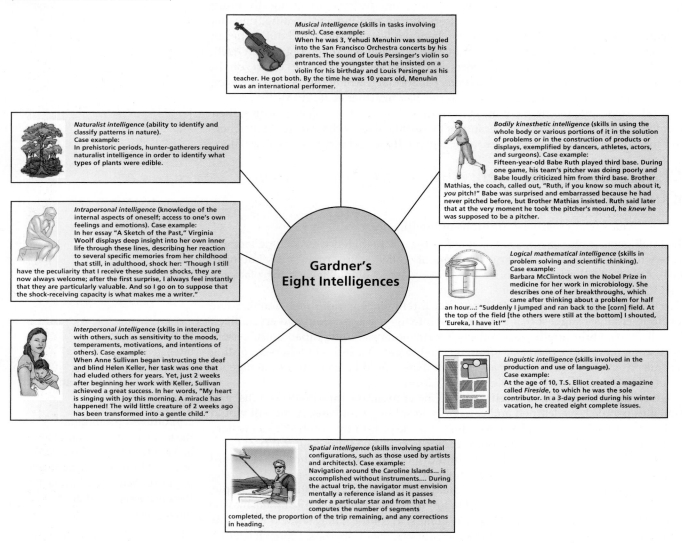

Musical intelligence (skills in tasks involving music). Case example:
When he was 3, Yehudi Menuhin was smuggled into the San Francisco Orchestra concerts by his parents. The sound of Louis Persinger's violin so entranced the youngster that he insisted on a violin for his birthday and Louis Persinger as his teacher. He got both. By the time he was 10 years old, Menuhin was an international performer.

Naturalist intelligence (ability to identify and classify patterns in nature).
Case example:
In prehistoric periods, hunter-gatherers required naturalist intelligence in order to identify what types of plants were edible.

Bodily kinesthetic intelligence (skills in using the whole body or various portions of it in the solution of problems or in the construction of products or displays, exemplified by dancers, athletes, actors, and surgeons). Case example:
Fifteen-year-old Babe Ruth played third base. During one game, his team's pitcher was doing poorly and Babe loudly criticized him from third base. Brother Mathias, the coach, called out, "Ruth, if you know so much about it, *you* pitch!" Babe was surprised and embarrassed because he had never pitched before, but Brother Mathias insisted. Ruth said later that at the very moment he took the pitcher's mound, he *knew* he was supposed to be a pitcher.

Intrapersonal intelligence (knowledge of the internal aspects of oneself; access to one's own feelings and emotions). Case example:
In her essay "A Sketch of the Past," Virginia Woolf displays deep insight into her own inner life through these lines, describing her reaction to several specific memories from her childhood that still, in adulthood, shock her: "Though I still have the peculiarity that I receive these sudden shocks, they are now always welcome; after the first surprise, I always feel instantly that they are particularly valuable. And so I go on to suppose that the shock-receiving capacity is what makes me a writer."

Gardner's Eight Intelligences

Logical mathematical intelligence (skills in problem solving and scientific thinking). Case example:
Barbara McClintock won the Nobel Prize in medicine for her work in microbiology. She describes one of her breakthroughs, which came after thinking about a problem for half an hour...: "Suddenly I jumped and ran back to the [corn] field. At the top of the field [the others were still at the bottom] I shouted, 'Eureka, I have it!'"

Interpersonal intelligence (skills in interacting with others, such as sensitivity to the moods, temperaments, motivations, and intentions of others). Case example:
When Anne Sullivan began instructing the deaf and blind Helen Keller, her task was one that had eluded others for years. Yet, just 2 weeks after beginning her work with Keller, Sullivan achieved a great success. In her words, "My heart is singing with joy this morning. A miracle has happened! The wild little creature of 2 weeks ago has been transformed into a gentle child."

Linguistic intelligence (skills involved in the production and use of language).
Case example:
At the age of 10, T.S. Elliot created a magazine called *Fireside*, to which he was the sole contributor. In a 3-day period during his winter vacation, he created eight complete issues.

Spatial intelligence (skills involving spatial configurations, such as those used by artists and architects). Case example:
Navigation around the Caroline Islands... is accomplished without instruments.... During the actual trip, the navigator must envision mentally a reference island as it passes under a particular star and from that he computes the number of segments completed, the proportion of the trip remaining, and any corrections in heading.

Studies of the nature and speed of problem-solving processes show that people with higher intelligence levels differ from others in the number of problems they solve and the methods they use. People with high IQ scores spend more time on the initial stages of problem solving, retrieving relevant information from memory. In contrast, those who score lower tend to skip ahead and make less informed guesses. The processes used in solving problems may reflect important differences in intelligence (Sternberg, Kaufman, & Grigorenko, 2008).

Sternberg's work on information processing approaches led him to develop the triarchic theory of intelligence, which we will look at next.

STERNBERG'S TRIARCHIC THEORY OF INTELLIGENCE

Your year on the job has been generally favorable. Performance ratings for your department are at least as good as they were before you took over, and perhaps even a little better. You have two assistants. One is quite capable. The other just seems to go through the motions and is of little real help. Even though you are well liked, you believe that there is little that would distinguish you in the eyes of your superiors from the nine other managers at a comparable level in the company. Your goal is rapid promotion to an executive position.

How do you meet your goal? (Based on Wagner & Sternberg, 1985, p. 447)

The way adults answer this question may affect their future success. The question is one of a series that Robert Sternberg designed to assess a particular type of intelligence that may have more of an impact on future success than the IQ measured by traditional tests (Sternberg, 2015).

In his **triarchic theory of intelligence**, Sternberg suggests that intelligence is made up of three major components: componential, experiential, and contextual. The *componential aspect* involves the mental components used to solve problems (e.g., selecting and using formulas, choosing problem-solving strategies, and in general making use of what has been learned in the past). The *experiential component* refers to the relationship between intelligence, prior experience, and the ability to cope with new situations. This is the insightful aspect of intelligence, which allows people to relate what they already know to a new situation and facts never before encountered. Finally, the *contextual component* of intelligence takes account of the demands of everyday, real-world environments. For instance, the contextual component is involved in adapting to on-the-job professional demands (Sternberg, 2005; Ekinci, 2014; Sternberg, 2016).

Traditional IQ tests tend to focus on the componential aspect. Yet increasing evidence suggests that a more useful measure, particularly when comparing and predicting adult success, is the contextual component—the aspect of intelligence that has come to be called practical intelligence.

triarchic theory of intelligence the belief that intelligence consists of three aspects of information processing: the componential element, the experiential element, and the contextual element.

From *an educator's* perspective

Do you think educators can teach people to be more intelligent? Are there components or varieties of intelligence that might be more "teachable" than others? If so, which ones: componential, experiential, contextual, practical, or emotional?

According to Sternberg, traditional IQ scores relate quite well to academic success but not to other types of achievement, such as career success. Although it is clear that success in business requires some level of the IQ sort of intelligence, the rate of career advancement and the ultimate success of business executives is only marginally related to IQ scores (Grigorenko et al., 2009; Ekinci, 2014; Joseph et al., 2015).

Sternberg contends that success in a career necessitates practical intelligence. While academic success is based on knowledge obtained largely from reading and listening, **practical intelligence** is learned primarily by observing others and modeling their behavior. People with practical intelligence have good "social radar." They understand and handle even new situations effectively, reading people and circumstances insightfully based on their previous experiences.

There is another related type of intelligence. **Emotional intelligence** is the set of skills that underlies the accurate assessment, evaluation, expression, and regulation of emotions. Emotional intelligence is what enables people to get along well with others, to understand what they are feeling and experiencing, and to respond appropriately to their needs. Emotional intelligence is of obvious value to career and personal success as a young adult (Nelis et al., 2009; Kross & Grossmann, 2012; Szczygieł & Mikolajczak, 2017).

practical intelligence according to Sternberg, intelligence that is learned primarily by observing others and modeling their behavior.

emotional intelligence the set of skills that underlies the accurate assessment, evaluation, expression, and regulation of emotions.

CREATIVITY. Although intelligence measures provide us with an important metric, they do not provide information about a related but significant trait, creativity. *Creativity* is the combination of ideas in novel ways.

Consider, for example, the case of composer Wolfgang Amadeus Mozart, widely acknowledged as one of the most creative and prolific composers of all time. The hundreds of musical compositions of Mozart, who died at age 35, were largely written during early adulthood. This pattern—major works produced during early adulthood—is true of many other creative individuals. Many mathematicians and physicists produce their major works during early adulthood. Overall, creative productivity seems to peak in the late 30s and early 40s, and then slowly decline. But there are many exceptions, and the most creative people maintain their creativity throughout their life span (Simonton, 2017; see Figure 8-6).

Neuroscience and Development

The Source of the Eureka Moment

The ancient Greek scientist Archimedes is said to have exclaimed "eureka!" ("I have found it!") when he solved the problem of estimating the volume of irregular objects after noticing that the level of water in his bath rose when he got in it. All of us have had "eureka" moments of our own when we suddenly gain new insight and are able to solve a problem over which we've been struggling. But how does the brain work to create such an insight?

To answer this, researchers conducted a study in which college students were asked to solve extremely difficult problems from various scientific fields. The next day, participants tackled the problems again, along with information that was designed either to provide insight into the problem, or in other cases, irrelevant information, while MRI images were taken of their brains. The researchers compared the brain activity of participants who solved the problem, experiencing a eureka moment, to those who did not solve it (Dandan et al., 2013).

Two areas of the brain showed greater activity during the students' eureka moments: the left dorsolateral prefrontal gyrus and the left angular gyrus (see Figure 8-5). The greater activity in the left dorsolateral prefrontal gyrus is consistent with what we know about the importance of the prefrontal cortex in memory retrieval and decision-making. The left angular gyrus is often linked to language comprehension and word recognition.

Research such as this can help us understand basic neurological processes. In addition, it also may lead to future therapies for people suffering from brain injury and dementia.

■ Think of a time when you were suddenly struck with a solution to a problem you had been stuck on. What new information or insight led to this solution? What areas of the brain do you think were likely involved in your eureka moment?

Figure 8-5 Brain activation while experiencing a eureka moment

In these different views of the brain, areas in orange represent increased activation in the group experiencing a eureka moment compared to the group that did not experience it.
(**Source:** Dandan et al., 2013.)

Figure 8-6 Creativity and Age

The period of maximum creativity differs depending on the particular field. The percentages refer to the percentage of total lifetime major works produced during the particular age period. Why do poets peak earlier than novelists?

(**Source:** Based on Dennis, 1966.)

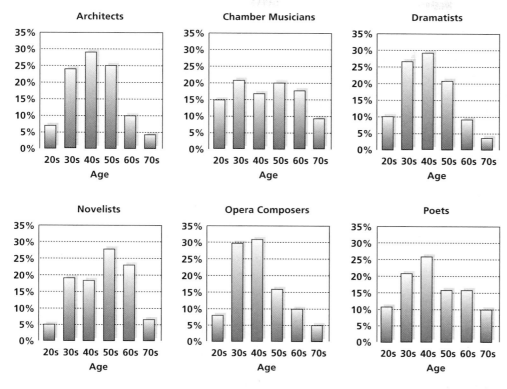

One reason for the higher creativity during early adulthood may be that after this period, creativity can be stifled by the fact that the more people know about a subject, the less likely they are to be creative. Early adulthood may be the peak of creativity because many problems encountered professionally are novel. As people get older, however, and become more familiar with the problems, their creativity may be stymied. In addition, as we age we become less flexible in our thinking, and we are less likely to adopt unfamiliar hypotheses and assumptions (Gopnik et al., 2017).

However, many people do not reach their pinnacle of creativity until much later in life. For instance, Buckminster Fuller did not devise the geodesic dome until he was in his 50s. Frank Lloyd Wright designed the Guggenheim Museum in New York at age 70. Charles Darwin and Jean Piaget were still writing influential works well into their 70s, and Pablo Picasso was painting in his 90s. Furthermore, overall productivity, as opposed to the period of a person's most important output, remains fairly steady throughout adulthood, particularly in the humanities (Simonton, 1989; Feist & Barron, 2003).

Overall, the study of creativity reveals few consistent developmental patterns. One reason is the difficulty of determining just what constitutes creativity, which is defined as combining responses or ideas in novel ways. Because definitions of what is "novel" may vary from one person to the next, it is hard to identify a particular behavior unambiguously as creative (Kaufman & Sternberg, 2006).

This hasn't stopped psychologists from trying. One suggested component of creativity is a person's willingness to take risks that may yield high payoffs. Creative people are like successful stock market investors who follow the "buy low, sell high" rule. Creative people develop and endorse ideas that are unfashionable or regarded as wrong ("buying low"), assuming that eventually others will see their value and embrace them ("selling high"). According to this theory, creative adults take a fresh look at ideas that were initially discarded, particularly if the problem is a familiar one. They are flexible enough to move away from tried-and-true ways of doing things and to consider new approaches (Sternberg, Kaufman, & Peretz, 2002; Sawyer, 2012).

Module 8.1 Review

LO 8.1   Describe traditional methods for measuring intelligence.

Pinning down the meaning of intelligence and measuring it accurately have proven to be challenging tasks that have occupied psychologists for many years. The measurement of intelligence began in the 20th century with the work of Alfred Binet, who took a trial-and-error approach to the question. His work is reflected in the most widely used IQ tests of today. To Binet we owe three legacies: his pragmatic, non-theoretical approach to intelligence testing; his linkage of intelligence to school success; and his derivation of a mathematical means of classifying children as more or less intelligent according to IQ scores.

LO 8.2   Examine current methods of intelligence testing.

Since the time of Binet, tests of intelligence have become increasingly accurate measures of IQ. One of the most widely used tests—the Stanford-Binet Intelligence Scale, Fifth Edition—began as an American revision of Binet's original test.

LO 8.3   Explore key issues surrounding intelligence testing.

Measurements must have both reliability (defined as consistency across persons and over time) and validity (defined as measuring what they claim to measure). Specific learning disorders are defined as difficulties in the acquisition and use of listening, speaking, reading, writing, reasoning, or mathematical abilities.

LO 8.4   Analyze alternative definitions of intelligence.

While they are reasonably predictive of school success, IQ scores fall short in other realms. As a result, a number of alternative conceptions of intelligence have emerged that differentiate different kinds of intelligence. One of the most successful alternative conceptions is Robert Sternberg's triarchic theory of intelligence, which breaks intelligence down into componential, experiential, and contextual components.

Journal Writing Prompt

Applying Lifespan Development: If a perfectly valid and reliable measure of intelligence were developed, how would it best be used? What uses would be inappropriate?

MODULE 8.2

CONTROVERSIES INVOLVING INTELLIGENCE

Maddy Rodriguez is a bundle of curiosity and energy. At 6 months of age, she cries heartily if she can't reach a toy, and when she sees a reflection of herself in a mirror, she gurgles and seems, in general, to find the situation quite amusing.

* * *

Jared Lynch, at 6 months, is a good deal more inhibited than Maddy. He doesn't seem to care much when a ball rolls out of his reach, losing interest in it rapidly. And, unlike Maddy, when he sees himself in a mirror, he pretty much ignores the reflection.

As anyone who has spent any time at all observing more than one baby can tell you, not all infants are alike. Some are full of energy and vitality, apparently displaying a natural-born curiosity, while others seem, by comparison, somewhat less interested in the world around them. Does this mean that such infants differ in intelligence? This turns out to be a highly controversial subject with potentially devastating effects on children judged less intelligent. Let's see what research tells us about this and several other issues that illustrate the difficulty in classifying children on the basis of intelligence.

What Is Infant Intelligence?

LO 8.5   Describe recent approaches to measuring intelligence in infants.

Given the difficulties we discussed earlier in defining intelligence in older children and adults, whose linguistic abilities allow a wide range of measurement techniques, the problem of defining intelligence in infants is even greater. Is infant intelligence the speed with which infants learn a new task through classical or operant conditioning?

Table 8-1 Approaches Used to Detect Differences in Intelligence During Infancy

Developmental quotient	Formulated by Arnold Gesell, the developmental quotient is an overall developmental score that relates to performance in four domains: motor skills (balance and sitting), language use, adaptive behavior (alertness and exploration), and personal–social behavior.
Bayley Scales of Infant Development	Developed by Nancy Bayley, the Bayley Scales of Infant Development evaluate an infant's development from 2 to 42 months. The Bayley Scales focus on two areas: mental (senses, perception, memory, learning, problem solving, and language) and motor abilities (fine and gross motor skills).
Visual-recognition memory measurement	Measures of visual-recognition memory (the memory of and recognition of a stimulus that has been previously seen) also relate to intelligence. The more quickly an infant can retrieve a representation of a stimulus from memory, the more efficient, presumably, is that infant's information processing.

The rapidity of habituation to stimuli? The age at which an infant learns to crawl or walk? Furthermore, even if we are able to identify particular behaviors that seem validly to differentiate one infant from another in terms of intelligence during infancy, we need to address a further, and probably more important, issue: How well do measures of infant intelligence relate to eventual adult intelligence?

Such questions are not simple, and no simple answers have been found. However, developmental specialists have devised several approaches (summarized in Table 8-1) to illuminate the nature of individual differences in intelligence during infancy.

DEVELOPMENTAL SCALES. Developmental psychologist Arnold Gesell formulated the earliest measure of infant development, which was designed to differentiate normally developing babies from those with atypical development (Gesell, 1946). Gesell based his scale on examinations of hundreds of babies. He compared their performance at different ages to learn what behaviors were most common at particular ages. If an infant varied significantly from the norms of a given age, he or she was considered to be developmentally either delayed or advanced.

Gesell's primary motivation in developing his norms was to screen out abnormally developing infants for purposes of adoption. Following the lead of researchers who sought to quantify intelligence through a specific score (an intelligence quotient, or IQ, score), Gesell developed a developmental quotient, or DQ, score. The **developmental quotient** is an overall developmental score that relates to performance in four domains: motor skills (e.g., balance and sitting), language use, adaptive behavior (such as alertness and exploration), and personal–social (e.g., feeding and dressing). Designed for infants age 2 to 30 months, the DQ provides a summary of an infant's overall competence in comparison to others of a similar age.

Later researchers were motivated by different goals. For instance, Nancy Bayley developed one of the most widely used measures for infants. Like Gesell's DQ, the **Bayley Scales of Infant Development** evaluate an infant's development from 2 to 30 months. The Bayley Scales concentrate on two areas: mental and motor abilities. The mental scale focuses on the senses, perception, memory, learning, problem solving, and language, while the motor scale evaluates fine and gross motor skills (see Table 8-2). Like Gesell's approach, Bayley's yields a developmental quotient (DQ). A child who scores at an average level—meaning average performance for other children at the same age—receives a score of 100 (Bos, 2013; Greene et al., 2013).

developmental quotient
an overall developmental score that relates to performance in four domains: motor skills, language use, adaptive behavior, and personal and social skills.

Bayley Scales of Infant Development
a measure that evaluates an infant's development from 2 to 42 months.

From *a nurse's* perspective

In what ways is the use of such developmental scales as Gesell's or Bayley's helpful? In what ways is it dangerous? How would you maximize the helpfulness and minimize the danger if you were advising a parent?

The virtue of approaches such as those taken by Gesell and Bayley is that they provide a good snapshot of an infant's current developmental level. Using these scales, we can tell in an objective manner whether a particular infant falls behind or is ahead of his or her same-age peers. The scales are particularly useful in identifying infants who are substantially behind their peers and who therefore need immediate special attention (Blaga et al., 2009; Sonne, 2012).

Table 8-2 Sample Items from the Bayley Scales of Infant Development

Age	2 months	6 months	12 months	17–19 months	23–25 months	38–42 months
Mental Scale	Turns head to locate origin of sound; Visibly responds to disappearance of face	Picks up cup by handle; Notices illustrations in a book	Constructs tower of 2 cubes; Can turn pages in a book	Mimics crayon stroke; Labels objects in photo	Pairs up pictures; Repeats a 2-word sentence	Can identify 4 colors; Past tense evident in speech; Distinguishes gender
Motor Scale	Can hold head steady and erect for 15 seconds; Sits with assistance	Sits up without aid for 30 seconds; Grasps foot with hands	Walks when holding onto someone's hand or furniture; Holds pencil in fist	Stands on right foot without help; Remains upright climbing stairs with assistance	Strings 3 beads; Jumps length of 4 inches	Can reproduce drawing of a circle; Hops two times on one foot; Descends stairs, alternating feet

(**Source:** Based on Bayley, 1993.)

However, except in extreme cases, such scales are not very good at all in predicting a child's future course of intellectual development. An individual whose development at the age of 1 year is relatively slow, as identified by these measures, does not necessarily display slow development at age 5, or 12, or 25. The association between most measures of behavior during infancy and adult intelligence is in fact minimal (Murray et al., 2007; Burakevych et al., 2017).

Because of the difficulties inherent in using these global measures to obtain measures of infant intelligence that are related to later intelligence, investigators have turned more recently to other techniques that may help assess intelligence in a meaningful way. Some have proven to be quite useful.

INFORMATION PROCESSING APPROACHES TO INFANT INTELLIGENCE. When we speak of intelligence in everyday parlance, we often differentiate between "quick" and "slow" individuals. According to research on the speed of infants' information processing, such terms hold some truth. Contemporary approaches to infant intelligence suggest that the speed with which infants process information may correlate most strongly with later intelligence, as measured by IQ tests administered during adulthood (Rose et al., 2012).

For instance, infants who process information efficiently ought to be able to learn about stimuli more quickly. Consequently, we would expect them to turn their attention away from a given stimulus more rapidly than those who are less efficient at information processing. This seems to be the case: Measures of how quickly infants lose interest in stimuli that they have previously seen, as well as their responsiveness to new stimuli, correlate moderately well with later measures of intelligence (Kavšek, 2004; Trainor, 2012; Fagan & Ployhart, 2015).

Similarly, measures of *visual-recognition memory*, the memory of and recognition of a stimulus that has been previously seen, as well as attention and representational competence, also relate to later IQ. The more quickly an infant can retrieve a representation of a stimulus from memory, the more efficient, presumably, is that infant's information processing. In general, then, infants who are more efficient information processors during the 6 months following birth tend to have higher intelligence scores between 2 and 12 years of age, as well as higher scores on other measures of cognitive competence (Robinson & Pascalis, 2005; Rose et al., 2012; Trainor, 2012).

Other research suggests that abilities related to the *multimodal approach to perception* may offer clues about later intelligence. For instance, the information processing skill of cross-modal transference is associated with intelligence. **Cross-modal transference** is the ability to identify a stimulus that has previously been experienced through only one sense by using another sense. For instance, a baby who is able to recognize by sight a screwdriver that she has previously touched, but not seen, is displaying cross-modal transference. Research has found that the degree of cross-modal transference displayed by an infant at age 1—which requires a high level of abstract thinking—is associated with intelligence scores several years later (Rose, Feldman, & Jankowski, 2015).

cross-modal transference
the ability to identify, using another sense, a stimulus that has previously been experienced only through one sense.

Although information processing efficiency and cross-modal transference abilities during infancy relate moderately well to later IQ scores, we need to keep in mind two qualifications. First, even though there is an association between early information processing capabilities and later measures of IQ, the correlation is only moderate in strength. Other factors, such as the degree of environmental stimulation, also play a crucial role in helping to determine adult intelligence. Consequently, we should not assume that intelligence is somehow permanently fixed in infancy.

Second, and perhaps even more important, intelligence measured by traditional IQ tests relates to a particular type of intelligence, one that emphasizes abilities that lead to academic, and certainly not artistic or professional, success. Consequently, predicting that a child may do well on IQ tests later in life is not the same as predicting that the child will be successful later in life.

Still, the findings that an association exists between efficiency of information processing and later IQ scores have changed how we view the consistency of cognitive development across the life span. Whereas the earlier reliance on scales such as the Bayley led to the misconception that little continuity existed, the more recent information processing approaches suggest that cognitive development unfolds in a more orderly, continuous manner from infancy to the later stages of life.

Achievement and Aptitude Tests: How Do They Differ from Intelligence Tests?

LO 8.6 **Define achievement and aptitude tests and compare their uses.**

IQ tests are not the only tests that children encounter during the course of their schooling. They also take achievement tests and aptitude tests, which are meant to assess characteristics that are somewhat different, though related, to IQ. An **achievement test** is a test intended to determine an individual's level of knowledge in a given subject area. Unlike intelligence tests, which are designed to measure overall, general ability, achievement tests are more targeted to specific areas. For instance, some achievement tests focus on mathematical progress, whereas others look at gains in knowledge of history.

Aptitude tests are designed to predict ability in a particular subject area or line of work. The emphasis in an aptitude test is on future performance; rather than looking at what children already know, an aptitude test is meant to identify how accomplished they are likely to be in the future. For instance, an aptitude test might be used to identify children who are particularly likely to excel in writing, and based on that information place them in special programs.

Almost all of us had to take one of the two best-known aptitude tests, the Scholastic Assessment Test (SAT) or the American College Test (ACT), before entering college. These tests are supposed to predict college-level performance, although the extent to which they predict future success as opposed to past achievement is controversial. The Educational Testing Service, which constructs the SAT, acknowledged the problem several years ago by changing the name of the test from Scholastic *Aptitude* Test to the current Scholastic *Assessment* Test.

Despite the change in name, the controversy continues over whether the SAT is really an aptitude test, predicting future college performance, or, in reality, an achievement test, measuring past performance. In short, the distinction between achievement, aptitude, and intelligence tests is often clearer in theory than in practice.

achievement test
a test designed to determine a person's level of knowledge in a given subject area.

aptitude test
a test designed to predict a person's ability in a particular area or line of work.

Group Differences in IQ

LO 8.7 **Analyze the sources of score differences achieved by different groups on IQ and other tests.**

A "jontry" is an example of a _____.

a. rulpow

b. flink

c. spudge

d. bakwoe

If you found an item composed of nonsense words such as this on an intelligence test, you would likely complain. What sort of intelligence test uses items that incorporate meaningless terms?

Yet for some people, the items used on traditional intelligence tests might appear nonsensical. As a hypothetical example, suppose rural children were asked details about subways, while urban students were asked about the mating practices of sheep. In both cases, we would expect the test-takers' prior experiences to substantially affect their ability to answer the questions. On an IQ test, such questions could rightly be seen as a measure of prior experience rather than of intelligence.

Although traditional IQ tests are not so obviously dependent on test-takers' prior experiences, cultural background and experience can affect test scores. In fact, many educators feel that traditional measures of intelligence subtly favor white, upper- and middle-class students over other cultural groups (Ortiz & Dynda, 2005).

EXPLAINING RACIAL DIFFERENCES IN IQ. How cultural background and experience affect IQ test scores has led to much debate among researchers, fueled by the finding that certain racial groups' IQ scores are consistently lower, on average, than those of other groups. For example, the mean score of African Americans tends to be about 15 points below the mean score of whites—although the measured difference varies a great deal depending on the IQ test employed (Maller, 2003; Saklofske et al., 2015; Sauce & Matzel, 2018).

The question that emerges from such differences is whether they reflect differences in intelligence or biases in intelligence tests. For example, if whites outperform African Americans on an IQ test because they are more familiar with the language of the test items, the test can hardly be adjudged a fair measure of African Americans' intelligence. Similarly, a test that solely used African American Vernacular English would not be an impartial measure of intelligence for whites.

How to interpret differences between the IQ test scores of different cultural groups is a major controversy in child development: To what degree is intelligence determined by heredity, and to what degree by environment? The social implications make this issue important. If intelligence is mostly hereditary and therefore largely fixed at birth, attempts to alter cognitive abilities, such as schooling, will have limited success. If intelligence is largely environmentally determined, modifying social and educational conditions is a more promising strategy to increase cognitive functioning (Weiss, 2003; Nisbett et al., 2012).

***THE BELL CURVE* CONTROVERSY.** Although the relative contributions of heredity and environment to intelligence have been investigated for decades, the smoldering debate became a raging fire in the 1990s with the publication of a book by Richard J. Herrnstein, Charles Murray (1994), titled *The Bell Curve*. Herrnstein and Murray argue that the average 15-point IQ difference between whites and African Americans is due primarily to heredity. They also argue that this difference accounts for the higher rates of poverty, lower employment, and higher use of welfare among minority groups.

These conclusions were met with outrage, and many researchers who examined the data used in the book came to quite different conclusions. Most developmentalists and psychologists argued that racial differences in measured IQ can be explained by environmental differences. In fact, mean IQ scores of black and white children are quite similar when a variety of economic and social factors are statistically taken into account simultaneously. For instance, children from similar middle-class backgrounds, whether African American or white, tend to have similar IQ scores (Alderfer, 2003).

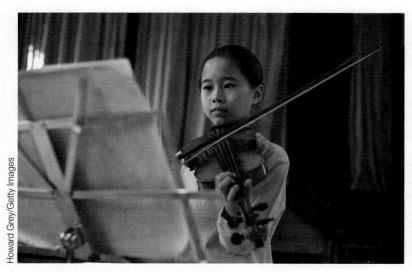

The issue of whether racial differences in IQ exist is highly controversial and ultimately relates to questions of the genetic and environmental determinants of intelligence.

Critics also maintained that there is little evidence that lower IQ causes poverty and other social ills. Some critics suggested, as mentioned earlier, that IQ scores were unrelated to later success in life (e.g., Sternberg, 1997; Reifman, 2000).

Finally, members of cultural and social minority groups may score lower than those in the majority group due to the biases of the tests. Traditional IQ tests may discriminate against minority groups who lack exposure to the environment majority group members have experienced.

Most traditional IQ tests are constructed using white, English-speaking, middle-class populations as their test subjects. Thus, children from different backgrounds may perform poorly on them—not because they are less intelligent, but because the questions are culturally biased in favor of the majority group. A classic study found that in one California school district, Mexican American students were 10 times more likely than whites to be placed in special education classes (Mercer, 1973). More recent findings show that nationally twice as many African American students as white students are classified as mildly intellectually disabled, a difference attributed primarily to cultural bias and poverty (Ebersole & Kapp, 2007). Although certain IQ tests (such as the System of Multicultural Pluralistic Assessment, or SOMPA) are designed to be valid regardless of cultural background, no test can be completely unbiased (Sandoval et al., 1998).

Most experts were not convinced by *The Bell Curve*'s contention that genetic factors largely determine differences in group IQ scores. Still, we cannot put the issue to rest because it is impossible to design a definitive experiment to determine the cause of these differences. (One cannot ethically assign children to different living conditions to find the effects of environment, nor genetically control or alter intelligence levels in unborn children.)

Today, IQ is seen as the product of both nature and nurture interacting in a complex manner. Genes are seen to affect experiences, and experiences are viewed as influencing the expression of genes. Psychologist Eric Turkheimer found evidence that while environmental factors play a larger role in the IQ of poor children, genes are more influential for affluent children (Harden, Turkheimer, & Loehlin, 2007; Turkheimer et al., 2017).

Ultimately, determining the absolute degree to which intelligence is influenced by genetic and environmental factors may be less important than improving children's living conditions and educational experiences. Enriching the quality of children's environments will better permit all children to reach their full potential and to maximize their contributions to society (Posthuma & de Geus, 2006).

Cognitive Functioning in Adulthood

LO 8.8   Describe the effects of aging on intelligence.

> *It began innocently enough. Forty-five-year-old Bina Clingman couldn't remember whether she had mailed the letter that her husband had given her, and she wondered, briefly, whether this was a sign of aging. The next day, the question recurred when she spent 20 minutes looking for a phone number she knew she had written down on a piece of paper— somewhere. By the time she found it, she was surprised and even a little anxious. "Am I losing my memory?" she asked herself, feeling both annoyance and a degree of concern.*

Many people in their 40s feel more absentminded than they did 20 years earlier, and they have some concern about becoming less mentally able as they age. Common wisdom suggests that people lose some mental sharpness in midlife. But how accurate is this notion, and how much of it is a stereotypical view of a much-maligned and much-dreaded age by those who secretly know they will one day soon achieve it—if they're lucky?

The status of intelligence and, more generally, of cognitive functioning as a whole during and beyond middle age remains a controversial topic—nowhere more than in the minds of people who write sitcoms, produce TV commercials, make up jokes, and produce movies. In those environs, people in their middle years are lampooned mercilessly. Among developmentalists, in contrast, the main controversy revolves around how people in middle age adapt to the changes in their cognitive processing and present themselves as the best representatives of their time.

DOES INTELLIGENCE DECLINE IN ADULTHOOD?

For years, experts provided an unwavering response when asked whether intelligence declined in adulthood: Intelligence peaks at age 18, stays fairly steady until the mid-20s, and then gradually declines until the end of life.

Today, developmentalists view questions about changes in intelligence across the life span as more complicated than that—and they have come to different, and more complex, conclusions.

CROSS-SECTIONAL RESEARCH.

The conclusion that intelligence starts to diminish in the mid-20s was based on extensive research. Cross-sectional studies—which test people of different ages at the same point in time—showed that older subjects were less likely to score well than younger subjects on traditional intelligence tests, of the sort we discussed earlier.

But consider the drawbacks of cross-sectional research in this context—in particular, the possibility that it may suffer from cohort effects—influences associated with growing up at a particular historical time that affect persons of a particular age. For instance, suppose that compared to younger subjects, the older people in a cross-sectional study had had a less adequate education or less stimulating jobs, or were less healthy. In that case, the lower IQ scores of the older group could not be attributed solely, or perhaps even partially, to differences in intelligence based on age. Because they do not control for cohort effects, cross-sectional studies may well underestimate intelligence in older subjects.

LONGITUDINAL RESEARCH.

To overcome the cohort problems of cross-sectional studies, developmentalists began to use longitudinal studies in which the same people are studied periodically over a span of time. These studies revealed a different developmental pattern for intelligence: Adults tended to show stable and even increasing intelligence test scores until their mid-30s, and in some cases up to their 50s. Then the scores began to decline (Bayley & Oden, 1955).

But let's consider the drawbacks of longitudinal studies, too. People taking an intelligence test repeatedly may perform better because they become familiar—and comfortable—with the testing situation. Similarly, through repeated exposure to the same test, they may begin to remember some of the test items. Consequently, practice effects may account for the superior performance of people on longitudinal measures of intelligence as opposed to cross-sectional measures.

It is also difficult for researchers using longitudinal studies to keep their samples intact. Participants may move away, decide they no longer want to participate, or become ill and die. Over time, the participants who remain may represent a healthier, more stable, and more psychologically positive group of people than those who are no longer part of the sample. If this is the case, longitudinal studies may overestimate intelligence in older subjects.

CRYSTALLIZED AND FLUID INTELLIGENCE.

Drawing conclusions about age-related changes in intelligence is complicated by the nature of cognitive measures. For instance, many IQ tests include sections based on physical performance, such as arranging a group of blocks. These sections are timed and scored on the basis of how quickly an item is completed. If older people take longer on physical tasks—reaction time does slow with age—then their poorer performance on IQ tests may result from physical rather than cognitive changes (Schroeders, Schipolowski, & Wilhelm, 2015).

To complicate the issue further, many researchers believe there are age-related changes in the two kinds of intelligence we discussed earlier: fluid intelligence and crystallized intelligence. As we noted earlier, fluid intelligence reflects information processing capabilities, reasoning, and memory. To arrange a series of letters according to some rule or to memorize a set of numbers uses fluid intelligence. In contrast, crystallized intelligence is the information, skills, and strategies that people have accumulated through experience and that they can apply to solve problems. Someone who is solving a crossword puzzle or attempting to identify the murderer in a mystery story is using crystallized intelligence, relying on past experience as a resource.

Frank Boston/Fotolia

It is difficult to evaluate cognitive abilities in middle adulthood. While some types of mental abilities may begin to decline, crystallized intelligence holds steady and actually may increase.

Figure 8-7 Changes in Crystallized and Fluid Intelligence

Although crystallized intelligence increases with age, fluid intelligence begins to decline in middle age.
THINKING ABOUT THE DATA: What are the implications for general competence in middle adulthood?
(**Source:** Schaie, 1985.)

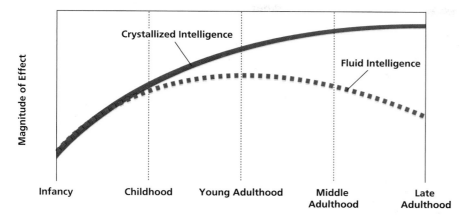

Researchers once believed that fluid intelligence was largely determined by genetic factors, and crystallized intelligence by experiential, environmental factors. They later abandoned this distinction when they found that crystallized intelligence is determined in part by fluid intelligence. For instance, a person's ability to solve a crossword puzzle (which involves crystallized intelligence) relies on that person's proficiency with letters and patterns (a manifestation of fluid intelligence).

When developmentalists examined the two kinds of intelligence separately, they discovered that there are two answers to the question of whether intelligence declines with age: yes and no. Yes, because fluid intelligence does decline with age; no, because crystallized intelligence holds steady and can actually improve (Salthouse, Pink, & Tucker-Drob, 2008; Manard et al., 2015; Wettstein et al., 2017; see Figure 8-7).

RECENT CONCLUSIONS ABOUT ADULT INTELLIGENCE. More recent research attempts to address these drawbacks. If we look at more specific types of intelligence, the true nature of age-related differences and developments begins to emerge.

According to developmental psychologist K. Warner Schaie, who has conducted extensive longitudinal research on adult intellectual development, we should consider many types of ability, such as spatial orientation, numeric ability, verbal ability, and so on, rather than the broad divisions of crystallized and fluid intelligence (Schaie, Willis, & Pennak, 2005; Schaie & Willis, 2011).).

In an ambitious study of intelligence in older people, Schaie used sequential methods, which combine cross-sectional and longitudinal methods by examining several different age groups at a number of points in time.

In Schaie's massive study, carried out in Seattle, Washington, 500 randomly chosen individuals took a battery of tests of cognitive ability. The people belonged to different age groups, starting at age 20 and extending at five-year intervals to age 70. The participants were tested, and continue to be tested, every seven years, and more people are recruited every year. At this point, more than 5,000 participants have been tested (Schaie & Willis, 2011).

The study, along with other research, supports several generalizations (Steinberg, 2018):

- Some abilities gradually decline starting at around age 25, while others stay relatively steady (see Figure 8-8). There is no uniform pattern of age-related intellectual changes. For example, fluid intelligence declines with age, while crystallized intelligence remains steady and in some cases improves.

- On average, some cognitive declines are found in all abilities by age 67, but they are minimal until the 80s. Even at age 81, less than half of the people tested showed consistent declines over the previous seven years.

Figure 8-8 Changes in Intellectual Functioning

Although some intellectual abilities decline across adulthood, others stay relatively steady.

(**Source:** Changes in Intellectual Functioning from Schaie, K. W. (1994.) "The course of adult intellectual development." P. 307, *American Psychologist*, 49, 403–313. Copyright © 1994 by the American Psychological Association. Reproduced by permission.)

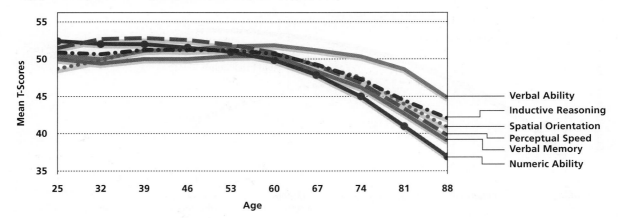

- There are also significant individual differences. Some people begin to show declines in their 30s, while others show no declines until their 70s. In fact, around a third of people in their 70s score higher than the average young adult.

- Environmental and cultural factors play a role. People with no chronic disease, higher socioeconomic status (SES), involvement in an intellectually stimulating environment, a flexible personality style, a bright spouse, good perceptual processing speed, and satisfaction with one's accomplishments in midlife or early old age showed less decline.

One reason these changes occur is that brain functioning begins to change in middle adulthood. Researchers have found that 20 genes that are vital to learning, memory, and mental flexibility begin to function less efficiently as early as age 40.

Furthermore, as people age, the specific areas of their brains used to accomplish particular tasks change. For instance, older adults use both brain hemispheres for tasks that in younger people involve just one hemisphere (Lu et al., 2004; Fling et al., 2011; Phillips, 2011).

Development in Your Life

Bulking Up the Brain

Research shows that continued intellectual stimulation keeps cognitive abilities sharp; the real threat to older people's cognitive functioning lies in a decline in their opportunities and motivation for cognitive challenges as they pass retirement age. Research provides some suggestions.

- A relatively small investment of time and effort in mental workouts can pay big dividends. Older people don't have to run mental marathons (unless, of course, they want to); they can benefit a great deal from ongoing mental exercise.

- Types of training that have proven effective include memory training, reasoning training, and processing speed training.

- Especially when backed up by booster sessions, the effects of such training appear to be remarkably durable.

- Ongoing mental exercise can result in improved confidence in the ability to perform daily tasks demanding cognition, such as housework, meal preparation, finances, and shopping.

- The self-confidence that may result from mental activities is associated with greater independence, less reliance on health services, and longer life.

- Mental exercise that is performed regularly appears to slow cognitive declines. The key is to perform some form of mental workout consistently and to increase the level of difficulty to sustain a sense of challenge.

REFRAMING THE ISSUE: FOCUSING ON COMPETENCE, NOT COGNITIVE ABILITIES. It is during midlife that people come to hold some of the most important and powerful positions in society, despite gradual declines in certain cognitive abilities. How do we explain such continuing, even growing, competence?

From *an educator's* perspective

How do you think the apparent discrepancy between declining IQ scores and continuing cognitive competence in middle adulthood would affect the learning ability of middle-aged adults who return to school?

Psychologist Timothy Salthouse (2006) suggests that this discrepancy between cognition and competence exists for four reasons. First, it is possible that typical measures of cognitive skills tap a different type of cognition than is required for success in certain occupations. Recall the earlier discussion of practical intelligence, in which we found that traditional IQ tests fail to measure cognitive abilities that are related to occupational success. Perhaps we would find no discrepancy between intelligence and cognitive abilities in midlife if we used measures of practical intelligence rather than traditional IQ tests to assess intelligence.

A second factor also relates to the measurement of IQ and occupational success. It is possible that the most successful middle-aged adults are not representative of midlife adults in general. It may be that only a small proportion of people are highly successful, and the rest, who experience only moderate or little success, have changed occupations, retired, or become sick and died. Highly successful people, then, may be an unrepresentative sample.

Third, the degree of cognitive ability required for professional success may simply not be that high. According to this argument, people can succeed professionally and still be on the decline in certain cognitive abilities. In other words, they have brains to spare.

Finally, perhaps older people are successful because they have developed specific kinds of expertise and particular competencies. Whereas IQ tests measure reactions to novel situations, occupational success may be influenced by very specific, well-practiced abilities. Consequently, middle-aged individuals may maintain and even expand the distinctive talents they need for professional accomplishment, despite a decline in overall intellectual skills.

For example, developmental psychologists Paul Baltes and Margaret Baltes have studied a strategy called selective optimization. *Selective optimization* is the process people use in concentrating on particular skill areas to compensate for losses in other areas. Baltes suggests that cognitive development during middle and later adulthood is a mixture of growth and decline. As people begin to lose certain abilities, they advance in other areas by strengthening skills in those areas. In so doing, they avoid showing any practical deterioration. Overall cognitive competence, then, remains stable and may even improve (Deary, 2012; Hahn & Lachman, 2015; Palmore, 2017).

Module 8.2 Review

LO 8.5 Describe recent approaches to measuring intelligence in infants.

Defining infant intelligence is especially challenging, and measuring it even more so. Approaches include developmental scales, which provide good snapshots of an infant's current level of development but are unable to predict future intellectual development. Information processing approaches—which have a quantitative rather than a qualitative orientation—differentiate more and less intelligent infants by observing the speed at which they process information and learn about stimuli.

Visual-recognition memory and cross-modal transference are also regarded as factors in infant intelligence.

LO 8.6 Define achievement and aptitude tests and compare their uses.

An achievement test is a test intended to determine an individual's level of knowledge in a given subject area. Aptitude tests are designed to predict ability in a particular subject area or line of work. The emphasis in an aptitude test is on future performance.

LO 8.7 **Analyze the sources of score differences achieved by different groups on IQ and other tests.**

A major controversy in the study of intelligence is the role of cultural background in determining IQ. If intelligence levels are determined by nature, academic interventions are of little use. This is the essence of the controversy over the book *The Bell Curve*. However, most developmentalists regard cultural background as unimportant when compared with economic and social background.

LO 8.8 **Describe the effects of aging on intelligence.**

The nature and extent of intellectual declines in adulthood and old age are another topic of heated discussion. Some areas of intellectual functioning show marked declines in adulthood, while others are less subject to decline. Cross-sectional

and longitudinal studies are used to address the question of intellectual decline, but both have significant drawbacks. A complicating factor is the fact that intelligence consists of crystallized and fluid components, which show different rates of decline. The most comprehensive study of the issue ever undertaken—a longitudinal study by developmental psychologist K. Warner Schaie—concludes that certain abilities begin to decline from age 25, while numeric ability increases until the mid-40s and verbal ability rises until about 40 and then holds steady.

Journal Writing Prompt

Applying Lifespan Development: Why is it important to measure intelligence in infants? What can we find out? What can we do with what we find out?

MODULE 8.3

INTELLECTUAL DISABILITIES AND THE INTELLECTUALLY GIFTED

Although Connie kept pace with her peers in kindergarten, by first grade, she was academically the slowest in almost every subject. She tried hard, but it took her longer than the others to absorb new material, and she regularly required special attention to keep up with the class.

In some areas, though, she excelled: When asked to draw or produce something with her hands, her performance exceeded her classmates'. She produced beautiful work that was much admired. The other students in the class felt that there was something different about Connie, but they couldn't identify the source of the difference and spent little time pondering the issue.

Connie's parents and teacher knew what made her special. Extensive testing in kindergarten had shown that Connie's intelligence was well below normal, and she was officially classified as a special needs student.

The Least Restrictive Environment

LO 8.9 **Explain the meaning of the term *least restrictive environment*.**

If Connie had been attending school before 1975, she would most likely have been placed in a special needs classroom as soon as her low IQ was identified. Such classes, consisting of students with a range of afflictions, including emotional difficulties, severe reading problems, and physical disabilities such as multiple sclerosis, as well those with lower IQs, were usually kept separate from the regular educational process.

All that changed in 1975 when Congress passed Public Law 94-142, the Education for All Handicapped Children Act. The intent of the law—an intent largely realized—was to ensure that special needs children were educated in the **least restrictive environment**, that is, the setting most similar to that of children without special needs (Yell & Drasgow, 2010; Yell, 2015).

In practice, the law has integrated children with special needs into regular classrooms and activities to the greatest extent possible, as long as doing so is educationally beneficial. Children are to be removed from the regular classroom only for those subjects specifically affected by their exceptionality; for all other subjects, they are to

least restrictive environment the setting most similar to that of children without special needs.

be taught in regular classrooms. Of course, some children with severe handicaps still need a mostly or entirely separate education. But the law integrates exceptional children and typical children to the fullest extent possible.

This approach to special education, designed to minimize the segregation of exceptional students, is called **mainstreaming**. In mainstreaming, exceptional children are integrated as much as possible into the regular education system and provided with a broad range of alternatives (Belkin, 2004; Crosland & Dunlap, 2012; Sailor, 2015).

Some professionals promote an alternative model known as **full inclusion**. Full inclusion is the integration of all students, even the most severely disabled, into regular classes, thereby eliminating separate special education programs. Full inclusion is controversial, and it remains to be seen how widespread it will become (Mangiatordi, 2012; Bešić et al., 2017).

Regardless of whether they are educated using mainstreaming or full inclusion, children whose intelligence is significantly beyond the typical range represent a challenge for educators. We will consider both those who are below and those who are above the norms.

mainstreaming

an educational approach in which exceptional children are integrated as much as possible into the traditional educational system and are provided with a broad range of educational alternatives.

full inclusion

the integration of all students, even those with the most severe disabilities, into regular classes and all other aspects of school and community life.

From *an educator's* perspective

What are some of the challenges of teaching a class that has been mainstreamed? What are some of the advantages?

Below the Norm: Intellectual Disability

LO 8.10 **Analyze the characteristics and effects of intellectual disability.**

Approximately 1 to 3 percent of the school-age population is considered to be intellectually disabled. Estimates vary so widely because the most commonly accepted definition of intellectual disability, which was previously referred to professionally as *mental retardation*, a term that is still used frequently, is one that leaves a great deal of room for interpretation. According to the American Association on Intellectual and Developmental Disabilities, **intellectual disability** is a disability characterized by significant limitations both in intellectual functioning and in adaptive behavior, which covers many everyday social and practical skills. (American Association on Intellectual and Developmental Disabilities, 2012).

Most cases of intellectual disability are classified as *familial intellectual disability*, in which no cause is apparent, but there is a history of intellectual disability in the family. In other cases, there is a clear biological cause. The most common biological causes are *fetal alcohol syndrome*, which is produced by a mother's use of alcohol while pregnant, and *Down syndrome*, which results from the presence of an extra chromosome. Birth complications, such as a temporary lack of oxygen, may also produce intellectual disabilities (Plomin, 2005; West & Blake, 2005; Manning & Hoyme, 2007).

Although cognitive limitations can be measured using standard IQ tests, it is more difficult to gauge limitations in other areas. This leads to imprecision in the ways the label "intellectual disability" is applied. It also means significant variation exists in the abilities of people categorized as experiencing intellectual disability, ranging from those who can be taught to work and function with little special attention to those who are virtually untrainable and who never develop speech or such basic motor skills as crawling or walking.

intellectual disability

a disability characterized by significant limitations both in intellectual functioning and in adaptive behavior, which covers many everyday social and practical skills.

This boy with intellectual disability is mainstreamed into this class.

From Research to Practice

The Tragic Impact of Child Neglect on Intelligence

In the mid-1960s, ill-advised government policies led to the abandonment of hundreds of thousands of children in Romania whose parents could not afford to feed them. Many of these children ended up in orphanages that were ill-equipped to provide even minimal care for the children.

To understand the consequences for the children of being placed in these substandard orphanages, a team of researchers investigated whether foster care, which was relatively nonexistent in Romania, improved outcomes for children compared to typical institutional care in orphanages (Zeanah, Fox, & Nelson, 2012).

Participants in the study were primarily very young children who had been abandoned by their parents, usually at birth, and were being raised in Romanian orphanages that were neglectful by most standards. Children received little attention and spent most of their days in cribs, largely ignored by overburdened caretakers. To study the effects of such neglect, researchers randomly assigned a group of these children, 21 months old on average, to two groups: half remained in the institution, while the other half were placed in foster homes (Nelson, et al., 2007).

Researchers tested the children's developmental quotient (DQ) using the Bayley Scales of Infant Development at 42 months, and then administered a Wechsler IQ test at 54 months. Results of the study indicated that the children in the foster care group had significantly higher DQ and IQ scores compared to the children who remained institutionalized. The researchers also found that the earlier children were removed from the orphanages and placed in foster care, the greater their cognitive gains.

Two important conclusions can be drawn from the results of this study. First, it is clear that high-quality foster care is much better for children and their cognitive development then orphanages in which children suffer from neglect. This is important, given that approximately 2.7 million children worldwide live in institutions, many of which provide substandard care. The second important conclusion is that the detrimental effects of neglect appear to be more difficult to overcome the longer the child is neglected. Thus, early intervention is paramount (Petrowski, Cappa, & Gross, 2017).

Shared Writing Prompt

What are the social policy implications from this study for children in the United States and around the world?

---

mild intellectual disability intellectual disability in which IQ scores fall in the range of 50 or 55 to 70.

moderate intellectual disability intellectual disability in which IQ scores range from around 35 or 40 to 50 or 55.

severe intellectual disability intellectual disability in which IQ scores range from around 20 or 25 to 35 or 40.

profound intellectual disability intellectual disability in which IQ scores fall below 20 or 25.

Some 90 percent of the intellectually disabled have relatively low deficit levels. Classified with **mild intellectual disability**, they score in the range of 50 or 55 to 70 on IQ tests. Their disability may not be identified before they reach school, although their early development is often slower than average. Once they enter school, their disability and need for special attention usually become apparent, as they did with Connie, the first-grader profiled at the beginning of the module. With appropriate training, these students can reach a third- to sixth-grade level. Although they cannot do complex intellectual tasks, they can hold jobs and function independently and successfully.

Intellectual and adaptive limitations become more apparent at higher levels of intellectual disability. People with IQ scores of 35 or 40 to 50 or 55 are classified with **moderate intellectual disability**. The moderately intellectually disabled— 5 to 10 percent of the intellectually disabled population—behave distinctively early in their lives (e.g., they are slow to develop language and motor skills). Regular schooling is seldom effective in teaching academic skills to the moderately intellectually disabled because they generally cannot progress beyond a second-grade level. Still, they can learn occupational and social skills, and they can learn to travel independently to familiar places. Typically, they require moderate levels of supervision.

For those classified with **severe intellectual disability** (IQs ranging from 20 or 25 to 35 or 40) and **profound intellectual disability** (IQs below 20 or 25), functioning is severely limited. Usually, such people have little or no speech, poor motor control, and may need 24-hour nursing care. At the same time, some people with severe intellectual disability are capable of learning basic self-care skills, such as dressing and eating, and they may become partially independent as adults. Still, they require relatively high levels of care throughout life, and most severely and profoundly intellectually disabled people are institutionalized for the majority of their lives.

Above the Norm: The Gifted and Talented

LO 8.11 Describe the characteristics and effects of giftedness.

Amy Leibowitz picked up reading at age 3. By 5, she was writing her own books. First grade bored her within a week. As her school had no program for gifted children, it was suggested she skip to second grade. From there, she went to fifth grade. Her parents were proud but concerned. When they asked the fifth-grade teacher where she felt Amy really belonged, the teacher said she was ready, academically, for high school.

It sometimes surprises people that the gifted and talented are considered to have a form of exceptionality. Yet the 3 to 5 percent of such children present special challenges of their own.

There is no formal definition of gifted and talented students. However, the federal government considers the term *gifted* to include "children who give evidence of high performance capability in areas such as intellectual, creative, artistic, leadership capacity, or specific academic fields, and who require services or activities not ordinarily provided by the school in order to fully develop such capabilities" (Sec 582, P.L. 97-35). Gifted and talented children, no less than students with low IQs, warrant special concern—although programs for them are often the first to be dropped when schools face budgetary problems (Mendoza, 2006; Olszewski-Kubilius & Thomson, 2013; Olszewski-Kubilius & Thomson, 2014).

UNSOCIABLE NERDS OR INTELLIGENT, WELL-ADJUSTED PEOPLE? Despite the stereotype that the gifted are "unsociable," "poorly adjusted," and "neurotic," research suggests that highly intelligent people tend to be outgoing, well adjusted, and popular (Howe, 2004; Bracken & Brown, 2006; Shaunessy et al., 2006).

For instance, one landmark, long-term study of 1,500 gifted students, which began in the 1920s, found that the gifted were healthier, better coordinated, and psychologically better adjusted than their less intelligent classmates. Furthermore, they received more awards and distinctions, earned more money, and made many more contributions in art and literature than the average person. By the time they had reached age 40, they had collectively produced more than 90 books, 375 plays and short stories, and 2,000 articles, and they had registered more than 200 patents. Perhaps not surprisingly, they reported greater satisfaction with their lives than the nongifted (Reis & Renzulli, 2004; Duggan & Friedman, 2014).

Yet being gifted and talented is no guarantee of school success. The verbal abilities that allow the expression of ideas and feelings can equally voice glib and persuasive statements that happen to be inaccurate. Furthermore, teachers sometimes misinterpret the humor, novelty, and creativity of unusually gifted children and regard their intellectual fervor as disruptive or inappropriate. And peers may be unsympathetic: Some very bright children try to hide their intelligence in an effort to fit in (Swiatek, 2002).

EDUCATING THE GIFTED AND TALENTED. Educators have devised two approaches to teaching the gifted and talented: acceleration and enrichment. **Acceleration** allows gifted students to move ahead at their own pace, even if this means skipping grade levels. The materials in acceleration programs are not always different; they may simply be provided at a faster pace than for the average student (Lee, Olszewski-Kubilius & Thomson, 2012).

An alternative approach is **enrichment**, through which students are kept at grade level but are enrolled in special programs and given individual activities to allow greater depth of study. In enrichment, the material differs not only in the timing of its presentation but in its sophistication as well. Thus, enrichment materials are designed to provide an intellectual challenge to the gifted student, encouraging higher-order thinking (Worrell, Szarko, & Gabelko, 2001).

acceleration
the provision of special programs that allow gifted students to move ahead at their own pace, even if this means skipping to higher grade levels.

enrichment
an approach whereby gifted students are kept at grade level but are enrolled in special programs and given individual activities to allow greater depth of study.

Module 8.3 Review

LO 8.9 **Explain the meaning of the term** *least restrictive environment.*

Students with various kinds of exceptionalities receive by federal mandate an education in the least restrictive environment. Two main ways of providing special education without unduly segregating special needs students are mainstreaming and full inclusion.

LO 8.10 **Analyze the characteristics and effects of intellectual disability.**

IQ scores are also used to classify children with intellectual disabilities. This approach is more useful in measuring cognitive limitations than other limitations. Individuals with intellectual disabilities vary widely across a range of performance and independence levels.

LO 8.11 **Describe the characteristics and effects of giftedness.**

A small but significant sector of students fit into the realm of the gifted and talented. To realize their potential in the school setting, they need special attention and programs, such as acceleration and enrichment programs. Contrary to stereotypes, gifted and talented individuals tend to be well adjusted and satisfied with their lives.

Journal Writing Prompt

Applying Lifespan Development: What are some advantages and disadvantages of mainstreaming versus full inclusion? Be sure to address multiple points of view (i.e., the student's, the teacher's, other students', the parents').

Epilogue

We opened the chapter with the question of what intelligence consists of and how it can be defined. We saw some of the ways in which intelligence has been measured, and we considered controversial topics such as group performance differences on IQ tests and the nature of cognitive decline that accompanies aging. Our discussion of intelligence concluded with a look at two groups with intellectual exceptionalities at opposite ends of the intelligence scale: people with intellectual disability and people who are gifted or talented.

Return to the prologue of this chapter, in which we met twins Darius and Jayden. In light of what you now know about intelligence, answer the following questions.

1. Given Darius and Jayden's differing "road to success," explain how other factors beyond intelligence can influence one's achievements in life.

2. Both boys took an IQ test that partly determined their placements in middle school. Jayden scored well above average and Darius well below. If you were an educator, what would you see as the benefits and limitations of these test results?

3. Is there a broader and more valid way to measure Darius's intelligence and capabilities? How might an assessment based on Sternberg's triarchic theory of intelligence produce more accurate results than a traditional IQ test?

4. How do you think Darius and Jayden might have performed on a test of practical intelligence? A test of emotional intelligence? A test of creativity?

5. How would you improve class offerings in high school for Darius and other similar children who may have skills that don't fit well into typical academic pursuits?

Looking Back

LO 8.1 **Describe traditional methods for measuring intelligence.**

It is difficult for developmental psychologists to define and measure intelligence. Alfred Binet is responsible for most 20th-century approaches to the study of intelligence. Binet left three major contributions to the field of intelligence measurement: using a practical, non-theoretical approach; linking intelligence to academic success; and using IQ scores to quantify intelligence.

LO 8.2 **Examine current methods of intelligence testing.**

Current IQ tests, including the Stanford-Binet Intelligence Scale, the Wechsler Intelligence Scale, and the Kaufman Assessment Battery for Children, while reliant on Binet's pioneering work, attempt to address some of the shortcomings and limitations of older tests. The Kaufman test, for example, permits paraphrasing of items by the administrator, use of the examinee's home language, and gestures to help examinees understand the content and do their best.

LO 8.3 **Explore key issues surrounding intelligence testing.**

Key issues that arise with intelligence testing include the merits of group administration versus individual administration and the avoidance of bias in test items. In addition, measurements must be consistent (i.e., have reliability) and measure what they are expected to measure (i.e., have validity). Test scores must also be interpretable in terms of the concept (i.e., intelligence) that they are testing.

LO 8.4 **Analyze alternative definitions of intelligence.**

Alternative conceptions of intelligence have sprung up to explain different kinds of intelligence, including Robert Sternberg's triarchic theory of intelligence, which claims that intelligence is composed of componential, experiential, and contextual components.

LO 8.5 **Describe recent approaches to measuring intelligence in infants.**

It is particularly difficult to define and measure infant intelligence. Approaches include developmental scales, which provide good cognitive snapshots, and information processing approaches, which focus on the speed at which infants process information and learn about stimuli.

LO 8.6 **Define achievement and aptitude tests and compare their uses.**

In addition to IQ tests, children face achievement tests, which measure their knowledge in particular subject areas, and aptitude tests, which attempt to predict ability in subject areas, college performance, or lines of work.

LO 8.7 **Analyze the sources of score differences achieved by different groups on IQ and other tests.**

A major controversy in the study of intelligence is the role of nature versus nurture in IQ. Most developmentalists regard nature as less important than nurture, especially economic and social background.

LO 8.8 **Describe the effects of aging on intelligence.**

Cross-sectional and longitudinal studies, which are used to study age-related intellectual decline, both have disadvantages. Developmental psychologist K. Warner Schaie used longitudinal methods and a sequential design to study intelligence declines comprehensively. Some areas of intellectual function decline in adulthood, but others are less subject to decline. A complicating factor is that the crystallized and fluid components of intelligence decline at different rates. Older people use selective optimization—the practice of concentrating on certain skills to compensate for areas of loss—to maintain high performance.

LO 8.9 **Explain the meaning of the term *least restrictive environment*.**

To comply with Public Law 94-142, schools are required to place students with exceptionalities in the least restrictive environment, which may mean mainstreaming or full inclusion.

LO 8.10 **Analyze the characteristics and effects of intellectual disability.**

Individuals with intellectual disability vary widely across a range of performance and independence levels, from those who can function and work independently to those who need constant care.

LO 8.11 **Describe the characteristics and effects of giftedness.**

A few students may be categorized as gifted or talented and can benefit from special programs, such as acceleration and enrichment programs. Contrary to stereotypes, gifted and talented people are usually well adjusted and satisfied with their lives.

Key Terms and Concepts

intelligence 242
intelligence quotient (IQ) 243
Stanford-Binet Intelligence Scale, Fifth Edition (SB5) 244
Wechsler Intelligence Scale for Children-IV (WISC-IV) 244
Wechsler Adult Intelligence Scale-IV (WAIS-IV) 244
Kaufman Assessment Battery for Children (KABC-II) 244
reliability 246
validity 246

specific learning disorders 246
fluid intelligence 247
crystallized intelligence 247
triarchic theory of intelligence 249
practical intelligence 249
emotional intelligence 249
developmental quotient 253
Bayley Scales of Infant Development 253
cross-modal transference 254
achievement test 255
aptitude test 255

least restrictive environment 262
mainstreaming 263
full inclusion 263
intellectual disability 263
mild intellectual disability 264
moderate intellectual disability 264
severe intellectual disability 264
profound intellectual disability 264
acceleration 265
enrichment 265

Chapter 9
Social and Emotional Development

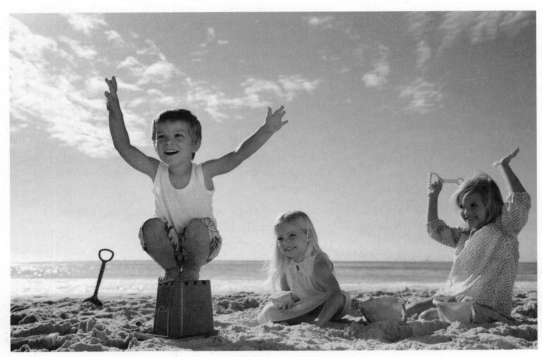

Tom Merton/Alamy

Learning Objectives

LO 9.1 Identify the four major patterns of infant attachment, and give examples of how the nature of attachment in infancy may influence relationships later in life.

LO 9.2 Describe how infants interact with peers, and explain the implications this has for their own development.

LO 9.3 Identify the emotions infants experience and their ability to decode the emotions of others.

LO 9.4 Define social referencing and theory of mind, and explain how they are related to a child's cognitive development.

LO 9.5 Summarize emotional development in middle childhood and adolescence, and give examples of emotional self-regulation.

LO 9.6 Identify the causes of adolescent anxiety and depression, and explain the role gender plays in both depression and suicide rates.

LO 9.7 Summarize how the determinants of happiness change throughout adulthood, and identify the three major theories regarding happiness in late adulthood.

LO 9.8 Identify the major dimensions of temperament, and explain how temperament is affected by a child's environment.

LO 9.9 Differentiate the eight stages of Erikson's theory of psychosocial development, and explain what factors determine the outcome at each stage.

LO 9.10 Summarize the contributions of Vaillant, Gould, Levinson, and Peck to our understanding of personality development in adulthood, and discuss the research on midlife crisis.

LO 9.11 Describe the Big Five personality traits, and summarize how genetics and environment interact in shaping personality.

Chapter Overview

Module 9.1 Forging Early Social Relationships
Attachment: Forming Social Bonds
Infants' Sociability with Their Peers: Infant–Infant Interaction

Module 9.2 Emotional Development
Emotions in Infancy: Do Infants Experience Emotional Highs and Lows?
Social Referencing: Feeling What Others Feel
Emotional Development in Middle Childhood and Adolescence

From Research to Practice: The Second Step Program
Emotional Difficulties in Adolescence: Anxiety, Depression, and Suicide

Neuroscience and Development: Therapy Can Change Your Brain

Development in Your Life: Preventing Suicide
Emotions in Adulthood: Fulfilling Psychological Needs

Module 9.3 Personality Development Across the Life Span
Temperament: Stabilities in Infant Behavior
Erikson's Theory of Psychosocial Development
Moving Beyond Erikson: Personality Development During Adulthood

Developmental Diversity and Your Life: Middle Age: In Some Cultures It Doesn't Exist
Trait Approaches to Personality

Prologue: Preventing Tears

Antonio's first day of volunteering at an after-school program for school-age children was eventful. After being the one to suggest that they all play tag together, he accidently ran right into a fourth-grader, Tyrone, and they both tumbled to the ground. Antonio could see the tears welling up in Tyrone's eyes.

Antonio quickly remembered something he'd just been taught in one of his college courses—kids often look to adults to see how they should react in uncertain situations. In a last-ditch effort to prevent the tears from escaping Tyrone's eyes, Antonio laughed and said, "That was awesome!" Still hesitant for a moment, Tyrone gathered himself together, and finally agreed, "Yeah, that was awesome." The tears dried up almost instantly.

Remembering how well this approach worked, Antonio tried the "That was awesome" trick again many years later when his own son, 8-year-old Henry, tripped as he was running across the lawn at a park. Unfortunately, this time the trick backfired and only seemed to infuriate his son, causing Henry to angrily scream, "No, it wasn't—I could have busted my head open!" Antonio realized some things learned in college might just work better on other people's children. ■

Looking Ahead

In this chapter, we consider the foundations of social relationships and how personality develops across the life span. We begin by examining the roots of children's earliest social relationships. We look at how bonds of attachment are forged in infancy and the ways in which children increasingly interact with peers. We also consider what makes a child popular or unpopular and how children can be helped to develop social competence.

Human beings are sociable from a very early age.

We then examine emotional development across the life span, beginning with the emotions infants feel and how well they can decode others' emotions. We look at how children use others to determine how to react, as Tyrone did, and the development of their ability to express emotions. Next, we discuss the nature and function of emotions in adolescence and see how adolescents learn to regulate their emotions. We also focus on the emotional difficulties adolescents may face, resulting in depression or even suicide, and how suicide can be prevented. We then turn to the relationship between fulfilling psychological needs and happiness in adulthood, and consider what constitutes successful aging.

Finally, we consider personality and the stages of human psychosocial development. We look at the differences among infants and evaluate the pros and cons of day care for young children. We then examine a variety of theories on how personality develops in adolescence. In closing we review the popular notion of midlife crisis—fact or fiction—and look at the stability of personality in adulthood.

MODULE 9.1

FORGING EARLY SOCIAL RELATIONSHIPS

Luis Camacho, now 38, clearly remembers the feelings that haunted him on the way to the hospital to meet his new sister Katy. Though he was only 4 at the time, that day of infamy is still vivid to him today. Luis would no longer be the only kid in the house; he would have to share his life with a baby sister. She would play with his toys, read his books, and be with him in the back seat of the car.

What really bothered him, of course, was that he would have to share his parents' love and attention with a new person. And not just any new person—a girl, who would automatically have a lot of advantages. Katy would be cuter, more needy, more demanding, more interesting—more everything—than he. He would be underfoot at best, neglected at worst.

Luis also knew that he was expected to be cheerful and welcoming. So he put on a brave face at the hospital and walked without hesitation to the room where his mother and Katy were waiting.

The arrival of a newborn brings a dramatic change to a family's dynamics. No matter how welcome a baby's birth, it causes a fundamental shift in the roles that people play within the family. Mothers and fathers must start to build a relationship with their infant, and older children must adjust to the presence of a new member of the family and build their own alliance with their infant brother or sister.

Although the process of social development during infancy is neither simple nor automatic, it is crucial: The bonds that grow between infants and their parents, siblings, family, and others provide the foundation for a lifetime's worth of social relationships.

Attachment: Forming Social Bonds

LO 9.1 Identify the four major patterns of infant attachment, and give examples of how the nature of attachment in infancy may influence relationships later in life.

The most important aspect of social development that takes place during infancy is the formation of attachment. **Attachment** is the positive emotional bond that develops between a child and a particular, special individual. When children experience attachment to a given person, they feel pleasure when they are with them and feel comforted by their presence in times of distress. As we'll see in a later chapter, the nature of

Attachment
the positive emotional bond that develops between a child and a particular individual.

our attachment during infancy affects how we relate to others throughout the rest of our lives (Fischer, 2012; Bergman et al., 2015; Kim et al., 2017).

To understand attachment, the earliest researchers turned to the bonds that form between parents and children in the nonhuman animal kingdom. For instance, ethologist Konrad Lorenz (1965) observed newborn goslings, which have an innate tendency to follow their mother, the first moving object to which they typically are exposed after birth. Lorenz found that goslings whose eggs were raised in an incubator and who viewed him just after hatching would follow his every movement, as if he were their mother. He labeled this process *imprinting*: behavior that takes place during a critical period and involves attachment to the first moving object that is observed.

Lorenz's findings suggested that attachment was based on biologically determined factors, and other theorists agreed. For instance, Freud suggested that attachment grew out of a mother's ability to satisfy a child's oral needs.

It turns out, however, that the ability to provide food and other physiological needs may not be as crucial as Freud and other theorists first thought. In a classic study, psychologist Harry Harlow gave infant monkeys the choice of cuddling a wire "monkey" that provided food or a soft, terry-cloth monkey that was warm but did not provide food (see Figure 9-1). Their preference was clear: Baby monkeys spent most of their time clinging to the cloth monkey, although they made occasional expeditions to the wire monkey to nurse. Harlow suggested that the warm cloth monkey provided *contact comfort* (Harlow & Zimmerman, 1959; Blum, 2002).

Harlow's work illustrates that food alone is not the basis for attachment. Given that the monkeys' preference for the soft cloth "mothers" developed some time after birth, these findings are consistent with research showing little support for the existence of a critical period for bonding between human mothers and infants immediately following birth.

The earliest work on human attachment, which is still highly influential, was carried out by British psychiatrist John Bowlby (1951). In Bowlby's view, attachment is based primarily on infants' needs for safety and security—their genetically determined motivation to avoid predators. As they develop, infants come to learn that their safety is best provided by a particular individual. This realization ultimately leads to the development of a special relationship with that individual, who is typically the mother. Bowlby suggested that this single relationship with the primary caregiver is qualitatively different from the bonds formed with others, including the father—a suggestion that, as we'll see later, has been a source of some disagreement.

According to Bowlby, attachment provides a type of home base. As children become more independent, they can progressively roam further away from their secure base.

THE AINSWORTH STRANGE SITUATION AND PATTERNS OF ATTACHMENT.
Developmental psychologist Mary Ainsworth built on Bowlby's theorizing to develop a widely used experimental technique to measure attachment (Ainsworth et al., 1978; Ainsworth, 1993). The **Ainsworth Strange Situation** consists of a sequence of staged episodes that illustrate the strength of attachment between a child and (typically) his or her mother. The "strange situation" follows this general eight-step pattern: (1) The mother and baby enter an unfamiliar room; (2) the mother sits down, leaving the baby free to explore; (3) an adult stranger enters the room and converses first with the mother and then with the baby; (4) the mother exits the room, leaving the baby alone with the stranger; (5) the mother returns, greeting and comforting the baby, and the stranger leaves; (6) the mother departs again, leaving the baby alone; (7) the stranger returns; and (8) the mother returns and the stranger leaves (Ainsworth, 1993; Pederson et al., 2014).

Infants' reactions to the various aspects of the Strange Situation vary considerably, depending on the nature of their attachment to their mothers. One-year-olds typically show one of four major patterns—avoidant, secure, ambivalent, and disorganized-disoriented (summarized in Table 9-1). Children who have a **secure attachment**

Figure 9-1 Monkey Mothers Matter

Harlow's research showed that monkeys preferred the terry-cloth, soft "mother" over the wire "monkey" that provided food.

Harlow Primate Laboratory

Ainsworth Strange Situation
a sequence of staged episodes that illustrate the strength of attachment between a child and (typically) his or her mother.

secure attachment pattern
a style of attachment in which children use the mother as a kind of home base and are at ease when she is present; when she leaves, they become upset.

Mary Ainsworth, who devised the Strange Situation to measure infant attachment.

JHU Sheridan Libraries/Getty Images

Table 9-1 Classification of Infant Attachment

	CLASSIFICATION CRITERIA			
Label	Seeking Proximity with Caregiver	Maintaining Contact with Caregiver	Avoiding Proximity with Caregiver	Resisting Contact with Caregiver
Avoidant	Low	Low	High	Low
Secure	High	High (if distressed)	Low	Low
Ambivalent	High	High (often pre-separation)	Low	High
Disorganized-disoriented	Inconsistent	Inconsistent	Inconsistent	Inconsistent

avoidant attachment pattern
a style of attachment in which children do not seek proximity to the mother; after the mother has left, they seem to avoid her when she returns.

ambivalent attachment pattern
a style of attachment in which children display a combination of positive and negative reactions to their mothers.

pattern use the mother as the type of home base that Bowlby described. These children seem at ease in the Strange Situation as long as their mothers are present. They explore independently, returning to her occasionally. Although they may or may not appear upset when she leaves, securely attached children immediately go to her when she returns and seek contact. Most North American children—about two-thirds—fall into the securely attached category.

In contrast, children with an **avoidant attachment pattern** do not seek proximity to the mother, and after she has left, they typically do not seem distressed. Furthermore, they seem to avoid her when she returns. It is as if they are indifferent to her behavior. Some 20 percent of 1-year-old children are in the avoidant category.

Children with an **ambivalent attachment pattern** display a combination of positive and negative reactions to their mothers. Initially, ambivalent children are in such close contact with the mother that they hardly explore their environment. They appear anxious even before the mother leaves, and when she does leave, they show great distress. But upon her return, they show ambivalent reactions, seeking to be close to her but also hitting and kicking, apparently in anger. About 10 to 15 percent of 1-year-olds fall into the ambivalent classification (Cassidy & Berlin, 1994).

Although Ainsworth identified only three categories, a more recent expansion of her work finds that there is a fourth category: disorganized-disoriented. Children who have a **disorganized-disoriented attachment pattern** show inconsistent, contradictory, and confused behavior. They may run to the mother when she returns but not look at her, or seem initially calm and then suddenly break into angry weeping. Their confusion suggests that they may be the least securely attached children of all. About 5 to 10 percent of all children fall into this category (Cole, 2005; Duschinsky, 2015).

A child's attachment style would be of only minor importance were it not for the fact that the quality of attachment between infants and their mothers has significant consequences for relationships at later stages of life. For example, boys who are securely attached at age 1 show fewer psychological difficulties at older ages than do avoidant or ambivalent children. Similarly, children who are securely attached as infants tend to be more socially and emotionally competent later, and others view them more positively. Adult romantic relationships are associated with the kind of attachment style developed during infancy (Mikulincer & Shaver, 2005; Simpson et al., 2007; Bergman, Blom, & Polyak, 2012).

At the same time, we cannot say that children who do not have a secure attachment style during infancy invariably experience difficulties later in life, nor can we

In this illustration of the Strange Situation, the infant first explores the playroom on his own, as long as his mother is present. But when she leaves, he begins to cry. On her return, however, he is immediately comforted and stops crying. The conclusion: He is securely attached.

state that those with a secure attachment at age 1 always have good adjustment later on. Some evidence suggests that children with avoidant and ambivalent attachment—as measured by the Strange Situation—do quite well (Fraley & Spieker, 2003; Alhusen, Hayat, & Gross, 2013; Smith-Nielsen et al., 2016).

In cases in which the development of attachment has been severely disrupted, children may suffer from *reactive attachment disorder*, a psychological problem characterized by extreme difficulty in forming attachments to others. In young children, it can be displayed in feeding difficulties, unresponsiveness to social overtures from others, and a general failure to thrive. Reactive attachment disorder is rare and typically the result of abuse or neglect (Hornor, 2008; Schechter & Willheim, 2009; Puckering, et al., 2011).

disorganized-disoriented attachment pattern
a style of attachment in which children show inconsistent, often contradictory behavior.

PRODUCING ATTACHMENT: THE ROLES OF THE MOTHER AND FATHER

As 5-month-old Annie cries passionately, her mother comes into the room and gently lifts her from her crib. After just a few moments, as her mother rocks Annie and speaks softly, Annie's cries cease, and she cuddles in her mother's arms. But the moment her mother places her back in the crib, Annie begins to wail, leading her mother to pick her up once again.

The pattern is familiar to most parents. The infant cries, the parent reacts, and the child responds in turn. Such seemingly insignificant sequences as these, repeatedly occurring in the lives of infants and parents, help pave the way for the development of relationships between children, their parents, and the rest of the social world. We'll consider how each of the major caregivers and the infant play a role in the development of attachment.

Mothers and Attachment. Sensitivity to their infants' needs and desires is the hallmark of mothers of securely attached infants. Such a mother tends to be aware of her child's moods, and she takes into account her child's feelings as they interact. She is also responsive during face-to-face interactions, provides feeding "on demand," and is warm and affectionate to her infant (McElwain & Booth-LaForce, 2006; Evans, Whittingham, & Boyd, 2012).

From *a social worker's* perspective

What might a social worker seeking to find a good home for a foster child look for when evaluating potential foster parents?

It is not only a matter of responding in *any* fashion to their infants' signals that separates mothers of securely attached and insecurely attached children. Mothers of secure infants tend to provide the appropriate level of response. In fact, overly responsive mothers are just as likely to have insecurely attached children as under-responsive mothers. In contrast, mothers whose communication involves *interactional synchrony*, in which caregivers respond to infants appropriately and both caregiver and child match emotional states, are more likely to produce secure attachment (Hane, Feldstein, & Dernetz, 2003; Pasiak & Menna, 2015).

Fathers and Attachment. Up to now, we've barely touched on one of the key players involved in the upbringing of a child: the father. If you were to look at the early theorizing and research on attachment, you'd find little mention of the father and his potential contributions to the life of the infant (Tamis-LeMonda & Cabrera, 1999; Tamis-LeMonda, 2004).

However, it has become increasingly clear that—despite societal norms that sometimes relegate fathers to secondary childrearing roles—infants can form their primary initial relationship with their fathers. For example, fathers' expressions of nurturance, warmth, affection, support, and concern are extremely important to their children's emotional and social well-being. Furthermore, some psychological disorders, such as

A growing body of research highlights the importance of a father's demonstration of love for his children. In fact, certain disorders such as depression and substance abuse have been found to be more related to fathers' than to mothers' behavior.

substance abuse and depression, have been found to be related more to fathers' than to mothers' behavior (Condon et al., 2013; Braungart-Rieker et al., 2014; Lickenbrock & Braungart-Rieker, 2015).

Infants' Sociability with Their Peers: Infant–Infant Interaction

LO 9.2 Describe how infants interact with peers, and explain the implications this has for their own development.

How sociable are infants with other children? Although it is clear that they do not form "friendships" in the traditional sense, babies do react positively to the presence of peers from early in life, and they engage in rudimentary forms of social interaction.

Infants' sociability is expressed in several ways. From the earliest months of life, they smile, laugh, and vocalize while looking at their peers. They show more interest in peers than in inanimate objects and pay greater attention to other infants than they do to a mirror image of themselves. They also begin to show preferences for peers with whom they are familiar compared with those they do not know. For example, studies of identical twins show that twins exhibit a higher level of social behavior toward each other than toward an unfamiliar infant (Sanefuji, Ohgami, & Hashiya, 2006; Legerstee, 2013; Kawakami, 2014).

Infants' level of sociability rises with age. For instance, 9- to 12-month-olds mutually present and accept toys, particularly if they know each other. They also play social games, such as peek-a-boo or crawl-and-chase. Such behavior is important, as it serves as a foundation for future social exchanges in which children will try to elicit responses from others and then offer reactions to those responses. These kinds of exchanges are important to learn because they continue even into adulthood. For example, someone who says, "Hi, what's up?" may be trying to elicit a response to which he or she can then reply (Eckerman & Peterman, 2001).

Finally, as infants age, they begin to imitate one another. For instance, 14-month-old infants who are familiar with one another sometimes reproduce each other's behavior. Such imitation serves a social function and can also be a powerful teaching tool (Ray & Heyes, 2011; Brownell, 2016).

According to Andrew Meltzoff, a developmental psychologist at the University of Washington, so-called expert babies are able to teach skills and information to other infants. According to the research of Meltzoff and his colleagues, the abilities learned from the "experts" are retained and later utilized to a remarkable degree. Learning by exposure starts early in life. Even 6-week-old infants can perform delayed imitation of a novel stimulus to which they have earlier been exposed, such as an adult sticking the tongue out the side of the mouth (Meltzoff, 2002; Meltzoff, Waismeyer, & Gopnik, 2012; Waismeyer & Meltzoff, 2017).

To some developmentalists, the capacity of young children to engage in imitation suggests that imitation may be inborn. In support of this view, research has identified a class of neurons in the brain that seems related to an innate ability to imitate. *Mirror neurons* are neurons that fire not only when an individual enacts a particular behavior but also when the individual simply observes *another* organism carrying out the same behavior (Falck-Ytter, 2006; Paulus, 2014).

For example, research on brain functioning shows activation of the inferior frontal gyrus both when an individual carries out a particular task and also when observing another individual carrying out the same task. Mirror neurons may help infants to understand others' actions, to develop a *theory of mind*, and to show goal-directed behavior from the time of birth. Dysfunction of mirror neurons may be related to the development of disorders involving children's theory of mind (a concept we'll discuss later) as well as autism, a psychological disorder involving significant emotional and linguistic problems (Martineau et al., 2008; Welsh et al., 2009; von Hofsten & Rosander, 2015).

Module 9.1 Review

LO 9.1 Identify the four major patterns of infant attachment, and give examples of how the nature of attachment in infancy may influence relationships later in life.

Attachment, the positive emotional bond between an infant and a significant individual, affects a person's later social competence as an adult.

LO 9.2 Describe how infants interact with peers, and explain the implications this has for their own development.

Infants and the persons with whom they interact engage in reciprocal socialization as they mutually adjust to one another's interactions.

Journal Writing Prompt

Applying Lifespan Development: In what sort of society might an avoidant attachment style be encouraged by cultural attitudes toward childrearing? In such a society, would characterizing the infant's consistent avoidance of its mother as anger be an accurate interpretation?

MODULE 9.2

EMOTIONAL DEVELOPMENT

Germaine smiles when he catches a glimpse of his mother. Tawanda looks angry when her mother takes away the spoon that she is playing with. Sydney scowls when a loud plane flies overhead.

A smile. A look of anger. A scowl. The emotions of infancy are written all over a baby's face. Yet do infants experience emotions in the same way that adults do? When do they become capable of understanding what others are experiencing emotionally? And how do they use others' emotional states to make sense of their environment? We consider some of these questions as we seek to understand how infants develop emotionally and socially.

Emotions in Infancy: Do Infants Experience Emotional Highs and Lows?

LO 9.3 Identify the emotions infants experience and their ability to decode the emotions of others.

Anyone who spends any time at all around infants knows they display facial expressions that seem indicative of their emotional states. In situations in which we expect them to be happy, they seem to smile; when we might assume they are frustrated, they show anger; and when we might expect them to be unhappy, they look sad.

These basic facial expressions are remarkably similar across the most diverse cultures. Whether we look at babies in India, the United States, or the jungles of New Guinea, the expression of basic emotions is the same (see Figure 9-2). Furthermore, the nonverbal expression of emotion, called *nonverbal encoding*, is fairly consistent among people of all ages. These consistencies have led researchers to conclude that we are born with the capacity to display basic emotions (Ackerman & Izard, 2004; Bornstein, Suwalsky, & Breakstone, 2012; Rajhans et al., 2016).

Infants display a fairly wide range of emotional expressions. According to research on what mothers see in their children's nonverbal behavior, almost all think that by the age of 1 month, their babies have expressed interest and joy. In addition, 84 percent of mothers think their infants have expressed anger, 75 percent surprise,

Figure 9-2 Universal Facial Expressions

Across every culture, infants show similar facial expressions relating to basic emotions. Do you think such expressions are similar in nonhuman animals?

58 percent fear, and 34 percent sadness. Research also finds that interest, distress, and disgust are present at birth, and that other emotions emerge over the next few months. Such findings are consistent with the work of the famous naturalist Charles Darwin, whose 1872 book *The Expression of the Emotions in Man and Animals* argued that humans and primates have an inborn, universal set of emotional expressions—a view consistent with today's evolutionary approach to development (Benson, 2003; MacLean et al., 2014).

Although infants display similar *kinds* of emotions, the *degree* of emotional expressivity varies among infants. Children in different cultures show reliable differences in emotional expressiveness, even during infancy. For example, by the age of 11 months, Chinese infants are generally less expressive than European, American, and Japanese infants (Camras, Meng, & Ujiie, 2002; Izard et al., 2003; Buss & Kiel, 2004).

STRANGER ANXIETY AND SEPARATION ANXIETY. "She used to be such a friendly baby," thought Erika's mother. "No matter who she encountered, she had a big smile. But almost the day she turned 7 months old, she began to react to strangers as if she were seeing a ghost. Her face crinkles up with a frown, and she either turns away or stares at them with suspicion. It's as if she has undergone a personality transplant."

What happened to Erika is, in fact, quite typical. By the end of the first year, infants often develop both stranger anxiety and separation anxiety. **Stranger anxiety** is the caution and wariness displayed by infants when encountering an unfamiliar person. Such anxiety typically appears in the second half of the first year.

What brings on stranger anxiety? Brain development and the increased cognitive abilities of infants play a role. As infants' memory develops, they are able to separate the people they know from the people they don't. The same cognitive advances that allow them to respond so positively to those people with whom they are familiar also give them

stranger anxiety

the caution and wariness displayed by infants when encountering an unfamiliar person.

the ability to recognize people who are unfamiliar. Furthermore, between 6 and 9 months, infants begin trying to make sense of their world, trying to anticipate and predict events. When something happens that they don't expect—such as the appearance of an unknown person—they experience fear (Volker, 2007; Mash, Bornstein, & Arterberry, 2013).

Separation anxiety is the distress displayed by infants when a customary care provider departs. Separation anxiety, which is also universal across cultures, usually begins at about 7 or 8 months (see Figure 9-3). It peaks around 14 months and then decreases. Separation anxiety is largely attributable to the same factors as stranger anxiety. Infants' growing cognitive skills allow them to ask reasonable questions, but they may be questions that they are too young to understand the answers to: "Why is my mother leaving?" "Where is she going?" and "Will she come back?"

Stranger anxiety and separation anxiety represent important social progress. They reflect both cognitive advances and the growing emotional and social bonds between infants and their caregivers—bonds that we'll consider later in the module when we discuss infants' social relationships.

separation anxiety
the distress displayed by infants when a customary care provider departs.

SMILING. As Luz lay sleeping in her crib, her mother and father caught a glimpse of the most beautiful smile crossing her face. Her parents were sure that Luz was having a pleasant dream. Were they right?

Probably not. The earliest smiles expressed during sleep probably have little meaning, although no one can be absolutely sure. By 6 to 9 weeks babies begin to smile reliably at the sight of stimuli that please them, including toys, mobiles, and—to the delight of parents—people. The first smiles tend to be relatively indiscriminate, as infants first begin to smile at the sight of almost anything they find amusing. However, as they get older, they become more selective in their smiles.

A baby's smile in response to another person, rather than to nonhuman stimuli, is considered a *social smile*. As babies get older, their social smiles become directed toward particular individuals, not just anyone. By the age of 18 months, social smiling, directed more toward mothers and other caregivers, becomes more frequent than smiling directed toward nonhuman objects. Moreover, if an adult is unresponsive to a child, the amount of smiling decreases. In short, by the end of the second year, children are quite purposefully using smiling to communicate their positive emotions, and they are sensitive to the emotional expressions of others (Reissland & Cohen, 2012; Wörmann et al., 2014; Planalp et al., 2016).

DECODING OTHERS' FACIAL EXPRESSIONS. Earlier, we discussed the possibility that neonates can imitate adults' facial expressions even minutes after birth. Although their imitative abilities certainly do not imply that they can understand the meaning of others' facial expressions, such imitation does pave the way for *nonverbal decoding* abilities, which begin to emerge fairly early. Using these abilities, infants can interpret others' facial and vocal expressions that carry emotional meaning. For example, they can tell when a caregiver is happy to see them and pick up on worry or fear in the faces of others (Hernandez-Reif et al., 2006; Striano & Vaish, 2006; Hoehl et al., 2012).

In the first 6 to 8 weeks, infants' visual precision is sufficiently limited that they cannot pay much attention to others' facial expressions. But they soon begin to discriminate among different facial expressions of emotion and even seem to be able to respond to differences in emotional intensity conveyed by facial expressions. By the time they reach the age of 4 months, infants already

Figure 9-3 Separation Anxiety

Separation anxiety, the distress displayed by infants when their usual care provider leaves their presence, is a universal phenomenon beginning at around the age of 7 or 8 months. It peaks at around 14 months and then begins to decline. Does separation anxiety have survival value for humans?

(**Source:** Kagan, Kearsley, & Zelazo, 1978.)

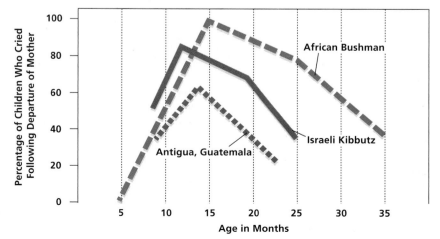

have begun to understand the emotions that lie behind the facial and vocal expressions of others (Bertin & Striano, 2006; Farroni et al., 2007; Safar & Moulson, 2017).

In sum, infants learn early both to produce and to decode emotions, and they begin to learn the effect of their own emotions on others. Such abilities play an important role not only in helping them experience their own emotions, but also—as we see next—in using others' emotions to understand the meaning of ambiguous social situations (Buss & Kiel, 2004; Messinger et al., 2012).

Social Referencing: Feeling What Others Feel

LO 9.4   Define social referencing and theory of mind, and explain how they are related to a child's cognitive development.

Twenty-three-month-old Stephania watches as her older brother Eric and his friend Chen argue loudly with each other and begin to wrestle. Uncertain of what is happening, Stephania glances at her mother. Her mother, though, wears a smile, knowing that Eric and Chen are just playing. On seeing her mother's reaction, Stephania smiles too, mimicking her mother's facial expression.

Like Stephania, most of us have been in situations in which we feel uncertain. In such cases, we sometimes turn to others to see how they are reacting. This reliance on others, known as social referencing, helps us decide what an appropriate response ought to be.

From *an educator's* perspective

In what situations do adults rely on social referencing to work out appropriate responses? How might social referencing be used to influence parents' behavior toward their children?

---

social referencing
the intentional search for information about others' feelings to help make sense of uncertain circumstances and events.

Social referencing is the intentional search for information about others' feelings to help explain the meaning of uncertain circumstances and events. Like Stephania, we use social referencing to clarify the meaning of a situation and so to reduce our uncertainty about what is occurring.

Social referencing first occurs around the age of 8 or 9 months. It is a fairly sophisticated social ability: Infants need it not only to understand the significance of others' behavior, by using such cues as their facial expressions, but also to understand the meaning of those behaviors within the context of a specific situation (Hepach & Westermann, 2013; Mireault et al., 2014; Walle, Reschke & Knothe, 2017).

THEORY OF MIND: UNDERSTANDING WHAT OTHERS ARE THINKING.   As the brain matures and myelination within the frontal lobes becomes more pronounced, children develop more emotional capacity involving self-awareness. In addition, hormonal changes seem to be related to emotions that are more evaluative in nature (Davidson, 2003; Schore, 2003).

As they develop, children become more insightful regarding the motives and reasons behind people's behavior. They begin to understand that their mother is angry because she was late for an appointment, even if they themselves haven't seen her be late. Furthermore, by age 4, preschool children's understanding that people can be fooled and mistaken by physical reality (such as magic tricks involving sleight of hand) becomes surprisingly sophisticated. This increase in understanding helps children become more socially skilled as they gain insight into what others are thinking (Fitzgerald & White, 2002; Eisbach, 2004; Fernández, 2013).

There are limits, however, to 3-year-olds' theory of mind. Although they understand the concept of "pretend," their understanding of "belief" is still not complete. The difficulty experienced by 3-year-olds in comprehending "belief" is illustrated by their performance on the *false belief* task. In the false belief task, preschoolers are shown a doll named Maxi who places chocolate in a cabinet and then leaves. After Maxi is gone, though, his mother moves the chocolate somewhere else.

After viewing these events, a preschooler is asked where Maxi will look for the chocolate when he returns. Three-year-olds answer (erroneously) that Maxi will look for it in the new location. In contrast, 4-year-olds correctly realize that Maxi has the erroneous false belief that the chocolate is still in the cabinet, and that's where he will look for it (Amsterlaw & Wellman, 2006; Brown & Bull, 2007; Lecce et al., 2014).

By the end of the preschool years, most children easily solve false belief problems. One group, however, has considerable difficulties throughout their lifetimes: children with autism spectrum disorder. Children with autism spectrum disorder find it particularly difficult to relate to others, in part because they find it difficult to understand what others are thinking. According to the Centers for Disease Control and Prevention, about 1 in 68 children (primarily males) has autism spectrum disorder, which is characterized by a lack of connection to other people, even parents, and an avoidance of interpersonal situations. Individuals with autism spectrum disorder are bewildered by false belief problems no matter how old they are (Begeer et al., 2012; Carey, 2012; Miller, 2012; Peterson, 2014).

Emotional Development in Middle Childhood and Adolescence

LO 9.5 Summarize emotional development in middle childhood and adolescence, and give examples of emotional self-regulation.

Let's examine some issues of emotional development in middle childhood and adolescence.

MIDDLE CHILDHOOD: EMOTIONAL CONTROL AND EMPATHY. During middle childhood, children's control of their emotions grows. They begin to understand their emotions better, and they are more successful in coping with their emotional highs and lows (Eisenberg, Spinrad, & Sadovsky, 2006; Rothbart, Posner, & Kieras, 2006).

In addition, children become more adept at hiding their emotions from others. Rather than showing their displeasure over a disappointing gift, they learn to hide it in a socially acceptable way. Similarly, they learn to hide their anger with a teacher who is treating them unfairly (Ruihe & Guoliang, 2006; Feldman, 2009).

Children also develop empathy, in which they genuinely experience the emotions of others. Because their cognitive abilities are growing, they are able to take

From Research to Practice
The Second Step Program

Children can vary widely in terms of their emotional control and empathy. Although many children demonstrate both of these skills early in middle childhood, others struggle with controlling their emotions and rarely show empathy, with some being identified as having "limited prosocial emotions" (American Psychiatric Association, 2013, p. 470).

Researchers have examined prevention programs aimed at improving children's understanding of emotions and empathy, including one called the Second Step program. For example, the elementary school version of the Second Step program consists of 22 lessons that focus on emotion management, empathy, problem solving, and skills for learning. This program uses group discussion, puppets, and role-play to keep children actively involved in the lessons. A recent study randomly assigned elementary schools to either the Second Step program or the control group. Results demonstrated that for children starting the school year with social-emotional deficits, the program improved several skills, including emotional management and empathy (Low et al., 2015).

The Second Step program has also been shown to decrease behavior problems and improve learning skills in elementary school children. It has been modified for use with younger and older children as well, and researchers have found the program to be effective for both preschoolers and children in middle school. Second Step is a commercially available program and is currently being used in schools across the United States and internationally (Espelage et al., 2015; Upshur, Heyman, & Wenz-Gross, 2017).

Shared Writing Prompt
What are other ways that a parent or teacher could try to increase emotional control and empathy in children?

the perspective of other children and understand how events are affecting them. For example, a 10-year-old boy may be able to understand the sadness experienced by a classmate whose father has died and feel that sadness himself (Eisenberg & Fabes, 2006; Oğuz & Akyol, 2008).

EMOTIONAL DEVELOPMENT IN ADOLESCENCE

> *Sometimes I have to stop and ask myself what kind of mood I'm in. Am I happy? sad? contemplative? usually contemplative, if I'm bothering to contemplate what kind of mood I'm in. I'm kind of sad because Kyle can't come tonight ... but kind of worried because he's sick. I'm kind of depressed feeling, too. It finally started sinking in a while ago that he's not coming back, that he has finally dropped out of my life as I feared he would.*

Happy ... sad ... contemplative ... worried ... depressed ... afraid. The feelings experienced by adolescents range from the positive to the negative, as this blog comment illustrates. Traditionally, the adolescent period is viewed as among the most emotionally volatile of the entire life span.

How accurate is this view? To answer the question, we first need to consider the role that emotions play during adolescence. For example, consider an adolescent girl who is experiencing sadness. As the definition suggests, sadness produces a feeling that can be differentiated from other emotions. She likely experiences physiological reactions, too, such as an increase in heart rate or sweating, that are part of her emotional reaction. In addition, the sadness has a cognitive element, in which her understanding and evaluation of the meaning of what is happening to her prompt her feelings of sadness.

It's also possible, however, to experience an emotion without the presence of cognitive elements. For example, adolescents may feel the sadness of depression without knowing why they are feeling that way. In the same way, they may react with fear to an unusual or a novel situation without having an awareness or understanding of what is so frightening.

The Instability of Emotions in Adolescence. Are adolescent emotions more volatile than emotions at other stages of life? That's certainly the stereotype. Adolescence has traditionally been seen as a period in which emotions run high and are easily triggered.

The stereotype does have some truth to it. Although not as extreme as the outmoded "storm and stress" view of adolescence would have us believe, emotions do tend to be more volatile during early adolescence. Younger adolescents experience emotional highs and lows, often in rapid succession. In addition, as they enter adolescence, teenagers report that they are less happy than in prior years. They are also more likely to experience mildly negative emotions as they move into adolescence (Rosenbaum & Lewis, 2003; Ackerman & Izard, 2004).

Not only are the emotions more negative than they were in middle childhood, but adolescents' emotional responses are often more extreme than one would expect from the nature of the situation. For example, an adolescent may react with fury to a parent's suggestion that he might consider wearing a jacket to school because it is chilly. Even seemingly innocuous suggestions may be viewed as critical and arouse extremes of emotion.

If there is a positive side to the more explosive nature of adolescents' emotions, it is that even though they may be extreme, they don't necessarily last very long. Partly because adolescents' moods change so frequently, any given emotional response is apt to be replaced by another before much time passes (Rosenbaum & Lewis, 2003).

Why are emotions so unstable during adolescence? One answer comes from work on the neurological underpinnings of emotion, which we discuss next.

The Neurological Basis of Emotion. Emotions produce activation of specific parts of the brain. For instance, the *amygdala*, located in the brain's temporal lobe, is central to the experience of emotions. It provides a link between the perception of an emotion-producing stimulus and later memory of that stimulus. For example, someone who was once frightened by a vicious dog is likely to respond with fear when he later sees the dog. Because of neural pathways connecting the amygdala, visual cortex, and the *hippocampus* (a part of the brain that is involved in the storage of memories), the emotion of fear is experienced almost instantly. The response occurs so quickly that rational thought may not be involved at first—the fear response is literally a kind of "gut reaction" produced by the brain. It is only later that the response will be evaluated more thoroughly using rational thought processes (Adolphs, 2002).

Studies of brain activity help explain the greater volatility of emotions in adolescence than later in life. For example, in one study, adolescents and adults repeatedly viewed faces showing different emotions. Although both age groups showed engagement of the *left ventrolateral prefrontal cortex*, adolescents showed more activity in certain other areas of the brain when viewing familiar faces, depending on the kind of emotion being displayed (see Figure 9-4). These differences suggest that emotional responses may be especially pronounced during adolescence and affect the rationality of adolescents' evaluation of the challenges they encounter and their responses to them (Nelson et al., 2003).

However, the physiological reactivity of emotions is not the full story of emotional responses during adolescence. As we'll see next, adolescents have considerable (and increasing) control over their emotions.

Figure 9-4 Brain Activity and Emotions

Although both adolescents and adults viewing pictures of faces displaying different emotions showed activation of the left ventrolateral prefrontal cortex, compared with adults, adolescents showed more activity than adults in other areas of the brain.
(**Source:** Nelson et al., 2003.)

National Institute of Mental Health

Emotional Self-Regulation. Throughout adolescence, both boys and girls become more adept at controlling their emotions. **Emotional self-regulation** is the ability to adjust emotions to a desired state and level of intensity. When adolescents seek to "keep cool," they are relying on emotional self-regulation.

It's not easy for any of us to regulate our emotions. For example, people asked to hide their responses to the observation of gruesome photos of accident victims show high levels of physiological reactivity as a result of their efforts to suppress their actual emotion. They also have difficulty later in recalling what they viewed. In short, emotional regulation takes both cognitive and physical effort (Richards, Butler, & Gross, 2003).

During childhood, emotional regulation skills improve considerably, and that trend continues throughout adolescence. The demands and challenges that adolescents face lead to improvements in emotion management (Zahn-Waxler et al., 2000; Eisenberg, Spinrad, & Smith, 2004; Graber, 2004).

Adolescents use several strategies to regulate their emotional responses. One is to try to cognitively reappraise events that produce emotional responses. Specifically, they may try to change the way they think about something they have encountered, making it seem less bothersome. For example, an adolescent might try to convince himself that his girlfriend's decision to break up is really a good thing because he didn't like being tied down. If he is able to convince himself of this rationale, his initial sadness or anger might be replaced with more positive (or at least neutral) emotions.

Another emotion-regulating strategy that adolescents can use is to suppress troubling emotions. Using such a strategy involves inhibiting outward signs of inner emotional states, despite experiencing particular emotions internally. Although such a strategy may not make the individuals who are suppressing the emotion feel better about negative emotions they might be experiencing, it can be effective in making others feel better. Learning to "put on" a face appropriate to a particular social situation is an important advance in emotional self-regulation that occurs during adolescence.

emotional self-regulation
the capability to adjust one's emotions to a desired state and level of intensity.

Emotional Difficulties in Adolescence: Anxiety, Depression, and Suicide

LO 9.6   **Identify the causes of adolescent anxiety and depression, and explain the role gender plays in both depression and suicide rates.**

One day in ninth grade it struck Leanne Taunton that she was stuck without hope inside a dreadful world. "It was like the air was a big weight pressing in on me from all sides. I couldn't shake the feeling and I couldn't ignore it. There was nothing I could do."

A friend listened to her sympathetically and invited her to her basement. "We started doing drugs, using whatever was in the medicine cabinet. At first it seemed to offer some relief, but in the end we both had to go home again, if you know what I mean."

One day Leanne grabbed her father's razor, filled up the tub, and slashed her wrists. At the ripe age of 14, she had had enough.

Although the vast majority of teenagers weather the search for identity—as well as other challenges of the age—without major difficulties, some find adolescence very stressful, and some develop severe emotional problems. Three of the most serious are adolescent anxiety, depression, and suicide.

ADOLESCENT ANXIETY.   All adolescents occasionally experience anxiety, a feeling of apprehension or tension in reaction to stressful situations; it is a totally normal reaction to stress.

In some cases, though, adolescents develop anxiety disorders, which are the most prevalent psychological disorder in the age group, striking around 8 percent of the population. *Anxiety disorders* develop when anxiety occurs without external justification, and it impacts normal, everyday functioning. Sometimes anxiety occurs as a result of exposure to a specific stimulus, such as fear of a specific animal or insect, or a fear of crowded places or heights. In other cases, though, anxiety is less specific and may be caused, for instance, by a fear of social situations in general (Merikangas et al., 2009; Stopa et al., 2013).

Adolescents with anxiety disorders can be hypervigilant, worried that their anxiety will be triggered by something in their environment and seeking to avoid situations that can produce anxiety. Moreover, if they cannot avoid anxiety-producing circumstances, they may become overwhelmed and experience physical symptoms such as panic attacks that produce a range of symptoms, including sweating, faintness, or gastric distress (Carleton et al., 2014).

ADOLESCENT DEPRESSION.   No one, including adolescents, is immune to periods of sadness, unhappiness, and feeling emotionally upset. The end of a relationship, failure at an important task, the death of a loved one—all may produce profound feelings of sadness, loss, and grief. In such situations, depression is a typical reaction.

More than a quarter of adolescents report feeling so sad or hopeless for two or more weeks in a row that they stop doing their normal activities. Almost two-thirds of teenagers say they have experienced such feelings at some point. In contrast, only a small minority of adolescents—some 3 percent—experience *major depression,* a full-blown psychological disorder, which is severe and lingers for long periods (Grunbaum, 2001; Galambos, Leadbeater, & Barker, 2004; Auerbach et al., 2015).

Gender, ethnic, and racial differences also affect depression rates. As is true for adults, adolescent girls experience depression more often than boys. Some studies show African American adolescents having a higher rate of depression than white adolescents, though not all research supports this conclusion. Native Americans, too, have higher rates of depression (Li, DiGiuseppe, & Froh, 2006; Sanchez, Lambert, & Ialongo, 2012; Blom et al., 2016).

In cases of severe, long-term depression, biological factors are often involved. Some adolescents do seem genetically predisposed to experience depression, but environmental and social factors related to the extraordinary changes in their social lives also have an impact. An adolescent who loses a loved one to death, for example, or who grows up with an alcoholic or a depressed parent, is at a higher risk of depression. Being unpopular, having few close friends, and being rejected are also associated with adolescent depression (Goldsmith et al., 2002; Eley, Liang, & Plomin, 2004; Zalsman et al., 2006).

Why the depression rate is higher for girls than boys is puzzling. There is little evidence of a link to hormone differences or a particular gene. Some psychologists speculate that stress is greater for girls in adolescence due to the many—often conflicting—demands of the traditional female role. Such conflict may make them feel helpless. Add to this the fact that traditional gender roles still give higher status to men than to women (Nolen-Hoeksema, 2003; Gilbert, 2004; Castelao & Kröner-Herwig, 2013).

Girls' higher levels of depression in adolescence may reflect gender differences in coping with stress rather than differences in mood. Girls may be more likely to react to stress by turning inward, resulting in a sense of helplessness and hopelessness. In contrast, boys more often externalize the stress and act more impulsively or aggressively, or turn to drugs and alcohol (Winstead & Sanchez, 2005; Brown et al., 2012; Anyan & Hjemdal, 2016).

ADOLESCENT SUICIDE.   Adolescent suicide in the United States has tripled in the past 30 years. Overall, one teenage suicide occurs every 90 minutes, for an annual rate of 12.2 suicides per 100,000 adolescents. The reported rate may actually understate the true number; parents and medical personnel often prefer to report a death as an accident rather than suicide (Joe & Marcus, 2003; Conner & Goldston, 2007; Healthychildren.org, 2016).

Even so, suicide is the third most common cause of death for 15- to 24-year-olds, after accidents and homicide. Despite this rise in suicide—more than for other age groups—the highest rate is still found in late adulthood (Healy, 2001; Grunbaum et al., 2002; Joe & Marcus, 2003; Conner & Goldston, 2007).

The rate of adolescent suicide is higher for boys, although girls *attempt* suicide more frequently. Attempts among males are more likely to be fatal because boys tend to use more violent means, such as guns, while girls usually resort to less violent means, such as drug overdose. Some estimates suggest there are as many as 200 attempted suicides by both sexes for every successful one (Dervic et al., 2006; Beauchaine, Crowell, & Hsiao, 2015).

The reasons for the increase in adolescent suicide are unclear. The most obvious explanation is that adolescent stress has increased (Elkind, 1984). But why should

Neuroscience and Development

Therapy Can Change Your Brain

Antidepressants are commonly used to treat mood disorders because they have been shown to make changes in areas of the brain that are associated with depression. For example, people who are depressed tend to have lower levels of a neurotransmitter called norepinephrine, and some antidepressants influence this and other neurotransmitters. However, antidepressants are not the only way to influence the brain. In recent years, researchers have begun investigating how psychosocial therapies can also alter the functioning of the brain (Amick et al., 2015).

One study examined how the brain might be affected when a patient undergoes cognitive-behavioral therapy (CBT), a type of talk therapy with a strong track record for treating depression by helping the patient learn to better challenge distorted negative thoughts (e.g., "I'm a horrible person"). The results of the study showed two important findings. First, after 12 weekly 90-minute sessions of CBT, patients reported being less depressed. Second, this decrease in depression was associated with changes in the brain. Before the therapy, the patients had elevated levels of activity in the medial prefrontal cortex, located in the front of the brain. After CBT, the levels of activity in the medial prefrontal cortex were decreased significantly (Yoshimura et al., 2014).

Overall, this study suggests that, like medication, CBT can alter the brains of people experiencing depression. CBT has also been shown to influence the brains of people experiencing other clinical issues, such as anxiety. In short, it is clear that both psychosocial therapy and medication are able to alter the functioning of the brain and provide effective treatment for a variety of disorders (Goldapple et al., 2004; Porto et al., 2009).

■ How might learning about this type of research affect the type of intervention that someone chooses?

Paul Kitagaki Jr/Newscom

The rate of adolescent suicide has tripled over the past 30 years. These students mourn following the suicide of a classmate.

stress have increased only for teenagers? The suicide rate for other age groups has remained fairly stable over the same period. Though we are not yet sure why adolescent suicide has increased, certain factors raise the risk. Depression is one. Depressed teenagers who feel profound hopelessness are at greater risk for suicide (although most depressed individuals do not commit suicide). Social inhibition, perfectionism, and high levels of stress and anxiety are also related to an increased risk. The easy availability of guns—more prevalent in the United States than in other industrialized nations—contributes to the suicide rate, too (Goldston, 2003; Hetrick et al., 2012).

Some suicide cases are associated with family conflicts and with relationship or school difficulties. Some stem from a history of abuse and neglect. The rate of suicide among drug and alcohol abusers is also relatively high. As shown in Figure 9-5, teens who called a hotline because they were considering suicide mentioned other factors as well (Bergen, Martin, & Richardson, 2003; Wilcox, Conner, & Caine, 2004; Jacobson et al., 2013). (Also see the *Development in Your Life* box.)

Figure 9-5 Adolescent Difficulties

Family, peer relationships, and self-esteem problems were most often mentioned by adolescents contemplating suicide, according to a review of phone calls to a telephone help line.
(**Source:** Boehm & Campbell, 1995.)

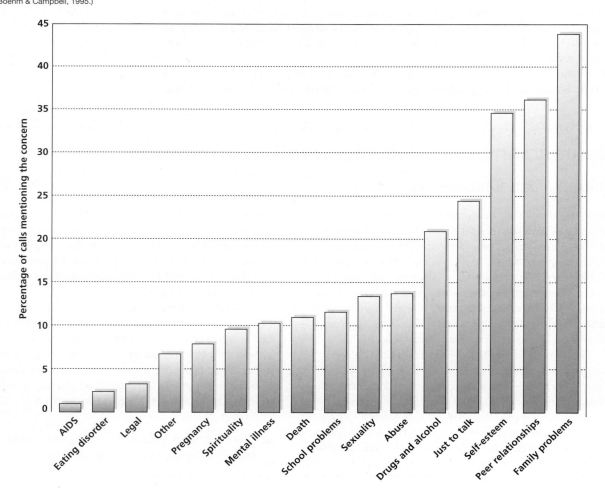

Development in Your Life

Preventing Suicide

If you suspect someone is contemplating suicide, act! Here are several suggestions:

- Talk to the person. Listen with understanding and without judging.

- Talk specifically about suicidal thoughts; ask questions such as: Do you have a plan? Have you bought a gun? Where is it? Have you stockpiled pills? Where are they? The Public Health Service notes that, "contrary to popular belief, such candor will not give a person dangerous ideas or encourage a suicidal act."

- Try to distinguish between general upset and more serious danger, such as when suicide plans *have* been made. If the crisis is acute, *do not leave the person alone*.

- Be supportive, let the person know you care, and try to break down his or her feelings of isolation.

- Take charge of finding help. Do not fear invading the person's privacy. Do not try to handle the problem alone. Get professional help immediately.

- Make the environment safe, removing (not just hiding) weapons, such as guns, razors, scissors, medication, and other potentially dangerous items.

- Do not keep suicide talk or threats secret; these are calls for help and require immediate action.

- Do not challenge, dare, or use verbal shock treatment on the person to correct his or her thinking.

- Make a contract with the person, getting a promise or commitment, preferably in writing, not to attempt suicide until you have talked further.

- Don't be overly reassured by a sudden improvement of mood. Such quick "recoveries" may be merely the relief of deciding to commit suicide or the temporary release of talking to someone; most likely, the underlying problems have not been resolved.

For immediate help with a suicide-related problem, call (800) 273-8255 (the National Suicide Prevention Lifeline) or (800) 621-4000 (the National Runaway Switchboard). Both hotlines are staffed with trained counselors. You can also contact the Lifeline Crisis chat line at http://chat.suicidepreventionlifeline. org/GetHelp/LifelineChat.aspx.

Emotions in Adulthood: Fulfilling Psychological Needs

LO 9.7   **Summarize how the determinants of happiness change throughout adulthood, and identify the three major theories regarding happiness in late adulthood.**

Think back over the past seven days of your life. What made you happiest?

According to research on young adults, it probably wasn't money or material objects. It was more likely the product of feelings of independence, competence, self-esteem, or relating well to other people (Bergsma & Ardelt, 2012; Bojanowska & Zalewska, 2015).

THE ROLE OF PSYCHOLOGICAL NEEDS IN DETERMINING HAPPINESS.   Asked to recall a time when they were happy, young adults are most likely to mention an experience or a moment when their psychological needs rather than material needs were satisfied. Typical answers include being chosen for a new job, developing a deep relationship, or moving into an apartment or a home of their own. Conversely, when they remember times when they were least satisfied, they mention incidents in which basic psychological needs were left unfulfilled.

Culture apparently influences which psychological needs are considered most important to happiness. For example, young adults in Korea more often associate satisfaction with experiences involving other people, whereas young adults in the United States associate satisfaction with experiences relating to the self and self-esteem (Sedikides, Gaertner, & Toguchi, 2003; Jongudomkarn & Camfield, 2006; Demir et al., 2012).

HAPPINESS IN LATE ADULTHOOD: WHAT IS THE SECRET?   At age 77, Elinor Reynolds spends most of her time at home, leading a quiet, routine existence. Never married, Elinor receives visits from her two sisters every few weeks, and some of her nieces and nephews stop by on occasion. But for the most part, she keeps to herself. When asked, she says she is quite happy.

In contrast, Carrie Masterson, also 77, is involved in something different almost every day. If she is not visiting the senior center and participating in some activity, she is out shopping. Her daughter complains that Carrie is "never home" when she tries to reach her by phone, and Carrie replies that she has never been busier—or happier.

Clearly, there is no single way to attain happiness during late adulthood. How people age depends on personality factors and people's circumstances. Some people become progressively less involved with the day-to-day, while others maintain active ties to people and their personal interests. Three major approaches provide explanations: disengagement theory, activity theory, and continuity theory.

disengagement theory

the period in late adulthood that marks a gradual withdrawal from the world on physical, psychological, and social levels.

Disengagement Theory: Gradual Retreat. According to **disengagement theory**, late adulthood often involves a gradual withdrawal from the world on physical, psychological, and social levels. On a physical level, older people have lower energy levels and slow down progressively. Psychologically, they begin to withdraw, showing less interest in the world around them and spending more time looking inward. Finally, on a social level, they engage in fewer interactions—both day-to-day, face-to-face encounters and participation in society as a whole. Older adults also become less involved and invested in the lives of others (Cummings & Henry, 1961; Bishop, 2008; Nair, 2008).

Disengagement theory suggests that withdrawal is a mutual process. Because of norms and expectations about aging, society begins to disengage from those in late adulthood. For example, mandatory retirement ages compel older people to withdraw from work, which accelerates disengagement.

Such withdrawal is not necessarily negative. In fact, most theorists who subscribe to the theory maintain that the outcomes of disengagement are largely positive. As people withdraw, they become more reflective about their lives and less constrained by social roles. Furthermore, they can become more discerning in their social relationships, focusing on those who best meet their needs. Thus, disengagement can be liberating (Settersten, 2002; Wrosch, Bauer, & Scheier, 2005; Liang & Luo, 2012).

Similarly, decreased emotional investment in others can be beneficial. By investing less emotional energy in others, people in late adulthood are better able to adjust to serious illness and death among their peers.

Evidence for disengagement comes from a pioneering study examining close to 300 people age 50 to 90, which found that specific events, such as retirement or the death of a spouse, were accompanied by a gradual disengagement in which the level of social interaction with others plummeted (Cummings & Henry, 1961). According to these results, disengagement was related to successful aging.

activity theory

the theory suggesting that successful aging occurs when people maintain the interests, activities, and social interactions with which they were involved during middle age.

Activity Theory: Continued Involvement. Although early findings were consistent with disengagement theory, later research was not so supportive. For example, a follow-up study found that although some of the subjects were happily disengaged, others, who had remained involved and active, were as happy as—and sometimes happier than—than those who disengaged. Furthermore, people in many non-Western cultures remain engaged, active, and busy throughout old age, and are expected to do so. Clearly, disengagement is not a universal process (Bergstrom & Holmes, 2000; Crosnoe & Elder, 2002; Kuykendall, Tay, & Ng, 2015).

The lack of support for disengagement theory led to an alternative. **Activity theory** suggests that successful aging occurs when people maintain the interests and activities of middle age, along with the amount and type of their social interactions. According to this perspective, happiness and satisfaction with life spring from involvement with the world (Consedine, Magai, & King, 2004; Hutchinson & Wexler, 2007; Rebok et al., 2014).

Activity theory suggests that continuation of activities is important. Even when continuation is no longer possible—such as continuing work after retirement—activity theory argues that successful aging occurs when replacement activities are found.

But activity theory is not the full story. For one thing, activity theory makes little distinction among activities. Not every activity will have an equal impact on a person's satisfaction with life; in fact, the nature and quality of the activities are likely to be more critical than mere quantity or frequency (Adams, 2004).

A more significant concern is that for some people in late adulthood, the principle of "less is more" holds: Less activity brings greater enjoyment because they can slow down and do only the things that bring them the greatest satisfaction. Some people view the ability to moderate their pace as one of the bounties of late adulthood. For them, a relatively inactive, and perhaps even solitary, existence is welcome (Stone, 2003; Hansson & Stroebe, 2007).

From *a social worker's* perspective

How might cultural factors affect an older person's likelihood of pursuing either the disengagement strategy or the activity strategy?

Continuity Theory: A Compromise Position. Neither disengagement theory nor activity theory provides a complete picture of successful aging (Ouwehand, de Ridder, & Bensing, 2007). Consequently, a compromise view has emerged, called continuity theory. **Continuity theory** suggests that people simply need to maintain their desired level of involvement in society in order to maximize their sense of well-being and self-esteem (Whitbourne, 2001; Atchley, 2003; Carmel, 2017).

According to continuity theory, those who were highly active and social will be happiest if they largely remain so. Those who enjoy solitude and solitary interests, such as reading or walks in the woods, will be happiest pursuing that level of sociability (Holahan & Chapman, 2002; Wang et al., 2014).

It is also clear that most older adults experience positive emotions as frequently as younger individuals. Furthermore, they become more skilled at regulating their emotions.

Other factors enhance happiness during late adulthood. The importance of physical and mental health cannot be overestimated, and having enough financial security to provide for basic needs is critical. In addition, a sense of autonomy, independence, and personal control over one's life is a significant advantage (Charles, Mather, & Carstensen, 2003; Vacha-Haase, Hill, & Bermingham, 2012).

continuity theory
the theory suggesting that people need to maintain their desired level of involvement in society in order to maximize their sense of well-being and self-esteem.

Module 9.2 Review

LO 9.3   Identify the emotions infants experience and their ability to decode the emotions of others.

Infants appear to express and to experience emotions, and their emotions broaden in range to reflect increasingly complex emotional states. The ability to decode the nonverbal facial and vocal expressions of others develops early in infants.

LO 9.4   Define social referencing and theory of mind, and explain how they are related to a child's cognitive development.

Social referencing is the intentional search for information about others' feelings to help explain the meaning of uncertain circumstances and events.

LO 9.5   Summarize emotional development in middle childhood and adolescence, and give examples of emotional self-regulation.

During middle childhood, children gain increasing control over their emotions, as well as showing greater empathy. Emotions in adolescence tend to be more changeable and more extreme than in other periods of life.

LO 9.6   Identify the causes of adolescent anxiety and depression, and explain the role gender plays in both depression and suicide rates.

One of the dangers that adolescents face is depression, which affects girls more than boys. Adolescent suicide in the United States has tripled in the past 30 years.

LO 9.7   Summarize how the determinants of happiness change throughout adulthood, and identify the three major theories regarding happiness in late adulthood.

Disengagement theory suggests that older people gradually withdraw from the world, while activity theory suggests that the happiest people continue to be engaged with the world. A compromise theory—continuity theory—may be the most useful approach to successful aging.

Journal Writing Prompt

Applying Lifespan Development: What are some advantages and disadvantages of emotional self-regulation? Are there dangers in too much self-regulation?

PERSONALITY DEVELOPMENT ACROSS THE LIFE SPAN

Lincoln was a difficult baby, his parents both agreed. For one thing, it seemed as if they could never get him to sleep at night. He cried at the slightest noise, a problem since his crib was near the windows facing a busy street. Worse yet, once he started crying, it seemed to take forever to calm him down again. One day his mother, Aisha, was telling her mother-in-law, Mary, about the challenges of being Lincoln's mom. Mary recalled that her own son, Lincoln's father Malcom, had been much the same way. "He was my first child, and I thought this was how all babies acted. So, we just kept trying different ways until we found out how he worked. I remember, we put his crib all over the apartment until we finally found out where he could sleep, and it ended up being in the hallway for a long time. Then his sister, Maleah, came along, and she was so quiet and easy, I didn't know what to do with my extra time!"

As the story of Lincoln's family shows, babies are not all alike, and neither are their families. As we'll see, some of the differences among people seem to be present from birth.

Temperament: Stabilities in Infant Behavior

LO 9.8 Identify the major dimensions of temperament, and explain how temperament is affected by a child's environment.

To understand how one individual differs from another, we need to consider the origins of **personality**, the sum total of the enduring characteristics that differentiate one person from another. From birth onward, children begin to show unique, stable traits and behaviors that ultimately lead to their development as distinct, special individuals.

The difference between Malcom and Maleah, described above, reflect differences in temperament. **Temperament** encompasses patterns of arousal and emotionality that are consistent and enduring characteristics of an individual (Kochanska et al., 2004; Chen & Schmidt, 2015; Gartstein et al., 2017).

Temperament refers to *how* children behave, as opposed to *what* they do or *why* they do it. Infants show temperamental differences in general disposition from the time of birth, largely due initially to genetic factors, and temperament tends to be fairly stable well into adolescence. However, temperament is not fixed and unchangeable: Childrearing practices can modify temperament significantly. In fact, some children show little consistency in temperament from one age to another (de Lauzon-Guillain et al., 2012; Kusangi, Nakano, & Kondo-Ikemura, 2014).

Temperament is reflected in several dimensions of behavior. One central dimension is *activity level*, which reflects the degree of overall movement. Some babies are relatively placid, and their movements are slow and almost leisurely. In contrast, the activity level of other infants is quite high, with strong, restless movements of the arms and legs.

Another important dimension of temperament is the nature and quality of an infant's mood, and in particular a child's *irritability*. Irritable infants fuss a great deal, and they are easily upset. They are also difficult to soothe when they do begin to cry. (Other aspects of temperament are listed in Table 9-2.)

CATEGORIZING TEMPERAMENT: EASY, DIFFICULT, AND SLOW-TO-WARM BABIES. Because temperament can be viewed along so many dimensions, some researchers have asked whether broader categories can be used to describe children's overall behavior. According to Alexander Thomas and Stella Chess, who carried out a large-scale study of a group of infants that has come to be known as the New York

personality
the sum total of the enduring characteristics that differentiate one individual from another.

temperament
patterns of arousal and emotionality that are consistent and enduring characteristics of an individual.

Table 9-2 Some Dimensions of Temperament in Infants, with Behavioral Indicators

Dimension	Definition
Activity level	**High:** wriggles while diaper is changed **Low:** lies still while being dressed
Approach-withdrawal	**Approach orientation:** accepts novel foods and toys easily **Withdrawal orientation:** cries when a stranger comes near
Quality of mood	**Negative:** cries when carriage is rocked **Positive:** smiles or smacks lips when tasting new food
Distractibility	**Low:** continues crying even when diaper is changed **High:** stops fussing when held and rocked
Rhythmicity	**Regular:** has consistent feeding schedule **Irregular:** has varying sleep and waking schedule
Threshold of responsiveness	**High:** not startled by sudden noises or bright lights **Low:** pauses sucking on bottle at approach of parent or slight noise

(**Source:** Thomas, Chess, & Birch, 1968.)

Longitudinal Study (Thomas & Chess, 1980), babies can be described according to one of several profiles:

- **Easy babies** have a positive disposition. Their body functions operate regularly, and they are adaptable. They are generally positive, showing curiosity about new situations, and their emotions are moderate or low in intensity. This category applies to about 40 percent (the largest number) of infants.
- **Difficult babies** have more negative moods and are slow to adapt to new situations. When confronted with a new situation, they tend to withdraw. About 10 percent of infants belong in this category.
- **Slow-to-warm babies** are inactive, showing relatively calm reactions to their environment. Their moods are generally negative, and they withdraw from new situations, adapting slowly. Approximately 15 percent of infants are slow to warm.

The remaining 35 percent of babies cannot be consistently categorized. These children show a variety of combinations of characteristics. For instance, one infant may have relatively sunny moods but react negatively to new situations, or another may show little stability of any sort in terms of general temperament.

THE CONSEQUENCES OF TEMPERAMENT: DOES TEMPERAMENT MATTER? One obvious question to emerge from the findings of the relative stability of temperament is whether a particular kind of temperament is beneficial. The answer seems to be that no single type of temperament is invariably good or bad. Instead, children's long-term adjustment depends on the **goodness of fit** of their particular temperament and the nature and demands of the environment in which they find themselves. For instance, children with a low activity level and low irritability may do particularly well in an environment in which they are left to explore on their own and are allowed largely to direct their own behavior. In contrast, high-activity-level, highly irritable children may do best with greater direction, which permits them to channel their energy in particular directions (Thomas & Chess, 1980; Schoppe-Sullivan et al., 2007).

Some research does suggest that certain temperaments are more adaptive than others. Difficult children, in general, are more likely to show behavior problems by school age than those classified in infancy as easy children. But not all difficult children experience problems. The key determinant seems to be the way parents react to their infant's difficult behavior. If they react by showing anger and inconsistency—responses that their child's difficult, demanding behavior readily evokes—then the child is more likely to experience behavior problems. In contrast, parents who display more warmth and consistency in their responses are more likely to have children who avoid later problems (Pauli-Pott, Mertesacker, & Bade, 2003; Salley, Miller, & Bell, 2013; Sayal et al., 2014).

easy babies
babies who have a positive disposition; their body functions operate regularly, and they are adaptable.

difficult babies
babies who have negative moods and are slow to adapt to new situations; when confronted with a new situation, they tend to withdraw.

slow-to-warm babies
babies who are inactive, showing relatively calm reactions to their environment; their moods are generally negative, and they withdraw from new situations, adapting slowly.

goodness of fit
the notion that development is dependent on the degree of match between children's temperament and the nature and demands of the environment in which they are being raised.

Erikson's Theory of Psychosocial Development

LO 9.9 Differentiate the eight stages of Erikson's theory of psychosocial development, and explain what factors determine the outcome at each stage.

Psychoanalyst Erik Erikson argued that personality starts in infancy and continues across the entire life span. **Erikson's theory of psychosocial development** considers how individuals come to understand themselves and the meaning of others'—and their own—behavior (Erikson, 1963). Building on the *psychodynamic perspective*, which suggests that unconscious influences affect behavior, Erikson's theory suggests that developmental change occurs throughout people's lives in eight distinct stages, starting in infancy.

PSYCHOSOCIAL DEVELOPMENT DURING INFANCY AND PRESCHOOL. According to Erikson, infants' early experiences are responsible for shaping one of the key aspects of their personalities: whether they will be basically trusting or mistrustful. The theory suggests that during the first 18 months of life, we pass through the **trust-versus-mistrust stage**, developing a sense of trust or mistrust, largely depending on how well our caretakers meet our needs.

Mary's attention to Malcom's needs, in the example at the beginning of the module, probably helped him develop a basic sense of trust in the world. Erikson suggests that if infants are able to develop trust, they experience a sense of hope, which permits them to feel they can fulfill their needs successfully. In contrast, feelings of mistrust lead infants to see the world as harsh and unfriendly, and they may have later difficulties in forming close bonds with others.

During the end of infancy, children enter the **autonomy-versus-shame-and-doubt stage**, which lasts from around 18 months to 3 years. In this period, children develop independence and autonomy if parents encourage exploration and freedom within safe boundaries. However, if children are restricted and overly protected, they feel shame, self-doubt, and unhappiness.

In the early part of the preschool period, children are ending the autonomy-versus-shame-and-doubt stage and entering what Erikson called the **initiative-versus-guilt stage**, which lasts from around age 3 to 6. It is during this period that children's views of themselves undergo major change as preschoolers face conflicts between the desire to act independently of their parents and the guilt that comes from the unintended consequences of their actions. In essence, preschoolers come to realize that they are persons in their own right, and they begin to make decisions and to shape the kind of persons that they will become.

Parents who react positively to this transformation toward independence can help their children resolve the opposing forces of initiative and guilt that characterize this period. By providing their children with opportunities to act with self-reliance, while still giving them direction and guidance, parents can support and encourage their children's initiative. However, parents who discourage their children's efforts to seek independence may contribute to a sense of guilt that persists throughout their lives.

PSYCHOSOCIAL DEVELOPMENT DURING MIDDLE CHILDHOOD AND ADOLESCENCE. Middle childhood encompasses the **industry-versus-inferiority stage**. Lasting from roughly age 6 to age 12, this stage is characterized by a focus on efforts to attain competence in meeting the challenges presented by parents, peers, school, clubs and groups to which they belong, and the other complexities of the modern world.

As they move through middle childhood, children direct their energies not only to mastering what they are presented in school—an enormous body of information—but to making a place for themselves in their social worlds. Success in these efforts brings with it feelings of mastery and proficiency and a growing sense of competence.

Erikson's theory of psychosocial development
the theory that considers how individuals come to understand themselves and the meaning of others'—and their own—behavior.

trust-versus-mistrust stage
according to Erikson, the period during which infants develop a sense of trust or mistrust, largely depending on how well their needs are met by their caregivers.

autonomy-versus-shame-and-doubt stage
the period during which, according to Erikson, toddlers (age 18 months to 3 years) develop independence and autonomy if they are allowed the freedom to explore, or shame and self-doubt if they are restricted and overprotected.

initiative-versus-guilt stage
according to Erikson, the period during which children age 3 to 6 experience conflict between independence of action and the sometimes negative results of that action.

industry-versus-inferiority stage
the period from age 6 to 12 characterized by a focus on efforts to attain competence in meeting the challenges presented by parents, peers, school, and the other complexities of the modern world.

However, difficulties in this stage lead to feelings of failure and inadequacy. Children may come to feel unskilled and incapable. As a result, they may withdraw both from academic pursuits, showing less interest and motivation to excel, and from interactions with peers.

Developing industriousness during the middle childhood years has lasting consequences. For example, one study examined how childhood industriousness and hard work were related to adult behavior by following a group of 450 men over a 35-year period, starting in early childhood. The men who were most industrious and hardworking during childhood were most successful as adults, both in occupational attainment and in their personal lives. Childhood industriousness was more closely associated with adult success than was intelligence or family background (Vaillant & Vaillant, 1981).

During adolescence, teenagers enter the **identity-versus-identity-confusion stage**. In this period, adolescents attempt to determine what is unique and distinctive about themselves and the roles they will play in their future lives. They may explore different roles, narrowing their choices and ideally finding out who they really are.

Adolescents with difficulties in resolving this stage may find it difficult to form and maintain close relationships. Alternatively, they may adopt socially inappropriate roles and fail to forge an acceptable identity.

identity-versus-identity-confusion stage
the period during which teenagers seek to determine what is unique and distinctive about themselves.

PSYCHOSOCIAL DEVELOPMENT DURING EARLY ADULTHOOD. Erikson regarded young adulthood as the time of the **intimacy-versus-isolation stage**, which spans the period of postadolescence into the early 30s. During this period, the focus is on developing close, intimate relationships with others.

To Erikson, intimacy comprises several aspects. One is selflessness, the sacrifice of one's own needs to those of another. Another is sexuality, the experience of joint pleasure from focusing not just on one's own gratification but also on that of one's partner. Finally, there is deep devotion, marked by efforts to fuse one's identity with the identity of a partner.

According to Erikson, those who experience difficulties during this stage are often lonely, isolated, and fearful of relationships. Their difficulties may stem from an earlier failure to develop a strong identity. In contrast, young adults who are able to form intimate relationships on a physical, intellectual, and emotional level successfully resolve the crisis of this stage of development.

intimacy-versus-isolation stage
according to Erikson, the period of postadolescence into the early 30s that focuses on developing close relationships with others.

PSYCHOSOCIAL DEVELOPMENT DURING MIDLIFE: ERIKSON'S STAGE OF GENERATIVITY VERSUS STAGNATION. Psychoanalyst Erik Erikson characterized midlife as a period of **generativity-versus-stagnation stage**, the seventh of his eight stages of psychosocial development. One's middle adulthood, according to Erikson, is either spent in generativity—making a contribution to family, community, work, and society—or in stagnation. Generative people strive to guide and encourage future generations. Often, people find generativity through parenting, but other roles can fill this need, such as working directly with young people, acting as mentors. Or the need for generativity may be satisfied through creative and artistic output, seeking to leave a lasting contribution. The focus of generativity, then, is beyond the self, as one looks toward the continuation of one's own life through others (Penningroth & Scott, 2012; Schoklitsch & Baumann, 2012; Serrat et al., 2017).

A lack of psychological growth in this period results in stagnation. Focusing on their own trivial activities, people may feel they have contributed little to the world, that their presence has counted for little. Some people find themselves floundering, still seeking new, potentially more fulfilling careers. Others become frustrated and bored.

generativity-versus-stagnation stage
according to Erikson, the stage during middle adulthood in which people consider their contributions to family and society.

EGO INTEGRITY VERSUS DESPAIR: ERIKSON'S FINAL STAGE. Erikson characterizes late adulthood as the time when people move into the last of life's eight stages of psychosocial development. Labeled the **ego-integrity-versus-despair stage**, this period is characterized by a process of looking back over one's life, evaluating it, and coming to terms with it.

ego-integrity-versus-despair stage
Erikson's final stage of life, characterized by a process of looking back over one's life, evaluating it, and coming to terms with it.

People who are successful in this stage of development experience satisfaction and accomplishment, which Erikson terms "integrity." When people achieve integrity, they feel they have fulfilled the possibilities that have come their way in life, and they have few regrets. Other people look back on their lives with dissatisfaction. They may feel that they have missed important opportunities and have not accomplished what they wished. Such individuals may be unhappy, depressed, angry, or despondent over what they have done, or failed to do, with their lives—in short, they despair.

ERIKSON'S APPROACH IN PERSPECTIVE. Erikson's approach has been enormously influential. His theory is comprehensive, covering the entire life span. It has received general support from subsequent research (Whitbourne et al., 1992).

Yet, like any theory, it has its weaknesses. Not everyone passes through the stages in the sequence that Erikson has laid out. In addition, the theory is troubling today because he limited healthy intimacy to heterosexuality. Same-sex partnerships, couples who are childless by choice, and other relationships different from Erikson's ideal were regarded as less than satisfactory. Erikson also focused more on men than on women and did not consider racial and ethnic identity, greatly limiting the applicability of his theory (Yip, Seaton, & Sellers, 2006). Furthermore, contemporary research has taken a more refined approach and has provided some alternatives. We'll discuss several alternative views of development, focusing on particular periods of life.

Moving Beyond Erikson: Personality Development During Adulthood

LO 9.10 Summarize the contributions of Vaillant, Gould, Levinson, and Peck to our understanding of personality development in adulthood, and discuss the research on midlife crisis.

Some theorists have paid particular attention to personality development and change during adulthood, building and moving beyond Erikson's psychosocial theory. We'll look at several approaches.

OTHER THEORISTS: VAILLANT AND GOULD. Developmentalist George Vaillant (1977) argues that an important period, which he calls *keeping the meaning versus rigidity*, takes place between the ages of about 45 and 55. During that period, adults seek to extract the meaning from their lives and to "keep the meaning" by developing an acceptance of the strengths and weaknesses of others. Although they recognize the world is not perfect and has many shortcomings, they strive to safeguard their world, and they are relatively content. People who are not able to keep the meaning in their lives risk becoming rigid and increasingly isolated from others.

Psychiatrist Roger Gould (1978, 1980) offered an alternative to Vaillant's views. While he agrees that people move through a series of stages and potential crises, he suggests that adults pass through a series of seven stages associated with specific age periods (see Table 9-3). According to Gould, people in their late 30s and early 40s begin to feel a sense of urgency in terms of attaining life's goals as they realize that their time is limited. Coming to grips with the reality that life is finite can propel people toward adult maturity.

Gould based his model of adult development on a relatively small sample and relied heavily on his own clinical judgments. In fact, little research has supported his description of the various stages, which was heavily influenced by the psychoanalytic perspective.

LEVINSON'S SEASONS OF LIFE. Another alternative to Erikson's work is psychologist Daniel Levinson's *seasons of life* theory. According to Levinson (1986, 1992), who intensively interviewed a group of men, the early 40s are a period of transition and crisis. Levinson suggests that adult men experience a series of stages beginning with their entry into early adulthood at around age 20 and continuing into middle adulthood. The beginning stages have to do with leaving one's family and entering the adult world.

Table 9-3 Summary of Gould's Transformations in Adult Development

Stage	Approximate Age Range	At This Stage, People Typically:
1	16 to 18	Plan to leave home and terminate parental control
2	18 to 22	Leave the family and begin to reorient toward peers
3	22 to 28	Become independent and commit to career and (often) spouse and children
4	29 to 34	Question themselves and experience confusion; they may become dissatisfied with marriage and career
5	35 to 43	Feel an urgent need to achieve life goals, becoming increasingly aware of the passage and limits of time; they often realign life goals
6	43 to 53	Settle down at last, with acceptance of their lives
7	53 to 60	Grow more tolerant, accepting their past; they become less negative and generally more mellow

(**Source:** Based on Gould, 1978.)

At around age 40 or 45, however, people move into a period that Levinson calls the midlife transition. The *midlife transition* is a time of questioning. People begin to focus on the finite nature of life, and they question some of their everyday, fundamental assumptions. They experience the first signs of aging, and they confront the knowledge that they will be unable to accomplish all their aims before they die.

In Levinson's view, this period of assessment may lead to a **midlife crisis**, a stage of uncertainty and indecision brought about by the realization that life is finite. Facing signs of physical aging, men may also discover that even the accomplishments of which they are proudest have brought them less satisfaction than they expected. Looking toward the past, they may seek to define what went wrong and look for ways to correct their past mistakes. The midlife crisis, then, is a painful and tumultuous period of questioning.

Levinson's view is that most people are susceptible to a fairly profound midlife crisis. But before accepting his perspective, we need to consider some critical drawbacks in his research. First, his initial theorizing was based on a group of only 40 men, and his work with women was carried out years later and once again on only a small sample. Furthermore, Levinson overstated the consistency and generality of the patterns he found in the samples he used to derive his theory. As we consider next, the notion of a universal midlife crisis has come under considerable criticism (McFadden & Rawson Swan, 2012; Thorpe et al., 2014).

THE MIDLIFE CRISIS: REALITY OR MYTH? Central to Levinson's model of the seasons of life is the concept of midlife crisis, a period in the early 40s presumed to be marked by intense psychological turmoil. The notion has taken on a life of its own: There is a general expectation in U.S. society that the age of 40 represents an important psychological juncture.

There's a problem, though, with such a view: The evidence for a widespread midlife crisis is simply lacking. In fact, most research suggests that for most people, the passage into middle age is relatively tranquil. The majority of people regard midlife as a particularly rewarding time. If they are parents, for example, their children often have passed the period when childrearing is physically demanding, and in some cases children have left the home altogether, allowing parents the opportunity to rekindle an intimacy that they may have lost. Many middle-aged people find that their careers have blossomed, and far from being in crisis, they may feel quite content with their lot in life. Rather than looking toward the future, they focus on the present, seeking to maximize their ongoing involvement with family, friends, and other social groups. Those who feel regret over the course of their lives may be motivated to change the direction of their lives, and those who do change their lives end up better off psychologically (Stewart & Vandewater, 1999; Robinson, Demetre & Litman, 2017).

Furthermore, how one feels about one's age is actually associated with health outcomes. People who feel younger than their chronological age are more likely to

midlife crisis
a stage of uncertainty and indecision brought about by the realization that life is finite.

Figure 9-6 Feeling Younger and Age of Death

People who said they felt younger than their chronological age were more likely to live longer than those who felt older than their chronological age.

(**Source:** Based on Rippon & Steptoe, 2015.)

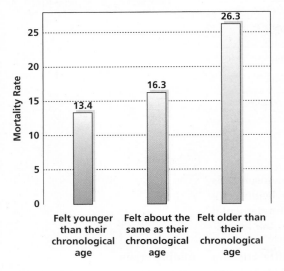

redefinition of self versus preoccupation with work role

the theory that those in old age must redefine themselves in ways that do not relate to their work roles or occupations.

body transcendence versus body preoccupation

a period in which people must learn to cope with and move beyond changes in physical capabilities as a result of aging.

ego transcendence versus ego preoccupation

the period in which elderly people must come to grips with their coming death.

avoid death than those who feel older than their chronological age (see Figure 9-6; Miche et al., 2014; Steptoe, Deaton, & Stone, 2015)

In short, the evidence for a midlife crisis experienced by most people is no more compelling than the evidence for a stormy adolescence. Yet, like that notion, the idea that the midlife crisis is nearly universal seems unusually well entrenched in "common wisdom." Why is this the case?

One reason may be that people who do experience turmoil during middle age tend to be relatively obvious and easily remembered by observers. For instance, a 40-year-old man who divorces his wife, replaces his sedate Ford station wagon with a red Audi convertible, and marries a much younger woman is likely to be more conspicuous than a happily married man who remains with his spouse (and Ford) throughout middle adulthood. As a consequence, we are more likely to notice and recall marital difficulties than the lack of them. In this way the myth of a blustery and universal midlife crisis is perpetuated. The reality, though, is quite different: For most people, a midlife crisis is more the stuff of fiction than of reality. For some people midlife may not bring many changes at all. And as we consider in the *Developmental Diversity and Your Life* feature, in some cultures, middle age is not even considered a separate period of life.

PERSONALITY IN LATE ADULTHOOD. Although Erikson's approach provides a picture of the broad possibilities of later adulthood, other theorists offer a more differentiated view of the final stage of life. Psychologist Robert Peck (1968) suggests that personality development in people in late adulthood is occupied by three major developmental tasks.

In Peck's view—part of a comprehensive description of change across adulthood—the first task in old age is to redefine oneself in ways that do not relate to work roles or occupations. He labels this stage the **redefinition of self versus preoccupation with work role**. As we will see, the changes that occur when people stop working can trigger a difficult adjustment in how they view themselves. Peck suggests that people must adjust their values to place less emphasis on themselves as workers or professionals and more on attributes that don't involve work, such as being a grandparent or a gardener.

The second major developmental task in late adulthood, according to Peck, is **body transcendence versus body preoccupation**. Elderly individuals can undergo significant changes in their physical abilities as a result of aging. In the body-transcendence-versus-body-preoccupation stage, people must learn to cope with and move beyond those physical changes (transcendence). If they don't, they become preoccupied with their physical deterioration, to the detriment of their personality development.

The third developmental task in old age is **ego transcendence versus ego preoccupation**, in which elderly people must come to grips with their coming death. They need to understand that, although death is inevitable and probably not too far off, they have made contributions to society. If they see these contributions, which can take the form of children or work and civic activities, as lasting beyond their own lives, they will experience ego transcendence. If not, they may become preoccupied with asking whether their lives had value and worth to society.

LEVINSON'S FINAL SEASON: THE WINTER OF LIFE. Daniel Levinson's theory of adult development does not focus as much on the challenges that aging adults must overcome. Instead, he looks at the processes that can lead to personality change as we grow old. According to Levinson, people enter late adulthood by passing through a transition stage that typically occurs around 60 to 65 (Levinson, 1986, 1992). During this stage, people come to view themselves as entering late adulthood—or, ultimately, as being "old." Knowing full well society's negative stereotypes about elderly individuals, they struggle with the notion that they are now in this category.

Developmental Diversity and Your Life

Middle Age: In Some Cultures It Doesn't Exist

There's no such thing as middle age.

At least one can draw that conclusion by looking at the lives of women living in the Oriya culture in Orissa, India. According to research carried out by developmental anthropologist Richard Shweder, who studied how high-caste Hindu women viewed the process of aging, a distinct period of middle age does not exist. These women view their life course not on the basis of chronological age but on the nature of one's social responsibility, family management issues, and moral sense at a given time (Shweder, 2003).

The model of aging of the Oriyan woman is based on two phases of life: life in her father's house (*bapa gharo*), followed by life in her husband's mother's house (*sasu gharo*). These two segments make sense in the context of Oriyan family life, which consists of multigenerational households in which marriages are arranged. After they are married, husbands remain with their parents, and wives are expected to move into the husband's parents' household. At the time of marriage, a wife's social status is seen as having changed from a child (someone's daughter) to a sexually active female (a daughter-in-law).

The shift from child to daughter-in-law typically occurs around age 18 to 20. However, chronological age per se does not mark significant boundaries in life for Oriyan women, nor do physical changes, such as the onset of menstruation and its cessation at menopause. Instead, it is the change from daughter to daughter-in-law that brings about a significant alteration in social responsibility. For instance, women must shift their focus from their own parents to the parents of their husband, and they must become sexually active in order to reproduce the husband's family line.

To a Western eye, the description of the life course of these Indian women suggests that they might perceive their lives as restricted because in most cases they have no careers outside the home, but they do not see themselves in this light. In fact, in the Oriya culture, domestic work is highly respected and valued. Furthermore, Oriyan women perceive themselves as more cultured and civilized than men, who must work outside the home.

In short, the notion of a separate middle age is clearly a cultural construction. The significance of a particular age range differs significantly depending on the culture in which one lives.

Shrikrishna Paranjpe/Alamy

Some women living in the Oriya culture in Orissa, India, view their life course not on the basis of chronological age, but on the nature of one's social responsibility, family management issues, and moral sense at a given period.

From *a health-care worker's* perspective

What approaches might a nursing home develop to meet the needs of elders with differing personalities?

According to Levinson, people come to realize that they are no longer on the center stage but are playing bit parts. This loss of power, respect, and authority may be difficult for individuals accustomed to having control in their lives.

However, people in late adulthood can serve as resources to younger individuals, and they may find that they are viewed as "venerated elders" whose advice is sought and relied upon. Furthermore, old age can bring a new freedom to do things simply for enjoyment and pleasure, rather than as obligations.

LIFE REVIEW AND REMINISCENCE: THE COMMON THEME OF ADULT PERSONALITY DEVELOPMENT. *Life review*, in which people examine and evaluate their lives, is a major thread running through the work of Erikson, Peck, and Levinson and a common theme among personality theorists who focus on late adulthood.

According to gerontologist Robert Butler (2002), life review is triggered by the increasingly obvious prospect of death. People look back on their lives, remembering and reconsidering what has happened to them. Far from being a harmful process of reliving the past, wallowing in past problems, and reviving old wounds, life review usually leads to a better understanding of the past. People may resolve lingering problems and conflicts with others, such as an estrangement from a child, and they may feel they can face their current lives with greater serenity (Korte, Westerhof, & Bohlmeijer, 2012; Latorre et al., 2015; Bergström, 2017).

Life review offers other benefits, including a sense of mutuality, a feeling of interconnectedness with others. Moreover, it can be a source of social interaction, as older adults share their experiences with others (Parks, Sanna, & Posey, 2003).

Reminiscence may even have cognitive benefits, improving memory. By reflecting on the past, people activate a variety of memories, which may trigger other memories and bring back sights, sounds, and even smells of the past. However, life review can sometimes produce declines in psychological functioning. If people become obsessive about the past, reliving old insults and mistakes that cannot be rectified, they may end up feeling guilt, depression, and anger against acquaintances who may not even still be alive.

Overall, however, the process of life review and reminiscence can play an important role by providing continuity between past and present and increasing awareness of the contemporary world. It can also lead to new insights into the past and into others, allowing people to continue personality growth and to function more effectively in the present (Coleman, 2005; Haber, 2006; Alwin, 2012).

Trait Approaches to Personality

LO 9.11 **Describe the Big Five personality traits, and summarize how genetics and environment interact in shaping personality.**

Roberto is moody, and it makes him hard to get along with.
Jake is a happy-go-lucky, cheerful kind of guy who has a lot of friends.
Rebecca is hardworking and conscientious, a very serious person, and that's why she's at the top of her high school class.

Moody … happy-go-lucky … cheerful … hardworking … conscientious. When we describe adolescents and seek to understand the reasons behind their behavior, we typically use specific traits to describe them. Furthermore, we usually assume that if someone is happy-go-lucky and cheerful in one situation, he or she is happy-go-lucky and cheerful in other situations (Gilbert, Miller, & Ross, 1998; Mischel, 2004).

But people have many traits. How do we decide which of the traits are the most important, the ones that are central to their personality? To answer the question, developmentalists have developed a perspective of personality known as *trait theory*. **Traits** are enduring dimensions of personality characteristics along which people differ.

traits
enduring dimensions of personality characteristics along which people differ.

Trait approaches—which offer an alternative to Erikson's stage theory and psychodynamic approach—do not assume that some people have a trait and others do not. Instead, they suggest that all individuals have certain traits, but to a greater or lesser degree. For example, all people might be assumed to have a "trustworthiness" trait, except that some are relatively trustworthy while others are relatively untrustworthy. In this case, the trustworthy people would be said to have the trait to a greater degree, while others have it to a lesser extent.

THE BIG FIVE PERSONALITY TRAITS: MAPPING PERSONALITY. Using a variety of sophisticated statistical techniques, personality research specialists have identified a set of five broad trait factors that describe basic personality. Known as the *Big Five personality traits* (which you can remember more easily by using the acronym OCEAN for the first letters of each trait), these traits are:

- Openness, a person's level of curiosity and interest in new experiences
- Conscientiousness, a person's tendencies to be organized and responsible
- Extraversion, how outgoing or shy a person is

- Agreeableness, how easygoing and helpful a person tends to be
- Neuroticism, the degree to which a person is moody, anxious, and self-critical

The Big Five have been found to reflect the basic core traits not only in adolescents but also in a variety of populations, including children, older adults, and non-English speakers. Furthermore, cross-cultural studies have found them in a variety of cultures ranging from across the Americas and Europe to the Middle East to Africa (Rossier, Dahourou, & McCrae, 2005; Hahn, Gottschling, & Spinath, 2012; Curtis, Windsor, & Soubelet, 2015).

Although most work examining the Big Five has involved adults, research involving children and adolescents has been highly supportive of the trait approach. For example, the Big Five trait of conscientiousness was associated with more decisiveness about career choices in adolescents in middle and high school. In addition, Big Five traits are related to deviant behavior in adolescents. For instance, one study found that low agreeableness is associated with impulsivity, instability, and social deviance in 13- and 16-year-old boys (Lounsbury, Hutchens, & Loveland, 2005; Lynam et al., 2005).

THE STABILITY OF PERSONALITY.   It's clear that the Big Five approach to personality, and trait approaches more broadly, provides a good description of personality. But an important question remains: How stable are personality traits across the life span? The answer is that although personality traits are somewhat less stable in childhood and adolescence than in the later stages of life, they are relatively consistent. The personality traits that children and adolescents hold may manifest themselves in different ways over the life span, but the particular constellation of traits that describes an individual is fairly consistent (Debast et al., 2014; Mõttus, Johnson, & Deary, 2012; Mõttus et al., 2017).

For example, an adolescent who is high on the Big Five trait of conscientiousness may be a highly organized student who takes pains to meet deadlines and carefully completes assignments. When he was in kindergarten, he may have carefully arranged his toys, neatly placing each of his action figures on shelves over his bed. As an older adult, he may demonstrate his high conscientiousness by precisely arranging the tools in his garage.

In the same way, we find that adolescents who are well adjusted tend to have been well adjusted during middle childhood—and are more likely to be well adjusted in later adulthood. Similarly, infants and toddlers who are easily frustrated and angered and who show more negative emotions as infants are more likely to evolve into adolescents who are easily frustrated and angered and behave more aggressively (Hart et al., 1998; Leve, Kim, & Pears, 2005; Baay et al., 2015).

PERSONALITY AND THE INTERACTION OF GENETICS AND THE ENVIRONMENT.   Traits related to temperament are not the only personality characteristics affected by heredity. The importance of genetics in shaping personality is highlighted by the work of behavioral geneticists and evolutionary psychologists. These scientists believe that personality is determined largely by combinations of inherited genes, similar to the way in which our height and eye color are largely an outcome of genetic contributions from our ancestors. The evolutionary approach argues that personality traits that were beneficial to the survival and reproductive success of our ancestors are more likely to be maintained and passed on to subsequent generations.

Studies of personality traits in genetically identical twins illustrate the importance of heredity in personality development (Tellegen et al., 1988). Identical twins who were raised apart from one another have similar personalities on a number of major dimensions, even when they were separated at an early age and experienced dissimilar upbringings. For example, the traits of social potency (the degree to which a person assumes mastery and leadership roles in social situations) and traditionalism (the tendency to follow authority) have particularly strong genetic components. In contrast, other traits, such as achievement and social closeness, have relatively weak genetic components (see Figure 2-8 for a list of personality traits that are strongly associated with genetic factors).

Although it is clear that genetics plays an important role in determining personality, environmental influences also have a significant effect in making these traits consistent throughout the life span. In fact, the environment tends to reinforce inherited traits. For example, a child who is active and aggressive might gravitate toward sports, whereas a more reserved child may be more engaged by academics or solitary pursuits, such as computer games or drawing. At the same time, both children may pay less attention to those aspects of the environment that are less compatible with their genetic endowments.

Thus, two adolescents may be checking out school announcements on their high school's website. One may notice an announcement advertising tryouts for an intramural baseball team, while her less coordinated but more musically endowed friend might be more apt to pay attention to the notice recruiting students for an after-school chorus. In each case, the adolescent is attending to those aspects of the environment in which her genetically determined temperament can flourish.

In other cases, the genetically driven temperament may *evoke* certain environmental influences. For instance, a child's demanding behavior may cause parents to be more attentive to the child's needs than would be the case if he or she were less demanding. In this case, the inherited traits are influencing the environment.

It is important to remember that temperament is not destiny. For instance, some individuals show relatively little consistency in temperament from one age to another.

Childrearing practices, too, can alter temperamental predispositions. An example is the temperamental trait of physiological reactivity, which we discussed earlier. A small percentage of individuals are born with temperaments that produce a high degree of physiological reactivity. Having a tendency to shrink from anything unusual, as infants they react to novel stimuli with a rapid increase in heartbeat and unusual excitability of the limbic system of the brain. Such heightened reactivity to stimuli at the start of life, which seems to be linked to inherited factors, is likely to cause them, by the time they are 4 or 5 and continuing through adolescence and later adulthood, to be considered shy by parents, teachers, and friends. But not always: Some of them behave indistinguishably from their peers at the same age (Kagan & Snidman, 1991; Kagan, Arcus, & Snidman, 1993; McCrae et al., 2000).

What makes the difference? The answer seems to be the environment in which they are raised. Those whose parents encourage them to be outgoing by arranging new opportunities for them may overcome their shyness by the time they reach adolescence. In contrast, children raised in a stressful environment marked by marital discord or a prolonged illness may retain their shyness into adolescence and later adulthood.

Module 9.3 Review

LO 9.8 **Identify the major dimensions of temperament, and explain how temperament is affected by a child's environment.**

Personality is the sum total of the enduring characteristics that differentiate one individual from another. Temperament encompasses enduring levels of arousal and emotionality that are characteristic of an individual.

LO 9.9 **Differentiate the eight stages of Erikson's theory of psychosocial development, and explain what factors determine the outcome at each stage.**

According to Erik Erikson, people move through eight stages between birth and late adulthood, with the necessity of resolving an important conflict characteristic of each stage.

LO 9.10 **Summarize the contributions of Vaillant, Gould, Levinson, and Peck to our understanding of personality development in adulthood, and discuss the research on midlife crisis.**

Vaillant, Gould, Levinson, and Peck have all made contributions to our understanding of personality development in adulthood. The evidence for a widespread midlife crisis is lacking.

LO 9.11 **Describe the Big Five personality traits, and summarize how genetics and environment interact in shaping personality.**

Personality research specialists have identified a set of five broad trait factors that describe basic personality. Known as the *Big Five personality traits*, these traits are openness, conscientiousness, extraversion, agreeableness, and neuroticism. In general, personality traits are fairly stable throughout life, with only slightly more volatility during adolescence than in other periods.

Journal Writing Prompt

Applying Lifespan Development: What are the educational implications of the finding that some personality traits are inherited and remain consistent over time? Is it wiser for schools to try to change personalities or accommodate to them? Why?

Epilogue

The road people travel as they develop as social individuals is a long and winding one. We began this chapter with an examination of the roots of children's earliest social relationships. We saw how bonds of attachment are forged in infancy and the ways in which children increasingly interact with peers as they move through the preschool years and into middle childhood. We considered, too, how emotional development proceeds, beginning with the decoding and encoding of emotions by infants, and the role social referencing plays in understanding what others may be feeling. We discussed the nature and function of emotions in adolescence and examined the ways in which adolescents learn to regulate their emotions.

We then looked at the emotional difficulties this age group may face, resulting in depression or even suicide. We explored the importance of fulfilling psychological needs to attaining happiness in adulthood. In conclusion, we discussed temperament and Erik Erikson's theory

of psychosocial development. We also considered the evidence for and against the popular notion of "midlife crisis," and discussed the stability of personality in adulthood.

Before moving on to the next chapter, take a moment to reread the prologue about Antonio, who used information from his college course to help prevent a child from crying. Then answer the following questions:

1. How did Antonio use his knowledge of social referencing to influence Tyrone?

2. In what ways do the actions of Tyrone indicate that he had developed a theory of mind?

3. How might feelings of anxiety or depression have influenced Tyrone's reaction to being knocked down?

4. Based on the story, how did Antonio, Tyrone, or Henry demonstrate emotional control or empathy?

Looking Back

LO 9.1   Identify the four major patterns of infant attachment, and give examples of how the nature of attachment in infancy may influence relationships later in life.

Attachment, a strong, positive emotional bond that forms between an infant and one or more significant persons, is a crucial factor in enabling individuals to develop social relationships. Early studies of attachment, particularly those by ethologist Konrad Lorenz, suggested that attachment was based on biological needs, such as food and safety. To these factors, psychologist Harry Harlow's experiments on attachment among monkeys added contact comfort.

The earliest work on human attachment was conducted by John Bowlby, who concluded that safety was the primary motivation behind attachment. According to Bowlby, attachment permits children to explore their world and gradually to become independent. The Ainsworth Strange Situation is an experimental technique used to classify children's attachment styles. The styles identified through this method and a more recent expansion of it are securely attached, avoidant, ambivalent, and disorganized-disoriented. Attachment styles during early childhood have significant effects on the types of relationships that people are able to form later in life.

However, attachment styles are not entirely universal and biologically determined; they are susceptible to strong cultural influences.

LO 9.2   Describe how infants interact with peers, and explain the implications this has for their own development.

From the earliest months of life, infants smile and vocalize while looking at peers. By 9 to 12 months, they enjoy mutually presenting and accepting toys, and like to engage in social games, such as peek-a-boo. By 14 months, children enjoy copying each other's behavior. While this serves a social function, it also can be a significant teaching tool. The capacity for children to engage in imitation suggests that imitation may be inborn. Research has identified a class of neurons in the brain that seems related to an innate ability to imitate the behavior of others. These so-called mirror neurons may even help infants to understand the actions of others.

LO 9.3   Identify the emotions infants experience and explain their ability to decode the emotions of others.

Infants display a variety of facial expressions, which are similar across cultures and appear to reflect basic emotional states. By the end of the first year, infants often develop both stranger anxiety, wariness around an unknown person, and separation anxiety, distress displayed when a customary care provider departs. Early in life, infants develop the capability of nonverbal decoding: determining the emotional states of others based on their facial and vocal expressions.

LO 9.4   Define social referencing and theory of mind, and explain how they are related to a child's cognitive development.

Through social referencing, infants from the age of 8 or 9 months use the expressions of others to clarify ambiguous situations and learn appropriate reactions to them. Children develop theory of mind as the brain matures, allowing them to become more insightful about the motives and reasons behind the behavior of others. Children with autism spectrum disorder have particular difficulty relating to others, in part because they find it hard to understand what others are thinking.

LO 9.5   Summarize emotional development in middle childhood and adolescence, and give examples of emotional self-regulation.

Empathy, the ability to experience the emotions of others, develops in middle childhood. During middle childhood and adolescence, the ability to self-regulate emotions increases dramatically. Emotions tend to be more volatile during adolescence. Alternating highs and lows can come in rapid succession. On the positive side, because adolescents' moods change rapidly, negative feelings usually pass without harm.

LO 9.6   Identify the causes of adolescent anxiety and depression, and explain the role gender plays in both depression and suicide rates.

Many adolescents have feelings of sadness and hopelessness, and some experience major depression. Biological, environmental, and social factors contribute to depression, and there are gender, ethnic, and racial differences in its occurrence. The rate of adolescent suicide is rising, with suicide now the third most common cause of death in the 15- to 24-year-old bracket. More boys than girls commit suicide, although girls make more suicide attempts.

LO 9.7   Summarize how the determinants of happiness change throughout adulthood, and identify the three major theories regarding happiness in late adulthood.

Young adults find happiness in feelings of independence, competence, self-esteem, and relating well to other people. Culture influences which psychological needs are considered most important to happiness. Disengagement theory and activity theory present opposite views of ways to deal successfully with aging. Continuity theory suggests a compromise between the two. People's choices depend partly on their prior habits and personalities.

LO 9.8   Identify the major dimensions of temperament, and explain how temperament is affected by a child's environment.

Temperament encompasses enduring levels of arousal and emotionality that are characteristic of an individual. Several dimensions, such as activity level and irritability, reflect temperament. Temperamental differences are reflected in the broad classification of infants into easy, difficult, and slow-to-warm categories. No single type of temperament is invariably bad or good. Long-term adjustment depends on the goodness of fit between a child's temperament and the environment in which she or he is raised.

LO 9.9   Differentiate the eight stages of Erikson's theory of psychosocial development, and explain what factors determine the outcome at each stage.

The origins of personality, the sum total of the enduring characteristics that differentiate one individual from another, are found during infancy. According to Erik Erikson's theory of psychosocial development, developmental change occurs throughout people's lives as they pass through eight stages in which they must confront and resolve characteristic crises. During infancy, children encounter the trust-versus-mistrust stage and the autonomy-versus-shame-and-doubt stage. Then, during early childhood, they pass through the initiative-versus-guilt stage, followed by the industry-versus-inferiority stage, which brings them to adolescence. In adolescence, they enter the identity-versus-identity-confusion stage. Early adulthood is characterized by the intimacy-versus-isolation stage, while middle adulthood is characterized by the generativity-versus-stagnation stage. The final stage of human psychosocial development, the ego-transcendence-versus-ego-preoccupation stage, occurs in late adulthood.

LO 9.10   Summarize the contributions of Vaillant, Gould, Levinson, and Peck to our understanding of personality development in adulthood, and discuss the research on midlife crisis.

Life review, in which people in late adulthood examine and evaluate their lives, is a major focus running through the work of Levinson and Peck, as well as Erikson, Vaillant, and Gould. Levinson's theory that people experience a midlife crisis in their 40s, as they confront the realization that life is finite, has largely been rejected by most research. While some people do experience turmoil and uncertainty at this age, most people transition through it smoothly.

LO 9.11   Describe the Big Five personality traits, and summarize how genetics and environment interact in shaping personality.

The Big Five personality traits are openness, conscientiousness, extraversion, agreeableness, and neuroticism. It appears that, in general, the broad personality may be relatively stable over time, with particular aspects changing in response to life changes. Although genetics play a powerful role in shaping personality, environment also plays a significant role, with a tendency toward reinforcing the traits we inherit.

Key Terms and Concepts

attachment   270
Ainsworth Strange Situation   271
secure attachment pattern   271
avoidant attachment pattern   272
ambivalent attachment pattern   272
disorganized-disoriented
    attachment pattern   272
stranger anxiety   276
separation anxiety   277
social referencing   278
emotional
    self-regulation   281
disengagement theory   286
activity theory   286
continuity theory   287
personality   288

temperament   288
easy babies   289
difficult babies   289
slow-to-warm babies   289
goodness of fit   289
Erikson's theory of psychosocial
    development   290
trust-versus-mistrust stage   290
autonomy-versus-shame-and-doubt
    stage   290
initiative-versus-guilt stage   290
industry-versus-inferiority
    stage   290
identity-versus-identity-confusion
    stage   291
intimacy-versus-isolation stage   291

generativity-versus-stagnation
    stage   291
ego-integrity-versus-despair
    stage   291
midlife crisis   293
redefinition of self versus
    preoccupation with work
    role   294
body transcendence versus body
    preoccupation   294
ego transcendence versus ego
    preoccupation   294
traits   296

Chapter 10
Development of the Self

PhotoAlto/Getty Images

Learning Objectives

LO 10.1 Describe the process by which young children develop an understanding of themselves.

LO 10.2 Trace the shift in self-understanding in the middle childhood and adolescent years.

LO 10.3 Explain how the process of self-definition continues in adulthood.

LO 10.4 Analyze the origins and effects of self-esteem.

LO 10.5 Explain how social comparison functions in childhood and adolescence.

LO 10.6 Analyze the methods by which people choose their careers and the ways in which career choices affect personal identity.

LO 10.7 Explore the varied reasons why people work.

LO 10.8 Examine some of the challenges that workers face today.

Chapter Overview

Prologue: All in the Family

At 25 years old, mechanical engineer Jim Aparicio thought he had it all. "I had graduated college early, married the girl of my dreams, and landed a great job with a big engineering firm," Jim reflects. But by the time Jim hit 40, things weren't so great. "I was really unhappy. I hated my job, the constant overwhelming pressure, the late nights away from my family. But most of all, I just didn't get any sense of fulfilment."

But one high point of his job was the way his co-workers interacted with him. "I'm not sure how this happened, but over the years I got the reputation for being the guy that you could tell your problems to. It was actually really nice to connect with people and listen to them as they talked about what they were struggling with. One time someone told me, 'You're a great listener—you should be a counselor,' and that night I couldn't think of anything else," Jim mused.

Now at 45, Jim talks about his newfound career and sense of purpose, "I went back to college and got my master's degree in counseling, and now my life has totally changed. I finally feel like I'm making a difference in people's lives. But if you had asked me at 25 what I would be doing at 45, I never would have guessed this. You just never know what the future holds." ■

Looking Ahead

Jim's career move at midlife is not unusual: Few lives follow a set, predictable pattern through middle adulthood. In fact, one of the remarkable characteristics of middle age is its variety, as the paths that different people take continue to diverge.

In this chapter, we consider the nature of the *self*, examining how we see and evaluate ourselves throughout our life span, and how we go about choosing our life's work. We start by tracing the first evidence that we have that infants are aware of their own existence. We consider how they come to understand that they are individuals distinct from the world around them. We examine how self-concept develops in preschool and middle childhood, and how children develop racial and ethnic awareness. We also consider how adolescents form their views of themselves in their search for identity.

We then turn to the ways that children and adolescents develop a positive—or negative—view of themselves. We discuss how social comparison provides a useful tool for self-evaluation by measuring one's abilities

During middle adulthood, people continue to develop a sense of self.

objectively within an appropriate context. We also consider how adolescents' ability to differentiate various aspects of the self leads them to evaluate those aspects in different ways.

Next, we turn to a discussion of how people make decisions about their future work—an important source of identity and self-esteem in adulthood. We see how people who begin with vague and often unrealistic thoughts during childhood begin to refine their options and make realistic choices regarding who they wish to be on a professional level. We consider the reasons people work—not only to earn money—and techniques for choosing a career. Finally, we examine the changing role of work in people's lives and some of the difficulties associated with work, such as burnout and unemployment.

MODULE 10.1

THE DEVELOPMENT OF THE SELF

Elysa, 8 months old, crawls past the full-length mirror that hangs on a door in her parents' bedroom. She barely pays any attention to her reflection as she moves by. In contrast, her cousin Brianna, who is almost 2 years old, stares at herself in the mirror as she passes and laughs as she notices, and then rubs off, a smear of jelly on her forehead.

Perhaps you have had the experience of catching a glimpse of yourself in a mirror and noticing a hair out of place. You probably reacted by attempting to push the unruly hair back into place. Your reaction shows more than that you care about how you look. It implies that you have a sense of yourself, the awareness and knowledge that you are an independent social entity to which others react, and which you attempt to present to the world in ways that reflect favorably on you.

The Roots of Self-Awareness

LO 10.1 Describe the process by which young children develop an understanding of themselves.

We are not born with the knowledge that we exist independently from others and the larger world. Very young infants do not have a sense of themselves as individuals; they do not recognize themselves in photos or mirrors. However, the roots of **self-awareness**, knowledge of oneself, begin to grow at around the age of 12 months.

We know this from a simple but ingenious experimental technique in which an infant's nose is secretly colored with a dab of red powder. Then the infant is seated in front of a mirror. If infants touch their noses or attempt to wipe off the rouge, we have evidence that they have at least some knowledge of their physical characteristics. For them, this awareness is one step in developing an understanding of themselves as independent beings. For instance, Brianna, in the example at the beginning of this section, showed her awareness of her independence when she tried to rub the jelly off her forehead (Rochat, Broesch, & Jayne, 2012).

Although some infants as young as 12 months seem startled on seeing the rouge spot, for most a reaction does not occur until between 17 and 24 months of age. It is also around this age that children begin to show awareness of their own capabilities. For instance, infants who participate in experiments when they are between the ages of 23 and 25 months sometimes begin to cry if the experimenter asks them to imitate a complicated sequence of behaviors involving toys, although they readily accomplish simpler sequences. Their reaction suggests that they are conscious that they lack the ability to carry out difficult tasks and are unhappy about it—a reaction that provides a clear indication of self-awareness (Asendorpf, 2002; Gergely, 2007; Waugh & Brownell, 2015).

Children's cultural upbringing also impacts the development of self-recognition. For instance, Greek children—who experience parenting practices that emphasize autonomy and separation—show self-recognition at an earlier age than children from

self-awareness
knowledge of oneself.

Cameroon in Africa. In the Cameroonian culture, parenting practices emphasize body contact and warmth, leading to more interdependence between infants and parents, and ultimately to later development of self-recognition (Keller et al., 2004; Keller, Voelker, & Yovsi, 2005; Ross et al., 2017).

In general, by age 18 to 24 months, infants in Western cultures have developed at least an awareness of their own physical characteristics and capabilities, and they understand that their appearance is stable over time. Although it is not clear how far this awareness extends, it is becoming increasingly evident that, as we discuss next, infants have not only a basic understanding of themselves but also the beginnings of an understanding of how the mind operates (Lewis & Ramsay, 2004; Lewis & Carmody, 2008; Langfur, 2013).

THEORY OF MIND: INFANTS' PERSPECTIVES ON THE MENTAL LIVES OF OTHERS—AND THEMSELVES. What are infants' thoughts about thinking? Infants begin to understand certain things about their own and others' mental processes at quite an early age, developing a *theory of mind*, which is their knowledge and beliefs about how the mind works and how it influences behavior. Theories of mind are the explanations that children use to explain how others think.

For instance, cognitive advances during infancy permit older infants to see people in a very different way from other objects. They learn to see other people as *compliant agents*, beings similar to themselves who behave under their own power and who have the capacity to respond to infants' requests (Rochat, 1999, 2004; Slaughter & Peterson, 2012).

In addition, children's capacity to understand intentionality and causality grows during infancy. For example, 10- and 13-month-olds are able to mentally represent social dominance, believing that larger size is related to the ability to dominate other, smaller-sized individuals and objects. Furthermore, infants have a kind of innate morality, in which they show a preference for helpfulness (Sloane, Baillargeon, & Premack, 2012; Ruffman, 2014; Yott & Poulin-Dubois, 2016).

Furthermore, as early as 18 months, they begin to understand that others' behaviors have meaning and that the behaviors they see people enacting are designed to accomplish particular goals, in contrast to the "behaviors" of inanimate objects. For example, a child comes to understand that his father has a specific goal when he is in the kitchen making sandwiches. In contrast, his father's car is simply parked in the driveway, having no mental life or goal (Ahn, Gelman, & Amsterlaw, 2000; Tomasello et al., 2005; Senju et al., 2011).

Another piece of evidence for infants' growing sense of mental activity is that by age 2, infants begin to demonstrate the rudiments of empathy—an emotional response that corresponds to the feelings of another person. At 24 months of age, infants sometimes comfort others or show concern for them. In order to do this, they need to be aware of the emotional states of others. For example, 1-year-olds are able to pick up emotional cues by observing the behavior of an actress on television (Legerstee, Haley, & Bornstein, 2013; Gredebäck et al., 2015; Xu, Saether, & Sommerville, 2016).

SELF-CONCEPT IN THE PRESCHOOL YEARS: THINKING ABOUT THE SELF. Although the question "Who am I?" is not explicitly posed by most preschool-age children, it underlies a considerable amount of development during the preschool years. During this period, children wonder about the nature of the self, and the way they answer the "Who am I?" question may affect them for the rest of their lives.

If you ask preschool-age children to specify what makes them different from other kids, they readily respond with answers like, "I'm a good runner" or "I like to color" or "I'm a big girl." Such answers relate to **self-concept**—their identity, or their set of beliefs about what they are like as individuals (Grace, David, & Ryan, 2008; Bhargava, 2014; Crampton & Hall, 2017).

The statements that describe children's self-concepts are not necessarily accurate. In fact, preschool children typically overestimate their skills and knowledge across all domains of expertise. Consequently, their view of the future is quite rosy: They expect to win the next game they play, to beat all opponents in an upcoming race, to write great

self-concept
a person's identity, or set of beliefs about what one is like as an individual.

stories when they grow up. Even when they have just experienced failure at a task, they are likely to expect to do well in the future. This optimistic view is held, in part, because they have not yet started to compare themselves and their performance against others. Their inaccuracy is also helpful, freeing them to take chances and try new activities (Verschueren, Doumen, & Buyse, 2012; Ehm, Lindberg, & Hasselhorn, 2013).

collectivistic orientation
a philosophy that promotes the notion of interdependence.

individualistic orientation
a philosophy that emphasizes personal identity and the uniqueness of the individual.

Culture and Self-Concept.   Preschool-age children's view of themselves also reflects the way their particular culture considers the self. For example, many Asian societies tend to have a **collectivistic orientation**, promoting the notion of interdependence. People in such cultures tend to regard themselves as parts of a larger social network in which they are interconnected with and responsible to others. In contrast, children in Western cultures are more likely to develop a view of the self reflecting an **individualistic orientation** that emphasizes personal identity and the uniqueness of the individual. They are more apt to see themselves as self-contained and autonomous, in competition with others for scarce resources. Consequently, children in Western cultures are more likely to focus on what sets them apart from others—what makes them special.

Such views pervade a culture, sometimes in subtle ways. For instance, one well-known saying in Western cultures states that "the squeaky wheel gets the grease." Preschoolers who are exposed to this perspective are encouraged to gain the attention of others by standing out and making their needs known. In contrast, children in Asian cultures are exposed to a different perspective; they are told that "the nail that stands out gets pounded down." This perspective suggests to preschoolers that they should attempt to blend in and refrain from making themselves distinctive (Lehman, Chiu, & Schaller, 2004; Wang, 2006).

race dissonance
the phenomenon in which minority children indicate preferences for majority values or people.

Self-Concept and Attitudes Toward Gender, Race, and Ethnicity.   Gender, the sense of being male or female, is well established by the time children reach the preschool years, and this, too, affects their self-concept.

Preschoolers' developing self-concepts can also be affected by their culture's attitudes toward various racial and ethnic groups. For most preschool-age children, racial awareness comes relatively early. Certainly, even infants are able to distinguish different skin colors; their perceptual abilities allow for such color distinctions quite early in life. However, it is only later that children begin to attribute meaning to different racial characteristics, a meaning that is subtly influenced by the attitudes of the people, schools, and other cultural institutions with which they come into contact in their community.

By the time they are 3 or 4 years old, preschool-age children notice differences among people based on skin color, and they begin to identify themselves as a member of a particular group such as "Hispanic" or "black." Although early in the preschool years they do not realize that ethnicity and race are enduring features of who they are, later they begin to develop an understanding of the significance that society places on ethnic and racial membership (Quintana & McKown, 2008; Guerrero, Enseco, & Lam, 2011; Setoh et al., 2017).

Some preschoolers have mixed feelings about their racial and ethnic identity. Some experience **race dissonance**, the phenomenon in which minority children indicate preferences for majority values or people. For instance, some studies find that as many as 90 percent of African American children, when asked about their reactions to drawings of black and white children, react more negatively to the drawings of black children than to those of white children. However, these negative reactions did not translate into lower self-esteem for the African American subjects. Instead, their preferences appear to be a result of the powerful influence of the dominant white culture rather than a disparagement of their own racial characteristics (Holland, 1994; Margie et al., 2005; Copping et al., 2013).

As children age, the number and depth of friendships outside their own racial group tend to decline. What are some ways in which schools can foster mutual acceptance?

Varina Patel/Fotolia

Ethnic identity emerges somewhat later than racial identity because it is usually less conspicuous than race. For instance, in one study of Mexican American ethnic awareness, preschoolers displayed only a limited knowledge of their ethnic identity. However, as they became older, they grew more aware of the significance of their ethnicity. Preschoolers who were bilingual, speaking both Spanish and English, were most apt to be aware of their ethnic identity (Bernal, 1994; Shi & Lu, 2007; Mesinas & Perez, 2016).

Furthermore, racial socialization is a particular issue for children who are adopted into families in which the parents and/or other siblings are of different races and ethnicities. Some researchers suggest that children in transracial families may hold more egalitarian attitudes regarding race (Langrehr, Thomas, & Morgan, 2016).

Preschool children are also sensitive to differences in socioeconomic status. Although they don't understand the abstract concepts of socioeconomic status, they can articulate a difference between those who are "rich" and those who are "poor" (Bienvenu & Ramsey, 2006; Goodman et al., 2007).

Understanding Oneself in Middle Childhood and Adolescence

LO 10.2 **Trace the shift in self-understanding in the middle childhood and adolescent years.**

Eight-year-old Sonia carefully removes her muddy garden clogs and proudly plops an armload of carrots in the kitchen sink to be rinsed and scrubbed. This year, she has taken over the care for a portion of the family's vegetable garden. Having worked beside her mother since she was 6, she was able to plant and tend the carrots, zucchini, and broccoli on her own this year. Sonia smiles as she washes the vegetables, thinking about how her family depends on her, too, now.

Sonia is coming to see herself as capable and reliable—someone her family can depend on. Conveying what psychologist Erik Erikson calls "industriousness," Sonia's quiet pride in her accomplishments illustrates one way children's views of themselves evolve and continue to develop.

During middle childhood, children actively seek to answer the question "Who am I?" Although the question will assume greater urgency in adolescence, elementary-age children still try to find their place in the world.

MIDDLE CHILDHOOD: THE SHIFT IN SELF-UNDERSTANDING FROM THE PHYSICAL TO THE PSYCHOLOGICAL. Cognitive advances aid school-age children in their quest for self-understanding. They begin to view themselves less in terms of external physical attributes and more in terms of psychological traits (Bosacki, 2014; Aronson & Bialostok, 2016; Thomaes, Brummelman & Sedikides, 2017).

For instance, 6-year-old Carey describes herself as "a fast runner and good at drawing"—characteristics dependent on motor skills in external activities. In contrast, 11-year-old Meiping characterizes herself as "pretty smart, friendly, and helpful to my friends." Because of her increasing cognitive skills, Meiping's view of herself is based on psychological characteristics, inner traits that are more abstract.

Children's views of who they are also become more complex. Erikson characterized psychosocial development in middle childhood as the industry-versus-inferiority stage. Children are seeking endeavors in which they can be successfully industrious. As they get older, children discover their strengths and weaknesses. Ten-year-old Ginny, for instance, comes to understand that she is good at arithmetic but not very good at spelling; 11-year-old Alberto decides he is good at softball but lacks the stamina to play soccer well.

Children's self-concepts become divided into personal and academic spheres. They evaluate themselves in four major areas, each of which can be broken down further; for example, the nonacademic self-concept includes physical appearance, peer relations, and physical ability, while the academic self-concept is similarly divided.

Research on students' self-concepts in English, mathematics, and nonacademic realms shows that the separate realms do not always correlate, although overlap exists. For example, a child who sees herself as a star math student will not necessarily feel she is great at English (Marsh & Hau, 2004; Ehm, Lindberg, & Hasselhorn, 2013).

ADOLESCENCE: THE SEARCH FOR IDENTITY

"You have no idea how much pressure a 13-year-old has to deal with. You've got to look cool, act cool, wear the right clothes, wear your hair a certain way—and your friends have different ideas about all these things than your parents, know what I mean? And you've got to have friends or you're nobody. And then some of your friends say you're not cool if you don't drink or do drugs, but what if you don't want that?"—Anton Merced

The thoughts of 13-year-old Anton Merced demonstrate a clear awareness—and self-consciousness—regarding his new place in society. During adolescence, questions like "Who am I?" and "Where do I belong in the world?" begin to take a front seat.

One reason issues of identity become so important is that adolescents' intellectual capacities become more adultlike. They see how they stack up to others and realize they are individuals, separate from everyone else. The dramatic physical changes of puberty make adolescents acutely aware of their own bodies and aware that others are reacting to them in new ways. Whatever the cause, adolescence brings major changes in teenagers' self-concepts and self-esteem—in sum, their views of their own identity.

Self-Concept: What Am I Like?   Valerie describes herself this way: "Others look at me as laid back, relaxed, and not worrying too much. But really, I'm often nervous and emotional."

The fact that Valerie distinguishes others' views from her own represents a developmental advance. In childhood, she would have characterized herself by traits that would not differentiate her view from the views of others. However, when adolescents describe who they are, they take into account both their own and others' perspectives (Preckel et al., 2013; McLean & Syed, 2015; Griffin, Adams & Little, 2017).

This broader view of themselves is one aspect of adolescents' increasing sense of identity. They can see various aspects of the self simultaneously, and this view becomes more organized and coherent. They look at the self from a psychological perspective, viewing traits not as concrete entities but as abstractions. For example, teenagers are more likely than younger children to define themselves by their ideology (e.g., "I'm an environmentalist") than by physical characteristics (e.g., "I'm the fastest runner in my class") (Yip, 2008).

This broader, multifaceted self-concept, however, can be a mixed blessing, especially during early adolescence. At that time, adolescents may be troubled by the complexity of their personalities. Younger adolescents may want to view themselves in a certain way ("I'm a sociable person and love to be with people"), and they may become concerned when their behavior contradicts that view ("Even though I want to be sociable, sometimes I can't stand being around my friends and just want to be alone"). By the end of adolescence, however, teenagers find it easier to accept that behaviors and feelings change with the situation (Trzesniewski, Donnellan, & Robins, 2003; Hitlin, Brown, & Elder, 2006; Raufelder et al., 2015).

Identity Formation: Change or Crisis?   According to Erikson, the search for identity inevitably leads some adolescents to an identity crisis involving substantial psychological turmoil (Erikson, 1963). Erikson's theory of this stage (the identity-versus-identity-confusion stage) suggests that teenagers try to figure out what is unique and distinctive about themselves—a task they manage with increasing sophistication due to the cognitive gains of adolescence.

Erikson argues that adolescents strive to discover their strengths and weaknesses and the roles that best suit their future lives. This often involves "trying on" different roles or choices to see if they fit their capabilities and views about themselves. In this process, adolescents seek

Adolescents' sense of who they are takes their own and others' views into account.

David Shopper/Getty Images

to understand who they are by narrowing and making choices about their personal, occupational, sexual, and political commitments.

In Erikson's view, adolescents who do not find a suitable identity may go off course in several ways. They may adopt socially unacceptable roles to express what they do *not* want to be. Forming and maintaining lasting close relationships may elude them. In general, their sense of self becomes "diffuse," failing to organize around a unified core identity.

In contrast, those who forge an appropriate identity set a foundation for future psychosocial development. They learn their unique capabilities and believe in them, and they develop an accurate sense of self. They are prepared to take full advantage of their unique strengths (Allison & Schultz, 2001; Merrell, 2008).

During the identity-versus-identity-confusion stage, U.S. teenagers seek to understand who they are by narrowing and making choices about their personal, occupational, sexual, and political commitments. Can this stage be applied to teenagers in other cultures? Why or why not?

Societal Pressures and Reliance on Friends and Peers. Societal pressures are also high during the identity-versus-identity-confusion stage. Adolescents feel pressure from parents and friends to decide whether their post-high-school plans include work or college and, if the decision is work, which occupation to follow. Up to this point, their educational lives have followed a universal track, laid out by U.S. society. However, the track ends at high school, leaving adolescents with difficult choices about which path to follow (Sampson & Chason, 2008).

During this period, friends and peers are increasingly sought as sources of information. Dependence on adults declines. As we discuss later, this increasing dependence on peers enables adolescents to forge close relationships. Comparing themselves to others helps to clarify their own identities.

Psychological Moratorium. Because of the pressures of the identity-versus-identity-confusion period, Erikson suggested that many adolescents pursue a *psychological moratorium*, a period during which they take time off from the upcoming responsibilities of adulthood to explore various roles and possibilities. For example, many college students take a semester or year off to travel, work, or find another way to examine their priorities.

Many adolescents, for practical reasons, cannot pursue a psychological moratorium to leisurely explore various identities. For economic reasons, some must work part-time after school and then take jobs immediately after high school, leaving them little time to experiment, and this seldom leads to psychological damage. Successfully holding a part-time job while attending school may offer a psychological reward that outweighs the lack of opportunity to try out various roles.

Marcia's Approach to Identity Development: Updating Erikson. Using Erikson's theory as a springboard, psychologist James Marcia suggests that identity can be seen in terms of which of two characteristics—crisis or commitment—is present or absent. *Crisis* is a period in which an adolescent consciously chooses between various alternatives and makes decisions. *Commitment* is psychological investment in a course of action or an ideology. One adolescent might career from one activity to another, with nothing lasting beyond a few weeks, while another becomes totally absorbed in volunteering at a homeless shelter (Peterson, Marcia, & Carpendale, 2004; Marcia, 2007; Crocetti, 2017).

From *a social worker's* perspective

Do you believe that all four of Marcia's identity statuses can lead to reassessment and different choices later in life? Are there stages in Marcia's theory of development that may be more difficult to achieve for adolescents who live in poverty? Why?

After conducting lengthy interviews with adolescents, Marcia proposed four categories of identity (see Table 10-1).

1. **Identity achievement**. Teenagers in this category have successfully explored and thought through who they are and what they want to do. Following a period of crisis during which they considered various alternatives, these adolescents have committed to a particular identity. Teens who have reached this identity status tend to be psychologically healthier, higher in achievement motivation and moral reasoning, than adolescents of any other status.

identity achievement
the status of adolescents who commit to a particular identity following a period of crisis during which they consider various alternatives.

Table 10-1 Marcia's Four Categories of Adolescent Development

		Commitment	
		Present	**Absent**
CRISIS/EXPLORATION — **PRESENT**		**Identity achievement** "I enjoyed working at an advertising company the last two summers, so I plan to go into advertising."	**Moratorium** "I'm taking a job at my mom's bookstore until I figure out what I really want to do."
CRISIS/EXPLORATION — **ABSENT**		**Identity foreclosure** "My dad says I'm good with kids and would be a good teacher, so I guess that's what I'll do."	**Identity diffusion** "Frankly, I have no idea what I'm going to do."

(**Source:** Based on Marcia, 1980).

---

identity foreclosure
the status of adolescents who prematurely commit to an identity without adequately exploring alternatives.

moratorium
the status of adolescents who may have explored various identity alternatives to some degree but have not yet committed themselves.

identity diffusion
the status of adolescents who consider various identity alternatives but never commit to one or never even consider identity options in any conscious way.

Emerging adulthood
the period beginning in the late teenage years and extending into the mid-20s.

2. **Identity foreclosure**. These are adolescents who have committed to an identity without passing through a period of crisis in which they explored alternatives. Instead, they accepted others' decisions about what was best for them. Typical of this category is a son who enters the family business because it is expected, or a daughter who becomes a physician because her mother is one. Foreclosers are not necessarily unhappy, but they tend to have something called "rigid strength": Happy and self-satisfied, they have a high need for social approval and tend to be authoritarian.

3. **Moratorium**. Adolescents in this category have explored some alternatives but have made no commitments. As a result, Marcia suggests, they show relatively high anxiety and experience psychological conflict, though they are often lively and appealing, seeking intimacy with others. Such adolescents typically settle on an identity but only after a struggle.

4. **Identity diffusion**. These adolescents neither explore nor commit to various alternatives. They tend to shift from one thing to the next. While appearing carefree, according to Marcia, their lack of commitment impairs their ability to form close relationships. They are often socially withdrawn.

Some adolescents shift among the four categories, for example, moving between moratorium and identity achievement in what is called a MAMA cycle (**m**oratorium—identity **a**chievement—**m**oratorium—identity **a**chievement). Or a forecloser who selected a career path without much thought in early adolescence may reassess and make a more active choice later. For some individuals, identity formation takes place beyond adolescence. However, for most people, identity gels in the late teens and early 20s (Kroger, 2000; Meeus, 2003; Duriez et al., 2012).

In some ways, Marcia's identity status perspective foreshadows what other researchers have called emerging adulthood. **Emerging adulthood** is the period beginning in the late teenage years and extending into the mid-20s. It is a transitional stage between adolescence and adulthood that spans the third decade of life (Arnett, 2011, 2016).

Emerging adulthood is a period in which teenagers have left adolescence, although brain growth continues and neural circuits become more complex. But it is typically a period of uncertainty, in which post-adolescents are working to determine who they are and their path forward (Verschueren et al., 2017).

Identity, Race, and Ethnicity.   Forming an identity is often difficult for adolescents, but it is especially challenging for members of racial and ethnic groups that face discrimination. Society's contradictory values tell adolescents that society should be color-blind, that race and ethnic background should not affect opportunities and achievement, and that if they do achieve, society will accept them. Based on a traditional *cultural assimilation model*, this view says individual cultural identities should be assimilated into a unified culture in the United States—the melting pot model.

In contrast, the *pluralistic society model* suggests that U.S. society is made up of diverse, coequal cultural groups that should preserve their individual features. This model grew from the belief that cultural assimilation denigrates the heritage of minorities and lowers their self-esteem. According to the pluralistic view, racial and ethnic factors form a central part of identity and are not submerged in an attempt to assimilate.

The middle ground says minority group members can form a *bicultural identity*, drawing from their own culture while integrating themselves into the dominant culture. This view suggests that an individual can hold two cultural identities, without having to prefer one over the other (LaFromboise, Coleman, & Gerton, 1993; Phinney, 2006, 2008).

The choice of a bicultural identity is increasingly common. In fact, the number of people who identify themselves as belonging to more than one race is considerable, increasing 134 percent from 2000 to 2010 (U.S. Bureau of the Census, 2011; see Figure 10-1).

The process of identity formation is always complex and may be twice as difficult for minority group members. Racial and ethnic identity takes time to form. For some, it may require a prolonged period, but the result can be a rich, multifaceted identity (Quintana, 2007; Jensen, 2008; Klimstra et al., 2012; Yoon et al., 2016).

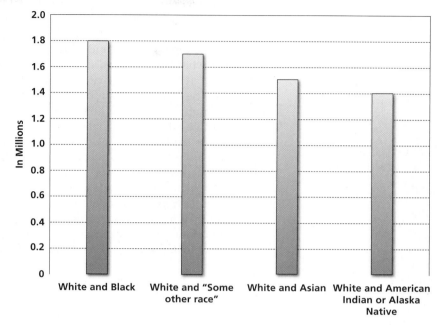

Figure 10-1 Bicultural Identity in the United States

The number of Americans who identified themselves as belonging to more than one race grew substantially between 2000 and 2010. Almost 10 percent report belonging to three or more races.

(**Source:** U.S. Bureau of the Census, 2011.)

Adulthood: Defining the Self Through Life Events

LO 10.3   **Explain how the process of self-definition continues in adulthood.**

> *At 21, Nadine defined herself, largely, as a college senior majoring in political science. At 23, her self-concept centered on the intelligence and persistence she brought to her work as an assistant in an ACLU office. A year later, Nadine added "wife" to her resume, and two years after that, "parent" trumped her former identity as a bright, young professional.*

Having children. Receiving a promotion. Getting divorced. Changing jobs. Each of these events marks a moment on what has been called the social clock of life. As Nadine's story illustrates, these life events also shape and reshape identity in early adulthood.

THE SOCIAL CLOCKS OF ADULTHOOD.   The **social clock** is a term used to describe the psychological timepiece that records the major milestones in people's lives. A personal social clock tells each of us whether we have reached the major benchmarks of life early, late, or right on time in comparison to our peers. Our social clocks are culturally determined, reflecting the expectations of the society in which we live.

Until the mid-20th century, the social clocks of adulthood were fairly uniform—at least for upper-class and middle-class people in Western societies. The typical man completed his education by his early 20s, started a career, married in his mid-20s, and was providing for a growing family by his 30s. Women also followed a set pattern, which focused on getting married and raising children—but not, in most cases, entering a profession and developing a career.

Today, there is considerably more heterogeneity in the social clocks of both men and women. The timing of major life events has changed, and women's social clocks have changed dramatically as a result of social and cultural changes (Goldberg, 2014).

WOMEN'S SOCIAL CLOCKS.   Developmental psychologist Ravenna Helson and colleagues suggest that people choose from several social clocks, and the selection they make has implications for personality development during middle adulthood.

social clock

the culturally determined psychological timepiece providing a sense of whether we have reached the major benchmarks of life at the appropriate time in comparison to our peers.

Focusing on a sample of women who graduated from college during the early 1960s, Helson's longitudinal research has examined women whose social clocks were focused either on their families, on careers, or on a more individualistic target (Helson, Jones, & Kwan, 2002; Society for Personality and Social Psychology, 2017).

Helson found that, over the course of the study, which assessed participants at ages 21, 27, and 43, the women generally became more self-disciplined and committed to their duties. They also felt greater independence and confidence and could cope with stress and adversity more effectively.

Finding a spouse and embarking on motherhood meant that many women exhibited what Helson called traditional feminine behavior from about age 21 to 27. But as children grew up and maternal duties diminished, women took on less traditional roles.

The study also found some intriguing similarities in women who chose to focus on family compared with those who focused on career. Both groups showed generally positive changes. In contrast, women who had no strong focus on either family or career tended to show either little change or more negative shifts in personality development, such as becoming less satisfied over time.

Helson's conclusion is that the critical factor in personality development is not which social clock a woman chooses, but the *process* of choosing a social clock, whether it involves motherhood or career. Whether the woman chooses a career first and then motherhood, or the opposite pattern—or an entirely different path—is less important than investing in and focusing on a particular trajectory.

It is important to keep in mind that social clocks are culturally determined. The timing of motherhood and the course of a woman's career are both influenced by the social, economic, and cultural worlds in which the woman lives.

THE ROLE OF WORK IN SHAPING IDENTITY DURING ADULTHOOD. According to psychiatrist George Vaillant, the stage of development that young adults reach is called career consolidation. During **career consolidation**, which begins between 20 and 40, young adults become centered on their careers. Vaillant based his conclusion on a comprehensive longitudinal study of male graduates of Harvard, begun when they were freshmen in the 1930s (Vaillant & Vaillant, 1990; Vaillant, 2003).

In their early 20s, the men tended to be influenced by their parents' authority. But in their late 20s and early 30s, they started to act with greater autonomy. They married, had children, and began to focus on their careers—the period of career consolidation.

Vaillant draws a relatively uninspiring portrait of people in this stage. His participants worked very hard as they climbed the corporate ladder. They tended to be rule-followers conforming to the norms of their professions. Rather than showing the independence and questioning that they had displayed in college, they threw themselves unquestioningly into their work.

Vaillant argues that work plays such an important role that the career consolidation stage should be seen as an addition to Erikson's intimacy-versus-isolation stage of psychosocial identity. In Vaillant's view, career concerns supplant the focus on intimacy, and the career consolidation stage marks a bridge between intimacy-versus-isolation and generativity-versus-stagnation. (*Generativity* refers to an individual's contribution to society, as we discussed earlier.)

Reactions to Vaillant's viewpoint are mixed. Critics point out that Vaillant's sample, though relatively large, comprised a highly restricted, unusually bright group of men. Furthermore, societal norms have changed considerably since the 1930s, and people's views of the importance of work may have shifted. Finally, the lack of women in the sample and the fact that there have been major changes in the role of work in *women's* lives make Vaillant's conclusions even less generalizable.

Furthermore, research on what has been called the *millennial generation*—those born after 1980 and who entered young adulthood around the millennium in 2000—seems to show a different view of work than that of earlier generations. Millennials are much more likely to expect to change jobs multiple times; the idea of working for life for a single company is less attractive than to previous generations. They also have high (and sometimes unrealistic) expectations about how successful they will be, but don't necessarily feel that they will need to work hard to achieve that success. In fact,

career consolidation

a stage that is entered between the ages of 20 and 40, when young adults become centered on their careers.

work-life balance is of considerable importance to millennials, who see employment as just one facet of a well-rounded life (Kuron et al., 2015; Deal & Levenson, 2016).

Still, whatever their attitudes about work, it is clear that employment plays an important role in young adults' lives and that it makes up a significant part of both men's and women's identity—if for no other reason than that many people spend more time working than they do on any other activity. We turn now to how people decide what careers to follow—and the implications of that decision.

Module 10.1 Review

LO 10.1 Describe the process by which young children develop an understanding of themselves.

Infants develop self-awareness, the knowledge that they exist separately from the rest of the world, after about 12 months of age, and by age 2, children have developed the rudiments of a theory of mind. During the preschool years, children develop their self-concepts, beliefs about themselves that they derive from their own perceptions, their parents' behaviors, and society. Racial, ethnic, and gender awareness begin to form in the preschool years.

LO 10.2 Trace the shift in self-understanding in the middle childhood and adolescent years.

In the middle childhood years, children begin to base their self-concept on psychological rather than physical characteristics. Self-concept during adolescence grows more differentiated as the view of the self becomes more organized, broader, and more abstract, and takes account of the views of others. James Marcia's four identity statuses focus on the adolescent's struggle to determine an identity and a role in society.

LO 10.3 Explain how the process of self-definition continues in adulthood.

Choosing a career is an important step in early adulthood, so important that developmental psychologist George Vaillant considers career consolidation a developmental stage on a par with Erik Erikson's intimacy-versus-isolation stage.

Journal Writing Prompt

Applying Lifespan Development: How might a child's developing sense of empathy be fostered by parents and other caregivers?

MODULE 10.2

EVALUATING THE SELF

Kieran had been given the part of "Frog" in the second-grade class play based on the popular Frog and Toad *stories. Somewhat shy, he was a bit nervous about this, his biggest challenge to date. His older sister helped him learn his lines, and his aunt made a frog costume. With so much support, Kieran's fear ebbed. He started to enjoy the rehearsals, and when he took his bow at the close of the performance, he received more applause than anyone else. Meeting his family backstage, he beamed. "I like doing plays. Everyone thought I was great!"*

Self-Esteem: Developing a Positive—or Negative—View of Oneself

LO 10.4 Analyze the origins and effects of self-esteem.

Although an awareness of *self* takes root in infancy, and preschoolers are able to form a self-concept, it is not until early middle childhood that children begin to evaluate themselves.

Children don't dispassionately view themselves just in terms of an itemization of physical and psychological characteristics. Instead, they make judgments about themselves as being good or bad in particular ways, as Kieran did. **Self-esteem** is an individual's overall and specific positive and negative self-evaluation. Whereas self-concept reflects beliefs and cognitions about the

self-esteem
an individual's overall and specific positive and negative self-evaluation.

self (*I am good at trumpet; I am not so good at social studies*), self-esteem is more emotionally oriented (*Everybody thinks I'm a nerd*) (Baumeister, 1993; Davis-Kean & Sandler, 2001; Bracken & Lamprecht, 2003).

Self-esteem develops in important ways during middle childhood. As we'll discuss shortly, children increasingly compare themselves to others, and as they do, they assess how well they measure up to society's standards. In addition, they increasingly develop their own internal standards of success, and they can see how well they compare to those.

One of the advances that occur during middle childhood is that, like self-concept, self-esteem becomes increasingly differentiated. At age 7, most children have self-esteem that reflects a global, fairly simple view of themselves. If their overall self-esteem is positive, they believe that they are relatively good at all things. Conversely, if their overall self-esteem is negative, they feel that they are inadequate at most things (Harter, 2006; Hoersting & Jenkins, 2011; Coelho, Marchante, & Jimerson, 2016).

From *an educator's* perspective

What can teachers do to help children whose low self-esteem is causing them to fail? How can this cycle of failure be broken?

As children progress into the middle childhood years, however, their self-esteem is higher for some areas and lower in others. For example, a boy's overall self-esteem may be composed of positive self-esteem in some areas (such as the positive feelings he gets from his artistic ability) and more negative self-esteem in others (such as the unhappiness he feels over his athletic skills).

Furthermore, self-esteem may be associated with social media use. Research on Facebook use with adults suggests that people who are frequently exposed to social media come to develop a distorted view of the world, a view that suggests that positive events are the norm. In turn, believing that others' lives are consistently positive (which is often the view they present on social media) suggests that their own lives pale in comparison. We don't yet know whether these findings hold for children, but it seems likely they do (Ozimek & Bierhoff, 2016; Chow & Wan, 2017).

SELF-ESTEEM IN ADOLESCENCE: HOW DO I LIKE MYSELF?   *Knowing* who you are and *liking* who you are are two different things. As children move into adolescence, they become increasingly accurate in understanding who they are (their self-concept). This knowledge, however, does not guarantee that they like themselves (their self-esteem) any better. In fact, their increasing accuracy in understanding themselves permits them to see themselves fully—warts and all. It's what they do with these perceptions that leads them to develop a sense of their self-esteem.

From Research to Practice

Is Anyone "Liking" Me? Social Comparison and Self-Esteem in the Digital Age

Social networking sites like Facebook have become a part of daily life. In fact, it's likely that you are reading this chapter on your laptop or smartphone while also checking your social media feed as well as those of your friends. But the quick pace of technology has left researchers racing to study how these social networking sites affect us. And not all of the news is good, as research has uncovered a "dark side" to social media use. For example, a recent review of 23 different studies of frequent and consistent Facebook users found a significant association with increased psychological distress. Similarly, one longitudinal study found that Facebook use over time led to lower self-ratings of life satisfaction and well-being (Kross et al., 2013; Marino et al., 2018).

But what could be the cause of the relationship between our use of social networking sites and our psychological well-being? One group of researchers gathered data from college students to find out how social comparison might affect self-esteem. In their study, participants were asked to view a fictitious social media profile of another student at their university. One group viewed a social media profile that consisted of photos of the person during a recent vacation. This profile showed "high activity," with a high number of "likes" and comments. The other group viewed a "low activity" version of the same profile and photos with many fewer "likes" and comments (Vogel et al., 2014).

The researchers hypothesized that self-esteem would be lower in those participants who made an upward social comparison to the high-activity profile than in those participants who made a downward social comparison to the low-activity profile. In fact, this was the case: Participant self-esteem was lower in those who had viewed the fictitious high-activity profile with more "likes" and comments. So as our personal relationships become reflected in the digital world of social networking sites, it seems that a symbolic thumbs-up is a key ingredient to one's self-esteem—for better or worse.

The practical implications of this research are many. For example, counselors working with teens or adults with depression should assess their client's social media use and how it might be negatively affecting their mood. And in turn, counselors could educate their clients regarding more adaptive social networking site practices. This research is also important to parents, teachers, counselors, and school psychologists, as they teach kids adaptive ways to use social networking sites and how to appropriately cope with online bullying or rejection.

Shared Writing Prompt

How do you think that receiving more "likes" and comments on one's social media posts affects people's relationships with others as well as their feelings about themselves?

The same cognitive sophistication that allows adolescents to differentiate various aspects of the self also leads them to evaluate those aspects in different ways (Bos et al., 2006). For instance, an adolescent may have high self-esteem in terms of academic performance but lower self-esteem in terms of relationships with others. (Also see the *From Research to Practice* box, above).

Race and Self-Esteem. If you were a member of a racial group whose members routinely experienced prejudice and discrimination, it seems reasonable to predict that your self-esteem would be affected. Early research confirmed that hypothesis and found that African Americans had lower self-esteem than whites. For example, as noted earlier, a set of pioneering studies a generation ago found that African American children shown black and white dolls preferred the white dolls over the black ones (Clark & Clark, 1947). The interpretation that was drawn from the study: The self-esteem of the African American children was low.

More recent research, however, has shown these early assumptions to be overstated. The picture is more complex regarding relative levels of self-esteem between members of different racial and ethnic groups. For example, although white children initially show higher self-esteem than black children, black children begin to show slightly higher self-esteem than white children around age 11. This shift occurs as African American children become more closely identified with their racial group, develop more complex views of racial identity, and increasingly view the positive aspects of their group membership (Tatum, 2007; Sprecher, Brooks & Avogo, 2013; Davis et al., 2017).

Hispanic children also show an increase in self-esteem toward the end of middle childhood, although even in adolescence their self-esteem still trails that of whites. In contrast, Asian American children show the opposite pattern: Their self-esteem in elementary school is higher than that of whites and blacks, but by the end of childhood, their self-esteem is lower than that of whites (Tropp & Wright, 2003; Verkuyten, 2008; Kapke, Gerdis & Lawton, 2017).

Social Identity Theory. One explanation for the complex relationship between self-esteem

Daniel M Ernst/Shutterstock

A strong sense of racial identity during adolescence is tied to higher levels of self-esteem.

and minority group status comes from *social identity theory*. According to the theory, members of a minority group are likely to accept the negative views held by a majority group only if they perceive that there is little realistic possibility of changing the power and status differences between the groups. If minority group members feel that prejudice and discrimination can be reduced, and they blame society for the prejudice and not themselves, self-esteem should not differ between majority and minority groups (Outten et al., 2009; Thompson, Briggs-King, & LaTouche-Howard, 2012).

As group pride and ethnic awareness among minority group members have grown, differences in self-esteem between members of different ethnic groups have narrowed. This trend has further been supported by an increased sensitivity to the importance of multiculturalism (Negy, Shreve, & Jensen, 2003; Lee, 2005; Tatum, 2007).

Another reason for the overall similarity in self-esteem levels found between adolescents of different racial groups is that teenagers in general focus their preferences and priorities on those aspects of their lives at which they excel. Consequently, African American youths may concentrate on the things that they find most satisfying—things that give them the highest degree of success and therefore self-esteem (Gray-Little & Hafdahl, 2000; Yang & Blodgett, 2000; Phinney, 2005).

Finally, self-esteem may be influenced not by race alone but by a complex combination of factors. For instance, some developmentalists have considered race and gender simultaneously, coining the term *ethgender* to refer to the joint influence of race and gender. One study that simultaneously took both race and gender into account found that African American and Hispanic males had the highest levels of self-esteem, while Asian and Native American females had the lowest levels (Saunders, Davis, & Williams, 2004; Biro et al., 2006; Park et al., 2012).

BEYOND ADOLESCENCE: SELF-ESTEEM IN ADULTHOOD.   Although discussions about identity and self-esteem often focus on middle childhood and adolescence, how we view and judge ourselves continues to be a central part of our development throughout our lives. Moving from being a child in our parents' home to being an adult in our own home (and perhaps a parent, too) dramatically alters our self-concept. How we feel we manage this transition can affect our self-esteem. Choosing our life's work and establishing a career, as we will discuss in the next module, also impact our identity and self-esteem. Even in late adulthood, self-esteem continues to play a significant role in how we experience our lives, as older people evaluate who they have been and how well they have managed their lives as they prepare for death.

GENDER DIFFERENCES IN SELF-ESTEEM.   Gender is another factor that affects self-esteem. Particularly during early adolescence, girls' self-esteem tends to be lower than that of boys, and girls tend to feel more vulnerable (Mäkinen et al., 2012).

One reason for the difference is that, compared to boys, girls tend to be more concerned about physical appearance and social success—in addition to academic achievement. Although boys are also concerned about these things, their attitudes are often more casual. In addition, societal messages suggesting that female academic achievement is a roadblock to social success can put girls in a difficult bind: If they do well academically, they jeopardize their social success. No wonder that the self-esteem of adolescent girls is more fragile than that of boys (Ayres & Leaper, 2013; Jenkins & Demaray, 2015; Ra & Cho, 2017).

Developmental Diversity and Your Life

Are Children of Immigrant Families Well Adjusted?

Immigration to the United States has risen significantly in the past 30 years. More than 13 million children in the United States are either foreign born or the children of immigrants—some one-fifth of the total population of children.

How well are these children of immigrants faring? Quite well. In fact, in some ways they are better off than their nonimmigrant peers. For example, they tend to have equal or better grades in school than children whose parents were born in the United

States. Psychologically, they also do quite well, showing similar levels of self-esteem to nonimmigrant children, although they do report feeling less popular and less in control of their lives (Kao, 2000; Driscoll, Russell, & Crockett, 2008; Jung & Zhang, 2016).

Why is the adjustment of immigrant children to U.S. culture so generally positive? One answer is that often their socioeconomic status is relatively higher. In spite of stereotypes that immigrant families come from lower social classes, many in fact are well educated and come to the United States seeking greater opportunities.

But socioeconomic status is only part of the story. Even the immigrant children who are not financially well off are often more highly motivated to succeed and place greater value on education than do children in nonimmigrant families. In addition, many immigrant children come from societies that emphasize collectivism, and consequently they may feel more obligation and duty toward their family to succeed. Finally, their country of origin may give some immigrant children a strong enough cultural identity to prevent them from adopting undesirable "American" qualities—such as materialism or selfishness (Fuligni & Yoshikawa, 2003).

During the middle childhood years, it thus appears that children in immigrant families typically do quite well

in the United States. The story is less clear, however, when children of immigrants reach adolescence and adulthood. For instance, some research shows higher rates of obesity (a key indicator of physical health) in adolescents. Research is just beginning to clarify how effectively immigrants cope over the course of the life span (Wiley, Perkins, & Deaux, 2008; Perreira & Ornelas, 2011; Fuligni, 2012).

Children of immigrant parents usually are well adjusted, academically and psychologically.

Although generally self-esteem is higher in adolescent boys than in girls, boys do have vulnerabilities of their own. For example, society's stereotypical gender expectations may lead boys to feel that they should be confident, tough, and fearless all the time. Boys facing difficulties, such as not making a sports team or being rejected by a girl they wanted to date, are likely to feel not only miserable about the defeat they face but also incompetent, since they don't measure up to the stereotype (Witt, Donnellan, & Trzesniewski, 2011; Levant et al., 2016).

SOCIOECONOMIC STATUS AND SELF-ESTEEM.   Socioeconomic status (SES) also influences self-esteem. Adolescents of higher SES generally have higher self-esteem than those of lower SES, particularly during middle and later adolescence. It may be that the social status factors that especially enhance one's standing and self-esteem— such as having more expensive clothes or a car—become more conspicuous in the later periods of adolescence (Dai et al., 2012).

As we shall see in the next module, socioeconomic status continues to play a role in how we view ourselves throughout our lives. For example, adults who hold jobs with a high status tend to be more satisfied with their work than those in low-status jobs. Since work is a major component of identity for adults, the status of a job may greatly influence an individual's self-esteem. (Also see the *Developmental Diversity and Your Life* feature.)

Social Comparison: Asking "How Do I Measure Up?"

LO 10.5   **Explain how social comparison functions in childhood and adolescence.**

If someone were to ask you how good you are at math, how would you respond? Most of us would compare our performance to that of others who are roughly the same age and educational level. It is unlikely that we'd answer the question by comparing ourselves either to Albert Einstein or to a kindergartner just learning about numbers.

social comparison

the desire to evaluate one's own behavior, abilities, expertise, and opinions by comparing them to those of others.

Elementary-school-age children begin to follow the same sort of reasoning when they seek to understand how able they are. When they were younger, they tended to consider their abilities in terms of some hypothetical standard, making a judgment that they are good or bad in an absolute sense. Now they begin to use social comparison processes, comparing themselves to others, to determine their levels of accomplishment during middle childhood (Malmberg, Wanner, & Little, 2008).

Social comparison is the desire to evaluate one's own behavior, abilities, expertise, and opinions by comparing them to those of others. According to a theory first suggested by psychologist Leon Festinger (1954), when concrete, objective measures of ability are lacking, people turn to *social reality* to evaluate themselves. Social reality refers to understanding that is derived from how others act, think, feel, and view the world.

But who provides the most adequate comparison? When they cannot objectively evaluate their ability, children during middle childhood increasingly look to others who are similar to themselves. In addition, children may use *upward social comparison*, in which they evaluate their abilities against those of people who appear to be more proficient and successful than they are. While using upward social comparison may provide aspirational models, it can sometimes make individuals feel worse about themselves as they fear they can never be as good as their more successful peers (Summers, Schallert, & Ritter, 2003; Boissicat et al., 2012).

DOWNWARD SOCIAL COMPARISON. Although children typically compare themselves to similar others, in some cases—particularly when their self-esteem is at stake—they choose to make *downward social comparisons* with others who are obviously less competent or successful (Vohs & Heatherton, 2004; Hosogi et al., 2012).

Downward social comparison protects children's self-esteem. By comparing themselves to those who are less able, children ensure that they will come out on top and thereby preserve an image of themselves as successful.

Downward social comparison helps explain why some students in elementary schools with generally low achievement levels are found to have stronger academic self-esteem than very capable students in schools with high achievement levels. The reason seems to be that students in the low-achievement schools observe others who are not doing terribly well academically, and they feel relatively good by comparison. In contrast, students in the high-achievement schools may find themselves competing with a more academically proficient group of students, and their perception of their performance may suffer in comparison. At least in terms of self-esteem, then, it is better to be a big fish in a small pond than a small fish in a big one (Marsh et al., 2008; Visconti, Kochenderfer-Ladd & Clifford, 2013; Lapan & Boseovski, 2017).

SOCIAL COMPARISON IN ADOLESCENCE: THE IMPORTANCE OF PEER GROUPS. Teenagers' seemingly compulsive need to communicate with friends, exemplified by social media and texting, demonstrates the role that peers play in adolescence. Continuing the trend that began in middle childhood, adolescents spend increasing amounts of time with their peers, and the importance of peer relationships grows as well. There is probably no period of life in which peer relationships are as important as they are in adolescence (Arnon, Shamai, & Ilatov, 2008; Shook et al., 2008).

Peers become more important in adolescence for a number of reasons. For one thing, they provide each other with the opportunity to compare and evaluate opinions, abilities, and even physical changes, extending the process of social comparison begun in middle childhood. Because physical and cognitive changes of adolescence are so unique to this age group and so pronounced, especially during the early stages of puberty, adolescents turn increasingly to others who share, and consequently can shed light on, their own experiences (Li & Wright, 2013; Schaefer & Salafia, 2014; Tian, Yu & Huebner, 2017).

Parents are unable to provide social comparison. Not only are they well beyond the changes that adolescents undergo, but adolescents' questioning of adult authority and their motivation to become more autonomous make parents, other family members, and adults in general inadequate and invalid sources of knowledge. Who is left to provide such information? Peers.

REFERENCE GROUPS.   As we have said, adolescence is a time of experimentation, of trying out new identities, roles, and conduct. Peers provide information about what roles and behavior are most acceptable by serving as a reference group. **Reference groups** are groups of people with whom one compares oneself. Just as a professional ballplayer is likely to compare his performance against that of other professional players, so do teenagers compare themselves to those who are similar to them.

Reference groups present a set of *norms*, or standards, against which adolescents can judge their abilities and social success. An adolescent need not even belong to a group for it to serve as a reference group. For instance, unpopular adolescents may find themselves belittled and rejected by members of a popular group, yet use that more popular group as a reference group (Berndt, 1999; Blanton & Burkley, 2008).

Reference groups
groups of people with whom one compares oneself.

THE CONSEQUENCES OF SELF-ESTEEM.   Although everyone occasionally goes through periods of low self-esteem, such as after an undeniable failure, some children have chronically low self-esteem. Children with low self-esteem face a tough road, in part because their self-esteem becomes enmeshed in a cycle of failure that grows increasingly difficult to break. Assume, for instance, that Harry, a student with chronically low self-esteem, is facing an important test. Because of his low self-esteem, he expects to do poorly. As a consequence, he is quite anxious—so anxious that he is unable to concentrate well and study effectively. Furthermore, he may decide not to study much because he figures that if he's going to do badly anyway, why bother studying?

Ultimately, of course, Harry's high anxiety and lack of effort bring about the result he expected: He does poorly on the test. This failure, which confirms Harry's expectation, reinforces his low self-esteem, and the cycle of failure continues (see Figure 10-2).

If a child continues to be chronically low in self-esteem in adolescence, life can be very painful. For instance, adolescents with low self-esteem respond more negatively to failure than those with high self-esteem, in part because those with low self-esteem focus on their shortcomings after experiencing failure. Like Harry, whose low expectations for his own performance led him to prepare poorly for a test—and thus fail it—adolescents with low self-esteem can become trapped in a cycle of failure. In addition, low self-esteem is related to higher levels of aggression, antisocial behavior, and delinquency in adolescence (Baumeister, 1993; Dodgson & Wood, 1998; Donnellan et al., 2005).

In contrast, students with high self-esteem travel a more positive path, falling into a cycle of success. Adolescents with high self-esteem focus on their strengths following failure. They hold more positive expectations about their future performance. Having higher expectations leads to increased effort and lower anxiety, increasing the probability of success. In turn, this helps affirm the higher self-esteem that began the cycle.

Clearly, positive self-esteem is associated with desirable consequences, and lower self-esteem is related to negative results. However, this doesn't mean that we should seek to boost the self-esteem of adolescents at any cost. For example, although higher self-esteem is associated with positive outcomes such as academic achievement, the relationship between the two factors is merely correlational. The association simply means that people with higher self-esteem are more likely to have better academic performance, and those with lower self-esteem are more likely to have poorer academic performance.

Figure 10-2 Cycles of Self-Esteem

Because children with low self-esteem may expect to do poorly on a test, they may experience high anxiety and not work as hard as those with higher self-esteem. As a result, they actually do perform badly on the test, which in turn confirms their negative view of themselves. In contrast, those with high self-esteem have more positive expectations, which lead to lower anxiety and higher motivation. As a consequence, they perform better, reinforcing their positive self-image. How would a teacher help students with low self-esteem break out of their negative cycle?

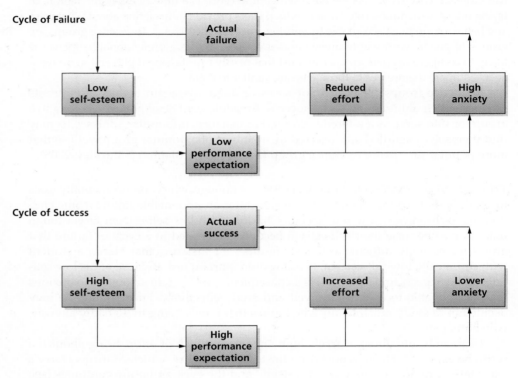

There are several possible explanations for the relationship between self-esteem and academic performance. On one hand, it may be that higher self-esteem indeed causes better academic performance. On the other hand, it may be the reverse: that doing well academically causes higher self-esteem. Or, finally, there may be some third factor (intelligence seems to be a reasonable possibility) that produces *both* higher self-esteem and better academic performance (Crocker & Knight, 2005).

Module 10.2 Review

LO 10.4 Analyze the origins and effects of self-esteem.

During the middle childhood years, self-esteem is based on comparisons with others and internal standards of success; if self-esteem is low, the result can be a cycle of failure. In adolescence, girls' self-esteem tends to be lower than boys' self-esteem, in part because girls are likely to be more concerned about physical appearance and social success—in addition to academic achievement. Self-esteem grows increasingly differentiated in adolescence as teens develop the ability to place different values on different aspects of the self.

LO 10.5 Explain how social comparison functions in childhood and adolescence.

Social comparison is the desire to evaluate one's own behavior, abilities, expertise, and opinions by comparing

them to those of others. Peer social groups serve as reference groups in adolescence and offer a ready means of social comparison. Chronic low self-esteem can lead to physical illness, psychological problems, and the inability to cope with stress. Low self-esteem is also related to aggression, antisocial behavior, and delinquency in adolescence.

Journal Writing Prompt

Applying Lifespan Development: How would you go about designing a program for elementary students who are academic underachievers to prevent them from falling into a "cycle of failure"?

MODULE **10.3**

PICKING AN OCCUPATION: CHOOSING LIFE'S WORK

Why did I decide that I wanted to be a lawyer? The answer is a bit embarrassing. When I got to my senior year of college, I began to worry about what I was going to do when I graduated. My parents were asking, with increasing frequency, what kind of work I was thinking about, and I felt the pressure rising with each phone call from home. So I began to think seriously about the problem. At the time, there was some big trial in the news all the time, and it got me to thinking about what it might be like to be an attorney. And I had always been fascinated by Law and Order *when it had been on television. For these reasons, and just about none other, I decided to take the law boards and apply to law school.*

Choosing a career represents an important milestone in people's lives. The choice we make goes well beyond determining how much money we will earn; it also relates to our status, our sense of self-worth, and the contributions that we will make in life. In sum, decisions about work go to the very core of our identity.

Embarking on a Career

LO 10.6   **Analyze the methods by which people choose their careers and the ways in which career choices affect personal identity.**

Some people know from childhood that they want to be physicians or firefighters or to go into business, and they follow invariant paths toward their goals. For others, the choice of a career is very much a matter of chance, of turning to job postings and seeing what's available. Many of us fall somewhere between these two extremes.

GINZBERG'S CAREER CHOICE THEORY.   According to Eli Ginzberg (1972), people typically move through a series of stages in choosing a career. The first stage is the **fantasy period**, which lasts until a person is around 11. During the fantasy period, career choices are made and discarded without regard to skills, abilities, or available job opportunities. Instead, choices are made solely on the basis of what sounds appealing. Thus, a child may decide he wants to be a rock star—despite the fact that she cannot carry a tune.

People begin to take practical considerations into account during the **tentative period**, which spans adolescence. They begin to think more practically about the requirements of various jobs and how their own abilities and interests might fit with them. They also consider their personal values and goals, exploring how well a particular occupation might satisfy them.

Finally, in early adulthood, people enter the realistic period. In the **realistic period**, young adults explore specific career options either through actual experience on the job or through training for a profession. After initially exploring what they might do, people begin to narrow their choices to a few alternative careers and eventually make a commitment to a particular one.

Although Ginzberg's theory makes sense, critics have charged that it oversimplifies the process of choosing a career. Because Ginzberg's research was based on subjects from middle socioeconomic levels, it may overstate the choices and options available to people in lower socioeconomic levels. Furthermore, the ages associated with the various stages may be too rigid. For instance, a person who does not attend college but begins to work immediately after high school graduation is likely to be making serious career decisions at a much earlier point than a person who attends college. In addition, economic shifts have caused many people to change careers at different points in their adult lives.

HOLLAND'S PERSONALITY TYPE THEORY.   Other theories of career choice emphasize how an individual's personality affects decisions about a career. According

fantasy period
according to Ginzberg, the period, lasting until about age 11, when career choices are made, and discarded, without regard to skills, abilities, or available job opportunities.

tentative period
the second stage of Ginzberg's theory, which spans adolescence, during which people begin to think in pragmatic terms about the requirements of various jobs and how their own abilities might fit with them.

realistic period
the third stage of Ginzberg's theory, which occurs in early adulthood, during which people begin to explore specific career options, and then narrow their choices and make a commitment.

According to one theory, people move through a series of life stages in choosing a career. The first stage is the fantasy period, which lasts until a person is around 11 years old.

Dschagunn/Getty Images

to John Holland, for instance, certain personality types match particularly well with certain careers. If the correspondence between personality and career is good, people will enjoy their careers more and be more likely to stay in them; but if the match is poor, they will be unhappy and more likely to shift into other careers (Holland, 1999).

According to Holland, six personality types are important in career choice:

- **Realistic.** These people are down-to-earth, practical problem-solvers, and physically strong, but their social skills are mediocre. They make good farmers, laborers, and truck drivers.

- **Intellectual.** Intellectual types are oriented toward the theoretical and abstract. Although not particularly good with people, they are well suited to careers in math and science.

- **Social.** The traits associated with the social personality type are related to verbal skills and interpersonal relations. Social types are good at working with people and consequently make good salespersons, teachers, and counselors.

- **Conventional.** Conventional individuals prefer highly structured tasks. They make good clerks, secretaries, and bank tellers.

- **Enterprising.** These individuals are risk-takers and take-charge types. They are good leaders and may be particularly effective as managers or politicians.

- **Artistic.** Artistic types use art to express themselves, and they often prefer the world of art to interactions with people. They are best suited to occupations involving art.

Although Holland's enumeration of personality types is sensible, it suffers from a central flaw: Not everyone fits neatly into particular personality types. Furthermore, there are certainly exceptions to the typology, with jobs being held by people who don't have the particular personality that Holland would predict. Still, the basic notions of the theory have been validated, and they form the foundation of several of the "job quizzes" that people can take to see what occupations they might especially enjoy (Deng, Armstrong, & Rounds, 2007).

GENDER AND CAREER CHOICES: WOMEN'S WORK

> *WANTED: Full-time employee for small family firm. DUTIES: Including but not limited to general cleaning, cooking, gardening, laundry, ironing and mending, purchasing, bookkeeping and money management. Child care may also be required. HOURS: Avg. 55/wk but standby duty required 24 hours/day, 7 days/wk. Extra workload on holidays. SALARY AND BENEFITS: No salary, but food, clothing, and shelter provided at employer's discretion; job security and benefits depend on continued goodwill of employer. No vacation. No retirement plan. No opportunities for advancement. REQUIREMENTS: No previous experience necessary, can learn on the job. Only women need apply. (Unger & Crawford, 1992, p. 446)*

Two generations ago, many women entering early adulthood assumed that this admittedly exaggerated job description matched the work for which they were best suited and to which they aspired: housewife. Even those women who sought work outside the home were relegated to certain professions. For instance, until the 1960s, employment ads in newspapers throughout the United States were almost always divided into two sections: "Help Wanted: Male" and "Help Wanted: Female." The men's job listings encompassed such professions as police officer, construction worker, and legal counsel; the women's listings were for secretaries, teachers, cashiers, and librarians.

The breakdown of jobs deemed appropriate for men and women reflected society's traditional view of what the two genders were best suited for. Traditionally, women were considered most appropriate for **communal professions**, occupations associated with relationships, like nursing. In contrast, men were perceived as best suited for **agentic professions**. Agentic professions are associated with getting things accomplished, like carpentry. It is probably no coincidence that communal professions typically have lower status and pay than agentic professions (Eagly & Steffen, 1986; Trapnell & Paulhus, 2012; Locke & Heller, 2017).

communal professions
occupations that are associated with relationships.

agentic professions
occupations that are associated with getting things accomplished.

Although discrimination based on gender is far less blatant today than it was several decades ago—it is now illegal, for instance, to advertise a position specifically for a man or a woman—remnants of traditional gender-role prejudice persist. Women are less likely to be found in traditionally male-dominated professions such as engineering and computer programming. As shown in Figure 10-3, although significant progress in closing the gender wage gap has been made in the past 30 years, women's weekly earnings still lag behind those of men. Women earn an average of 82 cents for every dollar that men earn. Women who are members of certain minority groups are even worse off: Black women earn 63 cents for every dollar that white men earn. And women in many professions earn significantly less than men in identical jobs (Frome et al., 2006; U.S. Bureau of Labor Statistics, 2017).

More women are working outside the home than ever before despite status and pay that are often lower than men's. Between 1950 and 2010, the percentage of the female population (age 16 and over) in the U.S. labor force increased from around 35 percent to over 47 percent. Almost all women expect to earn a living, and almost all do at some point in their lives. Furthermore, in about one-half of U.S. households, women earn about as much as their husbands (Bureau of Labor Statistics, 2012).

Opportunities for women are considerably greater than they were in earlier years. Women are more likely to be physicians, lawyers, insurance agents, and bus drivers than they were in the past. However, as noted earlier, within specific job categories, there are still notable gender differences. For example, female bus drivers are more apt to have part-time school bus routes, whereas men hold better-paying full-time routes in cities. Similarly, female pharmacists are more likely to work in hospitals, while men work in higher-paying jobs in retail stores (Unger & Crawford, 2003).

In the same way, women (and minorities, too) in high-status, visible professional roles may hit what has come to be called the *glass ceiling*. The glass ceiling is an invisible barrier within an organization that, because of discrimination, prevents individuals from being promoted beyond a certain level. It operates subtly, and often

Figure 10-3 The Gender Wage Gap

These occupations are those in which women's earnings as a percentage of men's earnings were the lowest.

(**Source:** Bureau of Labor Statistics, 2017.)

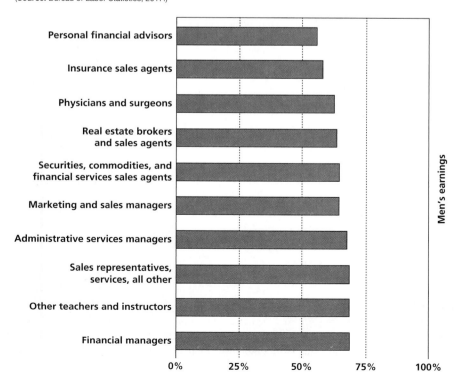

the people responsible for keeping the glass ceiling in place are unaware of how their actions perpetuate discrimination against women and minorities (Stockdale & Crosby, & Malden, 2004; Dobele, Rundle-Thiele, & Kopanidis, 2014).

IMMIGRANTS ON THE JOB: MAKING IT IN AMERICA. We saw earlier in the chapter that children of immigrants do quite well educationally and socially. But what about their parents? How are they doing?

If we rely solely on much of what we hear from anti-immigrant politicians in the United States, we would probably view immigrants to the United States as straining the educational, prison, welfare, and health-care systems while contributing little to U.S. society. But the assumptions that underlie anti-immigrant sentiment are in fact quite wrong.

Some 43 million people in the United States were born outside the country, representing close to around 14 percent of the population, nearly three times the percentage in 1970. First- and second-generation immigrants comprise almost a quarter of the population of the United States (see Figure 10-4; Congressional Budget Office, 2013).

Today's immigrants are somewhat different from the earlier waves at the beginning of the 20th century. Only a third are white, compared with almost 90 percent of immigrants who arrived before 1960. Critics argue that many new immigrants lack the skills that will allow them to make a contribution to the high-tech economy of the 21st century.

From *a social worker's* perspective

Why do you think immigrants' ambition and achievements are widely underestimated?

The critics are wrong in many fundamental respects. For instance, consider the following data (Flanigan, 2005; Gorman, 2010; Camarota & Zeigler, 2015):

- Most legal and illegal immigrants ultimately succeed financially. For example, although they initially experience higher rates of poverty than native-born Americans, immigrants who arrived in the United States prior to 1980 and

---

Figure 10-4 Immigrants in the United States

Since 1970, the number of immigrants in the United States has steadily climbed and, barring changes in immigration policy, immigrants who arrive in the future plus their descendants will account for roughly three-fourths of future U.S. population increases.

(**Source**: Data for 1900–2000 from Dicennial Census. For 2007, data from the March Current Population Survey. As cited in Camarota, 2007.)

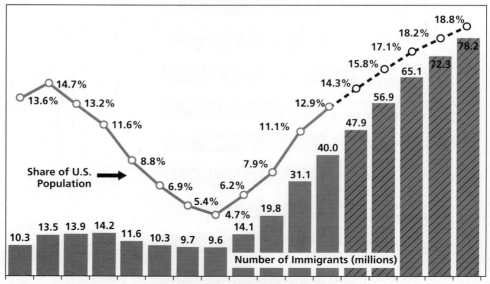

have had a chance to establish themselves actually have a higher family income than native-born Americans. Immigrants are twice as likely to start businesses as citizens born in the U.S. Furthermore, companies owned by immigrants are more likely to hire employees than companies owned by native-born citizens (ADL, 2017).

- Most of the projected increase in immigration comes from increases in legal immigrants, not illegal immigration.

- **Only a few immigrants come to the United States to get on welfare.** Instead, most say they come because of opportunities to work and prosper in the United States. Nonrefugee immigrants who are old enough to work are less likely to be on welfare than native-born U.S. citizens.

- **Given time, immigrants contribute more to the economy than they take away.** Although initially costly to the government, often because they hold low-paying jobs and therefore pay no income taxes, immigrants become more productive as they get older. Ultimately, immigrants pay $25 billion to $30 billion a year more in taxes than they use in government services.

Why are immigrants often ultimately financially successful? One explanation is that immigrants who voluntarily choose to leave their native countries are particularly motivated and driven to be successful, whereas those who choose *not* to immigrate may be relatively less motivated.

In short, the reality is that the majority of immigrants ultimately become contributing members of U.S. society. For instance, they may alleviate labor shortages, and the money they send to relatives who remain at home may invigorate the world economy (World Bank, 2003).

Why Do People Work? It's More Than Earning a Living

LO 10.7   Explore the varied reasons why people work.

Why do people work? This may seem an easy question to answer: People work to earn a living. Yet the reality is different, for young adults express many reasons for seeking a job, and middle-aged adults increasingly embark on new careers.

INTRINSIC AND EXTRINSIC MOTIVATION.   Certainly, people work in order to obtain various concrete rewards, or out of extrinsic motivation. **Extrinsic motivation** drives people to obtain tangible rewards, such as money and prestige (Vansteenkiste et al., 2007; D'Lima, Winsler, & Kitsantas, 2014).

People also work for their own enjoyment, for personal rewards, not just for the financial rewards a job may bring. This is known as **intrinsic motivation**. People in many Western societies tend to subscribe to the Puritan work ethic, the notion that work is important in and of itself. According to this view, working is a meaningful act that brings psychological and (at least in the traditional view) even spiritual well-being and satisfaction.

Work also brings a sense of personal identity. Consider, for instance, what people say about themselves when they first meet someone. After mentioning their names and where they live, they very typically tell what they do for a living. What people do is a large part of who they are.

Work may also be a central element in people's social lives. Because so much time is spent in work settings, work can be a source of adults' friends and social activities. Social relationships forged at work may spill over into other parts of people's lives. In addition, there are often social obligations—dinner with the boss, or the annual seasonal party in December—that are related to work.

Finally, the kind of work that people do is a factor in determining status. **Status** is the evaluation by society of the role a person plays. Various jobs are associated with a certain status. For example, traditionally, physicians and college teachers are near the top of the status hierarchy, while ushers and shoe shiners fall to the bottom.

extrinsic motivation
motivation that drives people to obtain tangible rewards, such as money and prestige.

intrinsic motivation
motivation that causes people to work for their own enjoyment not for the rewards work may bring.

status
the evaluation of a role or person by other relevant members of a group or society.

But the view of what professions have the highest status is changing. As Figure 10-5 indicates, 18- to 37-year-olds have considerably different views of what are high-status jobs from those in late adulthood. For example, 18- to 37-year-olds are more likely to view professions that provide fame, such as acting, as having high prestige (Harris Poll, 2014).

SATISFACTION ON THE JOB. The status associated with particular jobs affects people's satisfaction with their work. As might be expected, the higher the status of the job, the more satisfied people tend to be. Furthermore, the status of the job of the major wage earner can affect the status of the other members of the family (Schieman, McBrier, & van Gundy, 2003).

Status isn't everything, of course: Worker satisfaction depends on a number of factors, not the least of which is the nature of the job itself. For example, consider the plight of Patricia Alford, who worked at the Equitable Life Insurance Company. Her job consisted of entering data into a computer nine hours each day except for two 15-minute breaks and an hour off for lunch. She never knew how much she was earning because her salary depended on how many insurance claims she entered into the computer each day. The pay standards were so complicated that her pay varied from $217 to $400 a week, providing her with a weekly surprise at paycheck time (Booth, 1987; Ting, 1997; Hertel & Wittchen, 2008).

Other people who work at computers are monitored on a minute-by-minute basis; supervisors can consistently see how many keystrokes they are entering. In some

Figure 10-5 Status Hierarchy of Various Professions

Perception of occupational prestige. Young adults perceive occupational prestige differently from those in late adulthood. Bars to the right show the degree to which young adults rate a profession higher than those in late adulthood; bars to the left show the degree to which young adults rate a profession lower than those in late adulthood. (**Source:** Harris Poll, 2014.)

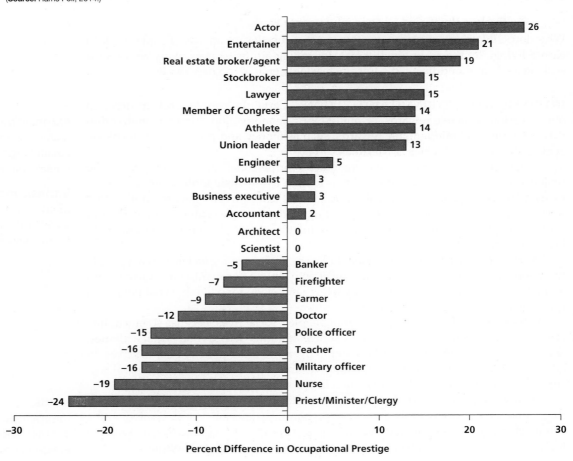

Percent Difference in Occupational Prestige

firms in which workers use the telephone for sales or to take customer orders, their conversations are monitored by supervisors. Workers' Internet use and email are also monitored or restricted by many employers. Not surprisingly, such forms of job stress produce worker dissatisfaction (MacDonald, 2003).

Job satisfaction is higher when workers have input into the nature of their jobs and feel their ideas and opinions are valued. They also prefer jobs that offer variety, requiring many different types of skills, over those that require only a few. Finally, the more influence employees have over others, either directly as supervisors or more informally, the greater their job satisfaction (Peterson & Wilson, 2004; Thompson & Prottas, 2006).

A CHANGE IN PERSPECTIVE: HOW ADULTS VIEW WORK AT MIDLIFE.   For many, middle age is the time of greatest productivity, success, and earning power. It is also a time when occupational success may become considerably less alluring than it once was. This is particularly the case for those who may not have achieved the occupational success they had hoped for when they began their careers. In such cases, work becomes less valued, while family and other off-the-job interests become more important (Grzywacz, Butler, & Almeida, 2008).

The factors that make a job satisfying change during middle age. Younger adults are interested in abstract and future-oriented concerns, such as the opportunity for advancement or the possibility of recognition and approval. Middle-aged employees care more about the here-and-now qualities of work. For instance, they are more concerned with pay, working conditions, and specific policies, such as the way vacation time is calculated. Furthermore, as at earlier stages of life, changes in overall job quality are associated with changes in stress levels for both men and women (Cohrs, Abele, & Dette, 2006; Rantanen et al., 2012; Hamlet & Herrick, 2014).

In general, though, the relationship between age and work seems to be positive: The older workers are, the more overall job satisfaction they experience. This pattern is not altogether surprising, since younger adults who are dissatisfied with their positions will quit them and find new positions that they like better. Furthermore, older workers have fewer opportunities to change positions. Consequently, they may learn to live with what they have and accept that the position they have is the best they are likely to get. Such acceptance may ultimately be translated into satisfaction (Tangri, Thomas, & Mednick, 2003).

Yet, as we shall see next, an increasing number of adults do embrace new careers in midlife.

SWITCHING—AND STARTING—CAREERS AT MIDLIFE.   When Perry Nicholas—a former boxer who also worked in construction—hit 50, he decided to go for a lifelong goal of becoming a full-time teacher. The once-amateur middleweight contender knocks 'em out with his poetry, having been nominated for a 2007 Pushcart [Poetry] Prize (Continelli, 2006, p. B3).

One of the remarkable characteristics of middle age is its variety, as the paths that different people travel continue to diverge. The twists and turns in Perry Nicholas's life path are not unusual: Few lives follow a set, predictable pattern through middle adulthood.

People who change careers in midlife do so for several reasons. It may be that their jobs offer little challenge; they have achieved mastery, and what was once difficult is now routine. Other people change because their jobs have changed in ways they do not like, or they may have lost their job. They may be asked to accomplish more with fewer resources, or technological advances may have resulted in such drastic changes in their day-to-day activities that they no longer enjoy what they do.

Still others are unhappy with the status they have achieved and wish to make a fresh start. Some are burned out or feel that they are on a treadmill. In addition, some people simply do not like to think of themselves doing the same thing for the rest of their lives. For them, middle age is seen as the last point at which they can make a meaningful occupational change (Grzywacz et al., 2008).

Finally, a significant number of people, almost all of them women, return to the job market after having taken time off to raise children. Some may need to find paying

Figure 10-6 Women at Work

The percentage of women age 55 to 64 who are in the labor force has steadily increased since the middle of the last century.
THINKING ABOUT THE DATA: What are some of the reasons why women's participation in the labor force has increased?
(**Source:** Hipple, 2016.)

work after a divorce. Since the mid-1980s, the number of women in the workforce who are in their 50s has grown significantly. Around half of women between the ages of 55 and 64—and an even larger percentage of those who graduated from college—are now in the workforce (see Figure 10-6).

People may enter new professions with unrealistically high expectations and be disappointed by the realities of the situation. Furthermore, middle-aged people who start new careers may find themselves in entry-level positions. As a consequence, their peers on the job may be considerably younger than they are. But in the long run, taking on a new career in middle adulthood can be invigorating. Those who switch or start new careers may be especially valued employees (Barnett & Hyde, 2001; Juntunen, Wegner, & Matthews, 2002).

Some forecasters suggest that career changes may become the rule rather than the exception. According to this point of view, technological advances will occur so rapidly that people will be forced periodically to change what they do to earn a living, often dramatically. In such a scenario, people will have not one but several careers during their lifetime.

Challenges of Work: Burnout, Unemployment, and Age Discrimination

LO 10.8 **Examine some of the challenges that workers face today.**

Mary Gehrig can't tolerate the thought of another "crisis" deadline in her job as an advertising executive. Twenty years ago, the panic in the office over a client's visit felt like excitement. Now it's just stressful, and Mary, age 42, is tired of missing her children's recitals, plays, and hockey games.

Bill Martin is still recovering from the shock he received last summer when the paper mill he had worked for since high school suddenly closed down. With two kids on the brink of college, Martin, 48, doesn't know where he'll find the money for their educations—or for that matter, where he'll find another job.

Arturo Albanez has worked since he was 15 in a variety of occupations. As none of his jobs provided for a pension, Albanez, 63, knows he will have to continue working the remainder of his life. But the opportunities are thinning out. "They want the young guys," he says.

Middle and late adulthood brings a variety of challenges for workers. A job that once held satisfactions becomes stressful or boring. Companies downsize or close, throwing people out of work overnight; these people are uncertain of where they'll land next. Advancing age narrows opportunities for finding new work. These challenges can pose threats to a worker's identity and self-esteem.

BURNOUT.   Job satisfaction is not universal in middle adulthood. For some people, work becomes increasingly stressful as dissatisfaction with working conditions or with the nature of the job mounts. In some cases, conditions become so bad that the result is burnout or a decision to change jobs.

For 44-year-old Peggy Augarten, early morning shifts in the intensive care unit of the suburban hospital where she worked were becoming increasingly difficult. Although it had always been hard to lose a patient, recently she found herself breaking into tears over her patients at the strangest moments: while she was doing the laundry, washing the dishes, or watching TV. When she began to dread going to work in the morning, she knew that her feelings about her job were undergoing a fundamental change.

Augarten's response can probably be traced to the phenomenon of burnout. **Burnout** occurs when workers experience dissatisfaction, disillusionment, frustration, and weariness from their jobs. It occurs most often in jobs that involve helping others, and it often strikes those who initially were the most idealistic and driven. In some ways, such workers may be overcommitted to their jobs, and the realization that they can make only minor dents in huge societal problems such as poverty and medical care can be disappointing and demoralizing. Furthermore, many such professions require long hours, and the difficulty of achieving success can lead to burnout (see Table 10-2; Dunford et al., 2012; Rössler et al., 2015; Miyasaki et al., 2017).

One of the consequences of burnout is a growing cynicism about one's work. For instance, an employee might say to himself, "What am I working so hard on this for? No one is even going to notice that I've come in on budget for the last two years." In addition, workers may feel indifference and lack of concern about how well they do their job. The idealism with which a worker may have entered a profession is replaced by pessimism and the attitude that it is impossible to provide any kind of meaningful solution to a problem (Schaufeli & Salanova, 2007; Oreyzi & Shapouri, 2015).

People can combat burnout, even those in professions with high demands and seemingly insurmountable burdens. For example, the nurse who despairs of not having enough time for every patient can be helped to realize that a more feasible goal— such as giving patients a quick backrub—can be equally important. Jobs can also be structured so that workers (and their supervisors) pay attention to small victories in their daily work, such as the pleasure of a client's gratitude, even though the "big picture" of disease, poverty, racism, and an inadequate educational system may look gloomy. Furthermore, engaging in "best practices" on the job, and knowing that one is doing one's best, can decrease burnout. Finally, mentally disengaging from work during leisure time is helpful in reducing the consequences of burnout (Peisah et al., 2009; Sonnentag, 2012; Wilkinson, Infantolino, & Wacha-Montes, 2017).

Burnout occurs when a worker experiences dissatisfaction, disillusionment, frustration, or weariness from his or her job. Those who experience it grow increasingly cynical or indifferent toward their work.

burnout
a situation that occurs when workers experience dissatisfaction, disillusionment, frustration, and weariness from their jobs.

Table 10-2 High Burnout Careers

1. Physician
2. Nurse
3. Social Worker
4. Teacher
5. School Principal
6. Attorney
7. Police Officer
8. Public Accountant
9. Fast Food Worker
10. Retail Worker

Source: White, 2017.

The loss of employment during midlife can be a shattering experience leading to pessimism, cynicism, and despondency.

UNEMPLOYMENT. For many workers, unemployment is a hard reality of life, and the implications of not being able to find work are as much psychological as they are economic. For those who have been fired, laid off by corporate downsizing, or forced out of jobs by technological advances, being out of work can be psychologically and even physically devastating (Winefield, 2002; Galic, 2007).

Unemployment can leave people feeling anxious, depressed, and irritable. Their self-confidence may plummet, and they may be unable to concentrate. According to one analysis, every time the unemployment rate goes up 1 percent, there is a 4 percent rise in suicide, and admissions to psychiatric facilities go up by some 4 percent for men and 2 percent for women (Inoue et al., 2006; Rizvi et al., 2015).

Even aspects of unemployment that might at first seem positive, such as having more time, can produce disagreeable consequences. Perhaps because of feelings of depression and having too much time on their hands, unemployed people are less apt to participate in community activities, use libraries, and read than employed people. They are more likely to be late for appointments and even for meals (Ball & Orford, 2002; Tyre & McGinn, 2003).

And these problems may linger. Middle-aged adults who lose their jobs tend to stay unemployed longer than younger workers and have fewer opportunities for gratifying work as they age. As we shall see next, employers may discriminate against older job applicants and make it more difficult to obtain new employment. Ironically, such discrimination is not only illegal but is also based on misguided assumptions: Research finds that older workers show less absenteeism than younger ones, hold their jobs longer, are more reliable, and are more willing to learn new skills (Menkens, 2005; Ng & Feldman, 2008).

In sum, midlife unemployment is a shattering experience. And for some people, especially those who never find meaningful work again, it taints their entire view of the world. For people forced into such involuntary—and premature—retirement, the loss of a job can lead to pessimism, cynicism, and despondency. Overcoming such feelings often takes time and a good deal of psychological adjustment to come to terms with the situation. In addition, there are challenges for those who *do* find a new career, too (Waters & Moore, 2002; Galic, 2007).

OLDER WORKERS: COMBATING AGE DISCRIMINATION. Many other people continue to work, either full- or part-time, for some part of late adulthood. That they can do so is largely because of legislation that was passed in the late 1970s, in which mandatory retirement ages were made illegal in almost every profession. Part of broader legislation that makes age discrimination illegal, these laws gave most workers the opportunity either to remain in jobs they held previously or to begin working in entirely different fields (Lindemann & Kadue, 2003; Lain, 2012).

Whether older adults continue to work because they enjoy the intellectual and social rewards that work provides or because they need to work for financial reasons, many encounter age discrimination. Age discrimination remains a reality despite laws making it illegal. Some employers encourage older workers to leave their jobs in order to replace them with younger employees whose salaries will be considerably lower. Furthermore, some employers believe that older workers are not up to the demands of the job or are less willing to adapt to a changing workplace—stereotypes about older adults that are enduring, despite legislative changes (Menkens, 2005).

There is little evidence to support the idea that older workers' ability to perform their jobs declines. In many fields, such as art, literature, science, politics, or even entertainment, it is easy to find examples of people who have made some of their greatest contributions during late adulthood. Even in those few professions that were specifically exempted from laws prohibiting mandatory retirement ages—those involving public safety—the evidence does not support the notion that workers should be retired at an arbitrary age.

For instance, one large-scale, careful study of older police officers, firefighters, and prison guards came to the conclusion that age was not a good predictor of whether a worker was likely to be incapacitated on the job, or the level of his or her general work performance. Instead, a case-by-case analysis of individual workers' performance was a more accurate predictor (Landy & Conte, 2004).

Development in Your Life

Choosing a Career

One of the greatest challenges people face is making a decision that will have lifelong implications: the choice of a career. Although there is no single correct choice—most people can be happy in any of several different jobs—the options can be daunting. Here are some guidelines for at least starting to come to grips with the question of what occupational path to follow.

- Systematically evaluate a variety of choices. Libraries contain a wealth of information about potential career paths, and most colleges and universities have career centers that can provide occupational data and guidance.

- Know yourself. Evaluate your strengths and weaknesses, perhaps by completing a questionnaire at a college career center that can provide insight into your interests, skills, and values.

- Create a "balance sheet," listing the potential gains and losses that you will incur from a particular profession. First list the gains and losses that you will experience directly, and then list gains and losses for others, such

as family members. Next, write down your projected self-approval or self-disapproval from the potential career. Finally, write down the projected social approval or disapproval you are likely to receive from others. By systematically evaluating a set of potential careers according to each of these criteria, you will be in a better position to compare different possibilities.

- "Try out" different careers through paid or unpaid internships. By seeing a job firsthand, interns are able to get a better sense of what an occupation is truly like.

- Remember that if you make a mistake, you can change careers. People today increasingly change careers in early adulthood and even beyond. No one should feel locked into a decision made earlier in life. As we have seen throughout this book, people develop substantially over the course of their lives.

- It is reasonable to expect that shifting values, interests, abilities, and life circumstances might make a different career more appropriate later in life than the one chosen during early adulthood.

Although age discrimination remains a problem, market forces may help reduce its severity. As baby boomers retire and the workforce drastically shrinks, companies may begin to offer incentives to older adults to either remain in the workforce or to return to it after they have retired. Although retirement remains the norm for most older adults, not everyone wants to—or can afford to—stop working. (Also see the *Development in Your Life* box, above.)

Module 10.3 Review

LO 10.6 **Analyze the methods by which people choose their careers and the ways in which career choices affect personal identity.**

According to Eli Ginzberg, people pass through three stages in considering careers: the fantasy period, the tentative period, and the realistic period. Gender stereotypes are changing, but women still experience subtle prejudice in career choices, roles, and wages. Given the time to establish themselves, most legal *and* illegal immigrants succeed financially, contributing more in taxes paid than they use in government services.

LO 10.7 **Explore the varied reasons why people work.**

People work because of both extrinsic and intrinsic motivation factors.

LO 10.8 **Examine some of the challenges that work presents in the present day.**

Midlife career changes are becoming more prevalent, motivated usually by dissatisfaction, the need for more challenge or status, or the desire to return to the workforce after childrearing. Unemployment in midlife can have negative economic, psychological, and physical effects.

Journal Writing Prompt

Applying Lifespan Development: How would you go about designing a course for high school or college students to assist them in choosing a career?

Epilogue

"Who am I?" and "How do I feel about myself?" are two key questions in an individual's ever-evolving sense of self across the life span. In this chapter, we considered the development of the self, examining how we understand and evaluate ourselves, and how we go about choosing our life's work. We began by tracing the evidence we have that infants are aware of their own existence—how they come to understand that they are individuals distinct from the world around them. We then focused on how self-concept develops in the years from preschool to early adulthood and how children develop racial and ethnic awareness. From there, we looked at self-esteem and discussed the ways that children and adolescents develop a positive—or negative—view of themselves.

We saw how social comparison provides a useful tool for evaluating one's abilities in light of the abilities of one's peers. We also considered how adolescents are able to differentiate various aspects of the self, which leads them to evaluate those aspects in different ways. Finally, we examined the stages people go through in choosing their careers, and the reasons they work, both extrinsic and intrinsic. We concluded with a look at the changing role of work in people's lives and the difficulties brought about by job burnout, unemployment, and age discrimination.

Before turning to the next chapter, recall the prologue to this one, about Jim Aparicio and his career change in middle adulthood. Using your knowledge of factors affecting career choice, the midlife period, and burnout, consider these questions.

1. How do you think that Jim's self-esteem and self-concept changed over time as he established his first career, experienced burnout, and then re-established his career in a new field?

2. Based on Jim's comments, what does he appear to value most in a job? How has this value system potentially changed over time?

3. What could Jim have done as an adolescent and college student to help him make a more informed career choice?

4. Apply your understanding of women's social clocks by describing other factors a woman would have to consider if she were in a situation similar to Jim's.

Looking Back

LO 10.1 Describe the process by which young children develop an understanding of themselves.

Infants begin to develop self-awareness at about the age of 12 months. They also begin to develop a theory of mind at this time: knowledge and beliefs about how they and others think. During the preschool years, children develop a self-concept, a set of beliefs about who they are as individuals. Typically, they overestimate their skills and knowledge in all areas. Preschool-age children's self-concept is also heavily influenced by the culture in which they are raised. Both the sense of gender and the sense of race develop in the preschool years.

LO 10.2 Trace the shift in self-understanding in the middle childhood and adolescent years.

According to Erik Erikson, children in the middle childhood years are in the industry-versus-inferiority stage, focusing on achieving competence and responding to a wide range of personal challenges. Children in the middle childhood years begin to view themselves in terms of psychological characteristics and to differentiate their self-concepts into separate areas. They develop a sense of both their strengths and their weaknesses. During adolescence, self-concept differentiates to encompass others' views as well as one's own and to include multiple aspects simultaneously. Differentiation of self-concept can cause confusion as behaviors reflect a complex definition of the self.

LO 10.3 Explain how the process of self-definition continues in adulthood.

Identity formation continues in adulthood, with a new focus on the major milestones that adults face. These are called the social clocks of adulthood. According to George Vaillant, career consolidation is a developmental stage in which young adults define their careers and themselves.

LO 10.4 Analyze the origins and effects of self-esteem.

Self-esteem is the emotional side of the self-concept, involving the self-evaluative feelings that people have about various aspects of themselves. In middle childhood, self-esteem is often differentiated with positive evaluations in some areas and negative in others. Adolescents' increasingly accurate self-concepts enable them to form self-evaluations that contain both positive and negative elements. Adolescent self-esteem changes over time, with boys and girls experiencing increases and decreases at different times. Males and females also differ in the aspects of themselves that they consider to be particularly important for self-esteem. Socioeconomic status, race, and ethnicity also affect self-esteem, with African American and white adolescents generally having higher self-esteem than other groups.

LO 10.5 Explain how social comparison functions in childhood and adolescence.

Through social comparison, people evaluate their behavior, abilities, expertise, and opinions by comparing them with those of other people. Some children choose to compare themselves with others who have less competence or ability, a phenomenon known as downward social comparison. Adolescents increasingly compare themselves with friends and peers as opposed to parents and other adults, using their peers as a reference group. Adolescents with chronically low self-esteem become victims of a cycle of failure that can lead to heightened aggression, antisocial behavior, and delinquency. Those with high self-esteem focus on their strengths and hold positive expectations for the future.

LO 10.6 Analyze the methods by which people choose their careers and the ways in which career choices affect personal identity.

A model developed by Eli Ginzberg suggests that people typically move through three stages in choosing a career: the fantasy period of youth, the tentative period of adolescence, and the realistic period of young adulthood. Other approaches, such as that of John Holland, attempt to match people's personality types with suitable careers. This sort of research underlies most career-related inventories and measures used in career counseling. Gender-role prejudice and stereotyping remain a problem in the workplace and in preparing for and selecting careers. Women tend to be pressured into certain occupations and out of others, and they earn less money for the same work.

LO 10.7 Explore the varied reasons why people work.

Extrinsic motivation causes people to work for concrete rewards, such as money or prestige, while intrinsic motivation views work as an important end in itself, providing benefits such as a personal identity and a sense of satisfaction. Work also provides a method for determining status, the societal evaluation of the role that a person plays. Status contributes to, but does not completely determine, the level of satisfaction that people feel about their jobs. While young adults focus on abstract and future-oriented concerns in their jobs, middle-aged workers care more about the reality of the job, including pay, working conditions, vacations, and so on. A growing number of people voluntarily change careers in midlife, some to increase job challenge, satisfaction, and status, and others to return to a workforce they left years earlier to rear children.

LO 10.8 Examine some of the challenges that workers face today.

For most people, midlife is a time of job satisfaction. Career ambition becomes less of a force in the lives of middle-aged workers, and outside interests begin to be more valued. Job dissatisfaction can result from disappointment with one's achievements and position in life or from the feeling that one has failed to make a difference in the insurmountable problems of the job. This latter phenomenon, termed *burnout*, often affects those in the helping professions. Some people in middle adulthood must face unexpected unemployment, which brings economic, psychological, and physical consequences. Older adults who continue to work, or who seek new jobs, often face subtle or overt age discrimination, even though this has been illegal since the 1970s.

Key Terms and Concepts

self-awareness 304
self-concept 305
collectivistic orientation 306
individualistic orientation 306
race dissonance 306
identity achievement 309
identity foreclosure 310
moratorium 310

identity diffusion 310
emerging adulthood 310
social clock 311
career consolidation 312
self-esteem 313
social comparison 318
reference groups 319
fantasy period 321

tentative period 321
realistic period 321
communal professions 322
agentic professions 322
extrinsic motivation 325
intrinsic motivation 325
status 325
burnout 329

Chapter 11
Moral Development and Aggression

SKA/Getty Images

Learning Objectives

LO 11.1 Compare and contrast the various approaches to moral development.

LO 11.2 Summarize Kohlberg's and Gilligan's theories of moral development, and explain how they differ.

LO 11.3 Identify the factors that influence moral and prosocial behaviors, including the roles played by gender and culture.

LO 11.4 Identify the four basic parenting styles, and summarize how each style influences a child's development.

LO 11.5 Summarize the development of religion in childhood and adolescence.

LO 11.6 Identify the purposes religion and spirituality serve in adulthood, and describe Fowler's stages of faith development.

LO 11.7 Explain the development of aggression in preschool children, and summarize the gender differences.

LO 11.8 Compare and contrast the different approaches that seek to explain the causes of aggression in children.

LO 11.9 Summarize the cycle of violence hypothesis, and identify the social and cultural factors that contribute to family violence.

Chapter Overview

Prologue: Drinking, Driving, and Recovery

Samantha Pevely's first Alcoholics Anonymous meeting didn't go very well. She didn't go by choice, and she exclaimed, "I don't really belong here! I'm not an alcoholic like the rest of you." The 22-year-old resented being forced to do anything, but after being convicted of her third DUI in the past 5 years, she knew that she was lucky to not be in prison.

Over the next few weeks, though, Samantha began to open up to the group about her problem drinking. "My dad was a cop in our small town," she explained, "He loved me a lot, but sometimes too much, I think. Ever since I was a little kid I could get away with anything at home. And as a teenager when my problems in school and with the law got more serious, he always managed to pull strings to get me out of trouble." After a few months, Samantha's perspective began to change. "I used to think my dad set me back in life by deciding he was going to give me every advantage he could as I was growing up," she says. "But now I see that he was just trying to ease my path through life and help me avoid some tough situations, because he really wanted me to make something out of my life. What he thought were good choices on his part actually ended up hurting me in the long run." ■

Looking Ahead

Making decisions—and the moral judgments that lie behind those decisions—among multiple possibilities is complicated. Moral decisions especially involve a complex process of weighing one value against another, and the outcome has profound consequences for the course of people's lives.

In this chapter, we examine two key aspects of social behavior: moral development and aggression. We begin by considering how children develop a sense of society's rights and wrongs and how that development can lead them to be helpful to others. We see how reasoning about moral dilemmas changes in adolescence and how the expression of moral and helping behavior develops. We look at a range of parenting styles and discuss how parents and other authority figures use discipline to shape children's behavior.

Next, we focus on religion and spirituality. We examine why religion is important to many people. We consider the comfort it provides in times of trouble and how it helps people make sense of their lives. We discuss how Jean Piaget's approach to cognitive development offers ways to think about the development of religious thought, and we look at the stages of faith development

Evaluating what is the right course of action becomes increasingly complicated as our ability to reason matures.

outlined by James Fowler. We examine the role religion plays in developing an iden-tity in adolescence. We also consider the relationship between religious belief and life satisfaction in late adulthood, and religion's special significance for older African Americans.

We then turn to aggression and violence, considering sources and consequences for both. We ask whether aggression is an innate, genetically determined behavior and/or a response a child learns from his or her environment while growing up. We look, too, at ways of decreasing aggression in children and increasing their moral be-haviors. Finally, we consider violence and abuse directed toward children, spouses, and elders by family members. We discuss ways of dealing with spousal abuse and look at the cultural roots of domestic violence.

MODULE 11.1

DEVELOPING MORALITY: FOLLOWING SOCIETY'S RIGHTS AND WRONGS

Lena and Carrie were part of a group of preschoolers who wanted to act out Goldilocks and The Three Bears. *The teacher began assigning parts. "Carrie, you can be Baby Bear. And Lena, you be Goldilocks." Tears welled up in Carrie's eyes. "I don't want to be Baby Bear," she sobbed. Lena put her arms around Carrie. "You can be Goldilocks, too. We'll be the Goldilocks twins." Carrie cheered up at once, grateful that Lena had understood her feelings and responded with kindness.*

In this short scenario, we see many of the key elements of morality as it is played out among preschool-age children. Changes in children's views of what is ethically right and what is the right way to behave involve a growing awareness of others and are an important element of growth during the preschool years and beyond.

Moral Development

LO 11.1 **Compare and contrast the various approaches to moral development.**

moral development
the changes in people's sense of justice and of what is right and wrong, and in their behavior re-lated to moral issues.

Moral development refers to changes in people's sense of justice and of what is right and wrong, and in their behavior related to moral issues. Developmentalists have considered moral development in terms of children's reasoning about morality, their attitudes toward moral lapses, and their behavior when faced with moral issues. In the process of studying moral development, several approaches have evolved (Hallpike, 2008; Sinnott-Armstrong, 2008).

SOCIAL LEARNING APPROACHES TO MORALITY. Social learning approaches to moral development focus on how the environment in which the individual operates produces moral behavior.

prosocial behavior
helping behavior that benefits others.

Social learning approaches build upon behavioral approaches. They acknowledge that some instances of an individual's **prosocial behavior** (helping behavior that ben-efits others) stem from situations in which they have received positive reinforcement for acting in a morally appropriate way. For instance, when Mia's mother tells her she has been "terrific" for helping her younger brother complete a difficult homework assignment, her mother has reinforced that helping behavior. As a consequence, Mia is more likely to engage in such prosocial behavior in the future (Schulz et al., 2013; Cuadrado, Tabernero, & Steinel, 2015; Buon, Habib, & Frey, 2017).

Social learning approaches go a step further, arguing that not all prosocial behav-ior has to be directly performed and subsequently reinforced for learning to occur. According to social learning approaches, we also learn moral behavior more indirectly by observing the behavior of others, called *models*. Children and adolescents imi-tate models who receive reinforcement for their behavior, and ultimately they learn to perform the behavior themselves. For example, when Mia's boyfriend David watches Mia help her brother with the assignment and be praised for it, David is more likely to engage in prosocial behavior himself at some later point (Bandura, 1977, 2004).

Quite a few studies illustrate the power of models and of social learning more generally in producing prosocial behavior in preschool-age children. For example, experiments have shown that children who view someone behaving generously or unselfishly are apt to follow the model's example, subsequently behaving in a generous or an unselfish manner themselves when put in a similar situation. The opposite also holds true: If a model behaves selfishly, children who observe such behavior tend to behave more selfishly themselves (Nielsen, 2006; Schönpflug & Bilz, 2009; Martin & Olson, 2015).

Studies have shown that children who view someone behaving generously are apt to follow the model's example.

Not all models are equally effective in producing prosocial responses. For instance, preschoolers are more apt to model the behavior of warm, responsive adults than of adults who appear colder. Furthermore, models viewed as highly competent or high in prestige are more effective than others (Ellis & Zarbatany, 2007).

Children do more than simply mimic unthinkingly behavior that they see rewarded in others. By observing moral conduct, they are reminded of society's norms about the importance of moral behavior as conveyed by parents, teachers, and other powerful authority figures. They notice the connections between particular situations and certain kinds of behavior. This increases the likelihood that similar situations will elicit similar behavior in the observer.

Consequently, modeling paves the way for the development of more general rules and principles in a process called **abstract modeling**. Rather than always modeling the particular behavior of others, children begin to develop generalized principles that underlie the behavior they observe. After observing repeated instances in which a model is rewarded for acting in a morally desirable way, children begin the process of inferring and learning the general principles of moral conduct (Bandura, 1991; Zimmerman & Schunk, 2003).

abstract modeling
the process in which modeling paves the way for the development of more general rules and principles.

EMPATHY IN ADOLESCENCE. Around the start of adolescence, more sophisticated kinds of empathy begin to emerge. Adolescents experience empathy not only in specific situations but also empathy for collective groups, such as people living in poverty or victims of racism (Hoffman, 2001; Eisenberg, Fabes, & Spinrad, 2006; Allemand, Steiger, & Fend, 2015).

For example, in early adolescence, a teenager may experience empathy when she learns a friend is ill. Understanding the emotions that the friend is experiencing—concerns about missing classes, fear about falling behind, and so forth—may lead the teenager to offer to help her classmate. However, when hearing about victims of an outbreak of bird flu in China, the same girl may be emotionally unmoved.

Later in adolescence, however, as her cognitive abilities increase and she can reason on more abstract levels, the same girl may feel empathy for collective groups. Not only may she feel emotionally involved over victims of specific situations (such as people who lost their homes as a consequence of a recent hurricane), but she may also experience deep emotional responses toward abstract groups such as the homeless, whose experiences may be completely unfamiliar to her.

GENETIC APPROACHES TO MORALITY. The newest, and most controversial, approach to morality suggests that particular genes may underlie some aspects of moral behavior. According to this view, preschoolers have a genetic predisposition to behave generously or selfishly.

In one study designed to illustrate this approach, researchers gave preschoolers the opportunity to behave generously by sharing stickers. Those who were more selfish and less generous were more likely to have a variation in a gene called AVPR1A, which regulates a hormone in the brain that is related to social behavior (Avinum et al., 2011; Pappa et al., 2016).

It is unlikely that the gene mutation fully accounts for the preschoolers' lack of generosity. The environment in which the children were raised also is likely to play a significant, and perhaps predominant, role in determining moral behavior. Still, the findings are provocative in showing that generosity may have genetic roots.

empathy
the understanding of what another individual feels.

EMPATHY AND MORAL BEHAVIOR. According to some developmentalists, **empathy**—the understanding of what another individual feels—lies at the heart of some kinds of moral behavior. The roots of empathy grow early. One-year-old infants cry when they hear other infants crying. By ages 2 and 3, toddlers will offer gifts and spontaneously share toys with other children and adults, even if they are strangers (Ruffman, Lorimer & Scarf, 2017).

During the preschool years, empathy continues to grow as children's ability to monitor and regulate their emotional and cognitive responses increases. Some theorists believe that increasing empathy—as well as other positive emotions, such as sympathy and admiration—leads children to behave in a more moral fashion. In addition, some negative emotions—such as anger at an unfair situation or shame over previous transgressions—also may promote moral behavior (Decety & Jackson, 2006; Bischof-Köhler, 2012; Eisenberg, Spinrad, & Morris, 2014).

The notion that negative emotions may promote moral development is one that Sigmund Freud first suggested in his theory of psychoanalytic personality development. Freud argued that a child's *superego*, the part of the personality that represents societal do's and don'ts, is developed through resolution of the *Oedipal conflict*. Children come to identify with their same-sex parent, incorporating that parent's standards of morality in order to avoid unconscious guilt raised by the Oedipal conflict.

Whether or not we accept Freud's account of the Oedipal conflict and the guilt it produces, his theory is consistent with more recent findings. These suggest that preschoolers' attempts to avoid experiencing negative emotions sometimes lead them to act in more moral, helpful ways. For instance, one reason children help others is to avoid the feelings of personal distress that they experience when they are confronted with another person's unhappiness or misfortune (Valiente, Eisenberg, & Fabes, 2004; Cushman et al., 2013).

Moral Reasoning and Prosocial Behavior

LO 11.2 **Summarize Kohlberg's and Gilligan's theories of moral development, and explain how they differ.**

> Your wife is near death from an unusual kind of cancer. One drug exists that the physicians think might save her—a form of radium that a scientist in a nearby city has recently developed. The drug, though, is expensive to manufacture, and the scientist is charging 10 times what the drug costs him to make. He pays $1,000 for the radium and charges $10,000 for a small dose. You have gone to everyone you know to borrow money, but you can get together only $2,500—one-quarter of what you need. You've told the scientist that your wife is dying and asked him to sell it more cheaply or let you pay later. But the scientist has said, "No, I discovered the drug and I'm going to make money from it." In desperation, you consider breaking into the scientist's laboratory to steal the drug for your wife. Should you do it?

According to developmental psychologist Lawrence Kohlberg and his colleagues, the answer that individuals give to this question reveals central aspects of their sense of morality and justice. He suggests that individuals' responses to moral dilemmas such as this one reveal the stage of moral development they have attained—and yield information about their general level of cognitive development (Kohlberg, 1984; Colby & Kohlberg, 1987; Buon, Habib & Frey, 2017).

Kohlberg contends that people pass through a series of stages as their sense of justice evolves and in the kind of reasoning they use to make moral judgments.

Primarily due to cognitive characteristics that we discussed earlier, younger school-age children tend to think either in terms of concrete, unvarying rules ("It is always wrong to steal" or "I'll be punished if I steal") or in terms of the rules of society ("Good people don't steal" or "What if everyone stole?").

By the time they reach adolescence, however, individuals are able to reason on a higher plane, typically having reached Piaget's stage of formal operations. They are capable of comprehending abstract, formal principles of morality, and they consider cases such as the one presented above in terms of broader issues of morality and of right and wrong ("Stealing may be acceptable if you are following your own conscience and doing the right thing").

Kohlberg suggests that moral development emerges in a three-level sequence, which is further subdivided into six stages (see Table 11-1). At the lowest level, **preconventional morality** (Stages 1 and 2), people follow rigid rules based on punishments or rewards. For example, a student at the preconventional level might evaluate the moral dilemma posed in the story by saying that it was not worth stealing the drug because if you were caught, you would go to jail.

In the next level, that of **conventional morality** (Stages 3 and 4), people approach moral problems in terms of their own position as good, responsible members of society. Some at this level would decide *against* stealing the drug because they think they would feel guilty or dishonest for violating social norms. Others would decide

preconventional morality
Kohlberg's first level of moral reasoning, in which the concrete interests of the individual are considered in terms of rewards and punishments.

conventional morality
Kohlberg's second level of moral reasoning, in which people approach moral problems as members of society.

Table 11-1 Kohlberg's Sequence of Moral Reasoning

Level	Stage	Sample Moral Reasoning	
		In Favor of Stealing	Against Stealing
LEVEL 1 Preconventional morality The main considerations are the avoidance of punishment and the desire for rewards.	**STAGE 1** Obedience and punishment orientation: People obey rules to avoid being punished. Obedience is its own reward.	"You shouldn't just let your wife die. People will blame you for not doing enough, and they'll blame the scientist for not selling you the drug for less money."	"You can't steal the drug because you'll be arrested and go to jail. Even if you aren't caught, you'll feel guilty, and you'll always worry that the police may figure out what you did."
	STAGE 2 Reward orientation: People obey rules in order to earn rewards for their own benefit.	"Even if you get caught, the jury will understand and give you a short sentence. Meanwhile, your wife is alive. And if you're stopped before you get the drug to your wife, you could probably just return the drug without penalty."	"You shouldn't steal the drug because you're not responsible for your wife's cancer. If you get caught, your wife will still die and you'll be in jail."
LEVEL 2 Conventional morality Membership in society becomes important. People behave in ways that will win the approval of others.	**STAGE 3** "Good boy" morality: People want to be respected by others and try to do what they're supposed to do.	"Who will blame you if you steal a lifesaving drug? But if you just let your wife die, you won't be able to hold your head up in front of your family or your neighbors."	"If you steal the drug, everyone will treat you like a criminal. They will wonder why you couldn't have found some other way to save your wife."
	STAGE 4 Authority and social-order-maintaining morality: People believe that only society, not individuals, can determine what is right. Obeying society's rules is right in itself.	"A husband has certain responsibilities toward his wife. If you want to live an honorable life, you can't let fear of the consequences get in the way of saving her. If you ever want to sleep again, you have to save her."	"You shouldn't let your concern for your wife cloud your judgment. Stealing the drug may feel right at the moment, but you'll live to regret breaking the law."
LEVEL 3 Postconventional morality People accept that there are certain ideals and principles of morality that must govern our actions. These ideals are more important than any particular society's rules.	**STAGE 5** Morality of contract, individual rights, and democratically accepted law: People rightly feel obligated to follow the agreed rules of society. But as societies develop over time, rules have to be updated to make societal changes reflect underlying social principles.	"If you simply follow the law, you will violate the underlying principle of saving your wife's life. If you do take the drug, society will understand your actions and respect them. You can't let an outdated law prevent you from doing the right thing."	"Rules represent society's thinking on the morality of actions. You can't let your short-term emotions interfere with the more permanent rules of society. If you do, society will judge you negatively, and in the end you will lose self-respect."
	STAGE 6 Morality of individual principles and conscience: People accept that laws are attempts to write down specific applications of universal moral principles. Individuals must test these laws against their consciences, which tend to express an inborn sense of those principles.	"If you allow your wife to die, you will have obeyed the letter of the law, but you will have violated the universal principle of life preservation that resides within your conscience. You will blame yourself forever if your wife dies because you obeyed an imperfect law."	"If you become a thief, your conscience will blame you for putting your own interpretation of moral issues above the legitimate rule of law. You will have betrayed your own standards of morality."

(**Source:** Based on Kohlberg, 1969.)

postconventional morality
Kohlberg's third level of moral reasoning, in which people use moral principles that are seen as broader than those of any particular society.

in favor of stealing the drug because if they did nothing in this situation, they would be unable to face others. All of these people would be reasoning at the conventional level of morality.

Finally, individuals using **postconventional morality** (Level 3; Stages 5 and 6) invoke universal moral principles that are considered broader than the rules of the particular society in which they live. People who feel that they would condemn themselves if they did not steal the drug because they would not be living up to their own moral principles would be reasoning at the postconventional level.

Kohlberg's theory proposes that people move through the periods of moral development in a fixed order and that they are unable to reach the highest stage until adolescence, due to deficits in cognitive development that are not overcome until then. However, not everyone is presumed to reach the highest stages: Kohlberg found that postconventional reasoning is relatively rare (Lapsley, 2006; Teo, 2015).

Although Kohlberg's theory provides a good account of the development of moral *judgments*, the links with moral *behavior* are less strong. Still, students at higher levels of moral reasoning are less likely to engage in antisocial behavior at school (such as breaking school rules) and in the community (engaging in juvenile delinquency; Carpendale, 2000; Wu & Liu, 2014).

Furthermore, one experiment found that 15 percent of students who reasoned at the postconventional level of morality—the highest category—cheated when given the opportunity, although they were not as likely to cheat as those at lower levels, where more than half of the students cheated. Clearly, though, knowing what is morally right does not always mean acting that way (Hart, Burock, & London, 2003; Semerci, 2006; Prohaska, 2012).

Kohlberg's theory has also been criticized because it is based solely on observations of members of Western cultures. In fact, cross-cultural research finds that members of more industrialized, technologically advanced cultures move through the stages more rapidly than members of nonindustrialized countries. Why? One explanation is that Kohlberg's higher stages are based on moral reasoning involving governmental and societal institutions like the police and court system. In less industrialized areas, morality may be based more on relationships between people in a particular village. In short, the nature of morality may differ in diverse cultures, and Kohlberg's theory is more suited for Western cultures (Fu et al., 2007).

An aspect of Kohlberg's theory that has proved even more problematic is the difficulty it has explaining *girls'* moral judgments. Because the theory initially was based largely on data from males, some researchers have argued that it does a better job describing boys' moral development than girls' moral development. This would explain the surprising finding that women typically score at a lower level than men on tests of moral judgments using Kohlberg's stage sequence. This result has led to an alternative account of moral development for girls.

GILLIGAN'S ACCOUNT OF MORAL DEVELOPMENT IN GIRLS. Psychologist Carol Gilligan (1982, 1987) has suggested that differences in the ways boys and girls are raised in our society lead to basic distinctions in how men and women view moral behavior. According to her, boys view morality primarily in terms of broad principles such as justice or fairness, whereas girls see it in terms of responsibility toward individuals and willingness to sacrifice themselves to help specific individuals within the context of particular relationships. Compassion for individuals, then, is a more prominent factor in moral behavior for women than it is for men (Gilligan, Lyons, & Hammer, 1990; Gump, Baker, & Roll, 2000; Van der Graaf et al., 2015).

Gilligan views morality as developing among females in a three-stage process (summarized in Table 11-2). In the first stage, called "orientation toward individual survival," females first concentrate on what is practical and best for them, gradually making a transition from selfishness to responsibility, in which they think about what would be best for others. In the second stage, termed "goodness as self-sacrifice," females begin to think that they must sacrifice their own wishes to what other people want.

Ideally, women make a transition from "goodness" to "truth," in which they take into account their own needs plus those of others. This transition leads to the third

Table 11-2 Gilligan's Three Stages of Moral Development for Women

Stage	Characteristics	Example
Stage 1 Orientation toward individual survival	Initial concentration is on what is practical and best for self. Gradual transition from selfishness to responsibility, which includes thinking about what would be best for others.	A first grader may insist on playing only games of her own choosing when playing with a friend.
Stage 2 Goodness as self-sacrifice	Initial view is that a woman must sacrifice her own wishes to what other people want. Gradual transition from "goodness" to "truth," which takes into account needs of both self and others.	Now older, the same girl may believe that to be a good friend, she must play the games her friend chooses, even if she herself doesn't like them.
Stage 3 Morality of nonviolence	A moral equivalence is established between self and others. Hurting anyone—including oneself—is seen as immoral. Most sophisticated form of reasoning, according to Gilligan.	The same girl may realize that both friends must enjoy their time together and look for activities that both she and her friend can enjoy.

stage, "morality of nonviolence," in which women come to see that hurting anyone is immoral—including hurting themselves. This realization establishes a moral equivalence between themselves and others and represents, according to Gilligan, the most sophisticated level of moral reasoning.

It is obvious that Gilligan's sequence of stages is quite different from Kohlberg's, and some developmentalists have suggested that her rejection of Kohlberg's work is too sweeping and that gender differences are not as pronounced as first thought. For instance, some researchers argue that both males and females use similar "justice" and "care" orientations in making moral judgments. Clearly, the question of how boys and girls differ in their moral orientations, as well as the nature of moral development in general, is far from settled (Tappan, 2006; Donleavy, 2008; Milanowicz & Bokus, 2013).

The lingering questions about the nature of moral reasoning have not deterred people from applying what has been learned about morality to everyday life.

From *an educator's* perspective

Should moral development be taught in public schools?

Moral Behavior and Moral Reasoning: Why the Disconnect?

LO 11.3 Identify the factors that influence moral and prosocial behaviors, including the roles played by gender and culture.

Except for social learning perspectives, most of the approaches to moral development (such as those of Kohlberg and Gilligan) focus on moral reasoning. Why has the research spotlight shone more brightly on reasoning about moral behavior, as opposed to examining *actual* behavior?

One reason is that the researchers have assumed that moral reasoning lies at the heart of moral behavior. If people don't have a clear internal moral compass, it seems unreasonable to expect that they will behave in a moral way. Unfortunately, though, there has been a persistent disconnect between prosocial *reasoning* and prosocial *behavior*. Obviously, we'd expect moral reasoning and judgments to be closely associated, but that doesn't seem to be the case. Why?

One reason is that in the real world there are often circumstances that override our internal moral compass. Although we may know and truly believe that it is wrong to break the law by not fully stopping at a stop sign, we may feel that because no one is around, we don't have to come to a complete stop. Or perhaps we're driving someone to a hospital emergency department, and our internal principles about aiding someone in distress are more salient at that moment than our principles about obeying traffic laws. Unlike when they are measured in experiments, moral principles in the real world occur in a particular context that brings its own situational pressures.

In addition, moral judgments are made in a variety of contexts, and it may be an oversimplification to expect that morality will be displayed in similar ways across different domains and situations. According to the **social domain approach**, moral reasoning needs to be considered in the context in which judgments are being made at a given time. Major contexts include the *moral domain* (contexts that focus on concerns about justice), the *social-conventional domain* (contexts involving the need for social groups to function well), and the *personal domain* (contexts involving matters of personal choice). The particular moral judgments are likely to vary according to the domain (Smetana & Turiel, 2003; Turiel, 2006; Smetana, Jambon, & Ball, 2014).

Finally, people sometimes look at situations through the lens of personal choices and freedom rather than in terms of ethical dilemmas. For example, consider the decision to engage in premarital sex. For some people, premarital sex is always ethically wrong and to engage in it is, by definition, an immoral act. But to others, premarital sex is a choice to be decided upon by the individuals who are involved. Similarly, alcohol use—while illegal for adolescents younger than a certain age—may be viewed in terms of a fairly rational cost-benefit analysis (drinking provides certain benefits but also accrues certain costs) rather than in terms of morality. The view that such activities as taking drugs, engaging in sex, and drinking are personal, not moral, choices helps explain the lack of relationship between risk-taking and moral reasoning (Kuther, 2000; Kuther & Higgins-D'Alessandro, 2003; Eisenberg & Morris, 2004).

PROSOCIAL REASONING AND PROSOCIAL BEHAVIOR: THE OTHER SIDE OF THE COIN. We've been focusing on situations in which people are faced with some form of wrongdoing—breaking a rule, violating a moral principle, disobeying a law. But what about the other side of the coin: doing positive, unselfish, or altruistic deeds that benefit others, sometimes at the expense of oneself?

Although there is considerably less research in this area, emerging work suggests that people generally become more sophisticated in their thinking about prosocial behavior. For example, their growing cognitive abilities allow them to distinguish between prosocial behavior that is self-serving (done to gain something, such as looking better in others' eyes) or truly *altruistic* (done to help others and requiring clear self-sacrifice).

Individuals who are unusually helpful to others tend to show more sophisticated moral reasoning than people who are less prosocially active. Furthermore, people who show more sophisticated levels of prosocial reasoning are generally more sympathetic. There's a persistent sex difference, too: Females tend to demonstrate higher levels of prosocial reasoning than males (Eisenberg & Morris, 2004).

However, it's harder to make generalizations about prosocial *behavior*. Although some people become increasingly helpful as they get older, others do not. In a way, the difficulty in finding a relationship between prosocial behavior and personal characteristics is not surprising, given the difficulty that researchers have had in finding any particular personality characteristics related to helpfulness. Most research suggests that people are not invariably helpful or, for that matter, unhelpful. Instead, whether particular individuals act in a prosocial manner depends on their personality *and* the specifics of the situation. Furthermore, no single pattern of specific, individual personality traits determines prosocial behavior. Rather, the way that specific personality factors fit together, as well as the demands of the particular situation, determines whether a person will help (Eisenberg & Morris, 2004).

GENDER AND CULTURAL DIFFERENCES IN PROSOCIAL BEHAVIOR. Both gender and culture are related to prosocial behavior. For example, quite consistently, girls are more helpful than boys. They are more caring about others, and they act in a more prosocial manner. By the way, not only are males less likely to provide

social domain approach
the concept that moral reasoning needs to be considered in the context in which judgments are being made at a given time.

help, they are less willing to ask for help than females—something we might call the males-hating-to-ask-for-directions-even-when-they-are-lost phenomenon (Eisenberg & Morris, 2004; Espinosa & Kovářík, 2015).

However, males don't always act less helpfully than females. If the situation is one in which their behavior is public and visible to others, and the person needing help is female, males are more likely to be helpful. Having the opportunity to act like a "knight in shining armor" and come to the rescue of a damsel in distress elevates the level of male helpfulness beyond its typically more modest level (Hyde & Grabe, 2008).

The typically higher levels of prosocial behavior displayed by females reflect their tendency to hold a *communal* orientation, centering on an interest in relationships and community. In contrast, males are more likely to have an *agentic* orientation, which focuses on individuality and getting things done. Communal orientations lead to greater prosocial behavior (Mosher & Danoff-Burg, 2005; Salmivalli et al., 2005).

Culture, too, affects the extent to which people behave prosocially. For instance, individuals living on Israeli kibbutzim, or collective farms, tend to show greater helpfulness and even different reasoning about morality than members of the dominant culture in the United States. Similarly, people raised in the United States use more rights-based reasoning about morality than people in other societies. In *rights-based reasoning*, certain rights (such as freedom of speech) are assumed; they don't have to be earned but are the birthright of every citizen. In contrast, people in India are more likely to use *duty-based reasoning*, in which people are expected to behave in a certain way because it is their responsibility (Shweder, Much, & Mahapatra, 1997; Verma, 2004).

Parents' childrearing practices, which we will discuss shortly, produce different forms of helping behavior, which emerge during childhood. For example, the level of helping behavior that children display while playing varies substantially in different cultures. Children raised in cultures in which they are taught to cooperate with other family members to do chores or to help in the upbringing of younger children (such as in Kenya, Mexico, and the Philippines) show relatively high levels of prosocial behavior. In contrast, cultures that promote competition—such as the United States—produce lower levels of prosocial behavior (Whiting & Edwards, 1988; Yablo & Field, 2007; Daniel et al., 2015).

Furthermore, the degree to which people view helping in the context of reciprocity—the view that we should help because we expect to receive help from others in the future—is related to cultural factors. For example, Hindu Indians see reciprocity as a moral obligation, whereas college students in the United States consider reciprocity as more of a personal choice (Miller, 1997; Chadha & Misra, 2004).

Effective Parenting: Teaching Desired Behavior

LO 11.4   Identify the four basic parenting styles, and summarize how each style influences a child's development.

While she thinks no one is looking, Maria goes into her brother Alejandro's bedroom, where he has been saving the last of his Halloween candy. Just as she takes his last Reese's Peanut Butter Cup, the children's mother walks into the room and immediately takes in the situation.

If you were Maria's mother, which of the following reactions seems most reasonable?

1. Tell Maria that she must go to her room and stay there for the rest of the day and that she is going to lose access to her favorite blanket, the one she sleeps with every night and during naps.

2. Mildly tell Maria that what she did was not such a good idea, and she shouldn't do it in the future.

What are the consequences of parents who are too permissive? Too authoritarian? Too uninvolved?

KidStock/Getty Images

3. Explain why her brother Alejandro was going to be upset, and tell her that she must go to her room for an hour as punishment.

4. Forget about it, and let the children sort it out themselves.

Each of these four alternative responses represents one of the major parenting styles identified by Diana Baumrind and updated by Eleanor Maccoby and colleagues (Maccoby & Martin, 1983; Baumrind, 1980, 2005).

Authoritarian parents respond as in the first alternative. They are controlling, punitive, rigid, and cold. Their word is law, and they value strict, unquestioning obedience from their children. They also do not tolerate expressions of disagreement.

Permissive parents, in contrast, provide lax and inconsistent feedback, as in the second alternative. They require little of their children, and they don't see themselves as holding much responsibility for how their children turn out. They place little or no limits or control on their children's behavior.

Authoritative parents are firm, setting clear and consistent limits. Although they tend to be relatively strict, like authoritarian parents, they are loving and emotionally supportive. They also try to reason with their children, giving explanations for why they should behave in a particular way ("Alejandro is going to be upset"), and communicating the rationale for any punishment they may impose. Authoritative parents encourage their children to be independent.

Finally, **uninvolved parents** show virtually no interest in their children, displaying indifferent, rejecting behavior. They are detached emotionally and see their role as no more than feeding, clothing, and providing shelter for their child. In its most extreme form, uninvolved parenting results in **neglect**, a form of child abuse. (The four patterns are summarized in Table 11-3.)

Does the particular style of discipline that parents use result in differences in children's behavior? The answer is very much yes (Cheah et al., 2009; Lin, Chiu, & Yeh, 2012; Flouri & Midouhas, 2017):

- Children of authoritarian parents tend to be withdrawn, showing relatively little sociability. They are not very friendly, often behaving uneasily around their peers. Girls who are raised by authoritarian parents are especially dependent on their parents, whereas boys are unusually hostile.

- Permissive parents have children who, in many ways, share the undesirable characteristics of children of authoritarian parents. Children with permissive parents tend to be dependent and moody, and they are low in social skills and self-control.

---

authoritarian parents
parents who are controlling, punitive, rigid, and cold, and whose word is law. They value strict, unquestioning obedience from their children and do not tolerate expressions of disagreement.

permissive parents
parents who provide lax and inconsistent feedback and require little of their children.

authoritative parents
parents who are firm, setting clear and consistent limits, but who try to reason with their children, giving explanations for why they should behave in a particular way.

uninvolved parents
parents who show almost no interest in their children and display indifferent, rejecting behavior.

neglect
a form of child abuse.

Table 11-3 Parenting Styles

How Demanding Parents Are of Children ▶	Demanding	Undemanding
How Responsive Parents Are to Children ▼	**Authoritative**	**Permissive**
Highly Responsive	**Characteristics:** firm, setting clear and consistent limits. **Relationship with Children:** Although they tend to be relatively strict, like authoritarian parents, they are loving and emotionally supportive and encourage their children to be independent. They also try to reason with their children, giving explanations for why they should behave in a particular way, and communicate the rationale for any punishment they may impose.	**Characteristics:** lax and inconsistent feedback. **Relationship with Children:** They require little of their children, and they don't see themselves as holding much responsibility for how their children turn out. They place few or no limits or controls on their children's behavior.
	Authoritarian	**Uninvolved**
Least Responsive	**Characteristics:** controlling, punitive, rigid, cold. **Relationship with Children:** Their word is law, and they value strict, unquestioning obedience from their children. They also do not tolerate expressions of disagreement.	**Characteristics:** displaying indifferent, rejecting behavior. **Relationship with Children:** They are detached emotionally and see their role as only providing food, clothing, and shelter. In its extreme form, this parenting style results in neglect, a form of child abuse.

(**Source:** Based on Baumrind, 1971; Maccoby & Martin, 1983.)

- Children of authoritative parents fare best. They generally are independent, friendly with their peers, self-assertive, and cooperative. They have strong motivation to achieve, and they are typically successful and likable. They regulate their own behavior effectively, both in terms of their relationships with others and emotional self-regulation.

  Some authoritative parents also display several characteristics that have come to be called *supportive parenting*, including parental warmth, proactive teaching, calm discussion during disciplinary episodes, and interest and involvement in children's peer activities. Children whose parents engage in such supportive parenting show better adjustment and are better protected from the consequences of later adversity they may encounter (Pettit, Bates, & Dodge, 1997; Belluck, 2000; Kaufmann et al., 2000).

- Children whose parents show uninvolved parenting styles are the worst off. Their parents' lack of involvement disrupts their emotional development considerably, leading them to feel unloved and emotionally detached, and impedes their physical and cognitive development as well.

Although such classification systems are useful ways of categorizing and describing parents' behavior, they are not a recipe for success. Parenting and growing up are more complicated than that! For instance, in a significant number of cases the children of authoritarian and permissive parents develop quite successfully. Furthermore, most parents are not entirely consistent: Although the authoritarian, permissive, authoritative, and uninvolved patterns describe general styles, sometimes parents switch from their dominant mode to one of the others. For instance, when a child darts into the street, even the most laid-back and permissive parent is likely to react in a harsh, authoritarian manner, laying down strict demands about safety. In such cases, authoritarian styles may be most effective (Eisenberg & Valiente, 2002; Gershoff, 2002).

CULTURAL DIFFERENCES IN CHILDREARING PRACTICES. It's important to keep in mind that the findings regarding childrearing styles we have been discussing are chiefly applicable to Western societies. The style of parenting that is most successful may depend quite heavily on the norms of a particular culture—and on what parents in a particular culture are taught regarding appropriate childrearing practices (Yagmurlu & Sanson, 2009; Calzada et al., 2012; Dotti Sani & Treas, 2016).

For example, the Chinese concept of *chiao shun* suggests that parents should be strict, firm, and in tight control of their children's behavior. Parents are seen to have a duty to train their children to adhere to socially and culturally desirable standards of behavior, particularly those manifested in good school performance. Children's acceptance of such an approach to discipline is seen as a sign of parental respect (Chao, 1994; Wu, Robinson, & Yang, 2002; Ng, Pomerantz, & Lam, 2007).

Parents in China are typically highly directive with their children, pushing them to excel and controlling their behavior to a considerably higher degree than parents typically do in Western countries. And it works: Children of Asian parents tend to be successful, particularly academically (Nelson et al., 2006; Kim et al., 2017).

In contrast, U.S. parents are generally advised to use authoritative methods and explicitly to avoid authoritarian measures. Interestingly, it wasn't always this way. Until World War II, the point of view that dominated the advice literature was authoritarian, apparently founded on Puritan religious influences that suggested that children had "original sin" or that they needed to have their wills broken (Smuts & Hagen, 1985).

For Hispanic parents, one central value relates to the concept of respect. Hispanic parents believe that children should listen to rules and should be obedient to authority figures (O'Connor et al., 2013).

In short, the childrearing practices that parents are urged to follow reflect cultural perspectives about the nature of children as well as about the appropriate role of parents and their support system. No single parenting pattern or style, then, is likely to be universally appropriate or invariably to produce successful children. For example, parents who are immigrants often hold different views of appropriate childrearing practices than natives in a country, and yet raise children who are quite successful (Wang, Pomerantz, & Chen 2007; Pomerantz et al., 2011; Chen, Sun, & Yu, 2017).

Similarly, it is important to keep in mind that childrearing practices are not the sole influence on children's development. For example, sibling and peer influences play a significant role in children's development. Furthermore, children's behavior is in part produced by their unique genetic endowment, and their behavior can in turn shape parental behavior. In sum, parents' childrearing practices are just one of a rich array of environmental and genetic influences that influence children (Boivin et al., 2005; Loehlin, Neiderhiser, & Reiss, 2005).

Module 11.1 Review

LO 11.1 Compare and contrast the various approaches to moral development.

Social learning approaches to moral development emphasize the importance of reinforcement for moral actions and the observation of models of moral conduct. Psychoanalytical and other theories focus on children's empathy with others and their wish to help others so they can avoid unpleasant feelings of guilt themselves.

LO 11.2 Summarize Kohlberg's and Gilligan's theories of moral development, and explain how they differ.

According to Kohlberg, moral development proceeds from a concern with rewards and punishments, through a focus on social conventions and rules, toward a sense of universal moral principles. Gilligan has suggested, however, that girls may follow a somewhat different progression of moral development.

LO 11.3 Identify the factors that influence moral and prosocial behaviors, including the roles played by gender and culture.

As people become more cognitively sophisticated, they are better able to consider and evaluate prosocial behavior. The

likelihood that a person will act prosocially depends on both the individual and the situation rather than on personality traits alone. There are clear gender and cultural differences in both empathy and prosocial behavior.

LO 11.4 Identify the four basic parenting styles, and summarize how each style influences a child's development.

There are several distinct childrearing styles, including authoritarian, permissive, authoritative, and uninvolved. Childrearing styles show strong cultural influences.

Journal Writing Prompt

Applying Lifespan Development: If high-prestige models of behavior are particularly effective in influencing moral attitudes and actions, are there implications for individuals in such industries as sports, advertising, and entertainment?

MODULE 11.2

VALUES, RELIGION, AND SPIRITUALITY: FOCUSING ON THE MEANING OF LIFE

The spirituality of old age is lovely. It takes one places that one needs to go to get ready to die, which is one of the biggest challenges that we, as human beings, face. I have found that my Unitarian Universalist [religion] helps me with this task in very satisfying ways. The idea that we are not a self but just a small part of an interdependent web of existence is a profound insight that contributes to a sense that death is not extinguishment but a transformation and that in some sense we all are eternal.

Reading this excerpt from the blog of a 63-year-old man makes it obvious that the search for meaning is something that has continued throughout his life. Indeed, the quest to understand who we are and our place in the universe is something that most people consider and often grapple with.

Religion in Childhood and Adolescence

LO 11.5   Summarize the development of religion in childhood and adolescence.

Only in relatively recent years have developmentalists focused on questions related to the meaning in life. They have sought first to understand how **values**, the qualities people see as most desirable and important, affect people's thinking and behavior. They have also begun to look at how religion and spirituality develop across the life span.

Values are part of each person's life, and they affect behavior in significant ways. They help determine how we feel about school, work, money, religion—just about every aspect of life. Values determine what goals we choose to pursue and what we see as important at every stage of our lives.

Surveys of college students show that the goal that they hold most important is raising a family (held by 77 percent of those surveyed). This was followed by "being very well off financially" (74 percent) and "helping others who are in difficulty" (70 percent). There also have been marked shifts in the values of college students over the past several decades. For example, finding a meaningful philosophy of life has declined in importance while being financially well off has increased significantly (see Figure 11-1; Pryor et al., 2007; Park & Bowman, 2015).

Religion often plays a central role in determining people's values. Only 16 percent of Americans do not have a religious affiliation, with the rest reporting a wide variety of different affiliations. However, religious affiliation is not fixed: Over a quarter of Americans report that they have left the religious faith in which they were raised and have become affiliated with another religion (Pew Forum on Religion & Public Life, 2008).

Religion is important to many people because it offers a formal means of satisfying spirituality needs. *Spirituality* is a sense of attachment to some higher power, such as God, nature, or a sacred entity. Although spirituality needs are typically tied to religious beliefs, they may be independent. Many people who consider themselves to be spiritual individuals do not participate in formal religious practices or are not tied to any particular religion.

values

the qualities people see as most desirable and important, affecting people's thinking and behavior.

Figure 11-1 Changes in Values

"Being very well off financially" is a value that has been of increasing importance to college students over the past 40 years, while "developing a meaningful philosophy of life" has been on the decline. Why do you think these trends have occurred?

(**Source:** Pryor et al., 2007.)

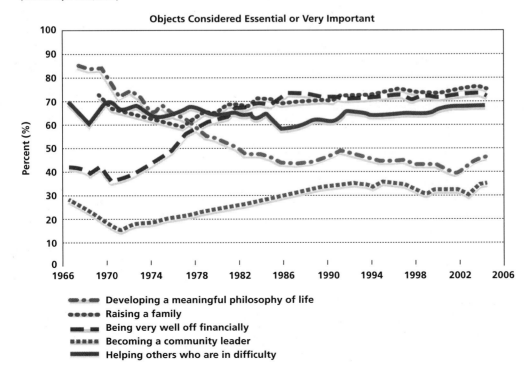

Piaget's approach to cognitive development offers a way of organizing how religious thinking develops through childhood and adolescence. Based on children's responses to Bible stories and pictures, children pass through three stages (Goldman, 1964):

- **Preoperational intuitive religious thought (up to age 7 or 8).** Children in this stage show religious thinking that is unsystematic. They don't understand religious stories very well, or they misinterpret their meaning altogether.

- **Concrete operational religious thought (ages 7 or 8 to 13 or 14).** Children focus on particular concrete details of the stories and pictures rather than the abstract lessons of the stories.

- **Formal operational religious thought (ages 13 or 14 and older).** In this stage, children are able to think more abstractly. They are able to understand the meaning of the stories and pictures, and draw inferences about them.

As teenagers grapple with questions of identity during adolescence, religious identity may be questioned. After having accepted their religious identity in an unquestioning manner during childhood, they may view it more critically and seek to distance themselves from formal religion. In other cases, they may be drawn to their religious affiliation because it offers answers to such abstract questions as "Why am I here on this earth?" and "What is the meaning of life?" Religion provides a way of viewing the world and universe as having intentional design—a place that was created by something or someone (Kiang, Yip, & Fuligni, 2008; Azar, 2010; Yonker, Schnabelrauch, & DeHaan, 2012).

From *an educator's* perspective

Given that teenagers are grappling with questions of identity and values during adolescence, should schools seek to teach values? And what values are most appropriately taught?

Religion and Spirituality in Adulthood

LO 11.6   Identify the purposes religion and spirituality serve in adulthood, and describe Fowler's stages of faith development.

Although it is rarely part of the formal college curriculum, surveys of college students show that many students seek discussions and information regarding spirituality, broadly defined. For example, surveys show that three-quarters of students report seeking meaning and purpose in life, and they think that college should help them in this quest. More than two-thirds say that it is "essential" or "very important" for their college experience to enhance their self-understanding (Higher Education Research Institute, 2005; Lindholm, 2006).

College students wanting greater coverage of spirituality are apt to be disappointed. Although 80 percent of faculty identify themselves as spiritual individuals, and more than two-thirds seek out opportunities to develop their own spirituality—they are unlikely to bring talk of spirituality and the meaning of life into the classroom. More than half of students say that their professors never offer opportunities to discuss topics related to spirituality.

There are probably several reasons for this lack of discussion of spirituality. Instructors at public, state-supported schools may feel that talk of spirituality veers into discussion of religious beliefs, something that many instructors feel violates the neutrality of their classes. In other cases, instructors may feel ill-equipped to discuss spirituality and the meaning of life, believing such talk should be left to philosophy and religion classes (Pingree, 2008).

RELIGION AND SPIRITUALITY IN MIDLIFE.   Religion plays a significant role in many adults' lives. For example, if you've ever suffered a death of a close relative or friend, you might have felt particularly motivated to attend religious services for a time after the death because of the comfort you derived from them.

Similarly, religion can help people make sense of catastrophes and events that otherwise appear to be senseless. It can offer an explanation of why things have happened and give people a sense of shared experience that can be comforting. It also provides perspective, showing people that their personal misfortunes can be viewed in a long-term, historical context (Cox, 2007).

Furthermore, religion may explain misfortunes as being due to some unseen, unknowable plan or simply as being "God's will." Even though people may not understand the "plan" that is unfolding, such a view may be more comforting than simply seeing events as random and without meaning (Marshall & Sutherland, 2008).

Finally, religion can provide direct social support to others. Traditionally, churches, synagogues, and mosques have provided both tangible and emotional help to members in time of need. Even if it is only providing meals to members who are experiencing illness, such social support can be both helpful and emotionally meaningful (Krause, 2008).

FOWLER'S STAGES OF FAITH DEVELOPMENT.   According to James Fowler, our understanding and practice of faith and spirituality proceeds through a series of stages that extend throughout the lifetime. During childhood, individuals hold a fairly literal view of God and biblical figures. For example, children may think of God as living at the top of the earth and being able to see what everyone is doing (Fowler & Dell, 2006).

In adolescence, the view of spirituality becomes more abstract. As they build their identity, adolescents typically develop a core set of beliefs and values. In many cases, however, they have not considered their views either in depth or systematically.

During early and middle adulthood, adults are in what Fowler calls the *individuative-reflective stage* of faith. During this time, people reflect on their beliefs and values. They understand that their views are one of many and that multiple views of God are possible. They do not simply accept the views of their religion, but seek to form a personal belief system that speaks to them.

Finally, in late adulthood, people may move into a final stage of faith development: the conjunctive stage. In the *conjunctive stage* of faith development, elderly individuals develop a broad, inclusive view of religion and all humanity. They see humanity as a whole, and they may work to promote a common good. In this stage, they may move beyond formal religion and hold a unified view of people across the globe.

It's important to note that Fowler does not believe that everyone attains each of these stages. Some people remain "stuck" at an earlier stage, depending on their degree of reflection and their exposure to religious and spiritual thinking.

RELIGION IN THE FINAL STAGES OF LIFE.   For many people in late adulthood, stronger religious beliefs are related to greater life satisfaction. For instance, one study found that older adults who found a sense of meaning in life from their religion also were more satisfied with their lives, had greater self-esteem, and were more optimistic (Krause, 2003a).

There are also some racial differences in the role that religion plays in people's lives during late adulthood. Older African American adults are more likely to find meaning in religion than older Caucasians. Furthermore, the relationship between religious meaning and life satisfaction, self-esteem, and optimism is stronger for African Americans than for Caucasians. These findings suggest that religious meaning may be an important source of resilience for older black adults (Krause, 2003a).

Prayer itself may produce positive benefits in older adults. For example, the negative effects of financial difficulties on health in older people are reduced in those who pray for others often. Furthermore, higher rates of prayer are associated with reports of greater happiness. However, the question of whether prayer actually extends life remains unanswered. Although some studies show a link between attendance at religious service and a healthier lifestyle, there is no evidence that religious involvement actually extends life (Gonnerman et al., 2008; Robbins et al., 2008; Michaelson et al., 2015).

Module 11.2 Review

LO 11.5 **Summarize the development of religion in childhood and adolescence.**

Surveys show that the goals of college students have undergone a shift in recent years. Finding a meaningful philosophy of life has decreased in importance, while being financially well off has increased. Although most Americans report having some religious affiliation, this affiliation is not fixed. One-fourth of Americans say they now have a different religious affiliation than the one with which they were raised. In adolescence, the question of religion and spiritual beliefs becomes part of the larger quest for an identity as teens seek to develop a core set of beliefs and values.

LO 11.6 **Identify the purposes religion and spirituality serve in adulthood, and describe Fowler's stages of faith development.**

In adulthood, religion can offer an explanation of why things happen and give people a long-term, historical perspective in which to view their personal problems and society's disasters. According to James Fowler, our understanding and practice of faith and spirituality proceeds through a series of stages that extend throughout the lifetime.

Journal Writing Prompt

Applying Lifespan Development: If formal religion provides people with a set of moral guidelines to live by, how might people not affiliated with any religion develop a moral framework and a set of core values?

MODULE 11.3

AGGRESSION AND VIOLENCE

Four-year-old Duane could not contain his anger and frustration anymore. Although he usually was mild-mannered, when Eshu began to tease him about the split in his pants and kept it up for several minutes, Duane finally snapped. Rushing over to Eshu, Duane pushed him to the ground and began to hit him with his small, closed fists. Because he was so distraught, Duane's punches were not terribly effective, but they were severe enough to hurt Eshu and bring him to tears before the preschool teachers could intervene.

Aggression among preschoolers is quite common, though attacks such as this are not. The potential for verbal hostility, shoving matches, kicking, and other forms of aggression is present throughout the preschool period, although the degree to which aggression is acted out changes as children become older.

Aggression and Violence in Children: Sources and Consequences

LO 11.7 **Explain the development of aggression in preschool children, and summarize the gender differences.**

aggression
intentional injury or harm to another person.

Eshu's taunting was also a form of aggression. **Aggression** is intentional injury or harm to another person. Infants don't act aggressively; it is hard to contend that their behavior is *intended* to hurt others, even if they inadvertently manage to do so. In contrast, by the time they reach preschool age, children demonstrate true aggression.

During the early preschool years, some of the aggression is addressed at attaining a desired goal, such as getting a toy away from another person or using a particular space occupied by another person. Consequently, in some ways the aggression is inadvertent, and minor scuffles may in fact be a typical part of early preschool life. It is the rare child who does not demonstrate at least an occasional act of aggression.

However, extreme and sustained aggression is a cause of concern. In most children, the amount of aggression declines as they move through the preschool years, as does the frequency and average length of episodes of aggressive behavior (Persson, 2005; DiCarlo et al., 2015).

The child's personality and social development contribute to this decline in aggression. Throughout the preschool years, children become better at controlling the emotions that they are experiencing. **Emotional self-regulation** is the capability to adjust emotions to a desired state and level of intensity. Starting at age 2, children are able to talk about their feelings, and they engage in strategies to regulate them. As they get older, they develop more effective strategies, learning to better cope with negative emotions. In addition to their increasing self-control, children are also, as we've seen, developing sophisticated social skills. Most learn to use language to express their wishes, and they become increasingly able to negotiate with others (Philippot & Feldman, 2005; Helmsen, Koglin, & Petermann, 2012; Rose et al., 2016).

Aggression, both physical and verbal, is present throughout the preschool period.

Despite these typical declines in aggression, some children remain aggressive throughout the preschool period. Furthermore, aggression is a relatively stable characteristic: The most aggressive preschoolers tend to be the most aggressive children during the school years, and the least aggressive preschoolers tend to be the least aggressive schoolchildren (Rosen, 1998; Tremblay, 2001; Schaeffer, Petras, & Ialongo, 2003).

Boys typically show higher levels of physical, instrumental aggression than girls. **Instrumental aggression** is aggression motivated by the desire to obtain a concrete goal, such as playing with a desirable toy that another child is playing with. Although girls show lower levels of instrumental aggression, they may be just as aggressive but in different ways from boys. Girls are more likely to practice **relational aggression**, which is nonphysical aggression intended to hurt another person's feelings. Such aggression may be demonstrated through name-calling, withholding friendship, or simply saying mean, hurtful things that make the recipient feel bad (Werner & Crick, 2004; Dailey, Frey & Walker, 2015).

SCHOOL VIOLENCE. Columbine ... Virginia Tech University ... Sandy Hook Elementary School. You may remember the names of these places where school shootings occurred, and you may conclude—like many Americans—that schools are particularly dangerous places.

The reality of school violence is different, however. Despite the public perception that school violence is on the upswing, there has in fact been an overall decline in violence. Less than 1 percent of youth homicides occur in schools, making them one of the safest places for children (Jimerson et al., 2006; Newsome & Kelly, 2006; Centers for Disease Control and Prevention, 2015).

The likelihood of injury from a school shooting is tiny (a child has about a one in a million chance of being killed in school). Nonetheless, parents and their children still worry about safety issues. Is it possible to identify beforehand students who pose a threat? It turns out that there are students who are prone to violence; for instance, the FBI has identified several characteristics of individuals who are at risk for carrying out violence in schools. These characteristics include a low tolerance for frustration, poor coping skills, a lack of resiliency, failed love relationships, resentment over perceived injustices, depression, self-centeredness, and alienation (O'Toole, 2000; Eisenbraun, 2007).

Furthermore, school shootings are rarely spontaneous. Attackers typically make plans, plotting out beforehand whom they wish to harm. Not only do they usually tell someone about their plans, they often are encouraged by others. In almost half the cases of school shootings, attackers were influenced or encouraged to act by friends or fellow students. They also have easy access to guns. In around two-thirds of school shootings, the attackers used guns from their own home or that of a relative (U.S. Secret Service, 2002).

emotional self-regulation
the capability to adjust emotions to a desired state and level of intensity.

instrumental aggression
aggression motivated by the desire to obtain a concrete goal, such as playing with a desirable toy that another child is playing with.

relational aggression
nonphysical aggression that is intended to hurt another person's feelings.

According to psychologist Elliot Aronson, students who carry out violence in schools frequently were the targets of bullying or have been rejected in some way. He notes that there are tremendous status differences in schools, and students who have been taunted and humiliated by students of higher status (or by their parents or other adults) may lash out in frustration (Aronson, 2000, 2004).

To respond to the potential of violence, many schools have instituted programs designed to prevent aggression among students. One of the most prominent programs is *Second Step*, which is designed to teach children to recognize and understand their feelings, experience empathy for others, make effective choices, and keep anger from escalating into violence. Carefully conducted studies have supported the program, finding improvements in students' social skills and a reduction in aggressive acts (Van Schoiack-Edstrom, Frey, & Beland, 2002; McMahon & Washburn, 2003).

Other school programs that involve cooperative learning, peer mediation, and communication skills training appear to be helpful. In addition, teaching students, parents, and educators to take threats seriously is important; many students who become violent threaten to commit violence before they actually engage in violent acts. Ultimately, schools need to be places where students feel comfortable discussing their feelings and problems, rather than sources of alienation and rejection (Aronson, 2004; Spencer, 2001; Eisenbraun, 2007).

The Roots of Aggression

LO 11.8 Compare and contrast the different approaches that seek to explain the causes of aggression in children.

How can we explain the aggression of children? Some theoreticians suggest that to behave aggressively is an instinct, part and parcel of the human condition. For instance, Freud's psychoanalytic theory suggests that we all are motivated by sexual and aggressive instincts (Freud, 1920). According to ethologist Konrad Lorenz, an expert in animal behavior, animals—including humans—share a fighting instinct that stems from primitive urges to preserve territory, maintain a steady supply of food, and weed out weaker animals (Lorenz, 1974).

Similar arguments are made by evolutionary theorists and sociobiologists, scientists who consider the biological roots of social behavior. They argue that aggression leads to increased opportunities to mate, improving the likelihood that one's genes will be passed on to future generations. In addition, aggression may help to strengthen the species and its gene pool as a whole because the strongest survive. Ultimately, then, aggressive instincts promote the survival of one's genes to pass on to future generations (Pellegrini, 2007; Farbiash et al., 2014).

Although instinctual explanations of aggression are logical, most developmentalists believe they are not the whole story. Not only do instinctual explanations fail to take into account the increasingly sophisticated cognitive abilities that humans develop as they get older, but they also have relatively little experimental support. Moreover, they provide little guidance in determining when and how children, as well as adults, will behave aggressively, other than noting that aggression is an inevitable part of the human condition. Consequently, developmentalists have turned to other approaches to explain aggression and violence.

SOCIAL LEARNING APPROACHES TO AGGRESSION. The day after Duane lashed out at Eshu, Lynn, who had watched the entire scene, got into an argument with Ilya. They verbally bickered for a while, and suddenly Lynn balled her hand into a fist and tried to punch Ilya. The preschool teachers were stunned: It was rare for Lynn to get upset, and she had never displayed aggression before.

Is there a connection between the two events? Most of us would answer yes, particularly if we subscribed to the view, suggested by social learning approaches, that aggression is largely a learned behavior. Social learning approaches to aggression contend that aggression is based on observation and prior learning. To understand the causes of aggressive behavior, then, we should look at the system of rewards and punishments that exists in a child's environment.

Social learning approaches to aggression emphasize how social and environmental conditions teach individuals to be aggressive. These ideas grow out of behavioral perspectives, which suggest that aggressive behavior is learned through direct reinforcement. For instance, preschool-age children may learn that they can continue to play with the most desirable toys by aggressively refusing their classmates' requests for sharing. In the parlance of traditional learning theory, they have been reinforced for acting aggressively (by continued use of the toy), and they are more likely to behave aggressively in the future.

But social learning approaches suggest that reinforcement also comes in less direct ways. A good deal of research suggests that exposure to aggressive models leads to increased aggression, particularly if the observers are themselves angered, insulted, or frustrated. For example, Albert Bandura and his colleagues illustrated the power of models in a classic study of preschool-age children (Bandura, Ross, & Ross, 1963). One group of children watched a film of an adult playing aggressively and violently with a Bobo doll (a large, inflated plastic clown designed as a punching bag for children that always returns to an upright position after being pushed down). In comparison, children in another condition watched a film of an adult playing sedately with a set of Tinkertoys (see Figure 11-2). Later, the preschool-age children were allowed to play with a number of toys, which included both the Bobo doll and the Tinkertoys. But first, the children were led to feel frustration by being refused the opportunity to play with a favorite toy.

As predicted by social learning approaches, the preschool-age children modeled the behavior of the adult. Those who had seen the aggressive model playing with the Bobo doll were considerably more aggressive than those who had watched the calm, unaggressive model playing with the Tinkertoys.

Figure 11-2 Modeling Aggression

This series of photos is from Albert Bandura's classic Bobo doll experiment, designed to illustrate the social learning of aggression. The photos clearly show how the adult model's aggressive behavior (in the first row) is imitated by children who had viewed the aggressive behavior (second and third rows).

(**Source:** Albert Bandura)

Later research has supported this early study, and it is clear that exposure to aggressive models increases the likelihood that aggression on the part of observers will follow. These findings have profound consequences, particularly for children who live in communities in which violence is prevalent. For instance, one survey conducted in a city public hospital found that 1 in 10 children under age 6 said they had witnessed a shooting or stabbing. Other research indicates that one-third of the children in some urban neighborhoods have seen a homicide and that two-thirds have seen a serious assault. Such frequent exposure to violence certainly increases the probability that observers will behave aggressively themselves (Farver et al., 1997; Evans, 2004; Dubow et al., 2016).

VIEWING VIOLENCE ON TV: DOES IT MATTER?   Even the majority of preschool-age children who are not witnesses to real-life violence are typically exposed to aggression via the medium of television. Children's television programs actually contain higher levels of violence (69 percent) than other types of programs (57 percent). In an average hour, children's programs contain more than twice as many violent incidents than other types of programs (Wilson et al., 2002).

This high level of televised violence, coupled with Bandura and others' research findings on modeling violence, raises a significant question: Does viewing aggression increase the likelihood that children (and later adults) will enact actual—and ultimately deadly—aggression? It is hard to answer the question definitively. Although it is clear that laboratory observation of aggression on television leads to higher levels of aggression, evidence showing that real-world viewing of aggression is associated with subsequent aggressive behavior is correlational. (Think, for a moment, of what would be required to conduct a true experiment involving children's viewing habits. It would require that we control children's viewing of television in their homes for extended periods, exposing some to a steady diet of violent shows and others to nonviolent ones—something that most parents would not agree to.)

Despite the fact, then, that the results are primarily correlational, the overwhelming weight of research evidence is clear in suggesting that observation of televised aggression does lead to subsequent aggression. Longitudinal studies have found that children's preferences for violent television shows at age 8 are related to the seriousness of criminal convictions by age 30. Other evidence supports the notion that observation of media violence can lead to a greater readiness to act aggressively, to bullying, and to an insensitivity to the suffering of victims of violence (Kirsh, 2012; Krahé, & Busching, 2015; Merritt et al., 2016).

Television is not the only source of media violence. Many video games contain a significant amount of aggressive behavior, and children are playing such games at high rates. For example, 14 percent of children age 3 and younger and around 50 percent of those 4 to 6 play video games. Because research conducted with adults shows that playing violent video games is associated with behaving aggressively, children who play video games containing violence may be at higher risk for behaving aggressively (Bushman, Gollwitzer, & Cruz, 2014; Linebarger, 2015).

Fortunately, social learning principles that lead preschoolers to learn aggression from television and video games suggest ways to reduce the negative influence of the medium. For instance, children can be explicitly taught to view violence with a more skeptical, critical eye. Being taught that violence is not representative of the real world, that the viewing of violence can affect them negatively, and that they should refrain from imitating the behavior they have seen on television can help children interpret the violent programs differently and be less influenced by them (Persson & Musher-Eizenman, 2003; Donnerstein, 2005).

From *a health-care provider's* perspective

What should you tell parents who are worried about their children's exposure to media violence?

Furthermore, just as exposure to aggressive models leads to aggression, observation of *non-aggressive* models can *reduce* aggression. Preschoolers don't just learn from others how to be aggressive; they can also learn how to avoid confrontation and to control their aggression, as we'll discuss later. (Also see the *From Research to Practice* box).

From Research to Practice

What Works with Teens Who Behave Aggressively?

Children who behave aggressively, no matter what their age, can certainly cause concern for their parents, teachers, and anyone who's the target of their aggression. Parents of youth who behave aggressively often feel at their wit's end and look everywhere for a way to help their child. And while a number of techniques have been shown by research to be effective, there are also a number of techniques that have no research support at all—and may even be harmful.

For example, television programs like *Beyond Scared Straight* tout scare tactics as an effective way to prevent kids from pursuing a life of crime. Scared Straight takes teens into adult prisons to meet with inmates who typically threaten and intimidate them. A review of research on scare-tactic programs like Scared Straight indicates that these types of programs actually make kids *more* likely to commit crimes (Petrosino et al., 2013).

So if intuitively appealing and popular programs like Scared Straight make kids more likely to commit crimes, what programs actually work to reduce aggression? Among the many research-based strategies to reduce aggression in youth, one of the most effective is family therapy. While several family therapy models exist, they often share a number of common goals. These goals include improving relationships between family members by increasing positive and decreasing negative interactions, improving communication between family members, and increasing structure in the home by teaching parents how to develop and apply consequences for child misbehavior.

A recent review examined the effectiveness of multidimensional family therapy (MDFT), an integrated and comprehensive form of therapy that involves the entire family. The review examined 19 different studies of young people (average age 15–16 years old) to determine whether MDFT is more effective than other types of therapy in treating youth with multiple behavior problems, including aggression. The authors averaged together the results of the studies and found that MDFT was significantly more effective than several other types treatment, including individual therapy focused on changing antisocial thinking, group therapy, and a combination of other treatments. In fact, the positive effects of MDFT were actually greatest for youth with the most severe behavior problems. The results of this study point to the importance of the family in treating children who are aggressive and violent (van der Pol et al., 2017).

Shared Writing Prompt

While family therapy has been found to be effective at treating youths who behave aggressively, what are some barriers to or difficulties in treating the entire family?

COGNITIVE APPROACHES TO AGGRESSION: THE THOUGHTS BEHIND VIOLENCE. Two children, waiting for their turn in a game of kickball, inadvertently knock into one another. One child's reaction is to apologize; the other's is to shove, saying angrily, "Cut it out."

Despite the fact that each child bears the same responsibility for the minor event, very different reactions result. The first child interprets the event as an accident, while the second sees it as a provocation and reacts with aggression.

The cognitive approach to aggression suggests that the key to understanding moral development is to examine preschoolers' interpretations of others' behavior and of the environmental context in which a behavior occurs. According to developmental psychologist Kenneth Dodge and his colleagues, some children are more prone than others to assume that actions are aggressively motivated. They are unable to pay attention to the appropriate cues in a situation and unable to interpret the behaviors in a given situation accurately. Instead, they assume—often erroneously—that what is happening is related to others' hostility. Subsequently, in deciding how to respond, they base their actions on their inaccurate interpretation of behavior. In sum, they may behave aggressively in response to a situation that never in fact existed (Dodge & Crick, 1990; Petit & Dodge, 2003).

For example, consider Jake, who is drawing at a table with Gary. Jake reaches over and takes the red crayon that Gary had just decided he was going to use next. Gary is instantly certain that Jake "knew" that he was going to use the red crayon and that Jake is taking it just to be mean. With this interpretation in mind, Gary hits Jake for "stealing" his crayon. Although the cognitive approach to aggression provides a description of the process that leads some children to behave aggressively, it is less successful in explaining how certain children come to be inaccurate perceivers of situations in the first place. Furthermore, it fails to explain why such inaccurate perceivers so readily respond with aggression, and why they assume that aggression is an appropriate and even desirable response.

However, cognitive approaches to aggression are useful in pointing out a means to reduce aggression: By teaching preschool-age children to be more accurate interpreters of a situation, we can induce them to be less prone to view others' behavior as motivated by hostility, and consequently less likely to respond with aggression themselves. (Also see the *Developmental Diversity and Your Life* feature on aggression in U.S. society.)

Developmental Diversity and Your Life

Is Aggression as American as Apple Pie?

Anyone who reads a daily newspaper is exposed to a constant stream of incidents of murder, rape, mugging, and other violence, often committed by teenagers and sometimes even by younger children. Does this perception of violence match the reality, and is aggression "as American as apple pie," as one expert on aggression put it (Berkowitz, 1993)? Unfortunately, in many ways, the perception matches reality.

For example, more men between the ages of 15 and 24 are murdered in the United States than in any other developed country in the world (see Figure 11-3).

Of course, aggression is hardly unique to the United States. In some cultures, aggression by children is substantial, whereas in others it is less pronounced. According to the findings of one classic study, childrearing practices help

Figure 11-3 Comparative Homicide Rates

The murder rate is far higher in the United States than in other developed countries. What features of U.S. society contribute to this state of affairs?
(**Source:** Based on UNODC, 2013.)

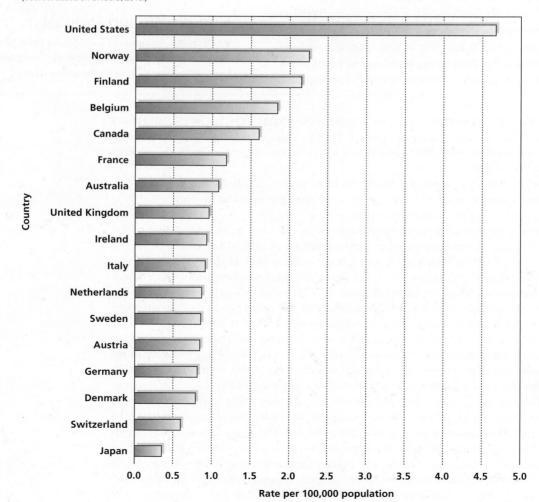

explain the substantial cross-cultural differences. In the study, researchers examined aggression in Kenya, India, Mexico, Japan, the Philippines, and the United States (Lambert, 1971).

The study first examined the reactions of mothers (who were the primary caregivers in each of the cultures) to their own children's aggression. The results showed that Mexican parents were the strictest, whereas U.S. mothers showed the greatest tolerance for aggressive behavior in their children. In contrast, for aggression against an adult, children living in Kenya, the Philippines, and Mexico received the greatest punishment, whereas children in India received the least punishment. Children living in the United States and Japan received a moderate degree of punishment.

As expected, mothers' reactions to aggression were related to their children's overall aggression levels, although the findings were complex. One important finding was that children with the highest activity levels learned the social values of their culture regarding aggression most effectively. Hence, active children in Mexico were less aggressive because their mothers reacted strongly to their aggression. In contrast, the more active children in the United States were more aggressive, a lesson they learned from their mother's lack of strong reactions to their aggression. In contrast, relatively inactive children, who had fewer opportunities to acquire the social values of their society, showed differing patterns of aggression from those of their more active counterparts.

Of course, the results don't show us why, in the first place, mothers in some cultures reacted more to their children's aggression than mothers in other cultures. Still, it is clear that cultures produce a particular set of childrearing practices that is associated with different patterns of aggression in their children.

Although there are substantial cultural differences in level of aggression, in some way patterns of aggression are similar across cultures. The most significant similarity is a gender difference: In every known culture, boys are more aggressive than girls, a pattern that is mirrored in adult behavior (LaFreniere et al., 2002; Verrity, 2007; Busching et al., 2015).

Why should boys be more aggressive than girls? Although it is tempting to look to biological or evolutionary explanations and suggest that boys are genetically preprogrammed to be aggressive, there are other possibilities. Parents and society in general hold different expectations about aggression for boys and girls, and in many cultures boys are explicitly encouraged to behave aggressively. In contrast, aggression in girls is typically discouraged (Zahn-Waxler & Polanichka, 2004; Letendre, 2007).

It is also possible that boys may behave aggressively in an effort to distinguish themselves from their female caregivers, given that males in almost all societies are reared primarily by women. Behaving aggressively may make boys believe that they are adopting a behavior that is similar to that of adults (Whiting, 1965).

Although such explanations are plausible, they remain theories, and there is no definitive explanation for the higher levels of male aggression found in every culture. In any case, we should not assume that the general pervasiveness of aggressive behavior is a necessary part of children's behavior.

Family Violence: The Hidden Epidemic

LO 11.9   **Summarize the cycle of violence hypothesis, and identify the social and cultural factors that contribute to family violence.**

After finding an unidentified earring, the wife accused her husband of being unfaithful. His reaction was to throw her against the wall of their apartment and then to toss her clothes out the window. In another incident, the husband became angry. Screaming at his wife, he threw her against a wall and then picked her up and literally threw her out of the house. Another time, the wife called 911, begging for the police to protect her. When the police came, the woman, with a black eye, a cut lip, and swollen cheeks, hysterically screamed, "He's going to kill me."

Unfortunately, the scene described above is far from rare. Violence, both physical and psychological, is part of many relationships.

THE PREVALENCE OF SPOUSAL ABUSE.   Domestic violence is one of the ugly truths about marriage in the United States, occurring at epidemic levels. Some form of violence happens in one-fourth of all marriages, and more than half the women who were murdered in one recent 10-year period were murdered by a partner. Between 21 and 34 percent of women will be slapped, kicked, beaten, choked, or threatened or attacked with a weapon at least once by an intimate partner. Close to 15 percent of all marriages in the United States are characterized by continuing, severe violence. Furthermore, domestic violence is a worldwide problem. Estimates suggest that one in three women throughout the globe experience some form of violent victimization during their lives (Walker, 1999; Garcia-Moreno et al., 2005).

Figure 11-4 The Stages of Domestic Violence
(**Source:** Adapted from Walker, 1979, 1984; Gondolf, 1985.)

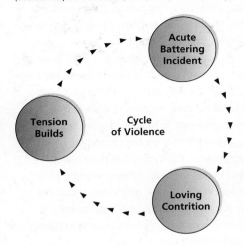

In the United States, no segment of society is immune from spousal abuse. Violence occurs across social strata, races, ethnic groups, and religions. Both gay and straight partnerships can be abusive. It also occurs across genders: Although in the vast majority of cases of abuse a husband batters a wife, in about 8 percent of the cases wives physically abuse their husbands (Cameron, 2003; Dixon & Browne, 2003; Yon et al., 2014).

Certain factors increase the likelihood of abuse. For instance, spousal abuse is more likely to occur in large families in which there is continuing economic concern and a high level of verbal aggression than in families in which such factors are not present. Those husbands and wives who grew up in families where violence was present are more likely to be violent themselves (Ehrensaft, Cohen, & Brown, 2003; Lackey, 2003).

Stages of Marital Aggression.   Marital aggression by a husband typically occurs in three stages (Walker, 1989; see Figure 11-4). The first is the *tension-building stage,* in which a batterer becomes upset and shows dissatisfaction initially through verbal abuse. He may also show some preliminary physical aggression in the form of shoving or grabbing. The wife may desperately try to avoid the impending violence, attempting to calm her spouse or withdraw from the situation. Such behavior may serve only to enrage the husband, who senses his wife's vulnerability, and her efforts to escape may lead to an escalation of his anger.

The next stage consists of an *acute battering incident*, when the physical abuse actually occurs. It may last from several minutes to hours. Wives may be shoved against walls, choked, slapped, punched, kicked, and stepped on. Their arms may be twisted or broken; they may be shaken severely, thrown down a flight of stairs, or burned with cigarettes or scalding liquids. About a quarter of wives are forced to engage in sexual activities during this period, which takes the form of aggressive sexual acts and rape.

Finally, in some—but not all—cases, the episode moves into the *loving contrition stage*. At this point, the husband feels remorse and apologizes for his actions. He may minister to his wife, providing first aid and sympathy, and assuring her that he will never act violently again. Because wives may feel that in some way they were partly at fault in triggering the aggression, they may be motivated to accept the apology and forgive their husbands. They want to believe that the aggression will never occur again.

The loving contrition stage helps explain why many wives remain with abusive husbands and are the continuing victims of abuse. Wishing desperately to keep their marriage intact, and believing that they have no good alternatives, some wives remain out of a vague sense that they are responsible for the abuse. Others remain out of fear: They are afraid their husbands may come after them if they leave.

The Cycle of Violence.   Still other wives stay with batterers because they, like their husbands, have learned a seemingly unforgettable lesson from childhood: that violence is an acceptable means of settling disputes.

Individuals who abuse their spouses and children were often as children the victims of abuse themselves. According to the **cycle of violence hypothesis**, abuse and neglect of children lead them to be predisposed to abusiveness as adults. In line with social learning theory, the cycle of violence hypothesis suggests that family aggression is perpetuated from one generation to another as family members follow the lead of the previous generation. It is a fact that individuals who abuse their wives often have been raised in households in which they have witnessed spousal abuse, just as parents who abuse their children frequently have been the victims of abuse themselves as children (Serbin & Karp, 2004; Renner & Slack, 2006; Alexander, 2015).

cycle of violence hypothesis
the theory that the abuse and neglect that children suffer predispose them as adults to abuse and neglect their own children.

What can be done to end the cycle of violence, in which people who were abused as children grow up to be abusers of others?

Growing up in a home where abuse occurs does not invariably lead to abusiveness as an adult. Only about one-third of people who were abused or neglected as children abuse their own children as adults, and two-thirds of abusers were not themselves abused as children. The cycle of violence, then, does not tell the full story of abuse (Hauser, Allen, & Golden, 2006; Eriksson & Mazerolle, 2015).

Whatever the causes of abuse, there are ways to deal with it, as we consider in the *Development in Your Life* box.

The Cultural Roots of Domestic Violence.   Although the tendency often is to see marital violence and aggression as a particularly North American phenomenon, in fact other cultures have traditions in which violence is regarded as acceptable (Abrahams et al., 2006; Wilson-Williams et al., 2008). For instance, wife battering is particularly prevalent in cultures in which women are viewed as inferior to men and are treated as property.

In Western societies too, wife beating was acceptable at one time. According to English common law, which formed the foundation of the legal system in the United States, husbands were allowed to beat their wives. In the 1800s this law was modified to permit only certain kinds of beating. It was not until the late 19th century that spousal abuse was made illegal in the United States (Davidson, 1977).

Some experts on abuse suggest that the traditional power structure under which women and men function is a root cause of abuse. They argue that the more a society differentiates between men and women in terms of status, the more likely it is that abuse will occur (Vandello & Cohen, 2003; Vandello et al., 2009).

Development in Your Life
Dealing with Spousal Abuse

Despite the fact that spousal abuse occurs in one-quarter of all marriages, efforts to deal with victims of abuse are underfunded and inadequate to meet current needs. Some psychologists argue that the same factors that led society to underestimate the magnitude of the problem for many years now hinder the development of effective interventions. Still, there are several measures available to help the victims of spousal abuse (Hamberger & Holtzworth-Munroe, 2007).

- **Teach both wives and husbands a basic premise.** Physical violence is *never*, under *any* circumstances, an acceptable means of resolving disagreements.

- **Call the police.** It is against the law to assault another person, including a spouse. Although it may be difficult to involve law enforcement officers, this is a realistic way of dealing with domestic abuse. Judges can also issue restraining orders requiring abusive husbands to stay away from their wives.

- **Understand that the remorse shown by a spouse, no matter how heartfelt, may have no bearing on the possibility of future violence.** Even if a husband shows loving regret after a battering session and vows that he will never be violent again, such a promise is no guarantee against future abuse.

- **If you are the victim of abuse, seek a safe haven.** Many communities have shelters for the victims of domestic violence that can house women and their children. Because addresses of shelters are kept confidential, an abusive spouse will not be able to find you. Telephone numbers are listed in the yellow or blue pages of phone books, and local police should also have the numbers.

- **If you feel in danger from an abusive partner, seek a restraining order** from a judge in court. Under a restraining order a spouse is forbidden to come near you, under penalty of law.

- **Call the National Domestic Violence Hotline at 1-800-799-7233** for immediate advice.

CHILD ABUSE. The figures are gloomy and disheartening: At least five children are killed by their parents or caretakers every day, and 140,000 others are physically injured every year. Around 3 million children are abused or neglected in the United States each year.

Child abuse can occur in any household, regardless of economic well-being or the social status of the parents. It is most frequent in families living in stressful environments. Poverty, single parenthood, and higher-than-average levels of marital conflict help create such environments. Stepfathers are more likely to commit abuse against stepchildren than genetic fathers are against their own offspring. Child abuse is also more likely when there is a history of violence between spouses (Osofsky, 2003; Evans, 2004; Ezzo & Young, 2012). Table 11-4 lists some of the warning signs of abuse.

Abused children are more likely to be fussy, resistant to control, and not readily adaptable to new situations. They have more headaches and stomachaches, experience more bedwetting, are generally more anxious, and may show developmental delays. Children in certain age groups are also more likely to be the targets of abuse: Three- and 4-year-olds and 15- to 17-year-olds are somewhat more likely to be abused by their parents than children of other ages (Haugaard, 2000; Ehrensaft et al., 2015).

As you consider this information about the characteristics of abused children, keep in mind that labeling children as being at higher risk for receiving abuse does not make them responsible for their abuse; the family members who carry out the abuse are at fault. Statistical findings simply suggest that children with such characteristics are more at risk of being the recipients of family violence.

Reasons for Physical Abuse.   Why does physical abuse occur? Most parents certainly do not intend to hurt their children. In fact, most parents who abuse their children later express bewilderment and regret about their own behavior.

One reason for child abuse is the vague demarcation between permissible and impermissible forms of physical violence. Societal folklore in the United States says that spanking is not merely acceptable but often necessary and desirable. Almost half of

Table 11-4 Recognizing Child Abuse

The following signs may signal the presence of child abuse or neglect.

The Child:

- Shows sudden changes in behavior or school performance
- Has not received help for physical or medical problems brought to the parents' attention
- Has learning problems (or difficulty concentrating) that cannot be attributed to specific physical or psychological causes
- Is always watchful, as though preparing for something bad to happen
- Lacks adult supervision
- Is overly compliant, passive, or withdrawn
- Comes to school or other activities early, stays late, and does not want to go home
- In cases of sexual abuse: the use of new words for private body parts, mimicking sexual acts with toys or stuffed animals, or resistance at removing clothes

The Parent:

- Shows little concern for the child
- Denies the existence of—or blames the child for—the child's problems in school or at home
- Asks teachers or other caregivers to use harsh physical discipline if the child misbehaves
- Sees the child as entirely bad, worthless, or burdensome
- Demands a level of physical or academic performance the child cannot achieve
- Looks primarily to the child for care, attention, and satisfaction of emotional needs

The Parent and Child:

- Rarely touch or look at each other
- Consider their relationship entirely negative
- State that they do not like each other

(**Source:** U.S. Department of Health & Human Services, Child Welfare Information Gateway, 2007.)

mothers with children less than 4 years of age have spanked their child in the previous week, and close to 20 percent of mothers believe it is appropriate to spank a child less than 1 year of age. In some other cultures, physical discipline is even more common (Lansford et al., 2005; Deb & Adak, 2006; Shor, 2006).

Unfortunately, the line between "spanking" and "beating" is not clear, and spankings begun in anger can escalate into abuse. In fact, there is increasing scientific evidence that spanking should be avoided entirely. Although physical punishment may produce immediate compliance—children typically stop the behavior spanking is meant to end—there are a number of long-term side effects. For example, spanking is associated with lower-quality parent–child relationships, poorer mental health for both child and parent, higher levels of delinquency, and more antisocial behavior. Spanking also teaches children that violence is an acceptable solution to problems by serving as a model of violent, aggressive behavior. Consequently, according to the American Academy of Pediatrics, the use of physical punishment of any sort is *not* recommended (Benjet & Kazdin, 2003; Gershoff et al., 2012; American Academy of Pediatrics, 2014).

Another factor that leads to high rates of abuse is the privacy in which child care is conducted in Western societies. In many other cultures, childrearing is seen as the joint responsibility of several people and even society as a whole. In most Western cultures—and particularly the United States—children are raised in private, isolated households. Because child care is seen as the sole responsibility of the parent, other people are typically not available to help out when a parent's patience is tested (Chaffin, 2006; Elliott & Urquiza, 2006).

Sometimes abuse is the result of an adult's unrealistically high expectations regarding children's abilities to be quiet and compliant at a particular age. Children's failure to meet these unrealistic expectations may provoke abuse.

Increasingly, spanking and other forms of physical violence are being seen as a human rights violation. The United Nations Committee on the Rights of the Child has called physical punishment "legalized violence against children," and it has called for its elimination. A treaty supporting this view has been ratified by 192 countries, with the exception of the United States and Somalia (Smith, 2012).

ELDER ABUSE: RELATIONSHIPS GONE WRONG. It would be easy to assume that abuse of elderly people by family members is even more rare than child abuse. The truth of the matter, however, is that such cases are considerably more common than we would like to believe. According to some estimates, **elder abuse**, the physical or psychological mistreatment or neglect of elderly individuals, may affect as many as 11 percent of the elderly. Even these estimates may be too low, since people who are abused are often too embarrassed or humiliated to report their plight. And as the number of elderly people increases, experts believe that the number of cases of elder abuse will also rise (Acierno et al., 2010; Dow & Joosten, 2012; Jackson, 2018).

Elder abuse is most frequently directed at family members and particularly at elderly parents. Those most at risk are likely to be less healthy and more isolated than the average person in late adulthood, and they are more likely to be living in a caregiver's home. Although there is no single cause for elder abuse, it often is the result of a combination of economic, psychological, and social pressures on caregivers who must provide high levels of care 24 hours a day. Thus, people with Alzheimer's disease or other sorts of dementia are particularly likely to be targets of abuse (Nahmiash, 2006; Tauriac & Scruggs, 2006; Baker, 2007).

The best approach to dealing with elder abuse is to prevent it from occurring in the first place. Family members caring for an older adult should take occasional breaks. Social support agencies can be contacted; they can provide both advice and concrete support. For instance, the National Family Caregivers Association (800-896-3650) maintains a caregivers' network and publishes a newsletter. Anyone suspecting that an elderly person is being abused should contact local authorities, such as their state's Adult Protective Services or Elder Protective Services.

elder abuse
the physical or psychological mistreatment or neglect of elderly individuals.

Module 11.3 Review

LO 11.7 Explain the development of aggression in preschool children, and summarize the gender differences.

Aggression typically declines in frequency and duration as children become more able to regulate their emotions and to use language to negotiate disputes. School violence receives a lot of attention from the media, but a school is in fact a safer environment for adolescents than any other.

LO 11.8 Compare and contrast the different approaches that seek to explain the causes of aggression in children.

Ethologists and sociobiologists regard aggression as an innate human characteristic, whereas proponents of social learning and cognitive approaches focus on learned aspects of aggression.

LO 11.9 Summarize the cycle of violence hypothesis, and identify the social and cultural factors that contribute to family violence.

Marital violence tends to pass through three stages: tension building, an acute battering incident, and loving contrition. The incidence of family violence is highest in families of lower socioeconomic status. A "cycle of violence" affords a partial explanation. Cultural norms may also play a role. Elder abuse typically involves a socially isolated elderly parent in poor health and a caregiver who feels burdened by the parent.

Journal Writing Prompt

Applying Lifespan Development: How might a preschool teacher or parent help children notice the violence in the programs they watch and protect them from its effects?

Epilogue

In this chapter, we considered both moral development and aggression, and explored the development of religious thought and the purpose of spiritual beliefs. First, we looked at a variety of theories about how children develop a sense of right and wrong. We discussed how reasoning about moral dilemmas grows more sophisticated as children move into adolescence. We also explored a range of parenting styles and discussed their implications for shaping children's behavior, both present and future.

Then we considered religion and spirituality and asked: Why is religion important to many people? We considered how religion helps people to find meaning in their lives and how it helps them cope with disasters. We also discussed the development of religious thought, using both Piaget's approach to cognitive development and Fowler's stages of faith development. We examined the relationship between religious belief and life satisfaction in late adulthood, and we discussed the special significance religion holds for older adults, especially African Americans.

In the final part of the chapter, we examined the sources of aggression and violence, and considered the question: Is nature or nurture more responsible for aggression? We explored ways of decreasing aggression in children and increasing their moral behaviors. We also considered the factors that predict a lifelong problem with aggression. In conclusion, we examined the epidemic of family violence involving abuse of children, spouses, and elders.

Before moving on to the next chapter, take a moment to reread the prologue to this chapter about Samantha and her problems with alcohol and the law, and answer the following questions:

1. Based on Samantha's comments, which parenting style do you think her father used? Why do you think that?

2. Samantha reported that her father often did everything he could to keep her out of trouble. Explain his moral reasoning in terms of the social domain approach.

3. Considering the social learning approach to morality, what models might Samantha have observed that support her belief that it's okay to break the law?

4. In what situations, if any, do you feel bending the rules to protect a family member or friend is justified? Where would you draw the line and why?

Looking Back

LO 11.1 Compare and contrast the various approaches to moral development.

Social learning approaches to morality emphasize interactions between environment and behavior in moral development in which models of behavior play an important role in development. The genetic approach to morality suggests that particular genes may underlie some aspects of moral behavior. Some developmentalists believe that moral behavior is rooted in a child's development of empathy. Other emotions, including the negative emotions of anger and shame, may also promote moral behavior.

LO 11.2 Summarize Kohlberg's and Gilligan's theories of moral development, and explain how they differ.

According to Lawrence Kohlberg, people pass from preconventional morality (motivated by rewards and punishments), through conventional morality (motivated by social reference), to postconventional morality (motivated by a sense of universal moral principles). Carol Gilligan has sketched out an alternative progression for girls, from an orientation toward individual survival, through goodness as self-sacrifice, to the morality of nonviolence.

LO 11.3 Identify the factors that influence moral and prosocial behaviors, including the roles played by gender and culture.

Moral reasoning is not the same as moral behavior, as researchers with a social learning orientation have noted. People who understand moral issues do not invariably behave in a moral manner. Adolescents' increasing cognitive abilities allow them to evaluate the motivations behind prosocial behavior, which may be altruistic or self-serving. The social domain approach suggests that moral reasoning needs to be considered in the context in which judgments are being made at any given time. Major contexts include the moral domain, the social-conventional domain, and the personal domain. People are not invariably helpful nor unhelpful. Whether individuals act in a prosocial manner depends on their personality and the specifics of the situation. There are gender and cultural differences in empathy and prosocial behavior. Girls tend to be more helpful and caring of others than boys. People raised in cultures that emphasize cooperation over competition show higher levels of prosocial behavior.

LO 11.4 Identify the four basic parenting styles, and summarize how each style influences a child's development.

Disciplinary styles differ both individually and culturally. In the United States and other Western societies, parents' styles tend to be mostly authoritarian, permissive, uninvolved, and authoritative, with the last regarded as the most effective. Children of authoritarian and permissive parents may develop dependency, hostility, and low self-control, whereas children of uninvolved parents may feel unloved and emotionally detached. Children of authoritative parents tend to be more independent, friendly, self-assertive, and cooperative.

LO 11.5 Summarize the development of religion in childhood and adolescence.

Using Jean Piaget's theory of cognitive development, you can view religious thinking as passing through three stages during childhood and adolescence: preoperational intuitive religious thought, in which children's religious thinking is unsystematic and the meanings of religious stories are often misinterpreted; concrete operational religious thought, during which school-age children focus more on the concrete details of religious stories rather than their abstract meanings; and formal operational religious thought, in which adolescents are able to understand the abstract meanings of stories and draw inferences from them.

LO 11.6 Identify the purposes religion and spirituality serve in adulthood, and describe Fowler's stages of faith development.

Religion helps people to grapple with who they are and what their purpose in life may be—one of the major challenges facing every individual. Many people turn to their religion or spiritual beliefs to provide comfort at the death of a loved one. They may look to their religion to make sense of disasters and other seemingly random events. Belonging to a religious group serves to give people a sense that they are part of a formal community. Religious groups often provide direct social support to their members in times of need. James Fowler suggested that faith development occurs in a series of stages over our life span. Children hold a literal view of God, while spirituality becomes more abstract in adolescence as teens develop a set of core values and beliefs. During adulthood, people reflect on their beliefs and values during the individuative-reflective stage. Near death, in the conjunctive stage, the elderly develop a broad, inclusive view of religion and humanity.

LO 11.7 Explain the development of aggression in preschool children, and summarize the gender differences.

Aggression, which involves intentional harm to another person, begins to emerge in the preschool years. As children age and improve their language skills, acts of aggression typically decline in frequency and duration. Boys typically show higher levels of physical, instrumental aggression, motivated by the desire to obtain a concrete goal. Girls may be just as aggressive, but they are likely to show more relational aggression, which uses name-calling or hurtful words and the withholding of friendship.

LO 11.8 Compare and contrast the different approaches that seek to explain the causes of aggression in children.

Some ethologists, such as Konrad Lorenz, believe that aggression is simply a biological fact of human life, a belief held also by many sociobiologists, who focus on competition within species to pass genes on to the next generation. Social learning theorists focus on the role of the environment, including the influence of models and social reinforcement as factors influencing aggressive behavior. The cognitive approach to aggression emphasizes the role of interpretations of the behaviors of others in determining aggressive or nonaggressive responses.

LO 11.9 Summarize the cycle of violence hypothesis, and identify the social and cultural factors that contribute to family violence.

Family violence in the United States has reached epidemic proportions, with some form of violence occurring in a quarter of all marriages. The likelihood of violence is highest in families that are subject to economic or emotional stresses. In addition, people who were abused as children have a higher likelihood of becoming abusers as adults—a phenomenon termed the

cycle of violence. Marital aggression typically proceeds through three stages: a tension-building stage, an acute battering incident, and a loving contrition stage. Despite contrition, abusers tend to remain abusers unless they get effective help.

Key Terms and Concepts

moral development   336
prosocial behavior   336
abstract modeling   337
empathy   338
preconventional morality   339
conventional morality   339
postconventional morality   340

social domain approach   342
authoritarian parents   344
permissive parents   344
authoritative parents   344
uninvolved parents   344
neglect   344
values   347

aggression   350
emotional self-regulation   351
instrumental aggression   351
relational aggression   351
cycle of violence hypothesis   358
elder abuse   361

Chapter 12
Gender and Sexuality

Ariel Skelley/Getty Images

Learning Objectives

LO 12.1 Explain the nature of gender differences and their effects on the roles people assume in life.

LO 12.2 Describe how an individual's gender identity develops in early childhood.

LO 12.3 Analyze the major theoretical explanations of gender differences.

LO 12.4 Explore the psychological implications of sexual maturation during adolescence.

LO 12.5 Describe how adolescents experience and explore their sexuality.

LO 12.6 Explain the role of sexuality during adulthood.

LO 12.7 Describe the functions and patterns of dating in adolescence.

LO 12.8 Analyze the nature of intimacy and relationships in early adulthood.

LO 12.9 Explain the process by which people choose their partners.

LO 12.10 Examine the varied forms of long-term relationships.

LO 12.11 Analyze why marriages work or don't work.

Chapter Overview

Prologue: Boys Don't Wear Dresses

Sondra Lewis and her husband knew their daughter Alexandra was a tomboy. Alexandra had always preferred her older brother Darren's toys, and now at age 3, she suddenly announced, "Dresses are funny. I want what Darren wears."

"You don't want dresses?" asked Sondra. "Don't you like them?" "Mommy," Alexandra replied firmly, "Boys don't wear dresses. I don't want them because I'm a boy."

This stopped Sondra cold. "Tomboy" was no longer the right word. But instead of trying to argue Alexandra out of her feelings, she held her tongue. She and her husband found a wealth of information on the Internet about "gender-nonconforming children" and learned that their daughter was not alone. Alexandra's family—Darren especially—decided to give their support.

Alexandra is now Alex, a happy fourth-grade boy at an understanding school. "Hormone treatments? Surgery?" says Sondra. "Who knows? That's for later. What I know now is that I have not one but two happy, healthy sons, and I love them both." ∎

Looking Ahead

Alex's conviction that he is a boy is an increasingly common phenomenon in this bold new century. In this chapter, we focus on gender, sexuality, and relationships. We begin by looking at gender, the sense of being male or female, and how children are both treated differently and behave differently on the basis of whether they are boys or girls. We also consider the various approaches that seek to explain gender differences.

We then turn to sexuality and its behavioral and psychological components. We consider how sexual maturation is tied up with body image, and we note that the timing of puberty has significant consequences for adolescents' psychological well-being. We also look at the nature of sexual relationships and sexual orientation, as well as considering the consequences of teen pregnancy. Then we explore the nature of sexuality in middle and late adulthood.

Finally, we consider the development and course of intimate relationships. We look at the role dating plays in adolescents' lives and the differences between liking and loving. We examine the different types of love and discuss how people choose partners. Then we consider the choice of whether to marry and the factors that influence the course and success of marriage throughout adulthood. We also look at some of the challenges of marriage, such as divorce and caring for an ill or dying spouse in late adulthood.

Anatoliy Samara/Fotolia

The ways girls and boys are treated differs from birth onward.

MODULE 12.1

GENDER: WHY DO BOYS WEAR BLUE AND GIRLS WEAR PINK?

"It's a boy." "It's a girl."

One of these two statements is probably the first announcement made after the birth of a child. From the moment of birth, girls and boys are treated differently. Their parents send out different kinds of birth announcements. They are dressed in different clothes and wrapped in different-colored blankets. They are given different toys (Serbin, Poulin-Dubois, & Colburne, 2001; Basow, 2006; Trawick-Smith et al., 2015). But just how profound are gender differences in babies, and what is their origin?

Gender Differences

LO 12.1 **Explain the nature of gender differences and their effects on the roles people assume in life.**

There is a considerable amount of disagreement over both the extent and causes of gender differences, even though most people agree that boys and girls do experience at least partially different worlds based on gender. Some gender differences are fairly clear from the time of birth. For example, male infants tend to be more active and fussier than female infants. Boys' sleep tends to be more disturbed than that of girls. Boys grimace more, although no gender difference exists in the overall amount of crying. There is also some evidence that male newborns are more irritable than female newborns, although the findings are inconsistent (Bornstein et al., 2008; Guinsburg et al., 2000; Losonczy-Marshall, 2008).

Innate differences between male and female infants, however, are generally minor. In most ways infants seem so similar that usually adults cannot discern whether a baby is a boy or a girl. Furthermore, it is important to keep in mind that there are much larger differences among individual boys and among individual girls than there are, on average, between boys and girls (Crawford & Unger, 2004; Chaplin & Aldao, 2013). The differences at this early stage of life may be more profound in parents than in their babies.

Parents play with boy and girl babies differently: From birth on, fathers tend to interact more with sons than daughters, while mothers interact more with daughters. Because mothers and fathers play in different ways (with fathers typically engaging in more physical, rough-and-tumble activities and mothers in traditional games such as peek-a-boo), male and female infants are clearly exposed to different styles of activity and interaction from their parents (Laflamme, Pomerleau, & Malcuit, 2002; Clearfield & Nelson, 2006).

The behavior exhibited by girls and boys is interpreted in very different ways by adults. For instance, when researchers showed adults a video of an infant whose name was given as either "John" or "Mary," adults perceived "John" as adventurous and inquisitive, while "Mary" was fearful and anxious, although it was the same baby performing a single set of behaviors (Condry & Condry, 1976). Clearly, adults view the behavior of children through the lens of gender. **Gender** refers to our sense of being male or female. The term *gender* is often used to mean the same thing as *sex*, but they are not actually the same. **Sex** typically refers to sexual anatomy and sexual behavior, while gender refers to the social perceptions of maleness or femaleness. All cultures prescribe *gender roles* for males and females, but these roles differ greatly from one culture to another.

gender
the sense of being male or female.

sex
typically refers to sexual anatomy and sexual behavior.

GENDER ROLES. Gender differences emerge more clearly as children age—and become increasingly influenced by the gender roles that society sets out for them. For instance, by the age of 1 year, infants are able to distinguish between males and females. Girls at this age prefer to play with dolls or stuffed animals, while

During the preschool period, differences in play according to gender become more pronounced. In addition, boys tend to play with boys, and girls with girls.

boys seek out blocks and trucks. Often, of course, these are the only options available to them due to the choices their parents and other adults have made in the toys they provide (Cherney, Kelly-Vance, & Glover, 2003; Alexander, Wilcox, & Woods, 2009).

Children's preferences for certain kinds of toys are reinforced by their parents. In general, however, parents of boys are more apt to be concerned about their child's choices than are parents of girls. Boys receive more reinforcement for playing with toys that society deems appropriate for boys, and this reinforcement increases with age. In contrast, a girl playing with a truck is viewed with considerably less concern than a boy playing with a doll might be. Girls who play with toys seen by society as "masculine" are less discouraged for their behavior than boys who play with toys seen as "feminine" (Schmalz & Kerstetter, 2006; Hill & Flom, 2007; Dinella, Weisgram, & Fulcher, 2017).

By the time they reach age 2, boys behave more independently and less compliantly than girls. Much of this behavior can be traced to parental reactions to earlier behavior. For instance, when a child takes his or her first steps, parents tend to react differently, depending on the child's gender: Boys are encouraged more to go off and explore the world, while girls are hugged and kept close. It is hardly surprising, then, that by age 2, girls tend to show less independence and greater compliance (Poulin-Dubois, Serbin, & Eichstedt, 2002; Laemmle, 2013).

Societal encouragement and reinforcement do not, however, completely explain differences in behavior between boys and girls. For example, one study examined girls who were exposed before birth to abnormally high levels of *androgen*, a male hormone, because their mothers unwittingly took a drug containing the hormone while pregnant. Later, these girls were more likely to play with toys stereotypically preferred by boys (such as cars) and less likely to play with toys stereotypically associated with girls (such as dolls). Although there are many alternative explanations for these results—you can probably think of several yourself—one possibility is that exposure to male hormones affected the brain development of the girls, leading them to favor toys that involve certain kinds of preferred skills (Mealey, 2000; Servin et al., 2003).

In sum, differences in behavior between boys and girls begin in infancy and continue throughout our lives. Although gender differences have complex causes, representing some combination of innate, biologically related factors and environmental factors, they play a profound role in the social and emotional development of infants.

Gender Identity: Developing Femaleness and Maleness

LO 12.2   Describe how an individual's gender identity develops in early childhood.

Boys' awards: Very Best Thinker, Most Eager Learner, Most Imaginative, Most Enthusiastic, Most Scientific, Best Friend, Mr. Personality, Hardest Worker, Best Sense of Humor.

Girls' awards: All-Around Sweetheart, Sweetest Personality, Cutest Personality, Best Sharer, Best Artist, Biggest Heart, Best Manners, Best Helper, Most Creative.

What's wrong with this picture? To one parent, whose daughter received one of the girls' awards during a kindergarten graduation ceremony, quite a bit (Deveny, 1994). While the girls were getting pats on the back for their pleasing personalities, the boys were receiving awards for their intellectual and analytic skills.

From *a preschool teacher's* perspective

How important is it to understand gender development in a multicultural class? Why?

Such a situation is not rare: Girls and boys often live in very different worlds. As we've discussed, differences in the ways males and females are treated begin at birth, continue during the preschool years, and extend into adolescence and beyond (Martin & Ruble, 2004; Bornstein et al., 2008; Ecklund, 2012).

Gender, the sense of being male or female, is well established by the time children reach the preschool years. By age 2, children consistently label themselves and those around them as male or female (Raag, 2003; Campbell, Shirley, & Candy, 2004; Dinella, Weisgram, & Fulcher, 2017).

One way gender shows up is in play. Preschool boys spend more time than girls in rough-and-tumble play, while preschool girls spend more time than boys in organized games and role-playing. Rough-and-tumble play is important because it promotes the development of the prefrontal cortex and helps teach preschoolers to regulate their emotions (Kestly, 2014).

During this time boys begin to play more with boys and girls play more with girls, a trend that increases during middle childhood. Girls begin to prefer same-sex playmates a little earlier than boys. They first have a clear preference for interacting with other girls at age 2, while boys don't show much preference for same-sex playmates until age 3 (Martin & Fabes, 2001; Raag, 2003; Bosacki, Woods, & Coplan, 2015).

Such same-sex preferences appear in many cultures. For instance, studies of kindergartners in mainland China show no examples of mixed-gender play. Similarly, gender "outweighs" ethnic variables when it comes to play: A Hispanic boy would rather play with a white boy than with a Hispanic girl (Whiting & Edwards, 1988; Aydt & Corsaro, 2003).

Preschool-age children often have very strict ideas about how boys and girls are supposed to act. Their expectations about gender-appropriate behavior are even more gender-stereotyped than those of adults and may be less flexible during the preschool years than at any other point in the life span. Beliefs in gender stereotypes become increasingly pronounced up to age 5, and although they become somewhat less rigid by age 7, they do not disappear. In fact, the gender stereotypes held by preschoolers resemble those held by traditional adults in society (Halim, Ruble, & Tamis-LeMonda, 2013; Halim et al., 2014; Emilson, Folkesson, & Lindberg, 2016).

And what is the nature of preschoolers' gender expectations? Like adults, preschoolers expect that males are more apt to have traits involving competence, independence, forcefulness, and competitiveness. In contrast, females are viewed as more likely to have traits such as warmth, expressiveness, nurturance, and submissiveness. Although these are *expectations*, and say nothing about the way that men and women actually behave, such expectations provide the lens through which preschool-age children view the world and affect their behavior as well as the way they interact with peers and adults (Blakemore, 2003; Gelman, Taylor, & Nguyen, 2004; Martin & Dinella, 2012).

From *a child-care provider's* perspective

If a girl in a preschool child-care setting loudly tells a boy that he can't play with the dolls in the play area because he's a boy, what is the best way to handle the situation?

Explaining Gender Differences

LO 12.3   Analyze the major theoretical explanations of gender differences.

The prevalence and strength of preschoolers' gender expectations, and differences in behavior between boys and girls, have proven puzzling. Why should gender play such a powerful role during the preschool years (as well as during the rest of the life span)? Developmentalists have proposed several explanations.

BIOLOGICAL PERSPECTIVES ON GENDER.   Because gender relates to the sense of being male or female, and sex refers to the physical characteristics that differentiate males and females, it would hardly be surprising to find that the biological characteristics associated with sex might themselves lead to gender differences. This has been shown to be true.

Hormones are one sex-related biological characteristic that has been found to affect gender-based behaviors. Girls exposed to unusually high levels of **androgens** (male hormones) prenatally are more likely to display behaviors associated with male stereotypes than are their sisters who were not exposed to androgens (Knickmeyer & Baron-Cohen, 2006; Burton et al., 2009; Mathews et al., 2009).

Androgen-exposed girls preferred boys as playmates and spent more time than other girls playing with toys associated with the male role, such as cars and trucks. Similarly, boys exposed prenatally to atypically high levels of female hormones are apt to display more behaviors that are stereotypically female than is usual (Servin et al., 2003; Knickmeyer & Baron-Cohen, 2006; Pasterski et al., 2014).

Moreover, as we noted earlier, some research suggests that biological differences exist in the structure of female and male brains. For instance, part of the **corpus callosum**, the bundle of nerves that connects the hemispheres of the brain, is proportionally larger in women than in men. To some theoreticians, this evidence suggests that gender differences may be produced by biological factors, such as hormones (Westerhausen et al., 2004).

Before accepting such contentions, however, it is important to note that alternative explanations abound. For example, the *corpus callosum* may be proportionally larger in women because of certain kinds of experiences that influence brain growth in particular ways. We know that girls are spoken to more than boys as infants, which might produce certain kinds of brain development. If this is true, environmental experience produces biological change—and not the other way around.

Other developmentalists see gender differences as serving the biological goal of survival of the species through reproduction. Basing their work on an evolutionary approach, these theorists suggest that our male ancestors who showed more stereotypically masculine qualities, such as forcefulness and competitiveness, may have been able to attract females who were able to provide them with hardy offspring. Females who excelled at stereotypically feminine tasks, such as nurturing, may have been valuable partners because they could increase the likelihood that children would survive the dangers of childhood (Browne, 2006; Ellis, 2006; McMillan, Frierson, & Campbell, 2011).

As in other domains that involve the interaction of inherited biological characteristics and environmental influences, it is difficult to attribute behavioral characteristics unambiguously to biological factors. Because of this problem, we must consider other explanations for gender differences.

PSYCHOANALYTIC PERSPECTIVES.   You may recall from earlier discussions that Sigmund Freud's psychoanalytic theory suggests that we move through a series of stages related to biological urges. To Freud, the preschool years encompass the *phallic stage*, in which the focus of a child's pleasure relates to genital sexuality.

Freud argued that the end of the phallic stage is marked by an important turning point in development: the Oedipal conflict. According to Freud, the *Oedipal conflict* occurs at around age 5, when the anatomical differences between males and females become particularly evident. Boys begin to develop sexual interests in their mothers, viewing their fathers as rivals. As a consequence, boys conceive a desire to kill their fathers—just as Oedipus did in the ancient Greek tragedy. However, because they view their fathers as all-powerful, boys develop a fear of retaliation, which takes the form of *castration anxiety*. In order to overcome this fear, boys repress their desires for their mothers and instead begin to identify with their fathers, attempting to be as similar to them as possible. *Identification* is the process in which children attempt to be similar to their same-sex parent, incorporating the parent's attitudes and values.

androgens
male hormones.

corpus callosum
the bundle of nerves that connects the hemispheres of the brain.

Koltsov/Shutterstock

Brad Killer/Getty Images

According to social learning approaches, children learn gender-related behavior and expectations from their observations of others.

Girls, according to Freud, go through a different process. They begin to feel sexual attraction toward their fathers and experience *penis envy—a* view that not unexpectedly has led to accusations that Freud viewed women as inferior to men. In order to resolve their penis envy, girls ultimately identify with their mothers, attempting to be as similar to them as possible.

In the cases of both boys and girls, the ultimate result of identifying with the same-sex parent is that the children adopt their parents' gender attitudes and values. In this way, says Freud, society's expectations about the ways females and males "ought" to behave are perpetuated into new generations.

You may find it difficult to accept Freud's elaborate explanation of gender differences. So do most developmentalists, who believe that gender development is best explained by other mechanisms. In part, they base their criticisms of Freud on the lack of scientific support for his theories. For example, children learn gender stereotypes much earlier than age 5. Furthermore, this learning occurs even in single-parent households. However, some aspects of psychoanalytic theory have been supported, such as findings indicating that preschool-age children whose same-sex parents support sex-stereotyped behavior tend to demonstrate that behavior also. Still, far simpler processes can account for this phenomenon, and many developmentalists have searched for explanations of gender differences other than Freud's (Martin & Ruble, 2004; Chen & Rao, 2011; Ju et al., 2015).

SOCIAL LEARNING APPROACHES. As their name implies, social learning approaches see children as learning gender-related behavior and expectations by observing others. Children watch the behavior of their parents, teachers, siblings, and even peers. A little boy sees the glory of a major league baseball player and becomes interested in sports. A little girl watches her high school neighbor practicing cheerleading moves and begins to try them herself. The observation of the rewards that these others attain for acting in a gender-appropriate manner leads children to conform to such behavior themselves (Rust et al., 2000).

Books and the media, and in particular television and video games, also play a role in perpetuating traditional views of gender-related behavior from which preschoolers may learn. Analyses of the most popular television shows, for example, find that male characters outnumber female characters by two to one. Furthermore, females are more apt to appear with males, whereas female–female relationships are relatively uncommon (Calvert et al., 2003; Chapman, 2016).

Television also presents men and women in traditional gender roles. Television shows typically define female characters in terms of their relationships with males. Females are more likely to appear as victims than males (Turner-Bowker, 1996). They are less likely to be presented as productive or as decision makers, and more likely to be portrayed as characters interested in romance, their homes, and their families. Such models, according to social learning theory, are apt to have a powerful influence on preschoolers' definitions of appropriate behavior (Nassif & Gunter, 2008; Prieler et al., 2011; Matthes, Prieler, & Adam, 2016).

In some cases, the learning of social roles does not involve models but occurs more directly. For example, most of us have heard preschool-age children being told by their parents to act like a "little girl" or "little man." What this generally means is that girls should behave politely and courteously, and boys should be tough and stoic—traits associated with society's traditional stereotypes of men and women. Such direct training sends a clear message about the behavior expected of a preschool-age child (Leaper, 2002).

gender identity

the perception of oneself as male or female.

gender schema

a cognitive framework that organizes information relevant to gender.

gender constancy

the belief that people are permanently males or females, depending on fixed, unchangeable biological factors.

COGNITIVE APPROACHES. In the view of some theorists, one aspect of the desire to form a clear sense of identity is the desire to establish a **gender identity**, a perception of oneself as male or female. To do this, we develop a **gender schema**, a cognitive framework that organizes information relevant to gender (Martin & Ruble, 2004; Signorella & Frieze, 2008; Halim et al., 2014).

Gender schemas are developed early in life and serve as a lens through which preschoolers view the world. For instance, preschoolers use their increasing cognitive abilities to develop "rules" about what is right and what is inappropriate for males and females. Thus, some girls decide that wearing pants is inappropriate for a female and apply the rule so rigidly that they refuse to wear anything but dresses. Or a preschool boy may reason that because makeup is typically worn by females, it is inappropriate for him to wear makeup even when he is in a preschool play and all the other boys and girls are wearing it (Frawley, 2008).

According to a cognitive-developmental theory proposed by Lawrence Kohlberg, this rigidity is in part a reflection of preschoolers' understanding of gender (Kohlberg, 1966). Rigid gender schemas are influenced by the preschooler's erroneous beliefs about sex differences. Specifically, young preschoolers believe that sex differences are based not on biological factors but on differences in appearance or behavior. Employing this view of the world, a girl may reason that she can be a father when she grows up or a boy may think he could turn into a girl if he put on a dress and tied his hair in a ponytail. However, by the time they reach 4 or 5, children develop an understanding of **gender constancy**, the awareness that people are permanently males or females, depending on fixed, unchangeable biological factors.

For some children, gender identification is particularly challenging. *Transgender children* believe that they are trapped in the body of the other gender. There are some reports of transgender children expressing to their parents that they believe their gender identity is different from that assigned at birth as early as they learn to talk, starting at 18 to 24 months. But there is relatively little research on the issue, and little guidance exists for parents about how to deal with preschoolers who express the conviction that they identify with the other gender (Prince-Embury & Saklofaske, 2014; Fast & Olson, 2017).

Interestingly, children's growing understanding of gender constancy during the preschool period has no particular effect on gender-related behavior. In fact, the appearance of gender schemas occurs well before children understand gender constancy. Even young preschool-age children assume that certain behaviors are appropriate—and others are not—on the basis of stereotypic views of gender (Martin, Ruble, & Szkrybalo, 2002; Martin & Ruble, 2004).

Like the other approaches to gender development (summarized in Table 12-1), the cognitive perspective does not imply that differences between the two sexes are in any way improper or inappropriate. Instead, it suggests that preschoolers should be taught to treat others as individuals. Furthermore, preschoolers need to learn the importance of fulfilling their own talents, acting as individuals and not as representatives of a particular gender.

Table 12-1 Four Approaches to Gender Development

Perspective	Key Concepts	Applying the Concepts to Preschool Children
Biological	Our ancestors who behaved in ways that are now stereotypically feminine or masculine may have been more successful in reproducing. Brain differences may lead to gender differences.	Girls may be genetically "programmed" by evolution to be more expressive and nurturing, while boys are "programmed" to be more competitive and forceful. Abnormal hormone exposure before birth has been linked to both boys and girls behaving in ways typically expected of the other gender.
Psychoanalytic	Gender development is the result of identification with the same-sex parent, achieved by moving through a series of stages related to biological urges.	Girls and boys whose parents of the same sex behave in stereotypically masculine or feminine ways are likely to do so, too, perhaps because they identify with those parents.
Social learning	Children learn gender-related behavior and expectations from their observation of others' behavior.	Children notice that other children and adults are rewarded for behaving in ways that conform to standard gender stereotypes—and sometimes punished for violating those stereotypes.
Cognitive	Through the use of gender schemas, developed early in life, preschoolers form a lens through which they view the world. They use their increasing cognitive abilities to develop "rules" about what is appropriate for males and females.	Preschoolers are more rigid in their rules about proper gender behavior than people at other ages, perhaps because they have just developed gender schemas that don't yet permit much variation from stereotypical expectations.

Module 12.1 Review

LO 12.1 Explain the nature of gender differences and their effects on the roles people assume in life.

Mothers and fathers interact with their babies differently, with mothers interacting more with their daughters and fathers interacting more with their sons. The types of interactions they engage in also differ. Some gender differences do exist in early infancy, but they are relatively minor. Gender differences become more pronounced as infants age.

LO 12.2 Describe how an individual's gender identity develops in early childhood.

Preference for same-sex playmates begins to appear in the preschool years. Such a preference occurs in many cultures.

LO 12.3 Analyze the major theoretical explanations of gender differences.

Gender awareness develops in the preschool years. Explanations of this phenomenon include biological, psychoanalytical, learning, and cognitive approaches. The books, television shows, movies, and video games young children see all play a role in perpetuating traditional stereotypes of gender-related behavior.

Journal Writing Prompt

Applying Lifespan Development: What sorts of activities might you encourage a preschool boy to undertake to encourage him to adopt a less stereotypical gender schema?

MODULE 12.2

SEXUAL MATURATION AND SEXUALITY

"I started having periods when I was just 9," Sharon Brewster, 16, recalls. By the time she entered seventh grade, Sharon was fully developed. She looked more like a mature woman in her 20s than a middle school student who struggled with French homework and what to say to boys. "Other girls envied me my very curvy figure, but I hated it," she says. "Guys—older guys, men really—followed me everywhere, and I knew it had nothing to do with who I was. It creeped me out."

Psychological Aspects of Sexual Maturation

LO 12.4 Explore the psychological implications of sexual maturation during adolescence.

Profound physical changes occur in children as they sexually mature. However, the nature and timing of these physical changes produce equally significant—and different—psychological consequences for boys and girls.

BODY IMAGE: REACTIONS TO PHYSICAL CHANGES IN ADOLESCENCE. Unlike infants, who also undergo extraordinarily rapid growth, adolescents are well aware of what is happening to their bodies, and they may react with horror or joy, spending long periods in front of mirrors. Few, though, are neutral about the changes they are witnessing (Mehran, 1997).

Some of the alterations of adolescence do not show up in physical changes but carry psychological weight. In the past, girls tended to react to menarche with anxiety because Western society tended to emphasize the more negative aspects of menstruation, such as the potential of cramps and messiness. Today, however, society's view of menstruation tends to be more positive, in part because menstruation has been demystified and is discussed more openly. (For instance, television commercials for tampons are commonplace.) As a consequence, menarche is typically accompanied by an increase in self-esteem, a rise in status, and greater self-awareness, as adolescent girls see themselves as becoming adults (Matlin, 2003; Yuan, 2012).

A boy's first ejaculation is roughly equivalent to menarche in a girl. However, while girls generally tell their mothers about the onset of menstruation, boys rarely mention their first ejaculation to their parents or even their friends (Stein & Reiser, 1994; Frankel, 2002). Why? One reason is that girls require tampons or sanitary napkins, and mothers provide them. It also may be that boys see the first ejaculation as an indication of their budding sexuality, an area about which they are quite uncertain and therefore reluctant to discuss with others.

Menstruation and ejaculations occur privately, but changes in body shape and size are quite public. Consequently, teenagers entering puberty frequently are embarrassed by the changes that are occurring. Girls, in particular, are often unhappy with their new bodies. Ideals of beauty in many Western countries call for an unrealistic thinness that is quite different from the actual shape of most women. Puberty brings a considerable increase in the amount of fatty tissue, as well as enlargement of the hips and buttocks—a far cry from the slenderness that society seems to demand (Cotrufo et al., 2007; Kretsch et al., 2016; Senín-Calderón et al., 2017).

How children react to the onset of puberty depends in part on when it happens. As we shall see next, girls and boys who mature either much earlier or later than most of their peers are especially affected by the timing of puberty.

THE TIMING OF PUBERTY: THE CONSEQUENCES OF EARLY AND LATE MATURATION. Why does it matter when a boy or girl reaches puberty? There are social consequences of early or late maturation. And as we shall see, social consequences are very important to adolescents.

Early Maturation.   For boys, early maturation is largely a plus. Early-maturing boys tend to be more successful at athletics, presumably because of their larger size. They also tend to be more popular and to have a more positive self-concept.

Early maturation in boys does have a downside, however. Boys who mature early are more apt to have difficulties in school, and they are more likely to become involved in delinquency and substance abuse. The reason: Their larger size makes it more likely that they will seek out the company of older boys who may involve them in activities that are inappropriate for their age. Furthermore, although early-maturers are more responsible and cooperative in later life, they are also more conforming and lacking in humor. Overall, though, the pluses seem to outweigh the minuses for early-maturing boys (Costello et al., 2007; Lynne et al., 2007; Natsuaki, 2014).

The story is a bit different for early-maturing girls. For them, the obvious changes in their bodies—such as the development of breasts—may lead them to feel uncomfortable and different from their peers. Moreover, because girls, in general, mature earlier than boys, early maturation tends to come at a very young age in the girl's life. Early-maturing girls may have to endure ridicule from their less mature classmates (Mendle, Turkheimer, & Emery, 2007; Hubley & Arim, 2012; Skoog & Özdemir, 2016).

Of course, early maturation is not a completely negative experience for girls. Girls who mature earlier tend to be sought after more as potential dates, and their popularity may enhance their self-concept. This attention has a price, however. They may not be socially ready to participate in the kind of one-on-one dating situations that most girls deal with at a later age, and such situations may be psychologically challenging for early-maturing girls. Moreover, the conspicuousness of their deviance from their later-maturing classmates may have a negative effect, producing anxiety, unhappiness, and depression (Kaltiala-Heino, Kosunen, & Rimpela, 2003; Galvao et al., 2013).

Cultural norms and standards regarding how women should look play a big role in how girls experience early maturation. For instance, in the United

Boys who mature early tend to be more successful in athletics and have a more positive self-concept. Why might there also be a downside to early maturation?

States, the notion of female sexuality is looked upon with a degree of ambivalence, being promoted in the media yet frowned upon socially. Girls who appear "sexy," like Sharon Brewster, attract both positive and negative attention. Consequently, unless a young girl who has developed secondary sex characteristics early can handle the disapproval she may encounter when she conspicuously displays her growing sexuality, the outcome of early maturation may be negative. In countries in which attitudes about sexuality are more liberal, the results of early maturation may be more positive. For example, in Germany, which has a more open view of sex, early-maturing girls have higher self-esteem than such girls in the United States. Furthermore, the consequences of early maturation vary even within the United States, depending on the views of girls' peer groups and on prevailing community standards regarding sex (Petersen, 2000; Dick & Mustanski, 2006).

Late Maturation.   As with early maturation, the situation with late maturation is mixed, although in this case boys fare worse than girls. For instance, boys who are smaller and lighter than their more physically mature peers tend to be viewed as less attractive. Because of their smaller size, they are at a disadvantage when it comes to sports activities. Furthermore, boys are expected to be bigger than their dates, so the social lives of late-maturing boys may suffer.

Ultimately, if the difficulties in adolescence lead to a decline in self-concept, the disadvantages of late maturation for boys could extend well into adulthood. However, coping with the challenges of late maturation may actually help males in some ways. For example, late-maturing boys grow up to have several positive qualities, such as assertiveness and insightfulness (Kaltiala-Heino, Kosunen, & Rimpela, 2003; Benoit, Lacourse, & Claes, 2014).

The picture for late-maturing girls is actually quite positive. In the short term, girls who mature later may be overlooked in dating and other mixed-sex activities during junior high school and middle school, and they may have relatively low social status (Clarke-Stewart & Friedman, 1987; Friedlander et al., 2007). However, by the time they are in the tenth grade and have begun to mature visibly, late-maturing-girls' satisfaction with themselves and their bodies may be greater than that of early-maturers. Late-maturing girls may end up with fewer emotional problems. The reason? Late-maturing girls are even more apt to fit the societal ideal of a slender, "leggy" body type than early-maturers, who tend to look heavier in comparison (Kaminaga, 2007; Leen-Feldner, Reardon, & Hayward, 2008).

In sum, the reactions to early and late maturation present a complex picture. As we have seen repeatedly, we need to take into consideration the complete constellation of factors affecting individuals in order to understand their development. Some developmentalists suggest that other factors, such as changes in peer groups, family dynamics, and particularly schools and other societal institutions, may be more pertinent in determining an adolescent's behavior than early and later maturation, and the effects of puberty in general (Stice, 2003; Mendle, Turkheimer, & Emery, 2007; Hubley & Arım, 2012).

Becoming Sexual

LO 12.5   Describe how adolescents experience and explore their sexuality.

When I started "tuning out," teachers thought I was sick—physically sick, that is. They kept sending me to the school nurse to have my temperature taken. If I'd told them I was carrying on with Beyoncé in their classes, while supposedly learning my Caesar and my Latin vocabulary, they'd have thought I was—well, delirious. I was! I'd even think of Beyoncé while jogging; I'd have to stop because it'd hurt down there! You can't run and have sex—or can you. (Based on Coles & Stokes, 1985, pp. 18–19)

Not every adolescent's sexual fantasies are as consuming as those of this teenage boy. But the hormonal changes of puberty not only trigger the maturation of the sexual organs but also produce a new range of feelings in the form of sexuality. Sexual behavior and thoughts are among the central concerns of adolescents. Almost all adolescents think about sex, and many think about it a good deal of the time (Kelly, 2001; Ponton, 2001; Allen, Seitz, & Apfel, 2007).

Adolescence is not the first time individuals think about sex. You probably know this from your own experiences. Perhaps you "played doctor" as a preschooler. Or maybe you had an erection as a child. Or perhaps you were curious about the pubic hair a sibling was growing.

Even infants and preschoolers experience some sort of sexuality because it is clear that they do take pleasure from touching their genitals and apparently enjoy the stimulation it produces. Later, preadolescents report experiencing sexual pleasure from kissing and touching themselves and others, and some even report going through the motions of sexual intercourse during middle childhood. But it is not until adolescence, and the onset of puberty, that sexuality becomes a central aspect of everyday life.

masturbation
sexual self-stimulation.

MASTURBATION.   The first type of sex in which adolescents engage is typically **masturbation**, sexual self-stimulation. By age 15, some 80 percent of teenage boys and 20 percent of teenage girls report that they have masturbated. The frequency of masturbation in males occurs more in the early teens and then begins to decline, while in females, the frequency is lower initially and increases throughout adolescence. In addition, patterns of masturbation frequency show differences according to race. For example, African American men and women masturbate less than whites (Oliver & Hyde, 1993; Schwartz, 1999; Hyde & DeLamater, 2003).

Although masturbation is widespread, it still may produce feelings of shame and guilt. There are several reasons for this. One is that adolescents may believe that masturbation signifies the inability to find a sexual partner—an erroneous assumption, since statistics show that three-quarters of married men and 68 percent of married women report masturbating between 10 and 24 times a year (Davidson, Darling, & Norton, 1995; Das, 2007; Gerressu et al., 2008).

For some, the sense of shame about masturbation is the result of a lingering legacy of misguided views of masturbation, in part based on religious prohibitions, cultural and social norms, and bad science. For instance, physician J. W. Kellogg believed in the 1800s that masturbation was detrimental to physical and emotional health. (One of his solutions: he invented corn flakes, thinking that certain grains would be less likely to provoke sexual excitation; Michael et al., 1994).

The reality of masturbation is different. Today, experts on sexual behavior view it as a normal, healthy, and harmless activity. Some suggest that it provides a useful way to learn about one's own sexuality (Hyde & DeLamater, 2007; Bowman, 2014).

SEXUAL INTERCOURSE. Although it may be preceded by many different types of sexual intimacy, including deep kissing, massaging, petting, and oral sex, sexual intercourse remains a major milestone in the perceptions of most adolescents. Consequently, the main focus of researchers investigating sexual behavior has been on the act of heterosexual intercourse.

From *a health-care provider's* perspective

A parent asks you how to prevent her 14-year-old son from engaging in sexual activity until he is older. What would you tell her?

The average age at which adolescents first have sexual intercourse has been steadily declining over the past 50 years, and about 13 percent of adolescents have had sex before age 15. Overall, the average age of first sexual intercourse is 17, and around 70 percent of adolescents have had sex before age 20 (see Figure 12-1). At the same time, though, many teenagers are postponing sex, and the number of adolescents who say they have never had sexual intercourse increased by 13 percent from 1991 to 2007 (MMWR, 2008; Guttmacher Institute, 2012).

It is impossible to consider sexual activities without also looking at the societal norms governing sexual conduct. The prevailing norm several decades ago was the **double standard** in which premarital sex was considered permissible for males but not for females. Women were told by society that "nice girls don't," while men heard that premarital sex was permissible—although they should be sure to marry virgins.

Today, however, the double standard largely has given way to a new norm, called **permissiveness with affection**. According to this standard, premarital intercourse is viewed as permissible for both men and women if it occurs in the context of a long-term, committed, or loving relationship (Hyde & Delamater, 2007).

The demise of the double standard is far from complete, however. Attitudes toward sexual conduct are still typically more lenient for males than for females, even in relatively socially liberal cultures. And in some cultures, the standards for men and women are quite distinct. For example, in North Africa, the Middle East, and the majority of Asian countries, most women conform to societal norms suggesting that they abstain from sexual intercourse until they are married. In Mexico, where there are strict standards against premarital sex, males are also considerably more likely than females to have premarital sex. In contrast, in sub-Saharan Africa, women are more likely to have sexual intercourse prior to marriage, and intercourse is common among unmarried teenage women (Johnson et al., 1992; Peltzer & Pengpid, 2006; Ghule, Balaiah, & Joshi, 2007).

double standard

the standard in which premarital sex is considered permissible for males but not for females.

permissiveness with affection

the standard in which premarital intercourse is viewed as permissible for both men and women if it occurs in the context of a long-term, committed, or loving relationship.

SEXUAL ORIENTATION: HETEROSEXUALITY, HOMOSEXUALITY, BISEXUALITY, AND TRANSGENDER INDIVIDUALS. When we consider adolescents' sexual development, the most frequent pattern is *heterosexuality*, sexual attraction and behavior directed to the other sex. Yet some teenagers are *homosexual*, in which their sexual attraction and behavior is oriented to members of their own sex. (Most male homosexuals prefer the term *gay* and female homosexuals the label *lesbian*, because they refer to a broader array of attitudes and lifestyle than the term *homosexual*, which focuses on the sexual act.) Other people find they are *bisexual*, sexually attracted to people of both sexes.

Many teens experiment with homosexuality. At one time or another, around 20 percent to 25 percent of adolescent boys and 10 percent of adolescent girls have at least one same-sex

Figure 12-1 Adolescents and Sexual Activity

The age at which adolescents have sexual intercourse for the first time is declining, and around three-quarters have had sex before age of 20.
(**Source:** Finer& Philbin, 2013.)

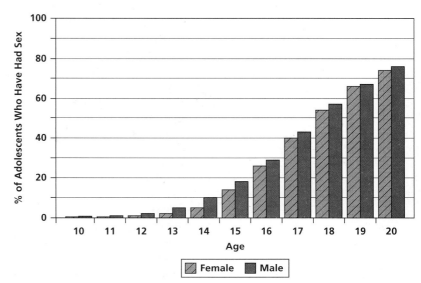

sexual encounter. In fact, homosexuality and heterosexuality are not completely distinct sexual orientations. Alfred Kinsey, a pioneer sex researcher, argued that sexual orientation should be viewed as a continuum in which "exclusively homosexual" is at one end and "exclusively heterosexual" at the other (Kinsey, Pomeroy, & Martin, 1948). In between are people who show both homosexual and heterosexual behavior. Although accurate figures are difficult to obtain, most experts believe that between 4 and 10 percent of both men and women are exclusively non-heterosexual during extended periods of their lives (Diamond, 2003a, 2003b; Russell & Consolacion, 2003; Pearson & Wilkinson, 2013).

The determination of sexual orientation is further complicated by distinctions between sexual orientation and gender identity. While sexual orientation relates to the object of one's sexual interests, as noted earlier, *gender identity* is the gender a person believes he or she is psychologically. Sexual orientation and gender identity are not necessarily related to one another: A man who has a strong masculine gender identity may be attracted to other men. Consequently, the extent to which men and women enact traditional "masculine" or "feminine" behavior is not necessarily related to their sexual orientation or gender identity. In fact, the range of gender labels now includes lesbian, gay, bisexual, transgender, cisgender, pansexual, asexual, queer, genderqueer, and others (Hunter & Mallon, 2000; Greydanus & Pratt, 2016).

For example, some individuals identify as transgender. *Transgender* individuals feel that the sex that were assigned at birth differs from their gender identity. Transgender individuals may seek sex-change operations in which their genitals are surgically removed and the genitals of the desired sex are created. It is a difficult path, one involving counseling, hormone injections, and living as a member of the desired sex for several years prior to surgery. Ultimately, though, the outcome can be very positive.

Transgender individuals are different from those who are called *intersex* or the older term *hermaphrodite*. An intersex person is born with an atypical combination of sexual organs or chromosomal or gene patterns. For instance, they may be born with both male and female sex organs or ambiguous organs. Only one in 4,500 births are intersex infants (Diamond, 2013).

WHAT DETERMINES SEXUAL ORIENTATION?　The factors that induce people to develop a particular sexual orientation are not well understood. Evidence suggests that genetic and biological factors may play an important role. For example, studies of twins show that identical twins are more likely to both be homosexual than pairs of siblings who don't share their genetic makeup. Other research finds that various structures of the brain are different in homosexuals and heterosexuals, and hormone production also seems to be linked to sexual orientation (Ellis et al., 2008; Fitzgerald, 2008; Santtila et al., 2008).

Other researchers have suggested that family or peer environmental factors play a role. For example, Freud argued that homosexuality was the result of inappropriate identification with the opposite-sex parent (Freud, 1922/1959). The difficulty with Freud's theoretical perspective and other, similar perspectives that followed is that there simply is no evidence to suggest that any particular family dynamic or child-rearing practice is consistently related to sexual orientation. Similarly, explanations based on learning theory, which suggest that homosexuality arises because of rewarding, pleasant homosexual experiences and unsatisfying heterosexual ones, do not appear to be the complete answer (Golombok & Tasker, 1996).

In short, there is no accepted explanation of why some adolescents develop a particular sexual orientation. Most experts believe that sexual orientation develops out of a complex interplay of genetic, physiological, and environmental factors (LeVay & Valente, 2003; Mustanski, Kuper, & Greene, 2014).

What is clear is that adolescents who find themselves attracted to members of the same sex may face a more difficult time than other teens. U.S. society still harbors great ignorance and prejudice regarding nontraditional sexual orientations, persisting in the belief that people have a choice in the matter—which they do not. Gay, lesbian, and transgender teens may be rejected by their family or peers, or even harassed and assaulted, if they are open about their orientation. The result is that adolescents who find themselves to have a nontraditional sexual orientation are at greater risk for depression, and suicide rates are significantly higher for homosexual adolescents than for heterosexual adolescents. Gays and lesbians who do not conform to gender stereotypes are particularly susceptible to victimization, and they have lower rates of adjustment (Toomey et al., 2010; Madsen & Green, 2012; Mitchell, Ybarra, & Korchmaros, 2014).

Most people ultimately come to grips with their sexual orientation and become comfortable with it. Although lesbian, gay, and bisexual individuals may experience mental health difficulties as a result of the stress, prejudice, and discrimination they face, homosexuality is not considered a psychological disorder by any major psychological or medical association. All of them endorse efforts to reduce discrimination against homosexuals. Furthermore, society's attitudes toward homosexuality are changing, particularly among younger individuals, and in 2015 the U.S. Supreme Court ruled that same-sex marriages are legal in all 50 states (Baker & Sussman, 2012; Patterson, 2013; Hu, Xu, & Tornello, 2016).

Disclosing Same-Sex Attraction to Parents.   As you might imagine, the decision to disclose to one's parents that one is attracted to persons of the same sex is not an easy one. For sexual minority adolescents, such disclosure is an important event in their sexual development. It's also an event that is fraught with anxiety; adolescents typically fear that their parents will react negatively to their coming out, possibly even by throwing them out of the house. Yet many sexual minority adolescents do tell at least one of their parents of their same-sex attraction, although the how, when, why, and to whom of disclosure vary from person to person (Rotheram-Borus & Langabeer, 2001; Hunter, 2007; Perrin-Wallqvist & Lindblom, 2015).

Research on the issue indicates that gender is an important factor in the disclosure of sexual orientation. Adolescents are more likely to disclose a same-sex attraction to their mothers than to their fathers, and if they disclose to both parents, they usually disclose to their mothers first. Most often this disclosure comes in a face-to-face meeting. Fathers, by contrast, are most likely to learn of their adolescent's same-sex attraction by accident or through someone else. Adolescents of both sexes disclose to their mothers because they share a closer relationship with them—in fact, in most cases, the mothers simply asked them whether they were gay. Their reasons for disclosing to their fathers differed, however; male adolescents most frequently did so to seek support, while female adolescents most often simply wanted to get it over with (Savin-Williams, 2003).

Adolescents' reasons for choosing *not* to come out to their parents differ for mothers versus fathers. Mothers are most often kept in the dark because adolescents perceive that the time is not yet right or because they fear damaging their relationship with their mother. Fathers, in contrast, are most frequently not told of their children's same-sex attractions because they are less important in their sons' or daughters' lives.

Are adolescents' fears of parental rejection well founded? Usually, no. Parental reactions typically are similar for male and female adolescents and for mothers and fathers, and both parents tend to be either supportive or slightly negative (a frequent reaction is to express disbelief). Moreover, in the overwhelming majority of cases, parent–child relations stay the same or even improve over time. In only about 5 percent of cases do adolescents report a decrease in relationship quality (Savin-Williams, 2003).

TEENAGE PREGNANCIES.   Feedings at 3 a.m., diaper changes, and visits to the pediatrician are not part of most people's vision of adolescence. Yet, every year, tens of thousands of adolescents in the United States give birth.

The good news, though, is that the number of teenage pregnancies has decreased significantly in the past two decades. In fact, in 2014, the birth rate for U.S. teenagers was the lowest level ever reported in the seven decades that the government has been tracking pregnancies (see Figure 12-2). Birth rates declined to historic lows in all racial and ethnic groups, but disparities remain, with non-Hispanic black and Hispanic teen birth rates more than two times greater than the rate for whites. In addition, American Indian/Alaska Native teen birth rates are more than 1.5 times higher than the white teen birth rate. Overall, the pregnancy rate of teenagers is 24.2 births per 1,000 (Hamilton & Ventura, 2012; CDC, 2016).

Figure 12-2 Teenage Pregnancy Rates

The rate of teenage pregnancy in the United States had declined significantly among all ethnic groups.
(**Source:** Hamilton et al., 2015.)

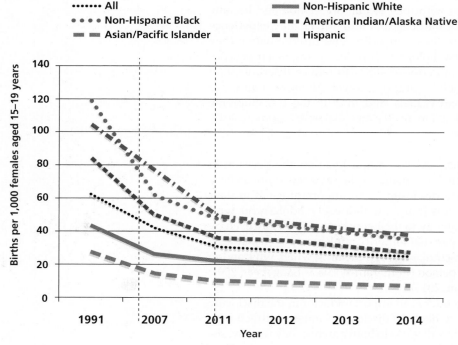

Several factors explain the drop in teenage pregnancies:

- New initiatives have raised awareness among teenagers of the risks of unprotected sex. For example, about two-thirds of high schools in the United States have established comprehensive sex education programs (Villarosa, 2003; Corcoran & Pillai, 2007).

- The rate of sexual intercourse among teenagers has declined. The percentage of teenage girls who have ever had sexual intercourse dropped from 51 percent in 1988 to 43 percent in 2006–2010 (Martinez, Copen, & Abma, 2011).

- The use of condoms and other forms of contraception has increased. For example, virtually all sexually experienced girls ages 15–19 have used some method of contraception (Martinez, Copen, & Abma, 2011).

- Substitutes for sexual intercourse may be more prevalent. For example, oral sex, which many teenagers do not even consider "sex," may increasingly be viewed as an alternative to sexual intercourse (Bernstein, 2004; Chandra et al., 2011).

One thing that apparently hasn't led to a reduction in teenage pregnancies is asking adolescents to take a virginity pledge. Public pledges to refrain from premarital sex—a centerpiece of some forms of sex education—apparently are ineffective. For example, in one study of 12,000 teenagers, 88 percent reported eventually having sexual intercourse. However, pledges did delay the start of sex an average of 18 months (Bearman & Bruckner, 2004). (Also see the *Development in Your Life* box.)

Even with the decline in the birthrate for U.S. teenagers, the rate of teenage pregnancy in the United States is two to 10 times higher compared to that of other industrialized countries. The results of an unintended pregnancy can be devastating to both mother and child. In comparison to earlier times, teenage mothers today are much less likely to be married. In a high percentage of cases, mothers care for their children without the help of the father. Without financial or emotional support, a mother may have to abandon her own education, and consequently she may be relegated to unskilled, poorly paying jobs for the rest of her life. In other cases, she may develop long-term dependency on welfare. An adolescent mother's physical and mental health may suffer as she faces unrelenting stress due to continual demands on her time (Manlove et al., 2004; Gillmore et al., 2006; Oxford et al., 2006).

Development in Your Life

Preventing Unwanted Pregnancy

If you're concerned about the possibility of an unwanted pregnancy and its harmful consequences, your first line of defense is to educate yourself on prevention methods. A number of birth control options are available that are appropriate for adolescents, each with its own advantages and disadvantages. A physician can help choose the method

that is best for each individual. Following are some effective recommendations (Food and Drug Administration, 2003; Knowles, 2005).

- **Abstinence.** Abstaining from sex is the only birth control method that is guaranteed to be 100 percent effective.

Abstinence requires no special equipment or medical supervision, costs nothing, and prevents sexually transmitted disease as well as unwanted pregnancy. The downside of abstinence is that people may find it difficult to refrain from sex, and if they have not explored alternative methods of birth control, they may not be prepared to protect themselves from unwanted pregnancy when they do become sexually active.

■ **Outercourse.** *Outercourse* is sexual activity that does not involve vaginal intercourse. It may include kissing, masturbation, massage, or oral sex. Outercourse is 100 percent effective against pregnancy as long as no semen comes in contact with the vaginal area.

■ **Condoms.** A condom, a sheath that covers the penis during intercourse, provides a barrier against the transmission of semen. Condoms are 85 to 98 percent effective against pregnancy, depending in part on how they are used (the addition of a spermicidal lubricant enhances their effectiveness). Condoms also provide protection against sexually transmitted diseases, and they are widely available and generally inexpensive. Relying on condoms to prevent unwanted pregnancy means that a condom must be used every time sexual intercourse occurs.

■ **Birth control pills.** Birth control pills contain hormones that prevent pregnancy by interfering with egg fertilization. They are 92 to 99 percent effective against pregnancy, but they must be prescribed by a physician. Birth control pills have the advantage of providing continuous protection against unwanted pregnancy—you don't have to remember to do anything special at the time of intercourse. Their main disadvantage is that they must be taken daily, whether or not one is having sex. Birth control pills do not provide protection against sexually transmitted diseases.

■ **Prescription barriers.** A prescription barrier, such as a diaphragm, is treated with spermicide and then inserted into the vagina before intercourse, where it blocks the transmission of semen. Prescription barriers are an alternative to daily hormone use for women who have intercourse only occasionally. They are available through a physician, and they are 84 to 94 percent effective against pregnancy. However, barriers can be difficult to use correctly, and like condoms, must be used every time one has intercourse. Barriers also do not provide protection against the spread of sexually transmitted diseases.

The Ongoing Sexuality of Adulthood

LO 12.6   Explain the role of sexuality during adulthood.

Despite a youth-oriented media, in which most portrayals of romance occur between young, fit, unwrinkled men and women, interest in sexual activity does not belong exclusively to the under-25 crowd. Indeed, it extends throughout the life span.

For example, sexuality remains an important part of life for most middle-aged people. Although the frequency of sexual intercourse declines with age (see Figure 12-3), sexual pleasure remains a vital part of most middle-aged adults' lives. About half of men and women age 45 to 59 report having sexual intercourse about once a week or more. Close to three-quarters of men and more than half of women age 50 to 59 report masturbating. Half of men age 50 to 59 and a third of women in that age group have received oral sex from a different-sex partner in the past year. Similarly, sex remains an important activity for gay and lesbian couples during middle adulthood (Duplassie & Daniluk, 2007; Herbenick et al., 2010; Koh & Sewell, 2015).

For many, middle adulthood brings a kind of sexual enjoyment and freedom that was missing during their earlier lives. With their children grown and away from home, middle-aged married couples have more time to engage in uninterrupted sexual activities. Women who have passed through menopause are liberated from the fear of pregnancy and no longer need to employ birth control techniques (Norman, 2008; DeLamater, 2012).

SEXUALITY IN OLD AGE: USE IT OR LOSE IT.   Do your grandparents have sex?

Quite possibly, yes. Although the answer may surprise you, increasing evidence suggests that people are sexually active well into their 80s and 90s. This happens in spite of societal stereotypes suggesting that it is somehow improper for two 75-year-olds to have sexual intercourse, and even worse for a 75-year-old to masturbate. Such negative attitudes are

Figure 12-3 Reported frequency of sexual intercourse.

As people age, the frequency of sexual intercourse declines.

(**Source:** Karraker, DeLamater, & Schwartz, 2011).

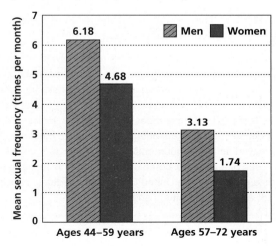

Figure 12-4 Attractiveness over Time

More than 50 percent of Americans over age 45 find their partners attractive, and as time goes on, more attractive.

(**Source:** AARP/Modern Maturity Sexuality Study, 1999.)

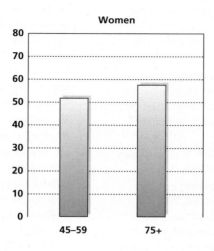

a function of societal expectations in the United States. In many other cultures, elderly people are expected to remain sexually active, and in some societies, people are expected to become less inhibited as they age (Hillman, 2000; Lindau et al., 2007; De Conto, 2017).

Two major factors determine whether an elderly person will engage in sexual activity (Papaharitou et al., 2008). One is good physical and mental health. People need to be physically healthy and to hold generally positive attitudes about sexual activity in order for sex to take place. The other determinant of sexual activity during old age is previous regular sexual activity. The longer elderly men and women have gone without sexual activity, the less likely is future sexual activity. "Use it or lose it" seems an accurate description of sexual functioning in older people. Sexual activity can and often does continue throughout the life span. Furthermore, there's some intriguing evidence that having sex may have some unexpected side benefits: One study found that having sex regularly is associated with a lower risk of death (Henry & McNab, 2003; Hillman, 2012; McCarthy & Pierpaoli, 2015)!

Masturbation is the most common sexual practice in late adulthood. One survey found that 43 percent of men and 33 percent of women over age 70 masturbated. The average frequency for those who masturbated was once per week. Around two-thirds of married men and women had sex with their spouses, again averaging around once per week. In addition, the percentage of people who view their sexual partners as physically attractive actually increases with age (see Figure 12-4; Herbenick et al., 2010).

Module 12.2 Review

LO 12.4 Explore the psychological implications of sexual maturation during adolescence.

Early or late maturation can bring advantages and disadvantages, depending on gender as well as emotional and psychological maturity.

LO 12.5 Describe how adolescents experience and explore their sexuality.

Masturbation, once viewed very negatively, is now generally regarded as a normal and harmless practice that continues into adulthood. Sexual intercourse is a major milestone that most people reach during adolescence. The age of first intercourse reflects cultural differences and has been declining over the past 50 years. Sexual orientation, which is most accurately viewed as a continuum rather than a category, develops as the result of a complex combination of factors. Teenage pregnancy is a problem in the United States, with negative consequences for adolescent mothers and their children.

LO 12.6 Explain the role of sexuality during adulthood.

Sexuality in middle adulthood changes slightly, but middle-aged couples, freed from concerns about children, can often progress to a new level of intimacy and enjoyment. Being in good physical and mental health and having a history of regular sexual activity are the key determinants of sexual activity during old age. In healthy adults sexuality can continue throughout the life span.

Journal Writing Prompt

Applying Lifespan Development: Do you think the double standard, which approved male sexual activity but condemned female sexual activity, has entirely disappeared? Does popular culture work to eliminate or perpetuate the double standard?

MODULE 12.3

RELATIONSHIPS

It took him almost a month, but Sylvester Chiu finally got up the courage to ask Jackie Durbin to go to the movies. It was hardly a surprise to Jackie, though. Sylvester had first told his friend Erik about his resolve to ask Jackie out, and Erik had told Jackie's friend Cynthia about Sylvester's plans. Cynthia, in turn, had told Jackie, who was primed to say "yes" when Sylvester finally did call.

Welcome to the complex world of dating, an important and changing ritual of adolescence.

Getting to Know You: Dating and Falling in Love in the 21st Century

LO 12.7   Describe the functions and patterns of dating in adolescence.

When and how adolescents begin to date is determined by cultural factors that change from one generation to another. Until fairly recently, exclusively dating a single individual was seen as something of a cultural ideal, viewed in the context of romance. In fact, society often encouraged dating in adolescence, in part as a way for adolescents to explore relationships that might eventually lead to marriage. Today, some adolescents believe that the concept of dating is outmoded and limiting, and in some places the practice of "hooking up"—a vague term that covers everything from kissing to sexual intercourse—is viewed as more appropriate. Still, despite changing cultural norms, dating remains the dominant form of social interaction that leads to intimacy among adolescents (Denizet-Lewis, 2004; Bogle, 2008; Rice, McGill, & Adler-Baeder, 2017).

Dating is also being changed through the use of social media. For example, although only 8 percent of teenagers have met a romantic partner online, expressing interest in a partner and flirting are common. Half of all teens ages 13 to 17 have let someone know they are interested in them by friending them on Facebook or another social media site, and 47 percent have expressed their attraction by liking or otherwise interacting with them on social media. Around a third have sent them flirtatious messages online. And in some cases, as we discuss in the *From Research to Practice* box, these messages become quite explicit (Lenhart, Smith, & Anderson, 2015).

From Research to Practice

When Texting Turns Explicit: Sexting

One day last winter Margarite posed naked before her bathroom mirror, held up her cell phone, and took a picture. Then she sent the full-length frontal photo to Isaiah, her new boyfriend. Both were in eighth grade. (Hoffman, 2011, p. A1).

For an increasing number of adolescents, *sexting* (the sending of texts that contain explicit, sexually provocative photos or text) is commonplace. It is easy to do and can be used in an effort to demonstrate one's affection or loyalty to a partner in an established relationship. Sexting also may be used

instead of having actual sex, or as a prelude to sex. In some cases, sexting is used to indicate interest in starting a relationship (Strassberg, Cann, & Velarde, 2017; Van Oosten & Vandenbosch, 2017).

Sexting has become commonplace: According to the results of one poll, 24 percent of 14- to 17-year-olds were involved in some form of naked sexting, either using cell phones or the Web. Another survey found that 4 percent of adolescents in the same age range admitted to sending naked photos or video by cell phone, and 15 percent had received them (Quaid, 2011; Lippman & Campbell, 2014; Vanden Abeele et al., 2014).

Sexting is also related to risky sexual behavior: Males who sext are four times more likely, and females twice as likely, to have had multiple sexual relationships at the same time compared to those who don't engage in sexting. In addition, males who sext are 40 percent less likely to regularly use condoms compared to those who don't sext. Moreover, compared with those who don't report sexting, teenagers who sext are considerably more likely to have low self-esteem (Ybarra & Mitchell, 2014).

The consequences of sexting can be devastating. It is not uncommon for texts to be forwarded, and there are numerous incidents in which recipients of explicit photos have sent the images to friends. Ultimately, a photo may be forwarded to hundreds of others. There is also a double standard at play: When boys are caught sending photos of themselves, they are typically viewed more positively than girls, who may be labeled as slutty (Hoffman, 2011; Lippman & Campbell, 2014; Van Oosten & Vandenbosch, 2017).

Sexting not only may produce considerable psychological harm to the person who is depicted in sexually explicit photos, but there can be legal consequences. If the image involves anyone under the age of 18 (including the subject depicted, the photographer, someone who forwards the text, or even the recipient), child pornography laws come into play. An increasing number of prosecutions have occurred as a result of sexting (Strohmaier, Murphy, & DeMatteo, 2014; Lorang, McNiel, & Binder, 2016).

Shared Writing Prompt

Why do you think there is a double standard for sexting, where boys who do it are viewed more favorably than girls?

Is it reasonable for prosecutors to use child pornography laws to deal with the problem of sexting?

THE FUNCTIONS OF DATING. Although on the surface, dating is part of a pattern of courtship that can potentially lead to marriage, it actually serves other functions as well, especially early on. Dating is a way to learn how to establish intimacy with another individual. It can provide entertainment and, depending on the status of the person one is dating, prestige. It even can be used to develop a sense of one's own identity (Friedlander et al., 2007; Paludi, 2012; Kreager et al., 2016).

Just how well dating serves such functions, particularly the development of psychological intimacy, is an open question. What specialists in adolescence do know, however, is surprising: Dating in early and middle adolescence is not terribly successful at facilitating intimacy. On the contrary, dating is often a superficial activity in which the participants so rarely let down their guards that they never become truly close and never expose themselves emotionally to each other. Psychological intimacy may be lacking even when sexual activity is part of the relationship (Collins, 2003; Furman & Shaffer, 2003).

True intimacy becomes more common during later adolescence. At that point, the dating relationship may be taken more seriously by both participants, and it may be seen as a way to select a mate and as a potential prelude to marriage.

For homosexual adolescents, dating presents special challenges. In some cases, blatant homophobic prejudice expressed by classmates may lead gays and lesbians to date members of the other sex in efforts to fit in. If they do seek relationships with other gays and lesbians, they may find it difficult to find partners who openly express their sexual orientation. Homosexual couples who do openly date face possible harassment, making the development of a relationship all the more difficult (Savin-Williams, 2003).

DATING, RACE, AND ETHNICITY. Culture influences dating patterns among adolescents of different racial and ethnic groups, particularly those whose parents have immigrated to the United States from other countries. Parents may try to control their children's dating behavior in an effort to preserve their culture's traditional values or ensure that their child dates within his or her racial or ethnic group.

For example, some immigrant parents may be especially conservative in their attitudes and values, in part because they themselves may have had no experience of dating and also because of religious considerations, such as in observant Muslim and Orthodox Jewish households. (In many cases, the parents' marriage was arranged by others, and the entire concept of dating is unfamiliar.) They may insist that dating be conducted with chaperones or not at all. As a consequence, they may find themselves involved in substantial conflict with their children (Hoelterk, Axinn, & Ghimire, 2004; Lau et al., 2009; Shenhav, Campos, & Goldbert, 2017).

Forging Relationships: Intimacy, Liking, and Loving During Early Adulthood

LO 12.8   Analyze the nature of intimacy and relationships in early adulthood.

> *Dianne Maher swept Thad Ramon off his feet—literally. "I was setting up the cafeteria for a dance, and she was sweeping the floor. Next thing I knew a push broom was under my heels and down I went. I didn't hurt myself or anything, and my pride wasn't injured, but you could say my heart took a beating. There she was, sly grin on her face, and all I could do was stare and laugh. We started talking and laughing some more, and soon we discovered we had a lot more than silliness in common. We've been together ever since."*

Thad followed his heart and in senior year publicly proposed to Dianne in that same cafeteria during lunch hour. They plan to get married beside the college duck pond and at the end of the ceremony march beneath crossed push brooms held by their ushers and bridesmaids.

Not everyone falls in love quite as easily as Dianne and Thad. For some, the road to love is tortuous, meandering through soured relationships and fallen dreams; for others, it is a road never taken. For some, love leads to marriage and a life befitting society's storybook view of home, children, and long years together as a couple. For many, it leads to a less happy ending, prematurely concluding in divorce and custody battles.

Erik Erikson regarded young adulthood as the **intimacy-versus-isolation stage**, a period focused on developing close, intimate relationships with others. Young adults' happiness stems, in part, from their relationships, and many worry about whether they are developing serious relationships "on time." Even those who are not interested in forming a long-term relationship typically are focused, to some extent, on connecting with others.

Erikson's work inspired other developmentalists to consider psychosocial growth during young adulthood and the range of intimate relationships we develop, from friendship to mates for life (Whitbourne, Sneed, & Sayer, 2009). For example, some developmentalists believe there is a unique developmental stage that begins at the end of the teenage years and extends through the early 20s, as we discuss in the *From Research to Practice* box.

intimacy-versus-isolation stage

according to Erikson, the period of postadolescence into the early 30s that focuses on developing close relationships with others.

FALLING IN LOVE: WHEN LIKING TURNS TO LOVING.   Whether one falls in love swiftly, as Dianne and Thad did, or more slowly, most relationships develop in a fairly similar way, following a surprisingly regular progression (Berscheid & Regan, 2005):

- Two people interact with each other more often and for longer periods of time. Furthermore, the range of settings increases.
- The two people increasingly seek out each other's company.
- They open up to each other more and more, disclosing more intimate information about themselves. They begin to share physical intimacies.
- The couple is more willing to share both positive and negative feelings, and they may offer criticism in addition to praise.
- They begin to agree on the goals they hold for the relationship.
- Their reactions to situations become more similar.
- They begin to feel that their own psychological well-being is tied to the success of the relationship, viewing it as unique, irreplaceable, and cherished.
- Finally, their definition of themselves and their behavior changes: They begin to see themselves and act as a couple rather than as two separate individuals.

From Research to Practice

Emerging Adulthood: Not Quite There Yet!

Do you feel as though you're not really an "adult," despite having reached an age where you are legally an adult? Are you still unsure of who you are and what you want to do with your life, and feeling unready to go out in the world on your own? If so, what you're experiencing is a developmental period known as emerging adulthood—a transitional stage between adolescence and adulthood that spans the third decade of life. Researchers are increasingly considering emerging adulthood to be a distinct developmental period during which the brain is still growing and modifying its neural pathways. It's typically a time of uncertainty and self-discovery during which the emerging adult is still figuring out the world and his or her place in it (Arnett, 2014a).

Emerging adulthood is marked by five features. *Identity exploration* entails learning to make important decisions about love, work, and one's core beliefs and values. In one comprehensive survey of over 1,000 diverse emerging adults ages 18 to 29 throughout the United States, 77 percent agreed with the statement "This is a time of life for finding out who I really am." Another feature of emerging adulthood is *instability*, which can be represented as changes in life plans or goals, fluctuating career and educational paths, rocky relationships, and even shifts in ideologies. In the survey, 83 percent of respondents agreed that "This time of my life is full of changes" (Arnett, 2014b).

A third feature of emerging adulthood is *self-focus*: It's a time of life that comes between parental control and the obligations of child-raising and career. With fewer people to answer to, emerging adults enjoy the luxury of focusing on themselves for a while before making any serious commitments. "This is a time of my life for focusing on myself" was a statement with which 71 percent of respondents to the survey agreed. Given all this, it's probably not surprising that a fourth feature of emerging adulthood is *feeling in-between*, a sense of being no longer an adolescent but not yet really an adult either. For some

emerging adults the feeling is enhanced by remaining dependent in some ways on their parents, and for others it's more a sense of uncertainty and hesitation in accepting full adulthood just yet. Half of the respondents to the survey were unwilling to agree completely that they had reached adulthood (Arnett, 2014b).

Finally, despite the stress and anxiety that are associated with the uncertainties of emerging adulthood, it is also a time of *optimism*. Nearly 90 percent of survey respondents agreed that "I am confident that someday I will get what I want out of life" and 83 percent agreed "At this time of my life, anything is possible." Part of the reason for this optimism is the tendency for young adults today to be better educated than their parents were, such that their optimism has a basis in reality. And happily, by the time they are 30, most emerging adults have found their way and have settled more comfortably into their adult roles (Arnett, 2014b, 2015; Ozmen, Brelsford, & Danieu, 2017).

The existence of the period of emerging adulthood is driven by the nature of economic changes in industrialized countries in the past several decades. As these economies have shifted toward technology and information, an increasing time has to be spent becoming educated. Furthermore, the age of marriage has risen, as has the timing of the birth of children (Arnett, 2016).

Furthermore, both men and women have increasing ambivalence about becoming adults. Surveys show that people in their late teens and early 20s respond with "yes and no" most frequently when asked if they have reached adulthood (Arnett, 2006; Verschueren et al., 2017).

Shared Writing Prompt

Do you think emerging adulthood is truly a universal life stage, or do you think it is a luxury enjoyed only by young adults who are more privileged? Why or why not?

PASSIONATE AND COMPANIONATE LOVE: THE TWO FACES OF LOVE. Is "love" just a lot of "liking"? Most developmental psychologists would answer negatively; love not only differs quantitatively from liking, it represents a qualitatively different state. For example, love, at least in its early stages, involves relatively intense physiological arousal, an all-encompassing interest in another individual, recurrent fantasies about the other individual, and rapid swings of emotion. As distinct from liking, love includes elements of closeness, passion, and exclusivity (Walster & Walster, 1978; Hendrick & Hendrick, 2003).

Not all love is the same. We don't love our mothers the same way we love girlfriends or boyfriends, brothers or sisters, or lifelong friends. What distinguishes these different types of love? Some psychologists suggest that our love relationships can fall into two different categories: passionate or companionate.

Passionate (or romantic) love is a state of powerful absorption in someone. It includes intense physiological interest and arousal, and caring for another's needs. In comparison, **companionate love** is the strong affection that we have for those with whom our lives are deeply involved (Hendrick & Hendrick, 2003; Barsade & O'Neill, 2014).

What is it that fuels the fires of passionate love? According to one theory, anything that produces strong emotions—even negative ones such as jealousy, anger, or fear of rejection—may be the source of deepening passionate love.

In psychologists Elaine Hatfield and Ellen Berscheid's **labeling theory of passionate love**, individuals experience romantic love when two events occur together: intense physiological arousal and situational cues indicating that "love" is the appropriate label for the feelings they are experiencing (Berscheid, 2006). The physiological arousal can be produced by sexual arousal, excitement, or even negative emotions such as jealousy. Whatever the cause, if that arousal is subsequently labeled as "I must be falling in love" or "she makes my heart flutter" or "he really turns me on," then the experience is attributed to passionate love.

The theory is particularly useful in explaining why people may feel deepened love even when they experience continual rejection or hurt from their assumed lover. It suggests that such negative emotions can produce strong physiological arousal. If this arousal is interpreted as being caused by "love," then people may decide that they are even more in love than they were before they experienced the negative emotions.

But why should people label an emotional experience as "love" when there are so many possible alternatives? One answer is that in Western cultures, romantic love is seen as possible, acceptable, desirable—an experience to be sought. The virtues of passion are extolled in love ballads, commercials, television shows, and films. Consequently, young adults are primed and ready to experience love in their lives (Florsheim, 2003; Hatfield, Mo, & Rapson, 2015).

It is interesting to note that this is not the way it is in every culture. For instance, in many cultures, passionate, romantic love is a foreign concept. Marriages may be arranged on the basis of economic and status considerations. Even in Western cultures, the concept of love is of relatively recent origin. For instance, the notion that couples need to be in love was not "invented" until the Middle Ages, when social philosophers first suggested that love ought to be a requirement for marriage. Their goal in making such a proposal: to provide an alternative to the raw sexual desire that had served as the primary basis for marriage before (Lewis, 1958; Haslett, 2004; Moore & Wei, 2012).

STERNBERG'S TRIANGULAR THEORY: THE THREE FACES OF LOVE. To psychologist Robert Sternberg, love is more complex than a simple division into passionate and companionate types. He suggests instead that love is made up of three components: intimacy, passion, and decision/commitment. The **intimacy component** encompasses feelings of closeness, affection, and connectedness. The **passion component** is exemplified by intense, physiologically arousing feelings of attraction. Finally, the third aspect of love, the **decision/commitment component**, embodies both the initial cognition that one loves another person and the longer-term determination to maintain that love (Sternberg, 2006).

These components can be combined to form eight different types of love depending on which of the three components is either present or missing from a relationship (see Table 12-2). For instance, *nonlove* refers to people who have only the most casual of relationships; it consists of the absence of the three components of intimacy, passion, and decision/commitment. *Liking* develops when only intimacy is present; *infatuated love* exists when only passion is felt; and *empty love* exists when only decision/commitment is present.

Other types of love involve a mix of two or more components. For instance, romantic love occurs when intimacy and passion are present, and *companionate love* when intimacy and decision/commitment occur jointly. When two people experience romantic love, they are drawn together physically and emotionally, but they do not necessarily view the relationship as lasting. Companionate love, however, may occur in long-lasting relationships in which physical passion has taken a back seat.

Fatuous love exists when passion and decision/commitment, without intimacy, are present. Fatuous love is a kind of mindless loving in which there is no emotional bond between the partners.

passionate (or romantic) love
a state of powerful absorption in someone.

companionate love
the strong affection for those with whom our lives are deeply involved.

labeling theory of passionate love
the theory that individuals experience romantic love when two events occur together: intense physiological arousal and situational cues suggesting that the arousal is due to love.

intimacy component
the component of love that encompasses feelings of closeness, affection, and connectedness.

passion component
the component of love that comprises the motivational drives relating to sex, physical closeness, and romance.

decision/commitment component
the third aspect of love, which embodies both the initial cognition that one loves another person and the longer-term determination to maintain that love.

Table 12-2 The Combinations of Love

			Component	
Type of Love	Intimacy	Passion	Decision/ Commitment	Example
Nonlove	Absent	Absent	Absent	The way you might feel about the person who takes your ticket at the movies
Liking	Present	Absent	Absent	Good friends who have lunch together at least once or twice a week
Infatuated love	Absent	Present	Absent	A "fling" or short-term relationship based only on sexual attraction
Empty love	Absent	Absent	Present	An arranged marriage or a couple who have decided to stay married "for the sake of the children"
Romantic love	Present	Present	Absent	A couple who have been happily dating a few months but have not made any plans for a future together
Companionate love	Present	Absent	Present	A couple who enjoy each other's company and their relationship, although they no longer feel much sexual interest in each other
Fatuous love	Absent	Present	Present	A couple who decides to move in together after knowing each other for only two weeks
Consummate love	Present	Present	Present	A loving, sexually vibrant, long-term relationship

Finally, the eighth kind of love is *consummate love*. In consummate love, all three components of love are present. Although we might assume that consummate love represents the "ideal" love, such a view may well be mistaken. Many long-lasting and entirely satisfactory relationships are based on types of love other than consummate love. Furthermore, the type of love that predominates in a relationship varies over time. As shown in Figure 12-5, in strong, loving relationships the level of decision/ commitment peaks and remains fairly stable. By contrast, passion tends to peak early in a relationship but then declines and levels off. Intimacy also increases fairly rapidly but can continue to grow over time.

Sternberg's triangular theory of love emphasizes both the complexity of love and its dynamic, evolving quality. As people and relationships develop and change over time, so does their love.

Choosing a Partner: Recognizing Mr. or Ms. Right

LO 12.9 **Explain the process by which people choose their partners.**

For many young adults, the search for a partner is a major pursuit during early adulthood. Certainly, society offers a great deal of advice on how to succeed in this endeavor, as a glance at the array of magazines at any supermarket checkout counter

Figure 12-5 The Shape of Love

Over the course of a relationship, the three aspects of love—intimacy, passion, and decision/commitment—vary in strength. How do these change as a relationship develops?
(**Source:** Sternberg, 1986.)

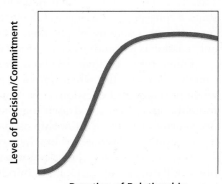

confirms. Despite all the counsel, however, the road to identifying an individual to share one's life is not always easy.

SEEKING A SPOUSE: IS LOVE THE ONLY THING THAT MATTERS?   Most people have no hesitation in stating that the major factor in choosing a husband or wife is love—most people in the United States, that is. If we ask people in other societies, love becomes a secondary consideration. For instance, consider the results of a survey in which college students were asked if they would marry someone they did not love. Hardly anyone in the United States, Japan, or Brazil would consider it. In contrast, a goodly proportion of college students in Pakistan and India would find it acceptable to marry without love (Levine, 1993; Madathil & Benshoff, 2008).

If love is not the only important factor, what else matters? The characteristics differ considerably from one culture to another. For instance, a survey of nearly 10,000 people from around the world found that although people in the United States believed that love and mutual attraction were the primary characteristics, in China men ranked good health most important, and women rated emotional stability and maturity most critical. In contrast, in South Africa men from a Zulu background rated emotional stability first, and Zulu women rated dependable character of greatest concern (Buss et al., 1990; Buss, 2003a).

At the same time, there are commonalities across cultures. For instance, love and mutual attraction, even if not at the top of a specific culture's list, were relatively highly desired across all cultures. Furthermore, traits such as dependability, emotional stability, pleasing disposition, and intelligence were highly valued almost universally.

Certain gender differences in the preferred characteristics of a mate were similar across cultures—findings that have been confirmed by other surveys (e.g., Sprecher, Sullivan, & Hatfield, 1994; Buss, 2004; Schmitt, 2004). Men, more than women, prefer a potential marriage partner who is physically attractive. In contrast, women, more than men, prefer a potential spouse who is ambitious and industrious.

One explanation for cross-cultural similarities in gender differences rests on evolutionary factors. According to psychologist David Buss and colleagues (Buss, 2004), human beings, as a species, seek out certain characteristics in their mates that are likely to maximize the availability of beneficial genes. He argues that males in

Developmental Diversity and Your Life

Gay and Lesbian Relationships

Most research conducted by developmental psychologists has examined heterosexual relationships, but an increasing number of studies have looked at relationships involving gay men and those involving lesbian women. The findings suggest that gay relationships are quite similar to relationships between heterosexuals.

For example, gay men describe successful relationships in ways that are similar to heterosexual couples' descriptions. They believe that successful relationships involve greater appreciation for the partner and the couple as a whole, less conflict, and more positive feelings toward the partner. Similarly, lesbian women in a relationship show high levels of attachment, caring, intimacy, affection, and respect (Beals, Impett, & Peplau, 2002; Kurdek, 2006).

Furthermore, the age preferences expressed in the marriage gradient for heterosexuals also extend to partner preferences for homosexual men. Like heterosexual men,

homosexual men prefer partners who are the same age or younger; lesbians' age preferences fall somewhere between those of heterosexual women and heterosexual men (Ni Bhrolcháin, 2006; Tadinac & Hromatko, 2007).

Finally, despite the stereotype that gay men, in particular, find it difficult to form relationships and are interested in only sexual alliances, the reality is different. Most gays and lesbians seek loving, long-term, and meaningful relationships that differ little qualitatively from those desired by heterosexuals. Furthermore, although there is less scientific data regarding gay and lesbian marriage, which was legalized across the United States by the Supreme Court in 2015, it is clear that children of gay and lesbian parents share the same degree of adjustment as children of heterosexual couples (Diamond & Savin-Williams, 2003; Kurdek, 2008; Barelds et al., 2017).

particular are genetically programmed to seek out mates with traits that indicate they have high reproductive capacity. Consequently, physically attractive, younger women might be more desirable since they are more capable of having children over a longer time period.

In contrast, women are genetically programmed to seek out men who have the potential to provide scarce resources in order to increase the likelihood that their off-spring will survive. Consequently, they are attracted to mates who offer the highest potential of providing economic well-being (Li et al., 2002; Brumbaugh & Wood, 2013).

The evolutionary explanation for gender differences has come under heavy fire from critics. First, there is the problem that the explanation is untestable. Furthermore, the similarities across cultures relating to different gender preferences may simply reflect similar patterns of gender stereotyping that have nothing to do with evolution. In addition, although some of the gender differences in what men and women prefer are consistent across cultures, there are numerous inconsistencies as well.

Finally, some critics of the evolutionary approach suggest that women prefer a partner who has good earning potential may have nothing to do with evolution and everything to do with the fact that men generally hold more power, status, and other resources fairly consistently across different cultures. Consequently, it is a rational choice for women to prefer a high-earning-potential spouse. In contrast, because men don't need to take economic considerations into account, they can use more inconsequential criteria—like physical attractiveness—in choosing a spouse. In short, the consistencies that are found across cultures may be due to the realities of economic life that are similar throughout different cultures (Eagly & Wood, 2003).

FILTERING MODELS: SIFTING OUT A SPOUSE.   While surveys assist in identifying the characteristics that are highly valued in a potential spouse, they are less helpful in determining how a specific individual is chosen as a partner. One approach that helps explain this is the filtering model developed by psychologists Louis Janda and Karen Klenke-Hamel (1980). They suggest that people seeking a mate screen potential candidates through successively finer-grained filters, just as we sift flour in order to remove undesirable material (see Figure 12-6).

The model assumes that people first filter for factors relating to broad determinants of attractiveness. Once these early screens have done their work, more sophisticated types of screening are used. The end result is a choice based on compatibility between the two individuals.

What determines compatibility? It is not only a matter of pleasing personality characteristics; several cultural factors also play an important role. For instance, people often marry according to the principle of homogamy. **Homogamy** is the tendency to marry someone who is similar in age, race, education, religion, and other basic demographic characteristics. Homogamy has traditionally been the dominant standard for most marriages in the United States.

The importance of homogamy is declining, however, particularly among certain ethnic and racial groups. For example, the rate of intermarriage among African American men increased by three-quarters in the 1990s and stood at 24 percent in 2010. Furthermore, 26 percent of Hispanics and 28 percent of Asians marry outside their own racial and ethnic group (also see Figure 12-7; Fu & Heaton, 2008; Taylor, et al., 2012; Mu & Xie, 2014).

The marriage gradient represents another societal standard that determines who marries whom. The **marriage gradient** is the tendency for men to marry women who are slightly younger, smaller, and lower in status, and women to marry men who are slightly older, larger, and higher in status (Bernard, 1982; Geary, 2006).

The marriage gradient, which has a powerful influence on marriage in the United States, has important, and

homogamy

the tendency to marry someone who is similar in age, race, education, religion, and other basic demographic characteristics.

marriage gradient

the tendency for men to marry women who are slightly younger, smaller, and lower in status, and women to marry men who are slightly older, larger, and higher in status.

Figure 12-6 Filtering Potential Marriage Partners

According to one approach, we screen potential mates through successively finer-grained filters in order to settle on an appropriate spouse.

(**Source:** Based on Janda & Klenke-Hamel, 1980.)

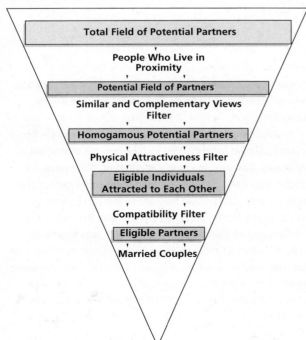

Total Field of Potential Partners

People Who Live in Proximity

Potential Field of Partners

Similar and Complementary Views Filter

Homogamous Potential Partners

Physical Attractiveness Filter

Eligible Individuals Attracted to Each Other

Compatibility Filter

Eligible Partners

Married Couples

unfortunate, effects on partner choice. For one thing, it limits the number of potential mates for women, especially as they age, while allowing men a wider choice of partners as their age increases. Furthermore, some men do not marry because they cannot find women of low enough status to meet the demands of the gradient or cannot find women of the same or higher status who are willing to accept them as mates. Consequently, they are, in the words of sociologist Jessie Bernard (1982), "bottom of the barrel" men. By the same token, some women will be unable to marry because they are higher in status or seek someone of higher status than anyone in the available pool of men—"cream of the crop" women, in Bernard's words.

The marriage gradient makes finding a spouse particularly difficult for well-educated African American women. Fewer African American men attend college than African American women, making the potential pool of men who are suitable—as defined by society and the marriage gradient—relatively small. Consequently, relative to women of other races, African American women are more apt to marry men who are less educated than they are—or not marry at all (Kiecolt & Fossett, 1997; Willie & Reddick, 2003).

ATTACHMENT STYLES AND ROMANTIC RELATIONSHIPS: DO ADULT LOVING STYLES REFLECT ATTACHMENT IN INFANCY?

"I want a girl just like the girl that married dear old Dad." So go the lyrics of an old song, suggesting that the songwriter would like to find someone who loves him as much as his mother did. Is this just a corny tune, or is there a kernel of truth in this sentiment? Put more broadly, is the kind of attachment that people experience during infancy reflected in their adult romantic relationships?

Increasing evidence suggests that it very well may be. *Attachment* refers to the positive emotional bond that develops between a child and a particular individual. Most infants fall into one of three attachment categories: securely attached children, who have healthy, positive, trusting relationships with their caregivers; avoidant infants, who are relatively indifferent to caregivers and who avoid interactions with them; and ambivalent infants, who show great distress when separated from a caregiver but who appear angry upon the caregiver's return.

According to psychologist Phillip Shaver and his colleagues, attachment styles continue into adulthood and affect the nature of romantic relationships (Dinero et al., 2008; Frías, Shaver, & Mikulincer, 2015; Shaver et al., 2017). For instance, consider the following statements:

1. I find it relatively easy to get close to others and am comfortable depending on them and having them depend on me. I don't often worry about being abandoned or about someone getting too close to me.

2. I am somewhat uncomfortable being close to others; I find it difficult to trust them completely, difficult to allow myself to depend on them. I am nervous when anyone gets too close, and often love partners want me to be more intimate than I feel comfortable being.

3. I find that others are reluctant to get as close as I would like. I often worry that my partner doesn't really love me or won't want to stay with me. I want to merge completely with another person, and this desire sometimes scares people away (Shaver, Hazan, & Bradshaw, 1988).

According to Shaver's research, agreement with the first statement reflects a secure attachment style. Adults who agree with this statement readily enter into relationships and feel happy, energized, and confident about the future success of their relationships. Most young adults—just over half—display the secure style of attachment (Hazan & Shaver, 1987; Luke, Sedikides, & Carnelley, 2012).

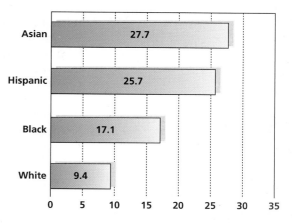

Figure 12-7 Marriage Outside of Racial/Ethnic Group

Although homogamy has been the standard for most marriages in the United States, the rate of marriages crossing ethnic and racial lines is substantial.
(**Source:** Based on data from Wang/Pew Research Center, 2012.)

Intermarriage Rates, by Race and Ethnicity, 2010
Percent of newlyweds married to someone of a different race/ethnicity

Group	Percent
Asian	27.7
Hispanic	25.7
Black	17.1
White	9.4

Note: Asians include Pacific Islanders. Whites, blacks, and Asians include only non-Hispanics. Hispanics are of any race.

In contrast, adults who agree with the second statement typically display the avoidant attachment style. These individuals, who make up about a quarter of the population, tend to be less invested in relationships, have higher break-up rates, and often feel lonely.

Finally, agreement with the third category is reflective of an ambivalent style. Adults with an ambivalent style have a tendency to become overly invested in relationships, have repeated breakups with the same partner, and have relatively low self-esteem. Around 20 percent of adults, gay and straight, fall into this category (Li & Chan, 2012).

Attachment style is also related to the nature of care that adults give to their romantic partners when they need assistance. For instance, secure adults tend to provide more sensitive and supportive care, being responsive to their partner's psychological needs. In comparison, anxious adults are more likely to provide compulsive, intrusive (and ultimately less helpful) aid to partners (Feeney & Collins, 2001, 2003; Gleason, Iida, & Bolger, 2003).

It seems clear that there are continuities between infants' attachment styles and their behavior as adults. People who are having difficulty in relationships might well look back to their infancy to identify the root of their problem (Rholes et al., 2007). Insight into the roots of our current behavior can sometimes help us learn more adaptive skills as adults.

The Course of Relationships

LO 12.10 Examine the varied forms of long-term relationships.

Relationships, like the individuals who make them up, face a variety of challenges. As men and women move through early adulthood, they encounter significant changes in their lives as they work at starting and building their careers, having children, and establishing, maintaining, and sometimes ending relationships with others. One of the primary questions young adults face is whether and when to marry.

COHABITATION, MARRIAGE, AND OTHER RELATIONSHIP CHOICES: SORTING OUT THE OPTIONS OF EARLY ADULTHOOD. For some people, the primary issue is not identifying a potential spouse but whether to marry at all. Although surveys show that most heterosexuals (and a growing number of gays and lesbians) say they want to get married, a significant number choose some other route. For instance, the past half-century has seen both a decline in the number of married couples and a huge, 1,500 percent rise in couples living together without being married, a status known as **cohabitation** (see Figure 12-8). Today, some 7.5 million people are cohabitating in the United States. In fact, married couples make up a minority of households.

Most young adults will live with a romantic partner for at least one period during their 20s. Furthermore, most marriages today occur after a period in which the couple has cohabited. Why do so many couples choose to cohabit rather than to marry? Some feel they are not ready to make a lifelong commitment. Others feel that cohabitation provides "practice" for marriage. (This is more likely for women than men. Women tend to see cohabitation as a step toward marriage; men are more likely to view it as a way to test a relationship (Jay, 2012; Perelli-Harris & Styrc, 2017). Some couples cohabitate because they reject the institution of marriage altogether, maintaining that marriage is outmoded and that it is unrealistic to expect a couple to spend a lifetime together (Martin, Martin, & Martin, 2001; Miller, Sassler, & Kusi-Appouh, 2011).

Statistics suggest that those who feel that cohabiting increases their subsequent chances of a happy marriage are incorrect. On the contrary, the chances of divorce are somewhat higher for those who have previously cohabited, according to data collected in both the United States and Western Europe (Rhoades, Stanley, & Markman, 2006; Tang, Curran, & Arroyo, 2014; Rhoades et al., 2015).

Despite the prevalence of cohabitation, marriage ultimately remains the preferred alternative for most people during early adulthood. Many see marriage as the appropriate culmination of a loving relationship, while others feel it is the "right" thing to do

cohabitation

couples living together without being married.

Figure 12-8 Cohabitation

The number of couples living together prior to marriage increased by 41 percent from the 2000 to 2010.

(**Source:** U.S. Bureau of the Census, 2010.)

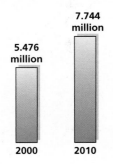

7.744 million

5.476 million

2000   2010

after reaching a particular age in early adulthood. Others seek marriage because of the various roles that a spouse can fill. For instance, a spouse can play an economic role, providing security and financial well-being. Spouses also fill a sexual role, offering a means of sexual gratification and fulfillment that is fully accepted by society. Another role is therapeutic and recreational: Spouses provide a sounding board to discuss one another's problems and act as partners for activities. Marriage also offers the only means of having children that is fully accepted by all segments of society. Finally, marriage offers legal benefits and protections, such as eligibility for medical insurance under a spouse's policy and eligibility for survivor benefits like Social Security benefits (Doherty, Carroll, & Waite, 2007).

Although marriage remains important, it is not a static institution. For example, fewer U.S. citizens are now married than at any time since the late 1890s. Part of this decline in marriage is attributable to higher divorce rates, but the decision of people to marry later in life is also a contributing factor. The median age of first marriage in the United States is now 28.7 for men and 26.5 for women—the oldest age for women since national statistics were first collected in the 1880s (see Figure 12-9; U.S. Census Bureau, 2012).

Figure 12-9 Postponing Marriage

The age at which women and men first marry is the highest since national statistics were first collected in the late 1800s. **THINKING ABOUT THE DATA:** How has the age differential between men and women changed over time? What factors account for the increasingly higher age at first marriage?

(**Source:** U.S. Bureau of the Census, Current Population Survey, 2011.)

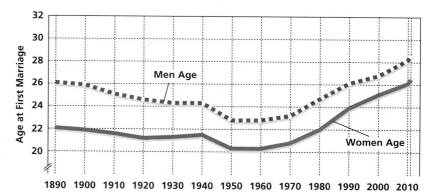

In many European countries, legal alternatives to marriage are growing. For instance, France offers "Civil Solidarity Pacts," in which couples receive many of the same legal rights as married couples. What differs is that there is no legal lifetime commitment that they would be asked to make if they married; Civil Solidarity Pacts can be dissolved more easily than marriages (Lyall, 2004).

Does this mean that marriage is losing its viability as a social institution? Probably not. Most people—some 90 percent—eventually do marry, and national polls find that almost everyone endorses the notion that a good family life is important (Newport & Wilke, 2013).

Why are people getting married later in life? The delay in part reflects economic concerns and the commitment to establishing a career. Choosing and starting a career presents an increasingly difficult series of decisions for young adults, and some feel that until they get a foothold on a career path and begin to earn an adequate salary, marriage plans should be put on hold (Hall, 2006).

From *a social worker's* perspective

Why do you think society has established such a powerful norm in favor of marriage? What effects might such a norm have on a person who prefers to remain single?

Staying Single: I Want to Be Alone.   For some people, neither marriage nor cohabitation is the preferred option. To them, living alone represents a good path, consciously chosen, through life. *Singlehood*, living alone without an intimate partner, has increased significantly in the past several decades, encompassing around 20 percent of women and 30 percent of men. Almost 20 percent will probably spend their entire lives in singlehood (U.S. Bureau of the Census, 2012).

People who choose not to marry or live with a partner give several reasons for their decision. One is that they view marriage negatively. Rather than seeing marriage in the idealized terms presented in the media of the 1950s, they focus more on high divorce rates and marital strife. Ultimately, they conclude that the risks of forming a lifetime union may be too high.

Others view marriage as too restrictive. These individuals place great value on personal change and growth, which would be impeded by the stable, long-term commitment implied by marriage. Finally, some people simply do not encounter anyone with whom they wish to spend the remainder of their lives. Instead, they value their independence, autonomy, and freedom (DePaulo, 2004, 2006).

Despite the advantages of singlehood, there are also drawbacks. Society often stigmatizes single individuals, particularly women, by holding up marriage as the idealized norm. Furthermore, there can be a lack of companionship and sexual outlets, and singles may feel that their future is less secure financially (Baumbusch, 2004; Pudrovska, Schieman, & Carr, 2006; Maier & McGeorge, 2014).

The Ups and Downs of Marriage

LO 12.11 Analyze why marriages work or don't work.

Fifty years ago, midlife was similar for most people. Men and women who had married during early adulthood were still married to one another. One hundred years ago, when life expectancy was much shorter than it is today, people in their 40s were most likely married—but not necessarily to the same persons they had first married. Spouses often died; people might be well into their second marriage by the time of middle age.

Today the story is different and more varied. More people are single during middle adulthood, having never married. Single people may live alone or with a partner. Gay and lesbian adults, for example, may have committed relationships even though marriage has not until recently been an option for them. Among heterosexuals, some have divorced, lived alone, and then remarried. During middle adulthood, many people's marriages end in divorce, and many families "blend" together into new households, containing children and stepchildren from previous marriages. Other couples still spend between 40 and 50 years together, the bulk of those years during middle adulthood. Many people experience the peak of marital satisfaction during middle age.

WHAT MAKES MARRIAGE WORK?   Partners in successful marriages display several characteristics. They visibly show affection to one another and communicate relatively little negativity. Happily married couples tend to perceive themselves as part of an interdependent couple rather than as one of two independent individuals. They also experience social homogamy, a similarity in leisure activity and role preferences. They hold similar interests, and they agree on a distribution of roles—such as who takes out the garbage and who takes care of the children (Carrere et al., 2000; Huston et al., 2001; Stutzer & Frey, 2006).

However, our awareness of the characteristics displayed by husbands and wives in successful marriages has not helped prevent what can only be called an epidemic of divorce. The statistics on divorce are grim: Only about half of all marriages in the United States remain intact. Over 800,000 marriages end in divorce each year, and there are 43.2 divorces for every 1,000 individuals. This figure actually represents a decline from the peak in the mid-1970s of 5.3 divorces per 1,000 people, and most experts think that the rate is leveling off (National Center for Health Statistics, 2017).

As we'll see next, divorce is a problem that has its roots in early adulthood and the early years of marriage. In fact, most divorces occur during the first 10 years of marriage.

EARLY MARITAL CONFLICT.   Conflict in marriage is not unusual. According to some statistics, nearly half of newly married couples experience a significant degree of conflict. One of the major reasons is that partners may initially idealize one another, perceiving each other through the proverbial "starry eyes." However, as the realities of day-to-day living together and interacting begin to sink in, they become more aware of flaws. In fact, perceptions of marital quality over the first 10 years of marriage on the part of both wives and husbands show a decline in the early years, followed by a period of stabilization, and then additional decline (see Figure 12-10; Huston et al., 2001; Karney & Bradbury, 2005; Kulik, Walfisch, & Liberman, 2016).

There are many sources of marital conflict. Husbands and wives may have difficulty making the transition from being children of their parents to autonomous adults. Others have difficulty developing an identity apart from their spouses, while some struggle to find a satisfactory allocation of time to share with the spouse, compared with time spent with friends and other family members (Crawford, Houts, & Huston, 2002; Murray, Bellavia, & Rose, 2003; Madigan, Plamondon, & Jenkins, 2017).

Most married couples, however, view the early years of marriage as deeply satisfying. For them, marriage can be a kind of extension of courtship. As they negotiate changes in their relationship and learn more about each other, many couples find themselves more deeply in love than before marriage. The newlywed period is for many couples one of the happiest of their entire married lives (McNulty & Karney, 2004).

THE COURSE OF MARITAL SATISFACTION. Even for happily married couples, marriage has its ups and downs, with satisfaction rising and falling over the course of the marriage. In the past, most research has suggested that marital satisfaction follows the U-shaped configuration shown in Figure 12-11 (Figley, 1973). Specifically, marital satisfaction begins to decline just after the marriage, and it continues to fall until it reaches its lowest point following the births of the couple's children. However, at that point, satisfaction begins to grow, eventually returning to the same level that it held before the marriage (Harvey & Weber, 2002; Stroope, McFarland, & Uecker, 2015).

However, newer research is calling the U-shaped pattern into question. Several recent studies, using more sophisticated research designs, suggest that the upturn in satisfaction that occurs later in life may be illusory and that marital satisfaction continues to decline across the life span. These recent studies have employed longitudinal research, in which the marital satisfaction of the same couples is tracked over substantial time periods, and the results of the studies are painting a somewhat different picture (VanLaningham, Johnson, & Amato, 2001; Umberson et al., 2005).

One longitudinal study assessed changes in marriage quality over a period of eight years, and another did the same over 17 years. Both studies confirmed earlier findings that marital satisfaction declines in the years just after marriage, but both also failed to find evidence of a subsequent upswing after the childbearing years. Rather, when assessed over time, marriage quality seems to continue to decline over the course of a marriage (or at best to reach a low point and level out) (Umberson et al., 2005).

It is too early to reject the U-shaped view of marital satisfaction, and it may be that individual differences in marriages account for the discrepancy in findings. What is clear is that middle-aged couples cite several sources of marital satisfaction. For instance, both men and women typically state that their spouse is "their best friend" and that they like their spouses

Figure 12-10 Perceptions of Marital Quality

At the beginning of marriage, partners see each other in a more idealized manner. But as time passes, the perception of the quality of the marriage declines.
(**Source:** Kurdek, 1999.)

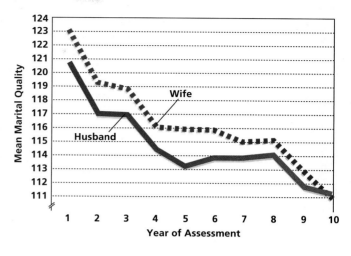

Figure 12-11 The Phases of Marital Satisfaction

For many couples, marital satisfaction falls and rises in a U-shaped configuration. It begins to decline after the birth of children but increases when the youngest child leaves home and eventually returns to a level of satisfaction similar to that at the start of marriage. Why do you think this pattern of satisfaction occurs?
(**Source:** Based on Rollins & Cannon, 1974.)

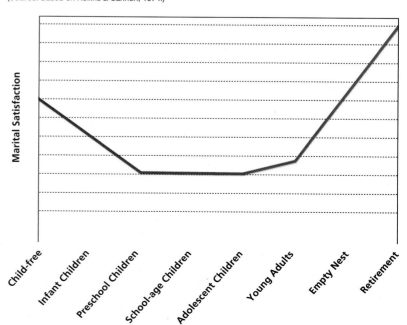

Figure 12-12 Rising Divorces in Middle Adulthood

Both the divorce rate and the number of people who experience divorce in the group that is 50 years and above have risen significantly, and the increases are projected to continue in the future.

(**Source:** Based on: Brown, S., & Lin, I-Fen. (2012, March). The gray divorce revolution: Rising divorce among middle-aged and older adults, 1990–2009. National Center for Family & Marriage Research, Bowling Green State University. Working Paper Series WP-12-04., Figure 1.)

as people. They also view marriage as a long-term commitment and agree on their aims and goals. Finally, most also feel that their spouses have grown more interesting over the course of the marriage (Levenson, Carstensen, & Gottman, 1993).

Are there "secrets" to successful marriages? Not really. However, there are proven coping mechanisms that allow couples to remain together happily. Among them (Orbuch, 2009; Bernstein, 2010):

- **Holding Realistic Expectations.** Successful couples understand that there are some things about your partner that you may not like all that much. They accept that their partner will do things that they don't like some of the time.

- **Focusing on the Positive.** Thinking about the things that they like about their partner helps them to accept the things that bother them.

- **Compromising.** Partners in successful marriages understand that they are not going to win every argument, and they don't keep score.

- **Avoiding Suffering in Silence.** If something does bother them, they let their partner know about it. But they don't bring it up in an accusatory way. Instead, they talk about it at a time when they are both calm.

DIVORCE. Although the overall divorce rate has declined in the past two decades, divorce among couples during midlife is actually rising. One woman in eight who is in her first marriage will get divorced after the age of 40, and one in four of all divorces are by people 50 and older. In fact, the divorce rate for people 50 and over has doubled since 1990. And for those over 65, the divorce rate has roughly tripled since 1990 (see Figure 12-12; Brown & Lin, 2012; Thomas, 2012; Stepler, 2017).

Why do marriages unravel in middle adulthood? There are many causes. One is that the decision to divorce is cumulative, and people may simply have increasingly grown apart or are dissatisfied with their marriage (Hawkins, Willoughby, & Doherty, 2012).

Furthermore, people in middle adulthood spend less time together than in earlier years. In individualistic Western cultures, people feel concerned with their own personal happiness and self-fulfillment. If their marriage is not satisfying, they feel that divorce may be the answer to increasing their happiness. Divorce is also more socially acceptable than in the past, and there are fewer legal impediments to divorces. In some cases—but certainly not all—the financial costs are not high. In fact, as more women enter the workforce, the economic reasons that would have otherwise kept women from divorcing their husbands are no longer strong enough to keep the marriage together. Consequently, as opportunities for women grow, wives may feel less dependent on their husbands, both from an emotional and an economic standpoint (Brown & Lin, 2012; Canham et al., 2014; Crowley, 2018).

Another reason for divorce is that, as we discussed earlier, feelings of romantic, passionate love may subside over time. Because Western culture emphasizes the importance of romance and passion, members of marriages in which passion has declined may feel that that is a sufficient reason to divorce. Finally, there is a great deal of stress in households in which both parents work, and this stress puts a strain on marriages. Much of the energy directed toward families and maintaining relationships in the past is now directed toward work and other institutions outside the home (Macionis, 2001).

Whatever the causes, divorce can be especially difficult for men and women in midlife. It can be particularly hard for women who have followed the traditional female role of staying with their children and never performing substantial work outside the home. They may face prejudice against older workers, finding that they are less likely to be hired than younger people, even in jobs with minimal requirements. Without a good deal of training and support, these divorced women, lacking recognized job skills, may remain virtually unemployable (Williams & Dunne-Bryant, 2006; Hilton & Anderson, 2009; Bowen & Jensen, 2017).

Of course, many people who divorce in midlife end up happy with the decision. Women, in particular, are apt to find that developing a new, independent self-identity is a positive outcome. Furthermore, both men and women who divorce during midlife are likely to enter new relationships, and—as we will see—they typically remarry (Enright, 2004).

REMARRIAGE.   Many of the people who divorce—some 75 to 80 percent—end up marrying again, usually within two to five years. They are most likely to marry people who have also been divorced, partly because divorced people tend to be the ones in the available pool but also because those who have gone through divorce share similar experiences (Pew Research Center, 2014; Lamidi & Cruz, 2014).

Around three-quarters of people who divorce remarry again, usually within two to five years.

Although the overall rate of remarriage is high, it is far higher in some groups than in others. For instance, it is harder for women to remarry than men, particularly older women. Whereas 90 percent of women under the age of 25 remarry after divorce, less than one-third of women over the age of 40 remarry (Besharov & West, 2002).

The reason for this age difference stems from the *marriage gradient* that we discussed earlier in this module: Societal norms push men to marry women who are younger, smaller, and lower in status than themselves. As a consequence, the older a woman is, the fewer the socially acceptable men she has available to her since those men her age are likely to be looking for younger women. In addition, women have the disadvantage of societal double standards regarding physical attractiveness. Older women tend to be perceived as unattractive, while older men tend to be seen as "distinguished" and "mature" (Buss, 2003b; Doyle, 2004b; Khodarahimi & Fathi, 2017).

There are several reasons divorced people may find getting married again more appealing than remaining single. One motivation to remarry is to avoid the social consequences of divorce. Even in the 21st century, when the breakup of marriages is common, divorce carries with it a certain stigma that people may attempt to overcome by remarrying. In addition, divorced people overall report lower levels of satisfaction with life than married people (Lucas, 2005).

Divorced people miss the companionship that marriage provides. Divorced men in particular report feeling lonely and experience an increase in physical and mental health problems following divorce. Finally, marriage provides clear economic benefits, such as sharing the cost of a house and medical benefits reserved for spouses (Thomas & Sawhill, 2005).

Second marriages are not the same as first marriages. Older couples tend to be more mature and realistic in their expectations of a partner and a marriage. They tend to look at marriage in less romantic terms than younger couples, and they are more cautious. They are also likely to show greater flexibility in terms of roles and duties; they share household chores more equitably and make decisions in a more participatory manner (Clarke, 2005; McCarthy & Ginsberg, 2007).

Unfortunately, though, this doesn't make second marriages more durable than first ones. In fact, the divorce rate for second marriages is slightly higher than for first marriages. Several factors explain this phenomenon. One is that second marriages may be subject to stresses that are not present in first marriages, such as the strain of blending different families. For another, having experienced and survived divorce before, partners in second marriages may be less committed to relationships and more ready to walk away from unsatisfactory ones. Finally, they may have personality and emotional characteristics that don't make them easy to live with (Warshak, 2000; Coleman, Ganong, & Weaver, 2001).

Despite the high divorce rate for second marriages, many people settle into remarriage quite successfully. In such cases, couples report as great a degree of satisfaction as those who were in successful first marriages (Michaels, 2006; Ayalon & Koren, 2015).

MARRIAGE IN THE LATER YEARS: TOGETHER, THEN ALONE.   It's a man's world—at least when it comes to marriage after age 65. The proportion of men who are married at that age is far greater than that of women (see Figure 12-13). One reason for this disparity is that 70 percent of women outlive their husbands by at least a few years. Because there are fewer men available (many have died), these women are unlikely to remarry (Bourque et al., 2005).

Figure 12-13 Living Patterns of Older Americans

What, if anything, do these patterns suggest about the relative health and adjustment of older men and women?
(**Source:** Administration on Aging, 2006.)

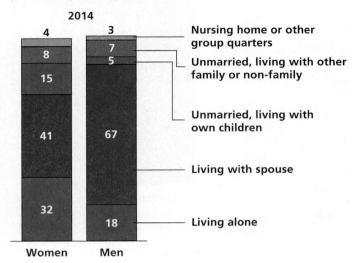

Furthermore, the marriage gradient that we discussed earlier is still a powerful influence. Reflecting societal norms that suggest that women should marry men older than themselves, the marriage gradient works to keep women single even in the later years of life. At the same time, it makes remarriage for men much easier, since the available pool of eligible partners is much larger (Clements & Swenson, 2003).

The vast majority of people who are still married in later life report that they are satisfied with their marriages. Their partners provide substantial companionship and emotional support. Because at this period in life they have typically been together for a long time, they have great insight into their partners (Jose & Alfons, 2007; Petrican, et al., 2015).

At the same time, not every aspect of marriage is equally satisfying, and marriages may undergo severe stress as spouses experience changes in their lives. For instance, the retirement of one or both spouses can bring about a shift in the nature of a couple's relationship (Henry, Miller, & Giarrusso, 2005).

For some couples, the stress is so great that one spouse or the other seeks a divorce. Some 15 percent of Americans over age 50 are divorced. The divorce rate has doubled since 1990 (Roberts, 2013). The reasons for divorce at such a late stage of life are varied. Often, women who divorce do so because their husbands are abusive or alcoholic. But in the more frequent case of a husband seeking a divorce from his wife, the reason is often that he has found a younger woman. Often the divorce occurs soon after retirement, when men who have been highly involved in their careers are in psychological turmoil (Pudrovska et al., 2006).

Divorce so late in life is particularly difficult for women. Between the marriage gradient and the limited size of the potential pool of eligible men, it is unlikely that an older divorced woman will remarry. Divorce in late adulthood can be devastating. For many women, their role as a marriage partner has been primary and the center of their identities, and they may view divorce as a major failure. As a consequence, happiness and the quality of life for divorced women often plummet (Davies & Denton, 2002).

Seeking a new relationship becomes a priority for many men and women who are divorced or whose spouses have died. As at earlier stages of life, people seeking to develop relationships use a variety of strategies to meet potential partners, such as joining singles organizations or using the Internet to seek out companionship (Durbin, 2003).

Some people enter late adulthood having never married. For those who have remained single throughout their lives—about 5 percent of the population—late adulthood may bring fewer transitions, since the status of living alone does not change. Never-married individuals report feeling less lonely than do most people their age, and they have a greater sense of independence (Cwikel, Gramotnev, & Lee, 2006).

Module 12.3 Review

LO 12.7 Describe the functions and patterns of dating in adolescence.

Dating in adolescence serves a number of functions, including intimacy, entertainment, and prestige.

LO 12.8 Analyze the nature of intimacy and relationships in early adulthood.

The course of relationships typically follows a pattern of increasing interaction, intimacy, and redefinition. Types of love include passionate and companionate love. Robert Sternberg's

triangular theory identifies three basic components (intimacy, passion, and decision/commitment).

LO 12.9 Explain the process by which people choose their partners.

According to filtering models, people apply increasingly fine filters to potential partners, eventually choosing a mate according to the principles of homogamy and the marriage gradient. In general, the values applied to relationships by heterosexual, gay, and lesbian couples are more similar than different.

LO 12.10 Examine the varied forms of long-term relationships.

Cohabitation is an increasingly popular option for young adults, but most still choose marriage.

LO 12.11 Analyze why marriages work or don't work.

Divorce is prevalent in the United States, particularly within the first 10 years of marriage. While marriages in older adulthood are generally happy, stresses due to aging can bring divorce.

Journal Writing Prompt

Applying Lifespan Development: Consider a long-term marriage with which you are familiar. Do you think the relationship involves passionate love or companionate love (or both)? What changes when a relationship moves from passionate to companionate love? From companionate to passionate love? In which direction is it more difficult for a relationship to move? Why?

Epilogue

In this chapter, we examined the development of gender awareness, sexuality, and intimate relationships. We saw how preschoolers have a strong sense of being male or female and of traditional gender roles and expectations. We discussed a range of theories that attempt to account for gender differences, including both biological and social theories. Then we considered the psychological aspects of sexual maturation in adolescence and also saw how sexual activity continues in healthy adults throughout the life span.

Next, we focused on intimate relationships, beginning with the role dating plays in adolescents' lives and how love develops in young adulthood. We considered, too, the questions of whether or not to marry and how people go about choosing a partner. In conclusion, we examined the ups and downs of marriage and the course of marriage—and divorce—from early to late adulthood.

Turn back to the prologue to this chapter, which describes Alex Lewis's insistence that although born a girl, he is really a boy, and answer the following questions.

1. Do you think Sondra Lewis was right in taking seriously Alex's assertion that he was a boy? How can a parent tell if a preference for jeans over dresses and trucks over dolls is more than just tomboyishness?

2. Would it have made any difference if Alex's parents had discouraged his tomboyishness early in life? How do you think a child like Alex manages to resist parental assignment into a particular gender role?

3. How would a biological approach to gender development explain Alex's situation? How would a social learning approach explain it? Do you think those explanations are adequate?

4. What challenges do you foresee for Alex as he enters adolescence? How do you think his gender identity will interact with his sexual development?

Looking Back

LO 12.1 Explain the nature of gender differences and their effects on the roles people assume in life.

From the moment of birth, girls and boys are treated differently and are subject to different expectations. Mothers and fathers display different interaction patterns with their children, and the toy and play preferences of boys and girls vary and are differently encouraged by their parents. Furthermore, boys' and girls' actions are interpreted differently by parents and other adults. Actual biologically based behavioral differences between boy and girl infants exist, but they are minor compared to the behavioral similarities between genders. However, as children age, gender differences become more pronounced, mostly because of environmental factors.

LO 12.2 Describe how an individual's gender identity develops in early childhood.

By the preschool years, gender is well established in terms of self-understanding and behavior. Preschoolers hold expectations about gender-appropriate behavior that are more rigid than at any other time during the life span, and they form ideas about the different careers that are appropriate for men and women.

LO 12.3 Analyze the major theoretical explanations of gender differences.

The strong gender expectations held by preschoolers are explained in different ways by different theorists. Some point to genetic factors as evidence for a biological explanation of gender expectations. Sigmund Freud's psychoanalytic theories use a framework based on the subconscious. Social learning theorists focus on environmental influences, including parents, teachers, peers, and the media, while cognitive theorists propose that children form gender schemas, cognitive frameworks that organize information that the children gather about gender.

LO 12.4 Explore the psychological implications of sexual maturation during adolescence.

The substantial body changes of adolescence bring psychological as well as physical effects. For example, menarche in adolescent girls can lead to increased self-esteem and greater self-awareness, but other physical changes can cause embarrassment and unhappiness with their bodies. The timing of puberty also has psychological implications. For both boys and girls, early maturation has many positive effects, but it can lead to dangers and disadvantages as well.

LO 12.5 Describe how adolescents experience and explore their sexuality.

For most adolescents, masturbation is often the first step into sexuality. The age of first intercourse, which is now in the teens, has declined as the double standard has faded and the norm of permissiveness with affection has gained ground. The most common sexual orientation among adolescents is heterosexuality, with a smaller number of adolescents having homosexual or bisexual orientations. Homosexuality and heterosexuality, rather than being distinct sexual orientations, are regarded by some researchers as a continuum along which people experience their individual sexuality, which may change over time. The number of teenage pregnancies has been decreasing in the United States, largely because of increased awareness of the risks of unprotected sex, more widespread use of condoms and other forms of contraception, and reliance on substitutes for intercourse.

LO 12.6 Explain the role of sexuality during adulthood.

Sexuality remains an important part of life for most middle-aged people. While frequency may decline, satisfaction with sexual activities is high, benefitting from increased freedom in a home without children. Continued sexuality depends on good physical and mental health and a history of ongoing sexual activity in the middle years.

LO 12.7 Describe the functions and patterns of dating in adolescence.

During adolescence, dating provides intimacy, entertainment, and prestige. Achieving psychological intimacy, difficult at first, becomes easier as adolescents mature, gain confidence, and take relationships more seriously.

LO 12.8 Analyze the nature of intimacy and relationships in early adulthood.

Young adults face Erik Erikson's intimacy-versus-isolation stage, a period focused on developing close, intimate relationships with others. Passionate love is characterized by intense physiological arousal, intimacy, and caring, while companionate love is characterized by respect, admiration, and affection. Psychologist Robert Sternberg suggests that three components of love (intimacy, passion, and decision/commitment) combine to form eight types of love, through which a relationship can dynamically evolve.

LO 12.9 Explain the process by which people choose their partners.

Although in Western cultures love tends to be the most important factor in selecting a partner, other cultures emphasize different factors. According to filtering models, people filter potential partners initially for attractiveness and then for compatibility, generally conforming to the principle of homogamy and the marriage gradient. Gays and lesbians generally seek the same qualities in relationships as heterosexual men and women: attachment, caring, intimacy, affection, and respect. In young adulthood, while cohabitation is popular, marriage remains the most attractive option. The median age of first marriage is rising for both men and women.

LO 12.10 Examine the varied forms of long-term relationships.

While the number of marriages in the United States has declined over the past half-century, the number of couples living together outside marriage, or cohabiting, has skyrocketed. Cohabitation is generally regarded by men as a way to test a relationship, and by women as practice for a future marriage. Most cohabiting couples eventually marry, but cohabitation itself does not prevent divorce. Instead of either cohabitation or marriage, some people choose singlehood, living alone without an intimate partner. The main reason appears to be a preference for independence.

LO 12.11 Analyze why marriages work or don't work.

Partners in successful marriages generally show affection for each other, accept that they are part of an interdependent entity, and enjoy similar likes and dislikes. They also share chores and agree on how to distribute roles in the household. Middle adulthood is, for most married couples, a time of satisfaction, but for many couples marital satisfaction declines steadily and divorce results. Divorce is prevalent in the United States, affecting nearly half of all marriages.

Most people who divorce remarry, usually to another divorced person. People who marry for a second time tend to be more realistic and mature than people in first marriages, and to share roles and responsibilities more equitably. However, second marriages end in divorce even more often than first marriages. Marriages in later life generally remain happy, although stresses brought about by major life changes that accompany aging can cause rifts. Divorce is usually harder on the woman than the man, partly because of the continuing influence of the marriage gradient.

Key Terms and Concepts

Chapter 13
Friends and Family

Cathy Yeulet/123RF GB Ltd

Learning Objectives

LO 13.1 Summarize the development of social relationships in the preschool years, and describe the types of play preschoolers engage in.

LO 13.2 Identify the three major stages of friendship in middle childhood, and explain how friendship patterns differ across gender.

LO 13.3 Explain the important role that peers play in adolescence, and describe the changes that occur in cross-race relationships.

LO 13.4 Identify the four categories of popularity, and summarize the qualities of popular adolescents.

LO 13.5 Explain how adolescents' quest for autonomy affects relationships in the family.

LO 13.6 Summarize the importance of friendships in adulthood, and identify the characteristics adults look for in a friend.

LO 13.7 Summarize the challenges couples face in deciding to have children, and identify successful coping strategies.

LO 13.8 Identify the changes that have occurred in family life in the past 50 years, and give examples of their impact on both parents and children.

LO 13.9 Identify the various family constellations, and summarize the impact of divorce on children.

LO 13.10 Compare the outcomes for children raised in a gay or lesbian household with those of children raised in a heterosexual household.

LO 13.11 Summarize what is meant by the empty nest syndrome, and identify the losses and gains associated with it.

LO 13.12 Define what is meant by the sandwich generation, and explain how those in the sandwich generation are affected by

LO 13.13 Identify the different styles of grandparenting, and explain the importance of family connections for older adults.

both boomerang children and caring for their own aging parents.

LO 13.14 Identify the different paths people take in retirement, and summarize the economic challenges this age group faces.

LO 13.15 Compare and contrast the variety of living arrangements available to older adults.

Chapter Overview

Prologue: New Roles in Retirement

Bernadine Connolly had been looking forward to retirement for several years. She had plenty of books and science podcasts to catch up on. She even thought she might like to start writing a blog for the first time.

But her plans for retirement were thwarted when she found that her three grown children increasingly asked for her help in caring for their own kids. Her five grandchildren ranged in age from 4 to 12 years old, and her help was especially needed with the youngest after his parents divorced and their schedules changed.

"I've never been busier in my whole life," she explained to her husband, Theodore, who had been contemplating retirement himself. "Don't retire," Bernadine started to warn him, but then she quickly changed her tune. "On second thought, please hurry up and retire because I need all the help I can get with our grandkids."

Eventually, Bernadine found a way to combine her increasing caretaker roles with her original retirement goals, and she started a blog about grandparenting in modern families. ▪

Looking Ahead

For people in late adulthood such as Bernadine, changing roles and opportunities offer new ways to stay active and connected with others, something that is true at every stage of life. In this chapter, we examine family and peer relationships throughout the life span. We begin by looking at the development of friendship and play in preschool and middle childhood and then consider the importance of peers and peer groups in adolescence. We also discuss the significance of the social support adult friendships offer, especially in later adulthood.

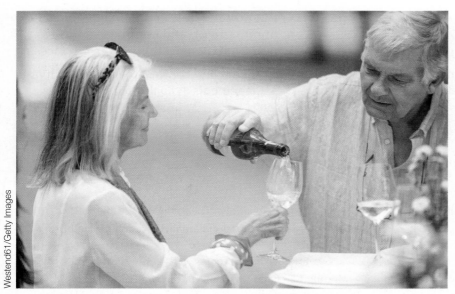

Social development is the way in which individuals' interactions with others and their social relationships grow, change, and remain stable over the course of life.

We then turn to a discussion of the family. We begin with a look at the decision to have a child and the consequences of such a choice on a couple's relationship. We then consider the nature of family life and discuss how it differs from earlier eras, considering a variety of family constellations. We also look at what it means to be a gay or lesbian parent today.

Finally, we look at the various familial ties that bind people together (or come unglued) during middle adulthood, and explore the importance of family in late adulthood. In doing so, we look at the lifestyles of people in late adulthood, including the paths they choose to pursue in retirement and their varied living arrangements.

MODULE 13.1

SOCIAL RELATIONSHIPS ACROSS THE LIFE SPAN

When Juan was 3, he had his first best friend, Emilio. Juan and Emilio, who lived in the same apartment building in San Jose, were inseparable. They played incessantly with toy cars, racing them up and down the apartment hallways until some of the neighbors began to complain about the noise. They pretended to read to one another, and sometimes they slept over at each other's home—a big step for a 3-year-old. Neither boy seemed more joyful than when he was with his "best friend"—the term each used of the other.

An infant's family can provide nearly all the social contact he or she needs. As preschoolers, however, many children, like Juan and Emilio, begin to discover the joys of peer friendships.

Preschoolers' Friendships

LO 13.1 Summarize the development of social relationships in the preschool years, and describe the types of play preschoolers engage in.

Before age 3, most social activity involves simply being in the same place at the same time, without real social interaction. However, at around age 3, children begin to develop real friendships as peers are seen as individuals who hold special qualities and rewards. While preschoolers' relations with adults reflect children's needs for care, protection, and direction, their relations with peers are based more on the desire for companionship, play, and fun. Gradually they come to view friendship as a continuing state that offers not just immediate pleasure but the promise of future activity (Proulx & Poulin, 2013; Paulus & Moore, 2014; Paulus, 2016).

Interactions with friends change during the preschool period. For 3-year-olds, the focus of friendship is the enjoyment of doing things together and playing jointly. Older preschoolers pay more attention to trust, support, and shared interests. Throughout the entire period, however, play remains an important part of friendship (Johnson & Foster, 2005; Rotenberg, Boulton, & Fox, 2005; Hoyte, Torr, & Degotardi, 2015).

PLAYING BY THE RULES: THE WORK OF PLAY.   In Rosie Graiff's class of 3-year-olds, Minnie bounces her doll's feet on the table as she sings softly to herself. Ben pushes his toy car across the floor, making motor noises. Sarah chases Abdul around and around the perimeter of the room.

Play is more than what children of preschool age do to pass the time. Instead, play helps preschoolers develop socially, cognitively, and physically (McGinnis, 2012; Holmes & Romeo, 2013; Fleer, 2017).

From *an educator's* perspective

How might a preschool teacher encourage a shy child to join a group of preschoolers who are playing?

CATEGORIZING PLAY.   At the beginning of the preschool years, children engage in **functional play**—simple, repetitive activities typical of 3-year-olds, such as pushing cars on the floor, skipping, and jumping. Functional play involves doing something to be active rather than to create something (Bober, Humphry, & Carswell, 2001; Kantrowitz & Evans, 2004).

By age 4, children become involved in a more sophisticated form of play. In **constructive play** children manipulate objects to produce or build something. A child who builds a house out of Legos or puts a puzzle together is involved in constructive play: He or she has an ultimate goal—to produce something. The creation need not be novel, since children may repeatedly build a house of blocks, let it fall, and then rebuild it.

Constructive play gives children a chance to practice their physical and cognitive skills and fine muscle movements. They gain experience in solving problems about the ways and the sequences in which things fit together. They also learn to cooperate with others as the social nature of play becomes more important to them (Edwards, 2000; Shi, 2003).

THE SOCIAL ASPECTS OF PLAY.   If two preschoolers sit side by side at a table, each assembling a different puzzle, are they engaged jointly in play?

According to pioneering work done by Mildred Parten (1932), the answer is yes. She suggests that these preschoolers are engaged in **parallel play**, in which children play with similar toys, in a similar manner, but do not interact with each other. Preschoolers also engage in another form of play, a highly passive one: onlooker play. In **onlooker play**, children simply watch others at play but do not actually participate themselves.

As they get older, however, preschool children engage in more sophisticated forms of social play that involve greater interaction. In **associative play**, two or more children interact with one another by sharing or borrowing toys or materials, although they do not do the same thing. In **cooperative play**, children genuinely play with one another, taking turns, playing games, or devising contests.

Solitary and onlooker play continues in the later stages of the preschool period. There are simply times when children prefer to play by themselves. And when newcomers join a group, one strategy for becoming part of the group—often successful—is to engage in onlooker play, waiting for an opportunity to join the play more actively (Lindsey & Colwell, 2003).

The nature of pretend, or make-believe, play also changes during the period, becoming in some ways more unrealistic—and imaginative—as preschoolers shift from using only realistic objects to using less concrete ones. Thus, at the start of the preschool period, children may pretend to listen to a radio only if they have a plastic radio on hand. Later, they may use an entirely different object, such as a cardboard box, as a pretend radio (Parsons & Howe, 2013; Russ, 2014; Thibodeau et al., 2016).

Russian developmentalist Lev Vygotsky (1930/1978) argued that pretend play, particularly if it involves social play, is an important means for expanding preschoolers' cognitive skills. Through make-believe play, children are able to "practice" activities (like pretending to use a computer or read a book) that are a part of their particular culture and broaden their understanding of the way the world functions.

functional play
play that involves simple, repetitive activities typical of 3-year-olds.

constructive play
play in which children manipulate objects to produce or build something.

parallel play
action in which children play with similar toys, in a similar manner, but do not interact with each other.

onlooker play
action in which children simply watch others at play but do not actually participate themselves.

associative play
play in which two or more children interact by sharing or borrowing toys or materials, although they do not do the same thing.

cooperative play
play in which children genuinely interact with one another, taking turns, playing games, or devising contests.

One reason that children's play changes is the continuing development of preschoolers' theory of mind—their knowledge and beliefs about how the mind operates. Using their theory of mind, preschool children increasingly see the world from others' perspectives. Even children as young as 2 are able to understand that others have emotions. By age 3 or 4, preschoolers know that they can imagine something that is not physically present, such as a zebra, and that others can do the same. They can also pretend that something has happened and react as if it really had occurred, a skill that becomes part of their imaginative play (Mauritzson & Saeljoe, 2001; Andrews, Halford, & Bunch, 2003; Wellman, 2012).

Building Friendships in Middle Childhood

LO 13.2 **Identify the three major stages of friendship in middle childhood, and explain how friendship patterns differ across gender.**

In Lunch Room Number Two, Jamillah and her new classmates chew slowly on sandwiches and sip quietly on straws from cartons of milk.... Boys and girls look timidly at the strange faces across the table from them, looking for someone who might play with them in the schoolyard, someone who might become a friend.

For these children, what happens in the schoolyard will be just as important as what happens in the school. And when they're out on the playground, there will be no one to protect them. No child will hold back to keep from beating them at a game, humiliating them in a test of skill, or harming them in a fight. No one will run interference or guarantee membership in a group. Out on the playground, it's sink or swim. No one automatically becomes your friend. (Kotre & Hall, 1990, pp. 112–113)

As Jamillah and her classmates demonstrate, friendship plays an increasingly important role in middle childhood, the period that lasts from the start of kindergarten through the start of adolescence. Building and maintaining friendships becomes a large part of social life and is a key developmental task for this age group.

Friends influence development in several ways. Friendships provide children with information about the world as well as themselves. Friends provide emotional support that allows children to respond more effectively to stress. Having friends makes a child a less likely target of aggression. It can teach children how to manage their emotions and help them interpret their own emotional experiences (Berndt, 2002; Lundby, 2013).

Friendships teach children how to communicate and interact with others. They also foster intellectual growth by increasing children's range of experiences (Nangle & Erdley, 2001; Gifford-Smith & Brownell, 2003; Majors, 2012).

Friends and other peers become increasingly influential at this stage, but parents and other family members remain significant. Most developmentalists believe that children's psychological functioning and their general development is the product of multiple factors, including peers and parents (Harris, 2000; Vandell, 2000; Parke, Simpkins, & McDowell, 2002).

STAGES OF FRIENDSHIP: CHANGING VIEWS OF FRIENDS. At this stage, a child's concept of friendship passes through three distinct stages, according to developmental psychologist William Damon (Damon & Hart, 1988).

Stage 1: Basing Friendship on Others' Behavior.   In this stage, from around ages 4 to 7, children see friends as others who like them and with whom they share toys and other activities. They view the children they spend the most time with as their friends.

What children in this stage seldom do, however, is consider others' personal qualities as the basis of friendships. Instead, they use a concrete approach, primarily choosing friends for their behavior. They like those who share, shunning those who don't share, who hit, or who don't play with them. In the first stage, friends are viewed largely as presenting opportunities for pleasant interactions.

Stage 2: Basing Friendship on Trust.   In the next stage, children's view of friendship becomes complicated. Lasting from around ages 8 to 10, this stage involves taking others' personal qualities and traits, as well as the rewards they provide, into consideration. But the centerpiece of friendship in this second stage is mutual trust. Friends are seen as those one can count on to help out when needed. Violations of trust are taken very seriously.

Stage 3: Basing Friendship on Psychological Closeness. The third stage of friendship begins toward the end of middle childhood, from ages 11 to 15, when children develop the view of friendship they will hold in adolescence. The main criteria for friendship shift toward intimacy and loyalty. Friendship becomes characterized by feelings of closeness, usually brought on by sharing personal thoughts and feelings. These friendships are also

Mutual trust is considered to be the centerpiece of friendship during middle childhood.

somewhat exclusive. By the end of middle childhood, children seek friends who will be loyal, and they view friendship less in terms of shared activities than in terms of the psychological benefits it brings (Güroglu et al., 2007).

GENDER AND FRIENDSHIPS: THE SEX SEGREGATION OF MIDDLE CHILDHOOD

> *Girls rule; boys drool.*
> *Boys are idiots. Girls have cooties.*
> *Boys go to college to get more knowledge; girls go to Jupiter to get more stupider.*

Those are some of the views of elementary school boys and girls regarding members of the other sex. Avoidance of the other sex becomes quite pronounced at this age, with social networks often consisting almost entirely of same-sex groupings (Rancourt et al., 2012; Zosuls et al., 2014; Braun & Davidson, 2016).

Interestingly, this segregation of friendships occurs in almost all societies. In non-industrialized societies, same-gender segregation may result from the types of activities children engage in. For instance, in many cultures, boys are assigned one type of chore and girls another. Participation in different activities may not wholly explain sex segregation, however: Children in more developed countries, who attend the same schools and participate in many of the same activities, still tend to avoid members of the other sex (Whiting & Edwards, 1988; Steinmetz et al., 2014).

When boys and girls make occasional forays into the other gender's territory, the action often has romantic overtones. For instance, girls may threaten to kiss a boy, or boys might try to lure girls into chasing them. Such behavior, termed "border work," emphasizes the clear boundaries between the two sexes. In addition, it may pave the way for adolescent interactions that do involve romantic or sexual interests, when cross-sex interactions become socially endorsed (Lindsey, 2012).

The lack of cross-gender interaction in middle childhood means that boys' and girls' friendships are restricted to their own sex. The nature of friendships within these two groups is quite different.

Boys typically have larger networks of friends, and they tend to play in groups rather than pairing off. Differences in status within the group are usually pronounced, with an acknowledged leader and a hierarchy of members. Because of the fairly rigid rankings that represent the relative social power of those in the group, known as the **dominance hierarchy**, members of higher status can safely question and oppose those lower in the hierarchy (Pedersen et al., 2007; Pun, Birch, & Baron, 2017).

Boys tend to be concerned with their place in the dominance hierarchy, and they attempt to maintain and improve their status. This makes for a style of play known as *restrictive*. In restrictive play, interactions are interrupted when a child feels his

dominance hierarchy
rankings that represent the relative social power of those in a group.

status is challenged. A boy who feels that he is unjustly challenged by a lower-status peer may attempt to end the interaction by scuffling over a toy or otherwise behaving assertively. Consequently, boys tend to play in bursts rather than in more extended, tranquil episodes (Fry, 2005; Estell et al., 2008; Cheng et al., 2016).

Friendship patterns among girls are quite different. Rather than a wide network of friends, girls focus on one or two "best friends." In contrast to boys, who seek out status differences, girls avoid differences, preferring to maintain equal-status friendships. Conflicts among girls are usually solved through compromise, by ignoring the situation, or by giving in rather than by seeking to make one's point of view prevail. The goal is to smooth over disagreements, making social interaction easy and nonconfrontational (Shute & Charlton, 2006).

The Role of Peers in Adolescence

LO 13.3 Explain the important role that peers play in adolescence, and describe the changes that occur in cross-race relationships.

Teenagers' seemingly compulsive need to communicate with friends, exemplified by Facebook, Twitter, and texting, demonstrates the important role that **peers**—individuals who are about the same age or level of maturity—play in adolescence. Continuing the trend that began in middle childhood, adolescents spend increasing amounts of time with their peers, and the importance of peer relationships grows as well. There is probably no period of life in which peer relationships are as important as they are in adolescence. Even peers who are not counted as friends become extraordinarily influential in the lives of adolescents (Engels, Kerr, & Stattin, 2007; Fortuin, van Geel, & Vedder, 2015).

Peers grow in importance in adolescence for a variety of reasons. Peers can help adolescents satisfy personal interests and can provide them with information that they feel they need for their own purposes. For instance, an interest in conservation may cause adolescents to become part of a group dedicated to stamping out pollution. Or they may join a high school Gay, Lesbian, and Bisexual Alliance not only because of their interest in supporting people with different sexual orientations but also because they themselves are questioning their sexual identity.

In addition, some groups provide prestige. Membership on a cheerleading squad or service on the school council may be an honor in some middle schools. (In others, membership on a cheerleading squad or school council may be a source of derision, with prestige reserved for other groups and activities.) Peers also provide a means of social comparison, allowing teens to compare and evaluate their opinions, abilities, and even physical changes with those of others. Peers and peer groups also fill another very important need for this age group: the need to *belong*. (Li & Wright, 2013; Schaefer & Salafia, 2014; Tian, Yu, & Huebner, 2017).

peers

individuals who are about the same age or level of maturity.

CLIQUES AND CROWDS: BELONGING TO A GROUP. When adolescents get together, they are likely to do so in larger groups than those in which they congregated during childhood. During middle and late childhood, typical groups consisted of pairs of children, or perhaps three or four others. In contrast, adolescent groups often consist of larger collectives.

One of the consequences of the increasing cognitive sophistication of adolescents is the ability to group others in more discriminating ways. These groups are characterized by the clothing they wear, their activities, the places they frequent, and even the vocabulary they use. Even

Cathy Yeulet/123RF GB Ltd

The sex segregation of childhood continues during the early stages of adolescence. However, by the time of middle adolescence, this segregation decreases, and boys' and girls' cliques begin to converge.

if they do not belong to the group that they use to compare themselves (*reference groups* present a set of *norms*, or standards, against which adolescents can judge their abilities and social success), adolescents typically are part of some identifiable group. Rather than defining people in concrete terms relating to what they do ("football players" or "musicians") as a younger school-age child might, adolescents use more abstract terms packed with greater subtleties ("jocks" or "skaters" or "stoners") (Cillessen & Borch, 2008).

There are actually two types of groups to which adolescents tend to belong: cliques and crowds. **Cliques** are groups of 2 to 12 people whose members have frequent social interactions with one another. In contrast, **crowds** are larger, comprising individuals who share particular characteristics but who may not interact with one another. For instance, "jocks" and "nerds" are representative of crowds found in many high schools.

Membership in particular cliques and crowds is often determined by the degree of similarity with members of the group. One of the most important dimensions of similarity relates to substance use; adolescents tend to choose friends who use alcohol and other drugs to the same extent that they do. Their friends are also often similar in terms of their academic success, although this is not always true. For instance, during early adolescence, attraction to peers who are particularly well behaved seems to decrease while, at the same time, those who behave more aggressively become more attractive (Hutchinson & Rapee, 2007; Kiuru et al., 2009; Pattiselanno et al., 2015).

Membership in cliques is most obvious during the early years of adolescence. In later stages, the number of liaisons and isolates—those who are not members of a clique—actually increases. In addition, cliques eventually become less distinctive and rigid, and membership in cliques shows a fair amount of turnover. In the later stages of adolescence, cliques become less stable, and social interactions revolve around more flexible groups that are tied together by liaisons who move between members of different groups (Brown & Klute, 2006).

GENDER RELATIONS. As children first enter adolescence, their groups of friends are composed almost universally of same-sex individuals. Boys hang out with boys; girls hang out with girls. Technically, this sex segregation is called the **sex cleavage**.

The situation changes as members of both sexes enter puberty. Boys and girls experience the hormonal surge that marks puberty and causes the maturation of the sex organs. At the same time, societal pressures suggest that the time is appropriate for romantic involvement. These developments lead to a change in the ways adolescents view the opposite sex. Whereas a 10-year-old is likely to see every member of the other sex as "annoying" and "a pain," heterosexual teenage boys and girls begin to regard each other with greater interest in terms of both personality and sexuality.

As they move into puberty, boys' and girls' cliques, which previously had moved along parallel but separate tracks, begin to converge. Adolescents begin to attend boy–girl dances or parties, although mostly the boys still spend their time with boys, and the girls with girls (Richards et al., 1998).

A little later, however, adolescents increasingly spend time with members of the other sex. New cliques emerge, composed of both males and females. Not everyone participates initially: Early on, the teenagers who are leaders of the same-sex cliques and who have the highest status lead the way. Eventually, however, most adolescents find themselves in cliques that include boys and girls.

Cliques and crowds undergo yet another transformation at the end of adolescence: They become less influential and may dissolve as a result of the increased pairing off that occurs.

ONLINE SOCIAL NETWORKS: CYBERSPACE PEERS. Adolescents are increasingly involved in groups comprising people that they've never met in person but with whom they are well acquainted online. Online social networks like Facebook are a growing aspect of adolescent social life, acting as virtual community centers where adolescents socialize, sometimes for hours at a time. Using such social networks, adolescents can make contact with people they know in real life as well as find new individuals with whom to network. However, social network communication does have its drawbacks: It is less personal, and emotion and other nuances of conversations are more difficult to convey.

cliques
(pronounced "kleeks") groups of 2 to 12 people whose members have frequent social interactions with one another.

crowds
in contrast to cliques, crowds are larger and looser groups, comprising individuals who share particular characteristics but who may not interact with one another.

sex cleavage
sex segregation in which boys interact primarily with boys and girls primarily with girls.

Neuroscience and Development
Good as Gold? How Positive Endorsements on Social Media Affect the Brain

What drives the attraction of adolescents and young adults to social media? Is it because these virtual communities stimulate the brain's reward centers in a manner analogous to the way that financial rewards activate the brain?

A recent study examined the social reward of endorsements on photos from Instagram, the commonly used social media site. Researchers wanted to know if these endorsements would activate the same part of the brain that responds to other types of rewards. In particular, they looked at how responses to social media activated the nucleus accumbens, a small structure in the brain that is considered a key hub involved in the neurological processing of rewards. Nucleus accumbens activation is associated with receiving monetary rewards, and this activation increases through childhood, peaking during the mid-to-late adolescent years (Sherman et al., 2016).

In the study, the experimenters showed high school and college student participants different photos from their Instagram accounts, and they manipulated how often the photos appeared to have been endorsed (i.e., "liked") by other users by making it seem as if some of the photos had a lot of endorsements while others had very few endorsements. During this process, the experimenters also measured activity in several areas of the brain, such as the nucleus accumbens (Sherman et al., 2018).

Results of the study demonstrated that when participants were led to believe their photos had received more endorsements, they had greater activation in the nucleus accumbens. In other words, perceived social rewards on social media appear to have a similar effect on the brain as do other types of reinforcement, such as monetary rewards. Overall, this study helps us better understand why young people are drawn to social media use.

■ Considering the finding that activation of some reward processing centers of the brain peak during the mid-to-late adolescent years, how might this help explain the behavior of some adolescents?

Popularity and Peer Pressure

LO 13.4 Identify the four categories of popularity, and summarize the qualities of popular adolescents.

Most adolescents have well-tuned antennae when it comes to determining who is popular and who is not. In fact, for some teenagers, concerns over popularity—or lack of it—may be a central focus of their lives.

PERSONAL QUALITIES AND POPULARITY. It's hardly surprising that adolescents' personal qualities—their personality, intelligence, and social skills—are significant factors in determining their level of popularity. Those with positive qualities are more popular than those with more disagreeable qualities.

What are the positive qualities that matter during adolescence? Popular boys and girls have high emotional intelligence, knowing how to act appropriately in a particular situation. They are enjoyable to be around—friendly, cheerful, smart, and with a good sense of humor.

But the sheer number of qualities is not the whole story. Sometimes adolescents prefer those who have at least a few negative qualities over those who are seemingly flawless. The negative aspects of their personality make them more human and approachable (Hawley, 2003).

Furthermore, some less-than-admirable qualities are associated with popularity. For example, adolescents who lie most effectively are more popular than those who lie less well. The explanation is not that lying produces popularity. Instead, effective lying may act as a kind of social skill, allowing an adolescent to say the right thing at the right moment. In contrast, adolescents who are always truthful may hurt others' feelings with their bluntness (Feldman, Tomasian, & Coats, 1999; Feldman, Forrest, & Happ, 2002).

Developmental Diversity and Your Life

Race Segregation: The Great Divide of Adolescence

When Robert Corker, a student at Tufts University, first stepped into the gym, he was immediately pulled into a pick-up basketball game. "The guys thought I'd be good at basketball just because I'm tall and black. Actually, I stink at sports and quickly changed their minds. Fortunately we all laughed about it later," Robert says.

* * *

When Sandra Cantú, a Puerto Rican nursing student at the University of Alabama, entered the cafeteria wearing her hospital whites, two female students assumed she was a cafeteria worker and asked her to clear off their table.

* * *

Race relations can also be difficult for white students to manage. Ted Connors, a white senior at Southern Methodist, recalls the day he asked a student in his dorm for help with his Spanish homework. "He laughed in my face," Ted recalls, "I assumed he spoke Spanish just because his name was Hector Gonzalez. Actually, he had grown up in Michigan and spoke only English. It took quite a while to live that one down."

The pattern of race segregation experienced by these students is repeated over and over in schools and colleges throughout the United States: Even when they attend desegregated schools with significant ethnic and racial diversity, people of different ethnicities and races interact relatively little. Moreover, even if they have a friend of a different ethnicity within the confines of a school, most adolescents don't interact with cross-race friends outside of school (Hamm, Brown, & Heck, 2005; Benner & Wang, 2017).

It doesn't start out this way. During elementary school and even during early adolescence, there is a fair amount of integration among students of differing ethnicities. However, by middle and late adolescence, the amount of segregation is striking (Mouw & Entwisle, 2006).

Why should racial and ethnic segregation be the rule, even in schools that have been desegregated for some time? One reason is that minority students may actively seek support from others who share their minority status (where "minority" is used in its sociological sense to indicate a subordinate group whose members lack power, compared to members of a dominant group). By associating primarily with other members of their own group, members of minority groups are able to affirm their own identity.

Members of different racial and ethnic groups may be segregated in the classroom as well. Adolescents who are members of groups that have been historically discriminated against tend to experience less school success than members of the majority group. It may be that ethnic and racial segregation in high school is based not on ethnicity itself but on academic achievement.

If minority group members experience less academic success, they may find themselves in classes with proportionally fewer majority group members. Similarly, majority students may be in classes with few minority students. Such class assignment practices, then, may inadvertently maintain and promote racial and ethnic segregation. This pattern would be particularly prevalent in schools where rigid academic tracking is practiced, with students assigned to "low," "medium," and "high" tracks depending on their prior achievement (Lucas & Berends, 2002).

The lack of contact among students of different racial and ethnic backgrounds in school may also reflect prejudice, both perceived and real, toward members of other groups. Students of color may feel that the white majority is prejudiced, discriminatory, and hostile, and they may prefer to stick to same-race groups. Conversely, white students may assume that minority group members are antagonistic and unfriendly. Such mutually destructive attitudes reduce the likelihood that meaningful interaction can take place (Phinney, Ferguson, & Tate, 1997; Tropp, 2003).

Is this sort of voluntary segregation along racial and ethnic lines found during adolescence inevitable? No. Adolescents who have interacted regularly and extensively with those of different races earlier in their lives are more likely to have friends of different races. Schools that actively promote contact among members of different ethnicities in classes help create an environment in which cross-race friendships can flourish. Furthermore, having friends of another race helps minority group members deal with discrimination they may encounter (Hewstone, 2003; Davies et al., 2011; Benner & Wang, 2017).

Still, the task is daunting. Many societal pressures act to keep members of different races from interacting with one another. Peer pressure, too, may encourage this as some cliques may actively promote norms that discourage group members from crossing racial and ethnic lines to form new friendships.

Figure 13-1 The Social World of Adolescence

An adolescent's popularity can fall into one of four categories, depending on the opinions of his or her peers. Popularity is related to differences in status, behavior, and adjustment.

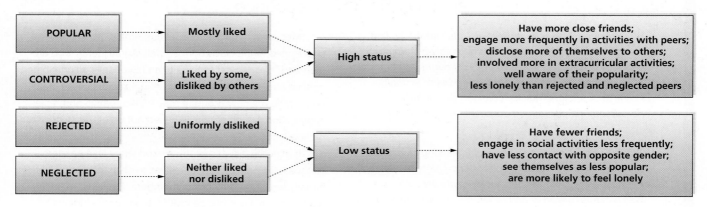

Culture also plays a role in determining what qualities are associated with popularity. In Western cultures, for example, extroversion is related to popularity, while introverted adolescents are generally less popular. In contrast, in Asian cultures, shyness is viewed as a desirable trait, and introversion is more closely related to popularity (Chen et al., 2002).

controversial adolescents
adolescents who are liked by some and disliked by others.

rejected adolescents
adolescents who are uniformly disliked.

neglected adolescents
adolescents who are neither liked nor disliked.

POPULARITY AND REJECTION. Actually, the social world of adolescents is divided not only into popular and unpopular individuals; the differentiations are more complex (see Figure 13-1). For instance, some adolescents are controversial; in contrast to *popular* adolescents, who are mostly liked, **controversial adolescents** are liked by some and disliked by others. For example, a controversial adolescent may be highly popular within a particular group such as the string orchestra but not popular among other classmates. Furthermore, there are **rejected adolescents**, who are uniformly disliked, and **neglected adolescents**, who are neither liked nor disliked. Neglected adolescents are the forgotten students—the ones whose status is so low that they are overlooked by almost everyone.

In most cases, popular and controversial adolescents tend to be similar in that their overall status is higher, while rejected and neglected adolescents share a generally lower status. Popular and controversial adolescents have more close friends, engage more frequently in activities with their peers, and disclose more about themselves to others than less popular students. They are also more involved in extracurricular school activities. In addition, they are well aware of their popularity, and they are less lonely than their less popular classmates (Zettergren, 2004; Becker & Luthar, 2007; Gommans et al., 2015).

In contrast, the social world of rejected and neglected adolescents is considerably less pleasant. They have fewer friends, engage in social activities less frequently, and have less contact with the opposite sex. They see themselves—accurately, it turns out—as less popular, and they are more likely to feel lonely (Woodhouse, Dykas, & Cassidy, 2012).

Changing Relations with Relations in Adolescence

LO 13.5 Explain how adolescents' quest for autonomy affects relationships in the family.

When Paco Lizzagara entered junior high school, his relationship with his parents changed drastically. What had been a good relationship had become tense by the middle of seventh grade. Paco felt his parents always seemed to "be on his case." Instead of giving him more freedom, they actually seemed to be becoming more restrictive.

Paco's parents would probably see things differently. They would likely suggest that they were not the source of the tension in the household—Paco was. From their point of view, Paco, with whom they'd established what seemed to be a close, stable, loving relationship throughout much of his childhood, suddenly seemed transformed. They felt he was shutting them out of his life, and when he did speak with them, it was merely to criticize their politics, their dress, their preferences in TV shows. To his parents, Paco's behavior was upsetting and bewildering.

THE QUEST FOR AUTONOMY.   Parents are sometimes angered, and even more frequently puzzled, by adolescents' conduct. Children who have previously accepted their parents' judgments, declarations, and guidelines begin to question—and sometimes rebel against—their parents' views of the world.

One reason for these clashes is the shift in roles that both children and parents must deal with during adolescence. Adolescents increasingly seek **autonomy**, independence, and a sense of control over their own lives. Most parents intellectually realize that this shift is a normal part of adolescence, representing one of the primary developmental tasks of the period, and in many ways they welcome it as a sign of their children's growth. However, in many cases, the day-to-day realities of adolescents' increasing autonomy may prove difficult for them to deal with. But understanding this growing independence intellectually and agreeing to allow a teen to attend a party when no parents will be present are two different things. To the adolescent, her parents' refusal indicates a lack of trust or confidence. To the parent, it's simply good sense.

In most families, teenagers' autonomy grows gradually over the course of adolescence. For instance, one study of changes in adolescents' views of their parents found that increasing autonomy led them to perceive parents less in idealized terms and more as persons in their own right. For example, rather than seeing their parents as authoritarian disciplinarians mindlessly reminding them to do their homework, they may come to see their parents' emphasis on excelling in school as evidence of parental regrets about their own lack of education and a wish to see their children have more options in life. At the same time, adolescents come to depend more on themselves and to feel more like separate individuals (see Figure 13-2).

The increase in adolescent autonomy changes the relationship between parents and teenagers. At the start of adolescence, the relationship tends to be asymmetrical: Parents hold most of the power and influence over the relationship. By the end of adolescence, power and influence have become more balanced, and parents and children end up in a more symmetrical, or egalitarian, relationship. Power and influence are shared, although parents typically retain the upper hand.

THE MYTH OF THE GENERATION GAP.   Teen movies often depict adolescents and their parents with totally opposing points of view about the world. For example, the parent of an environmentalist teen might turn out to own a polluting factory. These exaggerations are often funny because we assume there is a kernel of truth in them, in that parents and teenagers often don't see things the same way. According to this argument, there is a **generation gap**, a deep divide between parents and children in attitudes, values, aspirations, and worldviews.

The reality, however, is quite different. The generation gap, when it exists, is really quite narrow. Adolescents and their parents tend to see eye to eye in a variety of domains. Republican parents generally have Republican children; members of the Christian right have children who espouse similar views; parents who advocate for abortion rights have children who are similar. On social, political, and religious issues, parents and adolescents tend to be in synch, and children's worries mirror those of their parents. Adolescents' concerns about society's problems (see Figure 13-3) are those with which most adults would probably agree (Knafo & Schwartz, 2003; Smetana, 2005; Grønhøj & Thøgersen, 2012).

As we've said, most adolescents and their parents get along quite well. Despite their quest for autonomy and independence, most adolescents have deep love, affection, and respect for their parents—and parents feel

autonomy
the development and expression of independence.

generation gap
a divide between adolescence and other periods of life that supposedly reflects profound differences in behavior, values, attitudes, lifestyle choices, and experiences.

Figure 13-2 Changing Views of Parents

As adolescents become older, they come to perceive their parents in less idealized terms and more as individuals. What effect is this likely to have on family relations?
(**Source:** Based on Steinberg & Silverberg, 1986.)

- - - **Parents as people**
—— **Nondependent on parents**
- - - **Parents as less ideal**
— — **Parents as individuals**

Figure 13-3 What's the Problem?

Parents are likely to agree with their adolescent children's views of society's ills.
(**Source:** PRIMEDIA/Roper National Youth Survey, 1999.)

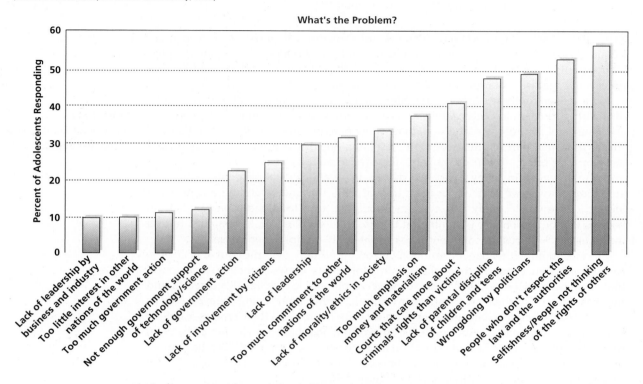

the same way about their children. Although some parent–adolescent relationships are seriously troubled, the majority of relationships are more positive than negative and help adolescents avoid peer pressure (Black, 2002; Jager et al., 2015).

Even though adolescents spend decreasing amounts of time with their families in general, the amount of time they spend alone with each parent remains remarkably stable across adolescence (see Figure 13-4). In short, there is no evidence suggesting

Figure 13-4 Time Spent by Adolescents with Parents

Despite their quest for autonomy and independence, most adolescents have deep love, affection, and respect for their parents, and the amount of time they spend alone with each parent (the lower two segments) remains remarkably stable across adolescence.
(**Source:** Larson et al., 1996.)

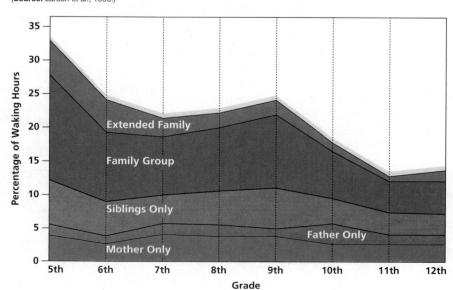

that family problems are worse during adolescence than at any other stage of development (Granic, Hollenstein, & Dishion, 2003).

Maintaining Social Networks: The Importance of Friendship in Adulthood

LO 13.6 **Summarize the importance of friendships in adulthood, and identify the characteristics adults look for in a friend.**

Tara Daley, a widow in her 50s, joined a writing workshop after her youngest child left home and her husband died. While she enjoys the writing exercises and respects the instructor, the real reason Tara signed up for the workshop was to meet new people. "There are 20 people in the class, so I figured I could probably find at least one friend among the group," she says. Tara ended up making three new friends, all women in their 50s and 60s whose children are grown and who have found themselves alone through widowhood or divorce. "I love to shop for antiques with Doreen, swap gardening tips with Anna, and go to concerts with Grace," Tara says. "I never have to be alone except when I want to be."

Like Tara, most of our relationships with others involve friends, and for most people, maintaining such relationships is an important part of adult life. Why? One reason is that the basic need for belonging we saw in adolescents continues to lead people to establish and maintain at least a minimum number of relationships with others throughout adulthood. Most people are driven toward forming and preserving relationships that allow them to experience a sense of belonging with others (Fiske & Yamamoto, 2005).

WHAT MAKES FOR FRIENDSHIP IN ADULTHOOD? How do particular people end up becoming our friends? One of the most important reasons is simple proximity—people form friendships with others who live nearby and with whom they come in contact most frequently. Because of their accessibility, people who are in close proximity can obtain rewards of friendship, such as companionship, social approval, and the occasional helping hand, at relatively little cost.

Similarity also plays an important role in friendship formation. Birds of a feather *do* flock together: People are more attracted to others who hold attitudes and values similar to their own (Morry, 2007; Preciado et al., 2012; Fiori & Denckla, 2015).

The importance of similarity becomes particularly evident when we consider cross-race friendships. As we noted earlier, by the time of adolescence, the number of cross-race close friendships dwindles, a pattern that continues throughout the remainder of the life span. In fact, although most adults who are surveyed claim to have a close friend of a different race, when they are queried regarding the names of close friends, few include a person of a different race (see Figure 13-5).

We also choose friends on the basis of their personal qualities. What's most important? People are most attracted to others who keep confidences and are loyal, warm, and affectionate. In addition, we like those who are supportive, helpful, and provide a sense of security (Hossfeld, 2008; You & Bellmore, 2012).

THE SOCIAL NETWORKS OF LATER ADULTHOOD. Older adults enjoy friends as much as younger people do, and friendships play an important role in the lives of those in late adulthood. Time spent with friends is often valued more highly during late adulthood than time spent with family, and friends are often seen as more important providers of support than family members. Furthermore, around a third of older persons report that they made a new friend within the past year, and many older adults engage in significant interaction with others.

Figure 13-5 Rephrasing the Question

Although a relatively high percentage of whites and blacks claim to have a close friend who is a member of a different race, only a small majority actually name a person of another race or ethnicity when asked to list the names of their close friends.
(**Source:** General Social Survey, 1998.)

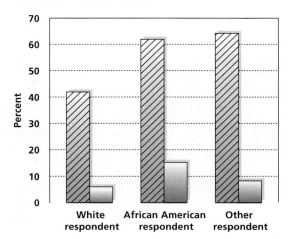

Percent who say they have a close friend who is black or white

Percent who name a close friend who is of a different race

Figure 13-6 Benefits of Growing Older

People 65 and older cite a number of aspects of growing old that are positive. Chief among them are more time with family.

(**Source:** Pew Research Center, 2009.)

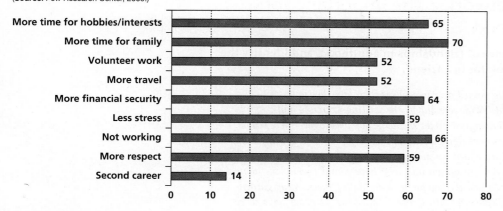

More time for hobbies/interests — 65
More time for family — 70
Volunteer work — 52
More travel — 52
More financial security — 64
Less stress — 59
Not working — 66
More respect — 59
Second career — 14

In fact, more time for friends and family is one of the biggest benefits of growing older (Pew Research Center, 2009; see Figure 13-6).

One reason for the importance of friendship relates to the element of control. In friendship relationships, unlike family relationships, we choose whom we like and whom we dislike, meaning that we have considerable control. Because late adulthood may bring with it a gradual loss of control in other areas, such as in one's health, the ability to maintain friendships may take on more importance than in other stages of life (Pruchno & Rosenbaum, 2003; Stevens, Martina, & Westerhof, 2006; Singh & Srivastava, 2014).

In addition, friendships—especially those that have developed recently—may be more flexible than family ties, given that recent friendships are not likely to have a history of obligations and past conflicts. In contrast, family ties may have a long and sometimes stormy record that can reduce the emotional sustenance they provide (Monsour, 2002; Hansson, Daleiden, & Hayslip, 2004; Lester et al., 2012).

Another reason for the importance of friendships in late adulthood relates to the increasing likelihood, over time, that one will be without a marital partner. When a spouse dies, people typically seek out the companionship of friends to help deal with their loss and also for some of the companionship that was provided by the deceased spouse.

Of course, it isn't only spouses who die during old age; friends die too. The way adults view friendship in late adulthood determines how vulnerable they are to the death of a friend. On the one hand, if the friendship has been defined as irreplaceable, then the loss of the friend may be quite difficult. On the other hand, if the friendship is defined as one of many friendships, then the death of a friend may be less traumatic. In such cases, older adults are more likely to become involved subsequently with new friends (Hansson et al., 2004).

social support

assistance and comfort supplied by a network of caring, interested people. Such support plays a critical role in successful aging.

It has been found that the benefits of social support are considerable for both the provider and the receiver. What is the importance of reciprocity as a factor of social support?

SOCIAL SUPPORT: THE SIGNIFICANCE OF OTHERS. Friendships also provide one of the basic social needs: social support. **Social support** is assistance and comfort supplied by a network of caring, interested people. Such support plays a critical role in successful aging (Gow et al., 2007; Evans, 2009; Li, Xu, & Li, 2014).

The benefits of social support are considerable. For instance, people can provide emotional support by lending a sympathetic ear and providing a sounding board for friends' concerns. Furthermore, social support from people who are experiencing similar problems—such as the loss of a spouse—can provide an unmatched degree of understanding and a pool of helpful suggestions for coping strategies that would be less credible coming from others.

Finally, people can furnish material support, such as helping with rides or picking up groceries. They can provide help in solving problems, such as dealing with a difficult landlord or fixing a broken appliance.

Module 13.1 Review

LO 13.1 Summarize the development of social relationships in the preschool years, and describe the types of play preschoolers engage in.

In the preschool years, children develop friendships on the basis of personal characteristics, trust, and shared interests. The character of preschoolers' play changes over time, growing more sophisticated, interactive, and cooperative, and relying increasingly on social skills.

LO 13.2 Identify the three major stages of friendship in middle childhood, and explain how friendship patterns differ across gender.

Children's understanding of friendship changes from the sharing of enjoyable activities, through the consideration of personal traits that can meet their needs, to a focus on intimacy and loyalty.

LO 13.3 Explain the important role that peers play in adolescence, and describe the changes that occur in cross-race relationships.

Peer groups are of great importance during adolescence, providing a way to meet personal interests, acquire information, and gain prestige. Cliques and crowds serve as reference groups in adolescence and offer a ready means of social comparison. Sex cleavage gradually diminishes, until boys and girls begin to pair off. Racial separation increases during adolescence, bolstered by socioeconomic status

differences, different academic experiences, and mutually distrustful attitudes.

LO 13.4 Identify the four categories of popularity, and summarize the qualities of popular adolescents.

Degrees of popularity in adolescence include popular, controversial, neglected, and rejected adolescents.

LO 13.5 Explain how adolescents' quest for autonomy affects relationships in the family.

Adolescents increasingly seek autonomy, independence, and a sense of control over their own lives. This can have effects on their family relationships.

LO 13.6 Summarize the importance of friendships in adulthood, and identify the characteristics adults look for in a friend.

Friendships are very important in adult life, providing social support and companionship from peers who are likely to understand the adult's feelings and problems.

Journal Writing Prompt

Applying Lifespan Development: Do you think TV and movie portrayals of popular and unpopular characters in high school settings are helpful or harmful to adolescents wrestling with popularity issues? Why?

MODULE 13.2

FAMILY LIFE

Consider this quote from a spouse who just became a parent:

> We had no idea what we were getting into when our first child was born. We certainly prepared for the event, reading magazine articles and books and even attending a class on childcare. But when Sheanna was actually born, the sheer enormity of the task of taking care of her, her presence at every moment of the day, and the awesome responsibility of raising another human being weighed on us like nothing else we'd ever faced. Not that it was a burden. But it did make us look at the world with an entirely different perspective.

There are no rehearsals for parenthood, no one-size-fits-all blueprint for creating a family. Family life in the 21st century, as we shall see, is diverse, complex, and often stressful. Nevertheless, most married couples choose to have children. And with that choice, they start down a road they will travel the rest of their lives.

Parenthood Today: Choosing to Have Children

LO 13.7 Summarize the challenges couples face in deciding to have children, and identify successful coping strategies.

Whether to have children is one of the most important decisions couples make. What makes a couple decide to have children? Childrearing certainly isn't economically advantageous: According to the U.S. government, a middle-class family with two children spends around $235,000 for each child by the time the child reaches age 18. Add in the costs of college and the figure comes to over $300,000 per child. And if you take into account the cost of care provided by families for their children, the total costs of caring for children are at least twice as high as the government estimates (Lino & Carlson, 2009; Folbre, 2012).

Instead, young adults typically cite psychological reasons for having children. They expect to derive pleasure from watching their children grow, fulfillment from their children's accomplishments, satisfaction from seeing them become successful, and enjoyment from forging a close bond with their children. But there also may be a self-serving element in the decision to have children. For example, parents-to-be may hope that their children will provide for them in their old age, maintain a family business or farm, or simply offer companionship. Others have children because to do so is such a strong societal norm: More than 90 percent of all married couples have at least one child, although most Americans prefer smaller families over larger ones (Saad, 2011).

For some couples, there is no decision to have children. Some children are unplanned, the result of the failure or absence of birth control methods. In some cases, the couple may have planned to have children at some point in the future, and so the pregnancy is not regarded as particularly undesirable and may even be welcomed. But in families that had actively not wanted to have children, or already had what they considered "enough" children, such a pregnancy can be viewed as problematic (Leathers & Kelley, 2000; Pajulo, Helenius, & MaYes, 2006).

The couples who are most likely to have unwanted pregnancies are often the most vulnerable in society. Unplanned pregnancies occur most frequently in younger, poorer, and less educated couples. Happily, the incidence of undesired pregnancies is considerably lower than it was several decades ago, largely due to a dramatic rise in the use and effectiveness of contraceptives. However, the rate of unwanted pregnancies in the United States is still higher than that for women in many other industrialized countries (Finer & Zola, 2016).

For many young adults, the decision to have children is independent of marriage. Although most women (59 percent) are married when they have children, more than half of births to women in the United States under age 30 now occur outside of marriage. The only demographic group for which this is not true is young adult women with a college education; they overwhelmingly still choose to be married before having children (DeParle & Tavernise, 2012).

THE TRANSITION TO PARENTHOOD: TWO'S A COUPLE, THREE'S A CROWD? The arrival of a child alters virtually every aspect of family life, in positive and sometimes negative ways. The addition of a child to a household brings about a dramatic shift in the roles spouses must play. They are suddenly placed in new roles—"mother" and "father"—and these new positions may overwhelm their ability to respond in their older, though continuing, roles of "wife" and "husband." In addition, the birth of a child produces significant physical and psychological demands, including near-constant fatigue, new financial responsibilities, and an increase in household chores (Meijer & van den Wittenboer, 2007).

Furthermore, in contrast to many non-Western cultures, in which childrearing is seen as a task that involves the entire community, Western culture's emphasis on individualism makes childrearing a primarily private enterprise. Thus, mothers and fathers in Western society are largely left to forge their own paths after the birth of a child, often without significant community support (Rubin & Chung, 2006; Lamm & Keller, 2007).

Consequently, for many couples, the strains accompanying the birth of a child produce the lowest level of marital satisfaction of any point in their marriage. This is particularly true for women, who tend to be more dissatisfied than men with their marriages after the arrival of children. The most likely reason for this gender difference is that wives often experience a greater increase in their responsibilities than husbands do, even in families in which parents seek to share childrearing chores (Laflamme, Pomerleau, & Malcuit, 2002; Lu, 2006; Falconier et al., 2015).

At the same time, not all couples experience a decrease in marital satisfaction upon the birth of a child. According to work by John Gottman and colleagues (Shapiro, Gottman, & Carrère, 2000; Wilson & Gottman, 2002), marital satisfaction can remain steady, and actually rise, with the birth of a child. They identified three factors that permitted couples to successfully weather the increased stress that follows the birth of a child:

- Working to build fondness and affection toward one's partner
- Remaining aware of events in one's spouse's life and responding to those events
- Considering problems as controllable and solvable

In particular, those couples who were well satisfied with their marriages as newlyweds were more likely to continue to be satisfied as they raised their children. Couples who harbor realistic expectations regarding the extent of childrearing effort and other household responsibilities they face when children are born also tend to be more satisfied after they become parents. Furthermore, parents who work together as a *co-parenting team,* in which they thoughtfully adopt common childrearing goals and strategies, are more apt to be satisfied with their parenting roles (Schoppe-Sullivan et al., 2006; McHale & Rotman, 2007).

In short, having children can well lead to greater marital satisfaction—at least for couples who are already satisfied with their marriage. For marriages in which satisfaction is low, having children may make a bad situation worse (Shapiro, Gottman, & Carrère, 2000; Driver, Tabares, & Shapiro, 2003).

POVERTY AND FAMILY LIFE.   Children living in families that are economically disadvantaged face significant hardships. Poor families have fewer basic everyday resources, and there are more disruptions in children's lives. For example, parents may be forced to look for less expensive housing or may move the entire household in order to find work. The result frequently is family environments in which parents are less responsive to their children's needs and provide less social support (Evans, 2004).

The stress of difficult family environments, along with other stress in the lives of poor children—such as living in unsafe neighborhoods with high rates of violence and attending inferior schools—ultimately takes its toll. Economically disadvantaged children are at risk for poorer academic performance, higher rates of aggression, and conduct problems. In addition, declines in economic well-being are linked to physical and mental health problems. Specifically, the chronic stress associated with poverty makes children more susceptible to cardiovascular disease, depression, and Type 2 diabetes (Morales & Guerra, 2006; Tracy et al., 2008; Duncan, Magnuson & Votruba-Drzal, 2017).

Changing Times: Family Life in the 21st Century

LO 13.8 Identify the changes that have occurred in family life in the past 50 years, and give examples of their impact on both parents and children.

A look back at television shows of the 1950s (such as *Leave It to Beaver*) finds a world of families portrayed in a way that today seems oddly old-fashioned and quaint: mothers and fathers, married for years, and their good-looking children making their way in a world that seems to have few, if any, serious problems.

Even in the 1950s such a view of family life was overly romantic and unrealistic. Today, however, it is broadly inaccurate, representing only a minority of families in the United States. A quick review tells the story:

- The number of single-parent families has increased significantly in the past three decades, as the number of two-parent households has declined. Currently, 65 percent of children ages 0–17 live with two married parents, down from 77 percent in 1980. Nearly a quarter of children live with only their mothers, 4 percent live with only their fathers, and 4 percent live with neither of their parents (Childstats.gov, 2017).

- The average size of families is shrinking. Today, on average, there are 2.58 persons per household, compared to 3.14 in 1970. The number of people living in nonfamily households (without any relatives) is 39 million (U.S. Census Bureau, 2017b).

- Although the number of adolescents giving birth has declined substantially over the past 20 years, there are still nearly 10 per 1,000 births to adolescent women ages 15 to 17, the vast majority of whom are unmarried (Childstats.gov, 2017).

- The labor force participation rate of mothers with infants is just under 60 percent (U.S. Bureau of Labor Statistics, 2017).

- In 2016, 41 percent of children under age 18 lived in low-income households, down from 45 percent in 2010. Sixty-one percent of black children, 59 percent of Hispanic children, and 60 percent of American Indian children live in low-income families (National Center for Children in Poverty, 2018).

At the very least, these statistics suggest that many children are being raised in environments in which substantial stressors are present. Such stress makes it unusually difficult to raise children—never easy even under the best circumstances.

However, society is adapting to the new realities of family life in the 21st century. Several kinds of social support exist for the parents of infants, and society is evolving new institutions to help in their care. One example is the growing array of child-care arrangements available to help working parents.

FAMILY SIZE. As we noted earlier, one of the major recent changes in family life is family size. The availability and use of effective contraceptives has dramatically decreased the number of children in the average American family. Almost 70 percent of Americans polled in the 1930s agreed that the ideal number of children was three or more, but by the 1990s the percentage had shrunk to less than 40 percent. Today, most families seek to have no more than two children—although most say that three or more is ideal if money is no object (see Figure 13-7; Gallup Poll, 2004; Saad, 2011).

Figure 13-7 Smaller Is Better

Continuing trends over the past 75 years, U.S. parents continue to prefer families with fewer children. What do you think is the ideal number of children for a family to have?
(**Source:** Saad, 2011.)

Americans' Ideal Number of Children for a Family, 1936–2011

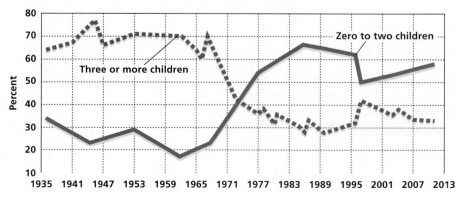

These preferences have been translated into changes in the actual birth rate. In 1957, the *fertility rate* reached a post–World War II peak in the United States of 3.7 children per woman and then began to decline. Today, the rate is at 1.9 children per woman, which is less than the *replacement level*, the number of children that one generation must produce to be able to replenish its numbers. In contrast, in some underdeveloped countries, such as Niger, the fertility rate is as high as 6.5 (*World Factbook*, 2017).

What has produced this decline in the fertility rate? In addition to the availability of more reliable birth control methods, one reason is that increasing numbers of women have joined the workforce. The pressures of simultaneously holding a job and raising a child have convinced many women to have fewer children.

Furthermore, many women who work outside the home are choosing to have children later in their child-bearing years in order to develop their careers. In fact, women between the ages of 30 and 34 are the only ones whose rate of births has actually increased over earlier de-cades. Still, because women who have their first children in their 30s have fewer years in which to have children, they ultimately cannot have as many children as women who begin childbearing in their 20s. In addition, research suggesting that there are health benefits for mothers in terms of spacing children further apart may lead families to ultimately have fewer children (Marcus, 2004).

Some of the traditional incentives for having children—such as their potential for providing economic support in old age—may also no longer be as attractive. Potential parents may view Social Security and other pensions as a more predictable means of support when they are elderly than relying on their children. There is also, as mentioned earlier, the sheer cost of raising a child, particularly the well-publicized increase in the cost of college. This, too, may act as a disincentive for bearing larger numbers of children.

Finally, some couples avoid having children because they fear they will not be good parents or simply don't want the work and responsibility involved in childrearing. Women may also fear that they will share a disproportionate amount of the effort involved in childrearing—a perception that may be an accurate reading of reality, as we will discuss next.

As increasing numbers of women have joined the workforce, more are choosing to have fewer children and have them later.

DUAL-EARNER COUPLES. One of the major historical shifts affecting young adults that began in the last half of the 20th century is the increase in families in which both parents work. Close to three-quarters of married women with school-age children are employed outside the home, and more than half of mothers with children under age 6 are working. In the mid-1960s, only 17 percent of mothers of 1-year-olds worked full time; now, more than 50 percent do. In the majority of families, both husband and wife work (Barnett & Hyde, 2001; Matias et al., 2017).

For married couples who both work and have no children, the combined total of paid (in the office) and unpaid work (the chores at home) is nearly identical, at 8 hours 11 minutes for men, and 8 hours 3 minutes for women. And even for those families who have children under age 18, women who are employed full time do only 20 minutes more of combined paid and unpaid work (Konigsberg, 2011). Of course, the nature of husbands' and wives' contributions to the household often differ. For instance, husbands tend to carry out chores such as mowing the lawn or house repairs that are more easily scheduled in advance (or some-times postponed) and often can be carried out on the weekend. In contrast, women's house-hold chores tend to be devoted to things that need immediate attention, such as child-care and meal preparation, and often can't be sched-uled on the weekend or put off. As a result, wives experience greater levels of anxiety and stress (Bureau of Labor Statistics, 2012; Ogolsky, Dennison, & Monk, 2014; see Figure 13-8).

Figure 13-8 Division of Labor

Although husbands and wives generally work at their paying jobs a similar number of hours each week, wives are apt to spend more time than their husbands doing home chores and in child-care activities. Why do you think this pattern exists?
(**Source:** Bureau of Labor Statistics, 2012.)

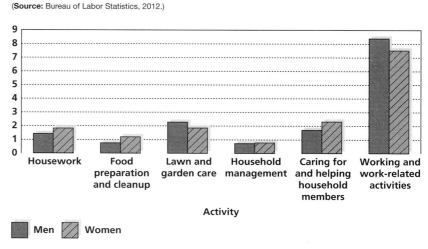

Note: Figures refer to average hours per day for persons who engaged in the activity.

Family Constellations: The Array of Possibilities

LO 13.9 Identify the various family constellations, and summarize the impact of divorce on children.

Tamara's mother, Brenda, waited outside the door of her second-grade classroom for the end of the school day. Tamara came over to greet her mother as soon as she spotted her. "Mom, can Anna come over to play today?" Tamara demanded. Brenda had been looking forward to spending some time alone with Tamara, who had spent the last three days at her dad's house. But, Brenda reflected, Tamara hardly ever got to ask kids over after school, so she agreed to the request. Unfortunately, it turned out today wouldn't work for Anna's family, so they tried to find an alternate date. "How about Thursday?" Anna's mother suggested. Before Tamara could reply, her mother reminded her, "You'll have to ask your dad. You're at his house that night." Tamara's expectant face fell. "OK," she mumbled.

How will Tamara's adjustment be affected from dividing her time between the two homes where she lives with her divorced parents? If her mother should remarry a man who also has children, will Tamara's life become more complicated even though there will be two adults in the house? These are just a few of the questions we need to consider as we look at the ways that children's home life affects their lives.

THE IMPACT OF DIVORCE ON CHILDREN. Having divorced parents, like Tamara, is no longer very distinctive. Only around half the children in the United States spend their entire childhoods living in the same household with both their parents. The rest will live in single-parent homes or with stepparents, grandparents, or other nonparental relatives, and some will end up in foster care (Harvey & Fine, 2004; Nicholson et al., 2014).

How do children react to divorce? The answer depends on how soon you ask the question following a divorce as well as how old the children are at the time of the divorce. Immediately after a divorce, both children and parents may show several types of psychological maladjustment for a period that may last from six months to two years. For instance, children may be anxious, experience depression, or show sleep disturbances and phobias. Even though children most often live with their mothers following a divorce, the quality of the mother–child relationship declines in the majority of cases, often because children see themselves caught in the middle between their mothers and fathers (Maes, De Mol, & Buysse, 2012).

During the early stage of middle childhood, children whose parents are divorcing often blame themselves for the breakup. By age 10, children feel pressure to choose sides, taking the position of either the mother or the father. As a result, they experience some degree of divided loyalty (Hipke, Wolchik, & Sandler, 2010).

Although researchers agree that the short-term consequences of divorce can be quite difficult, the longer-term consequences are less clear. Some studies have found that 18 months to 2 years later, most children begin to return to their predivorce state of psychological adjustment. For many children, there are minimal long-term consequences (Guttmann & Rosenberg, 2003; Harvey & Fine, 2004; Schaan & Vögele, 2016).

However, other evidence suggests that the fallout from divorce lingers. For example, twice as many children of divorced parents enter psychological counseling as children from intact families (although sometimes counseling is mandated by a judge as part of the divorce). In addition, people who have experienced parental divorce are more at risk for experiencing divorce themselves later in life (Uphold-Carrier & Utz, 2012; South, 2013; Mahrer & Wolchik, 2017).

How children react to divorce depends on several factors. One is the economic standing of the family the child is living with. In many cases, divorce brings a decline in both parents' standard of living. When this occurs, children may be thrown into poverty (Ozawa & Yoon, 2003).

In other cases, the negative consequences of divorce are less severe because the divorce reduces the hostility and anger in the home. If the household before the divorce was overwhelmed by parental strife—as is the case in around 30 percent of divorces—the greater calm of a post-divorce household may be beneficial to children. This is particularly true for children who maintain a close, positive relationship with the parent with whom they do not live (Davies et al., 2002).

For some children, then, divorce is an improvement over living with parents who have an intact but unhappy marriage that is high in conflict. But in about 70 percent of divorces, the predivorce level of conflict is not high, and children in these households may have a more difficult time adjusting to divorce (Lippman & Lewis, 2008; Amato & Afifi, 2006).

LIVING IN BLENDED FAMILIES.   For many children, the aftermath of divorce includes the subsequent remarriage of one or both parents. More than 10 million households in the United States contain at least one spouse who has remarried. More

Based on current trends, almost three-quarters of American children will spend some portion of their lives in a single-parent family. What are some possible consequences for a child in a single-parent family?

than 5 million remarried couples have at least one stepchild living with them in what have come to be called **blended families**. Overall, 17 percent of all children in the United States live in blended families (Bengtson et al., 2004; Zeleznikow & Zeleznikow, 2015).

Living in a blended family is challenging for the children involved. There often is a fair amount of *role ambiguity*, in which roles and expectations are unclear. Children may be uncertain about their responsibilities, how to behave toward stepparents and stepsiblings, and how to make a host of decisions that have wide-ranging implications for their role in the family. For instance, a child in a blended family may have to

blended families
a family consisting of remarried couples with at least one stepchild living with them.

From Research to Practice

Parent Education: Helping Children Cope with a Divorce

Most parents contemplating the possibility of divorce worry about the effect that this major life change will have on their children. The first year or two after the divorce can be a particularly challenging time for children. Fortunately, after this initial difficult period, many children begin to adjust to this new family dynamic without lasting psychological harm. However, some children may continue to experience negative emotional consequences (Kelly & Emery, 2003).

To address the challenges of this transition, several parent education programs have been developed to teach parents how to help their children cope during and after the divorce. For example, the Children First Program is a four-hour, two-session program for parents experiencing a divorce. The divorcing parents attend the program separately. The participants watch video clips involving parent–child interactions and then discuss how well the parents in the videos handled different challenging scenarios (Jewell et al., 2017).

A recent study compared the effectiveness of the latest edition of the program to the previous edition. Parents in the study filled out a questionnaire before and after participating in the program. Results of the study indicate that parents who completed either edition of the program had significant gains in knowledge of adaptive co-parenting skills, more favorable attitudes about adaptive co-parenting, and greater self-reported likelihood of using adaptive co-parenting strategies in the future. However, parents who received the newer edition (which included additional topics such as how to cope with stress, and more role-play, and emphasized teaching adaptive responses to challenging situations) had significantly greater gains on these measures than parents receiving the second edition. Overall, this study suggests that this parent education program has the potential to help family members cope with divorce-related challenges.

Shared Writing Prompt

In addition to teaching coping skills to divorcing parents, what are some specific skills that might be useful for children to learn themselves?

choose which parent to spend each vacation and holiday with or to decide between the conflicting advice coming from biological parent and stepparent (Belcher, 2003; Guadalupe & Welkley, 2012; Mundy & Wofsy, 2017).

In many cases, however, school-age children in blended families do surprisingly well. In comparison to adolescents, who have more difficulties, school-age children often adjust relatively smoothly to blended arrangements, for several reasons. For one thing, the family's financial situation is often improved after a parent remarries. In addition, in a blended family there are more people to share the burden of household chores. Finally, the simple fact that the family contains more individuals increases the opportunities for social interaction (Hetherington & Elmore, 2003; Purswell & Dillman Taylor, 2013).

Conversely, some children do not adjust well to life in a blended family. Some find the disruption of routine and of established networks of family relationships difficult. For instance, a child who is used to having her mother's complete attention may find it difficult to observe her mother showing interest and affection to a stepchild. The most successful blending of families occurs when the parents create an environment that supports children's self-esteem and helps all family members feel a sense of togetherness (Sage, 2003; Jeynes, 2006; Kirby, 2006).

From *a health-care worker's* perspective

How might the development of self-esteem in middle childhood be affected by a divorce? Can constant hostility and tension between parents lead to a child's health problems?

SINGLE-PARENT FAMILIES. Although the majority of children in the United States (69 percent) live with two parents, the remaining 31 percent live in some other arrangement, such as living with a single parent or with grandparents (see Figure 10-4). There are also some significant racial disparities: Seventy-four percent of white children live with two married parents, compared with 60 percent of Hispanic and 34 percent of black children (ChildStats.gov, 2017; also see Figure 13-9).

In rare cases, death is the reason for single parenthood. More frequently, either no spouse was ever present (that is, the mother never married), the spouses have

Figure 13-9 Living Arrangements of Children: 1960 to Present

Although the number of children living with single parents increased dramatically for several decades, it has leveled off in recent years.
(**Sources:** U.S. Census Bureau, 2017a)

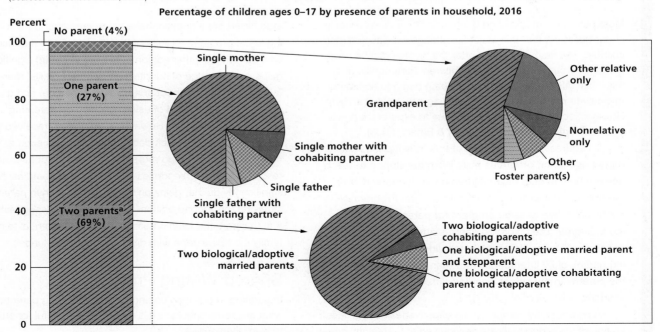

aChildren living with two stepparents are included here, in either of the categories where one parent is biological/adoptive and one is a stepparent.

divorced, or the spouse is absent. In the vast majority of cases, the single parent who is present is the mother.

What consequences are there for children living in homes with just one parent? This is a difficult question to answer. Much depends on whether a second parent was present earlier and the nature of the parents' relationship at that time. Furthermore, the economic status of the single-parent family plays a role in determining the consequences for children. Single-parent families are often less well-off financially than two-parent families, and living in relative poverty has a negative impact on children (Davis, 2003; Harvey & Fine, 2004).

In sum, the impact of living in a single-parent family is not, by itself, invariably negative or positive. Given the large number of single-parent households, the stigma that once existed toward such families has largely declined. The ultimate consequences for children depend on a variety of factors that accompany single parenthood, such as the economic status of the family, the amount of time that the parent is able to spend with the child, and the degree of stress in the household.

MULTIGENERATIONAL FAMILIES. Some households consist of several generations, in which children, parents, and grandparents live together. The number of multigenerational families is growing; some 19 percent of the U.S. population lived in households with multiple generations in 2014, up from 17 percent just five years earlier. The number of multigenerational families grew in part because of the economic downturn in 2008, as well as increases in the cost of housing (Carrns, 2016).

The prevalence of three-generation families who live together is greater among African Americans than among Caucasians. In addition, African American families, which are more likely than white families to be headed by single parents, often rely substantially on the help of grandparents in everyday child care, and cultural norms tend to be highly supportive of grandparents taking an active role (Baird, John, & Hayslip, 2000; Crowther & Rodriguez, 2003).

RACE AND FAMILY LIFE. Although there are as many types of families as there are individuals, research does find some consistencies related to race (Parke, 2004). For example, African Americans often have a particularly strong sense of family. Members of African American families are frequently willing to offer welcome and support to extended family members in their homes. Because there is a relatively high level of female-headed households among African Americans, the social and economic support of extended family often is critical. In addition, there is a relatively high proportion of families headed by older adults, such as grandparents, and some studies find that children in grandmother-headed households are particularly well-adjusted (McLoyd et al., 2000; Smith & Drew, 2002; Taylor, 2002).

Hispanic families also often stress the importance of family life as well as community and religious organizations. Children are taught to value their ties to their families, and they come to see themselves as a central part of an extended family. Ultimately, their sense of who they are becomes tied to the family. Hispanic families also tend to be relatively larger, with an average size of 3.71, compared to 2.97 for Caucasian families and 3.31 for African American families (U.S. Census Bureau, 2003; Halgunseth, Ispa, & Rudy, 2006).

Although relatively little research has been conducted on Asian American families, emerging findings suggest that fathers are more apt to be powerful figures, maintaining discipline. In keeping with the more collectivist orientation of Asian cultures, children tend to believe that family needs have a higher priority than personal needs, and males, in particular, are expected to care for their parents throughout their lifetimes (Ishii-Kuntz, 2000).

Gay and Lesbian Parents

LO 13.10 Compare the outcomes for children raised in a gay or lesbian household with those of children raised in a heterosexual household.

In increasing numbers, children are being raised in families in which there are two moms or two dads. Rough estimates suggest that between 1 million and 5 million families are headed by two lesbian or two gay parents in the United States, and some 6 million children have lesbian or gay parents (Patterson, 2007, 2009; Gates, 2013).

How do children in lesbian, gay, and transgender households fare? Although there is little data on the effects of children with a transgender parent, a growing body of research on the effects of same-sex parenting on children shows that children develop similarly to the children of heterosexual families. Their sexual orientation is unrelated to that of their parents, their behavior is no more or less gender-typed, and they seem equally well adjusted (Fulcher, Sutfin, & Patterson, 2008; Patterson, 2009; Goldberg, 2010).

One large-scale analysis that examined 33 studies of the effects of parental gender and sexual identity on their children's outcomes. No overall effects were found for children's sexual orientation cognitive abilities, or gender identity. There were some differences in terms of parent–child relationships, in which the relationship between parent and child was perceived to be *better* with same-gender parents, compared with different-gender parents. The research also found that children of same-gender parents showed more typical gender play and behavior than children in different-gender parents. Finally, children with lesbian or gay parents had higher levels of psychological adjustment than children with heterosexual parents (Fedewa, Black, & Ahn, 2015).

Other research shows that children of lesbian and gay parents have similar relationships with their peers as children of heterosexual parents. They also relate to adults—both those who are gay and those who are straight—no differently from children whose parents are heterosexual. And when they reach adolescence, their romantic relationships and sexual behavior are no different from those of adolescents living with opposite-sex parents (Patterson, 2009; Golombok et al., 2003; Wainright, Russell, & Patterson, 2004; Wainright & Patterson, 2008).

In short, research shows that there is little developmental difference between children whose parents are gay and lesbian and those who have heterosexual parents. There is insufficient research to make the same statement about transgender parenting; more studies need to be conducted before conclusions can be drawn. What is clearly different for children with same-sex parents is the possibility of discrimination and prejudice due to their parents' sexual orientation, although U.S. society has become considerably more tolerant of such unions. In fact, the 2015 U.S. Supreme Court ruling legalizing same-sex marriages should accelerate the trend of acceptance of such unions (Biblarz & Stacey, 2010; Kantor, 2015; Miller, Kors, & Macfie, 2017).

Module 13.2 Review

LO 13.7 Summarize the challenges couples face in deciding to have children, and identify successful coping strategies.

Most couples wish to produce children, although the availability of contraception and changes in women's roles in the workplace have combined to decrease average family size. Children bring pressures to relationships, causing changes in focus, roles, and responsibilities.

LO 13.8 Identify the changes that have occurred in family life in the past 50 years, and give examples of their impact on both parents and children.

The number of single-parent families has greatly increased in the past several decades. One in three children live in low-income households in the United States. Almost 75 percent of married women with school-age children work outside the home.

LO 13.9 Identify the various family constellations, and summarize the impact of divorce on children.

Children live in a variety of family constellations, including single-parent households, blended families, and multigenerational households. How divorce affects children depends on such factors as financial circumstances and the comparative levels of tension in the family before and after the divorce.

LO 13.10 Compare the outcomes for children raised in a gay or lesbian household with those of children raised in a heterosexual household.

Most research suggests that children who grow up in gay and lesbian households are as well-adjusted as their peers who grow up in heterosexual households.

Journal Writing Prompt

Applying Lifespan Development: Politicians often speak of "family values." How does this term relate to the diverse family situations covered in this chapter, including divorced parents, single parents, blended families, working parents, and gay and lesbian parents?

MODULE 13.3

FAMILY TIES IN MIDDLE AND LATE ADULTHOOD

> *For Kathy and Bob, accompanying their son Jon to his college orientation was like nothing they had ever experienced in the life of their family. When Jon had been accepted at a college on the other side of the country, the reality that he would be leaving home didn't really register. It wasn't until the time came to leave him on his new campus that it hit them that their family would be changing in ways they could barely fathom. It was a wrenching experience. Kathy and Bob felt a sense of profound loss—that, to a large extent, their job of raising their son was over. It was a thought that filled them with pride and anticipation for his future, but with great sadness as well.*

For members of many non-Western cultures who live in traditional extended families in which multiple generations spend their lives in the same household or village, middle adulthood is not particularly special. But in Western cultures, family dynamics undergo significant change during middle adulthood. It is in middle age that most parents experience major changes in their relationships not only with their children but with other family members as well. It is a period of shifting role relationships that, in 21st-century Western cultures, encompass an increasing number of combinations and permutations.

Family Evolutions: From Full House to Empty Nest

LO 13.11   Summarize what is meant by the empty nest syndrome, and identify the losses and gains associated with it.

For many parents, a major transition that typically occurs during middle adulthood is the departure of children, who may be going to college, getting married, joining the military, or taking a job far from home. Even people who become parents at relatively late ages are likely to experience this transition at some point during middle adulthood, since the period spans nearly a quarter century. As we saw in the description of Kathy and Bob, a child's departure can be a wrenching experience—so upsetting, in fact, that it has been labeled the "empty nest syndrome." The **empty nest syndrome** refers to instances in which parents experience unhappiness, worry, loneliness, and depression stemming from their children's departure from home (Rosen, Ackerman, & Zosky, 2002).

Many parents report that major adjustments are required. The loss can be particularly difficult for women who have stayed home to rear their children. Certainly, if traditional homemakers have little or nothing else in their lives except their children, they face a challenging period.

While coping with the feelings of loss can be difficult, some aspects of this era of middle adulthood can be quite positive for parents. Even mothers who have not worked outside the home find they have time for other outlets for their physical and psychological energies, such as community or recreational activities, when the children leave. Moreover, they may feel that they now have the opportunity to get a job or to go back to school. Finally, surveys show that most people feel that being a mother is harder than it used to be, and so these mothers may now feel liberated from a comparatively difficult set of responsibilities (Morfei et al., 2004; Chen, Yang, & Aagard, 2012).

empty nest syndrome
the experience that relates to parents' feelings of unhappiness, worry, loneliness, and depression resulting from their children's departure from home.

Leaving their youngest child at college marks the start of a significant transition for parents, who face an "empty nest."

Ariel Skelley/Getty Images

Although some feelings of loss over the departure of children are common for most people, there is little, if any, evidence to suggest that the departure of children produces anything more than temporary feelings of sadness and distress. This is especially true for women who have been working outside the home (Antonucci, 2001; Crowley, Hayslip, & Hobdy, 2003; Kadam, 2014).

In fact, some discernible benefits accrue when children leave home. Married spouses have more time for one another. Married or unmarried people can throw themselves into their own work without having to worry about helping the kids with homework, carpools, and the like. The house stays neater, and the telephone rings less often.

Keep in mind that most research examining the so-called empty nest syndrome has focused on women. Because men traditionally are not as involved as women in childrearing, it was assumed that the transition when children left home would be relatively smooth for men. However, at least some research suggests that men also experience feelings of loss when their children depart, although the nature of that loss may be different from that experienced by women.

One survey of fathers whose children had left home found that although most fathers expressed either happy or neutral feelings about the departure of their children, almost a quarter felt unhappy (Lewis, Freneau, & Roberts, 1979). Those fathers tended to mention lost opportunities, regretting things that they had not done with their children. For instance, some felt that they had been too busy for their children or hadn't been sufficiently nurturing or caring.

Some parents react to the departure of their children by becoming what has become known as *helicopter parents*, parents who intrusively intervene in their children's lives. Helicopter parenting is seen when parents micro-manage their children's college careers, complaining to instructors and administrators about poor grades that their children received or seeking to get them into certain classes. In some cases, the phenomenon has started earlier: parents of elementary school children sometimes exhibit the same tendencies.

In extreme cases, helicopter parenting extends to the workplace; some employers complain that parents call human relations departments to extol the virtues of their children as potential employees. Although statistics about the prevalence of helicopter parenting are hard to come by, it is clear that the phenomenon is real. One survey of employers found that nearly a third said that parents had submitted resumes for their child, sometimes not even informing their son or daughter. One-quarter said that parents had contacted them, urging them to hire their son or daughter. And 4 percent said that a parent had accompanied the child on a job interview. Some parents even help their children complete work assignments once they get a job (Gardner, 2007; Ludden, 2012).

In most cases, though, parents permit their children to develop independently once they leave home. Of course, children may not always leave home for good, and the empty nest sometimes becomes replenished with what have been called "boomerang children," as we discuss next.

Caught in the Middle at Midlife: Boomerang Children and Aging Parents

LO 13.12 Define what is meant by the sandwich generation, and explain how those in the sandwich generation are affected by both boomerang children and caring for their own aging parents.

Carole Olis doesn't know what to make of her 23-year-old son, Rob. He has been living at home since his graduation from college more than two years ago. Her six older children returned to the nest for just a few months and then bolted.

"I ask him, 'Why don't you move out with your friends?'" says Mrs. Olis, shaking her head. Rob has a ready answer: "They all live at home, too."

boomerang children
young adults who return, after leaving home for some period, to live in the homes of their middle-aged parents.

Carole Olis is not alone in being surprised and somewhat perplexed by the return of her son. There has been a significant increase in the United States in the number of young adults who come back to live in the homes of their middle-aged parents. Known as **boomerang children**, these returning offspring typically cite economic issues as the main reason for returning. Because of a difficult economy, many young adults cannot find jobs after college, or the positions they do find pay so little that they have difficulty making ends meet. Others return home after the breakup of a marriage. Overall, close to one-third of young adults ages 25 to 34 are living with their parents. In some European countries, the proportion is even higher (Roberts, 2009; Parker, 2012; Sandberg-Thoma, Snyder, & Jang, 2015).

Because about half of boomerang children pay rent to their parents, parental finances may benefit. The arrangement doesn't seem to affect social relationships within the family: Half say it makes no difference or is a plus. Only a quarter of boomerang children find the arrangement has been bad for their relationship with their parents (Parker, 2012; see Figure 13-10).

THE SANDWICH GENERATION: BETWEEN CHILDREN AND PARENTS.

At the same time children are leaving the nest, or perhaps even returning as boomerang children, many middle-aged adults face another challenge: growing responsibility for the care of their own aging parents. The term **sandwich generation** has come to be applied to these middle-aged adults who feel squeezed between the needs of their children and their aging parents (Grundy & Henretta, 2006; Chassin et al., 2009; Steiner & Fletcher, 2017).

Being part of the sandwich generation is a relatively new phenomenon, produced by several converging trends. First, both men and women are marrying later and having children at an older age. At the same time, people are living longer. Consequently, the likelihood is growing that those in middle adulthood will simultaneously have children who still require a significant amount of nurturing and parents who are still alive and in need of care.

The care of aging parents can be psychologically tricky. For one thing, there is a significant degree of role reversal, with children taking on the parental role and parents in a more dependent position. Older people, who were previously independent, may resent and resist their children's efforts to help. They certainly do not want to be burdens on their children. For instance, almost all older adults who live alone report that they do not wish to live with their children (O'Sullivan, 2015).

People in middle adulthood provide a range of care for their parents. In some cases, the care is merely financial, such as helping them make ends meet on meager pensions. In other situations, it takes the form of help in managing a household, such as taking down storm windows in the spring or shoveling snow in the winter.

In more extreme cases, elderly parents may be invited to live in the home of a son or daughter. Census data reveal that the multigenerational household, which includes three or more generations, is the fastest-growing household arrangement of any sort. Almost 20 percent of the U.S. population lives with multiple generations under the same roof—almost 61 million people. The number of multigenerational households has increased by more than 50 percent since 1980 (Carrns, 2016).

Multigenerational families present a difficult situation, as parental and children's roles are renegotiated. Typically, the adult children in the middle generation—who, after all, are no longer children—are in charge of the household. Both they and their parents must adjust to the changing relationships and find some common ground in making decisions. Older parents may find the loss of independence particularly difficult, and this can be disturbing for their adult child as well. The youngest generation may resist the inclusion of the oldest generation.

In many cases, the burden of caring for aging parents is not shared equally, with the larger share most often taken on by women. Even in married couples where both husband and wife are in the labor force, middle-aged women tend to be more involved in the day-to-day care of aging parents, even when the parent or parents are their in-laws (Putney & Bengtson, 2001; Corry et al., 2015).

Culture also influences how caregivers view their roles. For example, members of Asian cultures, which are more collectivistic, are more likely to view caregiving as a

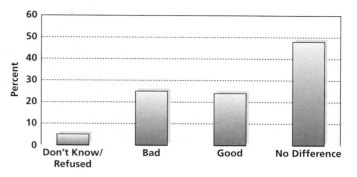

Figure 13-10 Boomerang Children's Views of Their Situation

The percentage of those saying that living with their parents at this stage of life has been bad, good, or no different in terms of their relationship.

(**Source:** Pew Research Center, 2012)

sandwich generation
adults who in middle adulthood must fulfill the needs of both their children and their aging parents.

traditional and not-out-of-the-ordinary duty. In contrast, members of more individualistic cultures may perceive familial ties as less central, and caring for a member of an older generation may be experienced as more burdensome (Ho et al., 2003; Kim & Lee, 2003; Ron, 2014).

Despite the burden of being sandwiched in the middle of two generations, which can stretch the caregiving child's resources, there are also significant rewards. The psychological attachment between middle-aged children and their elderly parents can continue to grow. Both partners in the relationship can see each other more realistically. They can become closer, more accepting of each other's weaknesses and more appreciative of each other's strengths (Vincent, Phillipson, & Downs, 2006). As we'll discuss next, family continues to play a significant role in the lives of older people.

Becoming a Grandparent: Generations Within the Family

LO 13.13 **Identify the different styles of grandparenting, and explain the importance of family connections for older adults.**

When her eldest son and daughter-in-law had their first child, Leah couldn't believe it. At age 54, she had become a grandmother! She kept telling herself that she felt far too young to be considered anybody's grandparent.

Middle adulthood often brings one of the unmistakable symbols of aging: becoming a grandparent. For some people, becoming a grandparent has been eagerly awaited. They may miss the energy and excitement and even demands of young children, and they may see grandparenthood as the next stage in the natural progression of life. Others are less pleased with the prospect of grandparenthood, seeing it as a clear signpost of aging.

Grandparenting tends to fall into different styles. *Involved* grandparents are actively engaged in grandparenting and have influence over their grandchildren's lives. They hold clear expectations about the ways their grandchildren should behave. A retired grandmother or grandfather who takes care of a grandchild several days a week while her parents are at work is an example of an involved grandparent (Mueller, Wilhelm, & Elder, 2002; Fergusson, Maughan, & Golding, 2008; Hayslip et al., 2015).

In contrast, *companionate* grandparents are more relaxed. Rather than taking responsibility for their grandchildren, companionate grandparents act as supporters and buddies to them. Grandparents who visit and call frequently, and perhaps occasionally take their grandchildren on vacations or invite them to visit without their parents, are practicing the companionate style of grandparenting.

Finally, the most aloof type of grandparents are *remote*. Remote grandparents are detached and distant, and they show little interest in their grandchildren. Remote grandparents, for example, would rarely make visits to see their grandchildren and might complain about their childish behavior when they did see them.

There are marked gender differences in the extent to which people enjoy grandparenthood. Generally, grandmothers are more interested and experience greater satisfaction than grandfathers, particularly when they have a high level of interaction with younger grandchildren (Smith & Drew, 2002).

African American grandparents are more apt to be involved with their grandchildren than white grandparents. The most reasonable explanation for this phenomenon is that the prevalence of three-generation families who live together is greater among African Americans than among Caucasians. In addition, African American families, which are more likely than white families to be headed by single parents, often rely substantially on the help of grandparents for everyday child care, and cultural norms tend to be highly supportive of grandparents taking an active role (Stevenson, Henderson, & Baugh, 2007; Keene, Prokos, & Held, 2012; Cox & Miner, 2014).

GREAT-GRANDCHILDREN. Great-grandchildren play less of a role in the lives of both white and African American great-grandparents. Most great-grandparents do not have close relationships with their great-grandchildren. Close relationships tend to occur only when the great-grandparents and great-grandchildren live relatively near one another (McConnell, 2012).

There are several explanations for the relative lack of involvement of great-grandparents with great-grandchildren. One is that by the time they reach great-grandparenthood, older adults are so old that they do not have much physical or psychological energy to expend on forming relationships with their great-grandchildren. Another is that there may be so many great-grandchildren that great-grandparents do not feel strong emotional ties to them. It is not uncommon for a great-grandparent who has had a large number of children to have so many great-grandchildren that they are difficult to keep track of.

Still, even though most great-grandparents may not have close relationships with their great-grandchildren, they profit emotionally from the mere fact that they have great-grandchildren. For instance, great-grandparents may see their great-grandchildren as representing both their own and their family's continuation, as well as providing a concrete sign of their longevity. Furthermore, as health advances in late adulthood continue to increase, great-grandparents are physically able to contribute more to the lives of their great-grandchildren (McConnell, 2012).

THE CONNECTION OF GENERATIONS.   Of course, it is not only grandchildren who provide important family connections for older adults. Some 75 percent of children live within a 30-minute drive of their aging parents, and parents and children visit and talk with one another frequently. Daughters tend to be in more frequent contact with their parents than sons, and mothers tend to receive more communication more frequently than fathers (Ji-liang, Li-qing, & Yan, 2003; Diamond, Fagundes, & Butterworth, 2010; Byrd-Craven et al., 2012).

Because the great majority of older adults have at least one child who lives fairly close by, family members still provide significant aid to one another. Moreover, parents and children tend to share similar views of how adult children should behave toward their parents (see Table 13-1). In particular, they expect children to help their parents understand their resources, provide emotional support, and talk over matters of importance, such as medical issues. Furthermore, as we noted earlier, it is most often children who end up caring for their aging parents when they require assistance (Dellmann-Jenkins & Brittain, 2003; Ron, 2006; Funk, 2010).

The bonds between parents and children are sometimes asymmetrical, with parents seeking a closer relationship and children a more distant one. Parents have a greater *developmental stake* in close ties, since they see their children as perpetuating their beliefs, values, and standards. For their part, children are motivated to maintain their autonomy and live independently from their parents. These divergent perspectives make parents more likely to minimize conflicts they experience with their children, and children more likely to maximize them (Pashos & McBurney, 2008).

For parents, their children remain a source of great interest and concern. Some surveys show, for instance, that even in late adulthood parents talk about their children nearly every day, particularly if the children are having some sort of problem. At the same time, children may turn to their aging parents for advice, information, and sometimes tangible help, such as money. And both adult generations have a stake in the next generation, as we see next (Ingersoll–Dayton, Neal, & Hammer, 2001; Diamond, Fagundes, & Butterworth, 2010).

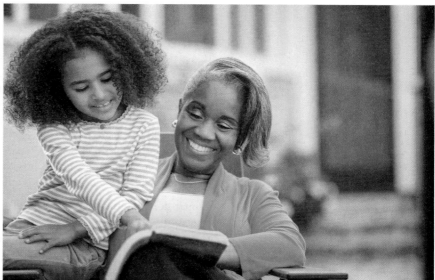

Sam Edwards/Getty Images

One reason that African American grandparents are more involved with their grandchildren than white grandparents is the greater prevalence of three-generation families living together in African American households.

Table 13-1 Views of Parents and Children Regarding Behavior of Adult Children Toward Parents

Rank	Children's Ranking	Parent's Ranking
1	Help understand resources	Discuss matters of importance
2	Give emotional support	Help understand resources
3	Discuss matters of importance	Give emotional support
4	Make room in home in emergency	Give parents advice
5	Sacrifice personal freedom	Be together on special occasions
6	Care when sick	Sacrifice personal freedom
7	Be together on special occasions	Make room in home in emergency
8	Provide financial help	Feel responsible for parent
9	Give parents advice	Care when sick
10	Adjust family schedule to help	Adjust family schedule to help
11	Feel responsible for parent	Visit once a week
12	Adjust work schedule to help	Adjust work schedule to help
13	Believe that parent should live with child	Provide financial help
14	Visit once a week	Write once a week
15	Live close to parent	Believe that parent should live with child
16	Write once a week	Live close to parent

(**Source:** Based on Hamon & Blieszner, 1990.)

Retirement

LO 13.14 Identify the different paths people take in retirement, and summarize the economic challenges this age group faces.

> *Before I retired 10 years ago, everyone told me I'd miss work, get lonely, and feel flat without the challenges of business. Baloney! This is the best time of my life! Miss work? No way. What's to miss? Meetings? Training sessions? Evaluations? Sure, there's less money and people, but I have all I need with my savings, my hobbies, and my traveling.*

This positive view of life in late adulthood was expressed by a 75-year-old retired insurance worker. Although the story is certainly not the same for all retirees, many, if not most, find their post-work lives happy and involving. We will consider some of the ways in which people lead their lives in late adulthood.

NEGOTIATING RETIREMENT: LIFESTYLE CHOICES. Many people think of retirement as a time of slowing down, perhaps of withdrawing from an active lifestyle to sit out the rest of one's days in a rocking chair. But the reality is that there are many different possible approaches to retirement, including options for staying just as active while retired as in the preretirement years. Rather than the closing of a book, retirement represents the opening of a new chapter—and the story that unfolds in that new chapter has a lot to do with the retiree's expectations, goals, and preretirement plans (Dittmann, 2004; Goodman, Schlossberg, & Anderson, 2006; Nuttman-Shwartz, 2007).

Based on an extensive series of interviews, psychologist Nancy Schlossberg (2004) has identified six basic paths of retirement:

- **Continuers** use part-time or volunteer work to remain at least partially active in their preretirement work.
- **Involved spectators** take more of a back-seat role in staying connected with their previous fields.
- **Adventurers** use retirement as a time to explore entirely new pursuits, perhaps including a new field of work.
- **Searchers** are trying different activities in search of a suitable way to spend their retirement.

- **Easy gliders** don't fret about retirement much and take each day as it comes.
- **Retreaters** become depressed and withdrawn and stop searching for a meaningful pathway through retirement.

The path that a person takes can change over the course of retirement, too, underscoring another fundamental point: Retirement is less of a destination than it is a journey. People who negotiate retirement most successfully are those who see it not as a time of withdrawal and stagnation but as an opportunity for development and exploration (Brucker & Leppel, 2013; Sherry et al., 2017).

For many people, retirement occurs in stages as they withdraw slowly from work—perhaps by dropping to part-time work for a period before retiring altogether. Others put off retirement as long as they can; some simply enjoy their work, while others are increasingly finding that they simply do not have the financial means to retire as employers scale back pension plans and health benefits for retirees (Harrison & Newman, 2013; Muratore & Earl, 2015).

Research suggests that it's just as important to prepare psychologically for retirement as it is to prepare financially. Some important considerations include the climate at work and the opportunities for future growth in one's career, relationships with family members, and community ties and activities. It's important for older adults to keep in mind that they don't just retire from work but they also retire to a new lifestyle. Planning for what that lifestyle will be like—whether it will include part-time work, volunteer work, travel, or other activities, for example—can make a difference in adjustment to retirement (Froidevaux, Hirschi, & Wang, 2016; Leandro-França et al., 2016). (Also see the *Development in Your Life* box).

FINANCIAL ISSUES: THE ECONOMICS OF LATE ADULTHOOD.   People in late adulthood, like people in all other stages of life, range from one end of the socioeconomic spectrum to the other. Those who were relatively affluent during their working years tend to remain relatively affluent, while those who were poor at earlier stages of life tend to remain poor when they reach late adulthood. However, the social inequities that various groups experience during their earlier lives become magnified with increasing age. At the same time, people who reach late adulthood today may

Development in Your Life

Planning for—and Living—a Good Retirement

What makes for a good retirement? Gerontologists suggest that several factors are related to successful retirement (Irving, 2015; Shultz & Fisher, 2017):

- **Plan ahead financially.**   Because most financial experts suggest that Social Security pensions will be inadequate in the future, personal savings are critical. Similarly, having adequate health-care insurance is essential.

- **Consider tapering off from work gradually.** Sometimes it is possible to enter into retirement by shifting from full-time to part-time work. Such a transition may be helpful in preparing for eventual full-time retirement.

- **Explore your interests before you retire.**   Assess what you like about your current job and think how that might be translated into leisure activities.

- **If you are married or in a long-term partnership, spend some time discussing your views of the ideal retirement with your partner.**   You may find that you need to negotiate a vision that will suit you both.

- **Consider where you want to live.**   Try out, temporarily, a community to which you are thinking of moving.

- **Determine the advantages and disadvantages of downsizing your current home.**

- **Plan to volunteer your time.**   People who retire have an enormous wealth of skills, and these are often needed by nonprofit organizations and small businesses. Organizations such as the Retired Senior Volunteer Program or the Foster Grandparent Program can help match your skills with people who need them.

experience growing economic pressure as a result of the ever-increasing human life span, which means it is more likely they will run through their savings.

Overall, 10 percent of people age 65 and older live in poverty, a proportion that is quite close to that for people under age 65. However, there are significant differences in gender and racial groups. For instance, women are almost twice as likely as men to be living in poverty. Of those older women living alone, around one-fourth live on incomes below the poverty line. A married woman may also slip into poverty if she becomes widowed, for she may have used up savings to pay for her husband's final illness, and the husband's pension may cease with his death (Spraggins, 2003; U.S. Census Bureau, Current Population Survey, 2015; see Figure 13-11).

Minority women fare the worst of any category. For example, divorced black women age 65 to 74 have a poverty rate of close to 50 percent (Federal Interagency Forum on Age-Related Statistics, 2000; U.S. Bureau of the Census, 2013).

One source of financial vulnerability for people in late adulthood is their reliance on a fixed income for support. Unlike the income of a younger person, that of an older person, which typically comes from a combination of Social Security benefits, pensions, and savings, rarely keeps up with inflation. Consequently, as inflation drives up the price of goods such as food and clothing, income does not rise as quickly. What may have been a reasonable income at age 65 is worth much less 20 years later, as the elderly person gradually slips into poverty.

The rising cost of health care is another source of financial vulnerability in older adults. The average older person spends close to 20 percent of his or her income for health-care costs. For those who require care in nursing home facilities, the financial costs can be staggering, running almost $100,000 a year.

Unless major changes are made in the way that Social Security and Medicare are financed, the costs borne by younger U.S. citizens in the workforce must rise significantly. Increasing expenditures mean that a larger proportion of younger people's pay must be taxed to fund benefits for the elderly. Such a situation is apt to lead to

Figure 13-11 Poverty in Late Adulthood

Although women are more likely than men to be living in poverty at every age after 18, women over age 75 are particularly at risk. Why do you think this discrepancy is so pronounced at this age?

Source: U.S. Census Bureau, Current Population Survey, 2015.

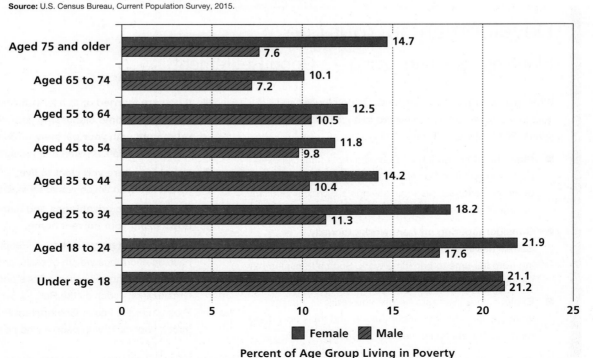

Percent of Age Group Living in Poverty

increasing friction and segregation between younger and older generations. Indeed, Social Security payments are one key factor in many people's decisions about how long to work.

Living Arrangements: The Places and Spaces of Their Lives

LO 13.15 Compare and contrast the variety of living arrangements available to older adults.

Think "old age," and if you are like most people, your thoughts soon turn to nursing homes. Popular stereotypes place most elderly people in lonely, unpleasant, institutional surroundings, under the care of strangers.

The reality is quite different. Although it is true that some people finish their lives in nursing homes, they are a tiny minority—only 5 percent. Most people live out their entire lives in home environments, typically in the company of at least one other family member.

LIVING AT HOME. A large number of older adults live alone. People over 65 represent a quarter of America's 9.6 million single-person households. Roughly two-thirds of people over age 65 live with other members of the family. In most cases they live with spouses. Some older adults live with their siblings, and others live in multigenerational settings with their children, grandchildren, and occasionally even great-grandchildren.

The consequences of living with a family member are quite varied, depending on the nature of the setting. For married couples, living with a spouse represents continuity with earlier life. For people who move in with their children, however, the adjustment to life in a multigenerational setting can be jarring. Not only is there a potential loss of independence and privacy, but older adults may feel uncomfortable with the way their children are raising their grandchildren. Unless there are some ground rules about the specific roles that people are to play in the household, conflicts can arise (Navarro, 2006).

For some groups, living in extended families is more typical than for other groups. For instance, African Americans are more likely than whites to live in multigenerational families. Furthermore, the amount of influence that family members have over one another and the interdependence of extended families are generally greater in African American, Asian American, and Hispanic families than in Caucasian families (Becker, Beyene, & Newsom, 2003).

SPECIALIZED LIVING ENVIRONMENTS. For some 10 percent of those in late adulthood, home is an institution. As we'll see, there is a broad range of different types of specialized environments in which elderly people live.

One of the more recent innovations in living arrangements is the **continuing-care community**. Such communities typically offer an environment in which all the residents are of retirement age or older. Residents may need various levels of care, which is provided by the community. Residents sign contracts under which the community makes a commitment to provide care at whatever level is needed. In many such communities, people start out living in separate houses or apartments, either independently or with occasional home care. As they age and their needs increase, residents may eventually move into *assisted living*, in which people live in independent housing but are supported by medical providers to the extent required. Continuing care ultimately extends all the way to full-time nursing care, which is often provided at an on-site nursing home.

Continuing-care communities tend to be fairly homogeneous in terms of religious, racial, and ethnic backgrounds, and they are often organized by private or religious organizations. Because joining may involve a substantial initial payment, members of such communities tend to be relatively well-off financially. Increasingly, though, continuing-care communities are making efforts to raise the level of diversity.

continuing-care community
a community that offers an environment in which all the residents are of retirement age or older and need various levels of care.

adult day-care facilities
a facility in which elderly individuals receive care only during the day but spend nights and weekends in their own homes.

skilled nursing facilities
facilities that provide full-time nursing care for people who have chronic illnesses or are recovering from a temporary medical condition.

Furthermore, they are attempting to increase opportunities for intergenerational interaction by establishing day-care centers on the premises and developing programs that involve younger populations (Chaker, 2003; Berkman, 2006; Howe, 2015).

Several types of nursing institutions exist, ranging from those that provide part-time day care to homes that offer 24-hour-a-day, live-in care. In **adult day-care facilities**, elderly individuals receive care only during the day but spend nights and weekends in their own homes. During the time that they are at the facility, people receive nursing care, take their meals, and participate in scheduled activities. Sometimes adult facilities are combined with infant and child day-care programs, an arrangement that allows for interaction between the old and the young (Gitlin et al., 2006; Dabelko & Zimmerman, 2008; Teitelman et al., 2017).

Other institutional settings offer more extensive care. The most intensive institutions are **skilled nursing facilities**, which provide full-time nursing care for people who have chronic illnesses or are recovering from a temporary medical condition. While only a small minority of those 65 and older live in nursing homes, the number increases dramatically with age. One percent of persons 65–74 years old live in a nursing home; 5 percent for those 75–84; and 18 percent for persons 85 and older. About half of those over age 95 live in nursing homes. Approximately 5 percent of the elderly live in a variety of self-described senior housing that offers a number of supportive services (Administration on Aging, 2006).

From *a health-care worker's* perspective

What policies might a nursing home institute to minimize the chances that its residents will develop "institutionalism"? Why are such policies relatively uncommon?

The greater the extent of nursing home care, the greater the adjustment required of residents. Although some newcomers adjust relatively rapidly, the loss of independence brought about by institutional life may lead to difficulties. In addition, elderly people are as susceptible as other members of society to society's stereotypes about nursing homes, and their expectations may be particularly negative. They may see themselves as just marking time until they eventually die, forgotten and discarded by a society that venerates youth (Biedenharn & Normoyle, 1991; Baltes, 1996; Golub & Langer, 2007).

institutionalism
a psychological state in which people in nursing homes develop apathy, indifference, and a lack of caring about themselves.

INSTITUTIONALISM AND LEARNED HELPLESSNESS. Although the fears of those in nursing homes may be exaggerated, they can lead to **institutionalism**, a psychological state in which people develop apathy, indifference, and a lack of caring about themselves. Institutionalism is brought about, in part, by a sense of *learned helplessness*, a belief that one has no control over one's environment (Peterson & Park, 2007).

The sense of helplessness brought about by institutionalism can literally have deadly consequences. Consider, for instance, what happens when people enter nursing homes in late adulthood. One of the most conspicuous changes from their independent past is that they no longer have control over their most basic activities. They may be told when and what to eat, their sleeping schedules may be arranged by others, and even their visits to the bathroom may be regulated (Wolinsky, Wyrwich, & Babu, 2003; Iecovich & Biderman, 2012; de Oliveira et al., 2014).

A classic experiment showed the consequences of such a loss of control. Psychologists Ellen Langer and Irving Janis (1979) divided elderly residents of a nursing home into two groups. One group of residents was encouraged to make a variety of choices about their day-to-day activities. The other group was given no choices and was encouraged to let the nursing home staff care for them. The results were clear. The participants who had choices were not only happier, they were also healthier. In fact, 18 months after the experiment began, only 15 percent of the choice group had died—compared to 30 percent of the comparison group.

In short, the loss of control over certain aspects of their daily life experienced by residents of nursing homes and other institutions can have a profound effect on their well-being. Keep in mind that not all nursing homes are the same, however. The best go out of their way to permit residents to make basic life decisions, and they attempt to give people in late adulthood a sense of control over their lives.

Module 13.3 Review

LO 13.11 **Summarize what is meant by the empty nest syndrome, and identify the losses and gains associated with it.**

Family changes in middle adulthood include the departure of children. The empty nest syndrome refers to instances in which parents experience unhappiness, worry, loneliness, and depression stemming from their children's departure from home. In some cases, though, the departure of children is experienced positively, as parents have new-found freedom.

LO 13.12 **Define what is meant by the sandwich generation, and explain how those in the sandwich generation are affected by both boomerang children and caring for their own aging parents.**

The "sandwich generation" refers to middle-aged adults who may have increasing responsibilities for their aging parents as well as their own children. In some cases, families experience boomerang children—young adults who come back to live in the homes of their middle-aged parents.

LO 13.13 **Identify the different styles of grandparenting, and explain the importance of family connections for older adults.**

Family ties continue to be important throughout late adulthood. Older adults remain emotionally invested in their children.

A further change is grandparenthood. Typically, grandparents may be involved, companionate, or remote.

LO 13.14 **Identify the different paths people take in retirement, and summarize the economic challenges this age group faces.**

Retirement is an important transition in later life. Financial issues can trouble older people, largely because their incomes are fixed, health-care costs are increasing, and the life span is lengthening.

LO 13.15 **Compare and contrast the variety of living arrangements available to older adults.**

Elderly people live in a variety of settings, although most live at home with a family member.

Journal Writing Prompt

Applying Lifespan Development: Why might it be desirable for older adults to move from working full time to part time at their jobs before retiring completely? How might traditional workplaces accommodate this change?

Epilogue

In this chapter, we focused on family and peer relationships across the life span and examined a variety of lifestyles. We looked at what determines popularity and the qualities children and adults seek in friends.

We then focused on the role family plays throughout our lives. We saw how the decision to have a child affects a couple's relationship, and how family life itself has changed in recent decades with the rise in divorce and the number of households where both parents work outside the home. We considered various family constellations and their effects on children.

Finally, we examined the continuing importance of family in late adulthood. We considered the lifestyles of older people as they enter retirement and examined the choices they face, the financial issues common to this age group, and their varied living arrangements.

Turn back to the prologue of this chapter, about Bernadine Connolly, the recently retired grandmother, and answer the following questions.

1. Which of Schlossberg's retirement paths most closely describes Bernadine? What are the benefits of such a path?

2. What might Bernadine gain if she decided to devote some time weekly to volunteer activities?

3. What type of grandparent do you imagine Bernadine is? Explain your thinking.

4. What effect will Bernadine have on helping one of her adult children cope with going through a divorce? What challenges might arise as she takes a more active role in helping to raise her youngest grandchild?

Looking Back

LO 13.1 **Summarize the development of social relationships in the preschool years, and describe the types of play preschoolers engage in.**

Preschool social relationships begin to encompass genuine friendships, which involve trust and endure over time. Older preschoolers engage in more constructive play than functional play. They also engage in more associative and cooperative play than younger preschoolers, who do more parallel and onlooker playing.

LO 13.2 Identify the three major stages of friend-ship in middle childhood, and explain how friendship patterns differ across gender.

Friendship plays an increasingly important role in middle childhood. Friendships teach children how to communicate and interact with others, and they provide emotional support. The three major stages of friendship include: basing friendship on others' behavior, basing friendship on trust, and basing friendship on psychological closeness. Boys and girls in middle childhood increasingly prefer same-gender friendships. Male friendships are characterized by groups, status hierarchies, and restrictive play. Female friendships tend to involve one or two close relationships, equal status, and a reliance on cooperation.

LO 13.3 Explain the important role that peers play in adolescence, and describe the changes that occur in cross-race relationships.

One of the most noticeable changes from childhood to adolescence is the greater reliance on friendships, which help adolescents define who they are. Peers influence one another in many ways during adolescence, providing support for academic achievement and prosocial behavior and compensation for negative school or family situations. Adolescents tend to belong to two types of groups: cliques and crowds. Cliques are composed of 2 to 12 people who have frequent social interaction with each other. Crowds are larger and composed of individuals who share particular characteristics such as being a "jock" or a "nerd." During adolescence, boys and girls begin to spend time together in groups and, toward the end of adolescence, to pair off. In general, segregation between people of different races and ethnicities increases in middle and late adolescence, even in schools with a diverse student body.

LO 13.4 Identify the four categories of popularity, and summarize the qualities of popular adolescents.

Many adolescents have concerns about their popularity, or lack of it. Popular teens tend to have a high level of emotional intelligence, knowing how to act in a variety of social situations. Degrees of popularity during adolescence include popular and controversial adolescents (on the high end of popularity) and neglected and rejected adolescents (on the low end).

LO 13.5 Explain how adolescents' quest for autonomy affects relationships in the family.

Adolescents' quest for autonomy often brings confusion and tension to their relationships with their parents, but the actual "generation gap" between parents' and teenagers' attitudes is usually small.

LO 13.6 Summarize the importance of friendships in adulthood, and identify the characteristics adults look for in a friend.

Friendships are important in later life because they offer personal control, companionship, and social support. Proximity plays a key role in adult friendships.

Most adults form friendships with people who live nearby or with whom they come into regular contact. Adults tend to seek friends who share their values and attitudes. They also look for friends who are loyal, supportive, warm, trustworthy, and have a good sense of humor.

LO 13.7 Summarize the challenges couples face in deciding to have children, and identify successful coping strategies.

Children bring pressures to any marriage, shifting the focus of the marriage partners, changing their roles, and increasing their responsibilities. Economic issues also arise. A middle-class family spends about $233,000 to raise each child to age 18. Poor families have fewer resources and their children experience more disruptions, putting them at risk for poor academic performance, higher rates of aggression, and conduct problems. Parents who work together as a co-parenting team, and those who continue to express affection for and take interest in their partner, are likely to successfully weather the increased stress of parenting.

LO 13.8 Identify the changes that have occurred in family life in the past 50 years, and give examples of their impact on both parents and children.

Single-parent families have increased significantly in the past several decades, rising to account for almost one-third of all families with children in the United States. One in three children lives in a low-income household. Family size continues to shrink for a variety of reasons, including economics and the dual demands placed on women by motherhood and working outside the home.

LO 13.9 Identify the various family constellations, and summarize the impact of divorce on children.

Children live in a variety of family constellations besides the traditional two-parent household: single-parent households (both by choice and by divorce or death), blended families, and multigenerational households. Immediately after a divorce, the effects on children in the middle childhood years can be serious, depending on the financial condition of the family and the hostility level between spouses before the divorce.

LO 13.10 Compare the outcomes for children raised in a gay or lesbian household with those of children raised in a heterosexual household.

Although gay and lesbian couples tend to divide household responsibilities more equally than their heterosexual counterparts, once they have a child, they often develop specialization of roles just as heterosexual couples do. Most research shows that children of gay and lesbian households are equally as well-adjusted as children raised in heterosexual households, although they may face prejudice or discrimination because of their parents' sexual orientation.

LO 13.11 Summarize what is meant by the empty nest syndrome, and identify the losses and gains associated with it.

The empty nest syndrome, a supposed psychological upheaval following the departure of children from the home, is probably exaggerated. Although parents, especially women who stayed home to raise their children, initially experience a sense of loss, there are a number of compensations, such as more time to pursue interests, work, or education, and the opportunity to rekindle the relationship with one's spouse.

LO 13.12 Define what is meant by the sandwich generation, and explain how those in the sandwich generation are affected by both boomerang children and caring for their own aging parents.

The permanent departure of children is often delayed as "boomerang" children return home for a number of years when faced with the harsh realities of economic life. The situation is helped if the children work and contribute to the household. Adults in the middle years often face responsibilities for both their children and their aging parents. Such adults, who have been called the sandwich generation, face significant challenges. Caring for elderly parents is psychologically tricky due to a major role reversal between the generations and can prove exhausting if the parents move in with their adult children. On the positive side, both parents and children can grow closer, accepting each other's weaknesses and appreciating each other's strengths.

LO 13.13 Identify the different styles of grandparenting, and explain the importance of family connections for older adults.

Many people become grandparents for the first time during middle age. Researchers have identified three grandparenting styles: involved, companionate, and remote. Styles tend to differ by gender and race. Family relationships provide a great deal of emotional support for people in later life.

LO 13.14 Identify the different paths people take in retirement, and summarize the economic challenges this age group faces.

Many retirees find their post-work lives satisfying and involving. Psychologist Nancy Schlossberg has identified six basic types of retirees: continuers, involved spectators, adventurers, searchers, easy gliders, and retreaters. However, financial issues can become challenging in late adulthood. Those who were affluent during their working years usually continue to be so, and those who lived in poverty tend to remain in poverty. Women age 65 and older fare worse than men, being almost twice as likely to live in poverty.

LO 13.15 Compare and contrast the variety of living arrangements available to older adults.

Living arrangement options include staying at home, living with family members, participating in adult day care, residing in continuing-care communities, and living in skilled nursing facilities. Older adults may become financially vulnerable because they must cope with rising health care and other costs on a fixed income.

Key Terms and Concepts

Chapter 14
Schooling, Culture, and Society: Living in a Multicultural World

Yellow Dog Production/Getty Images

Learning Objectives

LO 14.1 Analyze the functions and types of pre-school education in the United States.

LO 14.2 Explain how U.S. students generally progress from kindergarten through high school.

LO 14.3 Describe the nature of the U.S. college population.

LO 14.4 Describe how adolescents spend their leisure time.

LO 14.5 Explain how the use of time changes in early and middle adulthood.

LO 14.6 Analyze how cultural background affects individual self-definition.

LO 14.7 Examine the meaning and importance of an ethnic identity.

LO 14.8 Explain how socioeconomic status affects children and adolescents.

LO 14.9 Define prejudice, stereotypes, and discrimination, and explain their origins and effects.

Chapter Overview

Prologue: Too Many Choices

Niko and Jeff sat at the kitchen table with their smartphones, each searching though child-care options. Jeff had been staying home with their son Rex since he was born, but four years later he was eager to get back to work.

"Too many choices!" Niko exclaimed. "Child care or preschool? At a private home or at a school? How're we supposed to know the best way to go?"

Jeff agreed. There were so many possibilities nearby. "The Head Start program is so close to our house, but everyone I've spoken to really likes the Montessori program. I just don't understand how most of these options are different from each other. And I know it sounds crazy, but it feels like his future college opportunities are already hanging in the balance." ■

Looking Ahead

In this chapter, we focus on schooling, leisure, and what it means to live in a multicultural world. We begin by examining the different types of child care and preschool programs, and we consider what each has to offer young children. We then look at what makes children ready for school and discuss the transition from elementary to secondary school. We also consider the effectiveness of alternatives to traditional education such as home schooling and the factors that affect individual student achievement.

We then turn to looking at how people spend their leisure time. We focus on leisure during adolescence and later on in adulthood. We address this question: Does more leisure time necessarily mean a slower pace of life in the United States?

In the last part of the chapter, we look at culture and diversity. We discuss how a bicultural identity may be fostered in the schools. We examine the role that race, ethnicity, gender, and socioeconomic status play in determining culture. We also look at how members of different cultures relate to one another and how individuals develop an ethnic identity. Finally, we consider prejudice and discrimination.

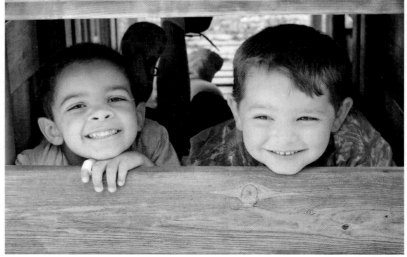

Schooling marks the beginning of an intellectual and social journey that continues for many years, shaping our development in significant ways.

Rob Hainer/Shutterstock

MODULE 14.1

SCHOOLING THROUGHOUT THE LIFE SPAN

On a Monday morning at Judi Wyler's family child-care center, six children, ages 3 to 5, gather around an incubator. Judi, a former preschool teacher, has turned off the lights so that she can candle the eggs in the incubator. The children stare, fascinated, as the high-powered flashlight turns the eggshell transparent. "Look! The baby chick is almost as big as the egg!" shouts one of the girls. "Yes, it won't be much longer before they hatch," Judi assures the children.

The children in Judi Wyler's child-care center are having fun, but they're also learning about how a chick develops in the egg. Such hands-on lessons are increasingly a part of many preschool programs, as we discuss here.

Early Childhood Education: Taking the Pre- Out of the Preschool Period

LO 14.1 Analyze the functions and types of preschool education in the United States.

The term *preschool period* is something of a misnomer because many children engage in some form of educational experiences during this period. Nearly 25 percent of children in the United States in this age group are enrolled in a preschool, Head Start center, or day-care facility. These child-care centers are typically designed either explicitly or implicitly to teach skills that will enhance intellectual as well as social abilities (see Figure 14-1). Another 10 percent of preschool children are cared for by a non-relative either in their own home or in another location. One important reason for the increase in the need for child care is the rise in the number of families in which both parents work outside the home (Laughlin, 2013).

However, there is another cause, one less tied to the practical considerations of child care: Developmentalists have found increasing evidence that children can benefit substantially from involvement in some form of educational activity before they enroll in formal schooling, which typically takes place at age 5 or 6 in the United States. When compared to children who stay at home and have no formal educational involvement, those children enrolled in *good* preschools experience clear cognitive and social benefits (National Association for the Education of Young Children, 2005; Auger et al., 2014).

THE VARIETY OF EARLY EDUCATION. The variety of early education alternatives is vast. Some outside-the-home care for children is little more than babysitting, while other options are designed to promote intellectual and social advances. Among the major choices of the latter type are the following:

- *Child-care centers* typically provide care for children all day, while their parents are at work. (Child-care centers were previously referred to as *day-care*

Figure 14-1 Care Outside the Home

Approximately 25 percent of children in the United States are enrolled in some form of preschool or day care outside the home—a trend that is the result of more parents being employed full time. Evidence suggests that children can benefit from early childhood education. What role might a caregiver provide that can help the educational development of a child?

(**Source:** Laughlin, 2013.)

Percentage of Children in Each Age Group*	less than 1 year	1–2 years old	3–4 years old
Children in relative care	82%	81%	72%
Children in center-based program	15.9%	30%	51%
Children in other non-relative care	20%	18%	15.4%
Multiple arrangements	22.4%	28.5%	27.2%

*Columns do not add up to 100 because some children participated in more than one type of day care.

centers. However, because a significant number of parents work nonstandard schedules and therefore require care for their children at times other than the day, the preferred label has changed to child-care centers.) Although many child-care centers were first established as safe, warm environments where children could be cared for and could interact with other children, today their purpose tends to be broader, aimed at providing some form of intellectual stimulation. Still, their primary purpose tends to be more social and emotional than cognitive.

- Some child care is provided in *family child-care centers*, small operations run in private homes. Because centers in some areas are unlicensed, the quality of care can be uneven, and parents should consider whether a family child-care center is licensed before enrolling their children. In contrast, providers of center-based care, which is offered in institutions such as school classrooms, community centers, and churches and synagogues, are typically licensed and regulated by governmental authorities. Because teachers in such programs are more often trained professionals than those who provide family child care, the quality of care is often higher.

- *Preschools* are explicitly designed to provide intellectual and social experiences for children. They tend to be more limited in their schedules than family care centers, typically providing care for only three to five hours per day. Because of this limitation, preschools mainly serve children from middle and higher socioeconomic levels, in cases where parents don't need to work full time.

    Like child-care centers, preschools vary enormously in the activities they provide. Some emphasize social skills, while others focus on intellectual development. Some do both. For instance, Montessori preschools, which use a method developed by Italian educator Maria Montessori, employ a carefully designed set of materials to create an environment that fosters sensory, motor, and language development through play. Children are provided with a variety of activities to choose from, with the option of moving from one to another (Gutek, 2003).

    Similarly, in the Reggio Emilia preschool approach—another Italian import—children participate in what is called a *negotiated curriculum* that emphasizes the joint participation of children and teachers. The curriculum builds on the interests of children, promoting their cognitive development through the integration of the arts and participation in week-long projects (Rankin, 2004; Paolella, 2013; Mages, 2016).

- *School child care* is provided by some local school systems in the United States. Almost half the states in the United States fund prekindergarten programs for 4-year-olds, often aimed at disadvantaged children. Because they typically are staffed by better-trained teachers than less-regulated child-care centers, school child-care programs are often of higher quality than other early education alternatives.

THE EFFECTIVENESS OF CHILD CARE.   How effective are such programs? Most research suggests that preschoolers enrolled in child-care centers show intellectual development that at least matches that of children at home, and often is better. For instance, some studies find that preschoolers in child care are more verbally fluent, show memory and comprehension advantages, and even achieve higher IQ scores than at-home children. Other studies find that early and long-term participation in child care is particularly helpful for children from impoverished home environments or for children who are otherwise at risk. Some research even shows that child-care programs can have positive consequences 25 years later (Mervis, 2011a; Reynolds et al., 2011; Vivanti et al., 2014).

Similar advantages are found for social development. Children in high-quality programs tend to be more self-confident, independent, and knowledgeable about the social world in which they live than those who do not participate. This is not to say that all the outcomes of outside-the-home care are positive: Children in child care have been found to be less polite, less compliant, less respectful of adults, and sometimes more competitive and aggressive than their peers (Belsky et al., 2007; Douglass & Klerman, 2012; Huston, Bobbitt, & Bentley, 2015).

Another way to consider the effectiveness of child care is to take an economic approach. For instance, one study of prekindergarten education in Texas found that every dollar invested in high-quality preschool programs produced $8.60 in benefits. Benefits included increased graduation rates, higher earnings, savings in juvenile crime, and reductions in child welfare costs (Aguirre et al., 2006; The Economics of Early Childhood Investments, 2014).

It is important to keep in mind that not all early childhood care programs are equally effective. One key factor is program *quality*: High-quality care provides intellectual and social benefits, while low-quality care not only is unlikely to furnish benefits but may actually may harm children (Votruba-Drzal, Coley, & Chase-Lansdale, 2004; NICHD Early Child Care Research Network, 2006).

THE QUALITY OF CHILD CARE.   How can we define "high quality"? Several characteristics are important; they are analogous to those that pertain to infant child care. The major characteristics of high-quality child care include the following (Lloyd, 2012; Huston, Bobbitt, & Bentley, 2015):

- The care providers are well trained, preferably with bachelor's degrees.
- The child-care center has an appropriate overall size and ratio of care providers to children. Single groups should not have many more than 14 to 20 children, and there should be no more than 5 to 10 3-year-olds per caregiver, or 7 to 10 4- or 5-year-olds per caregiver.
- The child–teacher ratio should be 10:1 or better.
- The curriculum of a child-care facility is not left to chance but is carefully planned out and coordinated among the teachers.
- The language environment is rich, with a great deal of conversation.
- The caregivers are sensitive to children's emotional and social needs, and they know when and when not to intervene.
- Materials and activities are age appropriate.
- Basic health and safety standards are followed.
- Children should be screened for vision, hearing, and health problems.
- At least one meal a day should be served.
- The facility should provide at least one family support service.

No one knows how many programs in the United States can be considered "high quality," but there are many fewer than are desirable. In fact, the United States lags behind almost every other industrialized country in the quality of its child care as well as in its quantity and affordability (Muenchow & Marsland, 2007; Pianta et al., 2009) (see also the *Developmental Diversity and Your Life* box).

PREPARING PRESCHOOLERS FOR ACADEMIC PURSUITS: DOES HEAD START TRULY PROVIDE A HEAD START? Although many programs designed for preschoolers focus primarily on social and emotional factors, some are geared primarily toward promoting cognitive gains and preparing preschoolers for the more formal instruction they will experience when they start kindergarten. In the United States, the best-known program designed to promote future academic success is Head Start. Born in the 1960s when the United States declared a "War on Poverty," the program has served over 30 million children and their families; each year, nearly 1 million children ages 3 and 4 are in Head Start. The program, which

Developmental Diversity and Your Life

Preschools Around the World: Why Does the United States Lag Behind?

In France and Belgium, access to preschool is a legal right. In Sweden and Finland, the governments provide child care to preschoolers whose parents work. Russia has an extensive system of state-run *yasli-sads*, nursery schools and kindergartens, attended by 75 percent of children ages 3 to 7 in urban areas.

In contrast, the United States has no coordinated national policy on preschool education—or on the care of children in general. There are several reasons for this. For one, decisions about education have traditionally been left to the states and local school districts. For another, the United States has no tradition of teaching preschoolers, unlike other countries in which preschool-age children have been enrolled in formal programs for decades. Finally, the status of preschools in the United States has been traditionally low. Consider, for instance, that preschool and nursery school teachers are the lowest paid of all teachers. (Teacher salaries increase as the age of students rises. Thus, college and high

school teachers are paid most, while preschool and elementary school teachers are paid least.)

Preschools also differ significantly from one country to another, reflecting their differing societal views on the purpose of early childhood education. For instance, in a cross-country comparison of preschools in China, Japan, and the United States, researchers found that parents in the three countries view the purpose of preschools very differently. Whereas parents in China tend to see preschools primarily as a way of giving children a good start academically, Japanese parents view them primarily as a way of giving children the opportunity to be members of a group. In the United States, in comparison, parents regard the primary purpose of preschools as making children more independent and self-reliant, although obtaining a good academic start and having group experience are also important (see Figure 14-2; Huntsinger et al., 1997; Roopnarine & Metindogan, 2006)

Figure 14-2 The Purpose of Preschool

To parents in China, Japan, and the United States, the main purpose of preschool is very different. As a preschool educator, how would you interpret these findings?
(**Source:** Based on Tobin, Wu, & Davidson, 1989.)

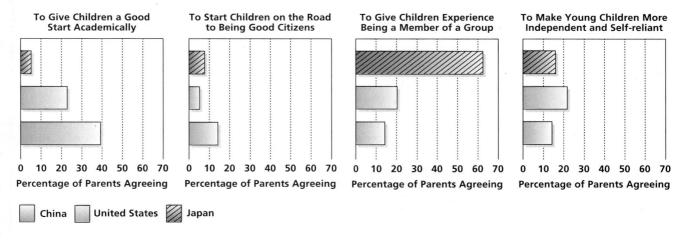

stresses parental involvement, was designed to serve the "whole child," including children's physical health, self-confidence, social responsibility, and social and emotional development (Zigler & Styfco, 2004; Zhai, Raver, & Jones, 2012; Zhang et al., 2015).

Whether or not Head Start is seen as successful depends on the lens through which one is looking. If, for instance, the program is expected to provide long-term increases in IQ scores, it is a disappointment. Although graduates of Head Start programs tend to show immediate IQ gains, these increases do not last.

However, it is clear that Head Start is meeting its goal of getting preschoolers ready for school. Preschoolers who participate in Head Start are better prepared for future schooling—in terms of health, social, emotional, and cognitive factors—than those who do not. Furthermore, graduates of Head Start programs have better future school adjustment than their peers, and they are less likely to be in special education classes or to be retained in grade. Finally, some research suggests that Head Start graduates even show higher academic performance at the end of high school, although the gains are modest (Bierman et al., 2009; Mervis, 2011b; Goble et al., 2017).

The most recent comprehensive evaluation of early intervention programs suggests that, taken as a group, they can provide significant benefits, and that government funds invested early in life may ultimately lead to a reduction in future costs. For instance, compared with children who did not participate in early intervention programs, participants in various programs showed gains in emotional or cognitive development, better educational outcomes, increased economic self-sufficiency, reduced levels of criminal activity, and improved health-related behaviors. Although not every program produced all these benefits, and not every child benefited to the same extent, the results of the evaluation suggested that the potential benefits of early intervention can be substantial (Izard et al., 2008; Mervis, 2011a; Harding, 2015).

Of course, traditional programs such as Head Start, which emphasize academic success brought about by traditional instruction, are not the only approach to early intervention that has proven effective. Montessori schools, which have their own unique philosophy and approach, have also proven valuable.

From Kindergarten to High School: Preparing Students for Success

LO 14.2 **Explain how U.S. students generally progress from kindergarten through high school.**

As the eyes of the six other children in his reading group turned to him, Glenn shifted uneasily in his chair. Reading had never come easily to him, and he always felt anxious when it was his turn to read aloud. But as his teacher nodded in encouragement, he plunged in, hesitantly at first, then gaining momentum as he read the story about a mother's first day on a new job. He found that he could read the passage quite nicely, and he felt a surge of happiness and pride at his accomplishment. When he was done, he broke into a broad smile as his teacher said simply, "Well done, Glenn."

Small moments such as these, repeated over and over, make—or break—a child's educational experience. Schooling marks a time when society formally attempts to transfer to new generations its accumulated body of knowledge, beliefs, values, and wisdom. The success with which this transfer is managed determines, in a very real sense, the future fortunes of the world.

WHAT MAKES CHILDREN READY FOR SCHOOL?   Many parents have a hard time deciding exactly when to enroll their children in school for the first time. Do children who are younger than most of the other children in their grade suffer as a result of the age difference? According to traditional wisdom, the answer is yes. Because younger children are assumed to be slightly less advanced developmentally than their peers, it has been assumed that such children would be at a competitive disadvantage. In some cases, teachers recommended that students delay entry into kindergarten in order to cope better academically and emotionally (Noel & Newman, 2008).

A massive study conducted by developmental psychologist Frederick Morrison contradicts this traditional view. He found that children who are among the youngest in first grade progress at the same rate as the oldest. Although they were slightly behind older first-graders in reading, the difference was negligible. It was also clear that parents who chose to hold their children back in kindergarten, thereby ensuring that they would be among the oldest in first grade and after, were not doing their children a favor. These older children did no better than their younger classmates (Vecchiotti, 2003; Morrison, Bachman, & Connor, 2005).

Other research has even identified some delayed negative reaction to delayed entry. For example, one longitudinal study examined adolescents whose entrance into kindergarten was delayed by a year. Even though many seemed to show no ill effects from the delay during elementary school, during adolescence a surprising number of these children had emotional and behavioral problems (Stipek, 2002).

In short, delaying children's entry into school does not necessarily provide an advantage and in some cases may actually be harmful. Ultimately, age per se is not a critical indicator of when children should begin school. Instead, the start of formal schooling is more reasonably tied to overall developmental readiness, which is the product of a complex combination of factors.

CREATING AN ATMOSPHERE THAT PROMOTES SCHOOL SUCCESS. What makes children succeed in school? Although there are many factors, several practical steps can be taken to maximize children's chances of success. Among them are these:

- **Promote a "literacy environment."** Parents should read to their children and familiarize them with books and reading. Adults should provide reading models so that children see that reading is an important activity in the lives of the adults with whom they interact.

- **Talk to children.** Discuss events in the news, talk about their friends, and share hobbies. Getting children to think about and discuss the world around them is one of the best preparations for school.

- **Provide a place for children to work.** This can be a desk, a corner of a table, or an area of a room. What's important is that it be a separate, designated area.

- **Encourage children's problem-solving skills.** To solve a problem, children should learn to identify their goal, what they know, and what they don't know; to design and carry out a strategy; and finally to evaluate their result.

HOMESCHOOLING: LIVING ROOMS AS CLASSROOMS

> *At 9 a.m. on a Wednesday, Damon Buchanan, 9 years old, sits on the couch going through one of his morning rituals: reading the horoscopes in the newspaper. In the kitchen his brothers, Jacob, age 7, and Logan, age 4, are performing one of their "experiments": dropping action figures and plastic toys into glasses of water, then freezing them. Another day of school has begun.*

For students like the Buchanan brothers, there is no distinction between their living room and classroom because they are among the close to 1 million students who are homeschooled. *Homeschooling* is a major educational phenomenon in which students are taught by their parents in their own homes.

There are a number of reasons why parents may choose to school their children at home. Some parents feel their children will thrive with the one-to-one attention that homeschooling can bring, whereas they might get lost in a larger public school. Other parents are dissatisfied with the nature of instruction and teachers in their local public schools and feel that they can do a better job teaching their children. And some parents engage in homeschooling for religious reasons, wishing to impart a particular religious ideology (and avoid exposing their children to aspects of the popular culture and values

There are a number of reasons why parents may choose to school their children at home, and it has been found that homeschooled children generally do as well on standardized tests as traditionally educated students.

Monkey Business Images/Shutterstock

with which they disagree) that would be impossible in a public school (Dennis, 2004; Jolly, Matthews, & Nester, 2013).

Homeschooling clearly works, in the sense that children who have been home-schooled generally do as well on standardized tests as students who have been educated traditionally. In addition, their acceptance rate into college appears to be no different from that of traditionally schooled children (Lauricella, 2001; Lines, 2001; Jones, 2013).

However, the apparent academic success of children schooled at home does not mean that homeschooling, per se, is effective, because their parents may be more affluent or have the kind of well-structured family situation in which children would succeed no matter what kind of schooling they had. In contrast, parents in dysfunctional and disorganized families are unlikely to have the motivation or interest to home-school their children. For children from families like these, the demands and structure of school may be a good thing.

Critics of homeschooling argue that it has considerable drawbacks. For example, the social interaction involving groups of children that is inherent in classrooms in traditional schools is largely missing for homeschooled children. Learning in an at-home environment, while perhaps strengthening family ties, hardly provides an environment that reflects the diversity of U.S. society. Furthermore, even the best-equipped home is unlikely to have sophisticated science and technology that is available at many schools. Finally, most parents do not have the preparation of well-trained teachers, and their teaching methods may be unsophisticated. Although parents may be successful in teaching subject areas in which their child is already interested, they may have more difficulty teaching subjects that their child seeks to avoid (Lois, 2006; Lubienski, Puckett, & Brewer, 2013).

Because homeschooling is relatively new, few controlled experiments have been conducted examining its effectiveness. More research needs to be done to determine how and when homeschooling is an effective means to educate children.

IN TRANSITION: MAKING THE MOVE FROM ELEMENTARY TO SECONDARY SCHOOL. The transition from elementary school into secondary education is a normative transition, meaning it is part of the life of almost all adolescents in the United States. However, the fact that nearly everyone is doing it doesn't make it easy. The transition can be particularly difficult because of the physical, intellectual, and social changes that are occurring at about the same time.

After leaving elementary school, most students enter a *middle school*, which typically comprises grades six to eight (see Figure 14-3). At the same time, most adolescents are beginning puberty and coming to grips with the changes taking place in their bodies. Furthermore, their thinking is becoming more sophisticated, and their relationships with their family and friends are becoming far more complicated than ever before.

For most adolescents, middle schools provide a very different educational structure from the one they grew

Figure 14-3 Middle School Configurations

The majority of middle schools are comprised of grades six to eight, particularly in suburban and urban locations.
(**Source:** Juvonen et al., 2004.)

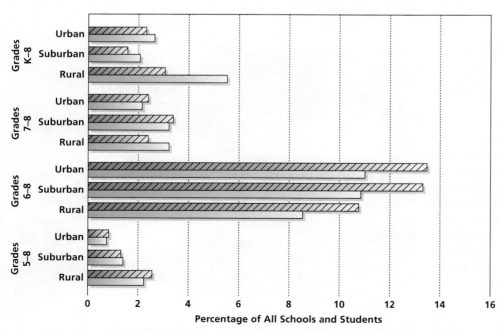

accustomed to in elementary school. Rather than spending the day in a self-contained classroom, students move from one class to another. Not only must they adapt to the demands of different teachers, but their classmates in each course may be different every class period. Those classmates may be more heterogeneous and diverse than those they encountered in their elementary schools.

Furthermore, because they are the youngest and least experienced, students in middle school enter an environment in which they suddenly find themselves at the bottom of the status hierarchy. Coming from elementary schools in which they were at the top of that status hierarchy (and at which they were physically and cognitively so different from the kindergarteners and first-graders who occupied the bottom of the hierarchy), students can find the middle school experience alarming and sometimes damaging.

In addition, middle schools are typically considerably larger than elementary schools. This factor alone makes the transition to middle school more difficult. A significant amount of research demonstrates quite clearly that students do better, both academically and psychologically, in smaller, less bureaucratic educational settings (Lee & Burkam, 2003; Suzuki, 2013).

SCHOOL PERFORMANCE IN ADOLESCENCE. Do the advances that occur in metacognition, reasoning, and other cognitive abilities during adolescence translate into improvements in school performance? If we use students' grades as the measure, the answer is yes. Grades awarded to high school students have shifted upward in the past decade. The mean high school grade point average went up from 3.27 to 3.38 from 1998 to 2016. And the greatest amount of grade inflation occurred in high schools with students who are wealthier, and where most students are white (College Board, 2005; Buckley, Letukas, & Wildavsky, 2018).

At the same time, though, independent measures of achievement, such as SAT scores, have not risen (U.S. Department of Education, 2016). Consequently, a more likely explanation for the higher grades is the phenomenon of grade inflation. According to this view, it is not that students have changed. Instead, instructors have become more lenient, awarding higher grades for the same performance (Cardman, 2004).

Further evidence for grade inflation comes from the relatively poor achievement of students in the United States when compared to students in other countries. For instance, students in the United States score lower on standardized math and science tests when compared to students in many other industrialized countries (see Figure 14-4; OECD, 2014; Pattison, Grodsky, & Muller, 2013).

But the lower scores of U.S. students go beyond grade inflation. For example, U.S. students spend less time in classes and receive less intensive instruction than students in many other countries. Furthermore, the broad diversity of the U.S. school population may affect performance relative to other countries, in which the population attending school is more homogeneous and affluent (Schemo, 2001).

The poorer showing of U.S. students is also reflected in high school graduation rates. Although the United States once stood first in the percentage of the population who graduates from high school, it has dropped to 24th among industrialized countries. Only 84 percent of U.S. high school students graduate—a rate considerably lower than rates in other developed countries (National Center for Education Statistics, 2018).

Figure 14-4 Not at the Top of the Class—U.S. Math Performance Lags

When compared to the math performance of students across the world, U.S. students perform at below-average levels. (**Source:** Adapted from OECD, 2014)

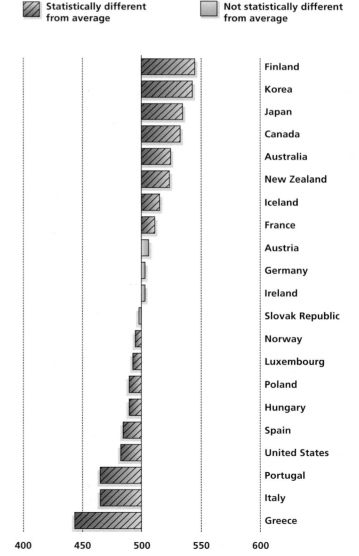

Figure 14-5 Achievement Test Results

Racial discrepancies between groups are apparent on a national test of reading and math achievement administered to a sample of 150,000 eighth-graders.

(**Source:** Donahue, Daane, & Jin, 2005; Perie, Grigg, & Dion, 2005.)

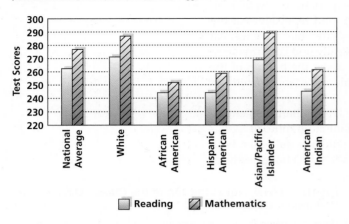

ETHNIC AND RACIAL DIFFERENCES IN SCHOOL ACHIEVEMENT.

Achievement differences between ethnic and racial groups are significant, and they paint a troubling picture of American education. For instance, data on school achievement indicate that, on average, African American and Hispanic students tend to perform at lower levels, receive lower grades, and score lower on standardized tests of achievement than Caucasian students (see Figure 14-5). In contrast, Asian American students tend to receive higher grades than Caucasian students (Byun & Park, 2012).

What is the source of such ethnic and racial differences in academic achievement? Aside from different attributional orientations, much of the difference is due to socioeconomic factors: Because a higher proportion of African American and Hispanic families live in poverty than the proportion of whites living in poverty, their economic disadvantage may be reflected in their school performance. When we take socioeconomic levels into account by comparing different ethnic and racial groups at the same socioeconomic level, achievement differences diminish, but they do not vanish (Cokley, 2003; Guerrero et al., 2006; Kurtz-Costes, Swinton, & Skinner, 2014).

Anthropologist John Ogbu (2003) argues that members of certain minority groups may perceive school success as relatively unimportant. They may believe that societal prejudice in the workplace will dictate that they will not succeed, no matter how much effort they expend. The conclusion is that hard work in school will have no eventual payoff.

Ogbu suggests that members of minority groups who enter a new culture voluntarily are more likely to be successful in school than those who are brought into a new culture against their will. For instance, he notes that Korean children who are the sons and daughters of voluntary immigrants to the United States tend to be, on average, quite successful in school. In contrast, Korean children in Japan whose parents were forced to immigrate during World War II and work as forced laborers tend to do relatively poorly in school. The reason for the disparity? The process of involuntary immigration apparently leaves lasting scars, reducing the motivation to succeed in subsequent generations. Ogbu suggests that in the United States, the involuntary immigration, as slaves, of the ancestors of many African American students might be related to their motivation to succeed (Ogbu, 2003; Jenkins et al., 2004).

Students' beliefs about the consequences of not doing well in school may also contribute to the racial and ethnic differences in school performance. Specifically, it may be that African American and Hispanic students tend to believe that they can succeed *despite* poor school performance. This belief may cause them to put less effort into their studies. In contrast, Asian American students tend to believe that if they do not do well in school, they are unlikely to get good jobs and be successful. Asian Americans, then, are motivated to work hard in school by a fear of the consequences of poor academic performance (Steinberg, Dornbusch, & Brown, 1992; Witkow & Fuligni, 2007; Kim & Lee, 2014).

DROPPING OUT OF SCHOOL.

Although most students complete high school, nearly one out of three public high school students drop out without graduating. The consequences of dropping out are severe. High school dropouts earn 42 percent less than high school graduates, and the unemployment rate for dropouts is 50 percent.

Adolescents who leave school do so for a variety of reasons. Some leave because of pregnancy or problems with the English language. Some leave for economic reasons, needing to support themselves or their families. Others leave because they are academically or socially disengaged (Croninger & Lee, 2001; Lee & Burkam, 2003; Bask & Salmela-Aro, 2013).

Figure 14-6 School Dropout Rates

Despite the fact that dropout rates have been falling for all ethnic groups, Hispanic and African American students are still less likely to graduate.
(**Source:** U.S. Department of Education, 2015.)

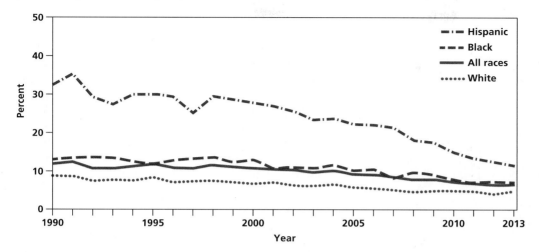

Dropout rates differ according to gender and ethnicity. Males are considerably more likely to drop out of school than females. In addition, although the dropout rate for all ethnicities has been declining somewhat over the past two decades, Hispanic and African American students still are more likely to leave high school before graduating than non-Hispanic white students (see Figure 14-6). However, not all minority groups show higher dropout rates: Asians, for instance, drop out at a lower rate than Caucasians (National Center for Education Statistics, 2003; Stearns & Glennie, 2006).

Poverty plays a large role in determining whether a student completes high school. Students from lower-income households are three times more likely to drop out than middle- and upper-income households. Because economic success is so dependent on education, dropping out often perpetuates a cycle of poverty (National Center for Education Statistics, 2002; Baydu, Kaplan, & Bayar, 2013).

Beyond High School: The Pursuit of Higher Education and Lifelong Learning

LO 14.3 Describe the nature of the U.S. college population.

For Enrico Vasquez, there was never any doubt: He was headed for college. Enrico, the son of a wealthy Cuban immigrant who had made a fortune in the medical supply business after fleeing Cuba five years before Enrico's birth, had had the importance of education constantly drummed into him by his family. In fact, the question was never whether he would go to college but what college he would be able to get into. As a consequence, Enrico found high school to be a pressure cooker: Every grade and extracurricular activity was evaluated in terms of its helping or hindering his chances of admission to a good college.

* * * *

Armando Williams's letter of acceptance to Dallas County Community College is framed on the wall of his mother's apartment. To her, the letter represents nothing short of a miracle, an answer to her prayers. Growing up in a neighborhood infamous for its drugs and drive-by shootings, Armando had always been a hard worker and a "good boy," in his mother's view. But when he was growing up, she never even entertained the possibility of his making it to college. To see him reach this stage in his education fills her with joy.

Figure 14-7 Who Goes to College?

The proportion of nonwhites who attend college is far lower than the proportion of whites.

(**Source:** U.S. Department of Commerce, Census Bureau, Current Population Survey (CPS), October, 1990–2013.)

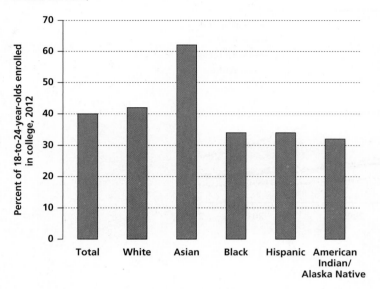

Whether a student's enrollment seems almost inevitable or signifies a triumph over the odds, attending college is a significant accomplishment. Although students already enrolled may feel that college attendance is nearly universal, this is not the case at all: Nationwide, only a minority of high school graduates enter college.

Furthermore, even for students for whom college was an inevitability, getting admitted to college may become a process that produces significant stress. Students who apply to colleges that accept only a small proportion of applicants may experience considerable anxiety as they await notification of which colleges will accept them. This stress, some of which is self-generated and some of which comes from family and peer pressure, can make the senior year of high school quite trying, as these blog excerpts suggest:

Desperately need help choosing college!!! Need advice please read!!! Can't sleep!!

Thank you O powerful (and treacherous) college gods for nothing but my current state of depression and anxiousness. (Saulny, 2006, p. 11)

We'll consider who goes to college and discuss some of the issues that relate to college attendance.

WHO GOES TO COLLEGE? As in the U.S. population as a whole, U.S. college students are primarily white and middle class. About 58 percent of the 18- to 24-year-old college population is white, compared with 17 percent Hispanic, 14 percent black, 7 percent Asian, and 2 percent other race/ethnicities (National Center for Education Statistics, 2018) (see Figure 14-7).

From Research to Practice

Does a Racially Diverse College Campus Make for a Richer Learning Environment?

One factor students sometimes consider in choosing a college to attend is the diversity of the student body. Some applicants—perhaps those seeking to learn about people from different backgrounds—are attracted to campuses with a diverse ethnic mixture. But the benefits of studying in a racially diverse environment may actually extend beyond learning about others, and may actually help students to think more effectively and critically.

It seems reasonable that diversity should stimulate critical thinking, and research has been supportive of this hypothesis. For example, in homogenous settings, in which students have similar backgrounds and perspectives, students bring similarities in thinking to situations in which they engage in problem solving. By contrast, diverse groups, whose members represent a variety of backgrounds and perspectives, bring greater variety in ideas and perspectives that the group must integrate in their discussions. This engagement with different outlooks on a problem tends to increase the complexity of the group members' thinking (Gurin et al., 2003; Roksa et al., 2017).

These findings are consistent with a growing body of research that finds that exposure to other students who represent the range of cultures, ethnicities, and races has important consequences. Not only do students benefit socially in terms of increased multicultural understanding, but their cognitive development is also enhanced. In short, diversity has significant cognitive benefits, leading to more critical thinking and other sorts of cognitive advances (Gurin, Nagda, & Lopez, 2004; Nagda, Gurin, & Johnson, 2005; Pascarella et al., 2014).

Shared Writing Prompt

How might you counter concerns that greater classroom diversity could make students feel less comfortable and therefore less willing to engage and able to learn effectively?

Furthermore, the proportion of students who enter college but ultimately never graduate is substantial. Only around 55 percent of those who start college complete a degree within six years. For some minorities, the picture is even worse: The national dropout rate for African American college students stands at 38 percent and at 46 percent for Hispanic students (Shapiro et al., 2017).

These observations notwithstanding, the number of students traditionally classified as "minorities" attending college is rising dramatically, and ethnic and racial minorities make up an increasingly larger proportion of the college population. Already at some colleges, such as the University of California at Berkeley, whites have shifted from the majority to the minority as diversity among the students has increased significantly. These trends, reflecting changes in the racial and ethnic composition of the United States, are significant, since higher education remains an important way for families to improve their economic well-being.

GENDER IN THE CLASSROOM

> I registered for a calculus course my first year at DePauw. Even 20 years ago I was not timid, so on the very first day I raised my hand and asked a question. I still have a vivid memory of the professor rolling his eyes, hitting his head with his hand in frustration, and announcing to everyone, "Why do they expect me to teach calculus to girls?" I never asked another question. (Sadker & Sadker, 1994, p. 162)

Although such incidents of blatant sexism are less likely to occur today, prejudice and discrimination directed at women are still a fact of college life. For instance, the next time you are in class, consider the gender of your classmates and the subject matter of the class. Although men and women attend college in roughly equal numbers, there is significant variation in the classes they take. Classes in education and the social sciences, for instance, typically have a larger proportion of women than men; and classes in engineering, the physical sciences, and mathematics tend to have more men than women.

The gender gap is also apparent when we look at college instructors. Although the number of female faculty members has increased, there is still evidence of apparent discrimination. For example, the more prestigious the institution, the smaller the proportion of women who have attained the highest rank. The situation is even more pronounced in the fields of math, science, and engineering, where women are significantly underrepresented (Wilson, 2004; Halpern, 2014; Lemaster et al., 2015).

The persistent differences in gender distribution across subject areas likely reflect the powerful influence of gender stereotypes that operate throughout the world of education and beyond. For instance, when women in their first year of college are asked to name a likely career choice, they are much less apt to choose careers that have traditionally been dominated by men, such as engineering or computer programming, and more likely to choose professions that have traditionally been populated by women, such as nursing and social work. Furthermore, even when they do choose to enter math- and science-related fields, they may face sex discrimination (Lane, Goh, & Driver-Linn, 2012; Jerrim & Schoon, 2014).

Male and female college students also have different expectations regarding their areas of competence. For instance, one survey asked first-year college students whether they were above or below average on a variety of traits and abilities. As can be seen in Figure 14-8, men were more likely than women to think of themselves as above average in overall academic and mathematical ability, competitiveness, and emotional health.

Both male and female college professors treat men and women differently in their classes, even though the different treatment is largely unintentional and often the professors are unaware of their actions. For instance, professors may call on men in class more frequently than women, and they make more eye contact with men than with women. Furthermore, male students are more likely to receive extra help from their professors than are female students. Finally, the male students often receive more positive reinforcement for their comments than female students, particularly in science and math fields (Sadker et al., 2007; D'Lima, Winsler, & Kitsantas, 2014).

Figure 14-8 Self-Perception of Ability

During their first year of college, men are more likely than women to view themselves as above average in areas relevant to academic success.

(**Source:** Data from Sax et al., 2000.)

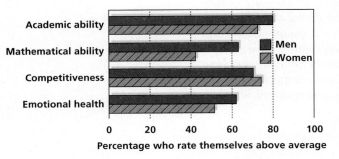

The different treatment of men and women in the classroom has led some educators to argue in favor of single-sex education for women. They point to evidence that the rate of participation and ultimately the success of women in the sciences is greater for graduates of women's colleges than for graduates of coeducational institutions. Furthermore, some research suggests that women who attend same-sex colleges may show higher self-esteem than those attending coeducational colleges, although the evidence is not entirely consistent on this count (Mael, 1998; Sax, 2005).

Why might women do better in single-sex environments? One reason is that they receive more attention than they would in coeducational settings, where professors are affected, however inadvertently, by societal biases. In addition, women's colleges tend to have more female professors than coeducational institutions, and they thereby provide more role models for women. Finally, women attending women's colleges may receive more encouragement for participation in nontraditional subjects such as mathematics and science than those in coeducational colleges (Robinson & Gillibrand, 2004).

THE OLDER, NONTRADITIONAL STUDENT. If you picture the "average college student" as an 18- or 19-year-old, it's time to rethink. Actually, around 40 percent of students taking college courses for credit in the United States are over age 25 (National Center for Education Statistics, 2018).

Why are so many older, nontraditional students taking college courses? One reason is economic. A college degree is becoming increasingly important for obtaining a job. Many employers encourage or require workers to undergo college-based training to learn new skills or update old ones.

In addition, as young adults age, they begin to feel the need to settle down with a family. This change in attitude can reduce their risk-taking behavior and make them focus more on acquiring the ability to support their family—a phenomenon that has been labeled *maturation reform.*

From *an educator's* perspective

How is the presence of older students likely to affect the college classroom, given what you know about human development? Why?

Several broad goals underlie adults' participation in learning. First, adults sometimes seek to understand their own aging, trying to figure out what is happening to them and what to expect in the future. Second, some adults seek to understand more fully the rapid technological and cultural changes of modern life. Third, some adult learners may be seeking a practical edge in combating obsolescence on the job by acquiring new vocational skills. Finally, education may be seen as helpful in preparing for future retirement. Concerned about shifting from a work orientation to a leisure orientation, they may see education as a means of broadening their possibilities (McGuire, 2017).

LEARNING IN LATER LIFE: NEVER TOO LATE TO LEARN

Martha Tilden and Jim Hertz, both 71, loved the Metropolitan Opera House tour, the talk by the famous tenor, the ballet, and the lectures they attended during the "Lincoln Center Festival" trip they are just finishing. Martha and Jim are veterans of Road Scholar (formerly Elderhostel), which has scrapped any suggestion of "elderness" or cheap student housing. All the educational programs they have taken have featured comfortable hotel or dorm rooms and mixed-age events. Now Martha and Jim are discussing their next program, trying to decide between a wildlife trip to Ontario and a "Building Bridges to Islam" program in Virginia.

More than 250,000 people enroll annually in thousands of classes organized by Road Scholar, the largest educational program for people in late adulthood. Represented on campuses across the world, the Road Scholar movement is further evidence that intellectual growth and change continue throughout people's lives. Although not everyone can afford Road Scholar tuitions, many public colleges encourage senior citizens to enroll in classes by offering free tuition. In addition, some retirement communities are located at or near college campuses, such as the University of Michigan and Penn State University (Spiers, 2014).

Although some elderly people are doubtful about their intellectual capabilities and consequently hesitate to compete with younger students in regular classes, their concern is largely misplaced. Older adults often have no trouble maintaining their standing in rigorous college classes. Furthermore, professors and other students generally find the presence of older people, with their varied and substantial life experiences, a real educational benefit (Simson, Wilson, & Harlow-Rosentraub, 2006).

Older adults have no trouble keeping up with college courses.

Module 14.1 Review

LO 14.1   Analyze the functions and types of preschool education in the United States.

A key factor in the effects of preschools is their level of quality. Montessori preschools, developed in Italy, employ a carefully designed set of materials to create an environment that fosters sensory, motor, and language development through play.

LO 14.2   Explain how U.S. students generally progress from kindergarten through high school.

Handling the transition from elementary to secondary school is especially difficult for young adolescents because of the other developmental issues that they face at around the same time. In recent years, homeschooling has emerged as a way for parents to educate their children at home while meeting district and state educational requirements. Performance in school depends on a number of factors, including socioeconomic status and race/ethnicity.

LO 14.3   Describe the nature of the U.S. college population.

African American and Hispanic high school graduates enroll in colleges in lower proportions than white high school graduates, but, overall, the number of students from minority groups attending college is on the rise and their proportions within the college population are growing. More than a quarter of all college students are 25 or older. These older, nontraditional students take college courses to learn new vocational skills, acquire technological knowledge, to achieve greater self-understanding, and to prepare for their future retirement.

Journal Writing Prompt

Applying Lifespan Development: In terms of the development of identity, what advantages and disadvantages would you predict for homeschooled adolescents?

MODULE 14.2

LEISURE

For fun I like doing things outside, like playing sports. I played football for my high school and I also did a lot of drama classes. I was in chorus. I love acting and singing and pretty much being on stage. I love hanging out with friends and going to parties and cookouts or camping—anything to do with a lot of people.... So anything fun that can make me laugh or make someone around me laugh I like. I also love going to the movies or out to eat.

The leisure time of this highly social adolescent (writing in an anonymous blog) is filled with a swirl of group activities. For others, leisure time is occupied by more solitary interests, with more hours spent in front of a computer screen than in the presence of other people. For still others, especially the many adolescents who are employed, leisure time is a rare commodity.

Almost everyone has a certain amount of leisure time at their disposal. How they carve out that time has important implications for the quality of life they enjoy. Let's examine how adolescents use leisure time, followed by a look at how older adults make choices about what to do in their spare time.

Time on Their Hands: Leisure in Adolescence

LO 14.4 Describe how adolescents spend their leisure time.

What *are* adolescents doing with their time? Surprisingly, it's a question that has been addressed systematically only recently because most adolescent specialists assumed that schooling was the predominant influence on adolescent development. But it's becoming increasingly clear that we need to better understand how adolescents spend their non-school-related time in order to get a complete picture of the major influences on adolescent development. To do that, adolescent scientists have used a variety of techniques designed to understand just what adolescents are doing.

SPENDING TIME. It's not easy to know with precision what adolescents are doing. The easiest technique—simply asking them what they've been doing—is not always the most precise. Consider, for example, how you would respond if you were asked to pinpoint to the minute what you did yesterday. Although you might be able to broadly define your activities, many of the details would probably be lost. (For instance, just how often and how long did you spend checking your messages or email throughout the day?)

To overcome the problem, social scientists have devised methodologies that go beyond mere questionnaires. For example, one increasingly common technique is the *experience sampling method* in which study participants wear an alarm watch that is remotely signaled to sound once every two hours during participants' waking hours. When the alarm sounds, participants complete a self-report form that asks what they are doing, the situation, and their emotional state. Because the experience sampling method relies less on memory and more on immediate self-report, it has proven a reliable measure of how adolescents use their time (Chen, 2006; Green et al., 2006; Maes et al., 2015).

Using the experience sampling method, researchers have found that suburban, middle-class white adolescents spend, on average, almost half their time in leisure activities. Furthermore, some 29 percent is spent in "productive" activities, such as school, homework, and paid work. Another quarter or so is spent on "maintenance" activities such as eating, transportation, chores and errands, and personal maintenance such as personal hygiene (Larson et al., 2001; see Figure 14-9).

Significant racial and cultural differences and individual differences have been found in use of time. For example, compared to their white suburban counterparts, poor African American adolescents living in urban areas spend somewhat less time on productive activities and somewhat more on leisure activities, especially viewing television (18 percent compared with 13 percent of the white sample) (Larson et al., 2001).

Furthermore, adolescents fall into several broad categories in terms of time use relating to the specific activities in which they participate. More than half are quite busy, spending significant amounts of time on homework, extracurricular activities, time with friends after school and on weekends, chores, and sometimes paid work. Around a third of adolescents, however, spend time on only one or just a few activities, such as primarily engaging in paid employment, with little or no engagement in extracurricular activities. Another group spends most of their time hanging out with friends, and neither work nor participate in extracurricular activities (Shanahan & Flaherty, 2001).

In addition, some adolescents' time investments change according to their age. For instance, as they become older, they are more likely

Figure 14-9 Spending Time

According to the experience sampling method, suburban, middle-class white adolescents differ from poor African Americans in terms of how they spend their time.

(**Source:** Data from Larson et al., 2001, Table 2.)

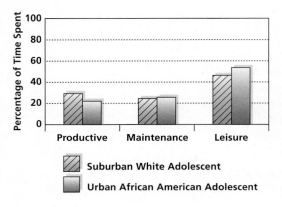

to spend a greater proportion of their time working. Individuals who were highly involved in many activities as younger adolescents usually remain busy throughout adolescence. Similarly, those who were less busy and were involved in a small number of domains continue to be involved in only a few domains. But the less busy adolescents often shift their interests over the course of adolescence (Shanahan & Flaherty, 2001).

The overall degree of time use is related to adolescent success. Busier adolescents tend to be more successful academically. They have higher grades and are better adjusted than those who are committed to fewer tasks. Busier adolescents are particularly better off than adolescents who spend minimal time in academic-related pursuits and more time in work (Shanahan & Flaherty, 2001; Mortimer, 2003).

Adolescents' use of time is not a zero-sum situation in which participation in one domain displaces participation in another domain. Instead, some adolescents are very busy, and others are not. Furthermore, some adolescents are carrying out multiple tasks simultaneously. Indeed, popular wisdom suggests that adolescents are particularly accomplished multitaskers. Is that true?

From *a high school administrator's* perspective

Are there any types of approaches that can be implemented in the school curriculum that can help students develop better uses of non-school-related time?

SHIFTING ATTENTION: THIS IS YOUR BRAIN ON MULTITASKING.   When an adolescent is simultaneously texting his friends, listening to Spotify, and writing a paper for class, is there a particular part of the brain that permits him to multitask in this way? More broadly, are adolescents, more than adults, adept at multitasking?

The answer to both questions is no. No one's brain—even one belonging to the most practiced multitasking adolescent—is designed to allow for the simultaneous processing of information in multiple channels. Instead, the brain switches back and forth between different media sources, prioritizing the information that is of greatest interest and importance. Although we can do some highly routine tasks simultaneously—like chewing gum and walking—most tasks are performed sequentially. Solving calculus problems while reading a history book, or even talking on the phone while driving, can be challenging propositions.

According to functional magnetic resonance imaging (fMRI) studies, the brain's anterior prefrontal cortex is responsible for switching attention from one task to another. One part of the brain in particular permits adolescents (as well as the rest of us) to return to tasks that they have already started and take up where they left off. The prefrontal cortex is one of the last areas of the brain to mature, suggesting that younger adolescents may be less efficient at multitasking than older ones (van der Schuur et al., 2018).

Even the most adept multitaskers, however, are limited by the hard-wired nature of the brain in their efforts to switch among different activities. The more tasks that individuals seek to accomplish, the greater the difficulties they encounter. Not only do errors increase, but efficiency plummets. Consequently, it takes longer to complete tasks when alternating between them than when doing them sequentially (Meyer et al., 2002; Luria & Meiran, 2005; Christensen et al., 2015).

In short, despite popular wisdom that contemporary adolescents are particularly proficient at multitasking, there's no evidence showing that they do it better than adults. They may multitask more frequently, but they suffer from the same limitations as older people. The brain simply does not have the wiring to allow great success at multitasking.

MEDIA AND TECHNOLOGY USE BY ADOLESCENTS

Prakash Subhani faces a choice: study for his chemistry final or check out Facebook. Prakash needs to do well on the test to raise his grade. But he also needs to keep up with his friends in India. Finally, he decides to compromise. He'll spend a half hour on Facebook and devote the rest of the night to study. But the next time he looks at his watch, nearly four hours have passed and he is too tired to study. Prakash has to face his chemistry test unprepared.

Figure 14-10 Teenagers and Social Media Use

Adolescents' use of social media is frequent even at the start of the teenage years and becomes more frequent as they become older.

(**Source:** Mary Madden et al., 2013. Amanda Lenhart, Sandra Cortesi, Urs Gasser, Maeve Duggan, Aaron Smith, and Meredith Beaton. (2013, May 21). Teens, Social Media, and Privacy. Pew Research Center: Internet & Technology.)

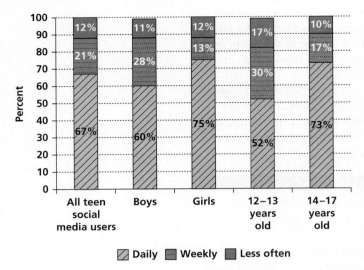

Facebook is only one of the enormous varieties of media and technologies available to adolescents, ranging from more traditional sorts, such as radio and television, to newer forms, such as text messaging and Twitter. And like Prakash Subhani, most adolescents make use of them—to a staggering degree.

According to a comprehensive survey using a sample of boys and girls ages 8 to 18 conducted by the Kaiser Family Foundation (a well-respected think tank), young people spend an average of 6.5 hours a day with media. Furthermore, because around a quarter of the time they are using more than one form of medium simultaneously, they are actually being exposed to the equivalent of 8.5 hours per day. Other, more recent research concurs, finding that teenagers spend around 9 hours a day using media (Rideout, Roberts, & Foehr, 2005; Tsukayama, 2015).

The amount of media use can be extraordinary. For example, some teenagers send nearly 30,000 texts a month, often carrying on multiple conversations simultaneously. The use of texting often supplants other forms of social interaction, such as telephone calls or even face-to-face interaction (Richtel, 2010; Blair, Fletcher, & Gaskin, 2015; also see Figure 14-10).

Adolescents are also likely to use multiple social platforms, with Facebook, Instagram, and Snapchat being most popular. There are also gender differences; boys are more likely to use Facebook, while girls are more likely to use visually oriented platforms such as Tumblr, Pinterest, and Instagram. Both boys and girls have few privacy concerns: Surveys show that nearly all share their names, birthdates, and photos of themselves. Finally, adolescents use social media to advance their romantic interests (Lenhart, Smith, & Anderson, 2015; Office of Adolescent Health, 2016).

For many adolescents, another form of social media involves engagement in online video games. In addition to their gaming aspects, video games provide a means to communicate with peers. Furthermore, some research suggests that video games provide cognitive stimulation. For example, even violent types of action or "shooter" video games produce improvements in attention, visual processing, spatial skills, and mental rotation abilities (Green & Bavelier, 2012; Uttal et al., 2013).

There are clear downsides to the social media use of adolescents. For example, some developmentalists suggest that high frequency of social media use is related to a decline in face-to-face social competence. In this view, online involvement reduces the opportunities to learn social skills. However, some aspects of social media use may actually help adolescents learn certain types of social skills and thereby enhance their overall social competence (Yang & Brown 2015; Reich, 2017).

Furthermore, some forms of online activities can be mean-spirited. For example, some teenagers make use of the Internet to bully others, repeatedly texting or emailing with hurtful messages. The source of such *cyberbullying* can remain anonymous, and the messages may be particularly abusive. Although they do not inflict physical harm, they can be psychologically damaging (Zacchilli & Valerio, 2011; Best, Manktelow, & Taylor, 2014; Bartlett et al., 2017).

Clearly, the media play a number of roles in adolescents' lives. Let's look at some of the specific types of media to which teenagers are exposed and consider their consequences.

Television.   Despite the proliferation of new technologies, television viewing remains the most frequent activity. Although figures on actual exposure to television vary significantly depending on how viewing is assessed, television use is substantial. On average, 8- to 18-year-olds watch 4.5 hours per day, and total daily media exposure is even higher, averaging 10 hours a day. Interestingly, that 10 hours is squeezed into about 7.5 hours per day due to multitasking (Roberts, Henriksen, & Foehr, 2004; Kaiser Family Foundation, 2010).

It's certainly easy for adolescents to watch television, given that two-thirds of U.S. 8- to 18-year-olds have television sets in their bedrooms. But not all of that viewing is particularly attentive. Sometimes adolescents leave the television on and only monitor what is going on rather than paying careful attention (Comstock & Scharrer, 1999; Rideout, Roberts, & Foehr, 2005).

When they do pay attention to what they are watching, though, adolescents are affected by their viewing in significant ways. For instance, television provides information about appropriateness of body image. In many ways, the television-based view of women's bodies is idealized in a way that barely approaches reality. Women with large breasts, small waists, and slender legs are represented as an ideal. Yet few adolescents (or anyone else) can achieve such a standard. Ultimately, the more adolescents watch television and are exposed to these idealized body images, the more negative is their own body image (Clay, Vignoles, & Dittmar, 2005; Ward & Friedman, 2006).

Television may also have an impact on the physical well-being of adolescents. For instance, according to the results of one survey, teenagers with the greatest number of electronic devices were twice as likely to fall asleep in school, suggesting that the availability of the equipment reduced the number of hours the most technologically well-equipped adolescents were sleeping. In addition, obesity has been linked to the level of television viewing: More hours spent viewing are associated with higher levels of adolescent obesity—largely due to the sedentary nature of television (Lawlor et al., 2005; National Sleep Foundation, 2006; Persch et al., 2015).

Computers and the Internet.   Despite the fact that adolescents are spending far more time using the Internet than they did a few decades ago—when the Internet was quite new and access was limited—we still don't know a great deal about its effects on adolescent development. Surveys are only recently telling us what, at least generally, adolescents are doing when they are online.

Most of the time, adolescents are visiting websites that have to do with entertainment and sports. Older adolescents also spend more substantial amounts of time on relationship-oriented sites like Facebook (Roberts & Foehr, 2003).

Although fears that cyberspace is overrun with child molesters are exaggerated, it is true that the Internet makes available material that many parents and other adults find highly objectionable. In addition, there is a growing problem with Internet gambling. High school and college students can easily bet on sports events and participate in games such as poker on the web using credit cards (Winters, Stinchfield, & Botzet, 2005; Floros et al., 2015).

The growing use of computers also presents a challenge involving socioeconomic status, race, and ethnicity. Poorer adolescents and members of minority groups have less access to computers than more affluent adolescents and members of socially advantaged groups—a phenomenon known as the *digital divide*. For example, 17 percent of households with school-age children lack regular access to the web. And there are stark racial and ethnic differences: 77 percent of African American students reported using a personal computer frequently, compared with 87 percent of white students and 81 percent of Hispanic/Latino students. Asian American students had the highest rates of computer use, at 91 percent (Sax et al., 2004; Fetterman, 2005). Furthermore, only 18 percent of teachers believe that their students have the digital resources available to complete assignments at home, and students agree: 42 percent of students say they received a lower grade on an assignment because they did not have Internet access. How society reduces these discrepancies is a matter of considerable importance (Olsen, 2009; Purcell et al., 2013; Hispanic Heritage Foundation, 2015).

Life Beyond Work: More Time for Leisure in Middle Adulthood

LO 14.5 Explain how the use of time changes in early and middle adulthood.

At 48, Marian Barnes felt the time had come to take on fewer "extra" projects at work. She was comfortable in her job and was no longer fixated on getting the next

For many adults, priorities change in midlife when they find the time to pursue dreams from early adulthood.

promotion. With the last of the kids off to college, Marian felt she could finally indulge in a few of the leisure activities she'd been dreaming of during the hectic years of full-time work and childrearing. She signed up for a weekly tennis group and collected the necessary signatures to run for Town Meeting, a civic activity that had always interested her.

Some of the busiest adults are young adults. As they build careers and families, they often feel as though they have little leisure time at their disposal. For many adults priorities change in midlife. Career ambitions begin to take a back seat to social relationships and personal interests. Children leave home. Midlife adults, like Marian Barnes, may find the time has come to live some of the dreams they formulated during the too-busy years of early adulthood.

THE EMPTY NEST: MORE FREE TIME. With the typical workweek hovering between 35 and 40 hours—and becoming shorter for most people—most middle-aged adults have some 70 waking hours per week at their disposal. What do they do with their leisure time?

For one thing—just as many adolescents do—they watch television. On average, middle-aged people watch around 15 hours of television each week. But middle-aged adults do much more with their leisure time than watch television. For many people, middle adulthood represents a renewed opportunity to become involved in activities outside the home. As children leave home, parents have substantial time freed up to participate more extensively in leisure activities such as taking up sports, or civic participation such as joining town committees. Middle-aged adults in the United States spend about six hours each week socializing (Lindstrom et al., 2005).

A significant number of people find the allure of leisure so great that they take early retirement. For those who make such a choice and who have adequate financial resources to last the dozens of years that likely remain to them, life can be quite gratifying. Early retirees tend to be in good health, and they may take up a variety of new activities (Litwin, 2007; deWind et al., 2015).

A MORE LEISURELY PACE? Although middle adulthood presents the opportunity for more leisure activities, most people report that the pace of their lives does not seem slower. Because they are involved in a variety of activities, much of their free time is scattered throughout the week in 15- and 30-minute chunks. Consequently, despite a documented increase of five hours of weekly leisure time since 1965, many people feel they have no more free time than they did earlier (Offer, 2016).

Because the pace of life in the United States is still considerably faster than in many countries, extra leisure time may not be noticeable. By measuring the length of time average pedestrians cover 60 feet, the time it takes for a customer to purchase a stamp, and the accuracy of public clocks, research has compared the tempo of living in a variety of countries. According to a composite of these measures, the United States has a quicker tempo than many other countries, particularly Latin American, Asian, Middle Eastern, and African countries. But many countries outpace the United States. For example, Western European countries and Japan operate more quickly than the United States, with Switzerland ranking first (see Table 14-1; Levine, 1997a).

Table 14-1 Comparative Pace of Life (Rank #1 = Highest Pace)

Rank	Overall Pace of Life	Time to Walk 60 Feet	Time to Buy a Postage Stamp	Accuracy of Public Clocks
1	Switzerland	Ireland	Germany	Switzerland
2	Ireland	Netherlands	Switzerland	Italy
3	Germany	Switzerland	Ireland	Austria
4	Japan	England	Japan	Singapore
5	Italy	Germany	Sweden	Romania
6	England	United States	Hong Kong	Japan
7	Sweden	Japan	Taiwan	Sweden
8	Austria	France	Austria	Germany
9	Netherlands	Kenya	England	Poland
10	Hong Kong	Italy	Costa Rica	France
11	France	Canada	Singapore	Ireland
12	Poland	Poland	Italy	China
13	Costa Rica	Sweden	Greece	England
14	Taiwan	Hong Kong	Netherlands	Hong Kong
15	Singapore	Greece	Poland	Costa Rica
16	United States	Costa Rica	El Salvador	South Korea
17	Canada	Mexico	Czech Republic	Bulgaria
18	South Korea	Taiwan	France	Hungary
19	Hungary	Hungary	Hungary	Jordan
20	Czech Republic	South Korea	South Korea	United States
21	Greece	Czech Republic	Canada	Taiwan
22	Kenya	El Salvador	Bulgaria	Canada
23	China	Austria	United States	Czech Republic
24	Bulgaria	China	Brazil	Kenya
25	Romania	Singapore	China	Netherlands
26	Jordan	Indonesia	Indonesia	Mexico
27	Syria	Bulgaria	Jordan	Syria
28	El Salvador	Jordan	Syria	Brazil
29	Brazil	Syria	Romania	Greece
30	Indonesia	Romania	Kenya	Indonesia
31	Mexico	Brazil	Mexico	El Salvador

Rank of 31 countries for overall pace of life and for three measures: minutes downtown pedestrians take to walk 60 feet; minutes it takes a postal clerk to complete a stamp purchase transaction; and accuracy in minutes of public clocks.

(**Source:** Based on Levine, 1997b.)

Module 14.2 Review

LO 14.4   Describe how adolescents spend their leisure time.

Adolescents spend almost half their time on leisure activities, with the rest divided between productive activities and maintenance activities. Adolescents can be categorized into two broad groups: busier and less busy, with busier adolescents tending to be more successful academically. True multitasking is no more possible for adolescents than for adults, although adolescents seem to prefer switching among a large number of activities. Adolescents have access to an enormous range of media and technologies, which can enhance entertainment and ease stress but can also enable excessive exposure to violence and sexual content.

LO 14.5   Explain how the use of time changes in early and middle adulthood.

Although people in early adulthood who are building careers and families often experience few opportunities for leisure activities, people in middle adulthood usually have more leisure time than previously. Often they use it to become more involved outside the home in recreational and community activities.

Journal Writing Prompt

Applying Lifespan Development: Do you think adolescents' increased access to technology and media simply continues a trend that began with radio and television, or is the abundance of new technologies likely to have significant psychological and societal effects? Why?

LIVING IN A MULTICULTURAL WORLD

"I can't go," said Chanthou when her teacher enthusiastically described a field trip down the Boone River. She explained that she was Cambodian, and her parents had strictly forbidden her to spend nights away from home.

Other students had additional reasons why they couldn't go on the trip. Zoya said that girls were not allowed to leave home for the night. Another student explained that her aunt was on trial, and she needed him to help translate. Yet another student said that he couldn't attend because his parents owned a convenience store, and he might be needed to work at the store. (Based on Chan, 2006).

For teachers in this eighth-grade classroom, composed of students whose families represent a variety of cultures, arranging a field trip is a complicated process.

As the U.S. population has become more diverse, schools have paid increased attention to issues involving student diversity and multiculturalism. And with good reason: Cultural as well as language differences affect both children and adults socially and educationally. The demographic makeup in the United States is undergoing an extraordinary shift. For instance, the proportion of Hispanics will in all likelihood more than double in the next 50 years. Moreover, by the year 2050, non-Hispanic Caucasians will likely become a minority of the total population of the United States (Colby & Ortman, 2014; see Figure 14-11).

How Culture Defines Us

LO 14.6 Analyze how cultural background affects individual self-definition.

An essential part of how people define themselves relates to their cultural background. Whether it involves race, ethnicity, gender, socioeconomic status, or a host of other factors, cultural background plays a central role in determining who they are, how they view themselves, and how others treat them.

For example, because of their knowledge of their own culture, people understand what clothes are appropriate to wear, are guided in their choice of what foods to choose and what to avoid, and know which sexual practices are likely to be acceptable on a date (kissing) and which are not (forced sexual intercourse). Such knowledge reflects basic cultural beliefs and values.

We can look at culture on various levels. At the broadest level, we all belong to the human culture, sharing certain customs that are brought about by particular biological necessities (sleeping every night or eating at various times during the day rather than once every few days, for example). All humans use language, which is a defining characteristic of human culture. Furthermore, there are other cultural universals such as cooking and funeral ceremonies that, although practiced in different ways, are found in every culture.

The United States has become a more diverse culture, as we discussed earlier. Furthermore, *globalization*—the integration of cultures, social movements, and financial markets around the world—has become increasingly common across a variety of dimensions, exposing adults and children to

Figure 14-11 The Changing Face of America

Current projections of the population makeup of the United States show that by the year 2050, the proportion of non-Hispanic whites will decline as the proportion of minority group members increases. What will be some of the impacts of changing demographics on social workers?

(**Source:** U.S. Bureau of the Census, 2000.)

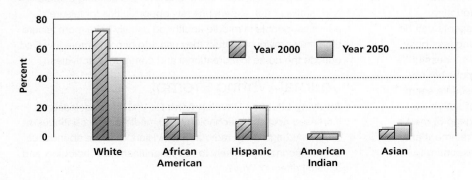

individuals with cultural backgrounds different from their own. Ultimately, it is clear that a full understanding of human development cannot be achieved without taking culture into account.

ACCULTURATION: WHEN CULTURES COLLIDE.   Let's begin our look at culture by considering the reactions of people when they encounter for sustained periods individuals from cultures other than their own, and how that experience may change them—a process called acculturation. **Acculturation** refers to the changes and adjustments that occur when groups of different people come into sustained firsthand contact.

The process of acculturation is particularly significant for people belonging to racial and ethnic minorities. They are faced with reconciling the demands of their own culture with those of the dominant culture. The issue of acculturation is particularly acute for adults and children who enter a new culture through immigration, an experience that typically involves leaving their native country and suddenly finding themselves in an entirely new culture. However, even members of racial and ethnic minorities who are raised their entire lives in the United States face pressures in reacting to their status as a subset of individuals living within a society in which they are a cultural minority.

The process of acculturation can produce one of four outcomes, depending on both the degree of identification with one's own culture and the strength of identification with the majority culture (illustrated in Figure 14-12):

- **Integration: Identifying with multiple cultures. Integration** is the process through which people maintain their own culture while simultaneously seeking to adapt to and incorporate the majority culture. By embracing the dominant culture, people are able to feel more secure and assimilated. People who employ integration often have a *bicultural identity* in which they see themselves as part of, and comfortable with, two different cultures.

- **Assimilation: Identifying with the majority culture. Assimilation** and rejecting the minority culture occurs when a person begins to identify with the mainstream culture and rejects the minority culture. Assimilated people not only may adopt the values and beliefs of the majority, but also, because they are only relatively weakly identified with their own culture, may reject the values and beliefs of their own culture (Unger et al., 2006).

- **Separation: Identifying with the minority culture and rejecting the majority culture. Separation** occurs when people identify with the ethnic minority culture to which they belong while rejecting or rebuffing the majority culture. Separation sometimes occurs with new immigrants, who may have difficulty integrating into their new society because they do not understand the dominant culture. Often, they eventually take on the norms and values of the dominant culture. But the process of acculturation can be slow and painful, producing anxiety and depression (Kim et al., 2005; Sawrikar & Hunt, 2005). Separation may also occur voluntarily, as a political act. Some people may wish to accentuate their racial or ethnic identity by actively separating themselves, both psychologically and physically, from members of the dominant culture. This strategy of separation, which can be used to bolster group identity, can have positive psychological benefits (Sue & Chu, 2003; Phinney, 2005).

- **Marginalization: Nonidentification with minority or majority cultures. Marginalization** occurs when people identify neither with their minority culture nor with the majority culture. Marginalized people may feel isolated from both their own cultural group and members of the majority culture, either because they have tried to connect and failed, or sometimes because they are rejected for personal reasons by others. Ultimately, they lack a clear cultural identity, and they typically feel isolated and alienated from society (Kosic, 2004; Arredondo et al., 2006).

Figure 14-12 Four Outcomes of Acculturation

Depending on both the degree of identification with one's own culture and the strength of identification with the majority culture, the process of acculturation can produce one of the four outcomes shown here.

(**Source:** Based on Phinney, Lochner, & Murphy 1990.)

Identification with One's Own Culture			
	WEAK	ASSIMILATION	MARGINALIZATION
	STRONG	INTEGRATION	SEPARATION
		STRONG	WEAK

Identification with
Majority Culture

acculturation
the changes and adjustments that occur when groups of different people come into sustained first-hand contact.

integration
the process in which people maintain their own culture while simultaneously seeking to adapt to and incorporate the majority culture.

assimilation
the process in which people begin to identify with the mainstream culture.

separation
the process in which people identify with the ethnic minority culture to which they belong while rejecting or rebuffing the majority culture.

marginalization
the process that occurs when people identify neither with their minority culture nor with the majority culture.

The particular type of identification found in racial and ethnic minorities has significant implications for their well-being. Some of the outcomes—including assimilation, integration, and occasionally even separation—can produce important psychological benefits.

Strongly identifying with the majority culture, however, may be seen negatively by one's minority peers. For example, although integration of majority and minority identities would seem to bring the benefits of belonging to both cultures, this may not always be true. Thus, blacks who seek to integrate the majority culture into their lives may be derided for trying to "act white"—that is, trying to act like something they are not.

Similarly, it can be stressful for members of nondominant cultures to try to integrate themselves into the majority culture if the majority culture resists their efforts. Minority members who are prevented from fully participating in the majority culture because of prejudice and discrimination may suffer psychological harm as a result (Schwartz, Montgomery, & Briones, 2006).

For some minority-culture members, the most successful approach may be to be highly adaptive, switching back and forth between the majority and minority cultures depending on the specific situation—a process called *code switching*. For example, in some cases, minority youth are so adept at code switching that they use different vocabulary and styles of speech depending on the group with which they are interacting (Cashman, 2005).

Developing an Ethnic Identity

LO 14.7 Examine the meaning and importance of an ethnic identity.

Think of how you would briefly describe yourself to someone who had never met you. Would you include your ethnic background? The country from which your ancestors emigrated?

If you are a member of a minority ethnic or racial group or a recent immigrant, it is very likely your description would prominently include that fact: "I'm a Korean American," "I'm black," or "I'm a Serb." But if you are a member of a group that is dominant in society or statistically in the majority, it might not even occur to you to say, for example, "I'm white."

ethnic identity
how members of ethnic, racial, and cultural minorities view themselves, both as members of their own group and in terms of their relationships with other groups.

The difference between the two responses reflects differences in ethnic identity and its salience in everyday life. **Ethnic identity** refers to how members of ethnic, racial, and cultural minorities view themselves, both as members of their own group and in terms of their relationships with other groups. Ethnic identity relates to the part of a person's self-concept that is derived from their awareness and knowledge that they are a member of a distinct social group (Umana-Taylor, Bhanot, & Shin, 2006; Else-Quest & Morse, 2015).

From *a social worker's* perspective

How important is it to understand the concept of ethnic identity when working in a multicultural community center? Why?

According to psychologist Jean Phinney, ethnic identity develops in several stages. The first stage is *unexamined ethnic identity*, which is characterized by a lack of consideration or exploration of one's ethnicity, as well as acceptance of the norms, beliefs, and attitudes of the dominant culture. In this stage, people might not even think about ethnicity or consider its impact on their lives. If they do think about their ethnicity, they may be embarrassed by it or reject it, believing that the dominant culture is superior (Phinney, 2003, 2006).

Although some people don't move beyond an unexamined ethnic identity, most reach the next stage, ethnic identity search. In *ethnic identity search*, people experience some sort of crisis that makes them become aware of ethnicity as a significant factor in their lives. It may be a shocking news event, such as a racially motivated killing, or they may be denied a job and suspect it's because of their race. In other cases, they may more gradually become aware that they are being treated differently by others because of their ethnicity.

Whatever the cause, people who enter the ethnic identity search phase become motivated to obtain a deeper understanding of their cultural identity. They may read books, attend ethnic celebrations and events, or—if their ethnic identity is tied to a religious group, such as Irish Catholics—they may begin to attend religious services.

The ethnic identity search may produce resentment toward dominant groups in society. As they learn more about the consequences of prejudice and discrimination, people may come to believe that the majority should make amends for its discriminatory behavior.

Finally, the last stage of ethnic identity development is *achieved ethnic identity*, in which people fully embrace their ethnic identity. People in this stage develop a clear sense of themselves as members of an ethnic minority and realize that this has become part of the way they view themselves. Their membership is viewed with pride, and they have a sense of belonging with others who share their ethnic identity.

Whereas people earlier may have experienced resentment or hostility regarding their ethnicity, directed either toward members of majority groups, others of their own ethnicity, or even themselves, they may feel more secure and optimistic after reaching the achieved ethnic identity stage. Furthermore, earlier feelings that they had two separate identities—one that identified with the majority culture and one that identified with their ethnic culture—are replaced with a more unified ethnic identity that draws on both parts of who they are (Shih & Sanchez, 2005).

ACHIEVING ETHNIC IDENTITY.   It's important to note that the stages of ethnic identity do not unfold according to any particular timetable. Some people may reach the achieved ethnic identity stage while still in adolescence, while for others it may occur later. Generally, the extent of identification with one's ethnicity increases with age.

Furthermore, some individuals may never enter the achieved ethnic identity stage or even the ethnic identity search stage at all. In such cases, ethnic identity is not perceived as part of the core of the individual. The danger is that a person will be treated differently (and sometimes discriminated against) by others due to his or her membership in an ethnic or racial group. Such treatment may be confusing at best and psychologically damaging at worst (Yasui, Dorham, & Dishion, 2004).

Ultimately, the nature and strength of a person's ethnic identity are determined both by parental socialization and by the particular experiences that an individual encounters. For example, ethnic minority parents teach their children, both explicitly and implicitly, about their own culture and about the dominant culture of the society in which they live. In addition, they may explicitly teach their children how to deal with the prejudice and discrimination that they are likely to encounter.

Finally, as we suggested earlier, ethnic identity is likely to be strongest for members of minority groups and weakest for members of the dominant societal group (which, in U.S. society, is whites). The reason: Members of the dominant group simply don't have to think as much about their ethnicity, given that they are not subject to the discrimination and prejudice experienced by members of ethnic minority groups. In contrast, members of minority groups expend more time and effort thinking not only about their own ethnicity but about the majority group. For ethnic minority group members, ethnicity becomes more a part of who they are (Guinote & Fiske, 2003; van de Vijver et al., 2015).

The fact that whites generally have less pronounced ethnic identities does not mean that ethnicity plays no role in their lives. Being a member of a particular nonracial ethnic or religious group (Italian, Jewish, or Irish, for example) may be a significant source of pride and may be perceived as a central part of identity. Furthermore, when whites find themselves in settings in which they are in the minority, their sense of racial identity may become magnified (Roberts et al., 1999; Romero & Roberts, 2003).

The Impact of Socioeconomic Status and Poverty on Children and Adolescents

LO 14.8 Explain how socioeconomic status affects children and adolescents.

One of the greatest cultural divides between people relates to their socioeconomic status. It is not a trivial problem that affects only a small part of the population: For example, some 15 million children in the United States—21 percent of all children—are living in poverty (with income levels below $28,290 per year for a family of four), and 35 percent live in low-income households. Furthermore, the discrepancy between the rich and the poor is also growing (Koball & Jiang, 2018).

Members of minority groups are proportionately more likely to be living in poverty than nonminority group members (see Figure 14-13). However, although Latino and black children and adolescents are disproportionately from low-income households, whites are the largest group of low-income individuals. More than half of the children of immigrant parents live in low-income families.

Poverty expands well beyond the stereotyped view of poor minority youth living in cities. Children and adolescents living in poverty are found throughout the United States in both urban and rural areas. According to Nobel Prize winner Robert Solow, the cost of child poverty in the United States runs between $36 billion and $177 billion each year.

Poverty affects children and adolescents in a number of ways. In some households, there is not enough food, and children and adolescents go to school and to bed hungry. Because many poor households lack health insurance, children and adolescents living in poverty are unable to afford good medical care, and minor illnesses, left untreated, become major ones. The greater the degree of poverty, the higher the health risks.

As we've discussed in many of the previous chapters, the impact of poverty on human development is profound. It impedes children's and adolescents' ability to learn and can slow their cognitive development, making academic success less likely. In addition, poverty is associated with behavioral and emotional difficulties. Children and adolescents living in persistent poverty are less well-adjusted and have more conduct problems, in part because their parents' emotional well-being is reduced, making them less successful caregivers (Maughan, 2001; Smokowski et al., 2004; Gutman, McLoyd, & Tokoyawa, 2005).

Poverty, of course, is not an insoluble problem, and solutions should be within the means of a country as affluent as the United States. However, the rate of poverty in the United States is actually higher than that in many other industrialized countries. Why? The answer has a good deal to do with aggressive antipoverty measures adopted by other nations. Compared with the United States, in other developed countries public assistance levels for poor families are often higher, health-care benefits are better, and governments have more programs to help those living in poverty (Rainwater & Smeeding, 2007).

The lower poverty rates in countries other than the United States offer a ray of hope even to poor people in this country, suggesting that the rate can be reduced. One route is clearly educational, for the higher the parental educational level, the less the chance of a child being raised in poverty. For example, only 28 percent of children living in poverty had at least one parent who had achieved an educational level beyond high school. In contrast, an astonishing 82 percent of children whose more educated parent did not graduate from high school lived in poverty (National Center for Children in Poverty, 2018).

Figure 14-13 The Cultural Divide of Socioeconomic Status

Socioeconomic status is one of the greatest cultural divides between adolescents. According to the National Center for Children in Poverty, members of minority groups are proportionately more likely to be living in poverty than nonminority group members. (**Source:** National Center for Children in Poverty, 2009.)

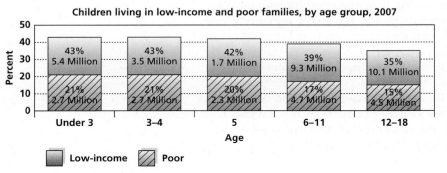

Children living in low-income and poor families, by age group, 2007

Age	Under 3	3–4	5	6–11	12–18
Low-income	43% 5.4 Million	43% 3.5 Million	42% 1.7 Million	39% 9.3 Million	35% 10.1 Million
Poor	21% 2.7 Million	21% 2.7 Million	20% 2.3 Million	17% 4.7 Million	15% 4.5 Million

Another route is through improvements in government programs and benefits targeted to the poor, and some government programs on the state and local levels have been successful in breaking the bonds of poverty. Ultimately, improvements in income levels will produce substantial benefits, not just for the poor, but for all children and for society in general.

Prejudice and Discrimination

LO 14.9 Define prejudice, stereotypes, and discrimination, and explain their origins and effects.

When I was 17, I wanted to be "authentic" too. I was a white, suburban, middle-class kid, and I wanted to be tough, street-smart and sexy. I wanted to be cool. Part of being cool was being, well—black. And since I had no hope of changing my skin color it meant listening to black music, reading black authors, and feeling, at least, a sense of solidarity with an oppressed and talented people. But in fact I had very little contact with actual black people.

* * * * *

Black and white kids did not play together in the schoolyard, and the black kids ate together in the cafeteria. We didn't socialize at all outside of school. This continued into high school and the only chance you might have to socialize with black people was in team sports. Even then, contact was largely limited to team activities. I did not know why this was so, and I never questioned it. It was just the way things were.

Although the number of youth living in low-income households began to decline in the early 1990s, it has been on the rise since 2000.

Navigating racial, ethnic, and other cultural differences is among the most difficult challenges that adolescents (and adults) face, as these anonymous blog excerpts imply. Learning how to accept and interact with individuals who are different in important ways from oneself represents an important developmental task for adolescents—the success or failure of which will have consequences throughout their lives.

For some, the challenge is too great, and their prejudiced attitudes and stereotypes guide their behavior. In this final part of the chapter, we examine the basic concepts of prejudice, stereotypes, and discrimination.

PREJUDICE, STEREOTYPES, AND DISCRIMINATION: THE FOUNDATIONS OF HATE. **Prejudice** refers to the negative (or positive) evaluations or judgments of members of a group that are based primarily on group membership, and not necessarily on the particular characteristics of individuals. For example, gender prejudice occurs when a person is evaluated on the basis of being a male or female and not because of his or her own specific characteristics or abilities.

Although prejudice is generally thought of as a negative evaluation of group members, it can also be positive: As we'll see, at the same time people dislike members of groups to which they don't belong, they may also positively evaluate members of their own group. In both cases, the assessment is unrelated to qualities of particular individuals; rather, it is due simply to membership in the specific group to which the individuals belong.

The mental framework that maintains prejudice is a stereotype. A **stereotype** is a set of beliefs and expectations about members of a group that are held simply because of their membership in the group. Stereotypes are oversimplifications that people employ in an effort to make sense of the complex social environment in which they live. They determine how information is interpreted, so that even when people are exposed to evidence contrary to their stereotypes, they may interpret the information in a way that supports their prejudice (Dovidio, Glick, & Rudman, 2005; Judd & Park, 2005; Fiske & North, 2015).

prejudice
the negative (or positive) evaluations or judgments of members of a group that are based primarily on group membership.

stereotype
a set of beliefs and expectations about members of a group that are held simply because of their membership in the group.

discrimination

the negative (or sometimes posi-tive) actions taken toward mem-bers of a particular group because of their membership in the group.

Ultimately, prejudice and stereotypes can lead to **discrimination**, the negative (or sometimes positive) actions taken toward members of a particular group because of their membership in the group. Although prejudice and discrimination often go hand in hand, one may be present without the other.

In the most extreme case, people's biases lead them to engage in self-fulfilling prophecies. *Self-fulfilling prophecies* reflect the tendency of people to act in ways that are consistent with their expectations, beliefs, or cognitions about an event or a behavior, thereby increasing the likelihood that the event or behavior will occur. Consequently, if a person thinks that members of a certain group are lazy, he or she may act in a way that actually elicits laziness from the members of that group.

THE ROOTS OF PREJUDICE.   Female. African American. Islamic fundamentalist. Gay. Quick: What images first come to mind when you read or hear each of these words? For most people, encountering a description of a person that includes such a label is enough to summon up a rich network of impressions, memories, and probably even predictions of how that person will behave in a given situation. The presence of such connections suggests that we are all susceptible to prejudice.

But where does prejudice originate? There are several sources.

Social Learning Explanations: The School of Stereotyping.   Children are not born feel-ing prejudice and showing discrimination to members of different religions, ethnic groups, or races. It is something that is taught to them, in much the same way that they learn that 2 + 2 = 4.

social learning view

the theory that suggests people develop prejudice and stereotypes about members of various groups in the same way they learn other attitudes, beliefs, and values.

The **social learning view** suggests that people develop prejudice and stereotypes about members of various groups in the same way they learn other attitudes, beliefs, and values. For instance, one important source of information for children regarding stereotypes and prejudice is the behavior and teaching of parents, other adults, and peers. Through direct reinforcement and through observation of the reinforcement given to others, people learn about members of other groups. Such learning begins at an early age: By the time they are preschoolers, children are able to distinguish between African Americans and whites, and even at that age they can possess pref-erential feelings for members of their own group over others (Ramsey & Myers, 1990; Cossman, 2004).

Children are not the only ones who learn stereotypes and prejudice from others. Although significant improvements have been made in the past decade, television and other media often portray minority group members in shallow, stereotyped ways. For instance, portrayals of African Americans perpetuate some of society's most dis-tasteful stereotypes, with many African American males being portrayed as sexually obsessed, shiftless, and speaking primarily in jive. Other groups are stereotyped in the media in equally derogatory ways, such as Godfather-like Italian mobsters, greedy Jewish bankers, and Hispanics in criminal or menial jobs (Alexander, Brewer, & Livingston, 2005; Jost et al., 2005).

Social Identity Theory: The Self-Esteem of Group Membership.   Think about your ethnic or religious identity for a moment. Are you proud of it? Does it make you feel good to be part of the group? Would you feel threatened if your group were criticized or attacked?

social identity theory

the theory that adolescents use group membership as a source of pride and self-worth.

Most people feel pride in the groups to which they belong. But this pride has a downside: It can lead to prejudice and discrimination. For example, according to **social identity theory**, adolescents use group membership as a source of pride and self-worth. However, to feel such pride, they must assume that their group is, in fact, superior to others. As a result, their quest for a positive social identity leads them to inflate the positive aspects of groups to which they belong and belittle groups to which they do not belong (Tajfel, 2001; Tajfel & Turner, 2004).

Certainly, there is ample evidence that members of various cultural groups tend to see their own groups in more positive terms than others. For instance, one cross-cultural investigation that examined 17 different societies found that, universally, people rated the group to which they belonged as more peace-loving, virtuous, and obedient than other groups (LeVine & Campble, 1972; Scheepers et al., 2006). Even countries in which national pride is relatively lower than that of other countries still are viewed quite positively by their citizens (see Table 14-2).

Of course, not all groups produce the same sense of self-worth as others. It is important for groups to be small enough so that people can feel somewhat unique and special. In fact, minority group membership sometimes produces stronger feelings of social identity than majority group membership. Minority group leaders of the past who used slogans such as "Black Is Beautiful" and "Gay Pride" reflected an awareness of the importance of instilling group pride. Research has supported this strategy: Ethnic group membership can be an important source of psychological support, particularly for minority group members (Mossakowski, 2003; González & Gándara, 2005).

Overall, membership in a group provides people with a sense of personal identity and self-esteem. When a group is successful, self-esteem can rise; conversely, when self-esteem is threatened, people feel enhanced attraction to their own group and increased hostility toward members of other groups (Garcia et al., 2005).

The use of group membership as a source of pride can lead to unfortunate consequences, however. For instance, in an effort to raise their own self-esteem, adolescents may come to think that their own group (known as the *ingroup*) is superior to groups to which they do not belong (the *outgroups*). Consequently, they inflate the positive aspects of the ingroup, and, at the same time, devalue outgroups and their members. Eventually they come to see members of outgroups as inferior to members of their ingroup. The ultimate result is prejudice toward members of groups of which they are not a part (Tajfel & Turner, 2004; Brown, Bradley, & Lang, 2006; Lam et al., 2006).

Table 14-2 National Pride by Country

Rank	Country	Score
1	Venezuela	18.4
2	United States	17.7
3	Australia	17.5
4	Austria	17.4
5	Chile	17.1
6	Canada	17.0
7	Russia	16.7
8	The Philippines	16.7
9	New Zealand	16.6
10	Spain	16.5
11	Israel	16.2
12	Slovenia	16.1
13	South Korea	16.0
14	Japan	15.9
15	Taiwan	15.6
16	Ireland	15.3
17	Poland	15.3
18	Great Britain	15.1
19	Czech Republic	15.1
20	Norway	14.9
21	Germany (Western area)	14.5
22	France	14.4
23	Switzerland	14.3
24	Germany (Eastern area)	14.2
25	Sweden	14.0

(**Source:** Data from Smith & Seokho, 2006.)

Development in Your Life

Taking a Stand Against Prejudice

Teachers and administrators can employ a number of strategies to combat prejudice in schools and create an atmosphere of respect and tolerance. But combating prejudice is everyone's responsibility, and students can do much to get actively involved in responding to hatred in their schools and communities. The Southern Poverty Law Center (2017) has put together a list of strategies for getting started, including the following:

- **Act.** The first step in combating hatred is being willing to take responsibility for doing something about it. Standing by and doing nothing sends a message to the perpetrators, the victims, and the community that prejudice is acceptable. Apathy encourages more hatred.

- **Join forces.** Get others involved in direct action, too. These could be family and friends, neighbors, church and civic group members, or teachers and administrators. Ways to get others involved range from informal discussions to writing letters to the editor of a local newspaper to organizing a community rally or event.

- **Support the victims.** Being a victim of prejudice can be a traumatic experience. Victims may feel frightened, intimidated, or alienated. Giving them your support and encouragement shows them that they are valued members of the community and that they are not alone. Even a kind word or a simple gesture can make a difference.

- **Speak up.** Prejudice has a voice; tolerance needs to have a voice as well. Condemning hateful messages is a good start, but letting others know that you actively value diversity is important, too. Create an atmosphere of tolerance by communicating your values.

- **Pressure leaders.** Students can do a lot to combat prejudice, but people in leadership positions enjoy special influence. The way that teachers, administrators, and other people in leadership roles respond to incidents of prejudice sends a strong message to others in the community. Quick, decisive action shows that prejudice is unacceptable; slow, uninspired action—or inaction—appears to condone it. Make sure that leaders know you expect them to respond decisively.

- **Examine your own prejudices.** Even tolerant people can harbor some prejudices. Are there any social groups you disparage or just don't know much about? Do you include people who are different from you in your circle of friends and in your group activities? Be continually on the lookout for ways to learn about different cultures and ethnicities and to build bridges across racial and ethnic divides.

Module 14.3 Review

LO 14.6 **Analyze how cultural background affects individual self-definition.**

Acculturation into a new culture can produce one of four outcomes: integration, assimilation, separation, or marginalization.

LO 14.7 **Examine the meaning and importance of an ethnic identity.**

Developing an ethnic identity, which is especially important to members of ethnic, racial, and cultural minorities, proceeds in stages from unexamined ethnic identity through ethnic identity search to achieved ethnic identity.

LO 14.8 **Explain how socioeconomic status affects children and adolescents.**

Members of minority groups are more likely to live in poverty than members of nonminority groups, with all the disadvantages and challenges that poverty brings. Poverty rates are higher in the United States than in many other industrialized countries largely because policymakers have not supported aggressive antipoverty programs.

LO 14.9 **Define prejudice, stereotypes, and discrimination, and explain their origins and effects.**

Children and adults must deal with prejudices (judgments of members of groups), stereotypes (beliefs and expectations about members of groups), and outright discrimination (actions taken toward members of groups). The social learning view suggests that people learn prejudice the same way they learn other attitudes, beliefs, and values: from other people. According to social identity theory, adolescents use group membership as a source of pride, dividing people into the ingroup and the outgroup, which is assumed to be inferior.

Journal Writing Prompt

Applying Lifespan Development: The United States has been called a "nation of immigrants," and yet feelings toward new immigrants are often negative. How might the phenomenon of cultural identity help to explain this?

Epilogue

In this chapter, we looked at schooling, leisure, and the ramifications of living in a multicultural world. We discussed the various options that are available in preschool education and considered their benefits to young children. We examined what makes children ready for school and how parents can increase the likelihood of academic success for their children. We also considered how race, ethnicity, gender, and socioeconomic status are related to academic performance. Then we discussed who goes to college and the increasing numbers of students over age 25 enrolled in courses.

We then turned to a look at how people spend their time, both in the United States and in other cultures. Next, we discussed the increased opportunities for leisure in midlife that adults enjoy as career pressure eases off and children leave home. We addressed the question of whether increased leisure time means a slower pace of life in the United States. In the closing pages of the chapter, we looked at culture and diversity, examining how race, ethnicity, gender, and socioeconomic

status shape culture. Finally, we discussed prejudice and discrimination.

Before moving on to the next chapter, turn back for a moment to this chapter's prologue, which describes Niko and Jeff's decision about what type of child care to choose for their son Rex. Consider these questions:

1. Niko and Jeff are contemplating several child-care options. What are some considerations they should keep in mind when it comes to the quality of the child-care options?

2. Why might Head Start be a good option for Rex?

3. What types of factors will influence how well Rex transitions into elementary school? Similarly, what factors could influence his transition into even later schools, including college?

4. How could the family's culture influence their choices regarding child care?

Looking Back

LO 14.1 Analyze the functions and types of preschool education in the United States.

A high proportion of U.S. children are engaged in some form of educational experiences during the preschool period. The types of early education include family child-care centers, preschools, and school child care. Preschool programs can be especially effective for children at risk of school failure. The United States lacks a coordinated national policy on preschool education. The major federal initiative in U.S. preschool education has been the Head Start program, which has yielded mixed, though promising, results.

LO 14.2 Explain how U.S. students generally progress from kindergarten through high school.

Many parents wrestle with deciding when to start their children in school. In general, delaying entry into schooling has no serious advantages and may have negative emotional and behavioral effects. Homeschooling has become a major educational reality, with parents choosing homeschooling for a variety of reasons. Homeschooled students generally perform well academically and are accepted into colleges at the same rate as non-homeschooled students. The transition from elementary school to secondary school can be challenging for students, who are experiencing the difficult bodily, cognitive, and psychological changes of adolescent at the time that they must navigate the transition. Many factors beyond simple ability and instructional quality influence student academic performance, including socioeconomic status (and the related factors of race and ethnicity), gender, and teacher

expectations. Dropping out of high school bears serious long-term consequences. While the motivation for dropping out varies from person to person, there are gender and ethnic differences in dropout rates.

LO 14.3 Describe the nature of the U.S. college population.

Despite a rise in the proportion of the college population represented by minority students, fewer African American and Hispanic high school graduates enroll in and graduate from college than white high school graduates. Even though women represent a majority of the students in colleges nationwide, gender stereotyping remains a persistent problem that affects choice of classes, treatment by professors, and student expectations for success. The average age of college students has risen beyond the traditional 18–22 age bracket. More than a quarter of students taking for-credit college courses in the United States are between 25 and 35. In addition, many older adults enroll each year in classes designed especially for them by organizations such as Road Scholar or by individual colleges.

LO 14.4 Describe how adolescents spend their leisure time.

While there are cultural, racial, and individual differences in the use of time, typical U.S. adolescents spend almost half their time in leisure activities, with the rest divided between productive and maintenance activities. Adolescents can be categorized as being more or less busy, with the busier adolescents experiencing the greater amount of academic success. While true multitasking is no more possible for adolescents than for adults, adolescents favor a style that involves the near-simultaneous performance of a great number of tasks and activities. Cross-cultural studies reveal that adolescents in developing societies have less free time and devote more time to household labor. New technologies and media have found ready consumers in adolescents, who use media for entertainment, coping with stress, and developing a sense of the norms that apply to their age group.

LO 14.5   Explain how the use of time changes in early and middle adulthood.

The priorities of many adults change in midlife, shifting from a focus on career advancement toward greater attention to social relationships and personal interests. Changes in work life, such as a lowering hours in the typical workweek, and in family life brought on by the departure of children, bring adults in midlife more leisure time for civic activities, sports, or socializing.

LO 14.6   Analyze how cultural background affects individual self-definition.

The demographic makeup of students in the United States is rapidly changing. By the year 2050, it is expected that non-Hispanic Caucasians will become a minority of the total population of the United States. Culture helps individuals define themselves and make decisions ranging from what clothes to wear to what sexual practices are appropriate. Acculturation is the process by which an individual of a different culture adjusts to a new culture

and may produce integration, assimilation, separation, or marginalization.

LO 14.7   Examine the meaning and importance of an ethnic identity.

It is especially important for members of minority cultures to develop an ethnic identity, a view of themselves as members of both a minority culture and a new culture.

LO 14.8   Explain how socioeconomic status affects children and adolescents.

Many of the problems faced by minority adolescents are more closely linked to socioeconomic status than to ethnicity or race. Half of adolescents in the United States live in poverty or in low-income households, and members of minority groups are disproportionately represented in these households.

LO 14.9   Define prejudice, stereotypes, and discrimination, and explain their origins and effects.

Evaluations of individuals on the basis of their membership in a group are reinforced by the existence of stereotypes, which are beliefs and expectations about group members. Prejudice and stereotypes can lead to discrimination, actions taken toward group members because of their membership in the group. Adolescents use group membership as a source of pride and self-worth, but the danger is that they will conclude that their group is better than others.

Key Terms and Concepts

acculturation 463
Integration 463
assimilation 463
separation 463

marginalization 463
ethnic identity 464
prejudice 467
stereotype 467

discrimination 468
social learning view 468
social identity theory 468

Chapter 15
Death and Dying

Danny E. Martindale/Getty Images

Learning Objectives

LO 15.1 Review the difficulties in defining death.

LO 15.2 Describe what death means at different stages of the life span.

LO 15.3 Describe how dying is affected by culture.

LO 15.4 Summarize how we can prepare for death.

LO 15.5 Describe ways in which people face the prospect of their own death.

LO 15.6 Describe ways in which people exercise control over the death decision.

LO 15.7 Compare and contrast the advantages of hospice and home care for the end of life.

LO 15.8 Describe how survivors react to and cope with death.

LO 15.9 Describe ways in which people experience grief and the functions it serves.

Chapter Overview

Prologue: A Good Death

Jackson LeRoi knew that he'd be dying soon—very soon. At age 71, he'd been diagnosed with a particularly aggressive form of brain cancer, and his doctors were clear that his time was limited.

LeRoi made a choice: Rather than endure grueling rounds of chemotherapy, which would only extend his life for a few months at best, he chose to refuse treatment, except for drugs that would keep his final days pain-free.

"I've led a good life. I'm happy with what I've accomplished," he said. And he had a lot of friends, many of whom attended a party he threw when his doctor told him he had less than two weeks to live. People laughed, people cried, but, for LeRoi, it's what he wanted: a celebration of a life well lived. ∎

Looking Ahead

Death will happen to all of us at some time. It is an experience as universal to the human condition as birth. As such, it is a milestone of life that is central to an understanding of the life span.

Only in the past several decades have lifespan developmentalists given serious study to the developmental implications of dying. In this chapter, we discuss death and dying from several perspectives. We begin by considering how we define death—a determination that is more complex than it seems. We then examine how people view and react to death at different points in the life span. We also consider the very different views of death held by various societies.

Next, we look at how people confront their own death. We discuss one theory that people move through several stages as they come to grips with their approaching death. We also look at how people use living wills and assisted suicide.

Finally, we consider bereavement and grief. We examine the difficulties in distinguishing normal from unhealthy grief, and we discuss the consequences of a loss. We also look at mourning and funerals, discussing how people can prepare themselves for the inevitability of death.

Quality of life becomes an increasingly important issue as people reach the end of the life span.

Lisa F. Young/Fotolia

DYING AND DEATH ACROSS THE LIFE SPAN

It took a major legal and political battle, but eventually Terri Schiavo's husband won the right to remove a feeding tube that had been keeping her alive for 15 years. Lying in a hospital bed all those years in what physicians called a "persistent vegetative state," Schiavo was never expected to regain consciousness after suffering brain damage due to respiratory and cardiac arrest. After a series of court battles, her husband—despite the wishes of her parents—was allowed to direct caretakers to remove the feeding tube; Schiavo died soon afterward.

Was Schiavo's husband right in seeking to remove her feeding tube? Was she already dead when it was removed? Were her constitutional rights unfairly ignored by her husband's action?

The difficulty of answering such questions illustrates the complexity of what are, literally, matters of life and death. Death is not only a biological event; it involves psychological aspects as well. We need to consider not only issues relating to the definition of death but also the ways in which our conception of death changes across various points in the life span.

Defining Death: Determining the Point at Which Life Ends

LO 15.1   Review the difficulties in defining death.

What is death? Although the question seems straightforward, defining the point at which life ceases and death occurs is surprisingly complex. Over the past few decades, medicine has advanced to the point where some people who would have been considered dead a few years ago would now be considered alive.

Functional death is defined by an absence of heartbeat and breathing. Although this definition seems unambiguous, it is not completely straightforward. For example, a person whose heart has stopped beating and whose breathing has ceased for as long as 5 minutes may be resuscitated and suffer little damage as a consequence of the experience. Does this mean that the person who is now alive was dead, as the functional definition would have it?

Because of this imprecision, heartbeat and respiration are no longer used to determine the moment of death. Medical experts now measure brain functioning. In **brain death**, all signs of brain activity, as measured by electrical brain waves, have ceased. When brain death occurs, there is no possibility of restoring brain functioning.

Some medical experts suggest that a definition of death that relies only on a lack of brain waves is too restrictive. They argue that losing the ability to think, reason, feel, and experience the world may be sufficient to declare a person dead. In this view, which takes psychological considerations into account, a person who suffers irreversible brain damage, who is in a coma, and who will never experience anything approaching a human life can be considered dead. In such a case, the argument goes, death can be judged to have arrived, even if some sort of primitive brain activity is still occurring (Burkle, Sharp, & Wijdicks, 2014; Wang et al., 2017).

Not surprisingly, such an argument, which moves us from strictly medical criteria to moral and philosophical considerations, is controversial. As a result, the legal definition of death in most localities in the United States relies on the absence of brain functioning, although some laws still include a definition relating to the absence of respiration and heartbeat. The reality is that no matter where a death occurs, in most cases people do not bother to measure brain waves. Usually, the brain waves are closely monitored only in certain circumstances—when the time of death is significant, when organs may potentially be transplanted, or when criminal or legal issues might be involved.

functional death
the absence of a heartbeat and breathing.

brain death
a diagnosis of death based on the cessation of all signs of brain activity, as measured by electrical brain waves.

The difficulty in establishing legal and medical definitions of death may reflect some of the changes in understanding and attitudes about death that occur over the course of people's lives.

Death Across the Life Span: Causes and Reactions

LO 15.2   Describe what death means at different stages of the life span.

Death is something we associate with old age. However, for many individuals, death comes earlier. In such cases, in part because it seems "unnatural" for a younger person to die, the reactions to death are particularly extreme. In the United States today, in fact, some people believe that children should be sheltered—that it is wrong for them to know much about death. Yet people of every age can experience the death of friends and family members, as well as their own death. How do our reactions to death evolve as we age? We will consider several age groups.

DEATH IN INFANCY AND CHILDHOOD.   Despite its economic wealth, the United States has a relatively high infant mortality rate. Some 55 countries have a smaller percentage of infants who die in the first year of birth than in the United States (*World Factbook*, 2017).

As these statistics indicate, the number of parents who experience the death of an infant is substantial, and their reactions may be profound. The loss of a child typically brings up all the same reactions one would experience on the death of an older person, and sometimes even more severe effects as family members struggle to deal with a death at such an early age. One of the most common reactions is extreme depression (Murphy, Johnson, & Wu, 2003).

One kind of death that is exceptionally difficult to deal with is prenatal death, or *miscarriage*, a topic touched on in Chapter 2. Parents typically form psychological bonds with their unborn child, and consequently they often feel profound grief if it dies before it is born. Moreover, friends and relatives often fail to understand the emotional impact of miscarriage on parents, making parents feel their loss all the more keenly (Wheeler & Austin, 2001; Nikčević & Nicolaides, 2014).

sudden infant death syndrome (SIDS)

the unexplained death of a seemingly healthy baby.

Another form of death that produces extreme stress, in part because it is so unanticipated, is sudden infant death syndrome. In **sudden infant death syndrome (SIDS)**, a seemingly healthy baby stops breathing and dies of unexplained causes. Usually occurring between the ages of 2 and 4 months, SIDS strikes unexpectedly; a robust, hardy baby is placed into a crib at naptime or nighttime and never wakes up.

In cases of SIDS, parents often feel intense guilt, and acquaintances may be suspicious of the "true" cause of death. As we discussed in Chapter 3, however, there is no known cause for SIDS, which seems to strike randomly, and parents' guilt is unwarranted (Kinney & Thach, 2009; Mitchell, 2009; Horne, 2017).

During childhood, the most frequent cause of death is accidents, most of them due to motor vehicle crashes, fires, and drowning. However, a substantial number of children in the United States are victims of homicides, which have nearly tripled in number since 1960. Homicide is the third- or fourth-leading cause of death for children between the ages of 1 and 24, and the leading cause of death for 15- to 24-year-old African Americans (Centers for Disease Control and Prevention, 2016).

For parents, the death of a child produces the most profound sense of loss and grief. In the eyes of most parents, there is no worse death, including the loss of a spouse or of one's own parents. Parents' extreme reaction is partly based on the sense that the natural order of the world, in which children "should" outlive their parents, has somehow collapsed. Their reaction is often coupled with the feeling that it is their primary responsibility to protect their children from any harm, and they may feel that they have failed in this task when a child dies (Granek et al., 2015).

Parents are almost never well equipped to deal with the death of a child, and they may obsessively ask themselves afterward, over and over, why the death occurred. Because the bond between children and parents is so strong, parents sometimes feel that a part of themselves has died as well. The stress is so profound that the loss of a child significantly increases the chances of admission to a hospital for a mental disorder (Feigelman, Jordan, & Gorman, 2009; Fox, Cacciatore, & Lacasse, 2014).

CHILDHOOD CONCEPTIONS OF DEATH.   Children themselves do not really begin to develop a concept of death until around age 5. Although they are well aware of death before that time, they are apt to think of it as a temporary state that involves a reduction in living, rather than a cessation. For instance, a preschool-age child might say, "Dead people don't get hungry—well, maybe a little" (Kastenbaum, 1985, p. 629).

Some preschool-age children think of death in terms of sleep—with the consequent possibility of waking up, just as Sleeping Beauty was awakened in the fairy tale. For children who believe this, death is not particularly fearsome; rather, it is something of a curiosity. If people merely tried hard enough—by administering medicine, providing food, or using magic—dead people might "return" (Russell, 2017).

From *an educator's* perspective

Given their developmental level and understanding of death, how do you think preschool children react to the death of a parent?

In some cases, children's misunderstanding of death can produce devastating emotional consequences. Children sometimes leap to the erroneous conclusion that they are somehow responsible for a person's death. For instance, they may assume they could have prevented the death by being better behaved. In the same way, they may think that if the person who died really wanted to, she or he could return.

Around age 5, children better understand the finality and irreversibility of death. In some cases, children personify death as some kind of ghostlike or devilish figure. At first, though, they do not think of death as universal but rather as something that happens only to certain people. By about age 9, however, they come to accept the universality of death and its finality (Nagy, 1948). By middle childhood, children also learn about some of the customs involved with death, such as funerals, cremation, and cemeteries (Hunter & Smith, 2008).

For children who are themselves dying, death can be a very real concept. In a groundbreaking study, anthropologist Myra Bluebond-Langner (2000) found that some children were able to articulate that they were dying very directly, saying, "I am going to die." Other children were more indirect, noting that they were never going back to school, expecting not to be around for someone's birthday party, or considering burying their dolls. Children also may be well aware that adults don't like to talk about their illness or of their possibility of dying.

DEATH IN ADOLESCENCE.   We might expect the significant advances in cognitive development that occur during adolescence to bring about a sophisticated, thoughtful, and reasoned view of death. However, in many ways, adolescents' views of death are as unrealistic as those of younger children, although along different lines.

Although adolescents clearly understand the finality and irreversibility of death, they tend not to think it can happen to them, a fact that can lead to risky behavior. Adolescents develop a *personal fable*, a set of beliefs that causes them to feel unique and special—so special, in fact, that they may believe they are invulnerable and that the bad things that happen to other people won't happen to them.

Many times, the risky behavior that results from these beliefs causes death in adolescence. For instance, the most frequent cause of death among adolescents is accidents, most often involving motor vehicles. Other frequent causes include homicide, suicide, cancer, and AIDS (National Center for Health Statistics, 2015).

When adolescents with feelings of invulnerability confront the likelihood of death due to an illness, the results can be shattering. Adolescents who learn that they have a terminal illness often feel angry and cheated—that life has been unjust to them. Because they feel—and act—so negatively, it may be difficult for medical personnel to treat them effectively.

In contrast, some adolescents diagnosed with a terminal illness react with total denial. Feeling indestructible, they may find it impossible to accept the seriousness of their illness. If it does not interfere with their acceptance of medical treatment, some degree of denial may actually be useful, as it allows adolescents to continue with their normal lives as long as possible (Beale, Baile, & Aaron, 2005; Cullen, 2017).

DEATH IN YOUNG ADULTHOOD.   Young adulthood is the time when most people feel primed to begin their lives. Past the preparatory time of childhood and adolescence, they are on the threshold of making their mark on the world. Because death at such a point in life seems close to unthinkable, its occurrence is particularly difficult. Actively pursuing their goals for life, they are angry and impatient with any illness that threatens their future.

In early adulthood, death is most likely to occur due to accidents, followed by suicide, homicide, AIDS, and cancer. By the end of early adulthood, however, disease becomes a more prevalent cause of death.

For those people facing death in early adulthood, several concerns are of particular importance. One is the desire to develop intimate relationships and express sexuality, both of which are inhibited, if not completely prevented, by a terminal illness. For instance, people who test positive for the AIDS virus may find it quite difficult to start new relationships. The role of sexual activities within evolving relationships presents even more challenging issues.

Another particular concern during young adulthood involves future planning. At a time when most people are mapping out their careers and deciding at what point to start a family, young adults who have a terminal illness face additional burdens. Should they marry, even though it is likely that the partner will soon end up widowed? Should a couple seek to conceive a child if the child is likely to be raised by only one parent? How soon should one's employer be told about a terminal illness, when it is clear that employers sometimes discriminate against unhealthy workers? None of these questions is easily answered.

Like adolescents, young adults sometimes make poor patients. They are outraged at their plight and feel the world is unfair, and they may direct their anger at care providers and loved ones. In addition, they may make the medical staff who provide direct care—nurses and orderlies—feel particularly vulnerable, since the staff themselves are often young.

DEATH IN MIDDLE ADULTHOOD.   For people in middle adulthood, the shock of a life-threatening disease—which is the most common cause of death in this period—is not so great. By this point, people are well aware that they are going to die sometime, and they may be able to consider the possibility of death in a fairly realistic manner.

Their sense of realism doesn't make the possibility of dying any easier, however. In fact, fears about death are often greater in middle adulthood than at any time previously—or even in later life. These fears may lead people to look at life in terms of the number of years they have remaining as opposed to their earlier orientation toward the number of years they have already lived.

The most frequent cause of death in middle adulthood is heart attack or stroke. Although the unexpectedness of such a death does not allow for preparation, in some ways it is easier than a slow and painful death from a disease such as cancer. It is certainly the kind of death that most people prefer: When asked, they say they would like an instant and painless death that does not involve loss of any body part (Taylor, 2015).

DEATH IN LATE ADULTHOOD.   By the time they reach late adulthood, people know with some certainty that their time is coming to an end. Furthermore, they face an increasing number of deaths in their environment. Spouses, siblings, and friends may have already died, leaving a constant reminder of their own mortality.

The most likely causes of death are cancer, stroke, and heart disease during late adulthood. What would happen if these causes of death were eliminated? According to demographers' estimates, the average 70-year-old's life expectancy would increase around 7 years (Hayward, Crimmins, & Saito, 1997).

The prevalence of death in the lives of elderly people makes them less anxious about dying than they were at earlier stages of life. This does not mean that people in late adulthood welcome death. Rather, it implies that they are more realistic and reflective about it. They think about death, and they may begin to make preparations for it. Some begin to pull away from the world due to diminishing physical and psychological energy.

Impending death is sometimes accompanied by acceleration of declines in cognitive functioning. In what is known as the *terminal decline*, a significant drop in performance in cognitive areas such as memory and reading may foreshadow death within the next few years (Thorvaldsson et al., 2008; Wilson et al., 2015; Brandmaier et al., 2017).

Some older adults actively seek out death, turning to suicide. In fact, the suicide rate for men climbs steadily during the course of late adulthood, and no age group has a higher rate of suicide than white men over age 85. (Adolescents and young adults commit suicide in greater numbers, but their *rate* of suicide—the number of suicides as a proportion of the general adolescent population—is actually lower.) Suicide is often a consequence of severe depression or some form of dementia, or it can be due to the loss of a spouse. And, as we will discuss, some individuals, struck down with a terminal illness, seek the assistance of others in committing suicide (Mezuk et al., 2008; Dombrovski et al., 2012; McCue & Balasubramaniam, 2017). One particularly important issue for older adults suffering from a terminal illness is whether their lives still have value. More than younger individuals, elderly people who are dying harbor concerns that they are a burden to their family or to society. Furthermore, they may be given the message, sometimes inadvertently, that their value to society has ended and that they have attained the status of "dying" as opposed to being "very sick" (Kastenbaum, 2000).

Do older people wish to know if death is impending? The answer, in most cases, is yes. Like younger patients, who usually state that they wish to know the true nature of an ailment, older people want the details of their illnesses. Ironically, candor is not something caregivers wish to provide: Physicians usually prefer to avoid telling dying patients that their illnesses are terminal (Goold, Williams, & Arnold, 2000; Hagerty et al., 2004). It should be noted, however, that not all people wish to learn the truth about their condition or to know that they are dying.

Cultural Responses to Death

LO 15.3 Describe how dying is affected by culture.

It is important to keep in mind that individuals react to death in substantially different ways. In part, their reaction is produced by personality factors. For example, people who are generally anxious are more concerned about death. In addition to personal differences, there are significant cultural differences in how people view and react to death (see the *Developmental Diversity and Your Life* feature).

People's responses to death take many forms across different cultures, but even within Western societies, reactions to death and dying are quite diverse. For instance, consider which is better: for a man to die after a full life in which he has raised a family and been successful in his job, or for a courageous and valiant young soldier to die defending his country in wartime. Has one person died a better death than the other? The answer depends on one's values, which are largely due to cultural and subcultural teachings, often shared through religious beliefs. For instance, some societies view death as a punishment or as a judgment about one's contributions to the world. Others see death as redemption from an earthly life of travail. Some view death as the start of an eternal life, while others believe that there is no heaven or hell and that an earthly life is all there is (Bryant, 2003).

Developmental Diversity and Your Life

Differing Conceptions of Death

In the midst of a tribal celebration, an older man waits for his oldest son to place a cord around his neck. The older man has been sick, and he is ready to relinquish his ties to this earthly world. He asks that his son lift him to his death, and the son complies.

To Hindus in India, death is not an ending, but rather part of a continual cycle. Because they believe in reincarnation, death is thought to be followed by rebirth into a new life. Death, then, is seen as a companion to life.

Given that religious teachings regarding the meaning of life and death are quite diverse, it is not surprising that views of death and dying vary substantially. For instance, one study found that Christian and Jewish 10-year-olds viewed death from a more "scientific" vantage point (in terms of the cessation of physical activity in the body) than Sunni Muslim and Druze children of the same age, who are more likely to see death in spiritual terms. We cannot be sure whether such differences are due to the different religious and cultural backgrounds of the children or whether differences in exposure to dying people influence the rate at which the understanding of death develops. However, it is clear that members of the various groups had very different conceptions of death (Thorson et al., 1997; Aiken, 2000; Xiao et al., 2012).

For members of Native American tribes, death is seen as a continuation of life. For example, Lakota parents will tell their children, "Be kind to your brother, for someday he will die." When people die, they are assumed to move to a spirit land called Wanagi Makoce, inhabited by all people and animals. Death, then, is not viewed with anger or seen as unfair (Huang, 2004).

Members of some cultures learn about death at an earlier age than others. For instance, exposure to high levels of violence and death may lead to an awareness of death earlier in some cultures than in cultures in which violence is less a part of everyday life. For example, children in Israel understand the finality, irreversibility, and inevitability of death at an earlier age than children in the United States and Britain (McWhirter, Young, & Majury, 1983; Atchley, 2000; Braun, Pietsch, & Blanchette, 2000).

Cultural differences are also reflected in the nature of care provided to the dying. For example, in traditional Thai cultures, members of the community participate in care by praying for the patient, and they attach strings to the patient, symbolically seeking to reattach the soul to the body. In some Native American cultures, spirit dancers may burn gifts for ancestors to help in treatment. (Putsch & Joyce, 2017).

Furthermore, in traditional multigenerational Asian families, who live together under one roof, younger generations were expected to provide care for dying older generations. But as modernization has occurred, more elderly people live by themselves, and there are fewer societal networks in place to care for the dying (Hatton, 2015).

Anne-Marie Palmer/Alamy

Differing conceptions of death lead to different rituals. For example, in India, bodies may be floated in the Ganges River following death.

Can Death Education Prepare Us for the Inevitable?

LO 15.4 Summarize how we can prepare for death.

"When will Mom come back from being dead?"
"Why did Barry have to die?"
"Did Grandpa die because I was bad?"

thanatologists
people who study death and dying.

Children's questions such as these illustrate why many developmentalists, as well as **thanatologists**, people who study death and dying, have suggested that death education should be an important component of everyone's schooling. Consequently, a relatively new area of instruction, termed death education, has emerged. *Death education* encompasses programs that teach about death, dying, and grief. Death education is designed to help people of all ages deal better with death and dying—both others' deaths and their own personal mortality.

Death education has evolved in part as a response to the way we hide death, at least in most Western societies. We typically give hospitals the task of dealing with dying people, and we do not talk to children about death or allow them to go to funerals for fear of upsetting them. Even those most familiar with death, such as emergency workers and medical specialists, are uncomfortable talking about the subject. Because it is discussed so little and is so removed from everyday life, people of all ages may have little opportunity to confront their feelings about death or to gain a more realistic sense of it (Kim & Lee, 2009; Waldrop & Kirkendall, 2009; Kellehear, 2015).

Several types of death education programs exist. Among them are the following:

- *Crisis intervention education.* After the December 2012 mass shooting at the Sandy Hook Elementary School, surviving children received crisis intervention designed to deal with their anxieties. Younger children, whose conceptions of death were shaky at best, needed explanations of the loss of life that day geared to their levels of cognitive development. Crisis intervention education is used in less extreme times as well. For example, it is common for schools to make emergency counseling available if a student is killed or commits suicide (Sandoval, Scott, & Padilla, 2009; Reeves & Fernandez, 2017).

- *Routine death education.* Although relatively little curricular material on death is available at the elementary school level, coursework in high schools is becoming increasingly common. For instance, some high schools have specific courses on death and dying. Furthermore, colleges and universities increasingly include courses relating to death in such departments as psychology, human development, sociology, and education (Eckerd, 2009; Corr, 2015).

- *Death education for members of the helping professions.* Professionals who will deal with death, dying, and grief as part of their careers have a special need for death education. Almost all medical and nursing schools now offer some form of death education to help their students. The most successful programs not only supply ways for providers to help patients deal with their own impending deaths and those of family members but also allow students to explore their feelings about the topic (Haas-Thompson, Alston, & Holbert, 2008; Kehl & McCarty, 2012).

Although no single form of death education will be sufficient to demystify death, the kinds of programs just described may help people come to grips more effectively with what is, along with birth, the most universal—and certain—of all human experiences.

Module 15.1 Review

LO 15.1   Review the difficulties in defining death.

Death has been defined as the cessation of heartbeat and respiration (functional death), the absence of electrical brain waves (brain death), and the loss of human qualities.

LO 15.2   Describe what death means at different stages of the life span.

The death of an infant or a young child can be particularly difficult for parents, and for an adolescent death appears to be unthinkable. Death in young adulthood can appear unfair, while people in middle adulthood have begun to understand the reality of death. By the time they reach late adulthood, people know they will die and begin to make preparations.

LO 15.3   Describe how dying is affected by culture.

Cultural differences in attitudes and beliefs about death strongly influence people's reactions to it.

LO 15.4   Summarize how we can prepare for death.

Thanatologists recommend that death education become a normal part of learning.

Journal Writing Prompt

Applying Lifespan Development: Do you think people who are going to die should be told? Does your response depend on the person's age?

MODULE 15.2

CONFRONTING DEATH

Carol Reyes had been active all her life. When she broke her pelvis at 89, she was determined to walk again. With six months of intensive physical therapy, she did. At 93, she came down with pneumonia. After a month in the hospital, she returned home to the things she loved—her cat, her books, and taking an active part in local politics—a little weaker but basically sound.

Three years later, Carol's doctor told her she had ALS, a disease in which the motor neurons in the brain and spinal cord slowly die. She could take a drug called Rilutek to slow its progress, but eventually her muscles would atrophy, making it hard to use her hands or walk. She'd have trouble speaking and swallowing. In the end, her lungs would be paralyzed.

Carol agreed to try the drug but told her doctor she wanted a DNR—a Do Not Resuscitate Order—for when her lungs began seizing up and breathing became difficult. "That's not a life I'd like to be living," she said.

Four months later, Carol Reyes found herself gasping for breath. She refused oxygen. She refused to go to the hospital. She died quickly, in her own bed.

Like other deaths, Reyes's raises a myriad of difficult questions. Was her refusal to take oxygen equivalent to suicide? Should the ambulance medic have complied with the request? Was she coping with her impending death effectively? How do people come to terms with death, and how do they react and adapt to it? Lifespan developmentalists and other specialists in death and dying have struggled to find answers to such questions.

Understanding the Process of Dying: Are There Steps Toward Death?

LO 15.5 Describe ways in which people face the prospect of their own death.

No individual has had a greater influence on our understanding of the way people confront death than Elisabeth Kübler-Ross. A psychiatrist, Kübler-Ross developed a theory of death and dying, built on extensive interviews with people who were dying and with those who cared for them (Kübler-Ross, 1969, 1982).

Based on her observations, Kübler-Ross initially suggested that people pass through five basic steps as they move toward death (summarized in Figure 15-1).

Figure 15-1 Moving Toward the End of Life

There are five steps toward death, according to Kübler-Ross (1975).

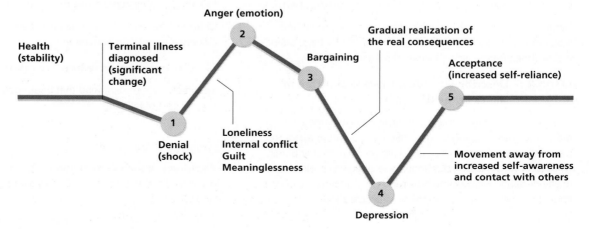

DENIAL. "No, I can't be dying. There must be some mistake." It is typical for people to protest in such a manner on learning that they have a terminal disease. Such objections represent the first stage of dying, *denial*. In denial, people resist the idea that they are going to die. They may argue that their test results have been mixed up, that an X-ray has been read incorrectly, or that their physician does not know what he or she is talking about (Teutsch, 2003).

ANGER. After they move beyond denial, people may be likely to express *anger*. A dying person may be angry at everyone: people who are in good health, their spouses and other family members, those who are caring for them, their children. They may lash out at others, and wonder—sometimes aloud—why *they* are dying and not someone else. They may be furious at God, reasoning that they have led good lives and that there are far worse people in the world who should be dying.

BARGAINING. "If you're good, you'll be rewarded." Most people learn this equation in childhood, and many try to apply it to their impending death. In this case, "good" means promising to be a better person, and the "reward" is staying alive.

In *bargaining*, dying people try to negotiate their way out of death. They may declare that they will dedicate their lives to the poor if God saves them. They may promise that if they can just live long enough to see a child get married, they will willingly accept death later.

However, the promises that are part of the bargaining process are rarely kept. If one request appears to be granted, people typically seek another, and yet another. Furthermore, they may be unable to fulfill their promises because their illnesses keep progressing and prevent them from achieving what they said they would do.

In the end, of course, all the bargaining in the world is unable to overcome the inevitability of death. When people eventually realize that death is unavoidable, they often move into a stage of depression.

From *an educator's* perspective

Do you think Kübler-Ross's five steps of dying might be subject to cultural influences? Age differences? Why or why not?

DEPRESSION. Many dying people experience phases of *depression*. Realizing that the issue is settled and they cannot bargain their way out of death, people are overwhelmed with a deep sense of loss. They know that they are losing their loved ones and that their lives really are coming to an end.

The depression they experience may be of two types. In *reactive depression*, the feelings of sadness are based on events that have already occurred: the loss of dignity that may accompany medical procedures, the end of a job, or the knowledge that one will never return from the hospital to one's home.

Dying people also experience preparatory depression. In *preparatory depression*, people feel sadness over future losses. They know that death will bring an end to their relationships with others and that they will never see future generations. The reality of death is inescapable in this stage, and it brings about profound sadness over the unalterable conclusion of one's life.

ACCEPTANCE. Kübler-Ross suggested that the final step of dying is *acceptance*. People who have developed a state of acceptance are fully aware that death is impending. Unemotional and uncommunicative, they have virtually no feelings—positive or negative—about the present or future. They have made peace with themselves, and they may wish to be left alone. For them, death holds no sting.

EVALUATING KÜBLER-ROSS'S THEORY. Kübler-Ross has had an enormous impact on the way we look at death. As one of the first people to observe systematically how people approach their own deaths, she is recognized as a pioneer. Kübler-Ross was almost single-handedly responsible for bringing into public awareness the phenomenon of death, which previously had languished out of sight in Western societies. Her contributions have been particularly influential among those who provide direct care to the dying.

However, her work has drawn significant criticism. For one thing, there are some obvious limitations to her conception of dying. It is largely limited to those who are aware that they are dying and who die in a relatively leisurely fashion. To people who suffer from diseases in which the prognosis is uncertain as to when or even if they will die, her theory is not applicable.

The most important criticisms, however, concern the stage-like nature of Kübler-Ross's theory. Not every person passes through every step on the way to death, and some people move through the steps in a different sequence. Some people even go through the same steps several times. Depressed patients may show bursts of anger, and an angry patient may bargain for more time (Larson, 2014; Jurecic, 2017; Stroebe, Schut, & Boerner, 2017).

Not everyone, then, proceeds through the stages in the same way. For example, a study of more than 200 recently bereaved people were interviewed immediately and then several months later. If Kübler-Ross's theory was correct, the final stage of acceptance comes at the end of a lengthy grieving process. But most of the participants expressed acceptance of the passing of their loved one right from the beginning. Moreover, rather than feeling anger or depression, two of the other putative stages of grief, participants reported mostly feeling a yearning for the deceased person. Rather than a series of fixed stages, grief looks more like an assortment of symptoms that rise and fall and eventually dissipate (Maciejewski et al., 2007; Genevro & Miller, 2010; Gamino & Ritter, 2012).

The finding that people often follow their own unique trajectories of grief has been especially important for medical and other caregivers who work with dying people. Because Kübler-Ross's stages have become so well known, well-meaning caregivers have sometimes tried to encourage patients to work through the steps in a prescribed order, without enough consideration for their individual needs.

Finally, there are substantial differences in people's reactions to impending death. The specific cause of dying; how long the process of dying lasts; a person's age, sex, and personality; and the social support available from family and friends all influence the course of dying and people's responses to it (Carver & Scheier, 2002).

Ultimately, there are significant concerns about the accuracy of Kübler-Ross's account of how people react to impending death. In response to some of these concerns, other theorists have developed alternative ideas. Psychologist Edwin Shneidman, for example, suggests that there are "themes" in people's reactions to dying that can occur—and recur—in any order throughout the dying process. These include such feelings and thoughts as incredulity, a sense of unfairness, fear of pain or even general terror, and fantasies of being rescued (Shneidman, 2007).

Another theorist, Charles Corr, suggests that, as in other periods of life, people who are dying face a set of psychological tasks. These include minimizing physical stress, maintaining the richness of life, continuing or deepening their relationships with other people, and fostering hope, often through spiritual searching (Corr, Nabe, & Corr, 2006; Corr, 2015).

Choosing the Nature of Death: Is DNR the Way to Go?

LO 15.6 Describe ways in which people exercise control over the death decision.

The letters "DNR" written on a patient's medical chart have a simple and clear meaning. Standing for "Do Not Resuscitate," DNR signifies that rather than administering any and every procedure that might possibly keep a patient alive, no extraordinary means are to be taken. For terminally ill patients, DNR may mean the difference between dying immediately or living additional days, months, or even years, kept alive only by the most extreme, invasive, and even painful medical procedures.

The decision to use or not to use extreme medical interventions entails several issues. One is the differentiation of "extreme" and "extraordinary" measures from those that are simply routine. There are no hard-and-fast rules; people making the decision must consider the needs of the specific patient, his or her prior medical history, and factors such as age and even religion. For instance, different standards might apply to a 12-year-old patient and an 85-year-old patient with the same medical condition.

Other questions concern quality of life. How can we determine an individual's current quality of life and whether it will be improved or diminished by a particular medical intervention? Who makes such decisions—the patient, a family member, or medical personnel?

One thing is clear: Medical personnel are reluctant to carry out the wishes of the terminally ill and their families to suspend aggressive treatment. Even when it is certain that a patient is going to die, and patients determine that they do not wish to receive further treatment, physicians often claim to be unaware of their patients' wishes. For instance, although one-third of patients ask not to be resuscitated, less than half of these people's physicians state that they know of their patients' preference (see Figure 15-2). In addition, only 49 percent of patients have their wishes entered on their medical charts. Physicians and other health-care providers may be reluctant to act on DNR requests in part because they are trained to save patients, not to permit them to die, and in part to avoid legal liability issues (Goold, Williams, & Arnold, 2000; McArdle, 2002).

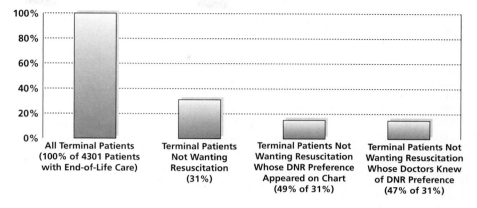

Figure 15-2 Dying Hard: Experiences of 4,301 Patients with End-of-Life Care

THINKING ABOUT THE DATA: What percent of the total patient sample has a preference to not be resuscitated? What factors would affect your personal decision to have or not have a do not resuscitate order?

(**Source:** Based on Knaus et al., 1995.)

LIVING WILLS. In order to gain more control over decisions regarding the nature of their death, people are increasingly signing living wills. A **living will** is a legal document that designates the medical treatments a person does or does not want if the person cannot express his or her wishes (see Figure 15-3).

Some people designate a specific person, called a *health care proxy*, to act as their representative in making health-care decisions. Health care proxies are authorized either in living wills or in a legal document known as *durable power of attorney*. Health care proxies may be authorized to deal with all medical care problems (such as a coma) or only terminal illnesses.

As with DNR orders, living wills are ineffective unless people take steps to make sure their health care proxies and doctors know their wishes. Although they may be reluctant to do so in advance, people should also have frank conversations clarifying their wishes with the representatives they choose as their health care proxies.

EUTHANASIA AND ASSISTED SUICIDE. Some three decades ago, Dr. Jack Kevorkian became well known for his invention and promotion of a "suicide machine," which allowed patients to push a button that releases anesthesia and a drug that stops the heart. By supplying the machine and the drugs, which patients administered themselves, Kevorkian was participating in a process known as *assisted suicide*, in which a person provides the means for a terminally ill individual to commit suicide. Kevorkian ended up spending eight years in prison after being convicted of second-degree murder for his participation in an assisted suicide that was shown on the television show *60 Minutes*.

living will
a legal document designating what medical treatments people want or do not want if they cannot express their wishes.

Figure 15-3 A Living Will

What steps can people take to make sure the wishes they write into their living wills are carried out?

I,_____,
being of sound mind, make this statement as a directive to be followed if I become permanently unable to participate in decisions regarding my medical care. These instructions reflect my firm and settled commitment to decline medical treatment under the circumstances indicated below:

I direct my attending physician to withhold or withdraw treatment that merely prolongs my dying, if I should be in **an incurable or irreversible mental or physical condition** with no reasonable expectation of recovery, including but not limited to: (a) a **terminal condition**; (b) a **permanently unconscious condition**; or (c) a **minimally conscious condition in which I am permanently unable to make decisions or express my wishes**.

I direct that treatment be limited to measures to keep me comfortable and to relieve pain, including any pain that might occur by withholding or withdrawing treatment.
While I understand that I am not legally required to be specific about future treatments, **if I am in the condition(s) described above I feel especially strongly about the following treatments**:

I do not want cardiac resuscitation.
I do not want mechanical respiration.
I do not want tube feeding.
I do not want antibiotics.

However, I **do want** maximum pain relief, even if it may hasten my death.

Other directions (insert personal instructions):

These directions express my legal right to refuse treatment under federal and state law. I intend my instructions to be carried out, unless I have revoked them in a new writing or by clearly indicating that I have changed my mind.

Signed:_____ Date:_____

Address:_____

- -

Statement by Witnesses
I declare that the person who signed this document appears to be at least eighteen (18) years of age, of sound mind, and under no constraint or undue influence. The person who signed this document appeared to do so willingly and free from duress. He or she signed (or asked another to sign for him or her) this document in my presence.

Witness:_____

Address:_____

- -

Witness:_____

Address:_____

- -

Assisted suicide continues to raise bitter conflict in the United States, and the practice is illegal in most states. Today, seven major jurisdictions (California, Colorado, Montana, Oregon, Vermont, Washington, and Washington, DC) have passed "right to die" laws, and Montana has legal physician-assisted suicide following a court order. In Oregon alone, more than 1,100 people have taken medication to end their own lives (Edwards, 2015; Oregon Death with Dignity Act, 2016).

In many countries, assisted suicide is an accepted practice. For instance, in the Netherlands, medical personnel may help end their patients' lives. However, several conditions must be met to make the practice permissible: At least two physicians must determine that the patient is terminally ill, there must be unbearable physical or mental suffering, the patient must give informed consent in writing, and relatives must be informed beforehand (Naik, 2002; Kleespies, 2004; Battin et al., 2007).

Assisted suicide is one form of **euthanasia**, the practice of assisting terminally ill people to die more quickly. Popularly known as "mercy killing," euthanasia can take a range of forms. *Passive euthanasia* involves removing respirators or other medical equipment that may be sustaining a patient's life, allowing the individual to die naturally. This happens when medical staff follow a DNR order, for example. In *voluntary active euthanasia*, caregivers or medical staff act to end a person's life before death would normally occur, perhaps by administering a dose of pain medication that they know will be fatal. Assisted suicide, as we have seen, lies between passive and voluntary active euthanasia. Euthanasia is an emotional and controversial—although surprisingly widespread—practice.

No one knows how widespread euthanasia truly is. However, one survey of nurses in intensive care units found that 20 percent had deliberately hastened a patient's death at least once, and other experts assert that euthanasia is far from rare (Asch, 1996).

Euthanasia is highly controversial, in part because it centers on decisions about who should control life. Does the right belong solely to an individual, a person's physicians, his or her dependents, the government, or some deity? Because, at least in the United States, we assume that we all have the absolute right to create lives by bringing children into the world, some people argue that we should also have the absolute right to end our lives (Allen et al., 2006; Goldney, 2012; Monteverde et al., 2017).

However, many opponents of euthanasia argue that the practice is morally wrong. In their view, prematurely ending someone's life, no matter how willing that person may be, is the equivalent of murder. Others point out that physicians are often inaccurate in predicting how long a person's life will last. For example, in some cases, patients have lived for years after being given no more than a 50 percent chance of living for six more months (Bishop, 2006; Peel & Harding, 2015; also see Figure 15-4).

euthanasia
the practice of assisting people who are terminally ill to die more quickly.

Figure 15-4 How Long Do "Terminal" Patients Really Live?

According to the large SUPPORT study, a significant percentage of a group of 3,693 patients given no more than a 50 percent chance of living for six months survived well beyond that period. Why do you think this happened?

(**Source:** Based on Lynn et al., 1997.)

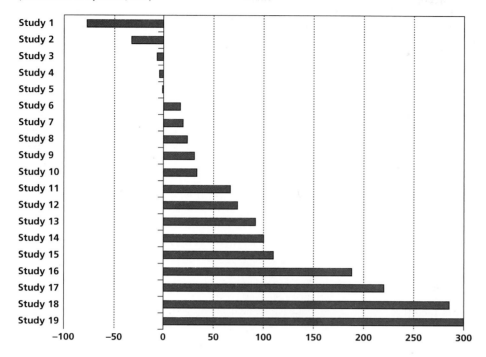

Another argument against euthanasia focuses on the emotional state of the patient. Even if patients ask or sometimes beg health-care providers to help them die, they may be suffering from a form of deep depression. In such cases, patients may be treated with antidepressant drugs that can alleviate the depression. Once the depression lifts, patients may change their minds about their earlier wish for death.

The debate over euthanasia is likely to continue. It is a highly personal issue, yet one that society increasingly must face as the world's elderly population increases (Becvar, 2000; Gostin, 2006; McLachlan, 2008).

Caring for the Terminally Ill: The Place of Death

LO 15.7   **Compare and contrast the advantages of hospice and home care for the end of life.**

About half the people in the United States who die do so in hospitals. It need not be that way. There are several reasons why hospitals are among the least desirable locales in which to face death. Hospitals are typically impersonal, with staff rotating throughout the day. Because visiting hours are limited, people frequently die alone, without the comfort of loved ones at their bedside.

Furthermore, hospitals are designed to make people better, not to deal with the dying, and it is extraordinarily expensive to provide custodial care for dying people. Consequently, hospitals typically don't have the resources needed to deal adequately with the emotional requirements of terminally ill patients and their families.

Because of the limitations of traditional hospitals in dealing with the dying, there are now several alternatives to hospitalization. In **home care**, dying people stay in their homes and receive treatment from their families and visiting medical staff. Many dying patients prefer home care because they can spend their final days in a familiar environment, with people they love and a lifetime accumulation of treasures around them.

home care
an alternative to hospitalization in which dying people stay in their homes and receive treatment from their families and visiting medical staff.

Although the dying may prefer home care, it can be quite difficult for family members. Furnishing final care can offer family members a good deal of emotional solace because they are giving something precious to people they love. But it is extraordinarily draining, both physically and emotionally, to be on call 24 hours a day. Furthermore, because most relatives are not trained in nursing, they may provide less than optimal medical care. Many people decide they just aren't equipped to care for a dying family member at home (Perreault, Fothergill-Bourbonnais, & Fiset, 2004).

hospice care

care provided for the dying in places devoted to those who are terminally ill.

For these families, another alternative to hospitalization that is becoming increasingly prevalent is hospice care. **Hospice care** is care for the dying provided in places devoted to those who are terminally ill. In the Middle Ages, hospices were facilities that provided comfort and hospitality to travelers. Drawing on that concept, today's hospices are designed to provide a warm, supportive environment for the dying. They do not focus on extending people's lives but rather on making their final days pleasant and meaningful. Typically, people who go to hospices are removed from treatments that are painful, and no extraordinary or invasive means are employed to make their lives longer. The emphasis is on making patients' lives as full as possible, not on squeezing out every possible moment of life at any cost (Corr, 2007; York et al., 2012; Prochaska et al., 2017).

Although the research is far from conclusive, hospice patients appear to be more satisfied with the care they receive than those who receive treatment in more traditional settings. Hospice care, then, provides a clear alternative to traditional hospitalization for the terminally ill (Seymour et al., 2007; Rhodes et al., 2008; Clark, 2015).

Module 15.2 Review

LO 15.5 Describe ways in which people face the prospect of their own death.

Elisabeth Kübler-Ross has identified five steps toward dying: denial, anger, bargaining, depression, and acceptance. The stage nature of her theory has been criticized as too inflexible, and other theorists have suggested alternatives.

LO 15.6 Describe ways in which people exercise control over the death decision.

Issues surrounding dying are highly controversial, including the degree of measures that physicians should apply to keep dying patients alive and who should make the decisions about those measures. Living wills are a way for people to take some control over the decision. Assisted suicide and, more generally,

euthanasia are highly controversial and are illegal in most of the United States, although many people believe they should be legalized if they are regulated.

LO 15.7 Compare and contrast the advantages of hospice and home care for the end of life.

Although most people in the United States die in hospitals, increasing numbers are choosing home care or hospice care for their final days.

Journal Writing Prompt

Applying Lifespan Development: Do you think assisted suicide should be permissible? What about other forms of euthanasia? Why or why not?

MODULE 15.3

GRIEF AND BEREAVEMENT

No one ever told me that grief felt so like fear. I am not afraid, but the sensation is like being afraid. The same fluttering in the stomach, the same restlessness, the yawning. I keep on swallowing.

At other times it feels like being mildly drunk, or concussed. There is a sort of invisible blanket between the world and me. I find it hard to take in what anyone says. Or perhaps, hard to want to take it in. It is so uninteresting. (Lewis, 1985, p. 394)

For something that is a universal experience, most of us are surprisingly ill-prepared for the grief that follows the death of a loved one. Particularly in Western societies, where life expectancy is long and mortality rates are lower than at any time in history, people are apt to view death as an atypical event rather than an expected part of life. This attitude makes grief all the more difficult to bear, particularly when we compare the present day with historical eras in which people lived shorter lives and the death rate was considerably higher. The first step in grieving, for most survivors in Western countries, is some sort of funeral (Bryant, 2003; Kleinman, 2012).

Mourning and Funerals: Final Rites

LO 15.8   Describe how survivors react to and cope with death.

Death is a big business in the United States. The average funeral and burial costs nearly $7,000. The purchase of an ornate, polished coffin; transportation to and from the cemetery in a limousine; and preparation of the body for preservation and viewing are among the services that people typically purchase in planning a funeral (Sheridan, 2013; Beard & Burger, 2017).

In part, the relatively grandiose nature of funerals is due to the vulnerability of those planning the funeral, who are typically close survivors of the deceased. Wishing to demonstrate love and affection, the survivors are susceptible to suggestions to "provide the best" for the deceased (Culver, 2003; Varga, 2014).

But it is not only the pressure of enterprising salespersons that leads many people to spend thousands of dollars on a funeral. In large measure, the nature of funerals, like that of weddings, is determined by social norms and customs. Because an individual's death represents an important transition, not only for loved ones but also for an entire community, the rites associated with death take on an added importance. In a sense, then, a funeral is not only a public acknowledgment that an individual has died but also a recognition of everyone's ultimate mortality and an acceptance of the cycle of life.

In Western societies, funeral rituals follow a typical pattern, despite some surface variations. Prior to the funeral, the body is prepared in some way and is dressed in special clothing. Funerals usually include the celebration of a religious rite, the delivery of a eulogy, a procession of some sort, and some formal period, such as the wake for Irish Catholics and Shiva for Jews, in which relatives and friends visit the mourning family and pay their respects. Military funerals typically include the firing of weapons and a flag draped over the coffin.

CULTURAL DIFFERENCES IN GRIEVING.   Non-Western cultures include funeral rituals of quite different sorts. For instance, in some societies mourners shave their heads as a sign of grief, while in others they allow the hair to grow, and men stop shaving for a period of time. In other cultures, mourners may be hired to wail and grieve. Sometimes noisy celebrations take place at funerals, while in other cultures silence is the norm. Even the nature of emotional displays, such as the amount and timing of crying, are determined culturally (Rosenblatt, 2001).

For example, mourners in Balinese funerals in Indonesia attempt to show little emotion because they believe they must be calm in order for the gods to hear their prayers. In contrast, mourners at African American funerals are encouraged to show their grief, and the funeral rituals are meant to allow attendees to display their feelings. Widows in Egypt are considered abnormal if they don't weep unconsolably, and Chinese mourners sometimes hire professional wailers (Collins & Doolittle, 2006; Walter, 2012; Carteret, 2017). Historically, some cultures have developed funeral rites that strike us as extreme. For example, in *suttee*, a traditional Hindu practice in India that is now illegal, a widow was expected to throw herself into the fire that consumed her husband's body. In ancient China, servants were sometimes buried (alive) with their masters' bodies.

Ultimately, no matter what the particular ritual, all funerals basically serve the same underlying function: They mark the endpoint of the life of the person who has died—and provide a formal forum for the feelings of the survivors, a place where they can come together and share their grief and comfort one another.

Bereavement and Grief: Adjusting to the Death of a Loved One

LO 15.9 Describe ways in which people experience grief and the functions it serves.

After the death of a loved one, a painful period of adjustment follows, involving bereavement and grief. **Bereavement** is acknowledgment of the objective fact that one has experienced a death, whereas **grief** is the emotional response to one's loss. Everyone's grief is different, but there are certain similarities in the ways people in Western societies adjust to the loss.

Survivors' first stage of grief typically entails shock, numbness, disbelief, or outright denial. People may avoid the reality of the situation, trying to carry on with the usual routines of their lives, although the pain may break through, causing anguish, fear, and deep sorrow and distress. If the pain is too severe, however, the person may cycle back to numbness. In some ways, such a psychological state may be beneficial, since it permits the survivor to make funeral arrangements and carry out other psychologically difficult tasks. Typically, people pass through this stage in a few days or weeks, although in some cases it lasts longer.

In the next phase, people begin to confront the death and realize the extent of their loss. They fully experience their grief, and they begin to acknowledge the reality that the separation from the dead person will be permanent. In so doing, mourners may suffer deep unhappiness or even depression, a normal feeling in this situation and not one necessarily requiring treatment. They may yearn for the dead individual. Emotions can range from impatient to lethargic. However, they also begin to view their past relationship with the deceased realistically, good and bad. In so doing, they begin to free themselves from some of the bonds that tied them to their loved ones (Norton & Gino, 2014; Rosenblatt, 2015).

Finally, people who have lost a loved one reach the accommodation stage. They begin to pick up the pieces of their lives and to construct new identities. For instance, rather than seeing herself as someone's widowed spouse, a woman whose husband has died may come to regard herself as a single person. Still, there are moments when intense feelings of grief occur.

Ultimately, most people are able to emerge from the grieving process and live new lives, independent from the person who has died. They form new relationships, and some even find that coping with the death has helped them to grow as individuals. They become more self-reliant and more appreciative of life.

It is important to keep in mind that not everyone passes through the stages of grief in the same manner and in the same order. People display vast individual differences, partly due to their personalities, the nature of the relationship with the deceased, and the opportunities that are available to them for continuing their lives after the loss. In fact, most bereaved people are quite resilient, experiencing strong positive emotions such as joy even soon after the death of a loved one. According to psychologist George Bonanno, who has studied bereavement extensively, humans are prepared in an evolutionary sense to move on after the death of someone close. He rejects the notion that there are fixed stages of mourning and argues that most people move on with their lives quite effectively (Bonanno, 2009; Mancini & Bonanno, 2012; Kosminsky, 2017).

DIFFERENTIATING UNHEALTHY GRIEF FROM NORMAL GRIEF. Although ideas abound about what separates normal grief from unhealthy grief, careful research has shown that many of the assumptions that both laypersons and clinicians hold are wrong. There is no particular timetable for grieving, particularly the common notion that grieving should be complete a year after a spouse has died. For some people (but not all), grieving may take considerably longer than a year. And some individuals experience *complicated grief* (or sometimes *prolonged grief disorder*), a type of mourning that continues unceasingly for months and years (as we discussed in the previous chapter). An estimated 15 percent of those who are bereaved suffer from complicated grief (Schumer, 2009; Zisook & Shear, 2009; Maercker, Neimeyer, & Simiola, 2017).

bereavement

acknowledgment of the objective fact that one has experienced a death.

grief

the emotional response to one's loss.

Research also contradicts the common assumption that depression following the death of a loved one is widespread. In fact, only 15 to 30 percent of people show relatively deep depression following the loss of a loved one (Bonanno et al., 2002; Hensley, 2006).

Why do you think the risk of death is so high for people who have recently lost a spouse? Why might remarriage lower the risk?

Similarly, it is often assumed that people who show little initial distress over a death are simply not facing up to reality, and that as a consequence they are likely to have problems later. This is not the case. In fact, those who show the most intense distress immediately after a death are the most apt to have adjustment difficulties and health problems later on (Boerner et al., 2005; also see the *From Research to Practice* box).

From Research to Practice

Moving On: Surviving the Loss of a Longtime Spouse

As you may well imagine, the death of a spouse is almost always a traumatic experience that is usually followed by intense grief and anguish. In the case of older couples who had been married for a very long time, losing a spouse can mean losing a lifelong companion and typically a partner's primary and sometimes sole source of emotional support. Intuition may therefore suggest that the period of grieving such a loss would be particularly prolonged for a surviving spouse who had enjoyed a close and happy marriage.

But a growing body of research suggests otherwise: It seems in fact that people who had a successful marriage are better able to work through their mourning of a lost spouse and get on with the rest of their lives than those with less successful marriages. In fact, research now suggests that around half of those who report having satisfying marriages are able to get past their grief within six months of the death of their spouses (Carr, Nesse, & Wortman, 2005; Carr, 2015; Carr, 2016).

One explanation for these findings is that people who enjoy close and happy marriages tend to have strong interpersonal skills on which to rely during their time of loss. They may be better equipped to call upon friends, family, and even a professional counselor if necessary to assist them through their grieving period. One way that others help the surviving spouse is by providing a diversion to keep him or her from dwelling on the loss and also by encouraging him or her to replace the void with new interests and activities. Strong interpersonal skills may also facilitate a positive approach to dating new people when the time is right (Carr, Nesse, & Wortman, 2005; Carr, 2015).

Another reason for the resiliency of surviving spouses of close marriages is the knowledge that they and their departed partner had culminated what they set out to achieve:

a successful and satisfying relationship. Surviving partners of strained marriages might feel more sadness over never having achieved a desired level of closeness, or they might regret not having an opportunity to resolve lingering conflicts, or they might feel guilty about not working harder to make their marriage better when they had the chance.

In contrast, surviving spouses who enjoyed a close marriage are more likely to have settled lingering issues and to have talked through what would happen after either of them died; they therefore are more likely to feel secure in knowing what their departed would have wanted for them in widowhood. Finally, spouses who have a close and secure relationship may simply have a better opportunity to say their final goodbyes as one of the partners' health fails (Mancini, Sinan, & Bonanno, 2015).

Of course, having a secure marriage is no guarantee that life as a widow or widower will be lacking in pain. Even very resilient survivors grieve deeply in the immediate months following the death of their spouses. And indeed, it's possible to be too close to one's spouse, making the loss more difficult; men in particular may be hit hard by the loss of a wife who was their only emotional confidant. But in many cases, the final gift of a close and loving spouse is the security to move on with one's life within a reasonable time after his or her death (Boerner, et al., 2005; Malgaroni, & Bonanno, 2017).

Shared Writing Prompt

Do you think that these same findings would apply in the case of losing a spouse earlier in life? Why or why not? What other factors besides interpersonal closeness might affect the duration of grief after losing a longtime spouse?

THE CONSEQUENCES OF GRIEF AND BEREAVEMENT. In a sense, death is catching, at least in terms of survivors' mortality. Widowed people are particularly at risk of death. Some studies find that the risk of death is as much as seven times higher than normal in the first year after the death of a spouse. At particular risk are men and younger women who have been widowed. Remarriage seems to lower the risk of death for survivors. This is particularly true for men who have lost their wives, although the reasons are not clear (Aiken, 2000; Elwert & Christakis, 2008).

Bereavement is more likely to produce depression or other negative consequences if the person who has lost a loved one is already insecure, anxious, or fearful and therefore is less able to cope effectively. Furthermore, people whose relationships were marked by ambivalence before death are more apt to suffer poor post-death outcomes than those who were secure in their relationships. Those who were highly dependent on the person who died, and who therefore feel more vulnerable without them, are apt to suffer more after the death, as are those who spend a great deal of time reflecting on a loved one's death and their feelings of grief.

Bereaved people who lack social support from family, friends, or a connection to some other group, religious or otherwise, are more likely to experience feelings of loneliness, and therefore are more at risk. Finally, people who are unable to make sense of the death or find meaning in it (such as a new appreciation of life) show less overall adjustment (Nolen-Hoeksema & Davis, 2002; Torges, Stewart, & Nolen-Hoeksema, 2008).

The suddenness of a loved one's death also appears to affect the course of grieving. People who unexpectedly lose their loved ones are less able to cope than those who were able to anticipate the death. For instance, in one study, people who experienced a sudden death still had not fully recovered four years later. In part, this may be because sudden, unanticipated deaths are often the result of violence, which occurs more frequently among younger individuals (Burton, Haley, & Small, 2006; De Leo et al., 2014). (Also see the *Development in Your Life* feature.)

Development in Your Life
Helping a Child Cope with Grief

Because of their limited understanding of death, younger children need special help in coping with grief. Among the strategies that can help are the following:

- Be honest. Don't say that a dead person is "sleeping" or "on a long trip." Use age-appropriate language to tell children the truth. Gently but clearly point out the irreversibility and the final and universal nature of death.

- Encourage expressions of grief. Don't tell children not to cry or show their feelings. Instead, tell them that it is understandable to feel terrible and that they may always miss the deceased. Encourage them to draw a picture, write a letter, or express their feelings in some other way. At the same time, assure them that they will always have good memories of the person who has died.

- Reassure children that they are not to blame for the death. Children sometimes attribute a loved one's death to their own behavior—if they had not misbehaved, they mistakenly reason, the person would not have died.

- Understand that children's grief may surface in unanticipated ways. Children may show little or no grief at the time of the death, but later they may become upset for no apparent reason or revert to behaviors such as sucking their thumb. Death can be overwhelming for a child, so try to be consistently loving and supportive.

- Talk to children about funerals, wakes, and other rituals associated with death, and what they should expect. You might give them a role to play, such as reading a poem, if they are old enough.

Module 15.3 Review

LO 15.8   Describe how survivors react to and cope with death.

Bereavement refers to the loss of a loved one; grief refers to the emotional response to that loss. Funeral rites play a significant role in helping people acknowledge the death of a loved one, recognize their own mortality, and proceed with their lives.

LO 15.9   Describe ways in which people experience grief and the functions it serves.

For many people, grief passes through denial, sorrow, and accommodation stages. Children need special help coping with grief.

Journal Writing Prompt

Applying Lifespan Development: Why do so many people in U.S. society feel reluctant to think and talk about death?

Epilogue

This chapter and the final part of the book focus on late adulthood and the end of life. Genuine physical and cognitive declines finally become the norm, but people can continue to lead healthy, engaged lives throughout most of the period—in defiance of stereotypes that characterize them as decrepit and doddering.

As in other periods of the life span, continuity and change are both evident in late adulthood. For example, we noticed that individual differences in cognitive performance, even as they show declines, reflect individual differences that were present in earlier years. We saw that lifestyle choices made earlier, such as participation in exercise, contribute to health and longevity during this time.

Social and personality development can continue throughout late adulthood. We saw that although most people show similar personality traits to those of their earlier years, late adulthood also affords a unique perspective on the more turbulent years that have gone before. People defy stereotypes of late adulthood in the varied ways they live and the rich relationships they sustain in this period.

We ended the book with a consideration of the inevitable end of life. Even here, as we considered death and its meaning at various stages in the life span and across cultures, we saw that there are challenges to be faced and satisfaction to be drawn from a graceful departure from

life whether in a hospital, hospice, or palliative or home care setting.

In sum, the story of the entire life span is one of fresh challenges and opportunities as we continuously undergo and adjust to physical and cognitive changes and learn to relate to new social situations. Development persists virtually to the point of death, and with preparation, we can appreciate and learn from all parts of the life span.

Before you leave the book, return to the chapter prologue, about Jackson LeRoi, the 71-year-old who refused treatment for his terminal cancer. Based on your understanding of death and dying, answer the following questions.

1. To what extent do you think LeRoi went through the stages described by Kübler-Ross?

2. How might LeRoi have reacted differently to his impending death if he were a young man in his early 20s?

3. How might LeRoi's celebratory attitude toward the ending of his life have affected the bereavement process for his family?

4. How might LeRoi's final days been different if he had elected to receive cancer treatment in the hospital? How might they have been different if he had required hospice care?

Looking Back

LO 15.1   Review the difficulties in defining death.

The precise point of death is difficult to define. Functional death refers to the absence of heartbeat and respiration, from which people can be resuscitated, while brain death refers to the absence of electrical activity in the brain, which is irreversible.

LO 15.2   Describe what death means at different stages of the life span.

The death of an infant or a young child is among the most devastating experiences for parents, largely because it seems unnatural and entirely incomprehensible. Adolescents have an unrealistic sense of invulnerability that makes them susceptible to accidental death. Denial often makes it impossible for terminally ill adolescents to accept the seriousness of their condition. For young adults, death is virtually unthinkable. Young adults who are terminally ill can be difficult patients because of their strong sense of the injustice of their fate. In middle adulthood, disease becomes the leading cause of death, and awareness of the reality of death can lead to a substantial fear of death. People in late adulthood begin to prepare for death. Older people generally prefer to know if death is near, and the main issue they have to deal with is whether their lives continue to have value.

LO 15.3   Describe how dying is affected by culture.

Responses to death are in part determined by culture. Death may be regarded as a release from the pains of the world, the beginning of a pleasurable afterlife, a punishment or judgment, or simply the end to life.

LO 15.4   Summarize how we can prepare for death.

Death education can help people learn about death and consider their own mortality realistically.

LO 15.5   Describe ways in which people face the prospect of their own death.

Elisabeth Kübler-Ross suggests that people pass through five basic stages on their way to death: denial, anger, bargaining, depression, and acceptance. The stage nature of her theory has been criticized, and other theorists have suggested alternatives.

LO 15.6   Describe ways in which people exercise control over the death decision.

A living will is a means of asserting control over decisions surrounding one's death through specification of desired medical treatments in life-threatening situations and designation of a health care proxy to enforce one's wishes. Assisted suicide, a form of euthanasia, is illegal in most of the United States.

LO 15.7   Compare and contrast the advantages of hospice and home care for the end of life.

Although most deaths in the United States occur in hospitals, an increasing number of terminal patients are opting for either home care or a hospice.

LO 15.8   Describe how survivors react to and cope with death.

Funeral rituals serve a dual function: acknowledging the death of a loved one and recognizing and anticipating the mortality of all who participate.

LO 15.9   Describe ways in which people experience grief and the functions it serves.

The death of a loved one brings a period of adjustment involving bereavement and grief. Grief may proceed through stages of shock and denial, the beginning of acceptance, and accommodation. One consequence of bereavement is an increase in the risk of death for the survivor. Children need particular help in dealing with death, including honesty, encouragement of expressions of grief, reassurance that the death was not caused by the child's behavior, and understanding that the child's grief may be delayed and indirect.

Key Terms and Concepts

functional death   475
brain death   475
sudden infant death syndrome
  (SIDS)   476

thanatologists   480
living will   485
euthanasia   486
home care   487

hospice care   488
bereavement   490
grief   490

References

AARP (American Association of Retired Persons)/Modern Maturity. (1999). *Sexuality survey.* Washington, DC: Author.

AARP (American Association of Retired Persons). (2005, October). I can see clearly now. *AARP Bulletin,* p. 34.

Abel, T., Havekes, R., Saletin, J. M., & Walker, M. P. (2013). Sleep, plasticity and memory from molecules to whole-brain networks. *Current Biology, 23*(17), R774–R788.

Abdo, C., Afif-Abdo, J., Otani, F., & Machado, A. (2008). Sexual satisfaction among patients with erectile dysfunction treated with counseling, sildenafil, or both. *Journal of Sexual Medicine, 5,* 1720–1726.

Abrahams, N., Jewkes, R., Laubscher, R., & Hoffman, M. (2006). Intimate partner violence: Prevalence and risk factors for men in Cape Town, South Africa. *Violence and Victims, 21*(2), 247–264.

Abril, C., & Gault, B. (2006, March). The state of music in the elementary school: The principal's perspective. *Journal of Research in Music Education, 54,* 6–20.

Acierno, R., Hernandez, M. A., Amstadter, A. B., Resnick, H. S., Steve, K., Muzzy, W., et al. (2010). Prevalence and correlates of emotional, physical, sexual, and financial abuse and potential neglect in the United States: The National Elder Mistreatment Study. *American Journal of Public Health, 100,* 292–297.

Ackerman, B. P., & Izard, C. E. (2004). Emotion cognition in children and adolescents: Introduction to the special issue. *Journal of Experimental Child Psychology, 89* [Special issue: Emotional cognition in children], 271–275.

Acocella, J. (2003, August 18 & 25). Little people. *New Yorker,* pp. 138–143.

ACOG (American Congress of Obstetricians and Gynecologists). (2002). *Guidelines for perinatal care.* Elk Grove, IN: Author.

Adams Hillard, P. J. (2001). Gynecologic disorders and surgery. In N. L. Stotland & D. E. Stewart (Eds.), *Psychological aspects of women's health care: The interface between psychiatry and obstetrics and gynecology* (2nd ed.). Washington, DC: American Psychiatric Publishing.

Adams, C., & Labouvie-Vief, G. (1986, November 20). *Modes of knowing and language processing. Symposium on developmental dimensions of adult adaptations. Perspectives in mind, self, and emotion.* Paper presented at the meeting of the Gerontological Association of America, Chicago.

Adams, K. B. (2004). Changing investment in activities and interests in elders' lives: Theory and measurement. *International Journal of Aging and Human Development, 58,* 87–108.

ADL. (2017) Myths and facts about immigrants and immigration. Accessed online, 11/29/17; https://www.adl.org/education/resources/fact-sheets/myths-and-facts-about-immigrants-and-immigration.

Administration on Aging. (2003). *A profile of older Americans: 2003.* Washington, DC: U.S. Department of Health and Human Services.

Administration on Aging. (2006). *Profiles of older Americans 2005: Research report.* Washington, DC: U.S. Department of Health and Human Resources.

Adolph, K. E., Kretch, K. S., & LoBue, V. (2014). Fear of heights in infants? *Current Directions in Psychological Science, 23,* 60–66.

Adolphs, R. (2002). Neural systems for recognizing emotion. *Current Opinion in Neurobiology, 12*(2), 169–177. doi:10.1016/S0959-4388(02)00301-X.

Agrawal, A., & Lynskey, M. (2008). Are there genetic influences on addiction? Evidence from family, adoption and twin studies. *Addiction, 103,* 1069–1081. Accessed online; http://search.ebsco-host.com, doi:10.1111/j.13 60-0443.2008.02213.x.

Aguirre, G. K. (2006). Interpretation of clinical functional neuroimaging studies. In M. D'Esposisto (Ed.), *Functional MRI: Applications in clinical neurology and psychiatry.* Boca Raton, FL: Informa Healthcare.

Ahn, W., Gelman, S., & Amsterlaw, J. (2000). Causal status effect in children's categorization. *Cognition, 76,* B35–B43.

Aiken, L. R. (2000). *Dying, death, and bereavement* (4th ed.). Mahwah, NJ: Lawrence Erlbaum.

Ainsworth, M. D. S. (1993). Attachment as related to mother-infant interaction. *Advances in Infancy Research, 8,* 1–50.

Ainsworth, M. D. S., Blehar, M. C., Waters, E., & Wall, S. (1978). *Patterns of attachment: A psychological study of the strange situation.* Hillsdale, NJ: Lawrence Erlbaum.

Alan Guttmacher Institute. (2004). *Report on viral sexual diseases.* Chicago: Author.

Albers, L. L., Migliaccio, L., Bedrick, E. J., Teaf, D., & Peralta, P. (2007). Does epidural analgesia affect the rate of spontaneous obstetric lacerations in normal births? *Journal of Midwifery and Women's Health, 52,* 31–36.

Alderfer, C. (2003). The science and nonscience of psychologists' responses to *The Bell Curve. Professional Psychology: Research & Practice, 34,* 287–293.

Aldwin, C., & Gilmer, D. (2004). *Health, illness, and optimal aging: Biological and psychosocial perspectives.* Thousand Oaks, CA: Sage Publications.

Alexander, B., Turnbull, D., & Cyna, A. (2009). The effect of pregnancy on hypnotizability. *American Journal of Clinical Hypnosis, 52,* 13–22.

Alexander, G., Wilcox, T., & Woods, R. (2009). Sex differences in infants' visual interest in toys. *Archives of Sexual Behavior, 38,* 427–433.

Alexander, M. G., Brewer, M. B., & Livingston, R. W. (2005). Putting stereotype content in context: Image theory and interethnic stereotypes. *Personality and Social Psychology Bulletin, 31,* 781–794.

Alexander, P. C. (2015). *Intergenerational cycles of trauma and violence: An attachment and family systems perspective.* New York: W. W. Norton & Co.

Alfred, M. V., & Chlup, D. T. (2010). Making the invisible, visible: Race matters in human resource development. *Advances in Developing Human Resources, 12,* 332–351.

Alhusen, J. L., Hayat, M. J., & Gross, D. (2013). A longitudinal study of maternal attachment and infant developmental outcomes. *Archives of Women's Mental Health, 16,* 521–529.

Alisky, J. M. (2007). The coming problem of HIV-associated Alzheimer's disease. *Medical Hypotheses, 12,* 47–55.

Allan, N. P., Joye, S. W., & Lonigan, C. J. (2017). Does gender moderate the relations between externalizing behavior and key emergent literacy abilities? Evidence from a longitudinal study. *Journal of Attention Disorders, 21,* 600–609.

Allemand, M., Steiger, A. E., & Fend, H. A. (2015). Empathy development in adolescence predicts social competencies in adulthood. *Journal of Personality, 83,* 229–241.

Allen, J., Chavez, S., DeSimone, S., Howard, D., Johnson, K., LaPierre, L., et al. (2006, June). Americans' attitudes toward euthanasia and physician-assisted suicide, 1936–2002. *Journal of Sociology & Social Welfare, 33,* 5–23.

Allen, J., Seitz, V., & Apfel, N. (2007). The sexually mature teen as a whole person: New directions in prevention and intervention for teen pregnancy and parenthood. *Child development and social policy: Knowledge for action* (pp. 185–199). Washington, DC: American Psychological Association.

Allison, B., & Schultz, J. (2001). Interpersonal identity formation during early adolescence. *Adolescence, 36,* 509–523.

Al-Namlah, A. S., Meins, E., & Fernyhough, C. (2012). Self-regulatory private speech relates to children's recall and organization of autobiographical memories. *Early Childhood Research Quarterly*. Accessed online, 7/18/12; http://www.sciencedirect.com/science/article/pii/S0885200612000300.

Alosco, M. L., Stanek, K. M., Galioto, R., Korgaonkar, M. S., Grieve, S. M., Brickman, A. M., & . . . Gunstad, J. (2014). Body mass index and brain structure in healthy children and adolescents. *International Journal of Neuroscience, 124*, 49–55.

Alshaarawy, O., & Anthony, J. C. (2014). Month-wise estimates of tobacco smoking during pregnancy for the United States, 2002–2009. *Maternal and Child Health Journal*. Accessed online, 3/14/15; http://www.ncbi.nlm.nih.gov/pubmed/25112459.

Altholz, S., & Golensky, M. (2004). Counseling, support, and advocacy for clients who stutter. *Health & Social Work, 29*, 197–205.

Alvarez-Leon, E. E., Roman-Vinas, B., & Serra-Majem, L. (2006). Dairy products and health: A review of the epidemiological evidence. *British Journal of Nutrition, 96*, Suppl. 1, S94–S99.

Alwin, D. F. (2012). Integrating varieties of life course concepts. *The Journals of Gerontology: Series B: Psychological Sciences and Social Sciences, 67B*, 206–220.

Alzheimer's Association (2017). 2017 Alzheimer's disease facts and figures. Accessed online; https://www.alz.org/documents_custom/2017-facts-and-figures.pdf.

Amato, P. R., & Afifi, T. D. (2006). Feeling caught between parents: Adult children's relations with parents and subjective well-being. *Journal of Marriage and Family, 68*, 222–235.

American Academy of Pediatrics. (2004, June 3). Sports programs. Accessed online; http://www.medem.com/medlb/article_detaillb_for_printer.cfm?article.

American Academy of Pediatrics. (2011). *SIDS and other sleep-related infant deaths: Expansion of recommendations for a safe infant sleeping environment*. Policy Statement accessed online; http://pediatrics.aappublications.org/content/early/2011/10/12/peds.2011-2284.

American Academy of Pediatrics. (2013). Prevalence and reasons for introducing infants early to solid foods: Variations by milk feeding type. *Pediatrics, 131*, Accessed online, 6/25/14; http://pediatrics.aappublications.org/content/131/4/e1108.

American Academy of Pediatrics. (2014). *Caring for your baby and young Child*. (5th ed.). New York: Bantam.

American Academy of Pediatrics (2016). *SIDS and other sleep-related infant deaths: Updated 2016 recommendations for a safe infant sleeping environment*. Policy Statement accessed online; http://pediatrics.aappublications.org/content/138/5/e20162938.

American Association of Neurological Surgeons. (2012). Shaken baby syndrome. Accessed online, 7/4/12; http://www.aans.org/Patient%20Information/Conditions%20and%20Treatments/Shaken%20Baby%20Syndrome.aspx.

American Association on Intellectual and Developmental Disabilities. (2012). Definition of intellectual disability. Accessed online, 7/23/12; www.aamr.org.

American Psychiatric Association. (2013). *Diagnostic and statistical manual of mental disorders*. Washington, DC: Author.

American Psychological Association. (2002). *Ethical principles of psychologists and code of conduct. Updated*. Washington, DC: Author.

American Speech-Language-Hearing Association. (2017). Typical speech and language development. Accessed online 12/21/17; http://www.asha.org/public/speech/development/.

Amick, H. R., Gartlehner, G., Gaynes, B. N., Forneris, C., Asher, G. N., Morgan, L. C., . . . & Bann, C. (2015). Comparative benefits and harms of second generation antidepressants and cognitive behavioral therapies in initial treatment of major depressive disorder: systematic review and meta-analysis. *BMJ, 351*, 1–10.

Amitai, Y., Haringman, M., Meiraz, H., Baram, N., & Leventhal, A. (2004). Increased awareness, knowledge and utilization of preconceptional folic acid in Israel following a national campaign. *Preventive Medicine: An International Journal Devoted to Practice and Theory, 39*, 731–737.

Amsterlaw, J., & Wellman, H. (2006). Theories of mind in transition: A microgenetic study of the development of false belief understanding. *Journal of Cognition and Development, 7*, 139–172.

An, R. (2015). Health care expenses in relation to obesity and smoking among U.S. adults by gender, race/ethnicity,and age group: 1998–2011. *Public Health, 129*(1), 29–36. doi:10.1016/j.puhe.2014.11.003.

Anderson, P., & Butcher, K. (2006, March). Childhood obesity: Trends and potential causes. *The Future of Children, 16*, 19–45.

Andreotti, C., Garrard, P., Venkatraman, S. L., & Compas, B. E. (2015). Stress-related changes in attentional bias to social threat in young adults: Psychobiological associations with the early family environment. *Cognitive Therapy and Research, 39*, 332–342.

Andrew, M., McCanlies, E., Burchfiel, C., Charles, L., Hartley, T., Fekedulegn, D., et al. (2008). Hardiness and psychological distress in a cohort of police officers. *International Journal of Emergency Mental Health, 10*, 137–148.

Andrews, B., d'Avossa, G., & Sapir, A. (2017). Aging changes 3D perception: Evidence for hemispheric rebalancing of lateralized processes. *Neuropsychologia, 99*, 121–127.

Andrews, G., Halford, G., & Bunch, K. (2003). Theory of mind and relational complexity. *Child Development, 74*, 1476–1499.

Andruski, J. E., Casielles, E., & Nathan, G. (2014). Is bilingual babbling language-specific? Some evidence from a case study of Spanish–English dual acquisition. *Bilingualism: Language and Cognition, 17*, 660–672.

Antonucci, T. C. (2001). Social relations: An examination of social networks, social support, and sense of control. In J. E. Birren & K. W. Schaie (Eds.), *Handbook of the psychology of aging* (5th ed.). San Diego: Academic Press.

Anyan, F., & Hjemdal, O. (2016). Adolescent stress and symptoms of anxiety and depression: Resilience explains and differentiates the relationships. *Journal of Affective Disorders, 203*, 213–220.

APA Reproductive Choice Working Group. (2000). *Reproductive choice and abortion: A resource packet*. Washington, DC: American Psychological Association.

Arai, J., Li, S., Hartley, D., and Feig, L. (2009). Transgenerational rescue of a genetic defect in long-term potentiation and memory formation by juvenile enrichment. *Journal of Neuroscience, 29*, 1496–1502.

Archimi, A., & Kuntsche, E. (2014). Do offenders and victims drink for different reasons? Testing mediation of drinking motives in the link between bullying subgroups and alcohol use in adolescence. *Addictive Behaviors, 39*, 713–716.

Ariès, P. (1962). *Centuries of childhood*. New York: Knopf.

Armstrong, J., Hutchinson, I., Laing, D., & Jinks, A. (2006). Facial electromyography: Responses of children to odor and taste stimuli. *Chemical Senses, 32*, 611–621.

Arnett, J. J. (2006). *Emerging adulthood: The winding road from the late teens through the twenties*. New York: Oxford University Press.

Arnett, J. (2011). Emerging adulthood(s): The cultural psychology of a new life stage. In L. Jensen (Ed.), *Bridging cultural and developmental approaches to psychology: New syntheses in theory, research, and policy*. New York: Oxford University Press.

Arnett, J. J. (2014a). *Emerging adulthood: The winding road from the late teens through the twenties* (2nd ed.). New York: Oxford University Press.

Arnett, J. J. (2014b). Presidential address: The emergence of emerging adulthood: A personal history. *Emerging Adulthood, 2*, 155–162.

Arnett, J. J. (2015). Identity development from adolescence to emerging adulthood: What we know and (especially) don't know. In K.C. McLean, M. Syed (Eds.), *The Oxford handbook of identity development*. New York: Oxford University Press.

Arnett, J. J. (2016). *The Oxford handbook of emerging adulthood*. New York: Oxford University Press.

Arnon, I., & Ramscar, M. (2012). Granularity and the acquisition of grammatical gender: How order of acquisition affects what gets learned. *Cognition, 122*, 292–305.

Arnon, S., Shamai, S., & Ilatov, Z. (2008). Socialization agents and activities of young adolescents. *Adolescence, 43*, 373–397.

Aronson, E. (2000). *Nobody left to hate: Teaching compassion after Columbine*. New York: Freeman.

Aronson, E. (2004). *The social animal (9th ed.).* New York: Worth Publishers.

Aronson, M., & Bialostok, S. (2016). 'Do some wondering': Children and their self-understanding selves in early elementary classrooms. *Symbolic Interaction, 39,* 229–251.

Arredondo, E., Elder, J., Ayala, G., Campbell, N., Baquero, B., & Duerksen, S. (2006, December). Is parenting style related to children's healthy eating and physical activity in Latino families? *Health Education Research, 21,* 862–871.

Asadi, S., Amiri, S., & Molavi, H. (2014). Development of post-formal thinking from adolescence through adulthood. *Journal of Iranian Psychologists, 10,* 161–174.

Asbury, K., & Plomin, R. (2014). *G is for genes: the impact of genetics on education and achievement.* Hoboken, NJ: Wiley-Blackwell.

Asch, D. A. (1996, May 23). The role of critical care nurses in euthanasia and assisted suicide. *New England Journal of Medicine, 334,* 1374–1379.

Asendorpf, J. (2002). Self-awareness, other-awareness, and secondary representation. In A. Meltzoffa & W. Prinz (Eds.), *The imitative mind: Development, evolution, and brain bases.* New York: Cambridge University Press.

Atchley, R. C. (2000). *Social forces and aging (9th ed.).* Belmont, CA: Wadsworth Thomson Learning.

Atchley, R. C. (2003). Why most people cope well with retirement. In J. Ronch & J. Goldfield (Eds.), *Mental wellness in aging: Strengths-based approaches.* Baltimore, MD: Health Professions Press.

Athanasiu, L., Giddaluru, S., Fernandes, C., Christoforou, A., Reinvang, I., Lundervold, A. J., & . . . Le Hellard, S. (2017). A genetic association study of CSMD1 and CSMD2 with cognitive function. *Brain, Behavior, and Immunity, 61,* 209–216.

Atkinson, R. C., & Shiffrin, R. M. (1968). Human memory: A proposed system and its control processes. In *The psychology of learning and motivation: II.* Oxford, England: Academic Press. doi:10.1016/S0079-7421(08)60422-3.

Athanasopoulou, E., & Fox, J. E. (2014). Effects of kangaroo mother care on maternal mood and interaction patterns between parents and their preterm, low birth weight infants: A systematic review. *Infant Mental Health Journal, 35,* 245–262.

Auerbach, R. P., Stanton, C. H., Proudfit, G. H., & Pizzagalli, D. A. (2015). Self-referential processing in depressed adolescents: A high-density event-related potential study. *Journal of Abnormal Psychology, 124,* 233–245.

Auger, A., Farkas, G., Burchinal, M. R., Duncan, G. J., & Vandell, D. L. (2014). Preschool center care quality effects on academic achievement: An instrumental variables analysis. *Developmental Psychology, 50,* 2559–2571.

Aureli, T. (2016). Object engagement and manipulation in extremely preterm and full term infants at 6 months of age. *Research in Developmental Disabilities, 55,* 173–184.

Austin, J. (2016). 2020 vision: Genetic counselors as acknowledged leaders in integrating genetics and genomics into healthcare. *Journal of Genetic Counseling, 25,* 1–5.

Auyeung, B., & Baron-Cohen, S. (2012). Fetal testosterone in mind: Human sex differences and autism. In F. M. de Waal & P. Ferrari (Eds.), *The primate mind: Built to connect with other minds.* Cambridge, MA: Harvard University Press.

Avinum, R., Israel, S., Shalev, I., Grtsenko, I., Bornstein, G., Ebstein, R. P., & Knafo, A. (2011). AVPRIA variant associated with preschoolers' lower altruistic behavior. *PLoS One, 6,* Accessed online, 7/5/12; http://www.sproutonline.com/kindnesscounts/dr-nancy-eisenberg/eight-tips-for-developing-caring-kids.

Ayalon, L., & Koren, C. (2015). Marriage, second couplehood, divorce, and singlehood in old age. In P. A. Lichtenberg, B. T. Mast, B. D. Carpenter, J. Loebach Wetherell (Eds.), *APA handbook of clinical geropsychology, Vol. 2: Assessment, treatment, and issues of later life.* Washington, DC: American Psychological Association.

Aydt, H., & Corsaro, W. (2003). Differences in children's construction of gender across culture: An interpretive approach. *American Behavioral Scientist, 46,* 1306–1325.

Ayers, B., Forshaw, M., & Hunger, M. S. (2010). The impact of attitudes towards the menopause on women's symptom experience: A systematic review. *Maturitas, 65,* 28–36.

Ayres, M. M., & Leaper, C. (2013). Adolescent girls' experiences of discrimination: An examination of coping strategies, social support, and self-esteem. *Journal of Adolescent Research, 28,* 479–508.

Ayoub, N. C. (2005, February 25). A pleasing birth: Midwives and maternity care in the Netherlands. *The Chronicle of Higher Education,* p. 9.

Azar, B. (2010, December). A reason to believe. *Monitor on Psychology,* pp. 53–56.

Aznar, A., & Tenenbaum, H. R. (2016). Parent–child positive touch: Gender, age, and task differences. *Journal of Nonverbal Behavior, 40,* 317–333.

Azari, S., & Gupta, R. (2015). Osteoporosis. In R. M. McCarron, G. L. Xiong, C. R. Keenan, H. A. Nasrallah (Eds.), *Preventive medical care in psychiatry: A practical guide for clinicians.* Arlington, VA: American Psychiatric Publishing, Inc.

Baay, P. E., van Aken, M. A., de Ridder, D. T., & van der Lippe, T. (2015). Understanding the role of social capital in adolescents' Big Five personality effects on school-to-work transitions. *Journal of Adolescence, 37,* 739–748.

Babenko, O., Kovalchuk, I., & Metz, G. S. (2015). Stress-induced perinatal and transgenerational epigenetic programming of brain development and mental health. *Neuroscience and Biobehavioral Reviews, 48,* 70–91.

Bacchus, L., Mezey, G., & Bewley, S. (2006). A qualitative exploration of the nature of domestic violence in pregnancy. *Violence Against Women, 12,* 588–604.

Baddeley, A., & Wilson, B. (1985). Phonological coding and short-term memory in patients without speech. *Journal of Memory and Language, 24,* 490–502.

Badenhorst, W., Riches, S., Turton, P., & Hughes, P. (2006). The psychological effects of stillbirth and neonatal death on fathers: Systematic review. *Journal of Psychosomatic Obstetrics & Gynecology, 27,* 245–256.

Baer, J. S., Sampson, P. D., & Barr, H. M. (2003). A 21-year longitudinal analysis of the effects of prenatal alcohol exposure on young adult drinking. *Archives of General Psychiatry, 60,* 377–385.

Bahrick, L. E., Todd, J. T., Castellanos, I., & Sorondo, B. M. (2016). Enhanced attention to speaking faces versus other event types emerges gradually across infancy. *Developmental Psychology, 52,* 1705–1720.

Baillargeon, R. (2008). Innate ideas revisited: For a principle of persistence in infants' physical reasoning. *Perspectives on Psychological Science, 3,* 2–13.

Baillargeon, R., & DeJong, G. F. (2017). Explanation-based learning in infancy. *Psychonomic Bulletin & Review.* Accessed online, 10/29/17; https://www.ncbi.nlm.nih.gov/pubmed/28698990.

Bainbridge, K. E., & Wallhagen, M. I. (2014). Hearing loss in an aging American population: Extent, impact, and management. *Annual Review of Public Health, 35,* 139–152.

Baird, A., John, R., & Hayslip, B., Jr. (2000). Custodial grandparenting among African Americans: A focus group perspective. In B. Hayslip, Jr., & R. Goldberg-Glen (Eds.), *Grandparents raising grandchildren: Theoretical, empirical, and clinical perspectives.* New York: Springer.

Baker, M. (2007, December). Elder mistreatment: Risk, vulnerability, and early mortality. *Journal of the American Psychiatric Nurses Association, 12,* 313–321.

Baker, P., & Sussman, D. (2012, May 15). Obama's switch on same-sex marriage stirs skepticism. *New York Times,* p. A17.

Baker, T., Brandon, T., & Chassin, L. (2004). Motivational influences on cigarette smoking. *Annual Review of Psychology, 55,* 463–491.

Bakoyiannis, I., Gkioka, E., Pergialiotis, V., Mastroleon, I., Prodromidou, A., Vlachos, G. D., & Perrea, D. (2014). Fetal alcohol spectrum disorders and cognitive functions of young children. *Reviews in the Neurosciences, 25,* 631–639.

Balakrishnan, V., & Claiborne, L. (2012). Vygotsky from ZPD to ZCD in moral education: Reshaping Western theory and practices in local context. *Journal of Moral Education, 41*, 225–243.

Ball, M., & Orford, J. (2002). Meaningful patterns of activity amongst the long-term inner city unemployed: A qualitative study. *Journal of Community & Applied Social Psychology, 12*, 377–396.

Ballesteros-Meseguer, C., Carrillo-García, C., Meseguer-de-Pedro, M., Canteras-Jordana, M., & Martínez-Roche, M. E. (2016). Episiotomy and its relationship to various clinical variables that influence its performance. *Revista Latino-Americana De Enfermagem, 24*, 22–27.

Baltes, M. M. (1996). *The many faces of dependency in old age.* New York: Cambridge University Press.

Bandura, A. (1977). *Social learning theory.* Englewood Cliffs, NJ: Prentice-Hall.

Bandura, A. (1986). *Social foundations of thought and action.* Englewood Cliffs, NJ: Prentice Hall.

Bandura, A. (1991). Social cognitive theory of moral thought and action. In W. M. Kurtines & J. L. Gewirtz (Eds.), *Handbook of moral behavior and development.* Hillsdale, NJ: Erlbaum.

Bandura, A. (1994). Social cognitive theory of mass communication. In J. Bryant & D. Zillmann (Eds.), *Media effects: Advances in theory and research. LEA's communication series.* Hillsdale, NJ: Lawrence Erlbaum.

Bandura, A. (2002). Social cognitive theory in cultural context. *Applied Psychology: An International Review, 51* [Special issue], 269–290.

Bandura, A. (2004). Model of causality in social learning theory. In A. Freeman, M. J. Mahoney, P. Devito, & D. Martin (Eds.), *Cognition and psychotherapy* (2nd ed.). New York: Springer Publishing Co.

Bandura, A., Grusec, J. E., & Menlove, F. L. (1967). Vicarious extinction of avoidance behavior. *Journal of Personality and Social Psychology, 5*, 16–23.

Bandura, A., Ross, D., & Ross, S. (1963). Vicarious extinction of avoidance behavior. *Journal of Personality and Social Psychology, 67*, 601–607.

Baptista, T., Aldana, E., Angeles, F., & Beaulieu, S. (2008). Evolution theory: An overview of its applications in psychiatry. *Psychopathology, 41*, 17–27.

Barbaro, N., Boutwell, B. B., Barnes, J. C., & Shackelford, T. K. (2017). Rethinking the transmission gap: What behavioral genetics and evolutionary psychology mean for attachment theory: A comment on Verhage et al. (2016). *Psychological Bulletin, 143*, 107–113.

Barber, A. D., Srinivasan, P., Joel, S. E., Caffo, B. S., Pekar, J. J., & Mostofsky, S. H. (2012). Motor "dexterity"?: Evidence that left hemisphere lateralization of motor circuit connectivity is associated with better motor performance in children. *Cerebral Cortex, 22*, 51–59.

Barelds, D. H., Dijkstra, P., Groothof, H. K., & Pastoor, C. D. (2017). The Dark Triad and three types of jealousy: Its relations among heterosexuals and homosexuals involved in a romantic relationship. *Personality and Individual Differences, 116*, 6–10.

Barlett, C., Chamberlin, K., & Witkower, Z. (2017). Predicting cyberbullying perpetration in emerging adults: A theoretical test of the Barlett Gentile Cyberbullying Model. *Aggressive Behavior, 43*, 147–154.

Bartlett, K., Kelley, E., Purdy, J., & Stein, M. T. (2017). Auditory processing disorder: What does it mean and what can be done? *Journal of Developmental and Behavioral Pediatrics, 38*, 349–351.

Barnes, J. C., & Boutwell, B. B. (2012). On the relationship of past to future involvement in crime and delinquency: A behavior genetic analysis. *Journal of Criminal Justice, 40*, 94–102.

Barnett, R. C., & Hyde, J. S. (2001). Women, men, work, and family. *American Psychologist, 56*, 781–796.

Barrouillet, P. (2015). Theories of cognitive development: From Piaget to today. *Developmental Review, 38*, 1–12.

Barrouillet, P., & Gaillard, V. (2011). *Cognitive development and working memory: A dialogue between neo-Piagetian theories and cognitive approaches.* New York: Psychology Press.

Barsade, S. G., & O'Neill, O. A. (2014). What's love got to do with it? A longitudinal study of the culture of companionate love and employee and client outcomes in a long-term care setting. *Administrative Science Quarterly, 59*, 551–598.

Bask, M., & Salmela-Aro, K. (2013). Burned out to drop out: Exploring the relationship between school burnout and school dropout. *European Journal of Psychology of Education, 28*, 511–528.

Basow, S. (2006). Gender role and gender identity development. In J. Worell & C. D. Goodheart (Eds.), *Handbook of girls' and women's psychological health: Gender and well-being across the lifespan* (pp. 242–251). New York: Oxford University Press.

Battin, M., van der Heide, A., Ganzini, L., van der Wal, F., & Onwuteaka-Philipsen, B. (2007). Legal physician-assisted dying in Oregon and the Netherlands: Evidence concerning the impact on patients in "vulnerable" groups. *Journal of Medical Ethics, 33*, 591–597.

Bauer, P. J. (2007). Recall in infancy: A neurodevelopmental account. *Current Directions in Psychological Science, 16*, 142–146.

Bauer, P. J., Wenner, J. A., Dropik, P. L., & Wewerka, S. S. (2000). Parameters of remembering and forgetting in the transition from infancy to early childhood. With commentary by Mark L. Howe. *Monographs of the Society for Research in Child Development, 65*, 4.

Baum, A. (1994). Behavioral, biological, and environmental interactions in disease processes. In S. Blumenthal, K. Matthews, & S. Weiss (Eds.), *New research frontiers in behavioral medicine: Proceedings of the National Conference.* Washington, DC: NIH Publications.

Baumbusch, J. (2004). Unclaimed treasures: Older women's reflections on lifelong singlehood. *Journal of Women & Aging, 16*, 105–121.

Baumeister, R. F. (Ed.). (1993). *Self-esteem: The puzzle of low self-regard.* New York: Plenum.

Baumrind, D. (1971). Current patterns of parental authority. *Developmental Psychology Monographs, 4* (1, pt. 2).

Baumrind, D. (1980). New directions in socialization research. *Psychological Bulletin, 35*, 639–652.

Baumrind, D. (2005). Patterns of parental authority. *New Directions in Child Adolescent Development, 108*, 61–69.

Baydu, M. M. & Kaplan, O., & Bayar, A. (2013). Facing the influence of poverty on graduation rates in public high schools. *Procedia—Social and Behavioral Sciences, 84*, 233–237.

Bayley, N. (1993.) *Bayley scales of infant development* [BSIDII]. 2nd ed. San Antonio, TX: The Psychological Corporation.

Bayley, N., & Oden, M. (1955). The maintenance of intellectual ability in gifted adults. *Journal of Gerontology, 10*, 91–107.

Bayliss, D. M., Jarrold, C., Baddeley, A. D., & Gunn, D. M. (2005a). The relationship between short-term memory and working memory: Complex span made simple? *Memory, 13*(3–4), 414–421. doi:10.1080/09658210344000332.

Bayliss, D. M., Jarrold, C., Baddeley, A. D., Gunn, D. M., & Leigh, E. (2005b). Mapping the developmental constraints on working memory span performance. *Developmental Psychology, 41*(4), 579–597. doi:10.1037/0012-1649.41.4.579.

Beale, E. A., Baile, W. F., & Aaron, J. (2005). Silence is not golden: Communicating with children dying from cancer. *Journal of Clinical Oncology, 23*, 3629–3631.

Beals, K., Impett, E., & Peplau, L. (2002). Lesbians in love: Why some relationships endure and others end. *Journal of Lesbian Studies, 6*, 53–63.

Bearce, K., & Rovee-Collier, C. (2006). Repeated priming increases memory accessibility in infants. *Journal of Experimental Child Psychology, 93*, 357–376.

Beard, V. R., & Burger, W. C. (2017). Change and innovation in the funeral industry: A typology of motivations. *Omega: Journal of Death and Dying, 75*, 47–68.

Bearman, P., & Bruckner, H. (2004). *Study on teenage virginity pledge.* Paper presented at meeting of the National STD Prevention Conference, Philadelphia, PA.

Beauchaine, T. P., Crowell, S. E., & Hsiao, R. C. (2015). Postdexamethasone cortisol, self-inflicted injury, and suicidal ideation among depressed adolescent girls. *Journal of Abnormal Child Psychology, 43*, 619–632.

Beck, M. (2012, June 5). Hormone use benefits may trump risks; age matters. *The Wall Street Journal*, pp. D1, D2.

Becker, B., & Luthar, S. (2007, March). Peer-perceived admiration and social preference: Contextual correlates of positive peer regard among suburban and urban adolescents. *Journal of Research on Adolescence, 17*, 117–144.

Becker, G., Beyene, Y., & Newsom, E. (2003). Creating continuity through mutual assistance: Intergenerational reciprocity in four ethnic groups. *Journals of Gerontology: Series B: Psychological Sciences & Social Sciences, 58B*, S151–S159.

Becvar, D. S. (2000). Euthanasia decisions. In F. W. Kaslow et al. (Eds.), *Handbook of couple and family forensics: A sourcebook for mental health and legal professionals*. New York: Wiley.

Begeer, S., Bernstein, D. M., van Wijhe, J., Schleeren, A. M., & Koot, H. (2012). A continuous false belief task reveals egocentric biases in children and adolescents with autism spectrum disorders. *Autism, 16*, 357–366.

Beilby, J. M., Byrnes, M. L., & Young, K. N. (2012). The experiences of living with a sibling who stutters: A preliminary study. *Journal of Fluency Disorders, 37*, 135–148.

Beitel, M., Bogus, S., Hutz, A., Green, D., Cecero, J. J., & Barry, D. T. (2014). Stillness and motion: An empirical investigation of mindfulness and self-actualization. *Person-Centered and Experiential Psychotherapies, 13*, 187–202.

Belcher, J. R. (2003). Stepparenting: Creating and recreating families in America today. *Journal of Nervous & Mental Disease, 191*, 837–838.

Belkin, L. (2004, September 12). The lessons of Classroom 506: What happens when a boy with cerebral palsy goes to kindergarten like all the other kids. *New York Times Magazine*, pp. 41–49.

Bell, M. (2012). A psychobiological perspective on working memory performance at 8 months of age. *Child Development, 83*, 251–265.

Belluck, P. (2000, October 18). New advice for parents: Saying "that's great!" may not be. *New York Times*, p. A14.

Belsky, J., Vandell, D. L., Burchinal, M., Clarke-Stewart, A. K., McCartney, K., & Owen, M. T. (2007). Are there long-term effects of early child care? *Child Development, 78*, 188–193.

Bengtson, V. L., Acock, A. C., Allen, K. R., & Dilworth-Anderson, P. (Eds.). (2004). *Sourcebook of family theory and research*. Thousand Oaks, CA: Sage Publications.

Benjet, C., & Kazdin, A. E. (2003). Spanking children: The controversies, findings and new directions. *Clinical Psychology Review, 23*, 197–224.

Benjuya, N., Melzer, I., & Kaplanski, J. (2004). Aging-induced shifts from a reliance on sensory input to muscle cocontraction during balanced standing. *Journal of Gerontology: Series A: Biological Sciences and Medical Sciences, 59*, 166–171.

Benner, A. D., & Wang, Y. (2017). Racial/ethnic discrimination and adolescents' well-being: The role of cross-ethnic friendships and friends' experiences of discrimination. *Child Development, 88*, 493–504.

Benoit, A., Lacourse, E., & Claes, M. (2013). Pubertal timing and depressive symptoms in late adolescence: The moderating role of individual, peer, and parental factors. *Development and Psychopathology, 25*, 455–471.

Benson, E. (2003, March). "Goo, gaa, grr?" *Monitor on Psychology*, pp. 50–51.

Benson, H. (1993). The relaxation response. In D. Goleman & J. Guerin (Eds.), *Mind-body medicine: How to use your mind for better health*. Yonkers, NY: Consumer Reports Publications.

Berenson, P. (2005). *Understand and treat alcoholism*. New York: Basic Books.

Bergelson, E., & Swingley, D. (2012). At 6–9 months, human infants know the meanings of many common nouns. *PNAS Proceedings of the National Academy of Sciences of the United States of America, 109*, 3253–3258.

Bergen, H., Martin, G., & Richardson, A. (2003). Sexual abuse and suicidal behavior: A model constructed from a large community sample of adolescents. *Journal of the American Academy of Child & Adolescent Psychiatry, 42*, 1301–1309.

Bergman, A., Blom, I., & Polyak, D. (2012). Attachment and separation-individuation: Two ways of looking at the mother/infant relationship. In S. Akhtar (Ed.), *The mother and her child: Clinical aspects of attachment, separation, and loss*. Lanham, MD: Jason Aronson.

Bergman, A., Blom, I., Polyak, D., & Mayers, L. (2015). Attachment and separation–individuation: Two ways of looking at the mother–infant relationship. *International Forum of Psychoanalysis, 24*, 16–21.

Bergmann, R. L., Bergman, K. E., & Dudenhausen, J. W. (2008). Undernutrition and growth restriction in pregnancy. *Nestle Nutritional Workshop Series; Pediatrics Program, 61*, 1030121.

Bergsma, A., & Ardelt, M. (2012). Self-reported wisdom and happiness: An empirical investigation. *Journal of Happiness Studies, 13*, 481–499.

Bergstrom, M. J., & Holmes, M. E. (2000). Lay theories of successful aging after the death of a spouse: A network text analysis of bereavement advice. *Health Communication, 12*, 377–406.

Bergström, M. (2017). 'I could've had a better life': Reflective life reviews told by late-middle-aged and older women and men with ongoing long-term alcohol problems. *NAT Nordisk Alkohol & Narkotikatidskrift, 34*, 6–17.

Berkman, R. (Ed.). (2006). *Handbook of social work in health and aging*. New York: Oxford University Press.

Berko, J. (1958). The child's learning of English morphology. *Word, 14*, 150–177.

Berkowitz, L. (1993). *Aggression: Its causes, consequences, and control*. New York: McGraw-Hill.

Bernal, M. E. (1994, August). *Ethnic identity of Mexican-American children*. Address at the annual meeting of the American Psychological Association, Los Angeles, CA.

Bernard, J. (1982). *The future of marriage*. New Haven, CT: Yale University Press.

Berndt, T. J. (1999). Friends' influence on students' adjustment to school. *Educational Psychologist, 34*, 15–28.

Berndt, T. J. (2002). Friendship quality and social development. *Current Directions in Psychological Science, 11*, 7–10.

Bernstein, E. (2010, April 20). Honey, do you have to . . . *Wall Street Journal*, pp. D1, D3.

Bernstein, N. (2004, March 7). Behind fall in pregnancy, a new teenage culture of restraint. *New York Times*, pp. 1, 20.

Berscheid, E. (2006). Searching for the meaning of "Love." In *The new psychology of love* (pp. 171–183). New Haven, CT: Yale University Press.

Berscheid, E., & Regan, P. C. (2005). *The psychology of interpersonal relationships*. New York: Psychology Press.

Bertin, E., & Striano, T. (2006, April). The still-face response in newborn, 1.5-, and 3-month-old infants. *Infant Behavior & Development, 29*, 294–297.

Besharov, D. J., & West, A. (2002). African American marriage patterns. In A. Thernstrom & S. Thernstrom (Eds.), *Beyond the color line: New perspectives on race and ethnicity in America*. Stanford, CA: Hoover Institution Press.

Bešić, E., Paleczek, L., Krammer, M., & Gasteiger-Klicpera, B. (2017). Inclusive practices at the teacher and class level: The experts' view. *European Journal of Special Needs Education, 32*, 329–345.

Best, P., Manktelow, R., & Taylor, B. (2014). Online communication, social media and adolescent wellbeing: A systematic narrative review. *Children and Youth Services Review, 41*, 27–36.

Betancourt, L. M., Brodsky, N. L., & Hurt, H. (2015). Socioeconomic (SES) differences in language are evident in female infants at 7 months of age. *Early Human Development, 91*(12), 719–724. doi:10.1016/j.earlhumdev.2015.08.002.

Bhagat, N., Laskar, A., & Sharma, N. (2012). Women's perception about sex selection in an urban slum in Delhi. *Journal of Reproductive and Infant Psychology, 30*, 92–104.

Bhargava, P. (2014). 'I have a family, therefore I am': Children's understanding of self and others. In N. Chaudhary, S. Anandalakshmy, J. Valsiner (Eds.), *Cultural realities of being: Abstract ideas within everyday lives*. New York: Routledge/Taylor & Francis Group.

Bhatia, P., Davis, A., & Shamas-Brandt, E. (2015). Educational gymnastics: The effectiveness of Montessori practical life activities in developing fine motor skills in kindergartners. *Early Education and Development, 26,* 594–607.

Bialystok, E., & Viswanathan, M. (2009). Components of executive control with advantages for bilingual children in two cultures. *Cognition, 112,* 494–500.

Bibace, R. (2013). Challenges in Piaget's legacy. *Integrative Psychological & Behavioral Science, 47,* 167–175.

Biblarz, T. J., & Stacey, J. (2010). How does the gender of parents matter? *Journal of Marriage and Family, 72,* 3–22.

Biedenharn, B. J., & Normoyle, J. B. (1991). Elderly community residents' reactions to the nursing home: An analysis of nursing home-related beliefs. *Gerontologist, 31,* 107–115.

Bienvenu, C., & Ramsey, C. J. (2006). The culture of socioeconomic disadvantage: Practical approaches to counseling. In C. C. Lee (Ed.), *Multicultural issues in counseling: New approaches to diversity, 3rd ed.* Alexandria, VA: American Counseling Association.

Bierman, K., Torres, M., Domitrovich, C., Welsh, J., & Gest, S. (2009). Behavioral and cognitive readiness for school: Cross-domain associations for children attending Head Start. *Social Development, 18,* 305–323.

Birch, E. E., Garfield, S., Hoffman, D. R., Uauy, R., & Birch, D. G. (2000). A randomized controlled trail of early dietary supply of long-chain polyunsaturated fatty acids and mental development in term infants. *Developmental Medicine and Child Neurology, 42,* 174–181.

Biro, F., Striegel-Moore, R., Franko, D., Padgett, J., & Bean, J. (2006, October). Self-esteem in adolescent females. *Journal of Adolescent Health, 39,* 501–507.

Bischof-Köhler, D. (2012). Empathy and self-recognition in phylogenetic and ontogenetic perspective. *Emotion Review, 4,* 40–48.

Bishop, A. (2008). Stress and depression among older residents in religious monasteries: Do friends and God matter? *International Journal of Aging & Human Development, 67,* 1–23.

Bishop, D. V. M., & Leonard, L. B. (Eds.). (2001). *Speech and language impairments in children: Causes, characteristics, intervention and outcome.* Philadelphia: Psychology Press.

Bishop, J. (2006, April). Euthanasia, efficiency, and the historical distinction between killing a patient and allowing a patient to die. *Journal of Medical Ethics, 32,* 220–224.

Bjorklund, D. F., & Ellis, B. (2005). Evolutionary psychology and child development: An emerging synthesis. In B. J. Ellis (Ed.), *Origins of the social mind: Evolutionary psychology and child development.* New York: Guilford Press.

Black, K. (2002). Associations between adolescent-mother and adolescent-best friend interactions. *Adolescence, 37,* 235–253.

Blaga, O., Shaddy, D., Anderson, C., Kannass, K., Little, T., & Colombo, J. (2009). Structure and continuity of intellectual development in early childhood. *Intelligence, 37,* 106–113.

Blaine, B. E., Rodman, J., & Newman, J. M. (2007). Weight loss treatment and psychological well-being: A review and meta-analysis. *Journal of Health Psychology, 12,* 66–82.

Blair, B. L., Fletcher, A. C., & Gaskin, E. R. (2015). Cell phone decision making: Adolescents' perceptions of how and why they make the choice to text or call. *Youth & Society, 47,* 395–411.

Blair, P., Sidebotham, P., Berry, P., Evans, M., & Fleming, P. (2006). Major epidemiological changes in sudden infant death syndrome: A 20-year population-based study in the UK. *Lancet, 367,* 314–319.

Blakemore, J. (2003). Children's beliefs about violating gender norms: Boys shouldn't look like girls, and girls shouldn't act like boys. *Sex Roles, 48,* 411–419.

Blakemore, S. (2012). Imaging brain development: The adolescent brain. *Neuroimage, 61,* 397–406.

Blanton, H., & Burkley, M. (2008). Deviance regulation theory: Applications to adolescent social influence. In *Understanding peer influence in children and adolescents.* New York: Guilford Press.

Blass, E. M., & Camp, C. A. (2015). The ontogeny of face recognition: Eye contact and sweet taste induce face preference in 9- and 12-week-old human infants. *Developmental Psychology, 37,* 762–774.

Blom, E. H., Ho, T. C., Connolly, C. G., LeWinn, K. Z., Sacchet, M. D., Tymofiyeva, O., & . . . Yang, T. T. (2016). The neuroscience and context of adolescent depression. *Acta Paediatrica, 105,* 358–365.

Blomqvist, Y. T., Nyqvist, K. H., Rubertsson, C., & Funkquist, E. (2017). Parents need support to find ways to optimise their own sleep without seeing their preterm infant's sleeping patterns as a problem. *Acta Paediatrica, 106,* 223–228.

Bleidorn, W., Kandler, C., & Caspi, A. (2014). The behavioural genetics of personality development in adulthood—Classic, contemporary, and future trends. *European Journal of Personality, 28,* 244–255.

Bloom, C., & Lamkin, D. (2006). The Olympian struggle to remember the cranial nerves: Mnemonics and student success. *Teaching of Psychology, 33,* 128–129.

Blount, B. G. (1982). Culture and the language of socialization: Parental speech. In D. A. Wagner & H. W. Stevenson (Eds.), *Cultural perspectives on child development.* San Francisco: Freeman.

Bluebond-Langner, M. (2000). *In the shadow of illness.* Princeton, NJ: Princeton University Press.

Blum, D. (2002). *Love at Goon Park: Harry Harlow and the science of affection.* New York: Perseus Publishing.

Blumberg, M., Coleman, C., Gerth, A., & McMurray, B. (2013). Spatiotemporal structure of REM sleep twitching reveals developmental origins of motor synergies. *Current Biology, 232,* 100–109.

Blumberg, M. S., Gall, A. J., & Todd, W. D. (2014). The development of sleep–wake rhythms and the search for elemental circuits in the infant brain. *Behavioral Neuroscience, 128,* 250–263.

Blumenshine, P. M., Egerter, S. A., Libet, M. L., & Braveman, P. A. (2011). Father's education: An independent marker of risk for preterm birth. *Maternal and Child Health Journal, 15,* 60–67.

Bober, S., Humphry, R., & Carswell, H. (2001). Toddlers' persistence in the emerging occupations of functional play and self-feeding. *American Journal of Occupational Therapy, 55,* 369–376.

Bodell, L. P., Joiner, T. E., & Ialongo, N. S. (2012). Longitudinal association between childhood impulsivity and bulimic symptoms in African American adolescent girls. *Journal of Consulting and Clinical Psychology, 80,* 313–316.

Boehm, K. E., & Campbell, N. B. (1995). Suicide: A review of calls to an adolescent peer listening phone service. *Child Psychiatry & Human Development, 26,* 61–66.

Boerner, K., Wortman, C. B., & Bonanno, G. A. (2005). Resilient or at risk? A 4-year study of older adults who initially showed high or low distress following conjugal loss. *Journals of Gerontology: Series B, Psychological Sciences and Social Sciences, 60,* P67–P73.

Bogle, K. A. (2008). 'Hooking up': What educators need to know. *Chronicle of Higher Education, 54,* A32.

Bohn, A., & Berntsen, D. (2014). Cultural life scripts and the development of personal memories. In P. J. Bauer, R. Fivush, P. J. Bauer, & R. Fivush (Eds.), *The Wiley handbook on the development of children's memory (Vols. I–II).* New York: Wiley-Blackwell.

Boissicat, N., Pansu, P., Bouffard, T. & Cottin, F. (2012). Relation between perceived scholastic competence and social comparison mechanisms among elementary school children. *Social Psychology of Education: An International Journal, 15*(4), 603–614.

Boivin, M., Perusse, D., Dionne, G., Saysset, V., Zoccolilo, M., Tarabulsy, G. M., et al. (2005). The genetic-environmental etiology of parents' perceptions and self-assessed behaviours toward their 5-month-old infants in a large twin and singleton sample. *Journal of Child Psychology and Psychiatry, 46,* 612–630.

Bojanowska, A., & Zalewska, A. M. (2015). Lay understanding of happiness and the experience of well-being: Are some conceptions of happiness more beneficial than others? *Journal of Happiness Studies.* Accessed online 6/21/15; http://link.springer.com/article/10.1007%2Fs10902-015-9620-1.

Bolhuis, J. J., Tattersal, I., Chomsky, N., & Berwick, R. C. (2014). How could language have evolved? *Plos Biology, 12,* 88–96.

Bonanno, G. A. (2009). *The other side of sadness.* New York: Basic Books.

Bonanno, G. A., Wortman, C. B., Lehman, D. R., Tweed, R. G., Haring, M., Sonnega, J., et al. (2002). Resilience to loss and chronic grief: A prospective study from preloss to 18-months postloss. *Journal of Personality and Social Psychology, 83,* 1150–1164.

Bonavita, S., & Tedeschi, G. (2017). Neural structure, connectivity, and cognition changes associated to physical exercise. In R. R.Watson (Ed.), *Physical activity and the aging brain: Effects of exercise on neurological function*. San Diego, CA: Elsevier Academic Press.

Bookheimer, S. Y., Strojwas, M. H., Cohen, M. S., Saunders, A. M., Pericak-Vance, M. A., Mazziotta, J. C., & Small, G. W. (2000). Patterns of brain activation in people at risk for Alzheimer's disease. *New England Journal of Medicine, 343*(7), 450–456. doi:10.1056/NEJM200008173430701.

Booth, W. (1987, October 2). Big Brother is counting your keystrokes. *Science, 238*, 17.

Bornstein, M. H. (2000). Infant into conversant: Language and non-language processes in developing early communication. In N. Budwig, I. C. Uzgiris, & J. V. Wertsch (Eds.), *Communication: An arena of development* (pp. 109–129). Stamford, CT: Ablex.

Bornstein, M. H., Cote, L., & Maital, S. (2004). Crosslinguistic analysis of vocabulary in young children: Spanish, Dutch, French, Hebrew, Italian, Korean, and American English. *Child Development, 75*, 1115–1139.

Bornstein, M. H., & Lamb, M. E. (1992). *Development in infancy: An introduction*. New York: McGraw-Hill.

Bornstein, M. H., Putnick, D. L., Suwalsky, T. D., & Gini, M. (2006). Maternal chronological age, prenatal and perinatal history, social support, and parenting of infants. *Child Development, 77*, 875–892.

Bornstein, M. H., Suwalsky, J. D., & Breakstone, D. A. (2012). Emotional relationships between mothers and infants: Knowns, unknowns, and unknown unknowns. *Development and Psychopathology, 24*, 113–123.

Bornstein, M. H., Tamis-LeMonda, C. S., Hahn, C., & Haynes, O. M. (2008). Maternal responsiveness to young children at three ages: Longitudinal analysis of a multidimensional, modular, and specific parenting construct. *Developmental Psychology, 44*, 867–874.

Bos, A. E. R., Muris, P., Mulkens, S., & Schaalma, H. P. (2006). Changing self-esteem in children and adolescents: A roadmap for future interventions. *Netherlands Journal of Psychology, 62*, 26–33.

Bos, A. F. (2013). Bayley-II or Bayley-III: What do the scores tell us? *Developmental Medicine & Child Neurology, 55*, 978–979.

Bos, H. W., Knox, J. R., van Rijn-van Gelderen, L., & Gartrell, N. K. (2016). Same-sex and different-sex parent households and child health outcomes: Findings from the National Survey of Children's Health. *Journal of Developmental and Behavioral Pediatrics, 37*, 179–187.

Bosacki, S. L. (2014). Brief report: The role of psychological language in children's theory of mind and self-concept development. *Psychology of Language and Communication, 18*, 41–52.

Bosacki, S., Woods, H., & Coplan, R. (2015). Canadian female and male early childhood educators' perceptions of child aggression and rough-and-tumble play. *Early Child Development and Care, 185*, 1134–1147.

Boseovski, J. J. (2012). Trust in testimony about strangers: Young children prefer reliable informants who make positive attributions. *Journal of Experimental Child Psychology, 111*, 543–551.

Bouchard, T. J., Jr. (1997, September/October). Whenever the twain shall meet. *The Sciences*, pp. 52–57.

Bouchard, T. J., Jr. (2004). Genetic influence on human psychological traits: A survey. *Current Directions in Psychological Science, 13*, 148–153.

Bouchard, T. J., Jr., Lykken, D. T., McGue, M., Segal, N. L., & Tellegen, A. (1990, October 12). Sources of human psychological differences: The Minnesota Study of twins reared apart. *Science, 250*, 223–228.

Bouchard, T. J., & McGue, M. (1981). Familial studies of intelligence: A review. *Science, 212*, 1055–1059.

Bourne, V., & Todd, B. (2004). When left means right: An explanation of the left cradling bias in terms of right hemisphere specializations. *Developmental Science, 7*, 19–24.

Bourque, P., Pushkar, D., Bonneville, L., & Beland, F. (2005). Contextual effects on life satisfaction of older men and women. *Canadian Journal on Aging, 24*, 31–44.

Bowen, G. L., & Jensen, T. M. (2017). Late-life divorce and postdivorce adult subjective well-being. *Journal of Family Issues, 38*, 1363–1388.

Bower, B. (1985). The left hand of math and verbal talent. *Science News, 127*, 263.

Bower, T. G. R. (1977). *A primer of infant development*. San Francisco: Freeman.

Bowlby, J. (1951). Maternal care and mental health. *Bulletin of the World Health Organization, 3*, 355–534.

Bowman, C. P. (2014). Women's masturbation: Experiences of sexual empowerment in a primarily sex-positive sample. *Psychology of Women Quarterly, 38*, 363–378.

Bracken, B., & Lamprecht, M. (2003). Positive self-concept: An equal opportunity construct. *School Psychology Quarterly, 18*, 103–121.

Bracken, B., & Brown, E. (2006, June). Behavioral identification and assessment of gifted and talented students. *Journal of Psychoeducational Assessment, 24*, 112–122.

Bradley, R., & Corwyn, R. (2008). Infant temperament, parenting, and externalizing behavior in first grade: A test of the differential susceptibility hypothesis. *Journal of Child Psychology and Psychiatry, 49*, 124–131. Accessed online; http://search.ebscohost.com.

Brady, S. A. (2011). Efficacy of phonics teaching for reading outcomes: Indications from post-NRP research. In S. A. Brady, D. Braze, & C. A. Fowler (Eds.), *Explaining individual differences in reading: Theory and evidence*. New York: Psychology Press.

Brandmaier, A. M., Ram, N., Wagner, G. G., & Gerstorf, D. (2017). Terminal decline in well-being: The role of multi-indicator constellations of physical health and psychosocial correlates. *Developmental Psychology, 53*, 996–1012.

Brandone, A. C. (2015). Infants' social and motor experience and the emerging understanding of intentional actions. *Developmental Psychology, 51*, 512–523.

Brandone, A. C., Cimpian, A., Leslie, S., & Gelman, S. A. (2012). Do lions have manes? For children, generics are about kinds rather than quantities. *Child Development, 83*, 423–433.

Branum, A. (2006). Teen maternal age and very preterm birth of twins. *Maternal & Child Health Journal, 10*, 229–233.

Braun, K. L., Pietsch, J. H., & Blanchette, P. L. (Eds.). (2000). *Cultural issues in end-of-life decision making*. Thousand Oaks, CA: Sage Publications.

Braun, S. S., & Davidson, A. J. (2016). Gender (non)conformity in middle childhood: A mixed methods approach to understanding gender-typed behavior, friendship, and peer preference. *Sex Roles*. Accessed online, 8/9/17; https://link.springer.com/article/10.1007/s11199-016-0693-z.

Braungart-Rieker, J. M., Zentall, S., Lickenbrock, D. M., Ekas, N. V., Oshio, T., & Planalp, E. (2014). Attachment in the making: Mother and father sensitivity and infants' responses during the still-face paradigm. *Journal of Experimental Child Psychology, 125*, 63–84.

Bredesen, D. (2009). Neurodegeneration in Alzheimer's disease: Caspases and synaptic element interdependence. *Molecular Neurodegeneration, 4*, 52–59.

Breheny, M., & Stephens, C. (2003). Healthy living and keeping busy: A discourse analysis of mid-aged women's attributions for menopausal experience. *Journal of Language & Social Psychology, 22*, 169–189.

Bremner, G., & Fogel, A. (Eds.). (2004). *Blackwell handbook of infant development*. Malden, MA: Blackwell Publishers.

Bremner, J. G., Slater, A. M., & Johnson, S. P. (2015). Perception of object persistence: The origins of object permanence in infancy. *Child Development Perspectives, 9*, 7–13.

Briley, D. A., & Tucker-Drob, E. M. (2017). Comparing the developmental genetics of cognition and personality over the life span. *Journal of Personality, 85*, 51-64.

Broesch, T. L., & Bryant, G. A. (2015). Prosody in infant-directed speech is similar across Western and traditional cultures. *Journal of Cognition and Development, 16*, 31–43.

Bronfenbrenner, U. (1989). Ecological systems theory. In R. Vasta (Ed.), *Six theories of child development*. Greenwich, CT: JAI Press.

Bronfenbrenner, U. (2000). Ecological theory. In A. Kazdin (Ed.), *Encyclopedia of psychology*. Washington, DC and New York: American Psychological Association/Oxford University Press.

Bronfenbrenner, U. (2002). Preparing a world for the infant in the twenty-first century: The research challenge. In J. Goes-Pedro, J. K. Nugent, J. G. Young, & T. B. Brazelton (Eds.), *The infant and family in the twenty- first century*. New York: Brunner-Routledge.

Brouwer, R. M., van Soelen, I. C., Swagerman, S. C., Schnack, H. G., Ehli, E. A., Kahn, R. S., & . . . Boomsma, D. I. (2014). Genetic associations between intelligence and cortical thickness emerge at the start of puberty. *Human Brain Mapping, 35*, 3760–3773.

Brown, B. B., & Klute, C. (2006). Friendships, cliques, and crowds. In G. Adams, & M. D. Berzonsky, *Blackwell handbook of adolescence*. Malden, MA: Blackwell Publishing.

Brown, D. L., Jewell, J. D., Stevens, A. L., Crawford, J. D., & Thompson, R. (2012). Suicidal risk in adolescent residential treatment: Being female is more important than a depression diagnosis. *Journal of Child and Family Studies, 21*, 359–367.

Brown, E. L., & Bull, R. (2007). Can task modifications influence children's performance on false belief tasks? *European Journal of Developmental Psychology, 4*, 273–292.

Brown, J. L., & Pollitt, E. (1996, February). Malnutrition, poverty and intellectual development. *Scientific American*, pp. 38–43.

Brown, L. M., Bradley, M. M., & Lang, P. J. (2006). Affective reactions to pictures of ingroup and outgroup members. *Biological Psychology, 71*, 303–311.

Brown, R., & Fraser, C. (1963). The acquisition of syntax. In C. N. Cofer & B. Musgrave (Eds.), *Verbal behavior and learning: Problems and processes*. New York: McGraw-Hill.

Brown, S., & Lin, I-Fen. (2012, March). *The gray divorce revolution: Rising divorce among middle-aged and older adults, 1990–2009*. Working Paper Series WP-12-04. National Center for Family & Marriage Research, Bowling Green State University.

Brown, W. M., Hines, M., & Fane, B. A. (2002). Masculinzed finger length patterns in human males and females with congenital adrenal hyperplasia. *Hormones and Behavior, 42*, 380–386.

Browne, K. (2006, March). Evolved sex differences and occupational segregation. *Journal of Organizational Behavior, 27*, 143–162.

Brownell, C. A. (2016). Prosocial behavior in infancy: The role of socialization. *Child Development Perspectives, 10*, 222–227.

Brucker, E., & Leppel, K. (2013). Retirement plans: Planners and non-planners. *Educational Gerontology, 39*(1), 1–11. doi:10.1080/03601277.2012.660859.

Brumbaugh, C. C., & Wood, D. (2013). Mate preferences across life and across the world. *Social Psychological and Personality Science, 4*, 100–107.

Bryant, C. D. (Ed.). (2003). *Handbook of death and dying*. Thousand Oaks, CA: Sage Publications.

Bucci, D., & Stanton, M. (2017). The ontogeny of learning and memory. *Neurobiology of Learning and Memory, 143*, 88–97.

Buckley, J., Letukas, L., & Wildavsky, B. (2018). *Measuring success: Testing, grades, and the future of college admissions*. Baltimore, MD: Johns Hopkins University Press.

Buon, M., Habib, M., & Frey, D. (2017). Moral development: Conflicts and compromises. In J. A. Sommerville, J. Decety (Eds.), *Social cognition: Development across the life span*. New York: Routledge/Taylor & Francis Group.

Burakevych, N., Mckinlay, C. D., Alsweiler, J. M., Wouldes, T. A., & Harding, J. E. (2017). Bayley-III motor scale and neurological examination at 2 years do not predict motor skills at 4.5 years. *Developmental Medicine & Child Neurology, 59*, 216–223.

Bureau of Labor Statistics. (2012, March 1). Labor force statistics from the current population survey. Accessed online, 7/10/12; http://www.bls.gov/cps/cpsaat37.htm.

Burgund, E., & Abernathy, A. (2008). Letter-specific processing in children and adults matched for reading level. *Acta Psychologica, 129*, 66–71.

Burkle, C. M., Sharp, R. R., & Wijdicks, E. F. (2014). Why brain death is considered death and why there should be no confusion. *Neurology, 83*, 1464–1469.

Burnham, M., Goodlin-Jones, B., & Gaylor, E. (2002). Nighttime sleep-wake patterns and self-soothing from birth to one year of age: A longitudinal intervention study. *Journal of Child Psychology & Psychiatry & Allied Disciplines, 43*, 713–725.

Burton, A., Haley, W., & Small, B. (2006, May). Bereavement after caregiving or unexpected death: Effects on elderly spouses. *Aging & Mental Health, 10*, 319–326.

Burton, L., Henninger, D., Hafetz, J., & Cofer, J. (2009). Aggression, gender-typical childhood play, and a prenatal hormonal index. *Social Behavior and Personality, 37*, 105–116.

Busching, R., Gentile, D. A., Krahé, B., Möller, I., Khoo, A., Walsh, D. A., & Anderson, C. A. (2015). Testing the reliability and validity of different measures of violent video game use in the United States, Singapore, and Germany. *Psychology of Popular Media Culture, 4*, 97–111.

Bushman, B. J., Gollwitzer, M., & Cruz, C. (2014). There is broad consensus: Media researchers agree that violent media increase aggression in children, and pediatricians and parents concur. *Psychology of Popular Media Culture*. Accessed online, 3/20/15; http://psycnet.apa.org/psycinfo/2014-41977-001/.

Busick, D., Brooks, J., Pernecky, S., Dawson, R., & Petzoldt, J. (2008). Parent food purchases as a measure of exposure and preschool-aged children's willingness to identify and taste fruit and vegetables. *Appetite, 51*, 468–473.

Buss, A. H. (2012). *Pathways to individuality: Evolution and development of personality traits*. Washington, DC: American Psychological Association.

Buss, D. M. (2003a). The dangerous passion: Why jealousy is as necessary as love and sex: Book review. *Archives of Sexual Behavior, 32*, 79–80.

Buss, D. M. (2003b). *The evolution of desire: Strategies of human mating* (Rev. ed.). New York: Basic Books.

Buss, D. M. (2004). *Evolutionary psychology: The new science of the mind* (2nd ed.). Boston: Allyn & Bacon.

Buss, D. M., Abbott, M., Angleitner, A., Asherian, A., Biaggio, A., Blanco-Villasenor, A., et al. (1990). International preferences in selecting mates: A study of 37 cultures. *Journal of Cross-Cultural Psychology, 21*, 5–7.

Buss, D. M., & Reeve, H. K. (2003). Evolutionary psychology and developmental dynamics: Comment on Lickliter and Honeycutt (2003). *Psychological Bulletin, 129*(6), 848–853. doi:10.1037/0033-2909.129.6.848.

Buss, K. A., & Kiel, E. J. (2004). Comparison of sadness, anger, and fear facial expressions when toddlers look at their mothers. *Child Development, 75*, 1761–1773.

Butler, R. J., Wilson, B. L., & Johnson, W. G. (2012). A modified measure of health care disparities applied to birth weight disparities and subsequent mortality. *Health Economics, 21*, 113–126.

Butler, R. N. (2002). The life review. *Journal of Geriatric Psychiatry, 35*, 7–10.

Byrd, M., Nelson, E., & Manthey, L. (2006). Oral-digital habits of childhood: Thumb sucking. In *Practitioner's guide to evidence-based psychotherapy*. New York: Springer Science + Business Media.

Byrd-Craven, J., Auer, B. J., Granger, D. A., & Massey, A. R. (2012). The father-daughter dance: The relationship between father-daughter relationship quality and daughters' stress response. *Journal of Family Psychology, 26*, 87–94.

Byrne, B., Shankweiler, D., & Hine, D. (2008). Reading development in children at risk for dyslexia. In *Brain, behavior, and learning in language and reading disorders*. New York: Guilford Press.

Byun, S., & Park, H. (2012). The academic success of East Asian American youth: The role of shadow education. *Sociology of Education, 85*, 40–60.

Cabera, N. J. (2013). Positive development of minority children. *SRCD Social Policy Report, 27*, 1–22.

Cacciatore, J., & Bushfield, S. (2007). Stillbirth: The mother's experience and implications for improving care. *Journal of Social Work in End-of-Life & Palliative Care, 3*, 59–79.

Caino, S., Kelmansky, D., Lejarraga, H., & Adamo, P. (2004). Short-term growth at adolescence in healthy girls. *Annals of Human Biology, 31*, 182–195.

Calhoun, F., & Warren, K. (2007). Fetal alcohol syndrome: Historical perspectives. *Neuroscience & Biobehavioral Reviews, 31*, 168–171.

Callaghan, B. L., Li, S., & Richardson, R. (2014). The elusive engram: What can infantile amnesia tell us about memory? *Trends in Neurosciences, 37*, 47–53.

Calvert, S. L., Kotler, J. A., Zehnder, S., & Shockey, E. (2003). Gender stereotyping in children's reports about educational and informational television programs. *Media Psychology, 5*, 139–162.

Calzada, E. J., Huang, K., Anicama, C., Fernandez, Y., & Brotman, L. (2012). Test of a cultural framework of parenting with Latino families of young children. *Cultural Diversity and Ethnic Minority Psychology, 18*, 285–296.

Camarota, S. A. (2007). *Immigrants in the United States—2007: A snapshot of America's foreign-born population.* Washington, DC: Center for Immigration Studies.

Camarota, S.A., & Zeigler, K. (2015, April 21). *Immigrant population to hit highest percentage ever in 8 years.* Washington, DC: Center for Immigration Studies.

Cameron, P. (2003). Domestic violence among homosexual partners. *Psychological Reports, 93*, 410–416.

Cami, J., & Farre, M. (2003). Drug addiction. *New England Journal of Medicine, 349*, 975–986.

Campbell, A., Shirley, L., & Candy, J. (2004). A longitudinal study of gender-related cognition and behaviour. *Developmental Science, 7*, 1–9.

Camras, L., Meng, Z., & Ujiie, T. (2002). Observing emotion in infants: Facial expression, body behavior, and rater judgments of responses to an expectancy violating event. *Emotion, 2*, 179–193.

Canals, J., Fernandez-Ballart, J., & Esparo, G. (2003). Evolution of neonatal behavior assessment scale scores in the first month of life. *Infant Behavior & Development, 26*, 227–237.

Canham, S. L., Mahmood, A., Stott, S., Sixsmith, J., & O'Rourke, N. (2014). 'Til divorce do us part: Marriage dissolution in later life. *Journal of Divorce & Remarriage, 55*, 591–612.

Cantin, V., Lavallière, M., Simoneau, M., & Teasdale, N. (2009). Mental workload when driving in a simulator: Effects of age and driving complexity. *Accident Analysis and Prevention, 41*, 763–771.

Caplan, L. J., & Barr, R. A. (1989). On the relationship between category intensions and extensions in children. *Journal of Experimental Child Psychology, 47*, 413–429.

Caplan, A., & Kunzler, N. (2015). Lessons from the genome. In G. Marcus, J. Freeman (Eds.), *The future of the brain: Essays by the world's leading neuroscientists.* Princeton, NJ: Princeton University Press.

Carbone, I., Lazzarotto, T., Ianni, M., Porcellini, E., Forti, P., Masliah, E., & . . . Licastro, F. (2014). Herpes virus in Alzheimer's disease: Relation to progression of the disease. *Neurobiology of Aging, 35*, 122–129.

Cardman, M. (2004). Rising GPAs, course loads a mystery to researchers. *Education Daily, 37*, 1–3.

Carey, B. (2012, March 29). Diagnoses of autism on the rise, report says. *New York Times*, p. A20.

Carleton, R. N., Duranceau, S., Freeston, M. H., Boelen, P. A., McCabe, R. E., & Antony, M. M. (2014). 'But it might be a heart attack': Intolerance of uncertainty and panic disorder symptoms. *Journal of Anxiety Disorders, 28*, 463–470.

Carmel, S. (2017). The will-to-live scale: Development, validation, and significance for elderly people. *Aging & Mental Health, 21*, 289–296.

Carnell, S., Benson, L., Pryor, K., & Driggin, E. (2013). Appetitive traits from infancy to adolescence: Using behavioral and neural measures to investigate obesity risk. *Physiology & Behavior.* doi: 10.1016/j.physbeh.2013.02.015.

Carpendale, J. I. M. (2000). Kohlberg and Piaget on stages and moral reasoning. *Developmental Review, 20*, 181–205.

Carr, D. (2015). Spousal/intimate partner loss and bereavement. In G. Christ, C. Messner, L. Behar (Eds.), *Handbook of oncology social work: Psychosocial care for people with cancer.* New York: Oxford University Press.

Carr, D. (2016). Is death 'the great equalizer'? The social stratification of death quality in the United States. *Annals of the American Academy of Political and Social Science, 663*, 331–354.

Carr, D. S., Nesse, R. M., & Wortman, C. B. (2005). *Spousal bereavement in late life.* New York: Springer.

Carrere, S., Buehlman, K. T., Gottman, J. M., Coan, J. A., & Ruckstuhl, L. (2000). Predicting marital stability and divorce in newlywed couples. *Journal of Family Psychology, 14*, 42–58.

Carrns, A. (2016, August 12). Multigenerational households: The benefits, and perils. *New York Times.* Accessed online, 11/29/17; https://www.nytimes.com/2016/08/12/your-money/multigenerational-households-financial-advice.html?_r=0.

Carson, A., Chabot, C., Greyson, D., Shannon, K., Duff, P., & Shoveller, J. (2016). A narrative analysis of the birth stories of early-age mothers. *Sociology of Health & Illness.* Accessed online, 3/3/17; http://onlinelibrary.wiley.com/doi/10.1111/1467-9566.12518/abstract.

Carteret, M. (2017). *Cultural aspects of death and dying.* Accessed online, 10/23/17; http://www.dimensionsofculture.com/2010/11/cultural-aspects-of-death-and-dying/.

Carver, C., & Scheier, M. (2002). Coping processes and adjustment to chronic illness. In A. Christensen & M. Antoni (Eds.), *Chronic physical disorders: Behavioral medicine's perspective* (pp. 47–68). Malden, MA: Blackwell Publishers.

Casalin, S., Luyten, P., Vliegen, N., & Meurs, P. (2012). The structure and stability of temperament from infancy to toddlerhood: A one-year prospective study. *Infant Behavior & Development, 35*, 94–108.

Casasanto, D. (2008). Who's afraid of the big bad whorf? Crosslinguistic differences in temporal language and thought. *Language Learning*, 63–79.

Case, R. (2007). Neo-Piagetian theory: Retrospect and prospect. *International Journal of Psychology, 22*(5–6), 773–791. doi:10.1080/00207598708246802.

Case, R., & Okamoto, Y. (1996). The role of central conceptual structures in the development of children's thought. *Monographs of the Society for Research in Child Development, 61*, v–265.

Case, R., Demetriou, A., & Platsidou, M. (2001). Integrating concepts and tests of intelligence from the differential and developmental traditions. *Intelligence, 29*, 307–336.

Caserta, M., O'Connor, T., Wyman, P., Wang, H., Moynihan, J., Cross, W., et al. (2008). The associations between psychosocial stress and the frequency of illness, and innate and adaptive immune function in children. *Brain, Behavior, and Immunity, 22*, 933–940.

Casey, B. J., Jones, R. M., & Somerville, L. H. (2011). Braking and accelerating of the adolescent brain. *Journal of Research on Adolescence, 21*, 21–33.

Cashman, H. R. (2005). Identities at play: Language preference and group membership in bilingual talk in interaction. *Journal of Pragmatics, 37, Special issue: Conversational* Code-Switching, 301–315.

Cassidy, J., & Berlin, L. J. (1994). The insecure/ambivalent pattern of attachment: Theory and research. *Child Development, 65*, 971–991.

Castelao, C., & Kröner-Herwig, B. (2013). Different trajectories of depressive symptoms in children and adolescents: Predictors and differences in girls and boys. *Journal of Youth and Adolescence, 42*, 1169–1182.

Cattell, R. (2004). The theory of fluid and crystallized intelligence; its relationship with "culture-free" tests and its verification with children aged 9–12 years. *European Review of Applied Psychology, 54*, 47–56.

Cauce, A. (2008). Parenting, culture, and context: Reflections on excavating culture. *Applied Developmental Science, 12*, 227–229. Accessed online; http://search.ebscohost.com, doi: 10.1080/10888690802388177.

Cavallini, A., Fazzi, E., & Viviani, V. (2002). Visual acuity in the first two years of life in healthy term newborns: An experience with the Teller Acuity Cards. *Functional Neurology: New Trends in Adaptive & Behavioral Disorders, 17*, 87–92.

CDC. (2016). *National Vital Statistics Report.* Hyattsville, MD: Centers for Disease Control.

Celera Genomics: International Human Genome Sequencing Consortium. (2001). Initial sequencing and analysis of the human genome. *Nature, 409*, 860–921.

Centers for Disease Control and Prevention. (2008). *HIV/AIDS surveillance report, 2006*. Vol. 18. Atlanta: U.S. Department of Health and Human Services, Centers for Disease Control and Prevention. Accessed online, 6/30/15; http://www.cdc.gov/hiv/topics/surveillance/resources/reports/.

Centers for Disease Control and Prevention. (2010). *Prevalence of obesity among children and adolescents; United States, trends 1963–1965 through 2007–2008*. Washington, DC: Author.

Centers for Disease Control and Prevention. (2015). *Current cigarette smoking among U.S. adults aged 18 and older*. Atlanta, GA: Centers for Disease Control. Accessed online, 6/30/15; http://www.cdc.gov/tobacco/campaign/tips/resources/data/cigarette-smoking-in-united-states.html.

Centers for Disease Control and Prevention. (2015). *Understanding school violence fact sheet*. Accessed online, 6/27/15; http://www.cdc.gov/violenceprevention/pdf/school_violence_fact_sheet-a.pdf.

Centers for Disease Control and Prevention. (2016). *10 Leading Causes of Death by Age Group, United States–2015*. Washington, DC: National Vital Statistics System, National Center for Health Statistics.

Centers for Disease Control and Prevention. (2017). Pregnancy. Accessed online, 10/25/17 https://www.cdc.gov/pregnancy/during.html.

Centers for Disease Control and Prevention. (2017). Sudden unexpected infant death and sudden infant death syndrome. Accessed online; www.cdc.gov.

Chabal, S., & Marian, V. (2015). Speakers of different languages process the visual world differently. *Journal of Experimental Psychology: General, 144*, 539–550.

Chadha, N., & Misra, G. (2004). Patterns of prosocial reasoning in Indian children. *Psychology and Developing Societies, 16*, 159–186.

Chaffin, M. (2006). The changing focus of child maltreatment research and practice within psychology. *Journal of Social Issues, 62*, 663–684.

Chaker, A. M. (2003, September 23). Putting toddlers in a nursing home. *Wall Street Journal*, p. D1.

Chandra, A., Mosher, W. D., Copen. C., & Sionean, C. (2011). Sexual behavior, sexual attraction, and sexual identity in the United States: Data from the 2006–2008 National Survey of Family Growth. *National health statistics reports, 36*. Hyattsville, MD: National Center for Health Statistics.

Channell, M. M., Thurman, A. J., Kover, S. T., & Abbeduto, L. (2014). Patterns of change in nonverbal cognition in adolescents with Down syndrome. *Research in Developmental Disabilities, 35*, 2933–2941.

Chao, R. K. (1994). Beyond parental control and authoritarian parenting style: Understanding Chinese parenting through the cultural notion of training. *Child Development, 65*, 1111–1119.

Chaplin, T. M., & Aldao, A. (2013). Gender differences in emotion expression in children: A meta-analytic review. *Psychological Bulletin, 139*, 735–765.

Chapman, R. (2016). A case study of gendered play in preschools: How early childhood educators' perceptions of gender influence children's play. *Early Child Development and Care, 186*, 1271–1284.

Charles, S. T., Mather, M., & Carstensen, L. L. (2003). Aging and emotional memory: The forgettable nature of negative images for older adults. *Journal of Experimental Psychology: General, 132*, 237–244.

Chassin, L., Macy, J., Seo, D., Presson, C., & Sherman, S. (2009). The association between membership in the sandwich generation and health behaviors: A longitudinal study. *Journal of Applied Developmental Psychology, 31*, 38–46.

Chaudhary, N., & Sharma, N. (2012). India. In J. Arnett (Ed.), *Adolescent psychology around the world*. New York: Psychology Press.

Cheah, C., Leung, C., Tahseen, M., & Schultz, D. (2009). Authoritative parenting among immigrant Chinese mothers of preschoolers. *Journal of Family Psychology, 23*, 311–320.

Chen, D., Yang, X., & Dale Aagard, S. (2012). The empty nest syndrome: Ways to enhance quality of life. *Educational Gerontology, 38*, 520–529.

Chen, E., & Rao, N. (2011). Gender socialization in Chinese kindergartens: Teachers' contributions. *Sex Roles, 64*, 103–116.

Chen, H. (2006). Digitization of the experience sampling method: Transformation, implementation, and assessment. *Social Science Computer Review, 24*, 106–118.

Chen, J. J, Chen, T., & Zheng, X. (2012). Parenting styles and practices among Chinese immigrant mothers with young children. *Early Child Development and Care, 182*, 1–21.

Chen, J. J., Sun, P., & Yu, Z. (2017). A comparative study on parenting of preschool children between the Chinese in China and Chinese immigrants in the United States. *Journal of Family Issues, 38*, 1262–1287.

Chen, J., & Gardner, H. (2005). Assessment based on multiple-intelligences theory. In D. P. Flanagan & P. L. Harrison (Eds.), *Contemporary intellectual assessment: Theories, tests, and issues*. New York: Guilford Press.

Chen, S. X., & Bond, M. H. (2007). Explaining language priming effects: Further evidence for ethnic affirmation among Chinese-English bilinguals. *Journal of Language and Social Psychology, 26*, 398–406.

Chen, X., & Schmidt, L. A. (2015). Temperament and personality. In & R. M. Lerner (Eds.), *Handbook of child psychology and developmental science, Vol. 3: Socioemotional processes* (7th ed.). Hoboken, NJ: John Wiley & Sons Inc.

Chen, X., Liu, M., Rubin, K. H., Cen, G., Gao, X., & Li, D. (2002). Sociability and prosocial orientation as predictors of youth adjustment: A seven-year longitudinal study in a Chinese sample. *International Journal of Behavioral Development, 26*, 128–136.

Cheng, J. T., Tracy, J. L., Ho, S., & Henrich, J. (2016). Listen, follow me: Dynamic vocal signals of dominance predict emergent social rank in humans. *Journal of Experimental Psychology: General, 145*, 536–547.

Cherney, I., Kelly-Vance, L., & Glover, K. (2003). The effects of stereotyped toys and gender on play assessment in children aged 18–47 months. *Educational Psychology, 23*, 95–105.

Cheung, W., Maio, G. R., Rees, K. J., Kamble, S., & Mane, S. (2016). Cultural differences in values as self-guides. *Personality and Social Psychology Bulletin, 42*, 769–781.

ChildStats.gov. (2017). *America's children: Key national indicators of well-being, 2017*. Accessed online, 10/27/17; https://www.childstats.gov/americaschildren/health2.asp.

Childers, J. (2009). Early verb learners: Creative or not? *Monographs of the Society for Research in Child Development, 74*, 133–139. http://search.ebscohost.com, doi:10.1111/j.1540-5834.2009.00524.x.

Chiodo, L. M., Bailey, B. A., Sokol, R. J., Janisse, J., Delaney-Black, V., & Hannigan, J. H. (2012). Recognized spontaneous abortion in mid-pregnancy and patterns of pregnancy alcohol use. *Alcohol, 46*, 261–267.

Chisolm, T., Willott, J., & Lister, J. (2003). The aging auditory system: Anatomic and physiologic changes and implications for rehabilitation. *International Journal of Audiology, 42*, 2S3–2S10.

Chiu, C., Leung, A., & Kwan, L. (2007). Language, cognition, and culture: Beyond the Whorfian hypothesis. *Handbook of cultural psychology*. New York: Guilford Press.

Choi, C. Q. (2017). Countries with most twins identified. *LiveScience*. Accessed online, 10/24/17; https://www.livescience.com/16469-twins-countries-twinning-rates.html.

Chomsky, N. (1999). On the nature, use, and acquisition of language. In W. C. Ritchie & T. J. Bhatia (Eds.), *Handbook of child language acquisition*. San Diego: Academic Press.

Chomsky, N. (2005). Editorial: Universals of human nature. *Psychotherapy and Psychosomatics [serial online], 74*, 263–268.

Choy, C. M., Yeung, Q. S., Briton-Jones, C. M., Cheung, C. K., Lam, C. W., & Haines, C. J. (2002). Relationship between semen parameters and mercury concentrations in blood and in seminal fluid from subfertile males in Hong Kong. *Fertility and Sterility, 78*, 426–428.

Chow, T. S., & Wan, H. Y. (2017). Is there any 'Facebook depression'? Exploring the moderating roles of neuroticism, Facebook social comparison and envy. *Personality and Individual Differences, 119,* 277–282.

Christensen, C. G., Bickham, D., Ross, C. S., & Rich, M. (2015). Multitasking with television among adolescents. *Journal of Broadcasting & Electronic Media, 59,* 130–148.

Cillessen, A., & Borch, C. (2008). Analyzing social networks in adolescence. *Modeling dyadic and interdependent data in the developmental and behavioral sciences* (pp. 61–85). New York: Routledge/Taylor & Francis Group.

Cina, V., & Fellmann, F. (2006). Implications of predictive testing in neurodegenerative disorders. *Schweizer Archiv für Neurologie und Psychiatrie, 157,* 359–365.

Cirulli, F., Berry, A., & Alleva, E. (2003). Early disruption of the mother-infant relationship: Effects on brain plasticity and implications for psychopathology. *Neuroscience & Biobehavioral Reviews, 27,* 73–82.

Clark, D. (2015). Hospice care of the dying. In J. M. Stillion, T. Attig (Eds.), *Death, dying, and bereavement: Contemporary perspectives, institutions, and practices.* New York: Springer.

Clark, K. B., & Clark, M. P. (1947). Racial identification and preference in Negro children. In T. M. Newcomb & E. L. Hartley (Eds.), *Readings in social psychology.* New York: Holt, Rinehart & Winston.

Clarke, L. H. (2005). Remarriage in later life: Older women's negotiation of power, resources and domestic labor. *Journal of Women & Aging, 17,* 21–41.

Clarke, L., & Griffin, M. (2007). The body natural and the body unnatural: Beauty work and aging. *Journal of Aging Studies, 21,* 187–201.

Clarke-Stewart, A., & Friedman, S. (1987). *Child development: Infancy through adolescence.* New York: Wiley.

Clay, D., Vignoles, V. L., & Dittmar, H. (2005). Body image and self-esteem among adolescent girls: Testing the influence of sociocultural factors. *Journal of Research on Adolescence, 15,* 451–477.

Clearfield, M., & Nelson, N. (2006, January). Sex differences in mothers' speech and play behavior with 6-, 9-, and 14-month-old infants. *Sex Roles, 54,* 127–137.

Clements, R., & Swenson, C. (2003). Commitment to one's spouse as a predictor of marital quality among older couples. *Love, romance, sexual interaction: Research perspectives from Current Psychology* (pp. 183–195). New Brunswick, NJ: Transaction Publishers.

Cline, K. D., & Edwards, C. P. (2017). Parent–child book-reading styles, emotional quality, and changes in early head start children's cognitive scores. *Early Education and Development, 28,* 41–58.

Coates, S. W. (2016). Can babies remember trauma? Symbolic forms of representation in traumatized infants. *Journal of the American Psychoanalytic Association, 64,* 751–776.

Close, F. T., Suther, S., Foster, A., El-Amin, S., & Battle, A. M. (2013). Community perceptions of Black infant mortality: A qualitative inquiry. *Journal of Health Care for the Poor and Underserved, 24,* 1089–1101.

Cockrill, K., & Gould, H. (2012). Letter to the editor: Response to "What women want from abortion counseling in the United States: A qualitative study of abortion patients in 2008." *Social Work in Health Care, 51,* 191–194.

Coelho, M., Ferreira, J., Dias, B., Sampaio, C., Martins, G., & Castro-Caldas, A. (2004). Assessment of time perception: The effect of aging. *Journal of the International Neuropsychological Society, 10,* 332–341.

Coelho, V. A., Marchante, M., & Jimerson, S. R. (2016). Promoting a positive middle school transition: A randomized-controlled treatment study examining self-concept and self-esteem. *Journal of Youth and Adolescence.* Accessed online, 6/13/16; http://www.ncbi.nlm.nih.gov/pubmed/27230119.

Cogan, L. W., Josberger, R. E., Gesten, F. C., & Roohan, P. J. (2012). Can prenatal care impact future well-child visits? The experience of a low income population in New York state Medicaid managed care. *Maternal and Child Health Journal, 16,* 92–99.

Cohen, L. B., & Cashon, C. H. (2003). Infant perception and cognition. In R. M. Lerner & M. A. Easterbrooks (Eds.), *Handbook of psychology: Developmental psychology,* Vol. 6. New York: Wiley.

Cohen, R. A., Mather, N., Schneider, D. A., & White, J. M. (2016). A comparison of schools: Teacher knowledge of explicit code-based reading instruction. *Reading and Writing.* Accessed online, 3/16/17; http://link.springer.com/article/10.1007/s11145-016-9694-0.

Cohen, S., Kamarck, T., & Mermelstein, R. (1983). A global measure of perceived stress. *Journal of Health and Social Behavior, 24*(4), 385–396. doi:10.2307/2136404.

Cohrs, J., Abele, A., & Dette, D. (2006, July). Integrating situational and dispositional determinants of job satisfaction: Findings from three samples of professionals. *Journal of Psychology: Interdisciplinary and Applied, 140,* 363–395.

Cokley, K. (2003). What do we know about the motivation of African American students? Challenging the "anti-intellectual" myth. *Harvard Educational Review, 73,* 524–558.

Colby, A., & Kohlberg, L. (1987). *The measurement of moral adjudgment* (Vols. 1–2). New York: Cambridge University Press.

Colby, S. L. & Ortman, J. M. (2014). Projections of the size and composition of the U.S. population: 2014 to 2060, *Current Population Reports, P25-1143.* Washington, DC: U.S. Census Bureau.

Cole, M. (1992). Culture in development. In M. H. Bornstein & M. E. Lamb (Eds.), *Developmental psychology: An advanced textbook* (3rd ed.). Hillsdale, NJ: Lawrence Erlbaum.

Cole, M., Gay, J., Glick, J. A., & Sharp, D. W. (Eds.). (1971). *The cultural context of learning and thinking.* New York: Basic Books.

Cole, S. A. (2005). Infants in foster care: Relational and environmental factors affecting attachment. *Journal of Reproductive & Infant Psychology, 23,* 43–61.

Coleman, H., Chan, C., Ferris, F., & Chew, E. (2008). Age-related macular degeneration. *Lancet, 372,* 1835–1845.

Coleman, M., Ganong, L., & Weaver, S. (2001). Relationship maintenance and enhancement in remarried families. In J. Harvey & A. Wenzel (Eds.), *Close romantic relationships: Maintenance and enhancement.* Mahwah, NJ: Lawrence Erlbaum.

Coleman, P. (2005, July). Editorial: Uses of reminiscence: Functions and benefits. *Aging & Mental Health, 9,* 291–294.

Coles, R., & Stokes, G. (1985). *Sex and the American teenager.* New York: Harper & Row.

Colibazzi, T., Zhu, H., Bansal, R., Schultz, R., Wang, Z., & Peterson, B. (2008). Latent volumetric structure of the human brain: Exploratory factor analysis and structural equation modeling of gray matter volumes in healthy children and adults. *Human Brain Mapping, 29,* 1302–1312.

College Board. (2005). *2001 College bound seniors are the largest, most diverse group in history.* New York: Author.

Collins, W. (2003). More than myth: The developmental significance of romantic relationships during adolescence. *Journal of Research on Adolescence, 13,* 1–24.

Collins, W., & Doolittle, A. (2006, December). Personal reflections of funeral rituals and spirituality in a Kentucky African American family. *Death Studies, 30,* 957–969.

Colom, R., Lluis-Font, J. M., & Andres-Pueyo, A. (2005). The generational intelligence gains are caused by decreasing variance in the lower half of the distribution: Supporting evidence for the nutrition hypothesis. *Intelligence, 33,* 83–91.

Colpin, H., & Soenen, S. (2004). Bonding through an adoptive mother's eyes. *Midwifery Today with International Midwife, 70,* 30–31.

Commons, M. L., & Richards, F. A. (2003). Four postformal stages. In J. Demick & C. Andreoletti (Eds.), *Handbook of adult development* (pp. 199–219). New York: Kluwer Academic/Plenum Publishers.

Comstock, G., & Scharrer, E. (1999). *Television: What's on, who's watching, and what it means.* San Diego: Academic Press.

Condon, J., Corkindale, C., Boyce, P., & Gamble, E. (2013). A longitudinal study of father-to-infant attachment: Antecedents and correlates. *Journal of Reproductive and Infant Psychology, 31,* 15–30.

Condry, J., & Condry, S. (1976). Sex differences: A study of the eye of the beholder. *Child Development, 47,* 812–819.

Conel, J. L. (1930/1975). *Postnatal development of the human cortex* (Vols. 1–6). Cambridge, MA: Harvard University Press.

Congressional Budget Office. (2013). *A description of the immigrant population: 2013 update*. Washington, DC: Congressional Budget Office.

Conn, V. S. (2003). Integrative review of physical activity intervention research with aging adults. *Journal of the American Geriatrics Society, 51*, 1159–1168.

Connell-Carrick, K. (2006). Early child care and early child development: Major findings of the NICHD Study of Early Child Care. *Child Welfare Journal, 85*, 819–836.

Conner, K., & Goldston, D. (2007, March). Rates of suicide among males increase steadily from age 11 to 21: Developmental framework and outline for prevention. *Aggression and Violent Behavior, 12*(2), 193–207.

Connor, T. (2008). Don't stress out your immune system—Just relax. *Brain, Behavior, and Immunity, 22*, 1128–1129.

Consedine, N., Magai, C., & King, A. (2004). Deconstructing positive affect in later life: A differential functionalist analysis of joy and interest. *International Journal of Aging & Human Development, 58*, 49–68.

Continelli, L. (2006, December 24). From boxing to books. *Buffalo News*, p. B3.

Coon, K. D., Myers, A. J., Craig, D. W., Webster, J. A., Pearson, J. V., Lince, D. H., et al. (2007). A high-density whole-genome association study reveals that APOE is the major susceptibility gene for sporadic late-onset Alzheimer's disease. *Journal of Clinical Psychiatry, 68*, 613–618.

Cooney, G., Dwan, K., & Mead, G. (2014). Exercise for depression. *JAMA, 311* (23), 2432–2433.

Cooper, H., & Valentine, J. (2001). Using research to answer practical questions about homework. *Educational Psychologist, 36*, 143–153.

Copping, K. E., Kurtz-Costes, B., Rowley, S. J., & Wood, D. (2013). Age and race differences in racial stereotype awareness and endorsement. *Journal of Applied Social Psychology, 43*, 971–980.

Corbin, C. (1973). *A textbook of motor development*. Dubuque, IA: Brown.

Corcoran, J., & Pillai, V. (2007, January). Effectiveness of secondary pregnancy prevention programs: A meta-analysis. *Research on Social Work Practice, 17*, 5–18.

Cordon, I. M., Pipe, M., Sayfan, L., Melinder, A., & Goodman, G. S. (2004). Memory for traumatic experiences in early childhood. *Developmental Review, 24*, 101–132.

Cornish, K., Turk, J., & Hagerman, R. (2008). The fragile X continuum: New advances and perspectives. *Journal of Intellectual Disability Research, 52*, 469–482.

Corr, C. (2007). Hospice: Achievements, legacies, and challenges. *Omega: Journal of Death and Dying, 56*, 111–120.

Corr, C. A. (2015). Death education at the college and university level in North America. In J. M. Stillion, T. Attig (Eds.), *Death, dying, and bereavement: Contemporary perspectives, institutions, and practices*. New York: Springer.

Corr, C., Nabe, C., & Corr, D. (2006). *Death & dying, life & living* (7th ed.). Belmont, CA: Thomson Wadsworth.

Corrow, S., Granrud, C. E., Mathison, J., & Yonas, A. (2012). Infants and adults use line junction information to perceive 3D shape. *Journal of Vision, 12*.

Corry, M., While, A., Neenan, K., & Smith, V. (2014) A systematic review of intervention for caregivers of people with chronic conditions. Accessed online, 1/1/15; http://onlinelibrary.wiley.com/doi/10.1111/jan.12523/abstract?deniedAccessCustomisedMessage=&userIsAuthenticated=false.

Cossman, J. S. (2004). Parents' heterosexism and children's attitudes toward people with AIDS. *Sociological Spectrum, 24*(3), 319–339. doi:10.1080/02732170490431322.

Costa-Martins, J. M., Pereira, M., Martins, H., Moura-Ramos, M., Coelho, R., & Tavares, J. (2014). The role of maternal attachment in the experience of labor pain: A prospective study. *Psychosomatic Medicine, 76*, 221–228.

Costello, E., Compton, S., & Keeler, G. (2003). Relationships between poverty and psychopathology: A natural experiment. *JAMA: The Journal of the American Medical Association, 290*, 2023–2029.

Costello, E., Sung, M., Worthman, C., & Angold, A. (2007, April). Pubertal maturation and the development of alcohol use and abuse. *Drug and Alcohol Dependence, 88*, S50–S59.

Cotrufo, P., Cella, S., Cremato, F., & Labella, A. G. (2007). Eating disorder attitude and abnormal behaviours in a sample of 11–13-year-old school children: The role of pubertal body transformation. *Eating Weight Disorders, 12*, 154–160.

Couperus, J., & Nelson, C. (2006). Early brain development and plasticity. In *Blackwell handbook of early childhood development*. New York: Blackwell Publishing.

Couzin, J. (2002, June 21). Quirks of fetal environment felt decades later. *Science, 296*, 2167–2169.

Cox, C., & Miner, J. (2014). Grandchildren raised by grandparents: Comparing the experiences of African-American and Tanzanian grandchildren. *Journal of Intergenerational Relationships, 12*, 9–24.

Cox, G. R. (2007). Religion, spirituality, and traumatic death. In D. Balk, C. Wogrin, G. Thornton, & D. Meagher (Eds.), *Handbook of thanatology: The essential body of knowledge for the study of death, dying, and bereavement*. New York: Routledge/Taylor & Francis Group.

Coyne, S. M. (2016). Effects of viewing relational aggression on television on aggressive behavior in adolescents: A three-year longitudinal study. *Developmental Psychology, 52*, 284–295.

Cramer, E. M., Song, H., & Drent, A. M. (2016). Social comparison on Facebook: Motivation, affective consequences, self-esteem, and Facebook fatigue. *Computers in Human Behavior, 64*, 739–746.

Crampton, A., & Hall, J. (2017). Unpacking socioeconomic risks for reading and academic self-concept in primary school: Differential effects and the role of the preschool home learning environment. *British Journal of Educational Psychology, 87*, 365–382.

Cratty, B. (1978). *Perceptual and motor development in infants and children* (2nd ed.). Englewood Cliffs, NJ: Prentice-Hall.

Cratty, B. (1979). *Perceptual and motor development in infants and children* (2nd ed.). Englewood Cliffs, NJ: Prentice-Hall.

Cratty, B. (1986). *Perceptual and motor development in infants and children* (3rd ed.). Englewood Cliffs, NJ: Prentice-Hall.

Crawford, D., Houts, R., & Huston, T. (2002). Compatibility, leisure, and satisfaction in marital relationships. *Journal of Marriage & Family, 64*, 433–449.

Crawford, M., & Unger, R. (2004). *Women and gender: A feminist psychology* (4th ed.). New York: McGraw-Hill.

Crews, D., Gillette, R., Scarpino, S. V., Manikkam, M., Savenkova, M. I., & Skinner, M. K. (2012). Epigenetic transgenerational inheritance of altered stress responses. *PNAS Proceedings of the National Academy of Sciences of the United States of America, 109*, 9143–9148.

Crisp, A., Gowers, S., Joughin, N., McClelland, L., Rooney, B., Nielsen, S., et al. (2006, May). Anorexia nervosa in males: Similarities and differences to anorexia nervosa in females. *European Eating Disorders Review, 14*, 163–167.

Critser, G. (2003). *Fat land: How Americans became the fattest people in the world*. Boston: Houghton Mifflin.

Crocetti, E. (2017). Identity formation in adolescence: The dynamic of forming and consolidating identity commitments. *Child Development Perspectives*. Accessed online, 3/22/17; http://onlinelibrary.wiley.com/doi/10.1111/cdep.12226/abstract.

Crocker, J., & Knight, K. M. (2005). Contingencies of self-worth. *Current Directions in Psychological Science, 14*, 200–203.

Croninger, R. G., & Lee, V. E. (2001). Social capital and dropping out of high school: Benefits to at-risk students of teachers' support and guidance. *Teachers College Record, 103*, 548–581.

Crosland, K., & Dunlap, G. (2012). Effective strategies for the inclusion of children with autism in general education classrooms. *Behavior Modification, 36*, 251–269.

Crosnoe, R., & Elder, G. H., Jr. (2002). Successful adaptation in the later years: A life course approach to aging. *Social Psychology Quarterly, 65*, 309–328.

Crowley, B., Hayslip, B., & Hobdy, J. (2003). Psychological hardiness and adjustment to life events in adulthood. *Journal of Adult Development, 10*, 237–248.

Crowley, J. (2018). *Gray divorce*. Berkeley, CA: University of California Press.

Crowley, K., Callaman, M. A., Tenenbaum, H. R., & Allen, E. (2001). Parents explain more often to boys than to girls during shared scientific thinking. *Psychological Science, 12*, 258–261.

Crowther, M., & Rodriguez, R. (2003). A stress and coping model of custodial grandparenting among African Americans. In B. Hayslip & J. Patrick (Eds.), *Working with custodial grandparents*. New York: Springer Publishing.

Crupi, R., & Brondolo, E. (2017). Posttraumatic stress disorder post 9/11: A review of the evidence and implications for public health policy. TPM-Testing, Psychometrics, *Methodology in Applied Psychology, 24*, 363–378.

Crozier, S., Robertson, N., & Dale, M. (2015). The psychological impact of predictive genetic testing for Huntington's disease: A systematic review of the literature. *Journal of Genetic Counseling, 24*, 29–39.

Cuadrado, E., Tabernero, C., & Steinel, W. (2015). Motivational determinants of prosocial behavior: What do included, hopeful excluded, and hopeless excluded individuals need to behave prosocially? *Motivation and Emotion, 39*, 344–358.

Cullen, C. (2017). Difficult conversations: Children, adolescents, and death. In R. G. Stevenson, G. R. Cox, R. (Eds.), *Children, adolescents and death: Questions and answers*. New York: Routledge/Taylor & Francis Group.

Culver, V. (2003, August 26). Funeral expenses overwhelm survivors: $10,000-plus tab often requires aid. *Denver Post*, p. B2.

Cummings, E. M., & Henry, W. E. (1961). *Growing old*. New York: Basic Books.

Curl, M. N., Davies, R., Lothian, S., Pascali-Bonaro, D., Scaer, R. M., & Walsh, A. (2004). Childbirth educators, doulas, nurses, and women respond to the six care practices for normal birth. *Journal of Perinatal Education, 13*, 42–50.

Curtin, C., Hubbard, K., Anderson, S. E., Mick, E., Must, A., & Bandini, L. G. (2015). Food selectivity, mealtime behavior problems, spousal stress, and family food choices in children with and without autism spectrum disorder. *Journal of Autism and Developmental Disorders, 45*(10), 3308–3315.

Curtis, R. G., Windsor, T. D., & Soubelet, A. (2015). The relationship between Big-5 personality traits and cognitive ability in older adults—A review. *Aging, Neuropsychology, and Cognition, 22*, 42–71.

Cushman, F., Sheketoff, R., Wharton, S., & Carey, S. (2013). The development of intent-based moral judgment. *Cognition, 127*, 6–21.

Cwikel, J., Gramotnev, H., & Lee, C. (2006). Never-married childless women in Australia: Health and social circumstances in older age. *Social Science & Medicine, 62*, 1991–2001.

D'Lima, G. M., Winsler, A., & Kitsantas, A. (2014). Ethnic and gender differences in first-year college students' goal orientation, self-efficacy, and extrinsic and intrinsic motivation. *The Journal of Educational Research, 107*, 341–356.

da Veiga, P., & Wilder, R. (2008). Maternal smoking during pregnancy and birthweight: A propensity score matching approach. *Maternal & Child Health Journal, 12*, 194–203.

Dabelko, H., & Zimmerman, J. (2008). Outcomes of adult day services for participants: A conceptual model. *Journal of Applied Gerontology, 27*, 78–92.

Dagys, N., McGlinchey, E. L., Talbot, L. S., Kaplan, I. A., Dahl, R. E., & Harvey, A. G. (2012). Double trouble? The effects of sleep deprivation and chronotype on adolescent affect. *Journal of Child Psychology and Psychiatry, 53*, 660–667.

Dahl, A., Satlof-Bedrick, E. S., Hammond, S. I., Drummond, J. K., Waugh, W. E., & Brownell, C. A. (2017). Explicit scaffolding increases simple helping in younger infants. *Developmental Psychology, 53*, 407–416.

Dai, D., Tan, X., Marathe, D., Valtcheva, A., Pruzek, R. M., & Shen, J. (2012). Influences of social and educational environments on creativity during adolescence: Does SES matter? *Creativity Research Journal, 24*, 191–199.

Dailey, A. L., Frey, A. J., & Walker, H. M. (2015). Relational aggression in school settings: Definition, development, strategies, and implications. *Children & Schools, 37*, 79–88.

Daley, K. C. (2004). Update on sudden infant death syndrome. *Current Opinion in Pediatrics, 16*, 227–232.

Daly, M., Boyce, C., & Wood, A. (2015). A social rank explanation of how money influences health. *Health Psychology, 34*, 222–230.

Damon, W., & Hart, D. (1988). *Self-understanding in childhood and adolescence*. New York: Cambridge University Press.

Dandan, T., Haixue, Z., Wenfu, L., Wenjing, Y., Jiang, Q., & Qinglin, Z. (2013). Brain activity in using heuristic prototype to solve insightful problems. *Behavioural Brain Research, 253*, 139–144.

Daniel, E., Bilgin, A. S., Brezina, I., Strohmeier, C. E., & Vainre, M. (2015). Values and helping behavior: A study in four cultures. *International Journal of Psychology, 50*, 186–192.

Daniels, H. (2006, February). The "Social" in post-Vygotskian theory. *Theory & Psychology, 16*, 37–49.

Dare, W. N., Noronha, C. C., Kusemiju, O. T., & Okanlawon, O. A. (2002). The effect of ethanol on spermatogenesis and fertility in male Sprague-Dawley rats pretreated with acetyl salicylic acid. *Nigeria Postgraduate Medical Journal, 9*, 194–198.

Darwin, Z., Green, J., McLeish, J., Willmot, H., & Spiby, H. (2017). Evaluation of trained volunteer doula services for disadvantaged women in five areas in England: Women's experiences. *Health & Social Care in the Community, 25*, 466–477.

Das, A. (2007). Masturbation in the United States. *Journal of Sex & Marital Therapy, 33*, 301–317.

Dasen, P., Inhelder, B., Lavallee, M., & Retschitzki, J. (1978). *Naissance de l'intelligence chez Tenfant Baoule de Cote d'Ivoire*. Berne, IN: Hans Huber.

Dasen, P., Ngini, L., & Lavallee, M. (1979). Crosscultural training studies of concrete operations. In J. H. Eckenberger, W. J. Lonner, & Y. H. Poortinga (Eds.), *Cross-cultural contributions to psychology*. Amsterdam: Swets & Zeilinger.

Daum, M. M., Prinz, W., & Aschersleben, G. (2011). Perception and production of object-related grasping in 6-month-olds. *Journal of Experimental Child Psychology, 108*, 810–818.

Davidson, J. K., Darling, C. A., & Norton, L. (1995). Religiosity and the sexuality of women: Sexual behavior and sexual satisfaction revisited. *Journal of Sex Research, 32*, 235–243.

Davidson, R. J. (2003). Affective neuroscience: A case for interdisciplinary research. In F. Kessel & P. L. Rosenfield (Eds.), *Expanding the boundaries of health and social science: Case studies in interdisciplinary innovation*. London: Oxford University Press.

Davidson, T. (1977). Wifebeating: A recurring phenomenon throughout history. In M. Roy (Ed.), *Battered women: A psychosociological study of domestic violence*. New York: Van Nostrand Reinhold.

Davies, K., Tropp, L. R., Aron, A. P., Thomas, F., & Wright, S. C. (2011). Cross-group friendships and intergroup attitudes: A meta-analytic review. *Personality and Social Psychology Review, 15*, 332–351.

Davies, S., & Denton, M. (2002). The economic wellbeing of older women who become divorced or separated in mid- or later life. *Canadian Journal on Aging, 21*, 477–493.

Davis, A. (2003). *Your divorce, your dollars: Financial planning before, during, and after divorce*. Bellingham, WA: Self-Counsel Press.

Davis, A. (2008). Children with Down syndrome: Implications for assessment and intervention in the school. *School Psychology Quarterly, 23*, 271–281. Accessed online; http://search.ebscohost.com, doi:10.1037/1045-3 830. 23.2.271.

Davis, B. L., Smith-Bynum, M. A., Saleem, F. T., Francois, T., & Lambert, S. F. (2017). Racial socialization, private regard, and behavior problems in African American youth: Global self-esteem as a mediator. *Journal of Child and Family Studies, 26*, 709–720.

Davis, M., Zautra, A., Younger, J., Motivala, S., Attrep, J., & Irwin, M. (2008). Chronic stress and regulation of cellular markers of inflammation in rheumatoid arthritis: Implications for fatigue. *Brain, Behavior, and Immunity, 22*, 24–32.

Davis, R. R., & Hofferth, S. L. (2012). The association between inadequate gestational weight gain and infant mortality among U.S. infants born in 2002. *Maternal and Child Health Journal, 16*, 119–124.

Davis-Kean, P. E., & Sandler, H. M. (2001). A metaanalysis of measures of self-esteem for young children: A framework for future measures. *Child Development, 72*, 887–906.

Dawson-Tunik, T., Fischer, K., & Stein, Z. (2004). Do stages belong at the center of developmental theory? A commentary on Piaget's stages. *New Ideas in Psychology, 22*, 255–263.

Daxinger L, Whitelaw E. (2012). Understanding transgenerational epigenetic inheritance via the gametes in mammals. *National Review of Genetics, 13*, 153–62.

de Bellis, M., Keshavan, M., Beers, S., Hall, J., Frustaci, K., Masalehdan, A., et al. (2001). Sex differences in brain maturation during childhood and adolescence. *Cerebral Cortex, 11*, 552–557.

De Conto, C. (2017). Intimité et sexualité en gériatrie. = Intimacy and sexuality in geriatrics. *NPG Neurologie - Psychiatrie - Gériatrie, 17*, 264–269.

de Dios, A. (2012). United States of America. In J. Arnett (Ed.), *Adolescent psychology around the world*. New York: Psychology Press.

de Graaf-Peters, V., & Hadders-Algra, M. (2006). Ontogeny of the human central nervous system: What is happening when? *Early Human Development, 82*, 257–266.

de Graag, J. A., Cox, R. A., Hasselman, F., Jansen, J., & de Weerth, C. (2012). Functioning within a relationship: Mother-infant synchrony and infant sleep. *Infant Behavior & Development, 35*, 252–263.

De Jesus-Zayas, S. R., Buigas, R., & Denney, R. L. (2012). Evaluation of culturally diverse populations. In D. Faust (Ed.), *Coping with psychiatric and psychological testimony: Based on the original work by Jay Ziskin* (6th ed.). New York: Oxford University Press.

de Lauzon-Guillain, B., Wijndaele, K., Clark, M., Acerini, C. L., Hughes, I. A., Dunger, D. B., et al. (2012). Breastfeeding and infant temperament at age three months. *Plos ONE, 7*, 182–190.

De Leo, D., Cimitan, A., Dyregrov, K., Grad, O., & Andriessen, K. (2014). *Bereavement after traumatic death: Helping the survivors*. Cambridge, MA: Hogrefe Publishing.

De Meersman, R., & Stein, P. (2007, February). Vagal modulation and aging. *Biological Psychology, 74*, 165–173.

de Oliveira Brito, L. V., Maranhao Neto, G. A., Moraes, H., Emerick, R. S., & Deslandes, A. C. (2014). Relationship between level of independence in activities of daily living and estimated cardiovascular capacity in elderly women. *Archives of Gerontology and Geriatrics, 59*, 367–371.

de Oliveira, E. A., & Jackson, E. A. (2017). The moderation role of self-perceived maternal empathy in observed mother–child collaborative problem solving. *Infant and Child Development, 26*, 1–13.

de Onis, M., Garza, C., Onyango, A. W., & Borghi, E. (2007). Comparison of the WHO child growth standards and the CDC 2000 growth charts. *Journal of Nutrition, 137*, 144–148.

De Pauw, S. W., & Mervielde, I. (2011). The role of temperament and personality in problem behaviors of children with ADHD. *Journal of Abnormal Child Psychology: An Official Publication of the International Society for Research in Child and Adolescent Psychopathology, 39*, 277–291.

De Roten, Y., Favez, N., & Drapeau, M. (2004). Two studies on autobiographical narratives about an emotional event by preschoolers: Influence of the emotions experienced and the affective closeness with the interlocutor. *Early Child Development & Care, 173*, 237–248.

de St. Aubin, E., & McAdams, D. P. (Eds.). (2004). *The generative society: Caring for future generations*. Washington, DC: American Psychological Association.

DeAngelis, T. (2010, March). Menopause, the makeover. *Monitor on Psychology*, pp. 41–43.

Deal, J. J., & Levenson, A. (2016). *What millennials want from work: How to maximize engagement in today's workforce*. New York: McGraw-Hill Education.

Deaner, R. O., Balish, S. M., & Lombardo, M. P. (2016). Sex differences in sports interest and motivation: An evolutionary perspective. *Evolutionary Behavioral Sciences, 10*, 73–97.

Deary, I. J. (2012). Intelligence. *Annual Review of Psychology, 63*, 453–482.

Deary, I., Ferguson, K., Bastin, M., Barrow, G., Reid, L., Seckl, J., et al. (2007). Skull size and intelligence, and King Robert Bruce's IQ. *Intelligence, 35*, 519–528.

Deater-Deckard, K., & Cahill, K. (2006). Nature and nurture in early childhood. In *Blackwell handbook of early childhood development* (pp. 3–21). New York: Blackwell Publishing.

Deb, S., & Adak, M. (2006, July). Corporal punishment of children: Attitude, practice and perception of parents. *Social Science International, 22*, 3–13.

Debast, I., van Alphen, S., Rossi, G., Tummers, J. A., Bolwerk, N., Derksen, J. L., & Rosowsky, E. (2014). Personality traits and personality disorders in late middle and old age: Do they remain stable? A literature review. *Clinical Gerontologist: The Journal of Aging and Mental Health, 37*, 253–271.

DeCasper, A. J., & Spence, M. J. (1986). Prenatal material speech influences newborns' perception of speech sounds. *Infant Behavior and Development, 9*, 133–150.

deCastro, J. (2002). Age-related changes in the social, psychological, and temporal influences on food intake in free-living, healthy, adult humans. *Journals of Gerontology: Series A: Biological Sciences & Medical Sciences, 57A*, M368–M377.

Decety, J., & Jackson, P. L. (2006). A social-neuroscience perspective on empathy. *Current Directions in Psychological Science, 15*, 54–61.

Dehaene-Lambertz, G., Hertz-Pannier, L., & Dubois, J. (2006). Nature and nurture in language acquisition: Anatomical and functional brain-imaging studies in infants. *Neurosciences, 29* [Special issue: Nature and nurture in brain development and neurological disorders], 367–373.

Dehaene-Lambertz, G. (2017). The human infant brain: A neural architecture able to learn language. *Psychonomic Bulletin & Review, 24*, 48–55.

DePietro, J. A. (2004). The role of prenatal maternal stress in child development. *Current Directions in Psychological Science, 13*, 71–73.

Dehaene, S., Pegado, F., Braga, L. W., Ventura, P., Nunes Filho, G., Jobert, A., Dehaenelambertz, G., Kolinsky, R., Morais, J., & Cohen, L. (2007). How learning to read changes the cortical networks for vision and language. *Science, 2010*(6009), 1359–1364.

Del Giudice, M. (2015). Self-regulation in an evolutionary perspective. In G. E. Gendolla, M. Tops, S. L. Koole (Eds.), *Handbook of biobehavioral approaches to self-regulation*. New York: Springer Science + Business Media.

Delamater, J. (2012). Sexual expression in later life: A review and synthesis. *Journal of Sex Research, 49*, 125–141.

Dellmann-Jenkins, M., & Brittain, L. (2003). Young adults' attitudes toward filial responsibility and actual assistance to elderly family members. *Journal of Applied Gerontology, 22*, 214–229.

DeLoache, J. S., Chiong, C., Sherman, K., Islam, N., Vanderborght, M., Troseth, G. L., Strouse, G. A., & O'Doherty, K. (2010). Do babies learn from baby media? *Psychological Science, 21*, 1570-1574.

Delpisheh, A., Attia, E., Drammond, S., & Brabin, B. (2006). Adolescent smoking in pregnancy and birth outcomes. *European Journal of Public Health, 16*, 168–172.

Delva, J., O'Malley, P., & Johnston, L. (2006, October). Racial/ethnic and socioeconomic status differences in overweight and health-related behaviors among American students: National trends 1986–2003. *Journal of Adolescent Health, 39*, 536–545.

Demir, M., Jaafar, J., Bilyk, N., & Ariff, M. (2012). Social skills, friendship and happiness: A cross-cultural investigation. *The Journal of Social Psychology, 152*, 379–385.

Dempster, F. N. (1981). Memory span: Sources of individual and developmental differences. *Psychological Bulletin, 89*, 63–100.

Deng, C., Armstrong, P., & Rounds, J. (2007). The fit of Holland's RIASEC model to US occupations. *Journal of Vocational Behavior, 71*, 1–22.

Denizet-Lewis, B. (2004, May 30). Friends, friends with benefits and the benefits of the local mall. *New York Times Magazine*, pp. 30–35, 54–58.

Dennis, J. G. (2004). *Homeschooling high school: Planning ahead for college admission*. Cambridge, MA: Emerald Press.

Dennis, W. (1966). Age and creative productivity. *Journal of Gerontology, 21,* 1–8.

Deon, M., Landgraf, S. S., Lamberty, J. F., Moura, D. J., Saffi, J., Wajner, M., & Vargas, C. R. (2015). Protective effect of L-carnitine on Phenylalanine-induced DNA damage. *Metabolic Brain Disease.* Accessed online, 3/14/15; http://www.ncbi.nlm.nih.gov/pubmed/25600689.

DeParle, J., & Tavernise, S. (2012, February 17). Unwed mothers now a majority before age of 30. *New York Times,* p. A1.

DePaulo, B. (2004). *The scientific study of people who are single: An annotated bibliography.* Glendale, CA: Unmarried America.

DePaulo, B. (2006). *Singled out: How singles are stereotyped, stigmatized, and ignored, and still live happily ever after.* New York: St Martin's Press.

Der, G., & Deary, I. (2006, March). Age and sex differences in reaction time in adulthood: Results from the United Kingdom Health and Lifestyle Survey. *Psychology and Aging, 21*(1), 62–73.

Dervic, K., Friedrich, E., Oquendo, M., Voracek, M., Friedrich, M., & Sonneck, G. (2006, October). Suicide in Austrian children and young adolescents aged 14 and younger. *European Child & Adolescent Psychiatry, 15,* 427–434.

Deshields, T., Tibbs, T., Fan, M. Y., & Taylor, M. (2005, August 12). Differences in patterns of depression after treatment for breast cancer. *PsychoOncology,* published online, John Wiley & Sons.

Deurenberg, P., Deurenberg-Yap, M., & Guricci, S. (2002). Asians are different from Caucasians and from each other in their body mass index/body fat percent relationship. *Obesity Review, 3,* 141–146.

Deurenberg, P., Deurenberg-Yap, M., Foo, L. F., Schmidt, G., & Wang, J. (2003). Differences in body composition between Singapore Chinese, Beijing Chinese and Dutch children. *European Journal of Clinical Nutrition, 57,* 405–409.

DeVader, S. R., Neeley, N. L., Myles, T. D., & Leet, T. L. (2007). Evaluation of gestational weight gain guidelines for women with normal prepregnancy body mass index. *Obstetrics and Gynecology, 110,* 745–751.

Deveny, K. (1994, December 5). Chart of kindergarten awards. *Wall Street Journal,* p. B1.

deVries, R. (2005). *A pleasing birth.* Philadelphia, PA: Temple University Press.

deWind, A., Geuskens, G. A., Ybema, J. F., Bongers, P. M., & van der Beek, A. J. (2015). The role of ability, motivation, and opportunity to work in the transition from work to early retirement—Testing and optimizing the Early Retirement Model. *Scandinavian Journal of Work, Environment & Health, 41*(1), 24–35.

Di Paolo, E. A., Buhrmann, T., & Barandiaran, X. E. (2017). *Sensorimotor life: An enactive proposal.* New York: Oxford University Press.

Diambra, L., & Menna-Barreto, L. (2004). Infradian rhythmicity in sleep/wake ratio in developing infants. *Chronobiology International, 21,* 217–227.

Diamond, L. (2003a). Love matters: Romantic relationships among sexual-minority adolescents. In P. Florsheim (Ed.), *Adolescent romantic relations and sexual behavior: Theory, research, and practical implications.* Mahwah, NJ: Lawrence Erlbaum.

Diamond, L. (2003b). Was it a phase? Young women's relinquishment of lesbian/bisexual identities over a 5-year period. *Journal of Personality & Social Psychology, 84,* 352–364.

Diamond, L. M., Fagundes, C. P., & Butterworth, M. R. (2010). Intimate relationships across the life span. In M. E. Lamb, A. Freund, & R. M. Lerner (Eds.), *The handbook of life-span development, Vol 2: Social and emotional development.* Hoboken, NJ: John Wiley & Sons Inc.

Diamond, L., & Savin-Williams, R. (2003). The intimate relationships of sexual-minority youths. In G. Adams & M. Berzonsky (Eds.), *Blackwell handbook of adolescence.* Malden, MA: Blackwell Publishers.

Diamond, M. (2013). Transsexuality among twins: Identity concordance, transition, rearing, and orientation. *International Journal of Transgenderism, 14,* 24–38.

DiCarlo, C. F., Baumgartner, J., Ota, C., & Jenkins, C. (2015). Preschool teachers' perceptions of rough and tumble play vs. aggression in preschool-aged boys. *Early Child Development and Care, 185,* 779–790.

Dick, D. M., & Mustanski, B. (2006). Pubertal development and health-related behavior. In *Socioemotional development and health from adolescence to adulthood* (pp. 108–125). New York: Cambridge University Press.

Dietrich, J. F., Huber, S., Dackermann, T., Moeller, K., & Fischer, U. (2016). Place-value understanding in number line estimation predicts future arithmetic performance. *British Journal of Developmental Psychology, 34,* 502–517.

DiNallo, J. M., Downs, D., & Le Masurier, G. (2012). Objectively assessing treadmill walking during the second and third pregnancy trimesters. *Journal of Physical Activity & Health, 9,* 21–28.

Dinella, L. M., Weisgram, E. S., & Fulcher, M. (2017). Children's gender-typed toy interests: Does propulsion matter? *Archives of Sexual Behavior, 46,* 1295–1305.

Dinero, R., Conger, R., Shaver, P., Widaman, K., & Larsen-Rife, D. (2008). Influence of family of origin and adult romantic partners on romantic attachment security. *Journal of Family Psychology, 22,* 622–632.

DiPietro, J. A., Bornstein, M. H., & Costigan, K. A. (2002). What does fetal movement predict about behavior during the first two years of life? *Developmental Psychobiology, 40,* 358–371.

DiPietro, J. A., Costigan, K. A., & Gurewitsch, E. D. (2005). Maternal psychophysiological change during the second half of gestation. *Biological Psychology, 69,* 23–39.

Dittmann, M. (2005). Generational differences at work. *Monitor on Psychology, 36,* 54–55.

Dittmann, M. (2004, November). A new face to retirement. *Monitor on Psychology, 35,* 78.

Dixon, L., & Browne, K. (2003). The heterogeneity of spouse abuse: A review. *Aggression & Violent Behavior, 8,* 107–130.

Dixon, W. E., Jr. (2004). There's a long, long way to go. *PsycCRITIQUES.*

Djurdjinovic, L., & Peters, J. A. (2017). Special issue introduction: Dealing with psychological and social complexity in genetic counseling. *Journal of Genetic Counseling, 26,* 1–4.

Dobele, A. R., Rundle-Thiele, S., & Kopanidis, F. (2014). The cracked glass ceiling: Equal work but unequal status. *Higher Education Research & Development, 33,* 456–468.

Dobrova-Krol, N., van IJzendoorn, M., Bakermans-Kranenburg, M., Cyr, C., & Juffer, F. (2008). Physical growth delays and stress dysregulation in stunted and non-stunted Ukrainian institution-reared children. *Infant Behavior & Development, 31,* 539–553.

Dodge, K. A., & Crick, N. R. (1990). Social information-processing bases of aggressive behavior in children. *Personality and Social Psychology Bulletin, 16,* 8–22.

Dodgson, P. G., & Wood, J. V. (1998). Self-esteem and the cognitive accessibility of strengths and weaknesses after failure. *Journal of Personality & Social Psychology, 75,* 178–197.

Doherty, W., Carroll, J., & Waite, L. (2007). Supporting the institution of marriage: Ideological, research, and ecological perspectives. In *The family in the new millennium: World voices supporting the "natural" clan Vol 2: Marriage and human dignity* (pp. 21–51). Westport, CT: Praeger Publishers/Greenwood Publishing Group.

Dombrovski, A. Y., Siegle, G. J., Szanto, K. K., Clark, L. L., Reynolds, C., & Aizenstein, H. H. (2012). The temptation of suicide: Striatal gray matter, discounting of delayed rewards, and suicide attempts in late-life depression. *Psychological Medicine, 42,* 1203–1215.

Donahue, P. L., Daane, M. C., & Jin, Y. (2005). The nation's report card: Reading 2003. Washington, DC: National Assessment of Educational Progress.

Donat, D. (2006, October). Reading their way: A balanced approach that increases achievement. *Reading & Writing Quarterly: Overcoming Learning Difficulties, 22,* 305–323.

Donini, L., Savina, C., & Cannella, C. (2003). Eating habits and appetite control in the elderly: The anorexia of aging. *International Psychogeriatrics, 15,* 73–87.

Donleavy, G. (2008). No man's land: Exploring the space between Gilligan and Kohlberg. *Journal of Business Ethics, 80,* 807–822.

Donnellan, M. B., Trzesniewski, K. H., Robins, R. W., Moffitt, T. E., & Caspi, A. (2005). Low self-esteem is related to aggression, antisocial behavior, and delinquency. *Psychological Science, 16,* 328–335.

Donnerstein, E. (2005, January). Media violence and children: What do we know, what do we do? Paper presented at the annual National Teaching of Psychology meeting, St. Petersburg Beach, FL.

Dotti Sani, G. M., & Treas, J. (2016). Educational gradients in parents' child-care time across countries, 1965–2012. *Journal of Marriage and Family, 78,* 1083–1096.

Douglass, A., & Klerman, L. (2012). The strengthening families initiative and child care quality improvement: How strengthening families influenced change in child care programs in one state. *Early Education and Development, 23,* 373–392.

Douglass, R., & McGadney-Douglass, B. (2008). The role of grandmothers and older women in the survival of children with kwashiorkor in urban Accra, Ghana. *Research in Human Development, 5,* 26–43.

Dovidio, J. F., Glick, P., & Rudman, L. A. (2005). *On the nature of prejudice: Fifty years after Allport.* Malden, MA: Blackwell Publishing.

Dow, B., & Joosten, M. (2012). Understanding elder abuse: A social rights perspective. *International Psychogeriatrics, 24,* 853–855.

Doyle, L. W., Victorian Infant Collaborative Study Group. (2004). Neonatal intensive care at borderline viability—Is it worth it? *Early Human Development, 80,* 103–113.

Dozor, A. J., & Amler, R. W. (2013). Children's environmental health. *Journal of Pediatrics, 162*(1), 6–7. doi:10.1016/j.jpeds.2012.10.004.

Driscoll, A. K., Russell, S. T., & Crockett, L. J. (2008). Parenting styles and youth well-being across immigrant generations. *Journal of Family Issues, 29,* 185–209.

Driver, J., Tabares, A., & Shapiro, A. (2003). Interactional patterns in marital success and failure: Gottman laboratory studies. In F. Walsh (Ed.), *Normal family processes: Growing diversity and complexity* (3rd ed.). New York: Guilford Press.

Dubow, E. F., Huesmann, L. R., Boxer, P., & Smith, C. (2016). Childhood and adolescent risk and protective factors for violence in adulthood. *Journal of Criminal Justice, 45,* 26–31.

Duggan, K. A., & Friedman, H. S. (2014). Lifetime biopsychosocial trajectories of the Terman gifted children: Health, well-being, and longevity. In D. K. Simonton (Ed.). *The Wiley handbook of genius.* New York: Wiley-Blackwell.

Dudding, T. C., Vaizey, C. J., & Kamm, M. A. (2008). Obstetric anal sphincter injury: Incidence, risk factors, and management. *Annals of Surgery, 247,* 224–237.

Duijts, L., Jaddoe, V. W. V., Hofman, A., & Moll, H. A. (2010, June 21). Prolonged and exclusive breastfeeding reduces the risk of infectious diseases in infancy. *Pediatrics.* doi:10.1542/peds.2008-3256.

Dumka, L., Gonzales, N., Bonds, D., & Millsap, R. (2009). Academic success of Mexican origin adolescent boys and girls: The role of mothers' and fathers' parenting and cultural orientation. *Sex Roles, 60,* 588–599. Accessed online; http://search.ebscohost.com, doi: 10.1007/s11199-008-9518-z.

Duncan, G. J., & Brooks-Gunn, J. (2000). Family poverty, welfare reform, and child development. *Child Development, 71,* 188–196.

Duncan, G. J., Magnuson, K., & Votruba-Drzal, E. (2014). Boosting family income to promote child development. *The Future of Children, 24,* 99–120.

Dundas, E. M., Plaut, D. C., & Behrmann, M. (2015). Variable left-hemisphere language and orthographic lateralization reduces right-hemisphere face lateralization. *Journal of Cognitive Neuroscience, 27,* 913–925.

Dunford, B. B., Shipp, A. J., Boss, R., Angermeier, I., & Boss, A. D. (2012). Is burnout static or dynamic? A career transition perspective of employee burnout trajectories. *Journal of Applied Psychology, 97,* 637–650.

Dunn, M., Thomas, J. O., Swift, W., & Burns, L. (2012). Elite athletes' estimates of the prevalence of illicit drug use: Evidence for the false consensus effect. *Drug and Alcohol Review, 31,* 27–32.

Duplassie, D., & Daniluk, J. C. (2007). Sexuality: Young and middle adulthood. In A. Owens & M. Tupper (Eds.), *Sexual health: Vol. 1,* Psychological foundations. Westport, CT: Praeger.

Durbin, J. (2003, October 6). Internet sex unzipped. *McCleans,* p. 18.

Duriez, B., Luyckx, K., Soenens, B., & Berzonsky, M. (2012). A process-content approach to adolescent identity formation: Examining longitudinal associations between identity styles and goal pursuits. *Journal of Personality, 80,* 135–161.

Duschinsky, R. (2015). The emergence of the disorganized/disoriented (D) attachment classification, 1979–1982. *History of Psychology, 18,* 32–46.

Dyson, A. H. (2003). "Welcome to the jam": Popular culture, school literacy and making of childhoods. *Harvard Educational Review, 73,* 328–361.

Eagly, A. H., & Steffen, V. J. (1986). Gender and aggressive behavior: A meta-analytic review of the social psychological literature. *Psychological Bulletin, 100,* 309–330.

Eagly, A. H., & Wood, W. (2003). In C. B. Travis, *Evolution, gender, and rape.* Cambridge, MA: MIT Press.

Earl, R., Burns, N., Nettelbeck, T., & Baghurst, P. (2016). Low-level environmental lead exposure still negatively associated with children's cognitive abilities. *Australian Journal of Psychology, 68,* 98–106.

Eastman, Q. (2003, June 20). Crib death exoneration in new gene tests. *Science, 300,* 1858.

Easton, J., Schipper, L., & Shackelford, T. (2007). Morbid jealousy from an evolutionary psychological perspective. *Evolution and Human Behavior, 28,* 399–402.

Eaves, B. J., Feldman, N. H., Griffiths, T. L., & Shafto, P. (2016). Infant-directed speech is consistent with teaching. *Psychological Review, 123,* 758–771.

Ebersole, J., & Kapp, S. (2007). Stemming the tide of overrepresentation: Ensuring accurate certification of African American students in programs for the mentally retarded. *School Social Work Journal, 31,* 1–16.

Eccles, J., Templeton, J., & Barber, B. (2003). Adolescence and emerging adulthood: The critical passage ways to adulthood. In M. Bornstein & L. Davidson (Eds.), *Well-being: Positive development across the life course.* Mahwah, NJ: Lawrence Erlbaum.

Eckerman, C., & Peterman, K. (2001). Peers and infant social/communicative development. In G. Bremner & A. Fogel (Eds.), *Blackwell handbook of infant development* (pp. 326–350). Malden, MA: Blackwell Publishers.

Ecklund, K. (2012). Intersectionality of identity in children: A case study. *Professional Psychology: Research and Practice, 43*(3), 256–264. doi:10.1037/a0028654.

The Economics of Early Childhood Investments. (2014, December). Accessed online, 3/27/18; https://obamawhitehouse.archives.gov/sites/default/files/docs/the_economics_of_early_childhood_investments.pdf.

Edwards, C. P. (2000). Children's play in cross-cultural perspective: A new look at the Six Cultures study. *Cross-Cultural Research: The Journal of Comparative Social Science, 34,* 318–338.

Edwards, J. G. (2015). Assisted dying bill calls for stricter safeguards. *Lancet, 385,* 686–687.

Ehm, J., Lindberg, S., & Hasselhorn, M. (2014). Reading, writing, and math self-concept in elementary school children: Influence of dimensional comparison processes. *European Journal of Psychology of Education, 29,* 277–294.

Ehrensaft, M., Cohen, P., & Brown, J. (2003). Intergenerational transmission of partner violence: A 20-year prospective study. *Journal of Consulting & Clinical Psychology, 71,* 741–753.

Ehrensaft, M. K., Knous-Westfall, H. M., Cohen, P., & Chen, H. (2015). How does child abuse history influence parenting of the next generation? *Psychology of Violence, 5,* 16–25.

Eisbach, A. O. (2004). Children's developing awareness of diversity in people's trains of thought. *Child Development, 75,* 1694–1707.

Eisenberg, N., & Fabes, R. A. (2006). Emotion regulation and children's socioemotional competence. In L. Baler & C. S. Tamis-

LeMonda (Eds.), *Child psychology: A handbook of contemporary issues* (2nd ed.). Philadelphia, PA: Psychology Press.

Eisenberg, N., & Morris, A. (2004). Moral cognitions and prosocial responding in adolescence. In R. Lerner & L. Steinberg (Eds.), *Handbook of adolescent psychology*. New York: Wiley.

Eisenberg, N., & Valiente, C. (2002). Parenting and children's prosocial and moral development. In M. Bornstein (Ed.), *Handbook of parenting: Vol. 5: Practical issues in parenting*. Mahwah, NJ: Lawrence Erlbaum.

Eisenberg, N., Fabes, R., & Spinrad, T. (2006). Prosocial development. In *Handbook of child psychology: Vol. 3, Social, emotional, and personality development* (6th ed.). Hoboken, NJ: John Wiley & Sons Inc.

Eisenberg, N., Spinrad, T. L, & Smith, C. L. (2004). Emotion-related regulation: Its conceptualization, relations to social functioning, and socialization. In P. Philippot, & R. S. Feldman (Eds.), *The regulation of emotion*. Mahwah, NJ: Lawrence Erlbaum Associates.

Eisenberg, N., Spinrad, T. L., & Morris, A. (2014). Empathy-related responding in children. In M. Killen, J. G. Smetana, M. Killen, & J. G. Smetana (Eds.), *Handbook of moral development* (2nd ed.). New York: Psychology Press.

Eisenberg, N., Spinrad, T. L., & Sadovsky, A. (2006). Empathy-related responding in children. In M. Killen & J. G. Smetana (Eds.), *Handbook of moral development*. Mahwah, NJ: Lawrence Erlbaum Associates.

Eisenbraun, K. (2007). Violence in schools: Prevalence, prediction, and prevention. *Aggression and Violent Behavior*, *12*, 459–469.

Ekinci, B. (2014). The relationships among Sternberg's Triarchic Abilities, Gardner's multiple intelligences, and academic achievement. *Social Behavior and Personality*, *42*, 625–633.

El Ayoubi, M., Patkai, J., Bordarier, C., Desfrere, L., Moriette, G., Jarreau, P., & Zeitlin, J. (2016). Impact of fetal growth restriction on neurodevelopmental outcome at 2 years for extremely preterm infants: A single institution study. *Developmental Medicine & Child Neurology*, *58*, 1249–1256.

Eley, T., Liang, H., & Plomin, R. (2004). Parental familial vulnerability, family environment, and their interactions as predictors of depressive symptoms in adolescents. *Child & Adolescent Social Work Journal*, *21*, 298–306.

Elkind, D. (1978). The children's reality: Three developmental themes. In S. Coren & L. M. Ward (Eds.), *Sensation and perception*. Hillsdale, NJ: Erlbaum.

Elkind, D. (1984). *All grown up and no place to go*. Reading, MA: Addison-Wesley.

Elkins, D. (2009). Why humanistic psychology lost its power and influence in American psychology: Implications for advancing humanistic psychology. *Journal of Humanistic Psychology*, *49*, 267–291. http://search.ebscohost.com, doi:10.1177/0022167808323575.

Elliott, K., & Urquiza, A. (2006). Ethnicity, culture, and child maltreatment. *Journal of Social Issues*, *62*, 787–809.

Ellis, B. H., MacDonald, H. Z., Lincoln, A. K., & Cabral, H. J. (2008). Mental health of Somali adolescent refugees: The role of trauma, stress, and perceived discrimination. *Journal of Consulting and Clinical Psychology*, *76*, 184–193.

Ellis, B. J. (2004). Timing of pubertal maturation in girls: An integrated life history approach. *Psychological Bulletin*, *130*, 920–958.

Ellis, L. (2006, July). Gender differences in smiling: An evolutionary neuroandrogenic theory. *Physiology & Behavior*, *88*, 303–308.

Ellis, W., & Zarbatany, L. (2007). Peer group status as a moderator of group influence on children's deviant, aggressive, and prosocial behavior. *Child Development*, *78*, 1240–1254.

Else-Quest, N. M., & Morse, E. (2015). Ethnic variations in parental ethnic socialization and adolescent ethnic identity: A longitudinal study. *Cultural Diversity and Ethnic Minority Psychology*, *21*(1), 54–64. doi:10.1037/a0037820.

Elwert, F., & Christakis, N. A. (2008). The effect of widowhood on mortality by the causes of death of both spouses. *American Journal of Public Health*, *98*(11), 2092–2098. doi:10.2105/AJPH.2007.114348.

Emack, J., Kostaki, A., Walker, C., & Matthews, S. (2008). Chronic maternal stress affects growth, behaviour and hypothalamo-pituitary-adrenal function in juvenile offspring. *Hormones and Behavior*, *54*, 514–520.

Emilson, A., Folkesson, A., & Lindberg, I. M. (2016). Gender beliefs and embedded gendered values in preschool. *International Journal of Early Childhood*, *48*, 225–240.

Enard, W., Przeworski, M., Fisher, S. E., Lai, C. S., Wiebe, V., Kitano, T., Monaco, A. P., & Pääbo, S. (2002, August 22). Molecular evolution of FOXP2, a gene involved in speech and language. *Nature*, *418*(6900), 869–872. Accessed online, 6/10/18; https://www.nature.com/articles/nature01025.

Endrass, T., Schreiber, M., & Kathmann, N. (2012). Speeding up older adults: Age-effects on error processing in speed and accuracy conditions. *Biological Psychology*, *89*, 426–432.

Engels, R., Kerr, M., & Stattin, H. (2007). *Friends, lovers and groups: Key relationships in adolescence*. New York: John Wiley & Sons Ltd.

Enright, E. (2004, July & August). A house divided. *AARP Magazine*, pp. 54, 57.

Erikson, E. H. (1963). *Childhood and society*. New York: Norton.

Eriksson, L., & Mazerolle, P. (2015). A cycle of violence? Examining family-of-origin violence, attitudes, and intimate partner violence perpetration. *Journal of Interpersonal Violence*, *30*, 945–964.

Espelage, D. L., Low, S., Polanin, J. R., & Brown, E. C. (2015). Clinical trial of Second Step© middle-school program: Impact on aggression & victimization. *Journal of Applied Developmental Psychology*, *37*, 52–63.

Espinosa, M. P., & Kovářík, J. (2015). Prosocial behavior and gender. *Frontiers in Behavioral Neuroscience*, *9*, 45–55.

Estell, D. B., Jones, M. H., Pearl, R., Van Acker, R., Farmer, T. W., & Rodkin, P. C. (2008). Peer groups, popularity, and social preference: Trajectories of social functioning among students with and without learning disabilities. *Journal of Learning Disabilities*, *41*, 5–14.

Evans, G. W. (2004). The environment of childhood poverty. *American Psychologist*, *59*, 77–92.

Evans, R. (2009). A comparison of rural and urban older adults in Iowa on specific markers of successful aging. *Journal of Gerontological Social Work*, *52*, 423–438.

Evans, T., Whittingham, K., & Boyd, R. (2012). What helps the mother of a preterm infant become securely attached, responsive and well-adjusted? *Infant Behavior & Development*, *35*, 1–11.

Evenson, K. R. (2011). Towards an understanding of change in physical activity from pregnancy through postpartum. *Psychology of Sport and Exercise*, *12*, 36–45.

Everson, M., & Boat, B. (2002). The utility of anatomical dolls and drawings in child forensic interviews. *Memory and suggestibility in the forensic interview*. Mahwah, NJ: Lawrence Erlbaum Associates Publishers.

Ezzo, F., & Young, K. (2012). Child Maltreatment Risk Inventory: Pilot data for the Cleveland child abuse potential scale. *Journal of Family Violence*, *27*, 145–155.

Facchini, C., & Rampazi, R. (2009). No longer young, not yet old: Biographical uncertainty in late-adult temporality. *Time & Society*, *18*, 351–372.

Fagan, J., & Ployhart, R. E. (2015). The information processing foundations of human capital resources: Leveraging insights from information processing approaches to intelligence. *Human Resource Management Review*, *25*, 4–11.

Fagan, M. (2009). Mean length of utterance before words and grammar: Longitudinal trends and developmental implications of infant vocalizations. *Journal of Child Language*, *36*, 495–527. http://search.ebscohost.com, doi:10.1017/S0305000908009070.

Falck-Ytter, T., Gredebäck, G., & von Hofsten, C. (2006). Infants predict other people's action goals. *Nature Neuroscience*, *9*, 878–879.

Falco, M. (2012, July 3). Since IVF began, 5 million babies born. *CNN News*. Accessed online, 7/3/12; http://www.10news.com/health/31243126/detail.html.

Falcone, G. J., Malik, R., Dichgans, M., & Rosand, J. (2014). Current concepts and clinical applications of stroke genetics. *Lancet Neurology*, *13*, 405–418.

Falconier, M. K., Nussbeck, F., Bodenmann, G., Schneider, H., & Bradbury, T. (2015). Stress from daily hassles in couples: Its effects on intradyadic stress, relationship satisfaction, and physical and psychological well-being. *Journal of Marital and Family Therapy, 41*, 221–235.

Falk, D. (2004). Prelinguistic evolution in early hominins: Whence motherese? *Behavioral and Brain Sciences, 27*, 491–503.

Fanger, S., Frankel, L., & Hazen, N. (2012). Peer exclusion in preschool children's play: Naturalistic observations in a playground setting. *Merrill-Palmer Quarterly, 58*, 224–254.

Fantz, R. (1963). Pattern vision in newborn infants. *Science, 140*, 296–297.

Fantz, R. L. (1961). The origin of form perception. *Scientific American, 72*.

Farbiash, T., Berger, A., Atzaba-Poria, N., & Auerbach, J. G. (2014). Prediction of preschool aggression from DRD4 risk, parental ADHD symptoms, and home chaos. *Journal of Abnormal Child Psychology, 42*, 489–499.

Farrell, A., & Danby, S. (2015). How does homework 'work' for young children? Children's accounts of homework in their everyday lives. *British Journal of Sociology of Education, 36*(2), 250–269. doi:10.1080/01425692.2013.814532.

Farroni, T., Menon, E., Rigato, S., & Johnson, M. (2007). The perception of facial expressions in newborns. *European Journal of Developmental Psychology, 4*, 2–13.

Farver, J. M., Welles-Nystrom, B., Frosch, D. L., & Wimbarti, S. (1997). Toy stories: Aggression in children's narratives in the United States, Sweden, Germany, and Indonesia. *Journal of Cross-Cultural Psychology, 28*, 393–420.

Farzin, F., Charles, E., & Rivera, S. (2009). Development of multimodal processing in infancy. *Infancy, 14*, 563–578.

Fast, A. A., & Olson, K. R. (2017). Gender development in transgender preschool children. *Child Development*. Accessed online, 11/10/17; https://www.ncbi.nlm.nih.gov/pubmed/28439873.

Fayers, T., Crowley, T., Jenkins, J. M., & Cahill, D. J. (2003). Medical student awareness of sexual health is poor. *International Journal STD/AIDS, 14*, 386–389.

Federal Interagency Forum on Age-Related Statistics. (2000). *Older Americans 2000: Key indicators of wellbeing*. Hyattsville, MD: Author.

Fedewa, A. L., Black, W. W., & Ahn, S. (2015). Children and adolescents with same-gender parents: A meta-analytic approach in assessing outcomes. *Journal of GLBT Family Studies, 11*, 1–34.

Feeney, B. C., & Collins, N. L. (2001). Predictors of caregiving in adult intimate relationships: An attachment theoretical perspective. *Journal of Personality & Social Psychology, 80*, 972–994.

Feeney, B. C., & Collins, N. L. (2003). Motivations for caregiving in adult intimate relationships: Influences on caregiving behavior and relationship functioning. *Personality and Social Psychology Bulletin, 29*, 950–968.

Feigelman, W., Jordan, J., & Gorman, B. (2009). How they died, time since loss, and bereavement outcomes. *Omega: Journal of Death and Dying, 58*, 251–273.

Feinberg, T. E. (2000). The nested hierarchy of consciousness: A neurobiological solution to the problem of mental unity. *Neurocase, 6*, 75–81.

Feist, G., & Barron, F. (2003). Predicting creativity from early to late adulthood: Intellect, potential, and personality. *Journal of Research in Personality, 37*, 62–88.

Feldman, R. S. (2009). *The liar in your life*. New York: Twelve.

Feldman, R. S., Forrest, J. A., & Happ, B. R. (2002.) Self-presentation and verbal deception: Do self-presenters lie more? *Basic and Applied Social Psychology, 24*, 163–170.

Feldman, R., & Masalha, S. (2007). The role of culture in moderating the links between early ecological risk and young children's adaptation. *Development and Psychopathology, 19*, 1–21.

Feldman, R. S., Tomasian, J., & Coats, E. J. (1999). Adolescents' social competence and nonverbal deception abilities: Adolescents with higher social skills are better liars. *Journal of Nonverbal Behavior, 23*, 237–249.

Feldman, R., Sussman, A., & Zigler, E. (2004). Parental leave and work adaptation at the transition to parenthood: Individual,

marital, and social correlates. *Journal of Applied Developmental Psychology, 25*, 459–479.

Fell, J., & Williams, A. (2008). The effect of aging on skeletal-muscle recovery from exercise: Possible implications for aging athletes. *Journal of Aging and Physical Activity, 16*, 97–115.

Fergusson, D. M., Horwood, L., Boden, J., & Jenkin, G. (2007, March). Childhood social disadvantage and smoking in adulthood: Results of a 25-year longitudinal study. *Addiction, 102*, 475–482.

Fergusson, E., Maughan, B., & Golding, J. (2008). Which children receive grandparental care and what effect does it have? *Journal of Child Psychology and Psychiatry, 49*, 161–169.

Fernald, A. (2001). Hearing, listening, and understanding: Auditory development in infancy. In G. Bremner & A. Fogel (Eds.), *Blackwell handbook of infant development*. Malden, MA: Blackwell Publishers.

Fernald, A., Marchman, V. A., & Weisleder, A. (2013). SES differences in language processing skill and vocabulary are evident at 18 months. *Developmental Science, 16*(2), 234–248. doi:10.1111/desc.12019.

Fernald, A., & Morikawa, H. (1993). Common themes and cultural variations in Japanese and American mothers' speech to infants. *Child Development, 64*, 637–656.

Fernald, A., Taeschner, T., Dunn, J., Papous ek, M., Boysson-Bardies, B., & Fukui, I. (1989). A cross-language study of prosodic modifications in mothers' and fathers' speech to preverbal infants. *Journal of Child Language, 16*, 477–501.

Fernández, C. (2013). Mindful storytellers: Emerging pragmatics and theory of mind development. *First Language, 33*, 20–46.

Ferri, R., Novelli, L., & Bruni, O. (2017). Sleep structure and scoring from infancy to adolescence. In S. Nevšímalová, O.Bruni (Eds.), *Sleep disorders in children*. Cham, Switzerland: Springer International Publishing.

Ferry, A. L., Hespos, S. J., & Gentner, D. (2015). Prelinguistic relational concepts: Investigating analogical processing in infants. *Child Development*, Accessed online, 6/18/15; http://onlinelibrary.wiley.com/doi/10.1111/cdev.12381/abstract.

Feshbach, S., & Tangney, J. (2008). Television viewing and aggression: Some alternative perspectives. *Perspectives on Psychological Science, 3*, 387–389. Accessed online; http://search.ebscohost.com, doi: 10.1111/j. 1745-6924.2008.00086.x.

Festinger, L. (1954). A theory of social comparison processes. *Human Relations, 7*, 117–140.

Fetterman, D. M. (2005). Empowerment evaluation: From the digital divide to academic distress. In D. Fetterman & A. Wandersman (Eds.), *Empowerment evaluation principles in practice*. New York: Guilford Press.

Fiedler, N. L. (2012). Gender (sex) differences in response to prenatal lead exposure. In M. Lewis L. Kestler (Eds.), *Gender differences in prenatal substance exposure*. Washington, DC: American Psychological Association.

Field, M. J., & Behrman, R. E. (Eds.). (2003). *When children die*. Washington, DC: National Academies Press.

Field, T., Diego, M., & Hernandez-Reif, M. (2009). Depressed mothers' infants are less responsive to faces and voices. *Infant Behavior & Development, 32*, 239–244.

Field, T., Diego, M., & Hernandez-Reif, M. (2008). Prematurity and potential predictors. *International Journal of Neuroscience, 118*, 277–289.

Figley, C. R. (1973). Child density and the marital relationship. *Journal of Marriage and the Family, 35*, 272–282.

Finer, L. B., and Philbin, J. M. (2013). Sexual initiation, contraceptive use, and pregnancy among young adolescents. *Pediatrics, 131*(5): 886–891.

Finer, L. B. & Zolna, M. R. (2016). Declines in unintended pregnancy in the United States, 2008–2011. *New England Journal of Medicine, 374*, 843–852.

Finn, C. (2008). Neuropsychiatric aspects of genetic disorders. *Psychiatric genetics: Applications in clinical practice*. Arlington, VA: American Psychiatric Publishing, Inc.

Finnegan, L. P., & Kandall, S. R. (2008). Perinatal substance abuse. In M. Galanter, H. D. Kleber (Eds.), *The American Psychiatric*

Publishing textbook of substance abuse treatment (pp. 565–580). Arlington, VA: American Psychiatric Publishing, Inc.

Fiori, K. L., & Denckla, C. A. (2015). Friendship and happiness among middle-aged adults. In M. Demir & M. Demir (Eds.), *Friendship and happiness: Across the life-span and cultures.* New York: Springer Science + Business Media.

Fischer, K. W., & Rose, S. P. (1995). Concurrent cycles in the dynamic development of brain and behavior. *Newsletter of the Society for Research in Child Development*, p. 16.

Fischer, N. (2012). Mother-infant attachment: The demystification of an enigma. In S. Akhtar (Ed.), *The mother and her child: Clinical aspects of attachment, separation, and loss.* Lanham, MD: Jason Aronson.

Fisher-Thompson, D. (2017). Contributions of look duration and gaze shift patterns to infants' novelty preferences. *Infancy, 22,* 190–222.

Fisher, C. B. (2004). Informed consent and clinical research involving children and adolescents: Implications of the revised APA Ethics Code and HIPAA. *Journal of Clinical Child & Adolescent Psychology, 33,* 832–839.

Fiske, S. T., & North, M. S. (2015). Measures of stereotyping and prejudice: Barometers of bias. In G. J. Boyle, D. H. Saklofske, G. Matthews (Eds.), *Measures of personality and social psychological constructs.* San Diego, CA: Elsevier Academic Press.

Fiske, S., & Yamamoto, M. (2005). Coping with rejection: Core social motives across cultures. In *The social outcast: Ostracism, social exclusion, rejection, and bullying* (pp. 185–198). New York: Psychology Press.

Fitzgerald, D., & White, K. (2002). Linking children's social worlds: Perspective-taking in parent-child and peer contexts. *Social Behavior & Personality, 31,* 509–522.

Fitzgerald, H. (2006). Cross cultural research during infancy: Methodological considerations. *Infant Mental Health Journal, 27,* 612–617.

Fitzgerald, P. (2008). A neurotransmitter system theory of sexual orientation. *Journal of Sexual Medicine, 5,* 746–748.

Fitzpatrick, E. M., Al-Essa, R. S., Whittingham, J., & Fitzpatrick, J. (2017). Characteristics of children with unilateral hearing loss. *International Journal of Audiology, 56,* 819–828.

Flanigan, J. (2005, July 3). Immigrants benefit U.S. economy now as ever. *Los Angeles Times.*

Fleer, M. (2017). Digital role-play: The changing conditions of children's play in preschool settings. *Mind, Culture, and Activity, 24,* 3–17.

Fleer, M., González Rey, F., & Veresov, N. (2017). *Perezhivanie, emotions and subjectivity: Advancing Vygotsky's legacy.* New York: Springer Science + Business Media.

Fling, B. W., Walsh, C. M., Bangert, A. S., Reuter-Lorenz, P. A., Welsh, R. C., & Seidler, R. D. (2011). Differential callosal contributions to bimanual control in young and older adults. *Journal of Cognitive Neuroscience, 23,* 2171–2185.

Flom, R., & Bahrick, L. (2007). The development of infant discrimination of affect in multimodal and unimodal stimulation: The role of intersensory redundancy. *Developmental Psychology, 43,* 238–252.

Floros, G., Siomos, K., Antoniadis, D., Bozikas, V., Hyphantis, T., & Garyfallos, G. (2015). Examining personality factors and character defenses assists in the differentiation between college students with Internet addiction and unaffected controls. *Personality and Individual Differences, 86,* 238–242. doi:10.1016/j.paid.2015.05.030.

Florsheim, P. (2003). Adolescent romantic and sexual behavior: What we know and where we go from here. In P. Florsheim (Ed.), *Adolescent romantic relations and sexual behavior: Theory, research, and practical implications.* Mahwah, NJ: Lawrence Erlbaum.

Flouri, E., & Midouhas, E. (2017). Environmental adversity and children's early trajectories of problem behavior: The role of harsh parental discipline. *Journal of Family Psychology, 31,* 234–243.

Fok, W. Y., Chan, L. Y., Tsui, M. H., Leung, T. N., Lau, T. K., & Chung, T. K. (2006). When to induce labor for post-term? A study of induction at 41 weeks versus 42 weeks. *European Journal of Obstetrics & Gynecology and Reproductive Biology, 125,* 206–210. doi: 10.1016/j.ejogrb.2005.07.005.

Folbre, N. (2012, July 2). Price tags for parents. *New York Times.* Accessed online, 7/7/12, *Economix;* http://economix.blogs.nytimes.com/2012//07/02/price-tags-for-parents.

Food and Drug Administration. (2003). Birth control guide. Accessed online, 4/1/06; http://www.fda.gov/fdac/features/1997/babyguide2.pdf.

Foroud, A., & Whishaw, I. Q. (2012). The consummatory origins of visually guided reaching in human infants: A dynamic integration of whole-body and upper-limb movements. *Behavioural Brain Research, 231,* 343–355.

Fortuin, J., van Geel, M., & Vedder, P. (2015). Peer influences on internalizing and externalizing problems among adolescents: A longitudinal social network analysis. *Journal of Youth and Adolescence, 44,* 887–897.

Fowler, J. W., & Dell, M. L. (2006). Stages of faith from infancy through adolescence: Reflections on three decades of faith development theory. In E. C. Roehlkepartain, P. E. King, L. Wagener, & P. L. Benson (Eds.), *The handbook of spiritual development in childhood and adolescence.* Thousand Oaks, CA: Sage Publications.

Fowler, R. C. (2017). Reframing the debate about the relationship between learning and development: An effort to resolve dilemmas and reestablish dialogue in a fractured field. *Early Childhood Education Journal, 45,* 155–162.

Fowler, W., Ogston, K., Roberts, G., & Swenson, A. (2006). The effects of early language enrichment. *Early Child Development and Care, 176*(8), 777–815. doi:10.1080/03004430500207211.

Fox, M., Cacciatore, J., & Lacasse, J. R. (2014). Child death in the United States: Productivity and the economic burden of parental grief. *Death Studies, 38,* 597–602.

Fraley, R. C., & Spieker, S. J. (2003). Are infant attachment patterns continuously or categorically distributed? A taxometric analysis of strange situation behavior. *Developmental Psychology, 39,* 387–404.

Frankel, L. (2002). "I've never thought about it": Contradictions and taboos surrounding American males' experiences of first ejaculation (semenarche). *Journal of Men's Studies, 11,* 37–54.

Frankenburg, W. K., Dodds, J., Archer, P., Shapiro, H., & Bresnick, B. (1992). The Denver II: A major revision and restandardization of the Denver Developmental Screening Test. *Pediatrics, 89,* 91–97.

Fransen, M., Meertens, R., & Schrander-Stumpel, C. (2006). Communication and risk presentation in genetic counseling: Development of a checklist. *Patient Education and Counseling, 61,* 126–133.

Frawley, T. (2008). Gender schema and prejudicial recall: How children misremember, fabricate, and distort gendered picture book information. *Journal of Research in Childhood Education, 22,* 291–303.

Frazier, L. M., Grainger, D. A., Schieve, L. A., & Toner, J. P. (2004). Follicle-stimulating hormone and estradiol levels independently predict the success of assisted reproductive technology treatment. *Fertility and Sterility, 82,* 834–840.

Fredriksen, K., Rhodes, J., Reddy, R., & Way, N. (2004). Sleepless in Chicago: Tracking the effects of adolescent sleep loss during the middle school years. *Child Development, 75,* 84–95.

Freedman, A. M., & Ellison, S. (2004, May 6). Testosterone patch for women shows promise. *Wall Street Journal,* pp. A1, B2.

Freedman, D. G. (1979, January). Ethnic differences in babies. *Human Nature,* pp. 15–20.

Freeman, E., Sammel, M., & Liu, L. (2004). Hormones and menopausal status as predictors of depression in women in transition to menopause. *Archives of General Psychiatry, 61,* 62–70.

Freeman, J. M. (2007). Beware: The misuse of technology and the law of unintended consequences. *Neurotherapeutics, 4,* 549–554.

Frerking, B. (October, 2006). I'm gonna keep that gray. *Slate.* Accessed online; http://www.slate.com/id/2147054/.

Freud, S. (1920). *A general introduction to psychoanalysis.* New York: Boni & Liveright.

Freud, S. (1922/1959). *Group psychology and the analysis of the ego.* London: Hogarth.

Frías, M. T., Shaver, P. R., & Mikulincer, M. (2015). Measures of adult attachment and related constructs. In G. J. Boyle, D. H. Saklofske, & G. Matthews (Eds.), *Measures of personality and social psychological constructs.* San Diego, CA: Elsevier Academic Press.

Friborg, O., Barlaug, D., Martinussen, M., Rosenvinge, J. H., & Hjemdal, O. (2005). Resilience in relation to personality and intelligence. *International Journal of Methods in Psychiatric Research, 14,* 29–42.

Fricke, S., Burgoyne, K., Bowyer-Crane, C., Kyriacou, M., Zosimidou, A., Maxwell, L., & . . . Hulme, C. (2017). The efficacy of early language intervention in mainstream school settings: A randomized controlled trial. *Journal of Child Psychology and Psychiatry, 58*(10), 1141–1151. doi:10.1111/jcpp.12737.

Frie, R. (2014). What is cultural psychoanalysis? Psychoanalytic anthropology and the interpersonal tradition. *Contemporary Psychoanalysis, 50,* 371–394.

Friedlander, L. J., Connolly, J. A., Pepler, D. J., & Craig, W. M. (2007). Biological, familial, and peer influences on dating in early adolescence. *Archives of Sexual Behavior, 36,* 821–830.

Friedman, L., Kahn, J., Middleman, A., Rosenthal, S., & Zimet, G. (2006, October). Human papillomavirus (HPV) vaccine: A position statement of the society for adolescent medicine. *Journal of Adolescent Health, 39,* 620–620.

Friedman, S., Heneghan, A., & Rosenthal, M. (2009). Characteristics of women who do not seek prenatal care and implications for prevention. *Journal of Obstetric, Gynecologic, & Neonatal Nursing: Clinical Scholarship for the Care of Women, Childbearing Families, & Newborns, 38,* 174–181.

Friedrich, J. (2014). Vygotsky's idea of psychological tools. In A. Yasnitsky, R. van der Veer, & M. Ferrari (Eds.), *The Cambridge handbook of cultural-historical psychology.* New York: Cambridge University Press.

Fritz, G., & Rockney, R. (2004). Summary of the practice parameter for the assessment and treatment of children and adolescents with enuresis. *Work Group on Quality Issues; Journal of the American Academy of Child & Adolescent Psychiatry, 43,* 123–125.

Froidevaux, A., Hirschi, A., & Wang, M. (2016). The role of mattering as an overlooked key challenge in retirement planning and adjustment. *Journal of Vocational Behavior, 94,* 57–69.

Frome, P., Alfeld, C., Eccles, J., & Barber, B. (2006, August). Why don't they want a male-dominated job? An investigation of young women who changed their occupational aspirations. *Educational Research and Evaluation, 12,* 359–372.

Fry, D. (2005). Rough-and-tumble social play in humans. In *The nature of play: Great apes and humans.* New York: Guilford Press.

Fu, G., Xu, F., Cameron, C., Heyman, G., & Lee, K. (2007, March). Cross-cultural differences in children's choices, categorizations, and evaluations of truths and lies. *Developmental Psychology, 43*(2), 278–293.

Fu, X., & Heaton, T. (2008). Racial and educational homogamy: 1980 to 2000. *Sociological Perspectives, 51,* 735–758.

Fujisawa, T. X., & Shinohara, K. (2011). Sex differences in the recognition of emotional prosody in late childhood and adolescence. *Journal of Physiological Science, 61,* 429–435.

Fulcher, M., Sutfin, E. L., & Patterson, C. J. (2008). Individual differences in gender development: Associations with parental sexual orientation, attitudes, and division of labor. *Sex Roles, 58,* 330–341.

Fuligni, A. J. (2012). The intersection of aspirations and resources in the development of children from immigrant families. In C. Coll & A. Marks (Eds.), *The immigrant paradox in children and adolescents: Is becoming American a developmental risk?* Washington, DC: American Psychological Association.

Fuligni, A., & Yoshikawa, H. (2003). Socioeconomic resources, parenting, and child development among immigrant families. In M. Bornstein & R. Bradley (Eds.), *Socioeconomic status, parenting, and child development.* Mahwah, NJ: Lawrence Erlbaum Associates.

Funk, L. (2010). Prioritizing parental autonomy: Adult children's accounts of feeling responsible and supporting aging parents. *Journal of Aging Studies, 24,* 57–64.

Furman, W., & Shaffer, L. (2003). The role of romantic relationships in adolescent development. In P. Florsheim (Ed.), *Adolescent romantic relations and sexual behavior: Theory, research, and practical implications.* Mahwah, NJ: Lawrence Erlbaum.

Fuso, A., Nicolia, V., Ricceri, L., Cavallaro, R. A., Isopi, E., Mangia, F., et al. (2012). S-adenosylmethionine reduces the progress of the Alzheimer-like features induced by B-vitamin deficiency in mice. *Neurobiology of Aging, 33,* e1–e16.

Gabler, E. (2011). Council bans sale of crib bumper pads in Chicago. Accessed online; www.chicagotribune.com.

Gagneux, P. (2016). *Assisted reproductive technologies: Evolution of human niche construction?* Paper presented at the annual meeting of the American Association for the Advancement of Science. Washington, DC.

Galambos, N., Leadbeater, B., & Barker, E. (2004). Gender differences in and risk factors for depression in adolescence: A 4-year longitudinal study. *International Journal of Behavioral Development, 28,* 16–25.

Galic, Z. (2007). Psychological consequences of unemployment: The moderating role of education. *Review of Psychology, 14,* 25–34.

Gallotta, M. C., Emerenziani, G. P., Franciosi, E., Meucci, M., Guidetti, L., & Baldari, C. (2015). Acute physical activity and delayed attention in primary school students. *Scandinavian Journal of Medicine & Science in Sports, 25,* e331–e338.

Galluccio, M., & Safran, J. D. (2015). Mindfulness-based training for negotiators: Fostering resilience in the face of stress. In M. Galluccio (Ed.), *Handbook of international negotiation: Interpersonal, intercultural, and diplomatic perspectives* (pp. 209–226). Cham, Switzerland: Springer International Publishing. doi:10.1007/978-3-319-10687-8_16.

Gallup Poll. (2004). How many children? *The Gallup Poll Monthly.*

Galvao, T. F., Silva, M. T., Zimmermann, I. R., Souza, K. M., Martins, S. S., & Pereira, M. G. (2014). Pubertal timing in girls and depression: A systematic review. *Journal of Affective Disorders, 155,* 13–19.

Gamino, L. A., & Ritter, R. R. (2012). Death competence: An ethical imperative. *Death Studies, 36,* 23–40.

Garcia, C., Baker, S., DeMayo, R., & Brown, G. (2005). Gestalt educational therapy. In *Gestalt therapy: History, theory, and practice.* Thousand Oaks, CA: Sage Publications, Inc.

Garcia-Moreno, C., Heise, L., Jansen, H. A. F. M., Ellsberg, M., & Watts, C. (2005, November 25). Violence against women. *Science, 310,* 1282–1283.

Gardner, H., & Moran, S. (2006). The science of multiple intelligences theory: A response to Lynn Waterhouse. *Educational Psychologist, 41,* 227–232.

Gardner, M. K. (2011). Theories of intelligence. In M. A. Bray, & T. J. Kehle (Eds.), *The Oxford handbook of school psychology.* New York: Oxford University Press.

Gardner, P. (2007). Parent involvement in the college recruiting process: To what extent? Research Brief 2-2007. Collegiate Employment Research Institute, Michigan State University.

Garlick, D. (2003). Integrating brain science research with intelligence research. *Current Directions in Psychological Science, 12,* 185–189.

Gartrell, N., & Bos, H. (2010). US national longitudinal lesbian family study: Psychological adjustment of 17-year-old adolescents. *Pediatrics, 126,* 28–36.

Gartstein, M. A., Prokasky, A., Bell, M. A., Calkins, S., Bridgett, D. J., Braungart-Rieker, J., & . . . Seamon, E. (2017). Latent profile and cluster analysis of infant temperament: Comparisons across person-centered approaches. *Developmental Psychology, 53,* 1811–1825.

Gates, G. J. (2013, February). *LGBT parenting in the United States.* Los Angeles: Williams Institute.

Gattringer, T., Enzinger, C., Ropele, S., Gorani, F., Petrovic, K., Schmidt, R., et al. (2012). Vascular risk factors, white matter hyperintensities and hippocampal volume in normal elderly individuals. *Dementia and Geriatric Cognitive Disorders, 33*(1), 29–34. doi:10.1159/000336052.

Gatz, M. (1997, August). Variations of depression in later life. Paper presented at the Annual Convention of the American Psychological Association, Chicago.

Gauvain, M. (1998). Cognitive development in social and cultural context. *Current Directions in Psychological Science, 7*, 188–194.

Gavin, T., & Myers, A. (2003). Characteristics, enrollment, attendance, and dropout patterns of older adults in beginner Tai-Chi and line-dancing programs. *Journal of Aging & Physical Activity, 11*, 123–141.

Gawande, A. (2007, April 30). The way we age now. *New Yorker*, pp. 49–59.

Geary, D. C. (2006). An evolutionary perspective on sexual and intimate relationships. *Sex and sexuality, Vol 2: Sexual function and dysfunction* (pp. 67–86). Westport, CT: Praeger Publishers/Greenwood Publishing Group.

Geary, D. C. (2015). Social competition and the evolution of fluid intelligence. In S. Goldstein, D. Princiotta, & J. A. Naglieri (Eds.), *Handbook of intelligence: Evolutionary theory, historical perspective, and current concepts.* New York: Springer Science + Business Media.

Geary, D. C., & Berch, D. B. (2016). *Evolutionary perspectives on child development and education.* Cham, Switzerland: Springer International Publishing.

Geirsdottir, O. G., Arnarson, A., Ramel, A., Briem, K., Jonsson, P. V., & Thorsdottir, I. (2015). Muscular strength and physical function in elderly adults 6–18 months after a 12-week resistance exercise program. *Scandinavian Journal of Public Health, 43*, 76–82.

Gelman, S. A., Taylor, M. G., & Nguyen, S. (2004). Mother-child conversations about gender. *Monographs of the Society for Research in Child Development, 69*.

General Social Survey. (1998). *National opinion research center.* Chicago: University of Chicago.

Genetics Home Reference. (2017). *Your guide to understanding genetic conditions.* Washington, DC: US National Library of Medicine. Accessed online, 10/25/17; https://ghr.nlm.nih.gov/.

Genevro, J. L., & Miller, T. L. (2010). The emotional and economic costs of bereavement in health care settings. *Psychologica Belgica, 50*, 69–88.

Genovese, J. (2006). Piaget, pedagogy, and evolutionary psychology. *Evolutionary Psychology, 4*, 127–137.

George, A. (2017). Ohio and Maryland only states to ban baby bumpers. Accessed online; http://wkbn.com.

Gergely, G. (2007). The social construction of the subjective self: The role of affect-mirroring, markedness, and ostensive communication in self-development. In *Developmental science and psychoanalysis: Integration and innovation.* London: Karnac Books.

Gerressu, M., Mercer, C., Graham, C., Wellings, K., & Johnson, A. (2008). Prevalence of masturbation and associated factors in a British national probability survey. *Archives of Sexual Behavior, 37*, 266–278.

Gershoff, E. T. (2002). Parental corporal punishment and associated child behaviors and experiences: A meta-analytic and theoretical review. *Psychological Bulletin, 128*, 539–579.

Gershoff, E. T., Lansford, J. E., Sexton, H. R., Davis-Kean, P., & Sameroff, A. J. (2012). Longitudinal links between spanking and children's externalizing behaviors in a national sample of White, Black, Hispanic, and Asian American families. *Clinical Psychology Review, 23*, 197–224.

Geschwind, D., & Iacoboni, M. (2007). Structural and functional asymmetries of the human frontal lobes. In B. L. Miller & J. L. Cummings (Eds.), *The human frontal lobes: Functions and disorders.* New York: Guilford Press.

Gesell, A. L. (1946). The ontogenesis of infant behavior. In L. Carmichael (Ed.), *Manual of child psychology.* New York: Harper.

Ghisletta, P., Kennedy, K., Rodrigue, K., Lindenberger, U., & Raz, N. (2010). Adult age differences and the role of cognitive resources in perceptual-motor skill acquisition: Application of a multilevel negative exponential model. *Journals of Gerontology: Series B: Psychological Sciences and Social Sciences, 65B*, 163–173.

Ghule, M., Balaiah, D., & Joshi, B. (2007). Attitude towards premarital sex among rural college youth in Maharashtra, India. *Sexuality & Culture, 11*, 1–17.

Gibbs, N. (2002, April 15). Making time for a baby. *Time*, pp. 48–54.

Gibson, E. J., & Walk, R. D. (1960). The "visual cliff." *Scientific American, 202*, 64–71.

Giedd, J. N. (2012). The digital revolution and adolescent brain evolution. *Journal of Adolescent Health, 51*, 101–105.

Gifford-Smith, M., & Brownell, C. (2003). Childhood peer relationships: Social acceptance, friendships, and peer networks. *Journal of School Psychology, 41*, 235–284.

Gilbert, D. T., Miller, A. G., & Ross, L. (1998). Speeding with Ned: A personal view of the correspondence bias. In J. M. Darley, J. Cooper et al. (Eds.), *Attribution and social interaction: The legacy of Edward E. Jones.* Washington, DC: American Psychological Association.

Gilbert, S. (2004, March 16). New clues to women veiled in black. *New York Times*, p. D1.

Gillham, A., Law, A., & Hickey, L. (2010). A psychodynamic perspective. In C. Cupitt (Ed.), *Reaching out: The psychology of assertive outreach.* New York, NY: Routledge/Taylor & Francis Group.

Gilligan, C. (1982). *In a different voice: Psychological theory and women's development.* Cambridge, MA: Harvard University Press.

Gilligan, C. (1987). Adolescent development reconsidered. In C. E. Irwin (Ed.), *Adolescent social behavior and health.* San Francisco: Jossey-Bass.

Gilligan, C., Lyons, N. P., & Hammer, T. J. (Eds.). (1990). *Making connections.* Cambridge, MA: Harvard University Press.

Gillmore, M., Gilchrist, L., Lee, J., & Oxford, M. (2006, August). Women who gave birth as unmarried adolescents: Trends in substance use from adolescence to adulthood. *Journal of Adolescent Health, 39*, 237–243.

Ginzberg, E. (1972). Toward a theory of occupational choice: A restatement. *Vocational Guidance Quarterly, 12*, 10–14.

Gitlin, L., Reever, K., Dennis, M., Mathieu, E., & Hauck, W. (2006, October). Enhancing quality of life of families who use adult day services: Short- and long-term effects of the Adult Day Services Plus Program. *The Gerontologist, 46*, 630–639.

Gitto, E., Aversa, S., Salpietro, C., Barberi, I., Arrigo, T., Trimarchi, G., et al. (2012). Pain in neonatal intensive care: Role of melatonin as an analgesic antioxidant. *Journal of Pineal Research: Molecular, Biological, Physiological and Clinical Aspects of Melatonin, 52*, 291–295.

Glaser, D. (2012). Effects of child maltreatment on the developing brain. In M. Garralda & J. Raynaud (Eds.), *Brain, mind, and developmental psychopathology in childhood.* Lanham, MD: Jason Aronson.

Glasson, E. J., Jacques, A., Wong, K., Bourke, J., & Leonard, H. (2016). Improved survival in Down syndrome over the last 60 years and the impact of perinatal factors in recent decades. *Journal of Pediatrics, 169*, 214–220.

Gleason, J. B., & Ely, R. (2002). Gender differences in language development. In A. McGillicuddy-De Lisi & R. De Lisi (Eds.), *Biology, society, and behavior: The development of sex differences in cognition* (pp. 127–154). Westport, CT: Ablex Publishing.

Gleason, J. B., Perlmann, R. U., Ely, R., & Evans, D. W. (1994). The babytalk register: Parents' use of diminutives. In J. L. Sokolov & C. E. Snow (Eds.), *Handbook of research in language development using CHILDES.* Mahwah, NJ: Lawrence Erlbaum.

Gleason, M., Iida, M., & Bolger, N. (2003). Daily supportive equity in close relationships. *Personality & Social Psychology Bulletin, 29*, 1036–1045.

Gleitman, L., & Papafragou, A. (2005). Language and thought. In *The Cambridge handbook of thinking and reasoning.* New York: Cambridge University Press.

Gliga, T., Elsabbagh, M., Andravizou, A., & Johnson, M. (2009). Faces attract infants' attention in complex displays. *Infancy, 14*, 550–562.

Glina, S., Cohen, D. J., & Vieira, M. (2014). Diagnosis of erectile dysfunction. *Current Opinion in Psychiatry, 27*, 394–399.

Goble, P., Eggum-Wilkens, N. D., Bryce, C. I., Foster, S. A., Hanish, L. D., Martin, C. L., & Fabes, R. A. (2017). The transition from preschool to first grade: A transactional model of development. *Journal of Applied Developmental Psychology, 49*, 55–67.

Goetz, A., & Shackelford, T. (2006). Modern application of evolutionary theory to psychology: Key concepts and clarifications. *American Journal of Psychology, 119*, 567–584.

Gogtay, N., Sporn, A., Clasen, L. S., Nugent, T. I., Greenstein, D., Nicolson, R., & ... Rapoport, J. L. (2004). Comparison of Progressive Cortical Gray Matter Loss in Childhood-Onset Schizophrenia with That in Childhood-Onset Atypical Psychoses. *Archives of General Psychiatry, 61*(1), 17–22. doi:10.1001/archpsyc.61.1.17

Goldapple, K., Segal, Z., Garson, C., Lau, M., Bieling, P., Kennedy, S., & Mayberg, H. (2004). Modulation of cortical-limbic pathways in major depression: treatment-specific effects of cognitive behavior therapy. *Archives of General Psychiatry, 61*(1), 34–41.

Goldberg, A. E. (2004). But do we need universal grammar? Comment on Lidz et al. *Cognition, 94*, 77–84.

Goldberg, A. E. (2010) *Gay and lesbian parents and their children: Research on the family life cycle.* Washington, DC: American Psychological Association.

Goldberg, W. A. (2014). *Father time: The social clock and the timing of fatherhood.* New York: Palgrave Macmillan.

Goldfield, G. S. (2012). Making access to TV contingent on physical activity: Effects on liking and relative reinforcing value of TV and physical activity in overweight and obese children. *Journal of Behavioral Medicine, 35*, 1–7.

Goldman, D., & Domschke, K. (2014). Making sense of deep sequencing. *International Journal of Neuropsychopharmacology, 17*, 1717–1725.

Goldman, R. (1964). *Religious thinking form childhood to adolescence.* London: Routledge & Kegan Paul.

Goldney, R. D. (2012). Neither euthanasia nor suicide, but rather assisted death. *Australian and New Zealand Journal of Psychiatry, 46*, 185–187.

Goldschmidt, L., Richardson, G., Willford, J., & Day, N. (2008). Prenatal marijuana exposure and intelligence test performance at age 6. *Journal of the American Academy of Child & Adolescent Psychiatry, 47*, 254–263.

Goldsmith, S. K., Pellman, T. C., Kleinman, A. M., & Bunney, W. E. (2002). *Reducing suicide: A national imperative.* Washington, DC: National Academies Press.

Goldston, D. B. (2003). *Measuring suicidal behavior and risk in children and adolescents.* Washington, DC: American Psychological Association.

Golmier, I., Cehbat, J. C., & Gelinas-Chebat, C. (2007). Can cigarette warnings counterbalance effects of smoking scenes in movies? *Psychological Reports, 100*, 3–18.

Golombok, S., Golding, J., Perry, B., Burston, A., Murray, C., Mooney-Somers, J., & Stevens, M. (2003). Children with lesbian parents: A community study. *Developmental Psychology, 39*, 20–33.

Golombok, S., & Tasker, F. (1996). Do parents influence the sexual orientation of their children? Findings from a longitudinal study of lesbian families. *Developmental Psychology, 32*, 3–11.

Golub, S., & Langer, E. (2007). Challenging assumptions about adult development: Implications for the health of older adults. In *Handbook of health psychology and aging* (pp. 9–29). New York: Guilford Press.

Golumb, C. (2002). *Child art in context.* Washington, DC: American Psychological Association.

Golumb, C. (2003). *The child's creation of a pictorial world* (2nd ed.). Mahwah, NJ: Erlbaum.

Gomez-Nicola, D., & Perry, V. H. (2015). Microglial dynamics and role in the healthy and diseased brain: A paradigm of functional plasticity. *The Neuroscientist, 21*, 169–184.

Gommans, R., Segers, E., Burk, W. J., & Scholte, R. J. (2015). The role of perceived popularity on collaborative learning: A dyadic perspective. *Journal of Educational Psychology, 107*, 599–608.

Göncü, A., & Gauvain, M. (2012). Sociocultural approaches to educational psychology: Theory, research, and application. In K. R. Harris, S. Graham, T. Urdan, C. B. McCormick, G. M. Sinatra, J. Sweller (Eds.), *APA educational psychology handbook, Vol 1: Theories, constructs, and critical issues* (pp. 125–154). Washington, DC: American Psychological Association. doi:10.1037/13273-006.

Gondolf, E. W. (1985). Fighting for control: A clinical assessment of men who batter. *Social Casework, 66*, 48–54.

Gonnerman, M. E., Jr., Lutz, G. M., Yehieli, M., & Meisinger, B. K. (2008). Religion and health connection: A study of African American, Protestant Christians. *Journal of Health Care for the Poor and Underserved, 19*, 193–199.

González, C., & Gándara, P. (2005). Why we like to call ourselves Latinas. *Journal of Hispanic Higher Education, 4*, 392–398.

Goodman, E., Huang, B., Schafer-Kalkhoff, T., & Adler, N. E. (2007). Perceived socioeconomic status: A new type of identity which influences adolescents' self-rated health. *The Journal of Adolescent Health: Official Publication of the Society for Adolescent Medicine, 41*, 479–487.

Goodman, G., & Melinder, A. (2007, February). Child witness research and forensic interviews of young children: A review. *Legal and Criminological Psychology, 12*, 1–19.

Goodman, G., & Quas, J. (2008). Repeated interviews and children's memory: It's more than just how many. *Current Directions in Psychological Science, 17*, 386–390.

Goodman, J. S., Schlossberg, N. K., & Anderson, M. L. (2006). *Counseling adults in transition: Linking practice with theory.* New York: Springer.

Goodnough, A., & Atkinson, S. (2016, April 30). A potent side effect to the Flint water crisis: Mental health problems. *New York Times*, A16.

Goold, S. D., Williams, B., & Arnold, R. M. (2000). Conflicts regarding decisions to limit treatment: A differential diagnosis. *JAMA: The Journal of the American Medical Association, 283*, 909–914.

Gopinath, B., Schneider, J., Hickson, L., McMahon, C. M., Burlutsky, G., Leeder, S. R., et al. (2012). Hearing handicap, rather than measured hearing impairment, predicts poorer quality of life over 10 years in older adults. *Maturitas, 72*, 146–151.

Gopnik, A. (2012, January 28). What's wrong with the teenage mind? *Wall Street Journal*, pp. C1–C2.

Gopnik, A. I., O'Grady, S., Lucas, C. G., Griffiths, T. L., Wente, A., et al. (2017). Changes in cognitive flexibility and hypothesis search across human life history from childhood to adolescence to adulthood. *PNAS, 114*, 892–899.

Gordon, I., Pratt, M., Bergunde, K., Zagoory-Sharon, O., & Feldman, R. (2017). Testosterone, oxytocin, and the development of human parental care. *Hormones and Behavior, 93*, 184–192.

Gorman, A. (2010, January 7). UCLA study says legalizing undocumented immigrants would help the economy. *Los Angeles Times*.

Gostin, L. (2006, April). Physician-assisted suicide A legitimate medical practice? *JAMA: The Journal of the American Medical Association, 295*, 1941–1943.

Gottlieb, G., & Blair, C. (2004). How early experience matters in intellectual development in the case of poverty. *Preventive Science, 5*, 245–252.

Gould, R. L. (1978). *Transformations: Growth and change in adult life.* New York: Simon & Schuster.

Gould, R. L. (1980). Transformations during adult years. In R. Smelzer & E. Erickson (Eds.), *Themes of love and work in adulthood.* Cambridge, MA: Harvard University Press.

Gow, A., Pattie, A., Whiteman, M., Whalley, L., & Deary, I. (2007). Social support and successful aging: Investigating the relationships between lifetime cognitive change and life satisfaction. *Journal of Individual Differences, 28*, 103–115.

Graber, J. A. (2004). Internalizing problems during adolescence. In R. M. Lerner & L. Steinberg (Eds.), *Handbook of adolescent psychology.* (2nd ed.). New York: Wiley.

Grace, D., David, B., & Ryan, M. (2008). Investigating preschoolers' categorical thinking about gender through imitation, attention, and the use of self-categories. *Child Development, 79*, 1928–1941.

Grady, D. (2006, November). Management of menopausal symptoms. *New England Journal of Medicine, 355*, 2338–2347.

Graf Estes, K. (2014). Learning builds on learning: Infants' use of native language sound patterns to learn words. *Journal of Experimental Child Psychology, 126*, 313–327.

Graf, E., Theakston, A., Lieven, E., & Tomasello, M. (2015). Subject and object omission in children's early transitive constructions: A discourse-pragmatic approach. *Applied Psycholinguistics, 36,* 701–727.

Granek, L., Barrera, M., Scheinemann, K., & Bartels, U. (2015). When a child dies: Pediatric oncologists' follow-up practices with families after the death of their child. *Psycho-Oncology.* Accessed online, 4/2/15; http://www.ncbi.nlm.nih.gov/pubmed/25707675.

Granic, I., Hollenstein, T., & Dishion, T. (2003). Longitudinal analysis of flexibility and reorganization in early adolescence: A dynamic systems study of family interactions. *Developmental Psychology, 39,* 606–617.

Grant, R. J. (2017). *Play-based intervention for autism spectrum disorder and other developmental disabilities.* New York: Routledge/Taylor & Francis Group.

Gray, E. (2013, September 30). This is not a cigarette. *Time,* pp. 38–46.

Gray-Little, B., & Hafdahl, A. R. (2000). Factors influencing racial comparisons of self-esteem: A quantitative review. *Psychological Bulletin, 126,* 26–54.

Gredebäck, G., Kaduk, K., Bakker, M., Gottwald, J., Ekberg, T., Elsner, C., & . . . Kenward, B. (2015). The neuropsychology of infants' pro-social preferences. *Developmental Cognitive Neuroscience, 12,* 106–113.

Green, A. S., Rafaeli, E., Bolger, N. Shrout, P. E., & Reis, H. T. (2006). Paper or plastic? Data equivalence in paper and electronic diaries. *Psychological Methods, 11,* 87–105.

Green, C. S., & Bavelier, D. (2012). Learning, attentional control, and action video games. *Current Biology, 22,* 197–206.

Green, M., DeCourville, N., & Sadava, S. (2012). Positive affect, negative affect, stress, and social support as mediators of the forgiveness-health relationship. *The Journal of Social Psychology, 152,* 288–307.

Greenberg, J. (2012). Psychoanalysis in North America after Freud. In G. O. Gabbard, B. E. Litowitz, & P. Williams (Eds.), *Textbook of psychoanalysis* (2nd ed.). Arlington, VA: American Psychiatric Publishing, Inc.

Greenberg, L. (2008). Emotion and cognition in psychotherapy: The transforming power of affect. *Canadian Psychology, 49,* 49–59.

Greenberg, L., Cwikel, J., & Mirsky, J. (2007, January). Cultural correlates of eating attitudes: A comparison between native-born and immigrant university students in Israel. *International Journal of Eating Disorders, 40,* 51–58.

Greene, M. M., Patra, K., Silvestri, J. M., & Nelson, M. N. (2013). Re-evaluating preterm infants with the Bayley-III: Patterns and predictors of change. *Research in Developmental Disabilities, 34*(7), 2107–2117.

Greenwood, D. N., & Pietromonaco, P. R. (2004). The interplay among attachment orientation, idealized media images of women, and body dissatisfaction: A social psychological analysis. In L. J. Shrum (Ed.), *Psychology of entertainment media: Blurring the lines between entertainment and persuasion.* Mahwah, NJ: Lawrence Erlbaum.

Gregory, K. (2005). Update on nutrition for preterm and full-term infants. *Journal of Obstetrics and Gynecological Neonatal Nursing, 34,* 98–108.

Greydanus, D. E., & Pratt, H. D. (2016). Human sexuality. *International Journal of Child and Adolescent Health, 9,* 291–312.

Griffin, L. K., Adams, N., & Little, T. D. (2017). Self-determination theory, identity development, and adolescence. In M. L. Wehmeyer, K. A. Shogren, T. D. Little, S. J. Lopez (Eds.), *Development of self-determination through the life-course.* New York: Springer Science + Business Media.

Grigorenko, E. (2003). Intraindividual fluctuations in intellectual functioning: Selected links between nutrition and the mind. In R. Sternberg & J. Lautrey (Eds.), *Models of intelligence: International perspectives.* Washington, DC: American Psychological Association.

Grigorenko, E., Jarvin, L., Diffley, R., Goodyear, J., Shanahan, E., & Sternberg, R. (2009). Are SSATS and GPA enough? A theory-based approach to predicting academic success in secondary school. *Journal of Educational Psychology, 101,* 964–981.

Grinkevičiūtė, D., Jankauskaitė, L., Kėvalas, R., & Gurskis, V. (2016). Shaken baby syndrome and consciousness. In G. Leisman, J. Merrick (Eds.), *Considering consciousness clinically.* Hauppauge, NY: Nova Biomedical Books.

Grønhøj, A., & Thøgersen, J. (2012). Action speaks louder than words: The effect of personal attitudes and family norms on adolescents' pro-environmental behaviour. *Journal of Economic Psychology, 33,* 292–302.

Grunbaum, J. A., Kann, L., Kinchen, S. A., Williams, B., Ross, J. G., Lowry, R., et al. (2002). *Youth risk behavior surveillance—United States, 2001.* Atlanta, GA: Centers for Disease Control.

Grundy, E., & Henretta, J. (2006, September). Between elderly parents and adult children: A new look at the intergenerational care provided by the "sandwich generation." *Ageing & Society, 26,* 707–722.

Grzywacz, J., Butler, A., & Almeida, D. (2008). Work, family, and health: Work-family balance as a protective factor against stresses of daily life. In *The changing realities of work and family: A multidisciplinary approach.* Wiley-Blackwell.

Guadalupe, K. L., & Welkley, D. L. (2012). *Diversity in family constellations: Implications for practice.* Chicago: Lyceum Books.

Guasti, M. T. (2002). *Language acquisition: The growth of grammar.* Cambridge, MA: MIT Press.

Guérin, E., Goldfield, G., & Prud'homme, D. (2017). Trajectories of mood and stress and relationships with protective factors during the transition to menopause: Results using latent class growth modeling in a Canadian cohort. *Archives of Women's Mental Health.* Accessed online 12/4/17; https://www.researchgate.net/publication/318411356_Trajectories_of_mood_and_stress_and_relationships_with_protective_factors_during_the_transition_to_menopause_results_using_latent_class_growth_modeling_in_a_Canadian_cohort.

Guerrero, A., Hishinuma, E., Andrade, N., Nishimura, S., & Cunanan, V. (2006, July). Correlations among socioeconomic and family factors and academic, behavioral, and emotional difficulties in Filipino adolescents in Hawaii. *International Journal of Social Psychiatry, 52,* 343–359.

Guerrero, S., Enesco, I., & Lam, V. (2011). Racial awareness, affect and sorting abilities: A study with preschool children. *Anales De Psicología, 27,* 639–646.

Guerrini, I., Thomson, A., & Gurling, H. (2007). The importance of alcohol misuse, malnutrition and genetic susceptibility on brain growth and plasticity. *Neuroscience & Biobehavioral Reviews, 31,* 212–220.

Guinote, A., & Fiske, S. T. (2003). Being in the outgroup territory increases stereotypic perceptions of outgroups: Situational sources of category activation. *Group Processes & Intergroup Relations, 6,* 323–331.

Guinsburg, R., de Araújo Peres, C., Branco de Almeida, M. F., Xavier Balda, R., Bereguel, R. C., Tonelotto, J., & Kopelman, B. I. (2000). Differences in pain expression between male and female newborn infants. *Pain, 85,* 127–133.

Gujral, S., Aizenstein, H., Reynolds, C. F., Butters, M. A., & Erickson, K. I. (2017). Exercise effects on depression: Possible neural mechanisms. *General Hospital Psychiatry, 49,* 2–10.

Gump, L. S., Baker, R. C., & Roll, S. (2000). Cultural and gender differences in moral judgment: A study of Mexican Americans and Anglo-Americans. *Hispanic Journal of Behavioral Sciences, 22,* 78–93.

Gurin, P., Nagda, B. A., & Lopez, G. E. (2004). The benefits of diversity in education for democratic citizenship. *Journal of Social Issues, 60*(1), 17-34. doi: 10.1111/j.0022-4537.2004.00097.x.

Gurin, P. Y., Dey, E. L., Gurin, G., & Hurtado, S. (2003). How does racial/ethnic diversity promote education? *Western Journal of Black Studies, 27,* 20–29.

Güroglu, B., van Lieshout, C., Haselager, G., & Scholte, R. (2007). Similarity and complementary of behavioral profiles of friendship types and types of friends: Friendships and psychosocial adjustment. *Journal of Research on Adolescence, 17,* 357–386.

Gutek, G. L. (2003). Maria Montessori: Contributions to educational psychology. In B. J. Zimmerman (Ed.), *Educational psychology: A century of contributions.* Mahwah, NJ: Lawrence Erlbaum.

Gutman, L. M., McLoyd, V. C., & Tokoyawa, T. (2005). Financial strain, neighborhood stress, parenting behaviors, and adolescent adjustment in urban African American families. *Journal of Research on Adolescence, 15*, 425–449.

Guttmacher Institute. (2012, February). *Facts on American teens' sexual and reproductive health*. New York: Guttmacher Institute.

Guttmacher Institute. (2017, September.) *Induced abortion worldwide*. New York: Guttmacher Institute.

Guttmann, J., & Rosenberg, M. (2003). Emotional intimacy and children's adjustment: A comparison between single-parent divorced and intact families. *Educational Psychology, 23*, 457–472.

Guttmannova, K., Hill, K. G., Bailey, J. A., Hartigan, L. A., Small, C. M., & Hawkins, J. D. (2016). Parental alcohol use, parenting, and child on-time development. *Infant and Child Development*. Accessed online, 10/25/17; http://onlinelibrary.wiley.com/doi/10.1002/icd.2013/abstract.

Haas-Thompson, T., Alston, P., & Holbert, D. (2008). The impact of education and death-related experiences on rehabilitation counselor attitudes toward death and dying. *Journal of Applied Rehabilitation Counseling, 39*, 20–27.

Haber, D. (2006). Life review: Implementation, theory, research, and therapy. *International Journal of Aging & Human Development, 63*, 153–171.

Habersaat, S., Pierrehumbert, B., Forcada-Guex, M., Nessi, J., Ansermet, F., Müller-Nix, C., & Borghini, A. (2014). Early stress exposure and later cortisol regulation: Impact of early intervention on mother–infant relationship in preterm infants. *Psychological Trauma: Theory, Research, Practice, and Policy, 6*, 457–464.

Haberstick, B. C., Timberlake, D., Ehringer, M. A., Lessem, J. M., Hopfer, C. J., Smolen, A., et al. (2007). Can cigarette warnings counterbalance effects of smoking scenes in movies? *Addiction, 102*, 655–665.

Hack, M., Flannery, D. J., Schluchter, M., Cartar, L., Borawski, E., & Klein, N. (2002). Outcomes in young adulthood for very low birth weight infants. *New England Journal of Medicine, 346*, 149–157.

Haeffel, G., Getchell, M., Koposov, R., Yrigollen, C., DeYoung, C., af Klinteberg, B., et al. (2008). Association between polymorphisms in the dopamine transporter gene and depression: Evidence for a gene-environment interaction in a sample of juvenile detainees. *Psychological Science, 19*, 62–69.

Hagan-Burke, S., Coyne, M. D., Kwok, O., Simmons, D. C., Kim, M., Simmons, L. E., & . . . McSparran Ruby, M. (2013). The effects and interactions of student, teacher, and setting variables on reading outcomes for kindergarteners receiving supplemental reading intervention. *Journal of Learning Disabilities, 46*, 260–277.

Hagen, Å. M., Melby-Lervåg, M., & Lervåg, A. (2017). Improving language comprehension in preschool children with language difficulties: A cluster randomized trial. *Journal of Child Psychology and Psychiatry, 58*(10), 1132–1140. doi:10.1111/jcpp.12762.

Hagerty, R. G., Butow, P. N., Ellis, P. A., Lobb, E. A., Pendlebury, S., Leighl, N., et al. (2004). Cancer patient preferences for communication of prognosis in the metastatic setting. *Journal of Clinical Oncology, 22*, 1721–1730.

Hahn, E. A., & Lachman, M. E. (2015). Everyday experiences of memory problems and control: The adaptive role of selective optimization with compensation in the context of memory decline. *Aging, Neuropsychology, and Cognition, 22*, 25–41.

Hahn, E., Gottschling, J., & Spinath, F. M. (2012). Short measurements of personality—Validity and reliability of the GSOEP Big Five Inventory (BFI-S). *Journal of Research in Personality, 46*, 355–359.

Haines, C. (2003). Sequencing, co-ordination and rhythm ability in young children, *Child: Care, Health & Development, 29*, 395–409.

Haith, M. H. (1986). Sensory and perceptual processes in early infancy. *Journal of Pediatrics, 109*(1), 158–171.

Halford, G. (2005). Development of Thinking. In *The Cambridge handbook of thinking and reasoning*. New York: Cambridge University Press.

Halford, G., & Andrews, G. (2006). Reasoning and problem Solving. In *Handbook of child psychology: Vol 2, Cognition, perception, and language* (6th ed.). Hoboken, NJ: John Wiley & Sons Inc.

Halgunseth, L. C., Ispa, J. M., & Rudy, D. (2006). Parental control in Latino families: An integrated review of the literature. *Child Development, 77*, 1282–1297.

Halim, M. L., Ruble, D. N., Tamis-LeMonda, C. S., Zosuls, K. M., Lurye, L. E., & Greulich, F. K. (2014). Pink frilly dresses and the avoidance of all things 'girly': Children's appearance rigidity and cognitive theories of gender development. *Developmental Psychology, 50*, 1091–1101.

Halim, M. L., Ruble, D. N., & Tamis-LeMonda, C. S. (2013). Four-year-olds' beliefs about how others regard males and females. *British Journal of Developmental Psychology, 31*, 128–135.

Hall, J. J., Neal, T., & Dean, R. S. (2008). Lateralization of cerebral functions. In A. M. McNeil & D. Wedding (Eds.), *The neuropsychology handbook* (3rd ed.). New York: Springer Publishing.

Hall, S. (2006). Marital meaning: Exploring young adults' belief systems about marriage. *Journal of Family Issues, 27*, 1437–1458.

Hallpike, C. (2008). The anthropology of moral development. In *Social life and social knowledge: Toward a process account of development*. New York: Taylor & Francis Group/Lawrence Erlbaum Associates.

Halkier, B. (2013). Review of the case study as research method: A practical handbook and how to do your case study: A guide for students & researchers. *Qualitative Research, 13*(1),107–110.

Halpern, D. F. (2014). It's complicated—in fact, it's complex: Explaining the gender gap in academic achievement in science and mathematics. *Psychological Science in the Public Interest, 15*, 72–74.

Hamberger, L., & Holtzworth-Munroe, A. (2007). Spousal abuse. *Cognitive-behavioral strategies in crisis intervention* (3rd ed.) (pp. 277–299). New York: Guilford Press.

Hamer, R., & van Rossum, E. J. (2016). Six languages in education—looking for postformal thinking. *Behavioral Development Bulletin*. Accessed online, 3/21/17; http://psycnet.apa.org/psycinfo/2016-59293-001/.

Hamilton, B. E., Martin, J. A., Osterman, M. J. K., Curtin, S. C., & Mathews, M. S. (2015). Births: Final data for 2014. *National Vital Statistics Report, 64*(12), 1–64.

Hamilton, B. E., Martin, J. A., Ventura, S. J. (2011). *Births: Preliminary data for 2010. National vital statistics reports* (Vol. 60, no. 2). Hyattsville, MD: National Center for Health Statistics.

Hamilton, B. S., & Ventura, S. J. (2012, April.) Birth rates for U.S. teenagers reach historic lows for all age and ethnic groups. *NCHS Data Brief, No. 89*. Washington, DC: National Center for Health Statistics.

Hamlet, H. S., & Herrick, M. (2014). Career challenges in midlife and beyond. In G. T. Eliason, T. Eliason, J. L. Samide, J. Patrick (Eds.), *Career development across the lifespan: Counseling for community, schools, higher education, and beyond*. Charlotte, NC: IAP Information Age Publishing.

Hamon, R. R., & Blieszner, R. (1990). Filial responsibility expectations among adult child-older parent pairs. *Journal of Gerontology, 45*, 110–112.

Hamm, J. V., Brown, B. B., and Heck, D. J. (2005). Bridging the ethnic divide: Student and school characteristics in African American, Asian-descent, Latino, and white adolescents' cross-ethnic friend nominations. *Journal of Research on Adolescence, 15*(1): 21–46.

Hane, A., Feldstein, S., & Dernetz, V. (2003). The relation between coordinated interpersonal timing and maternal sensitivity in four-month-old infants. *Journal of Psycholinguistic Research, 32*, 525–539.

Hanna, K., Davies, E., Henderson, E., & Hand, L. (2013). Questioning child witnesses: Exploring the benefits and risks of intermediary models in New Zealand. *Psychiatry, Psychology & Law, 20*(4), 527–542.

Hansen, C., Konradsen, H., Abrahamsen, B., & Pedersen, B. D. (2014). Women's experiences of their osteoporosis diagnosis at the time of diagnosis and 6 months later: A phenomenological hermeneutic study. *International Journal of Qualitative Studies on Health and Well-Being*, Accessed online, 6/23/15; http://www.ncbi.nlm.nih.gov/pubmed/24559545.

Hansson, R. O., & Stroebe, M. (2007). *Bereavement in late life: Coping, adaptation, and developmental influences*. Washington, DC: American Psychological Association.

Hansson, R. O., Daleiden, E., & Hayslip, B. (2004). Relational competence across the life span. In F. R. Lang & K. L. Fingerman (Eds.), *Growing together: Personal relationships across the lifespan* (pp. 317–340). New York: Cambridge University Press.

Harada, C. N, Natelson Love, M. C., & Triebold, K. (2013). Normal cognitive aging. *Clinical and Geriatric Medicine, 29,* 737–752.

Harden, K., Turkheimer, E., & Loehlin, J. (2007). Genotype by environment interaction in adolescents' cognitive aptitude. *Behavior Genetics, 37,* 273–283.

Harding, J. F. (2015). Increases in maternal education and low-income children's cognitive and behavioral outcomes. *Developmental Psychology, 51,* 583–599.

Harlow, H. F., & Zimmerman, R. R. (1959). Affectional responses in the infant monkey. *Science, 130,* 421–432.

Harris, A., Cronkite, R., & Moos, R. (2006, July). Physical activity, exercise coping, and depression in a 10-year cohort study of depressed patients. *Journal of Affective Disorders, 93,* 79–85.

Harris, J. R. (2000). Socialization, personality development, and the child's environments: Comment on Vandell. *Developmental Psychology, 36,* 711–723.

Harris, J. R., Vernon, P., & Jang, K. (2007). Rated personality and measured intelligence in young twin children. *Personality and Individual Differences, 42,* 75–86.

Harris, M., Prior, J., & Koehoorn, M. (2008). Age at menarche in the Canadian population: Secular trends and relationship to adulthood BMI. *Journal of Adolescent Health, 43,* 548–554.

Harris Poll. (2014, September 14.) *Doctors, military officers, firefighters, and scientists seen as among America's most prestigious occupations.* Accessed online, 11/28/17; http://www.theharrispoll.com/politics/Doctors__Military_Officers__Firefighters__and_Scientists_Seen_as_Among_America_s_Most_Prestigious_Occupations.html.

Harrison, D. A., & Newman, D. A. (2013). Absence, lateness, turnover, and retirement: Narrow and broad understandings of withdrawal and behavioral engagement. In N. W. Schmitt, S. Highhouse, I. B. Weiner (Eds.), *Handbook of psychology: Industrial and organizational psychology, Vol. 12.* (2nd ed.). Hoboken, NJ: John Wiley & Sons Inc.

Harrison, K., & Hefner, V. (2006, April). Media exposure, current and future body ideals, and disordered eating among preadolescent girls: A longitudinal panel study. *Journal of Youth and Adolescence, 35,* 153–163.

Hart, B. (2004). What toddlers talk about. *First Language, 24,* 91–106.

Hart, B., & Risley, T. R. (1995). *Meaningful differences in the everyday experience of young American children.* Baltimore, MD: Paul Brookes.

Hart, D., Burock, D., & London, B. (2003). Prosocial tendencies, antisocial behavior, and moral development. In A. Slater & G. Bremner (Eds.), *An introduction to developmental psychology.* Malden, MA: Blackwell Publishers.

Hart, D., Keller, M., Edelstein, W., & Hofmann, V. (1998). Childhood personality influences on social–cognitive development: A longitudinal study. *Journal of Personality and Social Psychology, 74(5),* 1278–1289.

Harter, S. (2006). *The development of self-esteem. Self-esteem issues and answers: A sourcebook of current perspectives.* New York: Psychology Press.

Hartley, C. A., & Lee, F. S. (2015). Sensitive periods in affective development: Nonlinear maturation of fear learning. *Neuropsychopharmacology, 40,* 50–60.

Hartman, K. M., Ratner, N. B., & Newman, R. S. (2017). Infant-directed speech (IDS) vowel clarity and child language outcomes. *Journal of Child Language, 44,* 1140–1162.

Hartshorne, J., & Ullman, M. (2006). Why girls say "holded" more than boys. *Developmental Science, 9,* 21–32.

Harvey, A., Mullin, B., & Hinshaw, S. (2006). Sleep and circadian rhythms in children and adolescents with bipolar disorder. *Development and Psychopathology, 18,* 1147–1168.

Harvey, J. H., & Fine, M. A. (2004). *Children of divorce: Stories of loss and growth.* Mahwah, NJ: Lawrence Erlbaum.

Harvey, J. H., & Weber, A. (2002). *Odyssey of the heart: Close relationships in the 21st century* (2nd ed.). Mahwah, NJ: Lawrence Erlbaum.

Harvey, S. B., Øverland, S., Hatch, S. L., Wessely, S., Mykletun, A., & Hotopf, M. (2017). Exercise and the prevention of depression: Results of the HUNT cohort study. *American Journal of Psychiatry, 175(1),* 28–36.

Haslam, C., & Lawrence, W. (2004). Health-related behavior and beliefs of pregnant smokers. *Health Psychology, 23,* 486–491.

Haslett, A. (2004, May 31). Love supreme. *New Yorker,* pp. 76–80.

Hatfield, E., Mo, Y., & Rapson, R. L. (2015). Love, sex, and marriage across cultures. In L. A. Jensen & L. A. Jensen (Eds.), *The Oxford handbook of human development and culture: An interdisciplinary perspective.* New York: Oxford University Press.

Hatton, C. (2015, December 21). Who will take care of China's elderly people? *BBC News Magazine.* Accessed online, 10/24/17; http://www.bbc.com/news/magazine-35155548.

Haugaard, J. J. (2000). The challenge of defining child sexual abuse. *American Psychologist, 55,* 1036–1039.

Hauser, S., Allen, J., & Golden, E. (2006). *Out of the woods: Tales of resilient teens.* Cambridge, MA: Harvard University Press.

Havard, C., & Memon, A. (2013). The mystery man can help reduce false identification for child witnesses: Evidence from video line-ups. *Applied Cognitive Psychology, 27,* 50–59.

Hawkins, A. J., Willoughby, B. J., & Doherty, W. J. (2012). Reasons for divorce and openness to marital reconciliation. *Journal of Divorce & Remarriage, 53,* 453–463.

Hawley, P. H. (2003). Prosocial and coercive configurations of resource control in early adolescence: A case for the well-adapted Machiavellian. *Merrill-Palmer Quarterly, 4, Special issue: Aggression and Adaptive Functioning: The bright side to bad behavior,* 279–309.

Hayashi, A., & Mazuka, R. (2017). Emergence of Japanese infants' prosodic preferences in infant-directed vocabulary. *Developmental Psychology, 53,* 28–37.

Hayslip, B. J., Maiden, R. J., Page, K. S., & Dolbin-MacNab, M. L. (2015). Grandparenting. In P. A. Lichtenberg, B. T. Mast, B. D. Carpenter, J. Loebach Wetherell (Eds.), *APA handbook of clinical geropsychology, Vol. 1: History and status of the field and perspectives on aging.* Washington, DC: American Psychological Association.

Hayward, M., Crimmins, E., & Saito, Y. (1997). Cause of death and active life expectancy in the older population of the United States. *Journal of Aging and Health,* 122–131.

Hazan, C., & Shaver, P. (1987). Romantic love conceptualized as an attachment process. *Journal of Personality and Social Psychology, 52,* 511–524.

Healthychildren.org. (2016, October 18.) Teen suicide statistics. Accessed online, 11/13/17; https://www.healthychildren.org/English/health-issues/conditions/emotional-problems/Pages/Teen-Suicide-Statistics.aspx.

Healy, P. (2001, March 3). Data on suicides set off alarm. *Boston Globe,* p. B1.

Heard, E., & Martienssen, R. A. (2014). Transgenerational epigenetic inheritance: myths and mechanisms. *Cell, 157,* 95–109.

Hecht, S. S., Carmella, S. G., Kotandeniya, D., Pillsbury, M. E., Chen, M., Ransom, B. S., & . . . Hatsukami, D. K. (2015). Evaluation of toxicant and carcinogen metabolites in the urine of e-cigarette users versus cigarette smokers. *Nicotine & Tobacco Research, 17,* 704–709.

Hedegaard, M., & Fleer, M. (2013). *Play, learning, and children's development: Everyday life in families and transition to school.* New York: Cambridge University Press.

Heimann, M., Strid, K., Smith, L., Tjus, T., Ulvund, S., & Meltzoff, A. (2006). Exploring the relation between memory, gestural communication, and the emergence of language in infancy: A longitudinal study. *Infant and Child Development, 15,* 233–249.

Helms, J. E., Jernigan, M., & Mascher, J. (2005). The meaning of race in psychology and how to change it: A methodological perspective. *American Psychologist, 60,* 27–36.

Helmsen, J., Koglin, U., & Petermann, F. (2012). Emotion regulation and aggressive behavior in preschoolers: The mediating role of social information processing. *Child Psychiatry and Human Development, 43,* 87–101.

Helson, R., Jones, C. J., & Kwan, V.S.Y. (2002). Personality change over 40 years of adulthood: HLM analyses of two longitudinal samples. *Journal of Personality and Social Psychology, 83*, 752–766.

Hendrick, C., & Hendrick, S. (2003). Romantic love: Measuring cupid's arrow. In S. Lopez & C. Snyder (Eds.), *Positive psychological assessment: A handbook of models and measures*. Washington, DC: American Psychological Association.

Henry, R., Miller, R., & Giarrusso, R. (2005). Difficulties, disagreements, and disappointments in late-life marriages. *International Journal of Aging & Human Development, 61*, 243–264.

Hensley, P. (2006, July). Treatment of bereavement-related depression and traumatic grief. *Journal of Affective Disorders, 92*, 117–124.

Hepach, R., & Westermann, G. (2013). Infants' sensitivity to the congruence of others' emotions and actions. *Journal of Experimental Child Psychology, 115*, 16–29.

Herbenick, D., Reece, M., Schick, V., Sanders, S., Dodge, B., & Fortenberry, J. D. (2010). Sexual behavior in the United States: Results from a national probability sample of men and women ages 14 to 94. *Journal of Sexual Medicine, 7*, Supplement 5, 255–265.

Herendeen, L. A., & MacDonald, A. (2014). Planning for healthy homes. In I. L. Rubin, J. Merrick, (Eds.), *Environmental health: Home, school and community*. Hauppauge, NY: Nova Biomedical Books.

Hermanto, N., Moreno, S., & Bialystok, E. (2012). Linguistic and metalinguistic outcomes of intense immersion education: How bilingual? *International Journal of Bilingual Education and Bilingualism, 15*, 131–145.

Hernandez-Reif, M., Field, T., Diego, M., Vera, Y., & Pickens, J. (2006, January). Brief report: Happy faces are habituated more slowly by infants of depressed mothers. *Infant Behavior & Development, 29*, 131–135.

Herrnstein, R. J., & Murray, C. (1994). *The bell curve: Intelligence and class structure in American life*. New York: Free Press.

Hertel, G., & Wittchen, M. (2008). Work motivation. *An introduction to work and organizational psychology: A European perspective* (2nd ed.). Malden, MA: Blackwell Publishing.

Hertenstein, M. J. (2002). Touch: Its communicative functions in infancy. *Human Development, 45*, 70–94.

Hertz, R., & Nelson, M. K. (2015). Introduction. *Journal of Family Issues, 36*, 447–460.

Hetherington, E. M., & Elmore, A. (2003). Risk and resilience in children coping with their parents' divorce and remarriage. In S. Luthar (Ed.), *Resilience and vulnerability: Adaptation in the context of childhood adversities*. New York: Cambridge University Press.

Hetrick, S. E., Parker, A. G., Robinson, J., Hall, N., & Vance, A. (2012). Predicting suicidal risk in a cohort of depressed children and adolescents. *Crisis: The Journal of Crisis Intervention and Suicide Prevention, 33*, 13–20.

Hewstone, M. (2003). Intergroup contact: Panacea for prejudice? *Psychologist, 16*, 352–355.

Higher Education Research Institute. (2005). *The spiritual life of college students: A national study of college students' search for meaning and purpose*. Los Angeles: Higher Education Research Institute.

Hill, B. D., Foster, J. D., Elliott, E. M., Shelton, J., McCain, J., & Gouvier, W. (2013). Need for cognition is related to higher general intelligence, fluid intelligence, and crystallized intelligence, but not working memory. *Journal of Research in Personality, 47*, 22–25.

Hill, S., & Flom, R. (2007, February). 18- and 24-month-olds' discrimination of gender-consistent and inconsistent activities. *Infant Behavior & Development, 30*, 168–173.

Hillman, J. (2000). *Clinical perspectives on elderly sexuality*. Dordrecht, Netherlands: Kluwer Academic Publishers.

Hillman, J. (2012). *Sexuality and aging: Clinical perspectives*. New York: Springer Science + Business Media.

Hilton, J., & Anderson, T. (2009). Characteristics of women with children who divorce in midlife compared to those who remain married. *Journal of Divorce & Remarriage, 50*, 309–329.

Hipke, K. N., Wolchik, S. A., & Sandler, I. N. (2010). Divorce, children of. In G. Fink (Ed.), *Stress consequences: Mental, neuropsychological and socioeconomic*. San Diego, CA: Elsevier Academic Press.

Hipple, S. F. (2016, September). Labor force participation: what has happened since the peak? *Monthly Labor Review, Bureau of Labor Statistics*. Accessed online, 11/29/17; https://www.bls.gov/opub/mlr/2016/article/labor-force-participation-what-has-happened-since-the-peak.htm#top.

Hiser, E., & Kobayashi, J. (2003). Hemisphere lateralization differences: A cross-cultural study of Japanese and American students in Japan. *Journal of Asian Pacific Communication, 13*, 197–229.

Hispanic Heritage Foundation. (2015, April 28). *HHF, MyCollege Options: Survey 3k students*. Accessed online, 11/9/17; http://hispanicheritage.org/hispanic-heritage-foundation-mycollegeoptions-family-online-safety-institute-and-other-partners-announce-findings-of-new-study-titled-taking-the-pulse-of-the-high-school-student-experience/.

Hitlin, S., Brown, J. S., & Elder, G. H., Jr. (2006). Racial self-categorization in adolescence: Multiracial development and social pathways. *Child Development, 77*, 1298–1308.

Hjelmstedt, A., Widstrom, A., & Collins, A. (2006). Psychological correlates of prenatal attachment in women who conceived after in vitro fertilization and women who conceived naturally. *Birth: Issues in Perinatal Care, 33*, 303–310.

Ho, B., Friedland, J., Rappolt, S., & Noh, S. (2003). Caregiving for relatives with Alzheimer's disease: Feelings of Chinese-Canadian women. *Journal of Aging Studies, 17*, 301–321.

Hocking, D. R., Kogan, C. S., & Cornish, K. M. (2012). Selective spatial processing deficits in an at-risk subgroup of the fragile X premutation. *Brain and Cognition, 79*, 39–44.

Hodgson, J. C., Hirst, R. J., & Hudson, J. M. (2016). Hemispheric speech lateralisation in the developing brain is related to motor praxis ability. *Developmental Cognitive Neuroscience, 22*, 9–17.

Hoehl, S., Wahl, S., Michel, C., & Striano, T. (2012). Effects of eye gaze cues provided by the caregiver compared to a stranger on infants' object processing. *Developmental Cognitive Neuroscience, 2*, 81–89.

Hoelterk, L. F., Axinn, W. G., & Ghimire, D. J. (2004). Social change, premarital nonfamily experiences, and marital dynamics. *Journal of Marriage & Family, 66*, 1131–1151.

Hoersting, R. C., & Jenkins, S. (2011). No place to call home: Cultural homelessness, self-esteem and cross-cultural identities. *International Journal of Intercultural Relations, 35*, 17–30.

Hoffman, J. (2011, March 27). A girl's nude photo and altered lives. *New York Times*, A1, A18–A19.

Hoffman, L. (2003). Why high schools don't change: What students and their yearbooks tell us. *High School Journal, 86*, 22–37.

Hoffman, M. L. (2001). Toward a comprehensive empathy-based theory of prosocial moral behavior. In A. C. Bohart, & D. J. Stipek (Eds.), *Constructive & destructive behavior: Implications for family, school, & society*. Washington, DC: American Psychological Association.

Holahan, C., & Chapman, J. (2002). Longitudinal predictors of proactive goals and activity participation at age 80. *Journals of Gerontology: Series B: Psychological Sciences & Social Sciences, 57B*, P418–P425.

Holland, A. (1999). Syndromes, phenotypes, and genotypes: Finding the links. *The Psychologist, 12*, 242–245.

Holland, N. (1994, August). Race dissonance—Implications for African American children. Paper presented at the annual meeting of the American Psychological Association, Los Angeles, CA.

Holmes, R. M., & Romeo, L. (2013). Gender, play, language, and creativity in preschoolers. *Early Child Development and Care, 183*, 1531–1543.

Homae, F., Watanabe, H., Nakano, T., & Taga, G. (2012). Functional development in the infant brain for auditory pitch processing. *Human Brain Mapping, 33*, 596–608.

Hong, D. S., Hoeft, F., Marzelli, M. J., Lepage, J., Roeltgen, D., Ross, J., & Reiss, A. L. (2014). Influence of the X-chromosome on neuroanatomy: Evidence from Turner and Klinefelter syndromes. *Journal of Neuroscience, 34*, 3509–3516.

Hooks, B., & Chen, C. (2008). Vision triggers an experience-dependent sensitive period at the retino-geniculate synapse. *The Journal of Neuroscience, 28*, 4807–4817. Accessed online; http://search.ebscohost.com, doi:10.1523/JNEUROSCI. 4667-07.2008.

Hopkins, B., & Westra, T. (1990). Motor development, maternal expectation, and the role of handling. *Infant Behavior and Development, 13*, 117–122.

Horne, R. C. (2017). Sleep disorders in newborns and infants. In S. Nevšímalová, O. Bruni (Eds.), *Sleep disorders in children*. Cham, Switzerland: Springer International Publishing.

Hornor, G. (2008). Reactive attachment disorder. *Journal of Pediatric Health Care, 22*, 234–239.

Horwitz, B. N., Luong, G., & Charles, G. T. (2008). Neuroticism and extraversion share genetic and environmental effects with negative and positive mood spillover in a nationally representative sample. *Personality and Individual Differences, 45*, 636–642.

Hosogi, M., Okada, A., Fuji, C., Noguchi, K., & Watanabe, K. (2012). Importance and usefulness of evaluating self-esteem in children. *Biopsychosocial Medicine, 6*, 80–88.

Hossfeld, B. (2008). Developing friendships and peer relationships: Building social support with the girls circle program. *Handbook of prevention and intervention programs for adolescent girls* (pp. 42–80). Hoboken, NJ: John Wiley & Sons Inc.

Hotelling, B. A., & Humenick, S. S. (2005). Advancing normal birth: Organizations, goals, and research. *Journal of Perinatal Education, 14*, 40–48.

Houwen, S., Visser, L., van der Putten, A., & Vlaskamp, C. (2016). The interrelationships between motor, cognitive, and language development in children with and without intellectual and developmental disabilities. *Research in Developmental Disabilities, 53*, 5419–5431.

Howard, J. S., Stanislaw, H., Green, G., Sparkman, C. R., & Cohen, H. G. (2014). Comparison of behavior analytic and eclectic early interventions for young children with autism after three years. *Research in Developmental Disabilities, 35*, 3326–3344.

Howe, B. B. (2015). Assisted living. In B. L. Bonham Howe (Ed.), *The gerontology nurse's guide to the community-based health network*. New York: Springer Publishing Co.

Howe, M. J. (2004). Some insights of geniuses into the causes of exceptional achievement. In L. V. Shavinina & M. Ferrari (Eds.), *Beyond knowledge: Extracognitive aspects of developing high ability*. Mahwah, NJ: Lawrence Erlbaum Associates.

Howe, M. L., Courage, M. L., & Edison, S. C. (2004). When autobiographical memory begins. In S. Algarabel, A. Pitarque, T. Bajo, S. E. Gathercole, & M. A. Conway (Eds.), *Theories of memory (Vol. 3)*. New York: Psychology Press.

Hoyte, F., Torr, J., & Degotardi, S. (2015). Creating pretence and sharing friendship: Modal expressions in children's play. *International Journal of Early Years Education, 23*, 17–30.

Hsin, L., & Snow, C. (2017). Social perspective taking: A benefit of bilingualism in academic writing. *Reading and Writing*. Accessed online, 3/16/17; http://link.springer.com/article/10.1007/s11145-016-9718-9.

Hsu, V., & Rovee-Collier, C. (2006). Memory reactivation in the second year of life. *Infant Behavior & Development, 29*, 91–107.

Hu, Y., Xu, Y., & Tornello, S. L. (2016). Stability of self-reported same-sex and both-sex attraction from adolescence to young adulthood. *Archives of Sexual Behavior, 45*, 651–659.

Huang, A., Subak, L., Thom, D., Van Den Eeden, S., Ragins, A., Kuppermann, M., . . . Brown, J. S. (2009). Sexual function and aging in racially and ethnically diverse women. *Journal of the American Geriatrics Society, 57*, 1362–1368.

Huang, C. T. (2012). Outcome-based observational learning in human infants. *Journal of Comparative Psychology, 126*, 139–149.

Huang, J. (2004). Death: Cultural traditions. From *On Our Own Terms: Moyers on Dying*. Accessed online, 05/ 24/2004, www.pbs.org.

Hubel, D. H., & Wiesel, T. N. (2004). *Brain and visual perception: The story of a 25-year collaboration*. New York: Oxford University Press.

Hubley, A. M., & Arim, R. G. (2012). Subjective age in early adolescence: Relationships with chronological age, pubertal timing, desired age, and problem behaviors. *Journal of Adolescence, 35*, 357–366.

Hueston, W., Geesey, M., & Diaz, V. (2008). Prenatal care initiation among pregnant teens in the United States: An analysis over 25 years. *Journal of Adolescent Health, 42*, 243–248.

Huh, S. Y., Rifas-Shiman, S. L., Zera, C. A., Rich Edwards, J. W., Oken, E., Weiss, S. T., & Gilmann, M. W. (2012). Delivery by caesarean section and risk of obesity in preschool age children: A prospective cohort study. *Archives of Disable Children, 34*, 66–79.

Huijbregts, S., Tavecchio, L., Leseman, P., & Hoffenaar, P. (2009). Child rearing in a group setting: Beliefs of Dutch, Caribbean Dutch, and Mediterranean Dutch caregivers in center-based child care. *Journal of Cross-Cultural Psychology, 40*, 797–815. Accessed online; http://search.ebscohost.com, doi:10.1177/0022022109338623.

Huizink, A., Mulder, E., & Buitelaar, J. (2004). Prenatal stress and risk for psychopathology: Specific effects or induction of general susceptibility? *Psychological Bulletin, 130*, 115–142.

Hülür, G., Gasimova, F., Robitzsch, A., & Wilhelm, O. (2017). Change in fluid and crystallized intelligence and student achievement: The role of intellectual engagement. *Child Development*. Accessed online, 11/16/17; https://www.ncbi.nlm.nih.gov/pubmed/28369877.

Hülür, G., Ram, N., Willis, S. L., Schaie, K. W., & Gerstorf, D. (2015). Cognitive dedifferentiation with increasing age and proximity of death: Within-person evidence from the Seattle Longitudinal Study. *Psychology and Aging, 30*, 311–323.

Human Genome Project. (2006). Accessed online; http://www.ornl.gov/sci/techresources/Human Genome/medicine/genetest.shtml.

Human Genome Project. (2010). Accessed online, 7/8/12, http://www.ornl.gov/sci/techresources/Human_Genome/medicine/genetest.shtml/.

Humphries, M. L., & Korfmacher, J. (2012). The good, the bad, and the ambivalent: Quality of alliance in a support program for young mothers. *Infant Mental Health Journal, 33*, 22–33.

Hungerford, A. (2005). The use of anatomically detailed dolls in forensic investigations: Developmental considerations. *Journal of Forensic Psychology Practice, 5*, 75–87.

Hunt, M. (1993). *The story of psychology*. New York: Doubleday.

Hunter, J., & Mallon, G. P. (2000). Lesbian, gay, and bisexual adolescent development: Dancing with your feet tied together. In B. Greene & G. L. Croom (Eds.), *Education, research, and practice in lesbian, gay, bisexual, and transgendered psychology: A resource manual (Vol. 5)*. Thousand Oaks, CA: Sage Publications.

Hunter, S. (2007). *Coming out and disclosures: LGBT persons across the life span*. New York: Haworth Press.

Hunter, S., & Smith, D. (2008). Predictors of children's understandings of death: Age, cognitive ability, death experience and maternal communicative competence. *Omega: Journal of Death and Dying, 57*, 143–162.

Huntsinger, C. S., Jose, P. E., Liaw, F., & Ching, W-D. (1997). Cultural differences in early mathematics learning: A comparison of Euro-American, Chinese-American, and Taiwan–Chinese families. *International Journal of Behavioral Development, 21*, 371–388.

Huster, R. J., Westerhausen, R. R., & Herrmann, C. S. (2011). Sex differences in cognitive control are associated with midcingulate and callosal morphology. *Brain Structure & Function, 215*, 225–235.

Huston, A. C., Bobbitt, K. C., & Bentley, A. (2015). Time spent in child care: How and why does it affect social development? *Developmental Psychology, 51*, 621–634.

Huston, T. L., Caughlin, J. P., Houts, R. M., & Smith, S. E. (2001). The connubial crucible: Newlywed years as predictors of marital delight, distress, and divorce. *Journal of Personality and Social Psychology, 80*, 237–252.

Hutchinson, D., & Rapee, R. (2007). Do friends share similar body image and eating problems? The role of social networks and peer influences in early adolescence. *Behaviour Research and Therapy, 45*, 1557–1577.

Hutchinson, S., & Wexler, B. (2007, January). Is "raging" good for health? Older women's participation in the Raging Grannies. *Health Care for Women International, 28*, 88–118.

Hutton, P. H. (2004). *Phillippe Ariès and the politics of French cultural history*. Amherst: University of Massachusetts Press.

Hyde, J. S., & DeLamater, J. D. (2003). *Understanding human sexuality* (8th ed.). New York: McGraw-Hill.

Hyde, J. S., & Grabe, S. (2008). Meta-analysis in the psychology of women. In *Psychology of women: A handbook of issues and theories* (2nd ed.). Westport, CT: Praeger Publishers/Greenwood Publishing Group.

Hyde, J. S., Mezulis, A., & Abramson, L. (2008). The ABCs of depression: Integrating affective, biological, and cognitive models to explain the emergence of the gender difference in depression. *Psychological Review, 115,* 291–313.

Iavarone, A., Ziello, A. R., Pastore, F., Fasanaro, A. M., & Poderico, C. (2014). Caregiver burden and coping strategies in caregivers of patients with Alzheimer's disease. *Neuropsychiatric Disease and Treatment, 10,* 88–97.

Ibbotson, P., & Tomasello, M. (2016). Language in a new key. *Scientific American,* 71–75.

Iecovich, E., & Biderman, A. (2012). Attendance in adult day care centers and its relation to loneliness among frail older adults. *International Psychogeriatrics, 24,* 439–448.

Ihle, A., Schnitzspahn, K., Rendell, P. G., Luong, C., & Kliegel, M. (2012). Age benefits in everyday prospective memory: The influence of personal task importance, use of reminders and everyday stress. *Aging, Neuropsychology, and Cognition, 19,* 84–101.

Ingersoll-Dayton, B., Neal, M., & Hammer, L. (2001). Aging parents helping adult children: The experience of the sandwiched generation. *Family Relations, 50,* 263–271.

Inoue, K., Tanii, H., Abe, S., Kaiya, H., Nata, M., & Fukunaga, T. (2006, December). The correlation between rates of unemployment and suicide rates in Japan between 1985 and 2002. *International Medical Journal, 13,* 261–263.

Institute of Medicine. 2007. *Preterm Birth: Causes, Consequences, and Prevention.* Washington, DC: National Academies Press. https://doi.org/10.17226/11622.

Irving, P. H. (2015, July 22). New frontier for successful aging. *Huffington Post.* https://www.huffingtonpost.com/paul-h-irving/new-frontier-for-successful-aging_b_7845022.html.

Irwin, M. R. (2015). Why sleep is important for health: A psychoneuroimmunology perspective. *Annual Review of Psychology, 66,* 143–172.

Isaacs, K. L., Barr, W. B., Nelson, P. K., & Devinsky, M. (2006). Degree of handedness and cerebral dominance. *Neurology, 66,* 1855–1858.

Ishii-Kuntz, M. (2000). Diversity within Asian-American families. In D. H. Demo, K. R. Allen, & M. A. Fine (Eds.), *Handbook of family diversity.* New York: Oxford.

Ishikawa, T., Fujiwara, H., Imai, O., & Okabe, A. (2008). Wayfinding with a GPS-based mobile navigation system: A comparison with maps and direct experience. *Journal of Environmental Psychology, 28*(1), 74–82.

Ishizuka, B., Kudo, Y., & Tango, T. (2008). Cross-sectional community survey of menopause symptoms among Japanese women. *Maturitas, 61,* 260–267.

Izard, C. E., King, K. A., Trentacosta, C. J., Morgan, J. K., Laurenceau, J., Krauthamer-Ewing, E., et al. (2008). Accelerating the development of emotion competence in Head Start children: Effects on adaptive and maladaptive behavior. *Development and Psychopathology, 20,* 369–397.

Izard, J., Haines, C., Crouch, R., Houston, S., & Neill, N. (2003). Assessing the impact of the teaching of modelling: Some implications. In S. Lamon, W. Parker, & K. Houston (Eds.), *Mathematical modelling: A way of life: ICTMA 11.* Chichester, England: Horwood Publishing.

Izawa, C., & Hayden, R. G. (1993). *Race against time: Toward the principle of optimization in learning and retention.* Hillside, NJ: Lawrence Erlbaum Associates.

Jack, F., Simcock, G., & Hayne, H. (2012). Magic memories: Young children's verbal recall after a 6-year delay. *Child Development, 83,* 159–172.

Jackson, S. L. (2018). Introduction and overview of elder abuse. In *Understanding elder abuse: A clinician's guide.* Washington, DC: American Psychological Association.

Jacobson, C., Batejan, K., Kleinman, M., & Gould, M. (2013). Reasons for attempting suicide among a community sample of adolescents. *Suicide and Life-Threatening Behavior, 43,* 646–662.

Jager, J., Yuen, C. X., Putnick, D. L., Hendricks, C., & Bornstein, M. H. (2015). Adolescent-peer relationships, separation and detachment from parents, and internalizing and externalizing behaviors: Linkages and interactions. *The Journal of Early Adolescence, 35,* 511–537.

Jager, R., Mieler, W., & Miller, J. (2008). Age-related macular degeneration. *New England Journal of Medicine, 358,* 2606–2617.

Jahagirdar, V. (2014). Hemispheric differences: The bilingual brain. In R. R. Heredia, J. Altarriba (Eds.), *Foundations of bilingual memory.* New York: Springer Science + Business Media.

Jalonick, M. C. (2011, January 13.) New guidelines would make school lunches healthier. *Washington Post.*

James, J., Ellis, B. J., Schlomer, G. L., & Garber, J. (2012). Sex-specific pathways to early puberty, sexual debut, and sexual risk taking: Tests of an integrated evolutionary-developmental model. *Developmental Psychology, 48,* 687–702.

James, W. (1890/1950). *The principles of psychology.* New York: Holt.

James-Roberts, I. S., Roberts, M., Hovish, K., & Owen, C. (2015). Video evidence that London infants can resettle themselves back to sleep after waking in the night, as well as sleep for long periods, by 3 months of age. *Journal of Developmental and Behavioral Pediatrics, 36,* 324–329.

Jäncke, K., Mérillat, S., Liem, F., & Hänggi, J. (2015). Brain size, sex, and the aging brain. *Human Brain Mapping, 36,* 150–169.

Janda, L. H., & Klenke-Hamel, K. E. (1980). *Human sexuality.* New York: Van Nostrand.

Janusek, L., Cooper, D., & Mathews, H. L. (2012). Stress, immunity, and health outcomes. In V. Rice (Ed.), *Handbook of stress, coping, and health: Implications for nursing research, theory, and practice* (2nd ed.). Thousand Oaks, CA: Sage Publications, Inc.

Jarrold, C., & Hall, D. (2013). The development of rehearsal in verbal short-term memory. *Child Development Perspectives, 7,* 182–186.

Jay, M. (2012, April 14). The downside of cohabiting before marriage. *New York Times,* p. SR4.

Jenkins, A., Harburg, E., Weissberg, N., & Donnelly, T. (2004). The influence of minority group cultural models on persistence in college. *Journal of Negro Education, 73,* 69–80.

Jenkins, L. N., & Demaray, M. K. (2015). Indirect effects in the peer victimization-academic achievement relation: The role of academic self-concept and gender. *Psychology in the Schools, 52,* 235–247.

Jensen, A. (2003). Do age-group differences on mental tests imitate racial differences? *Intelligence, 31,* 107–121.

Jensen, L. A. (2008). Coming of age in a multicultural world: Globalization and adolescent cultural identity formation. In D. L Browning (Ed.), *Adolescent identities: A collection of readings.* New York: The Analytic Press/Taylor & Francis Group.

Jerrim, J., & Schoon, I. (2014). Do teenagers want to become scientists? A comparison of gender differences in attitudes toward science, career expectations, and academic skill across 29 countries. In I. Schoon, & J. S. Eccles (Eds.), *Gender differences in aspirations and attainment: A life course perspective.* New York: Cambridge University Press.

Jewell, J., Schmittel, M., McCobin, A., Hupp, S., & Pomerantz, A. (2017). The Children First program: The effectiveness of a parent education program for divorcing parents. *Journal of Divorce & Remarriage, 58*(1), 16–28.

Jeynes, W. (2006). The impact of parental remarriage on children: A meta-analysis. *Marriage & Family Review, 40,* 75–102.

Ji-liang, S., Li-qing, Z., & Yan, T. (2003). The impact of intergenerational social support and filial expectation on the loneliness of elder parents. *Chinese Journal of Clinical Psychology, 11,* 167–169.

Jimerson, S., Morrison, G., Pletcher, S., & Furlong, M. (2006). Youth engaged in antisocial and aggressive behaviors: Who are they? In *Handbook of school violence and school safety: From research to practice* (pp. 3–19). Mahwah, NJ: Lawrence Erlbaum Associates Publishers.

Joe, S., & Marcus, S. (2003). Datapoints: Trends by race and gender in suicide attempts among U.S. adolescents, 1991–2001. *Psychiatric Services, 54,* 454.

Johnson, A. M., Wadsworth, J., Wellings, K., & Bradshaw, S. (1992). Sexual lifestyles and HIV risk. *Nature, 360*, 410–412.

Johnson, D. C., & Foster, S. (2005). The relationship between relational aggression in kindergarten children and friendship stability, mutuality, and peer liking. *Early Education and Development, 16*, 141–160.

Johnson, S. (2009). Developmental origins of object perception. In *Learning and the infant mind*. New York: Oxford University Press.

Johnson, W., & Penke, L. (2015). Genetics of social behavior. In B. Gawronski, G. V. Bodenhausen (Eds.), *Theory and explanation in social psychology*. New York: Guilford Press.

Johnston, L. D., O'Malley, P. M., Bachman, J. G., Schulenberg, J. E., & Miech, R. A. (2014). *Monitoring the future national survey results on drug use, 1975-2013: Volume II, college students and adults ages 19–55*. Ann Arbor, MI: Institute for Social Research, University of Michigan, pp. 424.

Johnston, L. D., O'Malley, P.M., Miech, R. A, Bachman, J. G., & Schulenberg, J. E. (2015). *Monitoring the Future national survey results on drug use: 1975–2014: Overview, key findings on adolescent drug use*. Ann Arbor, MI: Institute for Social Research, University of Michigan.

Joireman, J., & Van Lange, P. M. (2015). Ethical guidelines for data collection and analysis: A cornerstone for conducting high-quality research. In *How to publish high-quality research*. Washington, DC: American Psychological Association.

Jolly, J. L., Matthews, M. S., & Nester, J. (2013). Homeschooling the gifted: A parent's perspective. *Gifted Child Quarterly, 57*, 121–134.

Jones, D. E., Carson, K. A., Bleich, S. N., & Cooper, L. A. (2012). Patient trust in physicians and adoption of lifestyle behaviors to control high blood pressure. *Patient Education and Counseling*. Accessed online, 7/22/12; http://www.ncbi.nlm.nih.gov/pubmed/22770676.

Jones, J. (2008, December 1). Healthcare access, cost are top health concerns. Gallup Poll, accessed online; http://www.gallup.com/poll/112516/healthcare-access-cost-top-health-concerns.aspx.

Jones, N. A., & Mize, K. D. (2016). Introduction to the special issue: Psychophysiology and psychobiology in emotion development. *Journal of Experimental Child Psychology, 142*, 239–244.

Jones, P. R., Kalwarowsky, S., Braddick, O. J., Atkinson, J., & Nardini, M. (2015). Optimizing the rapid measurement of detection thresholds in infants. *Journal of Vision, 15*, 88–97.

Jones, T. (2013). Through the lens of home-educated children: Engagement in education. *Educational Psychology in Practice, 29*, 107–121.

Jongudomkarn, D., & Camfield, L. (2006, September). Exploring the quality of life of people in northeastern and southern Thailand. *Social Indicators Research, 78*, 489–529.

Jordan-Young, R. M. (2012). Hormones, context, and "brain gender": A review of evidence from congenital adrenal hyperplasia. *Social Science & Medicine, 74*, 1738–1744.

Jose, O., & Alfons, V. (2007). Do demographics affect marital satisfaction? *Journal of Sex and Marital Therapy, 33*, 73–85.

Joseph, D. L., Jin, J., Newman, D. A., & O'Boyle, E. H. (2015). Why does self-reported emotional intelligence predict job performance? A meta-analytic investigation of mixed EI. *Journal of Applied Psychology, 100*, 298–342.

Jost, J. T., Kivetz, Y., Rubini, M., Guermandi, G., & Mosso, C. (2005). System-justifying functions of complementary regional and ethnic stereotypes: Cross-national evidence. *Social Justice Research, 18*(3), 305–333. doi:10.1007/s11211-005-6827-z.

Ju, C., Zhao, F., Zhang, B., & Deng, J. (2015). Effects of fathering style on social problem-solving among Chinese teenagers: The roles of masculine gender stereotypes and identity. *Personality and Individual Differences, 77*, 124–130.

Judd, C. M., & Park, B. (2005). Group differences and stereotype accuracy. In J. F. Dovidio, P. Click, & L. A. Rudman (Eds.), *On the nature of prejudice: Fifty years after Allport*. Malden, MA: Blackwell Publishing.

Judge, T. A., Ilies, R., & Zhang, Z. (2012). Genetic influences on core self-evaluations, job satisfaction, and work stress: A behavioral genetics mediated model. *Organizational Behavior and Human Decision Processes, 117*, 208–220.

Julvez, J., Guxens, M., Carsin, A., Forns, J., Mendez, M., Turner, M. C., & Sunyer, J. (2014). A cohort study on full breastfeeding and child neuropsychological development: The role of maternal social, psychological, and nutritional factors. *Developmental Medicine & Child Neurology, 56*, 148–156.

Jung, E., & Zhang, Y. (2016). Parental involvement, children's aspirations, and achievement in new immigrant families. *The Journal of Educational Research, 109*, 333–350.

Juntunen, C., Wegner, K., & Matthews, L. (2002). Promoting positive career change in midlife. In *Counseling across the lifespan: Prevention and treatment*. Thousand Oaks, CA: Sage Publications.

Jurecic, A. (2017). Cautioning health-care professionals: Bereaved persons are misguided through the stages of grief. *Omega: Journal of Death and Dying, 75*(1), 92–93. doi:10.1177/0030222817701499.

Jurimae, T., & Saar, M. (2003). Self-perceived and actual indicators of motor abilities in children and adolescents. *Perception and Motor Skills, 97*, 862–866.

Juster, F., Ono, H., & Stafford, F. (2004). *Changing times of American youth: 1981–2003*. Ann Arbor, MI: Institute for Social Research.

Juvonen, J., Le, V-N., Kaganoff, T., Augustine, C. H., & Constand, L. (2004). *Focus on the wonder years: Challenges facing the American middle school*. Santa Monica, CA: Rand Corporation.

Kaffashi, F., Scher, M. S., Ludington-Hoe, S. M., & Loparo, K. A. (2013). An analysis of the kangaroo care intervention using neonatal EEG complexity: A preliminary study. *Clinical Neurophysiology, 124*, 238–246.

Kadam, G. (2014). Psychological health of parents whose children are away from them. *Indian Journal of Community Psychology, 10*, 358–363.

Kagan, J., Arcus, D., & Snidman, N. (1993). The idea of temperament: Where do we go from here? In R. Plomin & G. E. McClearn (Eds.), *Nature, nurture, and psychology*. Washington, DC: American Psychological Association.

Kagan, J. (2010). *The temperamental thread: How genes, culture, time, and luck make us who we are*. Washington, DC: Dana Press.

Kagan, J., Kearsley, R., & Zelazo, P. R. (1978). *Infancy: Its place in human development*. Cambridge, MA: Harvard University Press.

Kahn, J. (2007, February). Maximizing the potential public health impact of HPV vaccines: A focus on parents. *Journal of Adolescent Health, 40*, 101–103.

Kail, R. (1991). Developmental changes in speed of processing during childhood and adolescence. *Psychological Bulletin, 109*, 490–501.

Kail, R. V. (2004). Cognitive development includes global and domain-specific processes. *Merrill-Palmer Quarterly, 50* [Special issue: 50th anniversary issue: Part II, the maturing of the human development sciences: Appraising past, present, and prospective agendas], 445–455.

Kaiser Family Foundation. (2010). *Generation M2: Media in the lives of 8-18 year-olds*. Washington, DC: Kaiser Family Foundation.

Kalb, C. (1997, Spring/Summer). The top 10 health worries. *Newsweek Special Issue*, pp. 42–43.

Kalb, C. (2006). Peering into the Future. *Newsweek*. Accessed online, 5/30/18; http://www.newsweek.com/peering-future-105685.

Kalb, C. (2012, February). Fetal armor. *Scientific American*, p. 73.

Kalsi, M., Heron, G., & Charman, W. (2001). Changes in the static accommodation response with age. *Ophthalmic & Physiological Optics, 21*, 77–84.

Kaltiala-Heino, R., Kosunen, E., & Rimpela, M. (2003). Pubertal timing, sexual behaviour and self-reported depression in middle adolescence. *Journal of Adolescence, 26*, 531–545.

Kaminaga, M. (2007). Pubertal development and depression in adolescent boys and girls. *Japanese Journal of Educational Psychology, 55*, 21–33.

Kan, P., & Kohnert, K. (2009). Fast mapping by bilingual preschool children. *Journal of Child Language, 35*, 495–514.

Kandler, C., Bleidorn, W., & Riemann, R. (2012). Left or right? Sources of political orientation: The roles of genetic factors, cultural transmission, assortative mating, and personality. *Journal of Personality and Social Psychology, 102*, 633–645.

Kaneda, H., Maeshima, K., Goto, N., Kobayakawa, T., Ayabe-Kanamura, S., & Saito, S. (2000). Decline in taste and odor discrimination abilities with age, and relationship between gustation and olfaction. *Chemical Senses, 25*, 331–337.

Kanters, M. A., Bocarro, J. N., Edwards, M. B., Casper, J. M., & Floyd, M. F. (2013). School sport participation under two school sport policies: Comparisons by race/ethnicity, gender, and socioeconomic status. *Annals of Behavioral Medicine, 45*(Suppl 1), S113–S121.

Kantor, J. (2015, June 27). Historic day for gay rights, but a twinge of loss for gay culture. *New York Times*, A1.

Kantrowitz, E. J., & Evans, G. W. (2004). The relation between the ratio of children per activity area and off-task behavior and type of play in day care centers. *Environment & Behavior, 36*, 541–557.

Kao, G. (2000). Psychological well-being and educational achievement among immigrant youth. In D. J. Hernandez (Ed.), *Children of immigrants: Health, adjustment, and public assistance*. Washington, DC: National Academy Press.

Kapke, T. L., Gerdes, A. C., & Lawton, K. E. (2017). Global self-worth in Latino youth: The role of acculturation and acculturation risk factors. *Child & Youth Care Forum, 46*, 307–333.

Karney, B. R., & Bradbury, T. N. (2005). Contextual influences on marriage. *Current Directions in Psychological Science, 14*, 171–174.

Karpov, Y. (2006). Neo-Vygotskian activity theory: Merging Vygotsky's and Piaget's theories of cognitive development. In *Frontiers in Cognitive psychology*. Hauppauge, NY: Nova Science Publishers.

Karraker, A., DeLamater, J., & Schwartz, C. R. (2011). Sexual frequency decline from midlife to later life. *Journals of Gerontology, Series B, Psychological Sciences, 66B*, 502–512.

Kastenbaum, R. (1985). Dying and death: A life-span approach. In J. E. Birren & K. W. Schaie (Eds.), *Handbook of the psychology of aging*. New York: Van Nostrand Reinhold.

Kastenbaum, R. J. (2000). *The psychology of death* (3rd ed.). New York: Springer.

Kato, K., & Pedersen, N. L. (2005). Personality and coping: A study of twins reared apart and twins reared together. *Behavior Genetics, 35*, 147–158.

Katz, S., & Marshall, B. (2003). New sex for old: Lifestyle, consumerism, and the ethics of aging well. *Journal of Aging Studies, 17*, 3–16.

Kaufman, J. C., & Sternberg, R. (2006). *The international handbook of creativity*. New York: Cambridge University Press.

Kaufman, J. C., Kaufman, A. S., Kaufman-Singer, J., & Kaufman, N. L. (2005). The Kaufman assessment battery for children—Second Edition and the Kaufman adolescent and adult intelligence test. In D. P. Flanagan & P. L. Harrison (Eds.), *Contemporary intellectual assessment: Theories, tests, and issues*. New York: Guilford Press.

Kaufmann, D., Gesten, E., Santa Lucia, R. C., Salcedo, O., Rendina-Gobioff, G., & Gadd, R. (2000). The relationship between parenting style and children's adjustment: The parents' perspective. *Journal of Child & Family Studies, 9*, 231–245.

Kavšek, M. (2004). Predicting later IQ from infant visual habituation and dishabituation: A meta-analysis. *Journal of Applied Developmental Psychology, 25*, 369–393.

Kawakami, K. (2014). The early sociability of toddlers: The origins of teaching. *Infant Behavior & Development, 37*, 174–177.

Kaye, W. H., Devlin, B., Barbarich, N., Bulik, C. M., Thornton, L., Badanu, S. A., et al. (2004). Genetic analysis of bulimia nervosa: Methods and sample description. *Journal of Eating Disorders, 35*, 556–570.

Keating, D. P. (1980). Thinking processes in adolescence. In J. Adelson (Ed.), *Handbook of adolescent psychology*. New York: Wiley.

Keating, D. P. (1990). Adolescent thinking. In S. S. Feldman & G. R. Elliott (Eds.), *At the threshold*. Cambridge, MA: Harvard University Press.

Keene, J. R., Prokos, A. H., & Held, B. (2012). Grandfather caregivers: Race and ethnic differences in poverty. *Sociological Inquiry, 82*, 49–77.

Kehl, K. A., & McCarty, K. N. (2012). Readability of hospice materials to prepare families for caregiving at the time of death. *Research in Nursing & Health, 35*, 242–249.

Kellehear, A. (2015). Death education as a public health issue. In J. M. Stillion, T. Attig (Eds.), *Death, dying, and bereavement: Contemporary perspectives, institutions, and practices*. New York: Springer.

Keller, H., Voelker, S., & Yovsi, R. D. (2005). Conceptions of parenting in different cultural communities: The case of West African Nso and Northern German women. *Social Development, 14*, 158–180.

Keller, H., Yovsi, R., Borke, J., Kartner, J., Henning, J., & Papaligoura, Z. (2004). Developmental consequences of early parenting experiences: Self-recognition and self-regulation in three cultural communities. *Child Development, 75*, 1745–1760.

Kellman, P., & Arterberry, M. (2006). Infant visual perception. In W. Damon & R. M. Lerner (Eds.), *Handbook of child psychology: Vol. 2, Cognition, perception, and language* (6th ed.). New York: Wiley.

Kelloway, E., & Francis, L. (2013). Longitudinal research and data analysis. In R. R. Sinclair, M. Wang, & L. E. Tetrick (Eds.), *Research methods in occupational health psychology: Measurement, design, and data analysis*. New York: Routledge/Taylor & Francis Group.

Kelly, G. (2001). *Sexuality today: A human perspective* (7th ed.). New York: McGraw-Hill.

Kelly, J. B., & Emery, R. E. (2003). Children's adjustment following divorce: Risk and resilience perspectives. *Family Relations, 52*(4), 352–362.

Kemper, S. (2012). The interaction of linguistic constraints, working memory, and aging on language production and comprehension. In M. Naveh-Benjamin, N. Ohta (Eds.), *Memory and aging: Current issues and future directions*. New York: Psychology Press.

Kendler, K. S., Aggen, S. H., Gillespie, N., Neale, M. C., Knudsen, G. P., Krueger, R. F., & . . . Reichborn-Kjennerud, T. (2017). The genetic and environmental sources of resemblance between normative personality and personality disorder traits. *Journal of Personality Disorders, 31*, 193–207.

Kenett, Y. N., Beaty, R. E., Silvia, P. J., Anaki, D., & Faust, M. (2016). Structure and flexibility: Investigating the relation between the structure of the mental lexicon, fluid intelligence, and creative achievement. *Psychology of Aesthetics, Creativity, and the Arts, 10*, 377–388.

Kennedy-Hendricks, A., Barry, C. L., Gollust, S. E., Ensminger, M. E., Chisolm, M. S., & McGinty, E. E. (2017). Social stigma toward persons with prescription opioid use disorder: Associations with public support for punitive and public health–oriented policies. *Psychiatric Services, 68*, 462–469.

Kestly, T. A. (2014). *The interpersonal neurobiology of play: Brain-building interventions for emotional well-being*. New York: W. W. Norton & Co.

Kemps, E., & Tiggemann, M. (2007). Reducing the vividness and emotional impact of distressing autobiographical memories: The importance of modality-specific interference. *Memory, 15*(4), 412–422. doi:10.1080/09658210701262017.

Khodarahimi, S., & Fathi, R. (2017). Mate selection, meaning of marriage and positive cognitive constructs on younger and older married individuals. *Contemporary Family Therapy: An International Journal, 39*, 132–139.

Kiang, L., Yip, T., & Fuligni, A. J. (2008). Multiple social identities and adjustment in young adults from ethnically diverse backgrounds. *Journal of Research on Adolescence, 18*, 643–670.

Kiecolt, K. J., & Fossett, M. A. (1997). The effects of mate availability on marriage among black Americans: A contextual analysis. In R. J. Taylor, J. S. Jackson, & L. M. Chatters (Eds.), *Family life in black America* (pp. 63–78). Thousand Oaks, CA: Sage Publications.

Kim, B., Chow, S., Bray, B., & Teti, D. M. (2017). Trajectories of mothers' emotional availability: Relations with infant temperament in predicting attachment security. *Attachment & Human Development, 19*, 38–57.

Kim, E. H., & Lee, E. (2009). Effects of a death education program on life satisfaction and attitude toward death in college students. *Journal of Korean Academic Nursing, 39*, 1–9.

Kim, J., Bushway, S., & Tsao, H. (2016). Identifying classes of explanations for crime drop: Period and cohort effects for New York State. *Journal of Quantitative Criminology, 32*, 357–375.

Kim, J-S., & Lee, E-H. (2003). Cultural and noncultural predictors of health outcomes in Korean daughter and daughter-in-law caregivers. *Public Health Nursing, 20*, 111–119.

Kim, J. J., Fung, J., Wu, Q., Fang, C., & Lau, A. S. (2017). Parenting variables associated with growth mindset: An examination of three Chinese-heritage samples. *Asian American Journal of Psychology, 8*, 115–125.

Kim, M. T., Han, H-R., Shin, H. S., Kim, K. B., & Lee, H. B. (2005). Factors associated with depression experience of immigrant populations: A study of Korean immigrants. *Archives of Psychiatric Nursing, 19*, 217–225.

Kim, P. Y., & Lee, D. (2014). Internalized model minority myth, Asian values, and help-seeking attitudes among Asian American students. *Cultural Diversity and Ethnic Minority Psychology, 20*, 98–106.

Kim, Y. K., Curby, T. W., & Winsler, A. (2014). Child, family, and school characteristics related to English proficiency development among low-income, dual language learners. *Developmental Psychology, 50*, 2600–2613.

Kim-Cohen, J. (2007). Resilience and developmental psychopathology. *Child and Adolescent Psychiatric Clinics of North America, 16*, 271–283.

Kimm, S. Y., Glynn, N. W., Kriska, A. M., Barton, B. A., Kronsberg, S. S., Daniels, S. R., Crawford, P. B., Sabry, Z. I., & Liu, K. (2003). Decline in physical activity in black girls and white girls during adolescence. *New England Journal of Medicine, 347*, 709–715.

Kinney, H. C., Randall, L. L., Sleeper, L. A., Willinger, M., Beliveau, R. A., Zec, N., et al. (2003). Serotonergic brainstem abnormalities in Northern Plains Indians with the sudden infant death syndrome. *Journal of Neuropathology and Experimental Neurology, 62*, 1178–1191.

Kinney, H., & Thach, B. (2009). Medical progress: The sudden infant death syndrome. *The New England Journal of Medicine, 361*, 795–805.

Kinsey, A. C., Pomeroy, W. B., & Martin, C. E. (1948). *Sexual behavior in the human male*. Philadelphia: Saunders.

Kirby, J. (2006, May). From single-parent families to stepfamilies: Is the transition associated with adolescent alcohol initiation? *Journal of Family Issues, 27*, 685–711.

Kirchengast, S., & Hartmann, B. (2003). Impact of maternal age and maternal-somatic characteristics on newborn size. *American Journal of Human Biology, 15*, 220–228.

Kirkorian, H. L., Lavigne, H. J., Hanson, K. G., Troseth, G. L., Demers, L. B., & Anderson, D. R. (2016). Video deficit in toddlers' object retrieval: What eye movements reveal about online cognition. *Infancy, 21*, 37–64.

Kirsch, S. J. (2012). *Children, adolescents, and media violence: A critical look at the research* (2nd ed.). Thousand Oaks, CA: Sage Publications, Inc.

Kitamura, C., & Lam, C. (2009). Age-specific preferences for infant-directed affective intent. *Infancy, 14*, 77–100.

Kiuru, N., Nurmi, J., Aunola, K., & Salmela-Aro, K. (2009). Peer group homogeneity in adolescents' school adjustment varies according to peer group type and gender. *International Journal of Behavioral Development, 33*, 65–76.

Kjerulff, K. H., & Brubaker, L. H. (2017). New mothers' feelings of disappointment and failure after cesarean delivery. *Birth: Issues in Perinatal Care.* Accessed online, 10/29/17; https://www.ncbi.nlm.nih.gov/pubmed/?term=New+mothers%E2%80%99+feelings+of+disappointment+and+failure+after+cesarean+delivery.+Birth%3A+Issues+In+Perinatal+Care.

Kleespies, P. (2004). The wish to die: Assisted suicide and voluntary euthanasia. In P. Kleespies (Ed.), *Life and death decisions: Psychological and ethical considerations in end-of-life care*. Washington, DC: American Psychological Association.

Klein, M. C. (2012). The tyranny of meta-analysis and the misuse of randomized controlled trials in maternity care. *Birth: Issues in Perinatal Care, 39*, 80–82.

Kleinman, A. (2012). Culture, bereavement, and psychiatry. *The Lancet, 379*, 608–609.

Klibanoff, R., Levine, S., Huttenlocher, J., Vasilyeva, M., & Hedges, L. (2006). Preschool children's mathematical knowledge: The effect of teacher "math talk." *Developmental Psychology, 42*, 59–69.

Klimstra, T. A., Luyckx, K., Germeijs, V., Meeus, W. J., & Goossens, L. (2012). Personality traits and educational identity formation in late adolescents: Longitudinal associations and academic progress. *Journal of Youth and Adolescence, 41*, 346–361.

Klingner, J., & Artiles, A. J. (2006). English language learners struggling to learn to read: Emergent scholarship on linguistic differences and learning disabilities. *Journal of Learning Disabilities, 39*(5), 386–389. doi:10.1177/00222194060390050101.

Klitzman, R. L. (2012). *Am I my genes? Confronting fate and family secrets in the age of genetic testing*. New York: Oxford University Press.

Kloep, M., Güney, N., Çok, F., & Simsek, Ö. (2009). Motives for risk-taking in adolescence: A cross-cultural study. *Journal of Adolescence, 32*, 135–151.

Knafo, A., & Schwartz, S. H. (2003). Parenting and accuracy of perception of parental values by adolescents. *Child Development, 73*, 595–611.

Knaus, W. A., Conners, A. F., Dawson, N. V., Desbiens, N. A., Fulkerson, W. J., Jr., Goldman, L., et al. (1995, November 22). A controlled trial to improve care for seriously ill hospitalized patients: The study to understand prognoses and preferences for outcomes and risks of treatments (SUPPORT). *JAMA: The Journal of the American Medical Association, 273*, 1591–1598.

Knickmeyer, R., & Baron-Cohen, S. (2006, December). Fetal testosterone and sex differences. *Early Human Development, 82*, 755–760.

Knight, Z. G. (2017). A proposed model of psychodynamic psychotherapy linked to Erik Erikson's eight stages of psychosocial development. *Clinical Psychology & Psychotherapy.* Accessed online, 3/2/17; https://www.ncbi.nlm.nih.gov/pubmed/28124459.

Knowles, J. (2005). Birth control choices for teens. Accessed online, 5/1/06; http://www.plannedparenthood.org/pp2/portal/files/portal/medicalinfo/birthcontrol/pub-bc-choices-teens.xml.

Koball, H., & Jiang, Y. (2018, January). *Basic facts about low-income children*. New York: National Center for Children in Poverty.

Kochanska, G., Friesenborg, A. E., Lange, L. A., & Martel, M. M. (2004). Parents' personality and infants' temperament as contributors to their emerging relationship. *Journal of Personality and Social Psychology, 86*(5), 744–759. doi:10.1037/0022-3514.86.5.744.

Koenig, L. B., McGue, M., Krueger, R. F., & Bouchard, T. J., Jr. (2005). Genetic and environmental influences on religiousness: Findings for retrospective and current religiousness ratings. *Journal of Personality, 73*, 471–488.

Koenig, M., & Cole, C. (2013). Early word learning. In D. Reisberg (Ed.), *The Oxford handbook of cognitive psychology*. New York: Oxford University Press.

Koh, S., & Sewell, D. D. (2015). Sexual functions in older adults. *The American Journal of Geriatric Psychiatry, 23*, 223–226.

Kohlberg, L. (1966). A cognitive-developmental analysis of children's sex-role concepts and attitudes. In E. E. Maccoby (Ed.), *The development of sex differences*. Stanford, CA: Stanford University Press.

Kohlberg, L. (1969). Stage and sequence: The cognitive-developmental approach to socialization. In D. Goslin (Ed.), *Handbook of socialization theory and research*. Chicago: Rand McNally.

Kohlberg, L. (1984). *The psychology of moral development: Essays on moral development (Vol. 2)*. San Francisco: Harper & Row.

Kohut, S., & Riddell, R. (2009). Does the Neonatal Facial Coding System differentiate between infants experiencing pain-related and non-pain-related distress? *The Journal of Pain, 10*, 214–220.

Koike, K. J. (2014). *Everyday audiology: A practical guide for health care professionals* (2nd ed.). San Diego: Plural Publishing.

Kolata, G. (2004, May 11). The heart's desire. *New York Times*, p. D1.

Kolb, V. M. (1993). *Teratogens: Chemicals which cause birth defects*. New York: Elsevier Science Publishers.

Kosminsky, P. (2017). CBT for grief: Clearing cognitive obstacles to healing from loss. *Journal of Rational-Emotive & Cognitive-Behavior Therapy, 35*, 26–37.

Konigsberg R. D. (2011). Chore wars. *Time, 178*, pp. 44–49.

Konrad, K., Firk, C., & Uhlhaas, P. J. (2013). Brain development during adolescence. *Deutsches Przteblatt International, 110*, 425–431.

Koopmans, S., & Kooijman, A. (2006, November). Presbyopia correction and accommodative intraocular lenses. *Gerontechnology, 5*, 222–230.

Korotchikova, I., Stevenson, N. J., Livingstone, V., Ryan, C. A., & Boylan, G. B. (2016). Sleep–wake cycle of the healthy term newborn infant in the immediate postnatal period. *Clinical Neurophysiology, 127*, 2095–2101.

Korte, J., Westerhof, G. J., & Bohlmeijer, E. T. (2012). Mediating processes in an effective life-review intervention. *Psychology and Aging*. Accessed online, 7/24/12; http://psycnet.apa.org/psycinfo/2012-17923-001/.

Kosic, A. (2004). Acculturation strategies, coping process and acculturative stress. *Scandinavian Journal of Psychology, 45*, 269–278.

Koska, J., Ksinantova, L., Sebokova, E., Kvetnansky, R., Klimes, I., Chrousos, G., et al. (2002). Endocrine regulation of subcutaneous fat metabolism during cold exposure in humans. *Annals of the New York Academy of Science, 967*, 500–505.

Kotre, J., & Hall, E. (1990). *Seasons of life*. Boston: Little, Brown.

Kozey, M., & Siegel, L. (2008). Definitions of learning disabilities in Canadian provinces and territories. *Canadian Psychology/ Psychologie Canadienne, 49*, 162–171.

Krahé, B., & Busching, R. (2015). Breaking the vicious cycle of media violence use and aggression: A test of intervention effects over 30 months. *Psychology of Violence, 5*, 217–226.

Krause, N. (2003a). Religious meaning and subjective well-being in late life. *Journals of Gerontology: Series B: Psychological Sciences and Social Sciences, 58B*, S160–S170.

Krause, N. (2008). The social foundation of religious meaning in life. *Research on Aging, 30*, 395–427.

Kreager, D. A., Molloy, L. E., Moody, J., & Feinberg, M. E. (2016). Friends first? The peer network origins of adolescent dating. *Journal of Research on Adolescence, 26*, 257–269.

Kretch, K. S., & Adolph, K. E. (2013). Cliff or step? Posture-specific learning at the edge of a drop-off. *Child Development, 84*, 226–240.

Kretsch, N., Mendle, J., Cance, J. D., & Harden, K. P. (2016). Peer group similarity in perceptions of pubertal timing. *Journal of Youth and Adolescence, 45*, 1696–1710.

Krishnamoorthy, J. S., Hart, C., & Jelalian, E. (2006). The epidemic of childhood obesity: Review of research and implications for public policy. *Social Policy Report, 19*, 3–19.

Kroger, J. (2000). *Identity development: Adolescence through adulthood*. Thousand Oaks, CA: Sage Publications.

Kronenfeld, J. J. (2002). *Health care policy: Issues and trends*. New York: Prager.

Kross, E., & Grossmann, I. (2012). Boosting wisdom: Distance from the self enhances wise reasoning, attitudes, and behavior. *Journal of Experimental Psychology: General, 141*, 43–48.

Kross, E., Verduyn, P., Demiralp, E., Park, J., Lee, D. S., Lin, N., & . . . Ybarra, O. (2013). Facebook use predicts declines in subjective well-being in young adults. *Plos ONE, 8*, 22–29.

Krüger, O., Korsten, P., & Hoffman, J. I. (2017). The rise of behavioral genetics and the transition to behavioral genomics and beyond. In J. Call, G. M. Burghardt, I. M. Pepperberg, C. T. Snowdon, T. Zentall (Eds.), *APA handbook of comparative psychology: Basic concepts, methods, neural substrate, and behavior*. Washington, DC: American Psychological Association.

Kübler-Ross, E. (1969). *On death and dying*. New York: Macmillan.

Kübler-Ross, E. (1982). *Working it through*. New York: Macmillan.

Kuhn, D., & Franklin, S. (2006). The second decade: What develops (and how). In *Handbook of child psychology: Vol 2, Cognition,*

perception, and language (6th ed.). Hoboken, NJ: John Wiley & Sons Inc.

Kulik, L., Walfisch, S., & Liberman, G. (2016). Spousal conflict resolution strategies and marital relations in late adulthood. *Personal Relationships, 23*, 456–474.

Kurdek, L. (2008). Change in relationship quality for partners from lesbian, gay male, and heterosexual couples. *Journal of Family Psychology, 22*, 701–711.

Kurdek, L. A. (1999). The nature and predictors of the trajectory of change in marital quality for husbands and wives over the first 10 years of marriage. *Developmental Psychology, 35*, 1283–1296.

Kurdek, L. A. (2006, May). Differences between partners from heterosexual, gay, and lesbian cohabiting couples. *Journal of Marriage and Family, 68*, 509–528.

Kuron, L. J., Lyons, S. T., Schweitzer, L., & Ng, E. W. (2015). Millennials' work values: Differences across the school to work transition. *Personnel Review, 44*, 991–1009.

Kurtz-Costes, B., Swinton, A. D., & Skinner, O. D. (2014). Racial and ethnic gaps in the school performance of Latino, African American, and White students. In F. L. Leong, L. Comas-Díaz, G. C. Nagayama Hall, V. C. McLoyd, J. E. Trimble (Eds.), *APA handbook of multicultural psychology, Vol. 1: Theory and research.* Washington, DC: American Psychological Association.

Kusangi, E., Nakano, S., & Kondo-Ikemura, K. (2014). The development of infant temperament and its relationship with maternal temperament. *Psychologia: An International Journal of Psychological Sciences, 57*, 31–38.

Kuther, T. L. (2000). Moral reasoning, perceived competence, and adolescent engagement in risky activity. *Journal of Adolescence, 23*, 599–604.

Kuther, T. L., & Higgins-D'Alessandro, A. (2000). Bridging the gap between moral reasoning and adolescent engagement in risky behavior. *Journal of Adolescence, 23*, 409–422.

Kuykendall, L., Tay, L., & Ng, V. (2015). Leisure engagement and subjective well-being: A meta-analysis. *Psychological Bulletin, 141*, 364–403.

Labouvie-Vief, G. (2009). Cognition and equilibrium regulation in development and aging. *Restorative Neurology and Neuroscience, 27*, 551–565.

Labouvie-Vief, G. (2015). *Integrating emotions and cognition throughout the lifespan*. Cham, Switzerland: Springer International Publishing.

Lackey, C. (2003). Violent family heritage, the transition to adulthood, and later partner violence. *Journal of Family Issues, 24*, 74–98.

Laemmle, J. (2013). Review of Children at play: Learning gender in the early years. *Journal of Youth and Adolescence, 42*, 305–307.

Laflamme, D., Pomerleau, A., & Malcuit, G. (2002). A comparison of fathers' and mothers' involvement in childcare and stimulation behaviors during free-play with their infants at 9 and 15 months. *Sex Roles, 47*, 507–518.

LaFreniere, P., Masataka, N., Butovskaya, M., Chen, Q., Dessen, M., Atwanger, K., et al. (2002). Cross-cultural analysis of social competence and behavior problems in preschoolers. *Early Education and Development, 13*, 201–219.

LaFromboise, T., Coleman, H. L., & Gerton, J. (1993). Psychological impact of biculturalism: Evidence and theory. *Psychological Bulletin, 114*, 395–412.

Lahiri, D. K., Maloney, B., Basha, M. R., Ge, Y. W., & Zawia, N. H. (2007). How and when environmental agents and dietary factors affect the course of Alzheimer's disease: The "LEARn" model (latent early-life associated regulation) may explain the triggering of AD. *Current Alzheimer Research, 4*, 219–228.

Lain, D. (2012). Working past 65 in the UK and the USA: Segregation into "Lopaq" occupations? *Work, Employment and Society, 26*, 78–94.

Lam, S-F., Chiu, C-Y., Lau, I. Y., Chan, W-M., & Yim, P. (2006). Managing intergroup attitudes among Hong Kong adolescents: Effects of social category inclusiveness and time pressure. *Asian Journal of Social Psychology, 9*, 1–11.

Lambiase, A., Aloe, L., Centofanti, M., Parisi, V., Mantelli, F., Colafrancesco, V., et al. (2009). Experimental and clinical evidence of neuroprotection by nerve growth factor eye drops: Implications for glaucoma. *PNAS Proceedings of the National Academy of Sciences of the United States of America, 106,* 13469–13474.

Lamaze, F. (1970). *Painless childbirth: The Lamaze method.* Chicago: Regnery.

Lambert, W. W. (1971). Cross-cultural backgrounds to personality development and the socialization of aggression: Findings from the six culture study. In W. W. Lambert & R. Weisbrod (Eds.), *Comparative perspectives in social psychology.* Boston: Little Brown.

Lamidi, E., & Cruz, J. (2014). *Remarriage Rate in the U.S., 2012. (FP-14-10).* National Center for Family & Marriage Research. Accessed online, 11/29/17; https://www.bgsu.edu/content/dam/BGSU/college-of-arts-and-sciences/NCFMR/documents/FP/FP-14-10-remarriage-rate-2012.pdf.

Lamm, B., & Keller, H. (2007). Understanding cultural models of parenting: The role of intracultural variation and response style. *Journal of Cross-Cultural Psychology, 38,* 50–57.

Landstrom, S., Granhag, P., & Hartwig, M. (2007). Children's live and videotaped testimonies: How presentation mode affects observers' perception, assessment and memory. *Legal and Criminological Psychology, 12,* 333–347.

Landy, F., & Conte, J. M. (2004). *Work in the 21st century.* New York: McGraw-Hill.

Lane, K. A., Goh, J. X., & Driver-Linn, E. (2012). Implicit science stereotypes mediate the relationship between gender and academic participation. *Sex Roles, 66,* 220–234.

Langer, E., & Janis, I. (1979). *The psychology of control.* Beverly Hills, CA: Sage Publications.

Langfur, S. (2013). The You-I event: On the genesis of self-awareness. *Phenomenology and the Cognitive Sciences, 12,* 769–790.

Langrehr, K. J., Thomas, A. J., & Morgan, S. K. (2016). Confirmatory evidence for a multidimensional model of racial-ethnic socialization for transracially adoptive families. *Cultural Diversity and Ethnic Minority Psychology, 22,* 432–439.

Lansford, J. (2009). Parental divorce and children's adjustment. *Perspectives on Psychological Science, 4,* 140–152.

Lansford, J. E., Chang, L., Dodge, K. A., Malone, P. S., Oburu, P., Palmerus, K., et al. (2005). Physical discipline and children's adjustment: Cultural normativeness as a moderator. *Child Development, 76,* 1234–1246.

Lapan, C., & Boseovski, J. J. (2017). When peer performance matters: Effects of expertise and traits on children's self-evaluations after social comparison. *Child Development, 88,* 1860–1872.

LaPrairie, J. L., & Murphy, A. Z. (2009). Neonatal injury alters adult pain sensitivity by increasing opioid tone in the periaqueductal gray. *Frontiers in Behavioral Neuroscience.* Accessed online, 8/20/15; http://www.ncbi.nlm.nih.gov/pmc/articles/PMC2766783/.

Lapsley, D. (2006). Moral stage theory. In *Handbook of moral development.* Mahwah, NJ: Lawrence Erlbaum Associates Publishers.

Largo, R. H., Fischer, J. E., & Rousson, V. (2003). Neuromotor development from kindergarten age to adolescence: Developmental course and variability. *Swedish Medical Weekly, 133,* 193–199.

Larsen, K. E., O'Hara, M. W., & Brewer, K. K. (2001). A prospective study of self-efficacy expectancies and labor pain. *Journal of Reproductive and Infant Psychology, 19,* 203–214.

Larson, D. G. (2014). Taking stock: Past contributions and current thinking on death, dying, and grief. *Death Studies, 38,* 349–352.

Larson, R. W., Richards, M. H., Moneta, G., Holmbeck, G., & Duckett, E. (1996). Changes in adolescents' daily interactions with their families from ages 10 to 18: Disengagement and transformation. *Developmental Psychology, 32,* 744–754.

Larson, R. W., Richards, M. H., Sims, B., & Dworkin, J. (2001). How urban African American young adolescents spend their time: Time budgets for locations, activities, and companionship. *American Journal of Community Psychology, 29,* 565–597.

Latorre, J. M., Serrano, J. P., Ricarte, J., Bonete, B., Ros, L., & Sitges, E. (2015). Life review based on remembering specific positive events in active aging. *Journal of Aging and Health, 27,* 140–157.

Lau, I., Lee, S., & Chiu, C. (2004). Language, cognition, and reality: Constructing shared meanings through communication. In M. Schaller & C. Crandall (Eds.), *The psychological foundations of culture.* Mahwah, NJ: Lawrence Erlbaum.

Lau, M., Markham, C., Lin, H., Flores, G., & Chacko, M. (2009). Dating and sexual attitudes in Asian-American adolescents. *Journal of Adolescent Research, 24,* 91–113.

Lau, Y. C., Hinkley, L. N., Bukshpun, P., Strominger, Z. A., Wakahiro, M. J., Baron-Cohen, S., & . . . Marco, E. J. (2013). Autism traits in individuals with agenesis of the corpus callosum. *Journal of Autism and Developmental Disorders, 430,* 1106–1118.

Laugharne, J., Janca, A., & Widiger, T. (2007). Posttraumatic stress disorder and terrorism: 5 years after 9/11. *Current Opinion in Psychiatry, 20,* 36–41.

Laughlin, L. (2013). Who's minding the kids? Child care Arrangements: Spring 2011. *Current Population Reports,* P70-135. Washington, DC: U.S. Census Bureau.

Lauricella, T. (2001, November). The education of a home schooler. *Smart Money,* pp. 115–121.

Lavelle, J. S. (2015). Is a modular cognitive architecture compatible with the direct perception of mental states? *Consciousness and Cognition: An International Journal.* Accessed online, 6/17/15; http://www.ncbi.nlm.nih.gov/pubmed/25682016.

Lawlor, D. A., O'Callaghan, M. J., Mamun, A. A., Williams, G. M., Bor, W., & Najman, J. M. (2005), Socioeconomic position, cognitive function, and clustering of cardiovascular risk factors in adolescence: Findings from the Mater University study of pregnancy and its outcomes. *Psychosomatic Medicine, 67,* 862–868.

Lawson, C. A., Fisher, A. V., & Rakison, D. H. (2015). How children learn the ins and outs: A training study of toddlers' categorization of animals. *Journal of Cognition and Development, 16,* 236–251.

Lazarus, R. S. (1991). *Emotion and adaptation.* New York: Oxford University Press.

Lazarus, R. S., & Folkman, S. (1984). *Stress, appraisal, and coping.* New York: Springer.

Le, H., Oh, I., Shaffer, J., & Schmidt, F. (2010). Implications of methodological advances for the practice of personnel selection: How practitioners benefit from meta-analysis. In *Readings in organizational behavior.* New York: Routledge/Taylor & Francis.

Leandro-França, C., Murta, S. G., Hershey, D. A., & Martins, L. B. (2016). Evaluation of retirement planning programs: A qualitative analysis of methodologies and efficacy. *Educational Gerontology, 42,* 497–512.

Leaper, C. (2002). Parenting girls and boys. In M. Bornstein (Ed.), *Handbook of parenting: Vol. 1: Children and parenting.* Mahwah, NJ: Lawrence Erlbaum.

Leathers, H. D., & Foster, P. (2004). *The world food problem: Tackling causes of undernutrition in the third world.* Boulder, CO: Lynne Rienner Publishers.

Leathers, S., & Kelley, M. (2000). Unintended pregnancy and depressive symptoms among first-time mothers and fathers. *American Journal of Orthopsychiatry, 70,* 523–531.

Lecce, S., Bianco, F., Devine, R. T., Hughes, C., & Banerjee, R. (2014). Promoting theory of mind during middle childhood: A training program. *Journal of Experimental Child Psychology, 126,* 52–67.

Lee, G. Y., & Kisilevsky, B. S. (2014). Fetuses respond to father's voice but prefer mother's voice after birth. *Developmental Psychobiology, 56,* 1–11.

Lee, P. C. (2017). Maternal behavior. In J. Call, G. M. Burghardt, I. M. Pepperberg, C. T. Snowdon, T. Zentall (Eds.), *APA handbook of comparative psychology: Basic concepts, methods, neural substrate, and behavior.* Washington, DC: American Psychological Association.

Lee, R. M. (2005). Resilience against discrimination: Ethnic identity and other-group orientation as protective factors for Korean Americans. *Journal of Counseling Psychology, 52,* 36–44.

Lee, S., Olszewski-Kubilius, P., & Thomson, D. (2012). The social competence of highly gifted math and science adolescents. *Asia Pacific Education Review, 13,* 185–197.

Lee, V. E., & Burkam, D. T. (2003). Dropping out of high school: The role of school organization and structure. *American Educational Research Journal, 40,* 353–393.

Leen-Feldner, E. W., Reardon, L. E., Hayward, C., & Smith, R. C. (2008). The relation between puberty and adolescent anxiety: Theory and evidence. In M. J. Zvolensky & J. A. Smits (Eds.), *Anxiety in health behaviors and physical illness*. New York: Springer Science + Business Media.

Lefkowitz, E. S., Sigman, M., & Kit-fong Au, T. (2000). Helping mothers discuss sexuality and AIDS with adolescents. *Child Development, 71*, 1383–1394.

Legerstee, M. (2013). The developing social brain: Social connections and social bonds, social loss, and jealousy in infancy. In M. Legerstee, D. W. Haley, & M. H. Bornstein (Eds.), *The infant mind: Origins of the social brain*. New York: Guilford Press.

Legerstee, M., Haley, D. W., & Bornstein, M. H. (2013). *The infant mind: Origins of the social brain*. New York: Guilford Press.

Lehalle, H. (2006). Moral development in adolescence: How to integrate personal and social values? In *Handbook of adolescent development*. New York: Psychology Press.

Lehman, D., Chiu, C., & Schaller, M. (2004). Psychology and culture. *Annual Review of Psychology, 55*, 689–714.

Leis-Newman, E. (2012, June). Miscarriage and loss. *Monitor on Psychology*, pp. 57–59.

Lemaster, P., Strough, J., Stoiko, R., & DiDonato, L. (2015). To have and to do: Masculine facets of gender predict men's and women's attitudes about gender equality among college students. *Psychology of Men & Masculinity, 16*, 195–205.

Lenhart, A., Smith, A., and Anderson, M. (2015, October). *Teens, technology and romantic relationships*. Washington, DC: Pew Research Center.

Lerner, R. M., Fisher, C. B., & Weinberg, R. A. (2000). Toward a science for and of the people: Promoting civil society through the application of developmental science. *Child Development, 71*, 11–20.

Lesner, S. (2003). Candidacy and management of assistive listening devices: Special needs of the elderly. *International Journal of Audiology, 42*, 2S68–2S76.

Lesnoff-Caravaglia, G. (2007). Age-related changes within biological systems: Integumentary, skeletal, and muscular. In *Gerontechnology: Growing old in a technological society*. Springfield, IL: Charles C. Thomas Publisher.

Lester, H., Mead, N., Graham, C., Gask, L., & Reilly, S. (2012). An exploration of the value and mechanisms of befriending for older adults in England. *Ageing & Society, 32*, 307–328.

Lester, P., Paley, B., Saltzman, W., & Klosinski, L. E. (2013). Military service, war, and families: Considerations for child development, prevention and intervention, and public health policy—Part 2. *Clinical Child and Family Psychology Review, 16*, 345–347.

Letendre, J. (2007). "Sugar and spice but not always nice": Gender socialization and its impact on development and maintenance of aggression in adolescent girls. *Child & Adolescent Social Work Journal, 24*, 353–368.

LeVay, S., & Valente, S. M. (2003). *Human sexuality*. Sunderland, MA: Sinauer Associates.

Levant, R. F., McDermott, R. C., Hewitt, A. A., Alto, K. M., & Harris, K. T. (2016). Confirmatory factor analytic investigation of variance composition, gender invariance, and validity of the Male Role Norms Inventory-Adolescent-revised (MRNI-A-r). *Journal of Counseling Psychology, 63*, 543–556.

Leve, L. D., Kim, H. K., & Pears, K. C. (2005). Childhood temperament and family environment as predictors of internalizing and externalizing trajectories from ages 5 to 17. *Journal of Abnormal Child Psychology, 33*, 505–520.

Levenson, D. (2012). Genomic testing update: Whole genome sequencing may be worth the money. *Annals of Neurology, 71*, A7–A9.

Levenson, R. W., Carstensen, L. L., & Gottman, J. M. (1993). Long-term marriage: Age, gender, and satisfaction. *Psychology and Aging, 8*, 301–313.

Levin, R. J. (2015). Sexuality of the ageing female—The underlying physiology. *Sexual and Relationship Therapy, 30*, 25–36.

Levine, R. (1997a, November). The pace of life in 31 countries. *American Demographics*, pp. 20–29.

Levine, R. (1997b). *A geography of time: The temporal misadventures of a social psychologist, or how every culture keeps time just a little bit differently*. New York: HarperCollins.

LeVine, R. A., & Campble, D. T. (1972). *Ethnocentrism: Theories of conflict, ethnic attitudes, and group behavior*. Oxford, England: John Wiley & Sons.

Levine, R. V. (1993, February). Is love a luxury? *American Demographics*, pp. 29–37.

Levinson, D. J. (1986). A conception of adult development. *American Psychologist, 41*, 3–13.

Levinson, D. J. (1992). *The seasons of a woman's life*. New York: Knopf.

Levy, B. R., Slade, M. D., & Kasl, S. V. (2002). Longitudinal benefit of positive self-perceptions of aging on functioning health. *Journal of Gerontology: Psychological Sciences, 57*, 166–195.

Lewis, B., Legato, M., & Fisch, H. (2006). Medical implications of the male biological clock. *JAMA: The Journal of the American Medical Association, 296*, 2369–2371.

Lewis, C. S. (1958). *The allegory of love: A study in medieval traditions*. New York: Oxford University Press.

Lewis, C. S. (1985). A grief observed. In E. S. Shneidman (Ed.), *Death: Current perspectives* (3rd ed.). Palo Alto, CA: Mayfield.

Lewis, J., & Elman, J. (2008). Growth-related neural reorganization and the autism phenotype: A test of the hypothesis that altered brain growth leads to altered connectivity. *Developmental Science, 11*, 135–155.

Lewis, M., & Carmody, D. (2008). Self-representation and brain development. *Developmental Psychology, 44*, 1329–1334.

Lewis, M., & Ramsay, D. (2004). Development of self-recognition, personal pronoun use, and pretend play during the 2nd year. *Child Development, 75*, 1821–1831.

Lewis, R., Freneau, P., & Roberts, C. (1979). Fathers and the postparental transition. *Family Coordinator, 28*, 514–520.

Lewkowicz, D. (2002). Heterogeneity and heterochrony in the development of intersensory perception. *Cognitive Brain Research, 14*, 41–63.

Leyens, J. P., Camino, L., Parke, R. D., & Berkowitz, L. (1975). Effects of movie violence on aggression in a field setting as a function of group dominance and cohesion. *Journal of Personality and Social Psychology, 32*, 346–360.

Li, C., DiGiuseppe, R., & Froh, J. (2006, September). The roles of sex, gender, and coping in adolescent depression. *Adolescence, 41*, 409–415.

Li, M., Chen, H., Wang, J., Liu, F., Wang, Y., Lu, F., & . . . Chen, H. (2015). Increased cortical thickness and altered functional connectivity of the right superior temporal gyrus in left-handers. *Neuropsychologia, 67*, 27–34.

Li, N. P., Bailey, J. M., Kenrick, D. T., & Linsenmeier, J. A. W. (2002). The necessities and luxuries of mate preferences: Testing the tradeoffs. *Journal of Personality and Social Psychology, 82*, 947–955.

Li, Q., Xu, W., & Li, L. (2014). Elderly mental health quality and mental health condition: Mediating effect of social support. *Chinese Journal of Clinical Psychology, 22*, 688–690.

Li, S. (2003). Biocultural orchestration of developmental plasticity across levels: The interplay of biology and culture in shaping the mind and behavior across the life span. *Psychological Bulletin, 129*, 171–194.

Li, S. (2012). Neuromodulation of behavioral and cognitive development across the life span. *Developmental Psychology, 48*, 810–814.

Li, T., & Chan, D. K. (2012). How anxious and avoidant attachment affect romantic relationship quality differently: A meta-analytic review. *European Journal of Social Psychology, 42*(4), 406–419. doi:10.1002/ejsp.1842.

Li, Y., & Wright, M. F. (2013). Adolescents' social status goals: Relationships to social status insecurity, aggression, and prosocial behavior. *Journal of Youth and Adolescence, 43*, 146–160.

Lian, C., Wan Muda, W., Hussin, Z., & Thon, C. (2012). Factors associated with undernutrition among children in a rural district of Kelantan, Malaysia. *Asia-Pacific Journal of Public Health, 24*, 330–342.

Liang, J., & Luo, B. (2012). Toward a discourse shift in social gerontology: From successful aging to harmonious aging. *Journal of Aging Studies, 26*, 327–334.

Libertus, K., Joh, A. S., & Needham, A. W. (2016). Motor training at 3 months affects object exploration 12 months later. *Developmental Science, 19*, 1058–1066.

Lickenbrock, D. M., & Braungart-Rieker, J. M. (2015). Examining antecedents of infant attachment security with mothers and fathers: An ecological systems perspective. *Infant Behavior & Development, 39*, 173–187.

Lickliter, R., & Bahrick, L. E. (2000). The development of infant intersensory perception: Advantages of a comparative convergent-operations approach. *Psychological Bulletin, 126*, 260–280.

Lie, K. (2015). Hierarchical acquisition of visual specificity in spatial contextual cueing. *Attention, Perception, & Psychophysics, 77*, 160–172.

Lin, C., Chiang, S., Tzeng, W., & Chiang, L. (2014). Systematic review of impact of lifestyle modification programs on metabolic risks and patient-reported outcomes in adults with metabolic syndrome. *Worldviews on Evidence-Based Nursing, 11*, 361–368.

Lin, C., Chiu, H., & Yeh, C. (2012). Impact of socioeconomic backgrounds, experiences of being disciplined in early childhood, and parenting value on parenting styles of preschool children's parents. *Chinese Journal of Guidance and Counseling, 32*, 123–149.

Lindau, S., Schumm, L., Laumann, E., Levinson, W., O'Muircheartaigh, C., & Waite, L. (2007). A study of sexuality and health among older adults in the United States. *New England Journal of Medicine, 357*, 762–775.

Lindemann, B. T., & Kadue, D. D. (2003). *Age discrimination in employment law*. Washington, DC: BNA Books.

Lindholm, J. A. (2006). The "interior" lives of American college students: Preliminary findings from a national study. In J .L. Heft (Ed.), *Passing on the faith: Transforming traditions for the next generation of Jews, Christians, and Muslims*. New York: Fordham University Press.

Lindsey, E., & Colwell, M. (2003). Preschoolers' emotional competence: Links to pretend and physical play. *Child Study Journal, 33*, 39–52.

Lindsey, E. W. (2012). Girl's and boy's play form preferences and gender segregation in early childhood. In S. P. McGeown (Ed.), *Psychology of gender differences*. Hauppauge, NY: Nova Science Publishers.

Lindstrom, H., Fritsch, T., Petot, G., Smyth, K., Chen, C., Debanne, S., et al. (2005, July). The relationships between television viewing in midlife and the development of Alzheimer's disease in a case-control study. *Brain and Cognition, 58*, 157–165.

Linebarger, D. L. (2015). Contextualizing video game play: The moderating effects of cumulative risk and parenting styles on the relations among video game exposure and problem behaviors. *Psychology of Popular Media Culture, 4*, 375–396.

Lines, P. M. (2001). Homeschooling. *Eric Digest*, EDO-EA-10-08, 1–4.

Lino, M., & Carlson, A. (2009). *Expenditures on children by families*.

Lipina, S. J., & Evers, K. (2017). Neuroscience of childhood poverty: Evidence of impacts and mechanisms as vehicles of dialog with ethics. *Frontiers in Psychology, 8*, 88–97.

Lippman, J. R., & Campbell, S. W. (2014). Damned if you do, damned if you don't . . . if you're a girl: Relational and normative contexts of adolescent sexting in the United States. *Journal of Children and Media, 8*, 371–386.

Lippman, J., & Lewis, P. (2008). *Divorcing with children: Expert answers to tough questions from parents and children*. Westport, CT: Praeger Publishers/Greenwood Publishing Group.

Lipsitt, L. (2003). Crib death: A biobehavioral phenomenon? *Current Directions in Psychological Science, 12*, 164–170.

Lipsitt, L. P., & Rovee-Collier, C. (2012). The psychophysics of olfaction in the human newborn: Habituation and cross-adaptation. In G. M. Zucco, R. S. Herz, B. Schaal (Eds.), *Olfactory cognition: From perception and memory to environmental odours and neuroscience*. Amsterdam, Netherlands.: John Benjamins Publishing Company.

Litwin, H. (2007). Does early retirement lead to longer life? *Ageing & Society, 27*(5), pp 739–754. https://doi.org/10.1017/S0144686X07006216

Liu, N., Liang, Z., Li, Z., Yan, J., & Guo, W. (2012). Chronic stress on IL-2, IL-4, IL-18 content in SD rats. *Chinese Journal of Clinical Psychology, 20*, 35–36.

Lloyd, K. K. (2012). Health-related quality of life and children's happiness with their childcare. *Child: Care, Health and Development, 38*, 244–250.

Locke, K. D. & Heller, S. (2017). Communal and agentic interpersonal and intergroup motives predict preferences for status versus power. *Personality and Social Psychology Bulletin, 43*(1), 71–86. https://doi.org/10.1177/0146167216675333.

Loehlin, J. C., Neiderhiser, J. M., & Reiss, D. (2005). Genetic and environmental components of adolescent adjustment and parental behavior: A multivariate analysis. *Child Development, 76*, 1104–1115.

Loftus, E. F. (2004). Memories of things unseen. *Current Directions in Psychological Science, 13*, 145–147.

Loftus, E. F., & Bernstein, D. M. (2005). Rich false memories: The royal road to success. In A. F. Healy (Ed.), *Experimental cognitive psychology and its applications*. Washington, DC: American Psychological Association.

Loftus, E. F., & Palmer, J. C. (1974). Reconstruction of automobile destruction: An example of the interaction between language and memory. *Journal Of Verbal Learning & Verbal Behavior, 13*(5), 585-589. doi:10.1016/S0022-5371(74)80011-3.

Loggins, S., & Andrade, F. D. (2014). Despite an overall decline in U.S. infant mortality rates, the Black/White disparity persists: Recent trends and future projections. *Journal of Community Health: The Publication for Health Promotion and Disease Prevention, 39*, 118–123.

Lohman, D. (2005). Reasoning abilities. In *Cognition and intelligence: Identifying the mechanisms of the mind*. New York: Cambridge University Press.

Lois, J. (2006, September). Role strain, emotion management, and burnout: Homeschooling mothers' adjustment to the teacher role. *Symbolic Interaction, 29*(4), 507–530.

Lorang, M. R., McNiel, D. E., & Binder, R. L. (2016). Minors and sexting: Legal implications. *Journal of the American Academy of Psychiatry and the Law, 44*(1), 73–81.

Lorenz, K. Z. (1965). *Evolution and the modification of behavior*. Chicago: University of Chicago Press.

Lorenz, K. Z. (1974). *Civilized man's eight deadly sins*. New York: Harcourt Brace Jovanovich.

Losonczy-Marshall, M. (2008). Gender differences in latency and duration of emotional expression in 7- through 13-month-old infants. *Social Behavior and Personality, 36*, 267–274.

Louca, M., & Short, M. A. (2014). The effect of one night's sleep deprivation on adolescent neurobehavioral performance. *Sleep: Journal of Sleep and Sleep Disorders Research, 37*(11), 1799–1807. doi:10.5665/sleep.4174.

Lounsbury, J. W., Hutchens, T., & Loveland, J. M. (2005). An investigation of big five personality traits and career decidedness among early and middle adolescents. *Journal of Career Assessment, 13*, 25–39.

Low, S., Cook, C. R., Smolkowski, K., & Buntain-Ricklefs, J. (2015). Promoting social–emotional competence: An evaluation of the elementary version of Second Step®. *Journal of School Psychology, 53*(6), 463–477.

Lowe, M. R., Doshi, S. D., Katterman, S. N., & Feig, E. H. (2013). Dieting and restrained eating as prospective predictors of weight gain. *Frontiers in Psychology, 4*, 577–586.

Loewen, S. (2006). Exceptional intellectual performance: A neo-Piagetian perspective. *High Ability Studies, 17*, 159–181.

Lu, L. (2006). The transition to parenthood: Stress, resources, and gender differences in a Chinese society. *Journal of Community Psychology, 34*, 471–488.

Lu, T., Pan, Y., Lap. S-Y., Li, C., Kohane, I., Chang, J., et al. (2004, June 9). Gene regulation and DNA damage in the aging human brain. *Nature*, p. 1038.

Lubienski, C., Puckett, T., & Brewer, T. J. (2013). Does homeschooling 'work'? A critique of the empirical claims and agenda of advocacy organizations. *Peabody Journal of Education, 88*, 378–392.

Lubinski, D. (2004). Introduction to the special section on cognitive abilities: 100 years after Spearman's (1904) "General Intelligence," objectively determined and measured. *Journal of Personality and Social Psychology, 86*, 96–111.

Lucas, R. E. (2005). Time does not heal all wounds: A longitudinal study of reaction and adaptation to divorce. *Psychological Science, 16*, 945–951.

Lucas, S. R., & Berends, M. (2002). Sociodemographic diversity, correlated achievement, and de facto tracking. *Sociology of Education, 75*, 328–349.

Lucassen, A. (2012). Ethical implications of new genetic technologies. *Developmental Medicine & Child Neurology, 54*, 124–130.

Ludden, J. (2012, February 6). Helicopter parents hover in the workplace. *All Things Considered*. National Public Radio.

Luders, E., Toga, A. W., & Thompson, P. M. (2014). Why size matters: Differences in brain volume account for apparent sex differences in callosal anatomy: The sexual dimorphism of the corpus callosum. *Neuroimage, 84*, 820–824.

Luke, B., & Brown, M. B. (2008). Maternal morbidity and infant death in twin vs. triplet and quadruplet pregnancies. *American Journal of Obstetrics and Gynecology, 198*, 1–10.

Luke, M. A., Sedikides, C., & Carmelley, K. (2012). Your love lifts me higher! The energizing quality of secure relationships. *Personality and Social Psychology Bulletin, 38*, 721–735.

Lundberg, U. (2006, July). Stress, subjective and objective health. *International Journal of Social Welfare, 15*, S41–S48.

Lundby, E. (2013). 'You can't buy friends, but . . .' Children's perception of consumption and friendship. *Young Consumers, 14*, 360–374.

Luo, J., Derringer, J., Briley, D. A., & Roberts, B. W. (2017). Genetic and environmental pathways underlying personality traits and perceived stress: Concurrent and longitudinal twin studies. *European Journal of Personality*. Accessed online, 10/27/17; http://onlinelibrary.wiley.com/doi/10.1002/per.2127/abstract.

Luria, R., & Meiran, N. (2005). Increased control demand results in serial processing: Evidence from dual-task performance. *Psychological Science, 16*, 833–840.

Lyall, S. (2004, February 15). In Europe, lovers now propose: Marry me, a little. *New York Times*, p. D2.

Lynam, D. R., Caspi, A., Moffitt, T. E., Raine, A., Loeber, R., & Stouthamer-Loeber, M. (2005). Adolescent psychopathy and the big five: Results from two samples. *Journal of Abnormal Child Psychology, 33*(4), 431–443. doi:10.1007/s10648-005-5724-0.

Lynn, J., Teno, J. M., Phillips, R. S., Wu, A. W., Desbiens, N., Harrold, J., et al. (1997). Perceptions by family members of the dying experience of older and seriously ill patients. SUPPORT investigators. Study to understand prognoses and preferences for outcomes and risks of treatments [see comments]. *Annals of Internal Medicine, 126*, 164–165.

Lynne, S., Graber, J., Nichols, T., Brooks-Gunn, J., & Botvin, G. (2007, February). Links between pubertal timing, peer influences, and externalizing behaviors among urban students followed through middle school. *Journal of Adolescent Health, 40*, 35–44.

Mabbott, D. J., Noseworthy, M., Bouffet, E., Laughlin, S., & Rockel, C. (2006). White matter growth as a mechanism of cognitive development in children. *Neuroimaging, 15*, 936–946.

Maccallum, F., Malgaroli, M., & Bonanno, G. A. (2017). Networks of loss: Relationships among symptoms of prolonged grief following spousal and parental loss. *Journal of Abnormal Psychology, 126*, 652–662.

Maccoby, E. E., & Martin, J. A. (1983). Socialization in the context of the family: Parent-child interaction. In P. H. Mussen (Ed.) & E. M. Hetherington (Vol. Ed.), *Handbook of child psychology: Vol. 4. Socialization, personality, and social development* (4th ed., pp. 1–101). New York: Wiley.

MacDonald, W. (2003). The impact of job demands and workload stress and fatigue. *Australian Psychologist, 38*, 102–117.

MacDorman, M. F., Declercq, E., Menacker, F., & Malloy, M. (2008). Neonatal mortality for primary cesarean and vaginal births to low-risk women: Application of an "intention-to-treat" model. *Birth: Issues in Perinatal Care, 35*, 3–8.

MacDorman, M. F., Hoyert, D. L., & Mathews, T. J. (2013). Recent declines in infant mortality in the United States, 2005–2011. *NCHS data brief, no 120*. Hyattsville, MD: National Center for Health Statistics.

MacDorman, M. F., Martin, J. A., Mathews, T. J., Hoyert, D. L., & Ventura, S. J. (2005). Explaining the 2001–02 infant mortality increase: Data from the linked birth/infant death data set. *National Vital Statistics Report, 53*, 1–22.

MacDorman, M. F., & Matthews, T. J. (2009). Behind International Rankings of Infant Mortality: How the United States Compares with Europe. *NCHS Data Brief, # 23*.

Maciejewski, P. K., Zhang, B., Block, S. D., & Prigerson, H. G. (2007). An empirical examination of the stage theory of grief. *JAMA: Journal of the American Medical Association, 297*, 716–723.

Macionis, J. J. (2001). *Sociology*. Upper Saddle River, NJ: Prentice Hall.

MacLean, P. C., Rynes, K. N., Aragón, C., Caprihan, A., Phillips, J. P., & Lowe, J. R. (2014). Mother–infant mutual eye gaze supports emotion regulation in infancy during the Still-Face paradigm. *Infant Behavior & Development, 37*, 512–522.

Madathil, J., & Benshoff, J. (2008). Importance of marital characteristics and marital satisfaction: A comparison of Asian Indians in arranged marriages and Americans in marriages of choice. *Family Journal, 16*, 222–230.

Madden, M., Lenhart, A., Cortesi, S., Gasser, U., Duggan, M., Smith, A., & Beaton, M. (2013, May 21). Teens, social media, and privacy. Pew Research Center: Internet & Technology.

Maddi, S. R. (2014). Hardiness leads to meaningful growth through what is learned when resolving stressful circumstances. In A. Batthyany, P. Russo-Netzer (Eds.), *Meaning in positive and existential psychology* (pp. 291–302). New York: Springer Science + Business Media. doi:10.1007/978-1-4939-0308-5_17.

Madsen, P. B., & Green, R. (2012). Gay adolescent males' effective coping with discrimination: A qualitative study. *Journal of LGBT Issues in Counseling, 6*, 139–155.

Madigan, S., Plamondon, A., & Jenkins, J. M. (2017). Marital conflict trajectories and associations with children's disruptive behavior. *Journal of Marriage and Family, 79*, 437–450.

Madison, G., Mosing, M. A., Verweij, K. H., Pedersen, N. L., & Ullén, F. (2016). Common genetic influences on intelligence and auditory simple reaction time in a large Swedish sample. *Intelligence, 59*, 157–162.

Mael, F. A. (1998). Single-sex and coeducational schooling: Relationships to socioemotional and academic development. *Review of Education Research, 68*, 101–129.

Maercker, A., Neimeyer, R. A., & Simiola, V. (2017). Depression and complicated grief. In S. N. Gold (Ed.), *APA handbook of trauma psychology: Foundations in knowledge*. Washington, DC: American Psychological Association.

Maes, S. J., De Mol, J., & Buysse, A. (2012). Children's experiences and meaning construction on parental divorce: A focus group study. *Childhood: A Global Journal of Child Research, 19*, 266–279.

Maes, I. L., Delespaul, P. G., Peters, M. L., White, M. P., van Horn, Y., Schruers, K., . . . Joore, M. (2015). Measuring health-related quality of life by experiences: The experience sampling method. *Value in Health, 18*, 44–51.

Magee, C. A., Gordon, R., & Caputi, P. (2014). Distinct developmental trends in sleep duration during early childhood. *Pediatrics, 133*, e1561–e1567.

Mages, W. K. (2016). Taking inspiration from Reggio Emilia: An analysis of a professional development workshop on fostering authentic art in the early childhood classroom. *Journal of Early Childhood Teacher Education, 37*, 175–185.

Mahrer, N. E., & Wolchik, S. A. (2017). Moody child: Depression in the context of parental divorce. In C.A. Galanter, P. S. Jensen

(Eds.), *DSM-5® casebook and treatment guide for child mental health.* Arlington, VA: American Psychiatric Publishing, Inc.

Maier, C. A., & McGeorge, C. R. (2014). Positive attributes of never-married single mothers and fathers: Why gender matters and applications for family therapists. *Journal of Feminist Family Therapy: An International Forum, 26,* 163–190.

Majors, K. (2012). Friendships: The power of positive alliance. In S. Roffey (Ed.), *Positive relationships: Evidence based practice across the world.* New York: Springer Science + Business Media.

Mäkinen, M., Puukko-Viertomies, L., Lindberg, N., Siimes, M. A., & Aalberg, V. (2012). Body dissatisfaction and body mass in girls and boys transitioning from early to mid-adolescence: Additional role of self-esteem and eating habits. *BMC Psychiatry, 12,* 123–131.

Makino, M., Hashizume, M., Tsuboi, K., Yasushi, M., & Dennerstein, L. (2006, September). Comparative study of attitudes to eating between male and female students in the People's Republic of China. *Eating and Weight Disorders, 11,* 111–117.

Malchiodi, C. A. (2012). Humanistic approaches. In C. A. Malchiodi (Ed.), *Handbook of art therapy* (2nd ed.). New York, NY: Guilford Press.

Mallan, K. M., Sullivan, S. E., de Jersey, S. J., & Daniels, L. A. (2016). The relationship be-tween maternal feeding beliefs and practices and perceptions of infant eating behaviours at 4 months. *Appetite, 105,* 1–7.

Malik, R. D., Lapin, B., Wang, C. E., Lakeman, J. C., & Helfand, B. T. (2015). Are we testing appropriately for low testosterone? Characterization of tested men and compliance with current guidelines. *Journal of Sexual Medicine, 12,* 66–75.

Maller, S. (2003). Best practices in detecting bias in nonverbal tests. In R. McCallum (Ed.), *Handbook of nonverbal assessment.* New York: Kluwer Academic/Plenum Publishers.

Malmberg, L., Wanner, B., & Little, T. (2008). Age and school-type differences in children's beliefs about school performance. *International Journal of Behavioral Development, 32,* 531–541.

Malone, J. C., Liu, S. R., Vaillant, G. E., Rentz, D. M., & Waldinger, R. J. (2016). Midlife Eriksonian psychosocial development: Setting the stage for late-life cognitive and emotional health. *Developmental Psychology, 52,* 496–508.

Manard, M., Carabin, D., Jaspar, M., & Collette, F. (2015). Age-related decline in cognitive control: The role of fluid intelligence and processing speed. *BMC Neuroscience, 15,* 88–97.

Mancini, A. D., & Bonanno, G. A. (2012). Differential pathways to resilience after loss and trauma. In R. A. McMackin, E. Newman, J. M. Fogler, & T. M. Keane (Eds.), *Trauma therapy in context: The science and craft of evidence-based practice.* Washington, DC: American Psychological Association.

Mancini, A. D., Sinan, B., & Bonanno, G. A. (2015). Predictors of prolonged grief, resilience, and recovery among bereaved spouses. *Journal of Clinical Psychology, 71,* 1245–1258.

Madlensky, L., Trepanier, A. M., Cragun, D., Lerner, B., Shannon, K. M., & Zierhut, H. (2017). A rapid systematic review of outcomes studies in genetic counseling. *Journal of Genetic Counseling, 26,* 361–378.

Manfra, L., & Winsler, A. (2006). Preschool children's awareness of private speech. *International Journal of Behavioral Development, 30,* 537–549.

Mangan, P. A. (1997, November). Time perception. Paper presented at the annual meeting of the Society for Neuroscience, New Orleans.

Mangiatordi, A. (2012). Inclusion of mobility-impaired children in the one-to-one computing era: A case study. *Mind, Brain, and Education, 6,* 54–62.

Mangweth, B., Hausmann, A., & Walch, T. (2004). Body fat perception in eating-disordered men. *International Journal of Eating Disorders, 35,* 102–108.

Manlove, J., Franzetta, K., McKinney, K., Romano-Papillo, A., & Terry-Humen, E. (2004). *No time to waste: Programs to reduce teen pregnancy among middle school-aged youth.* Washington, DC: National Campaign to Prevent Teen Pregnancy.

Manning, R. C., Dickson, J. M., Palmier-Claus, J., Cunliffe, A., & Taylor, P. J. (2017). A systematic review of adult attachment and social anxiety. *Journal of Affective Disorders, 211,* 44–59.

Manning, M., & Hoyme, H. (2007). Fetal alcohol spectrum disorders: A practical clinical approach to diagnosis. *Neuroscience & Biobehavioral Reviews, 31,* 230–238.

Manzanares, S., Cobo, D., Moreno-Martínez, M., Sánchez-Gila, M., & Pineda, A. (2013). Risk of episiotomy and perineal lacerations recurring after first delivery. *Birth: Issues in Perinatal Care, 40,* 307–311.

Mao, A., Burnham, M. M., Goodlin-Jones, B. L., Gaylor, E. E., & Anders, T. F. (2004). A comparison of the sleep-wake patterns of cosleeping and solitary-sleeping infants. *Child Psychiatry and Human Development, 35,* 95–105.

Marcia, J. E. (1980). Identity in adolescence. In J. Adelson (Ed.), *Handbook of adolescent psychology.* New York: Wiley.

Marcia, J. E. (2007). Theory and measure: The identity status interview. In M. Watzlawik & A. Born (Eds.), *Capturing identity: Quantitative and qualitative methods.* Lanham, MD: University Press of America.

Marcovitch, S., Zelazo, P., & Schmuckler, M. (2003). The effect of the number of A trials on performance on the A-not-B task. *Infancy, 3,* 519–529.

Marcus, A. D. (2004, February 3). The new math on when to have kids. *Wall Street Journal,* pp. D1, D4.

Margie, N., Killen, M., Sinno, S., & McGlothlin, H. (2005). Minority children's intergroup attitudes about peer relationships. *British Journal of Developmental Psychology, 23,* 251–269.

Marin, T., Chen, E., Munch, J., & Miller, G. (2009). Double-exposure to acute stress and chronic family stress is associated with immune changes in children with asthma. *Psychosomatic Medicine, 71,* 378–384.

Marinellie, S. A., & Kneile, L. A. (2012). Acquiring knowledge of derived nominals and derived adjectives in context. *Language, Speech, and Hearing Services in Schools, 43,* 53–65.

Marino, C., Gini, G., Vieno, A., & Spada, M. M. (2018). The associations between problematic Facebook use, psychological distress and well-being among adolescents and young adults: A systematic review and meta-analysis. *Journal of Affective Disorders, 226,* 274–281.

Marques, A. H., Bjørke-Monsen, A., Teixeira, A. L., & Silverman, M. N. (2014). Maternal stress, nutrition and physical activity: Impact on immune function, CNS development and psychopathology. *Brain Research.* Accessed online, 6/22/15; http://www.ncbi.nlm.nih.gov/pubmed/25451133.

Marschark, M., Spencer, P. E., & Newsom, C. A. (Eds.). (2003). *Oxford handbook of deaf students, language, and education.* London: Oxford University Press.

Marsh, H., Seaton, M., Trautwein, U., Lüdtke, O., Hau, K., O'Mara, A., et al. (2008). The big-fish-little-pond-effect stands up to critical scrutiny: Implications for theory, methodology, and future research. *Educational Psychology Review, 20,* 319–350.

Marsh, H. W., & Hau, K. T. (2003). Big-fish-little-pond effect on academic self-concept. *American Psychologist, 58,* 364–376.

Marshall, R., & Sutherland, P. (2008). The social relations of bereavement in the Caribbean. *Omega: Journal of Death and Dying, 57,* 21–34.

Martin, C. L., & Dinella, L. M. (2012). Congruence between gender stereotypes and activity preference in self-identified tomboys and non-tomboys. *Archives of Sexual Behavior, 41,* 599–610.

Martin, C., & Fabes, R. (2001). The stability and consequences of young children's same-sex peer interactions. *Developmental Psychology, 37,* 431–446.

Martin, J. A., Hamilton, B. E., Sutton, P. D., Ventura, S. J., Menacker, F., & Munson, M. L. (2005). Births: Final data for 2003. *National Vital Statistics Reports, 54,* Table J, 21.

Martin, S., Li, Y., Casanueva, C., Harris-Britt, A., Kupper, L., & Cloutier, S. (2006). Intimate partner violence and women's depression before and during pregnancy. *Violence Against Women, 12,* 221–239.

Martin, P., Martin, D., & Martin, M. (2001). Adolescent premarital sexual activity, cohabitation, and attitudes toward marriage. *Adolescence, 36*, 601–609.

Martin, A., & Olson, K. R. (2015). Beyond good and evil: What motivations underlie children's prosocial behavior? *Perspectives on Psychological Science, 10*, 159–175.

Martin, A., Onishi, K. H., & Vouloumanos, A. (2012). Understanding the abstract role of speech in communication at 12 months. *Cognition, 123*, 50–60.

Martin, C. L., & Ruble, D. (2004). Children's search for gender cues: Cognitive perspectives on gender development. *Current Directions in Psychological Science, 13*, 67–70.

Martin, C. L., Ruble, D. N., & Szkrybalo, J. (2002). Cognitive theories of early gender development. *Psychological Bulletin, 128*, 903–933.

Martin, L., McNamara, M., Milot, A., Halle, T., & Hair, E. (2007). The effects of father involvement during pregnancy on receipt of prenatal care and maternal smoking. *Maternal and Child Health Journal, 11*, 595–602.

Martin-Prudent, A., Lartz, M., Borders, C., & Meehan, T. (2016). Early intervention practices for children with hearing loss: Impact of professional development. *Communication Disorders Quarterly, 38*, 13–23.

Martineau, J., Cochin, S., Magne, R., & Barthelemy, C. (2008). Impaired cortical activation in autistic children: Is the mirror neuron system involved? *International Journal of Psychophysiology, 68*, 35–40.

Martinez, G., Copen, C. E., & Abma, J. C. (2011). Teenagers in the United States: Sexual activity, contraceptive use, and childbearing, 2006–2010 National Survey of Family Growth. *National Center for Health Statistics. Vital Health Statistics*, 23.

Masapollo, M., Polka, L., & Ménard, L. (2015). When infants talk, infants listen: Pre-babbling infants prefer listening to speech with infant vocal properties. *Developmental Science*, accessed online 6/18/15; http://onlinelibrary.wiley.com/doi/10.1111/desc.12298/abstract

Masataka, N. (2000). The role of modality and input in the earliest stage of language acquisition: Studies of Japanese sign language. In C. Chamerlain & J. P. Morford (Eds.), *Language acquisition by eye*. Mahwah, NJ: Lawrence Erlbaum.

Masataka, N. (2003). *The onset of language*. Cambridge, England: Cambridge University Press.

Mash, C., Bornstein, M. H., & Arterberry, M. E. (2013). Brain dynamics in young infants' recognition of faces: EEG oscillatory activity in response to mother and stranger. *Neuroreport: For Rapid Communication of Neuroscience Research, 24*, 359–363.

Maslow, A. H. (1970). *Motivation and personality* (2nd ed.). New York: Harper & Row.

Master, S., Amodio, D., Stanton, A., Yee, C., Hilmert, C., & Taylor, S. (2009). Neurobiological correlates of coping through emotional approach. *Brain, Behavior, and Immunity, 23*, 27–35.

Mathews, G., Fane, B., Conway, G., Brook, C., & Hines, M. (2009). Personality and congenital adrenal hyperplasia: Possible effects of prenatal androgen exposure. *Hormones and Behavior, 55*, 285–291.

Matias, M., Ferreira, T., Vieira, J., Cadima, J., Leal, T., & Mena Matos, P. (2017). Workplace family support, parental satisfaction, and work–family conflict: Individual and crossover effects among dual-earner couples. *Applied Psychology: An International Review, 66*, 628–652.

Matlin, M. (2003). From menarche to menopause: Misconceptions about women's reproductive lives. *Psychology Science, 45*, 106–122.

Matsumoto, D., & Yoo, S. H. (2006). Toward a new generation of cross-cultural research. *Perspectives on Psychological Science, 1*, 234–250.

Matthes, J., Prieler, M., & Adam, K. (2016). Gender-role portrayals in television advertising across the globe. *Sex Roles*. Accessed online, 5/27/16; http://link.springer.com/article/10.1007/s11199-016-0617-y.

Matthews, K. A., Wing, R. R., Kuller, L. H., Meilahn, E. N., & Owens, J. F. (2000). Menopause as a turning point in midlife. In S. B. Manuck & R. Jennings et al. (Eds.), *Behavior, health, and aging*. Mahwah, NJ: Lawrence Erlbaum.

Mattson, S., Calarco, K., & Lang, A. (2006). Focused and shifting attention in children with heavy prenatal alcohol exposure. *Neuropsychology, 20*, 361–369.

Maughan, B. (2001). Conduct disorder in context. In J. Hill, & B. Maughan, Conduct disorders in childhood and adolescence. New York: Cambridge University Press.

Mauritzson, U., & Saeljoe, R. (2001). Adult questions and children's responses: Coordination of perspectives in studies of children's theories of other minds. *Scandinavian Journal of Educational Research, 45*, 213–231.

Maynard, A. (2008). What we thought we knew and how we came to know it: Four decades of cross-cultural research from a Piagetian point of view. *Human Development, 51*, 56–65.

Maynard, A., & Greenfield, P. (2003). Implicit cognitive development in cultural tools and children: Lessons from Maya Mexico. *Cognitive Development, 18*, 489–510.

Mazoyer, B., Houde, O., Joliot, M., Mellet, E., & Tzourio-Mazoyer, N. (2009). Regional cerebral blood flow increases during wakeful rest following cognitive training. *Brain Research Bulletin, 80*, 133–138. Accessed online; http://search.ebscohost.com, doi: 10.1016/j.brainres- bull.2009.06.021.

McAdams, S., & Drake, C. (2002). Auditory perception and cognition. In *Steven's handbook of experimental psychology (3rd ed.), Vol. 1: Sensation and perception*. Hoboken, NJ: John Wiley & Sons Inc.

McArdle, E. F. (2002). New York's Do-Not-Resuscitate law: Groundbreaking protection of patient autonomy or a physician's right to make medical futility determinations? *DePaul Journal of Health Care Law, 8*, 55–82.

McCarthy, B., & Ginsberg, R. (2007). Second marriages: Challenges and risks. *Family Journal, 15*, 119–123.

McCarthy, B., & Pierpaoli, C. (2015). Sexual challenges with aging: Integrating the GES approach in an elderly couple. *Journal of Sex & Marital Therapy, 41*, 72–82.

McConnell, V. (2012, February 16.) Great granny to the rescue! *Mail Online*. Accessed online, 07/ 13/2012; http://www.dailymail.co.uk/femail/article-2101720/As-live-work-longer-great-grandparents-filling-childcare-gap.html.

McCrae, R. R., Costa, P. T., Jr., Ostendorf, F., Angleitner, A., Hebikova, M., Avia, M. D., Sanz, J., Sanchez-Bernardos, M. L., Kusdil, M. E., Woodfield, R., Saunders, P. R., & Smith, P. B. (2000). Nature over nurture: Temperament, personality, and life span development. *Journal of Personality and Social Psychology, 78*, 173–186.

McCue, R. E., & Balasubramaniam, M. (2017). *Rational suicide in the elderly: Clinical, ethical, and sociocultural aspects*. Cham, Switzerland: Springer International Publishing.

McCullough, M. E., Tsang, J., & Brion, S. (2003). Personality traits in adolescence as predictors of religiousness in early maturity: Findings from the Terman longitudinal study. *Personality & Social Psychology Bulletin, 29*, 980–991.

McDonnell, C. G., Valentino, K., Comas, M., & Nuttall, A. K. (2016). Mother–child reminiscing at risk: Maternal attachment, elaboration, and child autobiographical memory specificity. *Journal of Experimental Child Psychology, 143*, 65–84.

McDonough, L. (2002). Basic-level nouns: First learned but misunderstood. *Journal of Child Language, 29*, 357–377.

McElwain, N., & Booth-LaForce, C. (2006, June). Maternal sensitivity to infant distress and nondistress as predictors of infant-mother attachment security. *Journal of Family Psychology, 20*, 247–255.

McFadden, J. R., & Rawson Swan, K. T. (2012). Women during midlife: Is it transition or crisis? *Family and Consumer Sciences Research Journal, 40*, 313–325.

McGillion, M., Herbert, J. S., Pine, J., Vihman, M., dePaolis, R., Keren-Portnoy, T., & Matthews, D. (2017). What paves the way to conventional language? The predictive value of babble, pointing, and socioeconomic status. *Child Development, 88*, 156–166.

McGinnis, E. (2012). *Skillstreaming in early childhood: A guide for teaching prosocial skills* (3rd ed.). Champaign, IL: Research Press.

McGonigle-Chalmers, M., Slater, H., & Smith, A. (2014). Rethinking private speech in preschoolers: The effects of social presence. *Developmental Psychology, 50*, 829–836.

McGrady, A. (2007). Relaxation and meditation. In *Low-cost approaches to promote physical and mental health: Theory, research, and practice*. New York: Springer Science + Business Media.

McGuire, S. L. (2017). Aging education: A worldwide imperative. *Creative Education, 8*, 1878–1891.

McGuffin, P., Riley, B., & Plomin, R. (2001, February 16.) Toward behavioral genomics. *Science, 291*, 1232–1233.

McHale, J. P., & Rotman, T. (2007). Is seeing believing? Expectant parents' outlooks on coparenting and later coparenting solidarity. *Infant Behavior & Development, 30*, 63–81.

McKinley, N. (2006). The developmental and cultural contexts of objectified body consciousness: A longitudinal analysis of two cohorts of women. *Developmental Psychology, 42*, 679–687.

McLachlan, H. (2008). The ethics of killing and letting die: Active and passive euthanasia. *Journal of Medical Ethics, 34*, 636–638.

McLean, K. C., & Syed, M. (2015). *The Oxford handbook of identity development*. New York: Oxford University Press.

McLoyd, V. C., Cauce, A. M., Takeuchi, D., & Wilson, L. (2000). Marital processes and parental socialization in families of color: A decade review of research. *Journal of Marriage and Family, 62*, 1070–1093.

McLoyd, V. C. (2006). The legacy of *Child Development's 1990 Special Issue on Minority Children*: An editorial retrospective. *Child Development, 77*, 1142–1148.

McMahon, S. D., & Washburn, J. J. (2003). Violence prevention: An evaluation of program effects with Urban African-American students. *Journal of Primary Prevention, 24*, 43–62.

McMillan, M. M., Frierson, H. T., & Campbell, F. A. (2011). Do gender differences exist in the academic identification of African American elementary school-age children? *Journal of Black Psychology, 37*, 78–98.

McMurray, B., Aslin, R. N., & Toscano, J. C. (2009). Statistical learning of phonetic categories: Insights from a computational approach. *Developmental Science, 12*, 369–378.

McNulty, J. K., & Karney, B. R. (2004). Positive expectations in the early years of marriage: Should couples expect the best or brace for the worst? *Journal of Personality and Social Psychology, 86*, 729–743.

McWhirter, L., Young, V., & Majury, Y. (1983). Belfast children's awareness of violent death. *British Journal of Psychology, 22*, 81–92.

Meador, K. J., Boyd, A., & Loring, D. W. (2017). Relationship of reaction time to perception of a stimulus and volitionally delayed response. *Cognitive and Behavioral Neurology, 30*, 57-61.

Mealey, L. (2000). *Sex differences: Developmental and evolutionary strategies*. Orlando, FL: Academic Press.

Medeiros, R., Prediger, R. D., Passos, G. F., Pandolfo, P., Duarte, F. S., Franco, J. L., et al. (2007). Connecting TNF-alpha signaling pathways to iNOS expression in a mouse model of Alzheimer's disease: Relevance for the behavioral and synaptic deficits induced by amyloid beta protein. *Journal of Neuroscience, 16*, 5394–5404.

Meeus, W. (2003). Parental and peer support, identity development and psychological well-being in adolescence. *Psychology: The Journal of the Hellenic Psychological Society, 10*, 192–201.

Mehran, K. (1997). Interferences in the move from adolescence to adulthood: The development of the male. In M. Laufer (Ed.), *Adolescent breakdown and beyond* (pp. 17–25). London, England: Karnac Books.

Meijer, A. M., & van den Wittenboer, G. L. H. (2007). Contribution of infants' sleep and crying to marital relationship of first-time parent couples in the first year after childbirth. *Journal of Family Psychology, 21*, 49–57.

Meinzen-Derr, J., Wiley, S., Grether, S., Phillips, J., Choo, D., Hibner, J., & Barnard, H. (2014). Functional communication of children who are deaf or hard-of-hearing. *Journal of Developmental and Behavioral Pediatrics, 35*, 197–206.

Meister, H., & von Wedel, H. (2003). Demands on hearing aid features—special signal processing for elderly users? *International Journal of Audiology, 42*, 2S58–2S62.

Meland, A., Ishimatsu, K., Pensgaard, A. M., Wagstaff, A., Fonne, V., Garde, A. H., & Harris, A. (2015). Impact of mindfulness training on physiological measures of stress and objective measures of attention control in a military helicopter unit. *International Journal of Aviation Psychology, 25*, 191–208.

Meltzoff, A. (2002). Elements of a developmental theory of imitation. In A. Meltzoff & W. Prinz (Eds.), *The imitative mind: Development, evolution, and brain bases* (pp. 19–41). New York: Cambridge University Press.

Meltzoff, A. N., Waismeyer, A., & Gopnik, A. (2012). Learning about causes from people: Observational causal learning in 24-month-old infants. *Developmental Psychology*. Accessed online, 7/18/12; http://www.alisongopnik.com/Papers_Alison/Observational%20Causal%20Learning.pdf.

Melzer, D., Hurst, A., & Frayling, T. (2007). Genetic variation and human aging: Progress and prospects. *The Journals of Gerontology: Series A: Biological Sciences and Medical Sciences, 62*, 301–307. Accessed online; http://search.ebsco-host.com.

Ménard, C., Pfau, M. L., Hodes, G. E., & Russo, S. J. (2017). Immune and neuroendocrine mechanisms of stress vulnerability and resilience. *Neuropsychopharmacology, 42*, 62–80.

Mendle, J., Turkheimer, E., & Emery, R. E. (2007). Detrimental psychological outcomes associated with early pubertal timing in adolescent girls. *Developmental Review, 27*, 151–171.

Mendonça, B., Sargent, B., & Fetters, L. (2016). Cross-cultural validity of standardized motor development screening and assessment tools: A systematic review. *Developmental Medicine & Child Neurology, 58*, 1213–1222.

Mendoza, C. (2006, September). Inside today's classrooms: Teacher voices on No Child Left Behind and the education of gifted children. *Roeper Review, 29*, 28–31.

Mendoza, J. A., Zimmerman, F. J., & Christakis, D. A. (2007). Television viewing, computer use, obesity, and adiposity in US preschool children. *International Journal of Behavioral Nutrition and Physical Activity, 4*, 44.

Menezes, C. B., Dalpiaz, N. R., Kiesow, L. G., Sperb, W., Hertzberg, J., & Oliveira, A. A. (2015). Yoga and emotion regulation: A review of primary psychological outcomes and their physiological correlates. *Psychology & Neuroscience, 8*(1), 82–101.

Meng, Z., & Jijia, Z. (2006). Effects of intonation on 6- to 10-year-old children's cognition of different types of irony. *Acta Psychologica Sinica, 38*, 197–206.

Menkens, K. (2005). Stereotyping older workers and retirement: The managers point of view. *Canadian Journal on Aging, 24*, 353–366.

Mensah, F. K., Bayer, J. K., Wake, M., Carlin, J. B., Allen, N. B., & Patton, G. C. (2013). Early puberty and childhood social and behavioral adjustment. *Journal of Adolescent Health, 53*, 118–124.

Menzel, J. C. (2008). Depression in the elderly after traumatic brain injury: A systematic review. *Brain Injury, 22*(5), 375–380. doi:10.1080/02699050802001492.

Mercer, J. R. (1973). *Labeling the mentally retarded*. Berkeley: University of California Press.

Merikangas, K. R., Nakamura, E. F. & Kessler, R. C. (2009). Epidemiology of mental disorders in children and adolescents. *Dialogues Clinical Neuroscience, 11*, 7–20.

Merrell, K. (2008). *Behavioral, social, and emotional assessment of children and adolescents* (3rd ed.). Mahwah, NJ: Lawrence Erlbaum Associates Publishers.

Merriman, W., & Lipko, A. (2008). A dual criterion account of the development of linguistic judgment in early childhood. *Journal of Memory and Language, 58*, 1012–1031.

Merritt, A., LaQuea, R., Cromwell, R., & Ferguson, C. J. (2016). Media managing mood: A look at the possible effects of violent media on affect. *Child & Youth Care Forum, 45*, 241–258.

Mervis, J. (2011a, August 19). Past successes shape effort to expand early intervention. *Science, 333*, 952–956.

Mervis, J. (2011b, August 19). Giving children a Head Start is possible—but it's not easy. *Science, 333*, 956–957.

Merwin, S. M., Smith, V. C., Kushner, M., Lemay, E. J., & Dougherty, L. R. (2017). Parent-child adrenocortical concordance in early childhood: The moderating role of parental depression and child temperament. *Biological Psychology, 124*, 100–110.

Mesinas, M., & Perez, W. (2016). Cultural involvement, indigenous identity, and language: An exploratory study of Zapotec adolescents and their parents. *Hispanic Journal of Behavioral Sciences, 38,* 482–506.

Messinger, D. S., Mattson, W. I., Mahoor, M. H., & Cohn, J. F. (2012). The eyes have it: Making positive expressions more positive and negative expressions more negative. *Emotion, 12,* 430–436.

Meyer, D. E., Kieras, D. E. Lauber, E., Schumacher, E. H., Glass, J., Zurbriggen, E., Gmeindl, L., & Apfelblat, D. (2002). Adaptive executive control: Flexible multiple-task performance without pervasive immutable response-selection bottlenecks. In T. A. Polk, & C. M. Seifert (Eds.), *Cognitive modeling.* Cambridge, MA: MIT Press.

Mezuk, B., Prescott, M., Tardiff, K., Vlahov, D., & Galea, S. (2008). Suicide in older adults in long-term care: 1990 to 2005. *Journal of the American Geriatrics Society, 56,* 2107–2111.

Michael, R. T., Gagnon, J. H., Laumann, E. O., & Kolata, G. (1994). *Sex in America: A definitive survey.* Boston: Little, Brown.

Michaels, M. (2006). Factors that contribute to step-family success: A qualitative analysis. *Journal of Divorce & Remarriage, 44,* 53–66.

Michaelson, V., Pickett, W., Robinson, P., & Cameron, L. (2015). Participation in church or religious groups and its association with health. Part 2: A qualitative, Canadian study. *Journal of Religion and Health, 54,* 1118–1133.

Miche, M., Elsässer, V. C., Schilling, O. K., & Wahl, H. (2014). Attitude toward own aging in midlife and early old age over a 12-year period: Examination of measurement equivalence and developmental trajectories. *Psychology and Aging, 29,* 588–600.

Mikulincer, M., & Shaver, P. R. (2005). Attachment security, compassion, and altruism. *Current Directions in Psychological Science, 14,* 34–38.

Milanowicz, A., & Bokus, B. (2013). Gender and moral judgments: The role of who is speaking to whom. *Journal of Gender Studies, 22,* 423–443.

Miles, R., Cowan, F., Glover, V., Stevenson, J., & Modi, N. (2006). A controlled trial of skin-to-skin contact in extremely preterm infants. *Early Human Development, 2*(7), 447–455.

Miller, A. J., Sassler, S., & Kus-Appough, D. (2011). The specter of divorce: Views from work and middle-class cohabitors. *Family Relations, 60,* 602–616.

Miller, B. (1997, April). Population update for April. *American Demographics,* p. 18.

Miller, B. G., Kors, S., & Macfie, J. (2017). No differences? Meta-analytic comparisons of psychological adjustment in children of gay fathers and heterosexual parents. *Psychology of Sexual Orientation and Gender Diversity, 4,* 14–22.

Miller, G. A. (1956). The magical number seven, plus or minus two: Some limits on our capacity for processing information. *Psychology Review, 63,* 81–97.

Miller, S. A. (2012). *Theory of mind: Beyond the preschool years.* New York: Psychology Press.

Miller, L., Bishop, J., Fischer, J., Geller, S., & Macmillan, C. (2008). Balancing risks: Dosing strategies for antidepressants near the end of pregnancy. *Journal of Clinical Psychiatry, 69,* 323–324.

Miltenberger, R. G. (2016). *Behavior modification: Principles and procedures* (6th ed.) Boston: Cengage Learning.

Mireault, G. C., Crockenberg, S. C., Sparrow, J. E., Pettinato, C. A., Woodard, K. C., & Malzac, K. (2014). Social looking, social referencing and humor perception in 6- and-12-month-old infants. *Infant Behavior & Development, 37,* 536–545.

Mischel, W. (2004). Toward an integrative science of the person. *Annual Review of Psychology, 55,* 1–22.

Missana, M., Altvater-Mackensen, N., & Grossmann, T. (2017). Neural correlates of infants' sensitivity to vocal expressions of peers. *Developmental Cognitive Neuroscience, 26,* 39–44.

Mistry, J., & Saraswathi, T. (2003). The cultural context of child development. In R. Lerner & M. Easterbrooks (Eds.), *Handbook of psychology: Developmental psychology* (Vol. 6, pp. 267–291). New York: Wiley.

Mitchell, E. (2009). What is the mechanism of SIDS? Clues from epidemiology. *Developmental Psychobiology, 51,* 215–222.

Mitchell, K. J., Ybarra, M. L., & Korchmaros, J. D. (2014). Sexual harassment among adolescents of different sexual orientations and gender identities. *Child Abuse & Neglect, 38,* 280–295.

Miyasaki, J. M., Rheaume, C., Gulya, L., Ellenstein, A., Schwarz, H. B., Vidic, T. R., & Busis, N. A. (2017). Qualitative study of burnout, career satisfaction, and well-being among U.S. neurologists in 2016. *Neurology, 89,* 1730–1738.

Mizuno, K., & Ueda, A. (2004). Antenatal olfactory learning influences infant feeding. *Early Human Development, 76,* 83–90.

MMWR. (2008, August 1). Trends in HIV- and STD-related risk behaviors among high school students—United States, 1991–2007. *Morbidity and Mortality Weekly Report, 57,* 817–822.

Mohammed, A., Attalla, B., Bashir, F., Ahmed, F., Hassan, A., Ibnauf, G., et al. (2006). Relationship of the sickle cell gene to the ethnic and geographic groups populating the Sudan. *Community Genetics, 9,* 113–120.

Moher, M., Tuerk, A. S., & Feigenson, L. (2012). Seven-month-old infants chunk items in memory. *Journal of Experimental Child Psychology.* Accessed online, 7/17/12; http://www.ncbi.nlm.nih.gov/pubmed/22575845.

Mølgaard-Nielsen, D., Pasternak, B., & Hviid, A. (2013). Use of oral fluconazole during pregnancy and the risk of birth defects. *New England Journal of Medicine, 369,* 830–839.

Monsour, M. (2002). *Women and men as friends: Relationships across the life span in the 21st century.* Mahwah, NJ: Lawrence Erlbaum Associates Publishers.

Monteverde, S., Terkamo-Moisio, A., Kvist, T., Kangasniemi, M., Laitila, T., Ryynänen, O., & Pietilä, A. (2017). Nurses' attitudes towards euthanasia in conflict with professional ethical guidelines. *Nursing Ethics, 24,* 70–86.

Montpetit, M., & Bergeman, C. (2007). Dimensions of control: Mediational analyses of the stress-health relationship. *Personality and Individual Differences, 43,* 2237–2248.

Moore, K. L. (1974). *Before we are born: Basic embryology and birth defects.* Philadelphia: Saunders.

Moore, L., Gao, D., & Bradlee, M. (2003). Does early physical activity predict body fat change throughout childhood? *Preventive Medicine: An International Journal Devoted to Practice & Theory, 37,* 10–17.

Moore, M. C. & de Costa, C. M. (2006). *Pregnancy and parenting after thirty-five: Mid-life, new life.* Baltimore, MD: Johns Hopkins University Press.

Moore, R. L., & Wei, L. (2012). Modern love in China. In M. A. Paludi (Ed.), *The psychology of love* (Vols. 1–4). Santa Barbara, CA: Praeger/ABC-CLIO.

Morales, J. R., & Guerra, N. F. (2006). Effects of multiple context and cumulative stress on urban children's adjustment in elementary school. *Child Development, 77,* 907–923.

Morfei, M. Z., Hooker, K., Carpenter, J., Blakeley, E., & Mix, C. (2004). Agentic and communal generative behavior in four areas of adult life: Implications for psychological well-being. *Journal of Adult Development, 11,* 55–58.

Morley, J. E. (2012). Sarcopenia in the elderly. *Family Practice, 29,* Supplement 1, I44–I48. doi:10.1093/fampra/cmr063.

Morra, S. (2008). Memory components and control processes in children's drawing. *Children's understanding and production of pictures, drawings, and art: Theoretical and empirical approaches* (pp. 53–85). Ashland, OH: Hogrefe & Huber Publishers.

Morris, P., & Fritz, C. (2006, October). How to improve your memory. *The Psychologist, 19,* 608–611.

Morrison, F. J., Bachman, H. J., Connor, C. M. (2005). *Improving literacy in America: Guidelines from research.* New Haven, CT: Yale University Press.

Morrison, F. J., Holmes, D. L., & Hairth, M. M. (1974). A developmental study of the effects of familiarity on short-term visual memory. *Journal of Experimental Child Psychology, 18,* 412–425.

Morrison, K. M., Shin, S., Tarnopolsky, M., & Taylor, V. H. (2015). Association of depression & health related quality of life with body composition in children and youth with obesity. *Journal of Affective Disorders, 172,* 18–23.

Morrongiello, B., & Hogg, K. (2004). Mothers' reactions to children misbehaving in ways that can lead to injury: Implications for gender differences in children's risk taking and injuries. *Sex Roles, 50,* 103–118.

Morrongiello, B., Midgett, C., & Stanton, K. (2000). Gender biases in children's appraisals of injury risk and other children's risk-taking behaviors. *Journal of Experimental Child Psychology, 77,* 317–336.

Morry, M. (2007, February). The attraction-similarity hypothesis among cross-sex friends: Relationship satisfaction, perceived similarities, and self-serving perceptions. *Journal of Social and Personal Relationships, 24,* 117–138.

Mortimer, J. (2003). *Working and growing up in America.* Cambridge, MA: Harvard University Press.

Mosher, C. E., & Danoff-Burg, S. (2005). Agentic and communal personality traits: Relations to attitudes toward sex and sexual experiences. *Sex Roles: A Journal of Research, 22,* 343–355.

Mossakowski, K. N. (2003). Coping with perceived discrimination: Does ethnic identity protect mental health? *Journal of Health and Social Behavior, 44,* Special issue: Race, Ethnicity and Mental Health, 318–331.

Motschnig, R., & Nykl, L. (2003). Toward a cognitive-emotional model of Rogers's person-centered approach. *Journal of Humanistic Psychology, 43,* 8–45.

Mõttus, R., Kandler, C., Bleidorn, W., Riemann, R., & McCrae, R. R. (2017). Personality traits below facets: The consensual validity, longitudinal stability, heritability, and utility of personality nuances. *Journal of Personality and Social Psychology, 112,* 474–490.

Mõttus, R., Johnson, W., & Deary, I. J. (2012). Personality traits in old age: Measurement and rank order stability and some mean-level change. *Psychology and Aging, 27,* 243–249.

Mouw, T., & Entwisle, B. (2006). Residential segregation and interracial friendship in schools. *American Journal of Sociology, 112,* 394–441.

Mrug, S., Elliott, M. N., Davies, S., Tortolero, S. R., Cuccaro, P., & Schuster, M. A. (2014). Early puberty, negative peer influence, and problem behaviors in adolescent girls. *Pediatrics, 133,* 7–14.

Mu, Z., & Xie, Y. (2014). Marital age homogamy in China: A reversal of trend in the reform era? *Social Science Research, 44,* 141–157.

Mueller, M., Wilhelm, B., & Elder, G. (2002). Variations in grandparenting. *Research on Aging, 24,* 360–388.

Muenchow, S., & Marsland, K. W. (2007). Beyond baby steps: Promoting the growth and development of U.S. child-care policy. In L. J. Aber et al. (Eds.), *Child development and social policy: Knowledge for action.* Washington, DC: American Psychological Association.

Muiños, M., & Ballesteros, S. (2014). Peripheral vision and perceptual asymmetries in young and older martial arts athletes and nonathletes. *Attention, Perception, & Psychophysics, 76,* 2465–2476.

Muldner, K. & Conati, C. (2010). Scaffolding meta-cognitive skills for effective analogical problem solving via tailored example selection. *International Journal of Artificial Intelligence in Education, 20,* 99–136.

Müller, L., Müller, E., Kornexl, E., & Raschner, C. (2015). The relationship between physical motor skills, gender and relative age effects in young Austrian alpine ski racers. *International Journal of Sports Science & Coaching, 10,* 69–85.

Muller, R. T. (2013). Not just a phase: Depression in preschoolers. Recognizing the signs and reducing the risk. *Psychology Today.* Accessed online, 2/27/14; http://www.psychologytoday.com/blog/talking-about-trauma/201306/not-just-phase-depression-in-preschoolers.

Müller, U., Ten Eycke, K., & Baker, L. (2015). Piaget's theory of intelligence. In S. Goldstein, D. Princiotta, & J. A. Naglieri (Eds.), *Handbook of intelligence: Evolutionary theory, historical perspective, and current concepts.* New York: Springer Science + Business Media.

Mundy, B., & Wofsy, M. (2017). Diverse couple and family forms and universal family processes. In S. Kelly (Ed.), *Diversity in couple and family therapy: Ethnicities, sexualities, and socioeconomics.* Santa Barbara, CA: Praeger/ABC-CLIO.

Munzar, P., Cami, J., & Farre, M. (2003). Mechanisms of drug addiction. *New England Journal of Medicine, 349,* 2365–2365.

Muratore, A. M., & Earl, J. K. (2015). Improving retirement outcomes: The role of resources, pre-retirement planning and transition characteristics. *Ageing & Society, 35,* 2100–2140.

Murasko, J. E. (2015). Overweight/obesity and human capital formation from infancy to adolescence: Evidence from two large US cohorts. *Journal of Biosocial Science, 47,* 220–237.

Murguia, A., Peterson, R. A., & Zea, M. C. (1997, August). Cultural health beliefs. Paper presented at the annual meeting of the American Psychological Association, Toronto, Canada.

Murphy, M. (2009). Language and literacy in individuals with Turner syndrome. *Topics in Language Disorders, 29,* 187–194. Accessed online; http://search.ebscohost.com.

Murphy, F. A., Lipp, A., & Powles, D. L. (2012, March 14). Follow-up for improving psychological well-being for women after a miscarriage. *Cochrane Database System Reviews.*

Murphy, S., Johnson, L., & Wu, L. (2003). Bereaved parents' outcomes 4 to 60 months after their children's death by accident, suicide, or homicide: A comparative study demonstrating differences. *Death Studies, 27,* 39–61.

Murray, L., Cooper, P., Creswell, C., Schofield, E., & Sack, C. (2007, January). The effects of maternal social phobia on mother–infant interactions and infant social responsiveness. *Journal of Child Psychology and Psychiatry, 48,* 45–52.

Murray, S., Bellavia, G., & Rose, P. (2003). Once hurt, twice hurtful: How perceived regard regulates daily marital interactions. *Journal of Personality & Social Psychology, 84,* 126–147.

Murray, T., & Lewis, V. (2014). Gender-role conflict and men's body satisfaction: The moderating role of age. *Psychology of Men & Masculinity, 15,* 40–48.

Musolino, J., & Lidz, J. (2006). Why children aren't universally successful with quantification. *Linguistics, 44,* 817–852.

Mychasiuk, R., & Metz, G. S. (2016). Epigenetic and gene expression changes in the adolescent brain: What have we learned from animal models? *Neuroscience and Biobehavioral Reviews, 70,* 189–197.

Mustanski, B., Kuper, L., & Greene, G. J. (2014). Development of sexual orientation and identity. In D. L. Tolman, L. M. Diamond, J. A. Bauermeister, W. H. George, J. G. Pfaus, L. M. Ward (Eds.), *APA handbook of sexuality and psychology, Vol. 1: Person-based approaches.* Washington, DC: American Psychological Association.

Myers, R. H. (2004). Huntington's disease genetics. *NeuroRx, 1,* 255–262.

Nagahashi, S. (2013). Meaning making by preschool children during pretend play and construction of play space. *Japanese Journal of Developmental Psychology, 24,* 88–98.

Nagda, B. R. A., Gurin, P., & Johnson, S. M. (2005). *Improving the first year of college: Research and practice* (pp. 73-108). Mahwah, NJ: Lawrence Erlbaum Associates Publishers.

Naglieri, J. A. (2015). Hundred years of intelligence testing: Moving from traditional IQ to second-generation intelligence tests. In S. Goldstein, D. Princiotta, J. A. Naglieri, S. Goldstein, D. Princiotta, & J. A. Naglieri (Eds.), *Handbook of intelligence: Evolutionary theory, historical perspective, and current concepts.* New York: Springer Science + Business Media.

Nagy, M. (1948). The child's theories concerning death. *Journal of Genetic Psychology, 73,* 3–27.

Nahmiash, D. (2006). *Abuse and neglect of older adults: What do we know about it and how can we identify it?* Westport, CT: Praeger Publishers/Greenwood Publishing Group.

Naik, G. (2002, November 22). The grim mission of a Swiss group: Visitor's suicides. *Wall Street Journal,* pp. A1, A6.

Nair, K. (2008). A plea for a holistic approach to aging. In *Discourses on aging and dying.* New Delhi: Sage Publications India.

Nanda, S., & Konnur, N. (2006, October). Adolescent drug & alcohol use in the 21st century. *Psychiatric Annals, 36,* 706–712.

Nangle, D. W., & Erdley, C. A. (Eds.). (2001). *The role of friendship in psychological adjustment.* San Francisco: Jossey-Bass.

Narang, S., & Clarke, J. (2014). Abusive head trauma: Past, present, and future. *Journal of Child Neurology, 29,* 1747–1756.

Nassif, A., & Gunter, B. (2008). Gender representation in television advertisements in Britain and Saudi Arabia. *Sex Roles, 58,* 752–760.

Nation, M., & Heflinger, C. (2006). Risk factors for serious alcohol and drug use: The role of psychosocial variables in predicting the frequency of substance use among adolescents. *American Journal of Drug and Alcohol Abuse, 32,* 415–433.

National Association for the Education of Young Children. (2005). Position statements of the NAEYC. Accessed online; http://www.naeyc.org/about/positions.asp#where.

National Center for Children in Poverty. (2009). *Basic facts about low-income children in the United States.* New York: National Center for Children in Poverty.

National Center for Children in Poverty (2013). *Poverty and the Achievement Gap.* New York: National Center for Children in Poverty, Columbia University, Mailman School of Public Health.

National Center for Children in Poverty. (2018). *Basic facts about low-income children in the United States.* New York: National Center for Children in Poverty. Accessed online, 3/11/18; http://www.nccp.org/publications/pub_1194.html.

National Center for Education Statistics. (2002). *Dropout rates in the United States: 2000.* Washington, DC: Author.

National Center for Education Statistics. (2003). *Public high school dropouts and completers from the common core of data: School year 2000–01 statistical analysis report.* Washington, DC: Author.

National Center for Education Statistics. (2018). *Digest of Education Statistics, 2016* (NCES 2017-094).

National Center for Health Statistics. (2000). *Health United States, 2000 with adolescent health chartbook.* Hyattsville, MD.

National Center for Health Statistics. (2015). *Leading causes of deaths among adolescents 15–19 years of age.* Atlanta, GA: Centers for Disease Control. Accessed online, 8/14/15; http://www.cdc.gov/nchs/fastats/adolescent-health.htm.

National Center for Health Statistics. (2017, November 25). National marriage and divorce trends. Accessed online, 11/25/17; https://www.cdc.gov/nchs/nvss/marriage_divorce_tables.htm.

National Health Interview Survey. (2015). Health status of children. Accessed online, 11/1/17; https://ftp.cdc.gov/pub/Health_Statistics/NCHS/NHIS/SHS/2015_SHS_Table_C-5.pdf.

National Institutes of Health. (2012, November 7). MRI and EEG could identify children at risk for epilepsy after febrile seizures. Accessed online; http://www.nih.gov/news/health/nov2012/nci-06.htm.

National Sleep Foundation. (2006). *Adolescents and sleep.* Washington, DC: Author.

National Sleep Foundation. (2013). Sleep and exercise. Accessed online, 3/10/18; https://sleepfoundation.org/sleep-polls-data/sleep-in-america-poll/2013-exercise-and-sleep.

Natsuaki, M. N. (2013). Puberty in context: Toward a more nuanced understanding of early maturation. *Journal of Adolescent Health, 53,* 677–678.

Navarro, M. (2006, May 25). Families add 3rd generation to households. *New York Times,* pp. A1, A22.

NCD Risk Factor Collaboration. (2017). Worldwide trends in body-mass index, underweight, overweight, and obesity from 1975 to 2016: A pooled analysis of 2416 population-based measurement studies in 128·9 million children, adolescents, and adults. doi: http://dx.doi.org/10.1016/S0140-6736(17)32129-3.

Needleman, H. L., Riess, J. A., Tobin, M. J., Biesecker, G. E., & Greenhouse, J. B. (1996, February 7). Bone lead levels and delinquent behavior. *JAMA: Journal of the American Medical Association, 2755,* 363–369.

Negy, C., Shreve, T., & Jensen, B. (2003). Ethnic identity, self-esteem, and ethnocentrism: A study of social identity versus multicultural theory of development. *Cultural Diversity & Ethnic Minority Psychology, 9,* 333–344.

Neisser, U. (2004). Memory development: New questions and old. *Developmental Review, 24,* 154–158.

Nelis, D., Quoidbach, J., Mikolajczak, M., & Hansenne, M. (2009). Increasing emotional intelligence: (How) is it possible? *Personality and Individual Differences, 47,* 36–41.

Nelson, C. A., Zeanah, C. H., Fox, N. A., Marshall, P. J., Smyke, A. T., & Guthrie, D. (2007). Cognitive recovery in socially deprived young children: The Bucharest Early Intervention Project. *Science, 318*(5858), 1937–1940.

Nelson, D. A., Hart, C. H., Yang, C., Olsen, J. A., & Jin, S. (2006). Aversive parenting in China: Associations with child physical and relational aggression. *Child Development, 77,* 554–572.

Nelson, E. E., McClure, E. B., Monk, C. S., Zarahn, E., Leibenluft, E., Pine, D. S., & Ernst, M. (2003). Developmental differences in neuronal engagement during implicit encoding of emotional faces: An event-related fMRI study. *Journal of Child Psychology and Psychiatry, 44*(7), 1015–1024. doi:10.1111/1469-7610.00186.

Nelson, K. (1996). *Language in cognitive development: Emergence of the mediated mind.* New York: Cambridge University Press.

Nelson, K., & Fivush, R. (2004). The emergence of autobiographical memory: A social cultural developmental theory. *Psychological Review, 111,* 486–511.

Nelson, L. D., Scheibel, K. E., & Ringman, J. M. (2007). An experimental approach to detecting dementia in Down syndrome: A paradigm for Alzheimer's disease. *Brain and Cognition, 64,* 92–103.

Nesheim, S., Henderson, S., Lindsay, M., Zuberi, J., Grimes, V., Buehler, J., et al. (2004). *Prenatal HIV testing and antiretroviral prophylaxis at an urban hospital—Atlanta, Georgia, 1997–2000.* Atlanta, GA: Centers for Disease Control.

Nestler, E. J. (2011, December). Hidden switches in the mind. *Scientific American,* pp. 77–83.

Nestler, E. J. (2016). Transgenerational epigenetic contributions to stress responses: Fact or fiction? *Plos Biology, 14,* 22–26.

Newport, F., & Wilke, J. (2013, October 28). Economy would benefit if marriage rate increases in U.S. *Gallup.* Accessed online, 8/8/15; http://www.gallup.com/poll/165599/economy-benefit-marriage-rate-increases.aspx.

Newsome, W., & Kelly, M. (2006). Bullying behavior and school violence. In *Fostering child & adolescent mental health in the classroom* (pp. 183–201). Thousand Oaks, CA: Sage Publications, Inc.

Ng, T., & Feldman, D. (2008). The relationship of age to ten dimensions of job performance. *Journal of Applied Psychology, 93,* 392–423.

Ng, F. F., Pomerantz, E. M., & Lam, S. (2007). European American and Chinese parents' responses to children's success and failure: Implications for children's responses. *Developmental Psychology, 43,* 1239–1255.

Ng, W., & Nicholas, H. (2010). A progressive pedagogy for online learning with high-ability secondary school students: A case study. *Gifted Child Quarterly, 54,* 239–251.

Ni Bhrolcháin, M. (2006). The age difference between partners: A matter of female choice? In *Human clocks: The bio-cultural meanings of age* (pp. 289–312). New York: Peter Lang Publishing.

NICHD Early Child Care Research Network. (2006). *Child care and child development: Results from the NICHD study of early child care and youth development.* New York: Guilford Press.

Nicholson, J. M., D'Esposito, F., Lucas, N., & Westrupp, E. M. (2014). Raising children in single-parent families. In A. Abela, J. Walker (Eds.), *Contemporary issues in family studies: Global perspectives on partnerships, parenting and support in a changing world.* New York: Wiley-Blackwell.

Nicholson, L. M., & Browning, C. R. (2012). Racial and ethnic disparities in obesity during the transition to adulthood: The contingent and nonlinear impact of neighborhood disadvantage. *Journal of Youth and Adolescence, 41,* 53–66.

Nicolson, R., & Fawcett, A. (2008). *Dyslexia, learning, and the brain.* Cambridge, MA: MIT Press.

Niederhofer, H. (2004). A longitudinal study: Some preliminary results of association of prenatal maternal stress and fetal movements, temperament factors in early childhood and behavior at age 2 years. *Psychological Reports, 95,* 767–770.

Nielsen, M. (2006). Copying actions and copying outcomes: Social learning through the second year. *Developmental Psychology, 42,* 555–565.

Nikčević, A. V., & Nicolaides, K. H. (2014). Search for meaning, finding meaning and adjustment in women following miscarriage: A longitudinal study. *Psychology & Health, 29,* 50–63.

Nikolas, M., Klump, K. L., & Burt, S. (2012). Youth appraisals of interparental conflict and genetic and environmental contributions to attention-deficit hyperactivity disorder: Examination of GxE effects in a twin sample. *Journal of Abnormal Child Psychology, 40,* 543–554.

Nilsen, E., & Graham, S. (2009). The relations between children's communicative perspective-taking and executive functioning. *Cognitive Psychology, 58,* 220–249.

Ninio, A. (2014). Variables and values in children's early word combinations. *Psychology of Language and Communication, 18,* 106–125.

Nisbett, R. E., Aronson, J., Blair, C., Dickens, W., Flynn, J., Halpern, D. F., et al. (2012). Intelligence: New findings and theoretical developments. *American Psychologist, 67,* 130–159.

Nixon-Cave, K. (2001). Influence of cultural/ethnic beliefs and behaviors and family environment on the motor development of infants 12–18 months of age in three ethnic groups: African-American, Hispanic/Latino and Anglo-European. Unpublished doctoral dissertation, Temple University, PA.

Nobre, R. G., de Azevedo, D. V., de Almeida, P. C., de Almeida, N. S., & de Lucena Feitosa, F. E. (2017). Weight-gain velocity in newborn infants managed with the kangaroo method and associated variables. *Maternal and Child Health Journal, 21,* 128–135.

Noel, A., & Newman, J. (2008). Mothers' plans for children during the kindergarten hold-out year. *Early Child Development and Care, 178*(3), 289–303.

Nolen-Hoeksema, S. (2001). Ruminative coping and adjustment to bereavement. In M. Stroebe & R. Hansson (Eds.), *Handbook of bereavement research: Consequences, coping, and care.* Washington, DC: American Psychological Association.

Nolen-Hoeksema, S., & Davis, C. (2002). Positive responses to loss: Perceiving benefits and growth. In C. Snyder & S. Lopez (Eds.), *Handbook of positive psychology.* London: Oxford University Press.

Nolen-Hoeksema, S., & Larson, J. (1999). *Coping with loss.* Mahwah, NJ: Lawrence Erlbaum.

Nordin, S., Razani, L., & Markison, S. (2003). Age-associated increases in intensity discrimination for taste. *Experimental Aging Research, 29,* 371–381.

Norman, R. (2008). Reproductive changes in the female lifespan. In *The active female: Health issues throughout the lifespan* (pp. 17–24). Totowa, NJ: Humana Press.

Norton, A., & D'Ambrosio, B. (2008). ZPC and ZPD: Zones of teaching and learning. *Journal for Research in Mathematics Education, 39,* 220–246.

Norton, M. I., & Gino, F. (2014). Rituals alleviate grieving for loved ones, lovers, and lotteries. *Journal of Experimental Psychology: General, 143,* 266–272.

Nosarti, C., Reichenberg, A., Murray, R. M., Cnattingius, S., Lambe, M. P., Yin, L., et al. (2012). Preterm birth and psychiatric disorders in young adult life preterm birth and psychiatric disorders. *Archives of General Psychiatry, 155,* 610–617.

Notaro, P., Gelman, S., & Zimmerman, M. (2002). Biases in reasoning about the consequences of psychogenic bodily reactions: Domain boundaries in cognitive development. *Merrill-Palmer Quarterly, 48,* 427–449.

Nugent, J. K., Lester, B. M., & Brazelton, T. B. (Eds.). (1989). *The cultural context of infancy, Vol. 1: Biology, culture, and infant development.* Norwood, NJ: Ablex.

Nuttman-Shwartz, O. (2007). Is there life without work? *International Journal of Aging & Human Development, 64,* 129–147.

Nygaard, E., Slinning, K., Moe, V., & Walhovd, K. B. (2017). Cognitive function of youths born to mothers with opioid and poly-substance abuse problems during pregnancy. *Child Neuropsychology, 23,* 159–187.

Nypaver, C. F., & Shambley-Ebron, D. (2016). Using community-based participatory research to investigate meaningful prenatal care among African American women. *Journal of Transcultural Nursing, 27,* 558–566.

O'Connor, M., & Whaley, S. (2006). Health care provider advice and risk factors associated with alcohol consumption following pregnancy recognition. *Journal of Studies on Alcohol, 67,* 22–31.

O'Connor, T. M., Cerin, E., Hughes, S. O., et al. (2013). What Hispanic parents do to encourage and discourage 3–5-year-old children to be active: A qualitative study using nominal group technique. *International Journal of Behavioral Nutrition and Physical Activity, 10,* 88–97.

O'Doherty, K. (2014). Review of Telling genes: The story of genetic counseling in America. *Journal of the History of the Behavioral Sciences, 50,* 115–117.

O'Grady, W., & Aitchison, J. (2005). *How children learn language.* New York: Cambridge University Press.

O'Neil, J. M., & Denke, R. (2016). An empirical review of gender role conflict research: New conceptual models and research paradigms. In Y. J. Wong & S. R. Wester (Eds.), *APA handbook of men and masculinities.* Washington, DC: American Psychological Association.

O'Sullivan, A. (2015). Pulled from all sides: The sandwich generation at work. *Work: Journal of Prevention, Assessment & Rehabilitation, 50,* 491–494.

O'Toole, M. E. (2000). *The school shooter: A threat assessment perspective.* Washington, DC: Federal Bureau of Investigation.

Oakes, L. M., & Kovack-Lesh, K. A. (2013). Infants' visual recognition memory for a series of categorically related items. *Journal of Cognition and Development, 14,* 63–86.

Ockerman, E. (2017, August 15). Pregnant women addicted to opioids face tough choices. *Washington Post.* Accessed online, 10/25/17; https://www.washingtonpost.com/national/pregnant-women-addicted-to-opioids-face-tough-choices-fear-treatment-can-lead-to-separation-and-harm/2017/08/13/8844e51a-6d78-11e7-b9e2-2056e768a7e5_story.html?utm_term=.8e1a5948eb1d.

OECD. (2014). *PISA 2012 results in focus: What 15-year-olds know and what they can do with what they know.* Paris: Organization for Economic Co-operation and Development (OECD).

Oesterdiekhoff, G. (2007). The reciprocal causation of intelligence and culture: A commentary based on a Piagetian perspective. *European Journal of Personality, 21,* 742–743.

Offer, S. (2016). Free time and emotional well-being: Do dual-earner mothers and fathers differ? *Gender & Society, 30*(2), 213–239.

Office of Adolescent Health. (2016, February). *Teens' social media use: How they connect and what it means for health.* U.S. Department of Health & Human Services. Accessed online, 11/9/17; https://www.hhs.gov/ash/oah/news/e-updates/february-2016-teens-social-media-use/index.html.

Ogbu, J. U. (2003). *Black American students in an affluent suburb: A study of academic disengagement.* Mahwah, NJ: Erlbaum.

Ogden, C. L., Carroll, M. D., Fryar, C. D., & Flegal, K. M. (2015). *Prevalence of obesity among adults and youth: United States, 2011–2014. NCHS data brief, no 219.* Hyattsville, MD: National Center for Health Statistics.

Ogolsky, B. G., Dennison, R. P., & Monk, J. K. (2014). The role of couple discrepancies in cognitive and behavioral egalitarianism in marital quality. *Sex Roles, 70,* 329–342.

Oğuz, V., & Akyol, A. K. (2008). Perspective-taking skills of 6-year-old children: Preschool attendance and mothers' and fathers' education and empathetic skills. *Perceptual and Motor Skills, 107*(2), 481–493. doi:10.2466/pms.107.2.481-493.

Ohta, H., & Ohgi, S. (2013). Review of 'The Neonatal Behavioral Assessment Scale.' *Brain & Development, 35,* 79–80.

Olds, T., Wake, M., Patton, G., Ridley, K., Waters, E., Williams, J., et al. (2009). How do school-day activity patterns differ with age and gender across adolescence? *Journal of Adolescent Health, 44*, 64–72.

Oliver, M. B., & Hyde, J. S. (1993). Gender differences in sexuality: A meta-analysis. *Psychological Bulletin, 114*, 29–51.

Olsen, S. (2009, October 30). Will the digital divide close by itself? *New York Times*. Accessed online, 11/23/09; http://bits.blogs.nytimes.com/2009/10/30/will-the-digital-divide-close-by-itself.

Olshansky, S. J., Passaro, D. J., Hershow, R. C., Layden, J., Carnes, B. A., Brody, J., et al. (2005, March 17). Special report: A potential decline in life expectancy in the United States in the 21st century. *The New England Journal of Medicine, 352*, 1138–1145.

Olson, E. (2006, April 27). You're in labor, and getting sleeeepy. *New York Times*, p. C2.

Olszewski-Kubilius, P., & Thomson, D. (2013). Gifted education programs and procedures. In W. M. Reynolds, G. E. Miller, I. B. Weiner, W. M. Reynolds, G. E. Miller, & I. B. Weiner (Eds.), *Handbook of psychology, Vol. 7: Educational psychology* (2nd ed.). Hoboken, NJ: John Wiley & Sons Inc.

Olszewski-Kubilius, P., & Thomson, D. (2014). Talent search. In J. A. Plucker, C. M. Callahan, J. A. Plucker, & C. M. Callahan (Eds.), *Critical issues and practices in gifted education: What the research says* (2nd ed.). Waco, TX: Prufrock Press.

Orbuch, T. (2009). *Five simple steps to take your marriage from good to great*. Oakland, CA: The Oakland Press.

Oregon Death with Dignity Act. (2016). Oregon Death with Dignity Act: Annual Report for 2016. Portland, OR: Death with Dignity National Center.

Oreyzi, H. R., & Shapouri, S. (2015). The effect of imbalance of reward relative to personnel effort on burnout via personal work goals mediation. *Journal of Psychology, 18*(4), 423–437.

Ormont, L. R. (2001). Developing emotional insulation (1994). In L. B. Fugeri (Ed.), *The technique of group treatment: The collected papers of Louis R. Ormont*. Madison, CT: Psychosocial Press.

Ortiz, S. O., & Dynda, A. M. (2005). Use of intelligence tests with culturally and linguistically diverse populations. In D. P. Flanagan & P. L. Harrison (Eds.), *Contemporary intellectual assessment: Theories, tests, and issues*. New York: Guilford Press.

Ortman, J. M., Velkoff, V. A., & Hogan, H. (2014) An aging nation: The older population in the United States population estimates and projections. *Current Population Reports, P25–1140*.

Osofsky, J. (2003). Prevalence of children's exposure to domestic violence and child maltreatment: Implications for prevention and intervention. *Clinical Child & Family Psychology Review, 6*, 161–170.

Osterman, M.J.K. & Martin, J.A. (2011). Epidural and spinal anesthesia use during labor: 27-state reporting area, 2008. *National vital statistics reports; vol. 59, no 5*. Hyattsville, MD: National Center for Health Statistics.

Ostrosky-Solis, F., & Oberg, G. (2006). Neuropsychological functions across the world—common and different features: From digit span to moral judgment. *International Journal of Psychology, 41*, 321–323.

Otsuka, Y., Hill, H. H., Kanazawa, S., Yamaguchi, M. K., & Spehar, B. (2012). Perception of Mooney faces by young infants: The role of local feature visibility, contrast polarity, and motion. *Journal of Experimental Child Psychology, 111*, 164–179.

Ott, C., Sanders, S., & Kelber, S. (2007). Grief and personal growth experience of spouses and adult-child caregivers of individuals with Alzheimer's disease and related dementias. *The Gerontologist, 47*, 798–809.

Outten, H., Schmitt, M., Garcia, D., & Branscombe, N. (2009). Coping options: Missing links between minority group identification and psychological well-being. *Applied Psychology: An International Review, 58*, 146–170.

Ouwehand, C., de Ridder, D. T., & Bensing, J. M. (2007). A review of successful aging models: Proposing proactive coping as an important additional strategy. *Clinical Psychology Review, 43*, 101–116.

Owens, J. (2008). Socio-cultural considerations and sleep practices in the pediatric population. *Sleep Medicine Clinics, 3*, 97–107.

Owsley, C., Stalvey, B., & Phillips, J. (2003). The efficacy of an educational intervention in promoting self-regulation among high-risk older drivers. *Accident Analysis & Prevention, 35*, 393–400.

Oxford, M., Gilchrist, L., Gillmore, M., & Lohr, M. (2006, July). Predicting variation in the life course of adolescent mothers as they enter adulthood. *Journal of Adolescent Health, 39*, 20–26.

Ozawa, M., & Yoon, H. (2003). Economic impact of marital disruption on children. *Children & Youth Services Review, 25*, 611–632.

Ozimek, P., & Bierhoff, H. (2016). Facebook use depending on age: The influence of social comparisons. *Computers in Human Behavior, 61*, 271–279.

Ozmen, C. B., Brelsford, G. M., & Danieu, C. R. (2017). Political affiliation, spirituality, and religiosity: Links to emerging adults' life satisfaction and optimism. *Journal of Religion and Health*. Accessed online, 12/3/17; https://www.ncbi.nlm.nih.gov/pubmed/28803368.

Pacala, J. T., & Yueh, B. (2012). Hearing deficits in the older patient: "I didn't notice anything." *JAMA: Journal of the American Medical Association, 307*(11), 1185–1194. doi:10.1001/jama.2012.305.

Paige, R. (2006, December). No Child Left Behind: The ongoing movement for public education reform. *Harvard Educational Review, 76*, 461–473.

Pajulo, M., Helenius, H., & MaYes, L. (2006, May). Prenatal views of baby and parenthood: Association with sociodemographic and pregnancy factors. *Infant Mental Health Journal, 27*, 229–250.

Palermo, L., Geberhiwot, T., MacDonald, A., Limback, E., Hall, S. K., & Romani, C. (2017). Cognitive outcomes in early-treated adults with phenylketonuria (PKU): A comprehensive picture across domains. *Neuropsychology, 31*, 255–267.

Palmore, E. B. (2017). Auto-gerontology: A personal odyssey. *Journal of Applied Gerontology, 36*, 1295–1305.

Paludi, M. A. (2012). *The psychology of love* (Vols 1–4). Santa Barbara, CA: Praeger/ABC-CLIO.

Panel, C. C., Watson, N. F., Badr, M. S., Belenky, G., Bliwise, D. L., Buxton, O. M., . . . & Kushida, C. (2015). Recommended amount of sleep for a healthy adult: a joint consensus statement of the American Academy of Sleep Medicine and Sleep Research Society. *Journal of Clinical Sleep Medicine: JCSM: Official Publication of the American Academy of Sleep Medicine, 11*(6), 591.

Paolella, F. (2013). La pedagogia di Loris Malaguzzi. Per una storia del Reggio Emiliaapproach. = The pedagogy of Malaguzzi. The Reggio Emilia approach. *Rivista Sperimentale Di Freniatria: La Rivista Della Salute Mentale, 137*, 95–112.

Papaharitou, S., Nakopoulou, E., Kirana, P., Giaglis, G., Moraitou, M., & Hatzichristou, D. (2008). Factors associated with sexuality in later life: An exploratory study in a group of Greek married older adults. *Archives of Gerontology and Geriatrics, 46*, 191–201.

Papousek, H., & Papousek, M. (1991). Innate and cultural guidance of infants' integrative competencies: China, the United States, and Germany. In M. H. Borstein (Ed.), *Cultural approaches to parenting*. Hillsdale, NJ: Lawrence Erlbaum.

Pappa, I., St. Pourcain, B., Benke, K., Cavadino, A., Hakulinen, C., Nivard, M. G., & . . . Tiemeier, H. (2016). A genome-wide approach to children's aggressive behavior: The EAGLE consortium. *American Journal of Medical Genetics Part B: Neuropsychiatric Genetics, 171*(5), 562–572. doi:10.1002/ajmg.b.32333.

Park, C. L., Riley, K. E., & Snyder, L. B. (2012). Meaning making coping, making sense, and posttraumatic growth following the 9/11 terrorist attacks. *The Journal of Positive Psychology, 7*, 198–207.

Park, H. K., Choi, S. H., Park, S. A., Kim, H. J., Lee, Y., Han, S., & . . . Lee, J. (2015). Cognitive profiles and neuropsychiatric symptoms in Korean early-onset Alzheimer's disease patients: A CREDOS study. *Journal of Alzheimer's Disease, 44*, 661–673.

Park, J. J., & Bowman, N. A. (2015). Religion as bridging or bonding social capital: Race, religion, and cross-racial interaction for college students. *Sociology of Education, 88*, 20–37.

Parke, R. D. (2004). Development in the family. *Annual Review of Psychology, 55*, 365–399.

Parke, R. D., Simpkins, S., & McDowell, D. (2002). Relative contributions of families and peers to children's social development. In

P. Smith & C. Hart (Eds.), *Blackwell handbook of childhood social development*. Malden, MA: Blackwell Publishers.

Parker, K. (2012). *The boomerang generation*. Washington, DC: Pew Research Center.

Parks, C., Sanna, L., & Posey, D. (2003). Retrospection in social dilemmas: How thinking about the past affects future cooperation. *Journal of Personality & Social Psychology*, 84, 988–996.

Parsons, A., & Howe, N. (2013). 'This is Spiderman's mask.' 'No, it's Green Goblin's': Shared meanings during boys' pretend play with superhero and generic toys. *Journal of Research in Childhood Education*, 27, 190–207.

Parten, M. B. (1932). Social participation among preschool children. *Journal of Abnormal and Social Psychology*, 27, 243–269.

Pascarella, E. T., Martin, G. L., Hanson, J. M., Trolian, T. L., Gillig, B., & Blaich, C. (2014). Effects of diversity experiences on critical thinking skills over 4 years of college. *Journal of College Student Development*, 55, 86–92.

Pascual-Leone, J., & Johnson, J. (2005). A dialectical constructivist view of developmental intelligence. In *Handbook of understanding and measuring intelligence*. Thousand Oaks, CA: Sage Publications, Inc.

Pashos, A., & McBurney, D. (2008). Kin relationships and the caregiving biases of grandparents, aunts, and uncles: A two-generational questionnaire study. *Human Nature*, 19, 311–330.

Pasiak, C., & Menna, R. (2015). Mother–child synchrony: Implications for young children's aggression and social competence. *Journal of Child and Family Studies*. Accessed online, 6/21/15; http://link.springer.com/article/10.1007%2Fs10826-015-0113-y#page-1.

Paterno, M. T., McElroy, K., & Regan, M. (2016). Electronic fetal monitoring and cesarean birth: A scoping review. *Birth: Issues in Perinatal Care*, 43, 277–284.

Pasterski, V., Zucker, K. J., Hindmarsh, P. C., Hughes, I. A., Acerini, C., Spencer, D., & . . . Hines, M. (2014). Increased cross-gender identification independent of gender role behavior in girls with congenital adrenal hyperplasia: Results from a standardized assessment of 4- to 11-year-old children. *Archives of Sexual Behavior*. Accessed online, 6/29/15; http://www.ncbi.nlm.nih.gov/pubmed/25239661.

Pathman, T., Larkina, M., Burch, M. M., & Bauer, P. J. (2013). Young children's memory for the times of personal past events. *Journal of Cognition and Development*, 14, 120–140.

Patterson, C. (2009). Children of lesbian and gay parents: Psychology, law, and policy. *American Psychologist*, (64), 727–736.

Patterson, C. J. (2007). Lesbian and gay family issues in the context of changing legal and social policy environments. In K. J. Bieschke, R. M. Perez, & K. A. DeBord (Eds.), *Handbook of counseling and psychotherapy with lesbian, gay, bisexual, and transgender clients* (2nd ed.). Washington, DC: American Psychological Association.

Patterson, C. J. (2013). Children of lesbian and gay parents: Psychology, law, and policy. *Psychology of Sexual Orientation and Gender Diversity*, 1(S), 27–34.

Pattiselanno, K., Dijkstra, J. K., Steglich, C., Vollebergh, W., & Veenstra, R. (2015). Structure matters: The role of clique hierarchy in the relationship between adolescent social status and aggression and prosociality. *Journal of Youth and Adolescence*, Accessed online, 6/30/15; http://www.ncbi.nlm.nih.gov/pubmed/26077559.

Pattison, E., Grodsky, E., & Muller, C. (2013). Is the sky falling? Grade inflation and the signaling power of grades. *Educational Researcher*, 42, 259–265.

Pauli-Pott, U., Mertesacker, B., & Bade, U. (2003). Parental perceptions and infant temperament development. *Infant Behavior & Development*, 26, 27–48.

Paulus, M. (2014). How and why do infants imitate? An ideomotor approach to social and imitative learning in infancy (and beyond). *Psychonomic Bulletin & Review*, 21, 1139–1156.

Paulus, M. (2016). Friendship trumps neediness: The impact of social relations and others' wealth on preschool children's sharing. *Journal of Experimental Child Psychology*, 146, 106–120.

Paulus, M., & Moore, C. (2014). The development of recipient-dependent sharing behavior and sharing expectations in preschool children. *Developmental Psychology*, 50, 914–921.

Pearson, J., & Wilkinson, L. (2013). Adolescent sexual experiences. In A. K. Baumle (Ed.), *International handbook on the demography of sexuality*. New York: Springer Science + Business Media.

Peck, R. C. (1968). Psychological developments in the second half of life. In B. L. Neugarten (Ed.), *Middle age and aging*. Chicago: University of Chicago Press.

Peel, E., & Harding, R. (2015). A right to 'dying well' with dementia? Capacity, 'choice' and relationality. *Feminism & Psychology*, 25, 137–142.

Pederson, D. R., Bailey, H. N., Tarabulsy, G. M., Bento, S., & Moran, G. (2014). Understanding sensitivity: Lessons learned from the legacy of Mary Ainsworth. *Attachment & Human Development*, 16, 261–270.

Pedersen, S., Vitaro, F., Barker, E. D., & Borge, A. I. H. (2007). The timing of middle-childhood peer rejection and friendship: Linking early behavior to early-adolescent adjustment. *Child Development*, 78, 1037–1051.

Peisah, C., Latif, E., Wilhelm, K., & Williams, B. (2009). Secrets to psychological success: Why older doctors might have lower psychological distress and burnout than younger doctors. *Aging & Mental Health*, 13, 300–307.

Pellegrini, A. (2007). Is aggression adaptive? Yes: Some kinds are and in some ways. In *Aggression and adaptation: The bright side to bad behavior*. Mahwah, NJ: Lawrence Erlbaum Associates Publishers.

Peltzer, K., & Pengpid, S. (2006). Sexuality of 16- to 17- year-old South Africans in the context of HIV/AIDS. *Social Behavior and Personality*, 34, 239–256.

Penido, A., de Souza Rezende, G., Abreu, R., de Oliveira, A., Guidine, P., Pereira, G., et al. (2012). Malnutrition during central nervous system growth and development impairs permanently the subcortical auditory pathway. *Nutritional Neuroscience*, 15, 31–36.

Penningroth, S., & Scott, W. D. (2012). Age-related differences in goals: Testing predictions, form selection, optimization, and compensation theory and socioemotional selectivity theory. *The International Journal of Aging & Human Development*, 74, 87–111.

Pennisi, E. (2000, May 19). And the gene number is . . .? *Science*, 288, 1146–1147.

Peralta, O., Salsa, A., del Rosario Maita, M., & Mareovich, F. (2013). Scaffolding young children's understanding of symbolic objects. *Early Years: An International Journal of Research and Development*, 33, 266–274.

Pereira, A. C., Huddleston, D. E., Brickman, A. M., Sosunov, A. A., Hen, R., McKhann, G. M., et al. (2007). An in vivo correlate of exercise-induced neurogenesis in the adult dentate gyrus. *Proceedings of the National Academy of Sciences*, 104, 5638–5643.

Perelli-Harris, B., & Styrc, M. (2017). Mental well being differences in cohabitation and marriage: The role of childhood selection. *Journal of Marriage and Family*. Accessed online, 12/3/17; http://onlinelibrary.wiley.com/doi/10.1111/jomf.12431/full.

Perlmann, R. Y., & Gleason, J. B. (1990, July). Patterns of prohibition in mothers' speech to children. Paper presented at the Fifth International Congress for the Study of Child Language, Budapest, Hungary.

Perie, M., Grigg, W. S., & Dion, G. S. (2005). The nation's report card: Mathematics 2005. Washington, DC: National Assessment of Educational Progress.

Perreault, A., Fothergill-Bourbonnais, F., & Fiset, V. (2004). The experience of family members caring for a dying loved one. *International Journal of Palliative Nursing*, 10, 133–143.

Perreira, K. M., & Ornelas, I. J. (2011, Spring). The physical and psychological well-being of immigrant children. *The Future of Children*, 21, 195–218.

Perrin-Wallqvist, R., & Lindblom, J. (2015). Coming out as gay: A phenomenological study about adolescents disclosing their homosexuality to their parents. *Social Behavior and Personality*, 43, 467–480.

Perry, W. G. (1981). Cognitive and ethical growth: The making of meaning. In A. W. Chickering and Associates (Eds.), *The Modern American College*. San Francisco: Jossey-Bass.

Persch, A. C., Lamb, A. J., Metzler, C. A., & Fristad, M. A. (2015). Healthy habits for children: Leveraging existing evidence to demonstrate value. *American Journal of Occupational Therapy, 69*(4), 1–5.

Persson, G. E. B. (2005). Developmental perspectives on prosocial and aggressive motives in preschoolers' peer interactions. *International Journal of Behavioral Development, 29*, 80–91.

Persson, A., & Musher-Eizenman, D. R. (2003). The impact of a prejudice-prevention television program on young children's ideas about race. *Early Childhood Research Quarterly, 18*, 530–546.

Pertzov, Y., Heider, M., Liang, Y., & Husain, M. (2015). Effects of healthy ageing on precision and binding of object location in visual short term memory. *Psychology and Aging, 30*(1), 26–35. doi:10.1037/a0038396.

Peter, C. J., Fischer, L. K., Kundakovic, M., Garg, P., Jakovcevski, M., Dincer, A., & . . . Akbarian, S. (2016). DNA methylation signatures of early childhood malnutrition associated with impairments in attention and cognition. *Biological Psychiatry, 80*, 765–774.

Petersen, A. (2000). A longitudinal investigation of adolescents' changing perceptions of pubertal timing. *Developmental Psychology, 36*, 37–43.

Peterson, C. (2014). Theory of mind understanding and empathic behavior in children with autism spectrum disorders. *International Journal of Developmental Neuroscience, 39*, 16–21.

Peterson, C., & Park, N. (2007). Explanatory style and emotion regulation. In J. J. Gross (Ed.), *Handbook of emotion regulation*. New York: Guilford Press.

Peterson, C., Wang, Q., & Hou, Y. (2009). "When I was little": Childhood recollections in Chinese and European Canadian grade school children. *Child Development, 80*, 506–518.

Peterson, R. A., & Brown, S. P. (2005). On the use of beta coefficients in meta-analysis. *Journal of Applied Psychology, 90*, 175–181.

Peterson, D. M., Marcia, J. E., & Carependale, J. I. (2004). Identity: Does thinking make it so? In C. Lightfood, C. Lalonde, & M. Chandler (Eds.), *Changing conceptions of psychological life*. Mahwah, NJ: Lawrence Erlbaum.

Peterson, M., & Wilson, J. F. (2004). Work stress in America. *International Journal of Stress Management, 11*, 91–113.

Petit, G., & Dodge, K. A. (2003). Violent children: Bridging development, intervention, and public policy. *Developmental Psychology, 39* [Special issue: Violent Children], 187–188.

Petrican, R., Todorov, A., Burris, C. T., Rosenbaum, R. S., & Grady, C. (2015). The look that binds: Partner-directed altruistic motivation and biased perception in married couples. *Journal of Nonverbal Behavior, 39*, 165–179.

Petrosino, A., Turpin-Petrosino, C., Hollis-Peel, M. E., & Lavenberg, J. G. (2013). 'Scared Straight' and other juvenile awareness programs for preventing juvenile delinquency. *Scientific Review of Mental Health Practice, 4*, 48–54.

Petrou, S. (2006). Preterm birth—What are the relevant economic issues? *Early Human Development, 82*(2), 75–76.

Petrowski, N., Cappa, C., & Gross, P. (2017). Estimating the number of children in formal alternative care: Challenges and results. *Child Abuse & Neglect, 70*, 388–398.

Pettit, G. S., Bates, J. E., & Dodge, K. A. (1997). Supportive parenting, ecological context, and children's adjustment: A 7-year longitudinal study. *Child Development, 68*, 908–923.

Pew Forum on Religion & Public Life. (2008). *U.S. religious landscape survey*. Washington, DC: Author.

Pew Research Center (2009, June 29). Growing old in America: Expectations vs. reality. Washington, DC: Pew Research Center.

Pew Research Center. (2014, November 14). *Four-in-ten couples are saying "I do" again*. Washington, DC: Pew Research Center. Accessed online, 7-23-15; http://www.pewsocialtrends.org/2014/11/14/four-in-ten-couples-are-saying-i-do-again/.

Pew Research Center. (2017). *Led by Baby Boomers, divorce rates climb for America's 50+ population*. Washington, DC: Pew Research Center. Accessed online, 11-13-18; http://www.pewresearch.org/fact-tank/2017/03/09/led-by-baby-boomers-divorce-rates-climb-for-americas-50-population/.

Philippot, P., & Feldman, R. S. (Eds.). (2005). *The regulation of emotion*. Mahwah, NJ: Lawrence Erlbaum Associates.

Phillips, B. M., Tabulda, G., Ingrole, S. A., Burris, P. W., Sedgwick, T. K., & Chen, S. (2016). Literate language intervention with high-need prekindergarten children: A randomized trial. *Journal of Speech, Language, and Hearing Research, 59*(6), 1409–1420. doi:10.1044/2016_JSLHR-L-15-0155.

Phillips, D., Gormley, W., & Anderson, S. (2016). The effects of Tulsa's CAP Head Start program on middle-school academic outcomes and progress. *Developmental Psychology, 52*, 1247–1261.

Phillips, M. L. (2011, April). The mind at midlife. *Monitor on Psychology*, pp. 39–41.

Phillips, L., & Henry, J. (2008). Adult aging and executive functioning. In *Executive functions and the frontal lobes: A lifespan perspective*. Philadelphia: Taylor & Francis.

Phinney, J. S. (2003). Ethic identity and acculturation. In K. M. Chun, P. Organista, & G. Marin, *Acculturation: Advances in theory, measurement, and applied research*. Washington, DC: American Psychological Association.

Phinney, J. S. (2005). Ethnic identity in late modern times: A response to Rattansi and Phoenix. *Identity, 5*, 187–194.

Phinney, J. S. (2008). Ethnic identity exploration in emerging adulthood. In D. L. Browning (Ed.), *Adolescent identities: A collection of readings* (pp. 47–66). New York: Analytic Press/Taylor & Francis Group.

Phinney, J. (2006). Ethnic identity exploration in emerging adulthood. In *Emerging adults in America: Coming of age in the 21st century*. Washington, DC: American Psychological Association.

Phinney, J. S., Ferguson, D. L., & Tate, J. D. (1997). Intergroup attitudes among ethnic minority adolescents: A causal model. *Child Development, 68*, 955–969.

Phinney, J., Lochner, B., & Murphy, R. (1990). Ethnic identity development and psychological adjustment in adolescence. In A. Stiffman & L. Davis (Eds.), *Advances in adolescent mental health: Vol. 5. Ethnic issues*. Greenwich, CT: JAI Press.

Phung, J. N., Milojevich, H. M., & Lukowski, A. F. (2014). Adult language use and infant comprehension of English: Associations with encoding and generalization across cues at 20 months. *Infant Behavior & Development, 37*, 465–479.

Piaget, J. (1954). *The construction of reality in the child*. New York. Basic Books.

Piaget, J. (1962). *Play, dreams and imitation in childhood*. New York: Norton.

Piaget, J. (1983). Piaget's theory. In W. Kessen (Ed.), P. H. Mussen (Series Ed.), *Handbook of child psychology: Vol 1. History, theory, and methods* (pp. 103–128). New York: Wiley.

Piaget, J., & Inhelder, B. (1958). *The growth of logical thinking from childhood to adolescence* (A. Parsons & S. Seagrin, Trans.). New York: Basic Books.

Pianta, R. C., Barnett, W. S., Burchinal, M., & Thornburg, K. R. (2009, August). The effects of preschool education: What we know, how public policy is or is not aligned with the evidence base, and what we need to know. *Psychological Science in the Public Interest, 10*, 49–88.

Pickles, A., Hill, J., Breen, G., Quinn, J., Abbott, K., Jones, H., & Sharp, H. (2013). Evidence for interplay between genes and parenting on infant temperament in the first year of life: Monoamine oxidase, a polymorphism, moderates effects of maternal sensitivity on infant anger proneness. *Journal of Child Psychology and Psychiatry, 54*, 1308–1317.

Pingree, A. (2008). Teaching, learning, and spirituality in the college classroom. *Teaching Excellence, 19*, 1–2.

Pinker, S. (1994). *The language instinct*. New York: William Morrow.

Planalp, E. M., Van Hulle, C., Lemery-Chalfant, K., & Goldsmith, H. H. (2016). Genetic and environmental contributions to the development of positive affect in infancy. Accessed online, 10/31/17; https://www.ncbi.nlm.nih.gov/pubmed/27797564.

Planinsec, J. (2001). A comparative analysis of the relations between the motor dimensions and cognitive ability of pre-school girls and boys. *Kinesiology, 33,* 56–68.

Plante, E., Schmithorst, V., Holland, S., & Byars, A. (2006). Sex differences in the activation of language cortex during childhood. *Neuropsychologia, 44,* 1210–1221.

Platt, I., Green, H. J., Jayasinghe, R., & Morrissey, S. A. (2014). Understanding adherence in patients with coronary heart disease: Illness representations and readiness to engage in healthy behaviours. *Australian Psychologist, 49,* 127–137.

Plomin, R. (2005). Finding genes in child psychology and psychiatry: When are we going to be there? *Journal of Child Psychology and Psychiatry, 46,* 1030–1038.

Plomin, R. (2007). *Genetics and developmental psychology.* Detroit, MI: Wayne State University Press.

Plomin, R. (2016). Bringing genetics into the mainstream of psychology. In R. J. Sternberg, S. T. Fiske, D. J. Foss (Eds.) *Scientists making a difference: One hundred eminent behavioral and brain scientists talk about their most important contributions.* New York: Cambridge University Press.

Plomin, R., DeFries, J. C., Knopik, V. S., & Neiderhiser, J. M. (2016). Top 10 replicated findings from behavioral genetics. *Perspectives on Psychological Science, 11,* 3–23.

Plosker, G., & Keam, S. (2006). Bimatoprost: A pharmacoeconomic review of its use in open-angle glaucoma and ocular hypertension. *PharmacoEconomics, 24,* 297–314.

Plummer, A. R., & Beckman, M. E. (2015). Framing a socio-indexical basis for the emergence and cultural transmission of phonological systems. *Journal of Phonetics, 53,* 66–78.

Pölkki, T., Korhonen, A., Axelin, A., Saarela, T., & Laukkala, H. (2014). Development and preliminary validation of the Neonatal Infant Acute Pain Assessment Scale (NIAPAS). *International Journal of Nursing Studies, 51,* 1585–1594.

Pollak, S., Holt, L., & Wismer Fries, A. (2004). Hemispheric asymmetries in children's perception of nonlinguistic human affective sounds. *Developmental Science, 7,* 10–18.

Pomares, C. G., Schirrer, J., & Abadie, V. (2002). Analysis of the olfactory capacity of healthy children before language acquisition. *Journal of Developmental Behavior and Pediatrics, 23,* 203–207.

Pomerantz, E. M., Qin, L., Wang, Q., & Chen, H. (2011). Changes in early adolescents' sense of responsibility to their parents in the United States and China: Implications for academic functioning. *Child Development, 82,* 1136–1151.

Ponton, L. E. (2001). *The sex lives of teenagers: Revealing the secret world of adolescent boys and girls.* New York: Penguin Putnam.

Porac, C. (2016). *Laterality: Exploring the enigma of left-handedness.* San Diego, CA: Elsevier Academic Press.

Porges, S. W., Lipsitt, & Lewis, P. (1993). Neonatal responsivity to gustatory stimulation: The gustatory-vagal hypothesis. *Infant Behavior & Development, 16,* 487–494.

Porter, M., van Teijlingen, E., Yip, L., & Bhattacharya, S. (2007). Satisfaction with cesarean section: Qualitative analysis of open-ended questions in a large postal survey. *Birth: Issues in Perinatal Care, 34,* 148–154.

Porto, P. R., Oliveira, L., Mari, J., Volchan, E., Figueira, I., & Ventura, P. (2009). Does cognitive behavioral therapy change the brain? A systematic review of neuroimaging in anxiety disorders. *The Journal of Neuropsychiatry and Clinical Neurosciences, 21*(2), 114–125.

Porzelius, L. K., Dinsmore, B. D., & Staffelbach, D. (2001). Eating disorders. In M. Hersen & V. B. Van Hasselt (Eds.), *Advanced abnormal psychology* (2nd ed.). New York: Kluwer Academic/Plenum Publishers.

Posthuma, D., & de Geus, E. (2006, August). Progress in the molecular-genetic study of intelligence. *Current Directions in Psychological Science, 15,* 151–155.

Poulin-Dubois, D., Serbin, L., & Eichstedt, J. (2002). Men don't put on make-up: Toddlers' knowledge of the gender stereotyping of household activities. *Social Development, 11,* 166–181.

Pozzi-Monzo, M. (2012). Ritalin for whom? Revisited: Further thinking on ADHD. *Journal of Child Psychotherapy, 38,* 49–60.

Preciado, P., Snijders, T. B., Burk, W. J., Stattin, H., & Kerr, M. (2012). Does proximity matter? Distance dependence of adolescent friendships. *Social Networks, 34,* 18–31.

Preckel, F., Niepel, C., Schneider, M., & Brunner, M. (2013). Self-concept in adolescence: A longitudinal study on reciprocal effects of self-perceptions in academic and social domains. *Journal of Adolescence, 36,* 1165–1175.

Prentice, A., Schoenmakers, I., Ann Laskey, M., De Bono, S., Ginty, F., & Goldberg, G. (2006). Symposium on 'Nutrition and health in children and adolescents' Session 1: Nutrition in growth and development. Nutrition and bone growth and development: A meeting of the Nutrition Society hosted by the Irish Section was held on 14–16 June 2006 at University College Cork, Cork, Republic of Ireland. *Proceedings of the Nutrition Society, 65*(4), 348–360. doi:10.1079/PNS2006519.

Pressley, M. (1987). Are keyword method effects limited to slow presentation rates? An empirically based reply to Hall and Fuson (1986). *Journal of Educational Psychology, 79,* 333–335.

Price, C. S., Thompson, W. W., Goodson, B., Weintraub, E. S., Croen, L. A., Hinrichsen, V. L., & DeStefano, F. (2010). Prenatal and infant exposure to thimerosal from vaccines and immunoglobulins and risk of autism. *Pediatrics, 126,* 656–664.

Prieler, M., Kohlbacher, F., Hagiwara, S., & Arima, A. (2011). Gender representation of older people in Japanese television advertisements. *Sex Roles, 64,* 405–415.

Prigerson, H. (2003). Costs to society of family caregiving for patients with end-stage Alzheimer's disease. *New England Journal of Medicine, 349,* 1891–1892.

PRIMEDIA/Roper. (1999). *Roper National Youth Survey.* Storrs, CT: Roper Center for Public Opinion Research.

Prince, C. B., Young, M. B., Sappenfield, W., & Parrish, J. W. (2016). Investigating the decline of fetal and infant mortality rates in Alaska during 2010 and 2011. *Maternal and Child Health Journal.* Accessed online, 10/27/17; http://www.ncbi.nlm.nih.gov/pubmed/26754348.

Prince, M. (2000, November 13). How technology has changed the way we have babies. *Wall Street Journal,* pp. R4, R13.

Prince-Embury, S., & Saklofske, D. H. (2014). *Resilience interventions for youth in diverse populations.* New York: Springer Science + Business Media.

Prochaska, M. T., Putman, M. S., Tak, H. J., Yoon, J. D., & Curlin, F. A. (2017). US physicians overwhelmingly endorse hospice as the better option for most patients at the end of life. *American Journal of Hospice & Palliative Medicine, 34,* 556–558

Proctor, C., Barnett, J., & Muilenburg, J. (2012). Investigating race, gender, and access to cigarettes in an adolescent population. *American Journal of Health Behavior, 36,* 513–521.

Prohaska, V. (2012). Strategies for encouraging ethical student behavior. In R. Landrum & M. A. McCarthy (Eds.), *Teaching ethically: Challenges and opportunities.* Washington, DC: American Psychological Association.

Proulx, M., & Poulin, F. (2013). Stability and change in kindergartners' friendships: Examination of links with social functioning. *Social Development, 22,* 111–125.

Pruchno, R., & Rosenbaum, J. (2003). Social relationships in adulthood and old age. In R. Lerner & M. Easterbrooks (Eds.), *Handbook of psychology, Vol. 6: Developmental psychology.* New York: Wiley.

Pryor, J. H., Hurtado, S., Saenz, V. B., Santos, J. L., & Korn, W. S. (2007). *The American freshman: National norms for fall 2007.* Los Angeles: Higher Education Research Institute, UCLA.

Puchalski, M., & Hummel, P. (2002). The reality of neonatal pain. *Advances in Neonatal Care, 2,* 245–247.

Puckering, C., Connolly, B., Werner, C., et al. (2011). Rebuilding relationships: A pilot study of the effectiveness of the Mellow Parenting Programme for children with reactive attachment disorder. *Clinical Child Psychology and Psychiatry, 16,* 73–87.

Pudrovska, T., Schieman, S., & Carr, D. (2006). Strains of singlehood in later life: Do race and gender matter? *Journals of Gerontology: Series B: Psychological Sciences and Social Sciences, 61B,* S315–S322.

Pun, A., Birch, S. A., & Baron, A. S. (2017). Foundations of reasoning about social dominance. *Child Development Perspectives*. Accessed online, 11/17/17; http://onlinelibrary.wiley.com/doi/10.1111/cdep.12235/full.

Pundir, A., Hameed, L., Dikshit, P. C., Kumar, P., Mohan, S., Radotra, B., et al. (2012). Expression of medium and heavy chain neurofilaments in the developing human auditory cortex. *Brain Structure & Function, 217*, 303–321.

Puntambekar, S., & Hübscher, R. (2005). Tools for scaffolding students in a complex learning environment: What have we gained and what have we missed? *Educational Psychologist, 40*, 1–12.

Purcell, K., Heaps, A., Buchanan, J., & Friedrich, L. (2013, February 28). *How teachers are using technology at home and in their classrooms.* Washington, DC: Pew Research Center.

Purswell, K. E., & Dillman Taylor, D. (2013). Creative use of sibling play therapy: An example of a blended family. *Journal of Creativity in Mental Health, 8*, 162–174.

Putney, N. M., & Bengtson, V. L. (2001). Families, intergenerational relationships and kinkeeping in midlife. In M. E. Lachman (Ed.), *Handbook of midlife development.* Hoboken, NJ: Wiley.

Putsch, R.W., III, and Joyce, M. (2017). *Clinical methods: The history, physical, and laboratory examinations.* (3rd ed.). Accessed online, 9/24/17; https://www.ncbi.nlm.nih.gov/books/NBK340/.

Qian, Z., Zhang, D., & Wang, L. (2013). Is aggressive trait responsible for violence? Priming effects of aggressive words and violent movies. *Psychology, 4*, 96–100.

Qiu, Z., Liu, C., Gao, Z., He, J., Liu, X., Wei, Q., & Chen, J. (2016). The inulin-type oligosaccharides extract from morinda officinalis, a traditional Chinese herb, ameliorated behavioral deficits in an animal model of post-traumatic stress disorder. *Metabolic Brain Disease, 31*, 1143–1149.

Quaid, L. (2011). Sexting puts teenagers and young adults at risk. In S. Kiesbye (Ed.), *Sexting.* Greenhaven Press.

Quinn, P., Uttley, L., Lee, K., Gibson, A., Smith, M., Slater, A., et al. (2008). Infant preference for female faces occurs for same- but not other-race faces. *Journal of Neuropsychology, 2*, 15–26.

Quintana, S. M. (2007). Racial and ethnic identity: Developmental perspectives and research. *Journal of Counseling Psychology, 54*, 259–270.

Quintana, S. M., & McKown, C. (2008). *Handbook of race, racism, and the developing child.* Hoboken, NJ: John Wiley & Sons.

Ra, J. S., & Cho, Y. H. (2017). Depression moderates the relationship between body image and health-related quality of life in adolescent girls. *Journal of Child and Family Studies, 26*, 1799–1807.

Raag, T. (2003). Racism, gender identities and young children: Social relations in a multi-ethnic, inner-city primary school. *Archives of Sexual Behavior, 32*, 392–393.

Rabin, R. (2006, June 13). Breast-feed or else. *New York Times*, p. D1.

Radford, J., Bosanquet, P., Webster, R., & Blatchford, P. (2015). Scaffolding learning for independence: Clarifying teacher and teaching assistant roles for children with special educational needs. *Learning and Instruction, 36*, 1–10.

Rainwater, L., & Smeeding, T. (2007). Is there hope for America's low-income children? *Shifting the center: Understanding contemporary families* (3rd ed.) (pp. 770–779). New York: McGraw-Hill.

Rajhans, P., Jessen, S., Missana, M., & Grossmann, T. (2016). Putting the face in context: Body expressions impact facial emotion processing in human infants. *Developmental Cognitive Neuroscience, 19*, 115–121.

Rakison, D. H., & Krogh, L. (2012). Does causal action facilitate causal perception in infants younger than 6 months of age? *Developmental Science, 15*, 43–53.

Raman, L., & Winer, G. (2002). Children's and adults' understanding of illness: Evidence in support of a coexistence model. *Genetic, Social, & General Psychology Monographs, 128*, 325–355.

Ramasubramanian, S. (2017). Mindfulness, stress coping and everyday resilience among emerging youth in a university setting: A mixed methods approach. *International Journal of Adolescence and Youth, 22*, 308–321.

Ramsey, P. G., & Myers, L. C. (1990). Salience of race in young children's cognitive, affective, and behavioral responses to social environments. *Journal of Applied Developmental Psychology, 11*, 49–67.

Rancourt, D., Conway, C. C., Burk, W. J., & Prinstein, M. J. (2012). Gender composition of preadolescents' friendship groups moderates peer socialization of body change behaviors. *Health Psychology*. Accessed online, 7/21/12; http://www.ncbi.nlm.nih.gov/pubmed/22545975.

Ranganath, C., Minzenberg, M., & Ragland, J. (2008). The cognitive neuroscience of memory function and dysfunction in schizophrenia. *Biological Psychiatry, 64*, 18–25. Accessed online, 6/6/18; http://search.ebscohost.com, doi:10.1016/j.biopsych.2008.04.011.

Rankin, B. (2004). The importance of intentional socialization among children in small groups: A conversation with Loris Malaguzzi. *Early Childhood Education Journal, 32*, 81–85.

Ransjö-Arvidson, A. B., Matthiesen, A. S., Lilja, G., Nissen, E., Widström, A. M., & Unväs-Moberg. (2001). Maternal analgesia during labor disturbs newborn behavior: Effects on breastfeeding, temperature, and crying. *Birth, 28*, 5–12.

Rantanen, J., Kinnunen, U., Pulkkinen, L., & Kokko, K. (2012). Developmental trajectories of work-family conflict for Finnish workers in midlife. *Journal of Occupational Health Psychology, 17*, 290–303.

Ratanachu-Ek, S. (2003). Effects of multivitamin and folic acid supplementation in malnourished children. *Journal of the Medical Association of Thailand, 4*, 86–91.

Raufelder, D., Sahabandu, D., Martínez, G. S., & Escobar, V. (2015). The mediating role of social relationships in the association of adolescents' individual school self-concept and their school engagement, belonging and helplessness in school. *Educational Psychology, 35*, 137–157.

Ray, L., Bryan, A., MacKillop, J., McGeary, J., Hesterberg, K., & Hutchison, K. (2009). The dopamine D receptor (4) gene exon III polymorphism, problematic alcohol use and novelty seeking: Direct and mediated genetic effects. *Addiction Biology, 14*, 238–244. Accessed online; http://search.ebscohost.com, doi:10.1111/j.1369-1600.2008.00120.x.

Ray, E., & Heyes, C. (2011). Imitation in infancy: The wealth of the stimulus. *Developmental Science, 14*, 92–105.

Rayner, K., Foorman, B. R., Perfetti, C. A., Pesetsky, D., & Seidenberg, M. S. (2002, March). How should reading be taught? *Scientific American*, pp. 85–91.

Raz, N., Rodrigue, K., Kennedy, K., & Acker, J. (2007, March). Vascular health and longitudinal changes in brain and cognition in middle-aged and older adults. *Neuropsychology, 21*, 149–157.

Raznahan, A., Shaw, P., Lalonde, F., Stockman, M., Wallace, G. L., Greenstein, D., Clasen, L., Gogtay, N., & Giedd, J. N. (2011). How does your cortex grow? *Journal of Neuroscience, 31*, 7174–7177.

Rebok, G. W., Ball, K., Guey, L. T., Jones, R. N., Kim, H., King, J. W., & . . . Willis, S. L. (2014). Ten-year effects of the advanced cognitive training for independent and vital elderly cognitive training trial on cognition and everyday functioning in older adults. *Journal of the American Geriatrics Society, 62*, 16–24.

Redcay, E., & Courchesne, E. (2008). When is the brain enlarged in Autism? A meta-analysis of all brain size reports. *Biological Psychiatry, 58*, 1–9.

Reed, R. K. (2005). *Birthing fathers: The transformation of men in American rites of birth.* New Brunswick, NJ: Rutgers University Press.

Reeves, M. L., & Fernandez, B. S. (2017). Evidence-based interventions for comprehensive school crises. In L. A. Theodore (Ed.), *Handbook of evidence-based interventions for children and adolescents.* New York: Springer Publishing Co.

Rego, A. (2006). The alphabetic principle, phonics, and spelling: Teaching students the code. In *Reading assessment and instruction for all learners* (pp. 118–162). New York: Guilford Press.

Reich, S. M. (2017). Connecting offline social competence to online peer interactions. *Psychology of Popular Media Culture, 6*, 291–310.

Reichborn-Kjennerud, T., Czajkowski, N., Ystrøm, E., Ørstavik, R., Aggen, S. H., Tambs, K., & . . . Kendler, K. S. (2015). A longitudinal twin study of borderline and antisocial personality disorder traits in early to middle adulthood. *Psychological Medicine*. Accessed online, 6/22/15; http://www.ncbi.nlm.nih.gov/pubmed/26050739.

Reifman, A. (2000). Revisiting *The Bell Curve*. *Psycoloquy*, 11.

Reis, S., & Renzulli, J. (2004). Current research on the social and emotional development of gifted and talented students: Good news and future possibilities. *Psychology in the Schools*, 41, 119–130.

Reissland, N., & Cohen, D. (2012). *The development of emotional intelligence: A case study*. New York: Routledge/Taylor & Francis Group.

Rembis, M. (2009). (Re)defining disability in the "genetic age": Behavioral genetics, "new" eugenics and the future of impairment. *Disability & Society*, 24, 585–597. Accessed online; http://search.ebscohost.com, doi:10.1080/09687590903010941.

Renner, L., & Slack, K. (2006, June). Intimate partner violence and child maltreatment: Understanding intra- and intergenerational connections. *Child Abuse & Neglect*, 30, 599–617.

Rentner, T. L., Dixon, L., & Lengel, L. (2012). Critiquing fetal alcohol syndrome health communication campaigns targeted to American Indians. *Journal of Health Communication*, 17, 6–21.

Reproductive Medicine Associates of New Jersey. (2002). *Older women and risks of pregnancy*. Princeton, NJ: American Society for Reproductive Medicine.

Reuters Health eLine. (2002, June 26). Baby's injuring points to danger of kids imitating television. *Reuters Health eLine*.

Reynolds, A. J., Temple, J. A., Ou, S. R., Arteaga, I. A., & White, B. A. (2011). School based early childhood education and age 28 well-being: Effects by timing, dosage, and subgroups. *Science*, 333, 360–364.

Rhoades, G., Stanley, S., & Markman, H. (2006, December). Pre-engagement cohabitation and gender asymmetry in marital commitment. *Journal of Family Psychology*, 20, 553–560.

Rhoades, G. K., Stanley, S. M., Markman, H. J., & Allen, E. S. (2015). Can marriage education mitigate the risks associated with premarital cohabitation? *Journal of Family Psychology*, 29, 500–506.

Rhodes, R., Mitchell, S., Miller, S., Connor, S., & Teno, J. (2008). Bereaved family members' evaluation of hospice care: What factors influence overall satisfaction with services? *Journal of Pain and Symptom Management*, 35, 365–371.

Rholes, W., Simpson, J., Tran, S., Martin, A., & Friedman, M. (2007, March). Attachment and information seeking in romantic relationships. *Personality and Social Psychology Bulletin*, 33, 422–438.

Ricciardelli, L. A., & McCabe, M. P. (2004). A biopsychosocial model of disordered eating and the pursuit of muscularity in adolescent boys. *Psychological Bulletin*, 130, 179–205.

Rice, T. M., McGill, J., & Adler-Baeder, F. (2017). Relationship education for youth in high school: Preliminary evidence from a non-controlled study on dating behavior and parent–adolescent relationships. *Child & Youth Care Forum*, 46, 51–68.

Rice, W. S., Goldfarb, S. S., Brisendine, A. E., Burrows, S., & Wingate, M. S. (2017). Disparities in infant mortality by race among Hispanic and non-Hispanic infants. *Maternal and Child Health Journal*. Accessed online, 10/29/17; https://www.ncbi.nlm.nih.gov/pubmed/28197819.

Richards, J. M., Butler, E. A., & Gross, J. J. (2003). Emotion regulation in romantic relationships: The cognitive consequences of concealing feelings. *Journal of Social and Personal Relationships*, 20, 599–620.

Richards, M. H., Crowe, P. A., Larson, R., & Swarr, A. (1998). Developmental patterns and gender differences in the experience of peer companionship during adolescence. *Child Development*, 69, 154–163.

Richtel, M. (2010, November 21). Growing up digital, wired for distraction. *New York Times*, pp. A1, A20.

Rideout, V., Roberts, D. F., & Foehr, U. G. (2005). *Generation M: Median in the lives of 8- to 18-year-olds*. Menlo Park, CA: The Henry J. Kaiser Family Foundation.

Riebe, D., Burbank, P., & Garber, C. (2002). Setting the stage for active older adults. In P. Burbank & D. Riebe (Eds.), *Promoting exercise and behavior change in older adults: Interventions with the transtheoretical mode*. New York: Springer Publishing Co.

Riley, K. (2008). Language socialization. In *The handbook of educational linguistics*. Malden, MA: Blackwell Publishing.

Rippon, I., & Steptoe, A. (2015). Feeling old vs being old: Associations between self-perceived age and mortality. *JAMA Intern Med*, 175(2): 307–309. doi:10.1001/jamainternmed.2014.6580.

Ritzen, E. M. (2003). Early puberty: What is normal and when is treatment indicated? *Hormone Research*, 60, Supplement 3, 31–34.

Rizvi, S. J., Cyriac, A., Grima, E., Tan, M., Lin, P., Gallaugher, L. A., & . . . Kennedy, S. H. (2015). Depression and employment status in primary and tertiary care settings. *The Canadian Journal of Psychiatry/La Revue Canadienne De Psychiatrie*, 60, 14–22.

Robbins, M. W., Francis, L. J., & Edwards, B. (2008). Prayer, personality and happiness: A study among undergraduate students in Wales. *Mental Health, Religion & Culture*, 11 [Special issue], 93–99.

Robb, M., Richert, R., & Wartella, E. (2009). Just a talking book? Word learning from watching baby videos. *British Journal of Developmental Psychology*, 27, 27–45. Accessed online; http://search.ebscohost.com, doi:10.1348/026151008X320156.

Roberts, S. (2013, September 22). Divorce after 50 grows more common. *New York Times*, p. ST26.

Roberts, S. (2009, November 24). Economy is forcing young adults back home in big numbers, survey finds. *New York Times*, p. A16.

Roberts, D. F., & Foehr, U. G. (2003). *Kids and media in America*. Cambridge University Press.

Roberts, D. F., Henriksen, L., & Foehr, U. G. (2004). Adolescents and media. In R. M. Lerner & L. Steinberg (Eds.), *Handbook of adolescent psychology* (2nd ed.). New York: John Wiley & Sons.

Roberts, R. D., & Lipnevich, A. A. (2012). From general intelligence to multiple intelligences: Meanings, models, and measures. In K. R. Harris, S. Graham, T. Urdan, S. Graham, J. M. Royer, M. Zeidner (Eds.), *APA educational psychology handbook, Vol 2: Individual differences and cultural and contextual factors*. Washington, DC: American Psychological Association.

Roberts, R. E., Phinney, J. S., Masse, L. C., Chen, Y. R., Roberts, C. R., & Romero, A. (1999). The structure of ethnic identity of young adolescents from diverse ethnocultural groups. *Journal of Early Adolescence*, 19, 301–322.

Roberts, R. E., Roberts, C. R., & Xing, Y. (2011). Restricted sleep among adolescents: Prevalence, incidence, persistence, and associated factors. *Behavioral Sleep Medicine*, 9, 18–30.

Robinson, A. J., & Pascalis, O. (2005). Development of flexible visual recognition memory in human infants. *Developmental Science*, 7, 527–533.

Robinson, G. E. (2004, April 16). Beyond nature and nurture. *Science*, 304, 397–399.

Robinson, O. C., Demetre, J. D., & Litman, J. A. (2017). Adult life stage and crisis as predictors of curiosity and authenticity: Testing inferences from Erikson's lifespan theory. *International Journal of Behavioral Development*, 41, 426–431.

Robinson, W. P., & Gillibrand, E. (2004, May 14). Single-sex teaching and achievement in science. *International Journal of Science Education*, 26, 659.

Rocha, N. F., de Campos, A. C., dos Santos Silva, F. P., & Tudella, E. (2013). Adaptive actions of young infants in the task of reaching for objects. *Developmental Psychobiology*, 55, 275–282.

Rochat, P. (Ed.). (1999). *Early social cognition: Understanding others in the first months of life*. Mahwah, NJ: Erlbaum.

Rochat, P. (2004). Emerging co-awareness. In G. Bremner & A. Slater (Eds.), *Theories of infant development*. Malden, MA: Blackwell Publishers.

Rochat, P., Broesch, T., & Jayne, K. (2012). Social awareness and early self-recognition. *Consciousness and Cognition: An International Journal*. Accessed online, 7/18/12; http://www.sciencedirect.com/science/article/pii/S1053810012001225.

Rodgers, J. L., Van Hulle, C., D'Onofrio, B., Rathouz, P., Beasley, W., Johnson, A., & . . . Lahey, B. B. (2015). Behavior problems and timing of menarche: A developmental longitudinal biometrical analysis using the NLSY-Children data. *Behavior Genetics*, 45, 51–70.

Rodkey, E. N., & Riddell, R. P. (2013). The infancy of infant pain research: The experimental origins of infant pain denial. *The Journal of Pain, 14*, 338–350.

Rodnitzky, R. L. (2012). Upcoming treatments in Parkinson's disease, including gene therapy. *Parkinsonism & Related Disorders, 18* (Suppl. 1), S37–S40.

Roffwarg, H. P., Muzio, J. N., & Dement, W. C. (1966). Ontogenic development of the human sleep dream cycle. *Science, 152*, 604–619.

Rogan, J. (2007). How much curriculum change is appropriate? Defining a zone of feasible innovation. *Science Education, 91*, 439–460.

Rogers, C. R. (1971). A theory of personality. In S. Maddi (Ed.), *Perspectives on personality*. Boston: Little, Brown.

Rogers, S. L., & Blissett, J. (2017). Breastfeeding duration and its relation to weight gain, eating behaviours and positive maternal feeding practices in infancy. *Appetite, 108*, 399–406.

Roggeveen, A. B., Prime, D. J., & Ward, L. M. (2007). Lateralized readiness potentials reveal motor slowing in the aging brain. *Journals of Gerontology: Series B: Psychological Science and Social Science, 62*, P78–P84.

Rohleder, N. (2012). Acute and chronic stress induced changes in sensitivity of peripheral inflammatory pathways to the signals of multiple stress systems—2011 Curt Richter Award Winner. *Psychoneuroendocrinology, 37*, 307–316.

Rohrer-Baumgartner, N., Zeiner, P., Egeland, J., Gustavson, K., Skogan, A. H., Reichborn-Kjennerud, T., & Aase, H. (2014). Does IQ influence associations between ADHD symptoms and other cognitive functions in young preschoolers? *Behavioral and Brain Functions, 10*. Accessed online, 6/18/15; http://www.behavioralandbrainfunctions.com/content/10/1/16.

Rolland, J., & Williams, J. (2006). Toward a psychosocial model for the new era of genetics. In S. M. Miller, S. H. McDaniel, J. S. Rolland, & S. L. Feetham (Eds.), *Individuals, families, and the new era of genetics: Biopsychosocial perspectives*. New York: W. W. Norton & Co.

Rollins, B. C. & Cannon, K. L. (1974). Marital satisfaction over the family life cycle: A reevaluation. *Journal of Family and Marriage, 36*, 271–282.

Rolls, E. (2000). Memory systems in the brain. *Annual Review of Psychology, 51*, 599–630.

Romero, S. T., Coulson, C. C., & Galvin, S. L. (2012). Cesarean delivery on maternal request: A western North Carolina perspective. *Maternal and Child Health Journal, 16*, 725–734.

Romero, A., & Roberts, R. (2003). The impact of multiple dimensions of ethnic identity on discrimination and adolescents' self-esteem. *Journal of Applied Social Psychology, 33*, 2288–2305.

Ron, P. (2006). Care giving offspring to aging parents: How it affects their marital relations, parenthood, and mental health. *Illness, Crisis, & Loss, 14*, 1–21.

Ron, P. (2014). Attitudes towards filial responsibility in a traditional vs modern culture: A comparison between three generations of Arabs in the Israeli society. *Gerontechnology, 13*, 31–38.

Roopnarine, J. L., & Metindogan, A. (2006). Early childhood education research in cross-national perspective. In B. Spodek, O. N. Saracho (Eds.), *Handbook of research on the education of young children* (pp. 555–571). Mahwah, NJ: Lawrence Erlbaum Associates Publishers.

Rosch, E. (1974). Linguistic relativity. In A. Silverstein (Ed.), *Human communication: Theoretical explorations* (pp. 95–121). New York: Halstead Press.

Rose, C. A., Richman, D. M., Fettig, K., Hayner, A., Slavin, C., & Preast, J. L. (2016). Peer reactions to early childhood aggression in a preschool setting: Defenders, encouragers, or neutral bystander. *Developmental Neurorehabilitation, 19*, 246–254.

Rose, S. A., Feldman, J. F., Jankowski, J. J., & Van Rossem, R. (2012). Information processing from infancy to 11 years: Continuities and prediction of IQ. *Intelligence, 40*, 445–457.

Rose, S. A., Feldman, J. F., & Jankowski, J. J. (2015). Pathways from toddler information processing to adolescent lexical proficiency. *Child Development, 86*, 1935–1947.

Rose, R. J., Viken, R. J., Dick, D. M., Bates, J. E., Pulkkinen, L., & Kaprio, J. (2003). It *does* take a village: Nonfamilial environments and children's behavior. *Psychological Science, 14*, 273–278.

Rosen, K. H. (1998). The family roots of aggression and violence: A life span perspective. In L. L'Abate (Ed.), *Family psychopathology: The relational roots of dysfunctional behavior*. New York: Guilford Press.

Rosen, E., Ackerman, L., & Zosky, D. (2002). The sibling empty nest syndrome: The experience of sadness as siblings leave the family home. *Journal of Human Behavior in the Social Environment, 6*, 65–80.

Rosenblum, G. D., & Lewis, M. (2003). Emotional development in adolescence. In G. R. Adams & M. D. Berzonsky (Eds.), *Blackwell handbooks of developmental psychology. Blackwell handbook of adolescence* (pp. 269–289). Malden: Blackwell Publishing.

Rosenblatt, P. C. (2001). A social constructionist perspective on cultural differences in grief. In M. S. Stroebe, R. O. Hansson, W. Stroebe, & H. Schut (Eds.), *Handbook of bereavement research: Consequences, coping, and care*. Washington, DC: American Psychological Association Press.

Rosenblatt, P. C. (2015). Death and bereavement in later adulthood: Cultural beliefs, behaviors, and emotions. In L. A. Jensen (Ed.), *The Oxford handbook of human development and culture: An interdisciplinary perspective* (pp. 697–709). New York: Oxford University Press. doi:10.1093/oxfordhb/9780199948550.013.43.

Rosenberg, T. (2013). The power of talking to your baby. *New York Times Opinionator Blog*. Accessed online, 2/27/14; http://opinionator.blogs.nytimes.com/2013/04/10/the-powerof-talking-to-your-baby/?_php=true&_type=blogs&_r=0.

Roksa, J., Trolian, T. L., Pascarella, E. T., Kilgo, C. A., Blaich, C., & Wise, K. S. (2017). Racial inequality in critical thinking skills: The role of academic and diversity experiences. *Research in Higher Education, 58*, 119–140.

Ross, J., Yilmaz, M., Dale, R., Cassidy, R., Yildirim, I., & Zeedyk, M. S. (2017). Cultural differences in self-recognition: The early development of autonomous and related selves? *Developmental Science, 20*, 27–33.

Ross, M., & Wilson, A. E. (2003). Autobiographical memory and conceptions of self: Getting better all the time. *Current Directions in Psychological Science, 12*, 66–69.

Rossi, S., Telkemeyer, S., Wartenburger, I., & Obrig, H. (2012). Shedding light on words and sentences: Near-infrared spectroscopy in language research. *Brain and Language, 121*, 152–163.

Rossier, J., Dahourou, D., & McCrae, R. R. (2005). Structural and mean level analyses of the Five-Factor Model and locus of control: Further evidence from Africa. *Journal of Cross-Cultural Psychology, 36*, 227–246.

Rössler, W., Hengartner, M. P., Ajdacic-Gross, V., & Angst, J. (2015). Predictors of burnout: Results from a prospective community study. *European Archives of Psychiatry and Clinical Neuroscience, 265*, 19–25.

Rossman, I. (1977). Anatomic and body composition changes with aging. In C. E. Finch & L. Hayflick (Eds.), *Handbook of the biology of aging*. New York: Van Nostrand Reinhold.

Ross-Sheehy, S., & Newman, R. S. (2015). Infant auditory short-term memory for non-linguistic sounds. *Journal of Experimental Child Psychology, 132*, 51–64.

Rotenberg, K., Boulton, M., & Fox, C. (2005). Cross-sectional and longitudinal relations among children's trust beliefs, psychological maladjustment and social relationships: Are very high as well as very low trusting children at risk? *Journal of Abnormal Child Psychology, 33*, 595–610.

Roth, D., Slone, M., & Dar, R. (2000). Which way cognitive development? An evaluation of the Piagetian and the domain-specific research programs. *Theory & Psychology, 10*, 353–373.

Roth, M. S. (2016). Psychoanalysis and history. *Psychoanalytic Psychology, 33* (Suppl 1), S19–S33.

Rothbart, M. K., Posner, M. I., & Kieras, J. (2006). Temperament, attention, and the development of self-regulation. In K. McCartney & D. Phillips (Eds.), *Blackwell handbook of early childhood development*. Malden, MA: Blackwell Publishing.

Rotheram-Borus, M., & Langabeer, K. (2001). Developmental trajectories of gay, lesbian, and bisexual youths. In A. D'Augelli & C. Patterson (Eds.), *Lesbian, gay, and bisexual identities and youth: Psychological perspectives* (pp. 97–128). New York: Oxford University Press.

Rothrauff, T., Middlemiss, W., & Jacobson, L. (2004). Comparison of American and Austrian infants' and toddlers' sleep habits: A retrospective, exploratory study. *North American Journal of Psychology, 6,* 125–144.

Rousseau, P. V., Matton, F., Lecuyer, R., & Lahaye, W. (2017). The Moro reaction: More than a reflex, a ritualized behavior of nonverbal communication. *Infant Behavior & Development, 46,* 169-177.

Roussotte, F. F., Gutman, B. A., Hibar, D. P., Madsen, S. K., Narr, K. L., & Thompson, P. M. (2014). Carriers of a common variant in the dopamine transporter gene have greater dementia risk, cognitive decline, and faster ventricular expansion. *Alzheimer's & Dementia: The Journal of the Alzheimer's Association.* Accessed online, 6/23/15; http://www.alzheimersanddementia.com/article/S1552-5260%2814%2902866-0/abstract.

Rubin, K. H., & Chung, O. B. (Eds.). (2006). *Parenting beliefs, behaviors, and parent-child relations: A crosscultural perspective.* New York: Psychology Press.

Rudowitz, R., & Antonisse, L. (2018, May 23). *Implications of the ACA Medicaid expansion: A look at the data and evidence.* San Francisco, CA: Henry J. Kaiser Family Foundation.

Ruffman, T., Slade, L., & Redman, J. (2006). Young infants' expectations about hidden objects. *Cognition [Serial Online], 97,* B35–B43.

Ruffman, T. (2014). To belief or not belief: Children's theory of mind. *Developmental Review, 34,* 265–293.

Ruffman, T., Lorimer, B., & Scarf, D. (2017). Do infants really experience emotional contagion? *Child Development Perspectives.* Accessed online, 11/13/17; http://onlinelibrary.wiley.com/doi/10.1111/cdep.12244/full.

Ruigrok, A. V., Salimi-Khorshidi, G., Lai, M., Baron-Cohen, S., Lombardo, M. V., Tait, R. J., & Suckling, J. (2014). A meta-analysis of sex differences in human brain structure. *Neuroscience and Biobehavioral Reviews, 39,* 34–50.

Ruihe, H., Guoliang, Y. (2006). Children's understanding of emotional display rules and use of strategies. *Psychological Science (China), 29,* 18–21.

Russ, S. W. (2014). Pretend play and creativity: An overview. In *Pretend play in childhood: Foundation of adult creativity.* Washington, DC: American Psychological Association.

Russell, J. (2017). 'Everything has to die one day:' Children's explorations of the meanings of death in human-animal-nature relationships. *Environmental Education Research, 23*(1), 75–90. doi:10.1080/13504622.2016.1144175.

Russell, S., & Consolacion, T. (2003). Adolescent romance and emotional health in the United States: Beyond binaries. *Journal of Clinical Child & Adolescent Psychology, 32,* 499–508.

Rust, J., Golombok, S., Hines, M., Johnston, K., & Golding, J., ALSPAC Study Team. (2000). The role of brothers and sisters in the gender development of preschool children. *Journal of Experimental Child Psychology, 77,* 292–303.

Rutter, M. (2006). *Genes and behavior: Nature—nurture interplay explained.* New York: Blackwell Publishing.

Ryan, B. P. (2001). *Programmed therapy for stuttering in children and adults* (2nd ed.). Springfield, IL: Charles C. Thomas.

Saad, L. (2011, June 30). *Americans' preference for smaller families edges higher.* Princeton, NJ: Gallup Poll.

Sachs, J. (2006, April 1). Will your child be fat? *Parenting, 20,* 112. Accessed online, 01/23/2007, LexisNexis Academic.

Sadeh, A., Flint-Ofir, E., Tirosh, T., & Tikotzky, L. (2007). Infant sleep and parental sleep-related cognitions. *Journal of Family Psychology, 21,* 74–87.

Sadker, D., Zittleman, K., Earley, P., McCormick, T., Strawn, C., & Preston, J. A. (2007). The treatment of gender equity in teacher education. In S. S. Klein, B. Richardson, D. A. Grayson, L. H. Fox, C. Kramarae, D. S. Pollard, . . . C. A. Dwyer (Eds.), *Handbook for achieving gender equity through education.* (2nd ed.) Mahwah, NJ: Lawrence Erlbaum Associates Publishers.

Sadker, M., & Sadker, D. (1994). *Failing at fairness: How America's schools cheat girls.* New York: Scribner's.

Safar, K., & Moulson, M. C. (2017). Recognizing facial expressions of emotion in infancy: A replication and extension. *Developmental Psychobiology, 59,* 507–514.

Sailor, W. (2015). Advances in schoolwide inclusive school reform. *Remedial and Special Education, 36,* 94–99.

Saklofske, D. H., van de Vijver, F. R., Oakland, T., Mpofu, E., & Suzuki, L. A. (2015). Intelligence and culture: History and assessment. In S. Goldstein, D. Princiotta, & J. A. Naglieri (Eds.), *Handbook of intelligence: Evolutionary theory, historical perspective, and current concepts.* New York: Springer Science + Business Media.

Salihu, H. M., August, E. M., de la Cruz, C., Mogos, M. F., Weldeselasse, H., & Alio, A. P. (2013). Infant mortality and the risk of small size for gestational age in the subsequent pregnancy: A retrospective cohort study. *Maternal and Child Health Journal, 17,* 1044–1051.

Salley, B., Miller, A., & Bell, M. (2013). Associations between temperament and social responsiveness in young children. *Infant and Child Development, 22,* 270–288.

Sallis, J., & Glanz, K. (2006, March). The role of built environments in physical activity, eating, and obesity in childhood. *The Future of Children, 16,* 89–108.

Salmivalli, C., Ojanen, T., Haanpaa, J., & Peets, K. (2005). "I'm OK but you're not" and other peer-relational schemas: Explaining individual differences in children's social goals. *Developmental Psychology, 41,* 363–375.

Salthouse, T. A. (2006). Mental exercise and mental aging: Evaluating the validity of the "Use it or lose it" hypothesis. *Perspectives on Psychological Science, 1,* 68–87.

Salthouse, T., Pink, J., & Tucker-Drob, E. (2008). Contextual analysis of fluid intelligence. *Intelligence, 36,* 464–486.

Samet, J. H., De Marini, D. M., & Malling, H. V. (2004, May 14). Do airborne particles induce heritable mutations? *Science, 304,* 971.

Sampson, J., & Chason, A. (2008). Helping gifted and talented adolescents and young adults: Make informed and careful career choices. In *Handbook of giftedness in children: Psychoeducational theory, research, and best practices.* New York: Springer Science + Business Media.

Sanchez, Y. M., Lambert, S. F., & Ialongo, N. S. (2012). Life events and depressive symptoms in African American adolescents: Do ecological domains and timing of life events matter? *Journal of Youth and Adolescence, 41,* 438–448.

Sánchez-Castañeda, C., Squitieri, F., Di Paola, M., Dayan, M., Petrollini, M., & Sabatini, U. (2015). The role of iron in gray matter degeneration in Huntington's disease: A magnetic resonance imaging study. *Human Brain Mapping, 36,* 50–66.

Sanchez-Garrido, M. A., & Tena-Sempere, M. (2013). Metabolic control of puberty: Roles of leptin and kisspeptins. *Hormones and Behavior, 64,* 187–194.

Sandall, J. (2014). The 30th international confederation of midwives triennial congress: Improving women's health globally. *Birth: Issues in Perinatal Care, 41,* 303–305.

Sandberg-Thoma, S. E., Snyder, A. R., & Jang, B. J. (2015). Exiting and returning to the parental home for boomerang kids. *Journal of Marriage and Family, 77,* 806–818.

Sanders, S., Ott, C., Kelber, S., & Noonan, P. (2008). The experience of high levels of grief in caregivers of persons with Alzheimer's disease and related dementia. *Death Studies, 32,* 495–523.

Sandis, E. (2000). The aging and their families: A cross-national review. In A. L. Comunian & U. P. Gielen (Eds.), *International perspectives on human development.* Lengerich, Germany: Pabst Science Publishers.

Sandoval, J., Frisby, C. L., Geisinger, K. F., Scheuneman, J. D., & Grenier, J. R. (Eds.). (1998). *Test interpretation and diversity: Achieving equity in assessment.* Washington, DC: APA Books.

Sanefuji, W., Ohgami, H., & Hashiya, K. (2006). Preference for peers in infancy. *Infant Behavior & Development, 29,* 584–593.

Santtila, P., Sandnabba, N. K., Harlaar, N., Varjonen, M., Alanko, K., & von der Pahlen, B. (2008). Potential for homosexual response is prevalent and genetic. *Biological Psychology, 77*(1), 102–105. doi:10.1016/j.biopsycho.2007.08.006.

Sargent, J. D., Tanski, S. E., & Gibson, J. (2007). Exposure to movie smoking among U.S. adolescents aged 10 to 14 years: A population estimate. *Pediatrics, 119,* 1167–1176.

Sargent-Cox, K. A., Anstey, K. J., & Luszcz, M. A. (2012). The relationship between change in self-perceptions of aging and physical functioning in older adults. *Psychology and Aging.* doi:10.1037/a0027578.

Sasisekaran, J. (2014). Exploring the link between stuttering and phonology: A review and implications for treatment. *Seminars in Speech and Language, 35,* 95–113.

Sauce, B., & Matzel, L. D. (2018). The paradox of intelligence: Heritability and malleability coexist in hidden gene-environment interplay. *Psychological Bulletin, 144*(1), 26–47.

Saul, S. (2009). The gift of life, and its price. *New York Times,* p. A1, A26–A27.

Saulny, S. (2006, March 3.) In baby boomlet, preschool derby is the fiercest yet. *New York Times,* p. C4.

Saunders, J., Davis, L., & Williams, T. (2004). Gender differences in self-perceptions and academic outcomes: A study of African American high school students. *Journal of Youth & Adolescence, 33,* 81–90.

Savin-Williams, R. C. (2003). Lesbian, gay, and bisexual youths' relationships with their parents. In L. Garnets & D. Kimme (Eds.), *Psychological perspectives on lesbian, gay, and bisexual experience* (2nd ed.). New York: Columbia University Press.

Sawatzky, J., & Naimark, B. (2002). Physical activity and cardiovascular health in aging women: A health- promotion perspective. *Journal of Aging & Physical Activity, 10,* 396–412.

Sawicka, M. (2016). Searching for a narrative of loss. Interactional ordering of ambiguous grief. *Symbolic Interaction.* Accessed online, 10/24/17; http://onlinelibrary.wiley.com/doi/10.1002/symb.270/full.

Sawyer, J. (2017). I think I can: Preschoolers' private speech and motivation in playful versus non-playful contexts. *Early Childhood Research Quarterly, 38,* 84–96.

Sawrikar, P., & Hunt, C. J. (2005). The relationship between mental health, cultural identity and cultural values in non-English-speaking background (NESB) Australian adolescents. *Behaviour Change, 22*(2), 97–113. doi:10.1375/bech.2005.22.2.97.

Sawyer, R. (2012). *Explaining creativity: The science of human innovation* (2nd ed.). New York: Oxford University Press.

Sax, L. (2005, March 2). The promise and peril of single-sex public education. *Education Week, 24,* 48–51.

Sax, L. J., Astin, A. W., Korn, W. S., & Mahoney, K. M. (2000). *The American freshman: National norms for fall 2000.* Los Angeles: University of California, Higher Education Research Institute.

Sax, L., Hurtado, S., Lindholm, J. A., Astin, A. W., Korn, W. S., & Mahoney, K. M. et al. (2004). *The American freshman: National norms for fall 2004.* Los Angeles: Higher Education Research Institute, UCLA.

Sayal, K., Heron, J., Maughan, B., Rowe, R., & Ramchandani, P. (2014). Infant temperament and childhood psychiatric disorder: Longitudinal study. *Child: Care, Health and Development, 40,* 292–297.

Scarborough, P., Nnoaham, K. E., Clarke, D., Capewell, S., & Rayner, M. (2012). Modelling the impact of a healthy diet on cardiovascular disease and cancer mortality. *Journal of Epidemiology and Community Health, 66,* 420–426.

Scarr, S. (1998). American child care today. *American Psychologist, 53,* 95–108.

Schaan, V. K., & Vögele, C. (2016). Resilience and rejection sensitivity mediate long-term outcomes of parental divorce. *European Child & Adolescent Psychiatry, 25,* 1267–1269.

Schachter, E. P. (2005). Erikson meets the postmodern: Can classic identity theory rise to the challenge? *Identity, 5,* 137–160.

Schaefer, M. K., & Salafia, E. B. (2014). The connection of teasing by parents, siblings, and peers with girls' body dissatisfaction and boys' drive for muscularity: The role of social comparison as a mediator. *Eating Behaviors, 15,* 599–608.

Schaeffer, C., Petras, H., & Ialongo, N. (2003). Modeling growth in boys' aggressive behavior across elementary school: Links to later criminal involvement, conduct disorder, and antisocial personality disorder. *Developmental Psychology, 39,* 1020–1035.

Schafer, D. P., & Stevens, B. (2013). Phagocytic glial cells: Sculpting synaptic circuits in the developing nervous system. *Current Opinion in Neurobiology, 23,* 1034–1040.

Schaie, K. W. (1977–1978). Toward a stage of adult theory of adult cognitive development. *Journal of Aging and Human Development, 8,* 129–138.

Schaie, K. W. (1985). *Longitudinal studies of adult psychological development.* New York, NY: Guilford Press.

Schaie, K. W. (1994). The course of adult intellectual development. *American Psychologist, 49,* 403–313

Schaie, K. W. (2016). The longitudinal study of adult cognitive development. In R. J. Sternberg, S. T. Fiske, D. J. Foss (Eds.), *Scientists making a difference: One hundred eminent behavioral and brain scientists talk about their most important contributions.* New York: Cambridge University Press.

Schaie, K. W., & Willis, S. L. (2011). *Handbook of the psychology of aging.* (7th ed.) San Diego, CA: Elsevier Academic Press.

Schaie, K. W., & Zanjani, F. A. K. (2006). Intellectual development across adulthood. In C. Hoare (Ed.), *Handbook of adult development and learning.* New York: Oxford University Press.

Schaie, W. K., Willis, S. L., & Pennak, S. (2005). An historical framework for cohort differences in intelligence. *Research in Human Development, 2,* 43–67.

Schatz, M. (1994). *A toddler's life.* New York: Oxford University Press.

Schaufeli, W., & Salanova, M. (2007). Efficacy or inefficacy, that's the question: Burnout and work engagement, and their relationships with efficacy beliefs. *Anxiety, Stress & Coping: An International Journal, 20,* 177–196.

Schechter, D., & Willheim, E. (2009). Disturbances of attachment and parental psychopathology in early childhood. *Child and Adolescent Psychiatric Clinics of North America, 18,* 665–686.

Schecklmann, M., Pfannstiel, C., Fallgatter, A. J., Warnke, A., Gerlach, M., & Romanos, M. (2012). Olfaction in child and adolescent anorexia nervosa. *Journal of Neural Transmission, 119,* 721–728.

Schecter, T., Finkelstein, Y., & Koren, G. (2005). Pregnant "DES daughters" and their offspring. *Canadian Family Physician, 51,* 493–494.

Scheepers, D., Spears, R., Doosje, B., & Manstead, A. (2006). The social functions of ingroup bias: Creating, confirming, or changing social reality. *European Review of Social Psychology, 17,* 359–396.

Scheers, N. J., Woodard, D. W., & Thach, B. T. (2016). Crib bumpers continue to cause infant deaths: a need for a new preventive approach. *Journal of Pediatrics, 169,* 93–97.

Schemo, D. J. (2001, December 5). U.S. students prove middling on 32-nation test. *New York Times,* p. A21.

Scherf, K. S., Sweeney, J. A., & Luna, B. (2006). Brain basis of developmental change in visuospatial working memory. *Journal of Cognitive Neuroscience, 18,* 1045–1058.

Schieman, S., McBrier, D. B., & van Gundy, K. (2003). Home-to-work conflict, work qualities, and emotional distress. *Sociological Forum, 18,* 137–164.

Schmalz, D., & Kerstetter, D. (2006). Girlie girls and manly men: Children's stigma consciousness of gender in sports and physical activities. *Journal of Leisure Research, 38,* 536–557.

Schmiedek, F. (2017). Development of cognition and intelligence. In J. Specht (Ed.), *Personality development across the lifespan.* San Diego, CA: Elsevier Academic Press.

Schmitt, D. (2004). Patterns and universals of mate poaching across 53 nations: The effects of sex, culture, and personality on romantically attracting another person's partner. *Journal of Personality and Social Psychology, 86,* 560–584.

Shneidman, E. (2007). Criteria for a good death. *Suicide and Life-Threatening Behavior, 37,* 245–247.

Schoklitsch, A., & Baumann, U. (2012). Generativity and aging: A promising future research topic? *Journal of Aging Studies, 26,* 262–272.

Schönpflug, U., & Bilz, L. (2009). The transmission process: Mechanisms and contexts. In *Cultural transmission: Psychological, developmental, social, and methodological aspects.* New York: Cambridge University Press.

Schoppe-Sullivan, S., Diener, M., Mangelsdorf, S., Brown, G., McHale, J., & Frosch, C. (2006, July). Attachment and sensitivity in family context: The roles of parent and infant gender. *Infant and Child Development, 15,* 367–385.

Schoppe-Sullivan, S., Mangelsdorf, S., Brown, G., & Sokolowski, M. (2007, February). Goodness-of-fit in family context: Infant temperament, marital quality, and early coparenting behavior. *Infant Behavior & Development, 30,* 82–96.

Schore, A. (2003). *Affect regulation and the repair of the self.* New York: Norton.

Schroeders, U., Schipolowski, S., & Wilhelm, O. (2015). Age-related changes in the mean and covariance structure of fluid and crystallized intelligence in childhood and adolescence. *Intelligence, 48,* 15–29.

Schulz, K., Rudolph, A., Tscharaktschiew, N., & Rudolph, U. (2013). Daniel has fallen into a muddy puddle—Schadenfreude or sympathy? *British Journal of Developmental Psychology, 31,* 363–378.

Schumer, F. (2009, September 29). After a death, the pain that doesn't go away. *New York Times,* p. D1.

Schutt, R. K. (2001). *Investigating the social world: The process and practice of research.* Thousand Oaks, CA: Sage Publications.

Schwab, S. (2014). Achievement goals in students with learning disabilities, emotional or behavioral disorders, and low IQ without special educational needs. *Journal of Cognitive Education and Psychology, 13,* 357–374.

Schwartz, I. M. (1999). Sexual activity prior to coital interaction: A comparison between males and females. *Archives of Sexual Behavior, 28,* 63–69.

Schwartz, S. J., Montgomery, M. J., & Briones, E. (2006). The role of identity in acculturation among immigrant people: Theoretical propositions, empirical questions, and applied recommendations. *Human Development, 49,* 1–30.

Schwarz, B., Mayer, B., Trommsdorff, G., Ben-Arieh, A., Friedlmeier, M., Lubiewska, K., et al. (2012). Does the importance of parent and peer relationships for adolescents' life satisfaction vary across cultures? *The Journal of Early Adolescence, 32,* 55–80.

Schwenkhagen, A. (2007). Hormonal changes in menopause and implications on sexual health. *The Journal of Sexual Medicine, 4,* Supplement 3, 220–226.

Scott, J. C., & Henderson, A. E. (2013). Language matters: Thirteen-month-olds understand that the language a speaker uses constrains conventionality. *Developmental Psychology, 49,* 2102–2111.

Seaton, S. E., King, S., Manktelow, B. N., Draper, E. S., & Field, D. J. (2012). Babies born at the threshold of viability: Changes in survival and workload over 20 years. *Archives of Disabled Children and Neonatal Education, 9,* 22–35.

Sedgh, G., Singh, S., Shah, I. H., Ahman, E., Henshaw, S. K., & Kankole, A. (2012). Induced abortion: Incidence and trends worldwide from 1995 to 2008. *The Lancet, 379,* 625–632.

Sedikides, C., Gaertner, L., & Toguchi, Y. (2003). Pancultural self-enhancement. *Journal of Personality and Social Psychology, 84,* 60–79.

Segal, N. L., Cortez, F. A., Zettel-Watson, L., Cherry, B. J., Mechanic, M., Munson, J. E., & . . . Reed, B. (2015). Genetic and experiential influences on behavior: Twins reunited at seventy-eight years. *Personality and Individual Differences, 73,* 110–117.

Segal, N. L. (2000). Virtual twins: New findings on within-family environmental influences on intelligence. *Journal of Educational Psychology, 92,* 188–194.

Segal, N. L., McGuire, S., Havlena, J., Gill, P., & Hershberger, S. (2007). Intellectual similarity of virtual twin pairs: Developmental trends. *Personality and Individual Differences, 42,* 1209–1219.

Segalowitz, S. J., & Rapin, I. (Eds.). (2003). *Child neuropsychology, Part I.* Amsterdam, The Netherlands: Elsevier Science.

Seidman, S. (2003). The aging male: Androgens, erectile dysfunction, and depression. *Journal of Clinical Psychiatry, 64,* 31–37.

Semerci, Ç. (2006). The opinions of medicine faculty students regarding cheating in relation to Kohlberg's moral development concept. *Social Behavior and Personality, 34,* 41–50.

Senín-Calderón, C., Rodríguez-Testal, J. F., Perona-Garcelán, S., & Perpiñá, C. (2017). Body image and adolescence: A behavioral impairment model. *Psychiatry Research, 248,* 121–126.

Senju, A., Southgate, V., Snape, C., Leonard, M., & Csibra, G. (2011). Do 18-month-olds really attribute mental states to others? A critical test. *Science, 331,* 477–480.

Sepehri, A., & Guliani, H. (2017). Regional gradients in institutional cesarean delivery rates: Evidence from five countries in Asia. *Birth: Issues in Perinatal Care, 44,* 11–20.

Serbin, L., & Karp, J. (2004). The intergenerational transfer of psychosocial risk: Mediators of vulnerability and resilience. *Annual Review of Psychology, 55,* 333–363.

Serbin, L., Poulin-Dubois, D., & Colburne, K. (2001). Gender stereotyping in infancy: Visual preferences for and knowledge of gender-stereotyped toys in the second year. *International Journal of Behavioral Development, 25,* 7–15.

Serrat, R., Villar, F., Pratt, M. W., & Stukas, A. A. (2017). On the quality of adjustment to retirement: The longitudinal role of personality traits and generativity. *Journal of Personality.* Accessed online, 12/12/17; https://www.ncbi.nlm.nih.gov/pubmed/28509366.

Servin, A., Nordenstrom, A., Larsson, A., & Bohlin, G. (2003). Prenatal androgens and gender-typed behavior: A study of girls with mild and severe forms of congenital adrenal hyperplasia. *Developmental Psychology, 39,* 440–450.

Setoh, P., Lee, K. J., Zhang, L., Qian, M. K., Quinn, P. C., Heyman, G. D., & Lee, K. (2017). Racial categorization predicts implicit racial bias in preschool children. *Child Development.* Accessed online, 11/13/17; https://www.ncbi.nlm.nih.gov/pubmed/28605007.

Settersten, R. (2002). Social sources of meaning in later life. In R. Weiss & S. Bass (Eds.), *Challenges of the third age: Meaning and purpose in later life.* London: Oxford University Press.

Seyfarth, R. M., & Cheney, D. L. (2013). The evolution of concepts about agents. In M. R. Banaji, S. A. Gelman (Eds.), *Navigating the social world: What infants, children, and other species can teach us.* New York: Oxford University Press.

Seymour, J., Payne, S., Chapman, A., & Holloway, M. (2007). Hospice or home? Expectations of end-of-life care among white and Chinese older people in the UK. *Sociology of Health & Illness, 29,* 872–890.

Shafto, C. L., Conway, C. M., Field, S. L., & Houston, D. M. (2012). Visual sequence learning in infancy: Domain-general and domain-specific associations with language. *Infancy, 17,* 247–271.

Shanahan, M. J., & Flaherty, B. P. (2001). Biobehavioral developments, perception, and action dynamic patterns of time use in adolescence. *Child Development, 72,* 385–401.

Shapiro, A. F., Gottman, J. M., & Carrère, S. (2000). The baby and the marriage: Identifying factors that buffer against decline in marital satisfaction after the first baby arrives. *Journal of Family Psychology, 14,* 124–130.

Shapiro, D., Dundar, A., Huie, F., Wakhungu, P., Yuan, X., Nathan, A & Hwang, Y. A. (2017, April). *Completing college: A national view of student attainment rates by race and ethnicity—Fall 2010 cohort* (Signature Report No. 12b). Herndon, VA: National Student Clearinghouse Research Center.

Shapiro, L., & Solity, J. (2008). Delivering phonological and phonics training within whole-class teaching. *British Journal of Educational Psychology, 78,* 597–620.

Shapiro, L. R., & Solity, J. (2016). Differing effects of two synthetic phonics programmes on early reading development. *British Journal of Educational Psychology, 86,* 182–203.

Sharkins, K. A., Leger, S. E., & Ernest, J. M. (2016). Examining effects of poverty, maternal depression, and children's self-regulation abilities on the development of language and cognition in early childhood: An early head start perspective. *Early Childhood Education Journal.* Accessed online, 3/12/17; http://link.springer.com/article/10.1007/s10643-016-0787-9.

Shaunessy, E., Suldo, S., Hardesty, R., & Shaffer, E. (2006, December). School functioning and psychological well-being of international baccalaureate and general education students: A preliminary examination. *Journal of Secondary Gifted Education, 17,* 76–89.

Shaver, P. R., Hazan, C., & Bradshaw, D. (1988). Love as attachment: The integration of three behavioral systems. In R. J. Sternberg & M. L. Barnes (Eds.), *The psychology of love* (pp. 68–99). New Haven, CT: Yale University Press.

Shaver, P. R., Mikulincer, M., Sahdra, B. K., & Gross, J. T. (2017). Attachment security as a foundation for kindness toward self and others. In K. W. Brown, M. R. Leary (Eds.), *The Oxford handbook of hypo-egoic phenomena.* New York: Oxford University Press.

Shaw, M. L. (2003). Creativity and whole language. In J. Houtz (Ed.), *The educational psychology of creativity.* Cresskill, NJ: Hampton Press.

Shea, J. (2006, September). Cross-cultural comparison of women's midlife symptom-reporting: A China study. *Culture, Medicine and Psychiatry, 30,* 331–362.

Sheldon, K. M., Joiner, T. E., Jr., & Pettit, J. W. (2003). Reconciling humanistic ideals and scientific clinical practice. *Clinical Psychology, 10,* 302–315.

Shelton, A. L., Cornish, K., Clough, M., Gajamange, S., Kolbe, S., & Fielding, J. (2017). Disassociation between brain activation and executive function in Fragile X premutation females. *Human Brain Mapping, 38,* 1056–1067.

Shen, Y., Hu, H., Taylor, B., Kan, H., & Xu, X. (2016). Early menarche and gestational diabetes mellitus at first live birth. *Maternal and Child Health Journal, 21,* 593–598.

Shenhav, S., Campos, B., & Goldberg, W. A. (2017). Dating out is intercultural: Experience and perceived parent disapproval by ethnicity and immigrant generation. *Journal of Social and Personal Relationships, 34,* 397–422.

Sherman, L. E., Greenfield, P. M., Hernandez, L. M., & Dapretto, M. (2018). Peer influence via Instagram: Effects on brain and behavior in adolescence and young adulthood. *Child Development, 89*(1), 37–47.

Sherman, L. E., Payton, A. A., Hernandez, L. M., Greenfield, P. M., & Dapretto, M. (2016). The power of the like in adolescence: Effects of peer influence on neural and behavioral responses to social media. *Psychological Science, 27*(7), 1027–1035.

Sheridan, T. (2013, April 11). 10 facts funeral directors won't tell you. Fox Business. Accessed online; http://www.foxbusiness.com/personal-finance/2013/04/11/10-facts-funeral-directors-may-not-tell/.

Sherry, A., Tomlinson, J. M., Loe, M., Johnston, K., & Feeney, B. C. (2017). Apprehensive about retirement: Women, life transitions, and relationships. *Journal of Women & Aging, 29,* 173–184.

Shi, L. (2003). Facilitating constructive parent-child play: Family therapy with young children. *Journal of Family Psychotherapy, 14,* 19–31.

Shi, X., & Lu, X. (2007). Bilingual and bicultural development of Chinese American adolescents and young adults: A comparative study. *Howard Journal of Communications, 18,* 313–333.

Shih, M., & Sanchez, D. T. (2005). Perspectives and research on the positive and negative implications of having multiple racial identities. *Psychological Bulletin, 131,* 569–591.

Shimizu, M., & Pelham, B. (2004). The unconscious cost of good fortune: Implicit and explicit self-esteem, positive life events, and health. *Health Psychology, 23,* 101–105.

Shoemark, H. (2014). Contingent singing as a therapeutic intervention for the hospitalised full term neonate. In C. Paul, F. Thomson-Salo, C. Paul, & F. Thomson-Salo (Eds.), *The baby as subject: Clinical studies in infant-parent therapy.* London: Karnac Books.

Shook, J., Vaughn, M., Litschge, C., Kolivoski, K., & Schelbe, L. (2009). The importance of friends among foster youth aging out of care: Cluster profiles of deviant peer affiliations. *Children and Youth Services Review, 31,* 284–291.

Shor, R. (2006, May). Physical punishment as perceived by parents in Russia: Implications for professionals involved in the care of children. *Early Child Development and Care, 176,* 429–439.

Shultz, K., & Fisher, G. (2017). Ageing and retirement behaviour. In L. Riby (Ed.), *Handbook of gerontology research methods: Understanding successful ageing* (pp. 118–136). New York: Routledge/Taylor & Francis Group.

Shute, R., & Charlton, K. (2006). Anger or compromise? Adolescents' conflict resolution strategies in relation to gender and type of peer relationship. *International Journal of Adolescence and Youth, 13,* 55–69.

Shweder, R. A., Much, N. C., & Mahapatra, M. (1997). The "big three" of morality (autonomy, community, divinity) and the "big three" explanations of suffering. In A. M. Brandt & P. Rozin (Eds.), *Morality and health.* Florence, KY: Taylor & Frances/Routledge.

Sieber, J. E. (2000). Planning research: Basic ethical decision-making. In B. D. Sales & S. Folkman (Eds.), *Ethics in research with human participants.* Washington, DC: American Psychological Association.

Siegel, S., Dittrich, R., & Vollmann, J. (2008). Ethical opinions and personal attitudes of young adults conceived by in vitro fertilisation. *Journal of Medical Ethics, 34,* 236–240.

Siegler, R. S. (1998). *Children's thinking* (3rd ed.). Upper Saddle River, NJ: Prentice Hall.

Siegler, R. S. (2012). From theory to application and back: Following in the giant footsteps of David Klahr. In J. Siegler, R. S. (2016). Continuity and change in the field of cognitive development and in the perspectives of one cognitive developmentalist. *Child Development Perspectives, 10,* 128–133.

Shrager, S. Carver (Eds.), *The journey from child to scientist: Integrating cognitive development and the education sciences.* Washington, DC: American Psychological Association.

Siegler, R. S. (2016). Continuity and change in the field of cognitive development and in the perspectives of one cognitive developmentalist. *Child Development Perspectives, 10,* 128–133.

Siegler, R. S., & Lortie-Forgues, H. (2014). An integrative theory of numerical development. *Child Development Perspectives, 8,* 144–150.

Signorella, M., & Frieze, I. (2008). Interrelations of gender schemas in children and adolescents: Attitudes, preferences, and self-perceptions. *Social Behavior and Personality, 36,* 941–954.

Silventoinen, K., Iacono, W. G., Krueger, R., & McGue, M. (2012). Genetic and environmental contributions to the association between anthropometric measures and IQ: A study of Minnesota twins at age 11 and 17. *Behavior Genetics, 42,* 393–401.

Sim, Z. L., & Xu, F. (2017). Infants preferentially approach and explore the unexpected. *British Journal of Developmental Psychology, 35,* 596–608.

Simcock, G., & Hayne, H. (2002). Breaking the barrier? Children fail to translate their preverbal memories into language. *Psychological Science, 13,* 225–231.

Simkin, P. (2014). Preventing primary cesareans: Implications for laboring women, their partners, nurses, educators, and doulas. *Birth: Issues in Perinatal Care, 41,* 220–222.

Simmons, S. W., Cyna, A. M., Dennis, A. T., & Hughes, D. (2007). Combined spinal-epidural versus epidural analgesia in labour. *Cochrane Database and Systematic Review, 18,* CD003401.

Simons, S. H., van Dijk, M., Anand, K. S., Roofthooft, D., van Lingen, R. A., & Tibboel. D. (2003). Do we still hurt newborn babies? A prospective study of procedural pain and analgesia in neonates. *Archives of Pediatrics and Adolescence, 157,* 1058–1064.

Simonton, D. K. (1989). The swan-song phenomenon: Last-works effects for 172 classical composers. *Psychology and Aging, 4,* 42–47.

Simonton, D. K. (2017). Creative productivity across the life span. In J. A. Plucker (Ed.), *Creativity and innovation: Theory, research, and practice.* Waco, TX: Prufrock Press.

Simpson, E. (2017, March 3). America's 1st test-tube baby, a Norfolk native, set to meet world's 1st test-tube baby. *Virginian-Pilot.*

Simpson, J., Collins, W., Tran, S., & Hay don, K. (2007, February). Attachment and the experience and expression of emotions in romantic relationships: A developmental perspective. *Journal of Personality and Social Psychology, 92,* 355–367.

Simson, S. P., Wilson, L. B., & Harlow-Rosentraub, K. (2006). Civic engagement and lifelong learning institutes: Current status and future directions. In L. Wilson & S. P. Simson (Eds.), *Civic engagement and the baby boomer generation: Research, policy, and practice perspectives.* New York: Haworth Press.

Singer, D. G., & Singer, J. L. (Eds.). (2000). *Handbook of children and the media*. Thousand Oaks, CA: Sage Publications.

Singer, J. K., Lichtenberger, E. O., Kaufman, J. C., Kaufman, A. S., & Kaufman, N. L. (2012). The Kaufman Assessment Battery for Children—Second Edition and the Kaufman Test of Educational Achievement—Second Edition. In D. P. Flanagan, P. L. Harrison, D. P. Flanagan, & P. L. Harrison (Eds.), *Contemporary intellectual assessment: Theories, tests, and issues* (3rd ed.). New York: Guilford Press.

Singh, K., & Srivastava, S. K. (2014). Mental health of runaway children. *Indian Journal of Community Psychology, 10*, 285–291.

Sinnott, J. (2014). *Adult development*. Oxford, England: Oxford University Press.

Sinnott, J. D. (1997). Developmental models of midlife and aging in women: Metaphors for transcendence and for individuality in community. In J. Coyle (Ed.), *Handbook on women and aging* (pp. 149–163). Westport, CT: Greenwood.

Sinnott, J. D. (2003). Postformal thought and adult development: Living in balance. In *Handbook of adult development*. New York: Kluwer Academic/Plenum Publishers.

Sinnott, J., Tobin, E., Chrzanowska, E., & Hilton, S. (2017). The relationship between attachment style and postformal thought. *Journal of Adult Development*. Accessed online, 11/30/17; https://link.springer.com/article/10.1007/s10804-017-9262-0.

Sinnott-Armstrong, W. (2008). *Moral psychology, Vol 3: The neuroscience of morality: Emotion, brain disorders, and development*. Cambridge, MA: MIT Press.

Skinner, B. F. (1957). *Verbal behavior*. New York: Appleton-Century-Crofts.

Skinner, B. F. (1975). The steep and thorny road to a science of behavior. *American Psychologist, 30*, 42–49.

Skinner, J. D., Ziegler, P., Pac, S., & Devaney, B. (2004). Meal and snack patterns of infants and toddlers. *Journal of the American Dietary Association, 104*, S65–S70.

Skinner, M. (2010). Metabolic disorders: Fathers' nutritional legacy. *Nature, 467*, 922–923.

Skledar, M., Nikolac, M., Dodig-Curkovic, K., Curkovic, M., Borovecki, F., & Pivac, N. (2012). Association between brain-derived neurotrophic factor Val66Met and obesity in children and adolescents. *Progress in Neuro-Psychopharmacology & Biological Psychiatry, 36*, 136–140.

Skoog, T., & Özdemir, S. B. (2016). Explaining why early-maturing girls are more exposed to sexual harassment in early adolescence. *Journal of Early Adolescence, 36*, 490–509.

Slaughter, V., & Peterson, C. C. (2012). How conversational input shapes theory of mind development in infancy and early childhood. In M. Siegal & L. Surian (Eds.), *Access to language and cognitive development*. New York: Oxford University Press.

Sleath, B., Sayner, R., Vitko, M., Carpenter, D. M., Blalock, S. J., Muir, K. W., & . . . Robin, A. L. (2017). Glaucoma patient-provider communication about vision quality-of-life. *Patient Education and Counseling, 100*, 703–709.

Sloane, S., Baillargeon, R., & Premack, D. (2012). Do infants have a sense of fairness? *Psychological Science, 23*, 196–207.

Slugocki, C., & Trainor, L. J. (2014). Cortical indices of sound localization mature monotonically in early infancy. *European Journal of Neuroscience, 40*, 3608–3619.

Smedley, A., & Smedley, B. D. (2005). Race as biology is fiction, racism as a social problem is real: Anthropological and historical perspectives on the social construction of race. *American Psychologist, 60*, 16–26.

Smedley, B. D., & Syme, S. L. (Eds.). (2000). *Promoting health: Intervention strategies from social and behavioral research*. Washington, DC: National Academy of Sciences.

Smetana, J. G. (2005). Adolescent-parent conflict: Resistance and subversion as developmental process. In L. Nucci (Ed.), *Conflict, contradiction, and contrarian elements in moral development and education*. Mahwah, NJ: Lawrence Erlbaum.

Smetana, J. G., Jambon, M., & Ball, C. (2014). The social domain approach to children's moral and social judgments. In M. Killen, J.

G. Smetana, M. Killen, & J. G. Smetana (Eds.), *Handbook of moral development* (2nd ed.). New York: Psychology Press.

Smetana, J. G., & Turiel, E. (2003). Moral development during adolescence. In G. R. Adams, & M. D. Berzonsky (Eds.), *Blackwell handbook of adolescence*. Malden, MA: Blackwell Publishing.

Smiley, P. A., Tan, S. J., Goldstein, A., & Sweda, J. (2016). Mother emotion, child temperament, and young children's helpless responses to failure. *Social Development, 25*, 285–303.

Smith, B. L. (2012, April.) The case against spanking. *Monitor on Psychology*, pp. 60–63.

Smith, R. J., Bale, J. F., Jr., & White, K. R. (2005, March 2). Sensorineural hearing loss in children. *Lancet, 365*, 879–890.

Smith, P. K., & Drew, L. M. (2002). Grandparenthood. In M. Bornstein (Ed.), *Handbook of parenting*. Mahwah, NJ: Lawrence Erlbaum.

Smith, S., Quandt, S., Arcury, T., Wetmore, L., Bell, R., & Vitolins, M. (2006, January). Aging and eating in the rural, Southern United States: Beliefs about salt and its effect on health. *Social Science & Medicine, 62*, 189–198.

Smith, T. W., & Kim, S. (2006). National pride in comparative perspective: 1995/96 and 2003/04. *International Journal of Public Opinion Research, 18*(1), 127–136. doi:10.1093/ijpor/edk007.

Smith-Nielsen, J., Tharner, A., Steele, H., Cordes, K., Mehlhase, H., & Vaever, M. S. (2016). Postpartum depression and infant-mother attachment security at one year: The impact of co-morbid maternal personality disorders. *Infant Behavior & Development, 44*, 148–158.

Smith-Rosenberg, C. (2010). *This violent empire: The birth of an American national identity*. Chapel Hill: University of North Carolina Press.

Smokowski, P. R. Mann, E, A. Reynolds, A. J., & Fraser, M. W. (2004). Childhood risk and protective factors and late adolescent adjustment in inner city minority youth. *Children and Youth Services Review, 26, Special issue: Promoting Well Being in Children and Youth: Findings from the Chicago Longitudinal Study*, 63–91.

Smorti, A. (2008). Everyday life reasoning, possible worlds and cultural processes. *Integrative Psychological & Behavioral Science, 42*, 224–232.

Smuts, A. B., & Hagen, J. W. (1985). History of the family and of child development: Introduction to Part 1. *Monographs of the Society for Research in Child Development, 50* (4–5, Serial No. 211).

Snowdon, C. T., & Burghardt, G. M. (2017). Studying animal behavior: Integration of field and laboratory approaches. In J. Call, G. M. Burghardt, I. M. Pepperberg, C. T. Snowdon, T. Zentall (Eds.), *APA handbook of comparative psychology: Basic concepts, methods, neural substrate, and behavior*. Washington, DC: American Psychological Association.

Society for Personality and Social Psychology. (2017). *A reflection on the legacy of Ravenna M. Helson's work*. Accessed online, 11/22/17; http://www.spsp.org/news-center/announcements/2017-convention-legacy-ravenna-m-helson.

Snyder, K. P., Barry, M., & Valentino, R. J. (2015). Cognitive impact of social stress and coping strategy throughout development. *Psychopharmacology, 232*(1), 185–195. doi:10.1007/s00213-014-3654-7.

Soderstrom, M., Blossom, M., Foygel, R., & Morgan, J. (2008). Acoustical cues and grammatical units in speech to two preverbal infants. *Journal of Child Language, 35*, 869–902.

Somerset, W., Newport, D., Ragan, K., & Stowe, Z. (2006). Depressive disorders in women: From menarche to beyond the menopause. In L. M. Keyes & S. H. Goodman (Eds.), *Women and depression: A handbook for the social, behavioral, and biomedical sciences*. New York: Cambridge University Press.

Sonne, J. L. (2012). Psychological assessment measures. In *PsycEssentials: A pocket resource for mental health practitioners*. Washington, DC: American Psychological Association.

Sonnentag, S. (2012). Psychological detachment from work during leisure time: The benefits of mentally disengaging from work. *Current Directions in Psychological Science, 21*, 114–118.

Sousa, D. L. (2005). *How the brain learns to read*. Thousand Oaks, CA: Corwin Press.

South, A. L. (2013). Perceptions of romantic relationships in adult children of divorce. *Journal of Divorce & Remarriage, 54*, 126–141.

South, S. C., Reichborn-Kjennerud, T., Eaton, N. R., & Krueger, R. F. (2015). Genetics of personality. In M. Mikulincer, P. R. Shaver, M. L. Cooper, R. J. Larsen (Eds.), *APA handbook of personality and social psychology, Volume 4: Personality processes and individual differences.* Washington, DC: American Psychological Association.

Southern Poverty Law Center. (2017, August 14). Ten ways to fight hate: A community response guide. Accessed online, 3/19/18; https://www.splcenter.org/20170814/ten-ways-fight-hate-community-response-guide.

Sowell, E. R., Peterson, B. S., Thompson, P. M., Welcome, S. E., Henkenius, A. L., & Toga, A. W. (2003). Mapping cortical change across the human life span. *Nature Neuroscience, 6*, 309–315.

Sowell, E. R., Thompson, P. M., Tessner, K. D., & Toga, A. W. (2001). Mapping continued brain growth and gray matter density reduction in dorsal frontal cortex: Inverse relationships during postadolescent brain maturation. *Journal of Neuroscience, 21*, 8819–8829.

Sparrow, J. (2016). Culture, community, and context in child development: Implications for family programs and policies. In D. Narvaez, J. M. Braungart-Rieker, L. E. Miller-Graff, L. T. Gettler, P. D. Hastings (Eds.), *Contexts for young child flourishing: Evolution, family, and society.* New York: Oxford University Press.

Spear, L. P. (2002). The adolescent brain and the college drinker: Biological basis of propensity to use and misuse alcohol. *Journal of Studies on Alcohol, Special Issue: College drinking, what it is, and what to do about it: Review of the state of the science*, Suppl 14, 71–81.

Spear, L. P. (2014). Adolescents and alcohol: Acute sensitivities, enhanced intake, and later consequences. *Neurotoxicology and Teratology, 41*, 51-59. doi:10.1016/j.ntt.2013.11.006.

Spearman, C. (1927). *The abilities of man.* London: Macmillan.

Spencer, J. (2001). How to battle school violence. *MSNBC News.* Accessed online; http://www.msnbc.com/news/.

Spinelli, L. (2015, September 14.) Fighting for every child. *Northern Virginia.* Accessed online, 10/24/17; https://www.northernvirginiamag.com/family/family-features/2015/09/14/fighting-for-every-child/.

Spraggins, R. E. (2003). *Women and men in the United States: March 2002.* Washington, DC: U.S. Department of Commerce.

Spessato, B., Gabbard, C., Valentini, N., & Rudisill, M. (2013). Gender differences in Brazilian children's fundamental movement skill performance. *Early Child Development and Care, 183*, 916–923.

Spiers, P. (2014). *Master class.* New York: Center Street.

Sprecher, S., Brooks, J. E., & Avogo, W. (2013). Self-esteem among young adults: Differences and similarities based on gender, race, and cohort (1990–2012). *Sex Roles, 69*, 264–275.

Sprecher, S., Sullivan, Q., & Hatfield, E. (1994). Mate selection preferences: Gender differences examined in a national sample. *Journal of Personality and Social Psychology, 66*, 1074–1080.

Squeglia, L. M., Sorg, S. F. Schweinsburg, A., Dager, W., Reagan, R., & Tapert, S. F. (2012). Binge drinking differentially affects adolescent male and female brain morphometry. *Psychopharmacology, 220*, 529–539.

Stacy, A. W., Suassman, S., Dent, C. W., Burton, D., Flay, B. R. (1992). Moderators of peer social influence in adolescent smoking. *Personality & Social Psychology Bulletin, 18*, 163–172.

Staudinger, U. M., & Leipold, B. (2003). The assessment of wisdom-related performance. In C. R. Snyder (Ed.), *Positive psychological assessment: A handbook of models and measures.* Washington, DC: American Psychological Association.

Staunton, H. (2005). Mammalian sleep. *Naturwissenschaften, 35*, 15.

Stearns, E., & Glennie, E. (2006, September). When and why dropouts leave high school. *Youth & Society, 38*, 29–57.

Stein, J. H., & Reiser, L. W. (1994). A study of white middle-class adolescent boys' responses to "semen-arche" (the first ejaculation). *Journal of Youth and Adolescence, 23*, 373–384.

Stein, Z., Susser, M., Saenger, G., & Marolla, F. (1975). *Famine and human development: The Dutch hunger winter of 1944–1945.* New York: Oxford University Press.

Steinberg, L. (2014). *Age of opportunity: Lessons from the new science of adolescence.* Boston: Houghton Mifflin Harcourt.

Steinberg, L., & Scott, S. S. (2003). Less guilty by reason of adolescence: Developmental immaturity, diminished responsibility, and the juvenile death penalty. *American Psychologist, 58*, 1009–1018.

Steinberg, L., & Silverberg, S. (1986). The vicissitudes of autonomy in early adolescence. *Child Development, 57*, 841–851.

Steinberg, L., Dornbusch, S., & Brown, B. B. (1992). Ethnic differences in adolescent achievement: An ecological perspective. *American Psychologist, 47*, 723–729.

Steiner, A. M., & Fletcher, P. C. (2017). Sandwich generation caregiving: A complex and dynamic role. *Journal of Adult Development, 24*, 133–143.

Steinmetz, J., Bosak, J., Sczesny, S., & Eagly, A. H. (2014). Social role effects on gender stereotyping in Germany and Japan. *Asian Journal of Social Psychology, 17*(1), 52–60. doi:10.1111/ajsp.12044.

Stella, L., Verreschi, l., & Lipay, M. (2008). Chimeric hermaphroditism: An overview. *International Journal of Child and Adolescent Health, 1*, 5–9.

Stepler, R. (2017). Led by baby boomers, divorce rates climb for America's 50+ population. Pew Research Center. Accessed online, 3/11/17; http://www.pewresearch.org/fact-tank/2017/03/09/led-by-baby-boomers-divorce-rates-climb-for-americas-50-population/.

Steptoe, A., Deaton, A., & Stone, A. A. (2015). Subjective wellbeing, health, and ageing. *The Lancet, 385*, 640–648.

Sternberg, R. J. (1986). Triangular theory of love. *Psychological Review, 93*, 119–135.

Sternberg, R. J. (1997). *Educating intelligence: Infusing the Triarchic Theory into school instruction.* New York: Cambridge University Press.

Sternberg, R. J. (2003). *Wisdom, intelligence, and creativity synthesized.* New York: Cambridge University Press.

Sternberg, R. J. (2005). The triarchic theory of successful intelligence. In D. P. Flanagan & P. L. Harrison (Eds.), *Contemporary intellectual assessment: Theories, tests, and issues.* New York: Guilford Press.

Sternberg, R. J. (2006). Intelligence. In K. Pawlik & G. d'Ydewalle (Eds.), *Psychological concepts: An international historical perspective.* Hove, England: Psychology Press/Taylor & Francis.

Sternberg, R. J. (2016). A triangular theory of creativity. *Psychology of Aesthetics, Creativity, and the Arts.* Accessed online, 3/16/17; http://psycnet.apa.org/index.cfm?fa=buy.optionToBuy&id=2016-60691-001.

Sternberg, R. J. (2018). Theories of intelligence. In S. I. Pfeiffer, E. Shaunessy-Dedrick, M. Foley-Nicpon (Eds.), *APA handbook of giftedness and talent* (pp. 145–161). Washington, DC: American Psychological Association.

Sternberg, R. J., & Grigorenko, E. L. (Eds.). (2002). *The general factor of intelligence: How general is it?* Mahwah, NJ: Lawrence Erlbaum.

Sternberg, R. J., Kaufman, J. C., & Grigorenko, E. (2008). *Applied intelligence.* New York: Cambridge University Press.

Sternberg, R. J., Kaufman, J. C., & Pretz, J. E. (2002). *The creativity conundrum: A propulsion model of creative contributions.* Philadelphia, PA: Psychology Press.

Stevens, J., Cai, J., Evenson, K. R., & Thomas, R. (2002). Fitness and fatness as predictors of mortality from all causes and from cardiovascular disease in men and women in the lipid research clinics study. *American Journal of Epidemiology, 156*, 832–841.

Stevens, N., Martina, C., & Westerhof, G. (2006, August). Meeting the need to belong: Predicting effects of a friendship enrichment program for older women. *The Gerontologist, 46*, 495–502.

Stevenson, C. E., Heiser, W. J., & Resing, W. M. (2016). Dynamic testing: Assessing cognitive potential of children with culturally diverse backgrounds. *Learning and Individual Differences, 47*, 27–36.

Stevenson, M., Henderson, T., & Baugh, E. (2007, February). Vital defenses: Social support appraisals of black grandmothers parenting grandchildren. *Journal of Family Issues, 28*, 182–211.

Stewart, A. J., & Vandewater, E. A. (1999). "If I had it to do over again . . ." Midlife review, midcourse corrections, and women's well-being in midlife. *Journal of Personality and Social Psychology, 76,* 270–283.

Stice, E. (2003). Puberty and body image. In C. Hayward (Ed.), *Gender differences at puberty.* New York: Cambridge University Press.

Stice, E., & Shaw, H. (2004). Eating disorder prevention programs: A meta-analytic review. *Psychological Bulletin, 130,* 206–227.

Stiles, J., & Jernigan, T. L. (2010). The basics of brain development. *Neuropsychology Review, 20,* 327–348.

Stipek, D. J. (2002). At what age should children enter kindergarten? A question for policy makers and parents. *Social Policy Report, 16,* 3–16.

Stock, P., Desoete, A., & Roeyers, H. (2007). Early markers for arithmetic difficulties. *Educational and Child Psychology, 24,* 28–39.

Stone, C. (2003). Counselors as advocates for gay, lesbian, and bisexual youth: A call for equity and action. *Journal of Multicultural Counseling & Development, 31,* 143–155.

Stopa, L., Denton, R., Wingfield, M., & Taylor, K. (2013). The fear of others: A qualitative analysis of interpersonal threat in social phobia and paranoia. *Behavioural and Cognitive Psychotherapy, 41,* 188–209.

Storm, B. C., & Stone, S. M. (2015). Saving-enhanced memory: The benefits of saving on the learning and remembering of new information. *Psychological Science, 26*(2), 182–188.

Strassberg, D. S., Cann, D., & Velarde, V. (2017). Sexting by high school students. *Archives of Sexual Behavior.* Accessed online, 8/9/17; https://www.ncbi.nlm.nih.gov/pubmed/28050742.

Strachan, E., Duncan, G., Horn, E., & Turkheimer, E. (2017). Neighborhood deprivation and depression in adult twins: Genetics and gene×environment interaction. *Psychological Medicine, 47,* 627–638.

Strauss, J. R. (2011). Contextual influences on women's health concerns and attitudes toward menopause. *Health & Social Work, 36,* 121–127.

Streissguth, A. (1997). *Fetal alcohol syndrome: A guide for families and communities.* Baltimore, MD: Paul H. Brookes.

Streri, A. (2003). Intermodal relations in infancy. In *Touching for knowing: Cognitive psychology of haptic manual perception.* Amsterdam, Netherlands: John Benjamins Publishing Company.

Striano, T., & Vaish, A. (2006, November). Seven- to 9-month-old infants use facial expressions to interpret others' actions. *British Journal of Developmental Psychology, 24,* 753–760.

Stright, A., Gallagher, K., & Kelley, K. (2008). Infant temperament moderates relations between maternal parenting in early childhood and children's adjustment in first grade. *Child Development, 79*(1), 186–200. Accessed online; http://search.ebscohost.com, doi:10.1111/j.1467-8624.2007.01119.x.

Stroebe, M., Schut, H., & Boerner, K. (2017). Cautioning health-care professionals: Bereaved persons are misguided through the stages of grief. *Omega: Journal of Death and Dying, 74,* 455–473.

Strobel, A., Dreisbach, G., Müller, J., Goschke, T., Brocke, B., & Lesch, K. (2007, December). Genetic variation of serotonin function and cognitive control. *Journal of Cognitive Neuroscience, 19,* 1923–1931.

Strohl, M., Bednar, C., & Longley, C. (2012). Residents' perceptions of food and nutrition services at assisted living facilities. *Family and Consumer Sciences Research Journal, 40,* 241–254.

Strohmaier, H., Murphy, M., & DeMatteo, D. (2014). Youth sexting: Prevalence rates, driving motivations, and the deterrent effect of legal consequences. *Sexuality Research & Social Policy: A Journal of the NSRC, 11*(3), 245–255. doi:10.1007/s13178-014-0162-9.

Stroope, S., McFarland, M. J., & Uecker, J. E. (2015). Marital characteristics and the sexual relationships of U.S. older adults: An analysis of National Social Life, Health, and Aging Project data. *Archives of Sexual Behavior, 44,* 233–247.

Struempler, B. J., Parmer, S. M., Mastropietro, L. M., Arsiwalla, D., & Bubb, R. R. (2014). Changes in fruit and vegetable consumption of third-grade students in body quest: Food of the warrior, a 17-class childhood obesity prevention program. *Journal of Nutrition Education and Behavior, 46,* 286–292.

Stuen, C., & Fischer, M. (2007). Gerontechnology and vision. In *Gerontechnology: Growing old in a technological society.* Springfield, IL: Charles C. Thomas Publisher.

Stutzer, A., & Frey, B. (2006, April). Does marriage make people happy, or do happy people get married? *Journal of Socio-Economics, 35,* 326–347.

Sudharsanan, N., Behrman, J. R., & Kohler, H. (2016). Limited common origins of multiple adult health-related behaviors: Evidence from U.S. twins. *Social Science & Medicine, 171,* 67–83.

Subotnik, R. (2006). Longitudinal studies: Answering our most important questions of prediction and effectiveness. *Journal for the Education of the Gifted, 29,* 379–383.

Sue, S., & Chu, J. Y. (2003). The mental health of ethnic minority groups: Challenges posed by the supplement to the Surgeon General's report on mental health. *Culture, Medicine and Psychiatry, 27,* Special issue: The Politics of Science: Culture, race, ethnicity, and the Supplement to the Surgeon General's Report on Mental Health. pp. 447–465.

Sugarmann, J. (2014, January 31). Murder rate for black Americans is four times the national average. *Huff Post Politics.* Accessed online, 6/13/15; http://www.huffingtonpost.com/josh-sugarmann/murder-rate-for-black-ame_b_4702228.html.

Sugarman, S. (1988). *Piaget's construction of the child's reality.* Cambridge, England: Cambridge University Press.

Suinn, R. M. (2001). The terrible twos—Anger and anxiety: Hazardous to your health. *American Psychologist, 56,* 27–36.

Summers, J., Schallert, D., & Ritter, P. (2003). The role of social comparison in students' perceptions of ability: An enriched view of academic motivation in middle school students. *Contemporary Educational Psychology, 28,* 510–523.

Sumner, R., Burrow, A. L., & Hill, P. L. (2015). Identity and purpose as predictors of subjective well-being in emerging adulthood. *Emerging Adulthood, 3,* 46–54.

Sun, B. H., Wu, C. W., & Kalunian, K. C. (2007). New developments in osteoarthritis. *Rheumatoid Disease Clinics of North America, 33,* 135–148.

Sun, Y., Mensah, F. K., Azzopardi, P., Patton, G. C., & Wake, M. (2017). Childhood social disadvantage and pubertal timing: A national birth cohort from Australia. *Pediatrics, 139,* 1–10.

Super, C. M. (1976). Environmental effects on motor development: A case of African infant precocity. *Developmental Medicine and Child Neurology, 18,* 561–576.

Super, C. M., & Harkness, S. (1982). The infant's niche in rural Kenya and metropolitan America. In L. Adler (Ed.), *Issues in cross-cultural research.* New York: Academic Press.

Sutherland, R., Pipe, M., & Schick, K. (2003). Knowing in advance: The impact of prior event information on memory and event knowledge. *Journal of Experimental Child Psychology, 84,* 244–263.

Suzuki, G. (2013). Grade-level differences in elementary and middle school students' conceptions of learning: Correlation with learning strategy use. *Japanese Journal of Educational Psychology, 61,* 17–31.

Swiatek, M. (2002). Social coping among gifted elementary school students. *Journal for the Education of the Gifted, 26,* 65–86.

Swingley, D. (2008). The roots of the early vocabulary in infants' learning from speech. *Current Directions in Psychological Science, 17,* 308–312.

Szaflarski, J. P., Rajagopal, A., Altaye, M., Byars, A. W., Jacola, L., Schmithorst, V. J., et al. (2012). Left-handedness and language lateralization in children. *Brain Research, 143385–97.* Accessed online, 7/18/12; http://www.ncbi.nlm.nih.gov/pubmed/22177775.

Szczygieł, D., & Mikolajczak, M. (2017). Why are people high in emotional intelligence happier? They make the most of their positive emotions. *Personality and Individual Differences, 117,* 177–181.

Tadic, I., Stevanovic, D., Tasic, L., & Stupar, N. (2012). Development of a shorter version of the osteoporosis knowledge assessment tool. *Women & Health, 52*(1), 18–31. doi:10.1080/03630242.2011.635246.

Tadinac, M., & Hromatko, I. (2007). Own mate value and relative importance of a potential mate's qualities. *Studia Psychologica, 49,* 251–264.

Tajfel, H. (2001). Experiments in intergroup discrimination. In M. A. Hogg, D. Abrams (Eds.), *Intergroup relations: Essential readings* (pp. 178–187). New York: Psychology Press.

Tajfel, H., & Turner, J. C. (2004). The social identity theory of intergroup behavior. In J. T. Jost & J. Sidanius (Eds.), *Political psychology: Key readings*. New York: Psychology Press.

Tamis-LeMonda, C. (2004). Conceptualizing fathers' roles: Playmates and more. *Human Development, 47*, 220–227.

Tamis-LeMonda, C. S., & Cabrera, N. (1999). Perspectives on father involvement: Research and policy. *Social Policy Report, 13*, 1–31.

Tamis-LeMonda, C. S., & Cabrera, N. (2002). *Handbook of father involvement: Multidisciplinary perspectives.* Mahwah, NJ: Lawrence Erlbaum.

Tamis-LeMonda, C. S., Song, L., Leavell, A., Kahana-Kalman, R., & Yoshikawa, H. (2012). Ethnic differences in mother-infant language and gestural communications are associated with specific skills in infants. *Developmental Science, 15*, 384–397.

Tang, C., Curran, M., & Arroyo, A. (2014). Cohabitors' reasons for living together, satisfaction with sacrifices, and relationship quality. *Marriage & Family Review, 50*, 598–620.

Tang, C., Wu, M., Liu, J., Lin, H., & Hsu, C. (2006). Delayed parenthood and the risk of cesarean delivery—Is paternal age an independent risk factor? *Birth: Issues in Perinatal Care, 33*, 18–26.

Tang, Z., & Orwin, R. (2009). Marijuana initiation among American youth and its risks as dynamic processes: Prospective findings from a national longitudinal study. *Substance Use & Misuse, 44*, 195–211.

Tangri, S., Thomas, V., & Mednick, M. (2003). Predictors of satisfaction among college-educated African American women in midlife. *Journal of Adult Development, 10*, 113–125.

Tanner, J. (1972). Sequence, tempo, and individual variation in growth and development of boys and girls aged twelve to sixteen. In J. Kagan & R. Coles (Eds.), *Twelve to sixteen: Early adolescence.* New York: Norton.

Tanner, J. M. (1978). *Education and physical growth* (2nd ed.). New York: International Universities Press.

Tanner, E., & Finn-Stevenson, M. (2002). Nutrition and brain development: Social policy implications. *American Journal of Orthopsychiatry, 72*, 182–193.

Tappan, M. B. (2006, March). Moral functioning as mediated action. *Journal of Moral Education, 35*, 1–18.

Tardif, T. (1996). Nouns are not always learned before verbs: Evidence from Mandarin speakers' early vocabularies. *Developmental Psychology, 32*, 492–504.

Tardif, T., Fletcher, P., Liang, W., Zhang, Z., Kaciroti, N., & Marchman, V. A. (2008). Baby's first 10 words. *Developmental Psychology, 44*, 929–938

Tardif, T., Gelman, S. A., Fu, X., & Zhu, L. (2012). Acquisition of generic noun phrases in Chinese: Learning about lions without an '-s.' *Journal of Child Language, 39*, 130–161.

Task Force on Sudden Infant Death Syndrome. (2005). The changing concept of sudden infant death syndrome: Diagnostic coding shifts, controversies regarding the sleeping environment, and new variables to consider in reducing risk. *Pediatrics, 105*, 650–656.

Tattersall, M., Cordeaux, Y., Charnock-Jones, D., & Smith, G. S. (2012). Expression of gastrin-releasing peptide is increased by prolonged stretch of human myometrium, and antagonists of its receptor inhibit contractility. *The Journal of Physiology, 590*, 2081–2093.

Tatum, B. (2007). *Can we talk about race? And other conversations in an era of school resegregation.* Boston: Beacon Press.

Tauriac, J., & Scruggs, N. (2006, January). Elder abuse among African Americans. *Educational Gerontology, 32*, 37–48.

Taveras, E., Sandora, T., Shih, M., Ross-Degnan, D., Goldmann, D., & Gillman, M. (2006, November). The association of television and video viewing with fast food intake by preschool-age children. *Obesity, 14*, 2034–2041.

Tavernise, S. (2013, September 5). Rise is seen in students who use e-cigarettes. *New York Times.* Accessed online, 5/24/18; https://www.nytimes.com/2013/09/06/health/e-cigarette-use-doubles-among-students-survey-shows.html.

Tavernise, S. (2014, February 22). A hot debate over e-cigarettes as a path to tobacco, or from it. *New York Times.* Accessed online, 5/24/18; https://www.nytimes.com/2014/02/23/health/a-hot-debate-over-e-cigarettes-as-a-path-to-tobacco-or-from-it.html.

Taylor, D. M. (2002). *The quest for identity: From minority groups to Generation Xers.* Westport, CT: Praeger Publishers/Greenwood Publishing.

Taylor, G., Liu, H., & Herbert, J. S. (2016). The role of verbal labels on flexible memory retrieval at 12 months of age. *Infant Behavior & Development, 45*(Part A), 11–17.

Taylor, P., Wang, W., Parker, K., Passei, J. S., Patten, E., & Motel, S. (2012). *The rise of intermarriage: Rates, characteristics vary by race and gender.* Washington, DC: Pew Research Center.

Taylor, S. E. (2010). Health psychology. In R. Baumeister, E. J. Finkel (Eds.), *Advanced social psychology.* New York: Oxford University Press

Taylor, S. E. (2015). *Health psychology* (9th ed.). New York: McGraw-Hill.

Taylor, W. D. (2014). Depression in the elderly. *New England Journal of Medicine, 371*, 1228–1235.

Teitelman, J., Hartman, G., Moossa, J., Uhl, K., & Vizzier, E. (2017). Assessing wellness outcomes for participants in adult day services: Options for activity professionals. *Activities, Adaptation & Aging, 41*, 258–267.

Teesson, M., & Mewton, L. (2015). Epidemiology of addiction. In M. Galanter, H. D. Kleber, K. T. Brady (Eds.), *The American Psychiatric Publishing textbook of substance abuse treatment* (pp. 47–58). Arlington, VA: American Psychiatric Publishing, Inc.

Tellegen, A., Lykken, D. T., Bouchard, T. J., Jr., Wilcox, K. J., Segal, N. L., & Rich, S. (1988). Personality similarity in twins reared apart and together. *Journal of Personality and Social Psychology, 54*, 1031–1039.

Tenenbaum, H. R., & Leaper, C. (2003). Parent-child conversations about science: The socialization of gender inequities? *Developmental Psychology, 39*, 34–47.

Teo, T. (2015). Are psychological 'ethics codes' morally oblique? *Journal of Theoretical and Philosophical Psychology, 35*, 78–89.

Teoli, D. A., Zullig, K. J., & Hendryx, M. S. (2015). Maternal fair/poor self-rated health and adverse infant birth outcomes. *Health Care for Women International, 36*, 108–120.

Terzidou, V. (2007). Preterm labour. Biochemical and endocrinological preparation for parturition. *Best Practices of Research in Clinical Obstetrics and Gynecology, 21*, 729–756.

Teutsch, C. (2003). Patient-doctor communication. *Medical Clinics of North America, 87*, 1115–1147.

Thach, B. T., Rutherford, G. W., & Harris, K. (2007). Deaths and injuries attributed to infant crib bumper pads. *Journal of Pediatrics, 151*(3), 271–274.

Tharp, R. G. (1989). Psychocultural variables and constants: Effects on teaching and learning in schools: Special issue: Children and their development: Knowledge base, research agenda, and social policy application. *American Psychologist, 44*, 349–359.

Thibodeau, R. B., Gilpin, A. T., Brown, M. M., & Meyer, B. A. (2016). The effects of fantastical pretend-play on the development of executive functions: An intervention study. *Journal of Experimental Child Psychology, 145*, 120–138.

Thoermer, C., Woodward, A., Sodian, B., Perst, H., & Kristen, S. (2013). To get the grasp: Seven-month-olds encode and selectively reproduce goal-directed grasping. *Journal of Experimental Child Psychology, 116*, 499–509.

Thomaes, S., Brummelman, E., & Sedikides, C. (2017). Why most children think well of themselves. *Child Development, 88*, 1873–1884.

Thoman, E. B., & Whitney, M. P. (1990). Sleep states of infants monitored in the home: Individual differences, developmental trends, and origins of diurnal cyclicity. *Infant Behavior and Development, 12*, 59–75.

Thomas, A., & Chess, S. (1980). *The dynamics of psychological development.* New York: Brunner-Mazel.

Thomas, A., Chess, S., & Birch, H. G. (1968). *Temperament and behavior disorders in children.* New York: New York University Press.

Thomas, A., & Sawhill, I. (2005). For love and money? The impact of family structure on family income. *The Future of Children, 15*(2), 57–74. doi:10.1353/foc.2005.0020.

Thomas, P., & Fenech, M. (2007). A review of genome mutation and Alzheimer's disease. *Mutagenesis, 22*, 15–33.

Thomas, R. M. (2001). *Recent human development theories*. Thousand Oaks, CA: Sage Publications.

Thomas, S. G. (2012, March 3). The gray divorces. *Wall Street Journal*, C1, C2.

Thompson, C., & Prottas, D. (2006, January). Relationships among organizational family support, job autonomy, perceived control, and employee wellbeing. *Journal of Occupational Health Psychology, 11*, 100–118.

Thompson, R. A., Briggs-King, E. C., & LaTouche-Howard, S. A. (2012). Psychology of African American children: Strengths and challenges. In E. C. Chang & C. A. Downey (Eds.), *Handbook of race and development in mental health*. New York: Springer Science + Business Media.

Thompson, R. A., & Nelson, C. A. (2001). Developmental science and the media. *American Psychologist, 56*, 5–15.

Thompson-Brenner, H. (2015). *Casebook of evidence-based therapy for eating disorders*. New York: Guilford Press.

Thoni, A., Mussner, K., & Ploner, F. (2010). Water birthing: Retrospective review of 2625 water births. Contamination of birth pool water and risk of microbial cross-infection. *Minerva Ginecologia, 62*, 203–211.

Thorpe, A. M., Pearson, J. F., Schluter, P. J., Spittlehouse, J. K., & Joyce, P. R. (2014). Attitudes to aging in midlife are related to health conditions and mood. *International Psychogeriatrics, 26*, 2061–2071.

Thorsen, C., Gustafsson, J., & Cliffordson, C. (2014). The influence of fluid and crystallized intelligence on the development of knowledge and skills. *British Journal of Educational Psychology, 84*, 556–570.

Thorson, J. A., Powell, F., Abdel-Khalek, A. M., & Beshai, J. A. (1997). Constructions of religiosity and death anxiety in two cultures: The United States and Kuwait. *Journal of Psychology and Theology, 25*, 374–383.

Thorvaldsson, V., Hofer, S., Berg, S., Skoog, I., Sacuiu, S., & Johansson, B. (2008). Onset of terminal decline in cognitive abilities in individuals without dementia. *Neurology, 71*, 882–887.

Tian, L., Yu, T., & Huebner, E. S. (2017). Achievement goal orientations and adolescents' subjective well-being in school: The mediating roles of academic social comparison directions. *Frontiers in Psychology, 8*, 27–37.

Tibben, A. (2007). Predictive testing for Huntington's disease. *Brain Research Bulletin, 72*, 165–171. Accessed online, 6/6/18; http://search.ebscohost.com, doi:10.1016/j.brainresbull.2006.10.023.

Tiesler, C. T., & Heinrich, J. (2014). Prenatal nicotine exposure and child behavioural problems. *European Child & Adolescent Psychiatry, 23*, 913–929.

Tine, M. (2014). Working memory differences between children living in rural and urban poverty. *Journal of Cognition and Development, 15*(4), 599–613.

Ting, Y. (1997). Determinants of job satisfaction of federal government employees. *Public Personnel Management, 26*, 313–334.

Tinsley, B., Lees, N., & Sumartojo, E. (2004). Child and adolescent HIV risk: Familial and cultural perspectives. *Journal of Family Psychology, 18*, 208–224.

Tobin, J. J., Wu, D. Y. H., & Davidson, D. H. (1989). *Preschool in three cultures: Japan, China, and the United States*. New Haven, CT: Yale University Press.

Toga, A. W., & Thompson, P. M. (2003). Temporal dynamics of brain anatomy. *Annual Review of Biomedical Engineering, 5*, 119–145.

Tomasello, M. (2011). Human culture in evolutionary perspective. In M. J. Gelfand, C. Chiu, & Y. Hong (Eds.), *Advances in culture and psychology* (Vol. 1). New York: Oxford University Press.

Tomasello, M., Carpenter, M., Call, J., Behne, T., & Moll, H. (2005). Understanding and sharing intentions: The origins of cultural cognition. *Behavioral and Brain Sciences, 28*, 675–735.

Tomasello, M., Carpenter, M., & Liszkowski, U. (2007). A new look at infant pointing. *Child Development, 78*, 705–722.

Tongsong, T., Iamthongin, A., Wanapirak, C., Piyamongkol, W., Sirichotiyakul, S., Boonyanurak, P., Tatiyapornkul, T., & Neelasri, C. (2005). Accuracy of fetal heart-rate variability interpretation by obstetricians using the criteria of the National Institute of Child Health and Human Development compared with computer-aided interpretation. *Journal of Obstetric and Gynaecological Research, 31*, 68–71.

Toomey, R. B., Ryan, C. D., Rafael, M., Card, N. A., & Russell, S. T. (2010). Gender-nonconforming lesbian, gay, bisexual, and transgender youth: School victimization and young adult psychosocial adjustment. *Developmental Psychology, 46*, 1580–1589.

Toporek, R. L., Kwan, K., Wlliams, R. A. (2012). Ethics and social justice in counseling psychology. In N. A. Fouad, J. A. Carter, & L. M. Subich (Eds.), *APA handbook of counseling psychology, vol. 1: Theories, research, and methods. APA handbooks in psychology*. Washington, DC: American Psychological Association.

Torges, C., Stewart, A., & Nolen-Hoeksema, S. (2008). Regret resolution, aging, and adapting to loss. *Psychology and Aging, 23*, 169–180.

Torvaldsen, S., Roberts, C. L, Simpson, J. M., Thompson, J. F., & Ellwood, D. A. (2006). Intrapartum epidural analgesia and breastfeeding: A prospective cohort study. *International Breastfeeding Journal, 24*, 1–24.

Tracy, M., Zimmerman, F., Galea, S., McCauley, E., & Vander Stoep, A. (2008). What explains the relation between family poverty and childhood depressive symptoms? *Journal of Psychiatric Research, 42*, 1163–1175.

Trainor, L. J. (2012). Predictive information processing is a fundamental learning mechanism present in early development: Evidence from infants. *International Journal of Psychophysiology, 83*, 256–258.

Trainor, L. J., & Desjardins, R. (2002). Pitch characteristics of infant-directed speech affect infants' ability to discriminate vowels. *Psychonomic Bulletin & Review, 9*, 335–340.

Trapnell, P. D., & Paulhus, D. L. (2012). Agentic and communal values: Their scope and measurement. *Journal of Personality Assessment, 94*, 39–52.

Trautwein, U., Ludtke, O., Kastens, C., & Koller, O. (2006). Effort on homework in grades 5–9: Development, motivational antecedents, and the association with effort on classwork. *Child Development, 77*, 1094–1111.

Trawick-Smith, J., Wolff, J., Koschel, M., & Vallarelli, J. (2015). Effects of toys on the play quality of preschool children: Influence of gender, ethnicity, and socioeconomic status. *Early Childhood Education Journal, 43*, 249–256.

Treat-Jacobson, D., Bronäs, U. G., & Salisbury, D. (2014). Exercise. In R. Lindquist, M. Snyder, M. F. Tracy (Eds.), *Complementary and alternative therapies in nursing* (7th ed.). New York: Springer Publishing Co.

Trehub, S. E. (2003). The developmental origins of musicality. *Nature Neuroscience, 6*, 669–673.

Tremblay, R. E. (2001). The development of physical aggression during childhood and the prediction of later dangerousness. In G. F. Pinard & L. Pagani (Eds.), *Clinical assessment of dangerousness: Empirical contributions*. New York: Cambridge University Press.

Tronick, E. Z. (1995). Touch in mother–infant interactions. In T. M. Field (Ed.), *Touch in early development*. Hillsdale, NJ: Lawrence Erlbaum.

Tropp, L. (2003). The psychological impact of prejudice: Implications for intergroup contact. *Group Processes & Intergroup Relations, 6*, 131–149.

Tropp, L., & Wright, S. (2003). Evaluations and perceptions of self, ingroup, and outgroup: Comparisons between Mexican-American and European-American children. *Self & Identity, 2*, 203–221.

Trzesniewski, K. H., Donnellan, M. B., & Robins, R. W. (2003). Stability of self-esteem across the life span. *Journal of Personality and Social Psychology, 84*, 205–220.

Tsantefski, M., Humphreys, C., & Jackson, A. C. (2014). Infant risk and safety in the context of maternal substance use. *Children and Youth Services Review, 47*, 10–17.

Tucker-Drob, E. M., & Briley, D. A. (2014). Continuity of genetic and environmental influences on cognition across the life span: A meta-analysis of longitudinal twin and adoption studies. *Psychological Bulletin, 140*, 949–979.

Tudge, J., & Scrimsher, S. (2003). Lev S. Vygotsky on education: A cultural-historical, interpersonal, and individual approach to development. In B. Zimmerman (Ed.), *Educational psychology: A century of contributions*. Mahwah, NJ: Lawrence Erlbaum.

Tulving, E., & Thompson, D. M. (1973). Encoding specificity and retrieval processes in episodic memory. *Psychological Review, 80*, 352–373.

Turati, C. (2008). Newborns' memory processes: A study on the effects of retroactive interference and repetition priming. *Infancy, 13*, 557–569.

Turiel, E. (2006). Thought, emotions, and social interactional processes in moral development. In M. Killen & J. G. Smetana (Eds.), *Handbook of moral development*. Mahwah, NJ: Lawrence Erlbaum Associates.

Turkheimer, E., Beam, C. R., Sundet, J. M., & Tambs, K. (2017). Interaction between parental education and twin correlations for cognitive ability in a Norwegian conscript sample. *Behavior Genetics, 47*, 507–515.

Turner, T. L., & Matlock, K. B. (2013). *Patient information: Toilet training (Beyond the basics)*. Accessed online, 8/22/15; http://www.upto-date.com/contents/toilet-training-beyond-the-basics.

Turner-Bowker, D. M. (1996). Gender stereotyped descriptors in children's picture books: Does "Curious Jane" exist in the literature? *Sex Roles, 35*, 461–488.

Turriff, A., Macnamara, E., Levy, H. P., & Biesecker, B. (2016). The impact of living with Klinefelter syndrome: A qualitative exploration of adolescents and adults. *Journal of Genetic Counseling*. Accessed online, 10/25/17; https://www.ncbi.nlm.nih.gov/pubmed/27832510.

Turton, P., Evans, C., & Hughes, P. (2009). Long-term psychosocial sequelae of stillbirth: Phase II of a nested case-control cohort study. *Archives of Women's Mental Health, 12*, 35–41.

Twomey, J. (2006). Issues in genetic testing of children. *MCN: The American Journal of Maternal/Child Nursing, 31*, 156–163.

Tyre, P. (2006, September 11). *The new first grade: Too much too soon? Newsweek*, 34–44.

Tyre, P., & McGinn, D. (2003, May 12). She works, he doesn't. *Newsweek*, pp. 45–52.

U.S. Bureau of the Census. (2000). *Current population reports*. Washington, DC: U.S. Government Printing Office.

U.S. Bureau of the Census. (2010). *Current population survey*. Washington, DC: Author.

U. S. Bureau of the Census. (2011). *Current population survey and annual social and economic supplements*. Washington, DC: Author.

U.S. Bureau of Labor Statistics. (2017). Employment characteristics of families summary. Accessed online, 3/11/18; https://www.bls.gov/news.release/famee.nr0.htm.

U.S. Bureau of Labor Statistics. (2017). *Highlights of women's earnings in 2016*. Washington, DC: Author.

U. S. Bureau of Labor Statistics, U.S. Department of Labor. (2017, March 8). Women's median earnings 82 percent of men's in 2016. *The Economics Daily*. Accessed online, 11/28/17; https://www.bls.gov/opub/ted/2017/womens-median-earnings-82-percent-of-mens-in-2016.htm.

U.S. Census Bureau. (2003). *Population reports*. Washington, DC: GPO.

U.S. Census Bureau. (2012). *Overview of race and Hispanic origin: 2010–2010 Census briefs* Washington, DC: U.S. Department of Commerce.

U.S. Census Bureau. (2017). Historical households tables. Accessed online, 3/11/18; https://www.census.gov/data/tables/time-series/demo/families/households.html.

U.S. Census Bureau. (2017a). Decennial census 1960 and current population Survey, annual social and economic supplements, 1968 to 2017. Accessed online, 6/21/18; https://www.census.gov/content/dam/Census/library/visualizations/time-series/demo/families-and-households/ch-1.pdf.

U.S. Census Bureau, (2017b). Historic household tables. Accessed online, 6/21/18; https://www.census.gov/data/tables/time-series/demo/families/households.html.

U.S. Census Bureau, Current Population Reports. (2013). *Income, poverty, and health insurance coverage in the United States: 2012*, Washington, DC: U.S. Government Printing Office.

U.S. Census Bureau, Current Population Survey. (2015). *Annual social and economic supplement*.

U.S. Department of Commerce, Census Bureau, *Current Population Survey (CPS)*, October, 1990–2013.)

U.S. Department of Education. (2015). *The condition of education, 2014*. Washington, DC: U.S. Department of Education.

U.S. Department of Education, National Center for Education Statistics. (2016). *Digest of education statistics, 2015* (NCES 2016–014).

U.S. Department of Health and Human Services Child Welfare Information Gateway. (2007, June). Recognizing child abuse and neglect: Signs and symptoms. Accessed online, 7/13/18; https://www.childwelfare.gov/pubPDFs/signs.pdf.

U.S. Secret Service. (2002). *The final report and findings of the safe school initiative: Implications for the prevention of school attacks in the United States*. Washington, DC: National Threat Assessment Center.

Umana-Taylor, A. J., Bhanot, R., & Shin, N. (2006). Ethnic identity formation during adolescence: The critical role of families. *Journal of Family Issues, 27*, 390–414.

Umberson, D., Williams, K., Powers, D., Chen, M., & Campbell, A. (2005). As good as it gets? A life course perspective on marital quality. *Social Forces, 81*, 493–511.

UNAIDS. (2011). *2011 World AIDS Day*. New York: United Nations.

Underwood, M. (2005). Introduction to the special section: Deception and observation. *Ethics & Behavior, 15*, 233–234.

Unger, J. B., Shakib, S., Gallaher, P., Ritt-Olson, A., Mouttapa, M., Palmer, P., & Johnson, C. A. (2006). Cultural/interpersonal values and smoking in an ethnically diverse sample of Southern California adolescents. *Journal of Cultural Diversity, 13*(1), 55–63.

Unger, R. K., & Crawford, M. (1992). *Women and gender: A feminist psychology* (2nd ed.). New York: McGraw-Hill.

Unger, R., & Crawford, M. (2003). *Women and gender: A feminist psychology*. New York: McGraw-Hill.

UNICEF, WHO. (2016). *World Bank joint child malnutrition set*. Geneva, Switzerland: UNICEF.

United Nations. (2015). *International survey of world hunger*. New York: United Nations.

UNODC. (2013). *Global study on homicide 2013*. United Nations publication, Sales No. 14.IV.1. Vienna: United Nations Office on Drugs and Crime.

United Nations Statistics Division. (2012). *Statistical Annex Table 2.A Health- United Nations Statistics Division*. Accessed online, 7/18/12; unstats.un.org/unsd/demographic/products/...%20 pdf/Table2A.pdf.

United Nations, Department of Economic and Social Affairs, Population Division. (2013). *World Population Aging 2013. ST/ESA/SER.A/348*. New York: United Nations.

United Nations World Food Programme. (2106). *Hunger statistics*. Rome: World Food Programme. Accessed online, 5/21/16; https://www.wfp.org/hunger/stats.

UNODC. (2013). *Global study on homicide 2013*. United Nations publication, Sales No. 14.IV.1. Vienna: United Nations Office on Drugs and Crime.

Unsworth, N., & Engle, R. W. (2005). Individual differences in working memory capacity and learning: Evidence from the serial reaction time task. *Memory & Cognition, 33*(2), 213–220. doi:10.3758/BF03195310.

Uphold-Carrier, H., & Utz, R. (2012). Parental divorce among young and adult children: A long-term quantitative analysis of mental health and family solidarity. *Journal of Divorce & Remarriage, 53*, 247–266. doi:1 0.1080/10502556.2012.663272.

Upshaw, M. B., Bernier, R. A., & Sommerville, J. A. (2015). Infants' grip strength predicts mu rhythm attenuation during observation of lifting actions with weighted blocks. *Developmental Science*. Accessed online, 6/23/15; http://www.ncbi.nlm.nih.gov/pubmed/25939632.

Upshur, C. C., Heyman, M., & Wenz-Gross, M. (2017). Efficacy trial of the Second Step Early Learning (SSEL) curriculum: Preliminary outcomes. *Journal of Applied Developmental Psychology, 50,* 15–25. doi:10.1016/j.appdev.2017.03.004.

Uttal, D. H., Meadow, N. G., Tipton, E., Hand, L. L., Alden, A. R., Warren, C., & Newcombe, N. S. (2013). The malleability of spatial skills: A meta-analysis of training studies. *Psychological Bulletin, 139,* 352–402.

Uttl, B. (2006). Age-related changes in event-cued visual and auditory prospective memory proper. *Aging, Neuropsychology, and Cognition, 13,* 141–172.

Uylings, H. (2006). Development of the human cortex and the concept of "critical" or "sensitive" periods. *Language Learning, 56,* 59–90.

Vacha-Haase, T., Hill, R. D., & Bermingham, D. W. (2012). Aging theory and research. In N. A. Fouad, J. A. Carter, L. M. Subich (Eds.), *APA handbook of counseling psychology, vol. 1: Theories, research, and methods.* Washington, DC: American Psychological Association.

Vaillant, G. (2003). Mental health. *American Journal of Psychiatry, 160,* 1373–1384.

Vaillant, G. E. (1977). *Adaptation to life.* Boston: Little, Brown.

Vaillant, G. E., & Vaillant, C. O. (1981). Natural history of male psychological health, X: Work as a predictor of positive mental health. *The American Journal of Psychiatry, 138,* 1433–1440.

Vaillant, G. E., & Vaillant, C. O. (1990). Natural history of male psychological health, XII: A 45-year study of predictors of successful aging. *American Journal of Psychiatry, 147*(1), 31–37.

Vaish, A., Carpenter, M., & Tomasello, M. (2009). Sympathy through affective perspective taking and its relation to prosocial behavior in toddlers. *Developmental Psychology, 45,* 534–543.

Vaish, V. (2014). Whole language versus code-based skills and interactional patterns in Singapore's early literacy program. *Cambridge Journal of Education, 44,* 199–215.

Valentino, K., Nuttall, A. K., Comas, M., McDonnell, C. G., Piper, B., Thomas, T. E. & Fanuele, S. (2014). *Developmental Psychology, 50,* 1197–1207.

Valeri, B. O., Holsti, L., & Linhares, M. M. (2015). Neonatal pain and developmental outcomes in children born preterm: A systematic review. *Clinical Journal of Pain, 31,* 355–362.

Valiente, C., Eisenberg, N., & Fabes, R. A. (2004). Prediction of children's empathy-related responding from their effortful control and parents' expressivity. *Developmental Psychology, 40,* 911–926.

Vallejo-Sánchez, B., & Pérez-García, A. M. (2015). Positividad y afrontamiento en pacientes con trastorno adaptativo. = Positivity and coping in patients with adjustment disorder. *Anales De Psicología, 31*(2), 462–471. doi:10.6018/analesps.31.2.176631.

Van Balen, F. (2005). The choice for sons or daughters. *Journal of Psychosomatic Obstetrics & Gynecology, 26,* 229–320.

Van de Graaf, K. (2000). *Human anatomy* (5th ed., p. 339). Boston: McGraw-Hill.

van de Vijver, F. R., Blommaert, J., Gkoumasi, G., & Stogianni, M. (2015). On the need to broaden the concept of ethnic identity. *International Journal of Intercultural Relations, 46,* 36–46.

Van den Bergh, B., Van Calster, B., Puissant, S., & Van Huffel, S. (2008). Self-reported symptoms of depressed mood, trait anxiety and aggressive behavior in post-pubertal adolescents: Associations with diurnal cortisol profiles. *Hormones and Behavior, 54,* 253–257.

van den Herik, J. C. (2017). Linguistic know-how and the orders of language. *Language Sciences, 61,* 17–27.

Van der Graaf, J., Branje, S., De Wied, M., Hawk, S., Van Lier, P., & Meeus, W. (2015). Perspective taking and empathic concern in adolescence: Gender differences in developmental changes. *Developmental Psychology, 50,* 881–888.

van der Pol, T. M., Hoeve, M., Noom, M. J., Stams, G. J. J., Doreleijers, T. A., Domburgh, L., & Vermeiren, R. R. (2017). Research review: The effectiveness of multidimensional family therapy in treating adolescents with multiple behavior problems–a meta-analysis. *Journal of Child Psychology and Psychiatry, 58*(5), 532–545

van der Veer, R., & Yasnitsky, A. (2016). Vygotsky the published: Who wrote Vygotsky and what Vygotsky actually wrote. In A. Yasnitsky & R. van der Veer (Eds.), *Revisionist revolution in Vygotsky studies.* New York: Routledge/Taylor & Francis Group.

van der Schuur, W. A., Baumgartner, S. E., Sumter, S. R., & Valkenburg, P. M. (2018). Media multitasking and sleep problems: A longitudinal study among adolescents. *Computers in Human Behavior, 81,* 316–324.

van Oosten, J. F., & Vandenbosch, L. (2017). Sexy online self-presentation on social network sites and the willingness to engage in sexting: A comparison of gender and age. *Journal of Adolescence, 54,* 42–50.

van Ditzhuijzen, J., ten Have, M., de Graaf, R., van Nijnatten, C. J., & Vollebergh, W. M. (2013). Psychiatric history of women who have had an abortion. *Journal of Psychiatric Research, 47,* 1737–1743.

Van Schoiack-Edstrom, L., Frey, K. S., & Beland, K. (2002). Changing adolescents' attitudes about relational and physical aggression. *School Psychology Review, 31,* 201–216.

Vandell, D. L. (2000). Parents, peer groups, and other socializing influences. *Developmental Psychology, 36,* 699–710.

Vandello, J., & Cohen, D. (2003). Male honor and female fidelity: Implicit cultural scripts that perpetuate domestic violence. *Journal of Personality & Social Psychology, 84,* 997–1010.

Vandello, J., Cohen, D., Grandon, R., & Franiuk, R. (2009). Stand by your man: Indirect prescriptions for honorable violence and feminine loyalty in Canada, Chile, and the United States. *Journal of Cross-Cultural Psychology, 40,* 81–104.

Vanden Abeele, M., Campbell, S. W., Eggermont, S., & Roe, K. (2014). Sexting, mobile porn use, and peer group dynamics: Boys' and girls' self-perceived popularity, need for popularity, and perceived peer pressure. *Media Psychology, 17,* 6–33.

VanLaningham, J., Johnson, D., & Amato, P. (2001). Marital happiness, marital duration, and the U-shaped curve: Evidence from a five-wave panel study. *Social Forces, 78,* 1313–1341.

Vansteenkiste, M., Neyrinck, B., Niemiec, C., Soenens, A., De Witte, H., & Van den Broeck, A. (2007). On the relations among work value orientations, psychological need satisfaction and job outcomes: A self-determination theory approach. *Journal of Occupational and Organizational Psychology, 80,* 251–277.

Varga, M. A. (2014). Why funerals matter: Death rituals across cultures. *Death Studies, 38,* 546–547.

Vecchiet, L. (2002). Muscle pain and aging. *Journal of Musculoskeletal Pain, 10,* 5–22.

Vecchiotti, S. (2003). Kindergarten: An overlooked educational policy priority. *Social Policy Report,* pp. 3–19.

Venker, C. E., Kover, S. T., & Weismer, S. E. (2016). Brief report: Fast mapping predicts differences in concurrent and later language abilities among children with ASD. *Journal of Autism and Developmental Disorders, 46,* 1118–1123.

Veraksa, N., Shiyan, O., Shiyan, I., Pramling, N., & Pramling-Samuelsson, I. (2016). Communication between teacher and child in early child education: Vygotskian theory and educational practice. *Infancia Y Aprendizaje/Journal for the Study of Education and Development, 39,* 221–243.

Veras, R. P., & Mattos, L. C. (2007). Audiology and aging: Literature review and current horizons. *Revista Brasileira de Otorrinolaringologia, 73,* 88–128.

Verhagen, J., Leseman, P., & Messer, M. (2015). Phonological memory and the acquisition of grammar in child l2 learners. *Language Learning, 65,* 417–448.

Verkuyten, M. (2008). Life satisfaction among ethnic minorities: The role of discrimination and group identification. *Social Indicators Research, 89*(3), 391–404.

Verma, J. (2004). *Social Values. Psychology in India revisited: Developments in the discipline, Vol 3: Applied social and organisational psychology.* Thousand Oaks, CA: Sage Publications, Inc.

Verrity, P. (2007). *Violence and aggression around the globe.* Hauppauge, NY: Nova Science Publishers.

Verschueren, K., Doumen, S., & Buyse, E. (2012). Relationships with mother, teacher, and peers: Unique and joint effects on young children's self-concept. *Attachment & Human Development, 14,* 233–248.

Verschueren, M., Rassart, J., Claes, L., Moons, P., & Luyckx, K. (2017). Identity statuses throughout adolescence and emerging adulthood: A large-scale study into gender, age, and contextual differences. *Psychologica Belgica, 57,* 32–42.

Veselka, L., Just, C., Jang, K. L., Johnson, A. M., & Vernon, P. A. (2012). The general factor of personality: A critical test. *Personality and Individual Differences, 52,* 261–264.

Victoria, N. C., Karom, M. C., & Murphy, A. Z. (2015). Analgesia for early-life pain prevents deficits in adult anxiety and stress in rats. *Developmental Neuroscience, 37,* 1–13.

Vidaver, R. M., Lafleur, B., Tong, C., Bradshaw, R., & Marts, S. A. (2000). Women subjects in NIH-funded clinical research literature: Lack of progress in both representation and analysis by sex. *Journal of Women's Health, Gender-Based Medicine, 9,* 495–504.

Vilette, B. (2002). Do young children grasp the inverse relationship between addition and subtraction? Evidence against early arithmetic. *Cognitive Development, 17,* 1365–1383.

Villarosa, L. (2003, December 23). More teenagers say no to sex, and experts are sure why. *New York Times,* p. D6.

Vincent, J. A., Phillipson, C. R., & Downs, M. (2006). *The futures of old age.* Thousand Oaks, CA: Sage Publications.

Vinik, D. (2015, May 5). Washington, DC, has the highest infant mortality rate of 25 rich world capitals. *New Republic.* Accessed online, 5/30/18; https://newrepublic.com/article/121719/washington-dc-highest-infant-mortality-rate-rich-world-capitals.

Vink, D., Aartsen, M. J., Comijs, H. C., Heymans, M. W., Penninx, B. H., Stek, M. L., & ... Beekman, A. F. (2009). Onset of anxiety and depression in the aging population: Comparison of risk factors in a 9-year prospective study. *American Journal of Geriatric Psychiatry, 17*(8), 642–652. doi:10.1097/JGP.0b013e3181a65228.

Vinukonda, G., Dohare, P., Arshad, A., Zia, M. T., Panda, S., Korumilli, R., & . . . Ballabh, P. (2016). Hyaluronidase and hyaluronan oligosaccharides promote neurological recovery after intraventricular hemorrhage. *Journal of Neuroscience, 36,* 872–889.

Visconti, K., Kochenderfer-Ladd, B., & Clifford, C. A. (2013). Children's attributions for peer victimization: A social comparison approach. *Journal of Applied Developmental Psychology, 34,* 277–287.

Vivanti, G., Paynter, J., Duncan, E., Fothergill, H., Dissanayake, C., & Rogers, S. J. (2014). Effectiveness and feasibility of the Early Start Denver Model implemented in a group-based community childcare setting. *Journal of Autism and Developmental Disorders, 44,* 3140–3153.

Vogel, E. A., Rose, J. P., Roberts, L. R., & Eckles, K. (2014). Social comparison, social media, and self-esteem. *Psychology of Popular Media Culture, 3*(4), 206.

Vohs, K. D., & Heatherton, T. (2004). Ego threats elicits different social comparison process among high and low self-esteem people: Implications for interpersonal perceptions. *Social Cognition, 22,* 168–191.

von Hofsten, C. & Rosander, K. (2015). On the development of the mirror neuron system. In: G. Rizolatti and P. Ferrari (Eds.), *New frontiers in mirror neuron research* (pp. 270–320). Oxford University Press.

Volker, S. (2007). Infants' vocal engagement oriented towards mother versus stranger at 3 months and avoidant attachment behavior at 12 months. *International Journal of Behavioral Development, 31,* 88–95.

Votruba-Drzal, E., Coley, R. L., & Chase-Lansdale, L. (2004). Child care and low-income children's development: Direct and moderated effects. *Child Development, 75,* 396–312.

Vreeswijk, C. M., Maas, A. M., Rijk, C. M., & van Bakel, H. A. (2013). Fathers' experiences during pregnancy: Paternal prenatal attachment and representations of the fetus. *Psychology of Men & Masculinity.* Accessed online, 10/25/17; http://psycnet.apa.org/psycinfo/2013-27681-001/.

Vurpillot, E. (1968). The development of scanning strategies and their relation to visual differentiation. *Journal of Experimental Child Psychology, 6,* 632–650.

Vygotsky, L. S. (1926/1997). *Educational psychology.* Delray Beach, FL: St. Lucie Press.

Vygotsky, L. S. (1930/1978). *Mind in society: The development of higher mental processes.* Cambridge, MA: Harvard University Press. (Original works published 1930, 1933, and 1935.)

Vygotsky, L. S. (1962). *Thought and language.* Cambridge, MA: MIT Press.

Waber, D. P., Bryce, C. P., Girard, J. M., Zichlin, M., Fitzmaurice, G. M., & Galler, J. R. (2014). Impaired IQ and academic skills in adults who experienced moderate to severe infantile malnutrition: A 40-year study. *Nutritional Neuroscience, 17,* 58–64.

Wachs, T. D. (2002). Nutritional deficiencies as a biological context for development. In W. Hartup, W. Silbereisen, & K. Rainer (Eds.), *Growing points in developmental science: An introduction.* Philadelphia, PA: Psychology Press.

Wade, N. (2001, October 4). Researchers say gene is linked to language. *New York Times,* p. A1.

Wade, T. D., & Watson, H. J. (2012). Psychotherapies in eating disorders. In J. Alexander & J. Treasure (Eds.), *A collaborative approach to eating disorders.* New York: Routledge/Taylor & Francis Group.

Wagner, R. K., & Sternberg, R. J. (1985). Alternate conceptions of intelligence and their implications for education. *Review of Educational Research, 54,* 179–223.

Wahlin, T. (2007). To know or not to know: A review of behaviour and suicidal ideation in preclinical Huntington's disease. *Patient Education and Counseling, 65,* 279–287.

Wainright, J. L., & Patterson, C. J. (2008). Peer relations among adolescents with female same-sex parents. *Developmental Psychology, 44,* 117–126.

Wainwright, J. L., Russell, S. T., & Patterson, C. J. (2004). Psychosocial adjustment, school outcomes, and romantic relationships of adolescents with same-sex parents. *Child Development, 75,* 1886–1898.

Waismeyer, A., & Meltzoff, A. N. (2017). Learning to make things happen: Infants' observational learning of social and physical causal events. *Journal of Experimental Child Psychology, 162,* 58–71.

Wałaszewska, E. (2011). Broadening and narrowing in lexical development: How relevance theory can account for children's overextensions and underextensions. *Journal of Pragmatics, 43,* 314–326.

Wakschlag, L. S., Pickett, K. E., Kasza, K. E., & Loeber, R. (2006). Is prenatal smoking associated with a developmental pattern of conduct problems in young boys? *Journal of the American Academy of Child & Adolescent Psychiatry, 45*(4), 461–467. doi:10.1097/01.chi.0000198597.53572.3e.

Waldfogel, J. (2001). International policies toward parental leave and child care. *Caring for Infants and Toddlers, 11,* 99–111.

Waldrop, D. P., & Kirkendall, A. M. (2009). Comfort measures: A qualitative study of nursing home-based end-of-life care. *Journal of Palliative Medicine, 12,* 718–724.

Walker, A. A. (1979). The development of relational concepts in three- and four-year-olds. *Journal of Educational Research, 73,* 37–40.

Walker, L. E. (1984). *The battered woman syndrome.* New York: Springer.

Walker, L. E. (1989). Psychology and violence against women. *American Psychologist, 44,* 695–702.

Walker, L. E. (1999). Psychology and domestic violence around the world. *American Psychologist, 54,* 21–29.

Walker, J., Anstey, K., & Lord, S. (2006, May). Psychological distress and visual functioning in relation to vision-related disability in older individuals with cataracts. *British Journal of Health Psychology, 11,* 303–317.

Walker, M. P., & Stickgold, R. (2006). Sleep, memory, and plasticity. *Annual Review of Psychology, 57,* 139-166.

Walker, W. R., Skowronski, J. J., & Thompson, C. P. (2003). Life is pleasant—and memory helps to keep it that way! *Review of General Psychology, 7*(2), 203–210. doi:10.1037/1089-2680.7.2.203.

Walle, E. A., Reschke, P. J., & Knothe, J. M. (2017). Social referencing: Defining and delineating a basic process of emotion. *Emotion Review, 9,* 245–252.

Walpole, S. C., Prieto-Merino, D., Edwards, P., Cleland, J., Stevens, G., & Roberts, I. (2012, June 18). The weight of nations: An estimation of adult human biomass. *BMC Public Health 2012.* Accessed online, 07/12/12; http://www.biomedcentral.com/1471-2458/12/439/abstract.

Walster, H. E., & Walster, G. W. (1978). *Love.* Reading, MA: Addison-Wesley.

Walter, T. (2012). Why different countries manage death differently: A comparative analysis of modern urban societies. *British Journal of Sociology, 63,* 123–145.

Walters, E., & Gardner, H. (1986). The theory of multiple intelligences: Some issues and answers. In R. J. Sternberg & R. K. Wagner (Eds.), *Practical intelligence*. New York: Cambridge University Press.

Wang, C., Tsai, C., Tseng, P., Yang, A. C., Lo, M., Peng, C., & . . . Liang, W. (2014). The association of physical activity to neural adaptability during visuo-spatial processing in healthy elderly adults: A multiscale entropy analysis. *Brain and Cognition, 92*, 73–83.

Wang, H. H., Varelas, P. N., Henderson, G. V., Wijdicks, E. M., & Greer, D. M. (2017). Improving uniformity in brain death determination policies over time. *Neurology, 88*, 562–568.

Wang, Q. (2006). Culture and the development of self-knowledge. *Current Directions in Psychological Science, 15*, 182–187.

Wang, Q., Pomerantz, E., & Chen, H. (2007). The role of parents' control in early adolescents' psychological functioning: A longitudinal investigation in the United States and China. *Child Development, 78*, 1592–1610.

Wang, S-H., Baillargeon, R., & Paterson, S. (2005). Detecting continuity violations in infancy: A new account and new evidence from covering and tube events. *Cognition, 95*, 129–173.

Wang, Y., Seidl, A., & Cristia, A. (2015). Acoustic-phonetic differences between infant- and adult-directed speech: The role of stress and utterance position. *Journal of Child Language, 42*, 821–842.

Wang, Z., Deater-Deckard, K., Cutting, L., Thompson, L. A., & Petrill, S. A. (2012). Working memory and parent-rated components of attention in middle childhood: A behavioral genetic study. *Behavior Genetics, 42*, 199–208.

Wang, Z., Devine, R. T., Wong, K. K., & Hughes, C. (2016). Theory of mind and executive function during middle childhood across cultures. *Journal of Experimental Child Psychology, 149*, 6–22.

Wang/Pew Research Center. (2012). *The rise of intermarriage: Rates characteristics vary by race and gender*. Washington, DC: Pew Research Center.

Ward, L. M., & Friedman, K. (2006). Using TV as a guide: Associations between television viewing and adolescents' sexual attitudes and behavior. *Journal of Research on Adolescence, 16*, 133–156.

Warford, M. K. (2011). The zone of proximal teacher development. *Teaching and Teacher Education, 27*, 252–258.

Warne, R. T., & Liu, J. K. (2017). Income differences among grade skippers and non-grade skippers across genders in the Terman sample, 1936–1976. *Learning and Instruction, 47*, 1–12.

Warshak, R. A. (2000). Remarriage as a trigger of parental alienation syndrome. *American Journal of Family Therapy, 28*, 229–241.

Warwick, P., & Maloch, B. (2003). Scaffolding speech and writing in the primary classroom: A consideration of work with literature and science pupil groups in the USA and UK. *Reading: Literacy & Language, 37*, 54–63.

Waterhouse, J. M., & DeCoursey, P. J. (2004). Human circadian organization. In J. C. Dunlap & J. J. Loros (Eds.), *Chronobiology: Biological timekeeping*. Sunderland, MA: Sinauer Associates.

Waterland, R. A., & Jirtle, R. L. (2004). Early nutrition, epigenetic changes at transposons and imprinted genes, and enhanced susceptibility to adult chronic diseases. *Nutrition*, 63–68.

Waters, L., & Moore, K. (2002). Predicting self-esteem during unemployment: The effect of gender financial deprivation, alternate roles and social support. *Journal of Employment Counseling, 39*, 171–189.

Watling, D., & Bourne, V. J. (2007). Linking children's neuropsychological processing of emotion with their knowledge of emotion expression regulation. *Laterality: Asymmetries of Body, Brain and Cognition, 12*, 381–396.

Watson, J. B. (1925). *Behaviorism*. New York: Norton.

Waugh, W. E., & Brownell, C. A. (2015). Development of body-part vocabulary in toddlers in relation to self-understanding. *Early Child Development and Care, 185*, 1166–1179.

Wechsler, H., Nelson, T. F., Lee, J. E., Seibring, M., Lewis, C., & Keeling, R. P. (2003). Perception and reality: A national evaluation of social norms marketing interventions to reduce college students' heavy alcohol use. *Journal of Studies on Alcohol, 64*, 484–494.

Weijerman, M., van Furth, A., Noordegraaf, A., van Wouwe, J., Broers, C., & Gemke, R. (2008). Prevalence, neonatal characteristics, and first-year mortality of Down syndrome: A national study. *Journal of Pediatrics, 152*, 15–19.

Weinstock, H., Berman, S., & Cates, W., Jr. (2004). Sexually transmitted diseases among American youth: Incidence and prevalence estimates, 2000. *Perspectives on Sexual and Reproductive Health, 36*, 182–191.

Weiss, R. (2003, September 2). Genes' sway over IQ may vary with class. *Washington Post*, p. A1.

Weiss, R., & Raz, I. (2006, July). Focus on childhood fitness, not just fatness. *Lancet, 368*, 261–262.

Weitzman, E., Nelson, T., & Wechsler, H. (2003). Taking up binge drinking in college: The influences of person, social group, and environment. *Journal of Adolescent Health, 32*, 26–35.

Wellman, H. M. (2012). Theory of mind: Better methods, clearer findings, more development. *European Journal of Developmental Psychology, 9*, 313–330.

Welsh, T., Ray, M., Weeks, D., Dewey, D., & Elliott, D. (2009). Does Joe influence Fred's action? Not if Fred has autism spectrum disorder. *Brain Research, 1248*, 141–148.

Wentzell, E. (2017). How did erectile dysfunction become 'natural'? A review of the critical social scientific literature on medical treatment for male sexual dysfunction. *Journal of Sex Research, 54*, 486–506.

Werker, J. F., & Fennell, C. (2009). Infant speech perception and later language acquisition: Methodological underpinnings. In *Infant pathways to language: Methods, models, and research disorders*. New York: Psychology Press.

Werker, J. F., Pons, F., Dietrich, C., Kajikawa, S., Fais, L., & Amano, S. (2007). Infant-directed speech supports phonetic category learning in English and Japanese. *Cognition, 103*, 147–162.

Werner, E. E. (2005). What can we learn about resilience from large-scale longitudinal studies? In S. Goldstein & R. B. Brooks (Eds.), *Handbook of resilience in children*. New York: Kluwer Academic/Plenum Publishers.

Werner, N. E., & Crick, N. R. (2004). Maladaptive peer relationships and the development of relational and physical aggression during middle childhood. *Social Development, 13*, 495–514.

Werner, E., Myers, M., Fifer, W., Cheng, B., Fang, Y., Allen, R., et al. (2007). Prenatal predictors of infant temperament. *Developmental Psychobiology, 49*, 474–484.

Wertsch, J. V. (2008). From social interaction to higher psychological processes: A clarification and application of Vygotsky's theory. *Human Development, 51*, 66–79.

West, J. R., & Blake, C. A. (2005). Fetal alcohol syndrome: An assessment of the field. *Experimental Biology and Medicine, 230*, 354–356.

Westerhausen, R., Kreuder, F., Sequeira Sdos, S., Walter, C., Woerner, W., Wittling, R. A., et al. (2004). Effects of handedness and gender on macro- and microstructure of the corpus callosum and its subregions: A combined high-resolution and diffusion-tensor MRI study. *Brain Research and Cognitive Brain Research, 21*, 418–426.

Westermann, G., Mareschal, D., Johnson, M. H., Sirois, S., Spratling, M. W., & Thomas, M. S. (2007). Neuroconstructivism. *Developmental Science, 10*, 75–83.

Wettstein, M., Tauber, B., Kuźma, E., & Wahl, H. (2017). The interplay between personality and cognitive ability across 12 years in middle and late adulthood: Evidence for reciprocal associations. *Psychology and Aging, 32*, 259–277.

Wexler, B. (2006). *Brain and culture: Neurobiology, ideology, and social change*. Cambridge, MA: MIT Press.

Whalen, D. J., Sylvester, C. M., and Luby, J. L. (2017). Depression and anxiety in preschoolers: A review of the past seven years. *Child and Adolescent Psychiatric Clinics of North America, 26*, 503–522.

Whalen, P., Davis, F. C., Oler, J. A., Kim, H. (2009). Human amygdala responses to facial expression of emotion. In P. J. Whalen & E. A. Phelps (Eds.), *The human amygdala*. New York: Guilford.

Wheeler, S., & Austin, J. (2001). The impact of early pregnancy loss. *American Journal of Maternal/Child Nursing, 26*, 154–159.

Whitaker, R. C., Wright, J. A., Pepe, M. S., Seidel, K. D., & Dietz, W. H. (1997, September 25). Predicting obesity in young adulthood from childhood and parental obesity. *New England Journal of Medicine, 337*, 869–873.

Whitbourne, S. K. (2001). *Adult development and aging: Biopsychosocial perspectives*. New York: Wiley.

Whitbourne, S., Sneed, J., & Sayer, A. (2009). Psychosocial development from college through midlife: A 34-year sequential study. *Developmental Psychology, 45*, 1328–1340.

Whitbourne, S. K., Zuschlag, M. K., Elliot, L. B., & Waterman, A. S. (1992). Psychosocial development in adulthood: A 22-year sequential study. *Journal of Personality and Social Psychology, 63*, 260–271.

White, K. (2007). Hypnobirthing: The Mongan method. *Australian Journal of Clinical Hypnotherapy and Hypnosis, 28*, 12–24.

White, M. G. (2017). *Which professionals are prone to burnout?* Accessed online, 11/29/17; http://stress.lovetoknow.com/Which_Professionals_are_Prone_to_Burnout.

Whiting, B. B. (1965). Sex identity conflict and physical violence: A comparative study. *American Anthropologist, 67*, 123–140.

Whiting, B. B., & Edwards, C. P. (1988). *Children of different worlds: The formation of social behavior*. Cambridge, MA: Harvard University Press.

Whiting, E., Chenery, H. J., & Copland, D. A. (2011). Effect of ageing on learning new names and descriptions for objects. *Aging, Neuropsychology and Cognition, 18*, 594–619.

Whorf, B. L. (1956). *Language, thought, and reality*. New York: Wiley.

Wielgosz, A. T., & Nolan, R. P. (2000). Biobehavioral factors in the context of ischemic cardiovascular disease. *Journal of Psychosomatic Research, 48*, 339–345.

Widaman, K. (2009). Phenylketonuria in children and mothers: Genes, environments, behavior. *Current Directions in Psychological Science, 18*, 48–52.

Wiggins, J. L., Bedoyan, J. K., Carrasco, M., Swartz, J. R., Martin, D. M., & Monk, C. S. (2014). Age-related effect of serotonin transporter genotype on amygdala and prefrontal cortex function in adolescence. *Human Brain Mapping, 35*, 646–658.

Wiggins, M., & Uwaydat, S. (2006, January). Age-related macular degeneration: Options for earlier detection and improved treatment. *Journal of Family Practice, 55*, 22–27.

Wilcox, H. C., Conner, K. R., & Caine, E. D. (2004). Association of alcohol and drug use disorders and completed suicide: An empirical review of cohort studies. *Drug & Alcohol Dependence, 76* [Special issue: Drug abuse and suicidal behavior], S11–S19.

Wilcox, T., Woods, R., Chapa, C., & McCurry, S. (2007). Multisensory exploration and object individuation in infancy. *Developmental Psychology, 43*, 479–495.

Wildberger, S. (2003, August). So you're having a baby. *Washingtonian*, pp. 85–86, 88–90.

Wiley, T. L., Nondahl, D. M., Cruickshanks, K. J., & Tweed, T. S. (2005). Five-year changes in middle ear function for older adults. *Journal of the American Academy of Audiology, 16*, 129–139.

Wiley, S., Perkins, K., & Deaux, K. (2008). Through the looking glass: Ethnic and generational patterns of immigrant identity. *International Journal of Intercultural Relations, 32*, 385–398.

Wilkinson, C. B., Infantolino, Z. P., & Wacha-Montes, A. (2017). Evidence-based practice as a potential solution to burnout in university counseling center clinicians. *Psychological Services, 14*, 543–548.

Willford, J. A., Richardson, G. A., & Day, N. L. (2012). Sex-specific effects of prenatal marijuana exposure on neurodevelopment and behavior. In M. Lewis, & L. Kestler (Eds.), *Gender differences in prenatal substance exposure*. Washington, DC: American Psychological Association.

Wilhoit, L. F., Scott, D. A., & Simecka, B. A. (2017). Fetal alcohol spectrum disorders: Characteristics, complications, and treatment. *Community Mental Health Journal*. Accessed online, 10/27/17; https://www.ncbi.nlm.nih.gov/pubmed/28168434.

Williams, J. M., & Binnie, L. (2002). Children's concept of illness: An intervention to improve knowledge. *British Journal of Health Psychology, 7*, 129–148.

Williams, K., & Dunne-Bryant, A. (2006, December). Divorce and adult psychological well-being: Clarifying the role of gender and child age. *Journal of Marriage and Family, 68*, 1178–1196.

Williams, H., & Monsma, E. (2007). Assessment of gross motor development. *Psychoeducational assessment of preschool children* (4th ed.). Mahwah, NJ: Lawrence Erlbaum Associates Publishers.

Williams, C., Povey, R., & White, D. (2008). Predicting women's intentions to use pain relief medication during childbirth using the theory of planned behaviour and self-efficacy theory. *Journal of Reproductive and Infant Psychology, 26*, 168–179.

Williams, J. M., & Ross, L. (2007). Consequences of prenatal toxin exposure for mental health in children and adolescents: A systematic review. *European Child & Adolescent Psychiatry, 16*, 243–253.

Willie, C., & Reddick, R. (2003). *A new look at black families* (5th ed.). Walnut Creek, CA: AltaMira Press.

Wilmer, H. H., Sherman, L. E., & Chein, J. M. (2017). Smartphones and cognition: A review of research exploring the links between mobile technology habits and cognitive functioning. *Frontiers in Psychology, 8*.

Wilson, B. J., Smith, S. L., Potter, W. J., Kunkel, D., Linz, D., Colvin, C. M., & Donnerstein, E. (2002). Violence in children's television programming: Assessing the risks. *Journal of Communication, 52*(1), 5–35. doi:10.1111/j.1460-2466.2002.tb02531.x.

Wilson, S. L. (2003). Post-institutionalization: The effects of early deprivation on development of Romanian adoptees. *Child & Adolescent Social Work Journal, 20*, 473–483.

Wilson, R. (2004, December 3). Where the elite teach, it's still a man's world. *Chronicle of Higher Education, 51*, A8.

Wilson, B., & Gottman, J. (2002). Marital conflict, repair, and parenting. *Handbook of parenting: Vol. 4: Social conditions and applied parenting* (2nd ed.) (pp. 227–258). Mahwah, NJ: Lawrence Erlbaum Associates Publishers.

Wilson-Williams, L., Stephenson, R., Juvekar, S., & Andes, K. (2008). Domestic violence and contraceptive use in a rural Indian village. *Violence Against Women, 14*, 1181–1198.

Winefield, A. (2002). *The psychology of unemployment. Psychology at the turn of the millennium, vol. 2: Social, developmental, and clinical perspectives*. Florence, KY: Taylor & Frances/Routledge.

Wines, M. (2006, August 24). Africa adds to miserable ranks for child workers. *New York Times*, p. D1.

Winger, G., & Woods, J. H. (2004). *A handbook on drug and alcohol abuse: The biomedical aspects*. Oxford, England: Oxford University Press.

Winkler, I., Haden, G. P., Nemeth, R., Haden, G. P., Winkler, I., & Toeroek, M. (2016). Processing of horizontal sound localization cues in newborn infants. *Ear and Hearing, 36*(5), 550–556.

Winner, E. (1989). Development in the visual arts. In W. Damon (Ed.), *Child development today and tomorrow*. San Francisco: Jossey-Bass.

Winner, E. (2006). Development in the arts: Drawing and music. In *Handbook of child psychology: Vol 2, Cognition, perception, and language* (6th ed.). Hoboken, NJ: John Wiley & Sons Inc.

Winsler, A. (2003). Introduction to special issue: Vygotskian perspectives in early childhood education. *Early Education and Development, 14* [Special issue], 253–269.

Winstead, B. A., & Sanchez, J. (2005). Gender and psychopathology. In J. Maddux (Ed.), *Psychopathology: Foundations for a contemporary understanding*. Mahwah, NJ: Lawrence Erlbaum.

Winterich, J. (2003). Sex, menopause, and culture: Sexual orientation and the meaning of menopause for women's sex lives. *Gender & Society, 17*, 627–642.

Winters, K. C., Stinchfield, R. D., & Botzet, A. (2005). Pathways of youth gambling problem severity. *Psychology of Addictive Behaviors, 19*, 104–107.

Wirth, A., Wabitsch, M., & Hauner, H. (2014). The prevention and treatment of obesity. *Deutsches Ärzteblatt International, 111*, 705–713.

Wisborg, K., Kesmodel, U., Bech, B. H., Hedegaard, M., & Henriksen, T. B. (2003). Maternal consumption of coffee during pregnancy and stillbirth and infant death in first year of life: Prospective study. *British Medical Journal, 326*, 420.

Wise, L., Adams-Campbell, L., Palmer, J., & Rosenberg, L. (2006, August). Leisure time physical activity in relation to depressive symptoms in the Black Women's Health Study. *Annals of Behavioral Medicine, 32*, 68–76.

Witkow, M., & Fuligni, A. (2007). Achievement goals and daily school experiences among adolescents with Asian, Latino, and European American backgrounds. *Journal of Educational Psychology, 99*, 584–596.

Witt, E. A., Donnellan, M., & Trzesniewski, K. H. (2011). Self-esteem, narcissism, and Machiavellianism: Implications for understanding antisocial behavior in adolescents and young adults. In C. T. Barry, P. K. Kerig, K. K. Stellwagen, & T. D. Barry (Eds.),

Narcissism and Machiavellianism in youth: Implications for the development of adaptive and maladaptive behavior. Washington, DC: American Psychological Association.

Woelfle, J. F., Harz, K., & Roth, C. (2007). Modulation of circulating IGF-I and IGFBP-3 levels by hormonal regulators of energy homeostasis in obese children. *Experimental and Clinical Endocrinology Diabetes, 115*, 17–23.

Wolfe, M. S. (2006, May). Shutting down Alzheimer's. *Scientific American*, pp. 73–79.

Wolfson, A. R., & Richards, M. (2011). Young adolescents: Struggles with insufficient sleep. In M. El-Sheikh (Ed.), *Sleep and development: Familial and socio-cultural considerations.* New York: Oxford University Press.

Wolinsky, F., Wyrwich, K., & Babu, A. (2003). Age, aging, and the sense of control among older adults: A longitudinal reconsideration. *Journals of Gerontology: Series B: Psychological Sciences & Social Sciences, 58B*, S212–S220.

Wolkorte, R., Kamphuis, J., & Zijdewind, I. (2014). Increased reaction times and reduced response preparation already starts at middle age. *Frontiers in Aging Neuroscience, 6*, 88–97.

Wonnacott, E; (2013) Learning: Statistical mechanisms in language acquisition. In: *The Language Phenomenon.* (pp. 65–92). Springer.

Wood, A. C., Saudino, K. J., Rogers, H., Asherson, P., & Kuntsi, J. (2007). Genetic influences on mechanically-assessed activity level in children. *Journal of Child Psychology and Psychiatry, 48*, 695–702.

Woodhouse, S. S., Dykas, M. J., & Cassidy, J. (2012). Loneliness and peer relations in adolescence. *Social Development, 21*, 273–293.

World Bank. (2003). *Global development finance 2003—Striving for stability in development finance.* Washington, DC: Author.

World Factbook. (2016). *Estimates of infant mortality.* Accessed online, 10/27/17, https://www.cia.gov/library/publications/the-world-factbook/fields/2091.html.

World Factbook. (2017). *Total fertility rate.* Accessed online, 11/22/17; https://www.cia.gov/library/publications/the-world-factbook/fields/2127.html.

World Factbook. (2017). *World Factbook.* Washington, DC: Central Intelligence Agency. Accessed online, 10/27/17; https://www.cia.gov/library/publications/the-world-factbook/rankorder/2091rank.html.

Wörmann, V., Holodynski, M., Kärtner, J., & Keller, H. (2014). The emergence of social smiling: The interplay of maternal and infant imitation during the first three months in cross-cultural comparison. *Journal of Cross-Cultural Psychology, 45*, 339–361.

Worrell, F., Szarko, J., & Gabelko, N. (2001). Multiyear persistence of nontraditional students in an academic talent development program. *Journal of Secondary Gifted Education, 12*, 80–89.

Wrosch, C., Bauer, I., & Scheier, M. (2005, December). Regret and quality of life across the adult life span: The influence of disengagement and available future goals. *Psychology and Aging, 20*, 657–670.

Wu, P., & Liu, H. (2014). Association between moral reasoning and moral behavior: A systematic review and meta-analysis. *Acta Psychologica Sinica, 46*, 1192–1207.

Wu, P., Robinson, C., & Yang, C. (2002). Similarities and differences in mothers' parenting of preschoolers in China and the United States. *International Journal of Behavioral Development, 26*, 481–491.

Wu, T., Treiber, F. A., & Snieder, H. (2013). Genetic influence on blood pressure and underlying hemodynamics measured at rest and during stress. *Psychosomatic Medicine, 75*, 404–412.

Wu, Y., Tsou, K., Hsu, C., Fang, L., Yao, G., & Jeng, S. (2008). Brief report: Taiwanese infants' mental and motor development—6–24 months. *Journal of Pediatric Psychology, 33*, 102–108.

Wupperman, P., Marlatt, G., Cunningham, A., Bowen, S., Berking, M., Mulvihill-Rivera, N., et al. (2012). Mindfulness and modification therapy for behavioral dysregulation: Results from a pilot study targeting alcohol use and aggression in women. *Journal of Clinical Psychology, 68*, 50–66.

Xiao, H., Kwong, E., Pang, S., & Mok, E. (2012). Perceptions of a life review programme among Chinese patients with advanced cancer. *Journal of Clinical Nursing, 21*, 564–572.

Xiao, N. G., Quinn, P. C., Liu, S., Ge, L., Pascalis, O., & Lee, K. (2015). Eye tracking reveals a crucial role for facial motion in recognition of faces by infants. *Developmental Psychology, 51*, 744–757.

Xie, R., Gaudet, L., Krewski, D., Graham, I. D., Walker, M. C., & Wen, S. W. (2015). Higher cesarean delivery rates are associated with higher infant mortality rates in industrialized countries. *Birth: Issues in Perinatal Care.* Accessed online, 3/14/15; http://onlinelibrary.wiley.com/doi/10.1111/birt.12153/pdf.

Xu, J., Saether, L., & Sommerville, J. A. (2016). Experience facilitates the emergence of sharing behavior among 7.5-month-old infants. *Developmental Psychology, 52*, 1732–1743.

Yablo, P., & Field, N. (2007). The role of culture in altruism: Thailand and the United States. *Psychologia: An International Journal of Psychology in the Orient, 50*, 236–251.

Yagmurlu, B., & Sanson, A. (2009). Parenting and temperament as predictors of prosocial behaviour in Australian and Turkish Australian children. *Australian Journal of Psychology, 61*, 77–88.

Yang, C., & Brown, B. B. (2015). Factors involved in associations between Facebook use and college adjustment: Social competence, perceived usefulness, and use patterns. *Computers in Human Behavior, 46*, 245–253.

Yang, C., Crain, S., Berwick, R. C., Chomsky, N., & Bolhuis, J. J. (2017). The growth of language: Universal grammar, experience, and principles of computation. *Neuroscience and Biobehavioral Reviews.* Accessed online, 10/29/17; http://www.sciencedirect.com/science/article/pii/S0149763416305656.

Yang, C. D. (2006). *The infinite gift: How children learn and unlearn the languages of the world.* New York: Scribner.

Yang, R., & Blodgett, B. (2000). Effects of race and adolescent decision-making on status attainment and self-esteem. *Journal of Ethnic & Cultural Diversity in Social Work, 9*, 135–153.

Yasui, M., Dorham, C., L., & Dishion, T. J. (2004). Ethnic identity and psychological adjustment: A validity analysis for European American and African American adolescents. *Journal of Adolescent Research, 19*, 807–825.

Ybarra, M. L., & Mitchell, K. J. (2014). 'Sexting' and its relation to sexual activity and sexual risk behavior in a national survey of adolescents. *Journal of Adolescent Health, 55*(6), 757–764. doi:10.1016/j.jadohealth.2014.07.012.

Yell, M. L. (2015). *Law and special education.* (4th ed.) Hoboken, NJ: Pearson.

Yell, M. L., & Drasgow, E. (2010). The continuing influence of the law in special education: Introduction to the special issue. *Exceptionality, 18*, 107–108.

Yildiz, O. (2007). Vascular smooth muscle and endothelial functions in aging. *Annals of the New York Academy of Sciences, 1100*, 353–360.

Yip, T. (2008). Everyday experiences of ethnic and racial identity among adolescents and young adults. In *Handbook of race, racism, and the developing child.* Hoboken, NJ: John Wiley & Sons Inc.

Yip, T., Sellers, R. M., & Seaton, E. K. (2006). African American racial identity across the lifespan: Identity status, identity content, and depressive symptoms. *Child Development, 77*, 1504–1517.

Yon, Y., Wister, A. V., Mitchell, B., & Gutman, G. (2014). A national comparison of spousal abuse in mid- and old age. *Journal of Elder Abuse & Neglect, 26*, 80–105.

Yonker, J. E., Schnabelrauch, C. A., & DeHaan, L. G. (2012). The relationship between spirituality and religiosity on psychological outcomes in adolescents and emerging adults: A meta-analytic review. *Journal of Adolescence, 35*, 299–314.

Yoo, S. S., Hu, P. T., Gujar, N., Jolesz, F. A., & Walker, M. P. (2007). A deficit in the ability to form new human memories without sleep. *Nature Neuroscience, 10*(3), 385–392.

Yoon, E., Adams, K., Clawson, A., Chang, H., Surya, S., & Jérémie-Brink, G. (2017). East Asian adolescents' ethnic identity development and cultural integration: A qualitative investigation. *Journal of Counseling Psychology, 64*, 65–79.

York, G. S., Churchman, R., Woodard, B., Wainright, C., & Rau-Foster, M. (2012). Free-text comments: Understanding the value in family member descriptions of hospice caregiver relationships. *American Journal of Hospice & Palliative Medicine, 29*, 98–105.

Yoshimura, S., Okamoto, Y., Onoda, K., Matsunaga, M., Okada, G., Kunisato, Y., & ... Yamawaki, S. (2014). Cognitive behavioral therapy for depression changes medial prefrontal and ventral anterior cingulate cortex activity associated with self-referential processing. *Social Cognitive and Affective Neuroscience, 9*(4), 487–493. doi:10.1093/scan/nst009.

Yoshinaga-Itano, C. (2003). From screening to early identification and intervention: Discovering predictors to successful outcomes for children with significant hearing loss. *Journal of Deaf Studies & Deaf Education, 8,* 11–30.

Yott, J., & Poulin-Dubois, D. (2016). Are infants' theory-of-mind abilities well integrated? Implicit understanding of intentions, desires, and beliefs. *Journal of Cognition and Development, 17,* 683–698.

You, J-I., & Bellmore, A. (2012). Relational peer victimization and psychosocial adjustment: The mediating role of best friendship qualities. *Personal Relationships, 19,* 340–353.

Young, A. M., Elliston, A., & Ruble, L. A. (2016). Children with autism and vaccinations. In J. Merrick (Ed.), *Children and childhood: Some international aspects.* Hauppauge, NY: Nova Biomedical Books.

Young, S., Rhee, S., Stallings, M., Corley, R., & Hewitt, J. (2006, July). Genetic and environmental vulnerabilities underlying adolescent substance use and problem use: General or specific? *Behavior Genetics, 36,* 603–615.

Yu, M., & Stiffman, A. (2007). Culture and environment as predictors of alcohol abuse/dependence symptoms in American Indian youths. *Addictive Behaviors, 32,* 2253–2259.

Yuan, A. (2012). Perceived breast development and adolescent girls' psychological well-being. *Sex Roles, 66,* 790–806.

Zacchilli, T. L., & Valerio, C. (2011). The knowledge and prevalence of cyber bullying in a college sample. *Journal of Scientific Psychology.*

Zafeiriou, D. I. (2004). Primitive reflexes and postural reactions in the neurodevelopmental examination. *Pediatric Neurology, 31,* 1–8.

Zagorsky, J. (2007). Do you have to be smart to be rich? The impact of IQ on wealth, income and financial distress. *Intelligence, 35,* 489–501.

Zahn-Waxler, C., Klimes-Dougan, B., & Slattery, M. J. (2000). Internalizing problems of childhood and adolescence: Prospects, pitfalls, and progress in understanding the development of anxiety and depression. *Development and Psychopathology, 12*(3), 443–466. doi:10.1017/S0954579400003102.

Zahn-Waxler, C., & Polanichka, N. (2004). All things interpersonal: Socialization and female aggression. In *Aggression, antisocial behavior, and violence among girls: A developmental perspective* (pp. 48–68). New York: Guilford Publications.

Zalenski, R., & Raspa, R. (2006). Maslow's hierarchy of needs: A framework for achieving human potential in hospice. *Journal of Palliative Medicine, 9,* 1120–1127.

Zalsman, G., Oquendo, M., Greenhill, L., Goldberg, P., Kamali, M., Martin, A., et al. (2006, October). Neurobiology of depression in children and adolescents. *Child and Adolescent Psychiatric Clinics of North America, 15,* 843–868.

Zampi, C., Fagioli, I., & Salzarulo, P. (2002). Time course of EEG background activity level before spontaneous awakening in infants. *Journal of Sleep Research, 11,* 283–287.

Zaporozhets, A. V. (1965). The development of perception in the preschool child. *Monographs of the Society for Research in Child Development, 30,* 82–101.

Zeanah, C. H., Fox, N. A., & Nelson, C. A. (2012). Case study in ethics of research: The Bucharest Early Intervention Project. *The Journal of Nervous and Mental Disease, 2012*(3), 243–247.

Zaragoza, M. S., Belli, R. F., & Payment, K. E. (2007). Misinformation effects and the suggestibility of eyewitness memory. In M. Garry, H. Hayne (Eds.), *Do justice and let the sky fall: Elizabeth Loftus and her contributions to science, law, and academic freedom* (pp. 35–63). Mahwah, NJ: Lawrence Erlbaum Associates Publishers.

Zeleznikow, L., & Zeleznikow, J. (2015). Supporting blended families to remain intact: A case study. *Journal of Divorce & Remarriage, 56,* 317–335.

Zellner, D., Loaiza, S., Gonzalez, Z., Pita, J., Morales, J., Pecora, D., et al. (2006, April). Food selection changes under stress. *Physiology & Behavior, 87,* 789–793.

Zettergren, P. (2004). School adjustment in adolescence for previously rejected, average and popular children. *British Journal of Educational Psychology, 73,* 207–221.

Zhai, F., Raver, C., & Jones, S. M. (2012). Academic performance of subsequent schools and impacts of early interventions: Evidence from a randomized controlled trial in Head Start settings. *Children and Youth Services Review, 34,* 946–954.

Zhang, C., Hur, J., Diamond, K. E., & Powell, D. (2015). Classroom writing environments and children's early writing skills: An observational study in Head Start classrooms. *Early Childhood Education Journal, 43,* 307–315.

Zhang, N., Baker, H. W., Tufts, M., Raymond, R. E., Salihu, H., & Elliott, M. R. (2013). Early childhood lead exposure and academic achievement: Evidence from Detroit Public Schools, 2008–2010. *American Journal of Public Health, 103*(3),e72–e77. http://doi.org/10.2105/AJPH.2012.301164.

Zhang, Q., He, X., & Zhang, J. (2007). A comparative study on the classification of basic color terms by undergraduates from Yi nationality, Bai nationality and Naxi nationality. *Acta Psychologica Sinica, 39,* 18–26.

Zhang, Q., & Wang, Y. (2004). Trends in the association between obesity and socioeconomic status in U.S. Adults: 1971 to 2000. *Obesity Research, 12,* 1622–1632.

Zhe, C., & Siegler, R. S. (2000). Across the great divide: Bridging the gap between understanding of toddlers' and older children's thinking. *Monographs of the Society for Research in Child Development, 65* (2, Serial No. 261).

Ziegler, M., Danay, E., Heene, M., Asendorpf, J., & Buhner, M. (2012). Openness, fluid intelligence, and crystallized intelligence: Toward an integrative model. *Journal of Research in Personality, 46,* 173–183.

Zigler, E. F., & Styfco, S. J. (2004). Moving Head Start to the states: One experiment too many. *Applied Developmental Science, 8,* 51–55.

Zimmerman, B., & Schunk, D. (2003). Albert Bandura: The scholar and his contributions to educational psychology. *Educational psychology: A century of contributions.* Mahwah, NJ: Lawrence Erlbaum Associates Publishers.

Zipke, M. (2007). The role of metalinguistic awareness in the reading comprehension of sixth and seventh graders. *Reading Psychology, 28,* 375–396.

Zisook, S., & Shear, K. (2009). Grief and bereavement: What psychiatrists need to know. *World Psychiatry, 8,* 67–74.

Zito, J. (2002). Five burning questions. *Journal of Developmental & Behavioral Pediatrics, 23,* S23–S30.

Zosuls, K. M., Field, R. D., Martin, C. L., Andrews, N. Z., & England, D. E. (2014). Gender-based relationship efficacy: Children's self-perceptions in intergroup contexts. *Child Development, 85,* 1663–1676.

Zuccarini, M., Sansavini, A., Iverson, J. M., Savini, S., Guarini, A., Alessandroni, R., & ... Aureli, T. (2016). Object engagement and manipulation in extremely preterm and full term infants at 6 months of age. *Research in Developmental Disabilities, 55,* 173–184.

Zucker, J. & Alexander-Tanner, R. (2017, May 11). Well illustrated: Childbirth. *New York Times.* Accessed online, 10/25/17; https://www.nytimes.com/2017/05/11/well/family/well-illustrated-childbirth.html?_r=0.

Zuckerman, G., & Shenfield, S. D. (2007). Child-adult interaction that creates a zone of proximal development. *Journal of Russian & East European Psychology, 45,* 43–69.

Zwelling, E. (2006). A challenging time in the history of Lamaze international: An interview with Francine Nichols. *Journal of Perinatal Education, 15,* 10–17.

Zyphur, M. J., Zhang, Z., Barsky, A. P., & Li, W. (2013). An ACE in the hole: Twin family models for applied behavioral genetics research. *Leadership Quarterly, 24,* 572–594.

Name Index

Subject Index